Fifth Edition

Accounting
An Introduction

Eddie McLaney
and
Peter Atrill

**Financial Times
Prentice Hall
is an imprint of**

PEARSON

Harlow, England • London • New York • Boston • San Francisco • Toronto
Sydney • Tokyo • Singapore • Hong Kong • Seoul • Taipei • New Delhi
Cape Town • Madrid • Mexico City • Amsterdam • Munich • Paris • Milan

Pearson Education Limited
Edinburgh Gate
Harlow
Essex CM20 2JE
England

and Associated Companies throughout the world

Visit us on the World Wide Web at:
www.pearsoned.co.uk

First published 1999 by Prentice Hall Europe
Second edition published 2002
Third edition published 2005
Fourth edition published 2008
Fifth edition published 2010

© Prentice Hall Europe 1999
© Pearson Education Limited 2002, 2005, 2008, 2010

ISBN: 978-0-273-73320-1

British Library Cataloguing-in-Publication Data
A catalogue record for this book is available from the British Library

Library of Congress Cataloging-in-Publication Data
McLaney, E. J.
   Accounting : an introduction / Eddie McLaney and Peter Atrill. — 5th ed.
     p. cm.
   Includes bibliographical references and index.
   ISBN 978-0-273-73320-1 (pbk.)
1. Accounting.   I. Atrill, Peter.   II. Title.
   HF5635.M48833 2010
   657—dc22

                                               2009053919

10   9   8   7   6   5   4   3   2   1
14   13   12   11   10

Typeset in 9.5/12.5pt Stone Serif by 35
Printed and bound by Rotolito Lombarda, Italy

The publisher's policy is to use paper manufactured from sustainable forests.

Brief contents

Detailed contents

Part 1 Financial accounting

5 Accounting for limited companies (2)   165

Part 2 Management accounting

11 Costing and performance evaluation in a competitive environment 393

Part 3 Financial management

Part 4 Supplementary information

Supporting resources

Visit **www.pearsoned.co.uk/mclaney** to find valuable online resources

For instructors
- Complete, downloadable Instructor's Manual
- PowerPoint slides that can be downloaded and used for presentations
- Case study material with solutions
- Progress tests, consisting of various questions and exercise material with solutions
- Tutorial/seminar questions and solutions
- Solutions to end of chapter review questions

Also: MyAccountingLab provides the following features:
- Search tool to help locate specific items of content
- E-mail results and profile tools to send results of quizzes to instructors
- Online help and support to assist with website usage and troubleshooting

For more information please contact your local Pearson Education sales representative or visit **www.pearsoned.co.uk/mclaney**

Preface

This text provides a comprehensive introduction to financial accounting, management accounting and core elements of financial management. It is aimed both at students who are not majoring in accounting or finance and at those who are. Those studying introductory-level accounting and/or financial management as part of their course in business, economics, hospitality management, tourism, engineering or some other area should find that the book provides complete coverage of the material at the level required. Students who are majoring in either accounting or finance should find the book useful as an introduction to the main principles, which can serve as a foundation for further study. The text does not focus on technical issues, but rather examines basic principles and underlying concepts. The primary concern throughout is the ways in which financial statements and information can be used to improve the quality of management decision making. To reinforce this practical emphasis, there are, throughout the text, numerous illustrative extracts with commentary from real life including company reports, survey data and other sources.

In this fifth edition, we have taken the opportunity to make improvements that have been suggested by students and lecturers who used the previous edition. We have also brought up to date and expanded the number of examples from real life. We have continued to reflect the latest developments in the international rules relating to the main financial statements. We have also made reference to changes in financing methods that have emerged recently and to the financial crisis that they have partly led to.

The text is written in an 'open-learning' style. This means that there are numerous integrated activities, worked examples and questions throughout the text to help you to understand the subject fully. You are encouraged to interact with the material and to check your progress continually. Irrespective of whether you are using the book as part of a taught course or for personal study, we have found that this approach is more 'user-friendly' and makes it easier for you to learn.

We recognise that most readers will not have studied accounting or finance before, and we have therefore tried to write in a concise and accessible style, minimising the use of technical jargon. We have also tried to introduce topics gradually, explaining everything as we go. Where technical terminology is unavoidable we try to provide clear explanations. In addition, you will find all of the key terms highlighted in the text. These are then listed at the end of each chapter with a page reference. They are also listed alphabetically, with a concise definition, in the glossary given in Appendix B towards the end of the book. This should provide a convenient point of reference from which to revise.

A further important consideration in helping you to understand and absorb the topics covered is the design of the text itself. The page layout and colour scheme have been carefully considered to allow for the easy navigation and digestion of material. The layout features a large page format, an open design, and clear signposting of the various features and assessment material.

More detail about the nature and use of these features is given in the 'How to use this book' section; and the main points are also summarised, using example pages from the text, in the guided tour on pages xxiv–xxv hereafter.

We hope that you will find the book readable and helpful.

Eddie McLaney
Peter Atrill

How to use this book

We have organised the chapters to reflect what we consider to be a logical sequence and, for this reason, we suggest that you work through the text in the order in which it is presented. We have tried to ensure that earlier chapters do not refer to concepts or terms that are not explained until a later chapter. If you work through the chapters in the 'wrong' order, you will probably encounter concepts and terms that were explained previously.

Irrespective of whether you are using the book as part of a lecture/tutorial-based course or as the basis for a more independent mode of study, we advocate following broadly the same approach.

Integrated assessment material

Interspersed throughout each chapter are numerous **Activities**. You are strongly advised to attempt all of these questions. They are designed to simulate the sort of quick-fire questions that your lecturer might throw at you during a lecture or tutorial. Activities serve two purposes:

- To give you the opportunity to check that you understand what has been covered so far.
- To encourage you to think about the topic just covered, either to see a link between that topic and others with which you are already familiar, or to link the topic just covered to the next.

The answer to each Activity is provided immediately after the question. This answer should be covered up until you have deduced your solution, which can then be compared with the one given.

Towards the middle/end of each chapter there is a **Self-assessment question**. This is more comprehensive and demanding than any of the Activities, and is designed to give you an opportunity to check and apply your understanding of the core coverage of the chapter. The solution to each of these questions is provided in Appendix C at the end of the book. As with the Activities, it is important that you attempt each question thoroughly before referring to the solution. If you have difficulty with a self-assessment question, you should go over the relevant chapter again.

End-of-chapter assessment material

At the end of each chapter there are four **Review questions**. These are short questions requiring a narrative answer or discussion within a tutorial group. They are intended to help you assess how well you can recall and critically evaluate the core terms and concepts covered in each chapter. Answers to these questions are provided in the MyAccountingLab as well as Appendix D at the end of the book. At the end of each chapter, except for Chapter 1, there are eight **Exercises**. These are mostly computational and are designed to reinforce your knowledge and understanding. Exercises are graded as 'basic' and 'more advanced', according to their level of difficulty. The basic-level questions are fairly straightforward; the more advanced ones can be quite demanding but are capable of being successfully completed if you have worked conscientiously through the chapter and have attempted the basic exercises. Solutions to five of the exercises in each chapter are provided in Appendix D at the end of the book. A coloured exercise number identifies these five questions. Here, too, a thorough attempt should be made to answer each exercise before referring to the solution. Solutions to the other three exercises and to the review questions in each chapter are provided in a separate Instructors' Manual.

To familiarise yourself with the main features and how they will benefit your study from this text, an illustrated Guided tour is provided on pages xxii–xxv.

Content and structure

The text comprises 16 chapters organised into three core parts: financial accounting, management accounting and financial management. A brief introductory outline of the coverage of each part and its component chapters is given in the opening pages of each part.

The market research for this text revealed a divergence of opinions, given the target market, on whether or not to include material on double-entry bookkeeping techniques. So as to not interrupt the flow and approach of the financial accounting chapters, Appendix A on recording financial transactions (including Activities and three Exercise questions) has been placed in Part 4.

MyAccountingLab

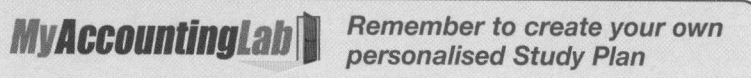

MyAccountingLab supports this book. This banner reminds students to complete the chapter pre-test to create their personal Study Plan. The results of the test determine the Study Plan going forward.

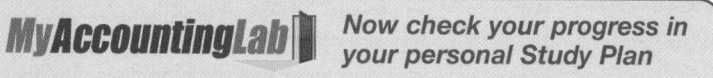

This banner reminds students to complete the chapter post-test in MyAccountingLab to track their progress and mastery of the topics included in each chapter. Their Study plan will adapt according to the results of the test.

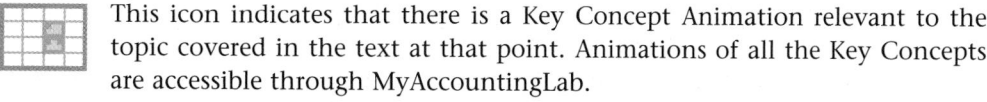

This icon indicates that there is a Key Concept Animation relevant to the topic covered in the text at that point. Animations of all the Key Concepts are accessible through MyAccountingLab.

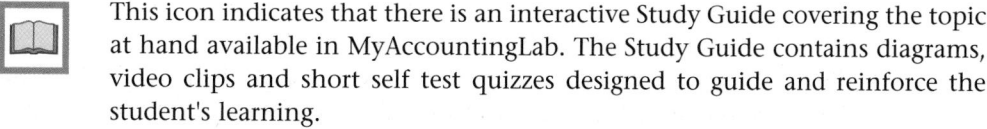

This icon indicates that there is an interactive Study Guide covering the topic at hand available in MyAccountingLab. The Study Guide contains diagrams, video clips and short self test quizzes designed to guide and reinforce the student's learning.

Guided tour of the book

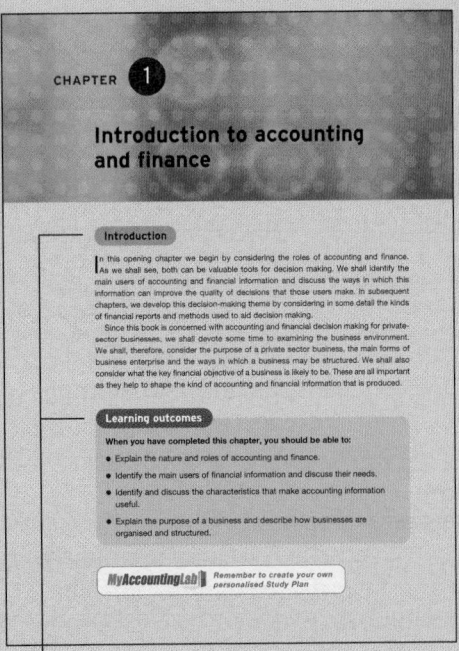

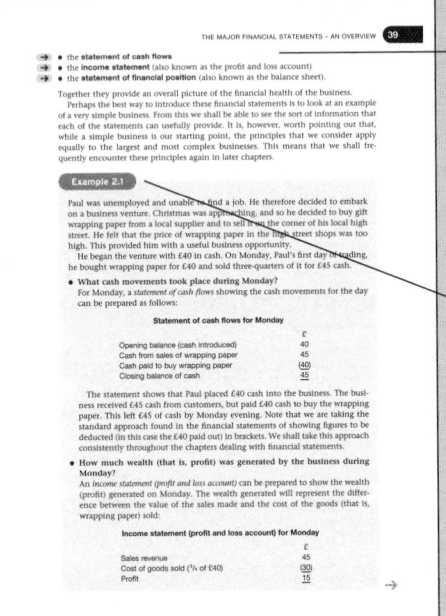

Key terms The key concepts and techniques in each chapter are highlighted in colour where they are first introduced, with an adjacent icon in the margin to help you refer back to them.

Examples At frequent intervals throughout most chapters, there are numerical examples that give you step-by-step workings to follow through to the solution.

Introductions A brief introduction, detailing the topics covered in the chapter, and also showing how chapters are linked together.

Learning outcomes Bullet points at the start of each chapter show what you can expect to learn from the chapter, and provide a brief checklist of the core issues.

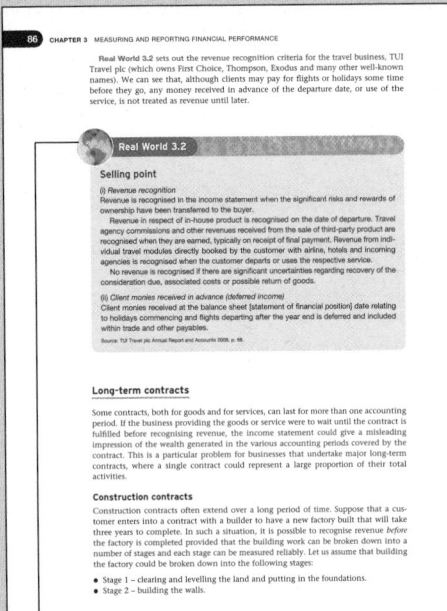

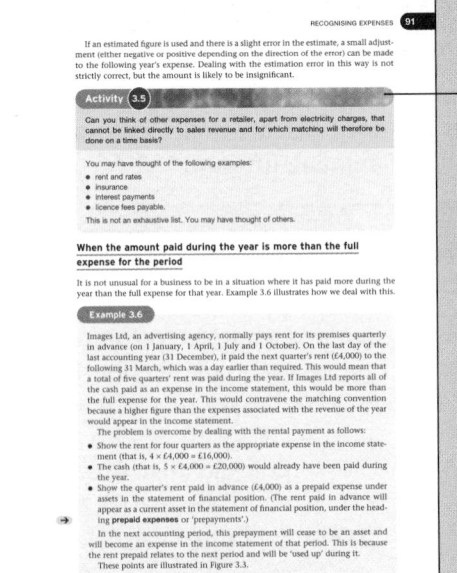

Activities These short questions, integrated throughout each chapter, allow you to check your understanding as you progress through the text. They comprise either a narrative question requiring you to review or critically consider topics, or a numerical problem requiring you to deduce a solution. A suggested answer is given immediately after each activity.

'Real World' illustrations Integrated throughout the text, these illustrative examples highlight the practical application of accounting concepts and techniques by real businesses, including extracts from company reports and financial statements, survey data and other insights from business.

Self-assessment questions Towards the end of most chapters you will encounter one of these questions, allowing you to attempt a comprehensive question before tackling the end-of-chapter assessment material. To check your understanding and progress, solutions are provided in Appendix C.

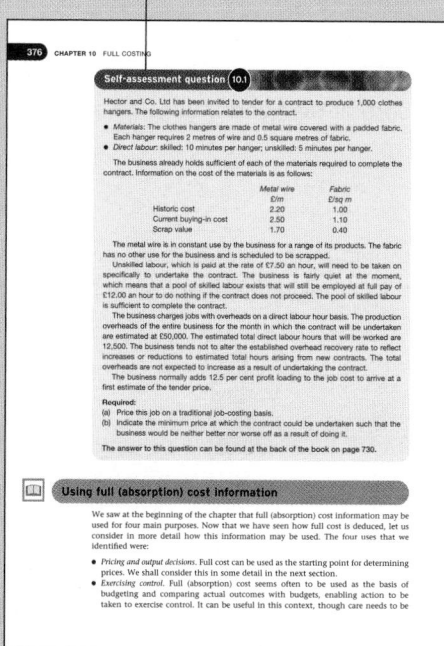

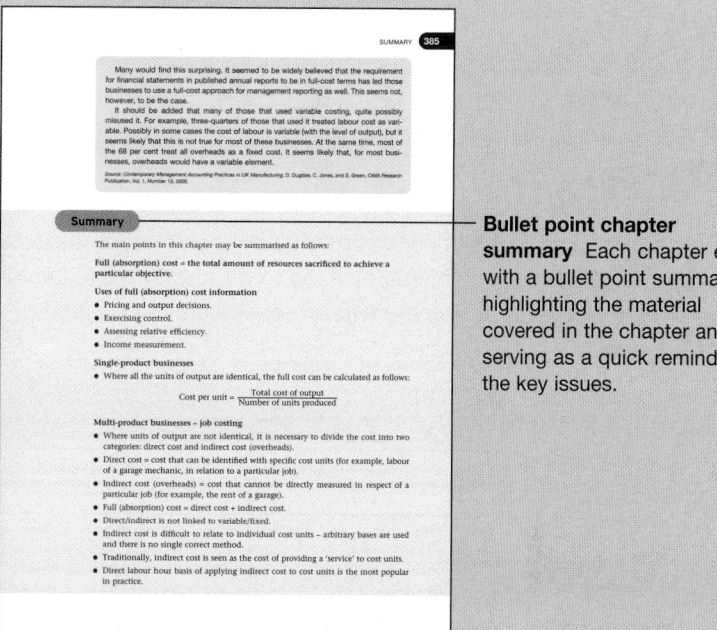

Bullet point chapter summary Each chapter ends with a bullet point summary, highlighting the material covered in the chapter and serving as a quick reminder of the key issues.

Key terms summary At the end of each chapter, there is a list (with page references) of all the key terms introduced in that chapter, allowing you to refer back easily to the essential points.

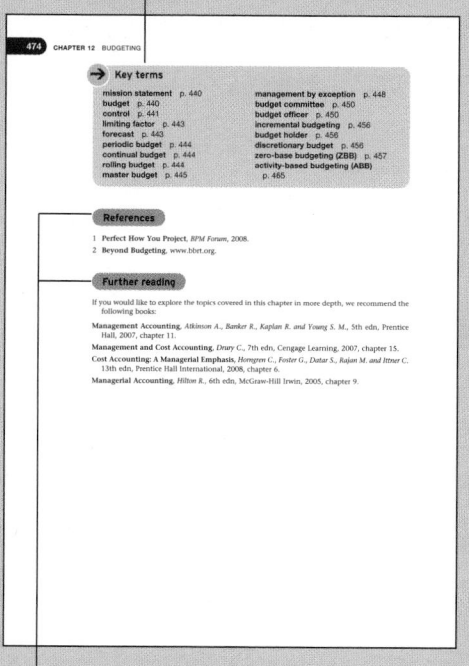

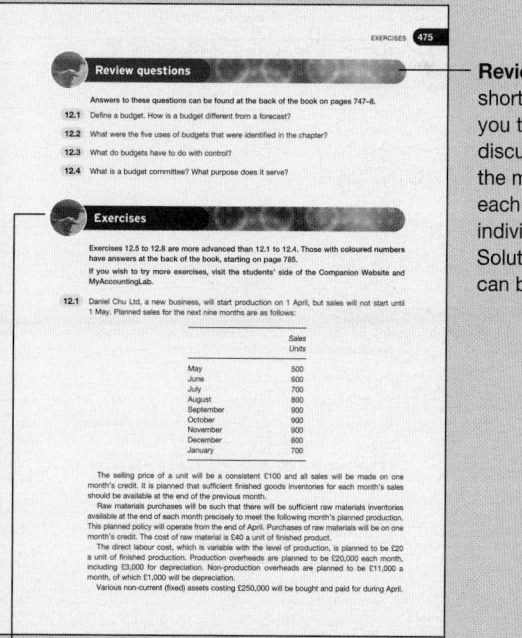

Review questions These short questions encourage you to review and/or critically discuss your understanding of the main topics covered in each chapter, either individually or in a group. Solutions to these questions can be found in Appendix D.

References Full details of the sources of information referred to in the chapter.

Further reading This section provides a list of relevant chapters in other textbooks that you might wish to refer to in order to pursue a topic in more depth or access an alternative perspective.

Exercises There are eight of these comprehensive questions at the end of most chapters. The more advanced questions are separately identified. Solutions to five questions (those with coloured numbers) are provided in Appendix E, enabling you to assess your progress. Solutions to the remaining questions are available for lecturers only. An additional exercise for each chapter can be found on the Companion Website at **www.pearsoned.co.uk/mclaney**.

Guided tour of MyAccountingLab

MyAccountingLab puts students in control of their own learning through a suite of study and practice tools tied to the online e-book and other media tools. At the core of **MyAccountingLab** are the following features:

Practice tests

Practice tests for each section of the textbook enable students to test their understanding and identify the areas in which they need to do further work. Lecturers can customise the practice tests or leave students to use the two pre-built tests per chapter.

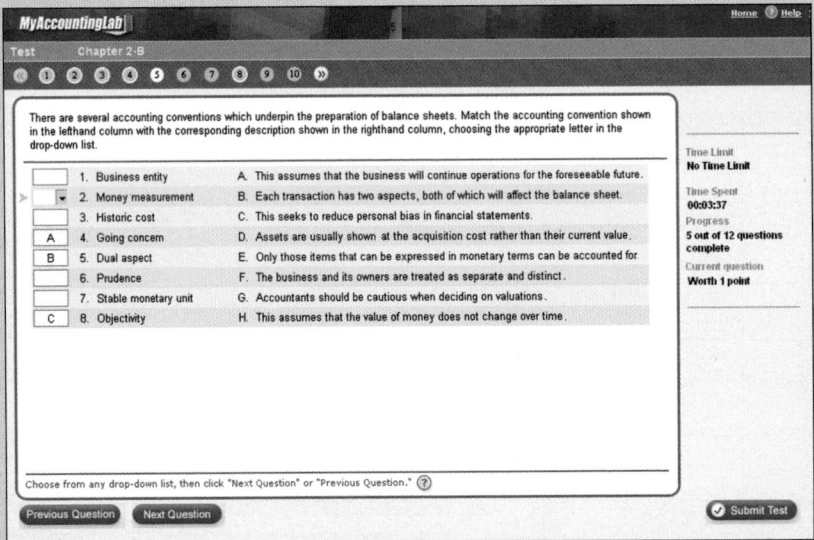

Personalised study plan

Based on a student's performance on a practice test, a personal study plan is generated that shows where further study needs to focus. This study plan consists of a series of additional practice exercises.

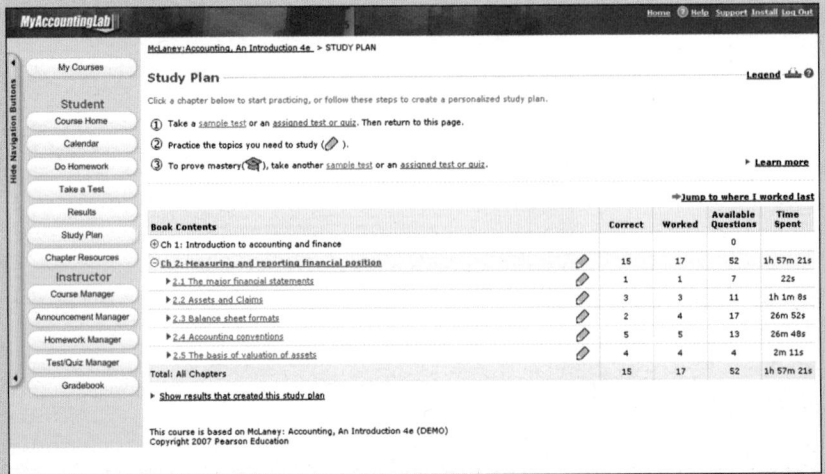

Additional practice exercises

Generated by the student's own performance on a practice test, additional practice exercises are keyed to the textbook and provide extensive practice and link students to the e-book and to other tutorial instruction resources.

Tutorial instruction

Launched from the additional practice exercises, tutorial instruction is provided in the form of solutions to problems, detailed differential feedback, step-by-step explanations, and other media-based explanations, including key concept animations.

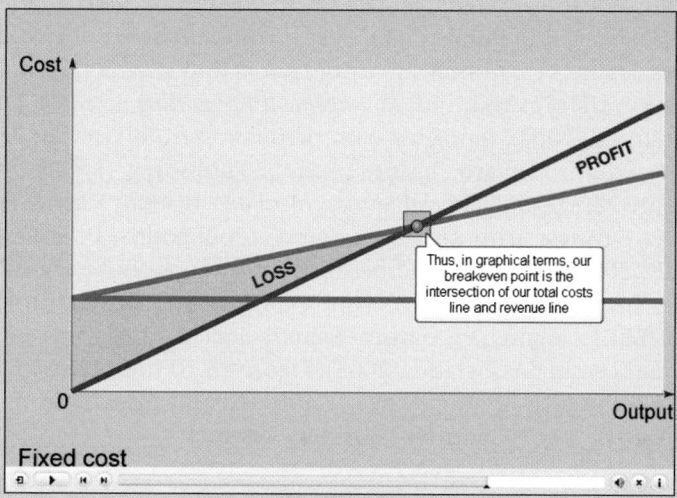

Additional MyAccountingLab tools

1. Interactive study guide
2. Electronic tutorials
3. Glossary – key terms from the textbook
4. Glossary flashcards
5. Links to the most useful accounting data and information sources on the Internet.

Lecturer training and support

We offer lecturers personalised training and support for MyAccountingLab. We have a dedicated team of Technology Specialists whose job it is to support lecturers in their use of our media products, including MyAccountingLab. To make contact with your Technology Specialist please email feedback-cw@pearson.com

For a visual walkthrough of how to make the most of MyAccountingLab, visit www.MyAcountingLab.com

To find details of your local sales representatives go to www.pearsoned.co.uk/replocater

Acknowledgements

We are grateful to the following for permission to reproduce copyright material:

Figures

Figure 5.3 from *Annual Report and Financial Statements* (Tesco Stores Limited 2008) p.4; Figure 7.6 from 'Financial ratios as predictors of failure', *Empirical Research in Accounting: Selected Studies*, a supplement to the *Journal of Accounting Research*, pp.71–111 (Beaver, W.H. 1966), Wiley-Blackwell; Figure 11.1 adapted from *Activity Based Costing: A Review with Case Studies*, CIMA Publishing (Innes, J. and Mitchell, F. 1990), copyright Professor John Innes; Figure 11.2 from A survey of factors influencing the choice of product costing systems in UK organisations, *Management Accounting Research*, December (Al-Omiri, M. and Drury, C. 2007), reprinted with permission from Elsevier; Figure 11.7 from *The Balanced Scorecard*, Harvard Business School Publishing (Kaplan, R. and Norton, D. 1996); Figure 12.7 from *Financial Management and Working Capital Practices in UK SMEs*, Manchester Business School (Chittenden, F., Poutziouris, P. and Michaelas, N. 1998) Fig.16, p.22. Reproduced by kind permission of the authors; Figure 12.8 from Beyond Budgeting, http//:www.bbrt.org/beyond-budgeting/bbmental.html, BBRT, source and copyright BBRT; Figure 15.4 from *Finance and Leasing Association Annual Review* (Finance and Leasing Association 2008); Figure 15.10 from *British Enterprise: Thriving or Surviving?*, University of Cambridge, Centre for Business Research (Cosh, A.D. and Hughes, A. (eds) 2007) Centre for Business Research.

Tables

Page 451 from *A Survey of Management Accounting Practices in UK Manufacturing Companies* (Drury, C., Braund, S., Osborne, P. and Tayles, M. 1993). With permission from Association of Chartered Certified Accountants (ACCA); Page 540 from *Unpacking the Black Box: An Econometric Analysis of Investment Strategies in Real World Firms*, CEPP Working Paper no. 08/05 (Baddeley, M. 2006), p.14. With permission from Cambridge Centre for Economic and Public Policy (CCEPP), p.14; Page 656 from *The Payment League*, Credit Management Research Centre (2008), www.paymentleague.com.

Text

Real World 1.2 from The thoughts of Warren Buffet, *The Times*, 26 September 2002, Business Section, p.25. © The Times 26 September 2002/nisyndication.com; Real World 1.4 from Business big shot, *The Times*, 27 January 2009, p. 39. © The Times 27 January 2009/nisyndication.com; Real World 1.5 from Investor FAQs, http://www.j-sainsbury.co.uk/index.asp?pageid=249, 8 January 2009; Real World 1.8 from We own Royal Bank, http://www.bbc.co.uk/blogs/thereporters/robertpeston/2008/11/we_own_royal_bank.html, Peston, R., 28 November 2008; Real World 2.1 adapted from Balance sheets: the basics, www.businesslink.gov.uk/balancesheets. Reproduced with permission of the copyright holder, Mr Sandeep Sud, Sanco Ltd, Hounslow; Real World 2.2 from Brandz Top 100 Brand Ranking 2009: Millward Brown Optimor 2009, p.2, www.millwardbrown.com; Real World 3.2 from *Annual Report and Accounts*, TUI Travel plc 2008, p.68; Real World 3.6 from JJB massages results to boost profits, *Accountancy Age*, 20 October 2005, p.3, copyright Incisive Media Ltd; Real World 3.7 from *Annual Report and Financial Statements* (J Sainsbury plc 2009) p.49; Real World 3.8 from Findel shares plunge as Yorkshire home shopping firm's bad debts rise *Yorkshire Evening Post*, 17 April 2008 (Scott, N.), www.yorkshireeveningpost.com; Real World 4.5 and 4.6 from *Annual Report and Accounts* (J D Wetherspoon plc 2008) p.28; Real World 4.7 from *Annual Report and Accounts* (J D Wetherspoon plc 2008) p.30; Real World 4.11 from *Annual Report and Accounts* (Rolls-Royce plc 2008) Note 14; Real World 4.12 from Eurotunnel pays first dividend since 1987 float, www.timesonline.co.uk, King, I., 4 March 2009 © The Times 4 March 2009/nisyndication.com; Real World 5.1 from *A Guide Through International Financial Reporting Standards (IFRSs)*, V and VI (IASC Foundation Education 2008), International Accounting Standards Committee Foundation; Real World 5.3 from *Annual Report and Financial Statements* (Tesco Stores Limited 2008) p.3; Real World 5.5 from *Annual Report and Financial Statements* (Tesco Stores Limited 2008) p.12; Real World 5.6 from *Annual Report and Financial Statements* (Tesco Stores Limited 2008) p.13; Real World 5.7 from *Annual Report and Financial Statements* (Tesco Stores Limited 2008) p.6; Real World 5.8 from *Annual Report and Financial Statements* (Tesco Stores Limited 2008) p.17; Real World 5.9 from Dirty laundry: how companies fudge the numbers, *The Times*, 22 September 2002, Business Section, © The Times 22 September 2002/nisyndication.com; Real World 5.12 from The rise and fall of Enron, *Journal of Accountancy*, 194(3) (Thomas, C.W. 2002); Real World 6.3 adapted from *LiDCO Group Plc Annual Report 2009* (LiDCO Group Plc 2009); Real World 7.10 from *Annual Report 2008* (Marks and Spencer plc 2008); Real World 7.11 from *Arnold Weinstock and the Making of GEC*, Aurum Press (Aris, S. 1998); Real World 9.3 from *Annual Report* (J Sainsbury plc 2008) p.4; Real World 10.8 from An empirical investigation of the importance of cost-plus pricing, *Managerial Auditing Journal*, 20(2) (Guilding, C., Drury, C. and Tayles, M. 2005); Real World 11.11 from *Internal control and risk management* (Tesco Stores Limited 2008); Real World 11.12 from *The Balanced Scorecard*, Harvard Business School Publishing (Kaplan, R. and Norton, D. 1996); Real World 12.8 from Transforming financial planning, D. Bunce, www.bbrt.org, BBRT, source and copyright BBRT; Real World 13.2 from *Annual Report* (Next plc 2008) p.24 and *Annual Report* (British Airways plc 2008) p.58; Real World 13.4 and 13.7 from *A Survey of Management Accounting Practices in UK Manufacturing Companies*, Chartered Association of Certified Accountants (Drury, C., Braund, S., Osborne, P., Tayles, M. 1993) (p.39, Table 5.7 for Real World 13.4); Real World 14.12 from *Annual Report* (Rolls-Royce plc 2008) p.59; Real World 14.16 from 2008 Corporate Governance Report, www.tescocorporate.com, Tesco Stores Limited, and 2007/8 Financial Review, www.kingfisher.co.uk; Real World 15.13 from Internet FD is in the money after flotation, *Accountancy Age*, 2 August 2007, p.3 (Jetuah, D.), copyright Incisive Media Ltd; Real World 16.10 from 13 August 2008, www.atradius.us/news/press-releases; Real World 16.12 and 16.14 from Dash for cash, *CFO Europe Magazine* (Karaian, J.), 8 July 2008, www.CFO.com. Reprinted with permission from CFO, July 2008. Visit our website at www.cfo.com. © CFO Publishing Corporation. All Rights Reserved. Foster Printing Service: 866-879-9144, www.marketingreprints.com. License #CFO-6053-JKK.

The Financial Times
Real World 1.1 from Morrison in uphill battle to integrate Safeway, *Financial Times*, Rigby, E., 27 May 2005; Real World 1.3 from Ask the Expert: Tesco's Sir Terry Leahy, *Financial Times*, 2 June 2006; Real World 1.6 from Fair shares?, FT.com, Skapinker, M., 11 June 2005; Real World 1.7 from Profit without honour, *Financial Times*, Kay, J.,

29/30 June 2002; Real World 2.5 from Akzo Nobel defends ICI takeover, Ft.com, Steen, M., 24 February 2009; Real World 4.1 from Monotub Industries in a spin as founder gets Titan for £1, *Financial Times/FT.com*, Urquhart, L., 23 January 2003; Real World 5.2 from Transfer pricing abuses criticised, FT.com, Politi, J., 13 August 2008; Real World 5.10 from Dell to lower writedowns on restated earnings, *Financial Times*, Allison, K., 30 October 2007; Real World 6.1 from Rations cut for army of buyers, FT.com, Mitchell, T. and Lau, J., 20 October 2008; Real World 7.4 from Investing in Bollywood, *Financial Times*, 25 June 2007, Lex Column; Real World 7.5 from Payment squeeze on suppliers, *Financial Times*, Grant, J., 22 December 2008; Real World 7.6 from Gearing levels set to plummet, *Financial Times*, Grant, J., 10 February 2009; Real World 11.8 from It is all about the value chain, FT.com, Bickerton, I., 23 February 2006; Real World 11.9 from Royal following but quality issues remain, FT.com, Reed, J., 3 October 2007; Real World 11.13 from When misuse leads to failure, FT.com, 24 May 2006; Real World 13.1 adapted from Watchdog warns on Olympic costs, FT.com, Eaglesham, J. 20 July 2007; Real World 14.6 adapted from Bond seeks funds in London to mine African diamonds, FT.com, Bream, R., 22 April 2007; Real World 14.7 from A hot topic, but poor returns, FT.com, Batchelor, C., 27 August 2005; Real World 14.11 from Satellites need space to earn, FT.com, Burt, T. 14 July 2003; Real World 14.13 from Easy ride, FT.com, Hughes, C. 26 October 2007; Real World 15.2 from BSkyB to raise $600m in bond issue, FT.com, Davoudi, S., 21 November 2008; Real World 15.5 from Wolesley shares plunge as net debt increases, *Financial Times*, 27 January 2009 (Cookson, R. and Fickling, D.); Real World 15.8 from Seeds of Woolworths' demise sown long ago, *Financial Times*, Rigby, E., 29 November 2008; Real World 15.14 from Greed and gullibility keep new issues afloat, *Financial Times*, 8 August 2003, p.22; Real World 16.4 from Wal-Mart aims for further inventory cuts, FT.com, Birchall, J., 19 April 2006; Real World 16.13 from NHS paying bills late in struggle to balance books, say suppliers, FT.com, Timmins, N. 13 February 2007.

In some instances we have been unable to trace the owners of copyright material, and we would appreciate any information that would enable us to do so.

CHAPTER 1

Introduction to accounting and finance

Introduction

In this opening chapter we begin by considering the roles of accounting and finance. As we shall see, both can be valuable tools for decision making. We shall identify the main users of accounting and financial information and discuss the ways in which this information can improve the quality of decisions that those users make. In subsequent chapters, we develop this decision-making theme by considering in some detail the kinds of financial reports and methods used to aid decision making.

Since this book is concerned with accounting and financial decision making for private-sector businesses, we shall devote some time to examining the business environment. We shall, therefore, consider the purpose of a private sector business, the main forms of business enterprise and the ways in which a business may be structured. We shall also consider what the key financial objective of a business is likely to be. These are all important as they help to shape the kind of accounting and financial information that is produced.

Learning outcomes

When you have completed this chapter, you should be able to:

● Explain the nature and roles of accounting and finance.

● Identify the main users of financial information and discuss their needs.

● Identify and discuss the characteristics that make accounting information useful.

● Explain the purpose of a business and describe how businesses are organised and structured.

 *Remember to create your own personalised Study Plan*

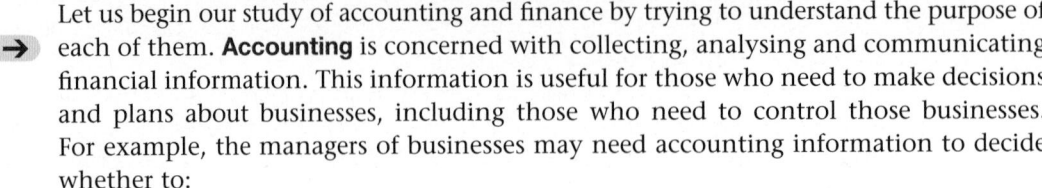

What are accounting and finance?

 Let us begin our study of accounting and finance by trying to understand the purpose of each of them. **Accounting** is concerned with collecting, analysing and communicating financial information. This information is useful for those who need to make decisions and plans about businesses, including those who need to control those businesses. For example, the managers of businesses may need accounting information to decide whether to:

- develop new products or services (such as a computer manufacturer developing a new range of computers);
- increase or decrease the price or quantity of existing products or services (such as a telecommunications business changing its mobile phone call and text charges);
- borrow money to help finance the business (such as a supermarket wishing to increase the number of stores it owns);
- increase or decrease the operating capacity of the business (such as a beef farming business reviewing the size of its herd); and
- change the methods of purchasing, production or distribution (such as a clothes retailer switching from UK to overseas suppliers).

The information provided should help in identifying and assessing the financial consequences of such decisions.

Though managers working within a business are likely to be significant users of accounting information about that particular business, they are by no means the only users. There are those outside the business (whom we shall identify later) who may need information to decide whether to:

- invest or disinvest in the ownership of the business (for example, buy or sell shares);
- lend money to the business;
- offer credit facilities (for example, a bank to grant an overdraft); and
- enter into contracts for the purchase of products or services.

Sometimes the impression is given that the purpose of accounting is simply to prepare financial reports on a regular basis. While it is true that accountants undertake this kind of work, the preparation of financial reports does not represent an end in itself. The ultimate purpose of the accountant's work is to give people better information on which to base their decisions. This decision-making perspective of accounting dictates the theme of this book and shapes the way in which we deal with each topic.

Finance (or **financial management**), like accounting, exists to help decision makers. It is concerned with the ways in which funds for a business are raised and invested. This lies at the very heart of what a business is about. In essence, a business exists to raise funds from investors (owners and lenders) and then to use those funds to make investments (equipment, premises, inventories and so on) in an attempt to make the business, and its owners, wealthier. It is important that funds are raised in a way that is appropriate to the particular needs of the business and an understanding of finance should help in identifying:

- the main forms of finance available;
- the costs and benefits of each form of finance;
- the risks associated with each form of finance; and
- the role of financial markets in supplying finance.

Once the funds are raised, they must be invested in ways that will provide the business with a worthwhile return. An understanding of finance should help in evaluating:

- the returns from an investment; and
- the risks associated with an investment.

Businesses often raise and invest funds in large amounts for long periods of time. The quality of the financing and investment decisions made can, therefore, have a profound impact on the fortunes of the business.

In this book, we shall not emphasise the distinctions between accounting and finance as there is little point in doing so. We have already seen that both are concerned with the financial aspects of decision making and there are many inter-connections. For example, accounting reports are a major source of information for financing and investment decision making.

Who are the users of accounting information?

For accounting information to be useful, the accountant must be clear *for whom* the information is being prepared and *for what purpose* the information will be used. There are likely to be various groups of people (known as 'user groups') with an interest in a particular organisation, in the sense of needing to make decisions about it. For the typical private sector business, the more important of these groups are shown in Figure 1.1. Take a look at this figure and then try Activity 1.1.

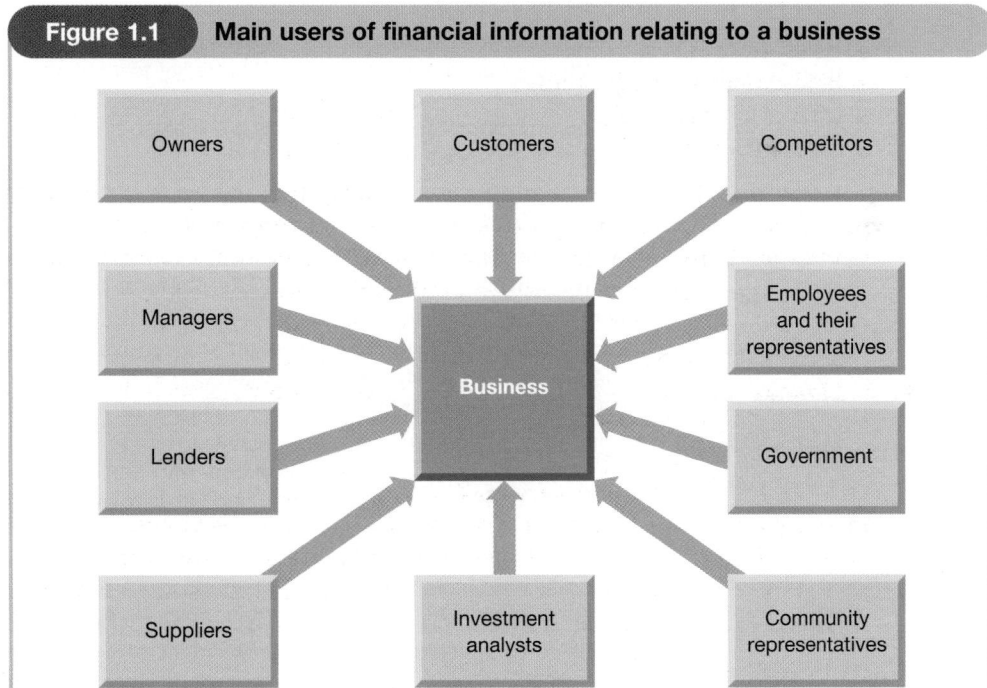

Figure 1.1 Main users of financial information relating to a business

Several user groups have an interest in accounting information relating to a business. The majority of these are outside the business but, nevertheless, have a stake in it. This is not meant to be an exhaustive list of potential users; however, the groups identified are normally the most important.

Activity (1.1)

Ptarmigan Insurance plc (PI) is a large motor insurance business. Taking the user groups identified above, suggest, for each group, the sorts of decisions likely to be made about PI and the factors to be taken into account when making these decisions.

Your answer may be along the following lines:

User group	Decision
Customers	Whether to take further motor policies with PI. This might involve an assessment of PI's ability to continue in business and to meet their needs, particularly in respect of any insurance claims made.
Competitors	How best to compete against PI or, perhaps, whether to leave the market on the grounds that it is not possible to compete profitably with PI. This might involve competitors using PI's performance in various aspects as a 'benchmark' when evaluating their own performance. They might also try to assess PI's financial strength and to identify significant changes that may signal PI's future actions (for example, raising funds as a prelude to market expansion).
Employees	Whether to continue working for PI and, if so, whether to demand higher rewards for doing so. The future plans, profits and financial strength of the business are likely to be of particular interest when making these decisions.
Government	Whether PI should pay tax and, if so, how much, whether it complies with agreed pricing policies, whether financial support is needed and so on. In making these decisions an assessment of its profits, sales revenues and financial strength would be made.
Community representatives	Whether to allow PI to expand its premises and/or whether to provide economic support for the business. PI's ability to continue to provide employment for the community, to use community resources and to help fund environmental improvements are likely to be considered when arriving at such decisions.
Investment analysts	Whether to advise clients to invest in PI. This would involve an assessment of the likely risks and future returns associated with PI.
Suppliers	Whether to continue to supply PI and, if so, whether to supply on credit. This would involve an assessment of PI's ability to pay for any goods and services supplied.
Lenders	Whether to lend money to PI and/or whether to require repayment of any existing loans. PI's ability to pay the interest and to repay the principal sum would be important factors in such decisions.
Managers	Whether the performance of the business needs to be improved. Performance to date would be compared with earlier plans or some other 'benchmark' to decide whether action needs to be taken. Managers may also wish to decide whether there should be a change in PI's future direction. This would involve looking at PI's ability to perform and at the opportunities available to it.
Owners	Whether to invest more in PI or to sell all, or part, of the investment currently held. This would involve an assessment of the likely risks and returns associated with PI. Owners may also be involved with decisions on rewarding senior managers. The financial performance of the business would normally be considered when making such a decision.

Although this answer covers many of the key points, you may have identified other decisions and/or other factors to be taken into account by each group.

The conflicting interests of users

We have seen above that each user group looks at a business from a different perspective and has its own particular interests. This means that there is always the risk that the interests of one group will collide with those of another group. Conflict between user groups is most likely to occur over the way in which the wealth of the business is generated and/or distributed. A good example is the conflict that may arise between the managers and the owners of the business. Although managers are appointed to act in the best interests of the owners, there is always a danger that they will not do so. Instead, managers may use the wealth of the business to award themselves large pay rises, to furnish large offices or to buy expensive cars for their own use. Accounting information has an important role to play in reporting the extent to which various groups have benefited from the business. Thus, owners may rely on accounting information to check whether the pay and benefits of managers are in line with agreed policy.

A further example is the potential conflict of interest between lenders and owners. There is a risk that the funds loaned to a business will not be used for purposes that have been agreed. Lenders may, therefore, rely on accounting information to check that the funds have been applied in an appropriate manner and that the terms of the loan agreement are not being broken.

Activity 1.2

Can you think of other examples where accounting information may be used to monitor potential conflicts of interest between the various user groups identified?

Two possible examples that spring to mind are:

- Employees (or their representatives) wishing to check that they are receiving a 'fair share' of the wealth created by the business and that agreed profit-sharing schemes are being adhered to.
- Government wishing to check that the profits made from a contract that it has given to a business are not excessive.

You may have thought of other examples.

How useful is accounting information?

No one would seriously claim that accounting information fully meets all of the needs of each of the various user groups. Accounting is still a developing subject and we still have much to learn about user needs and the ways in which these needs should be met. Nevertheless, the information contained in accounting reports should help users make decisions relating to the business. The information should reduce uncertainty about the financial position and performance of the business. It should help to answer questions concerning the availability of funds to pay owners a return, to repay loans, to reward employees and so on.

Typically, there is no close substitute for the information provided by the financial statements. Thus, if users cannot glean the required information from the financial statements, it is often unavailable to them. Other sources of information concerning the financial health of a business are normally much less useful.

Activity 1.3

What other sources of information might, say, an investment analayst use in an attempt to gain an impression of the financial position and performance of a business? What kind of information might be gleaned from these sources?

Other sources of information available include:

- meetings with managers of the business
- public announcements made by the business
- newspaper and magazine articles
- websites, including the website of the business
- radio and TV reports
- information-gathering agencies (for example, agencies that assess businesses' credit-worthiness or credit ratings)
- industry reports
- economy-wide reports.

These sources can provide information on various aspects of the business, such as new products or services being offered, management changes, new contracts offered or awarded, the competitive environment within which the business operates, the impact of new technology, changes in legislation, changes in interest rates and future levels of inflation. However, the various sources of information identified are not really substitutes for accounting reports. Rather, they are best used in conjunction with the reports in order to obtain a clearer picture of the financial health of a business.

Evidence on the usefulness of accounting

There are arguments and convincing evidence that accounting information is at least *perceived* as being useful to users. Numerous research surveys have asked users to rank the importance of accounting information, in relation to other sources of information, for decision-making purposes. Generally, these studies have found that users rank accounting information very highly. There is also considerable evidence that businesses choose to produce accounting information that exceeds the minimum requirements imposed by accounting regulations. (For example, businesses often produce a considerable amount of accounting information for managers, which is not required by any regulations.) Presumably, the cost of producing this additional accounting information is justified on the grounds that users find it useful. Such arguments and evidence, however, leave unanswered the question of whether the information produced is actually used for decision-making purposes, that is: does it affect people's behaviour?

It is normally very difficult to assess the impact of accounting on decision making. One situation arises, however, where the impact of accounting information can be observed and measured. This is where the **shares** (portions of ownership of a business) are traded on a stock exchange. The evidence reveals that, when a business makes an announcement concerning its accounting profits, the prices at which shares are traded and the volume of shares traded often change significantly. This suggests that investors are changing their views about the future prospects of the business as a result of this new information becoming available to them and that this, in turn, leads them to make a decision either to buy or to sell shares in the business.

Although there is evidence that accounting reports are perceived as being useful and are used for decision-making purposes, it is impossible to measure just how useful accounting reports are to users. As a result we cannot say with certainty whether the cost of producing those reports represents value for money. Accounting information will usually represent only one input to a particular decision and so the precise weight attached to the accounting information by the decision maker and the benefits which flow as a result cannot be accurately assessed. We shall now go on to see, however, that it is at least possible to identify the kinds of qualities which accounting information must possess in order to be useful. Where these qualities are lacking, the usefulness of the information will be diminished.

Providing a service

One way of viewing accounting is as a form of service. Accountants provide economic information to their 'clients', who are the various users identified in Figure 1.1. The quality of the service provided is determined by the extent to which the needs of the various user groups have been met. To meet these users' needs, it can be argued that accounting information should possess certain key qualities, or characteristics: relevance, reliability, comparability and understandability.

→ • **Relevance**. Accounting information must have the ability to influence decisions. Unless this characteristic is present, there is really no point in producing the information. The information may be relevant to the prediction of future events (for example, in predicting how much profit is likely to be earned next year) or relevant in helping to confirm past events (for example, in establishing how much profit was earned last year). The role of accounting in confirming past events is important because users often wish to check the accuracy of earlier predictions that they have made. The accuracy (or inaccuracy) of earlier predictions may help users to judge the accuracy of current predictions. To influence a decision, the information must, of course, be available when the decision is being made. Thus, relevant information must be timely.

→ • **Reliability**. Accounting should be free from significant error or bias. It should be capable of being relied upon by managers to represent what it is supposed to represent. Though both relevance and reliability are very important, the problem that we often face in accounting is that information that is highly relevant may not be very reliable, and that which is reliable may not be very relevant.

Activity 1.4

To illustrate this last point, let us assume that a manager has to sell a custom-built machine owned by the business and has recently received a bid for it. This machine is very unusual and there is no ready market for it.

What information would be relevant to the manager when deciding whether to accept the bid? How reliable would that information be?

→

> **Activity 1.4 continued**
>
> The manager would probably like to know the current market value of the machine before deciding whether or not to accept the bid. The current market value would be highly relevant to the final decision, but it might not be very reliable because the machine is unique and there is likely to be little information concerning market values.
>
> When seeking to strike the right balance between relevance and reliability, the needs of users should be the overriding consideration.

→ ● **Comparability**. This quality will enable users to identify changes in the business over time (for example, the trend in sales revenue over the past five years). It will also help them to evaluate the performance of the business in relation to similar businesses. Comparability is achieved by treating items that are basically the same in the same manner for accounting purposes. Comparability may also be enhanced by making clear the policies that have been adopted in measuring and presenting the information.

→ ● **Understandability**. Accounting reports should be expressed as clearly as possible and should be understood by those at whom the information is aimed.

> **Activity 1.5**
>
> Do you think that accounting reports should be understandable to those who have not studied accounting?
>
> It would be very useful if accounting reports could be understood by everyone. This, however, is unrealistic as complex financial events and transactions cannot normally be expressed in simple terms. It is probably best that we regard accounting reports in the same way that we regard a report written in a foreign language. To understand either of these, we need to have had some preparation. Generally speaking, accounting reports assume that the user not only has a reasonable knowledge of business and accounting but is also prepared to invest some time in studying the reports.

Despite the answer to Activity 1.5, the onus is clearly on accountants to provide information in a way that makes it as understandable as possible to non-accountants.

But . . . is it material?

The qualities, or characteristics, that have just been described will help us to decide whether accounting information is potentially useful. If a particular piece of information has these qualities then it may be useful. However, this does not automatically mean that it should be reported to users. We also have to consider whether the information is material, or significant. This means that we should ask whether its omission or misrepresentation in the accounting reports would really alter the decisions that users make. Thus, in addition to possessing the characteristics mentioned above, → accounting information must also cross the threshold of **materiality**. If the information is not regarded as material, it should not be included within the reports as it will merely clutter them up and, perhaps, interfere with the users' ability to interpret the financial results. The type of information and amounts involved will normally determine whether it is material.

Weighing up the costs and benefits

Having read the previous sections you may feel that, when considering a piece of accounting information, provided the four main qualities identified are present and it is material it should be gathered and made available to users. Unfortunately, there is one more hurdle to jump. Something may still exclude a piece of accounting information from the reports even when it is considered to be useful. Consider Activity 1.6.

Activity 1.6

Suppose an item of information is capable of being provided. It is relevant to a particular decision, it is also reliable, comparable, can be understood by the decision maker concerned and is material.

Can you think of a reason why, in practice, you might choose not to produce the information?

The reason that you may decide not to produce, or discover, the information is that you judge the cost of doing so to be greater than the potential benefit of having the information. This cost–benefit issue will limit the extent to which accounting information is provided.

In theory, a particular item of accounting information should only be produced if the costs of providing it are less than the benefits, or value, to be derived from its use. Figure 1.2 shows the relationship between the costs and value of providing additional accounting information.

The figure shows how the value of information received by the decision maker eventually begins to decline. This is, perhaps, because additional information becomes less relevant, or because of the problems that a decision maker may have in processing the sheer quantity of information provided. The costs of providing the information, however, will increase with each additional piece of information. The broken line indicates the point at which the gap between the value of information and the cost of providing that information is at its greatest. This represents the optimal amount of information that can be provided. This theoretical model, however, poses a number of problems in practice. We shall now go on to discuss these.

To illustrate the practical problems of establishing the value of information, let us assume that someone has collided with our car in a car park and dented and scraped the paint from one of the doors. We wish to have the dent taken out and the door resprayed at a local garage. We know that the nearest garage would charge £250 but believe that other local garages may offer to do the job for a lower price. The only way of finding out the prices at other garages is to visit them, so that they can see the extent of the damage. Visiting the garages will involve using some petrol and will take up some of our time. Is it worth the cost of finding out the price for the job at the various local garages? The answer, as we have seen, is that if the cost of discovering the price is less than the potential benefit, it is worth having that information.

Figure 1.2	Relationship between costs and the value of providing additional accounting information

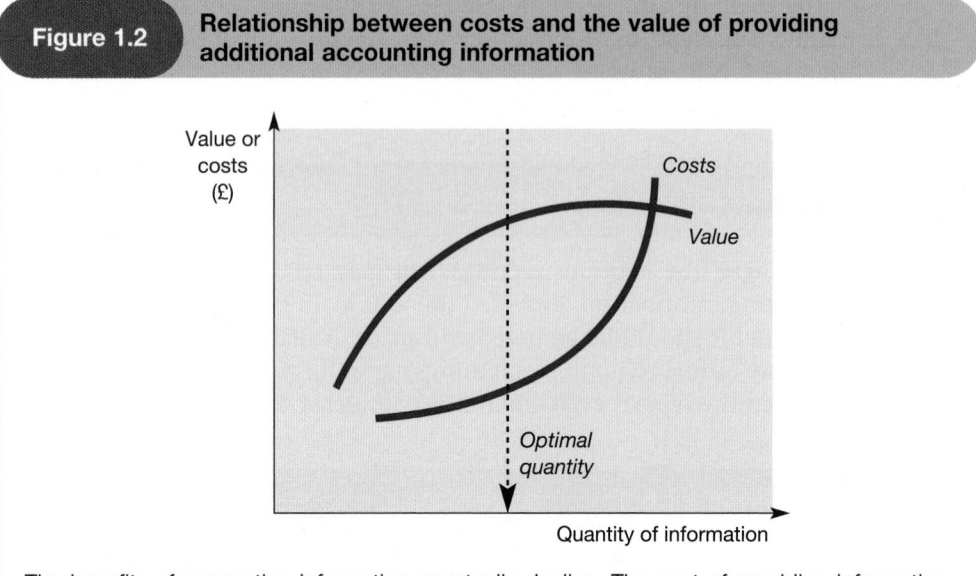

The benefits of accounting information eventually decline. The cost of providing information, however, will rise with each additional piece of information. The optimal level of information provision is where the gap between the value of the information and the cost of providing it is at its greatest.

To identify the various prices for the job, there are several points to be considered, including:

● How many garages shall we visit?
● What is the cost of petrol to visit each garage?
● How long will it take to make all the garage visits?
● At what price do we value our time?

The economic benefit of having the information on the price of the service is probably even harder to assess. The following points need to be considered:

● What is the cheapest price that we might be quoted for the job?
● How likely is it that we shall be quoted a price cheaper than £250?

As we can imagine, the answers to these questions may be far from clear – remember that we have only contacted the local garage so far. When assessing the value of accounting information we are confronted with similar problems.

The provision of accounting information can be very costly; however, the costs are often difficult to quantify. The direct, out-of-pocket, costs such as salaries of accounting staff are not really a problem to identify, but these are only part of the total costs involved. There are also less direct costs such as the cost of the user's time spent on analysing and interpreting the information contained in reports.

The economic benefit of having accounting information is even harder to assess. It is possible to apply some 'science' to the problem of weighing the costs and benefits, but a lot of subjective judgement is likely to be involved. No one would seriously advocate that the typical business should produce no accounting information. At the same time, no one would advocate that every item of information that could be seen as possessing one or more of the key characteristics should be produced, irrespective of the cost of producing it.

The characteristics that influence the usefulness of accounting information and which have been discussed in this section and the preceding section are set out in Figure 1.3.

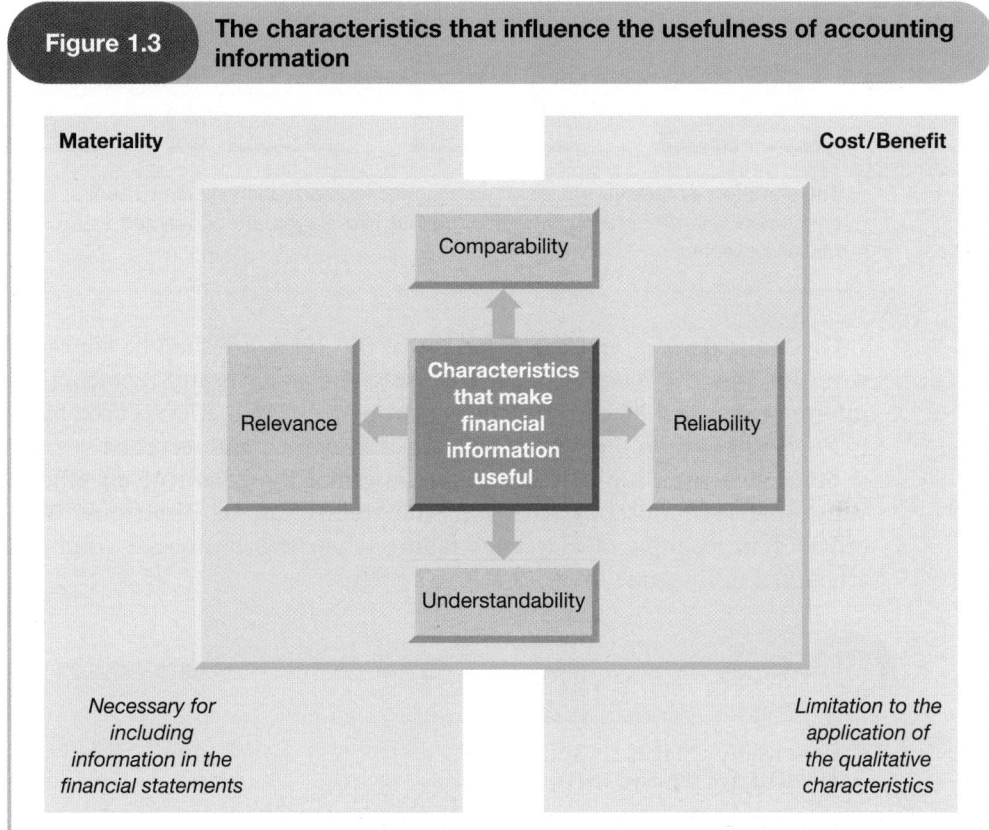

| Figure 1.3 | The characteristics that influence the usefulness of accounting information |

There are four main qualitative characteristics that influence the usefulness of accounting information. In addition, however, accounting information should be material and the benefits of providing the information should outweigh the costs.

Accounting as an information system

We have already seen that accounting can be seen as the provision of a service to 'clients'. Another way of viewing accounting is as a part of the business's total information system. Users, both inside and outside the business, have to make decisions concerning the allocation of scarce economic resources. To ensure that these resources are efficiently allocated, users need economic information on which to base decisions. It is the role of the accounting system to provide that information and this will involve information gathering and communication.

 The **accounting information system** should have certain features that are common to all valid information systems within a business. These are:

● identifying and capturing relevant information (in this case financial information);
● recording the information collected in a systematic manner;
● analysing and interpreting the information collected;
● reporting the information in a manner that suits the needs of users.

The relationship between these features is set out in Figure 1.4.

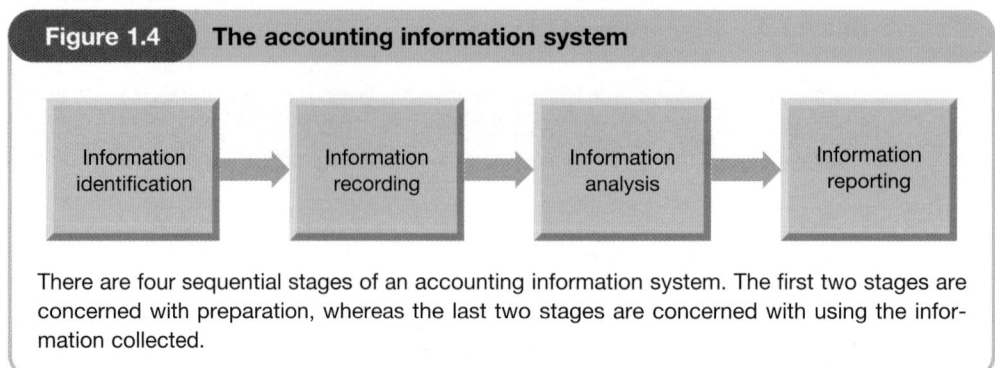

Figure 1.4 **The accounting information system**

Information identification → Information recording → Information analysis → Information reporting

There are four sequential stages of an accounting information system. The first two stages are concerned with preparation, whereas the last two stages are concerned with using the information collected.

Given the decision-making emphasis of this book, we shall be concerned primarily with the final two elements of the process: the analysis and reporting of accounting information. We shall consider the way in which information is used by, and is useful to, users rather than the way in which it is identified and recorded.

Efficient accounting systems are an essential ingredient of an efficient business. When the accounting systems fail, the results can be disastrous. **Real World 1.1** provides an example of a systems failure when two businesses combined and then attempted to integrate their respective systems.

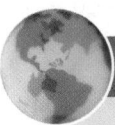

Real World 1.1

Blaming the system

FT

When Sir Ken Morrison bought Safeway for £3.35bn in March 2004, he almost doubled the size of his supermarket chain overnight and went from being a regional operator to a national force. His plan was simple enough. He had to sell off some Safeway stores – Morrison has to date sold off 184 stores for an estimated £1.3bn – and convert the remaining 230 Safeway stores into Morrison's. Sir Ken has about another 50 to sell. But, nearly 15 months on, and the integration process is proving harder in practice than it looked on paper. Morrison, once known for its robust performance, has issued four profit warnings in the past 10 months. Each time the retailer has blamed Safeway. Last July, it was because of a faster-than-expected sales decline in Safeway stores. In March – there were two warnings that month – it was the fault of Safeway's accounting systems, which left Morrison with lower supplier incomes. This month's warning was put down to higher-than-expected costs from running parallel store systems. At the time of the first warning last July, Simon Procter, of the stockbrokers Charles Stanley, noted that the news 'has blown all profit forecasts out of the water and visibility is very poor from here on out'. But if it was difficult then to predict where Morrison's profits were heading, it is impossible now. Morrison itself cannot give guidance. 'No one envisaged this,' says Mr Procter. 'When I made that comment about visibility last July, I was thinking on a 12-month time frame, not a two-year one.' Morrison says the complexity of the Safeway deal has put a 'significant strain' on its ability to cope with managing internal accounts. 'This is impacting the ability of the board to forecast likely trends in profitability and the directors are therefore not currently in a position to provide reliable guidance on the level of profitability as a whole,' admits the retailer.

Source: 'Morrison in uphill battle to integrate Safeway', Elizabeth Rigby, *Financial Times*, 27 May 2005.

As a footnote to Real World 1.1, though Morrisons had its problems, these were quickly overcome and the Safeway takeover has proved to be a success.

Management and financial accounting

Accounting is usually seen as having two distinct strands. These are:

→ • **Management accounting**, which seeks to meet the accounting needs of managers; and
→ • **Financial accounting**, which seeks to meet those of all of the other users identified earlier in the chapter (see Figure 1.1).

The difference in their targeted user groups has led to each strand of accounting developing along different lines. The main areas of difference are as follows.

- *Nature of the reports produced.* Financial accounting reports tend to be general purpose, that is, they contain financial information that will be useful for a broad range of users and decisions rather than being specifically designed for the needs of a particular group or set of decisions. Management accounting reports, on the other hand, are often specific-purpose reports. They are designed with a particular decision in mind and/or for a particular manager.
- *Level of detail.* Financial accounting reports provide users with a broad overview of the performance and position of the business for a period. As a result, information is aggregated and detail is often lost. Management accounting reports, however, often provide managers with considerable detail to help them with a particular operational decision.
- *Regulations.* Financial accounting reports, for many businesses, are subject to accounting regulations that try to ensure they are produced with standard content and in a standard format. The law and accounting rule makers impose these regulations. As management accounting reports are for internal use only, there are no regulations from external sources concerning the form and content of the reports. They can be designed to meet the needs of particular managers.
- *Reporting interval.* For most businesses, financial accounting reports are produced on an annual basis, though some large businesses produce half-yearly reports, and a few produce quarterly ones. Management accounting reports may be produced as frequently as required by managers. In many businesses, managers are provided with certain reports on a daily, weekly or monthly basis, which allows them to check progress frequently. In addition, special-purpose reports will be prepared when required (for example, to evaluate a proposal to purchase a piece of equipment).
- *Time orientation.* Financial accounting reports reflect the performance and position of the business for the past period. In essence, they are backward looking. Management accounting reports, on the other hand, often provide information concerning future performance as well as past performance. It is an oversimplification, however, to suggest that financial accounting reports never incorporate expectations concerning the future. Occasionally, businesses will release projected information to other users in an attempt to raise capital or to fight off unwanted takeover bids. Even preparation of the routine financial accounting reports typically requires making some judgements about the future, as we shall see in Chapter 3.
- *Range and quality of information.* Financial accounting reports concentrate on information that can be quantified in monetary terms. Management accounting also

produces such reports, but is also more likely to produce reports that contain information of a non-financial nature, such as physical volume of inventories, number of sales orders received, number of new products launched, physical output per employee and so on. Financial accounting places greater emphasis on the use of objective, verifiable evidence when preparing reports. Management accounting reports may use information that is less objective and verifiable, but nevertheless provide managers with the information they need.

We can see from this that management accounting is less constrained than financial accounting. It may draw from a variety of sources and use information that has varying degrees of reliability. The only real test to be applied when assessing the value of the information produced for managers is whether or not it improves the quality of the decisions made.

The distinction between management and financial accounting suggests that there are differences between the information needs of managers and those of other users. While differences undoubtedly exist, there is also a good deal of overlap between these needs.

Activity 1.7

Can you think of any areas of overlap between the information needs of managers and those of other users?

We thought of two points:

● Managers will, at times, be interested in receiving an historical overview of business operations of the sort provided to other users.
● Other users would be interested in receiving information relating to the future, such as the planned level of profits and non-financial information such as the state of the sales order book and the extent of product innovations.

The distinction between the two areas of accounting reflects, to some extent, the differences in access to financial information. Managers have much more control over the form and content of information they receive. Other users have to rely on what managers are prepared to provide or what the financial reporting regulations require to be provided. Though the scope of financial accounting reports has increased over time, fears concerning loss of competitive advantage and user ignorance concerning the reliability of forecast data have led businesses to resist providing other users with the same detailed and wide-ranging information available to managers.

In the past, it has been argued that accounting systems are far too geared to meeting the regulatory requirements of financial accounting to be able to provide the information most helpful to managers. This is to say that financial accounting requirements have been the main priority and management accounting has suffered as a result. Recent survey evidence suggests, however, that this argument has lost its force. Modern management accounting systems tend to provide managers with information that is relevant to their needs rather than what is determined by external reporting requirements. Financial reporting cycles, however, retain some influence over management accounting and managers are aware of expectations of external users (see reference 1 at the end of the chapter).

Scope of this book

This book covers both financial accounting and management accounting topics. The next six chapters (Part 1, Chapters 2 to 7) are broadly concerned with financial accounting and the next six (Part 2, Chapters 8 to 13) with management accounting. The final part of the book (Part 3, Chapters 14 to 16) is concerned with the financial management of the business, that is with issues relating to the financing and investing activities of the business. As we have seen, accounting information is usually vitally important for financial management decisions.

Has accounting become too interesting?

In recent years, accounting has become front-page news and has been a major talking point among those connected with the world of business. Unfortunately, the attention that accounting has attracted has been for all the wrong reasons. We have seen that investors rely on financial reports to help to keep an eye both on their investment and on the performance of the managers. What, though, if the managers provide misleading financial reports to investors? Recent revelations suggest that the managers of some large businesses have been doing just this.

Two of the most notorious cases have been those of:

● Enron, an energy-trading business based in Texas, which was accused of entering into complicated financial arrangements in an attempt to obscure losses and to inflate profits; and
● WorldCom, a major long-distance telephone operator in the US, which was accused of reclassifying $3.9 billion of expenses so as to falsely inflate the profit figures that the business reported to its owners (shareholders) and to others.

In the wake of these scandals, there was much closer scrutiny by investment analysts and investors of the financial reports that businesses produce. This led to further businesses, in both the US and Europe, being accused of using dubious accounting practices to bolster profits.

Accounting scandals can have a profound effect on all those connected with the business. The Enron scandal, for example, ultimately led to the collapse of the company, which, in turn, resulted in lost jobs and large financial losses for lenders, suppliers and investors. Confidence in the world of business can be badly shaken by such events and this can pose problems for society as a whole. Not surprisingly, therefore, the relevant authorities tend to be severe on those who perpetrate such scandals. In the US, Bernie Ebbers, the former chief executive of WorldCom, received 25 years in prison for his part in the fraud.

Various reasons have been put forward to explain this spate of scandals. Some may have been caused by the pressures on managers to meet unrealistic expectations of investors for continually rising profits, others by the greed of unscrupulous executives whose pay is linked to financial performance. However, they may all reflect a particular economic environment.

Real World 1.2 gives some comments suggesting that when all appears to be going well with a business, people can be quite gullible and over-trusting.

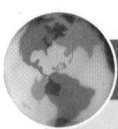

Real World 1.2

The thoughts of Warren Buffett

Warren Buffett is one of the world's shrewdest and most successful investors. He believes that the accounting scandals mentioned above were perpetrated during the 'new economy boom' of the late 1990s when confidence was high and exaggerated predictions were being made concerning the future. He states that during that period:

> You had an erosion of accounting standards. You had an erosion, to some extent, of executive behaviour. But during a period when everybody 'believes', people who are inclined to take advantage of other people can get away with a lot.

He believes that the worst is now over and that the 'dirty laundry' created during this heady period is being washed away and that the washing machine is now in the 'rinse cycle'.

Source: 'The thoughts of Warren Buffett', *The Times*, Business Section, 26 September 2002, p. 25. © The Times 26 September 2002/nisyndication.com.

Whatever the causes, the result of these accounting scandals has been to undermine the credibility of financial statements and to introduce much stricter regulations concerning the quality of financial information. We shall return to this issue in later chapters when we consider the financial statements.

The changing face of accounting

Over the past 25 years, the environment within which businesses operate has become increasingly turbulent and competitive. Various reasons have been identified to explain these changes, including:

● the increasing sophistication of customers;
● the development of a global economy where national frontiers become less important;
● rapid changes in technology;
● the deregulation of domestic markets (for example, electricity, water and gas);
● increasing pressure from owners (shareholders) for competitive economic returns;
● the increasing volatility of financial markets.

This new, more complex, environment has brought new challenges for managers and other users of accounting information. Their needs have changed and both financial accounting and management accounting have had to respond. To meet the changing needs of users there has been a radical review of the kind of information to be reported.

The changing business environment has given added impetus to the search for a clear framework and principles upon which to base financial accounting reports. Various attempts have been made to clarify the purpose of financial accounting reports and to provide a more solid foundation for the development of accounting rules. The frameworks and principles that have been developed try to address fundamental questions such as:

- Who are the users of financial accounting information?
- What kinds of financial accounting reports should be prepared and what should they contain?
- How should items (such as profit and asset values) be measured?

In response to criticisms that the financial reports of some businesses are not clear enough to users, accounting rule makers have tried to improve reporting rules to ensure that the accounting policies of businesses are more comparable and more transparent and that they portray economic reality more faithfully. While this has had a generally beneficial effect, the recent accounting scandals have highlighted the limitations of accounting rules in protecting investors and others.

The internationalisation of businesses has created a need for accounting rules to have an international reach. It can no longer be assumed that users of accounting information relating to a particular business are based in the country in which the business operates or are familiar with the accounting rules of that country. Thus, there has been increasing harmonisation of accounting rules across national frontiers. A more detailed review of these developments is included in Chapter 5.

Management accounting has also changed by becoming more outward looking in its focus. In the past, information provided to managers has been largely restricted to that collected within the business. However, the attitude and behaviour of customers and rival businesses have now become the object of much information gathering. Increasingly, successful businesses are those that are able to secure and maintain competitive advantage over their rivals.

To obtain this advantage, businesses have become more 'customer driven' (that is, concerned with satisfying customer needs). This has led to management accounting information that provides details of customers and the market, such as customer evaluation of services provided and market share. In addition, information about the costs and profits of rival businesses, which can be used as 'benchmarks' by which to gauge competitiveness, is gathered and reported.

To compete successfully, businesses must also find ways of managing costs. The cost base of modern businesses is under continual review and this, in turn, has led to the development of more sophisticated methods of measuring and controlling costs. These changes are considered in more detail in Chapter 11.

Why do I need to know anything about accounting and finance?

At this point you may be asking yourself 'Why do I need to study accounting and finance? I don't intend to become an accountant!' Well, from the explanation of what accounting and finance is about, which has broadly been the subject of this chapter so far, it should be clear that the accounting/finance function within a business is a central part of its management information system. On the basis of information provided by the system, managers make decisions concerning the allocation of resources. These decisions may concern whether to:

- continue with certain business operations;
- invest in particular projects; or
- sell particular products.

Such decisions can have a profound effect on all those connected with the business. It is important, therefore, that *all* those who intend to work in a business should have a fairly clear idea of certain important aspects of accounting and finance. These aspects include:

- how financial reports should be read and interpreted;
- how financial plans are made;
- how investment decisions are made;
- how businesses are financed.

Many, perhaps most, students have a career goal of being a manager within a business – perhaps a personnel manager, production manager, marketing manager or IT manager. If you are one of these students, an understanding of accounting and finance is very important. When you become a manager, even a junior one, it is almost certain that you will have to use financial reports to help you to carry out your management tasks. It is equally certain that it is largely on the basis of financial information and reports that your performance as a manager will be judged.

As part of your management role, it is likely that you will be expected to help in forward planning for the business. This will often involve the preparation of projected financial statements and setting of financial targets. If you do not understand what the financial statements really mean and the extent to which the financial information is reliable, you will find yourself at a distinct disadvantage to others who know their way round the system. Along with other managers, you will also be expected to help decide how the limited resources available to the business should be allocated between competing options. This will require an ability to evaluate the costs and benefits of the different options available. Once again, an understanding of accounting and finance is important to carrying out this management task.

This is not to say that you cannot be an effective and successful personnel, production, marketing or IT manager unless you are also a qualified accountant. It does mean, however, that you need to become a bit 'streetwise' in accounting and finance if you are to succeed. This book should give you that street wisdom.

Accounting for business

We have seen that the needs of the various user groups will determine the kind of accounting information to be provided; however, the forms of business ownership and the ways in which a business may be organised and structured will help to shape those needs. Thus, in the sections that follow, we consider the business environment within which accounting information is produced. A discussion of these topics should help our understanding of points that crop up in later chapters.

What is the purpose of a business?

Peter Drucker, an eminent management thinker, has argued that '*The purpose of business is to create and keep a customer*' (see reference 2 at the end of the chapter). Drucker defined the purpose of a business in this way in 1967, at a time when most businesses did not adopt this strong customer focus. His view therefore represented a radical challenge to the accepted view of what businesses do. More than 40 years on, however, his approach has become part of the conventional wisdom. It is now widely recognised that, in order to succeed, businesses must focus on satisfying the needs of the customer.

Although the customer has always provided the main source of revenue for a business, this has often been taken for granted. In the past, too many businesses have assumed that the customer would readily accept whatever services or products were on offer. When competition was weak and customers were passive, businesses could operate under this assumption and still make a profit. However, the era of weak competition has passed. Nowadays, customers have much greater choice and are much more assertive concerning their needs. They now demand higher quality services and goods at cheaper prices. They also require that services and goods be delivered faster with an increasing emphasis on the product being tailored to their individual needs. If a business cannot meet these needs, a competitor business often can. Thus the business mantra for the current era is '*the customer is king*'; most businesses now recognise this fact and organise themselves accordingly.

Real World 1.3 provides an illustration of how one very successful UK business recognises the supremacy of the customer.

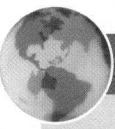

Real World 1.3

Checking out the customers

FT

Tesco plc, the UK supermarket business, has been highly successful at expanding its operations and generating wealth for its owners (the shareholders). In an interview with the *Financial Times*, the business's chief executive (most senior manager) Sir Terry Leahy explained how this profitable expansion is being achieved. He explained:

> The big change for Tesco came when we stopped being a company with a marketing department, and became a marketing company. We put the customer right at the heart of the business and their requirements drove everything we did. It's not too strong to say we became obsessed with customers. Real marketing, that is, understanding people's lives and needs and responding to them with products and services, I believe lies at the heart of business success.

Later in the interview Sir Terry added:

> We never forget customers have a choice of stores, and if we don't satisfy them they will go elsewhere.

Source: 'Ask the Expert: Tesco's Sir Terry Leahy', *Financial Times*, 2 June 2006.

What kinds of business ownership exist?

The particular form of business ownership has important implications for accounting purposes and so it is useful to be clear about the main forms of ownership that can arise.

There are basically three arrangements:

- sole proprietorship
- partnership
- limited company.

Each of these is considered below.

Sole proprietorship

→ **Sole proprietorship**, as the name suggests, is where an individual is the sole owner of a business. This type of business is often quite small in terms of size (as measured, for example, by sales revenue generated or number of staff employed); however, the number of such businesses is very large indeed. Examples of sole-proprietor businesses can be found in most industrial sectors but particularly within the service sector. Hence, services such as electrical repairs, picture framing, photography, driving instruction, retail shops and hotels have a large proportion of sole-proprietor businesses. The sole-proprietor business is easy to set up. No formal procedures are required and operations can often commence immediately (unless special permission is required because of the nature of the trade or service, such as running licensed premises). The owner can decide the way in which the business is to be conducted and has the flexibility to restructure or dissolve the business whenever it suits. The law does not recognise the sole-proprietor business as being separate from the owner, so the business will cease on the death of the owner.

Although the owner must produce accounting information to satisfy the taxation authorities, there is no legal requirement to produce accounting information relating to the business for other user groups. However, some user groups may demand accounting information about the business and may be in a position to have their demands met (for example, a bank requiring accounting information on a regular basis as a condition of a loan). The sole proprietor will have unlimited liability which means that no distinction will be made between the proprietor's personal wealth and that of the business if there are business debts that must be paid.

Partnership

→ A **partnership** exists where at least two individuals carry on a business together with the intention of making a profit. Partnerships have much in common with sole-proprietor businesses. They are usually quite small in size (although some, such as partnerships of accountants and solicitors, can be large). Partnerships are also easy to set up as no formal procedures are required (and it is not even necessary to have a written agreement between the partners). The partners can agree whatever arrangements suit them concerning the financial and management aspects of the business, and the partnership can be restructured or dissolved by agreement between the partners.

Partnerships are not recognised in law as separate entities and so contracts with third parties must be entered into in the name of individual partners. The partners of a business usually have unlimited liability.

Activity 1.8

What are the main advantages and disadvantages that should be considered when deciding between a sole proprietorship and a partnership?

The main advantages of a partnership over a sole-proprietor business are:

● sharing the burden of ownership;
● the opportunity to specialise rather than cover the whole range of services (for example, a solicitors' practice, where each partner tends to specialise in a different aspect of the law);
● the ability to raise capital where this is beyond the capacity of a single individual.

The main disadvantages of a partnership compared with a sole proprietorship are:

● the risks of sharing ownership of a business with unsuitable individuals;
● the limits placed on individual decision making that a partnership will impose.

Limited company

→ **Limited companies** can range in size from quite small to very large. The number of individuals who subscribe capital and become the owners may be unlimited, which provides the opportunity to create a very large-scale business. The liability of owners, however, is limited (hence 'limited' company), which means that those individuals subscribing capital to the company are liable only for debts incurred by the company up to the amount that they have agreed to invest. This cap on the liability of the owners is designed to limit risk and to produce greater confidence to invest. Without such limits on owner liability, it is difficult to see how a modern capitalist economy could operate. In many cases, the owners of a limited company are not involved in the day-to-day running of the business and will, therefore, invest in a business only if there is a clear limit set on the level of investment risk.

The benefit of limited liability, however, imposes certain obligations on such companies. To start up a limited company, documents of incorporation must be prepared that set out, among other things, the objectives of the business. Furthermore, a framework of regulations exists that places obligations on the way in which limited companies conduct their affairs. Part of this regulatory framework requires annual financial reports to be made available to owners and lenders and usually an annual general meeting of the owners has to be held to approve the reports. In addition, a copy of the annual financial reports must be lodged with the Registrar of Companies for public inspection. In this way, the financial affairs of a limited company enter the public domain. With the exception of small companies, there is also a requirement for the annual financial reports to be subject to an audit. This involves an independent firm of accountants examining the annual reports and underlying records to see whether the reports provide a true and fair view of the financial health of the company and whether they comply with the relevant accounting rules established by law and by accounting rule makers.

All of the large household-name UK businesses (Marks and Spencer, Tesco, Shell, BSkyB, BA, BT, easyJet and so on) are limited companies.

Limited companies are considered in more detail in Chapters 4 and 5.

Activity 1.9

What are the main advantages and disadvantages that should be considered when deciding between a partnership business and a limited liability company?

The main advantages of a partnership over a limited company are:

- the ease of setting up the business;
- the degree of flexibility concerning the way in which the business is conducted;
- the degree of flexibility concerning restructuring and dissolution of the business;
- freedom from administrative burdens imposed by law (for example, the annual general meeting and the need for an independent audit).

The main disadvantage of a partnership compared with a limited company is:

- the fact that it is not possible to limit the liability of all of the partners.

This book concentrates on the accounting aspects of limited liability companies because this type of business is by far the most important in economic terms. The early chapters will introduce accounting concepts through examples that do not draw a distinction between the different types of business. Once we have dealt with the basic accounting principles, which are the same for all three types of business, we can then go on to see how they are applied to limited companies. It must be emphasised that there are no differences in the way that all three of these forms of business keep their day-to-day accounting records. In preparing their periodic financial statements, there are certain differences that need to be considered. These differences are not ones of principle, however, but of detail.

How are businesses organised?

As we have just seen, nearly all businesses that involve more than a few owners and/or employees are set up as limited companies. This means that the finance will come from the owners (shareholders) both in the form of a direct cash investment to buy shares (in the ownership of the business) and through the owners allowing past profits, which belong to them, to be reinvested in the business. Finance will also come from lenders (banks, for example) who earn interest on their loans, and from suppliers of goods and services being prepared to supply on credit, with payment occurring a month or so after the date of supply, usually on an interest-free basis.

In larger limited companies, the owners (shareholders) are not involved in the daily running of the business; instead they appoint a board of directors to manage the business on their behalf. The board is charged with three major tasks:

● setting the overall direction and strategy for the business;
● monitoring and controlling its activities; and
● communicating with owners and others connected with the business.

Each board has a chairman, elected by the directors, who is responsible for running the board in an efficient manner. In addition, each board has a chief executive officer (CEO), or managing director, who is responsible for running the business on a day-to-day basis. Occasionally, the roles of chairman and CEO are combined, although it is usually considered to be a good idea to separate them in order to prevent a single individual having excessive power. We shall come back to consider the relationship between directors and shareholders in more detail in Chapter 4.

The board of directors represents the most senior level of management. Below this level, managers are employed, with each manager given responsibility for a particular part of the business's operations.

Activity (1.10)

Why are most larger businesses not managed as a single unit by one manager?

The three most obvious reasons are:

● the sheer volume of activity and/or number of staff employed makes it impossible for one person to manage everything;
● certain business operations may require specialised knowledge or expertise;
● geographical remoteness of part of the business operations may make it more practical to manage each location as a separate part, or set of separate parts.

The operations of a business may be divided for management purposes in different ways. For smaller businesses offering a single product or service, separate departments are often created, with each department responsible for a particular function (such as marketing, personnel, finance). The managers of each department will then be accountable to the board of directors. In some cases, individual board members may also be departmental managers.

A typical departmental structure, organised along functional lines, is set out in Figure 1.5.

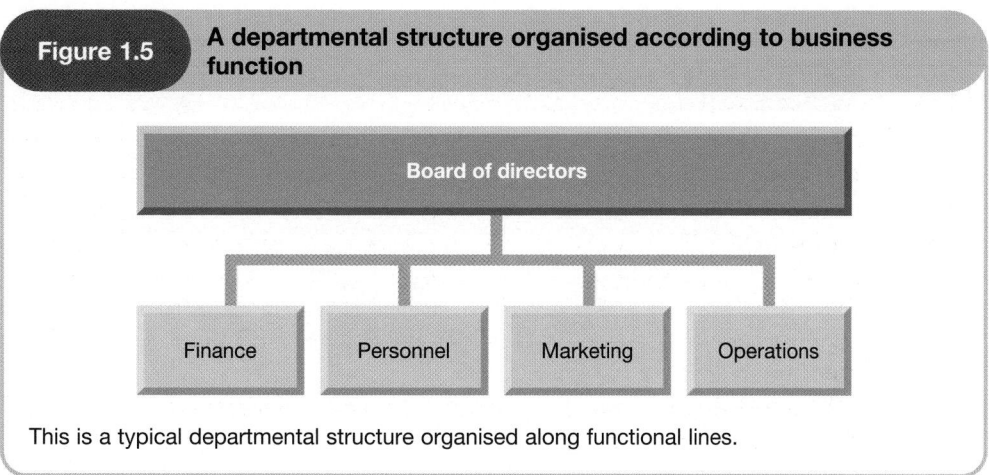

Figure 1.5   **A departmental structure organised according to business function**

Board of directors

Finance   Personnel   Marketing   Operations

This is a typical departmental structure organised along functional lines.

The structure set out in Figure 1.5 may be adapted according to the particular needs of the business. Where, for example, a business has few employees, the personnel function may not form a separate department but may form part of another department. Where business operations are specialised, separate departments may be formed to deal with each specialist area. Example 1.1 illustrates how Figure 1.5 may be modified to meet the needs of a particular business.

Example 1.1

Supercoach Ltd owns a small fleet of coaches that it hires out with drivers for private group travel. The business employs about 50 people. It might be departmentalised as follows:

- *marketing department*, dealing with advertising and with enquiries from potential customers, maintaining good relationships with existing customers and entering into contracts with customers;
- *routing and personnel department*, responsible for the coach drivers' routes, schedules, staff duties and rotas, problems that arise during a particular job or contract;
- *coach maintenance department*, looking after repair and maintenance of the coaches, buying spares, giving advice on the need to replace old or inefficient coaches;
- *finance department*, responsible for managing the cash flows, borrowing, use of spare funds, payment of wages and salaries, billing and collecting charges to customers, processing invoices from suppliers and paying the supplier.

For large businesses which have a diverse geographical spread and/or a wide product range, the simple departmental structure set out in Figure 1.5 will usually have to be adapted. Separate divisions are often created for each geographical area and/or major product group. Each division will be managed separately and will usually enjoy a degree of autonomy. Within each division, however, departments will often be created and organised along functional lines. Some functions providing support across the various divisions, such as personnel, may be undertaken at head office to avoid duplication. The managers of each division will be accountable to the board of directors. In some cases, individual board members may also be divisional managers. A typical divisional organisational structure is set out in Figure 1.6.

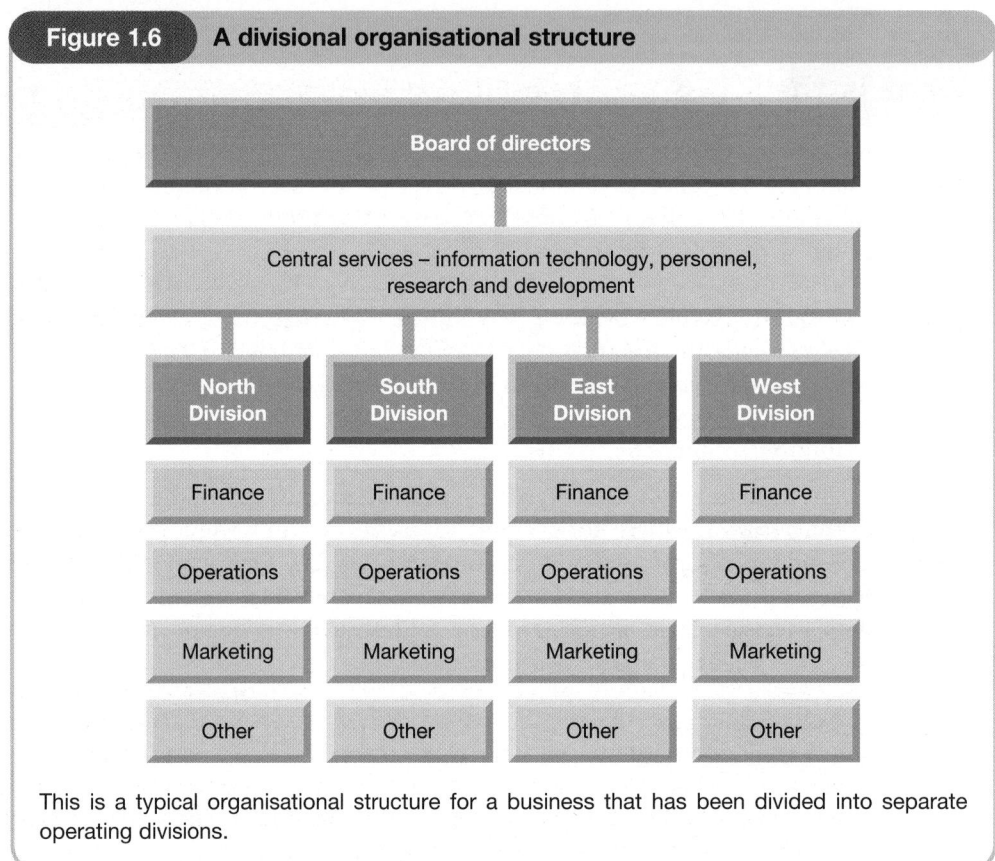

Figure 1.6 **A divisional organisational structure**

This is a typical organisational structure for a business that has been divided into separate operating divisions.

Both the divisional structure and departmental structure just described appear to be widely used, although it should be emphasised that other organisational structures may also be found in practice.

How are businesses managed?

We have already seen that the environment in which businesses operate has become increasingly turbulent and competitive. The effect of these environmental changes has been to make the role of managers more complex and demanding. It has meant that managers have had to find new ways to manage their business. This has increasingly led to the introduction of **strategic management**.

Strategic management seeks to provide a business with a clear sense of purpose and to ensure that appropriate action is taken to achieve that purpose. The action taken should link the internal resources of the business to the external environment of competitors, suppliers, customers and so on. This should be done in such a way that any business strengths, such as having a skilled workforce, are exploited and any weaknesses, such as being short of investment finance, are not exposed. To achieve this requires the development of strategies and plans that take account of the business's strengths and weaknesses, as well as the opportunities offered and threats posed by the external environment. Access to a new, expanding market is an example of an opportunity; the decision of a major competitor to reduce prices is an example of a threat. This topic will be considered in more depth in Chapter 12 when we consider business planning and budgeting.

What is the financial objective of a business?

A business is created to enhance the wealth of its owners, and throughout this book we shall assume that this is its main objective. This may come as a surprise, as there are other objectives that a business may pursue that are related to the needs of others associated with the business. For example, a business may seek to provide good working conditions for its employees, or it may seek to conserve the environment for the local community. While a business may pursue these objectives, it is normally set up with a view to increasing the wealth of its owners, and in practice the behaviour of businesses over time appears to be consistent with this objective.

Real World 1.4 reveals how one well-known business has changed its focus in order to improve profitability.

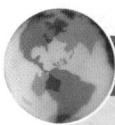 **Real World 1.4**

Profiting from change

It speaks volumes for the work done by Kate Swann in turning around W. H. Smith that when she became chief executive five years ago, the company was being spoken of in similar tems to Woolworths. Comments such as 'You wouldn't invent it if you were starting out today' and 'What is it actually for these days?' were typical among analysts, as they were with Woolies. Indeed, many thought that W. H. Smith was beyond help and argued that the supermarkets were eating away at sales.

Ms Swann has defied the sceptics, achieving an impressive turnaround. The company's magazine and newspaper distribution division was hived off as a separate entity and new outlets were opened at airports and railway stations – so much so that sales by W. H. Smith's travel unit now threaten to overtake those of its traditional high street stores. Lower (profit) margin lines, such as CDs and DVDs, have been cleared from the shelves to make way for higher (profit) margin items, such as stationery.

The last plank of the strategy was in evidence again in yesterday's update, in which Ms Swann reported that sales in the nine weeks to January 17 were down by 7 per cent in the high street stores and by 2 per cent in the travel stores, partly because W. H. Smith is continuing to reduce its exposure to the entertainment category.

That was the bad news. The good news was that, although sales overall were down, the reduced focus on entertainment was good for profits. W. H. Smith made an extra 2p of profit in every £1 of sales, compared with the same period a year earlier, a stunning achievement given the deflation hitting the high street.

Source: 'Business big shot', *The Times*, 27 January 2009, p. 39. © The Times 27 January 2009/nisyndication.com.

Within a market economy there are strong competitive forces at work that ensure that failure to enhance owners' wealth will not be tolerated for long. Competition for the funds provided by the owners and competition for managers' jobs will normally mean that the owners' interests will prevail. If the managers do not provide the expected increase in ownership wealth, the owners have the power to replace the existing management team with a new team that is more responsive to owners' needs.

Does this mean that the needs of other groups associated with the business (employees, customers, suppliers, the community and so on) are not really important? The answer to this question is certainly no, if the business wishes to survive and prosper over the longer term. Satisfying the needs of other groups will normally be consistent with increasing the wealth of the owners over the longer term.

The importance of customers to a business cannot be overstated. Dissatisfied customers will take their business to another supplier and this will, in turn, lead to a loss of wealth for the owners of the business losing the customers. **Real World 1.5** provides an illustration of the way in which one business acknowledges the link between customer satisfaction and creating wealth for its owners.

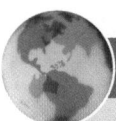

Real World 1.5

Checking out Sainsbury's objectives

J Sainsbury plc is a leading food retailer that recognises the importance of customers to increasing the wealth of the owners (shareholders) as follows:

> Our objective is to serve customers well and thereby provide shareholders with good, sustainable financial returns.

Source: Investor FAQs, www.j-sainsbury.co.uk, 8 January 2009, p. 1.

A dissatisfied workforce may result in low productivity, strikes and so forth, which will in turn have an adverse effect on owners' wealth. Similarly, a business that upsets the local community by unacceptable behaviour, such as polluting the environment, may attract bad publicity, resulting in a loss of customers and heavy fines.

Real World 1.6 provides an example of how two businesses responded to potentially damaging allegations.

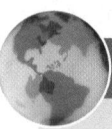

Real World 1.6

FT

The price of clothes

US clothing and sportswear manufacturers Gap and Nike have much of their clothes produced in Asia where labour tends to be cheap. However, some of the contractors that produce clothes on behalf of the two companies have been accused of unacceptable practices.

> Campaigners visited the factories and came up with damaging allegations. The factories were employing minors, they said, and managers were harassing female employees.

Nike and Gap reacted by allowing independent inspectors into the factories. They promised to ensure their contractors obeyed minimum standards of employment. Earlier this year, Nike took the extraordinary step of publishing the names and addresses of all its contractors' factories on the internet. The company said it could not be sure all the abuse had stopped. It said that if campaigners visited its contractors' factories and found examples of continued malpractice, it would take action.

Nike and Gap said the approach made business sense. They needed society's approval if they were to prosper. Nike said it was concerned about the reaction of potential US recruits to the campaigners' allegations. They would not want to work for a company that was constantly in the news because of the allegedly cruel treatment of those who made its products.

Source: 'Fair shares?', Michael Skapinker, FT.com, 11 June 2005.

It is important to recognise that generating wealth for the owners is not the same as seeking to maximise the current year's profit. Wealth creation is a longer-term concept, which relates not only to this year's profit but to that of future years as well. In the short term, corners can be cut and risks taken that improve current profit at the expense of future profit. **Real World 1.7** gives some examples of how emphasis on short-term profit can be damaging.

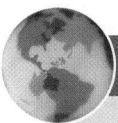

Real World 1.7

Short-term gains, long-term problems

FT

In recent years, many businesses have been criticised for failing to consider the long-term implications of their policies on the wealth of the owners. John Kay argues that some businesses have achieved short-term increases in wealth by sacrificing their longer-term prosperity. He points out that:

The business of Marks and Spencer, the retailer, was unparalleled in reputation but mature. To achieve earnings growth consistent with a glamour rating the company squeezed suppliers, gave less value for money, spent less on stores. In 1998, it achieved the highest (profit) margin in sales in the history of the business. It had also compromised its position to the point where sales and profits plummeted.

Banks and insurance companies have taken staff out of branches and retrained those that remain as sales people. The pharmaceuticals industry has taken advantage of mergers to consolidate its research and development facilities. Energy companies have cut back on exploration.

We know that these actions increased corporate earnings. We do not know what effect they have on the long-run strength of the business – and this is the key point – do the companies themselves know? Some rationalisations will genuinely lead to more productive businesses. Other companies will suffer the fate of Marks and Spencer.

Source: 'Profit without honour', John Kay, *Financial Times Weekend*, 29/30 June 2002.

Balancing risk and return

All decision making involves the future and business decision making is no exception. The only thing certain about the future, however, is that we cannot be sure what will happen. Things may not turn out as planned and this risk should be carefully considered when making financial decisions.

As in other aspects of life, risk and return tend to be related. Evidence shows that returns relate to risk in something like the way shown in Figure 1.7.

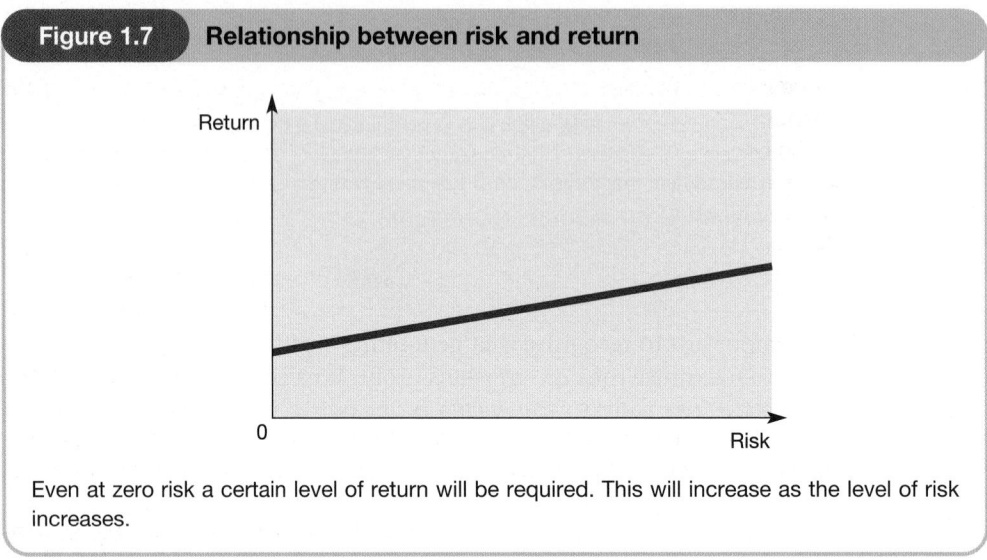

Figure 1.7   **Relationship between risk and return**

Even at zero risk a certain level of return will be required. This will increase as the level of risk increases.

This relationship between risk and return has important implications for setting financial objectives for a business. The owners will require a minimum return to induce them to invest at all, but will require an additional return to compensate for taking risks; the higher the risk, the higher the required return. Managers must be aware of this and must strike the appropriate balance between risk and return when setting objectives and pursuing particular courses of action.

The recent turmoil in the banking sector has shown, however, that the right balance is not always struck. Some banks have taken excessive risks in pursuit of higher returns and, as a consequence, have incurred massive losses. They are now being kept afloat with taxpayers' money. **Real World 1.8** mentions the collapse of one leading bank, in which the UK government took a majority stake, and argues that the risk appetite of banks must now change.

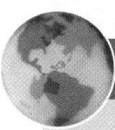

Real World 1.8

Banking on change

It's official. We the taxpayer own one of the world's biggest banks, Royal Bank of Scotland, or 58 per cent of it. Only a tiny number of RBS's shareholders chose to buy any of the new shares in Royal Bank that were being sold in order to strengthen its balance sheet. So the Treasury, on behalf of taxpayers, bought up the remaining 23bn shares at 65.5p each.

The commercial judgements of Royal Bank's management will inevitably be conditioned by the inescapable fact that we the taxpayers now own the bank. That's about a great deal more than whether it pays bonuses to senior executives or how much it lends to small business and homeowners (which is where the government has already exerted explicit pressure). It's about fundamental questions of culture and about how much risk the bank is prepared to take or is allowed to take by the new proprietor.

Those who run banks such as Royal Bank have for years seen themselves as creators and manufacturers of financial products, companies that can generate incremental wealth and can grow faster than the underlying rate of the economy. They didn't want to see themselves as the infrastructure of the economy, that couldn't and shouldn't attempt to push up their profits at an accelerating rate. Somehow it was a bit too humiliating to be no more than the pipework for the real generators of wealth, companies with genuinely new services, real products and real technology.

So bankers created and exploited new 'financial technology' that enriched themselves (for a while, at least) and was supposedly benefiting all of us by providing unlimited quantities of credit at astonishingly cheap rates. Much of that technology – the collateralised debt obligations, the collateralised loan obligations, the credit default swaps, the structured investment vehicles – generated colossal losses, hobbled the global banking system, and is part of the reason why taxpayers all over the world are now propping up wounded banks on a mindboggling scale.

So whether they like it or not, most banks and bankers are destined to lead a quieter, duller life for many years. Which, many taxpayers would say, isn't such a terrible thing. If our banks simply concentrated on the very basics – taking deposits, providing simple loans to customers they actually know, moving our money to where we want it to go – would that be so disastrous?

Throughout the entire history of banking there's always been a tension between their core function as public-service utilities and the desire of the bankers themselves to earn super-normal returns by speculating with their depositors' cash. Whether they like it or not, all our banks will for the next few years look a lot more like building societies and a lot less like Goldman Sachs.

Source: 'We own Royal Bank', Robert Peston, 28 November 2008, BBC News, www.bbc.co.uk.

Not-for-profit organisations

Though the focus of this book is accounting as it relates to private sector businesses, there are many organisations that do not exist mainly for the pursuit of profit. Examples include:

- charities
- clubs and associations
- universities
- local government authorities
- national government departments
- churches
- trade unions.

Such organisations also need to produce accounting information for decision-making purposes. Various user groups need accounting information about these types of organisation to help them to make decisions. These groups are often the same as, or similar to, those identified for private sector businesses. They may have a stake in the future viability of the organisation and may use accounting information to check that the wealth of the organisation is being properly controlled and used in a way that is consistent with its objectives.

Real World 1.9 provides an example of the importance of accounting to relief agencies.

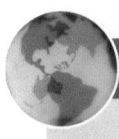

Real World 1.9

Accounting for disasters

FT

In the aftermath of the Asian tsunami more than £400m was raised from charitable donations. It was important that his huge amount of money for aid and reconstruction was
used as efficiently and effectively as possible. That did not just mean medical staff and
engineers. It also meant accountants.

The charity that exerts financial control over aid donations is Mango: Management
Accounting for Non-Governmental Organisations (NGOs). It provides accountants in the
field and it provides the back-up, such as financial training, and all the other services that
should result in really robust financial management in a disaster area.

The world of aid has changed completely as a result of the tsunami. According to
Mango's director, Alex Jacobs, 'Accounting is just as important as blankets. Agencies
have been aware of this for years. But when you move on to a bigger scale there is more
pressure to show the donations are being used appropriately.'

Source: Adapted from 'Tsunami: finding the right figures for disaster relief', Robert Bruce, FT.com, 7 March 2005; and 'The work of
Mango: coping with generous donations', Robert Bruce, FT.com, 27 February 2006.

Summary

The main points of this chapter may be summarised as follows.

What are accounting and finance?

- Accounting provides financial information for a range of users to help them make
better judgements and decisions concerning a business.

- Finance also helps users to make better decisions and is concerned with the financing and investing activities of the business.

Accounting and user needs

- For accounting to be useful, there must be a clear understanding of *for whom* and *for
what purpose* the information will be used.

- There may be conflicts of interest between users over the ways in which the wealth
of a business is generated or distributed.

- There is evidence to suggest that accounting is both used and useful for decision-
making purposes.

Providing a service

- Accounting can be viewed as a form of service as it involves providing financial
information required by the various users.

- To provide a useful service, accounting must possess certain qualities, or characteristics. These are relevance, reliability, comparability and understandability. In addition, accounting information must be material.

- Providing a service to users can be costly and financial information should be produced only if the cost of providing the information is less than the benefits gained.

Accounting information

- Accounting is part of the total information system within a business. It shares the features that are common to all information systems within a business, which are the identification, recording, analysis and reporting of information.

Management and financial accounting

- Accounting has two main strands: management accounting and financial accounting.
- Management accounting seeks to meet the needs of the business's managers and financial accounting seeks to meet the needs of the other user groups.
- These two strands differ in terms of the types of reports produced, the level of reporting detail, the time horizon, the degree of standardisation and the range and quality of information provided.

Is accounting too interesting?

- In recent years, there has been a wave of accounting scandals in the US and Europe.
- This appears to reflect a particular economic environment, although other factors may also play a part.

The changing face of accounting

- Changes in the economic environment have led to changes in the nature and scope of accounting.
- Financial accounting has improved its framework of rules and there has been greater international harmonisation of accounting rules.
- Management accounting has become more outward looking and new methods for managing costs have emerged.

Why study accounting?

- Everyone connected with business should be a little 'streetwise' about accounting and finance. Financial information and decisions exert an enormous influence over the ways in which a business operates.

What is the purpose of a business?

- To create and keep a customer.

What kinds of business ownership exist?

There are three main forms of business unit:

- Sole proprietorship – easy to set up and flexible to operate but the owner has unlimited liability.
- Partnership – easy to set up and spreads the burdens of ownership, but partners usually have unlimited liability and there are ownership risks if the partners are unsuitable.
- Limited company – limited liability for owners but obligations imposed on the way a company conducts its affairs.

How are businesses organised and managed?

- Most businesses of any size are set up as limited companies.
- A board of directors is appointed by owners (shareholders) to oversee the running of the business.

- Businesses are often divided into departments and organised along functional lines; however, larger businesses may be divisionalised along geographical and/or product lines.

- The move to strategic management has been caused by the changing and more competitive nature of business.

What is the financial objective of a business?

- A business may pursue a variety of objectives but the main objective for virtually all businesses is to enhance the wealth of its owners. This does not mean, however, that the needs of other groups connected with the business, such as employees, should be ignored.

- When setting financial objectives the right balance must be struck between risk and return.

 Now check your progress in your personal Study Plan

 Key terms

accounting p. 2	materiality p. 8
finance p. 2	accounting information system p. 11
financial management p. 2	management accounting p. 13
shares p. 6	financial accounting p. 13
relevance p. 7	sole proprietorship p. 19
reliability p. 7	partnership p. 20
comparability p. 8	limited company p. 21
understandability p. 8	strategic management p. 24

References

1 **Contemporary Management Accounting Practices in UK Manufacturing**, *Dugdale D., Jones C. and Green S.*, CIMA Research Publication, vol. 1, no. 13, 2005.

2 **Effective Executive**, *Drucker P.*, Heinemann, 1967.

Further reading

If you would like to explore the topics covered in this chapter in more depth, we recommend the following books:

Accounting Theory, *Riahi-Belkaoui A.*, 5th edn, Thomson Learning, 2004, chapters 1, 2 and 6.

Business Finance: Theory and Practice, *McLaney E.*, 8th edn, Financial Times Prentice Hall, 2009, chapters 1 and 2.

Management and Cost Accounting, *Drury C.*, 7th edn, Cengage Learning, 2007, chapter 1.

Cost Accounting: A Managerial Emphasis, *Horngren C., Foster G., Datar S., Rajan M. and Ittner C.*, 13th edn, Prentice Hall International, 2008, chapter 1.

Financial Accounting and Reporting, *Elliot B. and Elliot J.*, 13th edn, Financial Times Prentice Hall, 2010, chapter 7.

Review questions

Answers to these questions can be found at the back of the book on pages 738–9.

1.1 What is the purpose of producing accounting information?

1.2 Identify the main users of accounting information for a university. For what purposes would different user groups need information? Is there a major difference in the ways in which accounting information for a university would be used compared with that of a private sector business?

1.3 Management accounting has been described as 'the eyes and ears of management'. What do you think this expression means?

1.4 Financial accounting statements tend to reflect past events. In view of this, how can they be of any assistance to a user in making a decision when decisions, by their very nature, can only be made about future actions?

PART 1

Financial accounting

Part 1 of this book deals with the area of accounting and finance usually referred to as 'financial accounting'. Here we shall introduce three major financial statements:

● statement of financial position
● income statement
● statement of cash flows.

In Chapter 2, we provide an overview of these three statements and then go on to consider the first of these, the statement of financial position, in some detail. Included in our consideration of this statement will be an explanation of the accounting conventions used when preparing it. These 'conventions' are generally accepted rules that have evolved to help deal with practical problems experienced by preparers and users of the statement.

In Chapter 3 we examine the second of the major financial statements, the income statement. Here we shall be looking at such issues as how profit is measured and the point in time at which it is reported. Once again, there will be an explanation of the accounting conventions used when preparing this financial statement.

The limited company is the most important business form in the UK and in Chapters 4 and 5 we focus on this type of business. As far as accounting is concerned, there is nothing in essence that makes companies different from other types of private sector business, but there are some points of detail that we need to consider. Chapter 4 examines the nature of limited companies, the way in which they are financed and the accounting issues that specifically relate to this form of business. Chapter 5 considers the duty of directors of a limited company to account to its owners and to others and the regulatory framework imposed on limited companies. Some additional reports prepared by large limited companies are also considered.

Chapter 6 deals with the last of the three financial statements, the statement of cash flows. This financial statement sets out the sources and uses of cash during an accounting period. We shall see that making profit is not enough. A business must also be able to generate cash to pay its obligations and the statement of cash flows helps us to assess its ability to do this.

When taken together, the three financial statements provide useful information about the business's performance and position for the period concerned. It is possible, however, to gain even more helpful insights about the business by analysing these statements, using financial ratios and other techniques. Combining two figures from the financial statements in a ratio, and comparing this with a similar ratio for, say, another business, can often tell us much more than just reading the figures themselves. In Chapter 7 we consider some of the techniques for analysing financial statements.

CHAPTER 2

Measuring and reporting financial position

Introduction

We saw in Chapter 1 that accounting has two distinct strands: financial accounting and management accounting. This chapter, along with Chapters 3 to 7, examines the three major financial statements that form the core of financial accounting. We start by taking an overview of these statements to see how each contributes towards an assessment of the overall financial position and performance of a business.

Following this overview, we begin a more detailed examination by turning our attention towards one of these financial statements: the statement of financial position. We shall see how it is prepared, and examine the principles underpinning this statement. We shall also consider its value for decision-making purposes.

Learning outcomes

When you have completed this chapter, you should be able to:

● Explain the nature and purpose of the three major financial statements.

● Prepare a simple statement of financial position and interpret the information that it contains.

● Discuss the accounting conventions underpinning the statement of financial position.

● Discuss the uses and limitations of the statement of financial position for decision-making purposes.

 Remember to create your own personalised Study Plan

Making financial decisions

We have just seen that a key purpose of this chapter is to show how the statement of financial position is constructed and how it may help users. So, let us begin by considering a practical situation where this statement may be of benefit. **Real World 2.1** describes how the statement of financial position of a small business was used by a bank when deciding whether to grant a loan.

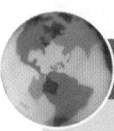

Real World 2.1

A sound education

Sandeep Sud is a qualified solicitor who also runs a school uniform business based in Hounslow, in partnership with his parents. The company, which has four full-time employees, uses its statement of financial position (balance sheet) to gauge how the business is progressing. It has also been a key factor in securing a bank loan for the improvement and expansion of the company premises.

According to Sandeep:

Having a strong statement of financial position helped when it came to borrowing. When we first applied for a refurbishment loan we couldn't provide up-to-date accounts to the bank manager. This could have been a problem, but we quickly got our accounts in order and the loan was approved straight away. Because our statement of financial position was strong, the bank thought we were a good risk. Although we decided not to draw down on the loan – because we used cash-flow instead – it did open our eyes to the importance of a strong statement of financial position.

Source: Adapted from 'Balance sheets: the basics', www.businesslink.gov.uk/balancesheets. Accessed 25 February 2009.

Before we consider the statement of financial position in detail, however, we shall first gain an overview of all three major financial accounting statements. This should help us to understand the role of each one as well as their interrelationships.

The major financial statements – an overview

The major financial accounting statements aim to provide a picture of the financial position and performance of a business. To achieve this, a business's accounting system will normally produce three particular statements on a regular, recurring basis. These three statements are concerned with answering the following questions:

● What cash movements (that is, cash in and cash out) took place over a particular period?
● How much wealth (that is, profit) was generated, or lost, by the business over that period? (Profit (or loss) is defined as the increase (or decrease) in wealth arising from trading activities.)
● What is the accumulated wealth of the business at the end of that period and what form does the wealth take?

To address each of the above questions, there is a separate financial statement. The financial statements are:

→ ● the **statement of cash flows**
→ ● the **income statement** (also known as the profit and loss account)
→ ● the **statement of financial position** (also known as the balance sheet).

Together they provide an overall picture of the financial health of the business.

Perhaps the best way to introduce these financial statements is to look at an example of a very simple business. From this we shall be able to see the sort of information that each of the statements can usefully provide. It is, however, worth pointing out that, while a simple business is our starting point, the principles that we consider apply equally to the largest and most complex businesses. This means that we shall frequently encounter these principles again in later chapters.

Example 2.1

Paul was unemployed and unable to find a job. He therefore decided to embark on a business venture. Christmas was approaching, and so he decided to buy gift wrapping paper from a local supplier and to sell it on the corner of his local high street. He felt that the price of wrapping paper in the high street shops was too high. This provided him with a useful business opportunity.

He began the venture with £40 in cash. On Monday, Paul's first day of trading, he bought wrapping paper for £40 and sold three-quarters of it for £45 cash.

● **What cash movements took place during Monday?**

For Monday, a *statement of cash flows* showing the cash movements for the day can be prepared as follows:

Statement of cash flows for Monday

	£
Opening balance (cash introduced)	40
Cash from sales of wrapping paper	45
Cash paid to buy wrapping paper	(40)
Closing balance of cash	45

The statement shows that Paul placed £40 cash into the business. The business received £45 cash from customers, but paid £40 cash to buy the wrapping paper. This left £45 of cash by Monday evening. Note that we are taking the standard approach found in the financial statements of showing figures to be deducted (in this case the £40 paid out) in brackets. We shall take this approach consistently throughout the chapters dealing with financial statements.

● **How much wealth (that is, profit) was generated by the business during Monday?**

An *income statement (profit and loss account)* can be prepared to show the wealth (profit) generated on Monday. The wealth generated will represent the difference between the value of the sales made and the cost of the goods (that is, wrapping paper) sold:

Income statement (profit and loss account) for Monday

	£
Sales revenue	45
Cost of goods sold (³/₄ of £40)	(30)
Profit	15

Note that it is only the cost of the wrapping paper *sold* that is matched against (and deducted from) the sales revenue in order to find the profit, and not the whole of the cost of wrapping paper acquired. Any unsold inventories (in this case ¼ of £40 = £10) will be charged against the future sales revenue that it generates.

● **What is the accumulated wealth at Monday evening?**

To establish the accumulated wealth at the end of Monday's trading, we can draw up a *statement of financial position (balance sheet)*. This will list the resources held at the end of that day:

Statement of financial position (balance sheet) as at Monday evening

	£
Cash (closing balance)	45
Inventories of goods for resale (¼ of £40)	10
Total assets	55
Equity	55

Note the terms 'assets' and 'equity' that appear in the above statement. 'Assets' are business resources (things of value to the business) and include cash and inventories. 'Equity' is the word used in accounting to describe the investment, or stake, of the owner(s) – in this case Paul – in the business. Both of these terms will be discussed in some detail a little later in this chapter.

We can see from the financial statements in Example 2.1 that each statement provides part of a picture portraying the financial performance and position of the business. We begin by showing the cash movements. Cash is a vital resource that is necessary for any business to function effectively. Cash is required to meet debts that may become due and to acquire other resources (such as inventories). Cash has been described as the 'lifeblood' of a business, and movements in cash are usually closely scrutinised by users of financial statements.

However, it is clear that reporting cash movements alone would not be enough to portray the financial health of the business. The changes in cash over time do not tell us how much profit was generated. The income statement provides us with information concerning this aspect of performance. For example, we saw that during Monday the cash balance increased by £5, but the profit generated, as shown in the income statement, was £15. The cash balance did not increase by the amount of the profit made because part of the wealth generated (£10) was held in the form of inventories.

The statement of financial position that was drawn up as at the end of Monday's trading provides an insight to the total wealth of the business. Cash is only one form in which wealth may be held. In the case of this business, wealth is also held in the form of inventories (also known as stock). Hence, when drawing up the statement of financial position, both forms of wealth held will be listed. In the case of a large business, there may be many other forms in which wealth will be held, such as land and buildings, equipment, motor vehicles and so on.

Let us now continue with our example.

Example 2.1 (continued)

On Tuesday, Paul bought more wrapping paper for £20 cash. He managed to sell all of the new inventories and all of the earlier inventories, for a total of £48.

The statement of cash flows for Tuesday will be as follows:

Statement of cash flows for Tuesday

	£
Opening balance (from Monday evening)	45
Cash from sales of wrapping paper	48
Cash paid to buy wrapping paper	(20)
Closing balance	73

The income statement for Tuesday will be as follows:

Income statement for Tuesday

	£
Sales revenue	48
Cost of goods sold (£20 + £10)	(30)
Profit	18

The statement of financial position as at Tuesday evening will be:

Statement of financial position as at Tuesday evening

	£
Cash (closing balance)	73
Inventories	–
Total assets	73
Equity	73

We can see that the total business wealth increased to £73 by Tuesday evening. This represents an increase of £18 (that is, £73 – £55) over Monday's figure – which, of course, is the amount of profit made during Tuesday as shown on the income statement.

Activity 2.1

On Wednesday, Paul bought more wrapping paper for £46 cash. However, it was raining hard for much of the day and sales were slow. After Paul had sold half of his total inventories for £32, he decided to stop trading until Thursday morning.

Have a go at drawing up the three financial statements for Paul's business for Wednesday.

Statement of cash flows for Wednesday

	£
Opening balance (from the Tuesday evening)	73
Cash from sales of wrapping paper	32
Cash paid to buy wrapping paper	(46)
Closing balance	59

Activity 2.1 continued

Income statement for Wednesday

	£
Sales revenue	32
Cost of goods sold (½ of £46)	(23)
Profit	9

Statement of financial position as at Wednesday evening

	£
Cash (closing balance)	59
Inventories (½ of £46)	23
Total assets	82
Equity	82

Note that the total business wealth had increased by £9 (that is, the amount of Wednesday's profit) even though the cash balance had declined. This is because the business is holding more of its wealth in the form of inventories rather than cash, compared with the position on Tuesday evening.

The equity by Wednesday evening stood at £82. This arose from Paul's initial investment of £40, plus his profits for Monday (£15), for Tuesday (£18) and for Wednesday (£9). This represents Paul's total investment in his business at that time. Typical of most businesses, the equity partly consists of specific injections of funds by the owner, plus profits that the owner has allowed to accumulate.

We can see that the income statement and statement of cash flows are both concerned with measuring flows (of wealth and cash respectively) during a particular period (for example, a particular day, a particular month or a particular year). The statement of financial position, however, is concerned with the financial position at a particular moment in time.

Figure 2.1 illustrates this point. The financial statements (income statement, statement of cash flows and statement of financial position) are often referred to as the **final accounts** of the business.

For external users (that is virtually all except the managers of the business concerned), these statements are normally backward looking because they are based on information concerning past events and transactions. This can be useful in providing feedback on past performance, and in identifying trends that provide clues to future performance. However, the statements can also be prepared using projected data to help assess likely future profits, cash flows and so on. The financial statements are normally prepared on a projected basis for internal decision-making purposes only, as we shall see in Chapter 12. Managers are usually reluctant to publish these projected statements for external users, as they may reveal valuable information to competitors.

Now that we have an overview of the financial statements, we shall consider each statement in more detail. We shall go straight on to look at the statement of financial position. Chapter 3 looks at the income statement, Chapter 6 goes into more detail on the statement of cash flows. (Chapters 4 and 5 consider the statements of financial position and income statements of limited companies.)

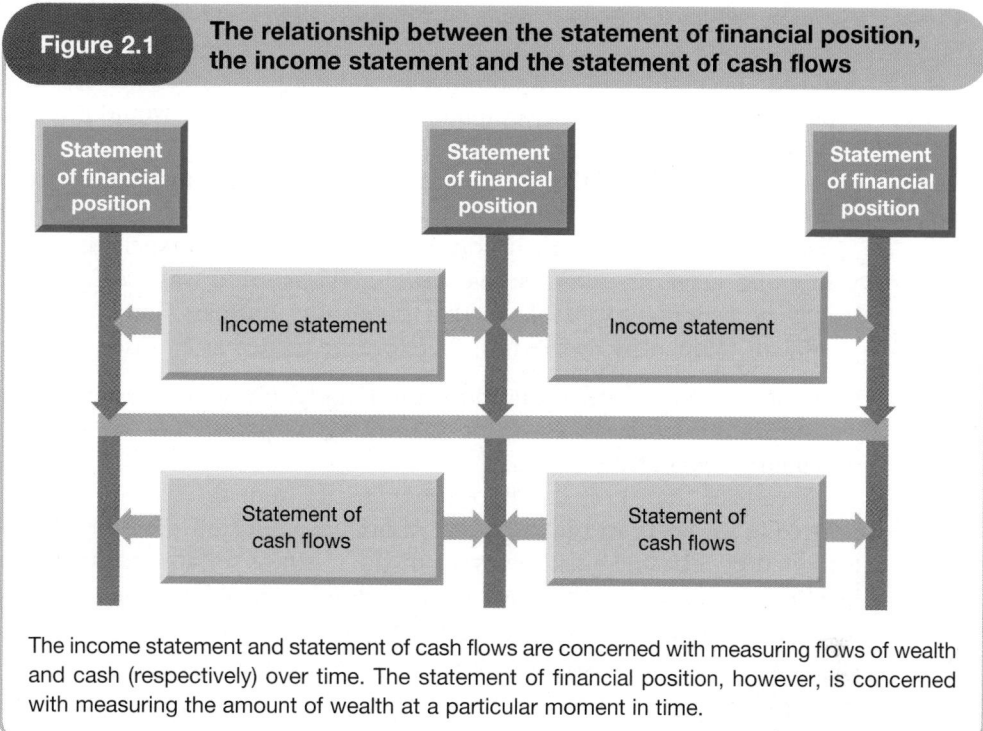

Figure 2.1 **The relationship between the statement of financial position, the income statement and the statement of cash flows**

The income statement and statement of cash flows are concerned with measuring flows of wealth and cash (respectively) over time. The statement of financial position, however, is concerned with measuring the amount of wealth at a particular moment in time.

The statement of financial position

This statement sets out the financial position of a business at a particular moment in time. We saw above that the statement of financial position sets out the forms in which the wealth of the business is held and how much wealth is held in each form. We can, however, be more specific about the nature of this statement by saying that it sets out the **assets** of the business on the one hand, and the **claims** against the business on the other. Before looking at the statement of financial position in more detail, we need to be clear about what these terms mean.

Assets

An asset is essentially a resource held by the business. For a particular item to be treated as an asset for accounting purposes it should have the following characteristics:

- *A probable future benefit must exist.* This simply means that the item must be expected to have some future monetary value. This value can arise through its use within the business or through its hire or sale. Thus, an obsolete piece of equipment that could be sold for scrap would still be considered an asset, whereas an obsolete piece of equipment that could not be sold for scrap would not be regarded as one.
- *The business must have the right to control the resource.* Unless the business controls the resource, it cannot be regarded as an asset for accounting purposes. Thus, for a business offering holidays on barges, the canal system may be a very valuable resource, but as the business will not be able to control the access of others to the canal system, it cannot be regarded as an asset of the business. (However, the barges owned by the business would be regarded as assets.)

- *The benefit must arise from some past transaction or event.* This means that the transaction (or other event) giving rise to the business's right to the benefit must have already occurred, and will not arise at some future date. Thus an agreement by a business to buy a piece of equipment at some future date would not mean the item is currently an asset of the business.
- *The asset must be capable of measurement in monetary terms.* Unless the item can be measured in monetary terms, with a reasonable degree of reliability, it will not be regarded as an asset for inclusion on the statement of financial position. Thus, the title of a magazine (for example *Hello!* or *Vogue*) that was created by its publisher may be extremely valuable to that publishing business, but this value is usually difficult to quantify. It will not, therefore, be treated as an asset.

Note that all four of these conditions must apply. If one of them is missing, the item will not be treated as an asset, for accounting purposes, and will not appear on the statement of financial position.

We can see that these conditions will strictly limit the kind of items that may be referred to as 'assets' in the statement of financial position. Certainly not all resources exploited by a business will be assets of the business for accounting purposes. Some, like the canal system or the magazine title *Hello!*, may well be assets in a broader sense, but not for accounting purposes. Once an asset has been acquired by a business, it will continue to be considered an asset until the benefits are exhausted or the business disposes of it in some way.

Activity 2.2

Indicate which of the following items could appear as an asset on the statement of financial position of a business. Explain your reasoning in each case.

1 £1,000 owed to the business by a customer who is unable to pay.
2 A patent, bought from an inventor, that gives the business the right to produce a new product. Production of the new product is expected to increase profits over the period during which the patent is held.
3 A new marketing director, whom the business had recently hired, who is confidently expected to increase profits by over 30 per cent during the next three years.
4 A recently purchased machine that will save the business £10,000 each year. It is already being used by the business but it has been acquired on credit and is not yet paid for.

Your answer should be along the following lines.

1 Under normal circumstances, a business would expect a customer to pay the amount owed. Such an amount is therefore typically shown as an asset under the heading 'trade receivables' (or 'debtors'). However, in this particular case the customer is unable to pay. Hence the item is incapable of providing future benefits, and the £1,000 owing would not be regarded as an asset. Debts that are not paid are referred to as 'bad debts'.
2 The patent would meet all of the conditions set out above and would therefore be regarded as an asset.
3 The new marketing director would not be considered as an asset. One argument for this is that the business does not have exclusive rights of control over the director. (Nevertheless, it may have an exclusive right to the services that the director provides.) Perhaps a stronger argument is that the value of the director cannot be measured in monetary terms with any degree of reliability.

4 The machine would be considered an asset even though it is not yet paid for. Once the business has agreed to buy the machine, and has accepted it, the machine represents an asset even though payment is still outstanding. (The amount outstanding would be shown as a claim, as we shall see below.)

The sorts of items that often appear as assets in the statement of financial position of a business include:

- property
- plant and equipment
- fixtures and fittings
- patents and trademarks
- trade receivables (debtors)
- investments.

Activity 2.3

Can you think of two additional items that might appear as assets in the statement of financial position of a typical business?

You may be able to think of a number of other items. Two that we have met so far, because they were the only types of asset that were held by Paul's wrapping paper business (in Example 2.1), are inventories and cash.

Note that an asset does not have to be a physical item – it may alternatively be a non-physical right to certain benefits. Assets that have a physical substance and can be touched (such as inventories) are referred to as **tangible assets**. Assets that have no physical substance but which, nevertheless, provide expected future benefits (such as patents) are referred to as **intangible assets**.

Claims

A claim is an obligation by the business to provide cash, or some other form of benefit, to an outside party. It will normally arise as a result of the outside party providing assets for use by the business. There are essentially two types of claim against a business:

- **Equity.** This represents the claim of the owner(s) against the business. This claim is sometimes referred to as the *owner's capital*. Some find it hard to understand how the owner can have a claim against the business, particularly when we consider the example of a sole-proprietor-type business where the owner *is*, in effect, the business. However, for accounting purposes, a clear distinction is made between the business (whatever its size and form) and the owner(s). The business is viewed as being quite separate from the owner and this is equally true for a sole proprietor like Paul, the wrapping-paper seller in Example 2.1, or a large company like Marks and Spencer plc. It is seen as a separate entity with its own separate existence and when financial statements are prepared, they relate to the business rather than to the owner(s). This means that the statement of financial position will reflect the position of the business as a separate entity. Viewed from this perspective, any funds contributed by the owner will be seen as coming from outside the business and will appear as a claim against the business in its statement of financial position.

As we have just seen, the business and the owner are separate for accounting purposes, irrespective of the type of business concerned. It is also true that the operation of the equity section of the statement of financial position is broadly the same irrespective of the type of business concerned. We shall see in Chapter 4 that, with limited companies, the owner's claim figure must be analysed according to how each part of it first arose. For example, companies must make a distinction between that part of the owner's claim that arose from retained profits and that part that arose from the owners putting in cash to start up the business, usually by buying shares in the company.

→ ● **Liabilities**. Liabilities represent the claims of all individuals and organisations, apart from the owner(s). They arise from past transactions or events such as supplying goods or lending money to the business. When a liability is settled it can only be through an outflow of assets (usually cash).

Once a claim from the owners or outsiders has been incurred by a business, it will remain as an obligation until it is settled.

Now that the meaning of the terms *assets*, *equity* and *liabilities* has been established, we can go on and discuss the relationship between them. This relationship is quite straightforward. If a business wishes to acquire assets, it will have to raise the necessary funds from somewhere. It may raise the funds from the owner(s) or from other outside parties or from both. Example 2.2 illustrates this relationship.

Example 2.2

Jerry and Company start a business by depositing £20,000 in a bank account on 1 March. This amount was raised partly from the owner (£6,000) and partly from borrowing (£14,000). Raising funds in this way will give rise to a claim on the business by both the owner (equity) and the lender (liability). If a statement of financial position of Jerry and Company is prepared following the above transactions, it will appear as follows:

Jerry and Company
Statement of financial position as at 1 March

	£
ASSETS	
Cash at bank	20,000
Total assets	20,000
EQUITY AND LIABILITIES	
Equity	6,000
Liabilities – borrowing	14,000
Total equity and liabilities	20,000

We can see from the statement of financial position that the total claims are the same as the total assets. Thus:

> **Assets = Equity + Liabilities**

This equation – which we shall refer to as the *accounting equation* – will always hold true. Whatever changes may occur to the assets of the business or the claims against it, there will be compensating changes elsewhere that will ensure that the statement of financial position always 'balances'. By way of illustration, consider the following transactions for Jerry and Company:

2 March	Bought a motor van for £5,000, paying by cheque.
3 March	Bought inventories (that is, goods to be sold) on one month's credit for £3,000. (This means that the inventories were bought on 3 March, but payment will not be made to the supplier until 3 April.)
4 March	Repaid £2,000 of the amount borrowed to the lender, by cheque.
6 March	Owner introduced another £4,000 into the business bank account.

A statement of financial position may be drawn up after each day in which transactions have taken place. In this way, the effect can be seen of each transaction on the assets and claims of the business. The statement of financial position as at 2 March will be:

Jerry and Company
Statement of financial position as at 2 March

	£
ASSETS	
Cash at bank (20,000 – 5,000)	15,000
Motor van	5,000
Total assets	20,000
EQUITY AND LIABILITIES	
Equity	6,000
Liabilities – borrowing	14,000
Total equity and liabilities	20,000

As can be seen, the effect of buying the motor van is to decrease the balance at the bank by £5,000 and to introduce a new asset – a motor van – to the statement of financial position. The total assets remain unchanged. It is only the 'mix' of assets that has changed. The claims against the business remain the same because there has been no change in the way in which the business has been funded.

The statement of financial position as at 3 March, following the purchase of inventories, will be:

Jerry and Company
Statement of financial position as at 3 March

	£
ASSETS	
Cash at bank	15,000
Motor van	5,000
Inventories	3,000
Total assets	23,000
EQUITY AND LIABILITIES	
Equity	6,000
Liabilities – borrowing	14,000
Liabilities – trade payable	3,000
Total equity and liabilities	23,000

The effect of buying inventories has been to introduce another new asset (inventories) to the statement of financial position. In addition, the fact that the goods have not yet been paid for means that the claims against the business will be increased by the £3,000 owed to the supplier, who is referred to as a *trade payable* (or trade creditor) on the statement of financial position.

Activity (2.4)

Try drawing up a statement of financial position for Jerry and Company as at 4 March.

The statement of financial postion as at 4 March, following the repayment of part of the borrowing, will be:

Jerry and Company
Statement of financial position as at 4 March

	£
ASSETS	
Cash at bank (15,000 – 2,000)	13,000
Motor van	5,000
Inventories	3,000
Total assets	21,000
EQUITY AND LIABILITIES	
Equity	6,000
Liabilities – borrowing (14,000 – 2,000)	12,000
Liabilities – trade payable	3,000
Total equity and liabilities	21,000

The repayment of £2,000 of the borrowing will result in a decrease in the balance at the bank of £2,000 and a decrease in the lender's claim against the business by the same amount.

Activity (2.5)

Try drawing up a statement of financial position as at 6 March for Jerry and Company.

The statement of financial position as at 6 March, following the introduction of more funds, will be:

Jerry and Company
Statement of financial position as at 6 March

	£
ASSETS	
Cash at bank (13,000 + 4,000)	17,000
Motor van	5,000
Inventories	3,000
Total assets	25,000
EQUITY AND LIABILITIES	
Equity (6,000 + 4,000)	10,000
Liabilities – borrowing	12,000
Liabilities – trade payable	3,000
Total equity and liabilities	25,000

The introduction of more funds by the owner will result in an increase in the equity of £4,000 and an increase in the cash at bank by the same amount.

Example 2.2 illustrates the point that the accounting equation (assets equals equity plus liabilities) will always hold true, because it reflects the fact that, if a business wishes to acquire more assets, it must raise funds equal to the cost of those assets. The funds raised must be provided by the owners (equity), or by others (liabilities) or by a combination of the two. Hence the total cost of assets acquired should always equal the total equity plus liabilities.

It is worth pointing out that in real life businesses do not normally draw up a statement of financial position after each day, as shown in the example above. Such an approach is not likely to be useful, given the relatively small number of transactions each day. We have done this in our examples to see the effect on the statement of financial position, transaction by transaction. In real life, a statement of financial position for the business is usually prepared at the end of a defined reporting period.

Determining the length of the reporting interval will involve weighing up the costs of producing the information against the perceived benefits of the information for decision-making purposes. In practice, the reporting interval will vary between businesses; it could be monthly, quarterly, half-yearly or annually. For external reporting purposes, an annual reporting cycle is the norm (although certain businesses, typically larger ones, report more frequently than this). However, for internal reporting purposes to managers, many businesses produce monthly financial statements.

The effect of trading transactions

In the example (Jerry and Company), we dealt with the effect on the statement of financial position of a number of different types of transactions that a business might undertake. These transactions covered the purchase of assets for cash and on credit, the repayment of borrowing and the injection of equity. However, one form of transaction, trading, has not yet been considered. To deal with the effect of trading transactions on the statement of financial position, let us return to our earlier example.

Example 2.2 (continued)

The statement of financial position that we drew up for Jerry and Company as at 6 March was as follows:

Jerry and Company
Statement of financial position as at 6 March

	£
ASSETS	
Cash at bank	17,000
Motor van	5,000
Inventories	3,000
Total assets	25,000
EQUITY AND LIABILITIES	
Equity	10,000
Liabilities – borrowing	12,000
Liabilities – trade payable	3,000
Total equity and liabilities	25,000

On 7 March, the business managed to sell all of the inventories for £5,000 and received a cheque immediately from the customer for this amount. The statement of financial position on 7 March, after this transaction has taken place, will be:

Jerry and Company
Statement of financial position as at 7 March

	£
ASSETS	
Cash at bank (17,000 + 5,000)	22,000
Motor van	5,000
Inventories (3,000 – 3,000)	–
Total assets	27,000
EQUITY AND LIABILITIES	
Equity (10,000 + (5,000 – 3,000))	12,000
Liabilities – borrowing	12,000
Liabilities – trade payable	3,000
Total equity and liabilities	27,000

We can see that the inventories (£3,000) have now disappeared from the statement of financial position, but the cash at bank has increased by the selling price of the inventories (£5,000). The net effect has therefore been to increase assets by £2,000 (that is, £5,000 less £3,000). This increase represents the net increase in wealth (the profit) that has arisen from trading. Also note that the equity of the business has increased by £2,000, in line with the increase in assets. This increase in equity reflects the fact that increases in wealth, as a result of trading or other operations, will be to the benefit of the owners and will increase their stake in the business.

Activity 2.6

What would have been the effect on the statement of financial position if the inventories had been sold on 7 March for £1,000 rather than £5,000?

The statement of financial position on 7 March would then have been:

Jerry and Company
Statement of financial position as at 7 March

	£
ASSETS	
Cash at bank (17,000 + 1,000)	18,000
Motor van	5,000
Inventories (3,000 – 3,000)	–
Total assets	23,000
EQUITY AND LIABILITIES	
Equity (10,000 + (1,000 – 3,000))	8,000
Liabilities – borrowing	12,000
Liabilities – trade payable	3,000
Total equity and liabilities	23,000

As we can see, the inventories (£3,000) will disappear from the statement of financial position but the cash at bank will rise by only £1,000. This will mean a net reduction in assets of £2,000. This reduction represents a loss arising from trading and will be reflected in a reduction in the equity of the owners.

We can see that any decrease in wealth (that is, a loss) arising from trading or other transactions will lead to a reduction in the owner's stake in the business. If the business wished to maintain the level of assets as at 6 March, it would be necessary to obtain further funds from the owners or from borrowing, or both.

What we have just seen means that the accounting equation can be extended as follows:

> Assets (at the end = Equity (amount at the start of the period
> of the period)　　　　+ profit (or – loss) for the period)
> 　　　　　　　　　　+ Liabilities (at the end of the period)

(This is assuming that the owner makes no injections or withdrawals of equity during the period.)

As we have seen, the profit (or loss) for the period is shown on the statement of financial position as an addition to (or a reduction of) equity. Any funds introduced or withdrawn by the owner for living expenses or other reasons also affect equity. If the owners withdrew £1,500 for their own use, the equity of the owners would be reduced by £1,500.

If the drawings were in cash, the balance of cash would decrease by £1,500 in the statement of financial position.

Note that, like all statement of financial position items, the amount of equity is cumulative. This means that any profit made that is not taken out as drawings by the owner(s) remains in the business. These retained (or 'ploughed-back') profits have the effect of expanding the business.

Classifying assets

If the items on the statement of financial position are listed haphazardly, with assets at the top of the statement and equity and liabilities underneath, it can be confusing, even though it may contain all of the information and be mathematically correct. To help users to understand the information, it is normally presented more clearly; assets and claims are usually grouped into categories. Assets may be categorised as being either current or non-current.

Current assets

→ **Current assets** are basically assets that are held for the short term. To be more precise, they are assets that meet any of the following conditions:

- they are held for sale or consumption during the business's normal operating cycle;
- they are expected to be sold within the next year;
- they are held principally for trading;
- they are cash, or near cash such as easily marketable, short-term investments.

The operating cycle of a business, mentioned above, is the time between buying and/or creating a product or service and receiving the cash on its sale. For most businesses, this will be less than a year.

The most common current assets are inventories (stock), customers who owe money for goods or services supplied on credit (trade receivables), and cash.

Perhaps it is worth making the point here that most sales made by most businesses are made on credit. This is to say that the goods pass to, or the service is rendered to, the customer at one point but the customer pays later. Retail sales are the only significant exception to this general point.

For businesses that sell goods, rather than render a service, the current assets of inventories, trade receivables and cash are interrelated. They circulate within a business as shown in Figure 2.2. We can see that cash can be used to buy inventories, which are then sold on credit. When the credit customers (trade receivables) pay, the business receives an injection of cash, and so on.

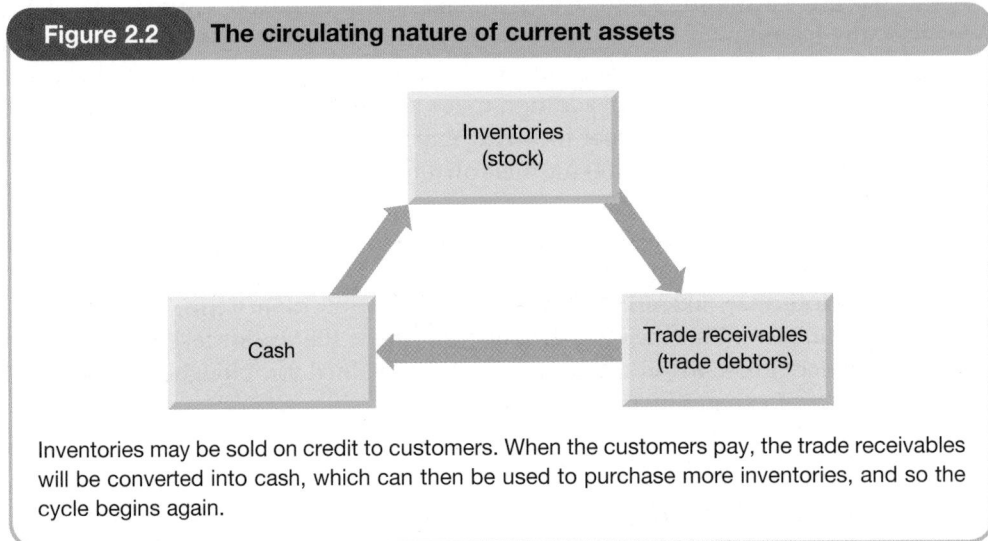

Figure 2.2 **The circulating nature of current assets**

Inventories may be sold on credit to customers. When the customers pay, the trade receivables will be converted into cash, which can then be used to purchase more inventories, and so the cycle begins again.

For purely service businesses, the situation is similar, except that inventories are not involved.

Non-current assets

→ **Non-current assets** (also called fixed assets) are simply assets that do not meet the definition of current assets. They tend to be held for long-term operations.

This distinction between assets that are continuously circulating within the business (current) and assets used for long-term operations (non-current) may be helpful when trying to assess the appropriateness of the mix of assets held. Most businesses will need a certain amount of both types of asset to operate effectively.

Activity (2.7)

Can you think of two examples of assets that may be classified as non-current assets for an insurance business?

Examples of assets that may be defined as being non-current are:

- property
- furniture
- motor vehicles
- computers
- computer software
- reference books.

This is not an exhaustive list. You may have thought of others.

It is important to appreciate that how a particular asset is classified (that is, between current and non-current) may vary according to the nature of the business. This is because the *purpose* for which a particular type of asset is held may differ from business to business. For example, a motor vehicle manufacturer will normally hold inventories of the finished motor vehicles produced for resale; it would, therefore, classify them as part of the current assets. On the other hand, a business that uses motor vehicles for delivering its goods to customers (that is, as part of its long-term operations) would classify them as non-current assets.

Activity (2.8)

The assets of Kunalun and Co., a large advertising agency, are as follows:

- cash at bank
- fixtures and fittings
- office equipment
- motor vehicles
- property
- computer equipment
- work in progress (that is, partly completed work for clients).

Which of these do you think should be defined as non-current assets and which should be defined as current assets?

Your answer should be as follows:

Non-current assets	*Current assets*
Fixtures and fittings	Cash at bank
Office equipment	Work in progress
Motor vehicles	
Property	
Computer equipment	

Classifying claims

As we have already seen, claims are normally classified into equity (owner's claim) and liabilities (claims of outsiders). Liabilities are further classified as either current or non-current.

Current liabilities

→ **Current liabilities** are basically amounts due for settlement in the short term. To be more precise, they are liabilities that meet any of the following conditions:

- they are expected to be settled within the business's normal operating cycle;
- they are held principally for trading purposes;
- they are due to be settled within a year after the end of the reporting period;
- there is no right to defer settlement beyond a year after the end of the reporting period.

Non-current liabilities

→ **Non-current liabilities** represent amounts due that do not meet the definition of current liabilities and so represent longer-term liabilities.

Note that it is quite common for non-current liabilities to become current liabilities. For example, borrowings that are due to be repaid within 18 months following the date of a particular statement of financial position will appear as a non-current liability, but if the borrowings have not been paid off in the meantime, they will appear as a current liability in the statement of financial position as at one year later.

This classification of liabilities can help gain a clearer impression of the ability of the business to meet its maturing obligations (that is, claims that must shortly be met). The value of the current liabilities (that is, the amounts that must be paid within the normal operating cycle) can be compared with the value of the current assets (that is, the assets that either are cash or will turn into cash within the normal operating cycle).

The classification of liabilities should also help to highlight how the long-term finance of the business is raised. If a business relies on long-term borrowings to finance the business, the financial risks associated with the business will increase. This is because these borrowings will bring a commitment to make periodic interest payments and capital repayments. The business may be forced to stop trading if this commitment is not fulfilled. Thus, when raising long-term finance, a business must try to strike the right balance between non-current liabilities and owner's equity. We shall consider this issue in more detail in Chapter 7.

Activity 2.9

Can you think of one example of a current liability and one of a non-current liability?

An example of a current liability would be amounts owing to suppliers for goods supplied on credit (known as trade payables or trade creditors) or a bank overdraft (a form of short-term bank borrowing that is repayable on demand). An example of a non-current liability would be long-term borrowings.

Statement layouts

Now that we have looked at the classification of assets and liabilities, we shall consider the layout of the statement of financial position. Although there is an almost infinite number of ways in which the same information on assets and claims could be presented, we shall consider two basic layouts. The first of these follows the style that we adopted with Jerry and Company earlier (see pages 46–51). A more comprehensive example of this style is shown in Example 2.3.

Example 2.3

Brie Manufacturing
Statement of financial position as at 31 December 2009

	£000
ASSETS	
Non-current assets	
Property	45
Plant and equipment	30
Motor vans	19
	94
Current assets	
Inventories	23
Trade receivables	18
Cash at bank	12
	53
Total assets	147
EQUITY AND LIABILITIES	
Equity	60
Non-current liabilities	
Long-term borrowings	50
Current liabilities	
Trade payables	37
Total equity and liabilities	147

The non-current assets have a total of £94,000, which together with the current assets total of £53,000 gives a total of £147,000 for assets. Similarly, the equity totals £60,000, which together with the £50,000 for non-current liabilities and £37,000 for current liabilities gives a total for equity and liabilities of £147,000.

Within each category of asset (non-current and current) shown in Example 2.3, the items are listed in reverse order of liquidity (nearness to cash). Thus, the assets that are furthest from cash are listed first and the assets that are closest to cash are listed last. In the case of non-current assets, property is listed first as this asset is usually the most difficult to turn into cash and motor vans are listed last as there is usually a ready market for them. In the case of current assets, we have already seen that inventories are converted to trade receivables and then trade receivables are converted to cash.

Hence, under the heading of current assets, inventories are listed first, followed by trade receivables and finally cash itself. This ordering of assets is a normal practice, which is followed irrespective of the layout used.

Note that, in addition to a grand total for assets held, subtotals for non-current assets and current assets are shown. Subtotals are also used for non-current liabilities and current liabilities when more than one item appears within these categories.

A slight variation from the standard layout illustrated in Example 2.3 is as shown in Example 2.4.

Example 2.4

Brie Manufacturing
Statement of financial position as at 31 December 2009

	£000
ASSETS	
Non-current assets	
Property	45
Plant and equipment	30
Motor vans	19
	94
Current assets	
Inventories	23
Trade receivables	18
Cash at bank	12
	53
Total assets	147
LIABILITIES	
Non-current liabilities	
Long-term borrowings	(50)
Current liabilities	
Trade payables	(37)
Total liabilities	(87)
Net assets	60
EQUITY	60

We can see that the total liabilities are deducted from the total assets. This derives a figure for net assets – which is equal to equity. Using this format, the basic accounting equation is rearranged so that:

$$\text{Assets} - \text{Liabilities} = \text{Equity}$$

This rearranged equation highlights the fact that equity represents the residual interest of the owner(s) after deducting all liabilities of the business.

Self-assessment question 2.1

The following information relates to Simonson Engineering as at 30 September 2009:

	£
Plant and equipment	25,000
Trade payables	18,000
Short-term borrowing	26,000
Inventories	45,000
Property	72,000
Long-term borrowing	51,000
Trade receivables	48,000
Equity at 1 October 2008	117,500
Cash in hand	1,500
Motor vehicles	15,000
Fixtures and fittings	9,000
Profit for the year to 30 September 2009	18,000
Drawings for the year to 30 September 2009	15,000

Required:

Prepare a statement of financial position for the business using the standard layout illustrated in Example 2.3.

The answer to this question can be found at the back of the book on page 722.

Capturing a moment in time

As we have already seen, the statement of financial position reflects the assets, equity and liabilities of a business at *a specified point in time*. It has been compared to a photograph. A photograph 'freezes' a particular moment in time and will represent the situation only at that moment. Hence, events may be quite different immediately before and immediately after the photograph was taken. When examining this statement, therefore, it is important to establish the date for which it has been drawn up. This information should be prominently displayed in the statement of financial position heading, as shown above in Example 2.4. When we are trying to assess current financial position, the more recent the statement of financial position date, the better.

A business will normally prepare a statement of financial position as at the close of business on the last day of its accounting year. In the UK, businesses are free to choose their accounting year. When making a decision on which year-end date to choose, commercial convenience can often be a deciding factor. For example, a business operating in the retail trade may choose to have a year-end date early in the calendar year (for example, 31 January) because trade tends to be slack during that period and more staff time is available to help with the tasks involved in the preparation of the annual financial statements (such as checking the amount of inventories held). Since trade is slack, it is also a time when the amount of inventories held by the retail business is likely to be unusually low as compared with other times of the year. Thus the statement of financial position, though showing a fair view of what it purports to show, may not show a picture of what is more typically the position of the business over the rest of the year.

The role of accounting conventions

Accounting has a number of rules or conventions that have evolved over time. They have evolved as attempts to deal with practical problems experienced by preparers and users of financial statements, rather than to reflect some theoretical ideal. In preparing the statements of financial position earlier, we have followed various **accounting conventions**, though they have not been explicitly mentioned. We shall now identify and discuss the major conventions that we have applied.

Business entity convention

For accounting purposes, the business and its owner(s) are treated as being quite separate and distinct. This is why owners are treated as being claimants against their own business in respect of their investment in the business. The **business entity convention** must be distinguished from the legal position that may exist between businesses and their owners. For sole proprietorships and partnerships, the law does not make any distinction between the business and its owner(s). For limited companies, on the other hand, there is a clear legal distinction between the business and its owners. (As we shall see in Chapter 4, the limited company is regarded as having a separate legal existence.) For accounting purposes these legal distinctions are irrelevant and the business entity convention applies to all businesses.

Historic cost convention

The **historic cost convention** holds that the value of assets shown on the statement of financial position should be based on their acquisition cost (that is, historic cost). This method of measuring asset value takes preference over other methods based on some form of current value. Many people, however, find the historic cost convention difficult to support, as outdated historic costs are unlikely to help in the assessment of current financial position. It is often argued that recording assets at their current value would provide a more realistic view of financial position and would be relevant for a wide range of decisions. However, a system of measurement based on current values can present a number of problems.

Activity (2.10)

Plumber and Company has some motor vans that are used by staff when visiting customers' premises to carry out work. It is now the last day of the business's accounting year.

If it were decided to show the vans on the statement of financial position at a current value (rather than a value based on their historic cost), how might the business arrive at a suitable value and how reliable would this figure be?

Two ways of deriving a current value are to find out:

● how much would have to be paid to buy vans of a similar type and condition;
● how much a motor van dealer would pay for the vans, were the business to sell them.

Both options will normally rely on opinion and so a range of possible values could be produced for each. For example, both the cost to replace the vans and the proceeds of selling them is likely to vary from one dealer to another. Moreover, the range of values for each option could be significantly different from one option to the other. (The selling prices of the vans are likely to be lower than the amount required to replace them.) Thus, any value finally decided upon could arouse some debate.

Activity 2.10 illustrates that the term 'current value' can be defined in different ways. It can be defined broadly as either the current replacement cost or the current realisable value (selling price) of an asset. These two types of valuation may result in quite different figures being produced to represent the current value of an item. Furthermore, the broad terms 'replacement cost' and 'realisable value' can be defined in different ways. We must therefore be clear about what kind of current value accounting we wish to use.

Activity 2.10 also illustrates the practical problems associated with current value accounting. Current values, however defined, are often difficult to establish with any real degree of objectivity. The figures produced may be heavily dependent on the opinion of managers. Unless current value figures are capable of some form of independent verification, there is a danger that the financial statements will lose their credibility among users. In fact, motor vans probably pose a less severe problem than do many other types of asset. This is because there tends to be a ready market for motor vans, which means that a value can be identified by contacting a dealer. For a highly specialised piece of equipment, perhaps one that was created to meet the precise needs of the particular business, identifying a replacement cost, or worse still a selling price, could be very difficult.

By reporting assets at their historic cost, it is argued that more reliable information is produced. Reporting in this way reduces the need for judgements, as the amount paid for a particular asset is usually a matter of demonstrable fact. Information based on past costs, however, may not always be relevant to the needs of users.

Later in the chapter, we shall consider the valuation of assets in the statement of financial position in more detail. We shall see that the historic cost convention is not always rigidly adhered to. Departures from this convention are becoming more frequent.

Prudence convention

→ The **prudence convention** holds that caution should be exercised when making accounting judgements. This means that liabilities and losses should not be understated while assets and profits should not be overstated. The application of this convention usually involves recording all losses at once and in full; this refers to both actual losses and expected losses. Profits, on the other hand, are recognised only when they actually arise. Greater emphasis is, therefore, placed on expected losses than on expected profits. To illustrate the application of this convention, let us assume that certain inventories held by a business prove unpopular with customers and so a decision is made to sell them below their original cost. The prudence convention requires that the expected loss from future sales be recognised immediately rather than when the goods are eventually sold. If, however, these inventories could have been sold above their original cost, profit would only be recognised at the time of sale.

The prudence convention evolved to counteract the excessive optimism of some managers and owners and is designed to prevent an overstatement of financial position. There is, however, a risk that it will introduce a bias towards understatement of both financial position and profit.

Activity (2.11)

What problems might arise if an excessively prudent view is taken of the financial position and performance of a business?

Excessive prudence will lead to an overstatement of losses and an understatement of profits and financial position. This will obscure the underlying financial reality and may lead users to make bad decisions. The owners, for example, may sell their stake in the business at a lower price than they would have received if a fairer picture of the financial health of the business had been presented.

In recent years, the prudence convention has weakened its grip on accounting and has become a less dominant force. Nevertheless, it remains an important convention.

Going concern convention

→ The **going concern convention** holds that the financial statements should be prepared on the assumption that the business will continue operations for the foreseeable future, unless this is known not to be true. In other words, it is assumed that there is no intention, or need, to sell off the non-current assets of the business. Such a sale may arise where the business is in financial difficulties and needs to pay amounts borrowed that are due for repayment. This convention is important because the market (sale) value of many non-current assets is often low in relation to the values at which they appear in the statement of financial position. This means that were a forced sale to occur, there is the likelihood that assets will be sold for less than their statement of financial position value. Such anticipated losses should be fully recorded as soon as the business's going concern status is called into question. However, where there is no expectation of a need to sell off the assets, the value of non-current assets can continue to be shown at their recorded values.

Dual aspect convention

→ The **dual aspect convention** asserts that each transaction has two aspects, both of which will affect the statement of financial position. Thus the purchase of a motor car for cash results in an increase in one asset (motor car) and a decrease in another (cash). The repayment of borrowings results in the decrease in a liability (borrowings) and the decrease in an asset (cash).

Activity 2.12

What are the two aspects of each of the following transactions?

1 Purchase £1,000 inventories on credit.
2 Owner withdraws £2,000 in cash.
3 Repayment of borrowings of £3,000.

Your answer should be as follows:

1 Inventories increase by £1,000, trade payables increase by £1,000.
2 Equity reduces by £2,000, cash reduces by £2,000.
3 Borrowings reduce by £3,000, cash reduces by £3,000.

Recording the dual aspect of each transaction ensures that the statement of financial position will continue to balance.

Figure 2.3 summarises the main accounting conventions that exert an influence on the construction of the statement of financial position.

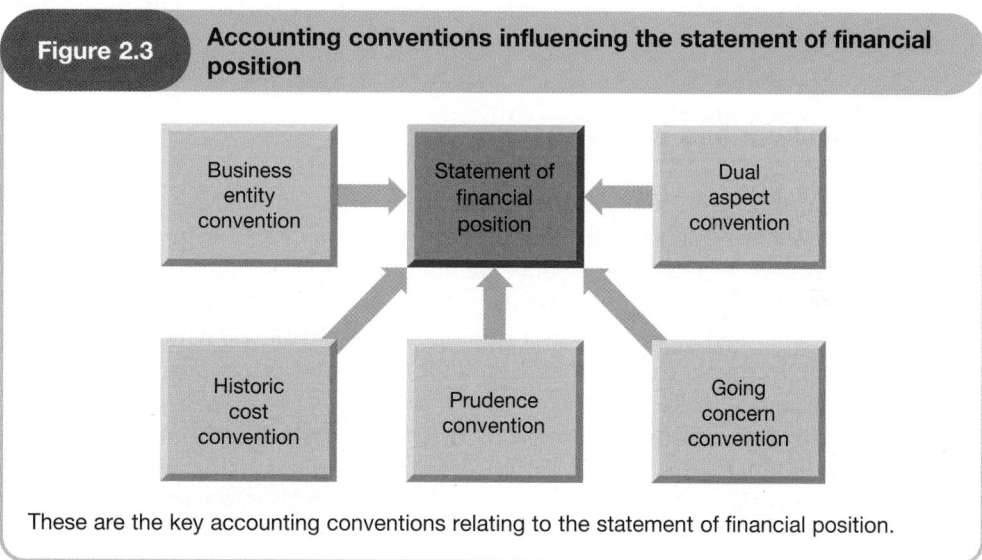

Figure 2.3 Accounting conventions influencing the statement of financial position

These are the key accounting conventions relating to the statement of financial position.

Money measurement

We saw earlier that a resource will only be regarded as an asset and included on the statement of financial position if it can be measured in monetary terms, with a reasonable degree of reliability. Some resources of a business, however, do not meet this criterion and so are excluded from the statement of financial position. As a result, the scope of this statement is limited.

Activity (2.13)

Can you think of resources of a business that cannot usually be measured reliably in monetary terms?

In answering this activity you may have thought of the following:

- the quality of the human resources of the business
- the reputation of the business's products
- the location of the business
- the relationship a business enjoys with its customers.

There have been occasional attempts to measure and report resources of a business that are normally excluded from the statement of financial position so as to provide a more complete picture of its financial position. These attempts, however, invariably fail the reliability test. We saw in Chapter 1 that a lack of reliability affects the quality of financial statements. Unreliable measurement can lead to inconsistency in reporting and can create uncertainty among users, which in turn undermines the credibility of the financial statements.

Some key resources of a business that normally defy reliable measurement are now discussed.

Goodwill and brands

Some intangible non-current assets are similar to tangible non-current assets: they have a clear and separate identity and the cost of acquiring the asset can be reliably measured. Examples normally include patents, trademarks, copyrights and licences. Other intangible non-current assets, however, are quite different. They lack a clear and separate identity and reflect a hotchpotch of attributes, which are part of the essence of the business. Goodwill and product brands are often examples of assets that lack a clear and separate identity.

The term 'goodwill' is often used to cover various attributes such as the quality of the products, the skill of employees and the relationship with customers. The term 'product brands' is also used to cover various attributes, such as the brand image, the quality of the product, the trademark and so on. Where goodwill and product brands have been generated internally by the business, it is often difficult to determine their cost or to measure their current market value or even to be clear that they really exist. They are, therefore, excluded from the statement of financial position.

When they are acquired through an arm's-length transaction, however, the problems of uncertainty about their existence and measurement are resolved. (An 'arm's-length' transaction is one that is undertaken between two unconnected parties.) If goodwill is acquired when taking over another business, or if a business acquires a particular product brand from another business, these items will be separately identified and a price agreed for them. Under these circumstances, they can be regarded as assets (for accounting purposes) by the business that acquired them and included on the statement of financial position.

To agree a price for acquiring goodwill or product brands means that some form of valuation must take place and this raises the question as to how it is done. Usually, the valuation will be based on estimates of future earnings from holding the asset, a process that is fraught with difficulties. Nevertheless, a number of specialist businesses now exist that are prepared to take on this challenge. **Real World 2.2** reveals how one specialist business ranked and valued the top ten brands in the world for 2009.

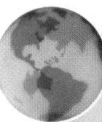

Real World 2.2

Brand leaders

Millward Brown Optimor, part of WPP marketing services group, recently produced a report that ranked and valued the top ten world brands for 2009 as follows.

Ranking	Brand	Value ($m)
1	Google	100,039
2	Microsoft	76,249
3	Coca-Cola	67,625
4	IBM	66,622
5	McDonalds	66,575
6	Apple	63,113
7	China Mobile	61,283
8	GE (General Electric)	59,793
9	Vodafone	53,727
10	Marlboro	49,460

We can see that the valuations placed on the brands owned are quite staggering.

Source: Brandz Top 100 Most Valuable Global Brands 2009, Millward Brown Optimor 2009, www.millwardbrown.com.

Human resources

Attempts have been made to place a monetary measurement on the human resources of a business, but without any real success. There are, however, certain limited circumstances in which human resources are measured and reported in the statement of financial position. These circumstances normally arise with professional football clubs. While football clubs cannot own players, they can own the rights to the players' services. Where these rights are acquired by compensating other clubs for releasing the players from their contracts, an arm's-length transaction arises and the amounts paid provide a reliable basis for measurement. This means that the rights to services can be regarded as an asset of the club for accounting purposes (assuming, of course, the player will also bring benefits to the club).

Real World 2.3 describes how one leading club reports its investment in players on the statement of financial position.

Real World 2.3

Spurs players appear on the pitch and on the statement of financial position

Tottenham Hotspur Football Club (Spurs) has acquired several key players as a result of paying transfer fees to other clubs. In common with most UK football clubs, Spurs reports the cost of acquiring the rights to the players' services on its statement of financial position. The club's statement as at 30 June 2008 shows the cost of registering its squad of players at about £121m. This figure does not include 'home-grown' players such as Ledley King, because Spurs did not pay a transfer fee for them and so no clear-cut value can be placed on their services. During the year to 30 June 2008, the club was very active in the transfer market and eight players, including Jonathan Woodgate, joined the club for a combined sum of £32.7m. Nine players left the club during the year for a combined sale price of £18.8m. One of the leavers, Jermain Defoe, returned to Spurs in January 2009.

The item of players' registrations is shown as an intangible asset in the statement of financial position as it is the rights to services, not the players, that are the assets.

Source: Tottenham Hotspur plc Annual Report 2008.

Monetary stability

When using money as the unit of measurement, we normally fail to recognise the fact that it will change in value over time. In the UK and throughout much of the world, however, inflation has been a persistent problem. This has meant that the value of money has declined in relation to other assets. In past years, high rates of inflation have resulted in statements of financial position, which were prepared on an historic cost basis, reflecting figures for assets that were much lower than if current values were employed. Rates of inflation have been relatively low in recent years and so the disparity between historic cost values and current values has been less pronounced. Nevertheless, it can still be significant and has added fuel to the debate concerning how to measure asset values on the statement of financial position. It is to this issue that we now turn.

Valuing assets

It was mentioned earlier that, when preparing the statement of financial position, the historic cost convention is normally applied for the reporting of assets. However, this point requires further elaboration as, in practice, it is not simply a matter of recording each asset on the statement of financial position at its original cost. We shall see that things are a little more complex than this. Before discussing the valuation rules in some detail, however, we should point out that these rules are based on international accounting standards, which are rules that are generally accepted throughout much of the world. The nature and role of accounting standards will be discussed in detail in Chapter 5.

Tangible non-current assets (property, plant and equipment)

→ Tangible non-current assets normally consist of **property, plant and equipment**, and we shall refer to them in this way from now on. This is a rather broad term that covers all items mentioned in its title plus other items such as motor vehicles and fixtures and fittings. All of these items are, in essence, the 'tools' used by the business to generate wealth, that is, they are used to produce or supply goods and services or for administration purposes. They tend to be held for the longer term, which means for more than one accounting period.

Initially these items are recorded at their historic cost, which will include any amounts spent on getting them ready for use. However, they will normally be used up over time as a result of wear and tear, obsolescence and so on. The amount used up, which is referred to as *depreciation*, must be measured for each accounting period for which the assets are held. Although we shall leave a detailed examination of depreciation until Chapter 3, we need to know that when an asset has been depreciated, this must be reflected in the statement of financial position.

The total depreciation that has accumulated over the period since the asset was acquired must be deducted from its cost. This net figure (that is, the cost of the asset less the total depreciation to date) is referred to as the *carrying amount, net book value*, or *written-down value*. The procedure just described is not really a contravention of the historic cost convention. It is simply recognition of the fact that a proportion of the historic cost of the non-current asset has been consumed in the process of generating benefits for the business.

Although using historic cost (less any depreciation) is the 'benchmark treatment' for recording these assets, an alternative is allowed. Property, plant and equipment can be
→ recorded using **fair values** provided that these values can be measured reliably. The fair values, in this case, are the current market values (that is, the exchange values in an arm's-length transaction). The use of fair values, rather than depreciated cost figures, can provide users with more up-to-date information, which may well be more relevant to their needs. It may also place the business in a better light, as assets such as property may have increased significantly in value over time. Of course, increasing the statement of financial position value of an asset does not make that asset more valuable. However, perceptions of the business may be altered by such a move.

One consequence of revaluing non-current assets is that the depreciation charge will be increased. This is because the depreciation charge is based on the increased value of the asset.

Real World 2.4 shows that one well-known business revalued its land and buildings and, by doing so, greatly improved the look of its statement of financial position.

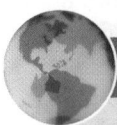 **Real World 2.4**

Marks marks up land and buildings

The statement of financial position of Marks and Spencer plc, a major high street retailer, as at 28 March 2009 reveals land and buildings at a carrying amount, or net book value, of £2,458m. These land and buildings were revalued by a firm of independent surveyors five years earlier and this has been reflected in subsequent statements of financial position. The effect of the revaluation was to give an uplift of £530.9m against the previous carrying amount.

Source: Marks and Spencer plc Annual Report 2009, Note 14 to the financial statements, annualreport.marksandspencer.com.

Activity (2.14)

Refer to the statement of financial position of Brie Manufacturing shown earlier in Example 2.3 (page 55). What would be the effect of revaluing the property to a figure of £110,000 on the statement of financial position?

The effect on the statement of financial position would be to increase the property to £110,000 and the gain on revaluation (that is, £110,000 – £45,000 = £65,000) would be added to the equity of the owner, as it is the owner who will benefit from the gain. The revised statement of financial position would therefore be as follows:

Brie Manufacturing
Statement of financial position as at 31 December 2009

	£000
ASSETS	
Non-current assets (property, plant and equipment)	
Property	110
Plant and equipment	30
Motor vans	19
	159
Current assets	
Inventories	23
Trade receivables	18
Cash at bank	12
	53
Total assets	212
EQUITY AND LIABILITIES	
Equity (60 + 65)	125
Non-current liabilities	
Long-term borrowings	50
Current liabilities	
Trade payables	37
Total equity and liabilities	212

Once assets are revalued, the frequency of revaluation then becomes an important issue as assets recorded at out-of-date values can mislead users. Using out-of-date revaluations on the statement of financial position is the worst of both worlds. It lacks the objectivity and verifiability of historic cost; it also lacks the realism of current values. Where fair values are used, revaluations should therefore be frequent enough to ensure that the carrying amount of the revalued asset does not differ materially from its fair value at the statement of financial position date.

When an item of property, or plant, or equipment is revalued on the basis of fair values, all assets within that particular group must be revalued. Thus, it is not acceptable to revalue some property but not others. Although this provides some degree of consistency within a particular group of assets, it does not, of course, prevent the statement of financial position from containing a mixture of valuations.

Intangible non-current assets

For these assets, the 'benchmark treatment' is, once again, that they are measured initially at historic cost. What follows, however, will depend on whether the asset has a finite or an infinite useful life. (Purchased goodwill can provide an example of an asset with an infinitely useful life, though its life can be limited.) Where the asset has a finite life, any depreciation (or *amortisation* as it is usually termed for intangible non-current assets) following acquisition will be deducted from its cost. Where, however, the asset has an infinite life, it will not be amortised. Instead, it will be tested annually to see whether there has been any fall in value. This point is discussed in more detail in the following section.

Once again, the alternative of revaluing intangible assets using fair values is available. However, this can only be used where an active market exists, which allows fair values to be properly determined. In practice, this is a rare occurrence.

The impairment of non-current assets

There is always a risk that both types of non-current asset (tangible and intangible) may suffer a significant fall in value. This may be due to factors such as changes in market conditions, technological obsolescence and so on. In some cases, this fall in value may lead to the carrying amount, or net book value, of the asset being higher than the amount that could be recovered from the asset through its continued use or through its sale. When this occurs, the asset value is said to be impaired and the general rule is to reduce the value on the statement of financial position to the recoverable amount. Unless this is done, the asset value will be overstated.

Activity (2.15)

With which one of the accounting conventions that we discussed earlier is this accounting treatment consistent?

The answer is the prudence convention, which states that actual or anticipated losses should be recognised in full.

In many situations, a business may use either historic cost, less any depreciation, or a value-based measure when reporting its non-current assets. However, where the value-based measure is the impaired value and is smaller than the historic-cost-based value, the business has no choice; the use of depreciated historic cost is not an option.

Real World 2.5 provides an example of where the application of the 'impairment rule', as it is called, resulted in huge write-downs (that is, reductions in the statement of financial position value of the assets) for one large business.

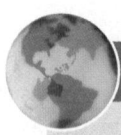

Real World 2.5

Painting a rosy picture

FT

Akzo Nobel, the Dutch paints and chemicals company, on Tuesday defended its £8bn ($11.6bn) acquisition of ICI in 2007 after it took a €1.2bn ($1.5bn) impairment charge on the former UK industrial giant because of sharply lower paint sales.

The company saw the volume of paint sold fall by 10 per cent in the fourth quarter, with even steeper declines in Asia, one of the areas where ICI had been strong. This prompted the move to slash growth estimates and fair value for ICI.

'It's not a world of high growth any more, it's a world with completely different challenges,' said Hans Wijers, chief executive. 'We expect 2009 to be an uncertain year with a lot of volatility [and] with challenging volume circumstances.'

The €1.2bn impairment charge cuts into the €4.4bn of goodwill the company recorded when it acquired ICI and its Dulux brand name, but Akzo defended its previous assumptions as conservative.

'Could we have anticipated that the world economy would go down so much?' Mr Wijers said. 'I'm not sorry about [the ICI] transaction. It was the right thing to do at the right time and the company has become much stronger because of it.'

Source: 'Akzo Nobel defends ICI takeover', Michael Steen, FT.com, 24 February 2009.

We saw earlier that intangible, non-current assets with infinite lives must be tested annually to see whether there has been any impairment. Other non-current assets, however, must be also tested where events suggest that impairment has taken place.

We should bear in mind that impairment reviews involve making judgements concerning the appropriate value to place on assets. Employing independent valuers to make these judgements may give users greater confidence in the information reported. There is always a risk that managers will manipulate impairment values to portray a picture that they would like users to see.

Inventories

It is not only non-current assets that run the risk of a significant fall in value. The inventories of a business could also suffer this fate, which could be caused by factors such as reduced selling prices, obsolescence, deterioration, damage and so on. Where a fall in value means that the amount likely to be recovered from the sale of the inventories will be lower than their cost, this loss must be reflected in the statement of financial position. Thus, if the net realisable value (that is, selling price less any selling costs) falls below the historic cost of inventories held, the former should be used as the basis of valuation. This reflects, once again, the influence of the prudence convention on the statement of financial position.

Real World 2.6 reveals how one well-known business wrote down the inventories of one of its products following a sharp reduction in selling prices.

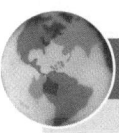

Real World 2.6

You're fired!

'You're fired!' is what some investors might like to tell Amstrad, run by *Apprentice* star Sir Alan Sugar. . . . Shares in the company fell nearly 10 per cent as it revealed that sales of its much-vaunted videophone have failed to take off.

Amstrad launched the E3, a phone allowing users to hold video calls with each other, in a blaze of publicity last year. But, after cutting the price from £99 to £49, Amstrad sold just 61,000 E3s in the year to June and has taken a £5.7m stock [inventories] write-down.

Source: 'Amstrad (AMT)', *Investors Chronicle*, 7 October 2005.

The published financial statements of large businesses will normally show the basis on which inventories are valued. **Real World 2.7** shows how one business reports this information.

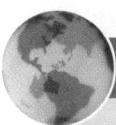

Real World 2.7

Reporting inventories

The 2009 annual report of Ted Baker plc, a leading designer clothes brand, includes the following explanation concerning inventories:

> Inventories and work in progress* are stated at the lower of cost and net realisable value. Cost includes materials, direct labour and inward transportation costs. Net realisable value is based on estimated selling price, less further costs expected to be incurred to completion and disposal. Provision is made for obsolete, slow moving or defective items where appropriate.
>
> *The term *work in progress* refers to partially-completed inventories.

Source: Ted Baker plc Report and Accounts 2009, p. 44.

Meeting user needs

The statement of financial position is the oldest of the three main financial statements and many businesses have prepared one on a regular basis, even when there was no regulation requiring it to be produced. This suggests that it is regarded as providing useful information. There are various ways in which the statement of financial position may help users, including the following:

● *It provides an insight into how the business is financed and how its funds are deployed.* We can see how much finance is contributed by the owners and how much is contributed by outside lenders. We can also see the different kinds of assets acquired and how much is invested in each kind.

● *It can provide a basis for assessing the value of the business.* Since the statement of financial position lists, and places a value on, the various assets and claims, it can provide a starting point for assessing the value of the business. It is, however, severely limited in the extent to which it can do this. We have seen earlier that accounting rules may result in assets being shown at their historic cost and that the restrictive definition of assets may exclude certain business resources from the statement of financial position. Ultimately, the value of a business will be based on its ability to generate wealth in the future. Because of this, assets need to be valued on the basis of their wealth-generating potential. Also, other business resources that do not meet the restrictive definition of assets, such as brand values, need to be similarly valued and included. In Chapter 14 we shall see how assets and other business resources can be valued on the basis of their future wealth-generating ability.

- *Relationships between assets and claims can be assessed.* It can be useful to look at relationships between statement of financial position items, for example the relationship between how much wealth is tied up in current assets and how much is owed in the short term (current liabilities). From this relationship, we can see whether the business has sufficient short-term assets to cover its maturing obligations. We shall look at this and other relationships between statement of financial position items in some detail in Chapter 7.
- *Performance can be assessed.* The effectiveness of a business in generating wealth (making a profit) can usefully be assessed against the amount of investment that was involved. The relationship between profit earned over a particular period and the value of the net assets involved can be very helpful to many of those involved with the business concerned. This is particularly likely to be of interest to the owners and the managers. This and similar relationships will also be explored in detail in Chapter 7.

Summary

The main points of this chapter may be summarised as follows.

The major financial statements

- There are three major financial statements: the statement of cash flows, the income statement (profit and loss account) and the statement of financial position (balance sheet).
- The statement of cash flows shows the cash movements over a particular period.
- The income statement shows the wealth (profit) generated over a particular period.
- The statement of financial position shows the accumulated wealth at a particular point in time.

The statement of financial position

- This sets out the assets of the business, on the one hand, and the claims against those assets, on the other.
- Assets are resources of the business that have certain characteristics, such as the ability to provide future benefits.
- Claims are obligations on the part of the business to provide cash, or some other benefit, to outside parties.
- Claims are of two types: equity and liabilities.
- Equity represents the claim(s) of the owner(s) and liabilities represent the claims of others, apart from the owner.

Classification of assets and liabilities

- Assets are normally categorised as being current or non-current.

- Current assets are cash or near cash or are held for sale or consumption in the normal course of business, or for trading, or for the short term.

- Non-current assets are assets that are not current assets. They are normally held for the long-term operations of the business.

- Liabilities are normally categorised as being current or non-current liabilities.

- Current liabilities represent amounts due in the normal course of the business's operating cycle, or are held for trading, or are to be settled within a year of, or cannot be deferred for at least a year after, the end of the reporting period.

- Non-current liabilities represent amounts due that are not current liabilities.

Statement of financial position layouts

- The standard layout begins with assets at the top of the statement of financial position and places equity and liabilities underneath.

- A variation of the standard layout begins with the assets at the top of the statement of financial position. From the total assets figure are deducted the non-current and current liabilities to arrive at a net assets figure. Equity is placed underneath.

Accounting conventions

- Accounting conventions are the rules of accounting that have evolved to deal with practical problems experienced by those preparing financial statements.

- The main conventions relating to the statement of financial position include business entity, historic cost, prudence, going concern and dual aspect.

Money measurement

- Using money as the unit of measurement limits the scope of the statement of financial position.

- Certain resources such as goodwill, product brands and human resources are difficult to measure. An 'arm's-length transaction' is normally required before such assets can be reliably measured and reported on the statement of financial position.

- Money is not a stable unit of measurement – it changes in value over time.

Asset valuation

- The 'benchmark treatment' is to show property, plant and equipment at historic cost less any amounts written off for depreciation. However, fair values may be used rather than depreciated cost.

- The 'benchmark treatment' for intangible non-current assets is to show the items at historic cost. Only assets with a finite life will be amortised (depreciated) and fair values will rarely be used.

- Where the recoverable amount from tangible non-current assets is below their carrying amount, this lower amount is reflected in the statement of financial position.

- Inventories are shown at the lower of cost or net realisable value.

The usefulness of the statement of financial position

- It shows how finance has been raised and how it has been been deployed.
- It provides a basis for valuing the business, though the conventional statement of financial position can only be a starting point.
- Relationships between various statement of financial position items can usefully be explored.
- Relationships between wealth generated and wealth invested can be helpful indicators of business effectiveness.

 Now check your progress in your personal Study Plan

→ **Key terms**

statement of cash flows p. 39	non-current (fixed) assets p. 52
income statement p. 39	current liabilities p. 54
statement of financial position p. 39	non-current liabilities p. 54
final accounts p. 42	accounting conventions p. 58
assets p. 43	business entity convention p. 58
claims p. 43	historic cost convention p. 58
tangible assets p. 45	prudence convention p. 59
intangible assets p. 45	going concern convention p. 60
equity p. 45	dual aspect convention p. 60
liabilities p. 46	property, plant and equipment p. 65
current assets p. 51	fair values p. 65

Further reading

If you would like to explore the topics covered in this chapter in more depth, we recommend the following books:

A Guide Through International Financial Reporting Standards (IFRSs) 2008, IASC Foundation Education, July 2008, IAS 16, IAS 36 and IAS 38.

Corporate Financial Accounting and Reporting, *Sutton T.*, 2nd edn, Financial Times Prentice Hall, 2004, chapters 2 and 8.

Financial Accounting and Reporting, *Elliott B. and Elliott J.*, 13th edn, Financial Times Prentice Hall, 2010, chapters 16 and 18.

Insights into IFRS, *KPMG*, 5th edn, 2008/9, Thomson, 2008, Sections 1.2, 3.2, 3.3, 3.8 and 3.10.

Review questions

Answers to these questions can be found at the back of the book on pages 739–40.

2.1 An accountant prepared a statement of financial position for a business. In this statement, the equity of the owner was shown next to the liabilities. This confused the owner, who argued: 'My equity is my major asset and so should be shown as an asset on the statement of financial position.' How would you explain this misunderstanding to the owner?

2.2 'The statement of financial position shows how much a business is worth.' Do you agree with this statement? Discuss.

2.3 What is meant by the accounting equation? How does the form of this equation differ between the two statement of financial position layouts mentioned in the chapter?

2.4 In recent years there have been attempts to place a value on the 'human assets' of a business in order to derive a figure that can be included on the statement of financial position. Do you think humans should be treated as assets? Would 'human assets' meet the conventional definition of an asset for inclusion on the statement of financial position?

Exercises

Exercises 2.5 to 2.8 are more advanced than 2.1 to 2.4. Those with **coloured numbers** have answers at the back of the book, starting on page 752.

If you wish to try more exercises, visit the students' side of the Companion Website and MyAccountingLab.

2.1 On Thursday, the fourth day of his business venture, Paul, the street trader in wrapping paper (see earlier in the chapter, pages 39–42), bought more inventories for £53 cash. During the day he sold inventories that had cost £33 for a total of £47.

Required:
Draw up the three financial statements for Paul's business venture for Thursday.

2.2 The equity belongs to Paul because he is the sole owner of the business. Can you explain how the figure for equity by Thursday evening has arisen? You will need to look back at the events of Monday, Tuesday and Wednesday (in this chapter on pages 39 to 42) to do this.

2.3 While on holiday in Bridlington, Helen had her credit cards and purse stolen from the beach while she was swimming. She was left with only £40, which she had kept in her hotel room, but she had three days of her holiday remaining. She was determined to continue her holiday and decided to make some money to enable her to do so. She decided to sell orange juice to holidaymakers using the local beach. On day 1 she bought 80 cartons of orange juice at £0.50 each for cash and sold 70 of these at £0.80 each. On the following day she bought 60 cartons at £0.50 each for cash and sold 65 at £0.80 each. On the third and final day she bought another 60 cartons at £0.50 each for cash. However, it rained and, as a result, business was poor. She managed to sell 20 at £0.80 each but sold off the rest of her inventories at £0.40 each.

Required:
Prepare an income statement and statement of cash flows for each day's trading and prepare a statement of financial position at the end of each day's trading.

2.4 On 1 March, Joe Conday started a new business. During March he carried out the following transactions:

1 March	Deposited £20,000 in a bank account.
2 March	Bought fixtures and fittings for £6,000 cash, and inventories £8,000 on credit.
3 March	Borrowed £5,000 from a relative and deposited it in the bank.
4 March	Bought a motor car for £7,000 cash and withdrew £200 in cash for his own use.
5 March	A further motor car costing £9,000 was bought. The motor car bought on 4 March was given in part exchange at a value of £6,500. The balance of purchase price for the new car was paid in cash.
6 March	Conday won £2,000 in a lottery and paid the amount into the business bank account. He also repaid £1,000 of the borrowings.

Required:

Draw up a statement of financial position for the business at the end of each day.

2.5 The following is a list of the assets and claims of Crafty Engineering Ltd at 30 June last year:

	£000
Trade payables	86
Motor vehicles	38
Long-term borrowing from Industrial Finance Co.	260
Equipment and tools	207
Short-term borrowings	116
Inventories	153
Property	320
Trade receivables	185

Required:

(a) Prepare the statement of financial position of the business as at 30 June last year from the above information using the standard layout. (*Hint*: There is a missing item that needs to be deduced and inserted.)

(b) Discuss the significant features revealed by this financial statement.

2.6 The statement of financial position of a business at the start of the week is as follows:

	£
ASSETS	
Property	145,000
Furniture and fittings	63,000
Inventories	28,000
Trade receivables	33,000
Total assets	269,000
EQUITY AND LIABILITIES	
Equity	203,000
Short-term borrowing (bank overdraft)	43,000
Trade payables	23,000
Total equity and liabilities	269,000

During the week the following transactions take place:

(a) Inventories sold for £11,000 cash; these inventories had cost £8,000.

(b) Sold inventories for £23,000 on credit; these inventories had cost £17,000.

(c) Received cash from trade receivables totalling £18,000.

(d) The owners of the business introduced £100,000 of their own money, which was placed in the business bank account.

(e) The owners brought a motor van, valued at £10,000, into the business.

(f) Bought inventories on credit for £14,000.

(g) Paid trade payables £13,000.

Required:

Show the statement of financial position after all of these transactions have been reflected.

2.7 The following is a list of assets and claims of a manufacturing business at a particular point in time:

	£
Short-term borrowing	22,000
Property	245,000
Inventories of raw materials	18,000
Trade payables	23,000
Plant and equipment	127,000
Loan from Manufacturing Finance Co. (long-term borrowing)	100,000
Inventories of finished goods	28,000
Delivery vans	54,000
Trade receivables	34,000

Required:

Write out a statement of financial position in the standard format incorporating these figures. (*Hint:* There is a missing item that needs to be deduced and inserted.)

2.8 You have been talking to someone who had read a few chapters of an accounting text some years ago. During your conversation the person made the following statements:

(a) The income statement shows how much cash has come into and left the business during the accounting period and the resulting balance at the end of the period.

(b) In order to be included in the statement of financial position as an asset, an item needs to be worth something in the market – that is all.

(c) The accounting equation is:

$$\text{Assets} + \text{Equity} = \text{Liabilities}$$

(d) Non-current assets are things that cannot be moved.

(e) Goodwill has an indefinite life and so should not be amortised.

Required:

Comment critically on each of the above statements, going into as much detail as you can.

CHAPTER 3

Measuring and reporting financial performance

Introduction

In this chapter, we continue our examination of the major financial statements by looking at the income statement. This statement was briefly considered in Chapter 2 and we shall now examine it in some detail. We shall see how it is prepared and how it links with the statement of financial position. We shall also consider some of the key measurement problems to be faced when preparing the income statement.

Learning outcomes

When you have completed this chapter, you should be able to:

● Discuss the nature and purpose of the income statement.

● Prepare an income statement from relevant financial information and interpret the information that it contains.

● Discuss the main recognition and measurement issues that must be considered when preparing the income statement.

● Explain the main accounting conventions underpinning the income statement.

 **Remember to create your own personalised Study Plan**

What does it mean?

Tate and Lyle plc, whose business is sweeteners, starches and sugar refining, reported sales revenue of £3,818 million and a profit of £187 million for the year ending on 31 March 2008. To understand fully the significance of these figures, we must be clear about the nature of revenue and profit. This means that we must be able to answer questions such as:

- Does the sales revenue of £3,818 million represent the cash generated from sales for the period?
- What is the relationship between the sales revenue and the profit for the period?
- Can the profit for the period of £187 million be measured with complete accuracy and certainty?
- Does the profit figure of £187 million mean that the business had £187 million *more* in the bank at the end of the year than it had at the beginning?
- How can the sales revenue and profit figures help in assessing performance?

The answers to these and other questions are covered in the chapter.

The income statement

In Chapter 2 we considered the statement of financial position (balance sheet). We saw that it sets out the wealth of a business, and who contributed that wealth, for a particular moment in time. However, it is not usually enough for users of financial statements to have information relating only to this aspect of financial health. Businesses exist for the primary purpose of generating wealth, or profit, and it is the profit generated *during a period* that is the concern of many users. The purpose of the income statement – or profit and loss account, as it is sometimes called – is to measure and report how much **profit** (wealth) the business has generated over a period. As with the statement of financial position, which we examined in Chapter 2, the principles of preparation are the same irrespective of whether the income statement is for a sole proprietorship business or for a limited company.

The measurement of profit requires that the total revenue of the business, generated during a particular period, be identified. **Revenue** is simply a measure of the inflow of economic benefits arising from the ordinary activities of a business. These benefits will result in either an increase in assets (such as cash or amounts owed to the business by its customers) or a decrease in liabilities. Different forms of business enterprise will generate different forms of revenue. Some examples of the different forms that revenue can take are as follows:

- sales of goods (for example, by a manufacturer)
- fees for services (for example, of a solicitor)
- subscriptions (for example, of a club)
- interest received (for example, on an investment fund).

Real World 3.1 shows the various forms of revenue generated by a leading football club.

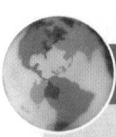

Real World 3.1

Gunning for revenue

Arsenal Football Club generated total revenue of £223 million for the year ended 31 May 2008. Like other leading clubs, it relies on various forms of revenue to sustain its success. Figure 3.1 shows the contribution of each form of revenue for the year.

Figure 3.1 **Arsenal's revenue for the year ended 31 May 2008**

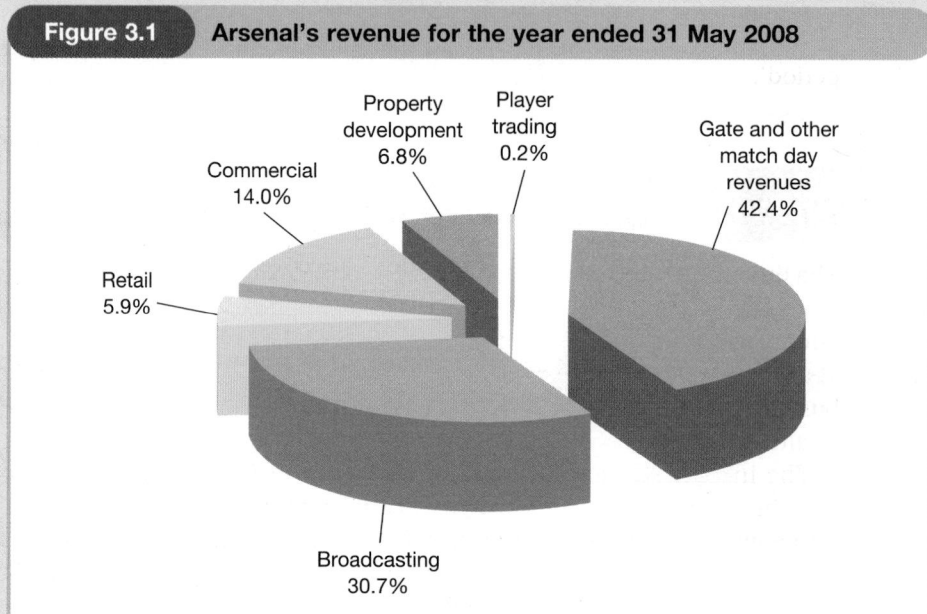

We can see that gate receipts and broadcasting are the main forms of revenue, although commercial activities (including sponsorship and events) are also significant. Together, these three account for more than 87 per cent of total revenue.

Source: Based on information in Arsenal Holdings plc Annual Report 2008, Notes to the Accounts, p. 36.

→   The total expenses relating to each period must also be identified. **Expense** is really the opposite of revenue. It represents the outflow of economic benefits arising from the ordinary activities of a business. This loss of benefits will result in either a decrease in assets (such as cash) or an increase in liabilities (such as amounts owed to suppliers). Expenses are incurred in the process of generating, or attempting to generate, revenue. The nature of the business will again determine the type of expenses that will be incurred. Examples of some of the more common types of expenses are:

● the cost of buying the goods that are sold during the period concerned – known as *cost of sales* or *cost of goods sold*
● salaries and wages
● rent and rates
● motor vehicle running expenses
● insurance
● printing and stationery
● heat and light
● telephone and postage.

→ The **income statement** simply shows the total revenue generated during a particular period and deducts from this the total expenses incurred in generating that revenue. The difference between the total revenue and total expenses will represent either profit (if revenue exceeds expenses) or loss (if expenses exceed revenue). Thus, we have:

> **Profit (or loss) for the period = Total revenue for the period less Total expenses incurred in generating that revenue**

→ The period over which profit or loss is normally measured is usually known as the **accounting period**, but it is sometimes called the 'reporting period' or 'financial period'.

Different roles

The income statement and the statement of financial position should not be viewed in any way as substitutes for one another. Rather they should be seen as performing different roles. The statement of financial position, as stated earlier, sets out the position at a single moment in time: it is a 'snapshot' of the make-up of the wealth held by the business. The income statement, on the other hand, is concerned with the *flow* of wealth over a period of time. The two statements are, however, closely related.

The income statement links the statements of financial position at the beginning and the end of an accounting period. Thus, at the start of a new accounting period, the statement of financial position shows the opening wealth position of the business. After an appropriate period, an income statement is prepared to show the wealth generated over that period. A statement of financial position is then also prepared to reveal the new wealth position at the end of the period. This statement of financial position will incorporate the changes in wealth that have occurred since the previous statement of financial position was drawn up.

We saw in Chapter 2 (page 51) that the effect on the statements of financial position of making a profit (or loss) means that the accounting equation can be extended as follows:

> **Assets (at the end of the period) = Equity (amount at the start of the period + profit (or – loss) for the period) + Liabilities (at the end of the period)**

(This is assuming that the owner makes no injections or withdrawals of equity during the period.)

The amount of profit or loss for the period affects the statement of financial position as an adjustment to equity.

The above equation can be extended to:

> **Assets (at the end of the period) = Equity (amount at the start of the period) + (sales revenue – expenses) + Liabilities (at the end of the period)**

In theory, it would be possible to calculate the profit (or loss) for the period by making all adjustments for revenue and expenses through the equity section of the statement of financial position. However, this would be rather cumbersome. A better solution is to have an 'appendix' to the equity section, in the form of an income statement. By deducting expenses from revenue for the period, the income statement derives the profit (or loss) for adjustment to the equity figure in the statement of financial position. This profit (or loss) figure represents the net effect of trading for the period. Through this 'appendix', users are presented with a detailed and more informative view of performance.

Income statement layout

The layout of the income statement will vary according to the type of business to which it relates. To illustrate an income statement, let us consider the case of a retail business (that is, a business that buys goods in their completed state and resells them). This type of business usually has straightforward operations and, as a result, the income statement is relatively easy to understand.

Example 3.1 sets out a typical layout for the income statement of a retail business.

Example 3.1

Better-Price Stores
Income statement for the year ended 31 October 2009

	£
Sales revenue	232,000
Cost of sales	(154,000)
Gross profit	78,000
Salaries and wages	(24,500)
Rent and rates	(14,200)
Heat and light	(7,500)
Telephone and postage	(1,200)
Insurance	(1,000)
Motor vehicle running expenses	(3,400)
Depreciation – fixtures and fittings	(1,000)
Depreciation – motor van	(600)
Operating profit	24,600
Interest received from investments	2,000
Interest on borrowings	(1,100)
Profit for the year	25,500

We saw in Chapter 2 that brackets are used to denote when an item is to be deducted. This convention is used by accountants in preference to + or – signs and will be used throughout the text.

Gross profit

→ The first part of the income statement is concerned with calculating the **gross profit** for the period. We can see that revenue, which arises from selling the goods, is the first item to appear. Deducted from this item is the cost of sales (also called cost of goods sold) during the period. This gives the gross profit, which represents the profit from buying and selling goods, without taking into account any other revenues or expenses associated with the business.

Operating profit

From the gross profit, other expenses (overheads) that have been incurred in operating the business (salaries and wages, rent and rates and so on) are deducted.

→ The resulting figure is known as the **operating profit** for the accounting period. This represents the wealth generated during the period from the normal activities of the business. It does not take account of any income that the business may have from activities that are not included in its normal operations. Better-Price Stores in Example 3.1 is a retailer, so the interest on some spare cash that the business has invested is not part of its operating profit. Costs of financing the business are also ignored in the calculation of the operating profit.

Profit for the year

Having established the operating profit, we add any non-operating income (such as interest receivable) and deduct any interest payable on borrowings made by the busi-

→ ness, to arrive at the **profit for the year** (or net profit). This is the income that is attributable to the owner(s) of the business and which will be added to the equity figure in the statement of financial position. As can be seen, profit for the year is a residual: that is, the amount remaining after deducting all expenses incurred in generating the sales revenue for the period and taking account of non-operating income.

Further issues

Having set out the main principles involved in preparing an income statement, we need to consider some further points.

Cost of sales

→ The **cost of sales** (or cost of goods sold) figure for a period can be identified in different ways. In some businesses, the cost of sales amount for each individual sale is identified at the time of the transaction. Each item of sales revenue is closely matched with the relevant cost of that sale and so identifying the cost of sales figure for inclusion in the income statement is not a problem. Many large retailers (for example, supermarkets) have point-of-sale (checkout) devices that not only record each sale but also simultaneously pick up the cost of the goods that are the subject of the particular sale. Other businesses that sell a relatively small number of high-value items (for example, an engineering business that produces custom-made equipment) also tend to match sales revenue with the cost of the goods sold, at the time of the sale. However, some businesses (for example, small retailers) do not usually find it practical to match each sale to a particular cost of sales figure as the accounting period progresses. Instead, therefore, they identify the cost of sales figure at the end of the accounting period.

Deriving the cost of sales after the end of the accounting period

To understand how this is done, we need to remember that the cost of sales figure represents the cost of goods that were *sold* by the business during the period rather than the cost of goods that were *bought* by that business during the period. Part of the goods bought during a particular period may remain in the business, as inventories, and not be sold until a later period. To derive the cost of sales for a period, we need to know the amount of opening and closing inventories for the period and the cost of goods bought during the period. Example 3.2 illustrates how the cost of sales is derived.

Example 3.2

Better-Price Stores, which we considered in Example 3.1 above, began the accounting year with unsold inventories of £40,000 and during that year bought inventories at a cost of £189,000. At the end of the year, unsold inventories of £75,000 were still held by the business.

The opening inventories at the beginning of the year *plus* the goods bought during the year will represent the total goods available for resale. Thus:

	£
Opening inventories	40,000
Purchases (goods bought)	189,000
Goods available for resale	229,000

The closing inventories will represent that portion of the total goods available for resale that remains unsold at the end of the period. Thus, the cost of goods actually sold during the period must be the total goods available for resale *less* the inventories remaining at the end of the period. That is:

	£
Goods available for resale	229,000
Closing inventories	(75,000)
Cost of sales (or cost of goods sold)	154,000

These calculations are sometimes shown on the face of the income statement as in Example 3.3.

Example 3.3

	£	£
Sales revenue		232,000
Cost of sales:		
Opening inventories	40,000	
Purchases (goods bought)	189,000	
Closing inventories	(75,000)	(154,000)
Gross profit		78,000

This is just an expanded version of the first section of the income statement for Better-Price Stores, as set out in Example 3.1. We have simply included the additional information concerning inventories balances and purchases for the year provided in Example 3.2.

Classifying expenses

The classifications for the revenue and expense items, as with the classifications of various assets and claims in the statement of financial position, are often a matter of judgement by those who design the accounting system. Thus, the income statement set out in Example 3.1 could have included the insurance expense with the telephone and postage expense under a single heading – say, 'general expenses'. Such decisions are normally based on how useful a particular classification will be to users. This will usually mean, however, that expense items of material size will be shown separately. For businesses that trade as limited companies, there are rules that dictate the classification of various items appearing in the financial statements for external reporting purposes. These rules will be discussed in Chapters 4 and 5.

Activity 3.1

The following information relates to the activities of H & S Retailers for the year ended 30 April 2009:

	£
Motor vehicle running expenses	1,200
Closing inventories	3,000
Rent and rates payable	5,000
Motor vans – cost less depreciation	6,300
Annual depreciation – motor vans	1,500
Heat and light	900
Telephone and postage	450
Sales revenue	97,400
Goods purchased	68,350
Insurance	750
Loan interest payable	620
Balance at bank	4,780
Salaries and wages	10,400
Opening inventories	4,000

Prepare an income statement for the year ended 30 April 2009. (*Hint*: Not all items listed should appear on this statement.)

Activity 3.1 continued

Your answer to this activity should be as follows:

H & S Retailers
Income statement for the year ended 30 April 2009

	£	£
Sales revenue		97,400
Cost of sales:		
Opening inventories	4,000	
Purchases	68,350	
Closing inventories	(3,000)	(69,350)
Gross profit		28,050
Salaries and wages		(10,400)
Rent and rates		(5,000)
Heat and light		(900)
Telephone and postage		(450)
Insurance		(750)
Motor vehicle running expenses		(1,200)
Depreciation – motor vans		(1,500)
Operating profit		7,850
Loan interest		(620)
Profit for the year		7,230

Note that neither the motor vans nor the bank balance are included in this statement, because they are both assets and so neither revenues nor expenses.

The accounting period

We have seen already that for reporting to those outside the business, a financial reporting cycle of one year is the norm, though some large businesses produce a half-yearly, or interim, financial statement to provide more frequent feedback on progress. For those who manage a business, however, it is probably essential to have much more frequent feedback on performance. Thus it is quite common for income statements to be prepared on a quarterly, monthly, weekly or even daily basis in order to show how things are progressing.

Recognising revenue

A key issue in the measurement of profit concerns the point at which revenue is recognised. Revenue arising from the sale of goods or provision of a service could be recognised at various points. Where, for example, a motor car dealer receives an order for a new car from one of its customers, the associated revenue could be recognised by the dealer

- at the time that the order is placed by the customer;
- at the time that the car is collected by the customer; or
- at the time that the customer pays the dealer.

These three points could well be quite far apart, particularly where the order relates to a specialist car that is sold to the customer on credit.

The point chosen is not simply a matter of academic interest: it can have a profound impact on the total revenues reported for a particular accounting period. This, in turn, could have a profound effect on profit. If the sale transaction straddled the end of an accounting period, the choice made between the three possible times for recognising the revenue could determine whether it is included as revenue of an earlier accounting period or a later one.

When dealing with the sale of goods or the provision of services, the main criteria for recognising revenue are that:

- the amount of revenue can be measured reliably, and
- it is probable that the economic benefits will be received.

An additional criterion, however, must be applied where the revenue comes from the sale of goods, which is that:

- ownership and control of the items should pass to the buyer.

Activity 3.2 provides an opportunity to apply these criteria to a practical problem.

Activity 3.2

A manufacturing business sells goods on credit (that is, the customer pays for the goods some time after they are received). Below are four points in the production/selling cycle at which revenue might be recognised by the business:

1. when the goods are produced;
2. when an order is received from the customer;
3. when the goods are delivered to, and accepted by, the customer;
4. when the cash is received from the customer.

A significant amount of time may elapse between these different points. At what point do you think the business should recognise revenue?

All of the three criteria mentioned above will usually be fulfilled at point 3: when the goods are passed to, and accepted by, the customer. This is because

- the selling price and the settlement terms will have been agreed and therefore the amount of revenue can be reliably measured;
- delivery and acceptance of the goods leads to ownership and control passing to the buyer;
- transferring ownership gives the seller legally enforceable rights that make it probable that the buyer will pay.

We can see that the effect of applying these criteria is that a sale on credit is usually recognised *before* the cash is received. Thus, the total sales revenue figure shown in the income statement may include sales transactions for which the cash has yet to be received. The total sales revenue figure in the income statement for a period will often, therefore, be different from the total cash received from sales during that period.

Where goods are sold for cash rather than on credit, the revenue will normally be recognised at the point of sale. It is at this point that all the criteria will usually be met. For cash sales, there will be no difference in timing between reporting sales revenue and cash received.

Real World 3.2 sets out the revenue recognition criteria for the travel business, TUI Travel plc (which owns First Choice, Thompson, Exodus and many other well-known names). We can see that, although clients may pay for flights or holidays some time before they go, any money received in advance of the departure date, or use of the service, is not treated as revenue until later.

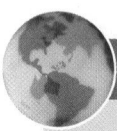

Real World 3.2

Selling point

(i) *Revenue recognition*
Revenue is recognised in the income statement when the significant risks and rewards of ownership have been transferred to the buyer.

Revenue in respect of in-house product is recognised on the date of departure. Travel agency commissions and other revenues received from the sale of third-party product are recognised when they are earned, typically on receipt of final payment. Revenue from individual travel modules directly booked by the customer with airline, hotels and incoming agencies is recognised when the customer departs or uses the respective service.

No revenue is recognised if there are significant uncertainties regarding recovery of the consideration due, associated costs or possible return of goods.

(ii) *Client monies received in advance (deferred income)*
Client monies received at the balance sheet [statement of financial position] date relating to holidays commencing and flights departing after the year end is deferred and included within trade and other payables.

Source: TUI Travel plc Annual Report and Accounts 2008, p. 68.

Long-term contracts

Some contracts, both for goods and for services, can last for more than one accounting period. If the business providing the goods or service were to wait until the contract is fulfilled before recognising revenue, the income statement could give a misleading impression of the wealth generated in the various accounting periods covered by the contract. This is a particular problem for businesses that undertake major long-term contracts, where a single contract could represent a large proportion of their total activities.

Construction contracts

Construction contracts often extend over a long period of time. Suppose that a customer enters into a contract with a builder to have a new factory built that will take three years to complete. In such a situation, it is possible to recognise revenue *before* the factory is completed provided that the building work can be broken down into a number of stages and each stage can be measured reliably. Let us assume that building the factory could be broken down into the following stages:

- Stage 1 – clearing and levelling the land and putting in the foundations.
- Stage 2 – building the walls.

- Stage 3 – putting on the roof.
- Stage 4 – putting in the windows and completing all the interior work.

Each stage can be awarded a separate price with the total for all the stages being equal to the total contract price for the factory. This means that, as each stage is completed, the builder can recognise the price for that stage as revenue and bill the customer accordingly. This is provided that the outcome of the contract as a whole can be estimated reliably.

If the builder were to wait until the factory was completed before recognising revenue, the income statement covering the final year of the contract would recognise all of the revenue on the contract and the income statements for each preceding year would recognise no revenue. This would give a misleading impression, as it would not reflect the work done during each period.

Real World 3.3 sets out the revenue recognition criteria for one large construction business.

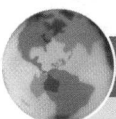

Real World 3.3

Tracking revenue

Jarvis plc is a business operating in the areas of road and rail infrastructure renewal, facilities management and plant hire. The point at which revenue on long-term contracts is recognised by the business is as follows:

> When the outcome of a long-term contract can be estimated reliably, contract revenue is recognised by reference to the degree of completion of each contract, based on the amounts certified and to be certified by the customer.

Source: Jarvis plc Annual Report and Accounts 2009, p. 41.

Services

Revenue from contracts for services may also be recognised in stages. Suppose a consultancy business has a contract to install a new computer system for the government, which will take several years to complete. Revenue can be recognised *before* the contract is completed as long as the contract can be broken down into stages and the particular stages of completion can be measured reliably. This is really the same approach as that used in the construction contract mentioned above.

Sometimes a continuous service is provided to a customer; for example, a telecommunications business may provide open access to the Internet to those who subscribe to the service. In this case, revenue is usually recognised as the service is rendered. Benefits from providing the service are usually assumed to flow evenly over time and so revenue is recognised evenly over the subscription period.

Where it is not possible to break down a service into particular stages of completion, or to assume that benefits from providing the service accrue evenly over time, revenue will not usually be recognised until the service is fully completed. A solicitor handling a house purchase for a client would normally be one such example.

Real World 3.4 provides an example of how one major business recognises revenue from providing services.

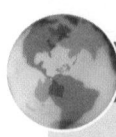

Real World 3.4

Sky-high broadcasting revenue

British Sky Broadcasting Group plc is a major satellite broadcaster that generates various forms of revenue. Here are the ways in which some of its revenues are recognised:

- Pay-per-view revenues – when the event (movie or football match) is viewed.
- Subscription services, including Sky TV and Sky Broadband – as the services are provided.
- Advertising revenues – when the advertising is broadcast.
- Installation, hardware and service revenue – when the goods and services are delivered.

Source: Based on information in British Sky Broadcasting Group plc Annual Report and Accounts 2009, p. 78.

When a service is provided, there will normally be a timing difference between the recognition of revenue and the receipt of cash. Revenue for providing services is often recognised *before* the cash is received, as with the sale of goods on credit. However, there are occasions when it is the other way around, usually because the business demands payment before providing the service.

Activity 3.3

Can you think of any examples where cash may be demanded in advance of a service being provided? (*Hint*: Try to think of services that you may use.)

Examples of cash being received in advance of the service being provided may include:

- rent received from letting premises
- telephone line rental charges
- TV licence (BBC) or subscription (for example, Sky) fees
- subscriptions received for the use of health clubs or golf clubs.

You may have thought of others.

Recognising expenses

Having decided on the point at which revenue is recognised, we can now turn to the issue of the recognition of expenses. The **matching convention** in accounting is designed to provide guidance concerning the recognition of expenses. This convention states that expenses should be matched to the revenue that they helped to generate. In other words, the expenses associated with a particular item of revenue must be taken into account in the same accounting period as that in which the item of revenue is included. Applying this convention may mean that a particular expense reported in the income statement for a period may not be the same figure as the cash paid for that item during the period. The expense reported might be either more or less than the cash paid during the period. Let us consider two examples that illustrate this point.

When the expense for the period is more than the cash paid during the period

Example 3.4

Domestic Ltd sells household electrical appliances. It pays its sales staff a commission of 2 per cent of sales revenue generated. Total sales revenue for last year amounted to £300,000. This will mean that the commission to be paid in respect of the sales for the year will be £6,000. However, by the end of the year, the amount of sales commission that had actually been paid to staff was £5,000. If the business reported only the amount paid, it would mean that the income statement would not reflect the full expense for the year. This would contravene the *matching convention* because not all of the expenses associated with the revenue of the year would have been matched in the income statement. This will be remedied as follows:

- Sales commission expense in the income statement will include the amount paid plus the amount outstanding (that is, £6,000 = £5,000 + £1,000).
- The amount outstanding (£1,000) represents an outstanding liability at the end of the year and will be included under the heading **accrued expenses**, or 'accruals', in the statement of financial position. As this item will have to be paid within 12 months of the year end, it will be treated as a current liability.
- The cash will already have been reduced to reflect the commission paid (£5,000) during the period.

These points are illustrated in Figure 3.2.

Figure 3.2 Accounting for sales commission

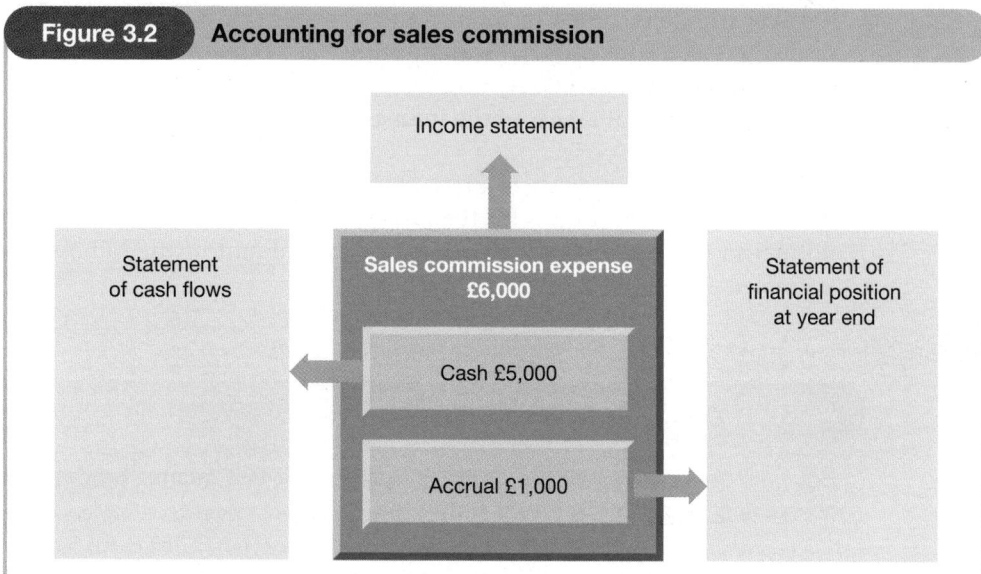

This illustrates the main points of Example 3.4. We can see that the sales commission expense of £6,000 (which appears in the income statement) is made up of a cash element of £5,000 and an accrued element of £1,000. The cash element appears in the statement of cash flows and the accrued element will appear as a year-end liability in the statement of financial position.

In principle, all expenses should be matched to the period in which the sales revenue to which they relate is reported. However, it is sometimes difficult to match certain expenses to sales revenue in the same precise way that we have matched sales commission to sales revenue. It is unlikely, for example, that electricity charges incurred can be linked directly to particular sales in this way. As a result, the electricity charges incurred by, say, a retailer would be matched to the *period* to which they relate. Example 3.5 illustrates this.

Example 3.5

Domestic Ltd, a retailer, has reached the end of its accounting year and has only paid for electricity for the first three-quarters of the year (amounting to £1,900). This is simply because the electricity company has yet to send out bills for the quarter that ends on the same date as Domestic Ltd's year end. The amount of Domestic Ltd's bill for the last quarter is £500. In this situation, the amount of the electricity expense outstanding is dealt with as follows:

- Electricity expense in the income statement will include the amount paid, plus the amount of the bill for the last quarter (that is, £1,900 + £500 = £2,400) in order to cover the whole year.
- The amount of the outstanding bill (£500) represents a liability at the end of the year and will be included under the heading 'accruals' or 'accrued expenses' in the statement of financial position. This item would normally have to be paid within 12 months of the year end and will, therefore, be treated as a current liability.
- The cash will already have been reduced to reflect the electricity paid (£1,900) during the period.

This treatment will mean that the correct figure for the electricity expense for the year will be included in the income statement. It will also have the effect of showing that, at the end of the accounting year, Domestic Ltd owed the amount of the last quarter's electricity bill. Dealing with the outstanding amount in this way reflects the dual aspect of the item and will ensure that the accounting equation is maintained.

Domestic Ltd may wish to draw up its income statement before it is able to discover how much it owes for the last quarter's electricity. In this case it is quite normal to make a reasonable estimate of the amount of the bill and to use this estimated amount as described above.

Activity (3.4)

How will the payment of the electricity bill for the last quarter be dealt with in the accounting records of Domestic Ltd?

When the electricity bill is eventually paid, it will be dealt with as follows:

- Reduce cash by the amount of the bill.
- Reduce the amount of the accrued expense as shown on the statement of financial position by the same amount.

If an estimated figure is used and there is a slight error in the estimate, a small adjustment (either negative or positive depending on the direction of the error) can be made to the following year's expense. Dealing with the estimation error in this way is not strictly correct, but the amount is likely to be insignificant.

Activity 3.5

Can you think of other expenses for a retailer, apart from electricity charges, that cannot be linked directly to sales revenue and for which matching will therefore be done on a time basis?

You may have thought of the following examples:

- rent and rates
- insurance
- interest payments
- licence fees payable.

This is not an exhaustive list. You may have thought of others.

When the amount paid during the period is more than the full expense for the period

It is not unusual for a business to be in a situation where it has paid more during the year than the full expense for that year. Example 3.6 illustrates how we deal with this.

Example 3.6

Images Ltd, an advertising agency, normally pays rent for its premises quarterly in advance (on 1 January, 1 April, 1 July and 1 October). On the last day of the last accounting year (31 December), it paid the next quarter's rent (£4,000) to the following 31 March, which was a day earlier than required. This would mean that a total of five quarters' rent was paid during the year. If Images Ltd reports all of the cash paid as an expense in the income statement, this would be more than the full expense for the year. This would contravene the matching convention because a higher figure than the expenses associated with the revenue of the year would appear in the income statement.

The problem is overcome by dealing with the rental payment as follows:

- Show the rent for four quarters as the appropriate expense in the income statement (that is, 4 × £4,000 = £16,000).
- The cash (that is, 5 × £4,000 = £20,000) would already have been paid during the year.
- Show the quarter's rent paid in advance (£4,000) as a prepaid expense under assets in the statement of financial position. (The rent paid in advance will appear as a current asset in the statement of financial position, under the heading **prepaid expenses** or 'prepayments'.)

In the next accounting period, this prepayment will cease to be an asset and will become an expense in the income statement of that period. This is because the rent prepaid relates to the next period and will be 'used up' during it.

These points are illustrated in Figure 3.3.

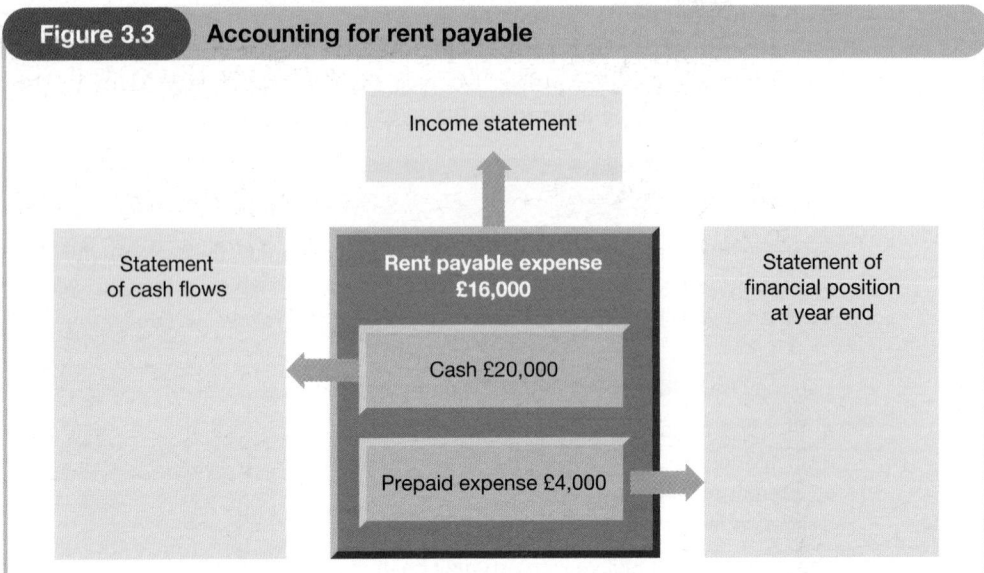

Figure 3.3   Accounting for rent payable

This illustrates the main points of Example 3.6. We can see that the rent expense of £16,000 (which appears in the income statement) is made up of four quarters' rent at £4,000 per quarter. This is the amount that relates to the period and is 'used up' during the period. The cash paid of £20,000 (which appears in the statement of cash flows) is made up of the cash paid during the period, which is five quarters at £4,000 per quarter. Finally, the prepayment of £4,000 (which appears on the statement of financial position) represents the payment made on 31 December and relates to the next financial year.

In practice, the treatment of accruals and prepayments will be subject to the **materiality convention** of accounting. This convention states that, where the amounts involved are immaterial, we should consider only what is reasonable. This may mean that an item will be treated as an expense in the period in which it is paid, rather than being strictly matched to the revenue to which it relates. For example, a business may find that, at the end of an accounting period, a bill of £5 has been paid for stationery that has yet to be delivered. For a business of any size, the time and effort involved in recording this as a prepayment would not be justified by the little effect that this would have on the measurement of profit or financial position. The amount would, therefore, be treated as an expense when preparing the income statement for the current period and ignored in the following period.

Profit, cash and accruals accounting

As we have just seen, revenue does not usually represent cash received, and expenses are not the same as cash paid. As a result, the profit figure (that is, total revenue minus total expenses) will not normally represent the net cash generated during a period. It is therefore important to distinguish between profit and liquidity. Profit is a measure of achievement, or productive effort, rather than a measure of cash generated. Although making a profit will increase wealth, as we have already seen in Chapter 2, cash is only one form in which that wealth may be held.

The above points are reflected in the **accruals convention** of accounting, which asserts that profit is the excess of revenue over expenses for a period, not the excess of cash receipts over cash payments. Leading on from this, the approach to accounting that is based on the accruals convention is frequently referred to as **accruals accounting**.

Thus, the statement of financial position and the income statement are both prepared on the basis of accruals accounting. The cash flow statement, on the other hand, is not, as it simply deals with cash receipts and payments.

Depreciation

→ The expense of **depreciation**, which appeared in the income statement in Activity 3.1, requires further explanation. Most non-current assets do not have a perpetual existence. They are eventually used up in the process of generating revenue for the business. In essence, depreciation is an attempt to measure that portion of the cost (or fair value) of a non-current asset that has been used up in generating the revenue recognised during a particular period. The depreciation charge is considered to be an expense of the period to which it relates. Depreciation tends to be relevant both to tangible non-current assets (property, plant and equipment) and to intangible non-current assets. We should be clear that the principle is the same for both types of non-current asset. We shall deal with each of the two in turn.

Tangible non-current assets (property, plant and equipment)

To calculate a depreciation charge for a period, four factors have to be considered:

- the cost (or fair value) of the asset
- the useful life of the asset
- the residual value of the asset
- the depreciation method.

The cost (or fair value) of the asset

The cost of an asset will include all costs incurred by the business to bring the asset to its required location and to make it ready for use. Thus, in addition to the costs of acquiring the asset, any delivery costs, installation costs (for example, setting up a new machine) and legal costs incurred in the transfer of legal title (for example, in purchasing property) will be included as part of the total cost of the asset. Similarly, any costs incurred in improving or altering an asset in order to make it suitable for its intended use within the business will also be included as part of the total cost.

Activity 3.6

Andrew Wu (Engineering) Ltd bought a new motor car for its marketing director. The invoice received from the motor car supplier showed the following:

	£
New BMW 325i	26,350
Delivery charge	80
Alloy wheels	660
Sun roof	200
Petrol	30
Number plates	130
Road fund licence	170
	27,620
Part exchange – Reliant Robin	(1,000)
Amount outstanding	26,620

→

Activity 3.6 continued

What is the total cost of the new car that will be treated as part of the business's property, plant and equipment?

The cost of the new car will be as follows:

	£
New BMW 325i	26,350
Delivery charge	80
Alloy wheels	660
Sun roof	200
Number plates	130
	27,420

This cost includes delivery charges, which are necessary to bring the asset into use, and it includes number plates, as they are a necessary and integral part of the asset. Improvements (alloy wheels and sun roof) are also regarded as part of the total cost of the motor car. The petrol and road fund licence, however, represent costs of operating the asset rather than a part of the total cost of acquiring it and making it ready for use: hence these amounts will be charged as an expense in the period incurred (although part of the cost of the licence may be regarded as a prepaid expense in the period incurred).

The part-exchange figure shown is part payment of the total amount outstanding and so is not relevant to a consideration of the total cost.

The fair value of an asset was defined in Chapter 2 as the exchange value that could be obtained in an arm's-length transaction. As we saw, assets may be revalued to fair value only if this can be measured reliably. When a revaluation is carried out, all items within the same class must be revalued and revaluations must be kept up to date.

The useful life of the asset

A tangible non-current asset has both a *physical life* and an *economic life*. The physical life will be exhausted through the effects of wear and tear and/or the passage of time. It is possible, however, for the physical life to be extended considerably through careful maintenance, improvements and so on. The economic life is decided by the effects of technological progress and by changes in demand. After a while, the benefits of using the asset may be less than the costs involved. This may be because the asset is unable to compete with newer assets, or because it is no longer relevant to the needs of the business. The economic life of a non-current tangible asset may be much shorter than its physical life. For example, a computer may have a physical life of eight years and an economic life of three years.

It is the economic life that will determine the expected useful life for the purpose of calculating depreciation. Forecasting the economic life, however, may be extremely difficult in practice: both the rate at which technology progresses and shifts in consumer tastes can be swift and unpredictable.

Residual value (disposal value)

 When a business disposes of a tangible non-current asset that may still be of value to others, some payment may be received. This payment will represent the **residual value,**

or *disposal value*, of the asset. To calculate the total amount to be depreciated, the residual value must be deducted from the cost of the asset. The likely amount to be received on disposal can, once again, be difficult to predict. The best guide is often past experience of similar assets sold.

Depreciation method

Once the amount to be depreciated (that is, the cost, or fair value, of the asset less any residual value) has been estimated, the business must select a method of allocating this depreciable amount between the accounting periods covering the asset's useful life. Although there are various ways in which the total depreciation may be allocated and, from this, a depreciation charge for each period derived, there are really only two methods that are commonly used in practice.

→ The first of these is known as the **straight-line method**. This method simply allocates the amount to be depreciated evenly over the useful life of the asset. In other words, an equal amount of depreciation is charged for each year that the asset is held.

Example 3.7

To illustrate this method, consider the following information:

Cost of machine	£78,124
Estimated residual value at the end of its useful life	£2,000
Estimated useful life	4 years

To calculate the depreciation charge for each year, the total amount to be depreciated must be calculated. This will be the total cost less the estimated residual value: that is, £78,124 − £2,000 = £76,124. Having done this, the annual depreciation charge can be derived by dividing the amount to be depreciated by the estimated useful life of the asset of four years. The calculation is therefore:

$$\frac{£76,124}{4} = £19,031$$

Thus, the annual depreciation charge that appears in the income statement in relation to this asset will be £19,031 for each of the four years of the asset's life.

The amount of depreciation relating to the asset will be accumulated for as long as the asset continues to be owned by the business. This accumulated depreciation figure will increase each year as a result of the annual depreciation amount charged to the income statement. This accumulated amount will be deducted from the cost of the asset on the statement of financial position. At the end of the second year, for example, the accumulated depreciation will be £19,031 × 2 = £38,062, and the asset details will appear on the statement of financial position as follows:

	£
Machine at cost	78,124
Accumulated depreciation	(38,062)
	40,062

→
→   The balance of £40,062 shown above is referred to as the **carrying amount** (sometimes also known as the **written-down value** or **net book value**) of the asset. It represents that portion of the cost (or fair value) of the asset that has still to be charged as an expense (written off) in future years. It must be emphasised that this figure does not represent the current market value, which may be quite different.

The straight-line method derives its name from the fact that the carrying amount of the asset at the end of each year, when plotted against time, will result in a straight line, as shown in Figure 3.4.

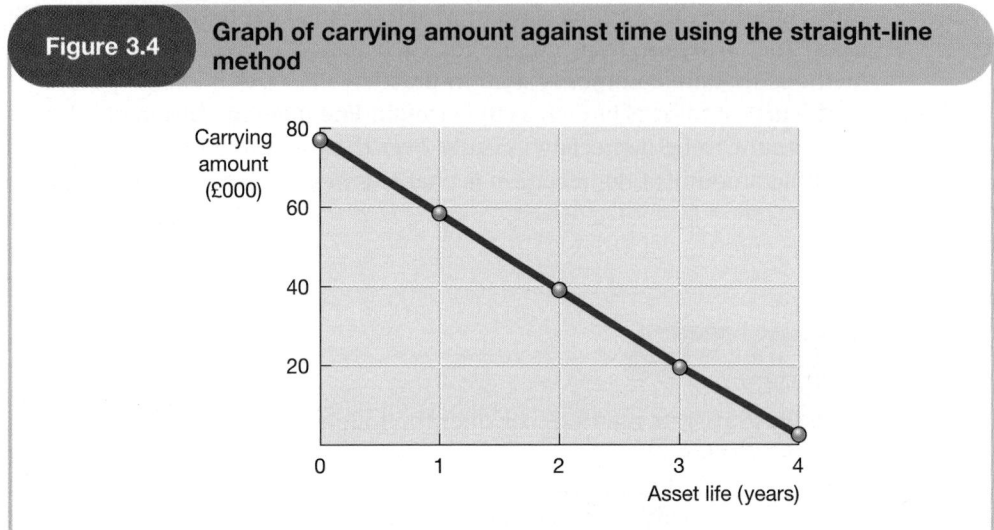

| Figure 3.4 | Graph of carrying amount against time using the straight-line method |

The carrying amount of the asset declines by a constant amount each year. This is because the straight-line method provides a constant depreciation charge each year. The result, when plotted on a graph, is a straight line.

→   The second approach to calculating depreciation for a period which is found in practice is referred to as the **reducing-balance method**. This method applies a fixed percentage rate of depreciation to the carrying amount of the asset each year. The effect of this will be high annual depreciation charges in the early years and lower charges in the later years. To illustrate this method, let us take the same information that was used in Example 3.7. By using a fixed percentage of 60 per cent of the carrying amount to determine the annual depreciation charge, the effect will be to reduce the carrying amount to £2,000 after four years.

The calculations will be as follows:

	£
Cost of machine	78,124
Year 1 Depreciation charge (60%* of cost)	(46,874)
Carrying amount	31,250
Year 2 Depreciation charge (60% of carrying amount)	(18,750)
Carrying amount	12,500
Year 3 Depreciation charge (60% of carrying amount)	(7,500)
Carrying amount	5,000
Year 4 Depreciation charge (60% of carrying amount)	(3,000)
Residual value	2,000

* See the following box for an explanation of how to derive the fixed percentage.

Deriving the fixed percentage

Deriving the fixed percentage to be applied requires the use of the following formula:

$$P = (1 - \sqrt[n]{R/C}) \times 100\%$$

where: P = the depreciation percentage
  n = the useful life of the asset (in years)
  R = the residual value of the asset
  C = the cost, or fair value, of the asset.

The fixed percentage rate will, however, be given in all examples used in this text.

We can see that the pattern of depreciation is quite different between the two methods. If we plot the carrying amount of the asset, which has been derived using the reducing-balance method, against time, the result will be as shown in Figure 3.5.

Figure 3.5	Graph of carrying amount against time using the reducing-balance method

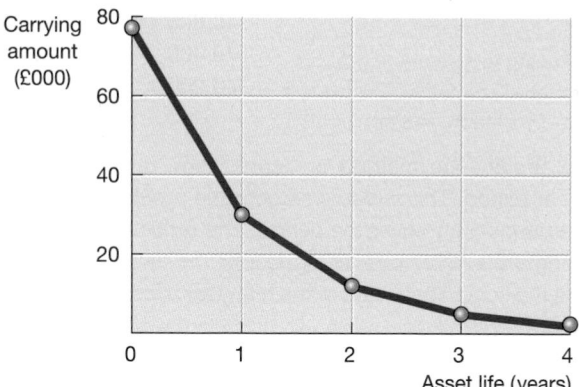

Under the reducing-balance method, the carrying amount of an asset falls by a larger amount in the earlier years than in the later years. This is because the depreciation charge is based on a fixed-rate percentage of the carrying amount.

Activity 3.7

Assume that the machine used in the example above was owned by a business that made a profit before depreciation of £40,000 for each of the four years in which the asset was held.

Calculate the profit for the business for each year under each depreciation method, and comment on your findings.

Activity 3.7 continued

Your answer should be as follows:

Straight-line method

	(a) Profit before depreciation £	(b) Depreciation £	(a – b) Profit £
Year 1	40,000	19,031	20,969
Year 2	40,000	19,031	20,969
Year 3	40,000	19,031	20,969
Year 4	40,000	19,031	20,969

Reducing-balance method

	(a) Profit before depreciation £	(b) Depreciation £	(a – b) Profit/(loss) £
Year 1	40,000	46,874	(6,874)
Year 2	40,000	18,750	21,250
Year 3	40,000	7,500	32,500
Year 4	40,000	3,000	37,000

The straight-line method of depreciation results in a constant profit figure over the four-year period. This is because both the profit before depreciation and the depreciation charge are constant over the period. The reducing-balance method, however, results in a changing profit figure over time, despite the fact that in this example the pre-depreciation profit is the same each year. In the first year a loss is reported, and thereafter a rising profit.

Although the *pattern* of profit over the four-year period will be quite different, depending on the depreciation method used, the *total* profit for the period (£83,876) will remain the same. This is because both methods of depreciating will allocate the same amount of total depreciation (£76,124) over the four-year period. It is only the amount allocated *between years* that will differ.

In practice, the use of different depreciation methods may not have such a dramatic effect on profits as suggested in Activity 3.7. This is because businesses typically have more than one depreciating non-current asset. Where a business replaces some of its assets each year, the total depreciation charge calculated under the reducing-balance method will reflect a range of charges (from high through to low), as assets will be at different points in the replacement cycle. This could mean that each year's total depreciation charge may not be significantly different from the total depreciation charge that would be derived under the straight-line method.

Selecting a depreciation method

How does a business choose which depreciation method to use for a particular asset? The answer is the one that best matches the depreciation expense to the pattern of economic benefits that the asset provides. Where these benefits are provided evenly over time (buildings, for example), the straight-line method is usually appropriate. Where assets lose their efficiency (as with certain types of machinery), the benefits provided will decline over time and so the reducing-balance method may be more appropriate. Where the pattern of economic benefits provided by the asset is uncertain, the straight-line method is normally chosen.

There is an international financial reporting standard (or international accounting standard) to deal with the depreciation of property, plant and equipment. As we shall see in Chapter 4, the purpose of accounting standards is to narrow areas of accounting difference and to try to ensure that information provided to users is transparent and comparable. The relevant standard endorses the view that the depreciation method chosen should reflect the pattern of economic benefits provided but does not specify particular methods to be used. It states that the useful life, depreciation method and residual values of non-current assets should be reviewed at least annually and adjustments made where appropriate.

Real World 3.5 sets out the depreciation policies of Thorntons plc.

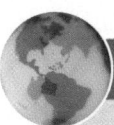

Real World 3.5

Sweet talk on depreciation policies

Thorntons plc, the manufacturer and retailer of confectionery, uses the straight-line method to depreciate all its property, plant and equipment, other than land and assets in the course of construction. The financial statements for the year ended 30 June 2009 show the period over which different classes of assets are depreciated as follows:

Long leasehold and freehold premises	50 years
Short leasehold land and buildings	Period of the lease
Other plant, vehicles and equipment	3 to 15 years
Retail fixtures and fittings	Up to 10 years

We can see that there are wide variations in the expected useful lives of the various assets held.

Source: Thorntons plc Annual Report and Accounts 2009, p. 49.

It seems that Thorntons plc is typical of UK businesses in that most use the straight-line approach. The reducing-balance method is not very much used.

The approach taken to calculating depreciation is summarised in Figure 3.6.

Depreciating intangible assets

Where an intangible asset has a finite life, the approach taken for the depreciation (or *amortisation* as it is usually called with intangibles) is broadly the same as that for property, plant and equipment (tangible non-current assets). The asset is amortised (depreciated) over its useful life and the amortisation method used should reflect the

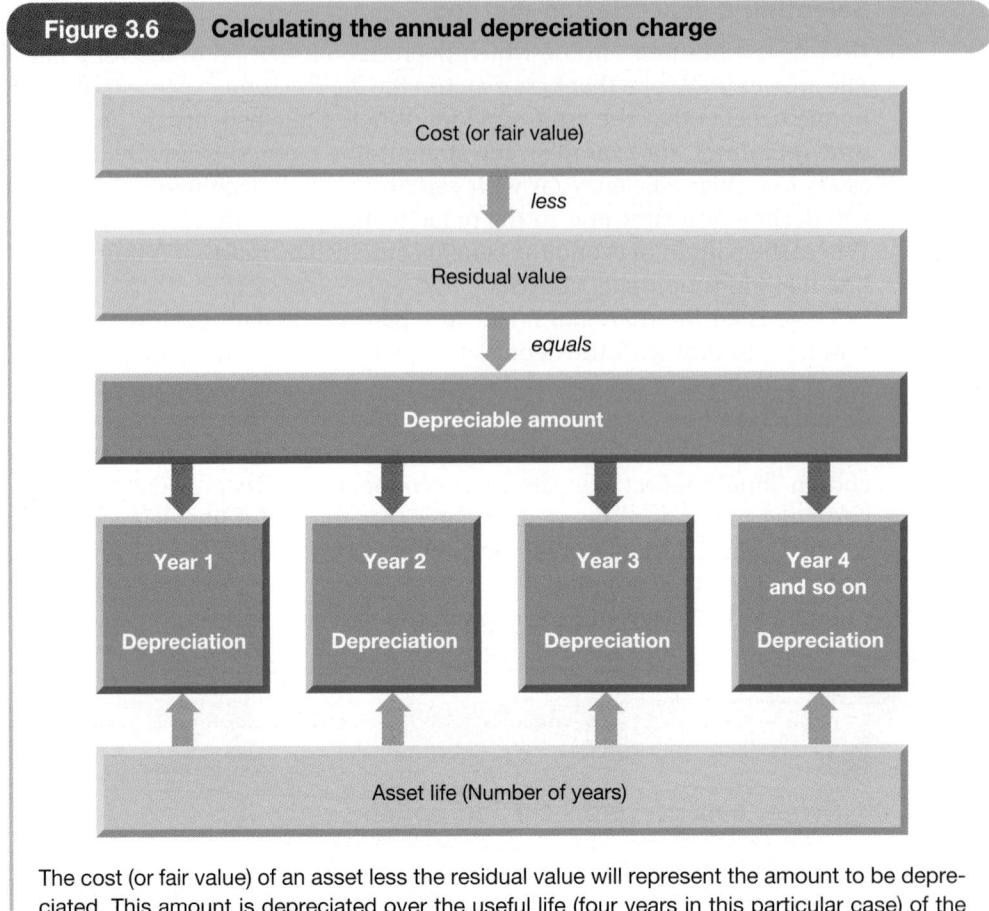

Figure 3.6   **Calculating the annual depreciation charge**

The cost (or fair value) of an asset less the residual value will represent the amount to be depreciated. This amount is depreciated over the useful life (four years in this particular case) of the asset using an appropriate depreciation method.

pattern of benefits provided. Some differences arise, however, because of the valuation problems surrounding these assets. Intangible assets are reported initially at cost but can, in principle, be revalued to fair value. However, this rarely occurs as there is usually no active market from which to establish fair values. For similar reasons, the residual value of an intangible asset is normally assumed to be zero.

We saw in Chapter 2 that some intangible assets, which may include acquired goodwill, have an indefinite useful life. These assets are not amortised but instead are tested for impairment at least annually. While intangible assets with finite lives and property, plant and equipment are also subject to impairment testing, this will only occur when there is some indication that impairment may actually have taken place.

Depreciation and asset replacement

There seems to be a misunderstanding in the minds of some people that the purpose of depreciation is to provide the funds for the replacement of a non-current asset when it reaches the end of its useful life. However, this is not the purpose of depreciation as conventionally defined. It was mentioned earlier that depreciation represents an attempt to allocate the cost, or fair value (less any residual value), of a non-current asset over its expected useful life. The resulting depreciation charge in each accounting period represents an expense, which is then used in the calculation of profit for the period. Calculating the depreciation charge for a period is therefore necessary for the proper measurement of financial performance, and must be done whether or not the business intends to replace the asset in the future.

If there is an intention to replace the asset, the depreciation charge in the income statement will not ensure that liquid funds are set aside by the business specifically for this purpose. Although the effect of a depreciation charge is to reduce profit, and therefore to reduce the amount available for withdrawal by the owners, the amounts retained within the business as a result may be invested in ways that are unrelated to the replacement of the particular asset.

Depreciation and judgement

When reading the above sections on depreciation, it may have struck you that accounting is not as precise and objective as it sometimes appears to be. There are areas where subjective judgement is required, and depreciation provides a good illustration of this.

Activity 3.8

What kinds of judgements must be made to calculate a depreciation charge for a period?

You may have thought of the following:

- the expected residual or disposal value of the asset
- the expected useful life of the asset
- the choice of depreciation method.

Making different judgements on these matters would result in a different pattern of depreciation charges over the life of the asset and, therefore, in a different pattern of reported profits. However, underestimations or overestimations that are made in relation to the above will be adjusted for in the final year of an asset's life, and so the total depreciation charge (and total profit) over the asset's life will not be affected by estimation errors.

Real World 3.6 describes the effect of extending the useful life of property, plant and equipment on the short-term profits of one large business.

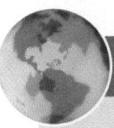

Real World 3.6

Sports massage

JJB Sports plc, a leading retailer, reported interim financial results for the six months ended 30 June 2005 that caused some disquiet among investors and analysts. The business changed the estimates for the useful life of its property, plant and equipment when calculating depreciation. It explained that this was due to new requirements to adopt International Financial Reporting Standards (IFRSs) when preparing financial statements. The article below, however, suggests that not everyone believed this.

Real World 3.6 continued

JJB massages results to boost profits

High street retailer JJB Sports massaged last week's disappointing interim results by changing its depreciation calculations, in order to boost flagging profits by £4.3m.

Analysts admitted that they were caught on the hop, as the company reported a 35.8% drop in operating profits from £27.4m to £17.6m for six months ended June 2005 on revenues down 6% to £340.4m. Operating profits would have plummeted even further to £13.3m had the company not changed its accounting for depreciation. 'The company explained the change as coming out of its IFRS conversion review, but it was clearly there for other reasons,' said Teather & Greenwood retail analyst Sanjay Vidyarthi.

JJB said that an impairment review ahead of its IFRS transition had forced a rethink on the carrying value of property, plant and equipment.

It concluded that these items had useful economic lives that more closely matched the length of the short-term lease of the property, rather than the 10-year economic life, which had formed the basis of the depreciation charge in previous accounting periods.

Richard Ratner, head of equity research at Seymour Pierce, said: 'They said the way they had depreciated assets previously was not correct but I haven't seen any other companies make this kind of change.'

JJB's share price fell from 168.2p before the results to 164.7p at the end of last week.

Source: 'JJB massages results to boost profits', *Accountancy Age*, 20 October 2005, p. 3.

Activity (3.9)

Sally Dalton (Packaging) Ltd bought a machine for £40,000. At the end of its useful life of four years, the amount received on sale was £4,000. When the asset was bought the business received two estimates of the likely residual value of the asset, which were: (a) £8,000, and (b) zero.

Show the pattern of annual depreciation charges over the four years and the total depreciation charges for the asset under each of the two estimates. The straight-line method should be used to calculate the annual depreciation charges.

The depreciation charge, assuming estimate (a), will be £8,000 a year ((that is, £40,000 – 8,000)/4). The depreciation charge, assuming estimate (b), will be £10,000 a year (that is, £40,000/4). As the actual residual value is £4,000, estimate (a) will lead to underdepreciation of £4,000 (that is, £8,000 – £4,000) over the life of the asset, and estimate (b) will lead to overdepreciation of £4,000 (that is, £0 – £4,000). These under- and overestimations will be dealt with in year 4.

The pattern of depreciation and total depreciation charges will therefore be:

| | | Estimate | |
| | | (a) | (b) |
Year		£	£
1	Annual depreciation	8,000	10,000
2	Annual depreciation	8,000	10,000
3	Annual depreciation	8,000	10,000
4	Annual depreciation	8,000	10,000
		32,000	40,000
4	Under/(over)depreciation	4,000	(4,000)
	Total depreciation	36,000	36,000

The final adjustment for underdepreciation of an asset is often referred to as 'loss (or deficit) on sale of non-current asset', as the amount actually received is less than the residual value. Similarly, the adjustment for overdepreciation is often referred to as 'profit (or surplus) on sale of non-current asset'. These final adjustments are normally made as an extra expense (or a reduction in the expense), for depreciation in the year of disposal of the asset.

Costing inventories

The way in which we measure the cost of inventories (or stock) is important because the cost of inventories sold during a period will affect the calculation of profit and the remaining inventories held at the end of the period will affect the portrayal of wealth in the statement of financial position. In the previous chapter, we saw that historic cost is often the basis for reporting assets, and so it is tempting to think that determining the cost of inventories held is very straightforward. However, in a period of changing prices, the costing of inventories can be a problem.

A business must determine the cost of the inventories sold during the period and the cost of the inventories remaining at the end of the period. To do this, some assumption must be made about the way in which the inventories are physically handled. The assumption made need have nothing to do with how the inventories are *actually* handled. The assumption is concerned only with providing useful accounting information.

Two common assumptions used are:

→ ● **first in, first out (FIFO)** – the earliest inventories held are the first to be used;
→ ● **last in, first out (LIFO)** – the latest inventories held are the first to be used.

Another approach to deriving the cost of inventories is to assume that inventories entering the business lose their separate identity and go into a 'pool'. Any issues of inventories then reflect the average cost of the inventories that are held. This is the
→ **weighted average cost (AVCO)** method, where the weights used in deriving the average cost figures are the quantities of each batch of inventories acquired. Example 3.8 provides a simple illustration of the way in which each method is applied.

Example 3.8

A business, which supplies grass seed to farmers and horticulturalists, has the following transactions during a period:

		Tonnes	Cost/tonne £
1 May	Opening inventories	100	100
2 May	Bought	500	110
3 May	Bought	800	120
		1,400	
6 May	Sold	(900)	
	Closing inventories	500	

First in, first out (FIFO)

Using the first in, first out approach, the first 900 tonnes of seed bought are treated as if these are the ones that are sold. This will consist of the opening inventories

(100 tonnes), the purchases made on 2 May (500 tonnes) and some of the purchases made on 3 May (300 tonnes). The remainder of the 3 May purchases (500 tonnes) will comprise the closing inventories. Thus we have:

	Cost of sales			Closing inventories		
	Tonnes	Cost/tonne £	Total £000	Tonnes	Cost/tonne £	Total £000
1 May	100	100	10.0			
2 May	500	110	55.0			
3 May	300	120	36.0	500	120	60.0
Cost of sales			101.0	Closing inventories		60.0

Last in, first out (LIFO)

Using the last in, first out approach, the later purchases will be treated as if these were the first to be sold. This is the 3 May purchases (800 tonnes) and some of the 2 May purchases (100 tonnes). The earlier purchases (the rest of the 2 May purchase and the opening inventories) will comprise the closing inventories. Thus we have:

	Cost of sales			Closing inventories		
	Tonnes	Cost/tonne £	Total £000	Tonnes	Cost/tonne £	Total £000
3 May	800	120	96.0			
2 May	100	110	11.0	400	110	44.0
1 May				100	100	10.0
Cost of sales			107.0	Closing inventories		54.0

Weighted average cost (AVCO)

Using this approach, a weighted average cost will be determined that will be used to derive both the cost of goods sold and the cost of the remaining inventories held. This simply means that the total cost of the opening inventories and the 2 May and 3 May purchases are added together and divided by the total number of tonnes to obtain the weighted average cost per tonne. Both the cost of sales and closing inventories values are based on that average cost per tonne. Thus we have:

	Purchases		
	Tonnes	Cost/tonne £	Total £000
1 May	100	100	10.0
2 May	500	110	55.0
3 May	800	120	96.0
	1,400		161.0

Average cost = £161,000/1,400 = £115 per tonne

	Cost of sales			Closing inventories	
Tonnes	Cost/tonne £	Total £000	Tonnes	Cost/tonne £	Total £000
900	115	103.5	500	115	57.5

Activity 3.10

Suppose the 900 tonnes of inventories in Example 3.8 were sold for £150 per tonne.

(a) Calculate the gross profit for the period under each of the three methods.
(b) What observations concerning the portrayal of financial position and performance can you make about each method when prices are rising?

Your answer should be along the following lines:

(a) Gross profit calculation:

	FIFO £000	LIFO £000	AVCO £000
Sales revenue (900 @ £150)	135.0	135.0	135.0
Cost of sales	(101.0)	(107.0)	(103.5)
Gross profit	34.0	28.0	31.5
Closing inventories figure	60.0	54.0	57.5

(b) These figures reveal that FIFO will give the highest gross profit during a period of rising prices. This is because sales revenue is matched with the earlier (and cheaper) purchases. LIFO will give the lowest gross profit because sales revenue is matched against the more recent (and dearer) purchases. The AVCO method will normally give a figure that is between these two extremes.

   The closing inventories figure in the statement of financial position will be highest with the FIFO method. This is because the cost of goods still held will be based on the more recent (and dearer) purchases. LIFO will give the lowest closing inventories figure as the goods held will be based on the earlier (and cheaper) purchases. Once again, the AVCO method will normally give a figure that is between these two extremes.

Activity 3.11

Assume that prices in Activity 3.10 are falling rather than rising. How would your observations concerning the portrayal of financial performance and position be different for the various costing methods?

→

Activity 3.11 continued

When prices are falling, the positions of FIFO and LIFO are reversed. FIFO will give the lowest gross profit as sales revenue is matched against the earlier (and dearer) goods bought. LIFO will give the highest gross profit as sales revenue is matched against the more recent (and cheaper) goods bought. AVCO will give a cost of sales figure between these two extremes. The closing inventories figure in the statement of financial position will be lowest under FIFO as the cost of inventories will be based on the more recent (and cheaper) purchases. LIFO will provide the highest closing inventories figure and AVCO will provide a figure between the two extremes.

The different costing methods will only have an effect on the reported profit from one year to the next. The figure derived for closing inventories will be carried forward and matched with sales revenue in a later period. Thus, if the cheaper purchases of inventories are matched to sales revenue in the current period, it will mean that the dearer purchases will be matched to sales revenue in a later period. Over the life of the business, therefore, the total profit will be the same whichever costing method has been used.

Inventories – some further issues

We saw in Chapter 2 that the convention of prudence requires that inventories be valued at the lower of cost and net realisable value. (The net realisable value of inventories is the estimated selling price less any further costs that may be necessary to complete the goods and any costs involved in selling and distributing the goods.) This rule may mean that the valuation method applied to inventories (cost or net realisable value) could switch each year, depending on which of cost and net realisable value is the lower. In practice, however, the cost of the inventories held is usually below the current net realisable value – particularly during a period of rising prices. It is, therefore, the cost figure that will normally appear in the statement of financial position.

Activity 3.12

Can you think of any circumstances where the net realisable value will be lower than the cost of inventories held, even during a period of generally rising prices?

The net realisable value may be lower where:

- goods have deteriorated or become obsolete;
- there has been a fall in the market price of the goods;
- the goods are being used as a 'loss leader';
- bad buying decisions have been made.

There is an international financial reporting standard that deals with inventories. It states that, when preparing financial statements for external reporting, the cost of inventories should normally be determined using either FIFO or AVCO. The LIFO approach is not an acceptable method to use for external reporting, but a business could use it for reports to management. The standard also requires the 'lower of cost and net realisable value' rule to be used and so endorses the application of the prudence convention.

Real World 3.7 sets out the inventories costing methods of one well known supermarket business.

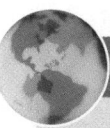

Real World 3.7

Buy one, get one free

J Sainsbury plc, the supermarket chain, employs two methods of costing inventories and the particular method applied depends on where the inventories are located. The business reports that:

> Inventories are valued at the lower of cost and net realisable value. Inventories at warehouses are valued on a first-in, first-out basis. Those at retail outlets are valued at calculated average cost prices.

Source: J Sainsbury plc Annual Report and Financial Statements 2009, p. 49.

→ Costing inventories and depreciation provide two examples where the **consistency convention** must be applied. This convention holds that once a particular method of accounting is selected, it should be applied consistently over time. Thus, it would not be acceptable to switch from, say, FIFO to AVCO between periods (unless exceptional circumstances make it appropriate). The purpose of this convention is to help users make valid comparisons of performance and position from one period to the next.

Activity 3.13

Reporting inventories in the financial statements provides a further example of the need to apply subjective judgement. For the inventories of a retail business, what are the main areas where judgement is required?

The main areas are:

- the choice of cost method (FIFO, LIFO, AVCO);
- deducing the net realisable value figure for inventories held.

Trade receivables problems

We have seen that, when businesses sell goods or services on credit, revenue will usually be recognised before the customer pays the amounts owing. Recording the dual aspect of a credit sale will involve increasing sales revenue and increasing trade receivables by the amount of the revenue from the credit sale.

With this type of sale there is always the risk that the customer will not pay the amount due, however reliable they might have appeared to be at the time of the sale. When it becomes reasonably certain that the customer will never pay, the debt owed

→ is considered to be a **bad debt** and this must be taken into account when preparing the financial statements.

Activity 3.14

When preparing the financial statements, what would be the effect on the income statement, and on the statement of financial position, of not taking into account the fact that a debt is bad?

The effect would be to overstate the assets (trade receivables) on the statement of financial position and to overstate profit in the income statement, as the revenue (which has been recognised) will not result in any future benefit.

To provide a more realistic picture of financial performance and position, the bad debt must be 'written off'. This will involve reducing the trade receivables and increasing expenses (by creating an expense known as 'bad debts written off') by the amount of the bad debt.

The matching convention requires that the bad debt is written off in the same period as the sale that gave rise to the debt is recognised.

Note that, when a debt is bad, the accounting response is not simply to cancel the original sale. If this were done, the income statement would not be so informative. Reporting the bad debts as an expense can be extremely useful in assessing management performance.

At the end of the accounting period, it may not be possible to identify with reasonable certainty all the bad debts that have been incurred during the period. It may be that some trade receivables appear doubtful, but only at some later point in time will the true position become clear. The uncertainty that exists does not mean that, when preparing the financial statements, we should ignore the possibility that some of the trade receivables outstanding will eventually prove to be bad. It would not be prudent to do so, nor would it comply with the need to match expenses to the period in which the associated sale is recognised. As a result, the business will normally try to identify all those trade receivables that, at the end of the period, can be classified as doubtful (that is, there is a possibility that they may eventually prove to be bad). This can be done by examining individual accounts of trade receivables or by taking a proportion of the total trade receivables outstanding based on past experience.

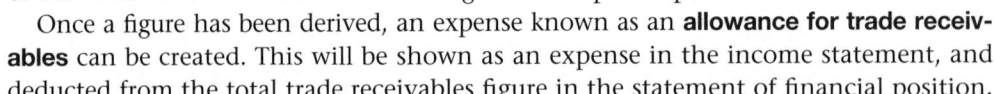 Once a figure has been derived, an expense known as an **allowance for trade receivables** can be created. This will be shown as an expense in the income statement, and deducted from the total trade receivables figure in the statement of financial position.

By doing this, full account is taken, in the appropriate accounting period, of those trade receivables where there is a risk of non-payment. This accounting treatment of these trade receivables will be in addition to the treatment of bad debts described above.

Example 3.9 illustrates the reporting of bad debts and allowances for trade receivables.

Example 3.9

Desai Enterprises had trade receivables of £350,000 outstanding at the end of the accounting year to 30 June 2009. Investigation of these trade receivables revealed that £10,000 would probably be irrecoverable and that a further £30,000 were doubtful of being recoverable.

Relevant extracts from the income statement for that year would be as follows:

Income statement (extracts) for the year ended 30 June 2009

	£
Bad debts written off	10,000
Allowances for trade receivables	30,000

Statement of financial position (extracts) as at 30 June 2009

	£
Trade receivables	340,000*
Allowances for trade receivables	(30,000)
	310,000

* That is, £350,000 – £10,000 irrecoverable trade receivables.

The allowances for trade receivables figure is, of course, an estimate, and it is quite likely that the actual amount of trade receivables that prove to be bad will be different from the estimate. Let us say that, during the next accounting period, it was discovered that, in fact, £26,000 of the trade receivables considered doubtful proved to be irrecoverable. These trade receivables must now be written off as follows:

● reduce trade receivables by £26,000, and
● reduce allowances for trade receivables by £26,000.

However, allowances for trade receivables of £4,000 will remain. This amount represents an overestimate made when creating the allowance as at 30 June 2009. As the allowance is no longer needed, it should be eliminated. Remember that the allowance was made by creating an expense in the income statement for the year to 30 June 2009. As the expense was too high, the amount of the overestimate should be 'written back' in the next accounting period. In other words, it will be treated as revenue for the year to 30 June 2010. This will mean:

● reducing the allowances for trade receivables by £4,000, and
● increasing revenue by £4,000.

Ideally, of course, the amount should be written back to the 2009 income statement; however, it is too late to do this. At the end of of the year to 30 June 2010, not only will 2009's overestimate be written back but a new allowance should be created to take account of the trade receivables arising from 2010's credit sales that are considered doubtful.

Activity 3.15

Clayton Conglomerates had trade receivables of £870,000 outstanding at the end of the accounting year to 31 March 2008. The chief accountant believed that £40,000 of those trade receivables were irrecoverable and that a further £60,000 were doubtful of being recoverable. In the subsequent year, it was found that an over-pessimistic estimate of those trade receivables considered doubtful had been made and that only a further £45,000 of trade receivables had actually proved to be bad.

→

Activity 3.15 continued

Show the relevant extracts in the income statement for both 2008 and 2009 to report the bad debts written off and the allowances for trade receivables. Also show the relevant statement of financial position extract as at 31 March 2008.

Your answer should be as follows:

Income statement (extracts) for the year ended 31 March 2008

	£
Bad debts written off	40,000
Allowances for trade receivables	60,000

Income statement (extracts) for the year ended 31 March 2009

	£
Allowances for trade receivables written back (revenue)	15,000

(*Note*: This figure will usually be netted off against any allowances for trade receivables created in respect of 2009.)

Statement of financial position (extracts) as at 31 March 2008

	£
Trade receivables	830,000
Allowances for trade receivables	(60,000)
	770,000

Activity 3.16

Bad debts and allowances for trade receivables are two further examples where judgement is needed to derive an appropriate expense figure.

What will be the effect of different judgements concerning the appropriate amount of bad debts expense and allowances for trade receivables expense on the profit for a particular period and on the total profit reported over the life of the business?

Judgement is often required in deriving a figure for bad debts incurred during a period. There may be situations where views will differ concerning whether or not a debt is irrecoverable. The decision concerning whether or not to write off a bad debt will have an effect on the expenses for the period and, hence, the reported profit. However, over the life of the business the total reported profit would not be affected, as incorrect judgements in one period will be adjusted for in a later period.

Suppose that a debt of £100 was written off in a period and that, in a later period, the amount owing was actually received. The increase in expenses of £100 in the period in which the bad debt was written off would be compensated for by an increase in revenue of £100 when the amount outstanding was finally received (bad debt recoverable). If, on the other hand, the amount owing of £100 was never written off in the first place, the profit for the two periods would not be affected by the bad debt adjustment and would, therefore, be different – but the total profit for the two periods would be the same.

A similar situation would apply where there are differences in judgements concerning allowances for trade receivables.

Real World 3.8 describes the rise in bad debts of one business.

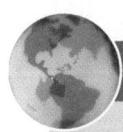

Real World 3.8

Shopping for bad debts

Shares in Yorkshire home shopping firm Findel dived by nearly 40 per cent after profits were hit by an increase in customers slipping behind on payments. The company, which sells a range of household goods under names such as the Cotswold Company, Kitbag and Ace, said it was adding £5m to its bad debt provision (allowances for trade receivables) for the year ended 31 March 2008, with profits hit as a result.

It comes after the group experienced a 'softening' in repayments from credit customers during the past two months. Around 1.5m customers use credit to buy goods through Findel's home shopping arm, with another 1m paying by cash. The group's bad debt provision (allowances for trade receivables) before the £5m change is understood to have been £83m.

Findel, which is based at Burley-in-Wharfedale, West Yorkshire, said: 'In light of the deteriorating economic climate the company has conducted a further review of the Home Shopping debt book and now estimates that the bad debt provision will be £5m higher than had previously been anticipated.'

The company warned profits would be down as a result, but would come in higher than last year's £56m.

Source: 'Findel shares plunge as Yorkshire home shopping firm's bad debts rise', Nigel Scott, *Yorkshire Evening Post*, www.yorkshireeveningpost.com, 17 April 2008.

Let us now try to bring together some of the points that we have raised in this chapter through a self-assessment question.

Self-assessment question 3.1

TT and Co. is a new business that started trading on 1 January 2008. The following is a summary of transactions that occurred during the first year of trading:

1. The owners introduced £50,000 of equity, which was paid into a bank account opened in the name of the business.
2. Premises were rented from 1 January 2008 at an annual rental of £20,000. During the year, rent of £25,000 was paid to the owner of the premises.
3. Rates (a tax on business premises) were paid during the year as follows:

    For the period 1 January 2008 to 31 March 2008   £500
    For the period 1 April 2008 to 31 March 2009   £1,200

4. A delivery van was bought on 1 January 2008 for £12,000. This is expected to be used in the business for four years and then to be sold for £2,000.
5. Wages totalling £33,500 were paid during the year. At the end of the year, the business owed £630 of wages for the last week of the year.
6. Electricity bills for the first three quarters of the year were paid totalling £1,650. After 31 December 2008, but before the financial statements had been finalised for the year, the bill for the last quarter arrived showing a charge of £620.

→

Self-assessment question 3.1 continued

7. Inventories totalling £143,000 were bought on credit.
8. Inventories totalling £12,000 were bought for cash.
9. Sales revenue on credit totalled £152,000 (cost of sales £74,000).
10. Cash sales revenue totalled £35,000 (cost of sales £16,000).
11. Receipts from trade receivables totalled £132,000.
12. Payments to trade payables totalled £121,000.
13. Van running expenses paid totalled £9,400.

At the end of the year it was clear that a credit customer (trade receivable) who owed £400 would not be able to pay any part of the debt. All of the other trade payables were expected to settle in full.

The business uses the straight-line method for depreciating non-current assets.

Required:
Prepare a statement of financial position as at 31 December 2008 and an income statement for the year to that date.

The answer to this question can be found at the back of the book on pages 723–4.

Uses and usefulness of the income statement

The income statement, like the statement of financial position, has been around for a long time. Most major businesses seem to prepare an income statement on a frequent basis (monthly or even more frequently). This is despite there being no rule requiring an income statement to be produced more frequently than once, or in some cases twice, a year. The income statement is, therefore, regarded as capable of providing useful information. In particular, this statement may help in providing information on:

● *How effective the business has been in generating wealth.* Since wealth generation is the primary reason for most businesses to exist, assessing how much wealth has been created is an important issue. Although we have seen that different judgements concerning depreciation, inventories and bad debts may affect the calculation of profit for a period, this problem should not be overstated. For most businesses in most years, the effect of making different judgements would probably not significantly affect the final profit figure.
● *How the profit was derived.* For some users, the only item of concern may be the final profit figure, or *bottom line* as it is sometimes called. While this is a primary measure of performance, and its importance is difficult to overstate, the income statement contains other information that should also be of interest. To evaluate business performance effectively, it is important to discover how the profit figure was derived. Thus the level of sales revenue, the nature and amount of expenses incurred, and the profit in relation to sales revenue are important factors in understanding the performance of the business over a period. The analysis and interpretation of financial statements is considered in detail in Chapter 7.

Summary

The main points of this chapter may be summarised as follows.

The income statement (profit and loss account)

- The income statement measures and reports how much profit (or loss) has been generated over a period.
- Profit (or loss) for the period is the difference between the total revenue and total expenses for the period.
- The income statement links the statements of financial position at the beginning and end of an accounting period.
- The income statement of a retail business will first calculate gross profit and then deduct any overheads for the period. The final figure derived is the profit (or loss) for the period.
- Gross profit represents the difference between the sales revenue for the period and the cost of sales.

Expenses and revenue

- Cost of sales may be identified either by matching the cost of each sale to the particular sale or by adjusting the goods bought during the period to take account of opening and closing inventories.
- Classifying expenses is often a matter of judgement, although there are rules for businesses that trade as limited companies.
- Revenue is recognised when the amount of revenue can be measured reliably and it is probable that the economic benefits will be received.
- Where there is a sale of goods, there is an additional criterion that ownership and control must pass to the buyer before revenue can be recognised.
- Revenue can be recognised after partial completion provided that a particular stage of completion can be measured reliably.
- The matching convention states that expenses should be matched to the revenue that they help generate.
- A particular expense reported in the income statement may not be the same as the cash paid. This will result in some adjustment for accruals or prepayments.
- The materiality convention states that where the amounts are immaterial, we should consider only what is expedient.
- 'Accruals accounting' is preparing the income statement and statement of financial position following the accruals convention, which says that profit = revenue less expenses (not cash receipts less cash payments).

Depreciation of non-current assets

- Depreciation requires a consideration of the cost (or fair value), useful life and residual value of an asset. It also requires a consideration of the method of depreciation.
- The straight-line method of depreciation allocates the amount to be depreciated evenly over the useful life of the asset.
- The reducing-balance method applies a fixed percentage rate of depreciation to the carrying amount of an asset each year.

- The depreciation method chosen should reflect the pattern of benefits associated with the asset.
- Depreciation is an attempt to allocate the cost (or fair value), less the residual value, of an asset over its useful life. It does not provide funds for replacement of the asset.

Costing inventories

- The way in which we derive the cost of inventories is important in the calculation of profit and the presentation of financial position.
- The first in, first out (FIFO) method approaches matters as if the earliest inventories held are the first to be used.
- The last in, first out (LIFO) method approaches matters as if the latest inventories are the first to be used.
- The weighted average cost (AVCO) method applies an average cost to all inventories used.
- When prices are rising, FIFO gives the lowest cost of sales figure and highest closing inventories figure and LIFO gives the highest cost of sales figure and the lowest closing inventories figure. AVCO gives figures for cost of sales and closing inventories that lie between FIFO and LIFO.
- When prices are falling, the positions of FIFO and LIFO are reversed.
- Inventories are shown at the lower of cost and net realisable value.
- When a particular method of accounting, such as an inventories costing method, is selected, it should be applied consistently over time.

Bad debts

- Where it is reasonably certain that a credit customer will not pay, the debt is regarded as 'bad' and written off.
- Where it is doubtful that a credit customer will pay, an allowance for trade receivables expense should be created.

Uses of the income statement

- It provides a profit figure.
- It provides information on how the profit was derived.

 *Now check your progress in your personal Study Plan*

→ Key terms

profit p. 77	accruals accounting p. 92
revenue p. 77	depreciation p. 93
expense p. 78	residual value p. 94
income statement p. 79	straight-line method p. 95
accounting period p. 79	carrying amount p. 96
gross profit p. 80	written-down value p. 96
operating profit p. 81	net book value p. 96
profit for the year p. 81	reducing-balance method p. 96
cost of sales p. 81	first in, first out (FIFO) p. 103
matching convention p. 88	last in, first out (LIFO) p. 103
accrued expenses p. 89	weighted average cost (AVCO) p. 103
prepaid expenses p. 91	consistency convention p. 107
materiality convention p. 92	bad debt p. 107
accruals convention p. 92	allowance for trade receivables p. 108

Further reading

If you would like to explore the topics covered in this chapter in more depth, we recommend the following books:

A Guide Through International Financial Reporting Standards (IFRSs) 2008, IASC Foundation Education, July 2008, IAS 2, IAS 16, IAS 18, IAS 36 and IAS 38.

Corporate Financial Accounting and Reporting, *Sutton T.*, 2nd edn, Financial Times Prentice Hall, 2004, chapters 2, 8, 9 and 10.

Financial Accounting and Reporting, *Elliott B. and Elliott J.*, 13th edn, Financial Times Prentice Hall, 2010, chapters 3, 18, 19 and 20.

Insights into IFRS, *KPMG*, 5th edn, 2008/9, Thomson, 2008, Sections 3.2, 3.3, 3.8, 3.10 and 4.2.

Review questions

Answers to these questions can be found at the back of the book on page 740.

3.1 'Although the income statement is a record of past achievement, the calculations required for certain expenses involve estimates of the future.' What does this statement mean? Can you think of examples where estimates of the future are used?

3.2 'Depreciation is a process of allocation and not valuation.' What do you think is meant by this statement?

3.3 What is the convention of consistency? Does this convention help users in making a more valid comparison between businesses?

3.4 'An asset is similar to an expense.' Do you agree?

Exercises

Exercises 3.6 to 3.8 are more advanced than Exercises 3.1 to 3.5. Those with **coloured numbers** have answers at the back of the book, starting on page 755.

If you wish to try more exercises, visit the students' side of the Companion Website and MyAccountingLab.

3.1 You have heard the following statements made. Comment critically on them.

(a) 'Equity only increases or decreases as a result of the owners putting more cash into the business or taking some out.'
(b) 'An accrued expense is one that relates to next year.'
(c) 'Unless we depreciate this asset we shall be unable to provide for its replacement.'
(d) 'There is no point in depreciating the factory building. It is appreciating in value each year.'

3.2 Singh Enterprises has an accounting year to 31 December and uses the straight-line method of depreciation. On 1 January 2006 the business bought a machine for £10,000. The machine had an expected useful life of four years and an estimated residual value of £2,000. On 1 January 2007 the business bought another machine for £15,000. This machine had an expected useful life of five years and an estimated residual value of £2,500. On 31 December 2008 the business sold the first machine bought for £3,000.

Required:
Show the relevant income statement extracts and statement of financial position extracts for the years 2006, 2007 and 2008.

3.3 The owner of a business is confused, and comes to you for help. The financial statements for the business, prepared by an accountant, for the last accounting period revealed a profit of £50,000. However, during the accounting period the bank balance declined by £30,000. What reasons might explain this apparent discrepancy?

3.4 Spratley Ltd is a builders' merchant. On 1 September the business had, as part of its inventories, 20 tonnes of sand at a cost of £18 per tonne and at a total cost of £360. During the first week in September, the business bought the following amounts of sand:

September	Tonnes	Cost per tonne £
2	48	20
4	15	24
6	10	25

On 7 September the business sold 60 tonnes of sand to a local builder.

Required:

Calculate the cost of goods sold and the closing inventories from the above information using the following costing methods:

(a) first in, first out
(b) last in, first out
(c) weighted average cost.

3.5 Fill in the values (a) to (f) in the following table on the assumption that there were no opening balances involved.

	Relating to period		At end of period	
	Paid/Received £	Expense/Revenue for period £	Prepaid £	Accruals/Deferred revenues £
Rent payable	10,000	a	1,000	
Rates and insurance	5,000	b		1,000
General expenses	c	6,000	1,000	
Interest (on borrowings) payable	3,000	2,500	d	
Salaries	e	9,000		3,000
Rent receivable	f	1,500		1,500

3.6 The following is the statement of financial position of TT and Co. at the end of its first year of trading (from Self-assessment question 3.1):

Statement of financial position as at 31 December 2008

	£
ASSETS	
Non-current assets	
Property, plant and equipment	
Delivery van at cost	12,000
Depreciation	(2,500)
	9,500
Current assets	
Inventories	65,000
Trade receivables	19,600
Prepaid expenses*	5,300
Cash	750
	90,650
Total assets	100,150
EQUITY AND LIABILITIES	
Equity	
Original	50,000
Retained earnings	26,900
	76,900
Current liabilities	
Trade payables	22,000
Accrued expenses†	1,250
	23,250
Total equity and liabilities	100,150

* The prepaid expenses consisted of rates (£300) and rent (£5,000).
† The accrued expenses consisted of wages (£630) and electricity (£620).

During 2009, the following transactions took place:

1 The owners withdrew equity in the form of cash of £20,000.
2 Premises continued to be rented at an annual rental of £20,000. During the year, rent of £15,000 was paid to the owner of the premises.
3 Rates on the premises were paid during the year as follows: for the period 1 April 2009 to 31 March 2010 £1,300.
4 A second delivery van was bought on 1 January 2009 for £13,000. This is expected to be used in the business for four years and then to be sold for £3,000.
5 Wages totalling £36,700 were paid during the year. At the end of the year, the business owed £860 of wages for the last week of the year.
6 Electricity bills for the first three quarters of the year and £620 for the last quarter of the previous year were paid totalling £1,820. After 31 December 2009, but before the financial statements had been finalised for the year, the bill for the last quarter arrived showing a charge of £690.
7 Inventories totalling £67,000 were bought on credit.
8 Inventories totalling £8,000 were bought for cash.
9 Sales revenue on credit totalled £179,000 (cost £89,000).
10 Cash sales revenue totalled £54,000 (cost £25,000).
11 Receipts from trade receivables totalled £178,000.
12 Payments to trade payables totalled £71,000.
13 Van running expenses paid totalled £16,200.

The business uses the straight-line method for depreciating non-current assets.

Required:
Prepare a statement of financial position as at 31 December 2009 and an income statement for the year to that date.

3.7 The following is the statement of financial position of WW Associates as at 31 December 2008:

Statement of financial position as at 31 December 2008

	£
ASSETS	
Non-current assets	
Machinery	25,300
Current assets	
Inventories	12,200
Trade receivables	21,300
Prepaid expenses (rates)	400
Cash	8,300
Total assets	67,500
EQUITY AND LIABILITIES	
Equity	
Original	25,000
Retained earnings	23,900
	48,900
Current liabilities	
Trade payables	16,900
Accrued expenses (wages)	1,700
	18,600
Total equity and liabilities	67,500

During 2009, the following transactions took place:

1. The owners withdrew equity in the form of cash of £23,000.
2. Premises were rented at an annual rental of £20,000. During the year, rent of £25,000 was paid to the owner of the premises.
3. Rates on the premises were paid during the year for the period 1 April 2009 to 31 March 2010 and amounted to £2,000.
4. Some machinery (a non-current asset), which was bought on 1 January 2008 for £13,000, has proved to be unsatisfactory. It was part-exchanged for some new machinery on 1 January 2009, and WW Associates paid a cash amount of £6,000. The new machinery would have cost £15,000 had the business bought it without the trade-in.
5. Wages totalling £23,800 were paid during the year. At the end of the year, the business owed £860 of wages.
6. Electricity bills for the four quarters of the year were paid totalling £2,700.
7. Inventories totalling £143,000 were bought on credit.
8. Inventories totalling £12,000 were bought for cash.
9. Sales revenue on credit totalled £211,000 (cost £127,000).
10. Cash sales revenue totalled £42,000 (cost £25,000).
11. Receipts from trade receivables totalled £198,000.
12. Payments to trade payables totalled £156,000.
13. Van running expenses paid totalled £17,500.

The business uses the reducing-balance method of depreciation for non-current assets at the rate of 30 per cent each year.

Required:
Prepare a statement of financial position as at 31 December 2009 and an income statement (profit and loss account) for the year to that date.

3.8 The following is the income statement for Nikov and Co. for the year ended 31 December 2009, along with information relating to the preceding year.

Income statement for the year ended 31 December

	2009	2008
	£000	£000
Sales revenue	420.2	382.5
Cost of sales	(126.1)	(114.8)
Gross profit	294.1	267.7
Salaries and wages	(92.6)	(86.4)
Selling and distribution costs	(98.9)	(75.4)
Rent and rates	(22.0)	(22.0)
Bad debts written off	(19.7)	(4.0)
Telephone and postage	(4.8)	(4.4)
Insurance	(2.9)	(2.8)
Motor vehicle expenses	(10.3)	(8.6)
Depreciation – Delivery van	(3.1)	(3.3)
– Fixtures and fittings	(4.3)	(4.5)
Operating profit	35.5	56.3
Loan interest	(4.6)	(5.4)
Profit for the year	30.9	50.9

Required:

Analyse the performance of the business for the year to 31 December 2009 in so far as the information allows.

Accounting for limited companies (1)

Introduction

Most businesses in the UK, except the very smallest, operate in the form of limited companies. More than 2 million limited companies now exist and they account for the majority of UK business activity and employment. The economic significance of this type of business is not confined to the UK; it can be seen in many of the world's developed countries.

In this chapter we consider the nature of limited companies and how they differ from sole proprietorship businesses and partnerships. We examine the ways in which the owners provide finance as well as the rules governing the way in which limited companies must account to their owners and to other interested parties. We shall also see how the financial statements, which were discussed in the previous two chapters, are prepared for this type of business.

Learning outcomes

When you have completed this chapter, you should be able to:

- Discuss the nature of the limited company.

- Describe the main features of the owners' claim in a limited company.

- Discuss the framework of rules designed to safeguard the interests of shareholders.

- Explain how the income statement and statement of financial position of a limited company differ in detail from those of sole proprietorships and partnerships.

 Remember to create your own personalised Study Plan

Why limited companies?

Although there are many businesses in the UK that trade as sole proprietorships, partnerships and other forms, overwhelmingly the most important business form is the limited company. In terms of sales revenue generated, wealth created, number of people employed, exports achieved and virtually any other measure, limited companies dominate the business scene. We shall be seeing in this chapter that limited companies are subject to a great deal of regulation, particularly in the areas of finance and accounting. This is particularly true of those limited companies whose shares are traded on the London Stock Exchange. All of this regulation can be very tiresome for the companies and, importantly, very expensive.

In this chapter we shall be looking at a number of issues, including:

● What is a limited company?
● Why are limited companies so popular?
● What regulation must limited companies accept?
● Why do some limited companies have their shares traded on the London Stock Exchange, when this leads to even more regulation, at great expense?

We shall be answering these and other questions during this chapter.

The main features of limited companies

Legal nature

Let us begin our examination of limited companies by discussing their legal nature. A → **limited company** has been described as an artificial person that has been created by law. This means that a company has many of the rights and obligations that 'real' people have. It can, for example, sue or be sued by others and can enter into contracts in its own name. This contrasts sharply with other types of businesses, such as sole proprietorships and partnerships (that is, unincorporated businesses), where it is the owner(s) rather than the business that must sue, enter into contracts and so on, because the business has no separate legal identity.

With the rare exceptions of those that are created by Act of Parliament or by Royal Charter, all UK companies are created (or *incorporated*) by registration. To create a company the person or persons wishing to create it (usually known as *promoters*) fill in a few simple forms and pay a modest registration fee. After having ensured that the necessary formalities have been met, the Registrar of Companies, a UK government official, enters the name of the new company on the Registry of Companies. Thus, in the UK, companies can be formed very easily and cheaply (for about £100).

A limited company may be owned by just one person, but most have more than one owner and some have many owners. The owners are usually known as *members* or *shareholders*. The ownership of a company is normally divided into a number, fre-
→ quently a large number, of **shares**, each of equal size. Each owner, or shareholder, owns one or more shares in the company. Large companies typically have a very large number of shareholders. For example, at 31 March 2008, BT Group plc, the telecommunications business, had nearly 1.2 million different shareholders.

As a limited company has its own legal identity, it is regarded as being quite separate from those that own and manage it. It is worth emphasising that this legal separateness of owners and the company has no connection whatsoever with the business entity convention of accounting, which we discussed in Chapter 2. This accounting convention applies equally well to all business types, including sole proprietorships and partnerships where there is certainly no legal distinction between the owner(s) and the business.

The legal separateness of the limited company and its shareholders leads to two important features of the limited company: perpetual life and limited liability. These are now explained.

Perpetual life

A company is normally granted a perpetual existence and so will continue even where an owner of some, or even all, of the shares in the company dies. The shares of the deceased person will simply pass to the beneficiary of his or her estate. The granting of perpetual existence means that the life of a company is quite separate from the lives of those individuals who own or manage it. It is not, therefore, affected by changes in ownership that arise when individuals buy and sell shares in the company.

Though a company may be granted a perpetual existence when it is first formed, it is possible for either the shareholders or the courts to bring this existence to an end. When this is done, the assets of the company are sold off to meet outstanding liabilities. Any surplus arising after all liabilities have been met will then be used to pay the shareholders. Shareholders may agree to end the life of a company where it has achieved the purpose for which it was formed or where they feel that the company has no real future. The courts may bring the life of a company to an end where creditors have applied to the courts for this to be done because they have not been paid amounts owing.

Where shareholders agree to end the life of a company, it is referred to as a 'voluntary liquidation'. **Real World 4.1** describes the demise of one company by this method.

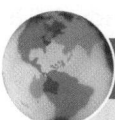

Real World 4.1

Monotub Industries in a spin as founder gets Titan for £1 **FT**

Monotub Industries, maker of the Titan washing machine, yesterday passed into corporate history with very little ceremony and with only a whimper of protest from minority shareholders.

At an extraordinary meeting held in a basement room of the group's West End headquarters, shareholders voted to put the company into voluntary liquidation and sell its assets and intellectual property to founder Martin Myerscough for £1. [The shares in the company were at one time worth 650p each.]

The only significant opposition came from Giuliano Gnagnatti who, along with other shareholders, has seen his investment shrink faster than a wool twin-set on a boil wash.

The not-so-proud owner of 100,000 Monotub shares, Mr Gnagnatti, the managing director of an online retailer . . . described the sale of Monotub as a 'free gift' to Mr Myerscough. This assessment was denied by Ian Green, the chairman of Monotub, who said the closest the beleaguered company had come to a sale was an offer for £60,000 that gave no guarantees against liabilities, which are thought to amount to £750,000.

The quiet passing of the washing machine, eventually dubbed the Titanic, was in strong contrast to its performance in many kitchens.

Originally touted as the 'great white goods hope' of the washing machine industry with its larger capacity and removable drum, the Titan ran into problems when it kept stopping during the spin cycle, causing it to emit a loud bang and leap into the air.

→

Real World 4.1 continued

Summing up the demise of the Titan, Mr Green said: 'Clearly the machine had some revolutionary aspects, but you can't get away from the fact that the machine was faulty and should not have been launched with those defects.'

The usually-vocal Mr Myerscough, who has promised to pump £250,000 into the company and give Monotub shareholders £4 for every machine sold, refused to comment on his plans for the Titan or reveal who his backers were. But . . . he did say that he intended to 'take the Titan forward'.

Source: 'Monotub Industries in a spin as founder gets Titan for £1', Lisa Urquhart, *Financial Times/FT.com*, 23 January 2003.

Limited liability

Since the company is a legal person in its own right, it must take responsibility for its own debts and losses. This means that once the shareholders have paid what they have agreed to pay for the shares, their obligation to the company, and to the company's creditors, is satisfied. Thus shareholders can limit their losses to the amount that they have paid, or agreed to pay, for their shares. This is of great practical importance to potential shareholders since they know that what they can lose, as part owners of the business, is limited.

Contrast this with the position of sole proprietors or partners. They cannot 'ring-fence' assets that they do not want to put into the business. If a sole proprietorship or partnership business finds itself in a position where liabilities exceed the business assets, the law gives unsatisfied creditors the right to demand payment out of what the sole proprietor or partner may have regarded as 'non-business' assets. Thus the sole proprietor or partner could lose everything – house, car, the lot. This is because the law sees Jill, the sole proprietor, as being the same as Jill the private individual. The shareholder, by contrast, can lose only the amount committed to that company. Legally, the business operating as a limited company, in which Jack owns shares, is not the same as Jack himself. This is true even if Jack were to own all of the shares in the company.

Real World 4.2 gives an example of a well-known case where the shareholders of a particular company were able to avoid any liability to those that had lost money as a result of dealing with the company.

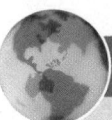

Real World 4.2

Carlton and Granada 1 – Nationwide Football League 0

Two television broadcasting companies, Carlton and Granada, each owned 50 per cent of a separate company, ITV Digital (formerly ON Digital). ITV Digital signed a contract to pay the Nationwide Football League (in effect the three divisions of English football below the Premiership) more than £89m on both 1 August 2002 and 1 August 2003 for the rights to broadcast football matches over three seasons. ITV Digital was unable to sell enough subscriptions for the broadcasts and collapsed because it was unable to meet its liabilities. The Nationwide Football League tried to force Carlton and Granada (ITV Digital's only shareholders) to meet ITV Digital's contractual obligations. It was unable to do so because the shareholders could not be held legally liable for the amounts owing.

Carlton and Granada merged into one business in 2003, but at the time of ITV Digital were two independent companies.

Activity (4.1)

The fact that shareholders can limit their losses to that which they have paid, or have agreed to pay, for their shares is of great practical importance to potential shareholders. Can you think of any practical benefit to a private sector economy, in general, of this ability of shareholders to limit losses?

Business is a risky venture – in some cases very risky. People with money to invest will usually be happier to do so when they know the limit of their liability. If investors are given limited liability, new businesses are more likely to be formed and existing ones are likely to find it easier to raise more finance. This is good for the private sector economy and may ultimately lead to the generation of greater wealth for society as a whole.

Although **limited liability** has this advantage to the providers of equity finance (the shareholders), it is not necessarily to the advantage of all others who have a stake in the business, like the Nationwide Football League clubs (see Real World 4.2). Limited liability is attractive to shareholders because they can, in effect, walk away from the unpaid debts of the company if their contribution has not been sufficient to meet those debts. This is likely to make any individual, or another business, that is considering entering into a contract, wary of dealing with the limited company. This can be a real problem for smaller, less established companies. Suppliers may insist on cash payment before delivery of goods or the rendering of a service. Alternatively, they may require a personal guarantee from a major shareholder that the debt will be paid before allowing trade credit. In the latter case, the supplier circumvents the company's limited liability status by demanding the personal liability of an individual. Larger, more established companies, on the other hand, tend to have built up the confidence of suppliers.

Legal safeguards

Various safeguards exist to protect individuals and businesses contemplating dealing with a limited company. These include the requirement to indicate limited liability status in the name of the company. By doing this, an alert is issued to prospective suppliers and lenders.

A further safeguard is the restrictions placed on the ability of shareholders to withdraw their equity from the company. These restrictions are designed to prevent shareholders from protecting their own investment and, as a result, leaving lenders and suppliers in an exposed position. We shall consider this point in more detail later in the chapter.

Finally, limited companies are required to produce annual financial statements (income statement, statement of financial position and statement of cash flows), and make them publicly available. This means that anyone interested can gain an impression of the financial performance and position of the company. The form and content of the first two of these statements are considered in some detail later in the chapter. Chapter 6 is devoted to the statement of cash flows.

Public and private companies

When a company is registered with the Registrar of Companies, it must be registered either as a public or as a private company. The main practical difference between these is that a **public limited company** can offer its shares for sale to the general public,

Figure 4.1 Comparison of public and private limited companies over five years

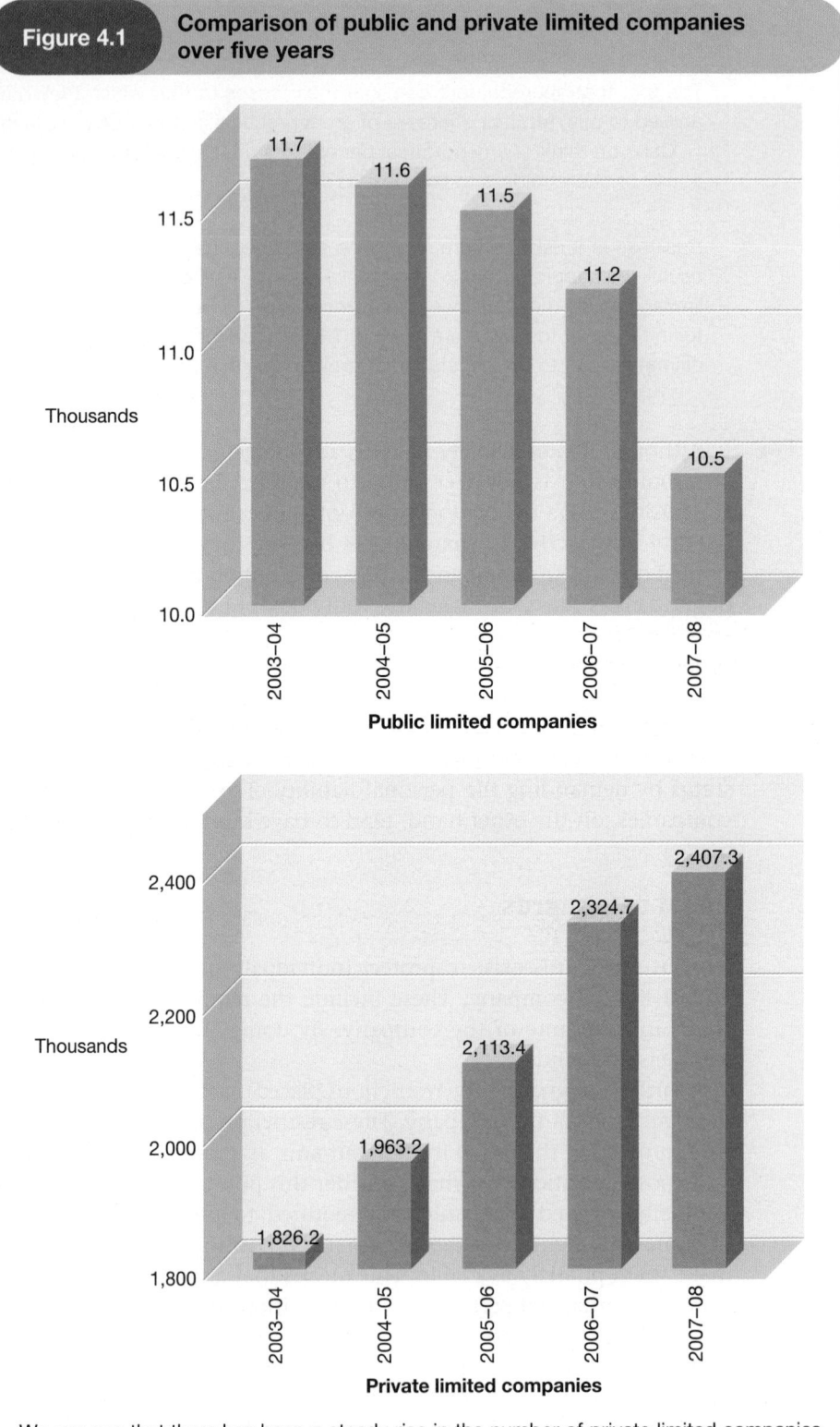

We can see that there has been a steady rise in the number of private limited companies over the five-year period. This has been matched by a gradual decline in the number of public limited companies.

Source: Based on information in *Companies Register Activities 2008*, Statistical tables on companies registration activities 2007–08, www.companieshouse.gov.uk.

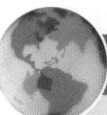 but a **private limited company** is restricted from doing so. A public limited company must signal its status to all interested parties by having the words 'public limited company', or its abbreviation 'plc', in its name. For a private limited company, the word 'limited' or 'Ltd' must appear as part of its name.

Private limited companies tend to be smaller businesses where the ownership is divided among relatively few shareholders who are usually fairly close to one another – for example, a family company. Numerically, there are vastly more private limited companies in the UK than there are public ones. Of the 2.4 million UK limited companies now in existence, only 10,500 (representing 0.4 per cent of the total) are public limited companies. Figure 4.1 shows the trend in the numbers of public and private limited companies in recent years.

Since individual public companies tend to be larger, they are often economically more important. In some industry sectors, such as banking, insurance, oil refining and grocery retailing, they are completely dominant. Although some large private limited companies exist, many private limited companies are little more than the vehicle through which one-person businesses operate.

Real World 4.3 shows the extent of market dominance of public limited companies in one particular business sector.

Real World 4.3

A big slice of the market

The grocery sector is dominated by four large players: Tesco, Sainsbury, Morrison and Asda. The first three are public limited companies and the fourth, Asda, is owned by a large US public company, Wal-Mart. Figure 4.2 shows the share of the grocery market enjoyed by each.

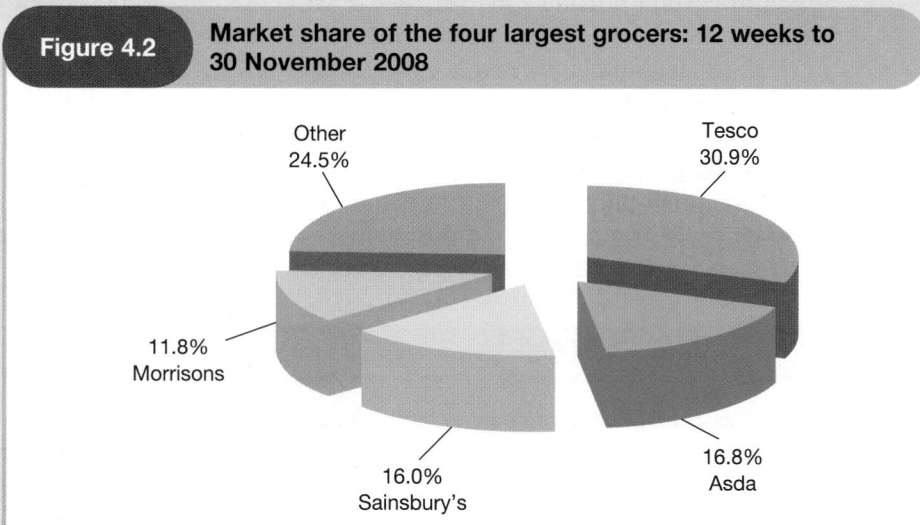

Figure 4.2 Market share of the four largest grocers: 12 weeks to 30 November 2008

Other 24.5%

Tesco 30.9%

11.8% Morrisons

16.0% Sainsbury's

16.8% Asda

Tesco had by far the largest market share and the four largest grocers, when taken together, had more than 75 per cent of the total market during the period.

Source: Compiled from information in 'Tesco and Waitrose lose market shares as grocery sector continues to slow', www.kamcity.com. Accessed 6 January 2009.

Source: 'Tesco and Waitrose lose market share as grocery sector begins to slow', www.kamcity.com, 6 January 2009.

Taxation

Another consequence of the legal separation of the limited company from its owners is that companies must be accountable to the tax authorities for tax on their profits and gains. This leads to the reporting of tax in the financial statements of limited companies. The charge for tax is shown in the income statement (profit and loss account). The tax charge for a particular year is based on that year's profit. Since only 50 per cent of a company's tax liability is due for payment during the year concerned, the other 50 per cent will appear on the end-of-year statement of financial position (balance sheet) as a short-term liability. This will be illustrated a little later in the chapter. The tax position of companies contrasts with that of sole proprietorships and partnerships, where tax is levied not on the business but on the owner(s). Thus tax does not impact on the financial statements of unincorporated businesses, but is an individual matter between the owner(s) and the tax authorities.

 Companies are charged **corporation tax** on their profits and gains. The percentage rates of tax tend to vary from year to year, but have recently been 28 per cent for larger companies and 21 per cent for smaller companies. These rates of tax are levied on the company's taxable profit, which is not necessarily the same as the profit shown on the income statement. This is because tax law does not, in every respect, follow the normal accounting rules. Generally, however, the taxable profit and the company's accounting profit are pretty close to one another.

Transferring share ownership: the role of the Stock Exchange

We have already seen that shares in a company may be transferred from one owner to another. The desire of some shareholders to sell their shares, coupled with the desire of others to buy those shares, has led to the existence of a formal market in which shares can be bought and sold. The London Stock Exchange and similar organisations around the world provide a marketplace in which shares in public companies may be bought and sold. Share prices are determined by the laws of supply and demand, which are, in turn, determined by investors' perceptions of the future economic prospects of the companies concerned. Only the shares of certain companies (*listed* companies) may be traded on the London Stock Exchange. Less than 1,100 UK companies are listed. This represents only about one in 2,200 of all UK companies (public and private) and about one in ten public limited companies. However, many of these listed companies are massive. Nearly all of the 'household-name' UK businesses (for example, Tesco, Next, BT, Vodafone, BP and so on) are listed companies.

Activity 4.2

If, as has been pointed out earlier, the change in ownership of shares does not directly affect the particular company, why do many public companies actively seek to have their shares traded in a recognised market?

The main reason is that investors are generally very reluctant to pledge their money unless they can see some way in which they can turn their investment back into cash. In theory, the shares of a particular company may be very valuable because the company has bright prospects. However, unless this value is capable of being turned into cash, the benefit to the shareholders is dubious. After all, we cannot spend shares; we normally need cash.

This means that potential shareholders are much more likely to be prepared to buy new shares from the company (thereby providing the company with new investment finance) where they can see a way of liquidating their investment (turning it into cash) as and when they wish. Stock Exchanges provide the means of liquidation.

Although the buying and selling of 'second-hand' shares does not provide the company with cash, the fact that the buying and selling facility exists will make it easier for the company to raise new share capital when it needs to do so.

Managing a company

A limited company may have legal personality, but it is not a human being capable of making decisions and plans about the business and exercising control over it. People must undertake these management tasks. The most senior level of management of a company is the board of directors.

→ The shareholders elect **directors** (by law there must be at least one director for a private limited company and two for a public limited company) to manage the company on a day-to-day basis on behalf of those shareholders. In a small company, the board may be the only level of management and consist of all of the shareholders. In larger companies, the board may consist of ten or so directors out of many thousands of shareholders. Indeed, directors are not even required to be shareholders. Below the board of directors of the typical large company could be several layers of management comprising thousands of people.

→ In recent years, the issue of **corporate governance** has generated much debate. The term is used to describe the ways in which companies are directed and controlled. The issue of corporate governance is important because, with larger companies, those who own the company (that is, the shareholders) are usually divorced from the day-to-day control of the business. The shareholders employ the directors to manage the company for them. Given this position, it may seem reasonable to assume that the best interests of shareholders will guide the directors' decisions. However, in practice this does not always occur. The directors may be more concerned with pursuing their own interests, such as increasing their pay and 'perks' (such as expensive motor cars, overseas visits and so on) and improving their job security and status. As a result, a conflict can occur between the interests of shareholders and the interests of directors.

Where directors pursue their own interests at the expense of the shareholders, there is clearly a problem for the shareholders. However, it may also be a problem for society as a whole. If shareholders feel that their funds are likely to be mismanaged, they will be reluctant to invest. A shortage of funds will mean that fewer investments can be made and the costs of funds will increase as businesses compete for what funds are available. Thus, a lack of concern for shareholders can have a profound effect on the performance of individual companies and, with this, the health of the economy. To avoid these problems, most competitive market economies have a framework of rules to help monitor and control the behaviour of directors.

These rules are usually based around three guiding principles:

● *Disclosure*. This lies at the heart of good corporate governance. An OECD report (see reference 1 at the end of the chapter) summed up the benefits of disclosure as follows:

> Adequate and timely information about corporate performance enables investors to make informed buy-and-sell decisions and thereby helps the market reflect the value of

a corporation under present management. If the market determines that present management is not performing, a decrease in stock [share] price will sanction management's failure and open the way to management change.

● *Accountability.* This involves defining the roles and duties of the directors and establishing an adequate monitoring process. In the UK, company law requires that the directors of a business act in the best interests of the shareholders. This means, among other things, that they must not try to use their position and knowledge to make gains at the expense of the shareholders. The law also requires larger companies to have their annual financial statements independently audited. The purpose of an independent audit is to lend credibility to the financial statements prepared by the directors. We shall take a brief look at audit later in Chapter 5.

● *Fairness.* Directors should not be able to benefit from access to 'inside' information that is not available to shareholders. As a result, both the law and the Stock Exchange place restrictions on the ability of directors to buy and sell the shares of the business. One example of these restrictions is that the directors cannot buy or sell shares immediately before the announcement of the annual trading results of the business or before the announcement of a significant event such as a planned merger or the loss of the chief executive.

Strengthening the framework of rules

The number of rules designed to safeguard shareholders has increased considerably over the years. This has been in response to weaknesses in corporate governance procedures, which have been exposed through well-publicised business failures and frauds, excessive pay increases to directors and evidence that some financial reports were being 'massaged' so as to mislead shareholders. (This last point will be discussed in the following chapter.) Some believe, however, that the shareholders must shoulder some of the blame for any weaknesses. Not all shareholders in large companies are private individuals owning just a few shares each. In fact, ownership, by market value, of the shares listed on the London Stock Exchange is dominated by investing institutions such as insurance businesses, banks and pension funds (see Real World 15.16, page 618). These are often massive operations, owning large quantities of the shares of the companies in which they invest. These institutional investors employ specialist staff to manage their portfolios of shares in various companies. It has been argued that the large institutional shareholders, despite their size and relative expertise, have not been very active in corporate governance matters. Thus there has been little monitoring of directors. However, things seem to be changing. There is increasing evidence that institutional investors are becoming more pro-active in relation to the companies in which they hold shares.

The Combined Code

During the 1990s there was a real effort by the accountancy profession and the London Stock Exchange to address the problems mentioned above. A Code of Best Practice on Corporate Governance emerged in 1992. This was concerned with accountability and financial reporting. In 1995, a separate code of practice emerged. This dealt with directors' pay and conditions. These two codes were revised, 'fine-tuned' and amalgamated to

 produce the **Combined Code**, which was issued in 1998.

The Combined Code was revised in 2003, following the recommendations of the Higgs Report, and modified slightly in 2006. These recommendations were mainly concerned with the roles of the company chairman (the senior director) and the other directors. The report was particularly concerned with the role of 'non-executive' directors. Non-executive directors do not work full-time in the company, but act solely in the role of director. This contrasts with 'executive' directors who are salaried employees. For example, the finance director of most large companies is a full-time employee. This person is a member of the board of directors and, as such, takes part in the key decision making at board level. At the same time, he or she is also responsible for managing the departments of the company that act on those board decisions as far as finance is concerned.

The view reflected in the 2003 Combined Code is that executive directors can become too embroiled in the day-to-day management of the company to be able to take a broad view. It also reflects the view that, for executive directors, conflicts can arise between their own interests and those of the shareholders. The advantage of non-executive directors can be that they are much more independent of the company than are their executive colleagues. Non-executive directors are remunerated by the company for their work, but this would normally form only a small proportion of their total income. This gives them an independence that the executive directors may lack. Non-executive directors are often senior managers in other businesses or people who have had good experience of such roles.

The Combined Code has the backing of the London Stock Exchange. This means that companies listed on the London Stock Exchange are expected to comply with the requirements of the Code or must give their shareholders good reason why they do not. Failure to do one or other of these can lead to the company's shares being suspended from listing. This is an important sanction against non-compliant directors.

The Combined Code sets out a number of principles relating to such matters as the role of the directors, their relations with shareholders, and their accountability. **Real World 4.4** outlines some of the more important of these.

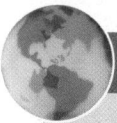

Real World 4.4

The Combined Code

Some of the key elements of the Combined Code are as follows:

- Every listed company should have a board of directors to lead and control the company.
- There should be a clear division of responsibilities between the chairman and the chief executive officer of the company to ensure that a single person does not have unbridled power.
- There should be a balance between executive and non-executive (who are often part-time and independent) members of the board, to ensure that small groups of individuals cannot dominate proceedings.
- The board should receive timely information that is of sufficient quality to enable them to carry out their duties.
- Appointments to the board should be the subject of rigorous, formal and transparent procedures.

Real World 4.4 continued

- All directors should submit themselves for re-election at regular intervals, subject to satisfactory performance.
- There should be formal and transparent procedures for developing policy on directors' remuneration.
- The board has a responsibility for ensuring that a satisfactory dialogue with shareholders occurs.
- Boards should use the annual general meeting to communicate with private investors and encourage their participation.
- Institutional shareholders have a responsibility to use their votes.
- The board should publish a balanced and understandable assessment of the company's position and performance.
- Internal controls should be in place to protect the shareholders' wealth.
- Formal and transparent arrangements for applying financial reporting and internal control principles and for maintaining an appropriate relationship with auditors should be in place.

Source: www.fsa.gov.uk.

Strengthening the framework of rules has improved the quality of information available to shareholders, resulted in better checks on the powers of directors, and provided greater transparency in corporate affairs. However, rules can only be a partial answer. A balance must be struck between the need to protect shareholders and the need to encourage the entrepreneurial spirit of directors, which could be stifled under a welter of rules. This implies that rules should not be too tight and so unscrupulous directors may still find ways around them.

Activity 4.3

Can you think of ways in which the shareholders themselves may try to ensure that the directors always act in the shareholders' best interests?

Two ways are commonly used in practice:

- The shareholders may insist on monitoring closely the actions of the directors and the way in which they use the resources of the company.
- The shareholders may introduce incentive plans for directors that link their pay to the share performance of the company. In this way, the interests of the directors and shareholders will become more closely aligned.

Implementing the code

A detailed study of how the various principles mentioned above are implemented is beyond the scope of this book. However, it is useful to have some idea as to how companies apply the code in practice. To achieve this, we can take a look at extracts from the statement on corporate governance made by the directors of J D Wetherspoon plc, the pub operator, which is set out in its 2008 annual report and accounts.

The first extract, which is set out in **Real World 4.5**, concerns the division of responsibilities between the chairman and the chief executive.

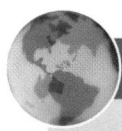

Real World 4.5

Divide and rule

Chairman's responsibility	Chief Executive's responsibility
The chairman is responsible for the smooth running of the board and ensuring that all directors are fully informed of matters relevant to their roles	The chief executive is responsible for the smooth daily running of the business
Delegated responsibility of authority from the company to exchange of contracts within controlled procedures	Developing and maintaining effective management controls, planning and performance measurements
Providing support, advice and feedback to the chief executive	Maintaining and developing an effective organisational structure
Supporting the company strategy and encouraging the chief executive with development of the strategy	External and internal communications in conjunction with the chairman on any issues facing the company
Chairing general meetings, board meetings, operational meetings and agreeing on board agendas	Implementing and monitoring compliance with board policies
Management of chief executive's contract, appraisal and remuneration by way of making recommendations to the remuneration committee	Timely and accurate reporting of the above to the board
Providing support to executive directors and senior managers of the company	Recruiting and managing senior managers in the business
Providing the 'ethos' and 'vision' of the company	Developing and maintaining effective risk management and regulatory controls
Providing operational presence across the estate	Maintaining primary relationships with shareholders and investors
	Chairing the management board responsible for implementing the company strategy

Source: J D Wetherspoon plc Annual Report and Accounts 2008, p. 28.

The next extract, which is set out in **Real World 4.6**, concerns the need for directors to receive timely information.

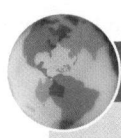

Real World 4.6

Time gentlemen, please!

All directors are provided with, and have full and timely access to, information which enables them to make informed decisions on corporate and business issues, including operational and financial performance. In particular, the board receives monthly information on the financial trading performance of the company and a comprehensive finance report which includes operational highlights. All directors receive sales and margin information for the company weekly by trading unit.

Source: J D Wetherspoon plc Annual Report and Accounts 2008, p. 28.

The final extract, which is set out in **Real World 4.7**, concerns the ways in which the directors seek to protect shareholder wealth through various internal controls.

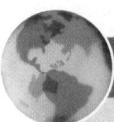

Real World 4.7

Exercising control

During the year, the company and the board continued to support and invest in resources to provide an internal audit and risk-management function. The system of internal control and risk mitigation is deeply embedded in the operations and culture of the company. The board is responsible for maintaining a sound system of internal control and reviewing its effectiveness. The function can only manage, rather than entirely eliminate the risk of failure to achieve business objectives. It can only provide reasonable and not absolute assurance against material misstatement or loss. Ongoing reviews and assessments took place continually throughout the year under review and up to the date of the approval of the annual report.

The company has an internal audit function which is discharged as follows:

- Adequate regular audits of the company stock (inventories)
- Unannounced visits to the retail units
- Monitoring systems which control the company cash
- Health and safety visits ensuring compliance with the company procedures
- Reviewing and assessing the impact of regulatory change
- Annually reviewing the company's strategy, including a review of risks facing the business
- Risk management process, identifying key risks facing the business.

The company has key controls as follows:

- Clearly defined authority limits and controls over cash-handling purchasing commitments and capital expenditure
- Comprehensive budgeting process, with a detailed operating 12-month plan and a mid-term financial plan, both approved by the board
- Business results are reported weekly (for key times), with a monthly comprehensive report in full, and compared with budget
- Forecasts are prepared regularly throughout the year for review by the board
- Complex treasury instruments are not used; decisions on treasury matters are reserved by the board

- The directors confirm that they have reviewed the effectiveness of the system of internal control
- Regular reviews of the amount of external insurance which it obtains, bearing in mind the availability of such cover, its costs and the likelihood of the risks involved
- Directors' insurance cover is maintained.

Source: J D Wetherspoon plc Annual Report and Accounts 2008, p. 30.

Financing limited companies

The owners' claim

The owner's claim of a sole proprietorship is normally encompassed in one figure on the statement of financial position, usually labelled 'equity' (or 'capital'). With companies, this is usually a little more complicated, although in essence the same broad principles apply. With a company, the owners' claim is divided between shares (for example, the original investment), on the one hand, and **reserves** (that is, profits and gains subsequently made), on the other. There is also the possibility that there will be more than one type of shares and of reserves. Thus, within the basic divisions of share capital and reserves, there might well be further subdivisions. This might seem quite complicated, but we shall shortly consider the reasons for these subdivisions and all should become clearer.

The basic division

When a company is first formed, those who take steps to form it (the promoters) will decide how much needs to be raised by the potential shareholders to set the company up with the necessary assets to operate. Example 4.1 acts as a basis for illustration.

Example 4.1

Some friends decide to form a company to operate an office cleaning business. They estimate that the company will need £50,000 to obtain the necessary assets. Between them, they raise the cash, which they use to buy shares in the company, on 31 March 2009, with a **nominal value** (or **par value**) of £1 each.

At this point the statement of financial position of the company would be:

Statement of financial position as at 31 March 2009

	£
Net assets (all in cash)	50,000
Equity	
Share capital	
50,000 shares of £1 each	50,000

→ The company now buys the necessary non-current assets (vacuum cleaners and so on) and inventories (cleaning materials) and starts to trade. During the first year, the company makes a profit of £10,000. This, by definition, means that the equity expands by £10,000. During the year, the shareholders (owners) make no drawings of their claim, so at the end of the year the summarised statement of financial position looks like this:

Statement of financial position as at 31 March 2010

	£
Net assets (various assets less liabilities*)	60,000
Equity	
Share capital	
50,000 shares of £1 each	50,000
Reserves (revenue reserve)	10,000
Total equity	60,000

* We saw in Chapter 2 that Assets = Equity + Liabilities. We also saw that this can be rearranged so that Assets − Liabilities = Equity.

→ The profit is shown in a reserve, known as a **revenue reserve**, because it arises from generating revenue (making sales). Note that we do not simply merge the profit with the share capital: we must keep the two amounts separate (to satisfy company law). The reason for this is that there is a legal restriction on the maximum drawings of the share-
→ holders' claim (or payment of a **dividend**) that the owners can make. This is defined by the amount of revenue reserves, and so it is helpful to show these separately. We shall look at why there is this restriction, and how it works, a little later in the chapter.

Share capital

Ordinary shares

Shares represent the basic units of ownership of a business. All companies issue
→ **ordinary shares**. Ordinary shares are often known as *equities*. The nominal value of such shares is at the discretion of the people who start up the company. For example, if the initial share capital is to be £50,000, this could be two shares of £25,000 each, 5 million shares of 1 penny each or any other combination that gives a total of £50,000. All shares must have equal value.

Activity (4.4)

The initial financial requirement for a new company is £50,000. There are to be two equal shareholders. Would you advise them to issue two shares of £25,000 each? Why?

Such large-denomination shares tend to be unwieldy. Suppose that one of the shareholders wanted to sell her shareholding. She would have to find one buyer. If there were shares of smaller denomination, it would be possible to sell part of the shareholding to various potential buyers. Furthermore, it would be possible to sell just part of the holding and retain a part.

In practice, £1 is the normal maximum nominal value for shares. Shares of 25 pence each and 50 pence each are probably the most common.

Altering the nominal value of shares

We have already seen that the promoters of a new company may make their own choice of the nominal or par value of the shares. This value need not be permanent. At a later date the shareholders can decide to change it.

Suppose that a company has 1 million ordinary shares of £1 each and a decision is made to change the nominal value of the shares from £1 to £0.50, in other words to halve the value. This would lead the company to issue each shareholder with a new share certificate (the shareholders' evidence of ownership of their shareholding) for exactly twice as many shares, each with half the nominal value. The result would be that each shareholder retains a holding of the same total nominal value. This process is known, not surprisingly, as **splitting** the shares. The opposite, reducing the number of shares and increasing their nominal value per share to compensate, is known as **consolidating**. Since each shareholder would be left, after a split or consolidation, with exactly the same proportion of ownership of the company's assets as before, the process should not increase the value of the total shares held.

Splitting is fairly common. The objective is probably to avoid individual shares becoming too valuable and making them a bit unwieldy, in the way discussed in the answer to Activity 4.4. If a company trades successfully, the value of each share is likely to rise, and in time could increase to a level that makes them less marketable. Splitting would solve this problem. Consolidating is relatively rare.

Real World 4.8 provides an example of a share split by one business.

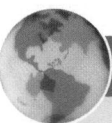

Real World 4.8

Doing the splits

A G Barr, the Scottish-based maker of soft drinks, including Tizer and Irn-Bru, had a share split in September 2009, as announced by the business in its half-yearly report:

> As previously announced, the 2 for 1 share split, which is aimed at improving liquidity and marketability of the company's shares became effective on 21 September.

Source: A G Barr plc Interim report page 3, August 2009.

Preference shares

Some companies not only issue ordinary shares, but also issue other classes of shares, **preference shares** being the most common. Preference shares guarantee that *if a dividend is paid*, the preference shareholders will be entitled to the first part of it up to a maximum value. This maximum is normally defined as a fixed percentage of the nominal value of the preference shares. If, for example, a company issues 10,000 preference shares of £1 each with a dividend rate of 6 per cent, this means that the preference shareholders are entitled to receive the first £600 (that is, 6 per cent of £10,000) of any dividend that is paid by the company for a year. The excess over £600 goes to the ordinary shareholders. Normally, any undistributed profits and gains also accrue to the ordinary shareholders.

The ordinary shareholders are the primary risk-takers as they are entitled to share in the profits of the company only after other claims have been satisfied. There are no upper limits, however, on the amount by which they may benefit. The potential rewards available to ordinary shareholders reflect the risks that they are prepared to take. Since ordinary shareholders take most of the risks, power normally resides in their hands. Usually, only the ordinary shareholders are able to vote on issues that affect the company, such as who the directors should be.

It is open to the company to issue shares of various classes – perhaps with some having unusual and exotic conditions – but in practice it is rare to find other than straightforward ordinary and preference shares. Although a company may have different classes of shares whose holders have different rights, within each class all shares must be treated equally. The rights of the various classes of shareholders, as well as other matters relating to a particular company, are contained in that company's set of rules, known as the 'articles and memorandum of association'. A copy of these rules must be lodged with the Registrar of Companies, who makes it available for inspection by the general public.

Reserves

As we have already seen, reserves are profits and gains that have been made by a company and which still form part of the shareholders' (owners') claim or equity. One reason that past profits and gains may not remain part of equity is that they have been paid out to shareholders (as dividends and so on). Another reason is that reserves will be reduced by the amount of any losses that the company might suffer. In the same way that profits increase equity, losses reduce it.

The shareholders' claim consists of share capital and reserves.

Activity (4.5)

Are reserves amounts of cash? Can you think of a reason why this is an odd question?

To deal with the second point first, it is an odd question because reserves are a claim, or part of one, on the assets of the company, whereas cash is an asset. So reserves cannot be cash.

→ Reserves are classified as either revenue reserves or **capital reserves**. In Example 4.1 we came across one type of reserve, the revenue reserve. We should recall that this reserve represents the company's retained trading profits and gains on the disposal of non-current assets. It is worth mentioning that retained profits, or earnings, as they are often called, represent overwhelmingly the largest source of new finance for UK companies. For most companies they amount to more than share issues and borrowings combined.

Capital reserves arise for two main reasons:

● issuing shares at above their nominal value (for example, issuing £1 shares at £1.50);
● revaluing (upwards) non-current assets.

Where a company issues shares at above their nominal value, UK law requires that the excess of the issue price over the nominal value be shown separately.

Activity 4.6

Can you think why shares might be issued at above their nominal value? (*Hint*: This would not usually happen when a company is first formed and the initial shares are being issued.)

Once a company has traded and has been successful, the shares would normally be worth more than the nominal value at which they were issued. If additional shares are to be issued to new shareholders to raise finance for further expansion, unless they are issued at a value higher than the nominal value, the new shareholders will be gaining at the expense of the original ones.

Example 4.2 shows how this works.

Example 4.2

Based on future prospects, the net assets of a company are worth £1.5 million. There are currently 1 million ordinary shares in the company, each with a face (nominal) value of £1. The company wishes to raise an additional £0.6 million of cash for expansion and has decided to raise it by issuing new shares. If the shares are issued for £1 each (that is 600,000 shares), the total number of shares will be

$$1.0m + 0.6m = 1.6m$$

and their total value will be the value of the existing net assets plus the new injection of cash:

$$£1.5m + £0.6m = £2.1m.$$

This means that the value of each share after the new issue will be

$$£2.1m/1.6m = £1.3125.$$

The current value of each share is

$$£1.5m/1.0m = £1.50$$

so the original shareholders will lose

$$£1.50 - £1.3125 = £0.1875 \text{ a share}$$

and the new shareholders will gain

$$£1.3125 - £1.0 = £0.3125 \text{ a share}.$$

The new shareholders will, no doubt, be delighted with this outcome; the original ones will not.

Things could be made fair between the two sets of shareholders described in Example 4.2 by issuing the new shares at £1.50 each. In this case it would be necessary to issue 400,000 shares to raise the necessary £0.6 million. £1 a share of the £1.50 is the nominal value and will be included with share capital in the statement of financial position (£400,000 in total). The remaining £0.50 is a share premium, which will be

 shown as a capital reserve known as the **share premium account** (£200,000 in total).

It is not clear why UK company law insists on the distinction between nominal share values and the premium. In some other countries (for example, the United States) with similar laws governing the corporate sector, there is not the necessity of distinguishing between share capital and share premium. Instead, the total value at which shares are issued is shown as one comprehensive figure on the company's statement of financial position. **Real World 4.9** shows the shareholders' claim of one well-known business.

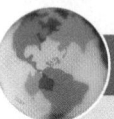

Real World 4.9

Funding Thorntons

Thorntons plc, the chocolate maker and retailer, had the following share capital and reserves as at 27 June 2009:

	£m
Share capital (10p ordinary shares)	6,835
Share premium	13,752
Retained earnings	8,151
Total equity	**28,738**

Note how the nominal share capital figure is only about one-half of the share premium account figure. This implies that Thorntons has issued shares at higher prices than the 10p a share nominal value. This reflects its trading success since the company was first formed. In 2008, retained earnings (profits) had made up over 40 per cent of the total for share capital and reserves. By 2009, this had reduced to around 28%. This reduction was mainly caused by a loss suffered by the company pension fund during the year.

Source: Thorntons plc Annual Report 2009, p. 45.

Bonus shares

It is always open to a company to take reserves of any kind (irrespective of whether they are capital or revenue) and turn them into share capital. This will involve transferring the desired amount from the reserve concerned to share capital and then distributing the appropriate number of new shares to the existing shareholders. New shares arising from such a conversion are known as **bonus shares**. Issues of bonus shares are quite frequently encountered in practice. Example 4.3 illustrates this aspect of share issues.

Example 4.3

The summary statement of financial position of a company is as follows:

Statement of financial position as at 31 March 2009

	£
Net assets (various assets less liabilities)	128,000
Equity	
Share capital	
50,000 shares of £1 each	50,000
Reserves	78,000
Total equity	**128,000**

The company decides that it will issue existing shareholders with one new share for every share currently owned by each shareholder. The statement of financial position immediately following this will appear as follows:

Statement of financial position as at 31 March 2009

	£
Net assets (various assets less liabilities)	128,000
Equity	
Share capital	
100,000 shares of £1 each (50,000 + 50,000)	100,000
Reserves (78,000 − 50,000)	28,000
Total equity	128,000

We can see that the reserves have decreased by £50,000 and share capital has increased by the same amount. Share certificates for the 50,000 ordinary shares of £1 each, that have been created from reserves, will be issued to the existing shareholders to complete the transaction.

Activity 4.7

A shareholder of the company in Example 4.3 owned 100 shares before the bonus issue. How will things change for this shareholder as regards the number of shares owned and the value of the shareholding?

The answer should be that the number of shares will double, from 100 to 200. Now the shareholder owns one five-hundredth of the company (that is, 200/100,000). Before the bonus issue, the shareholder also owned one five-hundredth of the company (that is, 100/50,000). The company's assets and liabilities have not changed as a result of the bonus issue and so, logically, one five-hundredth of the value of the company should be identical to what it was before. Thus, each share is worth half as much.

→ A **bonus issue** simply takes one part of the owners' claim (a reserve) and puts it into another part (share capital). The transaction has no effect on the company's assets or liabilities, so there is no effect on shareholders' wealth.

Note that a bonus issue is not the same as a share split. A split does not affect the reserves.

Activity 4.8

Can you think of any reasons why a company might want to make a bonus issue if it has no economic consequence?

We think that there are three possible reasons:

- *Share price.* To lower the value of each share without reducing the shareholders' collective or individual wealth. This has a similar effect to share splitting.
- *Shareholder confidence.* To provide the shareholders with a 'feel-good factor'. It is believed that shareholders like bonus issues because they seem to make them better off, although in practice they should not affect their wealth.

Activity 4.8 continued

● *Lender confidence.* Where reserves arising from operating profits and/or realised gains on the sale of non-current assets are used to make the bonus issue, it has the effect of taking part of that portion of the shareholders' equity that could be drawn by the shareholders, as drawings (or dividends), and locking it up. The amount transferred becomes part of the permanent equity base of the company. (We shall see a little later in this chapter that there are severe restrictions on the extent to which shareholders may make drawings from their claim.) An individual or business contemplating lending money to the company may insist that the dividend payment possibilities are restricted as a condition of making the loan. This point will be explained shortly.

Real World 4.10 provides an example of a bonus share issue.

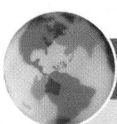

Real World 4.10

Bonus builder

Henry Boot plc is a leading property and construction business. In March 2007 the business announced a 4-for-1 bonus issue of shares. The bonus issue increased the number of shares in issue from 26 million to 130 million and left each shareholder with five times as many shares as before the issue. The directors believed that the bonus issue would benefit shareholders by enhancing the liquidity and marketability of the ordinary shares.

Source: Based on information contained in an announcement published by Henry Boot plc on 12 April 2007, www.henryboot.co.uk.

Share capital jargon

Before leaving our detailed discussion of share capital, it might be helpful to clarify some of the jargon relating to shares that is used in company financial statements.

→ Share capital that has been issued to shareholders is known as the **issued share**
→ **capital** (or **allotted share capital**). Sometimes, but not very often, a company may not require shareholders to pay the whole amount that is due to be paid for the shares at the time of issue. This may happen where the company does not need the money all at once. Some money would normally be paid at the time of issue and the company
→ would 'call' for further instalments until the shares were **fully paid shares**. That part of
→ the total issue price that has been 'called' is known as the **called-up share capital**. That
→ part that has been called and paid is known as the **paid-up share capital**.

Raising share capital

Once the company has made its initial share issue to start business (usually soon after the company is first formed) it may decide to make further issues of new shares. These may be:

● *Rights issues* – issues made to existing shareholders, in proportion to their existing shareholding.
● *Public issues* – issues made to the general investing public.
● *Private placings* – issues made to selected individuals who are usually approached and asked if they would be interested in taking up new shares.

During its lifetime a company may use all three of these approaches to raising funds through issuing new shares (although only public companies can make appeals to the general public). These approaches will be discussed in detail in Chapter 15.

Borrowings

Most companies borrow money to supplement that raised from share issues and ploughed-back profits. Company borrowing is often on a long-term basis, perhaps on a ten-year contract. Lenders may be banks and other professional providers of loan finance. Many companies borrow in such a way that small investors, including private individuals, are able to lend small amounts. This is particularly the case with the larger, Stock Exchange listed, companies and involves their making a **loan notes** issue, which, though large in total, can be taken up in small slices by individual investors, both private individuals and investing institutions, such as pension funds and insurance companies. In some cases, these slices of loans can be bought and sold through the Stock Exchange. This means that investors do not have to wait the full term of their loan to obtain repayment, but can sell their slice of it to another would-be lender at intermediate points in the term of the loan. Loan notes are often known as *loan stock* or *debentures*.

Some of the features of loan notes financing, particularly the possibility that the loan notes may be traded on the Stock Exchange, can lead to a confusion that loan notes are shares by another name. We should be clear that this is not the case. It is the shareholders who own the company and, therefore, who share in its losses and profits. Holders of loan notes lend money to the company under a legally binding contract that normally specifies the rate of interest, the interest payment dates and the date of repayment of the loan itself.

Usually, long-term loans are secured on assets of the company. This would give the lender the right to seize the assets concerned, sell them and satisfy the repayment obligation, should the company fail to pay either its interest payments or the repayment of the loan itself, on the dates specified in the contract between the company and the lender. A mortgage granted to a private individual buying a house or a flat is a very common example of a secured loan.

Long-term financing of companies can be depicted as in Figure 4.3.

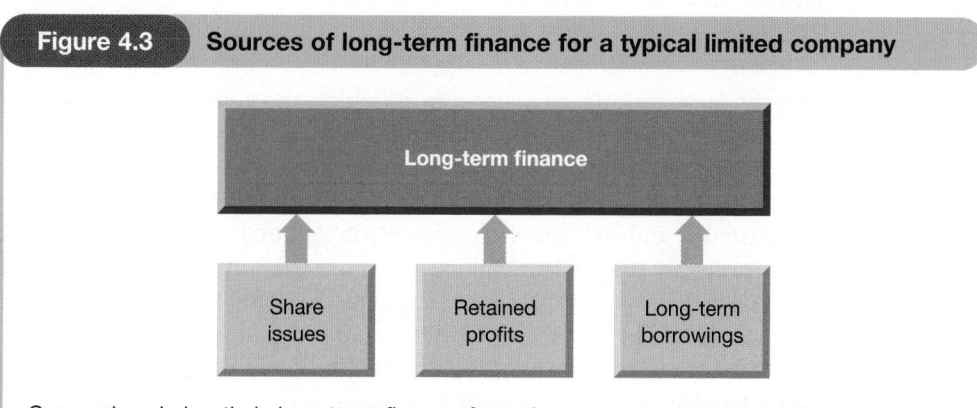

Figure 4.3   **Sources of long-term finance for a typical limited company**

Companies derive their long-term finance from three sources: new share issues, retained earnings and long-term borrowings. For a typical company, the sum of the first two (jointly known as 'equity finance') exceeds the third. Retained earnings usually exceeds either of the other two in terms of the amount of finance raised in most years.

It is important to the prosperity and stability of a company that it strikes a suitable balance between finance provided by the shareholders (equity) and from borrowing. This topic will be explored in Chapter 7. Equity and loan notes are, of course, not the only forms of finance available to a company. In Chapter 15, we consider other sources of finance available to businesses.

Real World 4.11 shows the long-term borrowings of Rolls-Royce plc, the engine-building business, at 31 December 2008.

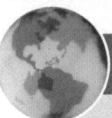

Real World 4.11

Borrowing at Rolls-Royce

The following extract from the annual financial statements of Rolls-Royce plc sets out the sources of the company's long-term borrowing as at 31 December 2008.

	£m
Unsecured	
Bank loans	5
$7^3/_8$% Notes 2016	200
5.84% Notes 2010	136
6.38% Notes 2013	178
6.55% Notes 2015	67
$4^1/_2$% Notes 2011	738
Secured	
Obligations under finance leases payable	
after five years	1
	1,325
Repayable	
Between one and two years – by instalments	2
– otherwise	136
Between two and five years – by instalments	1
– otherwise	916
After five years – by instalments	3
– otherwise	267
	1,325

Source: Rolls-Royce plc Annual Report and Accounts 2008, note 14.

Note the large number of sources from which the company borrows. This is typical of most large companies and probably reflects a desire to exploit all available means of raising finance, each of which may have some advantages and disadvantages. 'Secured' in this context means that the lender would have the right, should Rolls-Royce fail to meet its interest and/or capital repayment obligations, to seize a specified asset of the business (probably some land) and use it to raise the sums involved. Normally, a lender would accept a lower rate of interest where the loan is secured as there is less risk involved. It should be said that whether a loan to a company like Rolls-Royce is secured or unsecured is usually pretty academic. It is unlikely that such a large and profitable company would fail to meet its obligations.

'Finance leases' are, in effect, arrangements where Rolls-Royce needs the use of a non-current asset (such as an item of machinery) and, instead of buying the asset itself, it arranges for a financier to buy the asset. The financier then leases it to the business, probably for the entire economic life of the asset. Though legally it is the financier who owns the asset, from an accounting point of view the essence of the arrangement is that, in effect, Rolls-Royce has borrowed cash from the financier to buy the asset. Thus, the asset appears among the business's non-current assets and the financial obligation to the financier is shown here as long-term borrowing. This is a good example of how accounting tries to report the economic *substance* of a transaction, rather than its strict legal *form*. Finance leasing is a fairly popular means of raising long-term funds.

Chapter 15 considers in some detail the factors that a business must consider when deciding how to finance its operations.

Withdrawing equity

Companies, as we have seen, are legally obliged to distinguish, on the statement of financial position, between that part of the shareholders' equity that may be withdrawn and that part which may not. The withdrawable part consists of profits arising from trading and from the disposal of non-current assets. It is represented in the statement of financial position by *revenue reserves*.

It is important to appreciate that the total of revenue reserves appearing in the statement of financial position is rarely the total of all trading profits and profits on disposals of non-current assets generated by the company. This total will normally have been reduced by at least one of the following three factors:

- corporation tax paid on those profits
- any dividends paid
- any losses from trading and the disposal of non-current assets.

The non-withdrawable part consists of share capital plus profits arising from shareholders buying shares in the company and from upward revaluations of assets still held. It is represented in the statement of financial position by *share capital* and *capital reserves*.

The law does not specify how large the non-withdrawable part of a particular company's shareholders' equity should be. However, when seeking to impress prospective lenders and credit suppliers, the larger this part, the better. Those considering doing business with the company must be able to see from the company's statement of financial position how large it is.

Activity 4.9

Why are limited companies required to distinguish different parts of their shareholders' claim whereas sole proprietorship and partnership businesses are not?

The reason stems from the limited liability that company shareholders enjoy but which owners of unincorporated businesses do not. If a sole proprietor or partner withdraws all of the owners' claim, or even an amount in excess of this, the position of the lenders and credit suppliers of the business is not weakened since they can legally enforce their claims against the sole proprietor or partner as an individual. With a limited company, the business and the owners are legally separated and such a right to enforce claims against individuals does not exist. To protect the company's lenders and credit suppliers, however, the law insists that the shareholders cannot normally withdraw a specific part of their claim.

Let us now look at an example that illustrates how this protection of creditors works.

Example 4.4

The summary statement of financial position of a company at a particular date is as follows:

Statement of financial position

	£
Total assets	43,000
Equity	
Share capital	
20,000 shares of £1 each	20,000
Reserves (revenue)	23,000
Total equity	43,000

A bank has been asked to make a £25,000 long-term loan to the company. If the loan were to be made, the statement of financial position immediately following would appear as follows:

Statement of financial position (after the loan)

	£
Total assets (£43,000 + £25,000)	68,000
Equity	
Share capital	
20,000 shares of £1 each	20,000
Reserves (revenue)	23,000
	43,000
Non-current liability	
Borrowings – loan	25,000
Total equity and liabilities	68,000

As things stand, there are assets with a total carrying amount of £68,000 to meet the bank's claim of £25,000. It would be possible and perfectly legal, however, for the company to pay a dividend (withdraw part of the shareholders' claim) of £23,000. The statement of financial position would then appear as follows:

Statement of financial position

	£
Total assets (£68,000 – £23,000)	45,000
Equity	
Share capital	
20,000 shares of £1 each	20,000
Reserves [revenue (£23,000 – £23,000)]	–
	20,000
Non-current liabilities	
Borrowings – bank loan	25,000
Total equity and liabilities	45,000

This leaves the bank in a very much weaker position, in that there are now total assets with a carrying amount of £45,000 to meet a claim of £25,000. Note that the difference between the amount of the borrowings (bank loan) and the total assets equals the equity (share capital and reserves) total. Thus, the equity represents a margin of safety for lenders and suppliers. The larger the amount of the owners' claim withdrawable by the shareholders, the smaller is the potential margin of safety for lenders and suppliers.

As we have already seen, the law says nothing about how large the margin of safety must be. It is up to each company to decide what is appropriate.

As a practical footnote to Example 4.4, it is worth pointing out that long-term lenders would normally seek to secure a loan against an asset of the company, such as land.

Activity (4.10)

Would you expect a company to pay all of its revenue reserves as a dividend? What factors might be involved with a dividend decision?

It would be rare for a company to pay all of its revenue reserves as a dividend: the fact that it is legally possible does not necessarily make it a good idea. Most companies see ploughed-back profits as a major – usually *the* major – source of new finance. The factors that influence the dividend decision are likely to include:

- the availability of cash to pay a dividend; it would not be illegal to borrow to pay a dividend, but it would be unusual and, possibly, imprudent;
- the needs of the business for finance for new investment;
- the expectations of shareholders concerning the amount of dividends to be paid.

You may have thought of others.

If we look back at Real World 4.9 (page 140), we can see that at 27 June 2009, Thorntons plc could legally have paid a dividend totalling £8,151 million. Of course, the company did not do this, presumably because the funds concerned were tied up in property, plant and equipment and other assets, not lying around in the form of unused cash.

As we have seen, the law states that shareholders cannot, under normal circumstances, withdraw that part of their claim that is represented by shares and capital reserves. This means that potential lenders and credit suppliers know the maximum amount of the shareholders' equity that can be withdrawn. Figure 4.4 shows the important division between that part of the shareholders' equity that can be withdrawn as a dividend and that part which cannot.

Figure 4.4	Availability for dividends of various parts of the shareholders' claim

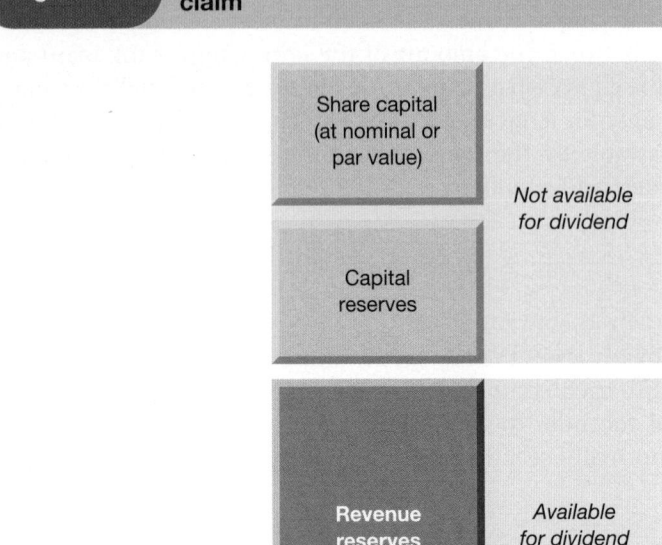

Total equity finance of limited companies consists of share capital, capital reserves and revenue reserves. Only the revenue reserves (which arise from realised profits and gains) can be used to fund a dividend. In other words, the maximum legal dividend is the amount of the revenue reserves.

Activity 4.11

Can you remember the circumstances where the non-withdrawable part of a company's capital could be reduced, without contravening the law? This was mentioned earlier in the chapter.

It can be reduced as a result of the company sustaining trading losses, or losses on disposal of non-current assets, which exceed the withdrawable amount of shareholders' equity. It cannot be reduced by shareholders making withdrawals.

Though payment of a cash dividend is the standard way for shareholders to withdraw equity from a company, it is not the only way. Provided that certain conditions are met, it is perfectly legal for a company to redeem some of its shares or to buy some of its shares from particular shareholders and cancel them. These conditions are generally not difficult to meet for profitable companies.

The main financial statements

As we might expect, the financial statements of a limited company are, in essence, the same as those of a sole proprietor or partnership. There are, however, some differences of detail, and we shall now consider these. Example 4.5 sets out the income statement and statement of financial position of a limited company.

Example 4.5

Da Silva plc

Income statement for the year ended 31 December 2009

	£m
Revenue	840
Cost of sales	(520)
Gross profit	320
Wages and salaries	(98)
Heat and light	(18)
Rent and rates	(24)
Motor vehicle expenses	(20)
Insurance	(4)
Printing and stationery	(12)
Depreciation	(45)
Audit fee	(4)
Operating profit	95
Interest payable	(10)
Profit before taxation	85
Taxation	(24)
Profit for the year	61

Statement of financial position as at 31 December 2009

	£m
ASSETS	
Non-current assets	
Property, plant and equipment	203
Intangible assets	100
	303
Current assets	
Inventories	65
Trade receivables	112
Cash	36
	213
Total assets	516
EQUITY AND LIABILITIES	
Equity	
Ordinary shares of £0.50 each	200
Share premium account	30
Other reserves	50
Retained earnings	25
	305
Non-current liabilities	
Borrowings	100
Current liabilities	
Trade payables	99
Taxation	12
	111
Total equity and liabilities	516

Let us now go through these statements and pick up those aspects that are unique to limited companies.

The income statement

There are several features in the income statement that need consideration.

Profit

We can see that, following the calculation of operating profit, two further measures of profit are shown.

→ ● The first of these is the **profit before taxation**. Interest charges are deducted from the operating profit to derive this figure. In the case of a sole proprietor or partnership business, the income statement would end here.

→ ● The second measure of profit is the **profit for the year**. As the company is a separate legal entity, it is liable to pay tax (known as corporation tax) on the profits generated. (This contrasts with the sole proprietor business where it is the owner rather than the business that is liable for the tax on profits, as we saw earlier in the chapter.) This measure of profit represents the amount that is available for the shareholders.

Audit fee

Companies beyond a certain size are required to have their financial statements audited by an independent firm of accountants, for which a fee is charged. As we shall see in Chapter 5, the purpose of the audit is to lend credibility to the financial statements. Although it is also open to sole proprietors and partnerships to have their financial statements audited, relatively few do, so this is an expense that is most often seen in the income statement of a company.

The statement of financial position

The main points for consideration in the statement of financial position are as follows.

Taxation

The amount that appears as part of the current liabilities represents 50 per cent of the tax on the profit for the year 2008. It is, therefore, 50 per cent (£12 million) of the charge that appears in the income statement (£24 million); the other 50 per cent (£12 million) will already have been paid. The unpaid 50 per cent will be paid shortly after the statement of financial position date. These payment dates are set down by law.

Other reserves

This will include any reserves that are not separately identified on the face of the statement of financial position. It may include a *general reserve*, which normally consists of trading profits that have been transferred to this separate reserve for reinvestment ('ploughing back') into the operations of the company. It is not at all necessary to set up a separate reserve for this purpose. The trading profits could remain unallocated and still swell the retained earnings of the company. It is not entirely clear why directors decide to make transfers to general reserves, since the profits concerned remain part of the revenue reserves, and are, therefore, still available for dividend. The most plausible explanation seems to be that directors feel that placing profits in a separate reserve indicates an intention to invest the funds, represented by the reserve, permanently in the company and, therefore, not to use them to pay a dividend. Of course, the retained earnings appearing on the statement of financial position are also a reserve, but that fact is not indicated in its title.

Dividends

We have already seen that dividends represent drawings by the shareholders of the company. Dividends are paid out of the revenue reserves and should be deducted from these reserves (usually retained earnings) when preparing the statement of financial position. Shareholders are often paid an annual dividend, perhaps in two parts. An 'interim' dividend may be paid part way through the year and a 'final' dividend shortly after the year end.

Dividends declared by the directors during the year but still unpaid at the year end *may* appear as a liability in the statement of financial position. To be recognised as a liability, however, they must be properly authorised before the year-end date. This normally means that the shareholders must approve the dividend.

Large companies tend to have a clear and consistent policy towards the payment of dividends. Any change in the policy provokes considerable interest and is usually interpreted by shareholders as a signal of the directors' views concerning the future. For example, an increase in dividends may be taken as a signal from the directors that future prospects are bright: a higher dividend being seen as tangible evidence of their confidence.

Real World 4.12 provides an example of one well-known business that paid a dividend after more than 20 years of trading.

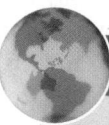

Real World 4.12

At last!

Eurotunnel is to pay its first-ever dividend to its long-suffering shareholders, it revealed today. The Channel tunnel operator announced the €0.04-a-share payout (3.56p) as it reported net profits for the year of €40 million (£35.6 million), compared with a loss for 2007 of €12 million.

Eurotunnel floated on the London stock market in November 1987 when it it raised £770 million from investors. This included some 574,000 small shareholders – who, if they invested more than £500 worth of shares at 350p each, were offered perks including free travel and discounts on hotels and car hire provided they held their shares beyond 1993 – when the tunnel was expected to open.

However, as the project over-ran more cash was required on top of the company's credit facilities, leading to a £532 million rights issue in December 1990.

Commenting on today's results, Jacques Gounon, the chairman and chief executive of Eurotunnel, said:

Despite the incident in September [following a fire in one of the tunnels], the year 2008 clearly marks the end of financial uncertainty for Eurotunnel. Through its efficiency and the control of its costs, the group has recorded a solid profit which, for the first time in our history, allows us to pay a dividend to our loyal shareholders.

Source: 'Eurotunnel pays first dividend since 1987 float', Ian King, www.timesonline.co.uk, 4 March 2009. © The Times 4 March 2009/www.nisyndication.com.

Accounting for groups of companies

Most large businesses, including nearly all of the well-known ones, operate not as a single company but as a group of companies. In these circumstances, one company (the **parent** or **holding company**) is able to control various subsidiary companies, normally by owning more than 50 per cent of their shares. Many larger businesses have numerous subsidiary companies, with each subsidiary operating some aspect of the group's activities. The reasons why many businesses operate in the form of groups include:

- a desire for each part of the business to have its own limited liability, so that financial problems in one part of a business cannot have an adverse effect on other parts;
- an attempt to make each part of the business have some sense of independence and autonomy and, perhaps, to create or perpetuate a market image of a smaller independent business.

Each company within a group will prepare its own independent annual financial statements. The law also requires, however, that the parent company prepares **consolidated** or **group financial statements**. These group financial statements amalgamate the financial statements of all of the group members. Thus, the group income statement includes the total revenue figure for all group companies, the statement of financial position includes the property, plant and equipment for all group companies and so on. This means that the group financial statements will look like the financial statements of the parent company had it owned and operated all of the assets of the business directly instead of through subsidiary companies.

Given the above, it may not be possible to detect whether the business operates through a single company or through a large number of subsidiaries simply by looking at a set of group financial statements. Only by referring to the heading at the top of each statement, which should mention the word 'consolidated' or 'group', might we find this out. In many cases, however, one or two items will be reported that are peculiar to group financial statements. These items are:

- *Goodwill arising on consolidation.* This occurs when a parent acquires a subsidiary from previous owners and pays more for the subsidiary than the subsidiary's individual assets (net of liabilities) appear to be worth. This excess may represent such things as the value of a good reputation that the new subsidiary already has in the market, or the value of its having a loyal and skilled workforce. Goodwill arising on consolidation will appear as an intangible non-current asset on the group statement of financial position.
- *Non-controlling interests (NCI).* One of the principles followed when preparing group financial statements is that all of the revenue, expenses, assets, liabilities and cash flows of each subsidiary are reflected to their full extent in the group financial statements. This is true whether or not the parent owns all of the shares in each subsidiary, provided that the parent has control. Control normally means owning more than 50 per cent of the subsidiary's ordinary shares. Where not all of the shares are owned by the parent, the investment of those shareholders in the subsidiary, other than the parent company, appears as part of the shareholders' equity in the group statement of financial position. This shows that, although the net assets of the group are being financed mainly by the parent company's shareholders, 'outside' shareholders also finance a part. Similarly, the group income statement reflects the fact that not all of the profit of the group is attributable to the shareholders of the parent company; a part of it is attributable to the 'outside' shareholders. The interests,

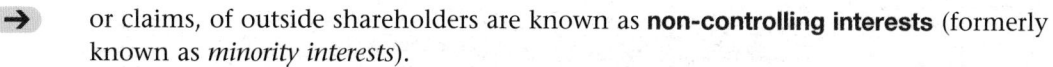

→ or claims, of outside shareholders are known as **non-controlling interests** (formerly known as *minority interests*).

Example 4.6 shows how the statement of financial position of Major plc and its subsidiary is drawn up. Note that the group statement of financial position closely resembles that of an individual company.

Major plc has just bought, from the previous shareholders, 45 million (out of 60 million) ordinary shares in Minor plc, paying £75 million for them. The remaining 15 million Minor plc shares are owned by other shareholders. These shareholders are now referred to by Major plc as the non-controlling interests. Minor plc is now a subsidiary of Major plc and, as is clear from Major plc's statement of financial position, its only subsidiary company.

→ The statements of financial position of the two companies immediately following the **takeover** (that is, the acquisition of control) of Minor plc by Major plc were as follows:

Statements of financial position

	Major plc £m	Minor plc £m
ASSETS		
Non-current assets		
Property, plant and equipment	63	67
Intangible – 45 million shares in Minor plc	75	
	138	67
Current assets		
Inventories	37	21
Trade receivables	22	12
Cash	16	2
	75	35
Total assets	213	102
EQUITY AND LIABILITIES		
Equity		
Ordinary shares of £1 each	100	60
Reserves	60	20
	160	80
Non-current liabilities		
Borrowings – Loan notes	35	13
Current liabilities		
Trade payables	18	9
Total equity and liabilities	213	102

As would be normal practice, the statement of financial position of the subsidiary (Minor plc) has been revised so that the values of the individual assets are based on *fair values*, rather than what Minor plc originally paid for them. Fair values are those that would be agreed as the selling price between a buyer and a seller, both of whom are knowledgable and willing. In this particuar context, they probably equate to the values that Major plc would have placed on the individual tangible assets when assessing Minor plc's value.

If a statement of financial position for the group were to be drawn up immediately following the takeover, it would be as follows:

Statements of financial position of Major plc and its subsidiary

	£m
ASSETS	
Non-current assets	
Property, plant and equipment (63 + 67)	130
Intangible – Goodwill [75 – ($^{45}/_{60}$ × 80)]	15
	145
Current assets	
Inventories (37 + 21)	58
Trade receivables (22 + 12)	34
Cash (16 + 2)	18
	110
Total assets	255
EQUITY AND LIABILITIES	
Equity	
Ordinary shares of £1 each	100
Reserves	60
Equity attributable to equity holders of the parent	160
Non-controlling interests ($^{15}/_{60}$ × 80)	20
Total equity	180
Non-current liabilities	
Borrowings – Loan notes (35 + 13)	48
Current liabilities	
Trade payables (18 + 9)	27
Total equity and liabilities	255

Note that all of the items, except two, in the group statement of financial position are simply the two figures for the item concerned added together. This is despite the fact that Major plc owns only three-quarters of the shares of Minor plc. The logic of group financial statements is that if the parent owns enough shares to control its subsidiary, all of the subsidiary's assets and claims should be reflected on the group statement of financial position.

As we have seen, there are two exceptions to this approach: goodwill and non-controlling interests.

Goodwill is simply the excess of what Major paid for the shares over their fair value, based on tangible assets. Major plc bought 45 million of 60 million shares, paying £75 million. According to Minor plc's statement of financial position, there were net assets (non-current and current assets, less current and non-current liabilities) of £80 million. So Major plc paid £75 million for £60 million (that is, $^{45}/_{60}$ × £80 million) of net assets – an excess of £15 million usually referred to as 'goodwill arising on consolidation'. This asset is seen as being the value of a loyal workforce, a regular and profitable customer base and so on, that a new business setting up would not have. The relevant International Financial Reporting Standard (IFRS 3) demands that goodwill be reviewed at least annually: if its value has been impaired, it must be written down to the lower value.

The non-controlling interests (NCI) take account of the fact that, although Major plc may control all of the assets and liabilities of Minor plc, it only provides the equity finance for three-quarters of them. The other quarter, £20 million (that is, $^{15}/_{60}$ × £80 million), is still provided by shareholders in Minor plc, other than Major plc. (Note that IFRS 3 allows an alternative method of calculating goodwill on consolidation and NCI for reporting purpose, but this is beyond the scope of this chapter.)

Example 4.7 shows the income statement of Major plc and its subsidiary (Minor plc) for the first year following the takeover. As with the statement of financial position, the various revenue and expense figures are simply the individual figures for each company added together. The non-controlling interests figure (£2 million) represents $^{15}/_{60} \times$ the after-tax profit of Minor plc, which is assumed to be £8 million.

Example 4.7

Income statement for the first year

	£m
Revenue	123
Cost of sales	(56)
Gross profit	67
Administration expenses	(28)
Distribution expenses	(9)
Profit before tax	30
Taxation	(12)
Profit for the year	18
Attributable to:	
Equity holders of the parent	16
Non-controlling interests	2
	18

Self-assessment question 4.1

The summarised statement of financial position of Dev Ltd is as follows:

Statement of financial position as at 31 December 2009

	£
Net assets (various assets less liabilities)	235,000
Equity	
Share capital: 100,000 shares of £1 each	100,000
Share premium account	30,000
Revaluation reserve	37,000
Retained earnings	68,000
Total equity	235,000

Required:

(a) Without any other transactions occurring at the same time, the company made a one-for-five rights share issue at £2 per share payable in cash. This means that each shareholder was offered one share for every five already held. All shareholders took up their rights. Immediately afterwards, the company made a one-for-two bonus issue. Show the statement of financial position immediately following the bonus issue, assuming that the directors wanted to retain the maximum dividend payment potential for the future.

(b) Explain what external influence might cause the directors to choose not to retain the maximum dividend payment possibilities.

→

Self-assessment question 4.1 continued

(c) Show the statement of financial position immediately following the bonus issue, assuming that the directors wanted to retain the *minimum* dividend payment potential for the future.

(d) What is the maximum dividend that could be paid before and after the events described in (a) if the minimum dividend payment potential is achieved?

(e) Lee owns 100 shares in Dev Ltd before the events described in (a). Assuming that the net assets of the company have a value equal to their carrying amount on the statement of financial position, show how these events will affect Lee's wealth.

(f) Looking at the original statement of financial position of Dev Ltd, shown above, what four things do we know about the company's status and history that are not specifically stated on the statement of financial position?

The answer to this question can be found at the back of the book on pages 724–5.

Summary

The main points of this chapter may be summarised as follows.

Main features of a limited company

- It is an artificial person that has been created by law.
- It has a separate life to its owners and is granted a perpetual existence.
- It must take responsibility for its own debts and losses but its owners are granted limited liability.
- A public company can offer its shares for sale to the public; a private company cannot.
- It is governed by a board of directors, which is elected by the shareholders.
- Corporate governance is a major issue; various scandals have led to the emergence of the Combined Code.

Financing the limited company

- The share capital of a company can be of two main types: ordinary shares and preference shares.
- Holders of ordinary shares (equities) are the main risk-takers and are given voting rights; they form the backbone of the company.
- Holders of preference shares are given a right to a fixed dividend before ordinary shareholders receive a dividend.
- Reserves are profits and gains made by the company and form part of the ordinary shareholders' claim.
- Borrowings provide another major source of finance.

Share issues

- Bonus shares are issued to existing shareholders when part of the reserves of the company is converted into share capital. No funds are raised.
- Rights issues give existing shareholders the right to buy new shares in proportion to their existing holding.

- Public issues are made direct to the general investing public.

- Private placings are share issues to particular investors.

- The shares of public companies may be bought and sold on a recognised Stock Exchange.

Reserves

- Reserves are of two types: revenue reserves and capital reserves.

- Revenue reserves arise from trading profits and from realised profits on the sale of non-current assets.

- Capital reserves arise from the issue of shares above their nominal value or from the upward revaluation of non-current assets.

- Revenue reserves can be withdrawn as dividends by the shareholders whereas capital reserves normally cannot.

Financial statements of limited companies

- The financial statements of limited companies are based on the same principles as those of sole proprietorship and partnership businesses. However, there are some differences in detail.

- The income statement has three measures of profit displayed after the gross profit figure: operating profit, profit before taxation and profit for the year.

- The income statement also shows audit fees and tax on profits for the year.

- Any unpaid tax and unpaid, but authorised, dividends will appear in the statement of financial position as current liabilities.

- The share capital plus the reserves make up 'equity'.

Groups of companies

- Parent companies are required to produce group financial statements incorporating the results of all companies controlled by the parent.

- A group statement of financial position is prepared by adding like items of assets and liabilities based on 'fair values' together, as if all of the trading is undertaken through the parent company.

- A 'goodwill arising on consolidation' figure often emerges in the group statement of financial position.

- Where the parent does not own all of the shares of each subsidiary, a non-controlling interests (NCI) figure will appear in the statement of financial position, representing the outside shareholders' investment.

- A group income statement is drawn up following similar logic to that applied to the group statement of financial position.

- The group income statement will contain a non-controlling interests figure if not all subsidiaries are fully owned by the parent, which represents the outside shareholders' share of the group profit.

MyAccountingLab | *Now check your progress in your personal Study Plan*

Key terms

limited company   p. 122
shares   p. 122
limited liability   p. 125
public limited company   p. 125
private limited company   p. 127
corporation tax   p. 128
directors   p. 129
corporate governance   p. 129
Combined Code   p. 130
reserves   p. 135
nominal value   p. 135
par value   p. 135
revenue reserve   p. 136
dividend   p. 136
ordinary shares   p. 136
splitting   p. 137
consolidating   p. 137
preference shares   p. 137

capital reserves   p. 138
share premium account   p. 139
bonus shares   p. 140
bonus issue   p. 141
issued share capital   p. 142
allotted share capital   p. 142
fully paid shares   p. 142
called-up share capital   p. 142
paid-up share capital   p. 142
loan notes   p. 143
profit before taxation   p. 150
profit for the year   p. 150
parent/holding company   p. 152
consolidated/group financial
   statements   p. 152
non-controlling interests
   (NCI)   p. 153
takeover   p. 153

Reference

1 **Corporate Governance: Improving Competitiveness and Access to Capital in Global Markets**, Business Sector Advisory Group on Corporate Governance, OECD, 1998, p. 14.

Further reading

If you would like to explore the topics covered in this chapter in more depth, we recommend the following books:

A Guide Through International Financial Reporting Standards (IFRSs) 2008, IASC Foundation Education, July 2008, IFRS 3.

Corporate Financial Accounting and Reporting, *Sutton T.*, 2nd edn, Financial Times Prentice Hall, 2004, chapters 6 and 12.

Financial Accounting and Reporting, *Elliott B. and Elliott J.*, 13th edn, Financial Times Prentice Hall, 2010, chapters 10 and 21.

Insights into IFRS, *KPMG*, 5th edn, 2008/9, Thomson, 2008, Sections 2.6 and 2.6A.

Review questions

Answers to these questions can be found at the back of the book on pages 740–1.

4.1 How does the liability of a limited company differ from the liability of a real person, in respect of amounts owed to others?

4.2 Some people are about to form a company, as a vehicle through which to run a new business. What are the advantages to them of forming a private limited company rather than a public one?

4.3 What is a reserve? Distinguish between a revenue reserve and a capital reserve.

4.4 What is a preference share? Compare the main features of a preference share with those of

(a) an ordinary share, and
(b) loan notes.

Exercises

Exercises 4.6 to 4.8 are more advanced than Exercises 4.1 to 4.5. Those with **coloured numbers** have answers at the back of the book, starting on page 758.

If you wish to try more exercises, visit the students' side of the Companion Website and MyAccountingLab.

4.1 Comment on the following quote:

> Limited companies can set a limit on the amount of debts that they will meet. They tend to have reserves of cash, as well as share capital and they can use these reserves to pay dividends to the shareholders. Many companies have preference as well as ordinary shares. The preference shares give a guaranteed dividend. The shares of many companies can be bought and sold on the Stock Exchange, and shareholders selling their shares can represent a useful source of new finance to the company.

4.2 Comment on the following quotes:

(a) 'Bonus shares increase the shareholders' wealth because, after the issue, they have more shares, but each one of the same nominal value as they had before.'
(b) 'By law, once shares have been issued at a particular nominal value, they must always be issued at that value in any future share issues.'
(c) 'By law, companies can pay as much as they like by way of dividends on their shares, provided that they have sufficient cash to do so.'
(d) 'Companies do not have to pay tax on their profits because the shareholders have to pay tax on their dividends.'

4.3 Briefly explain each of the following expressions that you have seen in the financial statements of a limited company:

(a) dividend
(b) audit fee
(c) share premium account.

4.4 Iqbal Ltd started trading on 1 January 2005. During the first five years of trading, the following occurred:

Year ended 31 December	Trading profit/ (loss) £	Profit/(loss) on sale of non-current assets £	Upward revaluation of non-current assets £
2005	(15,000)	–	–
2006	8,000	–	10,000
2007	15,000	5,000	–
2008	20,000	(6,000)	–
2009	22,000	–	–

Required:
Assume that the company paid the maximum legal dividend each year. Under normal circumstances, how much would each year's dividend be?

4.5 Hudson plc's outline statement of financial position as at a particular date was as follows:

	£m
Net assets (assets less liabilities)	72
Equity	
£1 ordinary shares	40
General reserve	32
Total equity	72

The directors made a one-for-four bonus issue, immediately followed by a one-for-four rights issue at a price of £1.80 per share.

Required:
Show the statement of financial position of Hudson plc immediately following the two share issues.

4.6 Presented below is a draft set of simplified financial statements for Pear Limited for the year ended 30 September 2009.

Income statement for the year ended 30 September 2009

	£000
Revenue	1,456
Cost of sales	(768)
Gross profit	688
Salaries	(220)
Depreciation	(249)
Other operating costs	(131)
Operating profit	88
Interest payable	(15)
Profit before taxation	73
Taxation at 30%	(22)
Profit for the year	51

Statement of financial position as at 30 September 2009

	£000
ASSETS	
Non-current assets	
Property, plant and equipment	
Cost	1,570
Depreciation	(690)
	880
Current assets	
Inventories	207
Trade receivables	182
Cash at bank	21
	410
Total assets	1,290
EQUITY AND LIABILITIES	
Equity	
Share capital	300
Share premium account	300
Retained earnings at beginning of year	104
Profit for year	51
	755
Non-current liabilities	
Borrowings (10% loan repayable 2012)	300
Current liabilities	
Trade payables	88
Other payables	20
Taxation	22
Borrowings (bank overdraft)	105
	235
Total equity and liabilities	1,290

The following information is available:

1 Depreciation has not been charged on office equipment with a carrying amount of £100,000. This class of assets is depreciated at 12 per cent a year using the reducing-balance method.

2 A new machine was purchased, on credit, for £30,000 and delivered on 29 September 2009 but has not been included in the financial statements. (Ignore depreciation.)

3 A sales invoice to the value of £18,000 for September 2009 has been omitted from the financial statements. (The cost of sales figure is stated correctly.)

4 A dividend of £25,000 had been approved by the shareholders before 30 September 2009, but was unpaid at that date. This is not reflected in the financial statements.

5 The interest payable on the loan for the second half-year was not paid until 1 October 2009 and has not been included in the financial statements.

6 An allowance for receivables is to be made at the level of 2 per cent of receivables.

7 An invoice for electricity to the value of £2,000 for the quarter ended 30 September 2009 arrived on 4 October and has not been included in the financial statements.

8 The charge for taxation will have to be amended to take account of the above information. Make the simplifying assumption that tax is payable shortly after the end of the year, at the rate of 30 per cent of the profit before tax.

Required:

Prepare a revised set of financial statements for the year ended 30 September 2009 incorporating the additional information in 1 to 8 above. (Work to the nearest £1,000.)

4.7 Presented below is a draft set of financial statements for Chips Limited.

Chips Limited
Income statement for the year ended 30 June 2009

	£000
Revenue	1,850
Cost of sales	(1,040)
Gross profit	810
Depreciation	(220)
Other operating costs	(375)
Operating profit	215
Interest payable	(35)
Profit before taxation	180
Taxation	(60)
Profit for the year	120

Statement of financial position as at 30 June 2009

	Cost £000	Depreciation £000	£000
ASSETS			
Non-current assets			
Property, plant and equipment			
Buildings	800	(112)	688
Plant and equipment	650	(367)	283
Motor vehicles	102	(53)	49
	1,552	(532)	1,020
Current assets			
Inventories			950
Trade receivables			420
Cash at bank			16
			1,386
Total assets			2,406
EQUITY AND LIABILITIES			
Equity			
Ordinary shares of £1, fully paid			800
Reserves at beginning of the year			248
Profit for the year			120
			1,168
Non-current liabilities			
Borrowings (secured 10% loan notes)			700
Current liabilities			
Trade payables			361
Other payables			117
Taxation			60
			538
Total equity and liabilities			2,406

The following additional information is available:

1 Purchase invoices for goods received on 29 June 2009 amounting to £23,000 have not been included. This means that the cost of sales figure in the income statement has been understated.
2 A motor vehicle costing £8,000 with depreciation amounting to £5,000 was sold on 30 June 2009 for £2,000, paid by cheque. This transaction has not been included in the company's records.

3 No depreciation on motor vehicles has been charged. The annual rate is 20 per cent of cost at the year end.

4 A sale on credit for £16,000 made on 1 July 2009 has been included in the financial statements in error. The cost of sales figure is correct in respect of this item.

5 A half-yearly payment of interest on the secured loan due on 30 June 2009 has not been paid.

6 The tax charge should be 30 per cent of the reported profit before taxation. Assume that it is payable, in full, shortly after the year end.

Required:

Prepare a revised set of financial statements incorporating the additional information in 1 to 6 above. (Work to the nearest £1,000.)

4.8 Rose Limited operates a small chain of retail shops that sell high quality teas and coffees. Approximately half of sales are on credit. Abbreviated and unaudited financial statements are given below.

Rose Limited
Income statement for the year ended 31 March 2009

	£000
Revenue	12,080
Cost of sales	(6,282)
Gross profit	5,798
Labour costs	(2,658)
Depreciation	(625)
Other operating costs	(1,003)
Operating profit	1,512
Interest payable	(66)
Profit before taxation	1,446
Taxation	(434)
Profit for the year	1,012

Statement of financial position as at 31 March 2009

	£000
ASSETS	
Non-current assets	2,728
Current assets	
Inventories	1,583
Trade receivables	996
Cash	26
	2,605
Total assets	5,333
EQUITY AND LIABILITIES	
Equity	
Share capital (50p shares, fully paid)	750
Share premium	250
Retained earnings	1,468
	2,468
Non-current liabilities	
Borrowings – Secured loan notes (2014)	300
Current liabilities	
Trade payables	1,118
Other payables	417
Tax	434
Borrowings – Overdraft	596
	2,565
Total equity and liabilities	5,333

Since the unaudited financial statements for Rose Limited were prepared, the following information has become available:

1 An additional £74,000 of depreciation should have been charged on fixtures and fittings.
2 Invoices for credit sales on 31 March 2009 amounting to £34,000 have not been included; cost of sales is not affected.
3 Trade receivables totalling £21,000 are recognised as having gone bad, but they have not yet been written off.
4 Inventories which had been purchased for £2,000 have been damaged and are unsaleable. This is not reflected in the financial statements.
5 Fixtures and fittings to the value of £16,000 were delivered just before 31 March 2009, but these assets were not included in the financial statements and the purchase invoice had not been processed.
6 Wages for Saturday-only staff, amounting to £1,000, have not been paid for the final Saturday of the year. This is not reflected in the financial statements.
7 Tax is payable at 30 per cent of profit after taxation. Assume that it is payable shortly after the year end.

Required:
Prepare revised financial statements for Rose Limited for the year ended 31 March 2009, incorporating the information in 1 to 7 above. (Work to the nearest £1,000.)

CHAPTER 5

Accounting for limited companies (2)

Introduction

This chapter continues our examination of the financial statements of limited companies. We begin by identifying the legal responsibilities of directors and then go on to discuss the main sources of accounting rules governing published financial statements. Although a detailed consideration of these accounting rules is beyond the scope of this book, the key rules that shape the form and content of the published financial statements are discussed. We also consider the efforts made to ensure that these rules are underpinned by a coherent framework of principles.

The increasing complexity of business and the added demands for information by financial report users have led to the publication of a number of additional financial reports. This chapter considers two of these, namely the segmental financial report and the business review. Both reports aim to provide users with a more complete picture of financial performance and position.

Despite the proliferation of accounting rules and the increasing supply of financial information to users of financial reports, concerns have been expressed over the quality of some published reports. This chapter ends by considering some well-publicised accounting scandals and the problem of creative accounting.

Learning outcomes

When you have completed this chapter, you should be able to:

- Describe the responsibilities of directors and auditors concerning the annual financial statements provided to shareholders and others.

- Discuss both the framework of regulation and the framework of principles that help to shape the form and content of annual financial statements.

- Prepare a statement of financial position, statement of comprehensive income and statement of changes in equity in accordance with International Financial Reporting Standards.

- Explain the purpose of two additional reports, segmental reports and the business review, and describe their main features.

- Discuss the threat posed by creative accounting and identify the areas that are vulnerable to creative accounting techniques.

 *Remember to create your own personalised Study Plan*

 ## The directors' duty to account

With most large companies, it is not possible for all shareholders to be involved in the management of the company, nor do most of them wish to be involved. Instead, they appoint directors to act on their behalf. This separation of ownership from day-to-day control creates a need for directors to be accountable for their stewardship (management) of the company's assets. To fulfil this need, the directors must prepare (or have prepared on their behalf) financial statements that provide a fair representation of the financial position and performance of the business. This means that they must select appropriate accounting policies, make reasonable accounting estimates and adhere to all relevant accounting rules when preparing the statements. To avoid misstatements on the financial statements, whether from fraud or error, the directors must also maintain appropriate internal control systems.

The financial statements produced by the directors are made available to the public by the company submitting a copy to the Companies Registry (Department of Trade and Industry), which allows anyone who wishes to do so to inspect them. In addition, listed companies are required to publish their financial statements on their website.

Activity 5.1

It can be argued that the publication of financial statements is vital to a well-functioning private sector. Why might this be the case?

There are at least two reasons:

- Unless shareholders receive regular information about the performance and position of a business they will have problems in appraising their investment. Under these circumstances, they would probably be reluctant to invest, which would adversely affect the functioning of a private enterprise economy.
- Suppliers of labour, goods, services and finance, particularly those supplying credit (loans) or goods and services on credit need information about the financial health of a business. They would be reluctant to engage in commercial relationships where a company does not provide information. The fact that a company has limited liability increases the risks involved in dealing with the company. An unwillingness to engage in commercial relationships with limited companies will, again, adversely affect the functioning of the private sector of the economy.

The need for accounting rules

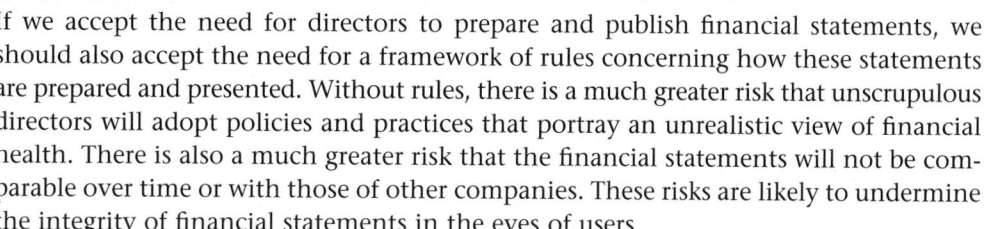

If we accept the need for directors to prepare and publish financial statements, we should also accept the need for a framework of rules concerning how these statements are prepared and presented. Without rules, there is a much greater risk that unscrupulous directors will adopt policies and practices that portray an unrealistic view of financial health. There is also a much greater risk that the financial statements will not be comparable over time or with those of other companies. These risks are likely to undermine the integrity of financial statements in the eyes of users.

Users must, however, be realistic about what can be achieved through regulation. Problems of manipulation and of concealment can still occur even within a highly regulated environment and some examples of both will be considered later in the chapter. The scale of these problems, however, should be reduced where there is a practical set of rules. Problems of comparability can also still occur, as accounting is not a precise science. Judgements and estimates must be made when preparing financial statements, and these may hinder comparisons. Furthermore, no two companies are identical and the accounting policies adopted may vary between companies for valid reasons.

Sources of accounting rules

In recent years there have been increasing trends towards the internationalisation of business and the integration of financial markets. These trends have helped to strengthen the case for the international harmonisation of accounting rules. With a common set of rules, users of financial statements should be better placed to compare the financial health of companies based in different countries. They should also relieve international companies of some of the burden of preparing financial statements as different financial statements would no longer have to be prepared to comply with the rules of different countries in which a particular company operates.

The International Accounting Standards Board (IASB) is an independent body that is at the forefront of the move towards harmonisation. The Board, which is based in the UK, is dedicated to developing a single set of high quality, global accounting rules that provide transparent and comparable information in financial statements. These rules, which are known as **International Accounting Standards** (IASs) or **International Financial Reporting Standards** (IFRSs), deal with key issues such as:

- what information should be disclosed;
- how information should be presented;
- how assets should be valued; and
- how profit should be measured.

We have already met several IASs and IFRSs in earlier chapters, including those that deal with:

- the valuation and impairment of assets (Chapter 2);
- depreciation and impairment of non-current assets (Chapter 3);
- the valuation of inventories (Chapter 3); and
- group financial statements (Chapter 4).

In recent years, several important developments have greatly increased the authority of the IASB. The first major boost came when the European Commission required nearly all companies listed on the stock exchanges of EU member states to adopt IFRSs for accounting periods commencing on or after 1 January 2005. As a result, nearly 7,000 companies in 25 different countries switched to IFRSs. This was followed in 2006 by the IASB and the US Financial Accounting Standards Board agreeing a roadmap for convergence between IFRSs and US accounting rules. In that same year, China closely aligned its accounting standards with IFRSs. Finally, in 2007, Brazil, Canada, Chile, India, Japan and Korea all announced their intention to adopt, or converge with, IFRSs.

There are now over 100 countries that either require or permit the use of IFRSs. Although non-listed UK companies are not currently required to adopt IFRSs, they have the option to do so. Some informed observers believe, however, that IFRSs will soon become a requirement for all UK companies.

The EU requirement to adopt IFRSs, mentioned earlier, overrides any laws in force in member states that could either hinder or restrict compliance with them. The ultimate aim is to achieve a single framework of accounting rules for companies from all member states. The EU recognises that this will be achieved only if individual governments do not add to the requirements imposed by the various IFRSs. Thus, it seems that accounting rules developed within individual EU member countries will eventually disappear. For the time being, however, the EU accepts that the governments of member states may need to impose additional disclosures for some corporate governance matters and regulatory requirements.

In the UK, company law requires disclosure relating to various corporate governance issues. There is, for example, a requirement to disclose details of directors' remuneration in the published financial statements, which goes beyond anything required by IFRSs. Furthermore, the Financial Services Authority (FSA), in its role as the UK (Stock Exchange) listing authority, imposes rules on Stock Exchange listed companies. These include the requirement to publish a condensed set of interim (half-year) financial statements in addition to the annual financial statements. (These statements are not required by the IASB, although there is a standard providing guidance on their form and content.)

Figure 5.1 sets out the main sources of accounting rules for Stock Exchange listed companies discussed above. While company law and the FSA still play an important role, in the longer term IFRSs seem set to become the sole source of company accounting rules.

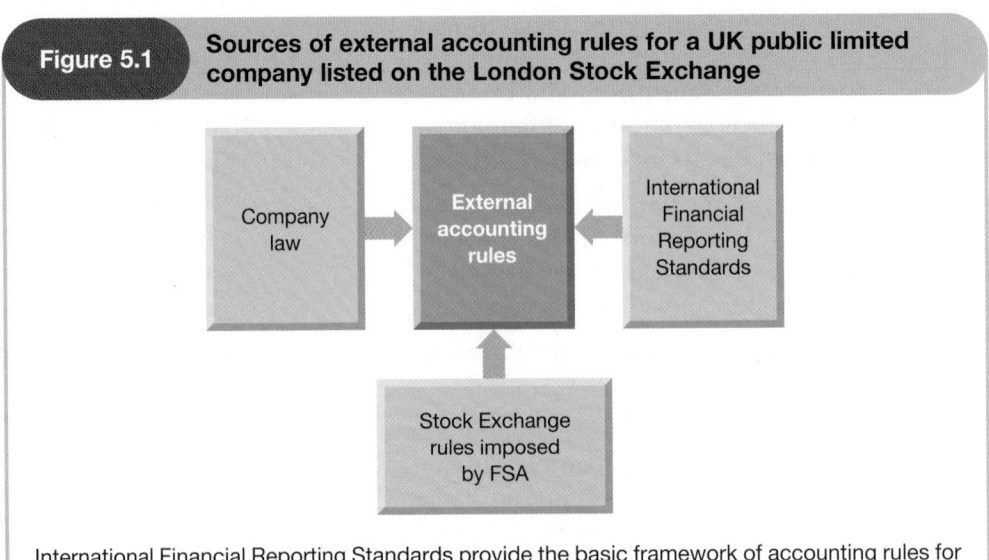

Figure 5.1 Sources of external accounting rules for a UK public limited company listed on the London Stock Exchange

International Financial Reporting Standards provide the basic framework of accounting rules for nearly all Stock Exchange listed companies. These rules are augmented by company law and by the Financial Services Authority (FSA) in its role as the UK listing authority.

Real World 5.1 is a list of IASB standards that are currently in force to give some idea of the range of topics that are covered.

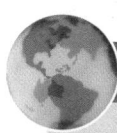

Real World 5.1

International standards

The following is a list of the International Accounting Standards (IASs) or International Financial Reporting Standards (IFRSs) in issue as at 1 July 2008. (The latter term is used for standards issued from 2003 onwards.) Several standards have been issued and subsequently withdrawn, which explains the gaps in the numerical sequence. In addition, several have been revised and reissued.

IAS 1	Presentation of Financial Statements
IAS 2	Inventories
IAS 7	Statement of Cash Flows
IAS 8	Accounting Policies, Changes in Accounting Estimates and Errors
IAS 10	Events after the Balance Sheet Date
IAS 11	Construction Contracts
IAS 12	Income Taxes
IAS 16	Property, Plant and Equipment
IAS 17	Leases
IAS 18	Revenue
IAS 19	Employee Benefits
IAS 20	Accounting for Government Grants and Disclosure of Government Assistance
IAS 21	The Effects of Changes in Foreign Exchange Rates
IAS 23	Borrowing Costs
IAS 24	Related Party Disclosures
IAS 26	Accounting and Reporting by Retirement Benefit Plans
IAS 27	Consolidated and Separate Financial Statements
IAS 28	Investments in Associates
IAS 29	Financial Reporting in Hyperinflationary Economies
IAS 31	Interests in Joint Ventures
IAS 32	Financial Instruments: Presentation
IAS 33	Earnings per Share
IAS 34	Interim Financial Reporting
IAS 36	Impairment of Assets
IAS 37	Provisions, Contingent Liabilities and Contingent Assets
IAS 38	Intangible Assets
IAS 39	Financial Instruments: Recognition and Measurement
IAS 40	Investment Property
IAS 41	Agriculture
IFRS 1	First-time Adoption of International Financial Reporting Standards
IFRS 2	Share-based Payments
IFRS 3	Business Combinations
IFRS 4	Insurance Contracts
IFRS 5	Non-current Assets Held for Sale and Discontinued Operations
IFRS 6	Exploration for and Evaluation of Mineral Resources
IFRS 7	Financial Instruments: Disclosures
IFRS 8	Operating Segments

Source: A Guide Through International Financial Reporting Standards (IFRSs), IASC Foundation Education, July 2008.

The IASB has an ambitious agenda and so significant changes to the above list are likely to occur in the future.

Presenting the financial statements

Now that we have gained an impression of the sources of rules affecting limited companies, let us turn our attention to the main rules to be followed in the presentation of financial statements. We shall focus on the IASB rules and, in particular, those contained in IAS 1 *Presentation of Financial Statements*. This standard is very important as it sets out the structure and content of financial statements and the principles to be followed in preparing these statements.

According to IAS 1, the financial statements consist of:

- a statement of financial position
- a statement of comprehensive income
- a statement of changes in equity
- a statement of cash flows
- notes on accounting policies and other explanatory notes.

The standard states that these financial statements should normally cover a one-year period and should be accompanied by comparative information for the previous year. Thus, at the end of each accounting year companies should normally produce two statements of financial position, two of each of the other statements and related notes. This is normally achieved by showing the equivalent figures for the previous year, in the current year's statements, in a separate column. See, for example, Example 5.1 (page 173).

Comparative narrative information should also be provided if needed for a better grasp of current period results – for example, as background to an ongoing legal dispute.

Fair representation

Before we consider the financial statements in detail, it is important to emphasise that the standard requires that they provide a fair representation of a company's financial position, financial performance and cash flows. There is a presumption that this will be achieved where they are drawn up in accordance with the various IASB standards that have been issued. It is only in very rare circumstances that compliance with a standard would not result in a fair representation of the financial health of a company. Where the financial statements have been prepared in accordance with IASB standards, it should be clearly stated in the notes.

Activity 5.2

IAS 1 does not say that the requirement is for the financial statements to show a 'correct' or an 'accurate' representation of financial health. Why, in your opinion, does it not use those words? (*Hint:* Think of depreciation of non-current assets.)

Accounting can never really be said to be 'correct' or 'accurate' as these words imply that there is a precise value that an asset, claim, revenue or expense could have. This is simply not true in many, if not most, cases.

> Depreciation provides a good example. The annual depreciation expense is based on judgements about the future concerning the expected useful life and residual value of an asset. If all relevant factors are taken into account and reasonable judgements are applied, it may be possible to achieve a fair representation of the amount of the cost or fair value of the asset that is consumed for a particular period. However, a precise figure for depreciation for a period cannot be achieved.

Let us now consider each of the financial statements in turn.

Statement of financial position

IAS 1 does not prescribe the format (or layout) for this financial statement but does set out the *minimum* information that should be presented on the face of the statement of financial position. This includes the following:

- property, plant and equipment
- investment property
- intangible assets
- financial assets (such as shares and loan notes of other companies held)
- inventories
- trade and other receivables
- cash and cash equivalents
- trade and other payables
- provisions
- financial liabilities (excluding payables and provisions shown above)
- tax liabilities
- issued share capital and reserves (equity).

Additional information should be also shown where it is relevant to an understanding of the financial position of the business.

The standard requires that a distinction is normally made, on the statement of financial position, between current assets and non-current assets and between current liabilities and non-current liabilities. However, for certain types of business, such as financial institutions, the standard accepts that it may be more appropriate to order items according to their liquidity.

Some of the items shown above may have to be sub-classified to comply with particular standards or because of their size or nature. Thus, sub-classifications are required for assets such as property, plant and equipment, receivables and inventories as well as for claims such as provisions and reserves. Certain details relating to share capital, such as the number of issued shares and their nominal value, must also be shown. To avoid cluttering up the statement of financial position, however, this additional information can be shown in the notes. In practice, most companies use notes for this purpose.

Statement of comprehensive income

This statement extends the conventional income statement to include certain other gains and losses that affect shareholders'equity. It may be presented either in the form of a single statement or as two separate statements, comprising an income statement and a **statement of comprehensive income**. This choice of presentation, however, seems to be a transitional arrangement as the IASB's clear preference is for a single statement.

Again the format of the statement of comprehensive income is not prescribed, but IAS 1 sets out the *minimum* information to be presented on the face of the statement. These items include:

● revenue
● finance costs
● profits or losses arising from discontinued operations
● tax expense
● profit or loss
● each component of other comprehensive income classified by its nature
● any share of the comprehensive income of associates or joint ventures
● total comprehensive income.

The standard makes it clear that further items should be shown on the face of the income statement where they are relevant to an understanding of performance. If, for example, a business is badly affected by flooding, and inventories are destroyed as a result, the cost of the flood damage should be shown.

As a further aid to understanding, all material expenses should be separately disclosed. However, they need not be shown on the face of the income statement: they can appear in the notes to the financial statements. The kind of material items that may require separate disclosure include:

● write-down of inventories to net realisable value
● write-down of property, plant and equipment
● disposals of investments
● restructuring costs
● discontinued operations
● litigation settlements.

This is not an exhaustive list and, in practice, other material expenses may require separate disclosure.

The standard suggests two possible ways in which expenses can be presented on the face of the income statement. Expenses can be presented either according to their nature, such as depreciation, employee expenses and so on, or according to business functions, such as administrative activities and distribution. The choice between the two will depend on which the directors believe will provide the more relevant and reliable information.

To understand what other information must be presented in this statement, apart from that already contained in a conventional income statement, we should remember that the conventional income statement shows all *realised* gains and losses for the period. However, any gains, and some losses, that remain *unrealised* (because the asset is still held) will not pass through the income statement, but will go, instead, directly to a reserve. We saw, in an earlier chapter, an example of an unrealised gain which does not pass through the conventional income statement.

Activity 5.3

Can you think of this example?

Where a business revalues its land and buildings, the gain arising is not shown in the conventional income statement. It is transferred to a revaluation reserve, which forms part of the equity. (We met this example in Activity 2.14 on page 66.) Land and buildings are not the only assets to which this rule relates, but these types of asset are, in practice, the most common examples of unrealised gains.

An example of an unrealised gain, or loss, that has not been mentioned so far, arises from exchange differences when the results of foreign operations are translated into UK currency. Any gain, or loss, bypasses the income statement and is taken directly to a currency translation reserve. A weakness of conventional accounting is that there is no robust principle that we can apply to determine precisely what should, and what should not, be included in the income statement. Nevertheless, the two examples mentioned reflect practice that is ingrained in conventional accounting.

The statement of comprehensive income includes all income and expenses for a period and so will take into account the unrealised gains or losses just described. It extends the conventional income statement by including these gains or losses immediately below the measure of profit for the year. An illustration of this statement is shown in Example 5.1. In this example, expenses are presented according to business function and comparative figures for the previous year are shown alongside the figures for the current year.

Example 5.1

Malik plc
Statement of comprehensive income for the year ended 31 December 2009

	2009 £m	2008 £m
Revenue	100.6	97.2
Cost of sales	(60.4)	(59.1)
Gross profit	40.2	38.1
Other income	4.0	3.5
Distribution expenses	(18.2)	(16.5)
Administration expenses	(10.3)	(11.2)
Other expenses	(2.1)	(2.4)
Operating profit	13.6	11.5
Finance charges	(2.0)	(1.8)
Profit before tax	11.6	9.7
Tax	(2.9)	(2.4)
Profit for the year	8.7	7.3
Other comprehensive income		
Revaluation of property, plant and equipment	20.3	6.6
Foreign currency translation differences for foreign operations	12.5	4.0
Tax on other comprehensive income	(6.0)	(2.6)
Other comprehensive income for the year, net of tax	26.8	8.0
Total comprehensive income for the year	35.5	15.3

This example adopts a single-statement approach to presenting comprehensive income. The alternative two-statement approach simply divides the information shown above into two separate parts. The income statement, which is the first statement, begins with the revenue for the year and ends with the profit for the year. The statement of comprehensive income, which is the second statement, begins with the profit for the year and ends with the total comprehensive income for the year.

Statement of changes in equity

→ The **statement of changes in equity** aims to help users to understand the changes in share capital and reserves that took place during the period. It reconciles the figures for these items at the beginning of the period with those at the end of the period. This is achieved by showing the effect on the share capital and reserves of total comprehensive income as well as the effect of share issues and purchases during the period. The effect of dividends during the period may also be shown in this statement, although dividends can be shown in the notes instead.

To see how a statement of changes in equity may be prepared, let us consider Example 5.2.

Example 5.2

At 1 January 2009 Miro plc had the following equity:

Miro plc

	£m
Share capital (£1 ordinary shares)	100
Revaluation reserve	20
Translation reserve	40
Retained earnings	150
Total equity	**310**

During 2009, the company made a profit for the year from normal business operations of £42 million and reported an upward revaluation of property, plant and equipment of £120 million (net of any corporation tax that would be payable were the unrealised gains to be realised). A loss on exchange differences on translating the results of foreign operations of £10 million was also reported. To strengthen its financial position, the company issued 50 million ordinary shares during the year at a premium of £0.40. Dividends for the year were £27 million.

The above information for 2009 can be set out in a statement of changes in equity as follows:

Statement of changes in equity for the year ended 31 December 2009

	Share capital £m	Share premium £m	Revaluation reserve £m	Translation reserve £m	Retained earnings £m	Total £m
Balance as at 1 January 2009	100	–	20	40	150	310
Changes in equity for 2009						
Issue of ordinary shares (Note 1)	50	20	–	–	–	70
Dividends (Note 2)	–	–	–	–	(27)	(27)
Total comprehensive income for the year (Note 3)	–	–	120	(10)	42	152
Balance at 31 December 2009	150	20	140	30	165	505

Notes:

(1) The premium on the share price is transferred to a specific reserve.

(2) We have chosen to show dividends in the statement of changes in equity rather than in the notes. They represent an appropriation of equity and are deducted from retained earnings.

(3) The effect of each component of comprehensive income on the various components of shareholders' equity must be separately disclosed. The revaluation gain and the loss on translating foreign operations are each allocated to a specific reserve. The profit for the year is added to retained earnings.

Statement of cash flows

The statement of cash flows should help users to assess the ability of a company to generate cash and to assess the company's need for cash. The presentation requirements for this statement are set out in IAS 7 *Statement of Cash Flows*, which we shall consider in some detail in the next chapter.

Notes

The notes play an important role in helping users to understand the financial statements. They will normally contain the following information:

- a statement that the financial statements comply with relevant IFRSs;
- a summary of the measurement bases used and other significant accounting policies applied (for example, the basis of inventories valuation);
- supporting information relating to items appearing on the statement of financial position, statement of comprehensive income, statement of changes in equity and statement of cash flows; and
- other significant disclosures such as future contractual commitments that have not been recognised and financial risk management objectives and policies.

General points

The standard provides support for three key accounting conventions when preparing the financial statements. These are:

- going concern
- accruals (except for the statement of cash flows)
- consistency.

These conventions were discussed in Chapters 2 and 3.

Finally, to improve the transparency of financial statements, the standard states that:

- offsetting liabilities against assets, or expenses against income, is not allowed. Thus it is not acceptable, for example, to offset a bank overdraft against a positive bank balance (where a company has both); and
- material items must be shown separately.

The framework of principles

In Chapters 2 and 3 we came across various accounting conventions such as prudence, historic cost and going concern. These conventions were developed as a practical response to particular problems that were confronted when preparing financial statements. They have stood the test of time and are still of value to preparers today. However, they do not provide, and were never designed to provide, a framework of principles to guide the development of financial statements. As we grapple with increasingly complex financial reporting problems, the need to have a sound understanding of *why* we account for things in a particular way becomes more pressing. Knowing *why* we account, rather than simply *how* we account, is vital if we are to improve the quality of financial statements.

In recent years, much effort has been expended in various countries, including the UK, to develop a clear **framework of principles** that will guide us in the development of accounting. Such a framework should provide clear answers to such fundamental questions as:

- Who are the main users of financial statements?
- What is the purpose of financial statements?
- What qualities should financial information possess?
- What are the main elements of financial statements?
- How should these elements be defined, recognised and measured?

If these questions can be answered, accounting rule makers, such as the IASB, will be in a stronger position to identify best practice and to develop more coherent rules. This should, in turn, increase the credibility of financial reports in the eyes of users. It may even help reduce the possible number of rules, because some issues may be resolved by reference to the application of general principles rather than by the generation of further rules.

The IASB framework

The quest for a framework of accounting principles began in earnest in the 1970s when the Financial Accounting Standards Board (FASB) in the US devoted a very large amount of time and resources to this endeavour. This resulted in a broad framework of principles, which other rule-making bodies, including the IASB, have drawn upon when developing their own frameworks.

The IASB has produced the *Framework for the Preparation and Presentation of Financial Statements*, which begins by discussing the main user groups and their needs. This is well-trodden territory and the various groups and needs identified are in line with those set out in the sections on this topic in Chapter 1. The framework goes on to identify the objective of financial statements, which is

> to provide information about the financial position, performance and changes in financial position of an enterprise that is useful to a wide range of users in making economic decisions.

This reflects the mainstream view and is similar to the objective of financial statements that others have developed in recent years.

The IASB framework sets out the qualitative characteristics that make financial statements useful. The main characteristics identified are relevance, reliability, comparability and understandability, all of which were discussed in Chapter 1. The framework also identifies the main elements of financial statements. These are assets, liabilities, equity, income and expense; and a definition of each element is provided. The definitions adopted hold no surprises and are similar to those adopted by other rule-making bodies and to those that we discussed earlier, in Chapters 2 and 3.

The IASB framework identifies different valuation bases in use such as historic cost, current cost and realisable value, but does not indicate a preference for a particular valuation method. It simply notes that historic cost is the most widely used method of valuation (although fair values are now increasingly used in International Financial Reporting Standards). Finally, the framework discusses the type of capital base that a business should try to maintain. It includes a discussion of the two main types of capital base – financial capital and physical capital – but, again, expresses no preference as to which should be maintained. The IASB framework does not have the same legal status as each of the IASB standards. Nevertheless, it offers guidance for dealing with accounting issues, particularly where no relevant accounting standard exists.

Overall, the IASB framework has provoked little debate and the principles and definitions adopted appear to enjoy widespread acceptance. There has been some criticism, mainly from academics, that the framework is really a descriptive document and does not provide theoretical underpinning to the financial statements. There has also been some criticism of the definitions of the elements of the financial statements. However, these criticisms have not sparked any major controversies.

In 2004, the IASB and the US Financial Accounting Standards Board agreed to undertake a joint project for the development of a common comceptual framework. This project revisits many of the areas covered by the existing IASB framework and has already led to the publication of various drafts and discussion papers. However, the project is still continuing.

The auditors' role

→ Shareholders are required to elect a qualified and independent person or, more usually, a firm to act as **auditors**. The auditors' main duty is to report whether, in their opinion, the financial statements do what they are supposed to do, namely to show a true and fair view of the financial performance, position and cash flows of the company. To be able to form such an opinion, auditors must carefully scrutinise the annual financial statements and the underlying evidence upon which they are based. In particular, they will examine the accounting principles followed, the accounting estimates made and the robustness of the company's internal control systems. The auditors' opinion must be included with the financial statements sent to the shareholders and to the Registrar of Companies.

The relationship between the shareholders, the directors and the auditors is illustrated in Figure 5.2. This shows that the shareholders elect the directors to act on their behalf, in the day-to-day running of the company. The directors are then required to 'account' to the shareholders on the performance, position and cash flows of the company, on an annual basis. The shareholders also elect auditors, whose role it is to give the shareholders an independent view of the truth and fairness of the financial statements prepared by the directors.

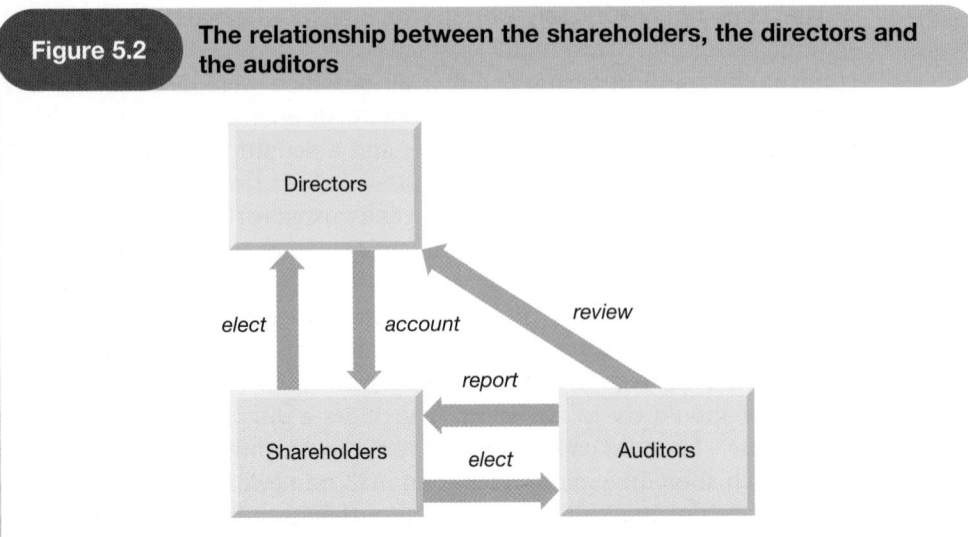

| Figure 5.2 | The relationship between the shareholders, the directors and the auditors |

The directors are appointed by the shareholders to manage the company on the shareholders' behalf. The directors are required to report each year to the shareholders, principally by means of financial statements, on the company's performance, position and cash flows. To give greater confidence in the statements, the shareholders also appoint auditors to investigate the reports and to express an opinion on their reliability.

Directors' report

In addition to preparing the financial statements, UK law requires the directors to prepare an annual report to shareholders and other interested parties. The **directors' report** will contain both financial and non-financial information, which goes beyond that contained in the financial statements. The information to be disclosed is diverse and will include the names of those who were directors during the year, the principal activities of the company and any recommended dividend. The most important element of the report, however, is probably the **business review**. This is aimed at helping shareholders to assess how well the directors have performed. It should provide an analysis of financial performance and position and should also set out the principal risks and uncertainties facing the business. We shall consider this review in some detail later in the chapter.

In addition to disclosing the above information, the directors' report must contain a declaration that the directors are not aware of any other information that the auditors might need in preparing their audit report. Furthermore, the report must declare that they have taken steps to ensure that the auditors are aware of all relevant information. The auditors do not carry out an audit of the directors' report. However, they will check to see that the information in the report is consistent with that contained in the audited financial statements.

For companies listed on the Stock Exchange, the law also requires the preparation of an annual directors' remuneration report. This should help shareholders assess whether the rewards received by directors are appropriate.

Segmental financial reports

Most large businesses are engaged in a number of different operations, with each having its own levels of risk, growth and profitability. Information relating to each type of business operation, however, is normally aggregated in the financial statements to provide an overall picture of financial performance and position. This aggregation (that is, adding together) of information makes it difficult to undertake comparisons over time or between businesses. Some idea of the range and scale of the various types of operation must be gained for a proper assessment of financial health. Thus, to undertake any meaningful analysis of financial performance and position, it is usually necessary to disaggregate the information contained within the financial statements.

By breaking down the financial information according to each type of business operation, or operating segment, we can evaluate the relative risks and profitability of each segment and make useful comparisons with other businesses or other business operating segments. We can also see the trend of performance for each operating segment over time and so determine more accurately the likely growth prospects for the business as a whole. We should also be able to assess more easily the impact on the overall business of changes in market conditions relating to particular operating segments.

Disclosure of information relating to the performance of each segment may also help to improve the efficiency of the business by keeping managers on their toes. Operating segments that are performing poorly will be revealed and this should put pressure on managers to take corrective action. Finally, where an operating segment has been sold, the shareholders will be better placed to assess the wisdom of the managers' decision.

Segmental reporting rules

An IASB standard (IFRS 8 *Operating Segments*) requires listed companies to disclose information about their various operating segments. Defining an operating segment, however, can be a tricky business. The IASB has opted for a 'management approach', which means that an operating segment is defined by reference to how management has segmented the business for internal reporting and monitoring purposes. An operating segment is, therefore, defined as a part of the business that:

- generates revenues and expenses,
- has its own separate financial statements, and
- has its results regularly reviewed for resource-allocation and assessment purposes.

Not all parts of the business will meet the criteria identified. The headquarters of the business, for example, is unlikely to do so.

Activity (5.4)

What do you think are the main advantages of adopting the management approach?

Under the management approach, shareholders will receive similar reports to the internal reports produced for management, which means that they can assess business performance from the same viewpoint as management. It should also mean that businesses will avoid heavy reporting costs as the information is already being produced.

There are, of course, other ways of identifying an operating segment. One approach would be to define a segment according to the industry to which it relates. This, however, may lead to endless definition and classification problems.

To be reported separately, an operating segment must be of significant size. This normally means that it must account for 10 per cent or more of the combined revenue, profits or assets of all operating segments. A segment that does not meet this size threshold may be combined with other similar segments to produce a reportable segment, or separately reported despite its size. If neither of these options is chosen, it should be reported with other segments under a separate category of 'all other segments'.

Segmental disclosure

Financial information to be disclosed includes a measure of profit (loss) for each segment along with the the following income statement items:

- revenue, distinguishing between revenue from external customers and revenue from other segments of the business;
- interest revenue and interest expense;
- depreciation, and other material non-cash items;
- material items of income and expense;
- any profit (loss) from associates or joint ventures;
- income tax (where it is separately reported for a segment).

The business must also disclose the total assets for each segment and, if they are reported to management, the total liabilities. Any additions to non-current assets during the period must also be reported.

Example 5.3 provides an illustrative **segmental financial report** for a business.

Example 5.3

Goya plc
Segmental report for the year ended 31 December 2009

	Publishing £m	Film making £m	All other £m	Totals £m
Revenues from external customers	150	200	25	375
Inter-segment revenues	20	10	–	30
Interest revenue	10	–	–	10
Interest expense	–	15	–	15
Depreciation	40	20	5	65
Reportable segment profit	15	19	4	38
Other material non-cash items				
Impairment of assets	–	10	–	10
Reportable segment assets	60	80	12	152
Expenditures for reportable				
segment non-current assets	12	18	2	32
Reportable segment liabilities	25	32	4	61

We can see that information relating to each segment as well as a combined total for all operating segments is shown. This information may be simply set out in the form of a table with no headings or totals.

Key items, which include revenues, profits, assets, liabilities and material items, must be reconciled with the corresponding amounts for the business as a whole. For example, the income statement should show revenue of £375 million for the business as a whole. When carrying out a reconciliation, we should bear in mind that:

- inter-segment revenues should be eliminated as no transaction with external parties occurs;
- any profit arising from inter-segment transfers should also be eliminated;
- assets and liabilities that have not been allocated to a particular segment should be taken into account.

The last item normally refers to assets and liabilities relating to business-wide activities. Thus, head office buildings may provide an example of unallocated assets and staff pension liabilities may provide an example of unallocated liabilities.

IFRS 8 requires certain non-financial information concerning segments to be disclosed including the basis for identifying operating segments and the types of products and services that each segment provides. It also requires business-wide information to be disclosed such as geographical areas of operations, and reliance on major customers.

Segmental reporting issues

Various issues arise when preparing segmental reports, not least of which is the problem of identifying a segment. We have already seen that the relevant IFRS identifies operating segments according to the internal reporting and monitoring procedures of the business. While this may be the most sensible course of action, comparisons between segments in other businesses may be impossible because of the different ways in which they are defined.

There may be a significant amount of sales between operating segments. Where this occurs, the **transfer price** of the goods or services between segments can have a substantial impact on the reported profits of each segment. (The transfer price is the price at which sales are made between different segments of the business.) A potential risk is that revenues and profits will be manipulated for each segment through the use of particular transfer pricing policies.

Activity (5.5)

Why might a business wish to do this?

Where a business operates in different countries, it may try to report high profits in a country that has low tax rates and to report low profits (or losses) in a country with high tax rates.

Real World 5.2 provides an example of where disappointing tax levies from large businesses has led to the finger of suspicion being pointed at transfer pricing.

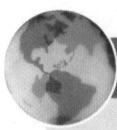

FT

A taxing issue

A majority of large businesses operating in the US reported no tax liability for at least one year between 1998 and 2005, according to a study released by the Government Accountability Office yesterday.

The finding could raise pressure on the US authorities to crack down more aggressively on abuses of transfer pricing – the price that units of the same company charge each other for internal transactions.

A number of senior US legislators have pointed to transfer-pricing violations as the vehicle by which companies have been shifting profits abroad and leaving US divisions with little or no tax liability.

Source: 'Transfer pricing abuses criticised', James Politi, FT.com, 13 August 2008.

IFRS 8 recognises the impact of transfer pricing policies on segmental revenues and profit by stating that the basis for accounting for transactions between segments must be disclosed.

Finally, some expenses and assets may relate to more than one operating segment and their allocation between segments may vary between businesses. Again, this may hinder comparisons of segmental profits and profitability between businesses.

Self-assessment question 5.1

Segmental information relating to Turner plc for the year to 30 April 2010 is shown below.

	Software £m	Electronics £m	Engineering £m	Totals £m
Revenues from external customers	250	230	52	532
Inter-segment revenues	45	25	–	70
Interest revenue	18	–	–	18
Interest expense	–	25	–	25
Depreciation	60	35	10	105
Reportable segment profit	10	34	12	56
Other material non-cash items				
Impairment of assets	–	5	–	5
Reportable segment assets	140	90	34	264
Expenditures for reportable segment				
non-current assets	22	12	10	44
Reportable segment liabilities	55	38	4	97

Required:

Analyse the performance of each of the three main business segments for the year and comment on your results.

The answer to this question can be found at the back of the book on page 726.

Business review

A business, particularly a large business, may have extremely complex organisational arrangements, financing methods and operating characteristics. The financial statements must, however, reflect this complexity if they are to provide a faithful portrayal of financial health. As a consequence, the statements can often be lengthy, detailed and difficult to understand.

To provide a clearer picture for users, a narrative report can be provided that reviews the business and its results. UK law now requires all except the smallest companies to include a business review in their annual financial report. This review, which is prepared by the directors, must provide a balanced and comprehensive analysis of performance during the year and the position at the year end. The review must also set out information concerning:

- the principal risks and uncertainties that are faced;
- key performance indicators;
- the main trends and factors likely to affect the future;
- the company's employees;
- environmental, social and community issues; and finally;
- persons with whom the company has essential contractual or other arrangements, unless disclosure is prejudicial to the person or to the public interest.

Activity 5.6

What do you think are the main qualitative characteristics that information contained within the business review should possess? (*Hint*: Think back to Chapter 1.)

To be useful, the information should contain the characteristics for accounting information in general, which we identified in Chapter 1. Thus the information should be relevant, understandable, reliable and comparable. The fact that we are dealing with narrative information does not alter the need for these characteristics to be present.

To contain the quality of reliability, the information provided must be complete. This means that it should include all significant information that will help assess business performance. Information that places the business in an unfavourable light must not be omitted.

The reporting framework

The particular form that a business review should take is left to the discretion of the directors. In searching for a suitable framework, the directors may look to the Reporting Statement (RS 1) issued by the UK Accounting Standards Board (ASB). This statement precedes the legal requirement for a business review but nevertheless covers the same sort of ground. It is not mandatory but aims rather to provide guidance on best practice.

The framework set out in RS 1 rests on the disclosure of information relating to four key elements of a business: the nature of the business; business performance; resources, risks and relationships; and finally, financial position. The information to be reported for each of these elements is discussed below.

1 The nature of the business

This part of the framework should describe the environment within which the business operates. As might be imagined, this can cover a wide range and may include a commentary on key operational matters such as the products sold, business processes, business structure and competitive position. It can also include a commentary on the legal, economic and social environment.

This part should also describe the objectives of the business and the strategy adopted to achieve those objectives. **Real World 5.3** indicates how one well-known business deals with this topic in its business review.

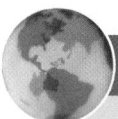

Real World 5.3

Tesco's strategy

The 2008 annual report of Tesco plc includes a 15-page business review, which deals with many areas. The strategy of the business is described in the review as follows:

> The strategy to diversify the business was laid down in 1997 and has been the foundation of Tesco's success in recent years. The new businesses which have been created and developed over the last decade as part of this strategy now have scale, they are competitive and profitable – in fact, the International business alone makes about the same profit as the entire Group did a decade ago. The Group has continued to make progress with this strategy, which now has five elements, reflecting our four established areas of focus, and also Tesco's long-term commitments on community and environment. The objectives of the strategy are:
>
> - to grow the core UK business;
> - to become a successful international retailer;
> - to be as strong in non-food as in food;
> - to develop retailing services – such as Tesco Personal Finance, Telecoms and tesco.com; and
> - to put community at the heart of what we do.

Source: Tesco plc Annual Report and Financial Statements 2008, p. 3.

Finally, this part should include a commentary on the key performance indicators (KPIs) used to assess the success of the business strategy. KPIs will vary between businesses but will normally comprise a combination of financial and non-financial measures. Key financial measures may be based upon sales revenue growth, profit, total shareholder return, dividends and so on. Key non-financial measures may relate to market share, employee satisfaction, product quality, supplier satisfaction and so on.

2 Business performance

This part of the framework considers the development and performance of the business for the year under review and for the future. It should include comments on anything affecting performance, such as changes in market conditions or the launch of new products or services. It should also identify trends and anything else that may affect future prospects. **Real World 5.4** provides an extract from Tesco's business review, which sets out diagrammatically key business trends.

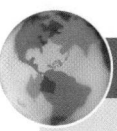

Real World 5.4

Foreign affairs

In line with the strategy mentioned above, Tesco plc has become increasingly international in its focus. The 2008 business review sets out the trend in sales, number of stores and retail space for its international and UK business over a five-year period as follows:

Figure 5.3   Key business trends of Tesco plc

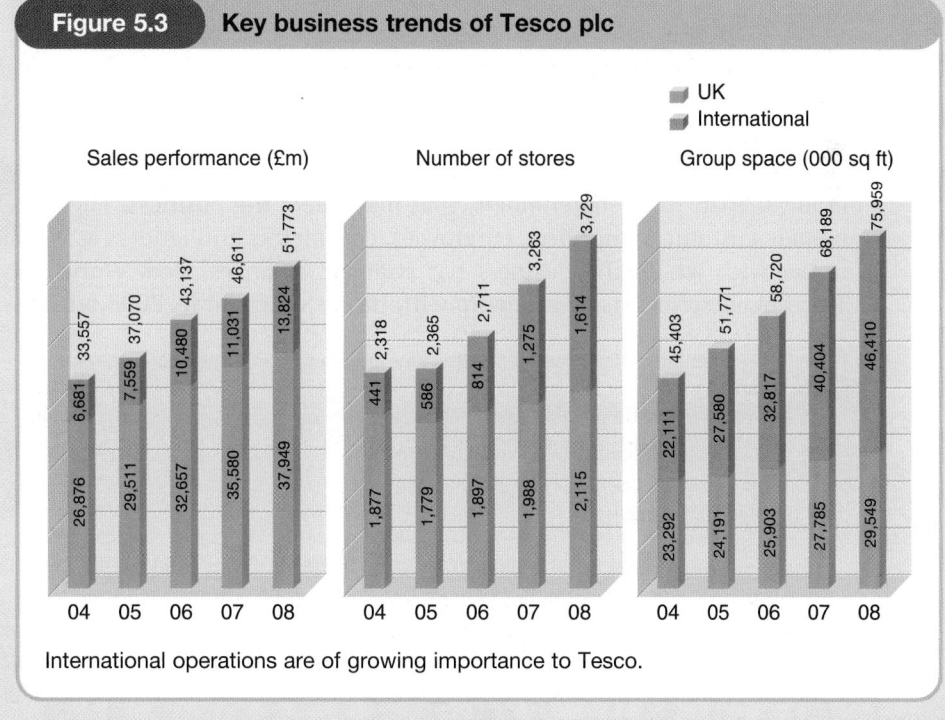

International operations are of growing importance to Tesco.

Source: Tesco plc Annual Report and Financial Statements 2008, p. 4.

3 Resources, risks and relationships

This part should comment on the resources of the business and how they are managed. The resources discussed should not be confined to items shown in the statement of financial position and may include such things as corporate reputation, patents, trade-marks, brand names, market position and the quality of employees.

This part should also include comments on the main risks and uncertainties facing the business and how they are managed. **Real World 5.5** reveals how Tesco plc comments on one important risk in its business review.

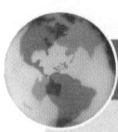

Real World 5.5

Risky business

In its 2008 business review, Tesco plc identifies more than twenty forms of risk that the business must consider. These cover a wide range and include competition, financial, environmental, product safety, terrorism and currency risks. The risk posed by competitors is described as follows:

> The retail industry is highly competitive. The Group competes with a wide variety of retailers of varying sizes and faces increased competition from UK retailers as well as international operators in the UK and overseas. Failure to compete with competitors on areas including price, product range, quality and service could have an adverse effect on the Group's financial results.
>
> We aim to have a broad appeal in price, range and store format in a way that allows us to compete in different markets. We track performance against a range of measures that customers tell us are critical to their shopping trip experience and we constantly monitor customer perceptions of ourselves and our competitors to ensure we can respond quickly if we need to.

Source: Tesco plc Annual Report and Financial Statements 2008, p. 12.

Finally, this part should include a commentary on key relationships with stakeholders, apart from shareholders, that may affect the business. The stakeholders may include customers, suppliers, employees, contractors and lenders as well as other businesses with which the business has strategic alliances. **Real World 5.6** reveals how Tesco plc describes its relationship with its customers in its 2008 business review.

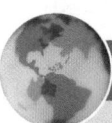

Real World 5.6

Every little helps

Our customers have told us what they want from an 'Every little helps' shopping trip and this year 300,000 shared their ideas on how to improve the shopping trip for all customers, including those who attended our in-store Customer Question Time sessions. Clubcard also helps us to understand what our customers want, whilst allowing us to thank them for shopping with us – this year we gave away over £380m in Clubcard vouchers. In the next year we plan to launch versions of Clubcard in Thailand, Hungary, Turkey, Slovakia and the Czech Republic. We don't always get it right but we try to make our customers' shopping trip as easy as possible, reduce prices where we can to help them spend less and give them the convenience of shopping when and where they want – in small stores, large stores or online.

Source: Tesco plc Annual Report and Financial Statements 2008, p. 13.

4 Financial position

This final part of the framework should describe events that have influenced the financial position of the business during the year and those that are likely to affect the business in the future. It should also include a discussion of the capital structure, cash flows and liquidity of the company. **Real World 5.7** reveals how Tesco plc comments on its cash flows and capital structure.

Real World 5.7

Tesco's cash

Tesco's 2008 business review contains the following comments concerning its cash flows and capital structure:

> Cash flow from operating activities, including an improvement of £194m within working capital, totalled £4.1bn (last year £3.5bn). Net borrowings rose to £6.2bn at the year end (last year £4.9bn). £0.6bn of this increase is attributable to the effect of unfavourable currency movements on our International balance sheet hedging (sterling has depreciated by 11.5% against the currencies of the countries in which we operate). A further £0.3bn relates to acquisitions, including our share of Dobbies Garden Centres plc. Gearing was 52%.

Source: Tesco plc Annual Report and Financial Statements 2008, p. 6.

This final part should also comment on the treasury policy of the business, which is concerned with managing cash, obtaining finance and managing relationships with financial institutions. Possible areas for discussion can include major financing transactions and the effects of interest charges, or interest rate changes, on the business. **Real World 5.8** reveals how Tesco plc comments on its funding arrangements.

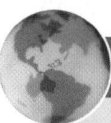

Real World 5.8

Funding Tesco

Tesco plc finances its operations by a combination of retained earnings, share issues, leases and borrowing of different forms. The 2008 business review includes the following comments concerning its funding:

> The objective is to ensure continuity of funding. The policy is to smooth the debt maturity profile, to arrange funding ahead of requirements and to maintain sufficient undrawn committed bank facilities, and a strong credit rating so that maturing debt may be refinanced as it falls due. The Group's long-term credit rating remained stable during the year. Tesco Group is rated A1 by Moody's and A+ by Standard and Poor's. New funding of £3.0bn was arranged during the year, including a net £0.9bn from property transactions, £1.1bn from an issue of US denominated senior notes and £1.0bn from medium-term notes (MTNs).

Source: Tesco plc Annual Report and Financial Statements 2008, p. 17.

The quality of business reviews

Narrative reports that review the business and its results are still at an early stage of development and problems relating to their quality are, perhaps, inevitable. In 2006, the ASB carried out a survey of narrative reporting practice. It found that, generally, businesses provided a good account of the nature of the business and its markets as well of their business strategy and objectives, but the reporting of principal risks, KPIs and the resources of the business needed improvement. The greatest problem area for businesses, however, was the reporting of forward-looking information. (See the reference at the end of the chapter.)

Activity 5.7

Why might the reporting of forward-looking information be a problem for the directors of a business?

The directors may be concerned that the information will be of use to competitors and so damage the competitive position of the business. There is also a risk that the information may turn out to be incorrect and users may then feel that they have been misled.

Summary financial statements

We saw earlier that the directors must provide each shareholder with a copy of the annual financial statements. For large businesses, these financial statements can be extremely detailed and complicated. Along with the accompanying notes, they may extend over many pages. It is possible, however, for the directors to provide a summarised version of the full financial statements as an alternative.

The main advantages of providing **summary financial statements** are that:

- many shareholders do not wish to receive the full version because they may not have the time, interest or skill necessary to be able to gain much from it;
- directors could improve their communication with their shareholders by providing something closer to the needs of many shareholders;
- reproducing and posting copies of the full version is expensive and a waste of resources where particular shareholders do not wish to receive it.

It has now become common practice for large businesses to send all of their private shareholders a copy of the summary financial statements, with a clear message that a copy of the full version is available on request.

Critics of summary financial statements, however, argue that it is dangerous for shareholders to receive financial reports that attempt to simplify complexity. Any attempt to do so runs the risk of forfeiting important information and distorting the message. If a shareholder is unwilling or unable to develop the necessary accounting skills, or to spend the necessary time to examine the full version of the financial statements, the proper solution is either to seek expert advice or to invest in mutual funds managed by experts. Viewed from this perspective, the best thing that a business can do to help private shareholders is to provide more detailed information to experts, such as investment analysts.

Creative accounting

Despite the proliferation of accounting rules and the independent checks that are imposed, concerns over the quality of published financial statements surface from time to time. There are occasions when directors apply particular accounting policies, or structure particular transactions, in such a way as to portray a picture of financial health that is in line with what they want users to see, rather than what is a true and fair view of financial position and performance. Misrepresenting the performance and position of a business in this way is referred to as **creative accounting** and it poses a major problem for accounting rule makers and for society generally.

Activity (5.8)

Why might the directors of a company engage in creative accounting?

There are many reasons, and these include:

- to get around restrictions (for example, to report sufficient profit to pay a dividend);
- to avoid government action (for example, the taxation of excessive profits);
- to hide poor management decisions;
- to achieve sales revenue or profit targets, thereby ensuring that performance bonuses are paid to the directors;
- to attract new share capital or long-term borrowing by showing an apparently healthy financial position;
- to satisfy the demands of major investors concerning levels of return.

Creative accounting methods

The ways in which unscrupulous directors can manipulate the financial statements are many and varied. However, they usually involve adopting novel or unorthodox practices for reporting key elements of the financial statements such as revenue, expenses, assets and liabilities. They may also involve the use of complicated or obscure transactions in an attempt to hide the underlying economic reality. The manipulation carried out may be designed either to bend the rules or to break them. Below we consider some of the more important ways in which rules may be bent or broken.

Misstating revenue

Some creative accounting methods are designed to overstate the revenue for a period. These methods often involve the early recognition of sales revenue or the reporting of sales transactions that have no real substance. **Real World 5.9** provides examples of both types of revenue manipulation.

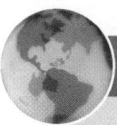 **Real World 5.9**

Overstating revenue

Hollow swaps: telecoms companies sell useless fibre optic capacity to each other in order to generate revenues on their income statements. Example: Global Crossing.

Channel stuffing: a company floods the market with more products than its distributors can sell, artificially boosting its sales. SSL, the condom maker, shifted £60 million in excess inventories on to trade customers. Also known as 'trade loading'.

Round tripping: also known as 'in-and-out trading'. Used to notorious effect by Enron. Two or more traders buy and sell energy among themselves for the same price and at the same time. Inflates trading volumes and makes participants appear to be doing more business than they really are.

Pre-dispatching: goods such as carpets are marked as 'sold' as soon as an order is placed. . . . This inflates sales and profits.

Real World 5.9 continued

Note that some of the techniques used, such as round tripping, may inflate the sales revenue for a period but will not inflate reported profits. Nevertheless, this may still benefit the business. Sales revenue growth has become an important yardstick of performance for some investors and can affect the value they place on the business.

Source: 'Dirty laundry: how companies fudge the numbers', *The Times*, Business Section, 22 September 2002. © The Times 22 September 2002/www.nisyndication.com.

The manipulation of revenue has been at the heart of many of the accounting scandals recently exposed. Given its critical role in the measurement of performance, this is, perhaps, not surprising. **Real World 5.10** provides an example of how the financial results of one well-known business were distorted by the overstatement of sales revenues.

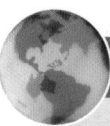

Real World 5.10

Recomputing the numbers

FT

In August 2007, Dell admitted that some unnamed 'senior executives' had been involved in a scheme to overstate sales revenue figures during the period 2003 to 2007. This was done in an attempt to make it appear that quarterly sales targets had been met, when in fact this was not the case. The overstatement of sales revenue was estimated to amount to $92m; about 1 per cent of total profit over the period concerned.

Source: 'Dell to lower writedowns on restated earnings', Kevin Allison, *Financial Times*, 30 October 2007.

Massaging expenses

Some creative accounting methods focus on the manipulation of expenses. Those expenses that rely on directors' estimates of the future or their choice of accounting policy are particularly vulnerable to manipulation.

Activity 5.9

Can you identify the kind of expenses where the directors make estimates or choices in the ways described?

These include certain expenses that we discussed in Chapter 3, such as:

● depreciation of property, plant and equipment;
● amortisation of intangible assets, such as goodwill;
● inventories costing methods;
● allowances for trade receivables.

By changing estimates about the future (for example, the useful life or residual value of an asset), or by changing accounting policies (for example, switching from FIFO to AVCO), it may be possible to derive an expense figure, and consequently a profit figure, that suits the directors.

The incorrect 'capitalisation' of expenses may also be used as a means of manipulation. This involves treating expenses as if they were amounts incurred to acquire or develop non-current assets, rather than amounts consumed during the period. Businesses that build their own assets are often best placed to undertake this form of malpractice.

Activity 5.10

What would be the effect on the profits and total assets of a business of incorrectly capitalising expenses?

Both would be artificially inflated. Reported profits would increase because expenses would be reduced. Total assets would be increased because the expenses would be incorrectly treated as non-current assets.

Real World 5.11 provides an example of one business that capitalised expenses on a huge scale.

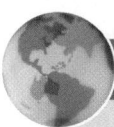

Real World 5.11

Sorry – wrong numbers

One particularly notorious case of capitalising expenses is alleged to have occurred in the financial statements of WorldCom (now renamed MCI). This company, which is a large US telecommunications business, is alleged to have overstated profits by treating certain operating expenses, such as basic network maintenance, as capital expenditure. This happened over a fifteen-month period during 2001 and 2002. To correct for this over-statement, profits had to be reduced by a massive $3.8bn.

Source: Based on two personal views on WorldCom posted on the FT.com site, 27 June 2002.

Concealing 'bad news'

Some creative accounting methods focus on the concealment of losses or liabilities. The financial statements can look much healthier if these can somehow be eliminated. One way of doing this is to create a 'separate' entity that will take over the losses or liabilities.

Real World 5.12 describes how one large business concealed losses and liabilities.

Real World 5.12

For a very special purpose

Perhaps the most well-known case of concealment of losses and liabilities concerned the Enron Corporation. This was a large US energy business that used 'special purpose entities' (SPEs) as a means of concealment. SPEs were used by Enron to rid itself of problem assets that were falling in value, such as its broadband operations. In addition, liabilities were transferred to these entities to help Enron's statement of financial position look

Real World 5.12 continued

healthier. The company had to keep its gearing ratios (the relationship between borrowing and equity) within particular limits to satisfy credit-rating agencies and SPEs were used to achieve this. The SPEs used for concealment purposes were not independent of the company and should have been consolidated in the statement of financial position of Enron, along with their losses and liabilities.

When these, and other accounting irregularities, were discovered in 2001, there was a restatement of Enron's financial performance and position to reflect the consolidation of the SPEs, which had previously been omitted. As a result of this restatement, the company recognised $591m in losses over the preceding four years and an additional $628m worth of liabilities at the end of 2000.

The company collapsed at the end of 2001.

Source: 'The rise and fall of Enron', C. W. Thomas, *Journal of Accountancy*, vol. 194, no. 3, 2002. This article represents the opinions of the author, which are not necessarily those of the Texas Society of Certified Public Accountants.

Misstating assets

There are various ways in which assets may be misstated. These include:

- using asset values that are higher than their fair market values;
- capitalising costs that should have been written off as expenses, as described earlier;
- recording assets that are not owned or which do not exist.

Real World 5.13 describes how one large business reported an asset that did not exist.

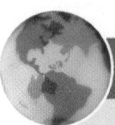

Real World 5.13

When things go sour

Parmalat, a large Italian dairy-and-food business, announced in December 2003 that a bank account held in the Cayman Islands with the Bank of America did not have, as had been previously reported, a balance of €3.95bn. The fake balance turned out to be part of a web of deception: it had simply been 'invented' in order to help offset more than $16 billion of outstanding borrowings. According to Italian prosecutors, the business had borrowed heavily on the strength of fictitious sales revenues.

A Cayman Islands subsidiary, which was supposed to hold the fake bank balance, engaged in fictitious trading in an attempt to conceal the true nature of the deception. This included the supply of 300,000 tonnes of milk powder from a fake Singapore-based business to a Cuban business through the subsidiary.

Source: Based on 'How it all went so sour', P. Gumbel, *Time Europe Magazine*, 21 November 2004.

Inadequate disclosure

Directors may misrepresent or try to conceal certain information. This may relate to commitments made, key changes in accounting policies or estimates, significant events and so on. The information may also relate to financial transactions between the directors and the business. **Real World 5.14** provides such an example.

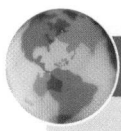

Real World 5.14

Banking on a loan

Anglo Irish Bank chairman Sean Fitzpatrick dramatically resigned last night, admitting he had hidden a massive €87m in loans from the bank. Mr Fitzpatrick's personal borrowings from the bank were more than twice the amount shown for loans to all 13 directors in last year's annual accounts. Another high-profile director, Lar Bradshaw, until recently chairman of Dublin Docklands Development Authority, also resigned from the board. Anglo Irish Bank said that a loan Mr Bradshaw held jointly with Mr Fitzpatrick was temporarily transferred to another bank prior to a year-end audit. 'While Mr Bradshaw was unaware that this transfer took place, he believed that it was in the bank's best interest that he should resign', Anglo said.

As required under accounting rules, company figures showed that directors had loans of €41m from Anglo Irish. Analysts were shocked to learn last night that the true figure of directors' borrowings at present is actually €150m. Mr Fitzpatrick's €87m makes up more than half of this. A statement from the bank said Mr Fitzpatrick would move his loans to another bank, understood to be Irish Nationwide, before the end of each financial year, so that they would not be recorded by the auditors. The loans were then moved back to Anglo Irish in a practice which continued for eight years.

Source: 'Anglo Irish bank chief quits over hiding €87m loans', www.belfasttelegraph.co.uk, 19 December 2008.

Checking for creative accounting

When examining the financial statements of a business, a number of checks may be carried out on the financial statements to help gain a feel for their reliability. These can include checks to see whether:

- the reported profits are significantly higher than the operating cash flows for the period, which may suggest that profits have been overstated;
- the tax charge is low in relation to reported profits, which may suggest, again, that profits are overstated, although there may be other, more innocent explanations;
- the valuation methods used for assets held are based on historic cost or fair values, and if the latter approach has been used why and how the fair values were determined;
- there have been changes in accounting policies over the period, particularly in key areas such as revenue recognition, inventories valuation and depreciation;
- the accounting policies adopted are in line with those adopted by the rest of the industry;
- the auditors' report gives a 'clean bill of health' to the financial statements; and
- the 'small print', that is the notes to the financial statements, is not being used to hide significant events or changes.

Real World 5.15 describes the emphasis that one analyst places on this last check.

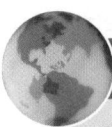

Real World 5.15

Taking note

FT

Alistair Hodgson, investment manager at private client stockbroker Pilling and Co, says:

> I almost look at the notes more than I look at the main figures at first. The notes tend to hold the key to anything that looks strange. I look to pick out things that the auditor has told the company to declare – the kind of thing they might not want to declare, but they have got to do so in order to make the accounts honest.

Source: 'It pays to read between the lines', FT.com, 17 September 2005.

Checks may also be carried out to provide confirmation of positive financial health. These may include checks to see whether:

● the business is paying increased dividends;
● the directors are buying shares in the business.

Although the various checks described are useful, they cannot be used to guarantee the reliability of the financial statements. Some creative accounting practices may be very deeply seated and may go undetected for years.

Creative accounting and economic growth

Some years ago there was a wave of creative accounting scandals, particularly in the US but also in Europe; however, it seems that this wave has now subsided. The quality of financial statements is improving and, it is to be hoped, trust among investors and others is being restored. As a result of the actions taken by various regulatory bodies and by accounting rule makers, creative accounting has become a more risky and difficult process for those who attempt it. However, it will never disappear completely and a further wave of creative accounting scandals may occur in the future.

The recent wave coincided with a period of strong economic growth, and during good economic times, investors and auditors become less vigilant. Thus, the opportunity to manipulate the figures becomes easier. We must not, therefore, become too complacent. Things may change again when we next experience a period of strong growth.

Summary

The main points of this chapter may be summarised as follows.

Directors' duty

● The directors have a duty to prepare and publish financial statements.
● These financial statements must provide a fair representation of the financial health of the business.

The need for accounting rules

- Accounting rules are necessary to:
  - avoid unacceptable accounting practices;
  - improve the comparability of financial statements.

Accounting rules

- The International Accounting Standards Board (IASB) has become an important source of rules.
- Company law and the London Stock Exchange are also sources of rules for UK companies.

Presenting financial statements

- IAS 1 sets out the structure and content of financial statements.
- It identifies four financial statements: the statement of financial position, statement of comprehensive income, statement of changes in equity and statement of cash flows. In addition notes will be required.
- The financial statements must provide a fair representation of the financial health of a company and this will only normally be achieved by adherence to relevant IASB standards.
- IAS 1 identifies information to be shown in the various financial statements and some of the principles to be followed in preparing the statements.

Framework of principles

- This helps to underpin accounting rules.
- The IASB framework identifies and discusses: the users of financial statements, the objective of financial statements, the qualitative characteristics of financial statements, the elements of financial statements, different valuation bases, and different capital maintenance bases.
- The IASB framework draws on earlier work by other rule-making bodies.

Other statutory reports

- The auditors' report provides an opinion by an independent auditor concerning whether the financial statements provide a true and fair view of the financial health of a business.
- The directors' report contains information of a financial and a non-financial nature, which goes beyond that contained in the financial statements.

Additional financial reports

- Segmental reports disaggregate information on the financial statements to help users to achieve a better understanding of financial health.
- An operating segment is defined by the IASB using the 'management approach'.
- IFRS 8 requires certain information relating to each segment to be shown.
- The way in which an operating segment is defined can hinder comparisons of segments between businesses.
- A business review is a narrative report that requires the directors to provide a balanced and comprehensive analysis of the development and performance of the business. It should also set out the principal risks.

- In the UK, the ASB has issued a Reporting Statement (RS 1) that provides useful guidance when producing a business review.
- Summary financial statements are available to investors who do not require the full set of financial statements.

Creative accounting

- Despite the accounting rules in place there have been examples of creative accounting by directors.
- This involves using accounting practices to show what the directors would like users to see rather than what is a fair representation of reality.
- There are various checks that can be carried out to the financial statements to see whether creative accounting practices may have been used.

 *Now check your progress in your personal Study Plan*

→ **Key terms**

International Accounting Standards p. 167	framework of principles p. 176
International Financial Reporting Standards p. 167	auditors p. 177
	directors' report p. 178
statement of comprehensive income p. 171	business review p. 178
	segmental financial report p. 180
statement of changes in equity p. 174	transfer price p. 181
	summary financial statements p. 188
	creative accounting p. 188

Reference

A Review of Narrative Reporting by UK Listed Companies in 2006, Accounting Standards Board, January 2007.

Further reading

If you would like to explore the topics covered in this chapter in more depth, we recommend the following books:

A Guide Through International Financial Reporting Standards (IFRSs) 2008, IASC Foundation Education, July 2008.

Corporate Financial Accounting and Reporting, *Sutton T.*, 2nd edn, Financial Times Prentice Hall, 2004, chapters 6 and 7.

Financial Accounting and Reporting, *Elliott B. and Elliott J.*, 13th edn, Financial Times Prentice Hall, 2010, chapters 5–8.

Insights into IFRS, *KPMG*, 5th edn, 2008/9, Thomson, 2008.

Reporting Statement 1 Operating and Financial Review, *Accounting Standards Board*, ASB 2006.

Review questions

Answers to these questions can be found at the back of the book on pages 741–2.

5.1 'Searching for an agreed framework of principles for accounting rules is likely to be a journey without an ending'. Discuss.

5.2 The size of annual financial reports published by limited companies has increased steadily over the years. Can you think of any reasons, apart from the increasing volume of accounting regulation, why this has occurred?

5.3 What problems does a user of segmental financial statements face when seeking to make comparisons between businesses?

5.4 'A business review should not be prepared by accountants but should be prepared by the board of directors.' Why should this be the case?

Exercises

Exercises 5.6 to 5.8 are more advanced than 5.1 to 5.5. Those with **coloured numbers** have answers at the back of the book, starting on page 760.

If you wish to try more exercises, visit the students' side of the Companion Website and MyAccountingLab.

5.1 It has been suggested that too much information might be as bad as too little information for users of annual reports. Explain.

5.2 What problems are likely to be encountered when preparing summary financial statements for shareholders?

5.3 The following information was extracted from the financial statements of I. Ching (Booksellers) plc for the year to 31 December 2009:

	£000
Finance charges	40
Cost of sales	460
Distribution expenses	110
Revenue	943
Administration expenses	212
Other expenses	25
Gain on revaluation of property, plant and equipment	20
Loss on foreign currency translations on foreign operations	15
Tax on profit for the year	24
Tax on other components of comprehensive income	1

Required:
Prepare a statement of comprehensive income for the year ended 31 December 2009 that is set out in accordance with the requirements of IAS 1 *Presentation of Financial Statements*.

5.4 Manet plc had the following share capital and reserves as at 1 January 2009:

	£m
Share capital (£0.25 ordinary shares)	250
Share premium account	50
Revaluation reserve	120
Currency translation reserve	15
Retained earnings	380
Total equity	815

During the year to 31 December 2009, the company revalued property, plant and equipment upwards by £30 million and made a loss on foreign exchange translation of foreign operations of £5 million. The company made a profit for the year from normal operations of £160 million during the year and the dividend was £80 million.

Required:

Prepare a statement of changes in equity in accordance with the requirements of IAS 1 *Presentation of Financial Statements*.

5.5 Professor Myddleton argues that accounting standards should be limited to disclosure requirements and should not impose rules on companies as to how to measure particular items in the financial statements. He states:

> The volume of accounting instructions is already high. If things go on like this, where will we be in 20 or 30 years' time? On balance I conclude we would be better off without any standards on accounting measurement. There could still be some disclosure requirements for listed companies, though probably less than now.

Do you agree with this idea? Discuss. (*Note*: This issue has not been directly covered in the chapter, but you should be able to use your knowledge to try to come up with some points on both sides of the argument.)

5.6 You have overheard the following statements:

(a) 'The role of independent auditors is to prepare the financial statements of the company.'
(b) 'International Accounting Standards (IASs) apply to all companies, but Stock Exchange listed companies must also adhere to International Financial Reporting Standards (IFRSs).'
(c) 'All listed companies in European Union states must follow IASs and IFRSs.'
(d) 'According to IAS 1, companies' financial statements must show an "accurate representation" of what they purport to show.'
(e) 'IAS 1 leaves it to individual companies to decide the format that they use in the statement of financial position.'
(f) 'The statement of changes in equity deals with unrealised profits and gains, for example an upward revaluation of a non-current asset.'
(g) 'If a majority of the shareholders of a listed company agree, the company need not produce a full set of financial statements, but can just produce summary financial statements.'

Critically comment on each of these statements.

5.7 Obtain a copy of the business review for two separate companies within the same industry. Compare the usefulness of each. In answering this question, consider the extent to which each of the two business reviews incorporate the recommendations made by the Accounting Standards Board in RS 1.

5.8 Segmental information relating to Dali plc for the year to 31 December 2009 is shown below.

	Car parts £m	Aircraft parts £m	Boat parts £m	Total £m
Revenues from external customers	360	210	85	655
Inter-segment revenues	95	40	–	135
Interest revenue	34	–	–	34
Interest expense	–	28	8	36
Depreciation	80	55	15	150
Reportable segment profit	20	24	18	62
Other material non-cash items				
Impairment of assets	–	39	–	39
Reportable segment assets	170	125	44	339
Expenditures for reportable segment				
non-current assets	28	23	26	77
Reportable segment liabilities	85	67	22	174

Required:

Analyse the performance of each of the three main business segments for the year and comment on your results.

CHAPTER 6

Measuring and reporting cash flows

Introduction

This chapter is devoted to the third major financial statement identified in Chapter 2: the statement of cash flows. This statement reports the movements of cash over a period and the effect of these movements on the cash position of the business. It is an important financial statement because cash is vital to the survival of a business. Without cash, a business cannot operate.

In this chapter, we shall see how the statement of cash flows is prepared and how the information that it contains may be interpreted. We shall also see why the deficiencies of the income statement in identifying and explaining cash flows make a separate statement necessary.

The statement of cash flows is being considered after the chapter on limited companies because the format of the statement requires an understanding of this type of business. Nearly all limited companies are required to provide a statement of cash flows for shareholders and other users as part of their annual financial reports.

Learning outcomes

When you have completed this chapter, you should be able to:

● Discuss the crucial importance of cash to a business.

● Explain the nature of the statement of cash flows and discuss how it can be helpful in identifying cash flow problems.

● Prepare a statement of cash flows.

● Interpret a statement of cash flows.

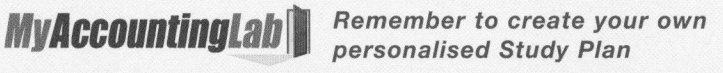

MyAccountingLab   *Remember to create your own personalised Study Plan*

The statement of cash flows

The statement of cash flows is a fairly recent addition to the annual published financial statements. Until recently companies were only required to publish an income statement and a statement of financial position (balance sheet). The prevailing view seems to have been that all the financial information needed by users would be contained within these two statements. This view may have been based partly on the assumption that if a business were profitable, it would also have plenty of cash. Although in the long run this is likely to be true, it is not necessarily true in the short to medium term.

We saw in Chapter 3 that the income statement sets out the revenue and expenses, rather than the cash receipts and cash payments, for the period. This means that profit (or loss), which represents the difference between the revenue and expenses for the period, may have little or no relation to the cash generated for the period. To illustrate this point, let us take the example of a business making a sale (generating a revenue). This may well lead to an increase in wealth that will be reflected in the income statement. However, if the sale is made on credit, no cash changes hands – at least not at the time of sale. Instead, the increase in wealth is reflected in another asset: an increase in trade receivables. Furthermore, if an item of inventories is the subject of the sale, wealth is lost to the business through the reduction in inventories. This means an expense is incurred in making the sale, which will be shown in the income statement. Once again, however, no cash has changed hands at the time of sale. For such reasons, the profit and the cash generated for a period will rarely go hand in hand.

The following activity should help to underline how profit and cash for a period may be affected differently by particular transactions or events.

Activity 6.1

The following is a list of business/accounting events. In each case, state the effect (increase, decrease or no effect) on both profit and cash:

		Effect	
		on profit	on cash
1	Repayment of borrowings	_____	_____
2	Making a sale on credit	_____	_____
3	Buying a current asset on credit	_____	_____
4	Receiving cash from a credit customer (trade receivable)	_____	_____
5	Depreciating a non-current asset	_____	_____
6	Buying some inventories for cash	_____	_____
7	Making a share issue for cash	_____	_____

You should have come up with the following:

		Effect	
		on profit	on cash
1	Repayment of borrowings	none	decrease
2	Making a sale on credit	increase	none
3	Buying a current asset on credit	none	none
4	Receiving cash from a credit customer (trade receivable)	none	increase
5	Depreciating a non-current asset	decrease	none
6	Buying some inventories for cash	none	decrease
7	Making a share issue for cash	none	increase

Activity 6.1 continued

The reasons for these answers are as follows:

1 Repaying borrowings requires that cash be paid to the lender. This means that two figures in the statement of financial position will be affected, but none in the income statement.
2 Making a sale on credit will increase the sales revenue figure (and a profit or a loss, unless the sale was made for a price that precisely equalled the expenses involved). No cash will change hands at this point, however.
3 Buying a current asset on credit affects neither the cash balance nor the profit figure.
4 Receiving cash from a credit customer increases the cash balance and reduces the credit customer's balance. Both of these figures are on the statement of financial position. The income statement is unaffected.
5 Depreciating a non-current asset means that an expense is recognised. This causes the carrying amount of the asset, as it is recorded on the statement of financial position, to fall by an amount equal to the amount of the expense. No cash is paid or received.
6 Buying some inventories for cash means that the value of the inventories will increase and the cash balance will decrease by a similar amount. Profit is not affected.
7 Making a share issue for cash increases the owners' claim and increases the cash balance; profit is unaffected.

It is clear from the above that if we are to gain insights about cash movements over time, the income statement is not the place to look. Instead we need a separate financial statement. This fact has become widely recognised in recent years, and in 1991 a UK financial reporting standard, FRS 1, emerged that required all but the smallest companies to produce and publish a statement of cash flows. This standard has been superseded for listed companies from 2005 by the International Financial Reporting (Accounting) Standard IAS 7. The two standards have broadly similar requirements. This chapter follows the provisions of IAS 7.

Why is cash so important?

It is worth asking why cash is so important. After all, cash is just an asset that the business needs to help it to function. In that sense, it is no different from inventories or non-current assets.

The reason for the importance of cash is that people and organisations will not normally accept anything other than cash in settlement of their claims. If a business wants to employ people, it must pay them in cash. If it wants to buy a new non-current asset to exploit a business opportunity, the seller of the asset will normally insist on being paid in cash, probably after a short period of credit. When businesses fail, it is their inability to find the cash to pay the amounts owed that really pushes them under. These factors lead to cash being the pre-eminent business asset. Cash is the one that analysts tend to watch most carefully when assessing the ability of businesses to survive and/or to take advantage of commercial opportunities.

During an economic downturn, the ability to generate cash takes on even greater importance. Banks become more cautious in their lending and those businesses with weak cash flows often find it difficult to obtain finance. **Real World 6.1** describes how the recent financial crisis has led banks in China to place greater emphasis on cash flows when considering loan applications.

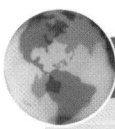

Real World 6.1

Cash flow is in top three places

FT

'The banks are tightening the screws,' says K. B. Chan, chairman of Surface Mount Technology, which supplies consumer electronics companies. 'A lot of companies are strapped for cash.'

Stanley Wong, business development director at Man Yue Electronics, the world's fifth largest maker of aluminium capacitors, says: 'Banks don't even trust each other. They are being a lot more careful.' Mr Wong says that companies such as his, with strong cash flows, will still get working capital and other loans but bankers who used to lend to Man Yue and other manufacturers sight unseen are now tramping out to their factories for a closer look.

'The banks only look at cash flow – number one is cash flow, number two is cash flow and number three is cash flow,' says Mr Chan. 'Profit is only an accounting statement.'

Source: 'Rations cut for army of buyers', Tom Mitchell and Justine Lau, FT.com, 20 October 2008.

The main features of the statement of cash flows

The statement of cash flows is a summary of the cash receipts and payments over the period concerned. All payments of a particular type, for example cash payments to acquire additional non-current assets or other investments, are added together to give just one figure that appears in the statement. The net total of the statement is the net increase or decrease of the cash (and cash equivalents) of the business over the period. The statement is basically an analysis of the business's cash (and cash equivalents) movements for the period.

A definition of cash and cash equivalents

IAS 7 defines cash as notes and coins in hand and deposits in banks and similar institutions that are accessible to the business on demand. Cash equivalents are short-term, highly liquid investments that are readily convertible to known amounts of cash and which are subject to an insignificant risk of changes of value. Cash equivalents are held for the purpose of meeting short-term cash commitments rather than for investment or other purposes.

Activity 6.2 should clarify the types of items that fall within the definition of 'cash equivalents'.

Activity 6.2

At the end of its accounting period, Zeneb plc's statement of financial position included the following items:

1 *A bank deposit account where one month's notice of withdrawal is required.* This deposit was made because the business has a temporary cash surplus that it will need to use in the short term for operating purposes;

Activity 6.2 continued

2 *Ordinary shares in Jones plc (a Stock Exchange listed business).* These were acquired because Zeneb plc has a temporary cash surplus and its directors believed that the share represents a good short-term investment. The funds invested will need to be used in the short term for operating purposes.

3 *A bank deposit account that is withdrawable instantly.* This represents an investment of surplus funds that are not seen as being needed in the short term.

4 *An overdraft on the business's bank current account.*

Which (if any) of these four items would be included in the figure for cash and cash equivalents?

Your response should have been as follows:

1 A cash equivalent because the deposit is part of the business's normal cash management activities and there is little doubt about how much cash will be obtained when the deposit is withdrawn.

2 Not a cash equivalent. Although the investment was made as part of normal cash management, there is a significant risk that the amount expected (hoped for!) when the shares are sold may not actually be forthcoming.

3 Not a cash equivalent because this represents an investment rather than a short-term surplus amount of cash.

4 This is cash itself, though a negative amount of it. The only exception to this classification would be where the business is financed in the longer term by an overdraft, when it would be part of the financing of the business, rather than negative cash.

As can be seen from the responses to Activity 6.2, whether a particular item falls within the definition of cash and cash equivalent depends on two factors:

● the nature of the item; and
● why it has arisen.

In practice, it is not usually difficult to decide whether an item is a cash equivalent.

The relationship between the main financial statements

The statement of cash flows is now accepted, along with the income statement and the statement of financial position, as a major financial statement. The relationship between the three statements is shown in Figure 6.1. The statement of financial position reflects the combination of assets (including cash) and claims (including the shareholders' equity) of the business *at a particular point in time*. The statement of cash flows and the income statement explain the *changes over a period* to two of the items in the statement of financial position. The statement of cash flows explains the changes to cash. The income statement explains changes to equity, arising from trading operations.

The form of the statement of cash flows

The standard layout of the statement of cash flows is summarised in Figure 6.2. Explanations of the terms used in the statement of cash flows are given below.

| Figure 6.1 | The relationship between the statement of financial position, the income statement and the statement of cash flows |

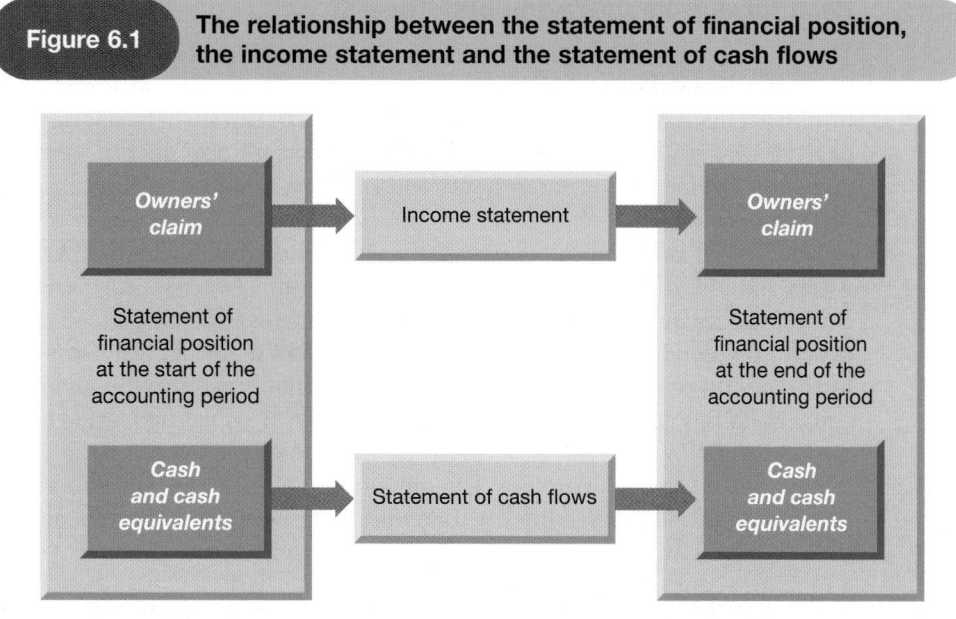

The statement of financial position shows the relationship, at a particular point in time, between the business's assets and claims. The income statement explains how, over a period between two statements of financial position, the owners' claim figure in the first statement of financial position has altered as a result of trading operations. The statement of cash flows also looks at changes over the accounting period, but this statement explains the alteration in the cash (and cash equivalent) balances from the first to the second of the two consecutive statements of financial position.

| Figure 6.2 | Standard layout of the statement of cash flows |

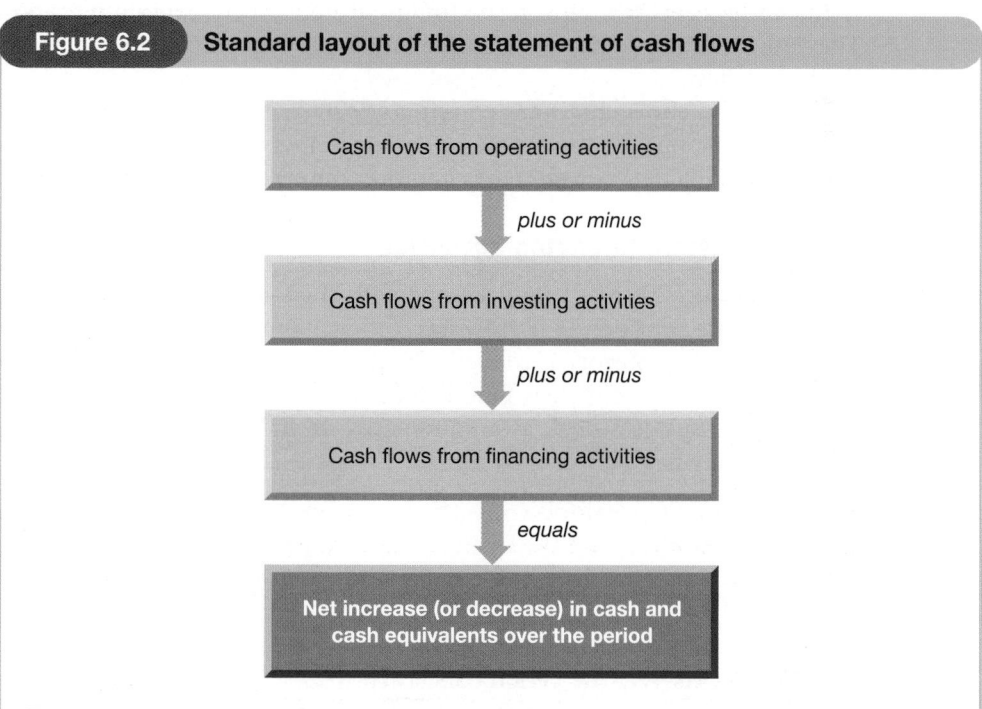

This is the standard layout for the statement of cash flows as required by IAS 7 *Statement of Cash Flows*.

Cash flows from operating activities

This is the net inflow or outflow from trading operations, after tax payments (or receipts) and cash paid to meet financing costs. It is equal to the sum of cash receipts from trade receivables, and cash receipts from cash sales where relevant, less the sums paid to buy inventories, to pay rent, to pay wages and so on. From this are also deducted payments for interest on the business's borrowings, corporation tax and dividends paid.

Note that it is the amounts of cash received and paid during the period that feature in the statement of cash flows, not the revenue and expenses for that period. It is, of course, the income statement that deals with the revenue and expenses. Similarly the tax and dividend payments that appear in the statement of cash flows are those made in the period of the statement. Companies normally pay tax on their profits in four equal instalments. Two of these are during the year concerned, and the other two are during the following year. As a result, by the end of each accounting year, one half of the tax will have been paid and the remainder will be a current liability at the end of the year, to be paid off during the following year. During any particular year, therefore, the tax payment would normally equal 50 per cent of the previous year's tax charge and 50 per cent of that of the current year.

The net figure for this section is intended to indicate the net cash flows for the period that arose from normal day-to-day trading activities after taking account of the tax that has to be paid on them and the cost of servicing the finance (equity and borrowings) needed to support them.

Cash flows from investing activities

This section of the statement is concerned with cash payments made to acquire additional non-current assets and with cash receipts from the disposal of non-current assets. These non-current assets will tend to be the usual items such as buildings and machinery. They might also be loans made by the business or shares in another company bought by the business.

This section also includes cash receipts arising from financial investments (loans and equities) made outside the business. These receipts are interest on loans made by the business and dividends from shares in other companies that are owned by the business.

Cash flows from financing activities

This part of the statement is concerned with the long-term financing of the business. So here we are considering borrowings (other than very short term) and finance from share issues. This category is concerned with repayment/redemption of finance as well as with the raising of it. It is permissible under IAS 7 to include dividend payments made by the business here, as an alternative to including them in 'Cash flows from operating activities' (above).

This section shows the net cash flows from raising and/or paying back long-term finance.

Net increase or decrease in cash and cash equivalents

The total of the statement must, of course, be the net increase or decrease in cash and cash equivalents over the period concerned.

The effect on a business's cash and cash equivalents of its various activities is shown in Figure 6.3. As explained, the arrows show the *normal* direction of cash flow for the typical healthy, profitable business in a typical year.

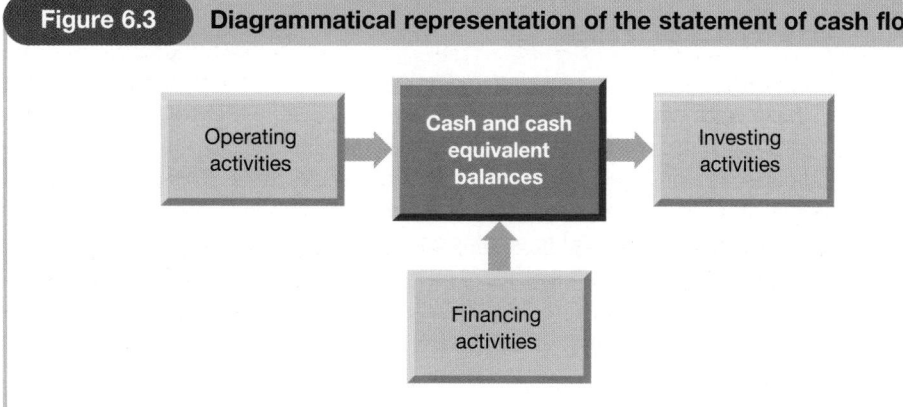

Figure 6.3 Diagrammatical representation of the statement of cash flows

Various activities of the business each have their own effect on its cash and cash equivalent balances, either positive (increasing them) or negative (reducing them). The net increase or decrease in the cash and cash equivalent balances over a period will be the sum of these individual effects, taking account of the direction (cash in or cash out) of each activity.

Note that the direction of the arrow shows the *normal* direction of the cash flow in respect of each activity. In certain circumstances, each of these arrows could be reversed in direction.

The normal direction of cash flows

Normally 'operating activities' provide positive cash flows, that is, they help to increase the business's cash resources. In fact, for most UK businesses, in most time periods, cash generated from day-to-day trading, even after deducting tax, interest and dividends, is overwhelmingly the most important source of new finance.

Activity 6.3

Last year's statement of cash flows for Angus plc showed a negative cash flow from operating activities. What could be the reason for this and should the business's management be alarmed by it? (*Hint*: We think that there are two broad possible reasons for a negative cash flow.)

The two reasons are:

- The business is unprofitable. This leads to more cash being paid out to employees, to suppliers of goods and services, for interest and so on, than is received from trade receivables in respect of sales. This would be particularly alarming, because a major expense for most businesses is depreciation of non-current assets. Since depreciation does not lead to a cash flow, it is not considered in 'net cash inflows from operating activities'. This means that, a negative operating cash flow might well indicate a very much larger trading loss – in other words, a significant loss of the business's wealth; something to concern management.
- The other reason might be less alarming. A business that is expanding its activities (level of sales revenue) would tend to spend quite a lot of cash relative to the amount of cash coming in from sales. This is because it will probably be expanding its assets (non-current and current) to accommodate the increased demand. For example, a business may well need to have inventories in place before additional sales can be made.

Activity 6.3 continued

Similarly staff have to be employed and paid. Even when the additional sales are made, those sales would normally be made on credit, with the cash inflow lagging behind the sale. All of this means that, in the first instance, in cash flow terms, the business would not necessarily benefit from the additional sales revenue. This is particularly likely to be true of a new business, which would be expanding inventories and other assets from zero. It would also need to employ and pay staff. Expansion typically causes cash flow strains for the reasons just explained. This can be a particular problem because the business's increased profitability might encourage a feeling of optimism, which could lead to lack of attention being paid to the cash flow problem.

Investing activities typically cause net negative cash flows. This is because many types of non-current asset wear out, and many that do not wear out become obsolete. Also, businesses tend to seek to expand their asset base. When a business sells some non-current assets, the sale will give rise to positive cash flows, but in net terms the cash flows are normally negative with cash spent on new assets outweighing that received from disposal of old ones.

Financing can go in either direction, depending on the financing strategy at the time. Since businesses seek to expand, there is a general tendency for this area to lead to cash coming into the business rather than leaving it.

Real World 6.2 shows the summarised statement of cash flows of Tesco plc, the UK-based supermarket.

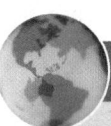

Real World 6.2

Cashing in

Like many larger companies, Tesco produces summary versions of its financial statements for users who do not want all of the detail. The summary statement of cash flows for the business for the year ended 28 February 2009 shows the cash flows of the business under each of the headings described above.

Summarised statement of cash flows for the year ended 28 February 2009

	£m
Cash generated from operations	4,978
Interest paid	(562)
Corporation tax paid	(456)
Net cash from operating activities	3,960
Net cash used in investing activities	(5,974)
Cash flows from financing activities	
Dividends paid	(883)
Other net cash flows from financing activities	4,498
Net cash from financing activities	3,615
Net increase in cash and cash equivalents	1,601

Source: Tesco Annual Review 2009, p. 24, www.tescocorporate.com.

As we shall see shortly, more detailed information under each of the main headings is provided in the statement of cash flows presented to shareholders and other users.

Preparing the statement of cash flows

Deducing net cash flows from operating activities

The first section of the statement of cash flows is the 'cash flows from operating activities'. There are two approaches that can be taken to deriving this figure: the direct method and the indirect method.

The direct method

→ The **direct method** involves an analysis of the cash records of the business for the period, picking out all payments and receipts relating to operating activities. These are summarised to give the total figures for inclusion in the statement of cash flows. Done on a computer, this would be a simple matter, but not many businesses adopt the direct method.

The indirect method

→ The **indirect method** is the more popular method. It relies on the fact that, broadly, sales revenue gives rise to cash inflows, and expenses give rise to outflows. This means that the profit for the year figure will be closely linked to the net cash flows from operating activities. Since businesses have to produce an income statement in any case, information from it can be used as a starting point to deduce the cash flows from operating activities.

Of course, within a particular accounting period, profit for the year will not normally equal the net cash inflows from operating activities. We saw in Chapter 3 that, when sales are made on credit, the cash receipt occurs some time after the sale. This means that sales revenue made towards the end of an accounting year will be included in that year's income statement, but most of the cash from those sales will flow into the business, and should be included in the statement of cash flows, in the following year. Fortunately it is easy to deduce the cash received from sales if we have the relevant income statement and statements of financial position, as we shall see in Activity 6.4.

Activity 6.4

How can we deduce the cash inflows from sales using the income statement and statement of financial position for the business?

The statement of financial position will tell us how much was owed in respect of credit sales at the beginning and end of the year (trade receivables). The income statement tells us the sales revenue figure. If we adjust the sales revenue figure by the increase or decrease in trade receivables over the year, we deduce the cash from sales for the year.

Example 6.1

The sales revenue figure for a business for the year was £34 million. The trade receivables totalled £4 million at the beginning of the year, but had increased to £5 million by the end of the year.

Basically, the trade receivables figure is affected by sales revenue and cash receipts. It is increased when a sale is made and decreased when cash is received from a credit customer. If, over the year, the sales revenue and the cash receipts had been equal, the beginning-of-year and end-of-year trade receivables figures would have been equal. Since the trade receivables figure increased, it must mean that less cash was received than sales revenues were made. This means that the cash receipts from sales must be £33 million (that is, 34 − (5 − 4)).

Put slightly differently, we can say that as a result of sales, assets of £34 million flowed into the business during the year. If £1 million of this went to increasing the asset of trade receivables, this leaves only £33 million that went to increase cash.

The same general point is true in respect of nearly all of the other items that are taken into account in deducing the operating profit figure. The exception is depreciation. This is not necessarily associated with any movement in cash during the accounting period.

All of this means that we can take the profit before taxation (that is, the profit after interest but before taxation) for the year, add back the depreciation and interest expense charged in arriving at that profit, and adjust this total by movements in inventories, trade (and other) receivables and payables. If we then go on to deduct payments made during the accounting period for taxation, interest on borrowings and dividends, we have the net cash from operating activities.

Example 6.2

The relevant information from the financial statements of Dido plc for last year is as follows:

	£m
Profit before taxation (after interest)	122
Depreciation charged in arriving at profit before taxation	34
Interest expense	6
At the beginning of the year:	
Inventories	15
Trade receivables	24
Trade payables	18
At the end of the year:	
Inventories	17
Trade receivables	21
Trade payables	19

The following further information is available about payments during last year:

	£m
Taxation paid	32
Interest paid	5
Dividends paid	9

The cash flow from operating activities is derived as follows:

	£m
Profit before taxation (after interest)	122
Depreciation	34
Interest expense	6
Increase in inventories (17 – 15)	(2)
Decrease in trade receivables (21 – 24)	3
Increase in trade payables (19 – 18)	1
Cash generated from operating activities	164
Interest paid	(5)
Taxation paid	(32)
Dividends paid	(9)
Net cash from operating activities	118

→   As we can see, the net increase in **working capital*** (that is current assets, less current liabilities), as a result of trading, was £162 million. Of this, £2 million went into increased inventories. More cash was received from trade receivables than sales revenue was made, and less cash was paid to trade payables than purchases of goods and services on credit. Both of these had a favourable effect on cash, which increased by £164 million. When account was taken of the payments for interest, tax and dividends, the net cash from operating activities was £118 million (inflow).

Note that we needed to adjust the profit before taxation (after interest) by the depreciation and interest expenses to derive the profit before depreciation, interest and taxation.

* Working capital is a term widely used in accounting and finance, not just in the context of the statement of cash flows. We shall encounter it several times in later chapters.

The indirect method of deducing the net cash flow from operating activities is summarised in Figure 6.4.

Activity 6.5

The relevant information from the financial statements of Pluto plc for last year is as follows:

	£m	
Profit before taxation (after interest)	165	
Depreciation charged in arriving at operating profit	41	
Interest expense	21	
At the beginning of the year:		
Inventories	22	(1)
Trade receivables	18	3
Trade payables	15	(2)
At the end of the year:		
Inventories	23	
Trade receivables	21	
Trade payables	17	

Activity 6.5 continued

The following further information is available about payments during last year:

	£m
Taxation paid	49
Interest paid	25
Dividends paid	28

What figure should appear in the statement of cash flows for 'Cash flows from operating activities'?

Net cash inflows from operating activities:

	£m
Profit before taxation (after interest)	165
Depreciation	41
Interest expense	21
Increase in inventories (23 – 22)	(1)
Increase in trade receivables (21 – 18)	(3)
Increase in trade payables (17 – 15)	2
Cash generated from operating activities	225
Interest paid	(25)
Taxation paid	(49)
Dividends paid	(28)
Net cash from operating activities	123

Deducing the other areas of the statement of cash flows

We can now go on to take a look at the preparation of a complete statement of cash flows through Example 6.3.

Example 6.3

Torbryan plc's income statement for the year ended 31 December 2009 and the statements of financial position as at 31 December 2008 and 2009 are as follows:

Income statement for the year ended 31 December 2009

	£m
Revenue	576
Cost of sales	(307)
Gross profit	269
Distribution expenses	(65)
Administrative expenses	(26)
	178
Other operating income	21
Operating profit	199
Interest receivable	17
	216
Interest payable	(23)
Profit before taxation	193
Taxation	(46)
Profit for the year	147

Figure 6.4	**The indirect method of deducing the net cash flows from operating activities**

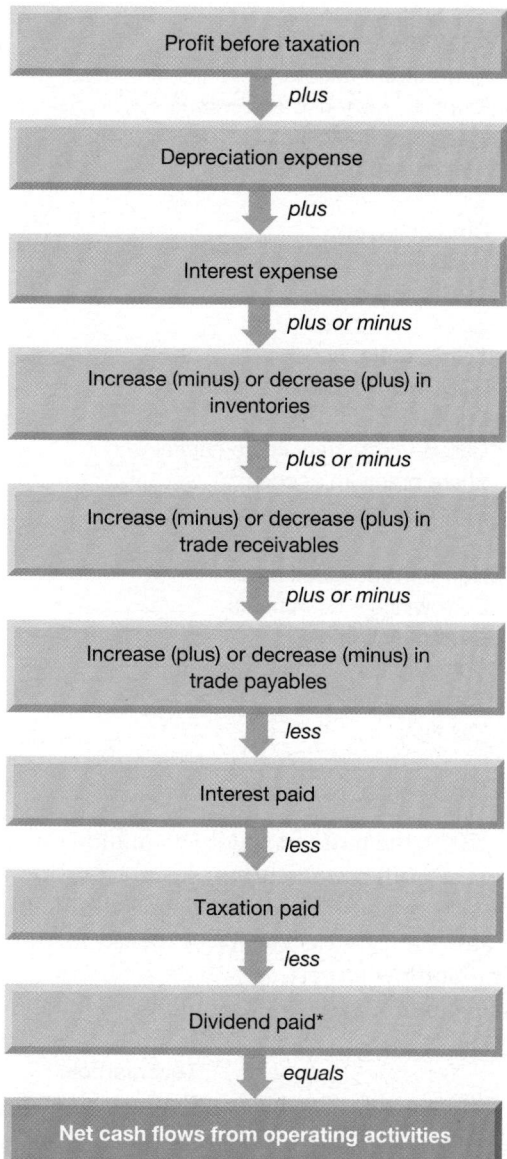

Determining the net cash from operating activities firstly involves adding back the depreciation and the interest expense to the profit before taxation. Next, adjustment is made for increases or decreases in inventories, trade receivables and trade payables. Lastly, cash paid for interest, taxation and dividends is deducted.

* Note that dividends could alternatively be included under the heading 'Cash flows from financing activities'.

Statements of financial position as at 31 December 2008 and 2009

	2008 £m	2009 £m
ASSETS		
Non-current assets		
Property, plant and equipment		
Land and buildings	241	241
Plant and machinery	309	325
	550	566
Current assets		
Inventories	44	41
Trade receivables	121	139
	165	180
Total assets	715	746
EQUITY AND LIABILITIES		
Equity		
Called-up ordinary share capital	150	200
Share premium account	–	40
Retained earnings	26	123
	176	363
Non-current liabilities		
Borrowings – Loan notes	400	250
Current liabilities		
Borrowings (all bank overdraft)	68	56
Trade payables	55	54
Taxation	16	23
	139	133
Total equity and liabilities	715	746

During 2009, the business spent £95 million on additional plant and machinery. There were no other non-current asset acquisitions or disposals. A dividend of £50 million was paid on ordinary shares during the year. The interest receivable revenue and the interest payable expense for the year were equal to the cash inflow and outflow respectively.

The statement of cash flows would be as follows:

Torbryan plc
Statement of cash flows for the year ended 31 December 2009

	£m
Cash flows from operating activities	
Profit before taxation (after interest) (see Note 1 below)	193
Adjustments for:	
Depreciation (Note 2)	79
Interest receivable (Note 3)	(17)
Interest payable (Note 4)	23
Increase in trade receivables (139 – 121)	(18)
Decrease in trade payables (55 – 54)	(1)
Decrease in inventories (44 – 41)	3
Cash generated from operations	262
Interest paid	(23)
Taxation paid (Note 5)	(39)

Dividend paid	(50)
Net cash from operating activities	150
Cash flows from investing activities	
Payments to acquire tangible non-current assets	(95)
Interest received (Note 3)	17
Net cash used in investing activities	(78)
Cash flows from financing activities	
Repayments of loan notes (Note 6)	(150)
Issue of ordinary shares (Note 7)	90
Net cash used in financing activities	(60)
Net increase in cash and cash equivalents	12
Cash and cash equivalents at 1 January 2009 (Note 8)	(68)
Cash and cash equivalents at 31 December 2009	(56)

To see how this relates to the cash of the business at the beginning and end of the year it can be useful to provide a reconciliation as follows:

Analysis of cash and cash equivalents during the year ended 31 December 2009

	£m
Overdraft balance at 1 January 2009	(68)
Net cash inflow	12
Overdraft balance at 31 December 2009	(56)

Notes:

(1) This is simply taken from the income statement for the year.

(2) Since there were no disposals, the depreciation charges must be the difference between the start and end of the year's plant and machinery (non-current assets) values, adjusted by the cost of any additions.

	£m
Carrying amount at 1 January 2009	309
Additions	95
	404
Depreciation (balancing figure)	(79)
Carrying amount at 31 December 2009	325

(3) Interest receivable must be taken away to work towards the profit before crediting it, because it is not part of operations but of investing activities. The cash inflow from this source appears under the 'Cash flows from investing activities' heading.

(4) Interest payable expense must be taken out, by adding it back to the profit figure. We subsequently deduct the cash paid for interest payable during the year. In this case the two figures are identical.

(5) Taxation is paid by companies 50 per cent during their accounting year and 50 per cent in the following year. As a result the 2009 payment would have been half the tax on the 2008 profit (that is, the figure that would have appeared in the current liabilities at the end of 2008), plus half of the 2009 taxation charge (that is, $16 + (\frac{1}{2} \times 46) = 39$). Probably the easiest way to deduce the amount paid during the year to 31 December 2009 is by following this approach:

	£m
Taxation owed at start of the year (from the statement of financial position as at 31 December 2008)	16
Taxation charge for the year (from the income statement)	46
	62
Less Taxation owed at the end of the year (from the statement of financial position as at 31 December 2009)	(23)
Taxation paid during the year	39

> This follows the logic that if we start with what the business owed at the beginning of the year, add the increase in what was owed as a result of the current year's taxation charge and then deduct what was owed at the end, the resulting figure must be what was paid during the year.
>
> (6) It has been assumed that the loan notes were redeemed for their statement of financial position value. This is not, however, always the case.
>
> (7) The share issue raised £90 million, of which £50 million went into the share capital total on the statement of financial position and £40 million into share premium.
>
> (8) There were no 'cash equivalents', just cash (though negative).

What does the statement of cash flows tell us?

The statement of cash flows tells us how the business has generated cash during the period and where that cash has gone. Since cash is properly regarded as the lifeblood of just about any business, this is potentially very useful information.

Tracking the sources and uses of cash over several years could show financing trends that a reader of the statements could use to help to make judgements about the likely future behaviour of the business.

Looking specifically at the statement of cash flows for Torbryan plc, in Example 6.3, we can see the following:

- Net cash flow from operations was strong, much larger than the profit for the year figure, after taking account of the dividend paid. This would be expected because depreciation is deducted in arriving at profit. Working capital has absorbed some cash, which would be unsurprising if there had been an expansion of activity (sales revenue) over the year. From the information supplied, however, we do not know whether there was an expansion or not. (We have only one year's income statement.)

- There were net outflows of cash for investing activities, but this would not be unusual. Many items of property, plant and equipment have limited lives and need to be replaced with new ones. The expenditure during the year was not out of line with the depreciation expense for the year, which is not unusual for a business with a regular replacement programme for non-current assets.

- There was a fairly major outflow of cash to redeem some borrowings, partly offset by the proceeds of a share issue. This presumably represents a change of financing strategy. Together with the ploughed-back profit from trading, there has been a significant shift in the equity/borrowings balance.

Real World 6.3 looks at the statement of cash flows of an emerging business, LiDCO Group plc, that is experiencing negative cash flows as it seeks to establish a profitable market for its products.

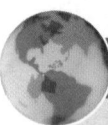

Real World 6.3

Not losing heart

LiDCO Group Plc has its shares quoted on the Alternative Investment Market (AIM). AIM is a junior market of the London Stock Exchange that specialises in the shares of smaller, up-and-coming companies.

LiDCO makes highly sophisticated equipment for monitoring the hearts of cardiac patients, typically in hospitals and clinics. The company was started by doctors and scientists. It has spent £6.8 million over ten years developing its products, obtaining registration for their use from both the UK and US authorities and creating manufacturing facilities.

LiDCO's statement of cash flows for the year to 31 January 2009 was as follows:

	£000
Net cash outflow from operating activities	(1,204)
Cash flows from investing activities	
Purchase of property, plant and equipment	(208)
Purchase of intangible fixed assets	(447)
Interest received	57
Net cash used in investing activities	(598)
Cash flows from financing activities	
Convertible loan repayment	(553)
Invoice discounting financing facility	364
Net cash outflow from financing activities	(189)
Net decrease in cash and cash equivalents	(1,991)

[Note that this was adapted from the statement that appeared in the company's annual report. Further details are provided in the notes to the accounts.]

To put these figures into context, the sales revenue for the year was £4.53 million. This means that the net cash outflow from operating activities was equal to 27 per cent of the revenue figure. (This was an improvement, since it was 30 per cent in 2008, nearly 40 per cent in 2007 and over 50 per cent in 2006.) Such cash flow profiles are fairly typical of 'high-tech' businesses that have enormous start-up costs to bring their products to the market in sufficient quantities to yield a profit. Of course, not all such businesses achieve this, but LiDCO seems confident of success.

Sources: LiDCO Group Plc Annual Report 2009 and AIM company profile, www.londonstockexchange.com.

Problems with IAS 7

IAS 7 *Statement of Cash Flows* does not enjoy universal acclaim. Its critics argue that the standard is too permissive in the description and classification of important items. One example is expenditure that does not produce a recognised asset but which may benefit future periods. This may include such things as advertising, exploration activities and research and development. In practice, these may be classified as either cash flows from operating activities or as cash flows from investing activities. Not only can this be confusing to users but by classifying this expenditure as investing activities it is possible to flatter cash flows from operating activities, which is a key measure.

Some believe that the standard would inspire greater confidence among users if it insisted that only the direct method be used to calculate cash flows from operating activities. Supporters of the direct method argue that, being cash-based, it provides greater clarity by setting out operating cash receipts and payments. No accrual-based adjustments are made and therefore it is less susceptible to manipulation than the indirect approach, which has been described as 'a gift to dodgy companies'. (See reference 1 at the end of the chapter.) In its defence, however, it should be said that the indirect approach may help to shed light on the quality of reported profits by reconciling profit with the net cash from operating activities for a period. A business must demonstrate an ability to convert profits into cash and so revealing the link between profits and cash is important.

IAS 7 is also criticised for failing to require cash flows to be reconciled with movements in net debt, which may be defined as borrowings less any cash and cash equivalents. This reconciliation, so it is argued, would help users to gain a better understanding of movements in net debt and the management of cash flows. Net debt is often seen as a useful indicator of business solvency and so linking movements in this figure to the statement of cash flows may be important. Although not required to do so, many listed UK businesses provide this reconciliation as additional information. This is, at least partly, for historical reasons: the standard that preceded IAS 7 required this information.

Example 6.4 below illustrates how this reconciliation may be carried out.

Example 6.4

Based on the information in the financial statements of Torbryan for the financial years ended 31 December 2008 and 2009 (see Example 6.3), the following reconciliation of net cash flow to movement in net debt for the year to 31 December 2009 can be carried out.

Reconciliation of net cash flow to movement in net debt for the year to 31 December 2009

	£m
Net increase in cash and cash equivalents during the year	12
Repayment of loan notes	150
Decrease in net debt during the year	162
Net debt at 1 January 2009 (400 + 68*)	468
Net debt at 31 December 2009 (250 + 56)	(306)
Decrease in net debt during the year	162

* We saw earlier that a bank overdraft is normally viewed as negative cash. An overdraft is added to other borrowings to derive the net debt, whereas a positive cash balance would be deducted.

We can see that the net debt has been reduced largely through the repayment of loan notes but partly through a reduction in the overdraft.

Self-assessment question 6.1

Touchstone plc's income statements for the years ended 31 December 2008 and 2009 and the statements of financial position as at 31 December 2008 and 2009 are as follows:

Income statements for the years ended 2008 and 2009

	2008 £m	2009 £m
Revenue	173	207
Cost of sales	(96)	(101)
Gross profit	77	106
Distribution expenses	(18)	(20)
Administrative expenses	(24)	(26)
Other operating income	3	4
Operating profit	38	64
Interest payable	(2)	(4)
Profit before taxation	36	60
Taxation	(8)	(16)
Profit for the year	28	44

Statements of financial position as at 31 December 2008 and 2009

	2008 £m	2009 £m
ASSETS		
Non-current assets		
Property, plant and equipment		
Land and buildings	94	110
Plant and machinery	53	62
	147	172
Current assets		
Inventories	25	24
Treasury bills (short-term investments)	–	15
Trade receivables	16	26
Cash at bank and in hand	4	4
	45	69
Total assets	192	241
EQUITY AND LIABILITIES		
Equity		
Called-up ordinary share capital	100	100
Retained earnings	30	56
	130	156
Non-current liabilities		
Borrowings – Loan notes (10%)	20	40
Current liabilities		
Trade payables	38	37
Taxation	4	8
	42	45
Total equity and liabilities	192	241

Included in 'cost of sales', 'distribution expenses' and 'administrative expenses', depreciation was as follows:

	2008 £m	2009 £m
Land and buildings	5	6
Plant and machinery	6	10

There were no non-current asset disposals in either year.

The interest payable expense equalled the cash payment made during the year, in both cases.

The business paid dividends on ordinary shares of £14 million during 2008 and £18 million during 2009.

The Treasury bills represent a short-term investment of funds that will be used shortly in operations. There is insignificant risk that this investment will lose value.

Required:

Prepare a statement of cash flows for the business for 2009.

The answer to this question can be found at the back of the book on pages 727–8.

Summary

The main points of this chapter may be summarised as follows:

The need for a statement of cash flows

- Cash is important because no business can operate without it.
- The statement of cash flows is specifically designed to reveal movements in cash over a period.
- Cash movements cannot be readily detected from the income statement, which focuses on revenue and expenses rather than on cash receipts and cash payments.
- Profit (or loss) and cash generated for the period are rarely equal.
- The statement of cash flows is a primary financial statement, along with the income statement and the statement of financial position.

Preparing the statement of cash flows

- The layout of the statement contains three categories of cash movement:
    - cash flows from operating activities;
    - cash flows from investing activities;
    - cash flows from financing activities.
- The total of the cash movements under these three categories will provide the net increase or decrease in cash and cash equivalents for the period.
- A reconciliation can be undertaken to check that the opening balance of cash and cash equivalents plus the net increase (or decrease) for the period equals the closing balance.

Calculating the cash generated from operations

- The net cash flows from operating activities can be derived by either the direct method or the indirect method.
- The direct method is based on an analysis of the cash records for the period, whereas the indirect method uses information contained within the income statement and statements of financial position of the business.
- The indirect method takes the net operating profit for the period, adds back any depreciation charge and then adjusts for changes in inventories, receivables and payables during the period.

Interpreting the statement of cash flows

- The statement of cash flows shows the main sources and uses of cash.
- Tracking the cash movements over several periods may reveal financing and investing patterns and may help predict future management action.

Problems with IAS 7

- IAS 7 has been criticised for being too permissive in the description and classification of important items and for allowing businesses to adopt the indirect method for determining net cash from operating activities.
- There have also been calls for movements in net debt to be reconciled with cash flows.

 Now check your progress in your personal Study Plan

→ **Key terms**

direct method   p. 209   working capital   p. 211
indirect method   p. 209

Reference

1 'Cash flow statements', *Financial Times*, 25 August 2005, FT.com.

Further reading

If you would like to explore the topics covered in this chapter in more depth, we recommend the following books:

A Guide Through International Financial Reporting Standards (IFRSs) 2008, IASC Foundation Education, July 2008.

Corporate Financial Accounting and Reporting, *Sutton, T.*, 2nd edn, Financial Times Prentice Hall, 2004, chapters 6 and 18.

Financial Accounting and Reporting, *Elliott B. and Elliott J.*, 13th edn, Financial Times Prentice Hall, 2010, chapter 27.

Insights into IFRS, *KPMG*, 5th edn, 2008/9, Thomson, 2008, Section 2.3.

Review questions

Answers to these questions can be found at the back of the book on pages 742–3.

6.1 The typical business outside the service sector has about 50 per cent more of its resources tied up in inventories than in cash, yet there is no call for an 'inventories flow statement' to be prepared. Why is cash regarded as more important than inventories?

6.2 What is the difference between the direct and indirect methods of deducing cash generated from operations?

6.3 Taking each of the categories of the statement of cash flows in turn, in which direction would you normally expect the cash flow to be? Explain your answer.

(a) Cash flows from operating activities.
(b) Cash flows from investing activities.
(c) Cash flows from financing activities.

6.4 What causes the profit for the year not to equal the net cash inflow?

Exercises

Exercises 6.3 to 6.8 are more advanced than 6.1 and 6.2. Those with **coloured numbers** have answers at the back of the book, starting on page 763.

If you wish to try more exercises, visit the students' side of the Companion Website and MyAccountingLab.

6.1 How will each of the following events ultimately affect the amount of cash?

(a) An increase in the level of inventories.
(b) A rights issue of ordinary shares.
(c) A bonus issue of ordinary shares.
(d) Writing off part of the value of some inventories.
(e) The disposal of a large number of the business's shares by a major shareholder.
(f) Depreciating a non-current asset.

6.2 The following information has been taken from the financial statements of Juno plc for last year and the year before last:

	Year before last £m	Last year £m
Operating profit	156	187
Depreciation charged in arriving at operating profit	47	55
Inventories held at the end of:	27	31
Trade receivables at the end of:	24	23
Trade payables at the end of:	15	17

Required:
What is the figure for cash generated from the operations for Juno plc for last year?

6.3   Torrent plc's income statement for the year ended 31 December 2009 and the statements of financial position as at 31 December 2008 and 2009 are as follows:

Income statement for the year ended 31 December 2009

	£m
Revenue	623
Cost of sales	(353)
Gross profit	270
Distribution expenses	(71)
Administrative expenses	(30)
Rental income	27
Operating profit	196
Interest payable	(26)
Profit before taxation	170
Taxation	(36)
Profit for the year	134

Statements of financial position as at 31 December 2008 and 2009

	2008 £m	2009 £m
ASSETS		
Non-current assets		
Property, plant and equipment		
Land and buildings	310	310
Plant and machinery	325	314
	635	624
Current assets		
Inventories	41	35
Trade receivables	139	145
	180	180
Total assets	815	804
EQUITY AND LIABILITIES		
Equity		
Called-up ordinary share capital	200	300
Share premium account	40	–
Revaluation reserve	69	9
Retained earnings	123	197
	432	506
Non-current liabilities		
Borrowings – Loan notes	250	150
Current liabilities		
Borrowings (all bank overdraft)	56	89
Trade payables	54	41
Taxation	23	18
	133	148
Total equity and liabilities	815	804

During 2009, the business spent £67 million on additional plant and machinery. There were no other non-current asset acquisitions or disposals.

There was no share issue for cash during the year. The interest payable expense was equal in amount to the cash outflow. A dividend of £60 million was paid.

Required:

Prepare the statement of cash flows for Torrent plc for the year ended 31 December 2009.

6.4   Chen plc's income statements for the years ended 31 December 2008 and 2009 and the statements of financial position as at 31 December 2008 and 2009 are as follows:

Income statements for the years ended 31 December 2008 and 2009

	2008 £m	2009 £m
Revenue	207	153
Cost of sales	(101)	(76)
Gross profit	106	77
Distribution expenses	(22)	(20)
Administrative expenses	(20)	(28)
Operating profit	64	29
Interest payable	(4)	(4)
Profit before taxation	60	25
Taxation	(16)	(6)
Profit for the year	44	19

Statements of financial position as at 31 December 2008 and 2009

	2008 £m	2009 £m
ASSETS		
Non-current assets		
Property, plant and equipment		
Land and buildings	110	130
Plant and machinery	62	56
	172	186
Current assets		
Inventories	24	25
Trade receivables	26	25
Cash at bank and in hand	19	–
	69	50
Total assets	241	236
EQUITY AND LIABILITIES		
Equity		
Called-up ordinary share capital	100	100
Retained earnings	56	57
	156	157
Non-current liabilities		
Borrowings – Loan notes (10%)	40	40
Current liabilities		
Borrowings (all bank overdraft)	–	2
Trade payables	37	34
Taxation	8	3
	45	39
Total equity and liabilities	241	236

Included in 'cost of sales', 'distribution expenses' and 'administrative expenses', depreciation was as follows:

	2008 £m	2009 £m
Land and buildings	6	10
Plant and machinery	10	12

There were no non-current asset disposals in either year. The amount of cash paid for interest equalled the expense in both years. Dividends were paid totalling £18 million in each year.

Required:

Prepare a statement of cash flows for the business for 2009.

6.5 The following are the financial statements for Nailsea plc for the years ended 30 June 2008 and 2009:

Income statement for years ended 30 June

	2008 £m	2009 £m
Revenue	1,230	2,280
Operating expenses	(722)	(1,618)
Depreciation	(270)	(320)
Operating profit	238	342
Interest payable	–	(27)
Profit before taxation	238	315
Taxation	(110)	(140)
Profit for the year	128	175

Statements of financial position as at 30 June

	2008 £m	2009 £m
ASSETS		
Non-current assets		
Property, plant and equipment (at carrying amount)		
Land and buildings	1,500	1,900
Plant and machinery	810	740
	2,310	2,640
Current assets		
Inventories	275	450
Trade receivables	100	250
Bank	–	118
	375	818
Total assets	2,685	3,458
EQUITY AND LIABILITIES		
Equity		
Share capital (fully paid £1 shares)	1,400	1,600
Share premium account	200	300
Retained profits	828	958
	2,428	2,858
Non-current liabilities		
Borrowings – 9% Loan notes (repayable 2011)	–	300
Current liabilities		
Borrowings (all bank overdraft)	32	–
Trade payables	170	230
Taxation	55	70
	257	300
Total equity and liabilities	2,685	3,458

There were no disposals of non-current assets in either year. Dividends were paid in 2008 and 2009 of £40 million and £45 million, respectively.

Required:

Prepare a statement of cash flows for Nailsea plc for the year ended 30 June 2009.

6.6 The following financial statements for Blackstone plc are a slightly simplified set of published accounts. Blackstone plc is an engineering business that developed a new range of products in 2007. These products now account for 60 per cent of its turnover.

Income statement for the years ended 31 March

	Notes	2008 £m	2009 £m
Revenue		7,003	11,205
Cost of sales		(3,748)	(5,809)
Gross profit		3,255	5,396
Operating expenses		(2,205)	(3,087)
Operating profit		1,050	2,309
Interest payable	1	(216)	(456)
Profit before taxation		834	1,853
Taxation		(210)	(390)
Profit for the year		624	1,463

Statements of financial position as at 31 March

	Notes	2008 £m	2009 £m
ASSETS			
Non-current assets			
Property, plant and equipment	2	4,300	7,535
Intangible assets	3	–	700
		4,300	8,235
Current assets			
Inventories		1,209	2,410
Trade receivables		641	1,173
Cash at bank		123	–
		1,973	3,583
Total assets		6,273	11,818
EQUITY AND LIABILITIES			
Equity			
Share capital		1,800	1,800
Share premium		600	600
Capital reserves		352	352
Retained profits		685	1,748
		3,437	4,500
Non-current liabilities			
Borrowings – Bank loan (repayable 2013)		1,800	3,800
Current liabilities			
Trade payables		931	1,507
Taxation		105	195
Borrowings (all bank overdraft)		–	1,816
		1,036	3,518
Total equity and liabilities		6,273	11,818

Notes:

(1) The expense and the cash outflow for interest payable are equal.

(2) The movements in property, plant and equipment during the year are set out below.

	Land and buildings £m	Plant and machinery £m	Fixtures and fittings £m	Total £m
Cost				
At 1 April 2008	4,500	3,850	2,120	10,470
Additions	–	2,970	1,608	4,578
Disposals	–	(365)	(216)	(581)
At 31 March 2009	4,500	6,455	3,512	14,467
Depreciation				
At 1 April 2008	1,275	3,080	1,815	6,170
Charge for year	225	745	281	1,251
Disposals	–	(305)	(184)	(489)
At 31 March 2009	1,500	3,520	1,912	6,932
Carrying amount				
At 31 March 2009	3,000	2,935	1,600	7,535

(3) Intangible assets represent the amounts paid for the goodwill of another engineering business acquired during the year.

(4) Proceeds from the sale of non-current assets in the year ended 31 March 2009 amounted to £54 million.

(5) Dividends were paid on ordinary shares of £300 million in 2008 and £400 million in 2009.

Required:

Prepare a statement of cash flows for Blackstone plc for the year ended 31 March 2009. (*Hint*: A loss (deficit) on disposal of non-current assets is simply an additional amount of depreciation and should be dealt with as such in preparing the statement of cash flows.)

6.7 Simplified financial statements for York plc are as follows:

Income statement for the year ended 30 September 2009

	£m
Revenue	290.0
Cost of sales	(215.0)
Gross profit	75.0
Operating expenses (Note 1)	(62.0)
Operating profit	13.0
Interest payable (Note 2)	(3.0)
Profit before taxation	10.0
Taxation	(2.6)
Profit for the year	7.4

Statement of financial position as at 30 September

	2008 £m	2009 £m
ASSETS		
Non-current assets (Note 4)	80.0	85.0
Current assets		
Inventories and trade receivables	119.8	122.1
Cash at bank	9.2	16.6
	129.0	138.7
Total assets	209.0	223.7
EQUITY AND LIABILITIES		
Equity		
Share capital	35.0	40.0
Share premium account	30.0	30.0
Reserves	31.0	34.9
	96.0	104.9
Non-current liabilities		
Borrowings	32.0	35.0
Current liabilities		
Trade payables	80.0	82.5
Taxation	1.0	1.3
	81.0	83.8
Total equity and liabilities	209.0	223.7

Notes:

(1) Operating expenses include depreciation of £13 million and a surplus of £3.2 million on the sale of non-current assets.

(2) The expense and the cash outflow for interest payable are equal.

(3) A dividend of £3.5 million was paid during 2009.

(4) Non-current asset costs and depreciation:

	Cost £m	Accumulated depreciation £m	Carrying amount £m
At 1 October 2008	120.0	40.0	80.0
Disposals	(10.0)	(8.0)	(2.0)
Additions	20.0		20.0
Depreciation		13.0	(13.0)
At 30 September 2009	130.0	45.0	85.0

Required:

Prepare a statement of cash flows for York plc for the year ended 30 September 2009.

6.8 The statements of financial position of Axis plc as at 31 December 2008 and 2009 and the income statement for the year ended 31 December 2009 were as follows:

Statements of financial position as at 31 December

	2008		2009	
	£m	£m	£m	£m
ASSETS				
Non-current assets				
Property, plant and equipment				
Land and building at cost	130		130	
Accumulated depreciation	(30)	100	(32)	98
Plant and machinery at cost	70		80	
Accumulated depreciation	(17)	53	(23)	57
		153		155
Current assets				
Inventories		25		24
Trade receivables		16		26
Short-term investments		–		12
Cash at bank and in hand		–		7
		41		69
Total assets		194		224
EQUITY AND LIABILITIES				
Equity				
Share capital		100		100
Retained earnings		36		40
		136		140
Non-current liabilities				
Borrowings – 10% loan notes		20		40
Current liabilities				
Trade payables		31		36
Taxation		7		8
		38		44
Total equity and liabilities		194		224

Income statement for the year ended 31 December 2009

	£m
Revenue	173
Cost of sales	(96)
Gross profit	77
Sundry operating expenses	(24)
Deficit on sale of non-current asset	(1)
Depreciation – buildings	(2)
– plant	(16)
Operating profit	34
Interest receivable	2
Interest payable	(2)
Profit before taxation	34
Taxation	(16)
Profit for the year	18

During the year, plant (a non-current asset) costing £15 million and with accumulated depreciation of £10 million was sold.

The short-term investments were government securities, where there was little or no risk of loss of value.

The expense and the cash outflow for interest payable were equal.

During 2009 a dividend of £14 million was paid.

Required:

Prepare a statement of cash flows for Axis plc for the year ended 31 December 2009.

CHAPTER 7

Analysing and interpreting financial statements

Introduction

In this chapter we shall consider the analysis and interpretation of the financial statements that we discussed in Chapters 2, 3 and 6. We shall see how financial (or accounting) ratios can help in assessing the financial health of a business. We shall also consider the problems that are encountered when applying this technique.

Financial ratios can be used to examine various aspects of financial position and performance and are widely used for planning and control purposes. As we shall see in later chapters, they can be very helpful to managers in a wide variety of decision areas, such as profit planning, pricing, working-capital management, financial structure and dividend policy.

Learning outcomes

When you have completed this chapter, you should be able to:

- Identify the major categories of ratios that can be used for analysis purposes.

- Calculate important ratios for assessing the financial performance and position of a business, and explain the significance of the ratios calculated.

- Discuss the limitations of ratios as a tool of financial analysis.

- Discuss the use of ratios in helping to predict financial failure.

MyAccountingLab *Remember to create your own personalised Study Plan*

Financial ratios

Financial ratios provide a quick and relatively simple means of assessing the financial health of a business. A ratio simply relates one figure appearing in the financial statements to some other figure appearing there (for example, operating profit in relation to capital employed) or, perhaps, to some resource of the business (for example, operating profit per employee, sales revenue per square metre of selling space, and so on).

Ratios can be very helpful when comparing the financial health of different businesses. Differences may exist between businesses in the scale of operations, and so a direct comparison of, say, the operating profit generated by each business may be misleading. By expressing operating profit in relation to some other measure (for example, capital [or funds] employed), the problem of scale is eliminated. A business with an operating profit of, say, £10,000 and capital employed of £100,000 can be compared with a much larger business with an operating profit of, say, £80,000 and capital employed of £1,000,000 by the use of a simple ratio. The operating profit to capital employed ratio for the smaller business is 10 per cent (that is, (10,000/100,000) × 100%) and the same ratio for the larger business is 8 per cent (that is, (80,000/1,000,000) × 100%). These ratios can be directly compared whereas comparison of the absolute operating profit figures would be much less meaningful. The need to eliminate differences in scale through the use of ratios can also apply when comparing the performance of the same business over time.

By calculating a small number of ratios it is often possible to build up a good picture of the position and performance of a business. It is not surprising, therefore, that ratios are widely used by those who have an interest in businesses and business performance. Although ratios are not difficult to calculate, they can be difficult to interpret, and so it is important to appreciate that they are really only the starting point for further analysis.

Ratios help to highlight the financial strengths and weaknesses of a business, but they cannot, by themselves, explain why those strengths or weaknesses exist or why certain changes have occurred. Only a detailed investigation will reveal these underlying reasons. Ratios tend to enable us to know which questions to ask, rather than provide the answers.

Ratios can be expressed in various forms, for example as a percentage or as a proportion. The way that a particular ratio is presented will depend on the needs of those who will use the information. Although it is possible to calculate a large number of ratios, only a few, based on key relationships, tend to be helpful to a particular user. Many ratios that could be calculated from the financial statements (for example, rent payable in relation to current assets) may not be considered because there is no clear or meaningful relationship between the two items.

There is no generally accepted list of ratios that can be applied to the financial statements, nor is there a standard method of calculating many ratios. Variations in both the choice of ratios and their calculation will be found in practice. However, it is important to be consistent in the way in which ratios are calculated for comparison purposes. The ratios that we shall discuss here are those that are widely used. They are popular because many consider them to be among the more important for decision-making purposes.

Financial ratio classifications

Ratios can be grouped into categories, each of which relates to a particular aspect of financial performance or position. The following broad categories provide a useful basis for explaining the nature of the financial ratios to be dealt with. There are five of them:

- *Profitability*. Businesses generally exist with the primary purpose of creating wealth for their owners. Profitability ratios provide insights relating to the degree of success in achieving this purpose. They express the profit made (or figures bearing on profit, such as sales revenue or overheads) in relation to other key figures in the financial statements or to some business resource.
- *Efficiency*. Ratios may be used to measure the efficiency with which particular resources have been used within the business. These ratios are also referred to as *activity* ratios.
- *Liquidity*. It is vital to the survival of a business that there are sufficient liquid resources available to meet maturing obligations (that is, amounts owing that must be paid in the near future). Some liquidity ratios examine the relationship between liquid resources held and amounts due for payment in the near future.
- *Financial gearing*. This is the relationship between the contribution to financing the business made by the owners of the business and the amount contributed by others, in the form of loans. The level of gearing has an important effect on the degree of risk associated with a business, as we shall see. Gearing is, therefore, something that managers must consider when making financing decisions. Gearing ratios tend to highlight the extent to which the business uses borrowings.
- *Investment*. Certain ratios are concerned with assessing the returns and performance of shares in a particular business from the perspective of shareholders who are not involved with the management of the business.

The analyst must be clear *who* the target users are and *why* they need the information. Different users of financial information are likely to have different information needs, which will in turn determine the ratios that they find useful. For example, shareholders are likely to be particularly interested in their returns in relation to the level of risk associated with their investment. Profitability, investment and gearing ratios will, therefore, be of particular interest. Long-term lenders are concerned with the long-term viability of the business and, to help them to assess this, the profitability and gearing ratios of the business are also likely to be of particular interest. Short-term lenders, such as suppliers of goods and services on credit, may be interested in the ability of the business to repay the amounts owing in the short term. As a result, the liquidity ratios should be of interest.

We shall consider ratios falling into each of the five categories (profitability, efficiency, liquidity, gearing and investment) a little later in the chapter.

The need for comparison

Merely calculating a ratio will not tell us very much about the position or performance of a business. For example, if a ratio revealed that the business was generating £100 in sales revenue per square metre of floor space, it would not be possible to deduce from this information alone whether this particular level of performance was good, bad or indifferent. It is only when we compare this ratio with some 'benchmark' that the information can be interpreted and evaluated.

Activity 7.1

Can you think of any bases that could be used to compare a ratio you have calculated from the financial statements of a particular period?
  We feel that there are three sensible possibilities.

You may have thought of the following bases:

- past periods for the same business
- similar businesses for the same or past periods
- planned performance for the business.

We shall now take a closer look at these three in turn.

Past periods

By comparing the ratio we have calculated with the same ratio, but for a previous period, it is possible to detect whether there has been an improvement or deterioration in performance. Indeed, it is often useful to track particular ratios over time (say, five or ten years) to see whether it is possible to detect trends. The comparison of ratios from different periods brings certain problems, however. In particular, there is always the possibility that trading conditions were quite different in the periods being compared. There is the further problem that, when comparing the performance of a single business over time, operating inefficiencies may not be clearly exposed. For example, the fact that sales revenue per employee has risen by 10 per cent over the previous period may at first sight appear to be satisfactory. This may not be the case, however, if similar businesses have shown an improvement of 50 per cent for the same period. Finally, there is the problem that inflation may have distorted the figures on which the ratios are based. Inflation can lead to an overstatement of profit and an understatement of asset values, as will be discussed later in the chapter.

Similar businesses

In a competitive environment, a business must consider its performance in relation to that of other businesses operating in the same industry. Survival may depend on its ability to achieve comparable levels of performance. A useful basis for comparing a particular ratio, therefore, is the ratio achieved by similar businesses during the same period. This basis is not, however, without its problems. Competitors may have different year ends, and therefore trading conditions may not be identical. They may also have different accounting policies, which can have a significant effect on reported profits and asset values (for example, different methods of calculating depreciation or valuing inventories). Finally, it may be difficult to obtain the financial statements of competitor businesses. Sole proprietorships and partnerships, for example, are not obliged to make their financial statements available to the public. In the case of limited companies, there is a legal obligation to do so. However, a diversified business may not provide a breakdown of activities that is sufficiently detailed to enable analysts to compare the activities with those of other businesses.

Planned performance

Ratios may be compared with the targets that management developed before the start of the period under review. The comparison of planned performance with actual performance may therefore be a useful way of revealing the level of achievement attained. However, the planned levels of performance must be based on realistic assumptions if they are to be useful for comparison purposes.

Planned performance is likely to be the most valuable benchmark against which managers may assess their own business. Businesses tend to develop planned ratios for each aspect of their activities. When formulating its plans, a business may usefully take account of its own past performance and that of other businesses. There is no reason, however, why a particular business should seek to achieve either its own previous performance or that of other businesses. Neither of these may be seen as an appropriate target.

Analysts outside the business do not normally have access to the business's plans. For these people, past performance and the performances of other, similar, businesses may provide the only practical benchmarks.

Calculating the ratios

Probably the best way to explain financial ratios is through an example. Example 7.1 provides a set of financial statements from which we can calculate important ratios.

Example 7.1

The following financial statements relate to Alexis plc, which operates a wholesale carpet business:

Statements of financial position (balance sheets) as at 31 March

	2008 £m	2009 £m
ASSETS		
Non-current assets		
Property, plant and equipment (at cost less depreciation)		
Land and buildings	381	427
Fixtures and fittings	129	160
	510	587
Current assets		
Inventories at cost	300	406
Trade receivables	240	273
Cash at bank	4	–
	544	679
Total assets	1,054	1,266
EQUITY AND LIABILITIES		
Equity		
£0.50 ordinary shares (Note 1)	300	300
Retained earnings	263	234
	563	534
Non-current liabilities		
Borrowings – 9% loan notes (secured)	200	300
Current liabilities		
Trade payables	261	354
Taxation	30	2
Short-term borrowings (all bank overdraft)	–	76
	291	432
Total equity and liabilities	1,054	1,266

Income statements for the year ended 31 March

	2008 £m	2009 £m
Revenue (Note 2)	2,240	2,681
Cost of sales (Note 3)	(1,745)	(2,272)
Gross profit	495	409
Operating expenses	(252)	(362)
Operating profit	243	47
Interest payable	(18)	(32)
Profit before taxation	225	15
Taxation	(60)	(4)
Profit for the year	165	11

Statement of cash flows for the year ended 31 March

	2008 £m	2008 £m	2009 £m	2009 £m
Cash flows from operating activities				
Profit, after interest, before taxation	225		15	
Adjustments for:				
Depreciation	26		33	
Interest expense	18		32	
	269		80	
Increase in inventories	(59)		(106)	
Increase in trade receivables	(17)		(33)	
Increase in trade payables	58		93	
Cash generated from operations	251		34	
Interest paid	(18)		(32)	
Taxation paid	(63)		(32)	
Dividend paid	(40)		(40)	
Net cash from/(used in) operating activities		130		(70)
Cash flows from investing activities				
Payments to acquire property, plant and equipment	(77)		(110)	
Net cash used in investing activities		(77)		(110)
Cash flows from financing activities				
Issue of loan notes	–		100	
Net cash from financing activities		–		100
Net increase in cash and cash equivalents		53		(80)
Cash and cash equivalents at start of year				
Cash/(overdraft)		(49)		4
Cash and cash equivalents at end of year				
Cash/(overdraft)		4		(76)

Notes:

(1) The market value of the shares of the business at the end of the year was £2.50 for 2008 and £1.50 for 2009.

(2) All sales and purchases are made on credit.

(3) The cost of sales figure can be analysed as follows:

	2008 £m	2009 £m
Opening inventories	241	300
Purchases (Note 2)	1,804	2,378
	2,045	2,678
Closing inventories	(300)	(406)
Cost of sales	1,745	2,272

(4) At 31 March 2007, the trade receivables stood at £223 million and the trade payables at £203 million.

(5) A dividend of £40 million had been paid to the shareholders in respect of each of the years.

(6) The business employed 13,995 staff at 31 March 2008 and 18,623 at 31 March 2009.

(7) The business expanded its capacity during 2009 by setting up a new warehouse and distribution centre in the north of England.

(8) At 1 April 2007, the total of equity stood at £438 million and the total of equity and non-current liabilities stood at £638 million.

A brief overview

Before we start our detailed look at the ratios for Alexis plc (in Example 7.1), it is help-ful to take a quick look at what information is obvious from the financial statements. This will usually pick up some issues that the ratios may not be able to identify. It may also highlight some points that could help us in our interpretation of the ratios. Starting at the top of the statement of financial position, the following points can be noted:

- *Expansion of non-current assets*. These have increased by about 15 per cent (from £510 million to £587 million). Note 7 mentions a new warehouse and distribution centre, which may account for much of the additional investment in non-current assets. We are not told when this new facility was established, but it is quite possible that it was well into the year. This could mean that not much benefit was reflected in terms of additional sales revenue or cost saving during 2009. Sales revenue, in fact, expanded by about 20 per cent (from £2,240 million to £2,681 million), greater than the expansion in non-current assets.

- *Major expansion in the elements of working capital*. Inventories increased by about 35 per cent, trade receivables by about 14 per cent and trade payables by about 36 per cent between 2008 and 2009. These are major increases, particularly in inven-tories and payables (which are linked because the inventories are all bought on credit – see Note 2).

- *Reduction in the cash balance*. The cash balance fell from £4 million (in funds) to a £76 million overdraft, between 2008 and 2009. The bank may be putting the business under pressure to reverse this, which could raise difficulties.

- *Apparent debt capacity*. Comparing the non-current assets with the long-term borrowings implies that the business may well be able to offer security on further borrowing. This is because potential lenders usually look at the value of assets that can be offered as security when assessing loan requests. Lenders seem particularly attracted to land and, to a lesser extent, buildings as security. For example, at 31 March 2009, non-current assets had a carrying amount (the value at which they appeared in the statement of financial position) of £587 million, but long-term bor-rowing was only £300 million (though there was also an overdraft of £76 million). Carrying amounts are not normally, of course, market values. On the other hand, land and buildings tend to have a market value higher than their statement of financial position value due to inflation in property values.

- *Lower operating profit*. Though sales revenue expanded by 20 per cent between 2008 and 2009, both cost of sales and operating expenses rose by a greater percentage, leaving both gross profit and, particularly, operating profit massively reduced. The level of staffing, which increased by about 33 per cent (from 13,995 to 18,623 employees), may have greatly affected the operating expenses. (Without knowing when the additional employees were recruited during 2009, we cannot be sure of the effect on operating expenses.) Increasing staffing by 33 per cent must put an enormous strain on management, at least in the short term. It is not surprising, therefore, that 2009 was not successful for the business.

Having had a quick look at what is fairly obvious without calculating the normal ratios, we shall now go on to calculate and interpret them.

Profitability

The following ratios may be used to evaluate the profitability of the business:

- return on ordinary shareholders' funds
- return on capital employed
- operating profit margin
- gross profit margin.

We shall now look at each of these in turn.

Return on ordinary shareholders' funds (ROSF)

→ The **return on ordinary shareholders' funds ratio** compares the amount of profit for the period available to the owners, with the owners' average stake in the business during that same period. The ratio (which is normally expressed in percentage terms) is as follows:

$$ROSF = \frac{\text{Profit for the year (net profit) less any preference dividend}}{\text{Ordinary share capital} + \text{Reserves}} \times 100$$

The profit for the year (less preference dividend (if any)) is used in calculating the ratio, as this figure represents the amount of profit that is attributable to the owners.

In the case of Alexis plc, the ratio for the year ended 31 March 2008 is:

$$ROSF = \frac{165}{(438 + 563)/2} \times 100 = 33.0\%$$

Note that, when calculating the ROSF, the average of the figures for ordinary shareholders' funds as at the beginning and at the end of the year has been used. It is preferable to use an average figure as this is likely to be more representative. This is because the shareholders' funds did not have the same total throughout the year, yet we want to compare it with the profit earned during the whole period. We know, from Note 8, that the total of the shareholders' funds at 1 April 2007 was £438 millon. By a year later, however, it had risen to £563 millon, according to the statement of financial position as at 31 March 2008.

The easiest approach to calculating the average amount of shareholders' funds is to take a simple average based on the opening and closing figures for the year. This is often the only information available, as is the case with Example 7.1. Averaging in this way is generally valid for all ratios that combine a figure for a period (such as profit for the year) with one taken at a point in time (such as shareholders' funds).

Where not even the beginning-of-year figure is available, it is usually acceptable to use just the year-end figure. This is not ideal but, provided that this approach is consistently adopted, it should provide ratios that are useful.

Activity 7.2

Calculate the ROSF for Alexis plc for the year to 31 March 2009.

The ratio for 2009 is:

$$ROSF = \frac{11}{(563 + 534)/2} \times 100 = 2.0\%$$

Broadly, businesses seek to generate as high a value as possible for this ratio, provided that it is not achieved at the expense of potential future returns by, for example, taking on more risky activities. In view of this, the 2009 ratio is very poor by any standards; a bank deposit account will normally yield a better return than this. We need to try to find out why things went so badly wrong in 2009. As we look at other ratios, we should find some clues.

Return on capital employed (ROCE)

→ The **return on capital employed ratio** is a fundamental measure of business performance. This ratio expresses the relationship between the operating profit generated during a period and the average long-term capital invested in the business during that period.

The ratio is expressed in percentage terms and is as follows:

$$\text{ROCE} = \frac{\text{Operating profit}}{\text{Share capital} + \text{Reserves} + \text{Non-current liabilities}} \times 100$$

Note, in this case, that the profit figure used is the operating profit (that is, the profit *before* interest and taxation), because the ratio attempts to measure the returns to all suppliers of long-term finance before any deductions for interest payable on borrowings, or payments of dividends to shareholders, are made.

For the year to 31 March 2008, the ratio for Alexis plc is:

$$\text{ROCE} = \frac{243}{(638 + 763)/2} \times 100 = 34.7\%$$

ROCE is considered by many to be a primary measure of profitability. It compares inputs (capital invested) with outputs (operating profit). This comparison is vital in assessing the effectiveness with which funds have been deployed. Once again, an average figure for capital employed may be used where the information is available.

Activity 7.3

Calculate the ROCE for Alexis plc for the year to 31 March 2009.

For 2009, the ratio is:

$$\text{ROCE} = \frac{47}{(763 + 834)/2} \times 100 = 5.9\%$$

This ratio tells much the same story as ROSF; namely a poor performance, with the return on the assets being less than the rate that the business has to pay for most of its borrowed funds (that is, 10 per cent for the loan notes).

Real World 7.1 shows how financial ratios are used by businesses as a basis for setting profitability targets.

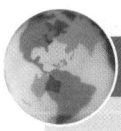

Real World 7.1

Targeting profitability

The ROCE ratio is widely used by businesses when establishing targets for profitability. These targets are sometimes made public and here are some examples:

Tesco plc, the supermarket business, in 2004 set a target to achieve a growth in ROCE of 2 per cent from its 2004 figure of 10.4 per cent. It achieved this with 12.5 per cent in 2006 and increased it further in 2007. Tesco then set a further 2 per cent target growth for ROCE for 2008 and beyond. The business achieved a 13 per cent rate of ROCE in 2009. Tesco uses performance against a target ROCE as a basis of rewarding its senior managers, indicating the importance that the business attaches to this measure of performance.

BSkyB plc, the satellite broadcaster, has a target ROCE of 15 per cent by 2011 for its broadband operation.

Air France-KLM, the world's largest airline (on the basis of sales revenue), has set itself the target of achieving a ROCE of 7 per cent.

Sources: Information taken from Tesco plc Annual Report 2009, 'BSkyB/triple play', *Financial Times*, 12 July 2006 and Air France-KLM, Press Release, 14 February 2008.

Real World 7.2 provides some indication of the levels of ROCE achieved by UK businesses.

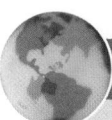

Real World 7.2

Achieving profitability

UK businesses reported an average ROCE of 11.6 per cent for the second quarter of 2009. This was down on the record rate of 15.1 per cent for the first quarter of 2007, the highest level of ROCE since the Office of National Statistics first kept records.

Service sector businesses were much the more successful with an average ROCE of 15.6 per cent, compared with 6.7 per cent among manufacturers. These compare with 15.7 per cent for service businesses and 10.2 per cent for manufacturers, averaged over 2006, 2007 and 2008. This suggests that despite the recession UK service businesses are maintaining their profitability quite well. Manufacturers, on the other hand, have suffered a large fall in profitability compared with that of recent years.

The difference in ROCE between the two sectors is accounted for by the higher capital intensity of manufacturing, according to the Office of National Statistics.

Source: Information taken from 'Corporate profitability', *Office of National Statistics*, www.statistics.gov.uk/cci, 17 October 2009.

Operating profit margin

The **operating profit margin ratio** relates the operating profit for the period to the sales revenue during that period. The ratio is expressed as follows:

$$\text{Operating profit margin} = \frac{\text{Operating profit}}{\text{Sales revenue}} \times 100$$

The operating profit (that is, profit before interest and taxation) is used in this ratio as it represents the profit from trading operations before the interest payable expense is taken into account. This is often regarded as the most appropriate measure of operational performance, when used as a basis of comparison, because differences arising from the way in which the business is financed will not influence the measure.

For the year ended 31 March 2008, Alexis plc's operating profit margin ratio is:

$$\text{Operating profit margin} = \frac{243}{2,240} \times 100 = 10.8\%$$

This ratio compares one output of the business (operating profit) with another output (sales revenue). The ratio can vary considerably between types of business. For example, supermarkets tend to operate on low prices and, therefore, low operating profit margins. This is done in an attempt to stimulate sales and thereby increase the total amount of operating profit generated. Jewellers, on the other hand, tend to have high operating profit margins but have much lower levels of sales volume. Factors such as the degree of competition, the type of customer, the economic climate and industry characteristics (such as the level of risk) will influence the operating profit margin of a business. This point is picked up again later in the chapter.

Activity 7.4

Calculate the operating profit margin for Alexis plc for the year to 31 March 2009.

The ratio for 2009 is:

$$\text{Operating profit margin} = \frac{47}{2,681} \times 100 = 1.8\%$$

Once again, a very weak performance compared with that of 2008. Whereas in 2008 for every £1 of sales revenue an average of 10.8p (that is, 10.8 per cent) was left as operating profit, after paying the cost of the carpets sold and other expenses of operating the business, for 2009 this had fallen to only 1.8p for every £1. It seems that the reason for the poor ROSF and ROCE ratios was partially, perhaps wholly, a high level of expenses relative to sales revenue. The next ratio should provide us with a clue as to how the sharp decline in this ratio occurred.

Real World 7.3 describes how one well-known business intends to increase its operating profit margin over time.

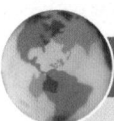

Real World 7.3

Operating profit margin taking off at BA

British Airways plc, the airline business, exceeded its 10 per cent operating profit margin target during the year to 31 March 2008. This target had been in existence since 2002.

The year to 31 March 2009 was rather less successful with the company sustaining an operating loss equal to 2.4 per cent of its sales revenue. The business put this down to 'incredibly difficult trading conditions' brought about by the recession.

Source: British Airways plc Annual Report 2009.

Gross profit margin

→ The **gross profit margin ratio** relates the gross profit of the business to the sales revenue generated for the same period. Gross profit represents the difference between sales revenue and the cost of sales. The ratio is therefore a measure of profitability in buying (or producing) and selling goods or services before any other expenses are taken into account. As cost of sales represents a major expense for many businesses, a change in this ratio can have a significant effect on the 'bottom line' (that is, the profit for the year). The gross profit margin ratio is calculated as follows:

$$\text{Gross profit margin} = \frac{\text{Gross profit}}{\text{Sales revenue}} \times 100$$

For the year to 31 March 2008, the ratio for Alexis plc is:

$$\text{Gross profit margin} = \frac{495}{2,240} \times 100 = 22.1\%$$

Activity 7.5

Calculate the gross profit margin for Alexis plc for the year to 31 March 2009.

The ratio for 2009 is:

$$\text{Gross profit margin} = \frac{409}{2,681} \times 100 = 15.3\%$$

The decline in this ratio means that gross profit was lower *relative* to sales revenue in 2009 than it had been in 2008. Bearing in mind that:

$$\text{Gross profit} = \text{Sales revenue} - \text{Cost of sales (or cost of goods sold)}$$

this means that cost of sales was higher *relative* to sales revenue in 2009, than in 2008. This could mean that sales prices were lower and/or that the purchase cost of carpets sold had increased. It is possible that both sales prices and carpets sold prices had reduced, but the former at a greater rate than the latter. Similarly they may both have increased, but with sales prices having increased at a lesser rate than the cost of the carpets.

Clearly, part of the decline in the operating profit margin ratio is linked to the dramatic decline in the gross profit margin ratio. Whereas, after paying for the carpets sold, for each £1 of sales revenue 22.1p was left to cover other operating expenses and leave an operating profit in 2008, this was only 15.3p in 2009.

The profitability ratios for the business over the two years can be set out as follows:

	2008 %	2009 %
ROSF	33.0	2.0
ROCE	34.7	5.9
Operating profit margin	10.8	1.8
Gross profit margin	22.1	15.3

Activity 7.6

What do you deduce from a comparison of the declines in the operating profit and gross profit margin ratios?

It occurs to us that the decline in the operating profit margin was 9 per cent (that is, 10.8 per cent to 1.8 per cent), whereas that of the gross profit margin was only 6.8 per cent (that is, from 22.1 per cent to 15.3 per cent). This can only mean that operating expenses were greater compared with sales revenue in 2009 than they had been in 2008. The declines in both ROSF and ROCE were caused partly, therefore, by the business incurring higher inventories purchasing costs relative to sales revenue and partly through higher operating expenses to sales revenue. We would need to compare these ratios with the planned levels for them before we could usefully assess the business's success.

The analyst must now carry out some investigation to discover what caused the increases in both cost of sales and operating expenses, relative to sales revenue, from 2008 to 2009. This will involve checking on what has happened with sales and inventories prices over the two years. Similarly, it will involve looking at each of the individual areas that make up operating expenses to discover which ones were responsible for the increase, relative to sales revenue. Here, further ratios, for example, staff expenses (wages and salaries) to sales revenue, could be calculated in an attempt to isolate the cause of the change from 2008 to 2009. In fact, as we discussed when we took an overview of the financial statements, the increase in staffing may well account for most of the increase in operating expenses.

Real World 7.4 is an article that discusses the reasons for improving profitability at 'Bollywood'.

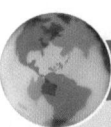

Real World 7.4

Investing in Bollywood

FT

Alas for investors, the economics of Bollywood have long been about as predictable as, but rather less uplifting than, the plotline of the average Hindi movie. The world's biggest movie market in terms of number of tickets sold – a massive 3.7bn – has traditionally offered miserable returns to its backers. Instead, revenues were swallowed up by a blend of piracy, taxes and inefficiencies.

Now the script appears to be changing. Big backers – in the shape of international entertainment giants such as Walt Disney and Viacom, and venture capitalists – are starting to enter Bollywood. With a brace of Indian film production companies listed on London's Alternative Investment Market and a third due to follow shortly, smaller investors are also getting in on the act. That is testament to improving industry dynamics. Digital technology and tougher regulation is helping reduce piracy while tax strains are being mitigated either by new rules at home – such as scrapping entertainment tax for multiplexes – or shifting production abroad.

Entertainment companies are also sharpening up their acts and evolving from one-stop shops to specialists in, say, production or distribution. Cleaner corporate structures enable them to access a broader range of financing. The economics of movie-making are improving too. Perhaps 40 per cent of Indian movies are now shot overseas, benefiting from tax breaks, 'captive' actors and producers and – in Europe – longer working days. As a result, a movie may be in the can in perhaps a quarter of the time it would normally take in India.

Evolution in other parts of the media world also plays into the hands of Bollywood moguls; for example, the growth in satellite TV means more channels to bid on movie licensing rights. Industry analysts reckon Bollywood now offers a return on capital employed of about 30 to 35 per cent, not too dissimilar from Hollywood. Years of tears followed by a happy ending? How Bollywood.

Source: 'Investing in Bollywood', Lex column, *Financial Times*, 25 June 2007.

Efficiency

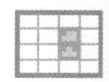

Efficiency ratios are used to try to assess how successfully the various resources of the business are managed. The following ratios consider some of the more important aspects of resource management:

- average inventories turnover period
- average settlement period for trade receivables
- average settlement period for trade payables
- sales revenue to capital employed
- sales revenue per employee.

We shall now look at each of these in turn.

Average inventories turnover period

Inventories often represent a significant investment for a business. For some types of business (for example, manufacturers and certain retailers), inventories may account for a substantial proportion of the total assets held (see Real World 16.1, page 640). The **average inventories turnover period ratio** measures the average period for which inventories are being held. The ratio is calculated as follows:

$$\text{Average inventories turnover period} = \frac{\text{Average inventories held}}{\text{Cost of sales}} \times 365$$

The average inventories for the period can be calculated as a simple average of the opening and closing inventories levels for the year. However, in the case of a highly seasonal business, where inventories levels may vary considerably over the year, a monthly average may be more appropriate.

In the case of Alexis plc, the inventories turnover period for the year ended 31 March 2008 is:

$$\text{Average inventories turnover period} = \frac{(241 + 300)/2}{1{,}745} \times 365 = 56.6 \text{ days}$$

(The opening inventories figure was taken from Note 3 to the financial statements.)

This means that, on average, the inventories held are being 'turned over' every 56.6 days. So, a carpet bought by the business on a particular day would, on average, have been sold about eight weeks later. A business will normally prefer a short inventories turnover period to a long one, because holding inventories has a cost, for example the opportunity cost of the funds tied up. When judging the amount of inventories to carry, the business must consider such things as the likely demand for the inventories, the possibility of supply shortages, the likelihood of price rises, the amount of storage space available and the perishability/susceptibility to obsolescence of the inventories. The management of inventories will be considered in more detail in Chapter 16.

This ratio is sometimes expressed in terms of weeks or months rather than days. Multiplying by 52 or 12, rather than 365, will achieve this.

Activity 7.7

Calculate the average inventories turnover period for Alexis plc for the year ended 31 March 2009.

The ratio for 2009 is:

$$\text{Average inventories turnover period} = \frac{(300 + 406)/2}{2,272} \times 365 = 56.7 \text{ days}$$

The inventories turnover period is virtually the same in both years.

Average settlement period for trade receivables

Selling on credit is the norm for most businesses, except for retailers. Trade receivables are a necessary evil. A business will naturally be concerned with the amount of funds tied up in trade receivables and try to keep this to a minimum. The speed of payment can have a significant effect on the business's cash flow. The **average settlement period for trade receivables ratio** calculates how long, on average, credit customers take to pay the amounts that they owe to the business. The ratio is as follows:

$$\frac{\text{Average settlement period}}{\text{for trade receivables}} = \frac{\text{Average trade receivables}}{\text{Credit sales revenue}} \times 365$$

A business will normally prefer a shorter average settlement period to a longer one as, once again, funds are being tied up that may be used for more profitable purposes. Although this ratio can be useful, it is important to remember that it produces an *average* figure for the number of days for which debts are outstanding. This average may be badly distorted by, for example, a few large customers who are very slow or very fast payers.

Since all sales made by Alexis plc are on credit, the average settlement period for trade receivables for the year ended 31 March 2008 is:

$$\text{Average settlement period for trade receivables} = \frac{(223 + 240)/2}{2,240} \times 365 = 37.7 \text{ days}$$

(The opening trade receivables figure was taken from Note 4 to the financial statements.)

Activity 7.8

Calculate the average settlement period for Alexis plc's trade receivables for the year ended 31 March 2009.

The ratio for 2009 is:

$$\text{Average settlement period for trade receivables} = \frac{(240 + 273)/2}{2{,}681} \times 365 = 34.9 \text{ days}$$

On the face of it, this reduction in the settlement period is welcome. It means that less cash was tied up in trade receivables for each £1 of sales revenue in 2009 than in 2008. Only if the reduction were achieved at the expense of customer goodwill or a high direct financial cost might the desirability of the reduction be questioned. For example, the reduction may have been due to chasing customers too vigorously or as a result of incurring higher expenses, such as discounts allowed to customers who pay quickly.

Real World 7.5 is an article that discusses how customers are unilaterally extending their payment terms as a result of the recession.

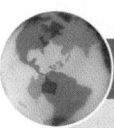

Real World 7.5

Taking too much credit

FT

Two-thirds of suppliers are being forced to accept arbitrary extensions of payment terms by their customers as pressure on businesses to conserve cash becomes more acute, a survey by the Institute of Credit Management has found.

The findings provide more evidence of the speed with which the recession is prompting many businesses to focus on preserving cash and managing working capital more tightly.

The findings come after the Department for Business, Enterprise and Regulatory Reform last week unveiled a voluntary 'prompt payment code', designed with the ICM. It aims to help small businesses by discouraging bigger companies from using their purchasing power to ease pressures on their cash flow by squeezing their supply chain.

In a poll of 600 members last month, the ICM asked whether any of their customers had tried arbitrarily to extend their payment terms in the previous three months. Sixty-seven per cent said Yes with the rest saying No.

For those answering Yes, 61 per cent said the extension applied retroactively as well as to future business, with 39 per cent saying it applied to all future business.

Philip King, ICM director general, said: 'We were certainly staggered by the volume and the proportion of respondents who said they had experienced that. It's no surprise that it's happening but for the number to be that high is a real surprise.'

The ICM is the largest organisation in Europe representing credit managers in trade credit, credit insurance and insolvency.

In some cases, it said, there was 'anecdotal evidence' that some companies were trying to delay paying their suppliers by challenging their invoices, but it stressed there was 'no scientific evidence' of an increase.

Challenging the accuracy of invoices is common practice, but there are signs it is being used more regularly to delay payment.

→

Real World 7.5 continued

The head of a global employment agency with operations in the UK said it had taken on more staff to process invoices. 'It used to be that if there was a mistake with one line, clients would pay the whole invoice and we'd resolve that one grey area. But now they're using one possible mistake as a way of withholding payment on the entire invoice,' said the executive.

Martin O'Donovan, an assistant director at the Association of Corporate Treasurers, said: 'People really are under strain and are pulling whatever levers they have got – even those that are not the most politic ones and perhaps not in the longer-term interest of the company.'

Source: 'Payment squeeze on suppliers', Jeremy Grant, *Financial Times*, 22 December 2008.

Average settlement period for trade payables

→ The **average settlement period for trade payables ratio** measures how long, on average, the business takes to pay those who have supplied goods and services on credit. The ratio is calculated as follows:

$$\text{Average settlement period for trade payables} = \frac{\text{Average trade payables}}{\text{Credit purchases}} \times 365$$

This ratio provides an average figure, which, like the average settlement period for trade receivables ratio, can be distorted by the payment period for one or two large suppliers.

As trade payables provide a free source of finance for the business, it is perhaps not surprising that some businesses attempt to increase their average settlement period for trade payables. However, such a policy can be taken too far and result in a loss of goodwill of suppliers. We shall return to the issues concerning the management of trade receivables and trade payables in Chapter 16.

For the year ended 31 March 2008, Alexis plc's average settlement period for trade payables is:

$$\text{Average settlement period for trade payables} = \frac{(203 + 261)/2}{1,804} \times 365 = 46.9 \text{ days}$$

(The opening trade payables figure was taken from Note 4 to the financial statements.)

Activity 7.9

Calculate the average settlement period for trade payables for Alexis plc for the year ended 31 March 2009.

The ratio for 2009 is:

$$\text{Average settlement period for trade payables} = \frac{(261 + 354)/2}{2,378} \times 365 = 47.2 \text{ days}$$

There was a very slight increase, between 2008 and 2009, in the average length of time that elapsed between buying inventories and services and paying for them. Had this increase been significant, it would, on the face of it, have been beneficial because the business is using free finance provided by suppliers. If, however, this is leading to a loss of supplier goodwill that could have adverse consequences for Alexis plc, it is not necessarily advantageous.

Sales revenue to capital employed

→ The **sales revenue to capital employed ratio** (or net asset turnover ratio) examines how effectively the assets of the business are being used to generate sales revenue. It is calculated as follows:

$$\text{Sales revenue to capital employed ratio} = \frac{\text{Sales revenue}}{\text{Share capital} + \text{Reserves} + \text{Non-current liabilities}}$$

Generally speaking, a higher net asset turnover ratio is preferred to a lower one. A higher ratio will normally suggest that assets are being used more productively in the generation of revenue. However, a very high ratio may suggest that the business is 'overtrading on its assets', that is, it has insufficient assets to sustain the level of sales revenue achieved. (Overtrading will be discussed in more detail later in the chapter.) When comparing this ratio for different businesses, factors such as the age and condition of assets held, the valuation bases for assets and whether assets are leased or owned outright can complicate interpretation.

A variation of this formula is to use the total assets less current liabilities (which is equivalent to long-term capital employed) in the denominator (lower part of the fraction). The identical result is obtained.

For the year ended 31 March 2008 this ratio for Alexis plc is:

$$\text{Sales revenue to capital employed} = \frac{2,240}{(638 + 763)/2} = 3.20 \text{ times}$$

Activity 7.10

Calculate the sales revenue to capital employed ratio for Alexis plc for the year ended 31 March 2009.

The sales revenue to capital employed ratio for 2009 is:

$$\text{Sales revenue to capital employed} = \frac{2,681}{(763 + 834)/2} = 3.36 \text{ times}$$

This seems to be an improvement, since in 2009 more sales revenue was being generated for each £1 of capital employed (£3.36) than was the case in 2008 (£3.20). Provided that overtrading is not an issue and that the additional sales are generating an acceptable profit, this is to be welcomed.

Sales revenue per employee

→ The **sales revenue per employee ratio** relates sales revenue generated to a particular business resource, that is, labour. It provides a measure of the productivity of the work-force. The ratio is:

$$\text{Sales revenue per employee} = \frac{\text{Sales revenue}}{\text{Number of employees}}$$

Generally, businesses would prefer to have a high value for this ratio, implying that they are using their staff efficiently.

For the year ended 31 March 2008, the ratio for Alexis plc is:

$$\text{Sales revenue per employee} = \frac{£2,240\text{m}}{13,995} = £160,057$$

Activity 7.11

Calculate the sales revenue per employee for Alexis plc for the year ended 31 March 2009.

The ratio for 2009 is:

$$\text{Sales revenue per employee} = \frac{£2,681\text{m}}{18,623} = £143,962$$

This represents a fairly significant decline and probably one that merits further investigation. As we discussed previously, the number of employees had increased quite notably (by about 33 per cent) during 2009 and the analyst will probably try to discover why this had not generated sufficient additional sales revenue to maintain the ratio at its 2008 level. It could be that the additional employees were not appointed until late in the year ended 31 March 2009.

The efficiency, or activity, ratios may be summarised as follows:

	2008	2009
Average inventories turnover period	56.6 days	56.7 days
Average settlement period for trade receivables	37.7 days	34.9 days
Average settlement period for trade payables	46.9 days	47.2 days
Sales revenue to capital employed (net asset turnover)	3.20 times	3.36 times
Sales revenue per employee	£160,057	£143,962

Activity 7.12

What do you deduce from a comparison of the efficiency ratios over the two years?

We feel that maintaining the inventories turnover period at the 2008 level might be reasonable, though whether this represents a satisfactory period can probably only be assessed by looking at the business's planned inventories period. The inventories holding period for other businesses operating in carpet retailing, particularly those regarded as the market leaders, may have been helpful in formulating the plans. On the face of things, a shorter receivables collection period and a longer payables payment period are both desirable. On the other hand, these may have been achieved at the cost of a loss of the goodwill of customers and suppliers, respectively. The increased net asset turnover ratio seems beneficial, provided that the business can manage this increase. The decline in the sales revenue per employee ratio is undesirable but, as we have already seen, is probably related to the dramatic increase in the level of staffing. As with the inventories turnover period, these other ratios need to be compared with the planned standard of efficiency.

Relationship between profitability and efficiency

In our earlier discussions concerning profitability ratios, we saw that return on capital employed (ROCE) is regarded as a key ratio by many businesses. The ratio is:

$$ROCE = \frac{\text{Operating profit}}{\text{Long-term capital employed}} \times 100$$

where long-term capital comprises share capital plus reserves plus long-term borrowings. This ratio can be broken down into two elements, as shown in Figure 7.1. The first ratio is the operating profit margin ratio, and the second is the sales revenue to capital employed (net asset turnover) ratio, both of which we discussed earlier.

Figure 7.1	The main elements of the ROCE ratio

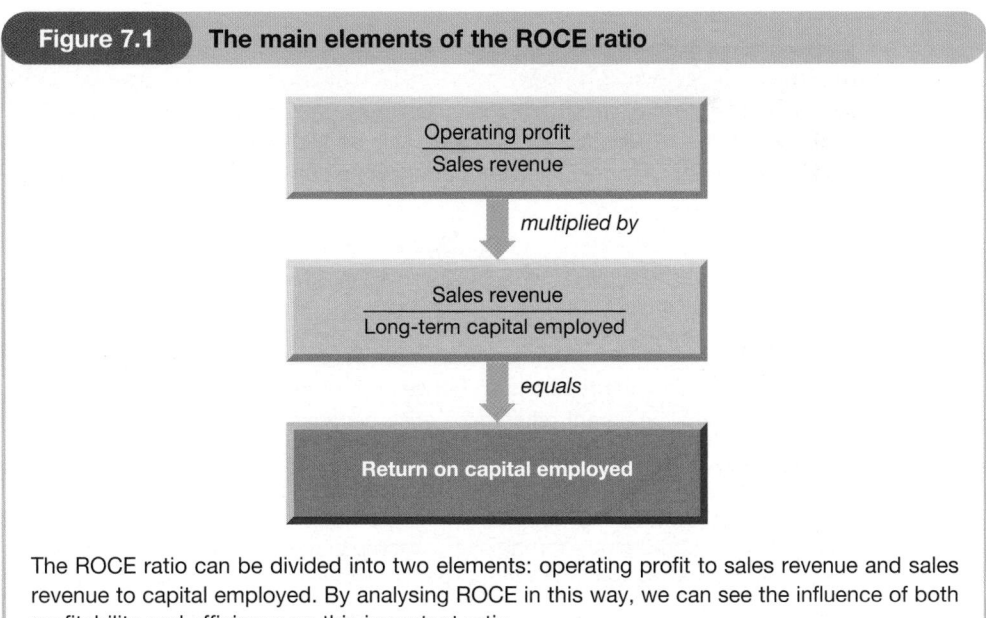

The ROCE ratio can be divided into two elements: operating profit to sales revenue and sales revenue to capital employed. By analysing ROCE in this way, we can see the influence of both profitability and efficiency on this important ratio.

By breaking down the ROCE ratio in this manner, we highlight the fact that the overall return on funds employed within the business will be determined both by the profitability of sales and by efficiency in the use of capital.

Example 7.2

Consider the following information, for last year, concerning two different businesses operating in the same industry:

	Antler plc	Baker plc
Operating profit	£20m	£15m
Average long-term capital employed	£100m	£75m
Sales revenue	£200m	£300m

The ROCE for each business is identical (20 per cent). However, the manner in which that return was achieved by each business was quite different. In the case of Antler plc, the operating profit margin is 10 per cent and the sales revenue to capital employed ratio is 2 times (so ROCE = 10% × 2 = 20%). In the case of Baker plc, the operating profit margin is 5 per cent and the sales revenue to capital employed ratio is 4 times (and so ROCE = 5% × 4 = 20%).

Example 7.2 demonstrates that a relatively high sales revenue to capital employed ratio can compensate for a relatively low operating profit margin. Similarly, a relatively low sales revenue to capital employed ratio can be overcome by a relatively high operating profit margin. In many areas of retail and distribution (for example, supermarkets and delivery services), the operating profit margins are quite low but the ROCE can be high, provided that the assets are used productively (that is, low margin, high turnover).

Activity 7.13

Show how the ROCE ratio for Alexis plc can be analysed into the two elements for each of the years 2008 and 2009. What conclusions can you draw from your figures?

	ROCE =	Operating profit margin	×	Sales revenue to capital employed
2008	34.7%	10.8%		3.20
2009	5.9%	1.8%		3.36

As we can see, the relationship between the three ratios holds for Alexis plc for both years. The small apparent differences arise because the three ratios are stated here only to one or two decimal places.

Although the business was more effective at generating sales revenue (sales revenue to capital employed ratio increased) in 2009 than in 2008, in 2009 it fell well below the level necessary to compensate for the sharp decline in the effectiveness of each sale (operating profit margin). As a result, the 2009 ROCE was well below the 2008 value.

Liquidity

Liquidity ratios are concerned with the ability of the business to meet its short-term financial obligations. The following ratios are widely used:

- current ratio
- acid test ratio
- operating cash flows to maturing obligations.

These three will now be considered.

Current ratio

→ The **current ratio** compares the 'liquid' assets (that is, cash and those assets held that will soon be turned into cash) of the business with the current liabilities. The ratio is calculated as follows:

$$\text{Current ratio} = \frac{\text{Current assets}}{\text{Current liabilities}}$$

Some people seem to believe that there is an 'ideal' current ratio (usually 2 times or 2:1) for all businesses. However, this fails to take into account the fact that different types of business require different current ratios. For example, a manufacturing business will often have a relatively high current ratio because it is necessary to hold inventories of finished goods, raw materials and work-in-progress. It will also normally sell goods on credit, thereby giving rise to trade receivables. A supermarket chain, on the other hand, will have a relatively low ratio, as it will hold only fast-moving inventories of finished goods and all of its sales will be made for cash (no credit sales). (See Real World 16.1 on page 640.)

The higher the ratio, the more liquid the business is considered to be. As liquidity is vital to the survival of a business, a higher current ratio might be thought to be preferable to a lower one. If a business has a very high ratio, however, it may be that funds are tied up in cash or other liquid assets and are not, therefore, being used as productively as they might otherwise be.

As at 31 March 2008, the current ratio of Alexis plc is:

$$\text{Current ratio} = \frac{544}{291} = 1.9 \text{ times (or 1.9:1)}$$

Activity 7.14

Calculate the current ratio for Alexis plc as at 31 March 2009.

The ratio as at 31 March 2009 is:

$$\text{Current ratio} = \frac{679}{432} = 1.6 \text{ times (or 1.6:1)}$$

Although this is a decline from 2008 to 2009, it is not necessarily a matter of concern. The next ratio may provide a clue as to whether there seems to be a problem.

Acid test ratio

→ The **acid test ratio** is very similar to the current ratio, but it represents a more stringent test of liquidity. It can be argued that, for many businesses, inventories cannot be converted into cash quickly. (Note that, in the case of Alexis plc, the inventories turnover period was about 57 days in both years (see page 244).) As a result, it may be better to exclude this particular asset from any measure of liquidity. The acid test ratio is a variation of the current ratio, but excluding inventories.

The minimum level for this ratio is often stated as 1.0 times (or 1:1; that is, current assets (excluding inventories) equals current liabilities). In many highly successful businesses that are regarded as having adequate liquidity, however, it is not unusual for the acid test ratio to be below 1.0 without causing particular liquidity problems. (See Real World 16.1 on page 640.)

The acid test ratio is calculated as follows:

$$\text{Acid test ratio} = \frac{\text{Current assets (excluding inventories)}}{\text{Current liabilities}}$$

The acid test ratio for Alexis plc as at 31 March 2008 is:

$$\text{Acid test ratio} = \frac{544 - 300}{291} = 0.8 \text{ times (or 0.8:1)}$$

We can see that the 'liquid' current assets do not quite cover the current liabilities, so the business may be experiencing some liquidity problems.

Activity 7.15

Calculate the acid test ratio for Alexis plc as at 31 March 2009.

The ratio as at 31 March 2009 is:

$$\text{Acid test ratio} = \frac{679 - 406}{432} = 0.6 \text{ times}$$

The 2009 ratio is significantly below that for 2008. The 2009 level may well be a cause for concern. The rapid decline in this ratio should lead to steps being taken, at least, to stop it falling further.

Cash generated from operations to maturing obligations ratio

The **cash generated from operations to maturing obligations ratio** compares the cash generated from operations (taken from the statement of cash flows) with the current liabilities of the business. It provides a further indication of the ability of the business to meet its maturing obligations. The ratio is expressed as:

$$\frac{\text{Cash generated from operations}}{\text{to maturing obligations ratio}} = \frac{\text{Cash generated from operations}}{\text{Current liabilities}}$$

The higher this ratio is, the better the liquidity of the business. This ratio has the advantage over the current ratio that the operating cash flows for a period usually provide a more reliable guide to the liquidity of a business than do the current assets held at the statement of financial position date. Alexis plc's ratio for the year ended 31 March 2008 is:

Cash generated from operations to maturing obligations ratio $= \dfrac{251}{291} = 0.9$ times

This ratio indicates that the operating cash flows for the year are not quite sufficient to cover the current liabilities at the end of the year.

Activity 7.16

Calculate the cash generated from operations to maturing obligations ratio for Alexis plc for the year ended 31 March 2009.

Cash generated from operations to maturing obligations ratio $= \dfrac{34}{432} = 0.1$ times

This ratio shows an alarming decline in the ability of the business to meet its maturing obligations from its operating cash flows. This confirms that liquidity is a real cause for concern for the business.

The liquidity ratios for the two-year period may be summarised as follows:

	2008	2009
Current ratio	1.9	1.6
Acid test ratio	0.8	0.6
Cash generated from operations to maturing obligations	0.9	0.1

Activity 7.17

What do you deduce from the liquidity ratios set out above?

Although it is probably not really possible to make a totally valid judgement without knowing the planned ratios, there appears to have been a worrying decline in liquidity. This is indicated by all three of these ratios. The most worrying is in the last ratio because it shows that the ability of the business to generate cash from trading operations has declined, relative to the short-term debts, from 2008 to 2009. The apparent liquidity problem may, however, be planned, short term and linked to the expansion in non-current assets and staffing. It may be that when the benefits of the expansion come on stream, liquidity will improve. On the other hand, short-term claimants may become anxious when they see signs of weak liquidity. This anxiety could lead to steps being taken to press for payment, and this could cause problems for Alexis plc.

Financial gearing

Financial gearing occurs when a business is financed, at least in part, by borrowing instead of by finance provided by the owners (the shareholders) as equity. A business's level of gearing (that is, the extent to which it is financed from sources that require a fixed return) is an important factor in assessing risk. Where a business borrows, it takes on a commitment to pay interest charges and make capital repayments. Where the borrowing is heavy, this can be a significant financial burden; it can increase the risk of the business becoming insolvent. Nevertheless, most businesses are geared to some extent. (Costain Group plc, the builders and construction business, is a rare example of a UK business with no borrowings.)

Given the risks involved, we may wonder why a business would want to take on gearing (that is, to borrow). One reason may be that the owners have insufficient funds, so the only way to finance the business adequately is to borrow from others. Another reason is that gearing can be used to increase the returns to owners. This is possible provided that the returns generated from borrowed funds exceed the cost of paying interest. Example 7.3 illustrates this point.

Example 7.3

The long-term capital structures of two new businesses, Lee Ltd and Nova Ltd, are as follows:

	Lee Ltd	Nova Ltd
	£	£
£1 ordinary shares	100,000	200,000
10% loan notes	200,000	100,000
	300,000	300,000

In their first year of operations, they each make an operating profit (that is, profit before interest and taxation) of £50,000. The tax rate is 30 per cent of the profit before taxation but after interest.

Lee Ltd would probably be considered relatively highly geared, as it has a high proportion of borrowed funds in its long-term capital structure. Nova Ltd is much lower geared. The profit available to the shareholders of each business in the first year of operations will be:

	Lee Ltd	Nova Ltd
	£	£
Operating profit	50,000	50,000
Interest payable	(20,000)	(10,000)
Profit before taxation	30,000	40,000
Taxation (30%)	(9,000)	(12,000)
Profit for the year (available to ordinary shareholders)	21,000	28,000

The return on ordinary shareholders' funds (ROSF) for each business will be:

Lee Ltd	Nova Ltd

$$\frac{21,000}{100,000} \times 100 = 21\% \qquad \frac{28,000}{200,000} \times 100 = 14\%$$

We can see that Lee Ltd, the more highly geared business, has generated a better ROSF than Nova Ltd. This is despite the fact that the ROCE (return on capital employed) is identical for both businesses (that is, (£50,000/£300,000) × 100 = 16.7%).

Note that at the £50,000 level of operating profit, the shareholders of both Lee Ltd and Nova Ltd benefit from gearing. Were the two businesses totally reliant on equity financing, the profit for the year (after taxation profit) would be £35,000 (that is, £50,000 less 30 per cent taxation), giving an ROSF of 11.7 per cent (that is, £35,000/£300,000). Both businesses generate higher ROSFs than this as a result of financial gearing.

An effect of gearing is that returns to shareholders become more sensitive to changes in operating profits. For a highly geared business, a change in operating profits will lead to a proportionately greater change in the ROSF ratio.

Activity 7.18

Assume that the operating profit was 20 per cent higher for each business than stated above (that is, an operating profit of £60,000). What would be the effect of this on ROSF?

The revised profit available to the shareholders of each business in the first year of operations will be:

	Lee Ltd	Nova Ltd
	£	£
Operating profit	60,000	60,000
Interest payable	(20,000)	(10,000)
Profit before taxation	40,000	50,000
Taxation (30%)	(12,000)	(15,000)
Profit for the year (available to ordinary shareholders)	28,000	35,000

The ROSF for each business will now be:

Lee Ltd

$$\frac{28,000}{100,000} \times 100 = 28\%$$

Nova Ltd

$$\frac{35,000}{200,000} \times 100 = 17.5\%$$

We can see that for Lee Ltd, the higher-geared business, the returns to shareholders have increased by one-third (from 21 per cent to 28 per cent), whereas for the lower-geared business, Nova Ltd, the benefits of gearing are less pronounced, increasing by only one-quarter (from 14 per cent to 17.5 per cent). The effect of gearing can, of course, work in both directions. So, for a highly geared business, a small decline in operating profit will bring about a much greater decline in the returns to shareholders.

The reason that gearing tends to be beneficial to shareholders is that interest rates for borrowings are low by comparison with the returns that the typical business can earn. On top of this, interest expenses are tax-deductible, in the way shown in Example 7.3 and Activity 7.18, which makes the effective cost of borrowing quite cheap. It is debatable whether the apparent low interest rates really are beneficial to the shareholders. Some argue that since borrowing increases the risk to shareholders, there is a hidden cost of borrowing. What are not illusory, however, are the benefits to the shareholders of the tax deductibility of interest on borrowings.

The effect of gearing is like that of two intermeshing cogwheels of unequal size (see Figure 7.2). The movement in the larger cog (operating profit) causes a more than proportionate movement in the smaller cog (returns to ordinary shareholders). The subject of gearing is discussed further in Chapter 15.

Two ratios are widely used to assess gearing:

- gearing ratio
- interest cover ratio.

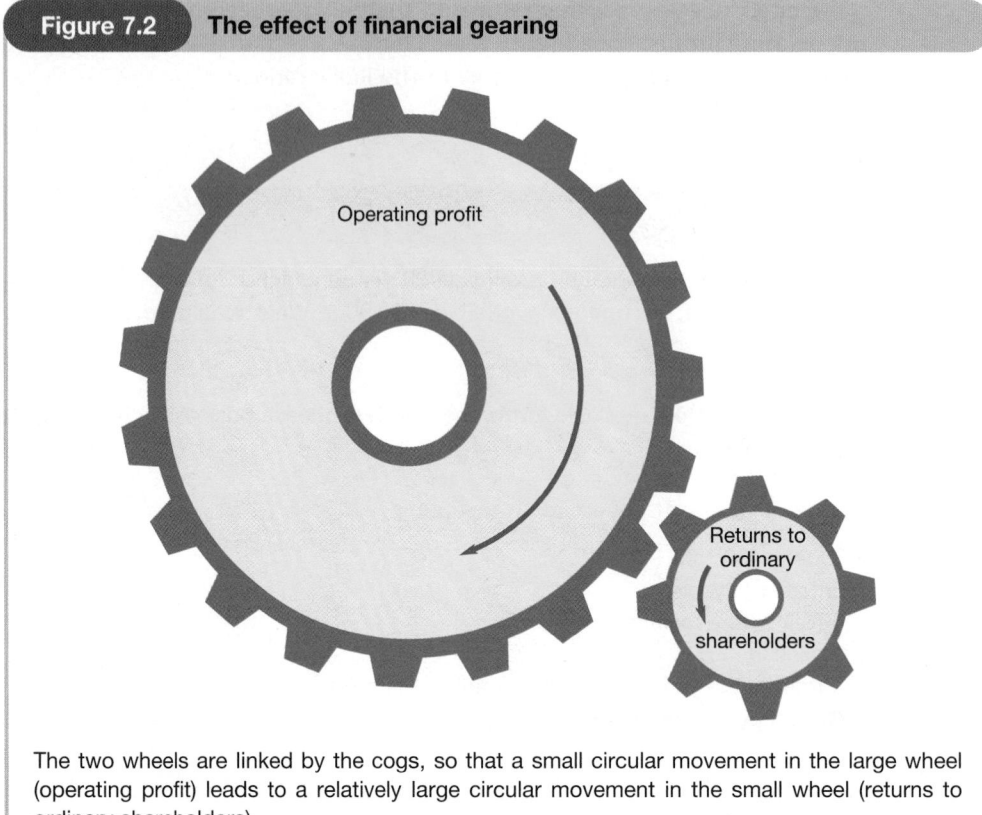

Figure 7.2 The effect of financial gearing

The two wheels are linked by the cogs, so that a small circular movement in the large wheel (operating profit) leads to a relatively large circular movement in the small wheel (returns to ordinary shareholders).

Gearing ratio

→ The **gearing ratio** measures the contribution of long-term lenders to the long-term capital structure of a business:

$$\text{Gearing ratio} = \frac{\text{Long-term (non-current) liabilities}}{\text{Share capital} + \text{Reserves} + \text{Long-term (non-current) liabilities}} \times 100$$

The gearing ratio for Alexis plc, as at 31 March 2008, is:

$$\text{Gearing ratio} = \frac{200}{(563 + 200)} \times 100 = 26.2\%$$

This is a level of gearing that would not normally be considered to be very high.

Activity (7.19)

Calculate the gearing ratio of Alexis plc as at 31 March 2009.

The ratio as at 31 March 2009 is:

$$\text{Gearing ratio} = \frac{300}{(534 + 300)} \times 100 = 36.0\%$$

This is a substantial increase in the level of gearing over the year.

Interest cover ratio

→ The **interest cover ratio** measures the amount of operating profit available to cover interest payable. The ratio may be calculated as follows:

$$\text{Interest cover ratio} = \frac{\text{Operating profit}}{\text{Interest payable}}$$

The ratio for Alexis plc for the year ended 31 March 2008 is:

$$\text{Interest cover ratio} = \frac{243}{18} = 13.5 \text{ times}$$

This ratio shows that the level of operating profit is considerably higher than the level of interest payable. This means that a significant fall in operating profit could occur before operating profit levels failed to cover interest payable. The lower the level of operating profit coverage, the greater the risk to lenders that interest payments will not be met, and the greater the risk to the shareholders that the lenders will take action against the business to recover the interest due.

Activity 7.20

Calculate the interest cover ratio of Alexis plc for the year ended 31 March 2009.

The ratio for the year ended 31 March 2009 is:

$$\text{Interest cover ratio} = \frac{47}{32} = 1.5 \text{ times}$$

Alexis plc's gearing ratios are:

	2008	2009
Gearing ratio	26.2%	36.0%
Interest cover ratio	13.5 times	1.5 times

Activity 7.21

What do you deduce from a comparison of Alexis plc's gearing ratios over the two years?

The gearing ratio altered significantly. This is mainly due to the substantial increase in the contribution of long-term lenders to the financing of the business.

The interest cover ratio has declined dramatically from a position where operating profit covered interest 13.5 times in 2008, to one where operating profit covered interest only 1.5 times in 2009. This was partly caused by the increase in borrowings in 2009, but mainly caused by the dramatic decline in profitability in that year. The later situation looks hazardous; only a small decline in future profitability would leave the business with insufficient operating profit to cover the interest payments. The gearing ratio at 31 March 2009 would not necessarily be considered to be very high for a business that was trading successfully. It is the low profitability that is the problem.

Without knowing what the business planned these ratios to be, it is not possible to reach a valid conclusion on Alexis plc's gearing.

Real World 7.6 is extracts from an article that discusses the likely lowering of gearing levels in the face of the recession. It explains that many businesses seem likely to issue additional ordinary shares (equity), either through making a rights issue or some public issue, and using the resulting funds to reduce borrowing as a means of reducing gearing.

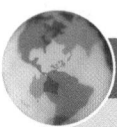

Real World 7.6

Changing gear

FT

When Stuart Siddall was corporate treasurer of Amec four years ago, analysts were critical when the engineering group swung from having substantial net debt on its balance sheet to sitting on a huge cash pile after completing disposals.

'The analysts were saying "this is inefficient balance sheet management",' says Mr Siddall.

Companies back then were expected to be highly geared, with net debt to shareholders' funds at historically high levels.

How times have changed. With a wave of rights issues and other equity issuance now expected from the UK's non-financial companies – and with funds from these being used to pay down debt – the pendulum is rapidly swinging back in favour of more conservative balance sheet management. Gearing levels are set to fall dramatically, analysts say. 'There is going to be an appreciable and material drop in gearing, by about a quarter or a third over the next three years,' predicts Mr Siddall, now chief executive of the Association of Corporate Treasurers.

Historically, gearing levels – as measured by net debt as a proportion of shareholders' funds – have run at an average of about 30 per cent over the past 20 years.

Peak levels (around 45 per cent) were reached in the past few years as companies took advantage of cheap credit. Current predictions see it coming down to about 20 per cent – and staying there for a good while to come.

Graham Secker, managing director of equity research at Morgan Stanley says: 'This is going to be a relatively long-term phenomenon.'

One of the most immediate concerns to heavily indebted companies is whether, in a recessionary environment, they will be able to generate the profit and cash flows to service their debts.

Gearing levels vary from sector to sector as well. Oil companies prefer low levels given their exposure to the volatility of oil prices. BP's net debt-shareholders' funds ratio of 21 per cent is at the low end of a 20–30 per cent range it considers prudent.

Miners' gearing is on a clear downward trend already. **Xstrata**, the mining group, stressed last month that its £4.1bn rights issue would cut gearing from 40 per cent to less than 30 per cent. A week later, **BHP** said its $13bn of first-half cash flows had cut gearing to less than 10 per cent. **Rio Tinto**, which had gearing of 130 per cent at the last count in August 2008, is desperately trying to cut it by raising fresh equity.

Utilities tend to be highly geared because they can afford to borrow more against their typically reliable cash flows. But even here the trend is downwards.

Severn Trent, the UK water group, says its appropriate long-term gearing level is 60 per cent. But 'given ongoing uncertainties . . . it is prudent in the near term to retain as much liquidity and flexibility as possible'. It does not expect to pursue that target until credit markets improve.

Reducing gearing is not easy, especially for the most indebted companies that need to the most: shareholders will be more reluctant to finance replacement equity in companies with highly leveraged balance sheets.

The supply of fresh equity will also be constrained, not only by a glut of demand from companies but by the squeeze on investor money from a wave of government bond issuance.

Richard Jeffrey, chief investment officer at Cazenove Capital Management, says there is a risk of the government making it more difficult to raise money to improve balance sheets. 'That is of extreme concern because that could become a limitation, longer term, in the capital that companies have to fund investment.'

Source: 'Gearing levels set to plummet', Jeremy Grant, *Financial Times*, 10 February 2009.

Investment ratios

There are various ratios available that are designed to help shareholders assess the returns on their investment. The following are widely used:

- dividend payout ratio
- dividend yield ratio
- earnings per share
- operating cash flow per share
- price/earnings ratio.

Dividend payout ratio

→ The **dividend payout ratio** measures the proportion of earnings that a business pays out to shareholders in the form of dividends. The ratio is calculated as follows:

$$\text{Dividend payout ratio} = \frac{\text{Dividends announced for the year}}{\text{Earnings for the year available for dividends}} \times 100$$

In the case of ordinary shares, the earnings available for dividend will normally be the profit for the year (that is, the profit after taxation) less any preference dividends relating to the year. This ratio is normally expressed as a percentage.

The dividend payout ratio for Alexis plc for the year ended 31 March 2008 is:

$$\text{Dividend payout ratio} = \frac{40}{165} \times 100 = 24.2\%$$

The information provided by this ratio is often expressed slightly differently as the
→ **dividend cover ratio**. Here the calculation is:

$$\text{Dividend cover ratio} = \frac{\text{Earnings for the year available for dividend}}{\text{Dividend announced for the year}}$$

In the case of Alexis plc (for 2008) it would be 165/40 = 4.1 times. That is to say, the earnings available for dividend cover the actual dividend by just over four times.

Activity 7.22

Calculate the dividend payout ratio of Alexis plc for the year ended 31 March 2009.

The ratio for 2009 is:

$$\text{Dividend payout ratio} = \frac{40}{11} \times 100 = 363.6\%$$

This would normally be considered to be a very alarming increase in the ratio over the two years. Paying a dividend of £40 million in 2009 would probably be widely regarded as very imprudent.

Dividend yield ratio

→ The **dividend yield ratio** relates the cash return from a share to its current market value. This can help investors to assess the cash return on their investment in the business. The ratio, expressed as a percentage, is:

$$\text{Dividend yield} = \frac{\text{Dividend per share}/(1 - t)}{\text{Market value per share}} \times 100$$

where t is the 'dividend tax credit' rate of income tax. This requires some explanation. In the UK, investors who receive a dividend from a business also receive a tax credit. As this tax credit can be offset against any tax liability arising from the dividends received, the dividends are effectively issued net of income tax, at the dividend tax credit rate.

Investors may wish to compare the returns from shares with the returns from other forms of investment. As these other forms of investment are often quoted on a 'gross' (that is, pre-tax) basis it is useful to 'gross up' the dividend to make comparison easier.

→ We can achieve this by dividing the **dividend per share** by $(1 - t)$, where t is the 'dividend tax credit' rate of income tax.

Using the 2007/08 dividend tax credit rate of 10 per cent, the dividend yield for Alexis plc for the year ended 31 March 2008 is:

$$\text{Dividend yield} = \frac{0.067*/(1 - 0.10)}{2.50} \times 100 = 3.0\%$$

* Dividend proposed/number of shares = 40/(300 × 2) = £0.067 dividend per share (the 300 is multiplied by 2 because they are £0.50 shares).

The share's market value is given in Note 1 to Example 7.1 (page 000).

Activity 7.23

Calculate the dividend yield for Alexis plc for the year ended 31 March 2009.

The ratio for 2009 is:

$$\text{Dividend yield} = \frac{0.067*/(1 - 0.10)}{1.50} \times 100 = 4.9\%$$

* 40/(300 × 2) = £0.067.

Earnings per share

→ The **earnings per share (EPS)** ratio relates the earnings generated by the business, and available to shareholders, during a period, to the number of shares in issue. For equity (ordinary) shareholders, the amount available will be represented by the profit for the year (profit after taxation) less any preference dividend, where applicable. The ratio for equity shareholders is calculated as follows:

$$\text{Earnings per share} = \frac{\text{Earnings available to ordinary shareholders}}{\text{Number of ordinary shares in issue}}$$

In the case of Alexis plc, the earnings per share for the year ended 31 March 2008 is as follows:

$$\text{EPS} = \frac{£165m}{600m} = 27.5p$$

Many investment analysts regard the EPS ratio as a fundamental measure of share performance. The trend in earnings per share over time is used to help assess the investment potential of a business's shares. Although it is possible to make total profit rise through ordinary shareholders investing more in the business, this will not necessarily mean that the profitability *per share* will rise as a result.

It is not usually very helpful to compare the EPS of one business with that of another. Differences in capital structure (for example, in the nominal value of shares issued) can render any such comparison meaningless. However, it can be very useful to monitor the changes that occur in this ratio for a particular business over time.

Activity 7.24

Calculate the earnings per share of Alexis plc for the year ended 31 March 2009.

The ratio for 2009 is:

$$\text{EPS} = \frac{£11m}{600m} = 1.8p$$

Cash generated from operations per share

It can be argued that, in the short term at least, cash generated from operations (found in the statement of cash flows) provides a better guide to the ability of a business to pay dividends and to undertake planned expenditures than the earnings per share figure.

→ The **cash generated from operations (CGO) per ordinary share ratio** is calculated as follows:

$$\text{Cash generated from operations per share} = \frac{\text{Cash generated from operations less preference dividend (if any)}}{\text{Number of ordinary shares in issue}}$$

The ratio for Alexis plc for the year ended 31 March 2008 is as follows:

$$\text{CGO per share} = \frac{£251m}{600m} = 41.8p$$

Activity 7.25

Calculate the CGO per ordinary share for Alexis plc for the year ended 31 March 2009.

The ratio for 2009 is:

$$\text{CGO per share} = \frac{£34m}{600m} = 5.7p$$

There has been a dramatic decrease in this ratio over the two-year period.

Note that, for both years, the CGO per share for Alexis plc is higher than the earnings per share. This is not unusual. The effect of adding back depreciation to derive the CGO figures will often ensure that a higher figure is derived.

Price/earnings (P/E) ratio

→ The **price/earnings ratio** relates the market value of a share to the earnings per share. This ratio can be calculated as follows:

$$\text{P/E ratio} = \frac{\text{Market value per share}}{\text{Earnings per share}}$$

The P/E ratio for Alexis plc as at 31 March 2008 is:

$$\text{P/E ratio} = \frac{£2.50}{27.5p^*} = 9.1 \text{ times}$$

* The EPS figure (27.5p) was calculated on page 261.

This ratio indicates that the market value of the share is 9.1 times higher than its current level of earnings. The ratio is a measure of market confidence in the future of a business. The higher the P/E ratio, the greater the confidence in the future earning power of the business and, consequently, the more investors are prepared to pay in relation to the earnings stream of the business.

P/E ratios provide a useful guide to market confidence concerning the future and they can, therefore, be helpful when comparing different businesses. However, differences in accounting policies between businesses can lead to different profit and earnings per share figures, and this can distort comparisons.

Activity 7.26

Calculate the P/E ratio of Alexis plc as at 31 March 2009.

The ratio for 2009 is:

$$\text{P/E ratio} = \frac{£1.50}{1.8p} = 83.3 \text{ times}$$

The investment ratios for Alexis plc over the two-year period are as follows:

	2008	2009
Dividend payout ratio	24.2%	363.6%
Dividend yield ratio	3.0%	4.9%
Earnings per share	27.5p	1.8p
Cash generated from operations per share	41.8p	5.7p
P/E ratio	9.1 times	83.3 times

Activity (7.27)

What do you deduce from the investment ratios set out above?
   Can you offer an explanation why the share price has not fallen as much as it might have done, bearing in mind the very poor (relative to 2008) trading performance in 2009?

We thought that, although the EPS has fallen dramatically and the dividend payment for 2009 seems very imprudent, the share price seems to have held up remarkably well (fallen from £2.50 to £1.50, see page 235). This means that dividend yield and P/E value for 2009 look better than those for 2008. This is an anomaly of these two ratios, which stems from using a forward-looking value (the share price) in conjunction with historic data (dividends and earnings). Share prices are based on investors' assessments of the business's future. It seems with Alexis plc that, at the end of 2009, the 'market' was not happy with the business, relative to 2008. This is evidenced by the fact that the share price had fallen by £1 a share. On the other hand, the share price has not fallen as much as profit for the year. It appears that investors believe that the business will perform better in the future than it did in 2009. This may well be because they believe that the large expansion in assets and employee numbers that occurred in 2009 will yield benefits in the future; benefits that the business was not able to generate during 2009.

Real World 7.7 gives some information about the shares of several large, well-known UK businesses. This type of information is provided on a daily basis by several newspapers, notably the *Financial Times*.

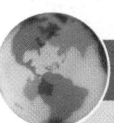

Real World 7.7

Market statistics for some well-known businesses

The following data was extracted from the *Financial Times* of 21 February 2009, relating to the previous day's trading of the shares of some well-known businesses on the London Stock Exchange:

Share	Price	Chng	2008/9		Y'ld	P/E	Volume
			High	Low			000s
BP	462.50	−20.75	657.25	370	9.3	5.7	50,446
J D Wetherspoon	402.50	+8.50	405	167.75	3.0	15.4	1,442
BSkyB	450	−8	621.50	310.50	3.8	16.3	7,707
Marks and Spencer	251.75	−0.25	572.50	191.90	8.9	6.4	9,553
Rolls-Royce	294	−12.50	529.88	237.27	4.5	5.2	11,569
Vodafone	125.50	−1.65	193.80	96.40	6.0	9.1	150,173

Real World 7.7 continued

The column headings are as follows:

Price   Mid-market price in pence (that is, the price midway between buying and selling price) of the shares at the end of trading on 21 February 2009.

Chng   Gain or loss in the mid-market price during 21 February 2009.

High/Low Highest and lowest prices reached by the share during the year ended on 21 February 2009.

Y'ld   Gross dividend yield, based on the most recent year's dividend and the current share price.

P/E   Price/earnings ratio, based on the most recent year's (after-tax) profit for the year and the current share price.

Volume   The number of shares (in thousands) that were bought/sold on 21 February 2009.

So, for example for BP, the oil business:

● the shares had a mid-market price of £4.625 each at the close of Stock Exchange trading on 21 February 2009;
● the shares had decreased in price by 20.75 pence during trading on 21 February 2009;
● the shares had highest and lowest prices during the previous year of £6.5725 and £3.70, respectively;
● the shares had a dividend yield, based on the 21 February 2009 price (and the dividend for the most recent year) of 9.3 per cent;
● the shares had a P/E ratio, based on the 21 February 2009 price (and the after-taxation earnings per share for the most recent year) of 5.7;
● during trading in the shares on 21 February 2009, 50,446,000 of the business's shares had changed hands from one investor to another.

Real World 7.8 shows how investment ratios can vary between different industry sectors.

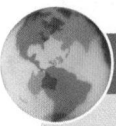

Real World 7.8

How investment ratios vary between industries

Investment ratios can vary significantly between businesses and between industries. To give some indication of the range of variations that occur, the average dividend yield ratios and average P/E ratios for listed businesses in twelve different industries are shown in Figures 7.3 and 7.4, respectively.

These dividend yield ratios are calculated from the current market value of the shares and the most recent year's dividend paid.

Some industries tend to pay out lower dividends than others, leading to lower dividend yield ratios. The average for all Stock Exchange listed businesses was 5.23 (as is shown in Figure 7.3), but there is a wide variation with Food and Drug Retailers at 3.11 and Life Insurance at 10.07.

| Figure 7.3 | Average dividend yield ratios for businesses in a range of industries |

Average dividend yield ratios for businesses in a range of industries

Industry	%
Oil and gas	4.83
Construction and materials	4.92
Chemicals	4.20
Industrial engineering	6.32
Pharmaceuticals and biotechnology	4.58
Tobacco	3.92
Travel and leisure	5.36
Media	4.95
Food and drug retailers	3.11
Electricity	4.88
Life insurance	10.07
Banks	8.38
Average for all SE listed businesses	5.23

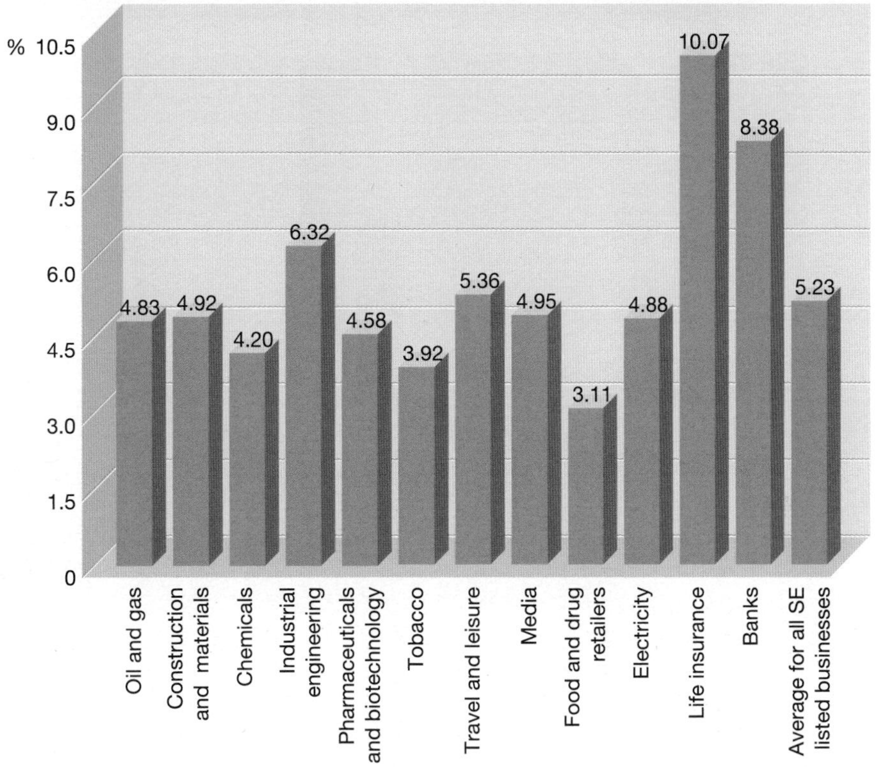

Average levels of dividend yield tend to vary from one industry to the next.

Source: Constructed from data appearing in *Financial Times*, 21 February 2009.

Pharmaceutical businesses tend to invest heavily in developing new drugs, hence their tendency to pay low dividends compared with their share prices. Some of the inter-industry differences in the dividend yield ratio can be explained by the nature of the calculation of the ratio. The prices of shares at any given moment are based on expectations of their economic futures; dividends are actual past events. A business that had a good trading year recently may have paid a dividend that, in the light of investors' assessment of the business's economic future, may be high (a high dividend yield).

These P/E ratios are calculated from the current market value of the shares and the most recent year's earnings per share (EPS).

Businesses that have a high share price relative to their recent historic earnings have high P/E ratios. This may be because their future is regarded as economically bright, which may be the result of investing heavily in the future at the expense of recent profits (earnings). On the other hand, high P/Es also arise where businesses have recent low earnings but investors believe that their future is brighter. The average P/E for all Stock Exchange listed businesses was 7.99, but Oil and Gas was as low as 6.32 and Tobacco as high as 20.78.

It should be noted that, as a result of a partial collapse of share prices during 2008/9, the dividend yield figures are unusually high. Similarly the P/E ratios are unusually low.

Real World 7.8 continued

Figure 7.4	Average price/earnings ratios for businesses in a range of industries

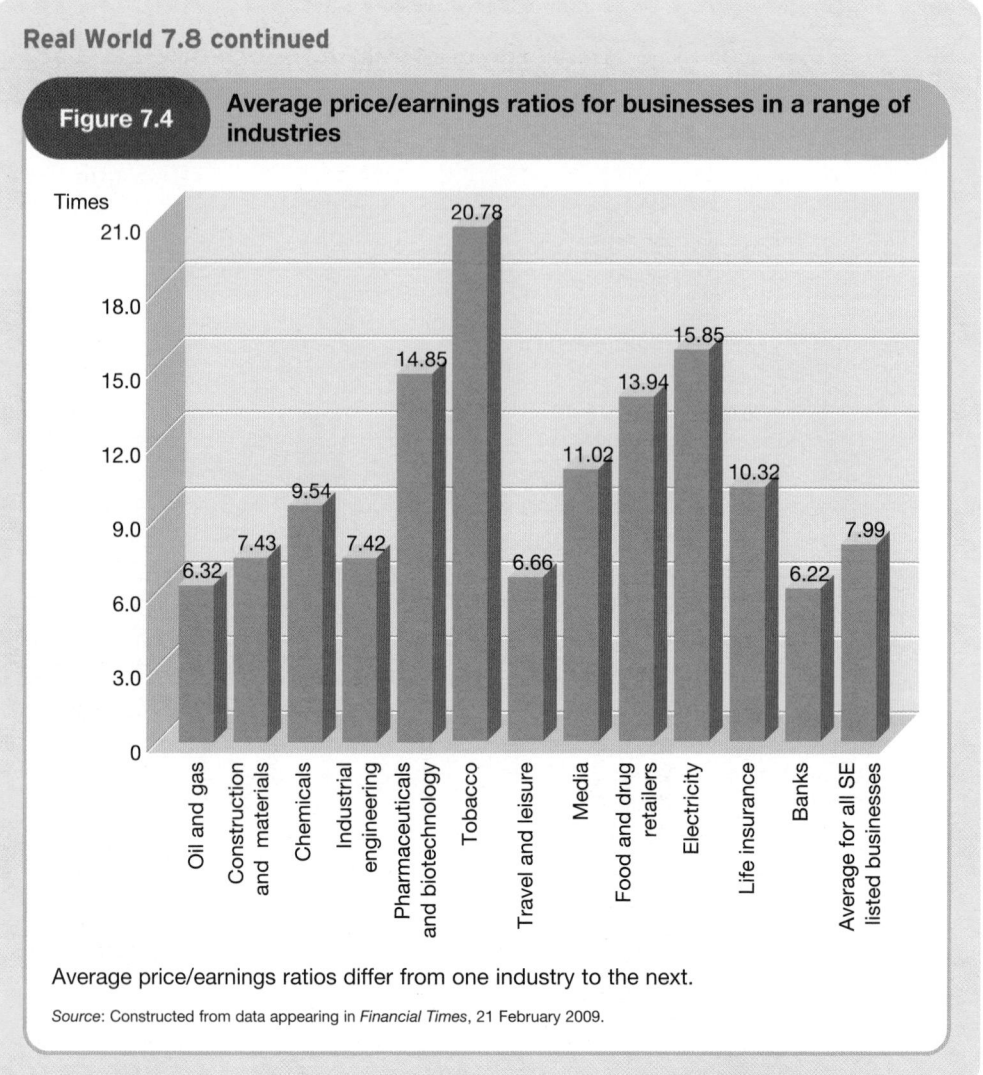

Average price/earnings ratios differ from one industry to the next.

Source: Constructed from data appearing in *Financial Times*, 21 February 2009.

Self-assessment question 7.1

Both Ali plc and Bhaskar plc operate electrical stores throughout the UK. The financial statements of each business for the year ended 30 June 2009 are as follows:

Statements of financial position as at 30 June 2009

	Ali plc £000	Bhaskar plc £000
ASSETS		
Non-current assets		
Property, plant and equipment		
(cost less depreciation)		
Land and buildings	360.0	510.0
Fixtures and fittings	87.0	91.2
	447.0	601.2

Current assets		
Inventories	592.0	403.0
Trade receivables	176.4	321.9
Cash at bank	84.6	91.6
	853.0	816.5
Total assets	1,300.0	1,417.7
EQUITY AND LIABILITIES		
Equity		
£1 ordinary shares	320.0	250.0
Retained earnings	367.6	624.6
	687.6	874.6
Non-current liabilities		
Borrowings – Loan notes	190.0	250.0
Current liabilities		
Trade payables	406.4	275.7
Taxation	16.0	17.4
	422.4	293.1
Total equity and liabilities	1,300.0	1,417.7

Income statements for the year ended 30 June 2009

	Ali plc	Bhaskar plc
	£000	£000
Revenue	1,478.1	1,790.4
Cost of sales	(1,018.3)	(1,214.9)
Gross profit	459.8	575.5
Operating expenses	(308.5)	(408.6)
Operating profit	151.3	166.9
Interest payable	(19.4)	(27.5)
Profit before taxation	131.9	139.4
Taxation	(32.0)	(34.8)
Profit for the year	99.9	104.6

All purchases and sales were on credit. Ali plc had announced its intention to pay a dividend of £135,000 and Bhaskar plc £95,000 in respect of the year. The market values of a share in Ali plc and Bhaskar plc at the end of the year were £6.50 and £8.20 respectively.

Required:
For each business, calculate two ratios that are concerned with liquidity, gearing and investment (six ratios in total). What can you conclude from the ratios that you have calculated?

The answer to this question can be found at the back of the book on page 728.

Financial ratios and the problem of overtrading

→ **Overtrading** occurs where a business is operating at a level of activity that cannot be supported by the amount of finance that has been committed. For example, the business has inadequate finance to fund the level of trade receivables and inventories necessary for the level of sales revenue that it is achieving. This situation usually reflects a poor level of financial control over the business. The reasons for overtrading are varied. It may occur:

- in young, expanding businesses that fail to prepare adequately for the rapid increase in demand for their goods or services;
- in businesses where the managers may have miscalculated the level of expected sales demand or have failed to control escalating project costs;
- as a result of a fall in the value of money (inflation), causing more finance to have to be committed to inventories and trade receivables, even where there is no expansion in the real volume of trade;
- where the owners are unable to inject further funds into the business themselves and/or they cannot persuade others to invest in the business.

Whatever the reason, the problems that it brings must be dealt with if the business is to survive over the longer term.

Overtrading results in liquidity problems such as exceeding borrowing limits, or slow repayment of borrowings and trade payables. It can also result in suppliers withholding supplies, thereby making it difficult to meet customer needs. The managers of the business might be forced to direct all of their efforts to dealing with immediate and pressing problems, such as finding cash to meet interest charges due or paying wages. Longer-term planning becomes difficult as managers spend their time going from crisis to crisis. At the extreme, a business may fail because it cannot meet its maturing obligations.

Activity (7.28)

If a business is overtrading, do you think the following ratios would be higher or lower than normally expected?

1 Current ratio.
2 Average inventories turnover period.
3 Average settlement period for trade receivables.
4 Average settlement period for trade payables.

Your answer should be as follows:

1 The current ratio would be lower than normally expected. This is a measure of liquidity, and lack of liquidity is an important symptom of overtrading.
2 The average inventories turnover period would be lower than normally expected. Where a business is overtrading, the level of inventories held will be low because of the problems of financing them. In the short term, sales revenue may not be badly affected by the low inventories levels and therefore inventories will be turned over more quickly.
3 The average settlement period for trade receivables may be lower than normally expected. Where a business is suffering from liquidity problems it may chase credit customers more vigorously in an attempt to improve cash flows.
4 The average settlement period for trade payables may be higher than normally expected. The business may try to delay payments to its suppliers because of the liquidity problems arising.

To deal with the overtrading problem, a business must ensure that the finance available is consistent with the level of operations. Thus, if a business that is overtrading is unable to raise new finance, it should cut back its level of operations in line with the finance available. Although this may mean lost sales and lost profits in the short term, it may be necessary to ensure survival over the longer term.

Trend analysis

It is often helpful to see whether ratios are indicating trends. Key ratios can be plotted on a graph to provide a simple visual display of changes occurring over time. The trends occurring within a business may, for example, be plotted against trends for rival businesses or for the industry as a whole for comparison purposes. An example of trend analysis is shown in **Real World 7.9**.

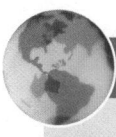

Real World 7.9

Trend setting

In Figure 7.5 the current ratio of three of the UK's leading supermarkets is plotted over time. We can see that the current ratio of Tesco plc has risen over the period but it was, nevertheless, consistently lower than that of its main rivals, until 2005, when it overtook Morrison.

Figure 7.5   Graph plotting current ratio against time

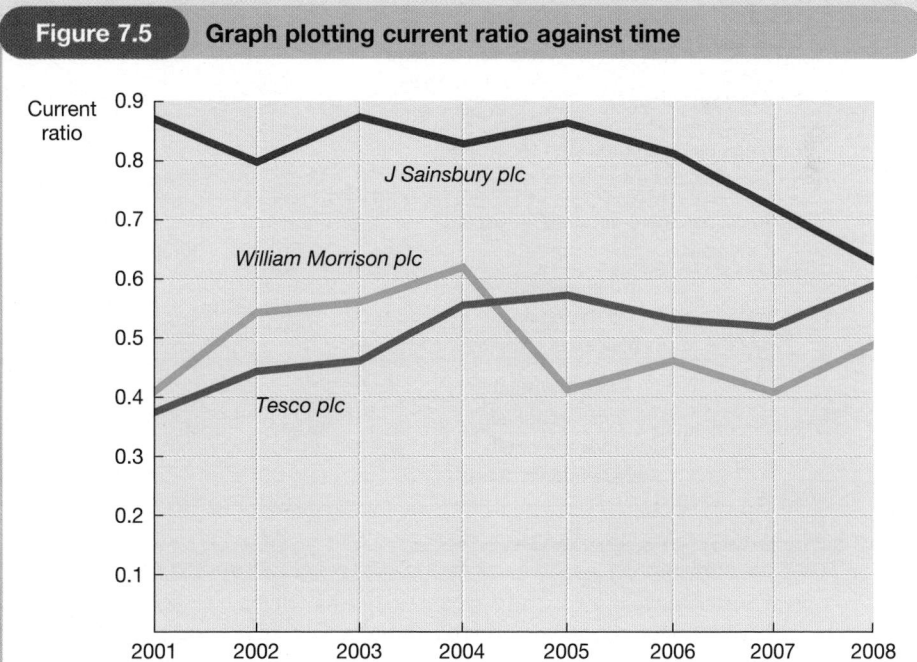

The current ratio for three leading UK supermarkets is plotted for the financial years ending 2001 to 2008. This enables comparison to be made regarding the ratio, both for each of the three businesses over time and between the businesses.

Many larger businesses publish certain key financial ratios as part of their annual reports to help users identify significant trends. These ratios typically cover several years' activities. **Real World 7.10** shows part of the table of 'key performance measures' of Marks and Spencer plc (M&S), the well-known UK high street store.

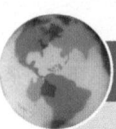

Real World 7.10

Key performance measures of Marks and Spencer plc

		2008 52 weeks	2007 52 weeks	2006 53 weeks	2005 52 weeks
Gross margin	$\dfrac{\text{Gross profit}}{\text{Revenue}}$	38.6%	38.9%	38.3%	34.7%
Net margin	$\dfrac{\text{Operating profit}}{\text{Revenue}}$	13.4%	12.2%	10.9%	8.0%
Net margin excluding property disposals and exceptional items		12.1%	12.2%	11.0%	8.7%
Profitability	$\dfrac{\text{Profit before tax}}{\text{Revenue}}$	12.5%	10.9%	9.6%	6.7%
Profitability excluding property disposals and exceptional items		11.2%	11.2%	9.6%	7.4%
Basic earnings per share	$\dfrac{\text{Basic earnings}}{\substack{\text{Weighted average} \\ \text{ordinary shares} \\ \text{in issue}}}$	49.2p	39.1p	31.3p	17.6p
Earnings per share adjusted for property disposals and exceptional items		43.6p	40.4p	31.4p	19.2p
Dividend per share declared in respect of the year		22.5p	18.3p	14.0p	12.1p
Dividend cover	$\dfrac{\substack{\text{Profit attributable} \\ \text{to shareholders}}}{\text{Dividends payable}}$	2.3×	2.1×	2.2×	2.9×
Return on equity	$\dfrac{\substack{\text{Profit attributable} \\ \text{to shareholders}}}{\substack{\text{Average equity} \\ \text{shareholders' funds}}}$	45.6%	46.3%	50.0%	35.1%

Source: Marks and Spencer plc Annual Report 2008.

M&S's return on equity (return on ordinary shareholders' funds) in 2006 was significantly better than for 2005, but dropped off a little for 2007 and 2008. The net margin has improved significantly for each of the four years, though the gross margin was fairly stable after 2005. This implies an improvement in controlling overheads in recent years.

Using ratios to predict financial failure

Financial ratios, based on current or past performance, are often used to help predict the future. However, both the choice of ratios and the interpretation of results are normally dependent on the judgement and opinion of the analyst. In recent years, however, attempts have been made to develop a more rigorous and systematic approach to the use of ratios for prediction purposes. In particular, researchers have shown an interest in the ability of ratios to predict the financial failure of a business.

By financial failure, we mean a business either being forced out of business or being severely adversely affected by its inability to meet its financial obligations. It is often referred to as 'going bust' or 'going bankrupt'. This, of course, is an area with which all those connected with the business are likely to be concerned.

Using single ratios

Many approaches that attempt to use ratios to predict future financial failure have been developed. Early research focused on the examination of ratios on an individual basis to see whether they were good or bad predictors of financial failure. Here, a particular ratio (for example the current ratio) for a business that had failed was tracked over several years leading up to the date of the failure. This was to see whether it was possible to say that the ratio had shown a trend that could have been taken as a warning sign.

Beaver (see reference 1 at the end of the chapter) carried out the first research in this area. He identified 79 businesses that had failed. He then calculated the average (mean) of various ratios for these 79 businesses, going back over the financial statements of each business for each of the ten years leading up to each one's failure. Beaver then compared these average ratios with similarly derived ratios for a sample of 79 businesses that did not fail over this period. (The research used a matched-pair design, where each failed business was matched with a non-failed business of similar size and industry type.) Beaver found that some ratios exhibited a marked difference between the failed and non-failed businesses for up to five years prior to failure. This is shown in Figure 7.6.

To explain Figure 7.6, let us take a closer look at graph (a). This plots the ratio, cash flow (presumably the operating cash flow figure, taken from the statement of cash flows) divided by total debt (borrowings). For the non-failed businesses this stayed fairly steady at just below +0.45 over the period. For the failed businesses, however, this was already well below the non-failed businesses, at about +0.15, even five years before those businesses eventually failed. It then declined steadily until, by one year before the failure, it was less than −0.15. Note that the scale of the horizontal axis shows the most recent year before actual failure (Year 1) on the left and the earliest one (Year 5) on the right. The other graphs in Figure 7.6 show a similar picture for five other ratios. In each case there is a deteriorating average ratio for the failed businesses as the time of failure approaches.

What is shown in Figure 7.6 implies that failure could be predicted by careful assessment of the trend shown by particular key ratios.

Research by Zmijewski (see reference 2 at the end of the chapter), using a sample of 72 failed and 3,573 non-failed businesses over a six-year period, found that businesses that ultimately went on to fail were characterised by lower rates of return, higher levels of gearing, lower levels of coverage for their fixed interest payments and more variable returns on shares. While we may not find these results very surprising, it is

| Figure 7.6 | Average (mean) ratios of failed and non-failed businesses plotted against the number of years before failure |

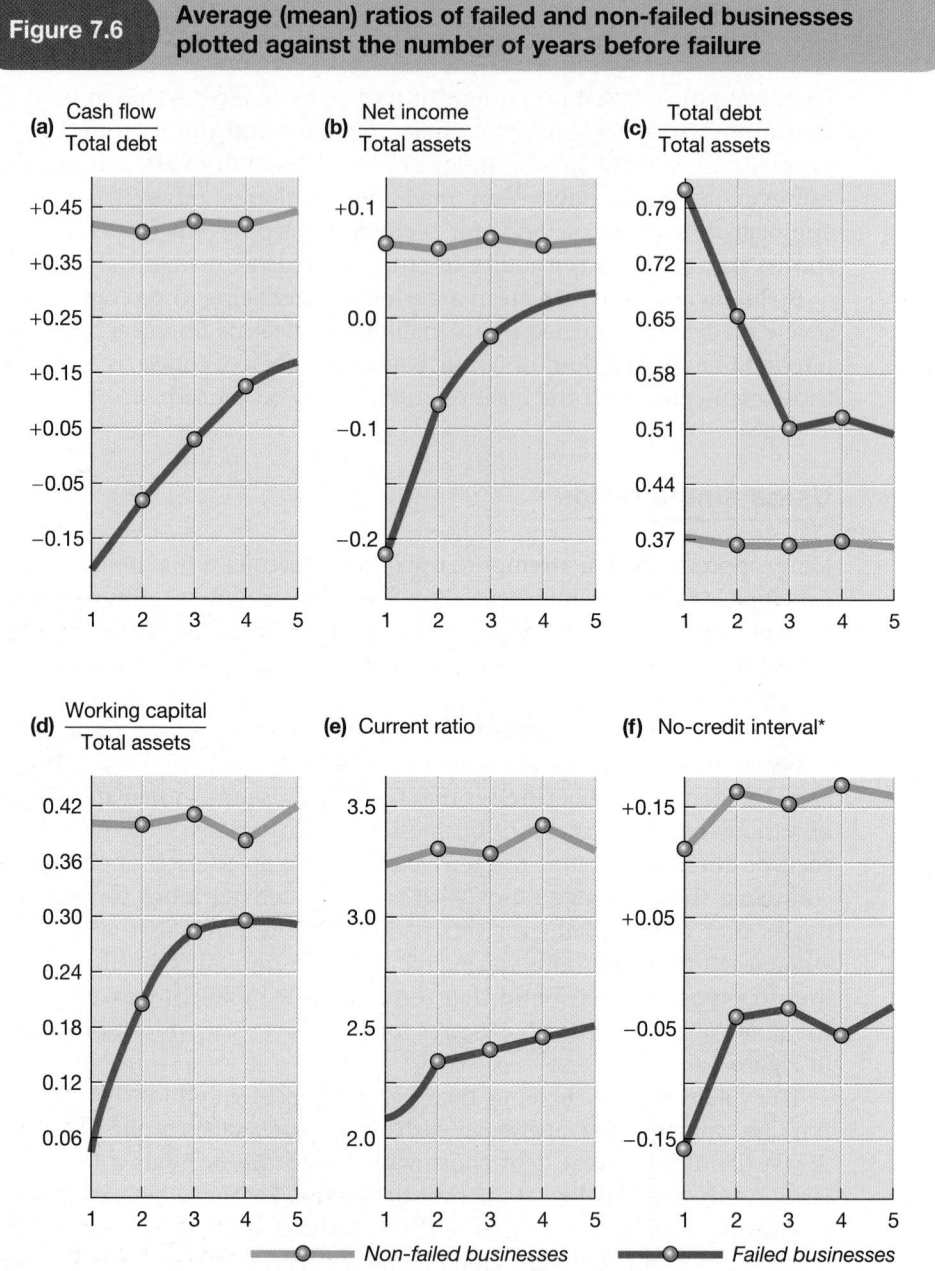

Each of the ratios (a) to (f) above indicates a marked difference in the average ratio between the sample of failed businesses and a matched sample of non-failed businesses. The vertical scale of each graph is the average value of the particular ratio for each group of businesses (failed and non-failed). The horizontal axis is the number of years before failure. Thus Year 1 is the most recent year and Year 5 the earliest of the years. For each of the six ratios, the difference between the average for the failed and the non-failed businesses can be detected five years prior to the failure of the former group.

* The no-credit interval is the same as the cash generated from operations to maturing obligations ratio discussed earlier in the chapter.

Source: Beaver (see reference 1 at the end of the chapter).

interesting to note that Zmijewski, like a number of other researchers in this area, did not find liquidity ratios particularly useful in predicting financial failure. Intuition might have led us (wrongly it seems) to believe that the liquidity ratios would have been particularly helpful in this context.

The approach adopted by Beaver and Zmijewski is referred to as **univariate analysis** because it looks at one ratio at a time. Although this approach can produce interesting results, there are practical problems associated with its use. Let us say, for example, that past research has identified two ratios as being good predictors of financial failure. When applied to a particular business, however, it may be found that one ratio predicts financial failure whereas the other does not. Given these conflicting signals, how should the decision maker interpret the results?

Using combinations of ratios

The weaknesses of univariate analysis have led researchers to develop models that combine ratios in such a way as to produce a single index that can be interpreted more clearly. One approach to model development, much favoured by researchers, applies **multiple discriminate analysis** (MDA). This is, in essence, a statistical technique that is similar to regression analysis and which can be used to draw a boundary between those businesses that fail and those businesses that do not. This boundary is referred to as the **discriminate function**. In this context, MDA attempts to identify those factors likely to influence financial failure. However, unlike regression analysis, MDA assumes that the observations come from two different populations (for example, failed and non-failed businesses) rather than from a single population.

To illustrate this approach, let us assume that we wish to test whether two ratios (say, the current ratio and the return on capital employed) can help to predict failure. To do this, we can calculate these ratios, first for a sample of failed businesses and then for a matched sample of non-failed ones. From these two sets of data we can produce a scatter diagram that plots each business according to these two ratios to produce a single co-ordinate. Figure 7.7 illustrates this approach.

Using the observations plotted on the diagram, we try to identify the boundary between the failed and the non-failed businesses. This is the diagonal line in Figure 7.7.

We can see that those businesses that fall below and to the left of the line are predominantly failed and those that fall to the right are predominantly non-failed ones. Note that there is some overlap between the two populations. The boundary produced is unlikely, in practice, to eliminate all errors. Some businesses that fail may fall on the side of the boundary with non-failed businesses, and the other way round as well. However, the analysis will *minimise* the misclassification errors.

The boundary shown in Figure 7.7 can be expressed in the form:

$$Z = a + (b \times \text{Current ratio}) + (c \times \text{ROCE})$$

where a is a constant and b and c are weights to be attached to each ratio. A weighted average or total score (Z) is then derived. The weights given to the two ratios will depend on the slope of the line and its absolute position.

Z score models

Altman (see reference 3 at the end of the chapter) was the first to develop a model (in 1968), using financial ratios, that was able to predict financial failure. In 2000

Figure 7.7	Scatter diagram showing the distribution of failed and non-failed businesses

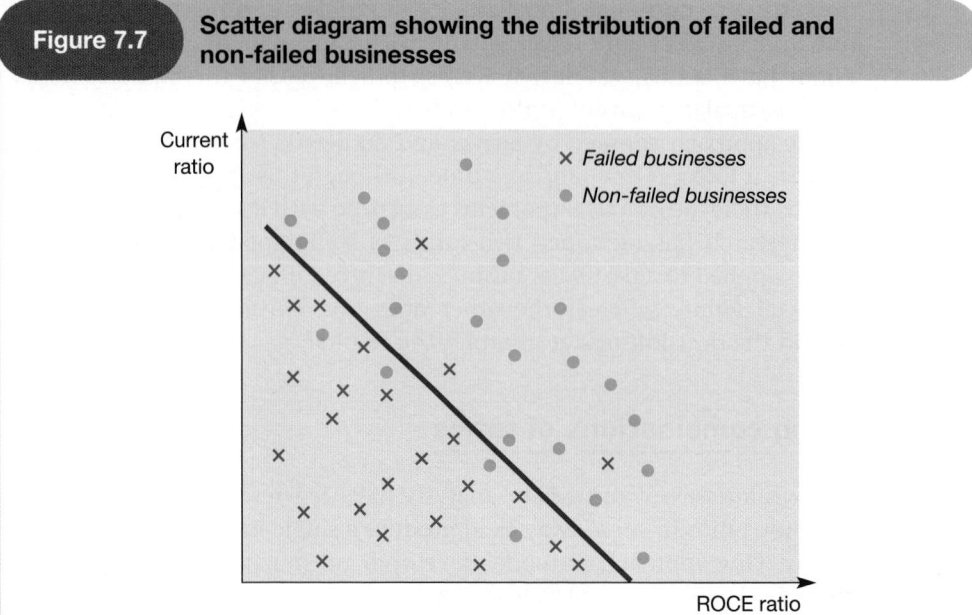

The distribution of failed and non-failed businesses is based on two ratios. The line represents a boundary between the samples of failed and non-failed businesses. Although there is some crossing of the boundary, the boundary represents the line that minimises the problem of mis-classifying particular businesses.

he revised that model. In fact, the revisions necessary to make the model effective in present times were quite minor. Altman's revised model, the Z score model, is based on five financial ratios and is as follows:

$$Z = 0.717a + 0.847b + 3.107c + 0.420d + 0.998e$$

where a = Working capital/Total assets
b = Accumulated retained profits/Total assets
c = Operating profit/Total assets
d = Book (statement of financial position) value of ordinary and preference shares/Total liabilities at book (statement of financial position) value
e = Sales revenue/Total assets

In developing and revising this model, Altman carried out experiments using a paired sample of failed businesses and non-failed businesses and collected relevant data for each business for five years prior to failure. He found that the model represented by the formula above was able to predict failure for up to two years before it occurred. However, the predictive accuracy of the model became weaker the longer the time before the date of the actual failure.

The ratios used in this model were identified by Altman through a process of trial and error, as there is no underlying theory of financial failure to help guide researchers in their selection of appropriate ratios. According to Altman, those businesses with a Z score of less than 1.23 tend to fail, and the lower the score the greater the probability of failure. Those with a Z score greater than 4.14 tend not to fail. Those businesses with a Z score between 1.23 and 4.14 occupied a 'zone of ignorance' and were difficult to classify. However, the model was able overall to classify 91 per cent of the businesses correctly. Altman based his model on US businesses.

In recent years, other models, using a similar approach, have been developed throughout the world. In the UK, Taffler has developed separate *Z* score models for different types of business. (See reference 4 at the end of the chapter for a discussion of the work of Taffler and others.)

The prediction of financial failure is not the only area where research into the predictive ability of ratios has taken place. Researchers have also developed ratio-based models that claim to assess the vulnerability of a business to takeover by another. This is another area that is of vital importance to all those connected with the business.

Limitations of ratio analysis

Although ratios offer a quick and useful method of analysing the position and performance of a business, they are not without their problems and limitations. We shall now review some of the shortcomings of financial ratio analysis.

Quality of financial statements

It must always be remembered that ratios are based on financial statements, and the results of ratio analysis are dependent on the quality of these underlying statements. Ratios will inherit the limitations of the financial statements on which they are based. In Chapter 2 we saw that one important limitation of financial statements is their failure to include all resources controlled by the business. Internally-generated goodwill and brands, for example, are excluded from the statement of financial position because they do not meet the strict definition of an asset. This means that, even though these resources may be of considerable value, key ratios such as ROSF, ROCE and the gearing ratio will fail to acknowledge their presence.

There is also the problem of deliberate attempts to make the financial statements misleading. We discussed this problem of *creative accounting* in Chapter 5.

Inflation

A persistent, though recently less severe, problem, in most Western countries is that the financial results of businesses can be distorted as a result of inflation. One effect of inflation is that the reported value of assets held for any length of time may bear little relation to current values. Generally speaking, the reported value of assets will be understated in current terms during a period of inflation as they are usually reported at their original cost (less any amounts written off for depreciation). This means that comparisons, either between businesses or between periods, will be hindered. A difference in, say, ROCE may simply be owing to the fact that assets in one of the statements of financial position being compared were acquired more recently (ignoring the effect of depreciation on the asset values). Another effect of inflation is to distort the measurement of profit. Sales revenue for a period is often matched against costs from an earlier period because there is often a time lag between acquiring a particular resource and using it to help generate sales revenue. For example, inventories may be acquired in one period and sold in a later period. During a period of inflation, this will mean that the expense does not reflect current prices. The cost of sales figure is usually based on the historic cost of the inventories concerned. As a result, expenses will be understated in the income statement and this, in turn, means that profit will be overstated. One effect of this will be to distort the profitability ratios discussed earlier.

The restricted vision of ratios

It is important not to rely exclusively on ratios, thereby losing sight of information contained in the underlying financial statements. As we saw earlier in the chapter, some items reported in these statements can be vital in assessing position and performance. For example, the total sales revenue, capital employed and profit figures may be useful in assessing changes in absolute size that occur over time, or in assessing differences in scale between businesses. Ratios do not provide such information. When comparing one figure with another, ratios measure *relative* performance and position, and therefore provide only part of the picture. When comparing two businesses, therefore, it will often be useful to assess the absolute size of profits, as well as the relative profitability of each business. For example, Business A may generate £1 million operating profit and have a ROCE of 15 per cent, and Business B may generate £100,000 operating profit and have a ROCE of 20 per cent. Although Business B has a higher level of *profitability*, as measured by ROCE, it generates lower total operating profits.

The basis for comparison

We saw earlier that if ratios are to be useful they require a basis for comparison. Moreover, it is important that the analyst compares like with like. However, no two businesses are identical, and the greater the differences between the businesses being compared, the greater the limitations of ratio analysis. Furthermore, any differences in accounting policies, financing methods (gearing levels) and financial year ends will add to the problems of making comparisons between businesses.

Ratios relating to the statement of financial position

Because the statement of financial position is only a 'snapshot' of the business at a particular moment in time, any ratios based on statement of financial position figures, such as the liquidity ratios, may not be representative of the financial position of the business for the year as a whole. For example, it is common for a seasonal business to have a financial year end that coincides with a low point in business activity. As a result, inventories and trade receivables may be low at the statement of financial position date, and so the liquidity ratios may also be low. A more representative picture of liquidity can only really be gained by taking additional measurements at other points in the year.

Real World 7.11 points out another way in which ratios are limited.

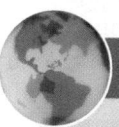

Real World 7.11

Remember, it's people that really count . . .

Lord Weinstock (1924 to 2002) was an influential industrialist whose management style and philosophy helped to shape management practice in many UK businesses. During his long and successful reign at GEC plc, a major engineering business, Lord Weinstock relied heavily on financial ratios to assess performance and to exercise control. In particular, he relied on ratios relating to sales revenue, expenses, trade receivables, profit margins and inventories turnover. However, he was keenly aware of the limitations of ratios and recognised that, ultimately, people produce profits.

In a memo written to GEC managers he pointed out that ratios are an aid to good management rather than a substitute for it. He wrote:

> The operating ratios are of great value as measures of efficiency but they are only the measures and not efficiency itself. Statistics will not design a product better, make it for a lower cost or increase sales. If ill-used, they may so guide action as to diminish resources for the sake of apparent but false signs of improvement.
>
> Management remains a matter of judgement, of knowledge of products and processes and of understanding and skill in dealing with people. The ratios will indicate how well all these things are being done and will show comparison with how they are done elsewhere. But they will tell us nothing about how to do them. That is what you are meant to do.

Source: Extract from *Arnold Weinstock and the Making of GEC*, S. Aris (Aurum Press, 1998), published in *The Sunday Times*, 22 February 1998, p. 3.

Summary

The main points of this chapter may be summarised as follows.

Ratio analysis

- Compares two related figures, usually both from the same set of financial statements.
- Is an aid to understanding what the financial statements really mean.
- Is an inexact science so results must be interpreted cautiously.
- Past periods, the performance of similar businesses and planned performance are often used to provide benchmark ratios.
- A brief overview of the financial statements can often provide insights that may not be revealed by ratios and/or may help in the interpretation of them.

Profitability ratios – concerned with effectiveness at generating profit

- Return on ordinary shareholders' funds (ROSF).
- Return on capital employed (ROCE).
- Operating profit margin.
- Gross profit margin.

Efficiency ratios – concerned with efficiency of using assets/resources

- Average inventories turnover period.
- Average settlement period for trade receivables.
- Average settlement period for trade payables.
- Sales revenue to capital employed.
- Sales revenue per employee.

Liquidity ratios – concerned with the ability to meet short-term obligations

- Current ratio.
- Acid test ratio.
- Cash generated from operations to maturing obligations ratio.

Gearing ratios – concerned with relationship between equity and debt financing

- Gearing ratio.
- Interest cover ratio.

Investment ratios – concerned with returns to shareholders

- Dividend payout ratio.
- Dividend yield ratio.
- Earnings per share.
- Cash generated from operations per share.
- Price/earnings ratio.

Trend analysis

- Individual ratios can be tracked (for example, plotted on a graph) to detect trends.

Ratios as predictors of financial failure

- Univariate analysis – looking at just one ratio over time in an attempt to predict financial failure.
- Multiple discriminate analysis – looking at several ratios, put together in a model, over time in an attempt to predict financial failure – *Z* scores.

Limitations of ratio analysis

- Ratios are only as reliable as the financial statements from which they derive.
- Inflation can distort the information.
- Ratios have restricted vision.
- It can be difficult to find a suitable benchmark (for example, another business) as comparator.
- Some ratios could mislead due to the 'snapshot' nature of the statement of financial position.

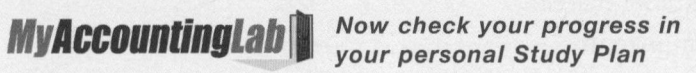

MyAccountingLab **Now check your progress in your personal Study Plan**

Key terms

References

1 'Financial ratios as predictors of failure', *Beaver W. H.*, **Empirical Research in Accounting: Selected Studies**, a supplement to the **Journal of Accounting Research**, 1966, pp. 71–111.

2 'Predicting corporate bankruptcy: an empirical comparison of the extent of financial distress models', *Zmijewski M.E.*, Research paper, State University of New York, 1983.

3 'Predicting financial distress of companies: revisiting the Z-score and Zeta models', *Altman E. I.*, Working paper, New York University, June 2000.

4 'Predicting corporate failure: empirical evidence for the UK', *Neophytou E., Charitou A. and Charalamnous C.*, Working Paper 01-173, Department of Accounting and Management Science, University of Southampton, 2001.

Further reading

If you would like to explore the topics covered in this chapter in more depth, we recommend the following books:

Corporate Financial Accounting and Reporting, *Sutton T.*, 2nd edn, Financial Times Prentice Hall, 2004, chapter 19.

Financial Accounting and Reporting, *Elliott B. and Elliott J.*, 13th edn, Financial Times Prentice Hall, 2010, chapters 28 and 29.

Financial Statement Analysis, *Wild J., Subramanyam K. and Halsey R.*, 9th edn, McGraw-Hill, 2006, chapters 8, 9 and 11.

Interpreting and Analyzing Financial Statements, *Schoenbebeck K.*, 4th edn, Prentice Hall, 2007, chapters 2–5.

Review questions

Answers to these questions can be found at the back of the book on pages 743–4.

7.1 Some businesses operate on a low operating profit margin (for example, a supermarket chain). Does this mean that the return on capital employed from the business will also be low?

7.2 What potential problems arise for the external analyst from the use of statement of financial position figures in the calculation of financial ratios?

7.3 Two businesses operate in the same industry. One has an inventories turnover period that is longer than the industry average. The other has an inventories turnover period that is shorter than the industry average. Give three possible explanations for each business's inventories turnover period ratio.

7.4 Identify and discuss three reasons why the P/E ratio of two businesses operating within the same industry may differ.

Exercises

Exercises 7.5 to 7.8 are more advanced than 7.1 to 7.4. Those with **coloured numbers** have answers at the back of the book, starting on page 768.

If you wish to try more exercises, visit the students' side of the Companion Website and MyAccountingLab.

7.1 I. Jiang (Western) Ltd has recently produced its financial statements for the current year. The directors are concerned that the return on capital employed (ROCE) had decreased from 14 per cent last year to 12 per cent for the current year.

The following reasons were suggested as to why this reduction in ROCE had occurred:

(1) an increase in the gross profit margin;
(2) a reduction in sales revenue;
(3) an increase in overhead expenses;
(4) an increase in amount of inventories held;
(5) the repayment of some borrowings at the year end; and
(6) an increase in the time taken for credit customers (trade receivables) to pay.

Required:
Taking each of these six suggested reasons in turn, state, with reasons, whether each of them could lead to a reduction in ROCE.

7.2 Amsterdam Ltd and Berlin Ltd are both engaged in retailing, but they seem to take a different approach to it according to the following information:

Ratio	Amsterdam Ltd	Berlin Ltd
Return on capital employed (ROCE)	20%	17%
Return on ordinary shareholders' funds (ROSF)	30%	18%
Average settlement period for trade receivables	63 days	21 days
Average settlement period for trade payables	50 days	45 days
Gross profit margin	40%	15%
Operating profit margin	10%	10%
Average inventories turnover period	52 days	25 days

Required:

Describe what this information indicates about the differences in approach between the two businesses. If one of them prides itself on personal service and one of them on competitive prices, which do you think is which and why?

7.3 Conday and Co. Ltd has been in operation for three years and produces antique reproduction furniture for the export market. The most recent set of financial statements for the business is set out as follows:

Statement of financial position as at 30 November

ASSETS	£000
Non-current assets	
Property, plant and equipment (Cost less depreciation)	
Land and buildings	228
Plant and machinery	762
	990
Current assets	
Inventories	600
Trade receivables	820
	1,420
Total assets	2,410
EQUITY AND LIABILITIES	
Equity	
Ordinary shares of £1 each	700
Retained earnings	365
	1,065
Non-current liabilities	
Borrowings – 9% loan notes (Note 1)	200
Current liabilities	
Trade payables	665
Taxation	48
Short-term borrowings (all bank overdraft)	432
	1,145
Total equity and liabilities	2,410

Income statement for the year ended 30 November

	£000
Revenue	2,600
Cost of sales	(1,620)
Gross profit	980
Selling and distribution expenses (Note 2)	(408)
Administration expenses	(194)
Operating profit	378
Finance expenses	(58)
Profit before taxation	320
Taxation	(95)
Profit for the year	225

Notes:

(1) The loan notes are secured on the freehold land and buildings.

(2) Selling and distribution expenses include £170,000 in respect of bad debts.

(3) A dividend of £160,000 was paid on the ordinary shares during the year.

(4) The directors have invited an investor to take up a new issue of ordinary shares in the business at £6.40 each making a total investment of £200,000. The directors wish to use the funds to finance a programme of further expansion.

Required:

(a) Analyse the financial position and performance of the business and comment on any features that you consider to be significant.

(b) State, with reasons, whether or not the investor should invest in the business on the terms outlined.

7.4 The directors of Helena Beauty Products Ltd have been presented with the following abridged financial statements:

Helena Beauty Products Ltd
Income statement for the year ended 30 September

	2008		2009	
	£000	£000	£000	£000
Sales revenue		3,600		3,840
Cost of sales				
Opening inventories	320		400	
Purchases	2,240		2,350	
	2,560		2,750	
Closing inventories	(400)	(2,160)	(500)	(2,250)
Gross profit		1,440		1,590
Expenses		(1,360)		(1,500)
Profit		80		90

Statement of financial position as at 30 September

	2008	2009
ASSETS	£000	£000
Non-current assets		
Property, plant and equipment	1,900	1,860
Current assets		
Inventories	400	500
Trade receivables	750	960
Cash at bank	8	4
	1,158	1,464
Total assets	3,058	3,324
EQUITY AND LIABILITIES		
Equity		
£1 ordinary shares	1,650	1,766
Reserves	1,018	1,108
Current liabilities	2,668	2,874
Total equity and liabilities	390	450
	3,058	3,324

Required:

Using six ratios, comment on the profitability (three ratios) and efficiency (three ratios) of the business as revealed by the statements shown above.

7.5 Threads Limited manufactures nuts and bolts, which are sold to industrial users. The abbreviated financial statements for 2008 and 2009 are as follows:

Income statements for the year ended 30 June

	2008	2009
	£000	£000
Revenue	1,180	1,200
Cost of sales	(680)	(750)
Gross profit	500	450
Operating expenses	(200)	(208)
Depreciation	(66)	(75)
Operating profit	234	167
Interest	(–)	(8)
Profit before taxation	234	159
Taxation	(80)	(48)
Profit for the year	154	111

Statements of financial position as at 30 June

	2008	2009
ASSETS	£000	£000
Non-current assets		
Property, plant and equipment	702	687
Current assets		
Inventories	148	236
Trade receivables	102	156
Cash	3	4
	253	396
Total assets	955	1,083
EQUITY AND LIABILITIES		
Equity		
Ordinary share capital of £1 (fully paid)	500	500
Retained earnings	256	295
	756	795
Non-current liabilities		
Borrowings – Bank loan	–	50
Current liabilities		
Trade payables	60	76
Other payables and accruals	18	16
Taxation	40	24
Short-term borrowings (all bank overdraft)	81	122
	199	238
Total equity and liabilities	955	1,083

Dividends were paid on ordinary shares of £70,000 and £72,000 in respect of 2008 and 2009, respectively.

Required:
(a) Calculate the following financial ratios for *both* 2008 and 2009 (using year-end figures for statement of financial position items):
  (1) return on capital employed
  (2) operating profit margin
  (3) gross profit margin
  (4) current ratio
  (5) acid test ratio
  (6) settlement period for trade receivables
  (7) settlement period for trade payables
  (8) inventories turnover period.

(b) Comment on the performance of Threads Limited from the viewpoint of a business considering supplying a substantial amount of goods to Threads Limited on usual trade credit terms.

7.6 Bradbury Ltd is a family-owned clothes manufacturer based in the south west of England. For a number of years the chairman and managing director was David Bradbury. During his period of office, sales revenue had grown steadily at a rate of 2–3 per cent each year. David Bradbury retired on 30 November 2008 and was succeeded by his son Simon. Soon after taking office, Simon decided to expand the business. Within weeks he had successfully negotiated a five-year contract with a large clothes retailer to make a range of sports and leisurewear items. The contract will result in an additional £2 million in sales revenue during each year of the contract. To fulfil the contract, Bradbury Ltd acquired new equipment and premises.

Financial information concerning the business is given below:

Income statements for the year ended 30 November

	2008 £000	2009 £000
Revenue	9,482	11,365
Operating profit	914	1,042
Interest charges	(22)	(81)
Profit before taxation	892	961
Taxation	(358)	(386)
Profit for the year	534	575

Statements of financial position as at 30 November

	2008 £000	2009 £000
ASSETS		
Non-current assets		
Property, plant and equipment		
Premises at cost	5,240	7,360
Plant and equipment (net)	2,375	4,057
	7,615	11,417
Current assets		
Inventories	2,386	3,420
Trade receivables	2,540	4,280
	4,926	7,700
Total assets	12,541	19,117
EQUITY AND LIABILITIES		
Equity		
Share capital	2,000	2,000
Reserves	7,813	8,268
	9,813	10,268
Non-current liabilities		
Borrowing – Loans	1,220	3,675
Current liabilities		
Trade payables	1,157	2,245
Taxation	179	193
Short-term borrowings (all bank overdraft)	172	2,736
	1,508	5,174
Total equity and liabilities	12,541	19,117

Dividends of £120,000 were paid on ordinary shares in respect of each of the two years.

Required:

(a) Calculate, for each year (using year-end figures for statement of financial position items), the following ratios:

   (1) operating profit margin

   (2) return on capital employed

   (3) current ratio

   (4) gearing ratio

   (5) trade receivables settlement period

   (6) sales revenue to capital employed.

(b) Using the above ratios, and any other ratios or information you consider relevant, comment on the results of the expansion programme.

7.7 The financial statements for Harridges Ltd are given below for the two years ended 30 June 2008 and 2009. Harridges Limited operates a department store in the centre of a small town.

Harridges Ltd Income statement for the years ended 30 June

	2008 £000	2009 £000
Sales revenue	2,600	3,500
Cost of sales	(1,560)	(2,350)
Gross profit	1,040	1,150
Wages and salaries	(320)	(350)
Overheads	(260)	(200)
Depreciation	(150)	(250)
Operating profit	310	350
Interest payable	(50)	(50)
Profit before taxation	260	300
Taxation	(105)	(125)
Profit for the year	155	175

Statement of financial position as at 30 June

ASSETS	2008 £000	2009 £000
Non-current assets		
Property, plant and equipment	1,265	1,525
Current assets		
Inventories	250	400
Trade receivables	105	145
Cash at bank	380	115
	735	660
Total assets	2,000	2,185
EQUITY AND LIABILITIES		
Equity		
Share capital: £1 shares fully paid	490	490
Share premium	260	260
Retained earnings	350	450
	1,100	1,200
Non-current liabilities		
Borrowings – 10% loan notes	500	500
Current liabilities		
Trade payables	300	375
Other payables	100	110
	400	485
Total equity and liabilities	2,000	2,185

Dividends were paid on ordinary shares of £65,000 and £75,000 in respect of 2008 and 2009, respectively.

Required:

(a) Choose and calculate eight ratios that would be helpful in assessing the performance of Harridges Ltd. Use end-of-year values and calculate ratios for both 2008 and 2009.

(b) Using the ratios calculated in (a) and any others you consider helpful, comment on the business's performance from the viewpoint of a prospective purchaser of a majority of shares.

7.8 Genesis Ltd was incorporated in 2006 and has grown rapidly over the past three years. The rapid rate of growth has created problems for the business, which the directors have found difficult to deal with. Recently, a firm of management consultants has been asked to help the directors to overcome these problems.

In a preliminary report to the board of directors, the management consultants state: 'Most of the difficulties faced by the business are symptoms of an underlying problem of overtrading.'

The most recent financial statements of the business are set out below:

Statement of financial position as at 31 October 2009

ASSETS	£000	£000
Non-current assets		
Property, plant and equipment		
Land and buildings at cost	530	
Accumulated depreciation	(88)	442
Fixtures and fittings at cost	168	
Accumulated depreciation	(52)	116
Motor vans at cost	118	
Accumulated depreciation	(54)	64
		622
Current assets		
Inventories		128
Trade receivables		104
		232
Total assets		854
EQUITY AND LIABILITIES		
Equity		
Ordinary £0.50 shares		60
General reserve		50
Retained earnings		74
		184
Non-current liabilities		
Borrowings – 10% loan notes (secured)		120
Current liabilities		
Trade payables		184
Taxation		8
Short-term borrowings (all bank overdraft)		358
		550
Total equity and liabilities		854

Income statement for the year ended 31 October 2009

	£000	£000
Revenue		1,640
Cost of sales		
Opening inventories	116	
Purchases	1,260	
	1,376	
Closing inventories	(128)	(1,248)
Gross profit		392
Selling and distribution expenses		(204)
Administration expenses		(92)
Operating profit		96
Interest payable		(44)
Profit before taxation		52
Taxation		(16)
Profit for the year		36

All purchases and sales were on credit.
A dividend was paid during the year on ordinary shares of £4,000.

Required:
(a) Explain the term 'overtrading' and state how overtrading might arise for a business.
(b) Discuss the kinds of problem that overtrading can create for a business.
(c) Calculate and discuss *five* financial ratios that might be used to establish whether the business is overtrading.
(d) State the ways in which a business may overcome the problem of overtrading.

PART 2

Management accounting

Part 2 deals with the area of accounting usually known as 'management accounting' or 'managerial accounting'. This area is concerned with providing information to help managers to manage the business: it is intended to help them to make decisions, to plan and to ensure that plans are actually achieved.

It is difficult to overestimate the extent to which management accounting, and with it the role of the management accountant, has changed over recent times. The advance of the computer has had an enormous influence. IT has released the management accountant from much of the routine work associated with preparation of management accounting reports and has provided the opportunity to take a more pro-active role within the business. This has led to the management accountant becoming part of the management team and, therefore, directly involved in planning and decision making.

At the same time, it has become increasingly obvious that businesses must be customer focused, outward looking and orientated towards value creation (as discussed in Chapter 1). This more strategic approach to management has required the management accountant to provide the types of information to managers that would have been unthought of, for the typical business, until fairly recently.

These new dimensions to the management accountant's role have implications for the kind of skills required to operate effectively. In particular, certain 'soft' skills are needed such as interpersonal skills for working as part of an effective team and communication skills to help influence the attitudes and behaviour of others.

Through working as part of a cross-functional team, the management accountant should gain a greater awareness of strategic and operational matters and an increased understanding of the information needs of managers. This is likely to have a positive effect on the design and development of management accounting systems. We should therefore see increasing evidence that management accounting systems are being designed to fit the particular structure and processes of the business rather than the other way round. By participating in planning, decision making and control of the business as well as providing management accounting information for these purposes, the management accountant plays a key role in achieving the objectives of the business. It is a role that should add value to the business and improve its competitive position.

Part 2 begins with a consideration of the basics of financial decision making. The first chapter in this part, Chapter 8, deals with how we identify information that is relevant to a particular decision. In practice, we may be confronted with a large volume of financial information and we must be able to discriminate between that which is relevant to a particular decision and that which can be ignored. Unless we can do this, we run the risk of making poor decisions. Chapter 9 continues our examination of the basics by considering the relationship between costs, volume of activity and profit. We shall see that an understanding of this relationship can be helpful in developing plans and in making a variety of decisions. This chapter incorporates an examination of break-even analysis, which is concerned with deducing the volume of activity at which the sales revenue equals the costs incurred so that neither profit nor loss is made by the activity. Knowledge of the break-even figure can be useful in assessing the degree of risk associated with the operations.

In Chapter 10 we look at how businesses can determine the full cost of each unit of their output. By 'full cost' we mean the figure that takes account of all of the costs of producing a product or service. This includes not just those costs that are directly caused by the unit of output, but those, like rent and administrative costs, which are indirectly involved. This topic is continued in Chapter 11, where we consider some recent developments in determining the full cost of a product or service. In this chapter we also consider how a business can set prices for its output and how costs can be controlled.

Chapter 12 deals with the way in which businesses convert their general objectives and long-term plans into workable short-term plans or budgets. Budgets are an important feature of business life and we shall be looking at the budgeting process in some detail. We shall examine the purpose of budgets and the way in which budgets are prepared. In Chapter 13 we shall consider how, after the period of the budget, the actual performance can be compared with the budgeted performance. This is done to assess performance and to help identify the reasons for any failure to meet budget targets. By finding out what has gone wrong, managers may be able to put things right for the future. The chapter concludes with a discussion of the impact of budgets on the attitudes and behaviour of managers.

Relevant costs for decision making

Introduction

This chapter considers the identification and use of costs in making management decisions. These decisions should be made in a way that will promote the business's achievement of its strategic objective. We shall see that not all of the costs that appear to be linked to a particular business decision are relevant to it. It is important to distinguish carefully between costs (and revenues) that are relevant and those that are not. Failure to do this could well lead to bad decisions being made. The principles outlined here will provide the basis for much of the rest of the book.

Learning outcomes

When you have completed this chapter, you should be able to:

● Define and distinguish between relevant costs, outlay costs and opportunity costs.

● Identify and quantify the costs that are relevant to a particular decision.

● Use relevant costs to make decisions.

● Set out the relevant cost analysis in a logical form so that the conclusion may be communicated to managers.

 *Remember to create your own personalised Study Plan*

What is meant by 'cost'?

→ **Cost** represents the amount sacrificed to achieve a particular business objective. Measuring cost may seem, at first sight, to be a straightforward process: it is simply the amount paid for the item of goods being supplied or the service being provided. When measuring cost *for decision-making purposes*, however, things are not quite that simple. The following activity illustrates why this is the case.

Activity 8.1

You own a motor car, for which you paid a purchase price of £5,000 – much below the list price – at a recent car auction. You have just been offered £6,000 for this car.

What is the cost to you of keeping the car for your own use? *Note:* Ignore running costs and so on; just consider the 'capital' cost of the car.

By retaining the car, you are forgoing a cash receipt of £6,000. Thus, the real sacrifice, or cost, incurred by keeping the car for your own use is £6,000. Any decision that you make with respect to the car's future should logically take account of this figure. This cost is known as the 'opportunity cost' since it is the value of the opportunity forgone in order to pursue the other course of action. (In this case, the other course of action is to retain the car.)

We can see that the cost of retaining the car is not the same as the purchase price. In one sense, of course, the cost of the car in Activity 8.1 is £5,000 because that is how much was paid for it. However, this cost, which for obvious reasons is known as the

→ **historic cost**, is only of academic interest. It cannot logically ever be used to make a decision on the car's future. If we disagree with this point, we should ask ourselves how we should assess an offer of £5,500, from another person, for the car. The answer is that

→ we should compare the offer price of £5,500 with the **opportunity cost** of £6,000. This should lead us to reject the offer as it is less than the £6,000 opportunity cost. In these circumstances, it would not be logical to accept the offer of £5,500 on the basis that it was more than the £5,000 that we originally paid. (The only other figure that should concern us is the value to us, in terms of pleasure, usefulness and so on, of retaining the car. If we valued this more highly than the £6,000 opportunity cost, we should reject both offers.)

We may still feel, however, that the £5,000 is relevant here because it will help us in assessing the profitability of the decision. If we sold the car, we should make a profit of either £500 (£5,500 – £5,000) or £1,000 (£6,000 – £5,000) depending on which offer we accept. Since we should seek to make the higher profit, the right decision is to sell the car for £6,000. However, we do not need to know the historic cost of the car to make the right decision. What decision should we make if the car cost us £4,000 to buy? Clearly we should still sell the car for £6,000 rather than for £5,500 as the important comparison is between the offer price and the opportunity cost. We should reach the same conclusion whatever the historic cost of the car.

To emphasise the above point, let us assume that the car cost £10,000. Even in this case the historic cost would still be irrelevant. Had we just bought a car for £10,000 and found that shortly after it is only worth £6,000, we may well be fuming with rage at our mistake, but this does not make the £10,000 a **relevant cost**. The only relevant factors, in a decision on whether to sell the car or to keep it, are the £6,000 opportunity cost and the value of the benefits of keeping it. Thus, the historic cost can never be relevant to a future decision.

To say that historic cost is an **irrelevant cost** is not to say that *the effects of having incurred that cost* are always irrelevant. The fact that we own the car, and are thus in a position to exercise choice as to how to use it, is not irrelevant.

Opportunity costs are rarely taken into account in the routine accounting process, as they do not involve any out-of-pocket expenditure. They are normally only calculated where they are relevant to a particular management decision. Historic costs, on the other hand, do involve out-of-pocket expenditure and are recorded. They are used in preparing the annual financial statements, such as the statement of financial position (balance sheet) and the income statement. This is logical, however, since these statements are intended to be accounts of what has actually happened and are drawn up after the event.

Real World 8.1 gives an example of linked decisions made by two English football clubs: Manchester City and Chelsea.

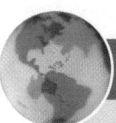

Real World 8.1

Transferring players: a game of two halves

In July 2005, Manchester City Football Club transferred one of its young players, Shaun Wright-Phillips, the England international, to Chelsea Football Club for a reported £21 million. City had signed the player eight years earlier (as a 15 year old) on a free transfer after Nottingham Forest had released him having decided that he was 'too small' to make a professional footballer.

In August 2008, Chelsea sold Wright-Phillips back to City for a fee believed to be around £8.5 million. During his three seasons with Chelsea, Wright-Phillips started only 43 games, though he was brought on as a substitute in some more.

As the transfer fee from Chelsea to City was rather less than half of the amount originally paid, Chelsea made a huge loss on the transaction. However, Chelsea must have viewed the offer of £8.5 million from City as being greater than the sacrifice, or cost, of losing Wright-Phillips's services for Chelsea to have agreed to the transfer. The original amount paid for the player's services should not have been a factor in arriving at the agreed transfer price.

Source: http://en.wikipedia.org.

It might be useful to formalise what we have discussed so far.

A definition of cost

Cost may be defined as the amount of resources, usually measured in monetary terms, sacrificed to achieve a particular objective. The objective might be to retain a car, to buy a particular house, to make a particular product or to render a particular service.

Relevant costs: opportunity and outlay costs

→ We have just seen that, when we are making decisions concerning the future, **past costs** (that is, historic costs) are irrelevant. It is future opportunity costs and future

→ **outlay costs** that are of concern. An opportunity cost can be defined as the value in monetary terms of being deprived of the next best opportunity in order to pursue the particular objective. An outlay cost is an amount of money that will have to be spent to achieve that objective. We shall shortly meet plenty of examples of both of these types of future cost.

To be relevant to a particular decision, a future outlay cost, or opportunity cost, must satisfy both of the following criteria:

● *It must relate to the objectives of the business.* Most businesses have enhancing owners' (shareholders') wealth as their key strategic objective. That is to say, they are seeking to become richer (see Chapter 1). Thus, to be relevant to a particular decision, a cost must have an effect on the wealth of the business.

● *It must differ from one possible decision outcome to the next.* Only costs (and revenues) that are different between outcomes can be used to distinguish between them. Thus the reason that the historic cost of the car that we discussed earlier is irrelevant is that it is the same whichever decision is taken about the future of the car. This means that all past costs are irrelevant because what has happened in the past must be the same for all possible future outcomes.

It is not only past costs that are the same from one decision outcome to the next; some future costs may also be the same. Take, for example, a road haulage business that has decided that it will buy a new lorry and the decision lies between two different models. The load capacity, the fuel and maintenance costs are different for each lorry. The potential costs and revenues associated with these are relevant items. The lorry will require a driver, so the business will need to employ one, but a suitably qualified driver could drive either lorry equally well, for the same wage. The cost of employing the driver is thus irrelevant to the decision as to which lorry to buy. This is despite the fact that this cost is a future one.

If, however, the decision did not concern a choice between two models of lorry but rather whether to operate an additional lorry or not, the cost of employing the additional driver would be relevant, because it would then be a cost that would vary with the decision made.

Activity 8.2

A garage business has an old car that it bought several months ago. The car needs a replacement engine before it can be driven. It is possible to buy a reconditioned engine for £300. This would take seven hours to fit by a mechanic who is paid £12 an hour. At present the garage is short of work, but the owners are reluctant to lay off any mechanics or even to cut down their basic working week because skilled labour is difficult to find and an upturn in repair work is expected soon.

The garage paid £3,000 to buy the car. Without the engine it could be sold for an estimated £3,500. What is the minimum price at which the garage should sell the car with a reconditioned engine fitted?

The minimum price is the amount required to cover the relevant costs of the job. At this price, the business will make neither a profit nor a loss. Any price that is lower than this amount will mean that the wealth of the business is reduced. Thus, the minimum price is:

	£
Opportunity cost of the car	3,500
Cost of the reconditioned engine	300
Total	3,800

The original cost of the car is irrelevant for reasons that have already been discussed; it is the opportunity cost of the car that concerns us. The cost of the new engine is relevant because, if the work is done, the garage will have to pay £300 for the engine; but will pay nothing if the job is not done. The £300 is an example of a future outlay cost.

The labour cost is irrelevant because the same cost will be incurred whether the mechanic undertakes the work or not. This is because the mechanic is being paid to do nothing if this job is not undertaken; thus the additional labour cost arising from this job is zero.

It should be emphasised that the garage will not seek to sell the car with its reconditioned engine for £3,800; it will attempt to charge as much as possible for it. However, any price above the £3,800 will make the garage better off financially than it would be by not undertaking the engine replacement.

Activity 8.3

Assume exactly the same circumstances as in Activity 8.2, except that the garage is quite busy at the moment. If a mechanic is to be put on the engine-replacement job, it will mean that other work that the mechanic could have done during the seven hours, all of which could be charged to a customer, will not be undertaken. The garage's labour charge is £40 an hour, though the mechanic is only paid £12 an hour.

What is the minimum price at which the garage should sell the car, with a reconditioned engine fitted, under these altered circumstances?

The minimum price is:

	£
Opportunity cost of the car	3,500
Cost of the reconditioned engine	300
Labour cost (7 × £40)	280
Total	4,080

We can see that the opportunity cost of the car and the cost of the engine are the same as in Activity 8.2 but now a charge for labour has been added to obtain the minimum price. The relevant labour cost here is that which the garage will have to sacrifice in making the time available to undertake the engine replacement job. While the mechanic is working on this job, the garage is losing the opportunity to do work for which a customer would pay £280. Note that the £12 an hour mechanic's wage is still not relevant. The mechanic will be paid £12 an hour irrespective of whether it is the engine-replacement work or some other job that is undertaken.

Activity (8.4)

A business is considering making a bid to undertake a contract. Fulfilment of the contract will require the use of two types of raw material. Quantities of both of these materials are held by the business. If it chose to, the business could sell the raw materials in their present state. All of the inventories of these two raw materials will need to be used on the contract. Information on the raw materials concerned is as follows:

Inventories item	Quantity	Historic cost	Sales value	Replacement cost
	Units	£/unit	£/unit	£/unit
A1	500	5	3	6
B2	800	7	8	10

Inventories item A1 is in frequent use in the business on a variety of work.

The inventories of item B2 were bought a year ago for a contract that was abandoned. It has recently become obvious that there is no likelihood of ever using this raw material if the contract currently being considered does not proceed.

Management wishes to deduce the minimum price at which the business could undertake the contract without reducing its wealth as a result. This can be used as the baseline in deducing the bid price.

How much should be included in the minimum price in respect of the two inventories items detailed above?

The relevant costs to be included in the minimum price are:

Inventories item: A1   £6 × 500 = £3,000
                   B2   £8 × 800 = £6,400

We are told that the item A1 is in frequent use and so, if it is used on the contract, it will need to be replaced. Sooner or later, the business will have to buy 500 units (currently costing £6 a unit) additional to those which would have been required had the contract not been undertaken.

We are told that item B2 will never be used by the business unless the contract is undertaken. Thus, if the contract is not undertaken, the only reasonable thing for the business to do is to sell the B2. This means that if the contract is undertaken and the B2 is used, it will have an opportunity cost equal to the potential proceeds from disposal, which is £8 a unit.

Note that the historic cost information about both materials is irrelevant and this will always be the case.

Activity (8.5)

HLA Ltd is in the process of preparing a quotation for a special job for a customer. The job will have the following material requirements:

Material	Units required	Units currently held in inventories			
		Quantity held	Historic cost £/unit	Sales value £/unit	Replacement cost £/unit
P	400	0	–	–	40
Q	230	100	62	50	64
R	350	200	48	23	59
S	170	140	33	12	49
T	120	120	40	0	68

Material Q is used consistently by the business on various jobs.

The business holds materials R, S and T as the result of previous overbuying. No other use (apart from this special job) can be found for R, but the 140 units of S could be used in another job as a substitute for 225 units of material V that are about to be purchased at a price of £10 a unit. Material T has no other use, it is a dangerous material that is difficult to store and the business has been informed that it will cost £160 to dispose of the material currently held.

If it chose to, the business could sell the raw materials Q, R and S already held in their present state.

What is the relevant cost of the materials for the job specified above?

The relevant cost is as follows:

	£
Material P	
This will have to be purchased at £40 a unit (400 × £40)	16,000
Material Q	
This will have to be replaced, therefore, the relevant price is (230 × £64)	14,720
Material R	
200 units of this are held and these could be sold. The relevant price of these is the sales revenue foregone (200 × £23)	4,600
The remaining 150 units of R would have to be purchased (150 × £59)	8,850
Material S	
This could be sold or used as a substitute for material V.	
The existing inventories could be sold for £1,680 (140 × £12); however, the saving on material V is higher and therefore should be taken as the relevant amount (225 × £10)	2,250
The remaining units of material S must be purchased (30 × £49)	1,470
A saving on disposal will be made if material T is used	(160)
Total relevant cost	47,730

Real World 8.2 gives an example of how opportunity costs can affect student demand for MBA courses.

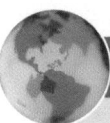

Sunk costs and committed costs

→ A **sunk cost** is simply another way of referring to a past cost and so the terms 'sunk
→ cost' and 'past cost' can be used interchangeably. A **committed cost** is also, in effect, a past cost to the extent that an irrevocable decision has been made to incur the cost because, for example, a business has entered into a binding contract. As a result, it is more or less a past cost despite the fact that the cash may not be paid in respect of it until some point in the future. Since the business has no choice as to whether it incurs the cost or not, a committed cost can never be a relevant cost for decision-making purposes.

It is important to remember that, to be relevant, a cost must be capable of varying according to the decision made. If the business is already committed by a legally binding contract to a cost, that cost cannot vary with the decision.

Figure 8.1 summarises the relationship between relevant, irrelevant, opportunity, outlay and past costs.

Activity 8.6

Past costs are irrelevant costs. Does this mean that what happened in the past is irrelevant?

No, it does not mean this. The fact that the business has an asset that it can deploy in the future is highly relevant. What is not relevant is how much it cost to acquire that asset. This point was examined in the discussion that followed Activity 8.1.

Another reason why the past is not irrelevant is that it generally – though not always – provides us with our best guide to the future. Suppose that we need to estimate the cost of doing something in the future to help us to decide whether it is worth doing. In these circumstances our own experience, or that of others, on how much it has cost to do the thing in the past may provide us with a valuable guide to how much it is likely to cost in the future.

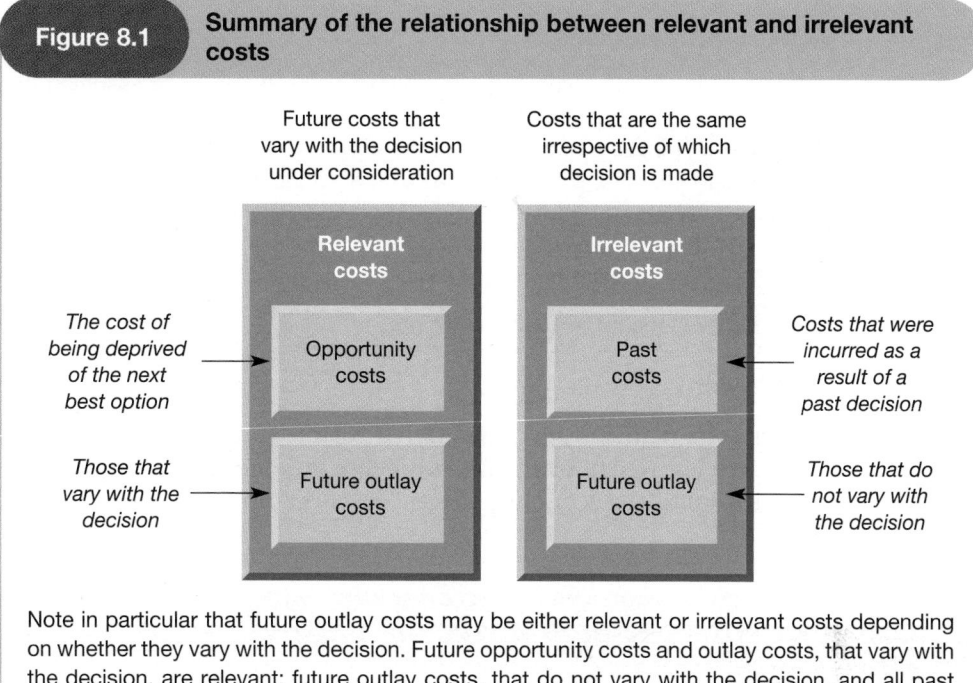

Figure 8.1 **Summary of the relationship between relevant and irrelevant costs**

Note in particular that future outlay costs may be either relevant or irrelevant costs depending on whether they vary with the decision. Future opportunity costs and outlay costs, that vary with the decision, are relevant; future outlay costs, that do not vary with the decision, and all past costs, are irrelevant.

Qualitative factors of decisions

Although businesses must look closely at the obvious financial effects when making decisions, they must also consider factors that are not directly economic. These are likely to be factors that have a broader, but less immediate, impact on the business. Ultimately, however, these factors are likely to have economic effect – that is, to affect the wealth of the business.

Activity 8.7

Activity 8.3 was concerned with the cost of putting a car into a marketable condition. Apart from whether the car could be sold for more than the relevant cost of doing this, are there any other factors that should be taken into account in making a decision as to whether or not to do the work?

We can think of three points:

● Turning away another job in order to do the engine replacement may lead to customer dissatisfaction.
● On the other hand, having the car available for sale may be useful commercially for the garage, beyond the profit that can be earned from that particular car sale. For example, having a good range of second-hand cars for sale may attract potential customers wanting to buy a car.

Activity 8.7 continued

● There is also a more immediate economic point. It has been assumed that the only opportunity cost concerns labour (the charge-out rate for the seven hours concerned). In practice, most car repairs involve the use of some materials and spare parts. These are usually charged to customers at a profit to the garage. Any such profit from a job turned away would be lost to the garage, and this lost profit would be an opportunity cost of the engine replacement and should, therefore, be included in the calculation of the minimum price to be charged for the sale of the car.

You may have thought of additional points.

It is important to consider 'qualitative' factors carefully. There is a risk that they may be given less weight by managers because they are virtually impossible to assess in terms of their ultimate economic effect. This effect can nevertheless be very significant.

Using relevant cost as a basis for setting prices

The relevant cost of some item or activity is the minimum price for which the business can offer it for sale. This minimum price will leave the business no better off as a result of making the sale than it would have been had it pursued the next best opportunity. To profit from the sale the business would need to add a profit margin.

This relevant cost approach to pricing would normally be used only where there is not the opportunity to sell at a price that will cover all of the business's cost, not just the relevant part. In the long run, the business must cover all of its costs if it is to generate value and increase its owners' wealth.

Self-assessment question 8.1

JB Limited is a small specialist manufacturer of electronic components. Makers of aircraft, for both civil and military purposes, use much of its output. One of the aircraft makers has offered a contract to JB Limited for the supply, over the next 12 months, of 400 identical components. The data relating to the production of each component are as follows:

● *Material requirements:*
  3 kg of material M1 (see Note 1 below)
  2 kg of material P2 (see Note 2 below)
  1 bought-in component (part number 678) (see Note 3 below)

  Note 1: Material M1 is in continuous use by the business; 1,000 kg are currently held by the business. The original cost was £4.70/kg, but it is known that future purchases will cost £5.50/kg.

  Note 2: 1,200 kg of material P2 are currently held. The original cost of this material was £4.30/kg. The material has not been required for the last two years. Its scrap value is £1.50/kg. The only foreseeable alternative use is as a substitute for material P4 (in constant use) but this would involve further processing costs of £1.60/kg. The current cost of material P4 is £3.60/kg.

Note 3: It is estimated that the component (part number 678) could be bought in for £50 each.

● *Labour requirements*: Each component would require five hours of skilled labour and five hours of semi-skilled. A skilled employee is available and is currently paid £14/hour. A replacement would, however, have to be obtained at a rate of £12/hour for the work which would otherwise be done by the skilled employee. The current rate for semi-skilled work is £10/hour and an additional employee could be appointed for this work.

● *General manufacturing costs*: It is JB Limited's policy to charge a share of the general costs (rent, heating and so on) to each contract undertaken at the rate of £20 for each machine hour used on the contract. If the contract is undertaken, the general costs are expected to increase as a result of undertaking the contract by £3,200.

Spare machine capacity is available and each component would require four machine hours. A price of £200 a component has been offered by the potential customer.

Required:

(a) Should the contract be accepted? Support your conclusion with appropriate figures to present to management.

(b) What other factors ought management to consider that might influence the decision?

The answer to this question can be found at the back of the book on page 729.

To end the chapter, **Real World 8.3** describes another case where the decision makers, quite correctly, ignored past costs and just concentrated on future options for the business concerned.

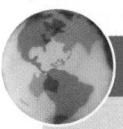

Real World 8.3

Pound shop

FT

In 2006 Merchant Equity Partners (MEP), a private equity group, bought the retail arm of MFI (the furniture business) for just £1. MEP planned to revive the loss-making furniture chain and sell it on for up to £500 million in around 2011. MFI management felt at the time that having it taken over by MEP might avoid the retail arm slipping further into financial difficulties.

The buy-out agreement included an arrangement that MFI would pay a 'dowry' of £75 million over three years to encourage MEP to take it off MFI's hands. MFI felt that it would then be able to concentrate on the profitable part of its business, Howden Joinery, which sells kitchen cabinets to the building trade.

In the event, MEP's plans for MFI retail were overtaken by the downturn in furniture sales and MEP allowed the business to be taken over by a group of its managers in 2008. The business collapsed completely and stopped trading late in 2008.

Source: Taken from 'MFI furniture retail arm bought for £1', E. Callan, FT.com, 12 July 2006; and 'Favell buy-out rescues MFI from administration', T. Braithwaite, *Financial Times*, 28 September 2008.

Summary

The main points in this chapter may be summarised as follows:

Cost = amount of resources, usually measured in monetary terms, sacrificed to achieve a particular objective.

Relevant and irrelevant costs

- Relevant costs must:
  - relate to the objective being pursued by the business;
  - differ from one possible decision outcome to the next.

- Relevant costs therefore include:
  - opportunity costs;
  - differential future outlay costs.

- Irrelevant costs therefore include:
  - all past (or sunk) costs;
  - all committed costs;
  - non-differential outlay costs.

Qualitative factors of decisions

- Financial/economic decisions almost inevitably have qualitative aspects that financial analysis cannot really handle, despite their importance.

Using relevant cost as a basis for setting prices

- Any price above the relevant cost will make the business and its owners wealthier.

- In the long run, the business must cover all of its costs, not just the relevant ones.

 **Now check your progress in your personal Study Plan**

→ Key terms

cost p. 292	**past cost** p. 294
historic cost p. 292	**outlay cost** p. 294
opportunity cost p. 292	**sunk cost** p. 298
relevant cost p. 293	**committed cost** p. 298
irrelevant cost p. 293	

Further reading

If you would like to explore the topics covered in this chapter in more depth, we recommend the following books:

Management Accounting, *Atkinson A., Banker R., Kaplan R., Young S. M. and Matsumura E.*, 5th edn, Prentice Hall, 2007, chapter 6.

Management and Cost Accounting, *Drury C.*, 7th edn, Cengage Learning, 2007, chapter 9.

Cost Accounting: A Managerial Emphasis, *Horngren C., Foster G., Datar S., Rajan M. and Ittner C.*, 13th edn, Prentice Hall International, 2008, chapter 11.

Managerial Accounting, *Hilton R.*, 6th edn, McGraw-Hill Irwin, 2005, chapter 14.

Review questions

Answers to these questions can be found at the back of the book on page 744.

8.1 To be relevant to a particular decision, a cost must have two attributes. What are they?

8.2 Distinguish between a sunk cost and an opportunity cost.

8.3 Define the word 'cost' in the context of management accounting.

8.4 What is meant by the expression 'committed cost'? How do committed costs arise?

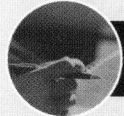

Exercises

Exercises 8.7 and 8.8 are more advanced than 8.1 to 8.6. Those with **coloured numbers** have answers at the back of the book, starting on page 772.

If you wish to try more exercises, visit the students' side of the Companion Website and MyAccountingLab.

8.1 Lombard Ltd has been offered a contract for which there is available production capacity. The contract is for 20,000 identical items, manufactured by an intricate assembly operation, to be produced and delivered in the next few months at a price of £80 each. The specification for one item is as follows:

Assembly labour	4 hours
Component X	4 units
Component Y	3 units

There would also be the need to hire equipment, for the duration of the contract, at an outlay cost of £200,000.

The assembly is a highly skilled operation and the workforce is currently underutilised. It is the business's policy to retain this workforce on full pay in anticipation of high demand next year, for a new product currently being developed. There is sufficient available skilled labour to undertake the contract now under consideration. Skilled workers are paid £15 an hour.

Component X is used in a number of other subassemblies produced by the business. It is readily available. 50,000 units of Component X are currently held in inventories. Component Y was a special purchase in anticipation of an order that did not in the end materialise. It is, therefore, surplus to requirements and the 100,000 units that are currently held may have to be sold at a loss. An estimate of various values for Components X and Y provided by the materials planning department is as follows:

Component	X	Y
	£/unit	*£/unit*
Historic cost	4	10
Replacement cost	5	11
Net realisable value	3	8

It is estimated that any additional relevant costs associated with the contract (beyond the above) will amount to £8 an item.

Required:
Analyse the information and advise Lombard Ltd on the desirability of the contract.

8.2 The local authority of a small town maintains a theatre and arts centre for the use of a local repertory company, other visiting groups and exhibitions. Management decisions are taken by a committee that meets regularly to review the financial statements and to plan the use of the facilities.

The theatre employs a full-time, non-performing staff and a number of artistes at total costs of £9,600 and £35,200 a month, respectively. The theatre mounts a new production every month for 20 performances. Other monthly costs of the theatre are as follows:

	£
Costumes	5,600
Scenery	3,300
Heat and light	10,300
A share of the administration costs of local authority	16,000
Casual staff	3,520
Refreshments	2,360

On average the theatre is half full for the performances of the repertory company. The capacity and seat prices in the theatre are:

200 seats at £24 each
500 seats at £16 each
300 seats at £12 each

In addition, the theatre sells refreshments during the performances for £7,760 a month. Programme sales cover their costs, but advertising in the programme generates £6,720 a month.

The management committee has been approached by a popular touring group, which would like to take over the theatre for one month (25 performances). The group is prepared to pay the local authority half of its ticket income as a fee for the use of the theatre. The group expects to fill the theatre for 10 nights and achieve two-thirds capacity on the remaining 15 nights. The prices charged are £2 less than normally applies in the theatre.

The local authority will, as normal, pay for heat and light costs and will still honour the contracts of all artistes and pay the non-performing employees who will sell refreshments, programmes and so on. The committee does not expect any change in the level of refreshments or programme sales if they agree to this booking.

Note: The committee includes the share of the local authority administration costs when making profit calculations. It assumes occupancy applies equally across all seat prices.

Required:
(a) On financial grounds should the management committee agree to the approach from the touring group? Support your answer with appropriate workings.
(b) What other factors may have a bearing on the decision by the committee?

8.3 Andrews and Co. Ltd has been invited to tender for a contract. It is to produce 10,000 metres of an electrical cable in which the business specialises. The estimating department of the business has produced the following information relating to the contract:

● *Materials*: The cable will require a steel core, which the business buys in. The steel core is to be coated with a special plastic, also bought in, using a special process. Plastic for the covering will be required at the rate of 0.10 kg/metre of completed cable.
● *Direct labour*:
Skilled: 10 minutes/metre
Unskilled: 5 minutes/metre

The business already holds sufficient of each of the materials required, to complete the contract. Information on the cost of the inventories is as follows:

	Steel core £/metre	Plastic £/kg
Historic cost	1.50	0.60
Current buying-in cost	2.10	0.70
Scrap value	1.40	0.10

The steel core is in constant use by the business for a variety of work that it regularly undertakes. The plastic is a surplus from a previous contract where a mistake was made and an excess quantity ordered. If the current contract does not go ahead, this plastic will be scrapped.

Unskilled labour, which is paid at the rate of £7.50 an hour, will need to be taken on specifically to undertake the contract. The business is fairly quiet at the moment which means that a pool of skilled labour exists that will still be employed at full pay of £12 an hour to do nothing if the contract does not proceed. The pool of skilled labour is sufficient to complete the contract.

Required:
Indicate the minimum price at which the contract could be undertaken, such that the business would be neither better nor worse off as a result of doing it.

8.4 SJ Services Ltd has been asked to quote a price for a special contract to render a service that will take the business one week to complete. Information relating to labour for the contract is as follows:

Grade of labour	Hours required	Basic rate/hour
Skilled	27	£12
Semi-skilled	14	£9
Unskilled	20	£7

A shortage of skilled labour means that the necessary staff to undertake the contract would have to be moved from other work that is currently yielding an excess of sales revenue over labour and other costs of £8 an hour.

Semi-skilled labour is currently being paid at semi-skilled rates to undertake unskilled work. If the relevant members of staff are moved to work on the contract, unskilled labour will have to be employed for the week to replace them.

The unskilled labour actually needed to work on the contract will be specifically employed for the week of the contract.

All labour is charged to contracts at 50 per cent above the rate paid to the employees, so as to cover the contract's fair share of the business's general costs (rent, heating and so on). It is estimated that these general costs will increase by £50 as a result of undertaking the contract.

Undertaking the contract will require the use of a specialised machine for the week. The business owns such a machine, which it depreciates at the rate of £120 a week. This machine is currently being hired out to another business at a weekly rental of £175 on a week-by-week contract.

To derive the above estimates, the business has had to spend £300 on a specialised study. If the contract does not proceed, the results of the study can be sold for £250.

An estimate of the contract's fair share of the business's rent is £150 a week.

Required:
Deduce the minimum price at which SJ Services Ltd could undertake the contract such that it would be neither better nor worse off as a result of undertaking it.

8.5 A business in the food industry is currently holding 2,000 tonnes of material in bulk storage. This material deteriorates with time, and so in the near future it needs to be repackaged for sale or sold in its present form.

The material was acquired in two batches: 800 tonnes at a price of £40 a tonne and 1,200 tonnes at a price of £44 a tonne. The current market price of any additional purchases is £48 a tonne. If the business were to dispose of the material, it could sell any quantity but only for £36 a tonne; it does not have the contacts or reputation to command a higher price.

Processing this material may be undertaken to develop either Product A or Product X. No weight loss occurs with the processing, that is, 1 tonne of material will make 1 tonne of A or X. For Product A, there is an additional cost of £60 a tonne, after which it will sell for £105 a tonne. The marketing department estimates that 500 tonnes could be sold in this way.

With Product X, the business incurs additional costs of £80 a tonne for processing. A market price for X is not known and no minimum price has been agreed. The management is currently engaged in discussions over the minimum price that may be charged for Product X in the current circumstances. Management wants to know the relevant cost per tonne for Product X so as to provide a basis for negotiating a profitable selling price for the product.

Required:
Identify the relevant cost per tonne for Product X, given sales volumes of X of:
(a)   up to 1,500 tonnes
(b)   over 1,500 tonnes, up to 2,000 tonnes
(c)   over 2,000 tonnes.

Explain your answer.

8.6 A local education authority is faced with a predicted decline in the demand for school places in its area. It is believed that some schools will have to close in order to remove up to 800 places from current capacity levels. The schools that may face closure are referenced as A, B, C and D. Their details are as follows:

● *School A* (capacity 200) was built 15 years ago at a cost of £1.2 million. It is situated in a 'socially disadvantaged' community area. The authority has been offered £14 million for the site by a property developer.
● *School B* (capacity 500) was built 20 years ago and cost £1 million. It was renovated only two years ago at a cost of £3 million to improve its facilities. An offer of £8 million has been made for the site by a business planning a shopping complex in this affluent part of the area.
● *School C* (capacity 600) cost £5 million to build five years ago. The land for this school is rented from a local business for an annual cost of £300,000. The land rented for School C is based on a 100-year lease. If the school closes, the property reverts immediately to the owner. If School C is not closed, it will require a £3 million investment to improve safety at the school.
● *School D* (800 capacity) cost £7 million to build eight years ago; last year £1.5 million was spent on an extension. It has a considerable amount of grounds, which is currently used for sporting events. This factor makes it popular with developers, who have recently offered £9 million for the site. If School D is closed, it will be necessary to pay £1.8 million to adapt facilities at other schools to accommodate the change.

In the accounting system, the local authority depreciates non-current assets based on 2 per cent a year on the original cost. It also differentiates between one-off, large items of capital expenditure or revenue, and annually recurring items.

The local authority has a central staff, which includes administrators for each school costing £200,000 a year for each school, and a chief education officer costing £80,000 a year in total.

Required:

(a) Prepare a summary of the relevant cash flows (costs and revenues, relative to not making any closures) under the following options:

  (1) closure of D only

  (2) closure of A and B

  (3) closure of A and C.

  Show separately the one-off effects and annually recurring items, rank the options open to the local authority, and briefly interpret your answer. *Note:* Various approaches are acceptable provided that they are logical.

(b) Identify and comment on any two different types of irrelevant cost contained in the information given in the question.

(c) Discuss other factors that might have a bearing on the decision.

8.7 Rob Otics Ltd, a small business that specialises in building electronic-control equipment, has just received an order from a customer for eight identical robotic units. These will be completed using Rob Otics's own labour force and factory capacity. The product specification prepared by the estimating department shows the following:

● Material and labour requirements for each robotic unit:

  Component X   2 per unit

  Component Y   1 per unit

  Component Z   4 per unit

● Other miscellaneous items:

  Assembly labour   25 hours per unit (but see below)

  Inspection labour   6 hours per unit

As part of the costing exercise, the business has collected the following information:

● *Component X.* This item is normally held by the business as it is in constant demand. The 10 units currently held were invoiced to Rob Otics at £150 a unit, but the sole supplier has announced a price rise of 20 per cent effective immediately. Rob Otics has not yet paid for the items currently held.

● *Component Y.* 25 units are currently held. This component is not normally used by Rob Otics but the units currently held are because of a cancelled order following the bankruptcy of a customer. The units originally cost the business £4,000 in total, although Rob Otics has recouped £1,500 from the liquidator of the bankrupt business. As Rob Otics can see no use for these units (apart from the possible use of some of them in the order now being considered), the finance director proposes to scrap all 25 units (zero proceeds).

● *Component Z.* This is in regular use by Rob Otics. There is none in inventories but an order is about to be sent to a supplier for 75 units, irrespective of this new proposal. The supplier charges £25 a unit on small orders but will reduce the price to £20 a unit for all units on any order over 100 units.

● Other miscellaneous items. These are expected to cost £250 in total.

Assembly labour is currently in short supply in the area and is paid at £10 an hour. If the order is accepted, all necessary labour will have to be transferred from existing work, and other orders will be lost. It is estimated that for each hour transferred to this contract £38 will be lost (calculated as lost sales revenue £60, less materials £12 and labour £10). The production director suggests that, owing to a learning process, the time taken to make each unit will reduce, from 25 hours to make the first one, by one hour a unit made.

Inspection labour can be provided by paying existing personnel overtime which is at a premium of 50 per cent over the standard rate of £12 an hour.

When the business is working out its contract prices, it normally adds an amount equal to £20 for each assembly hour to cover its general costs (such as rent and electricity). To the resulting total, 40 per cent is normally added as a profit mark-up.

Required:

(a) Prepare an estimate of the minimum price that you would recommend Rob Otics Ltd to charge for the proposed contract such that it would be neither better nor worse off as a result. Provide explanations for any items included.

(b) Identify any other factors that you would consider before fixing the final price.

8.8 A business places substantial emphasis on customer satisfaction and, to this end, delivers its product in special protective containers. These containers have been made in a department within the business. Management has recently become concerned that this internal supply of containers is very expensive. As a result, outside suppliers have been invited to submit tenders for the provision of these containers. A quote of £250,000 a year has been received for a volume that compares with current internal supply.

An investigation into the internal costs of container manufacture has been undertaken and the following emerges:

(a) The annual cost of material is £120,000, according to the stores records maintained, at actual historic cost. Three-quarters (by cost) of this represents material that is regularly stocked and replenished. The remaining 25 per cent of the material cost is a special foaming chemical that is not used for any other purpose. There are 40 tonnes of this chemical currently held. It was bought in bulk for £750 a tonne. Today's replacement price for this material is £1,050 a tonne but it is unlikely that the business could realise more than £600 a tonne if it had to be disposed of owing to the high handling costs and special transport facilities required.

(b) The annual labour cost is £80,000 for this department; however, most are casual employees or recent starters, and so, if an outside quote was accepted, little redundancy would be payable. There are, however, two long-serving employees who would each accept as a salary £15,000 a year until they reached retirement age in two years' time.

(c) The department manager has a salary of £30,000 a year. The closure of this department would release him to take over another department for which a vacancy is about to be advertised. The salary, status and prospects are similar.

(d) A rental charge of £9,750 a year, based on floor area, is allocated to the containers department. If the department were closed, the floor space released would be used for warehousing and, as a result, the business would give up the tenancy of an existing warehouse for which it is paying £15,750 a year.

(e) The plant cost £162,000 when it was bought five years ago. Its market value now is £28,000 and it could continue for another two years, at which time its market value would have fallen to zero. (The plant depreciates evenly over time.)

(f) Annual plant maintenance costs are £9,900 and allocated general administrative costs £33,750 for the coming year.

Required:

Calculate the annual cost of manufacturing containers for comparison with the quote using relevant figures for establishing the cost or benefit of accepting the quote. Indicate any assumptions or qualifications you wish to make.

CHAPTER 9

Cost-volume-profit analysis

Introduction

This chapter is concerned with the relationship between the volume of activity, cost and profit. Broadly, cost can be analysed between that element that is fixed, relative to the volume of activity, and that element that varies according to the volume of activity. We shall consider how we can use knowledge of this relationship to make decisions and to assess risk, particularly in the context of short-term decisions. This will help the business to work towards its strategic objectives. This continues the theme of Chapter 8, but in this chapter we shall be looking at situations where a whole class of cost – fixed cost – can be treated as being irrelevant for decision-making purposes.

Learning outcomes

When you have completed this chapter, you should be able to:

- Distinguish between fixed cost and variable cost and use this distinction to explain the relationship between cost, volume and profit.

- Prepare a break-even chart and deduce the break-even point for some activity.

- Discuss the weaknesses of break-even analysis.

- Demonstrate the way in which marginal analysis can be used when making short-term decisions.

MyAccountingLab   *Remember to create your own personalised Study Plan*

Cost behaviour

We saw in the previous chapter that cost represents the resources that have to be sacrificed to achieve a business objective. The objective may be to make a particular product, to provide a particular service, to operate an IT department and so on. The costs incurred by a business may be classified in various ways and one important way is according to how they behave in relation to changes in the volume of activity. Costs may be classified according to whether they:

● remain constant (fixed) when changes occur to the volume of activity; or
● vary according to the volume of activity.

→ These are known as **fixed costs** and **variable costs** respectively. Thus, in the case of a restaurant, the manager's salary would normally be a fixed cost while the cost of the unprepared food would be a variable cost.

As we shall see, knowing how much of each type of cost is associated with a particular activity can be of great value to the decision maker.

Fixed cost

The way in which a fixed cost behaves can be shown by preparing a graph that plots the fixed cost of a business against the level of activity, as in Figure 9.1. The distance 0F represents the amount of fixed cost, and this stays the same irrespective of the volume of activity.

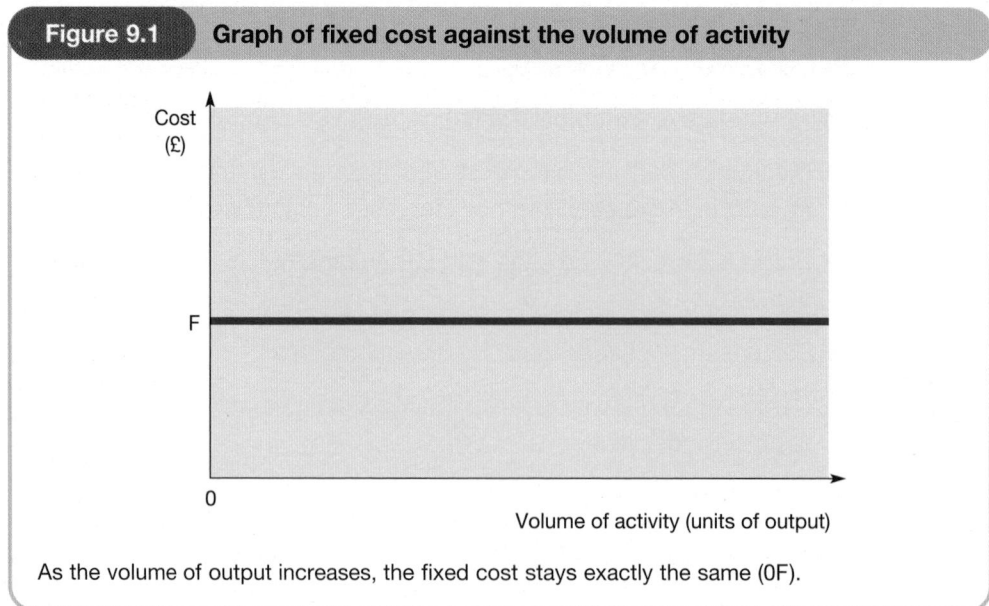

Figure 9.1 **Graph of fixed cost against the volume of activity**

As the volume of output increases, the fixed cost stays exactly the same (0F).

Activity 9.1

Can you give some examples of items of cost that are likely to be fixed for a hairdressing business?

We came up with the following:

- rent
- insurance
- cleaning cost
- staff salaries.

These items of cost are likely to be the same irrespective of the number of customers having their hair cut or styled.

Staff salaries (or wages) are often assumed to be a variable cost but in practice they tend to be fixed. Members of staff are not normally paid according to the volume of output and it is unusual to dismiss staff when there is a short-term downturn in activity. Where there is a long-term downturn, or at least it seems that way to management, redundancies may occur with fixed-cost savings. This, however, is true of all types of fixed cost. For example, management may also decide to close some branches to make rental cost savings.

There are circumstances in which the labour cost is variable (for example, where staff are paid according to how much output they produce), but this is unusual. Whether labour cost is fixed or variable depends on the circumstances in the particular case concerned.

It is important to be clear that 'fixed', in this context, means only that the cost is unaffected by changes in the volume of activity. Fixed cost is likely to be affected by inflation. If rent (a typical fixed cost) goes up because of inflation, a fixed cost will have increased, but not because of a change in the volume of activity.

Similarly, the level of fixed cost does not stay the same, irrespective of the time period involved. Fixed cost elements are almost always *time based*: that is, they vary with the length of time concerned. The rental charge for two months is normally twice that for one month. Thus, fixed cost normally varies with time, but (of course) not with the volume of output. This means that when we talk of fixed cost being, say, £1,000, we must add the period concerned, say, £1,000 a month.

Activity 9.2

Does fixed cost stay the same irrespective of the volume of output, even where there is a massive rise in that volume? Think in terms of the rent cost for the hairdressing business.

In fact, the rent is only fixed over a particular range (known as the 'relevant' range). If the number of people wanting to have their hair cut by the business increased, and the business wished to meet this increased demand, it would eventually have to expand its physical size. This might be achieved by opening an additional branch, or perhaps by moving the existing business to larger premises nearby. It may be possible to cope with relatively minor increases in activity by using existing space more efficiently, or by having longer opening hours. If activity continued to expand, however, increased rent charges would seem inevitable.

In practice, the situation described in Activity 9.2 would look something like Figure 9.2.

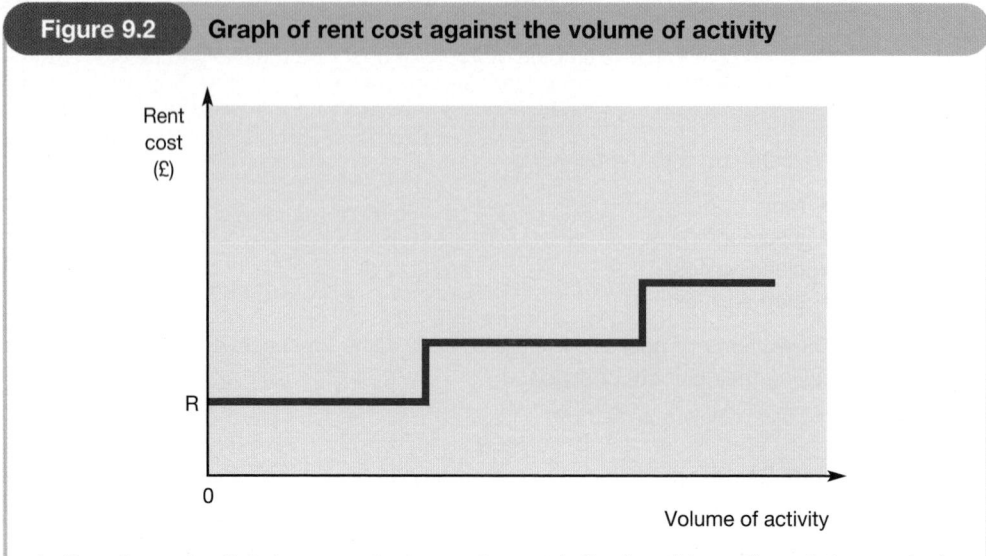

Figure 9.2	**Graph of rent cost against the volume of activity**

As the volume of activity increases from zero, the rent (a fixed cost) is unaffected. At a particular point, the volume of activity cannot increase further without additional space being rented. The cost of renting the additional space will cause a 'step' in the rent cost. The higher rent cost will continue unaffected if volume rises further until eventually another step point is reached.

At lower volumes of activity, the rent cost shown in Figure 9.2 would be 0R. As the volume of activity expands, the accommodation becomes inadequate and further expansion requires an increase in premises and, therefore, cost. This higher level of accommodation provision will enable further expansion to take place. Eventually, additional cost will need to be incurred if further expansion is to occur. Elements of fixed cost that behave in this way are often referred to as **stepped fixed costs**.

Variable cost

We saw earlier that variable cost varies with the volume of activity. In a manufacturing business, for example, this would include the cost of raw materials used.

Variable cost can be represented graphically as in Figure 9.3. At zero volume of activity, the variable cost is zero. It then increases in a straight line as activity increases.

Activity 9.3

Can you think of some examples of cost elements that are likely to be variable for a hairdressing business?

We can think of a couple:

● lotions, sprays and other materials used;
● laundry cost to wash towels used to dry customers' hair.

As with many types of business activity, the variable cost incurred by hairdressers tends to be low in comparison with the fixed cost: that is, fixed cost tends to make up the bulk of total cost.

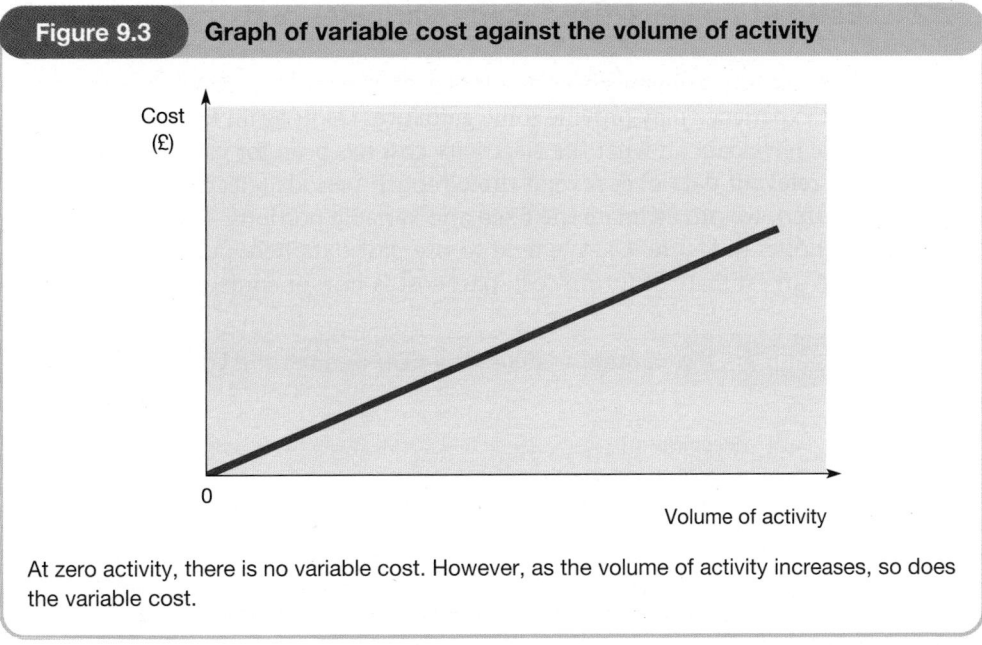

| Figure 9.3 | Graph of variable cost against the volume of activity |

At zero activity, there is no variable cost. However, as the volume of activity increases, so does the variable cost.

The straight line for variable cost on this graph implies that this type of cost will be the same per unit of activity, irrespective of the volume of activity. We shall consider the practicality of this assumption a little later in this chapter.

Semi-fixed (semi-variable) cost

In some cases, cost has an element of both fixed and variable cost. These can be described as **semi-fixed (semi-variable) costs**. An example might be the electricity cost for the hairdressing business. Some of this will be for heating and lighting, and this part is probably fixed, at least until the volume of activity expands to a point where longer opening hours or larger premises are necessary. The other part of the cost will vary with the volume of activity. Here we are talking about such things as power for hairdryers.

Activity 9.4

Can you suggest another cost for a hairdressing business that is likely to be semi-fixed (semi-variable)?

We thought of telephone charges for landlines. These tend to have a rental element, which is fixed, and there may also be certain calls that have to be made irrespective of the volume of activity involved. However, increased business would be likely to lead to the need to make more telephone calls and so to increased call charges.

Estimating semi-fixed (semi-variable) cost

Often, it is not obvious how much of each element a particular cost contains. However, past experience may provide some guidance. Let us again take the example of electricity. If we have data on what the electricity cost has been for various volumes of activity, say the relevant data over several three-month periods (electricity is usually billed by the quarter), we can estimate the fixed and variable portions. This may be done graphically, as shown in Figure 9.4. We tend to use past data here purely because they provide us with an estimate of future cost; past cost is not, of course, relevant for its own sake.

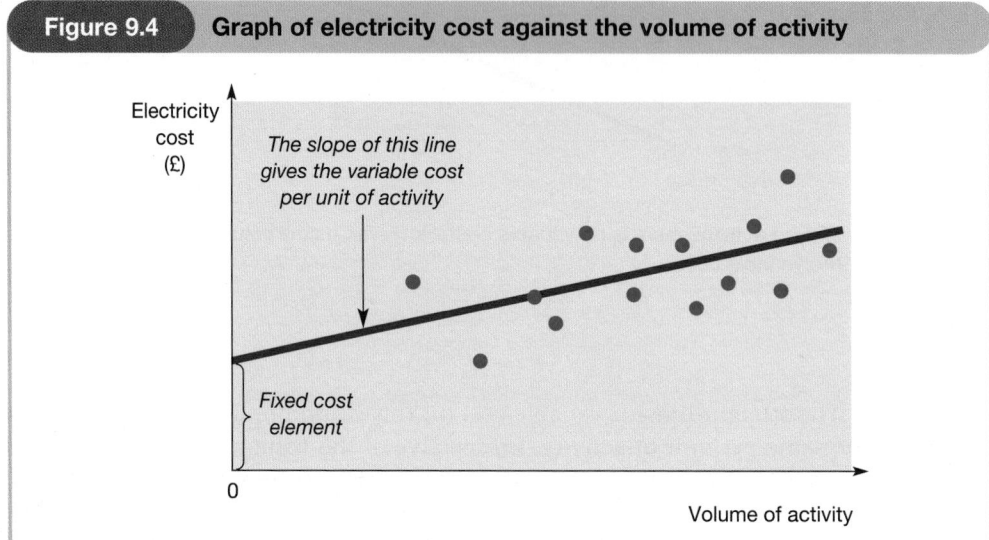

Figure 9.4   **Graph of electricity cost against the volume of activity**

Here the electricity bill for a time period (for example, three months) is plotted against the volume of activity for that same period. This is done for a series of periods. A line is then drawn that best 'fits' the various points on the graph. From this line we can then deduce both the cost at zero activity (the fixed element) and the slope of the line (the variable element).

Each of the dots in Figure 9.4 is the electricity charge for a particular quarter plotted against the volume of activity (probably measured in terms of sales revenue) for the same quarter. The diagonal line on the graph is the *line of best fit*. This means that this was the line that best seemed (to us, at least) to represent the data. A better estimate can usually be made using a statistical technique (*least squares regression*), which does not involve drawing graphs and making estimates. In practice though, it probably makes little difference which approach is taken.

From the graph we can say that the fixed element of the electricity cost is the amount represented by the vertical distance from the origin at zero (bottom left-hand corner) to the point where the line of best fit crosses the vertical axis of the graph. The variable cost per unit is the amount that the graph rises for each increase in the volume of activity.

By breaking down semi-fixed cost into its fixed and variable elements in this way, we are left with just two types of cost: fixed cost and variable cost.

Armed with knowledge of how much each element of cost represents for a particular product or service, it is possible to make predictions regarding total and per-unit cost at various projected levels of output. Such predictive information can be very useful to decision makers and much of the rest of this chapter will be devoted to seeing how, starting with **break-even analysis**.

Finding the break-even point

If, for a particular product or service, we know the fixed cost for a period and the variable cost per unit, we can produce a graph like the one shown in Figure 9.5. This graph shows the total cost over the possible range of volume of activity.

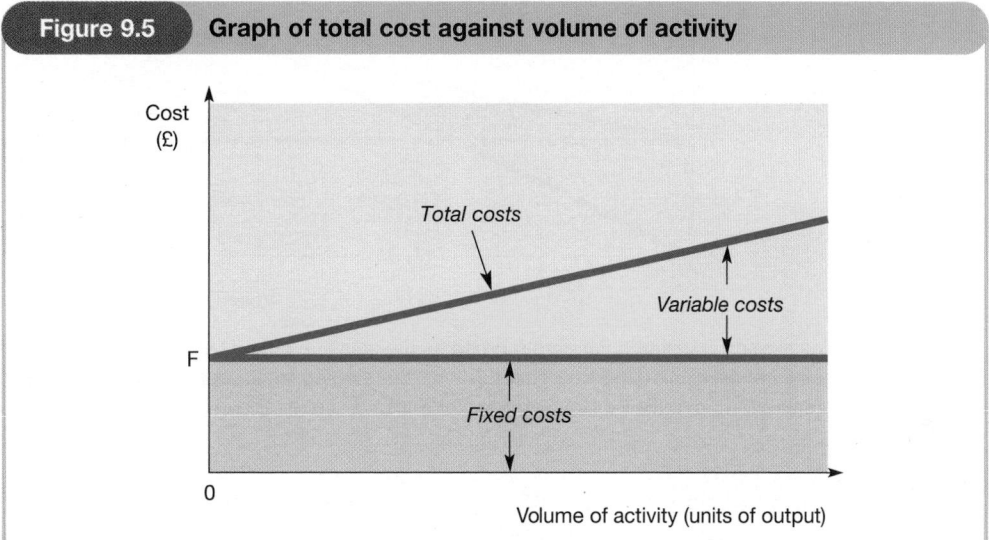

Figure 9.5 Graph of total cost against volume of activity

The bottom part of the graph represents the fixed cost element. To this is added the wedge-shaped top portion, which represents the variable cost. The two parts together represent total cost. At zero activity, the variable cost is zero, so total cost equals fixed cost. As activity increases so does total cost, but only because variable cost increases. We are assuming that there are no steps in the fixed cost.

The bottom part of Figure 9.5 shows the fixed cost area. Added to this is the variable cost, the wedge-shaped portion at the top of the graph. The uppermost line represents the total cost over a range of volume of activity. For any particular volume, the total cost can be measured by the vertical distance between the graph's horizontal axis and the relevant point on the uppermost line.

Logically, the total cost at zero activity is the amount of the fixed cost. This is because, even where there is nothing going on, the business will still be paying rent, salaries and so on, at least in the short term. As the volume of activity increases from zero, the fixed cost is augmented by the relevant variable cost to give the total cost.

If we take this total cost graph in Figure 9.5, and superimpose on it a line representing total revenue over the range of volume of activity, we obtain the **break-even chart**. This is shown in Figure 9.6.

Note in Figure 9.6 that, at zero volume of activity (zero sales), there is zero sales revenue. The profit (loss), which is the difference between total sales revenue and total cost, for a particular volume of activity, is the vertical distance between the total sales revenue line and the total cost line at that volume of activity. Where there is no vertical distance between these two lines (total sales revenue equals total cost) the volume of activity is at **break-even point (BEP)**. At this point there is neither profit nor loss; that is, the activity *breaks even*. Where the volume of activity is below BEP, a loss will be incurred because total cost exceeds total sales revenue. Where the business operates at

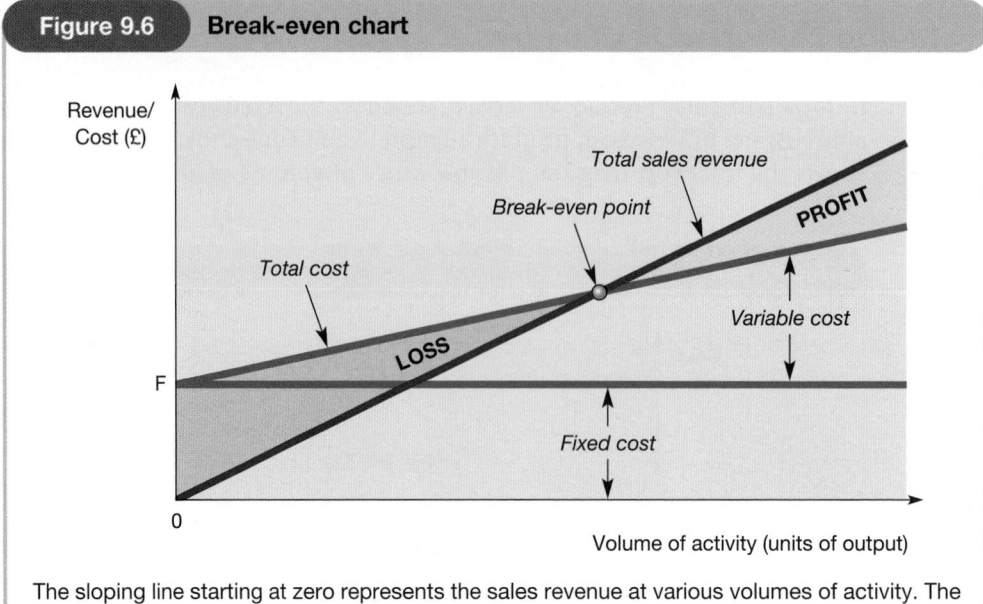

Figure 9.6 **Break-even chart**

The sloping line starting at zero represents the sales revenue at various volumes of activity. The point at which this finally catches up with the sloping total cost line, which starts at F, is the break-even point (BEP). Below this point a loss is made, above it a profit.

a volume of activity above BEP, there will be a profit because total sales revenue will exceed total cost. The further below BEP, the higher the loss: the further above BEP, the higher the profit.

Deducing BEPs by graphical means is a laborious business. Since the relationships in the graph are all linear (that is, the lines are all straight), however, it is easy to calculate the BEP.

We know that at BEP (but not at any other point):

$$\text{Total sales revenue} = \text{Total cost}$$

(At all other points except the BEP, either total sales revenue will exceed total cost or the other way round. Only at BEP are they equal.) The above formula can be expanded so that:

$$\text{Total sales revenue} = \text{Fixed cost} + \text{Total variable cost}$$

If we call the number of units of output at BEP b, then

$$b \times \text{Sales revenue per unit} = \text{Fixed cost} + (b \times \text{Variable cost per unit})$$

so:

$$(b \times \text{Sales revenue per unit}) - (b \times \text{Variable cost per unit}) = \text{Fixed cost}$$

and:

$$b \times (\text{Sales revenue per unit} - \text{Variable cost per unit}) = \text{Fixed cost}$$

giving:

$$b = \frac{\text{Fixed cost}}{\text{Sales revenue per unit} - \text{Variable cost per unit}}$$

If we look back at the break-even chart in Figure 9.6, this formula seems logical. The total cost line starts off at point F, higher than the starting point for the total sales revenues line (zero) by amount F (the amount of the fixed cost). Because the sales revenue per unit is greater than the variable cost per unit, the sales revenue line will gradually catch up with the total cost line. The rate at which it will catch up is dependent on the relative steepness of the two lines. Bearing in mind that the slopes of the two lines are the variable cost per unit and the selling price per unit, the above equation for calculating b looks perfectly logical.

Though the BEP can be calculated quickly and simply without resorting to graphs, this does not mean that the break-even chart is without value. The chart shows the relationship between cost, volume and profit over a range of activity and in a form that can easily be understood by non-financial managers. The break-even chart can therefore be a useful device for explaining this relationship.

Example 9.1

Cottage Industries Ltd makes baskets. The fixed costs of operating the workshop for a month totals £500. Each basket requires materials that cost £2 and takes one hour to make. The business pays the basket makers £10 an hour. The basket makers are all on contracts such that if they do not work for any reason, they are not paid. The baskets are sold to a wholesaler for £14 each.

What is the BEP for basket making for the business?

The BEP (in number of baskets) is:

$$\text{BEP} = \frac{\text{Fixed cost}}{(\text{Sales revenue per unit} - \text{Variable cost per unit})}$$

$$= \frac{£500}{£14 - (£2 + £10)}$$

$$= 250 \text{ baskets per month}$$

Note that the BEP must be expressed with respect to a period of time.

Real World 9.1 shows information on the BEPs of three well-known businesses.

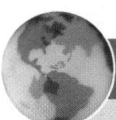

Real World 9.1

BE at BA, Ryanair and easyJet

Commercial airlines seem to pay a lot of attention to their BEPs and their 'load factors', that is, their actual level of activity. Figure 9.7 shows the BEP and load factor for three well-known airlines operating from the UK. British Airways (BA) is a traditional airline. Ryanair and easyJet both are 'no frills' carriers, which means that passengers receive lower levels of service in return for lower fares. All three operate flights within the UK and from the UK to other European countries. BA offers a much wider range of destinations than the other two airlines. We can see that all three airlines were making operating profits as each had a load factor greater than its BEP. We can see that easyJet has the highest load factor as well as the highest break-even point. Although Ryanair has nearly the same load factor as easyJet, it has a much lower break-even point.

→

Real World 9.1 continued

Figure 9.7 **Break-even and load factors in the airline industry**

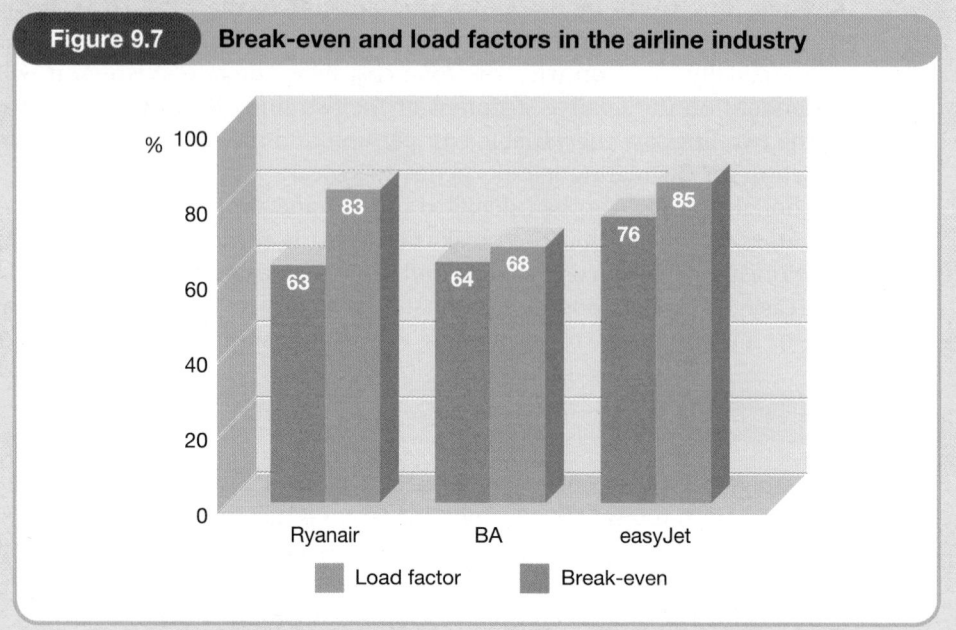

Source: Based on information contained in 'The battle for Europe's low-fare flyers', U. Binggeli and L. Pompeo, *The McKinsey Quarterly*, August 2005 (www.mckinseyquarterly.com). The data in the article are based on the year ended 31 March 2004.

Activity 9.5

Can you think of reasons why the managers of a business might find it useful to know the BEP of some activity that they are planning to undertake?

By knowing the BEP, it is possible to compare the expected, or planned, volume of activity with the BEP and so make a judgement about risk. If the volume of activity is expected only just to exceed the break-even point, this may suggest that it is a risky venture. Only a small fall from the expected volume of activity could lead to a loss.

Activity 9.6

Cottage Industries Ltd (see Example 9.1) expects to sell 500 baskets a month. The business has the opportunity to rent a basket-making machine. Doing so would increase the total fixed cost of operating the workshop for a month to £3,000. Using the machine would reduce the labour time to half an hour per basket. The basket makers would still be paid £10 an hour.

(a) How much profit would the business make each month from selling baskets
  - assuming that the basket-making machine is not rented; and
  - assuming that it is rented?
(b) What is the BEP if the machine is rented?
(c) What do you notice about the figures that you calculate?

(a) Estimated monthly profit from basket making:

	Without the machine		With the machine	
	£	£	£	£
Sales revenue (500 × £14)		7,000		7,000
Materials (500 × £2)	(1,000)		(1,000)	
Labour (500 × 1 × £10)	(5,000)			
(500 × ½ × £10)			(2,500)	
Fixed cost	(500)		(3,000)	
		(6,500)		(6,500)
Profit		500		500

(b) The BEP (in number of baskets) with the machine:

$$\text{BEP} = \frac{\text{Fixed cost}}{\text{Sales revenue per unit} - \text{Variable cost per unit}}$$

$$= \frac{£3,000}{£14 - (£2 + £5)}$$

$$= 429 \text{ baskets a month}$$

The BEP without the machine is 250 baskets per month (see Example 9.1).

(c) There seems to be nothing to choose between the two manufacturing strategies regarding profit, at the estimated sales volume. There is, however, a distinct difference between the two strategies regarding the BEP. Without the machine, the actual volume of sales could fall by a half of that which is expected (from 500 to 250) before the business would fail to make a profit. With the machine, however, just a 14 per cent fall (from 500 to 429) would be enough to cause the business to fail to make a profit. On the other hand, for each additional basket sold above the estimated 500, an additional profit of only £2 (that is, £14 – (£2 + £10)) would be made without the machine, whereas £7 (that is, £14 – (£2 + £5)) would be made with the machine. (Note that knowledge of the BEP and the planned volume of activity gives some basis for assessing the riskiness of the activity.)

We shall take a closer look at the relationship between fixed cost, variable cost and profit together with any advice that we might give the management of Cottage Industries Ltd after we have briefly considered the notion of contribution.

Contribution

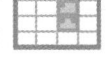

→ The bottom part of the break-even formula (sales revenue per unit less variable cost per unit) is known as the **contribution per unit**. Thus for the basket-making activity, without the machine the contribution per unit is £2, and with the machine it is £7. This can be quite a useful figure to know in a decision-making context. It is called 'contribution' because it contributes to meeting the fixed cost and, if there is any excess, it then contributes to profit.

We shall see, a little later in this chapter, how knowing the amount of the contribution generated by a particular activity can be valuable in making short-term decisions of various types, as well as being useful in the BEP calculation.

Contribution margin ratio

→ The **contribution margin ratio** is the contribution from an activity expressed as a percentage of the sales revenue, thus:

$$\text{Contribution margin ratio} = \frac{\text{Contribution}}{\text{Sales revenue}} \times 100\%$$

Contribution and sales revenue can both be expressed in per-unit or total terms. For Cottage Industries Ltd (Example 9.1 and Activity 9.6), the contribution margin ratios are:

Without the machine, $\dfrac{14 - 12}{14} \times 100\% = 14\%$

With the machine, $\dfrac{14 - 7}{14} \times 100\% = 50\%$

The ratio can provide an impression of the extent to which sales revenue is eaten away by variable cost.

Margin of safety

→ The **margin of safety** is the extent to which the planned volume of output or sales lies above the BEP. To illustrate how the margin of safety is calculated, we can use the information in Activity 9.6 relating to each option.

	Without the machine (number of baskets)	With the machine (number of baskets)
(a) Expected volume of sales	500	500
(b) BEP	250	429
Margin of safety (the difference between (a) and (b))	250	71
Expressed as a percentage of expected volume of sales	50%	14%

The margin of safety can be used as a partial measure of risk.

Activity 9.7

What advice would you give Cottage Industries Ltd about renting the machine, on the basis of the values for margin of safety?

It is a matter of personal judgement, which in turn is related to individual attitudes to risk, as to which strategy to adopt. Most people, however, would prefer the strategy of not renting the machine, since the margin of safety between the expected volume of activity and the BEP is much greater. Thus, for the same level of return, the risk will be lower without renting the machine.

The relative margins of safety are directly linked to the relationship between the selling price per basket, the variable cost per basket and the fixed cost per month. Without the machine the contribution (selling price less variable cost) per basket is £2; with the machine it is £7. On the other hand, without the machine the fixed cost is £500 a month; with the machine it is £3,000. This means that, with the machine, the contributions have more fixed cost to 'overcome' before the activity becomes profitable.

However, the rate at which the contributions can overcome fixed cost is higher with the machine, because variable cost is lower. Thus, one more, or one less, basket sold has a greater impact on profit than it does if the machine is not rented. The contrast between the two scenarios is shown graphically in Figures 9.8(a) and 9.8(b).

Figure 9.8	Break-even charts for Cottage Industries' basket-making activities (a) without the machine and (b) with the machine

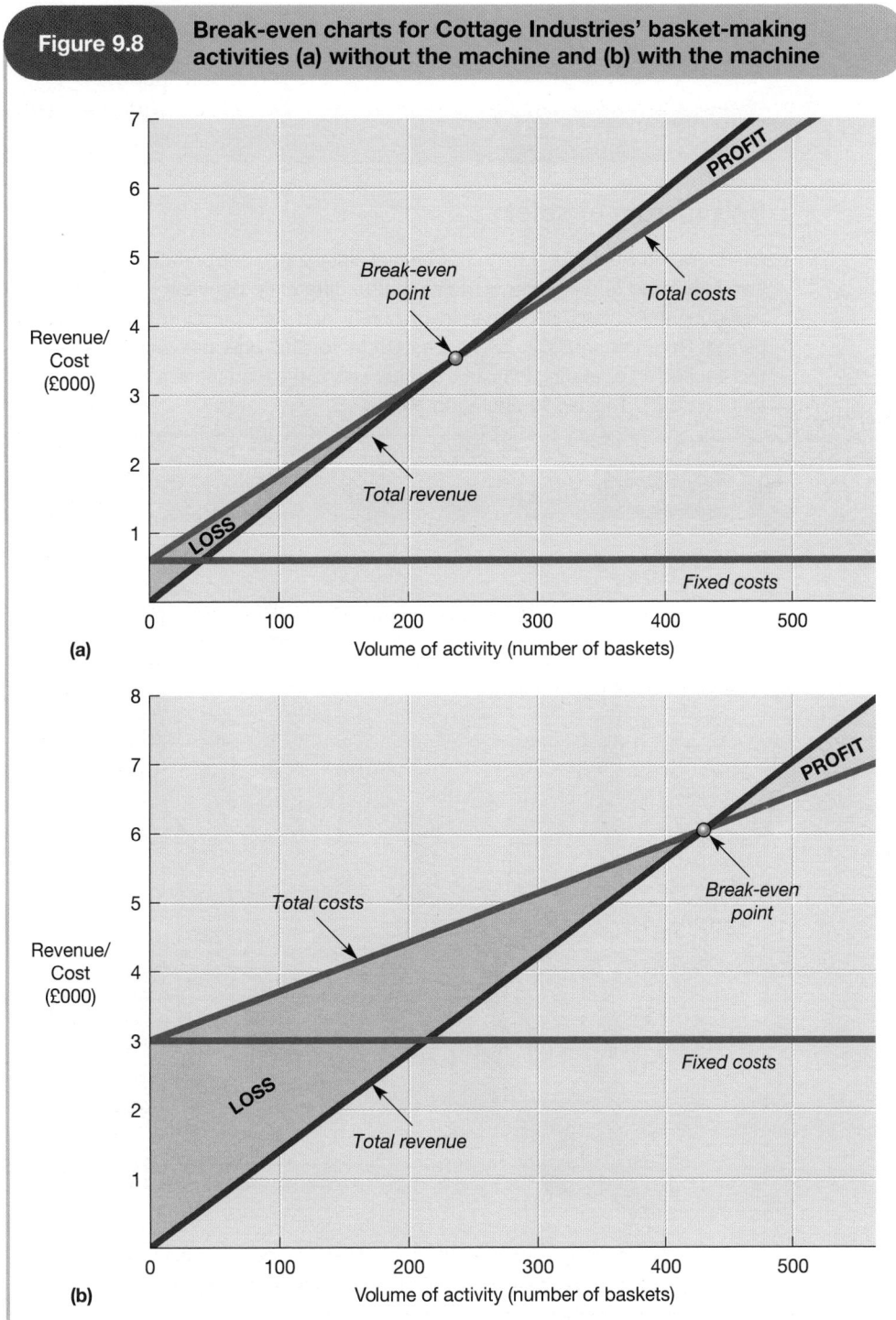

Without the machine the contribution per basket is low. Thus, each additional basket sold does not make a dramatic difference to the profit or loss. With the machine, however, the opposite is true, and small increases or decreases in the sales volume will have a great effect on the profit or loss.

If we look back to Real World 9.1 (pages 317–18), we can see that Ryanair had a much larger margin of safety than either BA or easyJet.

Real World 9.2 goes into more detail on the margin of safety and operating profit, over recent years, of one of the three airlines featured in Real World 9.1.

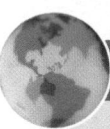

Real World 9.2

BA's margin of safety

As we saw in Real World 9.1, commercial airlines pay a lot of attention to BEPs. They are also interested in their margin of safety (the difference between load factor and BEP).

Figure 9.9 shows BA's margin of safety and its operating profit over a seven-year period. Note that in 2002, BA had a load factor that was below its break-even point and this caused an operating loss. In the other years, the load factors were comfortably greater than the BEP. This led to operating profits.

Figure 9.9   **BA's margin of safety**

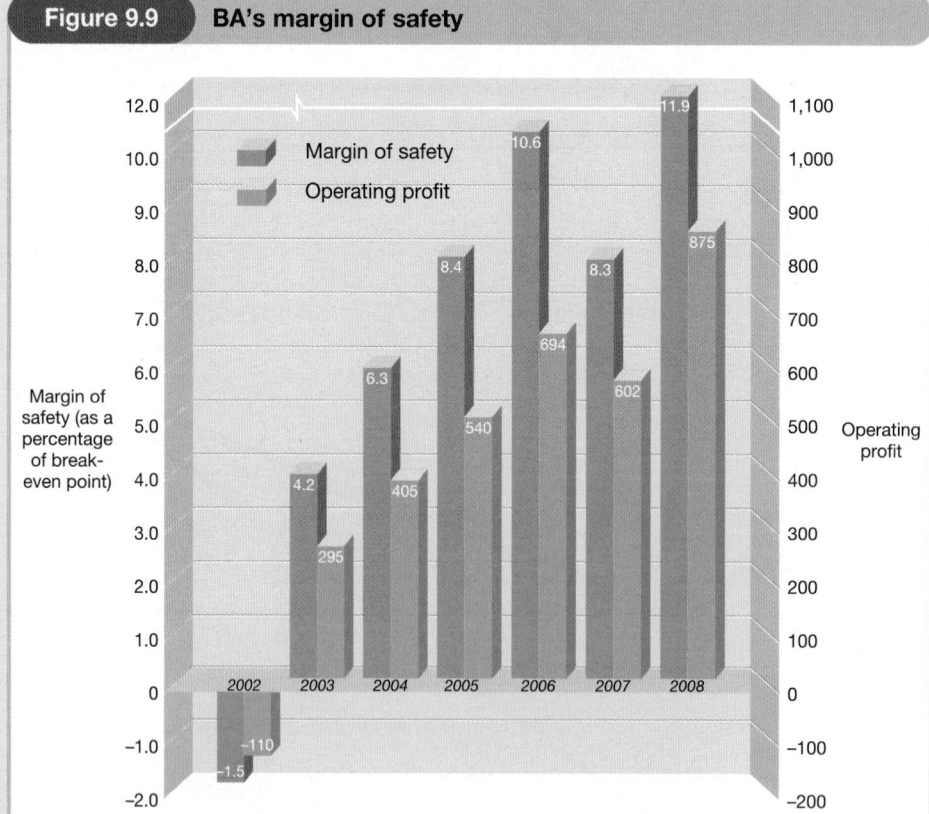

The margin of safety is expressed as the difference between the load factor and the BEP (for each year), expressed as a percentage of the BEP. Generally, the higher the margin of safety, the higher the operating profit.

Source: Derived from information contained in British Airways plc Annual Reports 2002 to 2008.

Achieving a target profit

In the same way as we can derive the number of units of output necessary to break even, we can calculate the volume of activity required to achieve a particular level of profit. We can expand the equation shown on page 316 so that:

> **Total sales revenue = Fixed cost + Total variable cost + Target profit**

If we let t be the required number of units of output to achieve the target profit, then

$t \times$ Sales revenue per unit = Fixed cost + ($t \times$ Variable cost per unit) + Target profit

so:

($t \times$ Sales revenue per unit) − ($t \times$ Variable cost per unit) = Fixed cost + Target profit

and:

$t \times$ (Sales revenue per unit − Variable cost per unit) = Fixed cost + Target profit

giving:

$$t = \frac{\text{Fixed cost} + \text{Target profit}}{\text{Sales revenue per unit} - \text{Variable cost per unit}}$$

Activity 9.8

What volume of activity is required by Cottage Industries Ltd (see Example 9.1 and Activity 9.6) in order to make a profit of £4,000 a month:
(a) assuming that the basket-making machine is not rented; and
(b) assuming that it is rented?

(a) Using the formula above, the required volume of activity without the machine:

$$\frac{\text{Fixed cost} + \text{Target profit}}{\text{Sales revenue per unit} - \text{Variable cost per unit}}$$

$$= \frac{£500 + £4,000}{£14 - (£2 + £10)}$$

= 2,250 baskets a month

(b) The required volume of activity with the machine:

$$\frac{£3,000 + £4,000}{£14 - (£2 + £5)}$$

= 1,000 baskets a month

Operating gearing

→ The relationship between contribution and fixed cost is known as **operating gearing** (or operational gearing). An activity with a relatively high fixed cost compared with its variable cost is said to have high operating gearing. Thus, Cottage Industries Ltd has higher operating gearing using the machine than it has if not using it. Renting the machine increases the level of operating gearing quite dramatically because it causes an increase in fixed cost, but at the same time it leads to a reduction in variable cost per basket.

Operating gearing and its effect on profit

The reason why the word 'gearing' is used in this context is that, as with intermeshing gear wheels of different circumferences, a movement in one of the factors (volume of output) causes a more-than-proportionate movement in the other (profit) as illustrated by Figure 9.10.

Figure 9.10 **The effect of operating gearing**

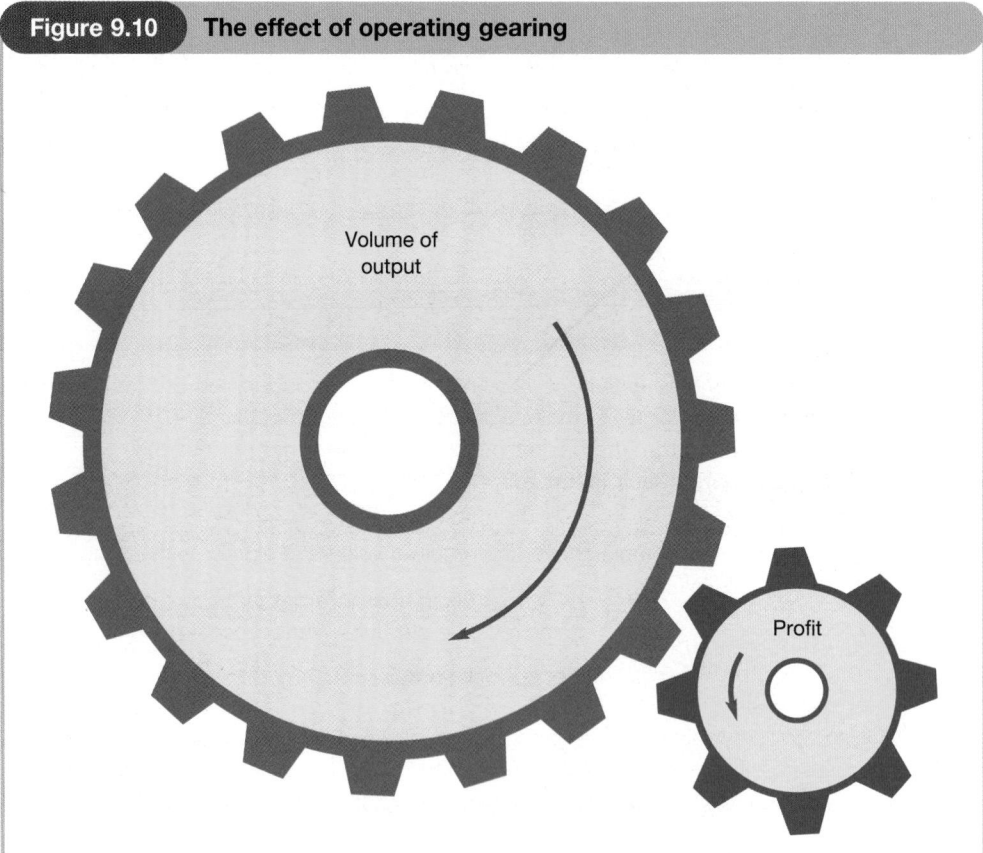

Where operating gearing is relatively high, as in the diagram, a small amount of motion in the volume wheel causes a relatively large amount of motion in the profit wheel. An increase in volume would cause a disproportionately greater increase in profit. The equivalent would also be true of a decrease in activity, however.

Increasing the level of operating gearing makes profit more sensitive to changes in the volume of activity. We can demonstrate operating gearing with Cottage Industries Ltd's basket-making activities as follows:

	Without the machine			With the machine		
Volume (number of baskets)	500	1,000	1,500	500	1,000	1,500
	£	£	£	£	£	£
Contributions*	1,000	2,000	3,000	3,500	7,000	10,500
Fixed cost	(500)	(500)	(500)	(3,000)	(3,000)	(3,000)
Profit	500	1,500	2,500	500	4,000	7,500

* £2 per basket without the machine and £7 per basket with it.

Note that, without the machine (low operating gearing), a doubling of the output from 500 to 1,000 units brings a trebling of the profit. With the machine (high operating gearing), doubling output causes profit to rise by eight times. At the same time, reductions in the volume of output tend to have a more damaging effect on profit where the operating gearing is higher.

Activity 9.9

What types of business activity are likely to have high operating gearing? (*Hint*: Cottage Industries Ltd might give you some idea.)

Activities that are capital intensive tend to have high operating gearing. This is because renting or owning capital equipment gives rise to additional fixed cost, but it can also give rise to lower variable cost.

Real World 9.3 shows how a very well-known business has benefited from high operating gearing.

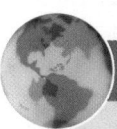

Real World 9.3

Check out operating gearing

After several years of disappointing trading and loss of market share, in 2004, J Sainsbury plc, the UK supermarket, set a plan to improve its profitability and gain market share. During the period from 2005 to 2008, Sainsbury's increased its sales revenue by 16 per cent, but this fed through to a 105 per cent increase in profit. This was partly due to relatively high operating gearing, which caused the profit to increase at a much greater rate than the sales revenue. Quite a lot of retailers' costs are fixed – rent, salaries, heat and light, training and advertising for example.

In its 2008 annual report Sainsbury's Chief Executive, Justin King, said 'Our sales growth is reflected in substantially improved profits and operational gearing is coming through.'

Source: J Sainsbury plc Annual Report 2008, p. 4.

Profit-volume charts

➜ A slight variant of the break-even chart is the **profit–volume (PV) chart**. A typical PV chart is shown in Figure 9.11.

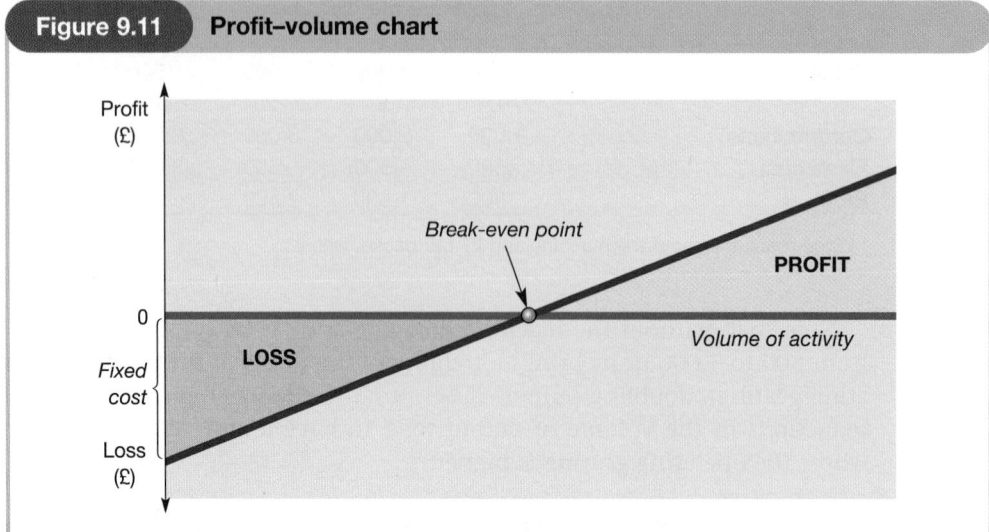

Figure 9.11 Profit–volume chart

The sloping line is profit (loss) plotted against activity. As activity increases, so does total contribution (sales revenue less variable cost). At zero activity there are no contributions, so there will be a loss equal in amount to the total fixed cost.

The PV chart is obtained by plotting loss or profit against volume of activity. The slope of the graph is equal to the contribution per unit, since each additional unit sold decreases the loss, or increases the profit, by the sales revenue per unit less the variable cost per unit. At zero volume of activity there are no contributions, so there is a loss equal to the amount of the fixed cost. As the volume of activity increases, the amount of the loss gradually decreases until BEP is reached. Beyond BEP a profit is made, which increases as activity increases.

As we can see, the PV chart does not tell us anything not shown by the break-even chart. It does, however, highlight key information concerning the profit (loss) arising at any volume of activity. The break-even chart shows this as the vertical distance between the total cost and total sales revenue lines. The PV chart, in effect, combines the total sales revenue and total variable cost lines, which means that profit (or loss) is directly readable.

The economist's view of the break-even chart

So far in this chapter we have treated all the relationships as linear – that is, all of the lines in the graphs have been straight. This is typically the approach taken in management accounting, though it may not be strictly valid.

Consider, for example, the variable cost line in the break-even chart; accountants would normally treat this as being a straight line. Strictly, however, the line should probably not be straight because at high levels of output **economies of scale** may be available to an extent not available at lower levels. For example, a raw material (a typical variable cost) may be able to be used more efficiently with higher volumes of activity. Similarly, buying large quantities of material and services may enable the business to benefit from bulk discounts and so lower the cost.

There is also a tendency for sales revenue per unit to reduce as volume is increased. To sell more of a particular product or service, it will usually be necessary to lower the price per unit.

Economists recognise that, in real life, the relationships portrayed in the break-even chart are usually non-linear. The typical economist's view of the chart is shown in Figure 9.12.

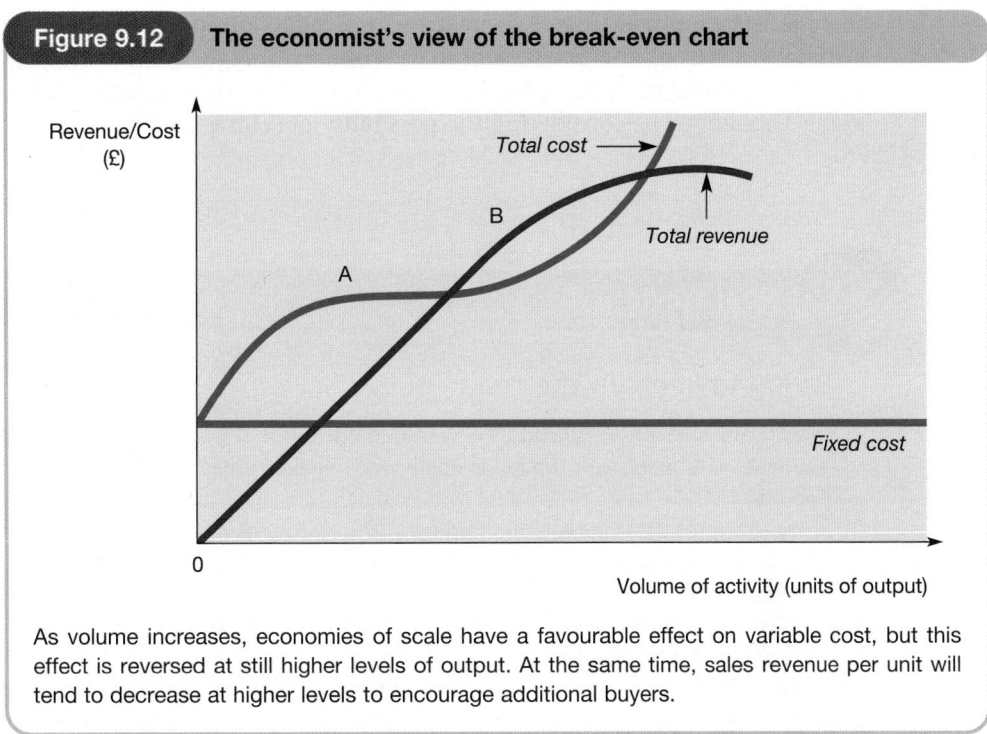

Figure 9.12 | **The economist's view of the break-even chart**

As volume increases, economies of scale have a favourable effect on variable cost, but this effect is reversed at still higher levels of output. At the same time, sales revenue per unit will tend to decrease at higher levels to encourage additional buyers.

Note, in Figure 9.12, that the total variable cost line starts to rise quite steeply with volume but, around point A, economies of scale start to take effect. With further increases in volume, total variable cost does not rise as steeply because the variable cost *for each additional unit of output* is lowered. These economies of scale continue to have a benign effect on cost until a point is reached where the business is operating towards the end of its efficient range. Beyond this range, problems will emerge that adversely affect variable cost. For example, the business may be unable to find cheap supplies of the variable-cost elements or may suffer production difficulties, such as machine breakdowns. As a result, the total variable cost line starts to rise more steeply.

At low levels of output, sales may be made at a relatively high price per unit. To increase sales output beyond point B, however, it may be necessary to lower the average sales price per unit. This will mean that the total revenue line will not rise as steeply, and may even curve downwards.

Note how this 'curvilinear' representation of the break-even chart can easily lead to the existence of two break-even points.

Accountants justify their approach to this topic by the fact that, though the lines may not, in practice, be perfectly straight, this defect is probably not worth taking into account in most cases. This is partly because all of the information used in the analysis is based on estimates of the future. As this will inevitably be flawed, it seems pointless to be pedantic about the minor approximation of treating the total cost and total revenue lines as straight when strictly this is not so. Only where significant economies or diseconomies of scale are involved should the non-linearity of the variable cost be taken into account. Also, for most businesses, the range of possible volumes of activity at which they are capable of operating (the **relevant range**) is pretty narrow. Over very short distances, it may be perfectly reasonable to treat a curved line as being straight.

Failing to break even

Where a business fails to reach its BEP, steps must be taken to remedy the problem: there must be an increase in sales revenue or a reduction in cost, or both of these. **Real World 9.4** discusses how Ford's subsidiary Volvo is struggling to reach its BEP. Ford has recently disposed of its three UK luxury brands (Aston Martin, Jaguar and Land Rover) and is thought to be considering the possibility of selling off Volvo as well.

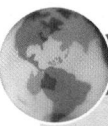

Real World 9.4

Trying to keep on the road   **FT**

Volvo Cars said on Wednesday it was cutting about 8 per cent of its global staff in response to soaring raw material costs and weaker sales on the US and European markets.

The axing of 2,000 jobs is the largest in the history of the premium brand, owned by Ford Motor, and created a stir in Sweden, where other exporters have also been hurt by the weak dollar.

Volvo reported a net loss of $151m in the first quarter of this year, compared with a profit of $94m a year ago.

Volvo has been hit harder than most other carmakers by the weakening of the dollar because it produces no cars in the US, unlike Japanese and Korean manufacturers or Germany's BMW and Mercedes-Benz brands. The brand sold 458,000 cars worldwide last year and the US is its largest market.

The pain at Volvo adds to mounting problems at Ford, which has abandoned pledges to break even next year and return to profit in 2010 due to a sharp contraction in US sales of its profitable large pick-ups and sport utility vehicles.

Source: Extracts from 'Volvo to cut 8 per cent of global staff', J. Reed and R. Anderson, FT.com, 25 June 2008.

Weaknesses of break-even analysis

As we have seen, break-even analysis can provide some useful insights concerning the important relationship between fixed cost, variable cost and the volume of activity. It does, however, have its weaknesses. There are three general problems:

● *Non-linear relationships*. The management accountant's normal approach to break-even analysis assumes that the relationships between sales revenues, variable cost and volume are strictly straight-line ones. In real life, this is unlikely to be the case. This is probably not a major problem, since, as we have just seen:

  – break-even analysis is normally conducted in advance of the activity actually taking place. Our ability to predict future cost, revenue and so on is somewhat limited, so what are probably minor variations from strict linearity are unlikely to be significant, compared with other forecasting errors; and

- most businesses operate within a narrow range of volume of activity; over short ranges, curved lines tend to be relatively straight.

- *Stepped fixed cost.* Most types of fixed cost are not fixed over all volumes of activity. They tend to be 'stepped' in the way depicted in Figure 9.2. This means that, in practice, great care must be taken in making assumptions about fixed cost. The problem is heightened because most activities will probably involve various types of fixed cost (for example rent, supervisory salaries, administration cost), all of which are likely to have steps at different points.

- *Multi-product businesses.* Most businesses do not offer just one product or service. This is a problem for break-even analysis since it raises the question of the effect of additional sales of one product or service on sales of another of the business's products or services. There is also the problem of identifying the fixed cost of one particular activity. Fixed cost tends to relate to more than one activity – for example, two activities may be carried out in the same rented premises. There are ways of dividing the fixed cost between activities, but these tend to be arbitrary, which calls into question the value of the break-even analysis and any conclusions reached.

Activity 9.10

We saw above that, in practice, relationships between costs, revenues and volumes of activity are not necessarily straight-line ones.

Can you think of at least three reasons, with examples, why this may be the case?

We thought of the following:

- *Economies of scale with labour.* A business may do things more economically where there is a high volume of activity than are possible at lower levels of activity. It may, for example, be possible for employees to specialise.
- *Economies of scale with buying goods or services.* A business may find it cheaper to buy in goods and services where it is buying in bulk as discounts are often given.
- *Diseconomies of scale.* This may mean that the per-unit cost of output is higher at higher levels of activity. For example, it may be necessary to pay higher rates of pay to workers to recruit the additional staff needed at higher volumes of activity.
- *Lower sales prices at high levels of activity.* Some consumers may only be prepared to buy the particular product or service at a lower price. Thus, it may not be possible to achieve high levels of sales activity without lowering the selling price.

Despite some practical problems, break-even analysis and BEP seem to be widely used. The media frequently refer to the BEP for businesses and activities. For example, there is seemingly constant discussion about Eurotunnel's BEP and whether it will ever be reached. Similarly, the number of people regularly needed to pay to watch a football team so that the club breaks even is often mentioned. This is illustrated in **Real World 9.5**, which is an extract from an article discussing the failure of Plymouth Argyle FC, the Coca Cola Championship football club, to spend all of its player transfer income on new players.

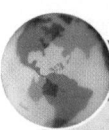

Real World 9.5

Pilgrims not progressing through the turnstiles

This year, Argyle have raked in plenty of income, in addition to their gate receipts. The sale of players has brought in over £8 million. Their expenditure has been nowhere near that sum.

The failure to sign adequate replacements for the departed players could put Argyle's Championship status in jeopardy. Yes, the Pilgrims have to retain some of their transfer income to help them cope with running costs – they do not break even on current gates – but the best way to increase attendances is to provide an attractive and successful team.

Source: Taken from 'Argyle viewpoint', R. Metcalf, *Western Morning News*, 15 September 2008.

Real World 9.6 shows specific references to break-even point for three well-known businesses.

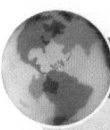

Real World 9.6

Breaking even is breaking out all over

FT

Setanta sets its break-even target

Setanta Sports Holdings Ltd, the satellite TV broadcaster and rival of BSkyB, has a break-even point of about 1.5 million subscribers. By April 2009, Setanta planned to have 4 million subscribers.

Source: Taken from 'Setanta chases fresh targets', B. Fenton, *Financial Times*, 23 July 2008.

Superjumbo break-even point grows

German industrial group EADS is developing the Airbus A380 aircraft. The aircraft can carry up to 555 passengers on each flight. When EADS approved development of the plane in 2000, it was estimated that the business would need to sell 250 of them to break even. By 2005, the break-even number had increased to 270, but by late 2008 the cost of development had increased to the point where it was estimated that it would require sales of 400 of the aircraft for it to break even. Expected total sales of the aircraft could be about 1,000 over its commercial lifetime.

Source: Taken from 'Boeing', *Financial Times*, 11 December 2008.

City Link to break even

City Link, the parcel delivery business owned by Rentokil Initial plc, was expected only to break even in 2008. This was as a result of inadequate management information systems, which led to loss of customers.

Source: Taken from 'Rentokil plunge spurs break-up fears', S. Davoudi and M. Urry, *Financial Times*, 28 February 2008.

Real World 9.7 provides a more formal insight to the extent that managers in practice use break-even analysis.

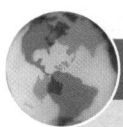

Real World 9.7

Break-even analysis in practice

A survey of management accounting practice in the United States was conducted in 2003. Nearly 2,000 businesses replied to the survey. These tended to be larger businesses, of which about 40 per cent were manufacturers and about 16 per cent financial services; the remainder were across a range of other industries.

The survey revealed that 62 per cent use break-even analysis extensively, with a further 22 per cent considering using the technique in the future.

Though the survey relates to the US and was undertaken several years ago, in the absence of UK evidence, it provides some insight to what is likely also to be current practice in the UK and elsewhere in the developed world.

Source: Taken from the 2003 Survey of Management Accounting by Ernst and Young, 2003.

Using contribution to make decisions: marginal analysis

If we cast our minds back to Chapter 8, where we discussed relevant costs for decision making, we should recall that when we are trying to decide between two or more possible courses of action, *only costs that vary with the decision should be included in the decision analysis.*

For many decisions that involve:

● relatively small variations from existing practice, and/or
● relatively limited periods of time,

fixed cost is not relevant to the decision, because it will be the same irrespective of the decision made.

This is because either:

● fixed cost elements tend to be impossible to alter in the short term, or
● managers are reluctant to alter them in the short term.

Activity 9.11

Ali plc owns premises from which it provides a PC repair and maintenance service. There is a downturn in demand for the service, and it would be possible for Ali plc to carry on the business from smaller, cheaper premises.

Can you think of any reasons why the business might not immediately move to smaller, cheaper premises?

We thought of broadly three reasons:

● It is not usually possible to find a buyer for existing premises at very short notice and it may be difficult to find available alternative premises quickly.
● It may be difficult to move premises quickly where there is, say, delicate equipment to be moved.
● Management may feel that the downturn might not be permanent, and would thus be reluctant to take such a dramatic step and deny itself the opportunity to benefit from a possible revival of trade.

We shall now consider some types of decisions where fixed cost can be regarded as irrelevant. In making these decisions, we should have as our key strategic objective the enhancement of owners' (shareholders') wealth. Since these decisions are short-term in nature, this means that wealth will normally be increased by trying to generate as much net cash inflow as possible.

→ In **marginal analysis** we concern ourselves just with costs and revenues that vary with the decision and so this usually means that fixed cost is ignored. This is because marginal analysis is usually applied to minor alterations in the level of activity, so it

→ tends to be true that the variable cost per unit will be equal to the **marginal cost**, which is the additional cost of producing one more unit of output. Whilst this is normally the case, there may be times when producing one more unit will involve a step in the fixed cost. If this occurs, the marginal cost is not just the variable cost; it will include the increment, or step, in the fixed cost as well.

Marginal analysis may be used in four key areas of decision making:

● pricing/assessing opportunities to enter contracts;
● determining the most efficient use of scarce resources;
● make-or-buy decisions;
● closing or continuation decisions.

We shall now consider each of these areas in turn.

Pricing/assessing opportunities to enter contracts

To understand how marginal analysis may be used in assessing an opportunity, let us consider the following activity.

Activity 9.12

Cottage Industries Ltd (see Example 9.1, page 317) has spare capacity in that its basket makers have some spare time. An overseas retail chain has offered the business an order for 300 baskets at a price of £13 each.

Without considering any wider issues, should the business accept the order? (Assume that the business does not rent the machine.)

Since the fixed cost will be incurred in any case, it is not relevant to this decision. All we need to do is see whether the price offered will yield a contribution. If it will, the business will be better off by accepting the contract than by refusing it.

	£
Additional revenue per unit	13
Additional cost per unit	(12)
Additional contribution per unit	1

For 300 units, the additional contribution will be £300 (that is, 300 × £1). Since no fixed cost increase is involved, irrespective of what else is happening to the business, it will be £300 better off by taking this contract than by refusing it.

As ever with decision making, there are other factors that are either difficult or impossible to quantify. These should be taken into account before reaching a final decision. In the case of Cottage Industries Ltd's decision concerning the overseas customer, these could include the following:

- The possibility that spare capacity will have been 'sold off' cheaply when there might be another potential customer who will offer a higher price, but, by that time, the capacity will be fully committed. It is a matter of commercial judgement as to how likely this will be.
- Selling the same product, but at different prices, could lead to a loss of customer good-will. The fact that a different price will be set for customers in different countries (that is, in different markets) may be sufficient to avoid this potential problem.
- If the business is going to suffer continually from being unable to sell its full production potential at the 'usual' price, it might be better, in the long run, to reduce capacity and make fixed cost savings. Using the spare capacity to produce marginal benefits may lead to the business failing to address this issue.
- On a more positive note, the business may see this as a way of breaking into the overseas market. This is something that might be impossible to achieve if the business charges its usual price.

The marginal cost is the minimum price at which the business can offer a product or service for sale such that the business will be no better off as a result of making the sale than it would have been had it not done so. Anything more than this minimum represents a profit (an increase in owners' wealth).

A marginal cost approach to pricing would only be used where there is not the opportunity to sell at a price that will cover the full cost. In the long run, the business must more than cover all of its costs, both variable and fixed, if it is to be profitable.

Activity 9.13

A commercial aircraft is due to take off in one hour's time with 20 seats unsold. What is the minimum price at which these seats could be sold such that the airline would be no worse off as a result?

The answer is that any price above the additional cost of carrying one more passenger would represent an acceptable minimum. If there are no such costs, the minimum price is zero.

This is not to say that the airline will seek to charge the minimum price; it will presumably seek to charge the highest price that the market will bear. The fact that the market will not bear the full cost, plus a profit margin, should not, in principle, be sufficient for the airline to refuse to sell seats, where there is spare passenger capacity.

In practice, airlines are major users of a marginal costing approach. They often offer low priced tickets for off-peak travel, where there are not sufficient customers willing to pay 'normal' prices. By insisting on a Saturday stopover for return tickets, they tend to exclude 'business' travellers, who are probably forced to travel, but for whom a Saturday stopover may be unattractive. UK train operators often offer substantial discounts for off-peak travel. Similarly, hotels often charge very low rates for off-peak rooms. A hotel mainly used by business travellers may well offer very low room rates for Friday and Saturday occupancy.

Relevant/marginal pricing must be regarded as a short-term or limited approach that can be adopted because a business finds itself in a particular position, for example, having spare aircraft seats. Ultimately, if the business is to be profitable, all costs must be covered by sales revenue.

Real World 9.8 provides an unusual example where humanitarian issues are the driving force for adopting marginal pricing.

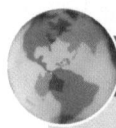

Real World 9.8

Drug prices in developing countries

Large pharmaceutical businesses have recently been under considerable pressure to provide cheap drugs to developing countries. It has been suggested that life-saving therapeutic drugs should be sold to these countries at a price that is close to their marginal cost. Indeed the Department for International Development would like to see HIV drugs sold at marginal cost in the poorest countries. However, a number of obstacles to such a pricing policy have been identified:

1. It may lead to customer revolts in the West [the 'loss of customer goodwill' referred to above].
2. There is a concern that the drugs may not reach their intended patients and could be re-exported to Western countries. A major cost of producing a new drug is the research and development costs incurred, and marginal costs of production are usually very low. Thus, a selling price based on marginal cost is likely to be considerably lower than the normal (full-cost) selling price in the West. This, it is feared, may lead to the cheap drugs provided leaking back into the West. Acquiring drugs at a price near to their marginal cost and reselling them at a figure close to the selling price in the West offers unscrupulous individuals an opportunity to make huge profits.
3. That compensation for any adverse consequences that may arise from the drugs sold will be sought in courts in the West, thereby creating the risk of huge payouts. This would make the risk to the pharmaceutical businesses of selling the drugs out of proportion to the benefits to them, in terms of the prices that would be charged.

The above problems are not insurmountable and are not the only problems surrounding this issue, but they do appear to have slowed progress towards a speedier response to a humanitarian crisis.

Source: Based on information from 'GSK varies prices to raise sales', A. Jack, FT.com, 16 March 2008; 'Drug pricing is a social problem', R. Epstein, FT.com, 16 June 2005; 'Pressure builds to cut price of HIV medicine', FT.com, 11 March 2006; and 'Patent nonsense', *Financial Times*, 24 August 2001.

Real World 9.9 is an extract from an article about the price for using a new high-speed rail line.

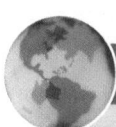

Real World 9.9

Fast track

FT

Rail freight operators will have to pay a premium rate for using the new 'High Speed 1' (HS1) line that links London to the Channel tunnel. With other lines on the UK rail network, freight operators are required to pay only the marginal cost of running each train. This would comprise the cost of the electricity, signalling and wear to the track that would not have been incurred had the train not run. For using the HS1 line, operators will be asked to pay twice the marginal cost of using the other lines. This is partly because HS1 has a higher maintenance cost, but also so that the owner of the line, London and Continental Railways, can make some profit from freight operations.

Source: Taken from 'Row over freight charges on fast rail line', R. Wright, *Financial Times*, 14 July 2008.

The most efficient use of scarce resources

Normally, the output of a business is determined by customer demand for the particular goods or services. In some cases, however, output will be restricted by the productive capacity of the business. Limited productive capacity might stem from a shortage of any factor of production – labour, raw materials, space, machine capacity and so on. Such scarce factors are often known as *key* or *limiting* factors.

Where productive capacity acts as a brake on output, management must decide on how best to meet customer demand. That is, it must decide which products, from the range available, should be produced and how many of each should be produced. Marginal analysis can be useful to management in such circumstances. The guiding principle is that the most profitable combination of products will occur where the *contribution per unit of the scarce factor* is maximised. Example 9.2 illustrates this point.

Example 9.2

A business provides three different services, the details of which are as follows:

Service (code name)	AX107	AX109	AX220
	£	£	£
Selling price per unit	50	40	65
Variable cost per unit	(25)	(20)	(35)
Contribution per unit	25	20	30
Labour time per unit	5 hours	3 hours	6 hours

Within reason, the market will take as many units of each service as can be provided, but the ability to provide the service is limited by the availability of labour, all of which needs to be skilled. Fixed cost is not affected by the choice of service provided because all three services use the same facilities.

The most profitable service is AX109 because it generates a contribution of £6.67 (£20/3) an hour. The other two generate only £5.00 each an hour (£25/5 and £30/6). So, to maximise profit, priority should be given to the production that maximises the contribution per unit of limiting factor.

Our first reaction might be that the business should provide only service AX220, as this is the one that yields the highest contribution per unit sold. If so, we would have been making the mistake of thinking that it is the ability to sell that is the limiting factor. If the above analysis is not convincing, we can take a random number of available labour hours and ask ourselves what is the maximum contribution (and, therefore, profit) that could be made by providing each service exclusively. Bear in mind that there is no shortage of anything else, including market demand, just a shortage of labour.

Activity 9.14

A business makes three different products, the details of which are as follows:

Product (code name)	B14	B17	B22
Selling price per unit (£)	25	20	23
Variable cost per unit (£)	10	8	12
Weekly demand (units)	25	20	30
Machine time per unit (hours)	4	3	4

Activity 9.14 continued

Fixed cost is not affected by the choice of product because all three products use the same machine. Machine time is limited to 148 hours a week.

Which combination of products should be manufactured if the business is to produce the highest profit?

Product (code name)	B14	B17	B22
	£	£	£
Selling price per unit	25	20	23
Variable cost per unit	(10)	(8)	(12)
Contribution per unit	15	12	11
Machine time per unit	4 hours	3 hours	4 hours
Contribution per machine hour	£3.75	£4.00	£2.75
Order of priority	2nd	1st	3rd

Therefore:

Produce		
20 units of product B17 using		60 hours
22 units of product B14 using		88 hours
		148 hours

This leaves unsatisfied the market demand for a further 3 units of product B14 and 30 units of product B22.

Activity 9.15

What steps could be taken that might lead to a higher level of contribution for the business in Activity 9.14?

The possibilities for improving matters that occurred to us are as follows:

- Consider obtaining additional machine time. This could mean obtaining a new machine, subcontracting the machining to another business or, perhaps, squeezing a few more hours a week out of the business's own machine. Perhaps a combination of two or more of these is a possibility.
- Redesign the products in a way that requires less time per unit on the machine.
- Increase the price per unit of the three products. This might well have the effect of dampening demand, but the existing demand cannot be met at present, and it may be more profitable in the long run to make a greater contribution on each unit sold than to take one of the other courses of action to overcome the problem.

Activity 9.16

Going back to Activity 9.14, what is the maximum price that the business concerned would logically be prepared to pay to have the remaining B14s machined by a subcontractor, assuming that no fixed or variable cost would be saved as a result of not doing the machining in-house?

Would there be a different maximum if we were considering the B22s?

If the remaining three B14s were subcontracted at no cost, the business would be able to earn a contribution of £15 a unit, which it would not otherwise be able to gain. Therefore, any price up to £15 a unit would be worth paying to a subcontractor to undertake the machining. Naturally, the business would prefer to pay as little as possible, but anything up to £15 would still make it worthwhile subcontracting the machining.

This would not be true of the B22s because they have a different contribution per unit; £11 would be the relevant figure in their case.

Make-or-buy decisions

Businesses are frequently confronted by the need to decide whether to produce the product or service that they sell themselves, or to buy it in from some other business. Thus, a producer of electrical appliances might decide to subcontract the manufacture of one of its products to another business, perhaps because there is a shortage of production capacity in the producer's own factory, or because it believes it to be cheaper to subcontract than to make the appliance itself.

It might just be part of a product or service that is subcontracted. For example, the producer may have a component for the appliance made by another manufacturer. In principle, there is hardly any limit to the scope of make-or-buy decisions. Virtually any part, component or service that is required in production of the main product or service, or the main product or service itself, could be the subject of a make-or-buy decision. So, for example, the personnel function of a business, which is normally performed in-house, could be subcontracted. At the same time, electrical power, which is typically provided by an outside electrical utility business, could be generated in-house. Obtaining services or products from a subcontractor is often called **outsourcing**.

Real World 9.10 provides an example of outsourcing by a well-known communications business.

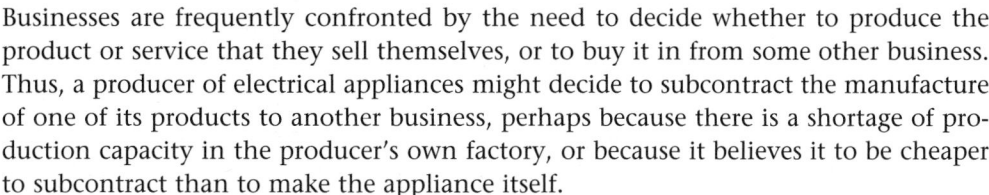

Real World 9.10

Vodafone subcontracts IT work

Vodafone is in the process of outsourcing all of its IT development and maintenance operations to a specialist organisation based in India. It is also outsourcing its internal helpdesks.

Source: Vodafone Group plc Annual Report 2008.

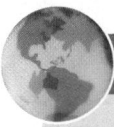

Activity 9.17

Shah Ltd needs a component for one of its products. It can subcontract production of the component to a subcontractor who will provide the components for £20 each. Shah Ltd can produce the components internally for a total variable cost of £15 per component. Shah Ltd has spare capacity.

Should the component be subcontracted or produced internally?

The answer is that Shah Ltd should produce the component internally, since the variable cost of subcontracting is greater by £5 (that is, £20 − £15) than the variable cost of internal manufacture.

Activity (9.18)

Now assume that Shah Ltd (Activity 9.17) has no spare capacity, so it can only produce the component internally by reducing its output of another of its products. While it is making each component, it will lose contributions of £12 from the other product.

Should the component be subcontracted or produced internally?

The answer is to subcontract. In this case, both the variable cost of production and the opportunity cost of lost contributions must be taken into account.

Thus, the relevant cost of internal production of each component is:

	£
Variable cost of production of the component	15
Opportunity cost of lost production of the other product	12
	27

This is obviously more costly than the £20 per component that will have to be paid to the subcontractor.

Activity (9.19)

What factors, other than the immediately financially quantifiable, would you consider when making a make-or-buy decision?

We feel that there are two major factors:

1. The general problems of subcontracting, particularly:
   (a) loss of control of quality;
   (b) potential unreliability of supply.
2. Expertise and specialisation. Generally, businesses should focus on their core competences. It is possible for most businesses, with sufficient determination, to do virtually everything in-house. This may, however, require a level of skill and facilities that most businesses neither have nor feel inclined to acquire. For example, though it is true that most businesses could generate their own electricity, their managements tend to take the view that this is better done by a specialist generator business. Specialists can often do things more cheaply, with less risk of things going wrong.

Closing or continuation decisions

It is quite common for businesses to produce separate financial statements for each department or section, to try to assess their relative performance. Example 9.3 considers how marginal analysis can help decide how to respond where it is found that a particular department underperforms.

Example 9.3

Goodsports Ltd is a retail shop that operates through three departments, all in the same premises. The three departments occupy roughly equal-sized areas of the premises. The trading results for the year just finished showed the following:

	Total	Sports equipment	Sports clothes	General clothes
	£000	£000	£000	£000
Sales revenue	534	254	183	97
Cost	(482)	(213)	(163)	(106)
Profit/(loss)	52	41	20	(9)

It would appear that if the general clothes department were to close, the business would be more profitable, by £9,000 a year, assuming last year's performance to be a reasonable indication of future performance.

When the cost is analysed between that part that is variable and that part that is fixed, however, the contribution of each department can be deduced and the following results obtained:

	Total	Sports equipment	Sports clothes	General clothes
	£000	£000	£000	£000
Sales revenue	534	254	183	97
Variable cost	(344)	(167)	(117)	(60)
Contribution	190	87	66	37
Fixed cost (rent and so on)	(138)	(46)	(46)	(46)
Profit/(loss)	52	41	20	(9)

Now it is obvious that closing the general clothes department, without any other developments, would make the business worse off by £37,000 (the department's contribution). The department should not be closed, because it makes a positive contribution. The fixed cost would continue whether the department was closed or not. As can be seen from the above analysis, distinguishing between variable and fixed cost, and deducing the contribution, can make the picture a great deal clearer.

Activity 9.20

In considering Goodsports Ltd (in Example 9.3), we saw that the general clothes department should not be closed 'without any other developments'.

What 'other developments' could affect this decision, making continuation either more attractive or less attractive?

The things that we could think of are as follows:

- Expansion of the other departments or replacing the general clothes department with a completely new activity. This would make sense only if the space currently occupied by the general clothes department could generate contributions totalling at least £37,000 a year.
- Subletting the space occupied by the general clothes department. Once again, this would need to generate a net rent greater than £37,000 a year to make it more financially beneficial than keeping the department open.
- Keeping the department open, even if it generated no contribution whatsoever (assuming that there is no other use for the space), may still be beneficial. If customers are attracted into the shop because it has general clothing, they may then buy something from one of the other departments. In the same way, the activity of a sub-tenant might attract customers into the shop. (On the other hand, it might drive them away!)

Self-assessment question 9.1

Khan Ltd can render three different types of service (Alpha, Beta and Gamma) using the same staff. Various estimates for next year have been made as follows:

Service	Alpha £/unit	Beta £/unit	Gamma £/unit
Selling price	30	39	20
Variable material cost	15	18	10
Other variable costs	6	10	5
Share of fixed cost	8 33.3%	12 50%	4 16.6%
Staff time required (hours)	2	3	1

Fixed cost for next year is expected to total £40,000.

Required:

(a) If the business were to render only service Alpha next year, how many units of the service would it need to provide in order to break even? (Assume for this part of the question that there is no effective limit to market size and staffing level.)

(b) If the business has a maximum of 10,000 staff hours next year, in which order of preference would the three services come?

(c) If the maximum market for next year for the three services is as follows:

Alpha	3,000 units
Beta	2,000 units
Gamma	5,000 units

what quantities of which service should the business provide next year and how much profit would this be expected to yield?

The answer to this question can be found at the back of the book on pages 729–30.

Summary

The main points in this chapter may be summarised as follows:

Cost behaviour

- Fixed cost is independent of the level of activity (for example, rent).
- Variable cost varies with the level of activity (for example, raw materials).
- Semi-fixed (semi-variable) cost is a mixture of fixed and variable costs (for example, electricity).

Break-even analysis

- The break-even point (BEP) is the level of activity (in units of output or sales revenue) at which total cost (fixed + variable) = total sales revenue.

- Calculation of BEP is as follows:

$$\text{BEP (in units of output)} = \frac{\text{Fixed cost for the period}}{\text{Contribution per unit}}$$

- Knowledge of the BEP for a particular activity can be used to help assess risk.
- Contribution per unit = sales revenue per unit less variable cost per unit.
- Contribution margin ratio = contribution/sales revenue ($\times$ 100%)
- Margin of safety = excess of planned volume of activity over BEP.
- Calculation of the volume of activity (t) required to achieve a target profit is as follows:

$$t = \frac{\text{Fixed cost + Target profit}}{(\text{Sales revenue per unit} - \text{Variable cost per unit})}$$

- Operating gearing = the extent to which the total cost of some activity is fixed rather than variable.
- The profit–volume (PV) chart is an alternative approach to the BE chart, which is easier to understand.
- Economists tend to take a different approach to BE, taking account of economies (and diseconomies) of scale and of the fact that, generally, to be able to sell large volumes, price per unit tends to fall.

Weaknesses of BE analysis

- There are non-linear relationships between costs, revenues and volume.
- There may be stepped fixed costs. Most fixed costs are not fixed over all volumes of activity.
- Multi-product businesses have problems in allocating fixed costs to particular activities.

Marginal analysis (ignores fixed costs where these are not affected by the decision)

- Accepting/rejecting special contracts – we consider only the effect on contributions.
- Using scarce resources – the limiting factor is most effectively used by maximising its contribution per unit.
- Make-or-buy decisions – we take the action that leads to the highest total contributions.
- Closing/continuing an activity – should be assessed by net effect on total contributions.

MyAccountingLab — *Now check your progress in your personal Study Plan*

Key terms

fixed cost   p. 310
variable cost   p. 310
stepped fixed cost   p. 312
semi-fixed (semi-variable) cost
   p. 313
break-even analysis   p. 314
break-even chart   p. 315
break-even point (BEP)   p. 315
contribution per unit   p. 319

contribution margin ratio   p. 320
margin of safety   p. 320
operating gearing   p. 323
profit–volume (PV) chart   p. 325
economies of scale   p. 326
relevant range   p. 327
marginal analysis   p. 332
marginal cost   p. 332
outsourcing   p. 337

Further reading

If you would like to explore the topics covered in this chapter in more depth, we recommend the
following books:

Cost Accounting: A Managerial Emphasis, *Horngren C., Foster G., Datar S., Rajan M. and
   Ittner C.,* 13th edn, Prentice Hall International, 2008, chapter 3.

Management Accounting: Analysis and Interpretation, *McWatters C., Zimmerman J. and
   Morse D.,* Financial Times Prentice Hall, 2008, chapter 5.

Management and Cost Accounting, *Drury C.,* 7th edn, Cengage Learning, 2007, chapter 8.

Managerial Accounting, *Hilton R.,* 6th edn, McGraw-Hill Irwin, 2005, chapter 8.

Review questions

Answers to these questions can be found at the back of the book on pages 744–5.

9.1 Define the terms *fixed cost* and *variable cost.* Explain how an understanding of the distinction between fixed cost and variable cost can be useful to managers.

9.2 What is meant by the *BEP* for an activity? How is the BEP calculated? Why is it useful to know the BEP?

9.3 When we say that some business activity has *high operating gearing*, what do we mean? What are the implications for the business of high operating gearing?

9.4 If there is a scarce resource that is restricting sales, how will the business maximise its profit? Explain the logic of the approach that you have identified for maximising profit.

Exercises

Exercises 9.4 to 9.8 are more advanced than 9.1 to 9.3. Those with **coloured numbers** have answers at the back of the book, starting on page 774.

If you wish to try more exercises, visit the students' side of the Companion Website and MyAccountingLab.

9.1 The management of a business is concerned about its inability to obtain enough fully trained labour to enable it to meet its present budget projection.

Service:	Alpha	Beta	Gamma	Total
	£000	£000	£000	£000
Variable costs				
Materials	6	4	5	15
Labour	9	6	12	27
Expenses	3	2	2	7
Allocated fixed costs	6	15	12	33
Total cost	24	27	31	82
Profit	15	2	2	19
Sales revenue	39	29	33	101

The amount of labour likely to be available amounts to £20,000. All of the variable labour is paid at the same hourly rate. You have been asked to prepare a statement of plans ensuring that at least 50 per cent of the budgeted sales revenues are achieved for each service, and the balance of labour is used to produce the greatest profit.

Required:

(a) Prepare the statement, with explanations, showing the greatest profit available from the limited amount of skilled labour available, within the constraint stated. *Hint*: Remember that all labour is paid at the same rate.

(b) What steps could the business take in an attempt to improve profitability, in the light of the labour shortage?

9.2 Lannion and Co. is engaged in providing and marketing a standard advice service. Summarised results for the past two months reveal the following:

	October	November
Sales (units of the service)	200	300
Sales revenue (£)	5,000	7,500
Operating profit (£)	1,000	2,200

There were no price changes of any description during these two months.

Required:
(a) Deduce the BEP (in units of the service) for Lannion and Co.
(b) State why the business might find it useful to know its BEP.

9.3 A hotel group prepares financial statements on a quarterly basis. The senior management is reviewing the performance of one hotel and making plans for next year.

The managers have in front of them the results for this year (based on some actual results and some forecasts to the end of this year):

Quarter	Sales revenue	Profit/(loss)
	£000	£000
1	400	(280)
2	1,200	360
3	1,600	680
4	800	40
Total	4,000	800

The total estimated number of visitors (guest nights) for this year is 50,000. The results follow a regular pattern; there are no unexpected cost fluctuations beyond the seasonal trading pattern shown above. For next year, management anticipates an increase in unit variable cost of 10 per cent and a profit target for the hotel of £1 million. These will be incorporated into its plans.

Required:
(a) Calculate the total variable and total fixed cost of the hotel for this year. Show the provisional annual results for this year in total, showing variable and fixed cost separately. Show also the revenue and cost per visitor.
(b) 1 If there is no increase in visitors for next year, what will be the required revenue rate per hotel visitor to meet the profit target?
2 If the required revenue rate per visitor is not raised above this year's level, how many visitors will be required to meet the profit target?
(c) Outline and briefly discuss the assumptions that are made in typical PV or break-even analysis, and assess whether they limit its usefulness.

9.4 Motormusic Ltd makes a standard model of car radio, which it sells to car manufacturers for £60 each. Next year the business plans to make and sell 20,000 radios. The business's costs are as follows:

Manufacturing	
Variable materials	£20 per radio
Variable labour	£14 per radio
Other variable costs	£12 per radio
Fixed cost	£80,000 per year
Administration and selling	
Variable	£3 per radio
Fixed	£60,000 per year

Required:

(a) Calculate the break-even point for next year, expressed both in quantity of radios and sales value.

(b) Calculate the margin of safety for next year, expressed both in quantity of radios and sales value.

9.5 A business makes three products, A, B and C. All three products require the use of two types of machine: cutting machines and assembling machines. Estimates for next year include the following:

Product	A	B	C
Selling price (£ per unit)	25	30	18
Sales demand (units)	2,500	3,400	5,100
Material cost (£ per unit)	12	13	10
Variable production cost (£ per unit)	7	4	3
Time required per unit on cutting machines (hours)	1.0	1.0	0.5
Time required per unit on assembling machines (hours)	0.5	1.0	0.5

Fixed cost for next year is expected to total £42,000. It is the business's policy for each unit of production to absorb this in proportion to its total variable cost.

The business has cutting machine capacity of 5,000 hours a year and assembling machine capacity of 8,000 hours a year.

Required:

(a) State, with supporting workings, which products in which quantities the business should plan to make next year on the basis of the above information. *Hint*: First determine which machines will be a limiting factor (scarce resource).

(b) State the maximum price per product that it would be worth the business paying to a sub-contractor to carry out that part of the work that could not be done internally.

9.6 Darmor Ltd has three products, which require the same production facilities. Information about the production cost for one unit of its products is as follows:

Product	X	Y	Z
	£	£	£
Labour: Skilled	6	9	3
Unskilled	2	4	10
Materials	12	25	14
Other variable costs	3	7	7
Fixed cost	5	10	10

All labour and materials are variable costs. Skilled labour is paid £12 an hour, and unskilled labour is paid £8 an hour. All references to labour cost above are based on basic rates of pay. Skilled labour is scarce, which means that the business could sell more than the maximum that it is able to make of any of the three products.

Product X is sold in a regulated market, and the regulators have set a price of £30 per unit for it.

Required:

(a) State, with supporting workings, the price that must be charged for products Y and Z, such that the business would find it equally profitable to make and sell any of the three products.

(b) State, with supporting workings, the maximum rate of overtime premium that the business would logically be prepared to pay its skilled workers to work beyond the basic time.

9.7 Intermediate Products Ltd produces four types of water pump. Two of these (A and B) are sold by the business. The other two (C and D) are incorporated, as components, into other of the business's products. Neither C nor D is incorporated into A or B. Costings (per unit) for the products are as follows:

	A	B	C	D
	£	£	£	£
Variable materials	15	20	16	17
Variable labour	25	10	10	15
Other variable costs	5	3	2	2
Fixed costs	20	8	8	12
	65	41	36	46
Selling price (per unit)	70	45		

There is an outside supplier who is prepared to supply unlimited quantities of products C and D to the business, charging £40 per unit for product C and £55 per unit for product D.

Next year's estimated demand for the products, from the market (in the case of A and B) and from other production requirements (in the case of C and D) is as follows:

	Units
A	5,000
B	6,000
C	4,000
D	3,000

For strategic reasons, the business wishes to supply a minimum of 50 per cent of the above demand for products A and B.

Manufacture of all four products requires the use of a special machine. The products require time on this machine as follows:

	Hours per unit
A	0.5
B	0.4
C	0.5
D	0.3

Next year there are expected to be a maximum of 6,000 special-machine hours available. There will be no shortage of any other factor of production.

Required:

(a) State, with supporting workings and assumptions, which quantities of which products the business should plan to make next year.

(b) Explain the maximum amount that it would be worth the business paying per hour to rent a second special machine.

(c) Suggest ways, other than renting an additional special machine, that could solve the problem of the shortage of special machine time.

9.8 Gandhi Ltd renders a promotional service to small retailing businesses. There are three levels of service: the 'basic', the 'standard' and the 'comprehensive'. On the basis of past experience, the business plans next year to work at absolute full capacity as follows:

Service	Number of units of the service	Selling price £	Variable cost per unit £
Basic	11,000	50	25
Standard	6,000	80	65
Comprehensive	16,000	120	90

The business's fixed cost totals £660,000 a year. Each service takes about the same length of time, irrespective of the level.

One of the accounts staff has just produced a report that seems to show that the standard service is unprofitable. The relevant extract from the report is as follows:

Standard service cost analysis

	£	
Selling price per unit	80	
Variable cost per unit	(65)	
Fixed cost per unit	(20)	(£660,000/(11,000 + 6,000 + 16,000))
Loss	(5)	

The producer of the report suggests that the business should not offer the standard service next year.

Required:

(a) Should the standard service be offered next year, assuming that the quantity of the other services could not be expanded to use the spare capacity?

(b) Should the standard service be offered next year, assuming that the released capacity could be used to render a new service, the 'nova', for which customers would be charged £75, and which would have variable cost of £50 and take twice as long as the other three services?

(c) What is the minimum price that could be accepted for the basic service, assuming that the necessary capacity to expand it will come only from not offering the standard service?

CHAPTER 10

Full costing

Introduction

Full (absorption) costing is a widely used approach to costing that takes account of all of the cost of producing a particular product or service. In this chapter, we shall see how this approach can be used to deduce the cost of some activity, such as making a unit of product (for example, a tin of baked beans), providing a unit of service (for example, a car repair) or creating a facility (for example, building an Olympic athletics stadium). The precise approach taken to deducing full cost will depend on whether each product or service is identical to the next or whether each job has its own individual characteristics. It will also depend on whether the business accounts for overheads on a segmental basis. We shall look at how full (or absorption) costing is carried out and we shall also consider its usefulness for management purposes.

This chapter considers the traditional, but still very widely used, form of full costing. In Chapter 11 we shall consider activity-based costing, which is a more recently developed approach.

Learning outcomes

When you have completed this chapter, you should be able to:

- Deduce the full (absorption) cost of a cost unit in a single-product environment.

- Deduce the full (absorption) cost of a cost unit in a multi-product environment.

- Discuss the problems of deducing full (absorption) cost in practice.

- Discuss the usefulness of full (absorption) cost information to managers.

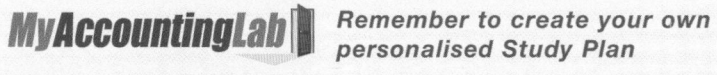
MyAccountingLab **Remember to create your own personalised Study Plan**

Why do managers want to know the full cost?

As we saw in Chapter 1, the only point in providing management accounting information is to help managers make more informed decisions. There are broadly four areas where managers use information concerning the full cost of the business's products or services. These are:

● *Pricing and output decisions.* Having full cost information can help managers to make decisions on the price to be charged to customers for the business's products or services. Linked to the pricing decisions are also decisions on the number of units of a product or service that the business should seek to provide to the market.

● *Exercising control.* Managers need information to help them make decisions that are aimed at keeping the business on course by trying to ensure that plans are met. Budgets are typically expressed in full cost terms. This means that periodic reports that compare actual performance with budgets need to be expressed in the same full cost terms.

● *Assessing relative efficiency.* Full cost information can help managers to compare the cost of doing something in one way, or place, with its cost if done in a different way, or place. For example, a motor car manufacturer may find it useful to compare the cost of building a particular model of car in one of its plants, rather than another. This could help the business decide on where to locate future production.

● *Assessing performance.* The level of profit, or income, generated over a period is an important measure of business performance. To measure profit, or income, we need to compare sales revenue with the associated expenses. Where a business produces a product or renders a service, a major expense will be the cost of making the product or rendering the service. Usually, this expense is based on the full cost of whatever is sold. Measuring income provides managers (and other users) with information that can help them make a whole range of decisions.

Later in the chapter we shall consider some of the issues surrounding these four purposes.

Figure 10.1 shows the four uses of full cost information.

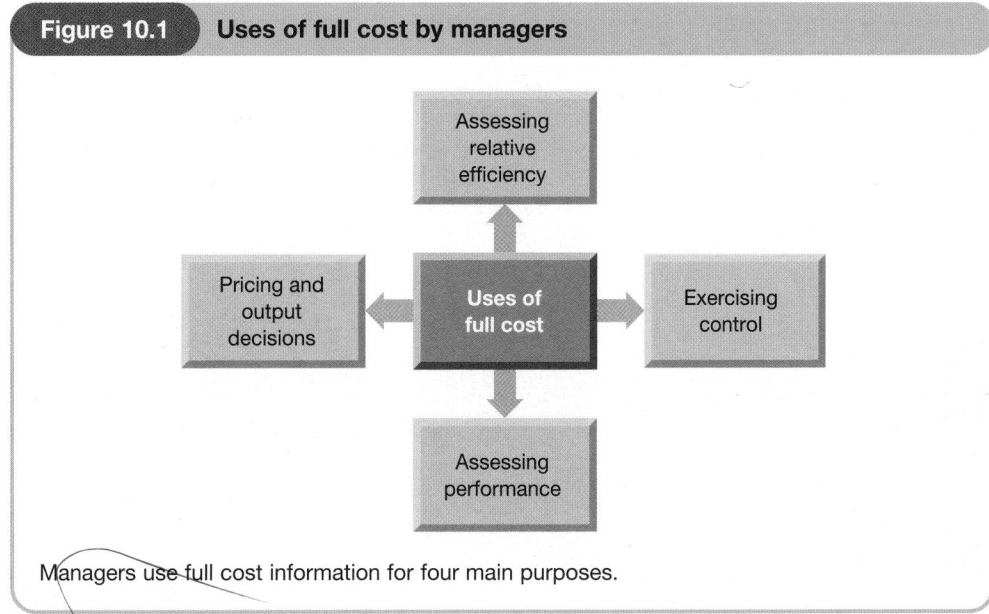

Figure 10.1   Uses of full cost by managers

Managers use full cost information for four main purposes.

Now let us consider **Real World 10.1**.

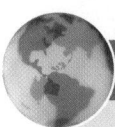

Real World 10.1

Operating cost

An interesting example of the use of full cost for pricing decisions occurs in the National Health Service (NHS). In recent years, the funding of hospitals has radically changed. A new system of Payment by Results (PBR) requires the Department of Health to produce a list of prices for an in-patient spell in hospital that covers different types of procedures. This list, which is revised annually, reflects the prices that hospitals will be paid by the government for carrying out the different procedures.

For 2007/8, the price list included the following figures:

- £4,967 for carrying out a hip replacement operation;
- £4,293 for treating a stroke.

These figures are based on the full cost of undertaking each type of procedure in 2006/7 (but adjusted for inflation). Full cost figures were submitted by all NHS hospitals for that year as part of their annual accounting process and an average for each type of procedure was then calculated. Figures for other procedures on the price list were derived in the same way.

Source: 'Payment by results – policy in focus', A. Cole and G. Robjent, *Frontline*, Chartered Society of Physiotherapists, 20 June 2007, pp. 26–30.

When considering the information in Real World 10.1, an important question that arises is 'what does the full cost of each type of procedure include?' Does it simply include the cost of the salaries earned by doctors and nurses during the time spent with the patient or does it also include the cost of other items? If the cost of other items is included, how is it determined? Would it include, for example, a charge for:

- the artificial hip and drugs provided for the patient;
- equipment used in the operating theatre;
- administrative and support staff within the hospital;
- heating and lighting;
- maintaining the hospital buildings;
- laundry and cleaning?

If the cost of such items is included, how can an appropriate charge be determined? If, on the other hand, it is not included, are the figures of £4,967 and £4,293 potentially misleading?

These questions are the subject of this chapter.

What is full costing?

Full cost is the total amount of resources, usually measured in monetary terms, sacrificed to achieve a given objective. It takes account of all resources sacrificed to achieve that objective. Thus, if the objective were to supply a customer with a product or service, the cost of all aspects relating to the making of the product or provision of the service would be included as part of the full cost. To derive the full cost figure, we must accumulate the elements of cost incurred and then assign them to the particular product or service.

→ The logic of **full costing** is that the entire cost of running a facility, say an office, is part of the cost of the output of that office. For example, the rent may be a cost that will not alter merely because we provide one more unit of the service. If the office were not rented, however, there would be nowhere for the staff to work, so rent is an impor-

→ tant element of the cost of that service. A **cost unit** is one unit of whatever is having its cost determined. This is usually one unit of output of a particular product or service.

In the sections that follow we shall see how full costing is applied to a single-product business and for a multi-product one.

Single-product businesses

The simplest case for which to deduce the full cost per unit is where the business has only one product or service, that is, each unit of its production is identical. Here it is simply a question of adding up all of the elements of cost of production incurred in a particular period (materials, labour, rent, fuel, power and so on) and dividing this total by the total number of units of output for that period.

Activity 10.1

Fruitjuice Ltd has just one product, a sparkling orange drink that is marketed as 'Orange Fizz'. During last month the business produced 7,300 litres of the drink. The cost incurred was made up as follows:

	£
Ingredients (oranges and so on)	390
Fuel	85
Rent of premises	350
Depreciation of equipment	75
Labour	880

What is the full cost per litre of producing 'Orange Fizz'?

This figure is found by simply adding together all of the elements of cost incurred and then dividing by the number of litres produced:

£(390 + 85 + 350 + 75 + 880)/7,300 = £0.24 per litre

In practice, there can be problems in deciding exactly how much cost was incurred. In the case of Fruitjuice Ltd, for example, how is the cost of depreciation deduced? As we saw in Chapter 3, it is certainly an estimate and so its reliability is open to question. The cost of raw materials may also be a problem. Should we use the 'relevant' cost of the raw materials (in this case, almost certainly the replacement cost), or the actual price paid for it (historic cost)? If the cost per litre is to be used for some decision-making purpose (which it should be), the replacement cost is probably more logical. In practice, however, it seems that historic cost is more often used to deduce full cost. It is not clear why this should be the case.

There can also be problems in deciding precisely how many units of output were produced. If making Orange Fizz is not a very fast process, some of the drink will probably be in the process of being made at any given moment. This, in turn, means that some of the cost incurred last month was for some Orange Fizz that was work in progress at the end of the month, so is not included in last month's output quantity of 7,300 litres. Similarly, part of the 7,300 litres might well have been started and incurred cost in the previous month, yet all of those litres were included in the 7,300 litres that we used in our calculation of the cost per litre. Work in progress is not a serious problem, but some adjustment for the value of opening and closing work in progress for the particular period needs to be made if reliable full cost information is to be obtained.

This approach to full costing, which can be taken where all of the output consists of identical, or near identical items (of goods or services), is often referred to as **process costing**.

Multi-product businesses

Most businesses produce more than one type of product or service. In this situation, the units of output of the product, or service, will not be identical and so the approach used with litres of 'Orange Fizz' in Activity 10.1 is inappropriate. Although it is reasonable to assign an identical cost to units of output that are identical, it is not reasonable to do this where the units of output are obviously different. It would not be reasonable, for example, to assign the same cost to each car repair carried out by a garage, irrespective of the complexity and size of the repair.

Direct and indirect cost

To provide full cost information, we need to have a systematic approach to accumulating the elements of cost and then assigning this total cost to particular cost units on some reasonable basis. Where cost units are not identical, the starting point is to separate cost into two categories: direct cost and indirect cost.

- **Direct cost**. This is the type of cost that can be identified with specific cost units. That is to say, the effect of the cost can be measured in respect of each particular cost unit. The main examples of a direct cost are direct materials and direct labour. Thus, in determining the cost of a motor car repair by a garage, both the cost of spare parts used in the repair and the cost of the mechanic's time would be part of the direct cost of that repair. Collecting elements of direct cost is a simple matter of having a cost-recording system that is capable of capturing the cost of direct materials used on each job and the cost, based on the hours worked and the rate of pay, of direct workers.
- **Indirect cost** (or **overheads**). This is all other elements of cost, that is, those items that cannot be directly measured in respect of each particular cost unit (job). Thus, the rent of the garage premises would be an indirect cost of a motor car repair.

We shall use the terms 'indirect cost' and 'overheads' interchangeably for the remainder of this book. Indirect cost is also sometimes known as **common cost** because it is common to all of the output of the production unit (for example, factory or department) for the period.

Real World 10.2 gives some indication of the relative importance of direct and indirect costs in practice.

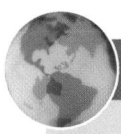

Real World 10.2

Counting the cost

A recent survey of 176 UK businesses operating in various industries, all with an annual turnover of more than £50 million, was conducted by Al-Omiri and Drury. They discovered that the total cost of the businesses' output on average is split between direct and indirect costs as follows:

	Direct cost Per cent	Indirect cost Per cent
All 176 businesses	69	31
Manufacturing businesses (91)	75	25
Service and retail businesses (85)	49	51

For the manufacturers, the 75 per cent direct cost was, on average, made up as follows:

	Per cent
Direct materials	52
Direct labour	14
Other direct costs	9

Source: 'A survey of factors influencing the choice of product costing systems in UK organisations', M. Al-Omiri and C. Drury, *Management Accounting Research*, December 2007, pp. 399–424.

A more extensive (nearly 2,000 responses) recent survey of management accounting practice in the US showed similar results. Like the UK survey (above), this tended to relate to larger businesses. About 40 per cent were manufacturers and about 16 per cent financial services; the remainder were from a range of other industries.

This survey revealed that, of total cost, indirect cost accounted for between:

- 34 per cent for retailers (lowest) and
- 42 per cent for manufacturers (highest),

with other industries' proportion of indirect cost falling within the 34 per cent to 42 per cent range. Financial and commercial businesses showed an average indirect cost percentage of 38 per cent.

Source: 2003 Survey of Management Accounting, Ernst and Young, 2003.

Activity 10.2

A garage bases its prices on the direct cost of each job (car repair) that it carries out. How could the garage collect the direct cost (labour and materials) information concerning a particular job?

Usually, direct workers are required to record how long was spent on each job. Thus, the mechanic doing the job would record the length of time worked on the car by direct workers (that is the mechanic concerned and any colleagues). The stores staff would normally be required to keep a record of the cost of parts and materials used on each job.

A 'job sheet' will normally be prepared – perhaps on the computer – for each individual job. Staff would need to get into the routine of faithfully recording all elements of direct labour and materials applied to the job.

Job costing

→ The term **job costing** is used to describe the way in which we identify the full cost per cost unit (unit of output or 'job') where the cost units differ. To cost (that is, deduce the full cost of) a particular cost unit, we first identify the direct cost of the cost unit, which, by the definition of direct cost, is fairly straightforward. We then seek to 'charge' each cost unit with a fair share of indirect cost (overheads). Put another way,
→ cost units will absorb overheads. This leads to full costing also being called **absorption costing**. The absorption process is shown graphically in Figure 10.2.

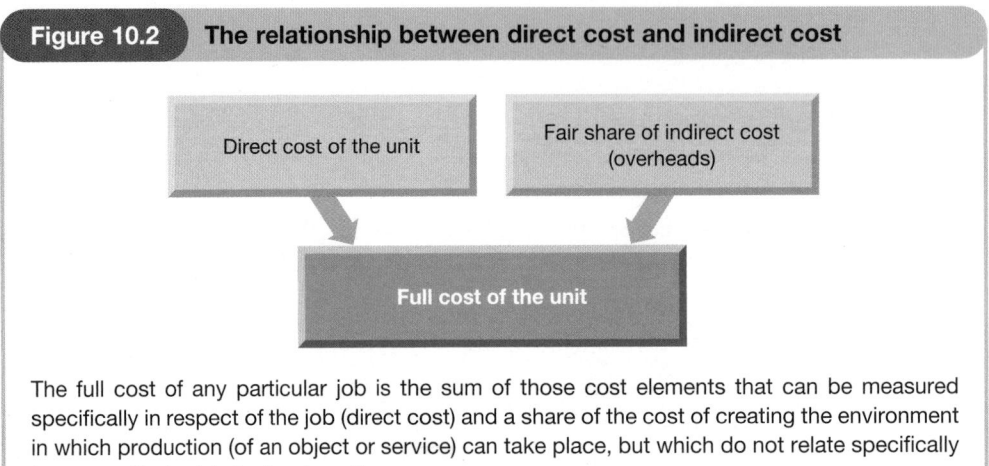

Figure 10.2 **The relationship between direct cost and indirect cost**

The full cost of any particular job is the sum of those cost elements that can be measured specifically in respect of the job (direct cost) and a share of the cost of creating the environment in which production (of an object or service) can take place, but which do not relate specifically to any particular job (indirect cost).

Activity 10.3

Sparky Ltd is a business that employs a number of electricians. The business undertakes a range of work for its customers, from replacing fuses to installing complete wiring systems in new houses.

In respect of a particular job done by Sparky Ltd, into which category (direct or indirect) would each of the following cost elements fall?

- the wages of the electrician who did the job;
- depreciation of the tools used by the electrician;
- the salary of Sparky Ltd's accountant;
- the cost of cable and other materials used on the job;
- rent of the premises where Sparky Ltd stores its inventories of cable and other materials.

Only the electrician's wages earned while working on the particular job and the cost of the materials used on the job are included in direct cost. This is because it is possible to measure how much time was spent on the particular job (and therefore its direct labour cost) and the amount of materials used (and therefore the direct material cost) in the job.

All of the others are included in the general cost of running the business and, as such, must form part of the indirect cost of doing the job, but they cannot be directly measured in respect of the particular job.

It is important to note that whether a cost is direct or indirect depends on the item being costed – the cost objective. To refer to indirect cost without identifying the cost objective is incorrect.

Activity (10.4)

Into which category, direct or indirect, would each of the elements of cost listed in Activity 10.3 fall, if we were seeking to find the cost of operating the entire business of Sparky Ltd for a month?

The answer is that all of them will form part of the direct cost, since they can all be related to, and measured in respect of, running the business for a month.

Naturally, broader-reaching cost objectives, such as operating Sparky Ltd for a month, tend to include a higher proportion of direct cost than do more limited ones, such as a particular job done by Sparky Ltd. As we shall see shortly, this makes costing broader cost objectives rather more straightforward than costing narrower ones. It is generally the case that direct cost is easier to deal with than indirect cost.

Full (absorption) costing and the behaviour of cost

We saw in Chapter 9 that the full cost of doing something (or total cost, as it is usually known in the context of marginal analysis) can be analysed between the fixed and the variable elements. This is illustrated in Figure 10.3.

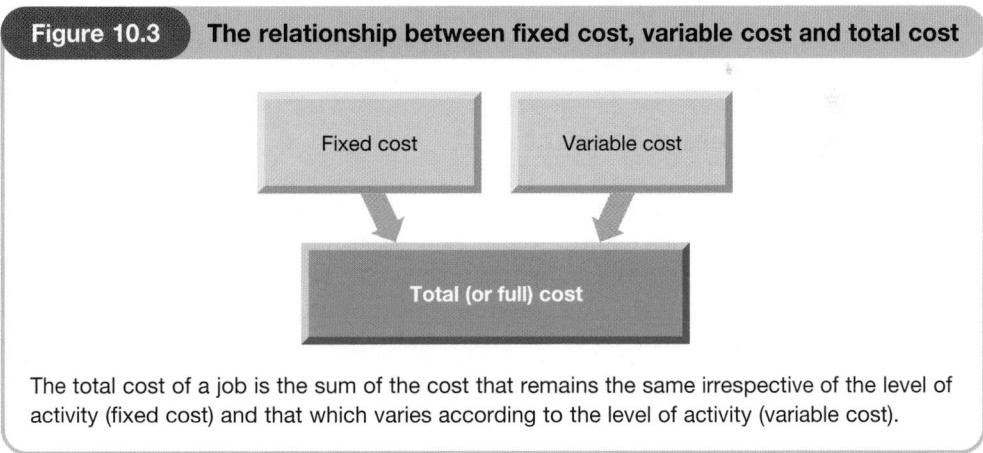

Figure 10.3 **The relationship between fixed cost, variable cost and total cost**

The total cost of a job is the sum of the cost that remains the same irrespective of the level of activity (fixed cost) and that which varies according to the level of activity (variable cost).

The apparent similarity of what is shown in Figure 10.3 to that depicted in Figure 10.2 seems to lead some to believe that variable cost and direct cost are the same, and that fixed cost and indirect cost (overheads) are the same. This is incorrect.

The notions of fixed and variable are concerned with **cost behaviour** in the face of changes in the volume of activity. The notions of direct and indirect, on the other hand, are concerned with the extent to which cost elements can be measured in respect of particular cost units (jobs). The two sets of notions are entirely different. Though it may be true that there is a tendency for fixed cost elements to be indirect (overheads) and for variable cost elements to be direct, there is no link, and there are many exceptions to this tendency. Most activities, for example, have variable indirect cost. Furthermore, labour is a significant element of direct cost in most types of business activity (14 per cent of the total cost of manufacture – see Real World 10.2) but is usually a fixed cost.

The relationship between the reaction of cost to volume changes (cost behaviour), on the one hand, and how cost elements need to be gathered to deduce the full cost (cost collection), on the other, in respect of a particular job is shown in Figure 10.4.

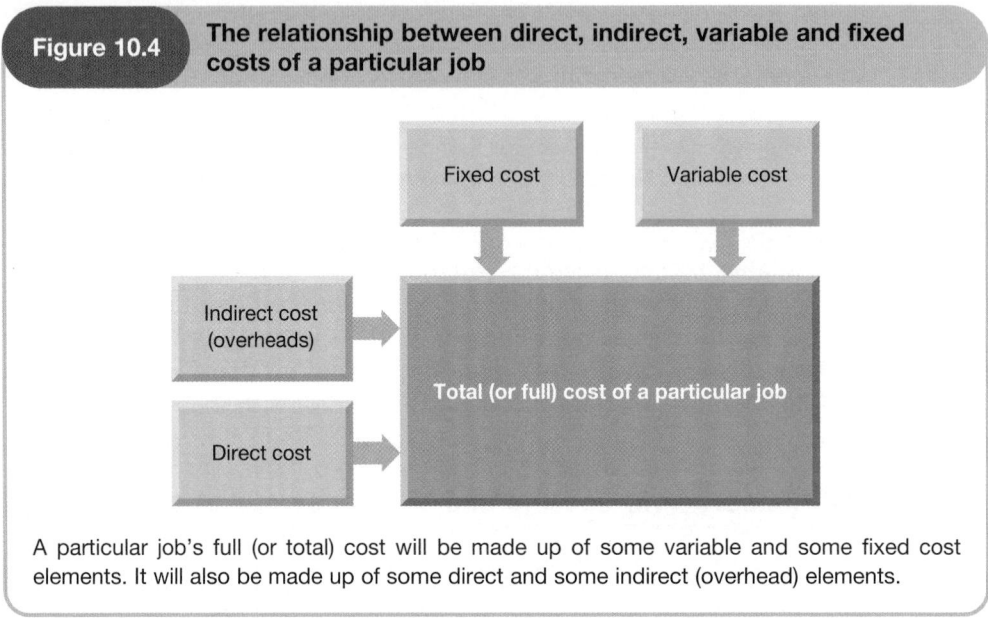

Figure 10.4 **The relationship between direct, indirect, variable and fixed costs of a particular job**

A particular job's full (or total) cost will be made up of some variable and some fixed cost elements. It will also be made up of some direct and some indirect (overhead) elements.

Total cost is the sum of direct and indirect costs. It is also the sum of fixed and variable costs. These two facts are independent of one another. Thus a particular element of cost may be fixed, but that tells us nothing about whether it is a direct or an indirect cost.

The problem of indirect cost

It is worth emphasising that the distinction between direct and indirect cost is only important in a job-costing environment, that is, where units of output differ. When we were considering costing a litre of 'Orange Fizz' drink in Activity 10.1, whether particular elements of cost were direct or indirect was of no consequence, because all elements of cost were shared equally between the individual litres of 'Orange Fizz'. Where we have units of output that are not identical, however, we have to look more closely at the make-up of the cost to achieve a fair measure of the full cost of a particular job.

Although the indirect cost of any activity must form part of the cost of each cost unit, it cannot, by definition, be directly related to individual cost units. This raises a major practical issue: how is the indirect cost to be apportioned to individual cost units?

Overheads as service renderers

It is reasonable to view the indirect cost (overheads) as rendering a service to the cost units. Take for example a legal case, undertaken by a firm of solicitors for a particular client. This job can be seen as being rendered a service by the office in which the work is done. In this sense, it is reasonable to charge each case (cost unit) with a share of the cost of running the office (rent, lighting, heating, cleaning, building maintenance and so on). It also seems reasonable to relate the charge for the 'use' of the office to the level of service that the particular case has received from the office.

The next step is the difficult one. How might the cost of running the office, which is a cost of all work done by the firm, be divided between individual cases that are not similar in size and complexity?

One possibility is sharing this overhead cost equally between each case handled by the firm within the period. This method, however, has little to commend it unless the cases were close to being identical in terms of the extent to which they had 'benefited' from the overheads.

If we are not to propose equal shares, we must identify something observable and measurable about the cases that we feel provides a reasonable basis for distinguishing between one case and the next. In practice, time spent working on each particular cost unit by direct labour is the most popular basis. It must be stressed that this is not the 'correct' way, and it certainly is not the only way.

Job costing: a worked example

To see how job costing (as it is usually called) works, let us consider Example 10.1.

Example 10.1

Johnson Ltd, a business that provides a personal computer maintenance and repair service to its customers, has overheads of £10,000 each month. Each month 1,000 direct labour hours are worked and charged to cost units (jobs carried out by the business). A particular PC repair undertaken by the business used direct materials costing £15. Direct labour worked on the repair was 3 hours and the wage rate is £16 an hour. Overheads are charged to jobs on a direct labour hour basis. What is the full (absorption) cost of the repair?

Solution

First, let us establish the **overhead absorption (recovery) rate**, that is, the rate at which individual repairs will be charged with overheads. This is £10 (that is, £10,000/1,000) per direct labour hour.

Thus, the full cost of the repair is:

	£
Direct materials	15
Direct labour (3 × £16)	48
	63
Overheads (3 × £10)	30
Full cost of the job	93

Note, in Example 10.1, that the number of labour hours (3 hours) appears twice in deducing the full cost: once to deduce the direct labour cost and a second time to deduce the overheads to be charged to the repair. These are really two separate issues, though they are both based on the same number of labour hours.

Note also that, if all the jobs undertaken during the month are assigned overheads in a similar manner, all £10,000 of overheads will be charged to the jobs between them. Jobs that involve a lot of direct labour will be assigned a large share of overheads, and jobs that involve little direct labour will be assigned a small share of overheads.

Activity (10.5)

Can you think of reasons why direct labour hours are regarded as the most logical basis for sharing overheads between cost units?

The reasons that occurred to us are as follows:

- Large jobs should logically attract large amounts of overheads because they are likely to have been rendered more 'service' by the overheads than small ones. The length of time that they are worked on by direct labour may be seen as a rough way of measuring relative size, though other means of doing this may be found – for example, relative physical size, where the cost unit is a physical object, like a manufactured product.
- Most overheads are related to time. Rent, heating, lighting, non-current asset depreciation, supervisors' and managers' salaries and interest on borrowings, which are all typical overheads, are all more or less time-based. That is to say that the overheads for one week tend to be about half of those for a similar two-week period. Thus, a basis of allotting overheads to jobs that takes account of the length of time that the units of output benefited from the 'service' rendered by the overheads seems logical.
- Direct labour hours are capable of being measured for each job. They will normally be measured to deduce the direct labour element of cost in any case. Thus, a direct labour hour basis of dealing with overheads is practical to apply in the real world.

It cannot be emphasised enough that there is no 'correct' way to allot overheads to jobs. Overheads, by definition, do not naturally relate to individual jobs. If, nevertheless, we wish to take account of the fact that overheads are part of the cost of all jobs, we must find some acceptable way of including a share of the total overheads in each job. If a particular means of doing this is accepted by those who use the full cost deduced, then the method is as good as any other method. Accounting is concerned only with providing useful information to decision makers. In practice, the method that seems to be regarded as being the most useful is the direct labour hour method. Real World 10.4, which we shall consider later in the chapter, provides some evidence of this.

Now let us consider **Real World 10.3**, which gives an example of one well-known organisation that does not use direct labour hours to cost its output.

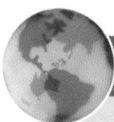 **Real World 10.3**

Operating cost

As we saw in Real World 10.1 the UK National Health Service (NHS) seeks to ascertain the cost of various medical and surgical procedures that it undertakes for its patients. In determining the costs of a procedure that requires time in hospital as an 'in patient', the NHS identifies the total direct cost of the particular procedure (staff time, medication and so on). To this it adds a share of the hospital overheads. The total overheads are absorbed by individual procedures by taking this overheads total and dividing it by the number of 'bed days' throughout the hospital for the period, to establish a 'bed-day rate'. A bed day is one patient spending one day occupying a bed in the hospital. To cost the procedure for a particular patient, the bed-day rate is applied to the cost of the procedure according to how many bed days the particular patient had.

Note that the NHS does not use the direct labour hour basis of absorption; however, the bed-day rate alternative is also a logical, time-based approach.

Source: NHS Costing Manual, Department of Health Gateway reference 9367, February 2008.

Activity (10.6)

Marine Suppliers Ltd undertakes a range of work, including making sails for small sailing boats on a made-to-measure basis.

The business expects the following to arise during the next month:

Direct labour cost	£60,000
Direct labour time	6,000 hours
Indirect labour cost	£9,000
Depreciation of machinery	£3,000
Rent and rates	£5,000
Heating, lighting and power	£2,000
Machine time	2,000 hours
Indirect materials	£500
Other miscellaneous indirect cost elements (overheads)	£200
Direct materials cost	£3,000

The business has received an enquiry about a sail. It is estimated that the particular sail will take 12 direct labour hours to make and will require 20 square metres of sailcloth, which costs £2 per square metre.

The business normally uses a direct labour hour basis of charging indirect cost (overheads) to individual jobs.

What is the full (absorption) cost of making the sail?

The direct cost of making the sail can be identified as follows:

	£
Direct materials (20 × £2)	40.00
Direct labour (12 × (£60,000/6,000))	120.00
	160.00

To deduce the indirect cost (overhead) element that must be added to derive the full cost of the sail, we first need to total these cost elements as follows:

	£
Indirect labour	9,000
Depreciation	3,000
Rent and rates	5,000
Heating, lighting and power	2,000
Indirect materials	500
Other miscellaneous indirect cost (overhead) elements	200
Total indirect cost (overheads)	19,700

Since the business uses a direct labour hour basis of charging indirect cost to jobs, we need to deduce the indirect cost (or overhead) recovery rate per direct labour hour. This is simply:

£19,700/6,000 = £3.28 per direct labour hour

Thus, the full cost of the sail would be expected to be:

	£
Direct materials (20 × £2)	40.00
Direct labour (12 × (£60,000/6,000))	120.00
Indirect cost (12 × £3.28)	39.36
Full cost	199.36

Figure 10.5 shows the process for applying indirect (overhead) and direct costs to the sail that was the subject of Activity 10.6.

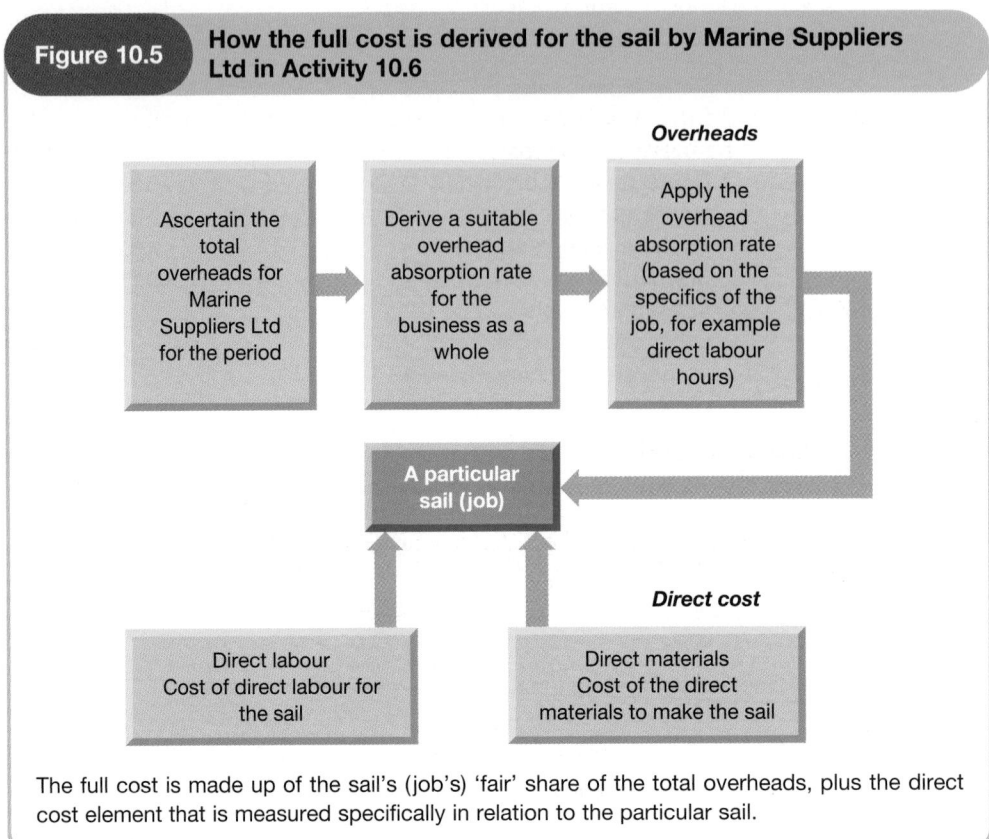

| Figure 10.5 | How the full cost is derived for the sail by Marine Suppliers Ltd in Activity 10.6 |

The full cost is made up of the sail's (job's) 'fair' share of the total overheads, plus the direct cost element that is measured specifically in relation to the particular sail.

Activity (10.7)

Suppose that Marine Suppliers Ltd (see Activity 10.6) used a machine hour basis of charging overheads to jobs. What would be the cost of the job detailed if it was expected to take 5 machine hours (as well as 12 direct labour hours)?

The total overheads of the business will of course be the same irrespective of the method of charging them to jobs. Thus, the overhead recovery rate, on a machine hour basis, will be:

£19,700/2,000 = £9.85 per machine hour

Thus, the full cost of the sail would be expected to be:

	£
Direct materials (20 × £2)	40.00
Direct labour (12 × (£60,000/6,000))	120.00
Indirect cost (5 × £9.85)	49.25
Full cost	209.25

Selecting a basis for charging overheads

We saw earlier that there is no single correct way of charging overheads. The final choice is a matter of judgement. It seems reasonable to say, however, that the nature of the overheads should influence the choice of the basis of charging the overheads to jobs. Where production is capital-intensive and overheads are primarily machine-based (such as depreciation, machine maintenance, power and so on), machine hours might be favoured. Otherwise direct labour hours might be preferred.

It would be irrational to choose one of these bases in preference to the other simply because it apportions either a higher or a lower amount of overheads to a particular job. The total overheads will be the same irrespective of the method of dividing that total between individual jobs and so a method that gives a higher share of overheads to one particular job must give a lower share to the remaining jobs. There is one cake of fixed size: if one person receives a relatively large slice, others must on average receive relatively small slices. To illustrate further this issue of apportioning overheads, consider Example 10.2.

Example 10.2

A business, that provides a service, expects to incur overheads totalling £20,000 next month. The total direct labour time worked is expected to be 1,600 hours and machines are expected to operate for a total of 1,000 hours.

During the next month, the business expects to do just two large jobs. Information concerning each job is as follows:

	Job 1	Job 2
Direct labour hours	800	800
Machine hours	700	300

How much of the total overheads will be charged to each job if overheads are to be charged on:

(a) a direct labour hour basis; and
(b) a machine hour basis?

What do you notice about the two sets of figures that you calculate?

(a) Direct labour hour basis

Overhead recovery rate = £20,000/1,600 = £12.50 per direct labour hour.

Job 1   £12.50 × 800 = £10,000
Job 2   £12.50 × 800 = £10,000

(b) Machine hour basis

Overhead recovery rate = £20,000/1,000 = £20.00 per machine hour.

Job 1   £20.00 × 700 = £14,000
Job 2   £20.00 × 300 = £6,000

It is clear from these calculations that the total overheads charged to jobs is the same (that is, £20,000) whichever method is used. So, whereas the machine hour basis gives Job 1 a higher share than does the direct labour hour method, the opposite is true for Job 2.

It is not practical to charge overheads on one basis to one job and on the other basis to the other job. This is because either total overheads will not be fully charged to the jobs, or the jobs will be overcharged with overheads. For example, using the direct labour hour method for Job 1 (£10,000) and the machine hour basis for Job 2 (£6,000) will mean that only £16,000 of a total £20,000 of overheads will be charged to jobs. As a result, the objective of full (absorption) costing, which is to charge all overheads to jobs done, will not be achieved. In this particular case, if selling prices are based on full cost, the business may not charge high enough prices to cover all of its costs.

Figure 10.6 shows the effect of the two different bases of charging overheads to Jobs 1 and 2.

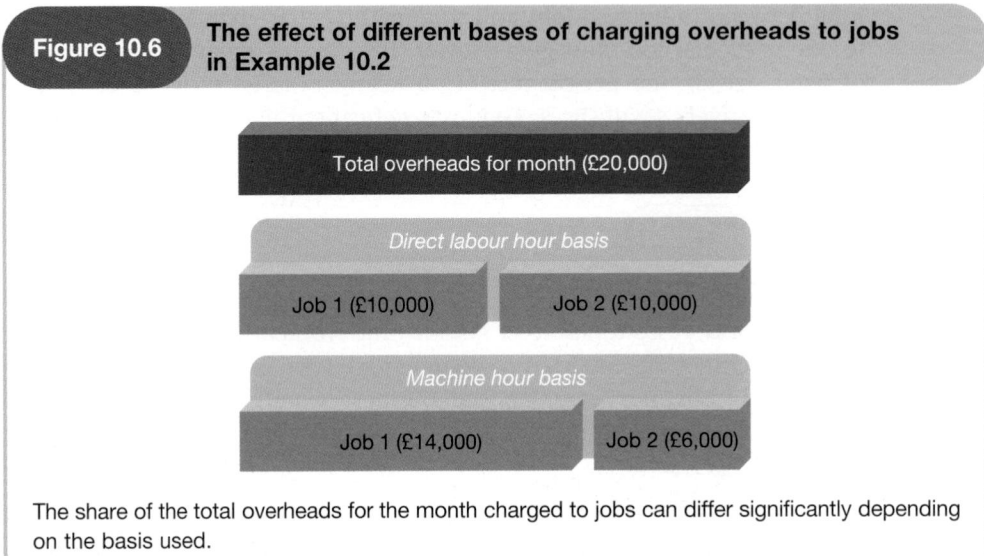

| Figure 10.6 | The effect of different bases of charging overheads to jobs in Example 10.2 |

The share of the total overheads for the month charged to jobs can differ significantly depending on the basis used.

Activity (10.8)

The point was made above that it would normally be irrational to prefer one basis of charging overheads to jobs simply because it apportions either a higher or a lower amount of overheads to a particular job. This is because the total overheads are the same irrespective of the method of charging the total to individual jobs. Can you think of any circumstances where it would not necessarily be so irrational?

This might apply where, for a particular job, a customer has agreed to pay a price based on full cost plus an agreed fixed percentage for profit. Here it would be beneficial to the producer for the total cost of the job to be as high as possible. This would be relatively unusual, but sometimes public sector organisations, particularly central and local government departments, have entered into contracts to have work done, with the price to be deduced, after the work has been completed, on a cost-plus basis. Such contracts are pretty rare these days, probably because they are open to abuse in the way described. Usually, contract prices are agreed in advance, typically in conjunction with competitive tendering. Despite this, in Real World 10.7 later in the chapter, we shall see an example of a business that makes many of its sales on a cost-plus basis.

Real World 10.4 provides some insight into the basis of overhead recovery in practice.

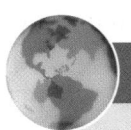

Real World 10.4

Overhead recovery rates in practice

A survey of 303 UK manufacturing businesses, published in 1993, showed that the direct labour hour basis of charging indirect cost (overheads) to cost units was overwhelmingly the most popular, used by 73 per cent of the respondents to the survey. Where the work has a strong labour element this seems reasonable, but the survey also showed that 68 per cent of businesses used this basis for automated activities. It is surprising that direct labour hours should have been used as the basis of charging overheads in an environment dominated by machines and machine-related cost.

Though this survey is not very recent and applied only to manufacturing businesses, in the absence of other information it provides some impression of what happens in practice. There is no reason to believe that current practice is very different from that which applied at the beginning of the 1990s.

Source: Based on information taken from *A Survey of Management Accounting Practices in UK Manufacturing Companies*, C. Drury, S. Braund, P. Osborne and M. Tayles, Chartered Association of Certified Accountants, 1993.

Segmenting the overheads

As we have just seen, charging the same overheads to different jobs on different bases is not logical. It is perfectly reasonable, however, to charge one segment of the total over-heads on one basis and another segment (or other segments) on another basis (or bases).

Activity 10.9

Taking the same business as in Example 10.2, on closer analysis we find that of the over-heads totalling £20,000 next month, £8,000 relate to machines (depreciation, maintenance, rent of the space occupied by the machines and so on) and the remaining £12,000 to more general overheads. The other information about the business is exactly as it was before.

How much of the total overheads will be charged to each job if the machine-related overheads are to be charged on a machine hour basis and the remaining overheads are charged on a direct labour hour basis?

Direct labour hour basis

Overhead recovery rate = £12,000/1,600 = £7.50 per direct labour hour

Machine hour basis

Overhead recovery rate = £8,000/1,000 = £8.00 per machine hour

Overheads charged to jobs

	Job 1	Job 2
	£	£
Direct labour hour basis:		
£7.50 × 800	6,000	
£7.50 × 800		6,000
Machine hour basis:		
£8.00 × 700	5,600	
£8.00 × 300		2,400
Total	11,600	8,400

We can see from this that the expected overheads of £20,000 are charged in total.

Segmenting the overheads in this way may well be seen as providing a better basis of charging overheads to jobs. This is quite often found in practice, usually by dividing a business into separate 'areas' for costing purposes, charging overheads differently from one area to the next, according to the nature of the work done in each.

Dealing with overheads on a cost centre basis

In general, as we saw in Chapter 1, all but the smallest businesses are divided into departments. Normally, each department deals with a separate activity. The reasons for dividing a business into departments include the following:

- *Size and complexity*. Many businesses are too large and complex to be managed as a single unit. It is usually more practical to operate each business as a series of relatively independent units with each one having its own manager.
- *Expertise*. Each department normally has its own area of specialism and is managed by a specialist.
- *Accountability*. Each department can have its own accounting records that enable its performance to be assessed. This can lead to greater management control and motivation among the staff.

As is shown in Real World 10.5, which we shall consider shortly, most businesses charge overheads to cost units on a department-by-department basis. They do this because they expect that it will give rise to a more useful way of charging overheads. It is probably only in a minority of cases that it leads to any great improvement in the usefulness of the resulting full cost figures. Though it may not be of enormous benefit in many cases, it is probably not an expensive exercise to apply overheads on a departmental basis. Since cost elements are collected department by department for other purposes (particularly control), to apply overheads on a department-by-department basis is a relatively simple matter.

We shall now take a look at how the departmental approach to deriving full cost works, in a service-industry context, through Example 10.3.

Example 10.3

Autosparkle Ltd offers a motor vehicle paint-respray service. The jobs that it undertakes range from painting a small part of a saloon car, usually following a minor accident, to a complete respray of a double-decker bus.

Each job starts life in the Preparation Department, where it is prepared for the Paintshop. In the Preparation Department the job is worked on by direct workers, in most cases taking some direct materials from the stores with which to treat the old paintwork to render the vehicle ready for respraying. Thus the job will be charged with direct materials, direct labour and with a share of the Preparation Department's overheads. The job then passes into the Paintshop Department, already valued at the cost that it picked up in the Preparation Department.

In the Paintshop, the staff draw direct materials (mainly paint) from the stores and direct workers spend time respraying the job, using sophisticated spraying apparatus as well as working by hand. So, in the Paintshop, the job is charged with direct materials, direct labour and a share of that department's overheads. The job now passes into the Finishing Department, valued at the cost of the materials, labour and overheads that it accumulated in the first two departments.

In the Finishing Department, jobs are cleaned and polished ready to go back to the customers. Further direct labour and, in some cases, materials are added. All jobs also pick up a share of that department's overheads. The job, now complete, passes back to the customer.

Figure 10.7 shows graphically how this works for a particular job.

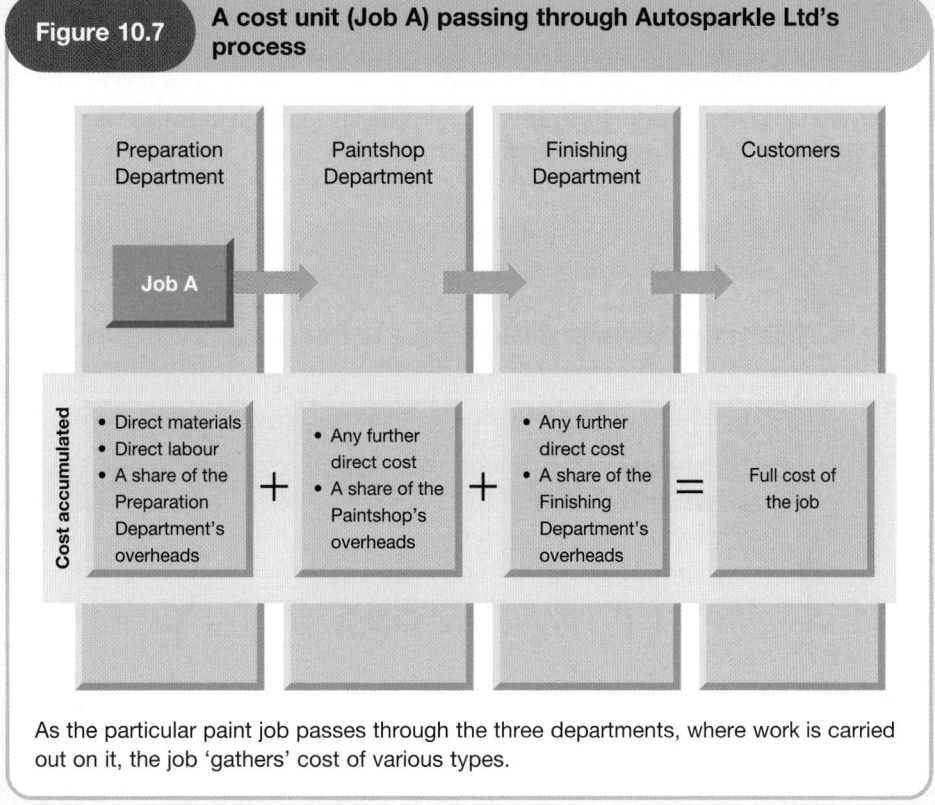

Figure 10.7 A cost unit (Job A) passing through Autosparkle Ltd's process

As the particular paint job passes through the three departments, where work is carried out on it, the job 'gathers' cost of various types.

The basis of charging overheads to jobs (for example, direct labour hours) might be the same for all three departments, or it might be different from one department to another. It is possible that spraying apparatus cost elements dominate the Paintshop cost, so that department's overheads might well be charged to jobs on a machine hour basis. The other two departments are probably labour intensive, so that direct labour hours may be seen as being appropriate there.

The passage of a job through the departments, picking up cost as it goes, can be compared to a snowball being rolled across snow: as it rolls, it picks up more and more snow.

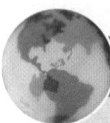 Where cost determination is dealt with departmentally, each department is known as a **cost centre**. This can be defined as a particular physical area or some activity or function for which the cost is separately identified. Charging direct cost to jobs, in a departmental system, is exactly the same as where the whole business is one single cost centre. It is simply a matter of keeping a record of:

- the number of hours of direct labour worked on the particular job and the grade of labour, assuming that there are different grades with different rates of pay;
- the cost of the direct materials taken from stores and applied to the job; and
- any other direct cost elements, for example some subcontracted work, associated with the job.

This record keeping will normally be done cost centre by cost centre.

It is obviously necessary to break down the production overheads of the entire business on a cost centre basis. This means that the total overheads of the business must be divided between the cost centres, such that the sum of the overheads of all of the cost centres equals the overheads for the entire business. By charging all of their overheads to jobs, the cost centres will, between them, charge all of the overheads of the business to jobs. **Real World 10.5** provides an indication of the number of different cost centres that businesses tend to use in practice.

Real World 10.5

Cost centres in practice

It is not unusual for businesses to have several cost centres. A recent survey of 186 larger UK businesses involved in various activities by Drury and Tayles showed the following:

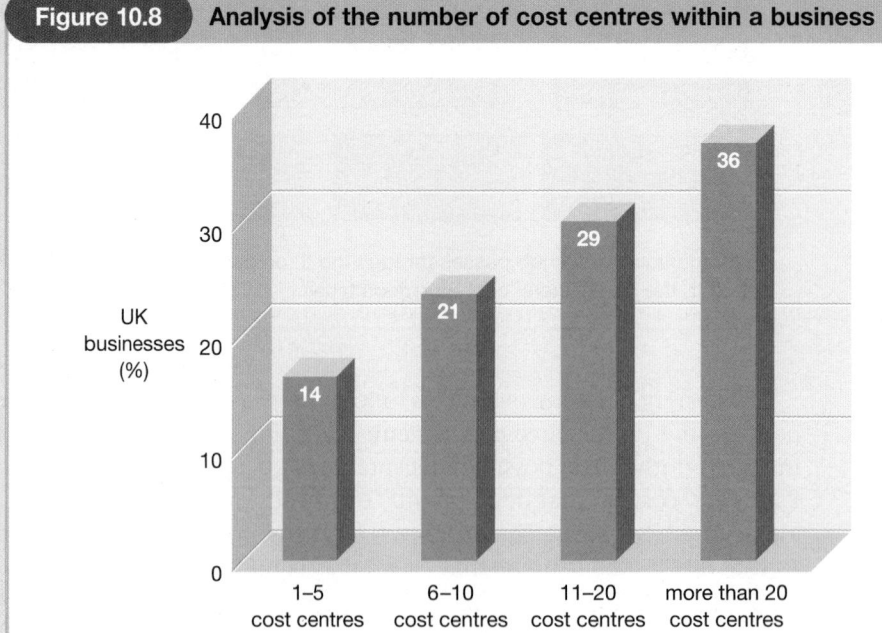

Figure 10.8 **Analysis of the number of cost centres within a business**

The survey of larger businesses shows, as might be expected, that they tend to have several cost centres.

We can see from Figure 10.8 that 85 per cent of businesses surveyed had six or more cost centres and that 36 per cent of businesses had more than 20 cost centres. Though not shown on the diagram, 3 per cent of businesses surveyed had a single cost centre (that is, there was a business-wide or overall overhead rate used). Clearly, businesses that deal with overheads on a business-wide basis are very rare.

Source: Based on information taken from 'Profitability analysis in UK organisations', C. Drury and M. Tayles, *British Accounting Review*, December 2006.

For purposes of cost assignment, it is necessary to distinguish between **product cost centres** and **service cost centres**. Product cost centres are those in which jobs are worked on by direct workers and/or where direct materials are added. Here jobs can be charged with a share of their overheads. The Preparation, Paintshop and Finishing Departments, discussed above in Example 10.3, are all examples of product cost centres.

Activity (10.10)

Can you guess what the definition of a service cost centre is?
Can you think of an example of a service cost centre?

A service cost centre is one where no direct cost is involved. It renders a service to other cost centres. Examples include:

- General administration
- Accounting
- Stores
- Maintenance
- Personnel
- Catering.

All of these render services to product cost centres and, possibly, to other service cost centres.

The service cost centre cost must be charged to product cost centres, and become part of the product cost centres' overheads, so that those overheads can be recharged to jobs. This must be done so that all of the overheads of the business find their way into the cost of the jobs. If this is not done, the 'full' cost derived will not really be the full cost of the jobs.

Logically, the cost of a service cost centre should be charged to product cost centres on the basis of the level of service provided to the product cost centre concerned. Thus, a product cost centre that has a higher level of machine maintenance carried out should be charged with a larger share of the maintenance cost centre's (department's) cost.

The process of dividing overheads between cost centres is as follows:

- **Cost allocation.** Allocate indirect cost elements that are specific to particular cost centres. These are items that relate to, and are specifically measurable in respect of, individual cost centres, that is, they are part of the direct cost of running the cost centre. Examples include:

    – salaries of indirect workers whose activities are wholly within the cost centre, for example the salary of the cost centre manager;

    – rent, where the cost centre is housed in its own premises for which rent can be separately identified;

    – electricity, where it is separately metered for each cost centre.

● **Cost apportionment**. Apportion the more general overheads to the cost centres. These are overheads that relate to more than one cost centre, perhaps to them all. It would include:

    – rent, where more than one cost centre is housed in the same premises;

    – electricity, where it is not separately metered;

    – salaries of cleaning staff who work in a variety of cost centres.

    These overheads would be apportioned to cost centres on the basis of the extent to which each cost centre benefits from the overheads concerned. For example, the rent cost might be apportioned on the basis of the square metres of floor area occupied by each cost centre. With electricity used to power machinery, the basis of apportionment might be the level of mechanisation of each cost centre. As with charging overheads to individual jobs, there is no correct basis of apportioning general overheads to cost centres.

● Having totalled, allocated and apportioned the cost to all cost centres, it is necessary to apportion the total cost of service cost centres to product cost centres. Logically, the basis of apportionment should be the level of service rendered by the individual service cost centre to the individual production cost centre. With the

Figure 10.9   **The steps in having overheads handled on a cost centre basis**

Step 1	Allocate specific cost centre overheads to the relevant cost centre
Step 2	Apportion general overheads between cost centres
Step 3	Total allocated and apportioned overheads to find the total for each cost centre
Step 4	Apportion service cost centre costs to product cost centres
Step 5	Total product cost centre overheads
Step 6	Calculate a cost centre overhead absorption rate for each product cost centre
Step 7	Cost units absorb overheads as they pass through product cost centres

There are seven steps involved with taking the overall business overheads to their effect on individual cost units, when dealt with on a cost centre basis.

personnel cost centre (department) cost, for example, the basis of apportionment might be the number of staff in each product cost centre, because it could be argued that the higher the number of staff, the more benefit the particular product cost centre would have derived from the personnel cost centre. This is, of course, rather a crude approach. A particular product cost centre may have severe personnel problems and a high staff turnover rate, which may make it a user of the personnel service that is way out of proportion to the number of staff it employs.

The final total for each product cost centre will be charged to jobs as they pass through. The process of applying overheads to cost units on a cost centre (departmental) basis is shown in Figure 10.9.

We shall now go on to consider Example 10.4, which deals with overheads on a cost centre (departmental) basis.

Example 10.4

A business consists of four cost centres:

- Preparation department
- Machining department
- Finishing department
- General administration (GA) department. (indirect workers)

The first three are product cost centres and the last renders a service to the other three. The level of service rendered is thought to be roughly in proportion to the number of employees in each product cost centre.

Overheads, and other data, for next month are expected to be as follows:

	£000
Rent	10,000
Electricity to power machines	3,000
Electricity for heating and lighting	800
Insurance of premises	200
Cleaning	600
Depreciation of machines	2,000
Total monthly salaries of the indirect workers:	
Preparation department	200
Machining department	240
Finishing department	180
General administration department	180

The general administration department has a staff consisting of only indirect workers (including managers). The other departments have both indirect workers (including managers) and direct workers. There are 100 indirect workers within each of the four departments and none does any 'direct' work.

Each direct worker is expected to work 160 hours next month. The number of direct workers in each department is:

Preparation department	600 £10
Machining department	900 £12
Finishing department	500 £10

Machining department direct workers are paid £12 an hour; other direct workers are paid £10 an hour.

→

→ All of the machinery is in the machining department. Machines are expected to operate for 120,000 hours next month.

The floorspace (in square metres) occupied by the departments is as follows:

Preparation department	16,000
Machining department	20,000
Finishing department	10,000
General administration department	2,000

Deducing the overheads, cost centre by cost centre, can be done, using a schedule, as follows:

	£000	Total £000	Prep'n £000	Mach'g £000	Fin'g £000	GA £000
Allocated cost:						
Machine power		3,000		3,000		
Machine depreciation		2,000		2,000		
Indirect salaries		800	200	240	180	180
Apportioned cost						
Rent	10,000					
Heating and lighting	800					
Insurance of premises	200					
Cleaning	600					
Apportioned by floor area		11,600	3,867	4,833	2,417	483
Cost centre overheads		17,400	4,067	10,073	2,597	663
Reapportion GA cost by number of staff (including the indirect workers)			202	288	173	(663)
		17,400	4,269	10,361	2,770	–

Activity 10.11

Assume that the machining department overheads (in Example 10.4) are to be charged to jobs on a machine hour basis, but that the direct labour hour basis is to be used for the other two departments. What will be the full (absorption) cost of a job with the following characteristics?

	Preparation	Machining	Finishing
Direct labour hours	10	7	5
Machine hours	–	6	–
Direct materials (£)	85	13	6

Hint: This should be tackled as if each cost centre were a separate business, then departmental cost elements are added together for the job so as to arrive at the total full cost.

First, we need to deduce the indirect (overhead) recovery rates for each cost centre:
Preparation department (direct labour hour based):

$$\frac{£4,269,000}{600 \times 160} = £44.47$$

Machining department (machine hour based):

$$\frac{£10,361,000}{120,000} = £86.34$$

Finishing department (direct labour hour based):

$$\frac{£2,770,000}{500 \times 160} = £34.63$$

The cost of the job is as follows:

	£	£
Direct labour:		
Preparation department (10 × £10)	100.00	
Machining department (7 × £12)	84.00	
Finishing department (5 × £10)	50.00	
		234.00
Direct materials:		
Preparation department	85.00	
Machining department	13.00	
Finishing department	6.00	
		104.00
Overheads:		
Preparation department (10 × £44.47)	444.70	
Machining department (6 × £86.34)	518.04	
Finishing department (5 × £34.63)	173.15	
		1,135.89
Full cost of the job		1,473.89

Activity 10.12

The manufacturing cost for Buccaneers Ltd for next year is expected to be made up as follows:

	£000
Direct materials:	
Forming department	450
Machining department	100
Finishing department	50
Direct labour: (£6)	
Forming department	180
Machining department	120
Finishing department	75

Activity 10.12 continued

Indirect materials:	
Forming department	40
Machining department	30
Finishing department	10
Administration department	10
Indirect labour:	
Forming department	80
Machining department	70
Finishing department	60
Administration department	60
Maintenance cost	50
Rent and rates	100
Heating and lighting	20
Building insurance	10
Machinery insurance	10
Depreciation of machinery	120
Total manufacturing cost	1,645

The following additional information is available:

(i)   Each of the four departments is treated as a separate cost centre.

(ii) All direct labour is paid £6 an hour for all hours worked.

(iii) The administration department renders personnel and general services to the production departments.

(iv) The area of the premises in which the business manufactures amounts to 50,000 square metres, divided as follows:

	Sq m
Forming department	20,000
Machining department	15,000
Finishing department	10,000
Administration department	5,000

(v) The maintenance employees are expected to divide their time between the production departments as follows:

	%
Forming department	15
Machining department	75
Finishing department	10

(vi) Machine hours are expected to be as follows:

	Hours
Forming department	5,000
Machining department	15,000
Finishing department	5,000

On the basis of this information:

(a) Allocate and apportion overheads to the three product cost centres.
(b) Deduce overhead recovery rates for each product cost centre using two different bases for each cost centre's overheads.
(c) Calculate the full cost of a job with the following characteristics:

Direct labour hours:	
Forming department	4 hours
Machining department	4 hours
Finishing department	1 hour
Machine hours:	
Forming department	1 hour
Machining department	2 hours
Finishing department	1 hour
Direct materials:	
Forming department	£40
Machining department	£9
Finishing department	£4

Use whichever of the two bases of overhead recovery, deduced in (b), that you consider more appropriate.

(d) Explain why you consider the basis used in (c) to be the more appropriate.

(a) Overheads can be allocated and apportioned as follows:

Cost	Basis of apport't	Total £000	Forming £000	Machining £000	Finishing £000	Admin. £000
Indirect materials	Specifically allocated	90	40	30	10	10
Indirect labour	Specifically allocated	270	80	70	60	60
Maintenance	Staff time	50	7.5	37.5	5	–
Rent/rates		100				
Heat/light		20				
Buildings insurance		10				
	Area	130	52	39	26	13
Machine insurance		10				
Machine depreciation		120				
	Machine hours	130	26	78	26	–
		670	205.5	254.5	127	83
Admin.	Direct labour		39.84	26.56	16.6	(83)
		670	245.34	281.06	143.6	–

Note: The direct cost is not included in the above because it is allocated *directly* to jobs.

Activity 10.12 continued

(b) Overhead recovery rates are as follows:

Basis 1: direct labour hours

$$\text{Forming} = \frac{£245,340}{£(180,000/6)} = £8.18 \text{ per direct labour hour}$$

$$\text{Machining} = \frac{£281,060}{£(120,000/6)} = £14.05 \text{ per direct labour hour}$$

$$\text{Finishing} = \frac{£143,600}{£(75,000/6)} = £11.49 \text{ per direct labour hour}$$

Basis 2: machine hours

$$\text{Forming} = \frac{£245,340}{5,000} = £49.07 \text{ per machine hour}$$

$$\text{Machining} = \frac{£281,060}{15,000} = £18.74 \text{ per machine hour}$$

$$\text{Finishing} = \frac{£143,600}{5,000} = £28.72 \text{ per machine hour}$$

(c) Full cost of job – on direct labour hour basis of overhead recovery

	£	£
Direct labour cost (9 × £6)		54.00
Direct materials (£40 + £9 + £4)		53.00
Overheads:		
Forming (4 × £8.18)	32.72	
Machining (4 × £14.05)	56.20	
Finishing (1 × £11.49)	11.49	100.41
Full cost		207.41

(d) The reason for using the direct labour hour basis rather than the machine hour basis was that labour is more important, in terms of the number of hours applied to output, than is machine time. Strong arguments could have been made for the use of the alternative basis; certainly, a machine hour basis could have been justified for the machining department.

It would be possible, and it may be reasonable, to use one basis in respect of one product cost centre's overheads and a different one for those of another. For example, machine hours could have been used for the machining department and a direct labour hours basis for the other two.

Batch costing

The production of many types of goods and services (particularly goods) involves producing in a batch of identical, or nearly identical, units of output, but where each batch is distinctly different from other batches. For example, a theatre may put on a production whose nature (and therefore cost) is very different from that of other productions. On the other hand, ignoring differences in the desirability of the various types of seating, all of the individual units of output (tickets to see the production) are identical.

In these circumstances, the cost per ticket would normally be deduced by:

● using a job costing approach (taking account of direct and indirect costs and so on) to find the cost of mounting the production; and then
● dividing the cost of mounting the production by the expected number of tickets to be sold to find the cost per ticket.

→ This is known as **batch costing**.

Figure 10.10 shows the process for deriving the cost of one cost unit (product) in a batch.

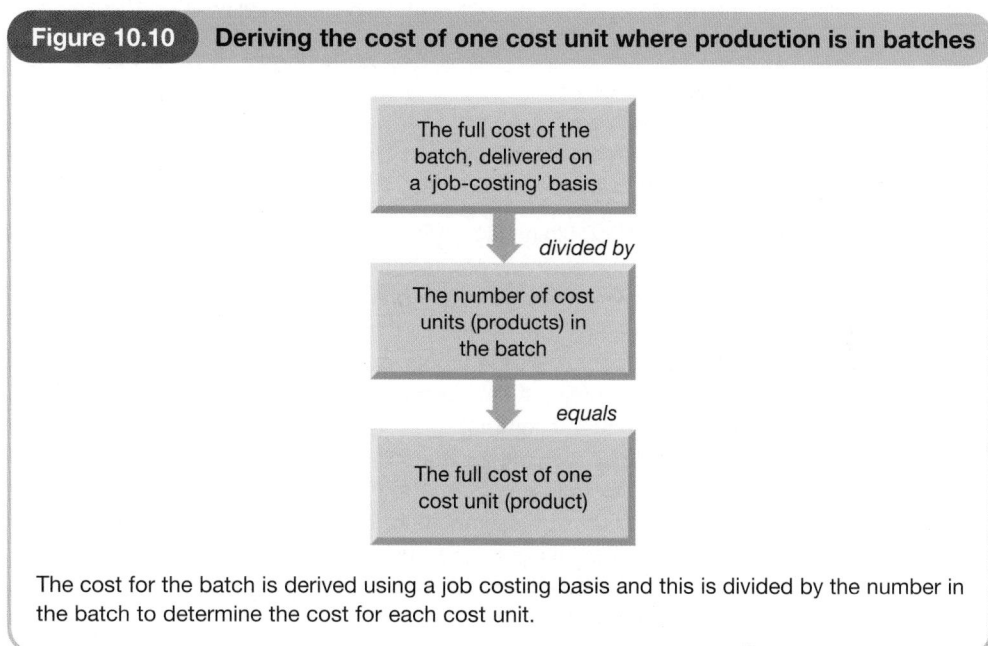

Figure 10.10   Deriving the cost of one cost unit where production is in batches

The full cost of the batch, delivered on a 'job-costing' basis

divided by

The number of cost units (products) in the batch

equals

The full cost of one cost unit (product)

The cost for the batch is derived using a job costing basis and this is divided by the number in the batch to determine the cost for each cost unit.

Full (absorption) cost as the break-even price

For decision-making purposes, it can be helpful to allocate non-manufacturing costs as well as manufacturing costs to products using some sensible basis of allocation. When this is done and everything proves to be as expected, then selling the output for its full cost should cause the business to break even exactly. Therefore, whatever profit (in total) is loaded onto full cost to set actual selling prices will, if plans are achieved, result in that level of profit being earned for the period.

The forward-looking nature of full (absorption) costing

Although deducing full cost can be done after the work has been completed, it is often done in advance. In other words, cost is frequently predicted. Where, for example, the full cost is needed as a basis on which to set a selling price, that price will usually need to be set before the customer will place the order. Even where no particular customer has been identified, some idea of the ultimate price will need to be known before the business will be able to make a judgement as to whether potential customers will buy the product, and in what quantities. There is a risk, of course, that the actual outcome will differ from that which was predicted. This risk is, however, one of the risks of being in business.

Self-assessment question (10.1)

Hector and Co. Ltd has been invited to tender for a contract to produce 1,000 clothes hangers. The following information relates to the contract.

- *Materials*: The clothes hangers are made of metal wire covered with a padded fabric. Each hanger requires 2 metres of wire and 0.5 square metres of fabric.
- *Direct labour*: skilled: 10 minutes per hanger; unskilled: 5 minutes per hanger.

The business already holds sufficient of each of the materials required to complete the contract. Information on the cost of the materials is as follows:

	Metal wire	Fabric
	£/m	£/sq m
Historic cost	2.20	1.00
Current buying-in cost	2.50	1.10
Scrap value	1.70	0.40

The metal wire is in constant use by the business for a range of its products. The fabric has no other use for the business and is scheduled to be scrapped.

Unskilled labour, which is paid at the rate of £7.50 an hour, will need to be taken on specifically to undertake the contract. The business is fairly quiet at the moment, which means that a pool of skilled labour exists that will still be employed at full pay of £12.00 an hour to do nothing if the contract does not proceed. The pool of skilled labour is sufficient to complete the contract.

The business charges jobs with overheads on a direct labour hour basis. The production overheads of the entire business for the month in which the contract will be undertaken are estimated at £50,000. The estimated total direct labour hours that will be worked are 12,500. The business tends not to alter the established overhead recovery rate to reflect increases or reductions to estimated total hours arising from new contracts. The total overheads are not expected to increase as a result of undertaking the contract.

The business normally adds 12.5 per cent profit loading to the job cost to arrive at a first estimate of the tender price.

Required:
(a) Price this job on a traditional job-costing basis.
(b) Indicate the minimum price at which the contract could be undertaken such that the business would be neither better nor worse off as a result of doing it.

The answer to this question can be found at the back of the book on page 730.

Using full (absorption) cost information

We saw at the beginning of the chapter that full (absorption) cost information may be used for four main purposes. Now that we have seen how full cost is deduced, let us consider in more detail how this information may be used. The four uses that we identified were:

- *Pricing and output decisions*. Full cost can be used as the starting point for determining prices. We shall consider this in some detail in the next section.
- *Exercising control*. Full (absorption) cost seems often to be used as the basis of budgeting and comparing actual outcomes with budgets, enabling action to be taken to exercise control. It can be useful in this context, though care needs to be

taken to try to ensure that individual managers are not being held responsible for cost elements, say overheads, that they are unable to control. This point will be raised again in Chapter 11, where we consider another approach to dealing with overheads in full costing. We shall look at budgeting and control in some detail in Chapters 12 and 13.

● *Assessing relative efficiency.* Full cost seems to be used as the basis of comparing relative efficiency in terms of the comparative cost of doing similar things. For example, as we saw in Real World 10.1 (page 350), the cost of carrying out a standard hospital in-patient procedure seems often compared on the basis of full cost between one hospital and another. The objective of this may well be to identify the cheaper hospital and encourage the other to copy its approach.

  As we saw in Chapters 8 and 9, including all aspects of cost (as full costing does) can lead to incorrect decisions. It is necessary to identify that part of the cost that is strictly relevant to a decision and ignore to the rest, be it direct or indirect in the full-costing context. Similarly, comparing the full cost of producing something, particularly when it is being produced in different organisations, can be confusing and can lead to bad decisions.

● *Assessing performance.* The conventional approach to measuring a business's income for a period requires that expenses be matched with the sales revenue to which they relate *in the same accounting period.* Thus, where a service is partially rendered in one accounting period but the revenue is recognised in the next, or where manufactured inventories are made, or partially made, in one period but sold in the next, the full cost (including an appropriate share of overheads) must be carried from the first accounting period to the second one.

  Deducing full cost is important because, unless we know the full cost of work done in one period that is sold in the next, the profit figures for each of the two periods concerned will be meaningless. Managers and others will not have a reliable means of assessing the effectiveness of the business as a whole, or the effectiveness of individual parts of it. Shortly, we shall take a quick look at an alternative approach to income measurement where full cost is not used.

The way in which full cost information is used to measure income can be illustrated by Example 10.5.

Example 10.5

During the accounting year that ended on 31 December last year, IT Modules Ltd developed a special piece of computer software for a customer, Kingsang Ltd. At the beginning of this year, after having a series of tests successfully completed by a subcontractor, the software was passed to Kingsang Ltd. IT Modules's normal practice (which is typical of most sales transactions by most businesses – see Chapter 3, page 85) is to take account of sales revenue when the product passes to the customer. The sale price of the Kingsang software was £45,000.

During last year, subcontract work costing £3,500 was used in developing the Kingsang software and 1,200 hours of direct labour, costing £24,300, were worked on it. The business uses a direct labour hour basis of charging overheads to jobs, which is believed to be fair because most of its work is labour intensive. The total production overheads for the business for last year were £77,000, and the total direct labour hours worked were 22,000. Testing the Kingsang software this year cost £1,000.

→

How much profit or loss did IT Modules make on the Kingsang software during last year? How much profit or loss did it make on the software during this year? At what value should IT Modules have included the software in its statement of financial position (balance sheet) at the end of last year so that the correct profit will be recorded for each of the two years?

The answers to these questions are as follows:

- No profit or loss was made during last year. This is because of IT Modules's (and the generally accepted) approach to recognising sales revenues and the need to match expenses with the revenues to which they relate in the same accounting period. The cost incurred during last year is carried forward to this year, which is the year of sale.
- As the sale is recognised this year, the cost of developing the software is treated as expenses in this year. This cost will include a reasonable share of overheads. Were IT Modules to draw up a 'mini' income statement for the Kingsang contract for this year, it would be as follows:

Kingsang software	£	£
Sales revenue		45,000
Cost:		
Direct labour	(24,300)	
Subcontract	(3,500)	
Overheads (1,200 × (£77,000/22,000))	(4,200)	
Total incurred last year	(32,000)	
Testing cost	(1,000)	
Total cost		(33,000)
This year's profit from the software		12,000

- The software needs to be shown as an asset of the business (valued at £32,000) in the statement of financial position as at 31 December last year. It represents the work in progress that is carried forward to this year.

Full cost (cost-plus) pricing

A business may seek to set its selling prices by simply adding a profit loading to the full cost of a product or service. The amount of profit is often calculated as a percentage of the full (absorption) cost figure. This approach to pricing is known as **cost-plus pricing**. The prices at which businesses are able to sell their output will usually be a major determinant of the quantity that they make available to the market. This is a perfectly logical approach. If a business charges the full cost of its output as a selling price, the business will, in theory, break even, because the sales revenue will exactly cover all of the costs. Charging something above full cost will yield a profit.

Garages, carrying out vehicle repairs, typically operate in this way. Solicitors and accountants doing work for clients also often use this approach.

If full cost (cost-plus) pricing is to be used, the required profit from each unit sold must be determined. This must logically be based on the total profit required for the period. In practice, this required profit is often set in relation to the amount of capital invested in the business. In other words, businesses seek to generate a target return on capital employed. It seems, therefore, that the profit loading on full cost should reflect the business's target profit and that the target should itself be based on a target return on capital employed.

Activity (10.13)

A business has just completed a service job whose full cost has been calculated at £112. For the current period, the total costs (direct and indirect) are estimated at £250,000. The profit target for the period is £100,000.

Suggest a selling price for the job.

If the profit is to be earned by jobs in proportion to their full cost, then the profit for each pound of full cost must be £0.40 (that is, £100,000/250,000). Thus, the target profit on the job must be:

$$£0.40 \times 112 = £44.80$$

This means that the target price for the job must be:

$$£112 + £44.80 = £156.80$$

Other ways could be found for apportioning a share of profit to jobs – for example, direct labour or machine hours. Such bases may be preferred where it is believed that these factors are better representatives of effort and, therefore, profitworthiness. It is clearly a matter of judgement as to how profit is apportioned to units of output.

Price makers and price takers

Despite the logic of basing selling prices on full cost, where there is a competitive market for the product or service, it is often not possible to set prices on a cost-plus basis. The problem with cost-plus pricing is that the market may not agree with the price. Businesses will usually have to accept the price that the market is prepared to pay. A business may fairly deduce the full cost of some product and then add what might be regarded as a reasonable level of profit, only to find that a rival producer is offering a similar product for a much lower price, or that the market simply will not buy at the cost-plus price.

Most suppliers are not strong enough in the market to dictate pricing. Most are *price takers* not *price makers*. They must accept the price offered by the market or they do not sell any of their products. Cost-plus pricing may be appropriate for price makers, but it has less relevance for price takers.

Real World 10.6 illustrates how adopting a cost-plus approach to pricing may lead to a situation where falling demand leads to price rises, which in turn lead to falling demand.

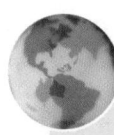

Real World 10.6

A vicious circle in the library

Librarians have long complained about the price rises of academic journals, and Derek Haan, chairman and chief executive of Elsevier Science, which publishes more than 1,600 journals, admits that journal price inflation has been a problem for the industry. He says the problem is due to falling subscription numbers as more readers make photocopies or use interlibrary lending. With fewer subscribers to share the cost of each publication, publishers have to increase prices. To stay within budgets, libraries start cancelling titles, which creates a vicious circle of dwindling subscriber numbers, soaring prices and reduced collections. Naturally, with fixed budgets, libraries will be forced to react to increasing journal prices.

Source: Adapted from 'Case study: Elsevier', FT.com, 19 June 2002.

Use of cost-plus information by price takers

The cost-plus price is not entirely without use to price takers. When contemplating entering a market, knowing the cost-plus price will give useful information. It will tell the price taker whether or not it can profitably enter the market. As mentioned earlier, the full cost can be seen as a long-run, break-even selling price. If entering a market means that this break-even price, plus an acceptable profit, cannot be achieved, then the business might be better to stay out. Having a breakdown of the full cost may put the business in a position to examine where costs might be capable of being cut in order to bring the full cost plus profit within a figure acceptable to the market. Here, the market would be providing the target price towards which the business can work, if it wishes to compete.

It is not necessary for a business to dominate a particular market for it to be a price maker. Many small businesses are, to some extent, price makers. This tends to be where buyers find it difficult to make clear distinctions between the prices offered by various suppliers. An example of this might be a car repair undertaken by a garage, where the nature and extent of the problem is not clear. As a result, garages normally charge cost-plus prices for car repairs.

In its 'pure' sense, cost-plus pricing implies that the seller sets the price that is then accepted by the customer. Often the price will not be finalised until after the product or service has been completed; as, for example, with a motor car or work done by a firm of accountants. Sometimes, however, cost-plus is used as a basis of negotiating a price in advance, which then becomes the fixed price. This is often the case with contracts with central or local government departments. Typically, with such public contracts, the price is determined by competitive tendering. Here each potential supplier offers a price for which it will perform the subject of the contract and the department concerned selects the supplier offering the lowest price, subject to quality safeguards. In some cases, however, particularly where only one supplier is capable of doing the work, a fixed cost-plus approach is used.

Cost-plus is also often the approach taken when monopoly suppliers of public utility services are negotiating a price, which they are legally allowed to charge their customers, with the government-appointed regulator. For example, the UK mains water suppliers, when agreeing the prices that they can charge customers, argue their case with Ofwat, the water industry regulator, on the basis of cost-plus information.

Real World 10.7 discusses how one business sees itself as partly protected from the recession that hit the UK from 2008 as a result of having contracts with its customers on a cost-plus price basis.

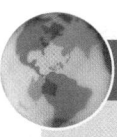

Real World 10.7

Adding Spice to cost-plus pricing

FT

Spice plc is a business that undertakes consultancy and other subcontract (outsourced) work for various UK public utilities (water and electricity suppliers). The business started when a group of managers bought Yorkshire Electricity's maintenance division to run it as a separate, independent unit.

Simon Rigby, Spice's chief executive, was very relaxed about the prospect of an economic recession. He said:

> I would not wish a recession on anybody, but if we have a recession it is going to throw Spice into very sharp focus. How do you think my 10-year cost-plus contracts are going to be affected by recession? The answer is not at all.

It must be said that Spice plc is very unusual in having so many 'cost-plus' priced contracts.

Source: 'Flexible business model helps Spice Holdings power ahead in outsource market', E. Jansson, *Financial Times*, 12 March 2008.

Real World 10.8 considers the extent to which cost-plus pricing seems to be used in practice.

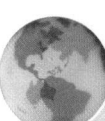

Real World 10.8

Counting the cost plus

A fairly recent study surveyed 267 large UK and Australian businesses during the period 1999 to 2002. Their findings were broadly as follows:

- Cost plus is regarded as important in determining selling prices by most of the businesses, but many businesses only use it for a small percentage of their total sales.
- Retailers base most of their sales prices on their costs. This is not surprising; we might expect that retailers add a mark-up on their cost prices to arrive at selling prices.
- Retailers and service businesses (both financial services and others) attach more importance to cost-plus pricing than do manufacturers and others.
- Cost-plus pricing tends to be more important in industries where competition is most intense. This is perhaps surprising because we might have expected fewer 'price makers' in more competitive markets.
- The extent of the importance of cost-plus pricing seems to have nothing to do with the size of the business. We might have imagined that larger businesses would have more power in the market and be more likely to be price makers, but the evidence does not support this. The reason could be that many larger businesses are, in effect, groups of smaller businesses. These smaller subsidiaries may not be bigger players in their markets than are small independent businesses. Also, cost-plus pricing tends to be particularly important in retailing and service businesses, where many businesses are quite small.

Source: 'An empirical investigation of the importance of cost-plus pricing', C. Guilding, C. Drury and M. Tayles, *Management Auditing Journal*, vol. 20, no. 2, 2005.

Criticisms of full (absorption) costing

Full costing has been criticised because, in practice, it tends to use past cost and to restrict its consideration of future cost to outlay cost. It can be argued that past cost is irrelevant, irrespective of the purpose for which the information is to be used. This is basically because it is not possible to make decisions about the past, only about the future. Similarly, it is argued that it is wrong to ignore opportunity costs. Advocates of full costing would argue, however, that it provides a useful guide to long-run average cost.

Despite the criticisms that are made of full costing, it is, according to research evidence, very widely practised. An international accounting standard (IAS 2 *Inventories*) requires that all inventories, including work in progress, be valued at full cost in the published financial statements. This means that virtually all businesses that have work in progress and/or inventories of finished goods at the end of their financial periods are obliged to apply full costing for income measurement purposes. This will include the many service providers that tend to have work in progress. Whether they use full cost information for other purposes is not clear.

Full (absorption) costing versus variable costing

→ An alternative to full (absorption) costing is **variable costing** – which we discussed in Chapter 9. We may recall that this approach distinguishes between fixed and variable costs and this distinction may be helpful when making short-term decisions. Where a business divides its cost between fixed and variable, it will measure its income in a different way to that described so far in this chapter. A variable costing approach will only include variable cost, including any variable indirect elements, as part of the cost of the goods or service. Fixed cost, both direct and indirect elements, is treated as a cost of the period in which it is incurred. Part of the philosophy of variable costing is that fixed cost is not linked to cost units in the way that it is with full costing. Thus, inventories of finished products, or work in progress, carried from one accounting period to the next, are valued only on the basis of their variable cost.

As we have seen, full costing includes in product cost not only the direct cost (whether fixed or variable) but also a 'fair' share of the indirect cost (both fixed and variable) that were incurred during the time that the product was being made or developed.

To illustrate the difference between the two approaches, let us consider Example 10.6.

Example 10.6

Lahore Ltd commenced operations on 1 June and makes a single product, which sells for £14 per unit. In the first two months of operations, the following results were achieved:

	June (Number of units)	July (Number of units)
Production output	6,000	6,000
Sales volume	4,000	5,000
Opening inventories	–	2,000
Closing inventories	2,000	3,000

The fixed manufacturing cost is £18,000 per month and variable manufacturing cost is £5 per unit. There is also a monthly fixed non-manufacturing cost (marketing and administration) of £5,000. There was no work in progress at the end of either June or July.

The operating profit for each month is calculated below, first using a variable costing approach and then a full costing approach.

Variable costing

In this case, only the variable costs are charged to the units produced and all the fixed cost (manufacturing and non-manufacturing) is charged to the period. Inventories will be carried forward at their variable cost.

	June		July	
	£	£	£	£
Sales revenue				
(4,000 × £14)		56,000		
(5,000 × £14)				70,000
Opening inventories				
(2,000 × £5)	–		10,000	
Cost of units produced				
(6,000 × £5)	30,000		30,000	
Closing inventories				
(2,000 × £5)	(10,000)	(20,000)		
(3,000 × £5)			(15,000)	(25,000)
Contribution margin		36,000		45,000
Fixed cost				
Manufacturing	(18,000)		(18,000)	
Non-manufacturing	(5,000)	(23,000)	(5,000)	(23,000)
Operating profit		13,000		22,000

Full costing

In this case, fixed manufacturing cost becomes part of the product cost and inventories are carried forward to the next period at their full cost (that is variable cost *plus* an appropriate fixed manufacturing cost element). There are 6,000 units produced in each period and the fixed manufacturing cost for each period is £18,000. Hence, the fixed manufacturing cost element per unit is £3 (that is, £18,000/6). The full cost per unit will therefore be £8 (that is, £5 + £3)

	June		July	
	£	£	£	£
Sales revenue				
(4,000 × £14)		56,000		
(5,000 × £14)				70,000
Opening inventories	–			
(2,000 × £8)			16,000	
Cost of units produced				
(6,000 × £8)	48,000		48,000	
Closing inventories				
(2,000 × £8)	(16,000)	(32,000)		
(3,000 × £8)			(24,000)	(40,000)
Gross profit		24,000		30,000
Non-manufacturing cost		(5,000)		(5,000)
Operating profit		19,000		25,000

→

We can see that the total operating profit over the two months is £35,000 (that is, £13,000 + £22,000) when derived on a variable cost basis. On a full cost basis it is £44,000 (that is, £19,000 + £25,000). This is a difference of £9,000 (that is £44,000 − £35,000). This is accounted for by the fact that the fixed manufacturing cost element of the inventories valuation at the end of July, on the full cost basis (that is, 3,000 × £3), has yet to be treated as an expense.

Which method is better?

In practice, the recorded profit of a particular business for each period is unlikely to be greatly affected by the choice of costing approach. If the level of fixed cost stays broadly the same from one year to the next and there are similar amounts of inventories and work in progress at year ends, reported profit will be similar between the two methods. This is because the same amount of fixed cost will be treated as an expense each year; all of it originating from the current year in the case of variable costing, some of it originating from past years in the case of full costing.

The significant differences in operating profit that we saw in Example 10.6 stem from the fact that inventories levels altered quite severely, from zero at the beginning of June to 2,000 units at the end of June to 3,000 units by the end of July. In practice, businesses do not tend to alter inventories levels so radically which means that the choice between full and variable costing may not make very much difference to operating profit levels.

Over the entire life of a particular business the total operating profit will be the same irrespective of which costing method has been applied. This is because, ultimately, all of the fixed costs will be charged as an expense.

Variable costing proponents might argue that it is a very prudent approach to measuring profit, as all fixed production costs are charged to the period in which they are incurred. Perhaps more importantly, they would argue that only variable cost is relevant to decision makers (as we discussed in Chapters 8 and 9) and that considering fixed cost obscures the issue.

Proponents of full (absorption) costing might counter that full costing provides a fairer measure of profit, job by job. Furthermore, in the long run, all elements of cost can be avoided and so to concentrate on only those that can be avoided in the short term (the variable cost) could be misleading.

In practice, management accountants can prepare their income statements taking either, or even both, approaches. We have already seen, however, that accounting rules insist that a full costing approach is taken when preparing published financial statements.

Real World 10.9 provides some indication of the extent to which variable costing is used in practice.

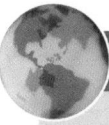 **Real World 10.9**

Variable costing in practice

A recent survey of 41 UK manufacturing businesses found that 68 per cent of them used a variable costing approach to management reporting.

Many would find this surprising. It seemed to be widely believed that the requirement for financial statements in published annual reports to be in full-cost terms has led those businesses to use a full-cost approach for management reporting as well. This seems not, however, to be the case.

It should be added that many of those that used variable costing, quite possibly misused it. For example, three-quarters of those that used it treated labour cost as variable. Possibly in some cases the cost of labour is variable (with the level of output), but it seems likely that this is not true for most of these businesses. At the same time, most of the 68 per cent treat all overheads as a fixed cost. It seems likely that, for most businesses, overheads would have a variable element.

Source: *Contemporary Management Accounting Practices in UK Manufacturing*, D. Dugdale, C. Jones, and S. Green, CIMA Research Publication, Vol. 1, Number 13, 2005.

Summary

The main points in this chapter may be summarised as follows:

Full (absorption) cost = the total amount of resources sacrificed to achieve a particular objective.

Uses of full (absorption) cost information

- Pricing and output decisions.
- Exercising control.
- Assessing relative efficiency.
- Income measurement.

Single-product businesses

- Where all the units of output are identical, the full cost can be calculated as follows:

$$\text{Cost per unit} = \frac{\text{Total cost of output}}{\text{Number of units produced}}$$

Multi-product businesses – job costing

- Where units of output are not identical, it is necessary to divide the cost into two categories: direct cost and indirect cost (overheads).
- Direct cost = cost that can be identified with specific cost units (for example, labour of a garage mechanic, in relation to a particular job).
- Indirect cost (overheads) = cost that cannot be directly measured in respect of a particular job (for example, the rent of a garage).
- Full (absorption) cost = direct cost + indirect cost.
- Direct/indirect is not linked to variable/fixed.
- Indirect cost is difficult to relate to individual cost units – arbitrary bases are used and there is no single correct method.
- Traditionally, indirect cost is seen as the cost of providing a 'service' to cost units.
- Direct labour hour basis of applying indirect cost to cost units is the most popular in practice.

Dealing with indirect cost on a cost centre (departmental) basis

- Indirect cost (overheads) can be segmented – usually on a cost centre basis – each product cost centre has its own overhead recovery rate.
- Cost centres are areas, activities or functions for which costs are separately determined.
- Overheads must be allocated or apportioned to cost centres.
- Service cost centre cost must then be apportioned to product cost centres and product cost centre overheads absorbed by cost units (jobs).

Batch costing

- A variation of job costing where each job consists of a number of identical (or near identical) cost units:

$$\text{Cost per unit} = \frac{\text{Cost of the batch (direct + indirect)}}{\text{Number of units in the batch}}$$

If the full (absorption) cost is charged as the sales price and things go according to plan, the business will break even.

Full cost information is seen by some as not very useful because it can be backward looking: it includes information irrelevant to decision making, but excludes some relevant information.

Full (absorption) costing versus variable costing

- With full costing, both fixed and variable costs are included in product cost and treated as expenses when the product is sold.
- With variable costing, only the variable product cost is linked to the products in this way, fixed cost is treated as an expense of the period in which it was incurred.
- Variable costing tends to be more straightforward and, according to proponents, more relevant for decision making.
- Supporters of full costing argue that it gives a more complete measure of the income generated from the sale of each unit of the product.
- Such evidence as there is about the use of variable costing in practice suggests that it is widely used. The evidence implies, however, that the values tend to be miscalculated in a large proportion of cases.

MyAccountingLab *Now check your progress in your personal Study Plan*

Key terms

full cost p. 350	total cost p. 356
full costing p. 351	overhead absorption (recovery)
cost unit p. 351	rate p. 357
process costing p. 352	cost centre p. 366
direct cost p. 352	product cost centre p. 367
indirect cost p. 352	service cost centre p. 367
overheads p. 352	cost allocation p. 367
common cost p. 352	cost apportionment p. 368
job costing p. 354	batch costing p. 375
absorption costing p. 354	cost-plus pricing p. 378
cost behaviour p. 355	variable costing p. 382

Further reading

If you would like to explore the topics covered in this chapter in more depth, we recommend the following books:

Cost Accounting: A Managerial Emphasis, *Horngren C., Foster G., Datar S., Rajan M. and Ittner C.*, 13th edn, Prentice Hall International, 2008, chapter 4.

Management and Cost Accounting, *Drury C.*, 7th edn, Cengage Learning, 2007, chapters 3, 4 and 5.

Management Accounting, *Atkinson A., Kaplan R., Young S. M. and Matsumura, E.* 5th edn, Prentice Hall, 2007, chapter 3.

Managerial Accounting, *Hilton R.*, 6th edn, McGraw-Hill Irwin, 2005, chapters 2 and 3.

Review questions

Answers to these questions can be found at the back of the book on pages 745–6.

10.1 What problem does the existence of work in progress cause in process costing?

10.2 What is the point of distinguishing direct cost from indirect cost? Why is this not necessary in process costing environments?

10.3 Are direct cost and variable cost the same thing? Explain your answer.

10.4 It is sometimes claimed that the full cost of pursuing some objective represents the long-run break-even selling price. Why is this said, and what does it mean?

Exercises

Exercises 10.4 to 10.8 are more advanced than 10.1 to 10.3. Those with **coloured numbers** have answers at the back of the book starting on page 777.

If you wish to try more exercises, visit the students' side of the Companion Website and MyAccountingLab.

10.1 Bodgers Ltd, a business that provides a market research service, operates a job costing system. Towards the end of each financial year, the overhead recovery rate (the rate at which indirect cost will be absorbed by jobs) is established for the forthcoming year.

(a) Why does the business bother to predetermine the recovery rate in the way outlined?
(b) What steps will be involved in predetermining the rate?
(c) What problems might arise with using a predetermined rate?

10.2 Athena Ltd is an engineering business doing work for its customers to their particular require-ments and specifications. It determines the full cost of each job taking a 'job-costing' approach, accounting for overheads on a cost centre (departmental) basis. It bases its prices to customers on this full cost figure. The business has two departments (both of which are cost centres): a Machining Department, where each job starts, and a Fitting Department, which completes all of the jobs. Machining Department overheads are charged to jobs on a machine hour basis and those of the Fitting Department on a direct labour hour basis. The budgeted information for next year is as follows:

Heating and lighting	£25,000	(allocated equally between the two departments)
Machine power	£10,000	(all allocated to the Machining Department)
Direct labour	£200,000	(£150,000 allocated to the Fitting Department and £50,000 to the Machining Department. All direct workers are paid £10 an hour)
Indirect labour	£50,000	(apportioned to the departments in proportion to the direct labour cost)
Direct materials	£120,000	(all applied to jobs in the Machining Department)
Depreciation	£30,000	(all relates to the Machining Department)
Machine time	20,000 hours	(all worked in the Machining Department)

Required:

(a) Prepare a statement showing the budgeted overheads for next year, analysed between the two cost centres. This should be in the form of three columns: one for the total figure for each type of overhead and one column each for the two cost centres, where each type of overhead is analysed between the two cost centres. Each column should also show the total of overheads for the year.

(b) Derive the appropriate rate for charging the overheads of each cost centre to jobs (that is, a separate rate for each cost centre).

(c) Athena Ltd has been asked by a customer to specify the price that it will charge for a particular job that will, if the job goes ahead, be undertaken early next year. The job is expected to use direct materials costing Athena Ltd £1,200, to need 50 hours of machining time, 10 hours of Machine Department direct labour and 20 hours of Fitting Department direct labour. Athena Ltd charges a profit loading of 20 per cent to the full cost of jobs to determine the selling price.

Show workings to derive the proposed selling price for this job.

10.3 Pieman Products Ltd makes road trailers to the precise specifications of individual customers. The following are predicted to occur during the forthcoming year, which is about to start:

Direct materials cost	£50,000
Direct labour cost	£160,000
Direct labour time	16,000 hours
Indirect labour cost	£25,000
Depreciation of machine	£8,000
Rent and rates	£10,000
Heating, lighting and power	£5,000
Indirect materials	£2,000
Other indirect cost (overhead) elements	£1,000
Machine time	3,000 hours

All direct labour is paid at the same hourly rate.

A customer has asked the business to build a trailer for transporting a racing motorcycle to race meetings. It is estimated that this will require materials and components that will cost £1,150. It will take 250 direct labour hours to do the job, of which 50 will involve the use of machinery.

Required:

Deduce a logical cost for the job, and explain the basis of dealing with overheads that you propose.

10.4 Promptprint Ltd, a printing business, has received an enquiry from a potential customer for the quotation of a price for a job. The pricing policy of the business is based on the plans for the next financial year shown below.

	£
Sales revenue (billings to customers)	196,000
Materials (direct)	(38,000)
Labour (direct)	(32,000)
Variable overheads	(2,400)
Advertising (for business)	(3,000)
Depreciation	(27,600)
Administration	(36,000)
Interest	(8,000)
Profit (before taxation)	49,000

A first estimate of the direct cost for the particular job is:

	£
Direct materials	4,000
Direct labour	3,600

Required:
(a) Prepare a recommended price for the job based on the plans, commenting on your method, ignoring the information given in the Appendix (below).
(b) Comment on the validity of using financial plans in pricing, and recommend any improvements you would consider desirable for the pricing policy used in (a).
(c) Incorporate the effects of the information shown in the Appendix (below) into your estimates of the direct material cost, explaining any changes you consider it necessary to make to the above direct material cost of £4,000.

Appendix to Exercise 10.4
Based on historic cost, direct material cost was computed as follows:

	£
Paper grade 1	1,200
Paper grade 2	2,000
Card (zenith grade)	500
Inks and other miscellaneous items	300
	4,000

Paper grade 1 is regularly used by the business. Enough of this paper to complete the job is currently held. Because it is imported, it is estimated that if it is used for this job, a new purchase order will have to be placed shortly. Sterling has depreciated against the foreign currency by 25 per cent since the last purchase.

Paper grade 2 is purchased from the same source as grade 1. The business holds exactly enough of it for the job, but this was bought in for a special order. This order was cancelled, although the defaulting customer was required to pay £500 towards the cost of the paper. The accountant has offset this against the original cost to arrive at the figure of £2,000 shown above. This paper is rarely used, and due to its special chemical coating will be unusable if it is not used on the job in question.

The card is another specialist item currently held by the business. There is no use foreseen, and it would cost £750 to replace if required. However, the inventories controller had planned to spend £130 on overprinting to use the card as a substitute for other materials costing £640.

Inks and other items are in regular use in the print shop.

10.5 Bookdon plc manufactures three products, X, Y and Z, in two product cost centres: a machine shop and a fitting section; it also has two service cost centres: a canteen and a machine maintenance section. Shown below are next year's planned production data and manufacturing cost for the business.

	X	Y	Z
Production	4,200 units	6,900 units	1,700 units
Direct materials	£11/unit	£14/unit	£17/unit
Direct labour			
Machine shop	£6/unit	£4/unit	£2/unit
Fitting section	£12/unit	£3/unit	£21/unit
Machine hours	6 hr/unit	3 hr/unit	4 hr/unit

Planned overheads are as follows:

	Machine shop	Fitting section	Canteen	Machine maintenance section	Total
Allocated overheads	£27,660	£19,470	£16,600	£26,650	£90,380
Rent, rates, heat and light					£17,000
Depreciation and insurance of equipment					£25,000
Additional data:					
Gross book value of equipment	£150,000	£75,000	£30,000	£45,000	
Number of employees	18	14	4	4	
Floor space occupied	3,600 sq m	1,400 sq m	1,000 sq m	800 sq m	

All machining is carried out in the machine shop. It has been estimated that approximately 70 per cent of the machine maintenance section's cost is incurred servicing the machine shop and the remainder servicing the fitting section.

Required:

(a) Calculate the following planned overhead absorption rates:
   (1) A machine hour rate for the machine shop.
   (2) A rate expressed as a percentage of direct wages for the fitting section.
(b) Calculate the planned full cost per unit of product X.

10.6 Shown below is an extract from next year's plans for a business manufacturing three products, A, B and C, in three product cost centres.

	A	B	C
Production	4,000 units	3,000 units	6,000 units
Direct material cost	£7 per unit	£4 per unit	£9 per unit
Direct labour requirements:			
Cutting department:			
Skilled operatives	3 hr/unit	5 hr/unit	2 hr/unit
Unskilled operatives	6 hr/unit	1 hr/unit	3 hr/unit
Machining department	$\frac{1}{2}$ hr/unit	$\frac{1}{4}$ hr/unit	$\frac{1}{3}$ hr/unit
Pressing department	2 hr/unit	3 hr/unit	4 hr/unit
Machine requirements:			
Machining department	2 hr/unit	$1\frac{1}{2}$ hr/unit	$2\frac{1}{2}$ hr/unit

The skilled operatives employed in the cutting department are paid £16 an hour and the unskilled operatives are paid £10 an hour. All the operatives in the machining and pressing departments are paid £12 an hour.

	Product cost centres			Service cost centres	
	Cutting	Machining	Pressing	Engineering	Personnel
Planned total overheads	£154,482	£64,316	£58,452	£56,000	£34,000
Service cost centre Cost incurred for the benefit of other cost centres, as follows:					
Engineering services	20%	45%	35%	–	–
Personnel services	55%	10%	20%	15%	–

The business operates a full absorption costing system.

Required:
Derive the total planned cost of:

(a) One completed unit of product A.
(b) One incomplete unit of product B, which has been processed by the cutting and machining departments but which has not yet been passed into the pressing department.

10.7 Consider this statement:
'In a job costing system, it is necessary to divide up the business into departments. Fixed costs (or overheads) will be collected for each department. Where a particular fixed cost relates to the business as a whole, it must be divided between the departments. Usually this is done on the basis of area of floor space occupied by each department relative to the entire business. When the total fixed costs for each department have been identified, this will be divided by the number of hours that were worked in each department to deduce an overhead recovery rate. Each job that was worked on in a department will have a share of fixed cost allotted to it according to how long it was worked on. The total cost for each job will therefore be the sum of the variable cost of the job and its share of the fixed cost. It is essential that this approach is taken in order to deduce a selling price for the business's output.'

Required:
Prepare a table of two columns. In the first column you should show any phrases or sentences in the above statement with which you do not agree, and in the second column you should show your reason for disagreeing with each one.

10.8 Many businesses charge overheads to jobs on a cost centre basis.

Required:
(a) What is the advantage that is claimed for charging overheads to jobs on a cost centre basis, and why is it claimed?
(b) What circumstances need to exist for it to make a difference to a particular job whether overheads are charged on a business-wide basis or on a cost centre basis? (Note that the answer to this part of the question is not specifically covered in the chapter. You should, nevertheless, be able to deduce the reason from what you know.)

CHAPTER 11

Costing and performance evaluation in a competitive environment

Introduction

In recent years we have seen major changes in the business world, including deregulation, privatisation, the growing expectations of shareholders and the impact of new technology. These have led to a much more fast-changing and competitive environment that has radically altered the way in which businesses are managed. In this chapter, we consider some of the management accounting techniques that have been developed to help businesses maintain their competitiveness in this new era.

We begin by considering the impact of this new environment on the full-costing approach that we considered in Chapter 10. We shall see that activity-based costing, which is a development of the traditional full-costing approach, takes a much more enquiring, much less accepting attitude towards overheads. We shall also examine some recent approaches to costing that can help lower costs and, therefore, increase the ability of a business to compete on price.

Management accounting embraces both financial and non-financial measures and, in this chapter, we shall consider the increasing importance of non-financial measures in managing a business. These include the balanced scorecard approach, which seeks to integrate financial and non-financial measures into a framework for the achievement of business objectives.

Finally, we consider the idea of shareholder value, which has been a 'hot' issue among managers in recent years. Many leading businesses now claim that the quest for shareholder value is the driving force behind strategic and operational decisions. We consider what the term 'shareholder value' means and we shall look at one of the main methods of measuring shareholder value.

Learning outcomes

When you have completed this chapter, you should be able to:

● Discuss the nature and usefulness of activity-based costing.

● Explain how new developments such as total life-cycle costing and target costing can be used to control costs.

● Discuss the importance of non-financial measures of performance in managing a business and the way in which the balanced scorecard attempts to integrate financial and non-financial measures.

● Explain the term 'shareholder value' and describe the role of EVA® in measuring and delivering shareholder value.

MyAccountingLab **Remember to create your own personalised Study Plan**

Cost determination in the changed business environment

Costing: the traditional way

The traditional, and still widely used, approach to job costing and product pricing developed when the notion of trying to determine the cost of industrial production first emerged. This was around the time of the UK Industrial Revolution when industry displayed the following characteristics:

● *Direct-labour-intensive and direct-labour-paced production.* Labour was at the heart of production. To the extent that machinery was used, it was to support the efforts of direct labour, and the speed of production was dictated by direct labour.

● *A low level of indirect cost relative to direct cost.* Little was spent on power, personnel services, machinery (leading to low depreciation charges) and other areas typical of the indirect cost (overheads) of modern businesses.

● *A relatively uncompetitive market.* Transport difficulties, limited industrial production worldwide and a lack of knowledge by customers of competitors' prices meant that businesses could prosper without being too scientific in costing and could add a margin for profit to arrive at the selling price (cost-plus pricing). Customers would have tended to accept what the supplier had to offer, rather than demanding precisely what they wanted.

Since overheads at that time represented a pretty small element of total cost, it was acceptable and practical to deal with them in a fairly arbitrary manner. Not too much effort was devoted to trying to control overheads because the potential rewards of better control were relatively small, certainly when compared with the benefits from firmer control of direct labour and material costs. It was also reasonable to charge overheads to individual jobs on a direct labour hour basis. Most of the overheads were incurred directly in support of direct labour: providing direct workers with a place to work, heating and lighting the workplace, employing people to supervise the direct workers, and so on. Direct workers, perhaps aided by machinery, carried out all production.

At that time, service industries were a relatively unimportant part of the economy and would have largely consisted of self-employed individuals. These individuals would probably have been uninterested in trying to do more than work out a rough hourly/daily rate for their time and to try to base prices on this.

Costing: the new environment

In recent years, the world of industrial production has fundamentally changed. Most of it is now characterised by:

- *Capital-intensive and machine-paced production.* Machines are at the heart of much production, including both the manufacture of goods and the rendering of services. Most labour supports the efforts of machines, for example, technically maintaining them. Also, machines often dictate the pace of production. According to evidence provided in Real World 10.2 (page 353), direct labour accounts on average for just 14 per cent of manufacturers' total cost.

- *A high level of indirect cost relative to direct costs.* Modern businesses tend to have very high depreciation, servicing and power costs. There are also high costs of personnel and staff welfare, which were scarcely envisaged in the early days of industrial production. At the same time, there are very low (sometimes no) direct labour costs. Although direct material cost often remains an important element of total cost, more efficient production methods lead to less waste and, therefore, to a lower total material cost, again tending to make indirect cost (overheads) more dominant. Again according to Real World 10.2, overheads account for 25 per cent of manufacturers' total cost and 51 per cent of service sector total cost.

- *A highly competitive international market.* Production, much of it highly sophisticated, is carried out worldwide. Transport, including fast airfreight, is relatively cheap. Fax, telephone and, particularly, the Internet ensure that potential customers can quickly and cheaply find the prices of a range of suppliers. Markets now tend to be highly price competitive. Customers increasingly demand products custom made to their own requirements. This means that businesses need to know their product costs with a greater degree of accuracy than historically has been the case. Businesses also need to take a considered and informed approach to pricing their output.

In the UK, as in many developed countries, service industries now dominate the economy, employing the great majority of the workforce and producing most of the value of productive output. Though there are many self-employed individuals supplying services, many service providers are vast businesses such as banks, insurance companies and cinema operators. For most of these larger service providers, the activities very closely resemble modern manufacturing activity. They too are characterised by high capital intensity, overheads dominating direct costs and a competitive international market.

Cost management systems

Changes in the competitive environment mean that businesses must now manage costs much more effectively than in the past. This, in turn, places an obligation on cost management systems to provide the information that will enable managers to do this. Traditional cost management systems have often proved inadequate for the task and, in recent years, new systems have gained in popularity. We shall now take a look at some of these systems.

The problem of overheads

In Chapter 10 we considered the traditional approach to job costing (deriving the full cost of output where one unit of output differs from another). We may recall that this approach involves collecting, for each job, those costs that can be clearly linked to, and measured in respect of, the particular job (direct costs). All indirect costs (overheads) are allocated or apportioned to product cost centres and then charged to individual jobs according to some formula. The evidence suggests that this formula is usually based on the number of direct labour hours worked on each particular job.

In the past, this approach has worked reasonably well, largely because overhead recovery rates (that is, rates at which overheads are absorbed by jobs) were typically of a much lower value for each direct labour hour than the rate paid to direct workers as wages or salaries. It is now, however, becoming increasingly common for overhead recovery rates to be between five and ten times the hourly rate of pay, because overheads are now much more significant. When production is dominated by direct labour paid, say, £8 an hour, it might be reasonable to have an overhead recovery rate of, say, £1 an hour. When, however, direct labour plays a relatively small part in production, to have an overhead recovery rate of, say, £50 for each direct labour hour is likely to lead to very arbitrary product costing. Even a small change in the amount of direct labour worked on a job could massively affect the total cost deduced: not because the direct worker is very highly paid, but because of the effect of the direct labour hours on the overhead cost loading. A further problem is that overheads are still typically charged on a direct labour hour basis even though the overheads may not be closely related to direct labour.

Real World 11.1 provides a rather disturbing view of costing and cost control in large banks.

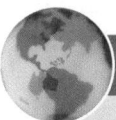

Real World 11.1

Bank accounts

In a study of the cost structures of 52 international banks, the German consultancy firm, Droege, found that indirect cost (overheads) could represent as much as 85 per cent of total cost. However, whilst direct costs were generally under tight management control, overheads were not. The overheads, which include such items as IT development, risk control, auditing, marketing and public relations, were often not allocated between operating divisions or were allocated in a rather arbitrary manner.

Source: Based on information in 'Banks have not tackled indirect costs', A. Skorecki, FT.com, 7 January 2004.

Taking a closer look

The changes in the competitive environment discussed above have led to much closer attention being paid to the issue of overheads, what causes them and how they are charged to jobs. Historically, businesses have been content to accept that overheads exist and, therefore, for job (product) costing purposes they must be dealt with in as practical a way as possible. In recent years, however, there has been increasing recognition of the fact that overheads do not just happen; something must be causing them. To illustrate this point, let us consider Example 11.1.

Example 11.1

Modern Producers Ltd has a storage area that is set aside for its inventories of finished goods. The cost of running the stores includes a share of the factory rent and other establishment costs, such as heating and lighting. It also includes the salaries of staff employed to look after the inventories and the cost of financing the inventories held in the stores.

The business has two product lines: A and B. Product A tends to be made in small batches and low levels of finished inventories are held. The business prides itself on its ability to supply Product B in relatively large quantities, instantly. As a consequence, most of the space in the finished goods store is filled with finished Product Bs, ready to be despatched immediately an order is received.

Traditionally, the whole cost of operating the stores would have been treated as a part of general overheads and included in the total of overheads charged to jobs, probably on a direct labour hour basis. This means that, when assessing the cost of Products A and B, the cost of operating the stores has fallen on them according to the number of direct labour hours worked on manufacturing each one; a factor that has nothing to do with storage. In fact, most of the stores' cost should be charged to Product B, since this product causes (and benefits from) the stores' cost much more than Product A.

Failure to account more precisely for the cost of running the stores is masking the fact that Product B is not as profitable as it seems to be. It may even be leading to losses as a result of the relatively high stores-operating cost that it causes. However, much of this cost is charged to Product A, without regard to the fact that Product A causes little of it.

Activity-based costing

→ **Activity-based costing (ABC)** aims to overcome the kind of problem just described by directly tracing the cost of all support activities to particular products or services. For a manufacturing business, these support activities may include materials ordering, materials handling, storage, inspection and so on. The cost of the support activities makes up the total overheads cost. The outcome of this tracing exercise is to provide a more realistic, and more finely measured, account of the overhead cost element for a particular product or service.

To implement a system of ABC, managers must begin by carefully examining the business's operations. They will need to identify:

- each of the various support activities involved in the process of making products or providing services;
- the costs to be attributed to each support activity; and
→ - the factors that cause a change in the costs of each support activity, that is the **cost drivers**.

Identifying the cost drivers is a vital element of a successful ABC system. They have a cause-and-effect relationship with activity costs and so are used as a basis for attaching activity costs to a particular product or service. This point is discussed further below.

Attributing overheads

Once the various support activities, their costs and the factors that drive these costs, have been identified, ABC requires:

- An overhead **cost pool** to be established for each activity. Thus, the business in Example 11.1 will create a cost pool for operating the finished goods store.
- The total cost associated with each support activity to be allocated to the relevant cost pool.
- The total cost in each pool to then be charged to output (Products A and B, in the case of Example 11.1) using the relevant cost driver.

The final step identified involves dividing the amount in each cost pool by the estimated total usage of the cost driver to derive a cost per unit of the cost driver. This unit cost figure is then multiplied by the number of units of the cost driver used by a particular product, or service, to determine the amount of overhead cost to be attached to it.

Example 11.2 should make this last step clear.

Example 11.2

The management accountant at Modern Producers Ltd (see Example 11.1) has estimated that the cost of running the finished goods stores for next year will be £90,000. This will be the amount allocated to the 'finished goods stores cost pool'.

It is estimated that each Product A will spend an average of one week in the stores before being sold. With Product B, the equivalent period is four weeks. Both products are of roughly similar size and have very similar storage needs. It is felt, therefore, that the period spent in the stores ('product weeks') is the cost driver.

Next year, 50,000 Product As and 25,000 Product Bs are expected to pass through the stores. The estimated total usage of the cost driver will be the total number of 'product weeks' that the products will be in store. For next year, this will be:

Product	A	50,000 × 1 week	=	50,000
	B	25,000 × 4 weeks	=	100,000
				150,000

The cost per unit of cost driver is the total cost of the stores divided by the number of 'product weeks', as calculated above. This is:

$$£90,000/150,000 = £0.60$$

To determine the cost to be attached to a particular unit of product, the figure of £0.60 must be multiplied by the number of 'product weeks' that a product stays in the finished goods store. Thus, each unit of Product A will be charged with £0.60 (that is, £0.60 × 1), and each Product B with £2.40 (that is, £0.60 × 4).

Benefits of ABC

Through the direct tracing of cost to products in the way described, ABC seeks to establish more accurate costs for each unit of product or service. This should help managers in assessing product profitability and in making decisions concerning pricing and the appropriate product mix. Other benefits, however, may also flow from adopting an ABC approach.

Activity (11.1)

Can you think of any other benefits that an ABC approach to costing may provide?

By identifying the various support activities' costs and analysing what causes them to change, managers should gain a better understanding of the business. This, in turn, should help them in controlling costs and improving efficiency. It should also help them in forward planning. They may, for example, be in a better position to assess the likely effect of new products and processes on activities and costs.

ABC versus the traditional approach

We can see that there is a basic philosophical difference between the traditional and the ABC approaches. The traditional approach views overheads as *rendering a service to cost units*, the cost of which must be charged to those units. ABC, on the other hand, views overheads as being *caused by activities*, and so it is the cost units that cause these activities that must be charged with the costs that they cause.

With the traditional approach, overheads are apportioned to product cost centres. Each product cost centre would then derive an overhead recovery rate, typically overheads per direct labour hour. Overheads would then be applied to units of output according to how many direct labour hours were worked on them.

With ABC, the overheads are analysed into cost pools, with one cost pool for each cost-driving activity. The overheads are then charged to units of output, through activity cost driver rates. These rates are an attempt to represent the extent to which each particular cost unit is believed to cause the particular part of the overheads.

Cost pools are much the same as cost centres, except that each cost pool is linked to a particular *activity* (operating the stores in Examples 11.1 and 11.2), rather than being more general, as is the case with cost centres in traditional job (or product) costing.

The two different approaches are illustrated in Figure 11.1.

ABC and service industries

Much of our discussion of ABC has concentrated on the manufacturing industry, perhaps because early users of ABC were manufacturing businesses. In fact, ABC is possibly even more relevant to service industries because, in the absence of a direct material element, a service business's total cost is likely to be largely made up of overheads (see Real World 10.2 on page 353). There is certainly evidence that ABC has been adopted more readily by businesses that sell services rather than products, as we shall see later.

Activity (11.2)

What is the difference in the way in which direct costs are accounted for when using ABC, relative to their treatment taking a traditional approach to full costing?

The answer is no difference at all. ABC is concerned only with the way in which overheads are charged to jobs to derive the full cost.

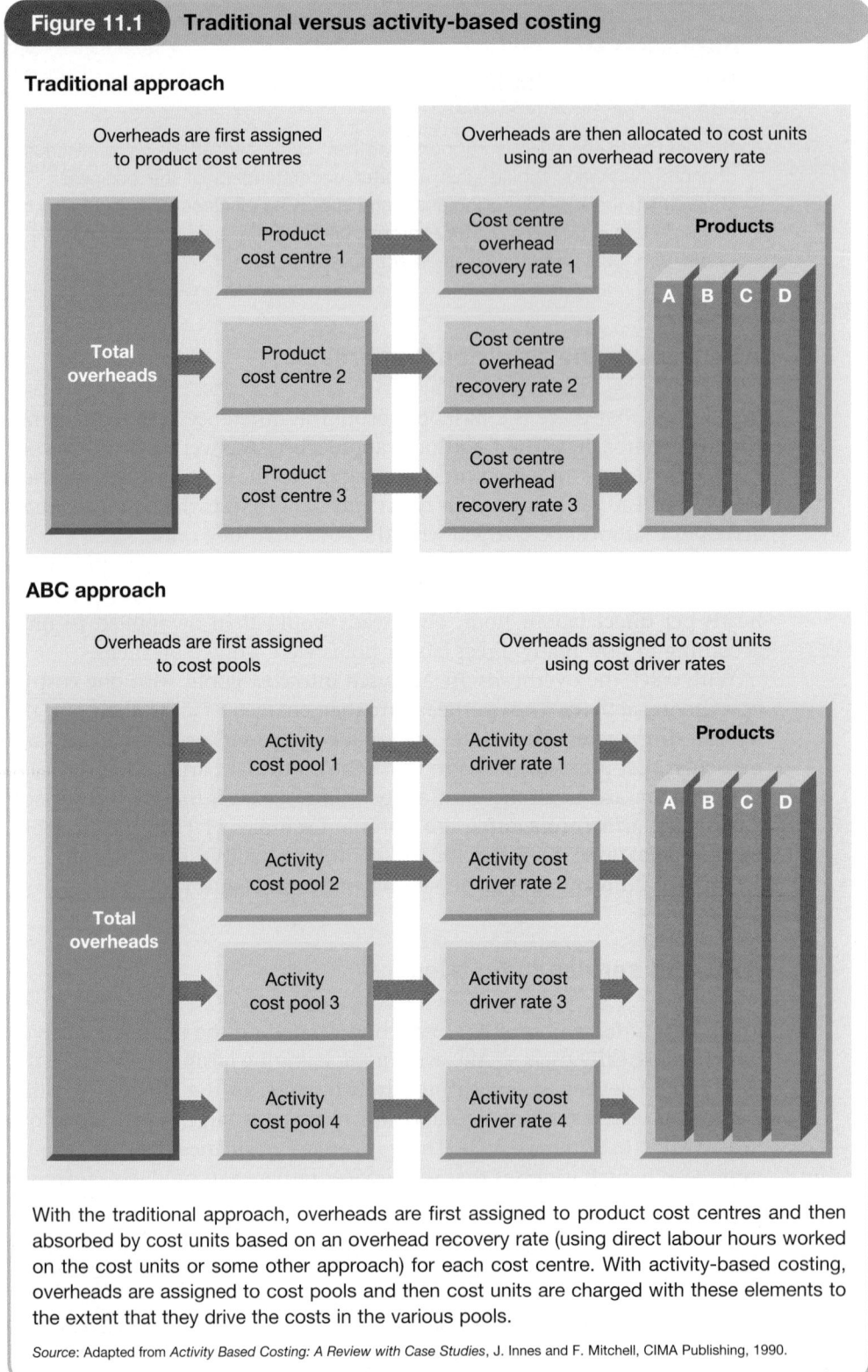

Figure 11.1 Traditional versus activity-based costing

With the traditional approach, overheads are first assigned to product cost centres and then absorbed by cost units based on an overhead recovery rate (using direct labour hours worked on the cost units or some other approach) for each cost centre. With activity-based costing, overheads are assigned to cost pools and then cost units are charged with these elements to the extent that they drive the costs in the various pools.

Source: Adapted from *Activity Based Costing: A Review with Case Studies*, J. Innes and F. Mitchell, CIMA Publishing, 1990.

Example 11.3 provides an example of activity-based costing and brings together the points that have been raised so far.

Example 11.3

Comma Ltd manufactures two types of Sprizzer – Standard and Deluxe. Each product requires the incorporation of a difficult-to-handle special part (one of them for a Standard and four for a Deluxe). Both of these products are made in batches (large batches for Standards and small ones for Deluxes). Each new batch requires that the production facilities are 'set up'.

Details of the two products are:

	Standard	Deluxe
Annual production and sales – units	12,000	12,000
Sales price per unit	£65	£87
Batch size – units	1,000	50
Direct labour time per unit – hours	2	2½
Direct labour rate per hour	£8	£8
Direct material cost per unit	£22	£32
Number of special parts per unit	1	4
Number of set-ups per batch	1	3
Number of separate material issues from stores per batch	1	1
Number of sales invoices issued per year	50	240

In recent months, Comma Ltd has been trying to persuade customers who buy the Standard to purchase the Deluxe instead. An analysis of overhead costs for Comma Ltd has provided the following information.

Overhead cost analysis	£	Cost driver
Set-up cost	73,200	Number of set-ups
Special part handling cost	60,000	Number of special parts
Customer invoicing cost	29,000	Number of invoices
Material handling cost	63,000	Number of batches
Other overheads	108,000	Labour hours

Required:

(a) Calculate the profit per unit and the return on sales for Standard and Deluxe Sprizzers using both:
- the traditional direct-labour-hour-based absorption of overheads; and
- activity-based costing methods.

(b) Comment on the managerial implications for Comma Ltd of the results in (a) above.

Solution

Using the traditional full (absorption) costing approach that we considered in Chapter 10, the overheads are added together and an overheads recovery rate deduced as follows:

Overheads	£
Set-up cost	73,200
Special part handling cost	60,000
Customer invoicing cost	29,000
Material handling cost	63,000
Other overheads	108,000
	333,200

→

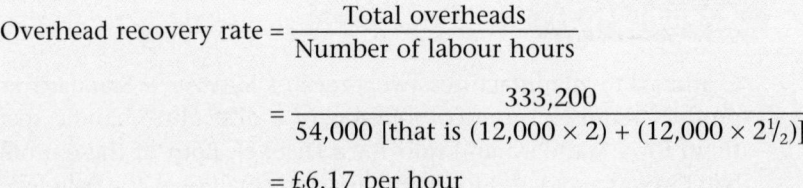

$$\text{Overhead recovery rate} = \frac{\text{Total overheads}}{\text{Number of labour hours}}$$

$$= \frac{333,200}{54,000 \ [\text{that is } (12,000 \times 2) + (12,000 \times 2\frac{1}{2})]}$$

$$= £6.17 \text{ per hour}$$

The total cost per unit of each type of Sprizzer is calculated by adding the direct cost to the overheads cost per unit. The overheads cost per unit is calculated by multiplying the number of direct labour hours spent on the product (2 hours for each Standard and $2\frac{1}{2}$ hours for each Deluxe) by the overheads recovery rate calculated above. Hence:

	Standard £	Deluxe £
Direct costs		
Labour	16.00	20.00
Material	22.00	32.00
Indirect cost		
Overheads (£6.17 per hour)	12.34	15.43
Total cost per unit	50.34	67.43

The return on sales is calculated as follows:

	Standard £ per unit	Deluxe £ per unit
Sales price	65.00	87.00
Total cost (see above)	50.34	67.43
Profit	14.66	19.57
Return on sales [(profit/sales) × 100%]	22.55%	22.49%

Using the ABC costing approach, the activity cost driver rates will be calculated as follows:

Overhead cost pool	Driver	(a) Standard driver volume	(b) Deluxe driver volume	(c) Total driver volume (a + b)	(d) Costs £	(e) Driver rate £ (d/c)
Set-up	Set-ups per batch	12	720	732	73,200	100
Special part	Special parts per unit	12,000	48,000	60,000	60,000	1
Customer invoices	Invoices per year	50	240	290	29,000	100
Material handling	Number of batches	12	240	252	63,000	250
Other overheads	Labour hours	24,000	30,000	54,000	108,000	2

The activity-based costs are derived as follows:

Overhead cost pool	(f) Total costs Standard (a × e) £	(g) Total costs Deluxe (b × e) £	Unit costs Standard (f/12,000) £	Unit costs Deluxe (g/12,000) £
Set-up	1,200	72,000	0.10	6.00
Special part	12,000	48,000	1.00	4.00
Customer invoices	5,000	24,000	0.42	2.00
Material handling	3,000	60,000	0.25	5.00
Other overheads	48,000	60,000	4.00	5.00
Total overheads			5.77	22.00

The total cost per unit is calculated as follows:

	Standard £ per unit	Deluxe £ per unit
Direct costs:		
Labour	16.00	20.00
Material	22.00	32.00
Indirect costs		
See above	5.77	22.00
Total cost per unit	43.77	74.00

The return on sales is calculated as follows:

	Standard £ per unit	Deluxe £ per unit
Sales price	65.00	87.00
Total cost (see above)	43.77	74.00
Profit	21.23	13.00
Return on sales		
[(profit/sales) × 100%]	32.67%	14.94%

The figures show that under the traditional approach the returns on sales for each product are broadly equal. However, the ABC approach shows that the Standard product is far more profitable. Hence, the business should reconsider its policy of trying to persuade customers to switch to the Deluxe product.

Criticisms of ABC

Although many businesses now adopt a system of ABC, its critics point out that ABC can be time-consuming and costly. The cost of setting up the ABC system, as well as costs of running and updating it, must be incurred. These costs can be very high, particularly where the business's operations are complex and involve a large number of activities and cost drivers. Furthermore, ABC information produced under the scenario just described may be complex. If managers find ABC reports difficult to understand, there is a risk that the potential benefits of ABC will be lost.

Not all businesses are likely to benefit from ABC. Where a business sells products or services that all have similar levels of output and involve similar activities and processes, it is unlikely that the finer measurements provided by ABC will lead to strikingly different outcomes than under the traditional approach. As a result, opportunities for better pricing, planning and cost control may not be great and may not justify the cost of switching to an ABC system.

Measurement and tracing problems can arise with ABC, which may undermine any potential benefits. Not all costs can be easily identified with a particular activity and some may have to be allocated to cost pools. This can often be done on some sensible basis. For example, factory rent may be allocated on the basis of square metres of space used. In some cases, however, a lack of data concerning a particular cost may lead to fairly arbitrary cost allocations between activities. There is also the problem that the relationship between activity costs and their cost drivers may be difficult to determine. Identifying a cause-and-effect relationship can be difficult where a large proportion of activity costs are fixed and so do not vary with changes in usage.

ABC is also criticised for the same reason that full costing generally is criticised: because it does not provide very relevant information for decision making. The point was made in Chapter 10 that full costing tends to use past costs and to ignore opportunity costs. Since past costs are always irrelevant in decision making and opportunity costs can be significant, full costing information is seen as an expensive irrelevance. In contrast, advocates of full costing claim that it *is* relevant, in that it provides a long-run average cost, whereas 'relevant costing', which we considered in Chapter 8, relates only to the specific circumstances of the short term. The use of ABC, rather than the traditional approach to job (or product) costing, does not affect the validity of this irrelevance argument.

Real World 11.2 shows how ABC came to be used at the Royal Mail.

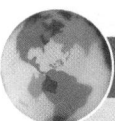

Real World 11.2

Delivering ABC

Early in the 2000s the publicly-owned Royal Mail adopted ABC and used it to find the cost of making postal deliveries. Royal Mail identified 340 activities that gave rise to costs, created a cost pool and identified a cost driver for each of these.

Roger Tabour, Royal Mail's Enterprise Systems Programme Director, explained, 'A new regulatory and competitive environment, plus a down-turned economy, led management to seek out more reliable sources of information on performance and profitability,' and this led to the introduction of ABC.

The Royal Mail is a public sector organisation that is subject to supervision by Postcomm, the UK government appointed regulatory body. The government requires the Royal Mail to operate on a commercial basis and to make profits.

Source: www.sas.com.

Real World 11.3 provides some indication of the extent to which ABC is used in practice.

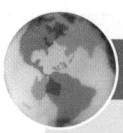

Real World 11.3

ABC in practice

A recent survey of 176 UK businesses operating in various industries, all with an annual turnover of more than £50 million, was conducted by Al-Omiri and Drury. This indicated that 29 per cent of larger UK businesses use ABC.

The adoption of ABC in the UK varies widely between industries, as is shown in Figure 11.2.

Figure 11.2   **ABC in practice**

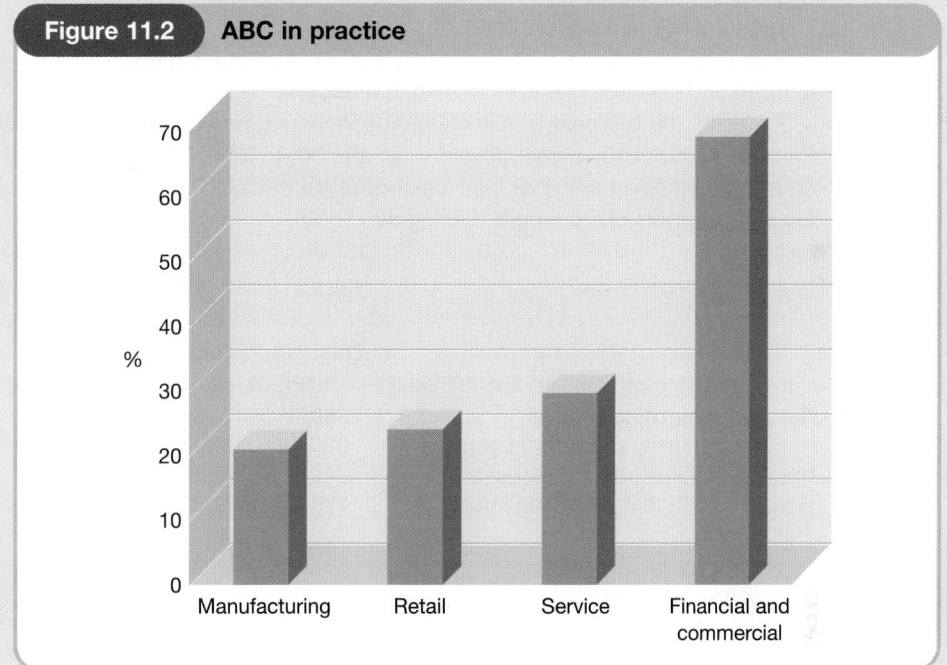

Al-Omiri and Drury took their analysis a step further by looking at the factors that apparently tend to lead a particular business to adopt ABC. They found that businesses that used ABC tended to be:

- large;
- sophisticated, in terms of using advanced management accounting techniques generally;
- in an intensely competitive market for their products;
- operating in a service industry, particularly in the financial services.

All of these findings are broadly in line with other recent research evidence involving businesses from around the world.

Source: 'A survey of factors influencing the choice of product costing systems in UK organisations', M. Al-Omiri and C. Drury, *Management Accounting Research*, December 2007.

Self-assessment question 11.1

Psilis Ltd makes a product in two qualities, called 'Basic' and 'Super'. The business is able to sell these products at a price that gives a standard profit mark-up of 25 per cent of full cost. Management is concerned by the lack of profit.

Full cost for one unit of a product is calculated by charging overheads to each type of product on the basis of direct labour hours. The costs are as follows:

	Basic	Super
	£	£
Direct labour (all £10/hour)	40	60
Direct material	15	20

The total overheads are £1,000,000.

Based on experience over recent years, in the forthcoming year the business expects to make and sell 40,000 Basics and 10,000 Supers.

Recently, the business's management accountant has undertaken an exercise to try to identify activities and cost drivers in an attempt to be able to deal with the overheads on a more precise basis than had been possible before. This exercise has revealed the following analysis of the annual overheads:

Activity (and cost driver)	Cost	Annual number of activities		
	£000	Total	Basic	Super
Number of machine set-ups	280	100	20	80
Number of quality-control inspections	220	2,000	500	1,500
Number of sales orders processed	240	5,000	1,500	3,500
General production (machine hours)	260	500,000	350,000	150,000
Total	1,000			

The management accountant explained the analysis of the £1,000,000 overheads as follows:

- The two products are made in relatively small batches, so that the amount of the finished product held in inventories is negligible. The Supers are made in very small batches because their demand is relatively low. Each time a new batch is produced, the machines have to be reset by skilled staff. Resetting for Basic production occurs about 20 times a year and for Supers about 80 times: about 100 times in total. The cost of employing the machine-setting staff is about £280,000 a year. It is clear that the more set-ups that occur, the higher the total set-up costs; in other words, the number of set-ups is the factor that drives set-up costs.
- All production has to be inspected for quality and this costs about £220,000 a year. The higher specifications of the Supers mean that there is more chance that there will be quality problems. Thus the Supers are inspected in total 1,500 times annually, whereas the Basics only need about 500 inspections. The number of inspections is the factor that drives these costs.
- Sales order processing (dealing with customers' orders, from receiving the original order to dispatching the products) costs about £240,000 a year. Despite the larger amount of Basic production, there are only 1,500 sales orders each year because the Basics are sold to wholesalers in relatively large-sized orders. The Supers are sold mainly direct to the public by mail order, usually in very small-sized orders. It is believed that the number of orders drives the costs of processing orders.

Required:

(a) Deduce the full cost of each of the two products on the basis used at present and, from these, deduce the current selling price.

(b) Deduce the full cost of each product on an ABC basis, taking account of the management accountant's recent investigations.

(c) What conclusions do you draw? What advice would you offer the management of the business?

The answer to this question can be found at the back of the book on pages 731–2.

Other costing approaches in the modern environment

The increasingly competitive environment in which modern businesses operate is leading to greater effort being applied in trying to manage costs. Businesses need to keep costs to a minimum so that they can supply goods and services at a price that customers will be prepared to pay and, at the same time, generate a level of profit necessary to meet the businesses' objectives of enhancing shareholder wealth. We have just seen how ABC can help manage costs. We shall now go on to outline some other techniques that have recently emerged in an attempt to meet these goals of competitiveness and profitability. These can be used in conjunction with ABC.

Total (or whole) life-cycle costing

This approach to costing starts from the premise that the total (or whole) life cycle of a product or service that the business provides for sale has three phases. These are:

1 The *pre-production phase*. This is the period that precedes production of the product or service. During this phase, research and development – both of the product or service and of the market – is conducted. The product or service is invented/designed and so is the means of production. The phase culminates with acquiring and setting up the necessary production facilities and with advertising and promotion.

2 The *production phase* comes next, being the one in which the product is made and sold or the service is rendered to customers.

3 The *post-production phase* comes last. During this phase, any costs necessary to correct faults that arose with products or services that have been sold (after-sales service) are incurred. There would also be the costs of closing production at the end of the product's or service's life cycle, such as the cost of decommissioning production facilities. Since after-sales service will tend to arise from as early as the first product or service being sold and probably, therefore, well before the last one is sold, this phase would typically overlap with the production phase.

Businesses often seem to consider environmental costs alongside the more obvious financial costs involved in the life of a product.

The total life cycle is shown in Figure 11.3.

In some types of business, particularly those engaged in an advanced manufacturing environment, it is estimated that a very high proportion (as much as 80 per cent) of the total costs that will be incurred over the total life of a particular product are either incurred or committed at the pre-production phase. For example, a motor car

Figure 11.3 The total life cycle of a product or service

Total life cycle of a product or service

Research and development, production set-up, pre-production marketing costs → **Pre-production phase**

Manufacturing and marketing costs → **Production phase**

After-sales service and production facility decommissioning costs → **Post-production phase**

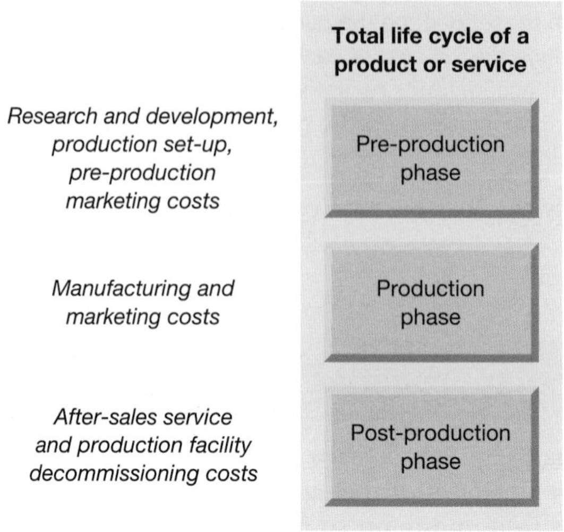

From the producer's viewpoint, the life of a product can be seen as having three distinct phases. During the first the product is developed and everything is prepared so that production and marketing can start. Next come production and sales. Lastly, dealing with post-production activities is undertaken.

manufacturer, when designing, developing and setting up production of a new model, incurs a high proportion of the total costs that will be incurred on that model during the whole of its life. Not only are pre-production costs specifically incurred during this phase, but the need to incur particular costs during the production phase is also established. This is because the design will incorporate features that will lead to particular manufacturing costs. Once the design of the car has been finalised and the manufacturing plant set up, it may be too late to 'design out' a costly feature without incurring another large cost.

Activity 11.3

A decision taken at the design stage (during the pre-production phase) could well commit the business to costs during the post-production phase. Can you suggest a potential cost that could be built in at the design stage that will show itself *after* the manufacture of the product?

After-sales service costs could be incurred as a result of some design fault. Once the manufacturing facilities have been established, it may not be economic to revise the design but merely to deal with the problem through after-sales service procedures.

→ **Total life-cycle costing** seeks to focus management's attention on the fact that it is not just during the production phase that attention needs to be paid to cost management. By the start of the production phase it may be too late to try to manage a large element of the product's or service's total life-cycle cost. Efforts need to be made to assess the costs of alternative designs.

There needs to be a review of the product or service over its entire life cycle, which could be a period of 20 or more years. Traditional management accounting, however, tends to be concerned with assessing performance over periods of just one year or less.

Real World 11.4 provides some idea of the extent to which total life-cycle costing is used in practice.

Real World 11.4

Total (whole) life-cycle costing in practice

A survey of management accounting practice in the US was conducted in 2003. Nearly 2,000 businesses replied to the survey. These tended to be larger businesses, of which about 40 per cent were manufacturers and about 16 per cent financial services; the remainder were across a range of other industries.

The survey revealed that 22 per cent extensively use a total life-cycle approach to cost control, with a further 37 per cent considering using the technique in the future.

Though the survey relates to the US, in the absence of UK evidence, it provides some insight into what is likely also to be practised in the UK and elsewhere in the developed world.

Source: *2003 Survey of Management Accounting*, Ernst and Young, 2003.

Real World 11.5 shows how a well-known international car maker uses total life-cycle costing.

Real World 11.5

Total life-cycle costing at Renault

According to Renault, the French motor vehicle manufacturer:

The life of a vehicle is long and comprises several phases:

Design: Creating a vehicle
Manufacturing: Extracting and producing materials, manufacturing and assembling the components, and then the whole vehicle
Distribution: Transition between the vehicle's departure from the production plant and its purchase by a customer
Vehicle service life: The use by the motorist, the longest phase **recycling.**

These phases make up the life cycle. Why the word 'cycle'? Because the end of a vehicle's service life is factored in right from the design phase.

Source: www.renault.com.

Note that Renault divides the *production phase* into two sections: manufacturing and distribution. It also divides the *post-production phase* into vehicle service life and recycling.

Target costing

With traditional cost-plus pricing, costs are totalled for a product or service and a percentage is added for profit to arrive at a selling price. We saw in Chapter 10 that this is not a very practical basis on which to price output for many businesses – certainly not those operating in a price-competitive market (price takers). The cost-plus price may well be totally unacceptable to the market.

→ **Target costing** approaches the problem from the other direction. First, with the help of market research or other means, a unit selling price is identified at which the market is expected to buy the product. The business will also estimate the sales volume that could be sold at the identified selling price. An amount for profit is deducted from this target unit selling price. This unit profit figure must be such as to be acceptable to meet the business's profit objective. The resulting figure is the target cost. The target cost may well be less than the 'current' cost; there may be a 'cost gap'. Efforts are then made to bridge this gap, that is, to provide the service or produce the product in a way that will enable the target cost to be met. These efforts may involve revising the design, finding more efficient means of production or requiring suppliers of goods and services to supply more cheaply.

Target costing is seen as a part of a total life-cycle costing approach, in that cost savings are sought at a very early stage in the life cycle, during the pre-production phase.

Real World 11.6 indicates the level of usage of target costing. This shows quite a low level of usage in the US. In contrast, other survey evidence shows that target costing is very widely used by Japanese manufacturing businesses.

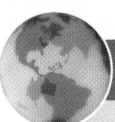

Real World 11.6

On target

The Ernst and Young survey of management accounting practice in the US, conducted in 2003, revealed that 27 per cent use target costing extensively, with a further 41 per cent considering using the technique in the future.

Source: 2003 Survey of Management Accounting, Ernst and Young, 2003.

Activity 11.4

Though target costing seems effective and has its enthusiasts, some people feel it has its problems. Can you suggest what these problems might be?

There seem to be three main problem areas:

● It can lead to various conflicts – for example, between the business, its suppliers and its own staff.
● It can cause a great deal of stress for employees who are trying to meet target costs that are sometimes extremely difficult to achieve.
● Although, in the end, ways may be found to meet a target cost (through product or service redesign, negotiating lower prices with suppliers, and so on), the whole process can be very expensive.

Costing quality control

Such is the importance that their customers place on quality that businesses are forced to make sure that their output is of a high quality. In the competitive environment in which most businesses operate, a failure to deliver quality will lead to customers going to another supplier. Businesses, therefore, need to establish procedures that promote the quality of their output, either by preventing quality problems in the first place or by dealing with them when they occur. These procedures have a cost. It has been estimated that these **quality costs** can amount to up to 30 per cent of total processing costs. These costs tend to be incurred during the production phase of the product life cycle. They have been seen as falling into four main categories:

- *Prevention costs.* These are involved with procedures to try to prevent products being produced that are not up to the required quality. Such procedures might include staff training on quality issues. Some types of prevention costs might be incurred during the *Pre-production phase* of the product life cycle, where the production process could be designed in such a way as to avoid potential quality problems with the output.
- *Appraisal costs.* These are concerned with monitoring raw materials, work in progress and finished products to try to avoid substandard production from reaching the customer.
- *Internal failure costs.* These include the costs of rectifying substandard products before they pass to the customer and the costs of scrap arising from quality failures.
- *External failure costs.* These are involved with rectifying quality problems with products that have passed to the customer. There is also the cost to the business of its loss of reputation from having passed substandard products to the customer.

Figure 11.4 sets these out in diagram form.

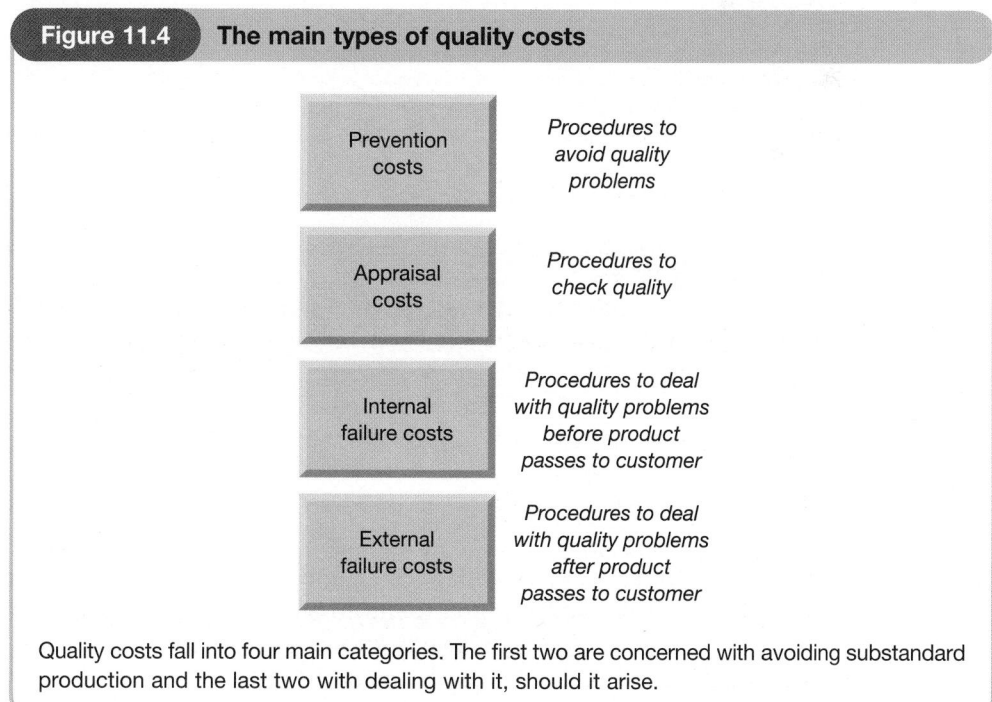

| Figure 11.4 | The main types of quality costs |

Prevention costs — *Procedures to avoid quality problems*

Appraisal costs — *Procedures to check quality*

Internal failure costs — *Procedures to deal with quality problems before product passes to customer*

External failure costs — *Procedures to deal with quality problems after product passes to customer*

Quality costs fall into four main categories. The first two are concerned with avoiding substandard production and the last two with dealing with it, should it arise.

Kaizen costing

→ ***Kaizen* costing** is linked to total life-cycle costing and focuses on cost saving during the production phase. The Japanese word *kaizen* implies 'continuous changes'. The application of the *kaizen* costing approach involves continuous improvement, in terms of cost saving, throughout the production phase. Since this phase is at a relatively late stage in the life cycle (from a cost control point of view) only relatively small cost savings can usually be made. The major production-phase cost savings should already have been made through target costing.

With *kaizen* costing, efforts are made to reduce the unit manufacturing cost of the particular product or service under review, if possible taking it below the unit cost in the previous period. Target percentage reductions can be set. Usually, production workers are encouraged to identify ways of reducing costs. This is something that the 'hands on' experience of these workers may enable them to do. Even though the scope to reduce costs is limited at the production stage, valuable savings can still be made.

Real World 11.7 explains how a major UK manufacturer used *kaizen* costing to advantage.

Real World 11.7

Kaizen costing is part of the package

Kappa Packaging is a major UK packaging business. It has a factory at Stalybridge where it makes, among other things, packaging (cardboard cartons) for glass bottles containing alcoholic drinks. In 2002, Kappa introduced a new approach to reducing the amount of waste paper and cardboard. Before this, the business wasted 14.6 per cent of its raw materials used. This figure was taken as the base against which improvements would be measured.

Improvements were made at Kappa as a result of:

● making staff more aware of the waste problem;
● requiring staff to monitor the amount of waste for which they were individually responsible; and
● establishing a *kaizen* team to find ways of reducing waste.

As a result of *kaizen* savings, Kappa was able to reduce waste from 14.6 per cent to 13.1 per cent in 2002 and 11 per cent in 2003. The business estimates that each 1 per cent waste saving was worth £110,000 a year. So by the end of 2003, Kappa was saving about £400,000 a year, relative to 2001: that is, over £2,000 per employee each year.

Source: Taken from 'Accurate measurement of process waste leads to reduced costs', www.envirowise.gov.uk, 2003.

Value chain analysis

Another approach that seeks to manage costs, and which recognises the total life-cycle
→ concept, is **value chain analysis**. It is useful to analyse a business into a sequence of value-creating activities. This sequence is known as the value chain and value chain analysis examines the potential for each link in the chain to add value. The value chain is the linking sequence of activities, through the three phases of the product life cycle

from research and development to after-sales activities. In a wealth-seeking business, the objective for the product is that it should create value for the business and its owners.

Each link in the value chain represents a particular activity. All of the activities will lead to a cost. Ideally, each link should add value to the product, making the product more valuable to the customer. Any links in the chain that fail to add value should be examined very critically. The objective of this examination is to assess whether the particular link could be eliminated completely or, at least, have its cost reduced.

An example of a typical non-value-added activity is inspection of the completed product or service by a quality controller. This activity does not add value to the product or service, yet it adds cost. This inspection cost might well be capable of being reduced, or even completely eliminated. The introduction of a 'quality' culture in the business could lead to all output being reliable and not needing to be inspected. This is a development that many modern businesses have achieved.

An example of a value-added activity would be the rendering of a service to a customer for which the customer is prepared to pay more than it cost.

For a manufacturing business, the value-creating sequence begins with the acquisition of inputs, such as raw materials and energy, and ends with the sale of completed goods and after-sales service. Figure 11.5 sets out the main 'links' in the value chain for a manufacturing business.

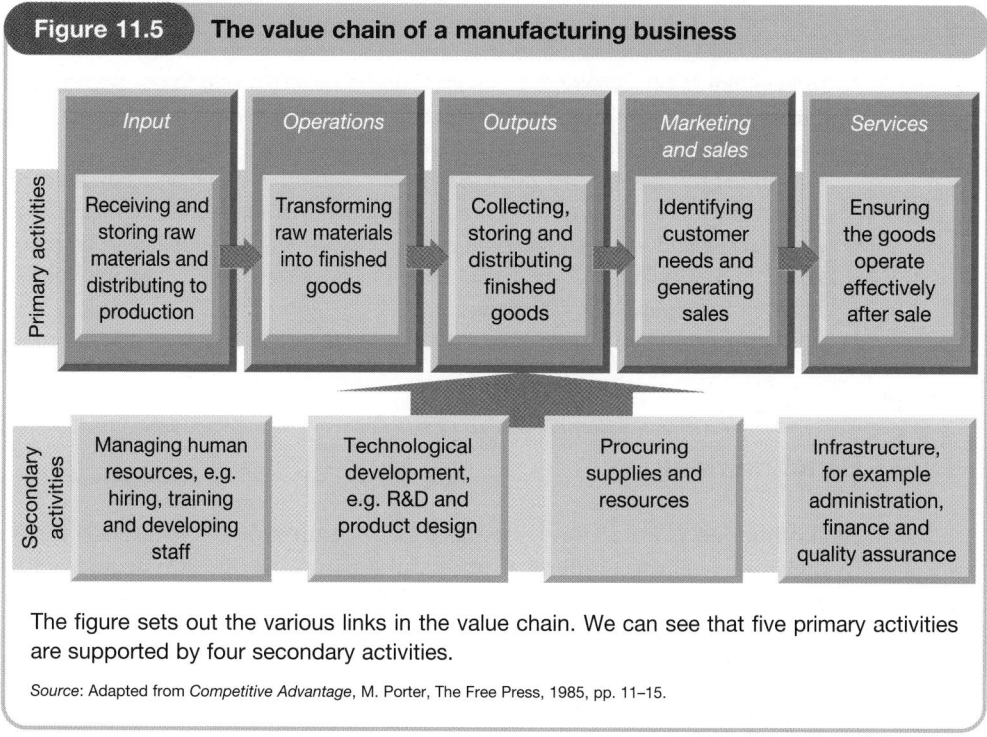

Figure 11.5   The value chain of a manufacturing business

The figure sets out the various links in the value chain. We can see that five primary activities are supported by four secondary activities.

Source: Adapted from *Competitive Advantage*, M. Porter, The Free Press, 1985, pp. 11–15.

Value chain analysis applies as much to service-providing businesses as it does to manufacturers. Service providers similarly have a sequence of activities leading to provision of the service to their customers. Analysing these activities in an attempt to identify and eliminate non-value added activities is very important.

Real World 11.8 provides an example of how focusing on the value chain may help transform the performance of a business.

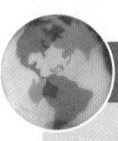

Real World 11.8

What a sauce

FT

Ahold is a major Dutch retailer that has recently been recovering its fortunes, under its chief executive Anders Moberg. The business has a recovery plan that involves 're-engineering the value chain' and according to Mr Moberg, the key is a detailed analysis of the cost of goods sold. 'That is probably the single biggest opportunity [for savings] that we have.'

Take a bottle of tomato ketchup. 'What are the costs of the growers of the tomatoes? What are the components of the value chain, production, marketing, packaging and distribution? Can you add a component in a different way, for example with standardised bottles? You are looking at how to re-engineer the value chain [in order] to lower the price.'

Manufacturers' brands do this, he says, 'but they keep the savings, hence they have a better return on capital'. With supermarket own-label brands on the rise – they account for 50 per cent of Ahold Dutch store sales, and 15 per cent in the US – Mr Moberg can reduce what it costs him to make products while at the same time lowering prices, attracting more shoppers to Ahold stores and thereby raising volumes.

Armed with intricate knowledge of supply chain costs, Ahold can press big brand manufacturers to cut the prices they ask of the retailer. It is a delicate balancing act. Both Grolsch, the Dutch brewer, and Peijnenburg, a bakery group, have quarrelled with Ahold about the damage inflicted on their brands by pricing policy, while Unilever, the consumer goods group, took Ahold to court, claiming it had copied its packaging.

It appears, however, to be a battle Mr Moberg is winning. Not only is customer perception of the quality of own-label products rising – a fact confirmed by independent industry research – but Ahold has a strong position with big consumer brands through its control of distribution channels, especially in the Netherlands, where its Albert Heijn chain is market leader and has 700 stores.

Source: 'It is all about the value chain', Ian Bickerton, FT.com, 23 February 2004.

Benchmarking

→ **Benchmarking** is an activity – usually a continuing one – where a business, or one of its divisions, seeks to emulate a successful business or division and so achieve a similar level of success. The successful business or division provides a benchmark against which the business can measure its own performance, as well as examples of approaches that can lead to success. Sometimes the benchmark business will help with the activity, but even where no cooperation is given, outside observers can still learn quite a lot about what makes that business successful.

Businesses are under no statutory obligation to benchmark and are understandably reluctant to divulge commercially sensitive information to competitor businesses. They may, however, benchmark internally, with one division or department comparing itself with another part of the same business. They may also benchmark with businesses with which they are not directly competing but which may have similar functions.

Real World 11.9 provides an example of two well-known divisions, of an equally well-known parent business, that were able to benchmark, one against the other.

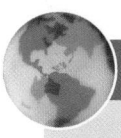

Real World 11.9

Tracking the Jaguar

FT

The solid off-road qualities of Land Rover vehicles inspire devotion among many of their owners, who include members of Britain's royal family. But the brand has been plagued by quality problems, setting spurious warning lights flashing in some of its vehicles and putting it last in consultancy JD Power's 2007 Initial Quality Study in the US.

Land Rover is now benchmarking the quality levels of Jaguar, its sister brand, and clawing its way back up the league tables. 'They're still below the average, but improving relative to the competition,' said Brian Walters, JD Power's vice-president of European operations. Lewis Booth, head of Ford Motor's premium-brands group, told the *Financial Times*: 'We want to get Land Rover to Jaguar quality levels.'

The problems owe something to the complexity of the vehicles, packed with electronic control units aimed at keeping them stable off road.

Land Rover, formerly owned by BMW and now up for sale by Ford, has seen a flurry of new vehicle launches in recent years, even as it changed owners.

Source: 'Royal following but quality issues remain', John Reed, FT.com, 3 October 2007.

Ford sold Jaguar and Land Rover to the Indian motor business, Tata, in March 2008, but no doubt the inter-divisional benchmarking still continues.

Non-financial measures of performance

Financial measures have long been seen as the most important ones for a business. They provide us with a valuable means of summarising and evaluating business achievement and there is no real doubt about the continued importance of financial measures in this role. In recent years, however, there has been increasing recognition that financial measures alone will not provide managers with sufficient information to manage a business effectively. Non-financial measures must also be used to gain a deeper understanding of the business and to achieve the objectives of the business, including the financial objectives.

Financial measures portray various aspects of business achievement (for example, sales revenues, profits and return on capital employed) that can help managers determine whether the business is increasing the wealth of its owners. These measures are vitally important but, in an increasingly competitive environment, managers also need to understand what drives the creation of wealth. These **value drivers** may be such things as employee satisfaction, customer loyalty and the level of product innovation. Often they do not lend themselves to financial measurement, although non-financial measures may provide some means of assessment.

Activity (11.5)

How might we measure:

(a) employee satisfaction
(b) customer loyalty
(c) the level of product innovation?

(a) Employee satisfaction may be measured through the use of an employee survey. This could examine attitudes towards various aspects of the job, the degree of autonomy that is permitted, the level of recognition and reward received, the level of participation in decision making, the degree of support received in carrying out tasks and so on. Less direct measures of satisfaction may include employee turnover rates and employee productivity. However, other factors may have a significant influence on these measures.

(b) Customer loyalty may be measured through the proportion of total sales generated from existing customers, the number of repeat sales made to customers, the percentage of customers renewing subscriptions or other contracts and so on.

(c) The level of product innovation may be measured through the number of innovations during a period compared to those of competitors, the percentage of sales attributable to recent product innovations, the number of innovations that are brought successfully to market and so on.

Real World 11.10 provides some insight into the kind of non-financial measures that are regarded as important by management accountants in manufacturing businesses.

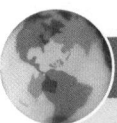

Real World 11.10

Measure for measure

A study by Abdel-Maksoud and others asked management accountants employed in 313 UK manufacturing businesses to assess the importance of 19 'shop floor' non-financial measures. The accountants were asked to rank the measures on a scale ranging from 1 (low) to 7 (high). The mean importance of each of the 19 measures is set out in Figure 11.6.

We can see that the first three measures relate to customers. This is followed by three measures relating to cost control and the efficiency of processes.

Source: 'Non-financial performance measurement in manufacturing companies', A. Abdel-Maksoud, D. Dugdale and R. Luther, *The British Accounting Review*, 37, 2005, pp. 261–97.

Figure 11.6   The mean importance of non-financial measures

% of businesses using measure	Measure	Mean importance
92	On-time delivery	6.4
95	Number of complaints from customers	6.2
91	Number of customer returns	5.9
90	Efficiency (std hrs produced/worked)	5.8
87	Defects (% of total production)	5.8
90	Scrap (% of total production)	5.7
97	Absenteeism	5.5
70	Number of warranty claims	5.5
62	Manufacturing cycle efficiency	5.3
86	Activity (std hrs produced/budgeted std hrs)	5.3
84	Capacity utilisation (hrs worked/budgeted hrs)	5.3
92	Proportion of overtime worked	5.3
68	% schedule adherence	5.2
76	% on-time production	5.2
84	Rework (% of total production)	5.2
90	Employee lateness	4.9
89	Staff turnover	4.6
63	Employee attitudes	4.5
56	Batches (% adjusted)	4.1

We can see that the degree of importance attached to the 19 'shop floor' financial measures identified varies, but all are located at the upper end of the scale.

Financial measures are normally 'lag' indicators, in that they tell us about outcomes. In other words, they measure the consequences arising from management decisions that were made earlier. Non-financial measures can also be used as lag indicators, of course. However, they can also be used as 'lead' indicators by focusing on those things that drive performance. It is argued that if we measure changes in these value drivers, we may be able to predict changes in future financial performance. For example, a business may find from experience that a 10 per cent fall in levels of product innovation during one period will lead to a 20 per cent fall in sales revenues over the next three periods. In this case, the levels of product innovation can be regarded as a lead indicator that can warn managers of a future decline in sales unless corrective action is taken. Thus, by using this lead indicator, managers can identify key changes at an early stage and can respond quickly.

The balanced scorecard

One of the most impressive attempts to integrate the use of financial and non-financial measures has been the **balanced scorecard**, developed by Robert Kaplan and David Norton (see reference 1 at the end of the chapter). The balanced scorecard is both a management system and a measurement system. In essence, it provides a framework that translates the aims and objectives of a business into a series of key performance measures and targets. This framework is intended to make the strategy of the business more coherent by tightly linking it to particular targets and initiatives. As a result, managers should be able to see more clearly whether the objectives that have been set have actually been achieved.

The balanced scorecard approach involves setting objectives and developing appropriate measures and targets in four main areas:

- *Financial.* This area will specify the financial returns required by shareholders and may involve the use of financial measures such as return on capital employed, operating profit margin, percentage sales revenue growth and so on.
- *Customer.* This area will specify the kind of customer and/or markets that the business wishes to service and will establish appropriate measures such as customer satisfaction, new customer growth levels and so on.
- *Internal business process.* This area will specify those business processes (for example, innovation, types of operation and after-sales service) that are important to the success of the business and will establish appropriate measures such as percentage of sales from new products, time to market for new products, product cycle times, and speed of response to customer complaints.
- *Learning and growth.* This area will specify the kind of people, the systems and the procedures that are necessary to deliver long-term business growth. This area is often the most difficult for the development of appropriate measures. However, examples of measures may include employee motivation, employee skills profiles and information systems capabilities.

These four areas are shown in Figure 11.7.

The balanced scorecard approach does not prescribe the particular objectives, measures or targets that a business should adopt; this is a matter for the individual business to decide upon. There are differences between businesses in terms of technology employed, organisational structure, management philosophy and business environment, so each business should develop objectives and measures that reflect its unique circumstances. The balanced scorecard simply sets out the framework for developing a

| Figure 11.7 | The balanced scorecard – for translating a strategy into operational processes |

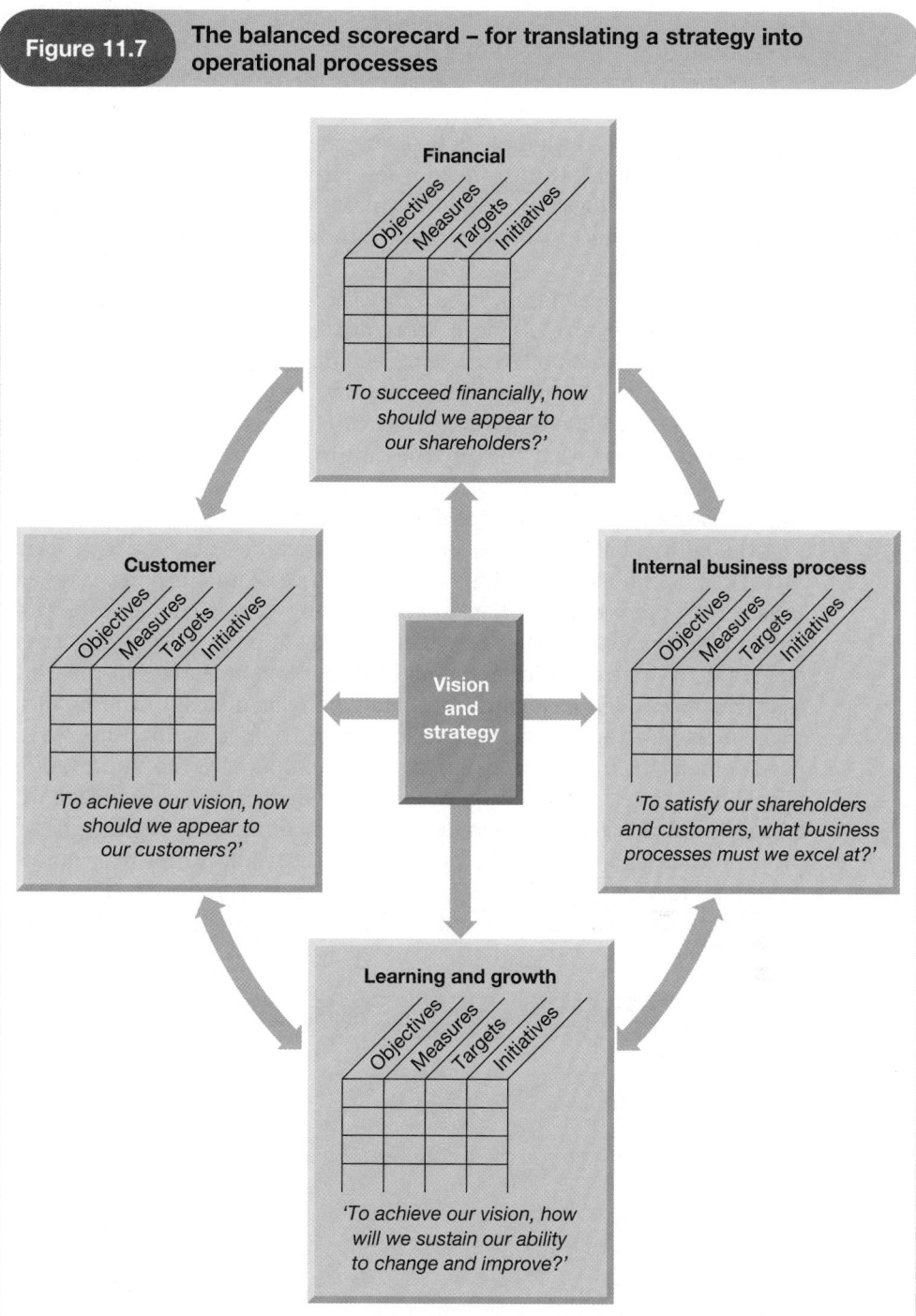

There are four main areas covered by the balanced scorecard. Note that, for each area, a fundamental question must be addressed. By answering these questions, managers should be able to develop the key objectives of the business. Once this has been done, suitable measures and targets can be developed that are relevant to those objectives. Finally, appropriate management initiatives will be developed to achieve the targets set.

Source: The Balanced Scorecard (see reference 1 at the end of the chapter).

coherent set of objectives for the business and for ensuring that these objectives are then linked to specific targets and initiatives.

A balanced scorecard will be prepared for the business as a whole or, in the case of large, diverse businesses, for each strategic business unit. However, having prepared an overall scorecard, it is then possible to prepare a balanced scorecard for each sub-unit, such as a department, within the business. Thus, the balanced scorecard approach can cascade down the business, resulting in a pyramid of balanced scorecards that are linked to the 'master' balanced scorecard through an alignment of the objectives and measures employed.

Though a very large number of measures, both financial and non-financial, exist and so could be used in a balanced scorecard, only a handful of measures should be employed. A maximum of 20 measures will normally be sufficient to enable the factors that are critical to the success of the business to be captured. (If a business has come up with more than 20 measures, it is usually because the managers have not thought hard enough about what the key measures really are.) The key measures developed should be a mix of lagging indicators (those relating to outcomes) and lead indicators (those relating to the things that drive performance).

Although the balanced scorecard employs measures across a wide range of business activity, it does not seek to dilute the importance of financial measures and objectives. In fact, the opposite is true. Kaplan and Norton (see reference 1 at the end of the chapter) emphasise the point that a balanced scorecard must reflect a concern for the financial objectives of the business and so measures and objectives in the other three areas that have been identified must ultimately be related back to the financial objectives. There must be a cause-and-effect relationship. So, for example, an investment in staff development (in the learning and growth area) may lead to improved levels of after-sales service (internal business process area), which, in turn, may lead to higher levels of customer satisfaction (customer area) and, ultimately, higher sales revenues and profits (financial area). At first, cause-and-effect relationships may not be very clearly identified. However, by gathering information over time, the business can improve its understanding of the linkages and thereby improve the effectiveness of the scorecard.

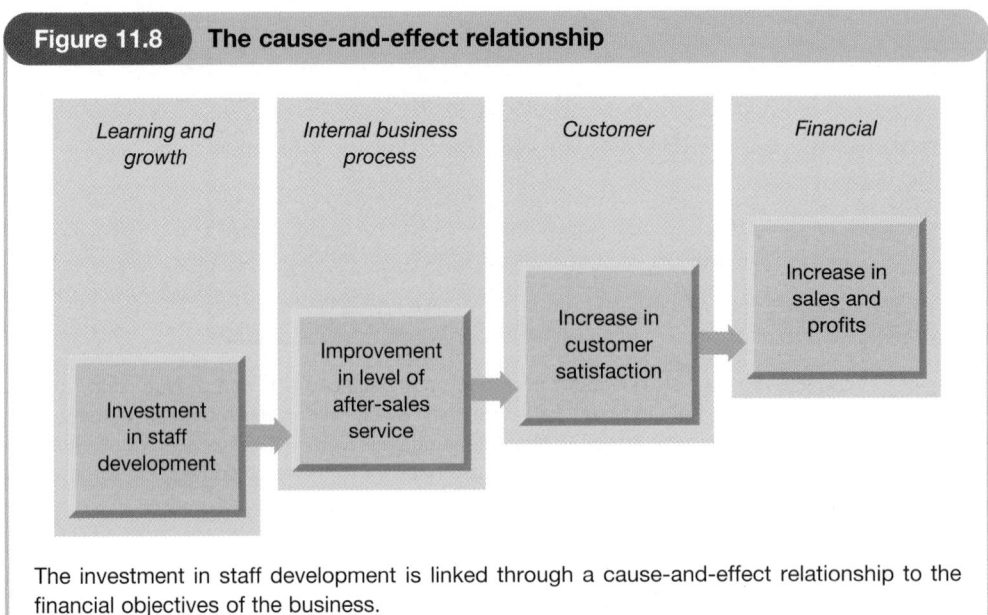

Figure 11.8   **The cause-and-effect relationship**

The investment in staff development is linked through a cause-and-effect relationship to the financial objectives of the business.

Figure 11.8 shows the cause-and-effect relationship between the investment in staff development and the business's financial objectives.

Activity 11.6

Do you think this is a rather hard-nosed approach to dealing with staff development? Should staff development always have to be justified in terms of the financial results achieved?

This approach may seem rather hard-nosed. However, Kaplan and Norton argue that unless this kind of link between staff development and increased financial returns can be demonstrated, managers are likely to become cynical about the benefits of staff development and so the result may be that there will be no investment in staff.

Why is this framework referred to as a *balanced* scorecard? According to Kaplan and Norton there are various reasons. First, it is because it aims to strike a balance between *external* measures relating to customers and shareholders, and *internal* measures relating to business process, learning and growth. Secondly, it aims to strike a balance between the measures that reflect *outcomes* (lag indicators) and measures that help *predict future performance* (lead indicators). Finally, the framework aims to strike a balance between *hard* financial measures and *soft* non-financial measures.

It is possible to adapt the balanced scorecard to fit the needs of the particular business. **Real World 11.11** shows how this has been done by Tesco plc, a large retailer.

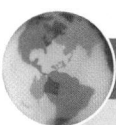 **Real World 11.11**

Every little helps

Tesco plc has modified the balanced scorecard approach to meet its particular needs. It has added a fifth dimension, the community, to demonstrate its commitment to the communities that it serves. There is frequent monitoring of the various performance measures against the scorecard targets. The business states:

> We operate a balanced scorecard approach which is known within the Group as our Steering Wheel. This unites the Group's resources around our customers, people, operations, community and finance. The scorecard operates at every level within the Group, from ground level business units, through to country level operations. It enables the business to be operated and monitored on a balanced basis with due regard for all stakeholders.

> . . . the Steering Wheel is reviewed quarterly. Steering Wheels are operated in business units across the Group, and reports are prepared of performance against target KPIs (key performance indicators) on a quarterly basis enabling management to measure performance.

Source: Tesco plc Internal Control and Risk Management 2008, www.tesco.com.

As a footnote to our consideration of the balanced scorecard, **Real World 11.12** provides an interesting analogy with aeroplane pilots limiting themselves to just one control device.

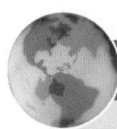

(UN)Real World 11.12

Fear of flying

Kaplan and Norton invite us to imagine the following conversation between a passenger and the pilot of a jet aeroplane during a flight:

Q: I'm surprised to see you operating the plane with only a single instrument. What does it measure?

A: Airspeed. I'm really working on airspeed this flight.

Q: That's good. Airspeed certainly seems important. But what about altitude? Wouldn't an altimeter be helpful?

A: I worked on altitude for the last few flights and I've gotten pretty good on it. Now I have to concentrate on proper airspeed.

Q: But I notice you don't even have a fuel gauge. Wouldn't that be useful?

A: You're right; fuel is significant, but I can't concentrate on doing too many things well at the same time. So on this flight I'm focusing on airspeed. Once I get to be excellent at airspeed, as well as altitude, I intend to concentrate on fuel consumption on the next set of flights.

The point they are trying to make (apart from warning against flying with a pilot like this!) is that to fly an aeroplane, which is a complex activity, a wide range of navigation instruments is required. A business, however, can be even more complex to manage than an aeroplane and so a wide range of measures, both financial and non-financial, is necessary. Reliance on financial measures is not enough and so the balanced scorecard aims to provide managers with a more complete navigation system.

Source: Kaplan and Norton (see reference 1 at the end of the chapter).

The above story makes the point that, by concentrating only on a few areas of performance, other important areas may be ignored. Too narrow a focus can adversely affect behaviour and distort performance. This may, in turn, mean that the business fails to meet its strategic objectives. Perhaps we should bear in mind another apocryphal story concerning a factory in Russia which, under the former communist regime, produced nails. The factory had its output measured according only to the weight of nails manufactured. For one financial period, it achieved its output target by producing one very large nail!

Scorecard problems

Not all attempts to embed the balanced scorecard approach within a business are successful. Why do things go wrong? It has been suggested that often too many measures are employed, thereby making the scorecard too complex and unwieldy. It has also been suggested that managers are confronted with trade-off decisions between the four different dimensions and struggle because they lack a clear compass. Imagine a manager who has a limited budget and therefore has to decide whether to invest in either staff training or product innovation. If both add value to the business, which choice will be optimal for the business?

Whilst such problems exist, David Norton believes that there are two main reasons why the balanced scorecard fails to take root within a business, as **Real World 11.13** explains.

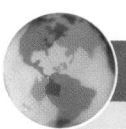

Real World 11.13

When misuse leads to failure

FT

There are two main reasons why companies go wrong with the widely used balanced scorecard, according to David Norton, the consultant who created the concept with Robert Kaplan, a Harvard Business School Professor.

'The number one cause of failure is that you don't have leadership at the executive levels of the organisation,' says Mr Norton. 'They don't embrace it and use it for managing their strategy.'

The second is that some companies treat it purely as a measurement tool, a problem he admits stems partly from its name. The concept has evolved since its inception, he says. The latest Kaplan-Norton thinking is that companies need a unit at corporate level – they call it an 'office of strategy management' – dedicated to ensuring that strategy is communicated to every employee and translated into plans, targets and incentives in each business unit and department.

Incentives are crucial, Mr Norton believes. Managers who have achieved breakthroughs in performance with the scorecard say they would tie it to executive compensation sooner if they were doing it again. 'There's so much change in organisations that managers don't always believe you mean what you say. The balanced scorecard may just be "flavour of the month". Tying it to compensation shows that you mean it.'

Source: 'When misuse leads to failure', FT.com, 24 May 2006.

Measuring shareholder value

Traditional measures of financial performance have been subject to much criticism in recent years and new measures have been advocated to guide and to assess strategic management decisions. In this section we shall consider one such measure, which is based on the idea of increasing shareholder value. Before examining this method, we shall first consider why increasing shareholder value is regarded as the ultimate financial objective of a business.

The quest for shareholder value

For some years, shareholder value has been a 'hot' issue among managers. Many leading businesses now claim that the quest for shareholder value is the driving force behind their strategic and operational decisions. As a starting point, we shall consider what is meant by the term 'shareholder value' and in the sections that follow we shall look at one of the main approaches to measuring shareholder value.

In simple terms, 'shareholder value' is about putting the needs of shareholders at the heart of management decisions. It is argued that shareholders invest in a business with a view to maximising their financial returns in relation to the risks that they are prepared to take. As managers are appointed by the shareholders to act on their behalf, management decisions and actions should therefore reflect a concern for maximising shareholder returns. Though the business may have other 'stakeholder' groups, such as employees, customers and suppliers, it is the shareholders that should be seen as the most important group.

This, of course, is not a new idea. As we discussed in Chapter 1, maximising shareholder wealth is assumed to be the key objective of a business. However, not everyone accepts this idea. Some believe that a balance must be struck between the competing claims of the various stakeholders. A debate concerning the merits of each viewpoint is beyond the scope of this book; however, it is worth pointing out that, in recent years, the business environment has radically changed.

In the past, shareholders have been accused of being too passive and of accepting too readily the profits and dividends that managers have delivered. However, this has changed. Shareholders are now much more assertive, and, as owners of the business, are in a position to insist that their needs are given priority. Since the 1980s we have witnessed the deregulation and globalisation of business, as well as enormous changes in technology. The effect has been to create a much more competitive world. This has meant not only competition for products and services but also competition for funds. Businesses must now compete more strongly for shareholder funds and so must offer competitive rates of return.

Thus, self-interest may be the most powerful reason for managers to commit themselves to maximising shareholder returns. If they do not do this, there is a real risk that shareholders will either replace them with managers who will, or shareholders will allow the business to be taken over by another business that has managers who are dedicated to maximising shareholder returns.

How can shareholder value be created?

Creating shareholder value involves a four-stage process. The first stage is to set objectives for the business that recognise the central importance of maximising shareholder returns. This will set a clear direction for the business. The second stage is to establish an appropriate means of measuring the returns, or value, that have been generated for shareholders. For reasons that we shall discuss later, the traditional methods of measuring returns to shareholders are inadequate for this purpose. The third stage is to manage the business in such a manner as to ensure that shareholder returns are maximised. This means setting demanding targets and then achieving them through the best possible use of resources, the use of incentive systems and the embedding of a shareholder value culture throughout the business. The final stage is to measure the shareholder returns over a period of time to see whether the objectives have actually been achieved.

Figure 11.9 shows the shareholder value creation process.

The need for new measures

Given a commitment to maximise shareholder returns, we must select an appropriate measure that will help us assess the returns to shareholders over time. It is argued that the traditional methods for measuring shareholder returns are seriously flawed and so should not be used for this purpose.

Figure 11.9 **The four-stage process for creating shareholder value**

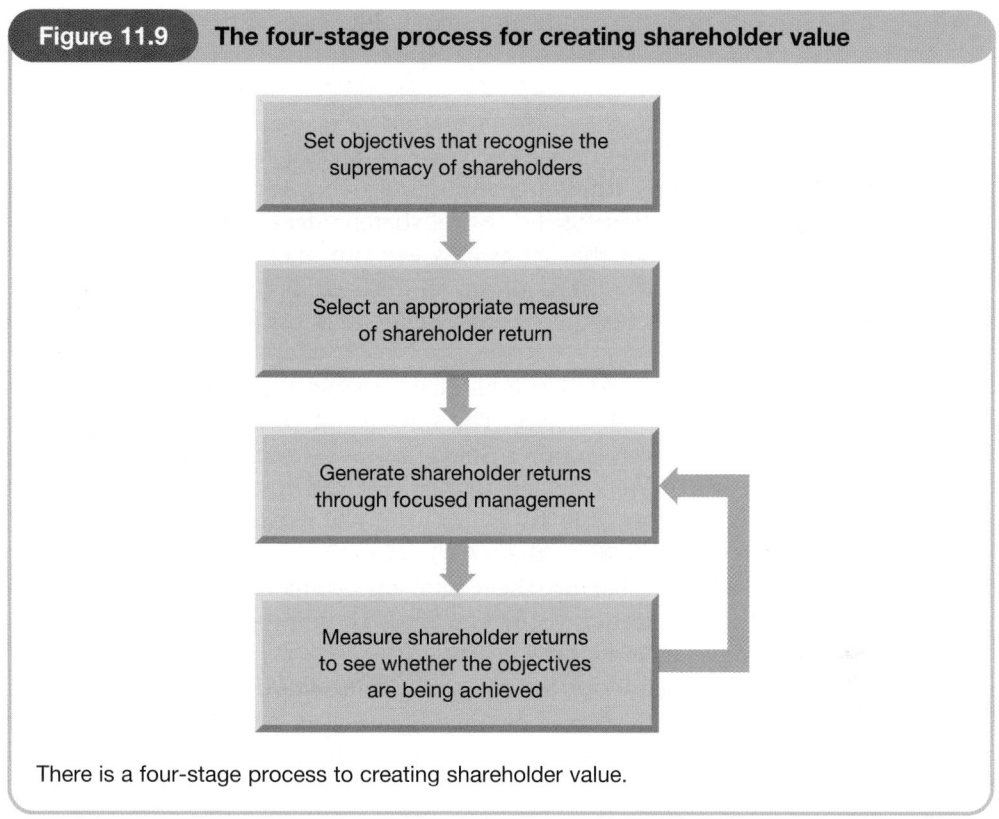

There is a four-stage process to creating shareholder value.

Activity (11.7)

What are the traditional methods of measuring shareholder returns?

The traditional approach is to use accounting profit or some ratio that is based on accounting profit, such as return on shareholders' funds or earnings per share.

There are broadly four problems with using accounting profit, or a ratio based on profit, to assess shareholder returns. These are:

- *Profit is measured over a relatively short period of time* (usually one year). However, when we talk about maximising shareholder returns, we are concerned with maximising returns over the *long term*. It has been suggested that using profit as the key measure will run the risk that managers will take decisions that improve performance in the short term, but which may have an adverse effect on long-term performance. For example, profits may be increased in the short term by cutting back on staff training and research expenditure. However, this type of expenditure may be vital to long-term survival.
- *Risk is ignored.* A fundamental business reality is that there is a clear relationship between the level of returns achieved and the level of risk that must be taken to achieve those returns. The higher the level of returns required, the higher the level of risk that must be taken to achieve the returns. A management strategy that produces

an increase in profits can reduce shareholder value if the increase in profits achieved is not commensurate with the increase in the level of risk. Thus, profit alone is not enough.

● *Accounting profit does not take account of all of the costs of the capital invested by the business.* The conventional approach to measuring profit will deduct the cost of borrowing (that is, interest charges) in arriving at profit for the period, but there is no similar deduction for the cost of shareholder funds. Critics of the conventional approach point out that a business will not make a profit, in an economic sense, unless it covers the cost of all capital invested, including shareholder funds. Unless the business achieves this, it will operate at a loss and so shareholder value will be reduced.

● *Accounting profit reported by a business can vary according to the particular accounting policies that have been adopted.* The way that accounting profit is measured can vary from one business to another. Some businesses adopt a very conservative approach, which would be reflected in particular accounting policies such as immediately treating some intangible assets (for example, research and development and good-will) as expenses ('writing them off') rather than retaining them on the statement of financial position (balance sheet) as assets. Similarly, the use of the reducing-balance method of depreciation (which means high depreciation charges in the early years) reduces profit in those early years.

Businesses that adopt less conservative accounting policies would report higher profits in the early years of owning depreciating assets. Writing off intangible assets over a long time period (or perhaps, not writing off intangible assets at all), the use of the straight-line method of depreciation and so on will have this effect. In addition, there may be some businesses that adopt particular accounting policies or carry out particular transactions in a way that paints a picture of financial health that is in line with what those who prepared the financial statements would like share-holders and other users to see, rather than what is a true and fair view of financial performance and position. This practice, known as 'creative accounting', was discussed in Chapter 5. It has been a major problem for accounting rule makers and for society generally.

Economic value added (EVA®)

→ **Economic value added (EVA®)** has been developed and trademarked by a US manage-ment consultancy firm, Stern Stewart. However, EVA® is based on the idea of economic profit, which has been around for many years. The measure reflects the point made earlier that, for a business to be profitable in an economic sense, it must generate returns that exceed the required returns of investors. It is not enough simply to make an accounting profit, because this measure does not take full account of the returns required by investors.

EVA® indicates whether or not the returns generated exceed the required returns by investors. The formula is as follows:

$$EVA® = NOPAT - (R \times C)$$

where:

NOPAT = net operating profit after tax
R = required returns of investors
C = capital invested (that is, the net assets of the business).

Only when EVA® is positive can we say that the business is increasing shareholder wealth. The higher the EVA®, the greater the increase in shareholder wealth.

Activity 11.8

Can you suggest what managers might do in order to increase EVA®? (*Hint*: Use the formula shown above as your starting point.)

The formula suggests that in order to increase EVA® managers may try to:

- Increase NOPAT. This may be done by reducing expenses and/or by increasing sales revenue.
- Reduce capital invested by using assets more efficiently. This means selling off any assets that are not generating adequate returns and investing in assets that are generating a satisfactory NOPAT.
- Reduce the required rates of return for investors. This may be achieved by changing the capital structure in favour of borrowing (which tends to be cheaper to service than share capital). However, this strategy can create problems.

EVA® relies on conventional financial statements (income statement and statement of financial position) to measure the wealth created for shareholders. However, the NOPAT and capital figures shown on these statements are used only as a starting point. They have to be adjusted because of the problems and limitations of conventional measures. According to Stern Stewart, the major problem is that both profit and capital tend to be understated because of the conservative bias in accounting measurement.

Profit is understated as a result of judgemental write-offs (such as goodwill written off or research and development expenditure written off) and as a result of excessive provisions being created (such as an allowance for trade receivables (bad debt provision)). Both of these stem from taking an unrealistically pessimistic view of the value of some of the business's assets.

Capital is also understated because assets are reported at their original cost (less amounts written off for depreciation and so on), which can produce figures considerably below current market values. In addition, certain assets, such as internally generated goodwill and brand names, are omitted from the financial statements because no external transactions have occurred.

Stern Stewart has identified more than 100 adjustments that could be made to the conventional financial statements in order to eliminate the conservative bias. However, it is believed that, in practice, only a handful of adjustments will usually have to be made to the accounting figures of any particular business. Unless an adjustment is going to have a significant effect on the calculation of EVA® it is really not worth making. The adjustments made should reflect the nature of the particular business. Each business is unique and so must customise the calculation of EVA® to its particular circumstances. (This aspect of EVA® can be seen as either indicating flexibility or as being open to manipulation depending on whether or not you support this measure.)

The most common adjustments that have to be made include:

- *Research and development (R&D) costs and marketing costs*. These costs should be written off over the period that they benefit. In practice, however, they are often written off in the period in which they are incurred. This means that any amounts written off immediately should be added back to the assets on the statement of financial position, thereby increasing invested capital, and then written off over time.
- *Restructuring costs*. This item can be viewed as an investment in the future rather than an expense to be written off. Supporters of EVA® argue that by restructuring, the business is better placed to meet future challenges and so any amounts incurred should be added back to assets.
- *Marketable investments*. Investment in shares and loan notes of other businesses are not included as part of the capital invested in the business. This is because the income from marketable investments is not included in the calculation of operating profit. (Income from this source will be added in the income statement *after* operating profit has been calculated.)

Let us now consider a simple example to show how EVA® may be calculated.

Example 11.4

Scorpio plc was established two years ago and has produced the following statement of financial position and income statement at the end of the second year of trading.

Statement of financial position as at the end of the second year

ASSETS	£m
Non-current assets	
Plant and equipment	80.0
Motor vehicles	12.4
Marketable investments	6.6
	99.0
Current assets	
Inventories	34.5
Receivables	29.3
Cash	2.1
	65.9
Total assets	164.9
EQUITY AND LIABILITIES	
Equity	
Share capital	60.0
Retained earnings	23.7
	83.7
Non-current liabilities	
Loan notes	50.0
Current liabilities	
Trade payables	30.3
Taxation	0.9
	31.2
Total equity and liabilities	164.9

Income statement for the second year

	£m
Sales revenue	148.6
Cost of sales	(76.2)
Gross profit	72.4
Wages	(24.5)
Depreciation of plant and equipment	(12.8)
Marketing costs	(22.5)
Allowances for trade receivables	(4.5)
Operating profit	8.1
Income from investments	0.4
	8.5
Interest payable	(0.5)
Ordinary profit before taxation	8.0
Restructuring costs	(2.0)
Profit before taxation	6.0
Tax	(1.8)
Profit for the year	4.2

Discussions with the finance director reveal the following:

1 Marketing costs relate to the launch of a new product. The benefits of the marketing campaign are expected to last for three years (including this most recent year).

2 The allowance for trade receivables was created this year and the amount is considered to be very high. A more realistic figure for the allowance would be £2.0 million.

3 Restructuring costs were incurred as a result of a collapse in a particular product market. As a result of the restructuring, benefits are expected to flow for an infinite period.

4 The business has a 10 per cent required rate of return for investors.

The first step in calculating EVA® is to adjust the net operating profit after tax to take account of the various points revealed from the discussion with the finance director. The revised figure is calculated as follows:

NOPAT adjustment	£m	£m
Operating profit		8.1
Less Tax		(1.8)
		6.3
EVA® adjustments (to be added back to profit)		
Marketing costs ($^2/_3 \times 22.5$)	15.0	
Excess allowance	2.5	17.5
Adjusted NOPAT		23.8

The next step is to adjust the net assets (as represented by equity and loan notes) to take account of the points revealed.

→

Adjusted net assets (or capital invested)

	£m	£m
Net assets per statement of financial position		133.7
Marketing costs (Note 1)	15.0	
Allowance for trade receivables	2.5	
Restructuring costs (Note 2)	2.0	19.5
		153.2
Marketable investments (Note 3)		(6.6)
Adjusted net assets		146.6

Notes:

(1) The marketing costs represent two years' benefits added back ($^2/_3 \times$ £22.5m).

(2) The restructuring costs are added back to the net assets as they provide benefits over an infinite period. (Note they were not added back to the operating profit as these costs were deducted after arriving at operating profit in the income statement.)

(3) The marketable investments do not form part of the operating assets of the business and the income from these investments is not part of the operating income.

Activity 11.9

Can you work out the EVA® for the second year of the business in Example 11.4?

EVA® can be calculated as follows:

$$EVA^{®} = NOPAT - (R \times C)$$
$$= £23.8m - (10\% \times £146.6m)$$
$$= £9.1m \text{ (to one decimal place)}$$

We can see that EVA® is positive and so the business increased shareholder wealth during the year.

The main advantage of this measure is the discipline to which managers are subjected as a result of the charge for capital that has been invested. Before any increase in shareholder wealth can be recognised, an appropriate deduction is made for the use of business resources. Thus, EVA® encourages managers to use these resources efficiently. Where managers are focused simply on increasing profits, there is a danger that the resources used to achieve any increase in profits will not be taken into proper account.

Although EVA® is used by many large businesses, both in the US and Europe, it tends to be used for management purposes only: few businesses report this measure to shareholders. One business that does, however, is Whole Foods Market, a leading retailer of natural and organic foods, which operates more than 270 stores in the US and the UK. **Real World 11.14** below describes the way in which the business uses EVA® and the results of doing so.

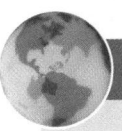

Real World 11.14

The whole picture

Whole Foods Market aims to improve its business by achieving improvements to EVA®. To encourage managers along this path, an incentive plan based on improvements to EVA® has been introduced. The plan embraces senior executives, regional managers and store managers and the bonuses awarded form a significant part of their total remuneration. To make the incentive plan work, measures of EVA® based on the whole business, the regional level and the store level are calculated. More than five hundred managers are already included in the incentive plan and this number is expected to increase in the future.

EVA® is used to evaluate capital investment decisions such as the acquisition of new stores and the refurbishment of existing stores. Unless there is clear evidence that value will be added, investment proposals are rejected. EVA® is also used to improve operational efficiency. It was mentioned earlier that one way in which EVA® can be increased is through an improvement in NOPAT. The business is, therefore, continually seeking ways to improve sales and profit margins and to bear down on costs.

EVA® for 2005 and 2006 are shown below. The relevant tax rate for each year was 40% and the cost of capital was 9%.

Years ended:	24 September 2006	25 September 2005
	$000	$000
NOPAT	215,281	165,579
Capital cost	(150,871)	(139,793)
EVA®	64,410	25,786
Improvement in EVA®	38,624	

Source: www.wholefoodsmarket.com.

Summary

The main points of this chapter may be summarised as follows:

Activity-based costing is an approach to dealing with overheads (in full costing) that treats all costs as being caused or 'driven' by activities. Advocates argue that it is more relevant to the modern commercial environment than is the traditional approach.

● It involves identifying the support activities and their costs and then analysing these costs to see what drives them.

● The costs of each support activity enter a cost pool and the relevant cost drivers are used to attach an amount of overheads from this pool to each unit of output.

● ABC should help provide more accurate costs for each unit of output and should help in better control of overheads.

● ABC is however time-consuming and costly, can involve measurement problems and is not likely to suit all businesses.

Other costing methods

- Total (whole) life-cycle costing takes account of all of the costs incurred over a product's entire life.
- The life cycle of a product can be broken down into three phases: pre-production, production and post-production.
- A high proportion of costs is incurred and/or committed during the pre-production phase.
- Target costing attempts to reduce costs so that the market price covers the cost plus an acceptable profit.
- Ensuring quality output has costs, known as *quality costs*, typically divided into four aspects: prevention costs, appraisal costs, internal failure costs and external failure costs.
- *Kaizen* costing attempts to reduce costs at the production stage.
- Since most costs will have been saved at the pre-production phase and through target costing, only small cost savings are likely to be possible.
- Value chain analysis involves analysing the various activities in the product life cycle to identify and to try to eliminate non-value-added activities.
- Benchmarking attempts to emulate a successful aspect of, for example, another business or division.

Non-financial measures of performance

- Non-financial measures are increasingly being used to manage the business.
- The balanced scorecard is a management tool that uses financial and non-financial measures to assess progress towards objectives.
- It has four aspects: financial, customer, internal business process, and learning and growth.
- It encourages a balanced approach to managing the business.

Value-based management

- Shareholder value is seen as the key objective of most businesses.
- One approach used to measure shareholder value is economic value added (EVA®).
- Economic value added is a means of measuring whether the returns generated by the business exceed the required returns of investors.

$$EVA^{®} = NOPAT - (R \times C)$$

where:

NOPAT = net operating profit after tax
  R = required returns from investors
  C = capital invested (that is, the net assets of the business).

MyAccountingLab | *Now check your progress in your personal Study Plan*

Key terms

activity-based costing (ABC) p. 397	*kaizen* **costing** p. 412
cost driver p. 397	**value chain analysis** p. 412
cost pool p. 398	**benchmarking** p. 414
total life-cycle costing p. 408	**value driver** p. 415
target costing p. 410	**balanced scorecard** p. 418
quality costs p. 411	**economic value added (EVA®)** p. 426

Reference

1 **The Balanced Scorecard**, *Kaplan R. and Norton D.*, Harvard Business School Press, 1996.

Further reading

If you would like to explore the topics covered in this chapter in more depth, we recommend the following books:

Cost Accounting: A Managerial Emphasis, *Horngren C., Foster G., Datar S., Rajan M. and Ittner C.*, 13th edn, Prentice Hall International, 2008, chapters 5 and 12.

Management Accounting, *Atkinson A., Banker R., Kaplan R. and Young S. M.*, 5th edn, Prentice Hall, 2007, chapters 4, 5, 6 and 9.

Management and Cost Accounting, *Drury C.*, 7th edn, Cengage Learning, 2007, chapters 10 and 11.

Managerial Accounting, *Hilton R.*, 6th edn, McGraw-Hill Irwin, 2005, chapters 4, 5, 6 and 15.

Review questions

Answers to these questions can be found at the back of the book on pages 746–7.

11.1 How does activity-based costing differ from the traditional approach? What is the underlying difference in the philosophy of each of them?

11.2 The use of activity-based costing in helping to deduce full costs has been criticised. What has tended to be the basis of this criticism?

11.3 What are the four main areas on which the balanced scorecard is based?

11.4 Derry and Co. is a large computer consultancy business that has a division specialising in robotics. Can you identify three *non-financial measures* that might be used to help assess the performance of this division?

Exercises

Exercises 11.4 and 11.6 to 11.8 are more advanced than 11.1, 11.2, 11.3 and 11.5. Those with **coloured numbers** have answers at the back of the book, starting on page 782.

If you wish to try more exercises, visit the students' side of the Companion Website and MyAccountingLab.

11.1 Aires plc was recently formed and issued 80 million £0.50 shares at nominal value and loan notes of £24 million. The business used the proceeds from the capital issues to purchase the remaining lease on some commercial properties that are rented out to small businesses. The lease will expire in four years' time and during that period the operating profits are expected to be £12 million each year. At the end of the four years, the business will be wound up and the lease will have no residual value.

The required rate of return by investors is 12 per cent.

Required:
Calculate the expected shareholder value generated by the business in each of the four years, using the EVA® approach.

11.2 Comment critically on the following statements that you have overheard:

(a) 'The balanced scorecard is another name for the statement of financial position.'
(b) 'The financial area of the balanced scorecard is, in effect the income statement of the business and measures the profit for the period.'
(c) 'Adopting the balanced scorecard approach means accepting a particular set of targets that were set out by Kaplan and Norton.'
(d) 'The balanced scorecard approach tends to take little notice of financial objectives.'

11.3 Kaplan plc makes a range of suitcases of various sizes and shapes. There are 10 different models of suitcase produced by the business. In order to keep inventories of finished suitcases to a minimum, each model is made in a small batch. Each batch is costed as a separate job and the cost for each suitcase deduced by dividing the batch cost by the number of suitcases in the batch.

At present, the business derives the cost of each batch using a traditional job-costing approach. Recently, however, a new management accountant was appointed, who is advocating the use of activity-based costing (ABC) to deduce the cost of the batches. The management accountant claims that ABC leads to much more reliable and relevant costs and that it has other benefits.

Required:

(a) Explain how the business deduces the cost of each suitcase at present.

(b) Explain how ABC could be applied to costing the suitcases, highlighting the differences between ABC and the traditional approach.

(c) Explain what advantages the new management accountant probably believes ABC to have over the traditional approach.

11.4 Pisces plc produced the following statement of financial position and income statement at the end of the third year of trading:

Statement of financial position (balance sheet) as at the end of the third year

	£m
ASSETS	
Non-current assets	
Property	40.0
Machinery and equipment	80.0
Motor vans	18.6
Marketable investments	9.0
	147.6
Current assets	
Inventories	45.8
Trade receivables	64.6
Cash	1.0
	111.4
Total assets	259.0
EQUITY AND LIABILITIES	
Equity	
Share capital	80.0
Reserves	36.5
	116.5
Non-current liabilities	
Loan notes	80.0
Current liabilities	
Trade payables	62.5
	259.0

Income statement for the third year

	£m
Sales revenue	231.5
Cost of sales	(143.2)
Gross profit	88.3
Wages	(43.5)
Depreciation of machinery and equipment	(14.8)
R&D costs	(40.0)
Allowance for trade receivables	(10.5)
Operating loss	(20.5)
Income from investments	0.6
	(19.9)
Interest payable	(0.8)
Ordinary loss before taxation	(20.7)
Restructuring costs	(6.0)
Loss before taxation	(26.7)
Tax	–
Loss for the year	(26.7)

An analysis of the underlying records reveals the following:

(1) R&D costs relate to the development of a new product in the previous year. These costs are written off over a two-year period (starting last year). However, this is a prudent approach and the benefits are expected to last for 16 years.

(2) The allowance for trade receivables (bad debts) was created this year and the amount of the provision is very high. A more realistic figure for the allowance would be £4 million.

(3) Restructuring costs were incurred at the beginning of the year and are expected to provide benefits for an infinite period.

(4) The business has a 7 per cent required rate of return for investors.

Required:
Calculate the EVA® for the business for the third year of trading.

11.5 Comment critically on the following statements that you have overheard:

(a) 'Direct labour hours are the most appropriate basis to use to charge indirect cost (overheads) to jobs in the modern manufacturing environment where people are so important.'

(b) 'Activity-based costing is a means of more accurately accounting for direct labour cost.'

(c) 'Activity-based costing cannot really be applied to the service sector because the "activities" that it seeks to analyse tend to be related to manufacturing.'

(d) '*Kaizen* costing is an approach where great efforts are made to reduce the costs of developing a new product and setting up its production processes.'

(e) 'Benchmarking is an approach to job costing where each direct worker keeps a record of the time spent on each job on his or her workbench before it is passed on to the next direct worker or into finished inventories (stock) stores.'

11.6 Badger Ltd (Badger) manufactures plastic building materials. After a recent analysis Badger has decided to classify its products into two varieties: Largeflo and Smallflo. There are several products in each of these two categories. Largeflo are produced on large machines by a simple process. Smallflo are manufactured on small machines by a more complex process with more production stages. The previous pricing policy has been to absorb all overheads using direct labour hours to obtain total cost. Price is then calculated as total cost plus a 35 per cent mark-up.

The recent analysis has also examined overhead costs; the results are shown below. Set-up costs are incurred for each production stage for each batch. The ordering costs for bought-in parts are incurred initially for each production type.

Analysis of overhead costs

	cost per month £	monthly volume
Large machine cost	96,000	480 hours
Small machine cost	44,800	1,280 hours
Set-up costs	32,500	260 set-ups
Ordering bought-in parts	10,800	120 different parts
Handling charges	45,600	380 movements
Other overheads	50,300	
	280,000	–

There are 4,000 direct labour hours available each month.

Details for a typical Largeflo product (one of several Largeflo products) and a typical Smallflo product (again, one of several Smallflo products) are shown below.

	Largeflo	Smallflo
Monthly volume	1,000 units	500 units
Batch size	1,000 units	50 units
Machine time per batch		
– large	100 hours	–
– small	–	25 hours
Number of bought-in parts	–	3 per product type
Set-ups	1 per batch	2 per batch
Handling charges	1 movement per batch	5 movements per batch
Materials per unit	£16	£15
Direct labour per unit	½ hour	½ hour

Direct labour is charged at £16 per hour.

Required:

(a) Calculate the price for each of the Largeflo and Smallflo products detailed above, using traditional absorption costing based on direct labour hours.

(b) Calculate the price for the Largeflo and Smallflo products using activity-based costing. Assume that 'Other overheads' are allocated using direct labour hours.

(c) Outline the points that you would raise with the management of Badger in the light of your answers to (a) and (b).

(d) Outline the practical problems that may be encountered in implementing activity-based techniques and comment on how they may be overcome.

11.7 Sillycon Ltd is a business engaged in the development of new products in the electronics industry. Subtotals on the spreadsheet of planned overheads reveal:

	Electronics department	Testing department	Service department
Overheads: variable (£000)	1,200	600	700
fixed (£000)	2,000	500	800
Planned activity: Direct labour hours ('000)	800	600	

The three departments are cost centres.

For the purposes of reallocation of service department's overheads, it is agreed that variable overhead costs vary with the direct labour hours worked in each cost centre. Fixed overheads of the service cost centre are to be reallocated on the basis of maximum practical capacity of the two product cost centres, which is the same for each.

The business has a long-standing practice of marking up full manufacturing costs by between 25 per cent and 35 per cent in order to establish selling prices.

One new product, which is in a final development stage, is hoped to offer some improvement over competitors' products, which are currently marketed at between £90 and £110 each. Product development engineers have determined that the direct material content is £7 a unit. The product will take 2 labour hours in the electronics department and 1½ hours in testing. Hourly labour rates are £20 and £12, respectively.

Management estimates that the fixed costs that would be specifically incurred in relation to the product are: supervision £13,000, depreciation of a recently acquired machine £100,000 and advertising £37,000 a year. These fixed costs are included in the table given above.

Market research indicates that the business could expect to obtain and hold about 25 per cent of the market or, optimistically, 30 per cent. The total market is estimated at 20,000 units.

Note: It may be assumed that the existing plan has been prepared to cater for a range of products and no single product decision will cause the business to amend it.

Required:
(a) Prepare a summary of information that would help with the pricing decision for the new product. Such information should include marginal cost and full cost implications after allocation of service department overheads.
(b) Explain and elaborate on the information prepared.

11.8 A business manufactures refrigerators for domestic use. There are three models: Lo, Mid and Hi. The models, their quality and their price are aimed at different markets.

Product costs are computed on a blanket (business-wide) overhead-rate basis using a labour hour method. Prices as a general rule are set based on cost plus 20 per cent. The following information is provided:

	Lo	Mid	Hi
Material cost (£/unit)	25	62.5	105
Direct labour hours (per unit)	½	1	1
Budget production/sales (units)	20,000	1,000	10,000

The budgeted overheads for the business amount to £4,410,000. Direct labour is costed at £8 an hour.

The business is currently facing increasing competition, especially from imported goods. As a result, the selling price of Lo has been reduced to a level that produces a very low profit margin. To address this problem, an activity-based costing approach has been suggested. The overheads are examined and these are grouped around main business activities of machining (£2,780,000), logistics (£590,000) and establishment (£1,040,000) costs. It is maintained that these costs could be allocated based respectively on cost drivers of machine hours, material orders and space, to reflect the use of resources in each of these areas. After analysis, the following proportionate statistics are available related to the total volume of products:

	Lo	Mid	Hi
	%	%	%
Machine hours	40	15	45
Material orders	47	6	47
Space	42	18	40

Required:
(a) Calculate for each product the full cost and selling price determined by:
  (1) The original costing method.
  (2) The activity-based costing method.
(b) What are the implications of the two systems of costing in the situation given?
(c) What business/strategic options exist for the business in the light of the new information?

CHAPTER 12

Budgeting

Introduction

In this chapter we consider the role and nature of budgets. In its 2008 annual report, BSkyB Group plc, the satellite television broadcaster, said:

> There is a comprehensive budgeting and forecasting process, and the annual budget, which is regularly reviewed and updated, is approved by the board [of directors].

As we shall see later, the practice at BSkyB is typical of businesses of all sizes.

What is a budget? What is it for? How is it prepared? Who prepares it? Why does the board regard it as important enough to concern itself with? We will be looking at the answers to each of these questions in the course of this chapter. In addition, we will see that budgets set out short-term plans that help managers to run the business. They provide the means to assess whether actual performance has gone as planned and, where it has not, to identify the reasons for this.

It is important to recognise that budgets do not exist in a vacuum; they are an integral part of a planning framework that is adopted by well-run businesses. To understand fully the nature of budgets we must, therefore, understand the strategic planning framework within which they are set.

Preparing budgets relies on an understanding of many of the issues relating to the behaviour of costs and full costing, topics that we explored in Chapters 9 and 10. The chapter begins with a discussion of the budgeting framework and then goes on to consider detailed aspects of the budgeting process.

Learning outcomes

When you have completed this chapter, you should be able to:

- Define a budget and show how budgets, strategic objectives and strategic plans are related.
- Explain the budgeting process and the interlinking of the various budgets within the business.
- Indicate the uses of budgeting and construct various budgets, including the cash budget, from relevant data.
- Discuss the criticisms that are made of budgeting.

 Remember to create your own personalised Study Plan

How budgets link with strategic plans and objectives

It is vital that businesses develop plans for the future. Whatever a business is trying to achieve, it is unlikely to come about unless its managers are clear what the future direction of the business is going to be. The development of plans involves five key steps:

1 *Establish mission and objectives*

→ The **mission statement** sets out the ultimate purpose of the business. It is a broad statement of intent, whereas the strategic objectives are more specific and will usually include quantifiable goals.

2 *Undertake a position analysis*

This involves an assessment of where the business is currently placed in relation to where it wants to be, as set out in its mission and strategic objectives.

3 *Identify and assess the strategic options*

The business must explore the various ways in which it might move from where it is now (identified in step 2) to where it wants to be (identified in step 1).

4 *Select strategic options and formulate plans*

This involves selecting what seems to be the best of the courses of action or strategies (identified in step 3) and formulating a long-term strategic plan. This strategic plan is then normally broken down into a series of short-term plans, one

→ for each element of the business. These plans are the budgets. Thus, a **budget** is a business plan for the short term – typically one year – and is expressed mainly in financial terms. Its role is to convert the strategic plans into actionable blueprints for the immediate future. Budgets will define precise targets concerning such things as:

● Cash receipts and payments
● Sales volumes and revenues, broken down into amounts and prices for each of the products or services provided by the business
● Detailed inventories requirements
● Detailed labour requirements
● Specific production requirements.

5 *Perform, review and control*

Here the business pursues the budgets derived in step 4. By comparing the actual outcome with the budgets, managers can see if things are going according to plan or not. Action would be taken to exercise control where actual performance appears not to be matching the budgets.

Activity 12.1

The approach described in step 3 above suggests that managers will systematically collect information and then carefully evaluate all the options available. Do you think this is what managers really do?

In practice, managers may not be as rational and capable as implied in the process described. They may find it difficult to handle a wealth of information relating to a wide range of options. To avoid becoming overloaded, they may restrict their range of possible options and/or discard some information. Managers may also adopt rather simple approaches to evaluating the mass of information provided. These approaches might not lead to the best decisions being made.

From the above description of the planning process, we can see that the relationship between the mission, strategic objectives, strategic plans and budgets can be summarised as follows:

- the mission sets the overall direction and, once set, is likely to last for quite a long time – perhaps throughout the life of the business;
- the strategic objectives, which are also long-term, will set out how the mission can be achieved;
- the strategic plans identify how each objective will be pursued; and
- the budgets set out, in detail, the short-term plans and targets necessary to fulfil the strategic objectives.

An analogy might be found in terms of a student enrolling on a course of study. His or her mission might be to have a happy and fulfilling life. A key strategic objective flowing from this mission might be to embark on a career that will be rewarding in various ways. He or she might have identified the particular study course as the most effective way to work towards this objective. Successfully completing the course would then be the strategic plan. In working towards this strategic plan, passing a particular stage of the course might be identified as the target for the forthcoming year. This short-term target is analogous to the budget. Having achieved the 'budget' for the first year, the budget for the second year becomes passing the second stage.

Collecting information on performance and exercising control

However well planned the activities of a business might be, they will come to nothing unless steps are taken to try to achieve them in practice. The process of making planned events actually occur is known as **control**. This is part of step 5 (above).

Control can be defined as compelling events to conform to plan. This definition is valid in any context. For example, when we talk about controlling a motor car, we mean making the car do what we plan that it should do. In a business context, management accounting is very useful in the control process. This is because it is possible to state many plans in accounting terms (as budgets). Since it is also possible to state *actual* outcomes in the same terms, making comparison between actual and planned outcomes is a relatively simple matter. Where actual outcomes are at variance with budgets, this variance should be highlighted by accounting information. Managers can then take steps to get the business back on track towards the achievement of the budgets. We shall be looking quite closely at the control aspect of budgeting in Chapter 13.

Figure 12.1 shows the planning and control process in diagrammatic form.

It should be emphasised that planning (including budgeting) is the responsibility of managers rather than accountants. Though accountants should play a role in the planning process, by supplying relevant information to managers and by contributing to decision making as part of the management team, they should not dominate the process. In practice, it seems that the budgeting aspect of planning is often in danger of being dominated by accountants, perhaps because most budgets are expressed in financial terms. However, managers are failing in their responsibilities if they allow this to happen.

Figure 12.1   The planning and control process

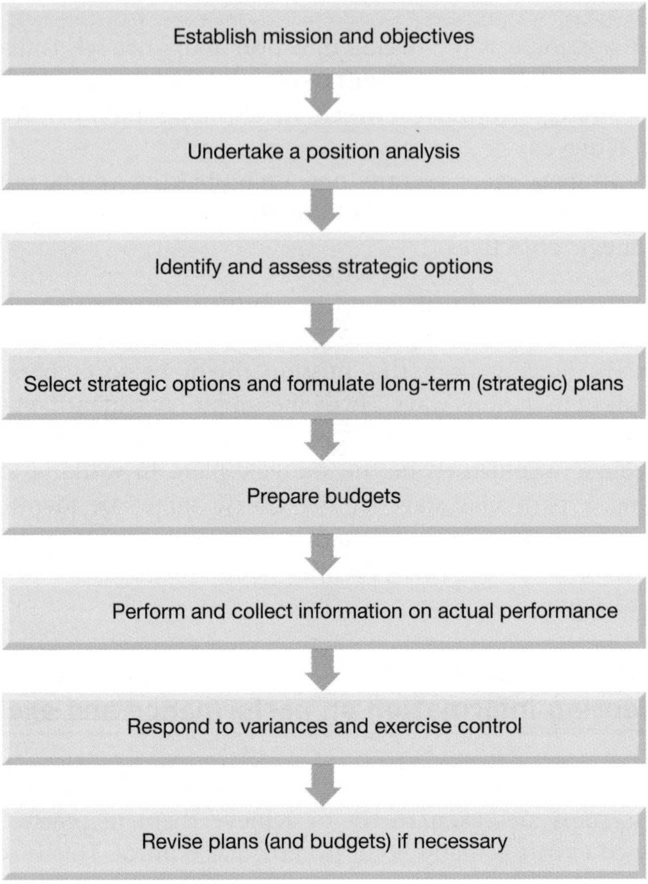

Establish mission and objectives

↓

Undertake a position analysis

↓

Identify and assess strategic options

↓

Select strategic options and formulate long-term (strategic) plans

↓

Prepare budgets

↓

Perform and collect information on actual performance

↓

Respond to variances and exercise control

↓

Revise plans (and budgets) if necessary

Once the mission and objectives of the business have been determined, the various strategic options available must be considered and evaluated in order to derive a strategic plan. The budget is a short-term financial plan for the business that is prepared within the framework of the strategic plan. Control can be exercised through the comparison of budgeted and actual performance. Where a significant divergence emerges, some form of corrective action should be taken. If the budget figures prove to be based on incorrect assumptions about the future, it might be necessary to revise the budget.

Time horizon of plans and budgets

Setting strategic plans is typically a major exercise performed about every five years and budgets are usually set annually for the forthcoming year. It need not necessarily be the case that strategic plans are set for five years and that budgets are set for one year; it is up to the management of the business concerned. Businesses involved in certain industries – say, information technology – may feel that five years is too long a planning period since new developments can, and do, occur virtually overnight. Here, a planning horizon of two or three years is more feasible. Similarly, a budget need not be set for one year, although this appears to be a widely used time horizon.

Activity (12.2)

Can you think of any reason why most businesses prepare detailed budgets for the forthcoming year, rather than for a shorter or longer period?

The reason is probably that a year represents a long enough time for the budget preparation exercise to be worthwhile, yet short enough into the future for detailed plans to be capable of being made. As we shall see later in this chapter, the process of formulating budgets can be a time-consuming exercise, but there are economies of scale – for example, preparing the budget for the next year would not normally take twice as much time and effort as preparing the budget for the next six months.

An annual budget sets targets for the forthcoming year for all aspects of the business. It is usually broken down into monthly budgets, which define monthly targets. Indeed, in many instances, the annual budget will be built up from monthly figures. For example, the sales staff may be required to set sales targets for each month of the budget period. In many cases the sales target will differ from month to month – many businesses experience seasonal demand variations. Other budgets will be set for each month of the budget period, as we shall explain below.

Limiting factors

Some aspect of the business will, inevitably, stop it achieving its objectives to the maximum extent. This is often a limited ability of the business to sell its products. Sometimes, it is some production shortage (such as labour, materials or plant) that is the **limiting factor**, or, linked to these, a shortage of funds. Often, production shortages can be overcome by an increase in funds – for example, more plant can be bought or leased. This is not always a practical solution, because no amount of money will buy certain labour skills or increase the world supply of some raw material.

Easing an initial limiting factor may sometimes be possible. For example, subcontracting can eliminate a plant capacity problem. This means that some other factor, perhaps lack of sales demand, will replace the production problem, though at a higher level of output. Ultimately, however, the business will hit a ceiling; some limiting factor will prove impossible to ease.

The limiting factor must be identified. Ultimately, most, if not all, budgets will be affected by the limiting factor, and so if it can be identified at the outset, all managers can be informed of the restriction early in the process. When preparing the budgets, account can then be taken of the limiting factor.

Budgets and forecasts

A budget may, as we have already seen, be defined as a business plan for the short term. Budgets are, to a great extent, expressed in financial terms. Note particularly that a budget is a *plan*, not a forecast. To talk of a plan suggests an intention or determination to achieve the targets; **forecasts** tend to be predictions of the future state of the environment.

Clearly, forecasts are very helpful to the planner/budget-setter. If, for example, a reputable forecaster has predicted the number of new cars to be purchased in the UK during next year, it will be valuable for a manager in a car manufacturing business to take account of this information when setting next year's sales budgets. However, a forecast and a budget are distinctly different.

Periodic and continual budgets

→ Budgeting can be undertaken on a periodic or a continual basis. A **periodic budget** is prepared for a particular period (usually one year). Managers will agree the budget for the year and then allow the budget to run its course. Although it may be necessary to revise the budget on occasions, preparing the budget is in essence a one-off exercise

→ during each financial year. A **continual budget**, as the name suggests, is continually updated. We have seen that an annual budget will normally be broken down into smaller time intervals (usually monthly periods) to help control the activities of a business. A continual budget will add a new month to replace the month that has just passed, thereby ensuring that, at all times, there will be a budget for a full planning

→ period. Continual budgets are also referred to as **rolling budgets**.

Activity (12.3)

Which method of budgeting do you think is likely to be more costly and which method is likely to be more beneficial for forward planning?

Periodic budgeting will usually take less time and effort and will, therefore, be less costly. However, as time passes, the budget period shortens and towards the end of the financial year managers will be working to a very short planning period indeed. Continual budgeting, on the other hand, will ensure that managers always have a full year's budget to help them make decisions. It is claimed that continual budgeting ensures that managers plan throughout the year rather than just once each year. In this way it encourages a forward-looking attitude.

While continual budgeting encourages a forward-looking attitude, there is a danger that budgeting will become a mechanical exercise, as managers may not have time to step back from their other tasks each month and consider the future carefully. Continually taking this future-oriented perspective may be difficult for managers to sustain.

Continual budgets do not appear to be very popular in practice. A recent study of 340 senior financial staff of small, medium and large businesses in North America revealed that only 9 per cent of businesses use them (see reference 1 at the end of the chapter).

How budgets link to one another

A business will prepare more than one budget for a particular period. Each budget prepared will relate to a specific aspect of the business. The ideal situation is probably that there should be a separate operating budget for each person who is in a managerial position, no matter how junior. The contents of all of the individual operating budgets will be summarised in **master budgets** usually consisting of a budgeted income statement and statement of financial position (balance sheet). The cash budget is considered by some to be a third master budget.

Figure 12.2 illustrates the interrelationship and interlinking of individual operating budgets, in this particular case using a manufacturing business as an example.

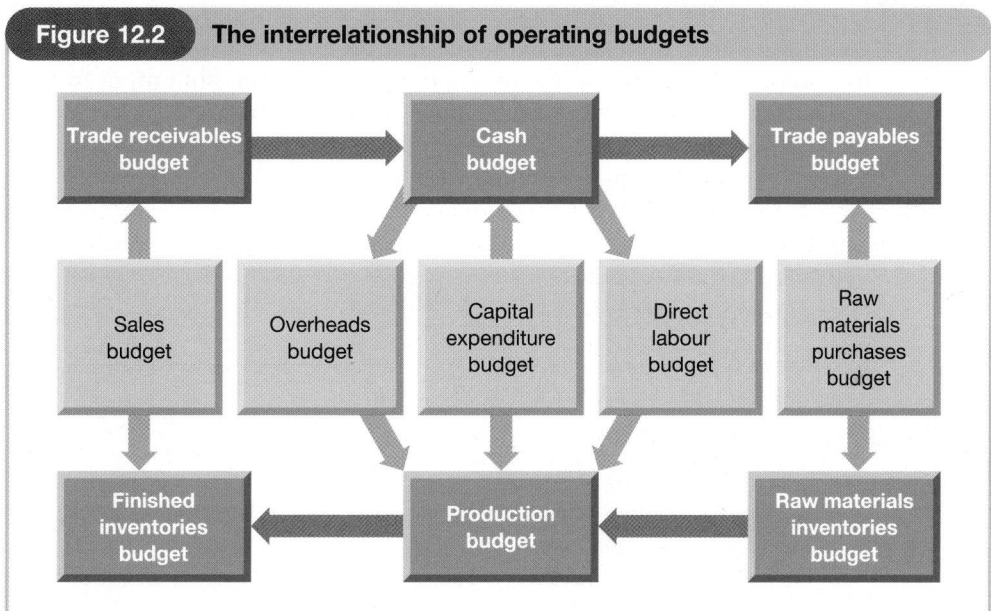

Figure 12.2   The interrelationship of operating budgets

The starting point is usually the sales budget. The expected level of sales normally defines the overall level of activity for the business, and the other operating budgets will be drawn up in accordance with this. Thus, the sales budget will largely define the finished inventories requirements, and from this we can define the production requirements and so on. This shows the interrelationship of operating budgets for a manufacturing business.

The sales budget is usually the first one to be prepared (at the left of Figure 12.2), as the level of sales often determines the overall level of activity for the forthcoming period. This is because it is probably the most common limiting factor (see page 443). The finished inventories requirement tends to be set by the level of sales, though it would also be dictated by the policy of the business on the level of the finished products inventories. The requirement for finished inventories will define the required production levels, which will, in turn, dictate the requirements of the individual production departments or sections. The demands of manufacturing, in conjunction with the business's policy on how long it holds raw materials before they enter production, define the raw materials inventories budget. The purchases budget will be dictated by the materials inventories budget, which will, in conjunction with the policy of the business on taking credit from suppliers, dictate the trade payables budget. One of the determinants of the cash budget will be the trade payables budget; another will be the trade receivables budget, which itself derives, through the business's policy on credit periods granted to credit customers, from the sales budget. Cash will also be affected by overheads and direct labour costs (themselves linked to production) and by capital expenditure. Cash will also be affected by new finance and redemption of existing sources. (This is not shown in Figure 12.2 because the diagram focuses only on budgets concerned with operational matters.) The factors that affect policies on matters such as inventories holding, trade receivables collection and trade payables payment periods will be discussed in some detail in Chapter 16.

A manufacturing business has been used as the example in Figure 12.2 simply because it has all of the types of operating budgets found in practice. Service businesses have similar arrangements of budgets, but obviously may not have inventories budgets. All of the issues relating to budgets apply equally well to all types of business.

Sales demand is not necessarily the limiting factor. Assuming that the budgeting process takes the order just described, it might be found in practice that there is some constraint other than sales demand. The production capacity of the business may, for example, be incapable of meeting the necessary levels of output to match the sales budget for one or more months. Finding a practical way of overcoming the problem may be possible. As a last resort, it might be necessary to revise the sales budget to a lower level to match the production limitation.

Activity 12.4

Can you think of any ways in which a short-term shortage of production facilities of a manufacturer might be overcome?

We thought of the following:

- Higher production in previous months and increasing inventories ('stockpiling') to meet periods of higher demand.
- Increasing production capacity, perhaps by working overtime and/or acquiring (buying or leasing) additional plant.
- Subcontracting some production.
- Encouraging potential customers to change the timing of their purchases by offering discounts or other special terms during the months that have been identified as quiet.

You might well have thought of other approaches.

There will be the horizontal relationships between budgets, which we have just looked at, but there will usually be vertical ones as well. Breaking down the sales budget into a number of subsidiary budgets, perhaps one for each regional sales manager, is a common approach. The overall sales budget will be a summary of the subsidiary ones. The same may be true of virtually all of the other budgets, most particularly the production budget.

Figure 12.3 shows the vertical relationship of the sales budgets for a business. The business has four geographical sales regions, each one the responsibility of a separate manager, who is probably located in the region concerned. Each regional manager is responsible to the overall sales manager of the business. The overall sales budget is the sum of the budgets for the four sales regions.

Although sales are often managed on a geographical basis, and so their budgets reflect this, sales may be managed on some other basis. For example, a business that sells a range of products may manage sales on a product-type basis, with a specialist manager responsible for each type of product. Thus, an insurance business may have separate sales managers, and so separate sales budgets, for life insurance, household

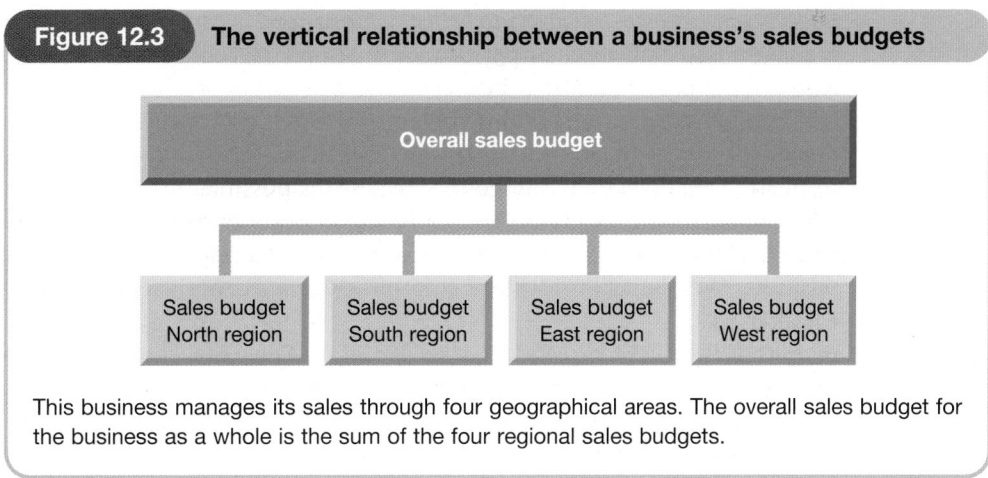

Figure 12.3 **The vertical relationship between a business's sales budgets**

This business manages its sales through four geographical areas. The overall sales budget for the business as a whole is the sum of the four regional sales budgets.

insurance, motor insurance and so on. Very large businesses may even have separate product-type managers for each geographical region. Each of these managers would have a separate budget, which would combine to form the overall sales budget for the business as a whole.

All of the operating budgets that we have just reviewed must mesh with the master budgets, that is, the budgeted income statement and statement of financial position.

How budgets help managers

Budgets are generally regarded as having five areas of usefulness. These are:

- *Budgets tend to promote forward thinking and the possible identification of short-term problems.* We saw above that a shortage of production capacity might be identified during the budgeting process. Making this discovery in good time could leave a number of means of overcoming the problem open to exploration. If the potential production problem is picked up early enough, all of the suggestions in the answer to Activity 12.4 and, possibly, other ways of overcoming the problem can be explored. Identifying the potential problem early gives managers time for calm and rational consideration of the best way of overcoming it. The best solution to the potential problem possibly may only be feasible if action can be taken well in advance. This would be true of all of the suggestions made in the answer to Activity 12.4.
- *Budgets can be used to help co-ordination between the various sections of the business.* It is crucially important that the activities of the various departments and sections of the business are linked so that the activities of one are complementary to those of another. The activities of the purchasing/procurement department of a manufacturing business, for example, should dovetail with the raw materials needs of the production departments. If they do not, production could run out of raw materials, leading to expensive production stoppages. Possibly, just as undesirable, excessive amounts of raw materials could be bought, leading to large and unnecessary inventories holding costs. We shall see how this co-ordination tends to work in practice later in this chapter.

- *Budgets can motivate managers to better performance.* Having a stated task can motivate managers and staff in their performance. Simply to tell a manager to do his or her best is not very motivating, but to define a required level of achievement is more likely to be so. Managers will be better motivated by being able to relate their particular role in the business to its overall objectives. Since budgets are directly derived from strategic objectives, budgeting makes this possible. It is clearly not possible to allow managers to operate in an unconstrained environment. Having to operate in a way that matches the goals of the business is a price of working in an effective business. We shall consider the role of budgets as motivators, in more detail, in Chapter 13.

- *Budgets can provide a basis for a system of control.* As we saw earlier in the chapter, control is concerned with ensuring that events conform to plans. If senior management wishes to control and to monitor the performance of more junior staff, it needs some yardstick against which to measure and assess performance. Current performance could possibly be compared with past performance or perhaps with what happens in another business. However, planned performance is usually the most logical yardstick. If there is information available concerning the actual performance for a period, and this can be compared with the planned performance, then a basis for control will have been established. This will enable the use of **management by exception**, a technique where senior managers can spend most of their time dealing with those staff or activities that have failed to achieve the budget (the exceptions). Thus senior managers do not have to spend too much time on those that are performing well. It also allows junior managers to exercise self-control. By knowing what is expected of themselves and what they have actually achieved, they can assess how well they are performing and take steps to correct matters where they are failing to achieve. We shall consider the effect of making plans and being held accountable for their achievement in Chapter 13.

- *Budgets can provide a system of authorisation for managers to spend up to a particular limit.* Some activities (for example, staff development and research expenditure) are allocated a fixed amount of funds at the discretion of senior management. This provides the authority to spend.

Figure 12.4 shows the benefits of budgets in diagrammatic form.

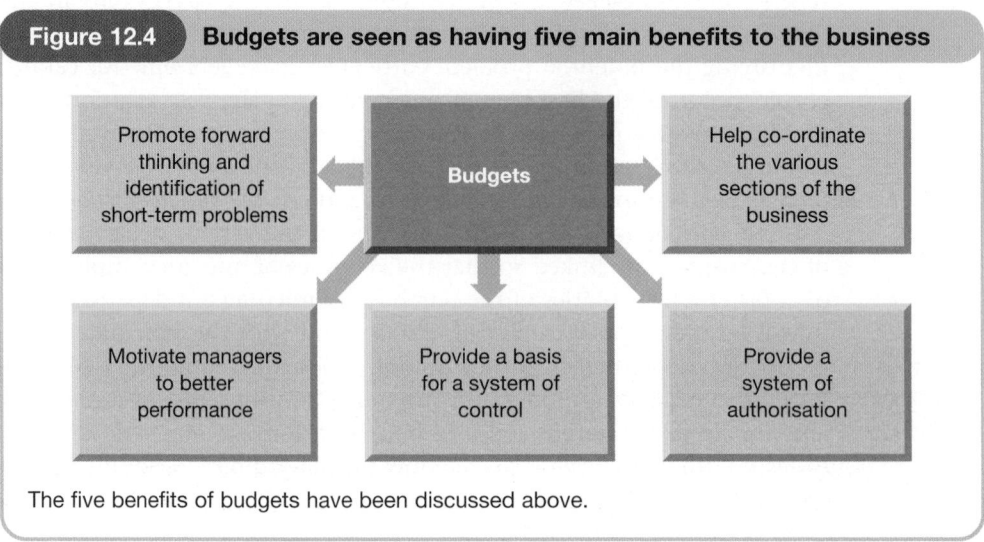

Figure 12.4 **Budgets are seen as having five main benefits to the business**

| Promote forward thinking and identification of short-term problems | Budgets | Help co-ordinate the various sections of the business |

| Motivate managers to better performance | Provide a basis for a system of control | Provide a system of authorisation |

The five benefits of budgets have been discussed above.

The following two activities pick up issues that relate to some of the uses of budgets.

Activity 12.5

The third point on the above list of the uses of budgets (motivation) implies that managers are set stated tasks. Do you think there is a danger that requiring managers to work towards such predetermined targets will stifle their skill, flair and enthusiasm?

If the budgets are set in such a way as to offer challenging yet achievable targets, the manager is still required to show skill, flair and enthusiasm. There is the danger, however, that if targets are badly set (either unreasonably demanding or too easy to achieve), they could be demotivating and have a stifling effect.

Activity 12.6

The fourth point on the above list of the uses of budgets (control) implies that current management performance is compared with some yardstick. What is wrong with comparing actual performance with past performance, or the performance of others, in an effort to exercise control?

What happened in the past, or is happening elsewhere, does not necessarily represent a sensible target for this year in this business. Considering what happened last year, and in other businesses, may help in the formulation of plans, but past events and the performance of others should not automatically be seen as the target.

The five identified uses of budgets can conflict with one another on occasion.

Using the budget as a motivational device provides a possible example of this. Some businesses set the budget targets at a more difficult level than the managers are expected to achieve in an attempt to motivate managers to strive to reach their targets. For control purposes, however, the budget becomes less meaningful as a benchmark against which to compare actual performance. Incidentally, there is good reason to doubt the effectiveness of setting excessive targets as a motivational device, as we shall see in Chapter 13.

Conflict between the different uses will mean that managers must decide which particular uses for budgets should be given priority. Managers must be prepared, if necessary, to trade off the benefits resulting from one particular use for the benefits of another.

The budget-setting process

Budgeting is such an important area for businesses, and other organisations, that it tends to be approached in a fairly methodical and formal way. This usually involves a number of steps, as described below.

Step 1: Establish who will take responsibility

Those responsible for the budget-setting process must have real authority within the organisation.

Activity 12.7

Why would those responsible for the budget-setting process need to have real authority?

One of the crucial aspects of the process is establishing co-ordination between budgets so that the plans of one department match and are complementary to those of other departments. This usually requires compromise where adjustment of initial budgets must be undertaken. This in turn means that someone on the board of directors (or a senior manager) has to be closely involved; only people of this rank are likely to have the necessary moral and, if needed, formal managerial authority to force departmental managers to compromise.

→ A **budget committee** is usually formed to supervise and take responsibility for the budget-setting process. This committee usually includes a senior representative of most of the functional areas of the business – marketing, production, human resources and
→ so on. Often, a **budget officer** is appointed to carry out the technical tasks of the committee, or to supervise others carrying them out. Not surprisingly, given their technical expertise in the activity, accountants are often required to take budget officer roles.

Step 2: Communicate budget guidelines to relevant managers

Budgets are intended to be the short-term plans that seek to work towards the achievement of strategic plans and to the overall objectives of the business. It is therefore important that, in drawing up budgets, managers are well aware of what the strategic plans are and how the forthcoming budget period is intended to work towards them. Managers also need to be made well aware of the commercial/economic environment in which they will be operating. This may include awareness of market trends, future rates of inflation, predicted changes in technology and so on. It is the budget committee's responsibility to see that managers have all the necessary information.

Step 3: Identify the key, or limiting, factor

There will be a limiting factor that will restrict the business from achieving its objectives to the maximum extent, as we saw earlier in the chapter (page 443). Identifying the limiting factor at the earliest stage in the budget-setting process will be helpful.

Step 4: Prepare the budget for the area of the limiting factor

The limiting factor will determine the overall level of activity for the business. The limiting-factor budget will, as we have already seen, usually be the sales budget, since the ability to sell is normally the constraint on future growth. (When discussing the interrelationship of budgets earlier in the chapter, we started with the sales budget for this reason.) Sales demand, however, is not always the limiting factor.

Real World 12.1 looks at the methods favoured by businesses of different sizes to determine their sales budgets.

Real World 12.1

Sources of the sales budget in practice

Determining the future level of sales can be a difficult problem. In practice, a business may rely on the judgements of sales staff, statistical techniques or market surveys (or some combination of these) to arrive at a sales budget. A survey of UK manufacturing businesses provides the following insights concerning the use of such techniques and methods.

	All respondents	Small businesses	Large businesses
Number of respondents	281	47	46
	%	%	%
Technique			
Statistical forecasting	31	19	29
Market research	36	13	54
Subjective estimates based on sales staff experience	85	97	80

We can see that the most popular approach by far is the opinion of sales staff. We can also see that there are differences between largest and smallest businesses surveyed, particularly concerning the use of market surveys. This evidence is now pretty old, but in the absence of more up-to-date research, it provides some idea of how businesses determine their sales targets.

Source: *A Survey of Management Accounting Practices in UK Manufacturing Companies*, C. Drury, S. Braund, P. Osborne and M. Tayles, Chartered Association of Certified Accountants, 1993.

Step 5: Prepare draft budgets for all other areas

The other budgets are prepared, consistent with the budget for the area of the limiting factor. In all budget preparation, the computer has become an almost indispensable tool. Much of the work of preparing budgets is repetitive and tedious, yet the resultant budget has to be a reliable representation of the plans made. Computers are ideally suited to such tasks and human beings are not. Budgets often have to be redrafted several times because of some minor alteration; computers do this without complaint.

Setting individual budgets may be approached in one of two broad ways. The *top-down approach* is where the senior management of each budget area originates the budget targets, perhaps discussing them with lower levels of management and, as a result, refining them before the final version is produced. With the *bottom-up approach*, the targets are fed upwards from the lowest level. For example, junior sales managers will be asked to set their own sales targets, which then become incorporated into the budgets of higher levels of management until the overall sales budget emerges.

Where the bottom-up approach is adopted, it is usually necessary to haggle and negotiate at different levels of authority to achieve agreement. Perhaps the plans of some departments do not fit in with those of others or the targets set by junior managers are not acceptable to their superiors. The bottom-up approach seems rarely to be found in practice.

Activity (12.8)

What are the advantages and disadvantages of each type of budgeting approach (bottom-up and top-down)?

The bottom-up approach allows greater involvement among managers in the budgeting process and this, in turn, may increase the level of commitment to the targets set. It also allows the business to draw more fully on the local knowledge and expertise of its managers. However, this can be time-consuming and may result in some managers setting undemanding targets for themselves in order to have an easy life.

The top-down approach enables senior management to communicate plans to employees and to co-ordinate the activities of the business more easily. It may also help in establishing more demanding targets for managers. However, the level of commitment to the budget may be lower as many of those responsible for achieving the budgets will have been excluded from the budget-setting process.

There will be further discussion of the benefits of participation in target setting in Chapter 13.

Step 6: Review and co-ordinate budgets

The budget committee must, at this stage, review the various budgets and satisfy itself that the budgets are consistent with one another. Where there is a lack of co-ordination, steps must be taken to ensure that the budgets mesh. Since this will require that at least one budget must be revised, this activity normally benefits from a diplomatic approach. Ultimately, however, the committee may be forced to assert its authority and insist that alterations are made.

Step 7: Prepare the master budgets

The master budgets are the budgeted income statement and budgeted statement of financial position – and perhaps a summarised cash budget. The individual operating budgets, that have already been prepared, should provide all of the information required to prepare the master budgets. The budget committee usually undertakes the task of preparing the master budgets.

Step 8: Communicate the budgets to all interested parties

The formally agreed operating budgets are now passed to the individual managers who will be responsible for their implementation. This is, in effect, senior management formally communicating to the other managers the targets that they are expected to achieve.

Step 9: Monitor performance relative to the budget

Much of the budget-setting activity will have been pointless unless each manager's actual performance is compared with the benchmark of planned performance, which is embodied in the budget. This issue is examined in detail in Chapter 13.

The steps in the budget-setting process are shown in diagrammatic form in Figure 12.5.

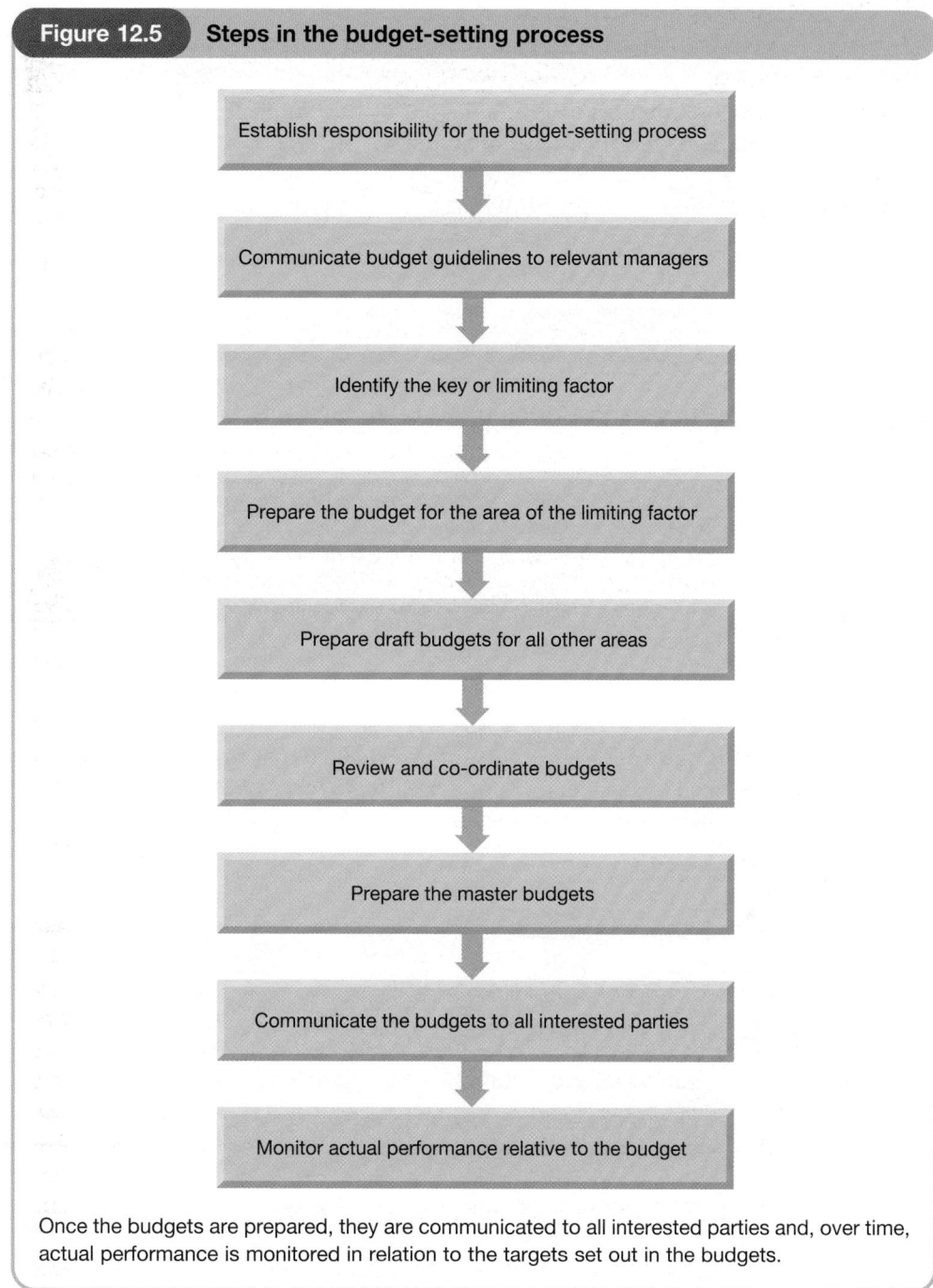

Figure 12.5 Steps in the budget-setting process

Establish responsibility for the budget-setting process

Communicate budget guidelines to relevant managers

Identify the key or limiting factor

Prepare the budget for the area of the limiting factor

Prepare draft budgets for all other areas

Review and co-ordinate budgets

Prepare the master budgets

Communicate the budgets to all interested parties

Monitor actual performance relative to the budget

Once the budgets are prepared, they are communicated to all interested parties and, over time, actual performance is monitored in relation to the targets set out in the budgets.

Where the established budgets are proving to be unrealistic, it is usually helpful to revise them. They may be unrealistic because certain assumptions made when the budgets were first set have turned out to be incorrect. This may occur where managers (budget-setters) have made poor judgements or where the environment has changed unexpectedly from what was, quite reasonably, assumed. Irrespective of the cause, unrealistic budgets are of little value and revising them may be the only logical approach to take. Nevertheless, revising budgets should be regarded as exceptional and only undertaken after very careful consideration.

Using budgets in practice

This section attempts to give a flavour of how budgets are used, the extent to which they are used, and their level of accuracy.

Real World 12.2 shows how the UK-based international engineering and support services business, Babcock International Group plc, undertakes its budgeting process.

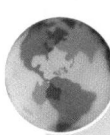

Real World 12.2

Budgeting at Babcock

According to its annual report, Babcock has the following arrangements:

> Comprehensive systems are in place to develop annual budgets and medium-term financial plans. The budgets are reviewed by central management before being submitted to the Board for approval. Updated forecasts for the year are prepared at least quarterly. The Board is provided with details of actual performance each month compared with budgets, forecasts and the prior year, and is given a written commentary on significant variances from approved plans.

Source: Babcock International Group plc Annual Report 2008.

There is quite a lot of recent survey evidence that reveals the extent to which budgeting is used by businesses in practice. **Real World 12.3** reviews some of this evidence, which shows that most businesses prepare and use budgets.

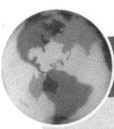

Real World 12.3

Budgeting in practice

A fairly recent survey of 41 UK manufacturing businesses found that 40 of the 41 surveyed prepared budgets.

Source: Contemporary Management Accounting Practices in UK Manufacturing, D. Dugdale, C. Jones and S. Green, CIMA Publication, Elsevier, 2006.

Another fairly recent survey of UK businesses, but this time businesses involved in the food and drink sector, found that virtually all of them used budgets.

Source: An Empirical Investigation of the Evolution of Management Accounting Practices, M. Abdel-Kader and R. Luther, Working paper No. 04/06, University of Essex, October 2004.

A survey of the opinions of senior finance staff at 340 businesses of various sizes and operating in a wide range of industries in North America revealed that 97 per cent of those businesses had a formal budgeting process.

Source: 'Perfect how you project', BPM Forum, 2008.

Though these three surveys relate to UK and North American businesses, they provide some idea of what is likely also to be the practice elsewhere in the developed world.

Real World 12.4 below gives some insight to the accuracy of budgets.

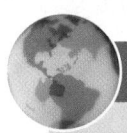

Real World 12.4

Budget accuracy

The survey of senior finance staff of North American businesses, mentioned in Real World 12.3 above, asked them to compare the actual revenues with the budgeted revenues for 2007. Figure 12.6 shows the results:

Figure 12.6   The accuracy of revenue budgets for 2007

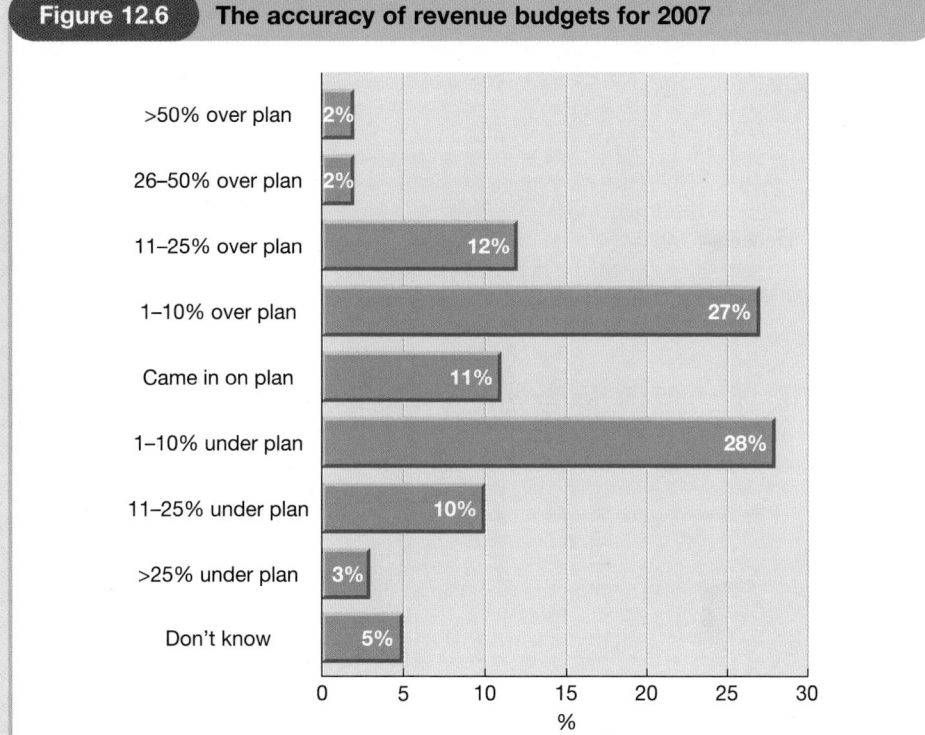

The figure reveals that 66 per cent of revenue budgets were accurate within a range of 10 per cent.

We can see that only 66 per cent of revenue budgets were accurate within 10 per cent. The survey revealed that budgets for expenses were generally more accurate, with 74 per cent being accurate within 10 per cent.

Source: 'Perfect how you project', BPM Forum, 2008.

A survey of budgeting practice in small and medium-sized enterprises (SMEs) (see **Real World 12.5**) revealed that not all such businesses fully use budgeting. It seems that some smaller businesses prepare budgets only for what they see as key areas. The budget that is most frequently prepared by such businesses is the sales budget, followed by the budgeted income statement and the overheads budget. Perhaps surprisingly, the cash budget is prepared by less than two-thirds of the small businesses surveyed.

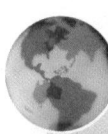

Real World 12.5

Preparation of budgets in SMEs

A study of budgeting practice in small and medium-sized enterprises (SMEs) revealed that the budget that the most businesses prepare is the sales budget (78 per cent prepared it), followed by the budgeted income statement and the overheads budget as is shown in Figure 12.7.

Figure 12.7 **Budgeting practice in SMEs**

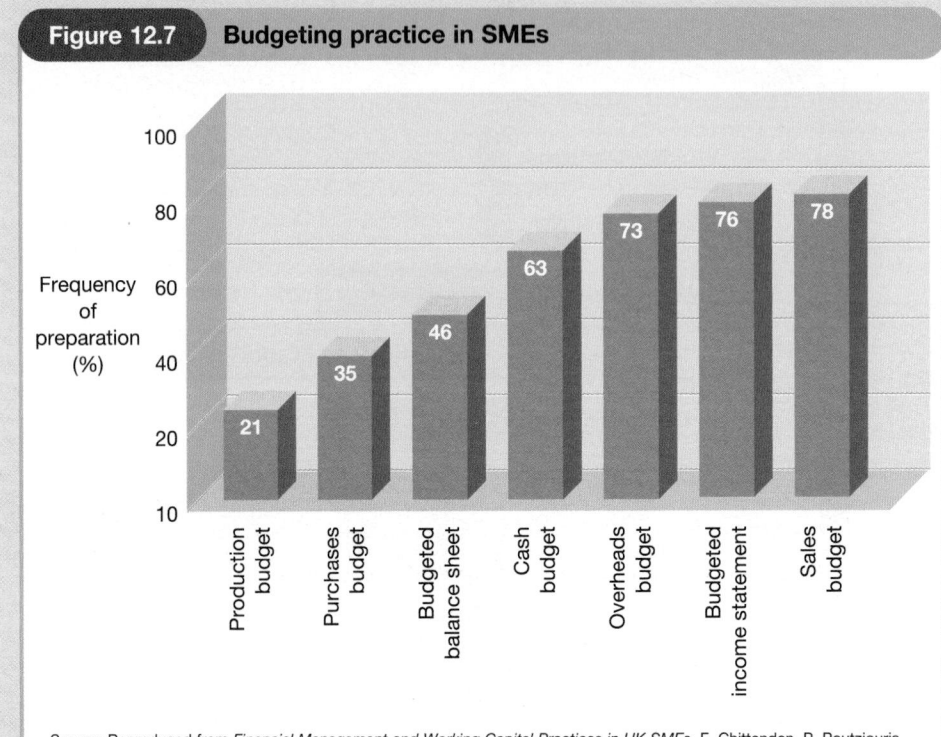

Source: Reproduced from *Financial Management and Working Capital Practices in UK SMEs*, F. Chittenden, P. Poutziouris and N. Michaelas, Manchester Business School, 1998, p. 22, Figure 16. By kind permission of the authors.

Incremental and zero-base budgeting

Budget setting is often done on the basis of what happened last year, with some adjustment for any changes in factors that are expected to affect the forthcoming budget period (for example, inflation). This approach is known as **incremental budgeting** and is often used for 'discretionary' budgets, such as research and development and staff training. With this type of budget, the **budget holder** (the manager responsible for the budget) is allocated a sum of money to be spent in the area of activity concerned. Such budgets are referred to as **discretionary budgets** because the sum allocated is normally at the discretion of senior management. These budgets are very common in local and central government (and in other public bodies), but are also used in commercial businesses to cover the types of activity that we have just referred to.

Discretionary budgets are often found in areas where there is no clear relationship between inputs (resources applied) and outputs (benefits). Compare this with, say, a raw materials usage budget in a manufacturing business, where the amount of material used and, therefore, the amount of funds involved, is clearly related to the level of production and, ultimately, to sales volumes. Discretionary budgets can easily eat up funds, with no clear benefit being derived. It is often only the proposed periodic increases in these budgets that are closely scrutinised.

→ **Zero-base budgeting (ZBB)** rests on the philosophy that all spending needs to be justified. Thus, when establishing, say, the training budget each year, it is not automatically accepted that training courses should be financed in the future simply because they were undertaken this year. The training budget will start from a zero base (that is no resources at all) and will only be increased above zero if a good case can be made for the scarce resources of the business to be allocated to this form of activity. Top management will need to be convinced that the proposed activities represent 'value for money'.

ZBB encourages managers to adopt a more questioning approach to their areas of responsibility. To justify the allocation of resources, managers are often forced to think carefully about the particular activities and the ways in which they are undertaken. This questioning approach should result in a more efficient use of business resources. With an increasing portion of the total costs of most businesses being in areas where the link between outputs and inputs is not always clear, and where commitment of resources is discretionary rather than demonstrably essential to production, ZBB is increasingly relevant.

Activity (12.9)

Can you think of any disadvantages of using ZBB?

The principal problems with ZBB are:

- It is time-consuming and therefore expensive to undertake.
- Managers whose sphere of responsibility is subjected to ZBB can feel threatened by it.

The benefits of a ZBB approach can be gained to some extent – perhaps at not too great a cost – by using the approach on a selective basis. For example, a particular budget area could be subjected to ZBB-type scrutiny only every third or fourth year. In any case, if ZBB is used more frequently, there is the danger that managers will use the same arguments each year to justify their activities. The process will simply become a mechanical exercise and the benefits will be lost. For a typical business, some areas are likely to benefit from ZBB more than others. As mentioned earlier, the areas most likely to benefit from ZBB involve discretionary spending, such as training, advertising, and research and development.

If senior management is aware that their subordinates are likely to feel threatened by the nature of this form of budgeting, care can be taken to apply ZBB with sensitivity. However, in the quest for cost control and value for money, the application of ZBB can result in some tough decisions being made.

Real World 12.6 provides some insight into the extent to which ZBB is used in practice.

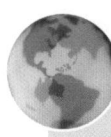

Real World 12.6

ZBB is not food and drink to many businesses

The fairly recent survey of businesses in the UK food and drink sector found that ZBB is not much used by them. Only 48 per cent ever use it and only 16 per cent use it 'often' or 'very often'.

ZBB seems to be most appropriate, however, with 'spending' budgets, such as training, advertising and so on. Such budgets probably represent a minority for the types of business in this survey.

Source: An Empirical Investigation of the Evolution of Management Accounting Practices, M. Abdel-Kader and R. Luther, Working paper No. 04/06, University of Essex, October 2004.

Preparing the cash budget

We shall now look in some detail at how the various budgets used by the typical business are prepared, starting with the cash budget and then looking at the others. It is helpful for us to start with the cash budget because:

- it is a key budget (some people see it as a 'master budget' along with the budgeted income statement and budgeted statement of financial position); most economic aspects of a business are reflected in cash sooner or later, so that for a typical business the cash budget reflects the whole business more comprehensively than any other single budget;
- a very small, unsophisticated business (for example, a corner shop) may feel that full-scale budgeting is not appropriate to its needs, but almost certainly it should prepare a cash budget as a minimum (despite the survey evidence mentioned in Real World 12.5 above).

Since budgets are documents that are to be used only internally by a business, their style is a question of management choice and will vary from one business to the next. However, as managers, irrespective of the business, are likely to be using budgets for similar purposes, some consistency of approach tends to be found. In most businesses, the cash budget will probably possess the following features:

1. the budget period would be broken down into sub-periods, typically months;
2. the budget would be in columnar form, with one column for each month;
3. receipts of cash would be identified under various headings and a total for each month's receipts shown;
4. payments of cash would be identified under various headings and a total for each month's payments shown;
5. the surplus of total cash receipts over payments, or of payments over receipts, for each month would be identified;
6. the running cash balance would be identified. This would be achieved by taking the balance at the end of the previous month and adjusting it for the surplus or deficit of receipts over payments (or payments over receipts) for the current month.

Typically, all of the pieces of information in points 3 to 6 in this list would be useful to management for one reason or another.

Probably the best way to deal with this topic is through an example.

Example 12.1

Vierra Popova Ltd is a wholesale business. The budgeted income statements for each of the next six months are as follows:

	Jan £000	Feb £000	Mar £000	Apr £000	May £000	June £000
Sales revenue	52	55	55	60	55	53
Cost of goods sold	(30)	(31)	(31)	(35)	(31)	(32)
Salaries and wages	(10)	(10)	(10)	(10)	(10)	(10)
Electricity	(5)	(5)	(4)	(3)	(3)	(3)
Depreciation	(3)	(3)	(3)	(3)	(3)	(3)
Other overheads	(2)	(2)	(2)	(2)	(2)	(2)
Total expenses	(50)	(51)	(50)	(53)	(49)	(50)
Profit for the month	2	4	5	7	6	3

The business allows all of its customers one month's credit (this means, for example, that cash from January sales will be received in February). Sales revenue during December totalled £60,000.

The business plans to maintain inventories at their existing level until some time in March, when they are to be reduced by £5,000. Inventories will remain at this lower level indefinitely. Inventories purchases are made on one month's credit. December purchases totalled £30,000. Salaries, wages and 'other overheads' are paid in the month concerned. Electricity is paid quarterly in arrears in March and June. The business plans to buy and pay for a new delivery van in March. This will cost a total of £15,000, but an existing van will be traded in for £4,000 as part of the deal.

The business expects to have £12,000 in cash at the beginning of January.

The cash budget for the six months ending in June will look as follows:

	Jan £000	Feb £000	Mar £000	Apr £000	May £000	June £000
Receipts						
Trade receivables (Note 1)	60	52	55	55	60	55
Payments						
Trade payables (Note 2)	(30)	(30)	(31)	(26)	(35)	(31)
Salaries and wages	(10)	(10)	(10)	(10)	(10)	(10)
Electricity			(14)			(9)
Other overheads	(2)	(2)	(2)	(2)	(2)	(2)
Van purchase	–	–	(11)	–	–	–
Total payments	(42)	(42)	(68)	(38)	(47)	(52)
Cash surplus for the month	18	10	(13)	17	13	3
Opening balance (Note 3)	12	30	40	27	44	57
Closing balance	30	40	27	44	57	60

Notes:

(1) The cash receipts from trade receivables lag a month behind sales because customers are given a month in which to pay for their purchases. So, December sales will be paid for in January, and so on.

(2) In most months, the purchases of inventories will equal the cost of goods sold. This is because the business maintains a constant level of inventories. For inventories to remain constant at the end of each month, the business must replace exactly the amount that has been used. During March, however, the business plans to reduce its inventories by £5,000. This means that inventories purchases will be lower than inventories usage in that month. The payments for inventories purchases lag a month behind purchases because the business expects to be allowed a month to pay for what it buys.

(3) Each month's cash balance is the previous month's figure plus the cash surplus (or minus the cash deficit) for the current month. The balance at the start of January is £12,000 according to the information provided earlier.

(4) Depreciation does not give rise to a cash payment. In the context of profit measurement (in the income statement), depreciation is a very important aspect. Here, however, we are interested only in cash.

Activity (12.10)

Looking at the cash budget of Vierra Popova Ltd, what conclusions do you draw and what possible course of action do you recommend regarding the cash balance over the period concerned?

There appears to be a fairly large cash balance, given the size of the business, and it seems to be increasing. Management might give consideration to putting some of the cash into an income-yielding deposit. Alternatively, it could be used to expand the trading activities of the business by, for example, increasing the investment in non-current (fixed) assets.

Activity (12.11)

Vierra Popova Ltd (Example 12.1) now wishes to prepare its cash budget for the second six months of the year. The budgeted income statements for each month of the second half of the year are as follows:

	July £000	Aug £000	Sept £000	Oct £000	Nov £000	Dec £000
Sales revenue	57	59	62	57	53	51
Cost of goods sold	(32)	(33)	(35)	(32)	(30)	(29)
Salaries and wages	(10)	(10)	(10)	(10)	(10)	(10)
Electricity	(3)	(3)	(4)	(5)	(6)	(6)
Depreciation	(3)	(3)	(3)	(3)	(3)	(3)
Other overheads	(2)	(2)	(2)	(2)	(2)	(2)
Total expenses	(50)	(51)	(54)	(52)	(51)	(50)
Profit for the month	7	8	8	5	2	1

The business will continue to allow all of its customers one month's credit.

It plans to increase inventories from the 30 June level by £1,000 each month until, and including, September. During the following three months, inventories levels will be decreased by £1,000 each month.

Inventories purchases, which had been made on one month's credit until the June payment, will, starting with the purchases made in June, be made on two months' credit.

Salaries, wages and 'other overheads' will continue to be paid in the month concerned. Electricity is paid quarterly in arrears in September and December.

At the end of December, the business intends to pay off part of some borrowings. This payment is to be such that it will leave the business with a cash balance of £5,000 with which to start next year.

Prepare the cash budget for the six months ending in December. (Remember that any information you need that relates to the first six months of the year, including the cash balance that is expected to be brought forward on 1 July, is given in Example 12.1.)

The cash budget for the six months ended 31 December is:

	July £000	Aug £000	Sept £000	Oct £000	Nov £000	Dec £000
Receipts						
Trade receivables	53	57	59	62	57	53
Payments						
Trade payables (Note 1)	–	(32)	(33)	(34)	(36)	(31)
Salaries and wages	(10)	(10)	(10)	(10)	(10)	(10)
Electricity	–	–	(10)	–	–	(17)
Other overheads	(2)	(2)	(2)	(2)	(2)	(2)
Borrowings repayment (Note 2)	–	–	–	–	–	(131)
Total payments	(12)	(44)	(55)	(46)	(48)	(191)
Cash surplus for the month	41	13	4	16	9	(138)
Opening balance	60	101	114	118	134	143
Closing balance	101	114	118	134	143	5

Notes:
(1) There will be no payment to suppliers (trade payables) in July because the June purchases will be made on two months' credit and will therefore be paid in August. The July purchases, which will equal the July cost of sales figure plus the increase in inventories made in July, will be paid for in September and so on.
(2) The borrowings repayment is simply the amount that will cause the balance at 31 December to be £5,000.

Preparing other budgets

Though each one will have its own particular features, other budgets will tend to follow the same sort of pattern as the cash budget, that is, they will show inflows and outflows during each month and the opening and closing balances in each month.

Example 12.2

To illustrate some of the other budgets, we shall continue to use the example of Vierra Popova Ltd that we considered in Example 12.1. To the information given there, we need to add the fact that the inventories balance at 1 January was £30,000.

Trade receivables budget

This would normally show the planned amount owed to the business by credit customers at the beginning and at the end of each month, the planned total credit sales revenue for each month and the planned total cash receipts from credit customers (trade receivables). The layout would be something like this:

	Jan £000	Feb £000	Mar £000	Apr £000	May £000	June £000
Opening balance	60	52	55	55	60	55
Sales revenue	52	55	55	60	55	53
Cash receipts	(60)	(52)	(55)	(55)	(60)	(55)
Closing balance	52	55	55	60	55	53

The opening and closing balances represent the amount that the business plans to be owed (in total) by credit customers (trade receivables) at the beginning and end of each month, respectively.

Trade payables budget

Typically this shows the planned amount owed to suppliers by the business at the beginning and at the end of each month, the planned credit purchases for each month and the planned total cash payments to trade payables. The layout would be something like this:

	Jan £000	Feb £000	Mar £000	Apr £000	May £000	June £000
Opening balance	30	30	31	26	35	31
Purchases	30	31	26	35	31	32
Cash payment	(30)	(30)	(31)	(26)	(35)	(31)
Closing balance	30	31	26	35	31	32

The opening and closing balances represent the amount planned to be owed (in total) by the business to suppliers (trade payables), at the beginning and end of each month respectively.

Inventories budget

This would normally show the planned amount of inventories to be held by the business at the beginning and at the end of each month, the planned total inventories purchases for each month and the planned total monthly inventories usage. The layout would be something like this:

	Jan £000	Feb £000	Mar £000	Apr £000	May £000	June £000
Opening balance	30	30	30	25	25	25
Purchases	30	31	26	35	31	32
Inventories used	(30)	(31)	(31)	(35)	(31)	(32)
Closing balance	30	30	25	25	25	25

The opening and closing balances represent the amount of inventories, at cost, planned to be held by the business at the beginning and end of each month respectively.

A *raw materials inventories budget*, for a manufacturing business, would follow a similar pattern, with the 'inventories usage' being the cost of the inventories put into production. A *finished inventories budget* for a manufacturer would also be similar to the above, except that 'inventories manufactured' would replace 'purchases'. A manufacturing business would normally prepare both a raw materials inventories budget and a finished inventories budget. Both of these would typically be based on the full cost of the inventories (that is, including overheads). There is no reason why the inventories should not be valued on the basis of either variable cost or direct costs, should managers feel that this would provide more useful information.

The inventories budget will normally be expressed in financial terms, but may also be expressed in physical terms (for example, kg or metres) for individual inventories items.

Note how the trade receivables, trade payables and inventories budgets in Example 12.2 link to one another, and to the cash budget for the same business in Example 12.1. Note particularly that:

● the purchases figures in the trade payables budget and in the inventories budget are identical;
● the cash payments figures in the trade payables budget and in the cash budget are identical;
● the cash receipts figures in the trade receivables budget and in the cash budget are identical.

Other values would link different budgets in a similar way. For example, the row of sales revenue figures in the trade receivables budget would be identical to the sales revenue figures that will be found in the sales budget. This is how the linking (co-ordination), that was discussed earlier in this chapter, is achieved.

Activity (12.12)

Have a go at preparing the trade receivables budget for Vierra Popova Ltd for the six months from July to December (see Activity 12.11).

The trade receivables budget for the six months ended 31 December is:

	July £000	Aug £000	Sept £000	Oct £000	Nov £000	Dec £000
Opening balance (Note 1)	53	57	59	62	57	53
Sales revenue (Note 2)	57	59	62	57	53	51
Cash receipts (Note 3)	(53)	(57)	(59)	(62)	(57)	(53)
Closing balance (Note 4)	57	59	62	57	53	51

Notes:

(1) The opening trade receivables figure is the previous month's sales revenue figure (sales are on one month's credit).
(2) The sales revenue is the current month's figure.
(3) The cash received each month is equal to the previous month's sales revenue figure.
(4) The closing balance is equal to the current month's sales revenue figure.

Note that if we knew any three of the four figures each month, we could deduce the fourth.

This budget could be set out in any manner that would have given the sort of information that management would require in respect of planned levels of trade receivables and associated transactions.

Activity (12.13)

Have a go at preparing the trade payables budget for Vierra Popova Ltd for the six months from July to December (see Activity 12.12). (*Hint*: Remember that the trade payables payment period alters from the June purchases onwards.)

The trade payables budget for the six months ended 31 December is:

	July £000	Aug £000	Sept £000	Oct £000	Nov £000	Dec £000
Opening balance	32	65	67	70	67	60
Purchases	33	34	36	31	29	28
Cash payments	–	(32)	(33)	(34)	(36)	(31)
Closing balance	65	67	70	67	60	57

This, again, could be set out in any manner that would have given the sort of information that management would require in respect of planned levels of trade payables and associated transactions.

Activity-based budgeting

→ **Activity-based budgeting (ABB)** extends the principles of activity-based costing (ABC), that we discussed in Chapter 11, to budgeting. Under a system of ABB, the budgeted sales of products or services are determined and the activities necessary to achieve the budgeted sales are then identified. Budgets for each of the various activities are prepared by multiplying the budgeted usage of the cost driver for a particular activity (as determined by the sales budget) by the budgeted rate for the relevant cost driver. The following example should help to make the process clear.

Example 12.3

Danube Ltd produces two products, the Gamma and the Delta. The sales budget for next year shows that 60,000 units of Gamma and 80,000 units of Delta are expected to be sold. Each type of product spends time in the finished goods stores. Both products are of roughly similar size and have very similar storage needs. It is felt, therefore, that the period spent in the stores ('product weeks') is the cost driver and so a budget for this cost-driving activity is created. It is estimated that Product Gamma will spend an average of two weeks in the stores before being sold and, for Product Delta, the average period is five weeks.

To calculate the activity budget for the finished goods stores, the estimated total usage of the cost driver must be calculated. This will be the total number of 'product weeks' that the products will be in store.

Based on previous years' data, the budgeted rate for the cost driver has been set at £1.50 per product week.

Product			*Product weeks*
Delta	60,000 × 2 weeks	=	120,000
Gamma	80,000 × 5 weeks	=	400,000
			520,000

The number of product weeks will then be multiplied by the budgeted rate for the cost driver to derive the activity budget figure. That is:

$$520,000 \times £1.50 = £780,000$$

The same process will be carried out for the other activities identified.

Note that budgets are prepared according to the cost-driving activity rather than function, as is the case with the traditional approach to budgeting.

Through the application of ABC principles, the factors that cause costs are known and there is a direct linking of costs with outputs. This means that ABB should provide a better understanding of future resource needs and more accurate budgets. It should also provide a better understanding of the effect on budgeted costs of changes in the usage of the cost driver because of the explicit relationship between cost drivers, activities and costs.

Control should be improved within an ABB environment for two reasons:

● By developing more accurate budgets, managers should be provided with demanding yet achievable targets.

● ABB should ensure that costs are closely linked to responsibilities. Managers who have control over particular cost drivers will become accountable for the costs that are caused. An important principle of effective budgeting is that those responsible for meeting a particular budget (budget holders) should have control over the events that affect performance in their area.

Real World 12.7 provides some indication of the extent to which ABB is used in practice.

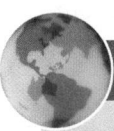

Real World 12.7

ABB is not often on the menu

The fairly recent survey of UK food and drink businesses found that ABB is not much used by them. Only 19 per cent use it 'often' or 'very often'. Not surprisingly, businesses that use ABC are much more likely to use ABB as well.

Interestingly, ABB seems to be used by more businesses than those that use ABC for product costing. This implies that the 'activity-based' approach is more used in cost management than in determining product costs.

Source: An Empirical Investigation of the Evolution of Management Accounting Practices, M. Abdel-Kader and R. Luther, Working paper No. 04/06, University of Essex, October 2004.

Self-assessment question 12.1 pulls together what we have just seen about preparing budgets.

Self-assessment question 12.1

Antonio Ltd has planned production and sales for the next nine months as follows:

	Production Units	Sales Units
May	350	350
June	400	400
July	500	400
August	600	500
September	600	600
October	700	650
November	750	700
December	750	800
January	750	750

During the period, the business plans to advertise so as to generate these increases in sales. Payments for advertising of £1,000 and £1,500 will be made in July and October respectively.

The selling price per unit will be £20 throughout the period. Forty per cent of sales are normally made on two months' credit. The other 60 per cent are settled within the month of the sale.

Raw materials will be held for one month before they are taken into production. Purchases of raw materials will be on one month's credit (buy one month, pay the next). The cost of raw materials is £8 per unit of production.

Other direct production expenses, including labour, are £6 per unit of production. These will be paid in the month concerned.

Various production overheads, which during the period to 30 June had run at £1,800 a month, are expected to rise to £2,000 each month from 1 July to 31 October. These are expected to rise again from 1 November to £2,400 a month and to remain at that level for the foreseeable future. These overheads include a steady £400 each month for depreciation. Overheads are planned to be paid 80 per cent in the month of production and 20 per cent in the following month.

To help to meet the planned increased production, a new item of plant will be bought and delivered in August. The cost of this item is £6,600; the contract with the supplier will specify that this will be paid in three equal amounts in September, October and November.

Raw materials inventories is planned to be 500 units on 1 July. The balance at the bank on the same day is planned to be £7,500.

Required:
(a) Draw up the following for the six months ending 31 December:
   (1) A raw materials inventories budget, showing both physical quantities and financial values.
   (2) A trade payables budget.
   (3) A cash budget.
(b) The cash budget reveals a potential cash deficiency during October and November. Can you suggest any ways in which a modification of plans could overcome this problem?

The answer to this question can be found at the back of the book on pages 732–3.

Non-financial measures in budgeting

The efficiency of internal operations and customer satisfaction levels have become of critical importance to businesses striving to survive in an increasingly competitive environment. Non-financial performance indicators have an important role to play in assessing performance in such key areas as customer/supplier delivery times, set-up times, defect levels and customer satisfaction levels.

There is no reason why budgeting need be confined to financial targets and measures. As we saw in Chapter 11, non-financial measures can also be used as the basis for targets and these can be brought into the budgeting process and reported alongside the financial targets for the business.

Budgets and management behaviour

All accounting statements and reports are intended to affect the behaviour of one or another group of people. Budgets are intended to affect the behaviour of managers, for example, to encourage them to work towards the business's objectives and to do this in a co-ordinated manner.

Whether budgets are effective and how they could be made more effective are crucial issues for managers. We shall examine this topic in detail in Chapter 13, after we have seen, in the earlier part of that chapter, how budgets can be used to help managers to exercise control.

Who needs budgets?

Until recently it would have been a heresy to suggest that budgeting was not of central importance to any business. The benefits of budgeting, mentioned earlier in this chapter, have been widely recognised and the vast majority of businesses prepare annual budgets (see Real World 12.3 on page 454). However, there is increasing concern that, in today's highly dynamic and competitive environment, budgets may actually be harmful to the achievement of business objectives. This has led a small but growing number of businesses to abandon traditional budgets as a tool of planning and control.

Various charges have been levelled against the conventional budgeting process. It is claimed that:

- Budgets cannot deal with a fast-changing environment and they are often out of date before the start of the budget period.
- They focus too much management attention on the achievement of short-term financial targets. Instead, managers should focus on the things that create value for the business (for example, innovation, building brand loyalty, responding quickly to competitive threats, and so on).
- They reinforce a 'command and control' structure that concentrates power in the hands of senior managers and prevents junior managers from exercising autonomy. This may be particularly true where a top-down approach, that allocates budgets to managers, is being used. Where managers feel constrained, attempts to retain and recruit able managers can be difficult.
- Budgeting take up an enormous amount of management time that could be better used. In practice, budgeting can be a lengthy process that may involve much negotiation, reworking and updating. However, this may add little to the achievement of business objectives.
- Budgets are based around business functions (sales, marketing, production, and so on). To achieve the business's objectives, however, the focus should be on business processes that cut across functional boundaries and reflect the needs of the customer.
- They encourage incremental thinking by employing a 'last year plus x per cent' approach to planning. This can inhibit the development of 'break out' strategies that may be necessary in a fast-changing environment.
- They can protect costs rather than lower costs, particularly in the area of discretionary budgets. In some cases, a fixed budget for an activity, such as research and development, is allocated to a manager. If the amount is not spent, the budget may be taken away and, in future periods, the budget for this activity may be either reduced or eliminated. Such a response to unused budget allocations can encourage managers to spend the whole of the budget, irrespective of need, in order to protect the allocations they receive.
- They promote 'sharp' practice among managers. In order to meet budget targets, managers may try to negotiate lower sales targets or higher cost allocations than they feel is really necessary. This helps them to build some 'slack' into the budgets and so meeting the budget becomes easier (see reference 2 at the end of the chapter).

Although some believe that many of the problems identified can be solved by better budgeting systems such as activity-based budgeting and zero-base budgeting and by taking a more flexible approach, others believe that a more radical solution is required.

Beyond conventional budgeting

In recent years, a few businesses have abandoned budgeting, although they still recognise the need for forward planning. No one seriously doubts that there must be appropriate systems in place to steer a business towards its objectives. It is claimed, however, that the systems adopted should reflect a broader, more integrated approach to planning. The new systems that have been implemented are often based around a 'leaner' financial planning process that is more closely linked to other measurement and reward systems. Emphasis is placed on the use of rolling forecasts, key performance indicators (such as market share, customer satisfaction and innovations) and/or 'scorecards' (like the balanced scorecard, which we met in Chapter 11) that identify both monetary and non-monetary targets to be achieved over the long term and short term. These are often very demanding ('stretch') targets, based on benchmarks that have been set by world-class businesses.

The new 'beyond budgeting' model promotes a more decentralised, participative approach to managing the business. It is claimed that the traditional hierarchical management structure, where decision making is concentrated at the higher levels of the hierarchy, encourages a culture of dependency where meeting the budget targets set by senior managers is the key to managerial success. This traditional structure is replaced by a network structure where decision making is devolved to 'front-line' managers. A more open, questioning attitude among employees is encouraged by the new structure. There is a sharing of knowledge and best practice, and protective behaviour by managers is discouraged. In addition, rewards are linked to targets based on improvement in relative performance rather than to meeting the budget. It is claimed that this new approach allows greater adaptability to changing conditions, increases performance and increases motivation among staff.

Figure 12.8 sets out the main differences between the traditional and 'beyond budgeting' planning models.

Real World 12.8 looks at the management planning systems at Toyota, the well-known Japanese motor vehicle business, a business that does not use conventional budgets.

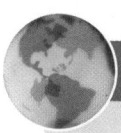 **Real World 12.8**

Steering Toyota

Peter Bunce is at the forefront of those who argue that budgeting systems have an adverse effect on the ability of businesses to compete effectively. The following is an outline of Toyota's planning and control systems, written by him:

> Toyota is a well-known example of a sense-and-respond organisation. Instead of pushing products through rigid processes to meet sales targets, its operating systems start from the customer – it is the customer order that drives operating processes and the work that people do. The point is that in sense-and-respond companies, predetermined plans and performance contracts are an anathema and represent insurmountable barriers; which is why adaptive organisations like Toyota don't have them. However, in industries such as manufacturing, planning has a vital role to play as they have to ensure that they will have sufficient capacity for expected levels of customer orders and they have to manage and coordinate the supply chain. Every year Toyota Motor Europe develops what it calls its Original Business Plan (OBP). The OBP is just a forecast (or financial plan) for the year and provides a baseline for understanding actuals and changes, for communicating, discussion and reaching consensus (a key element of Toyota's way of working) and also for

Real World 12.8 continued

management reviews. The OBP doesn't have any of the toxic elements of a traditional budget such as agreeing and coordinating fixed targets, rewards and resources for the year ahead, and the measuring and controlling performance against such an agreement. Nor is it a reference for bonuses as it doesn't contain any targets or goals (aspirational goals are set separately by Toyota). Toyota Motors Europe also undertakes quarterly forecasts to update the OBP. These are much lighter than the OBP and don't go into much detail.

Source: 'Transforming financial planning', P. Bunce, www.bbrt.org, June 2007.

Figure 12.8 **Traditional versus 'beyond budgeting' planning model**

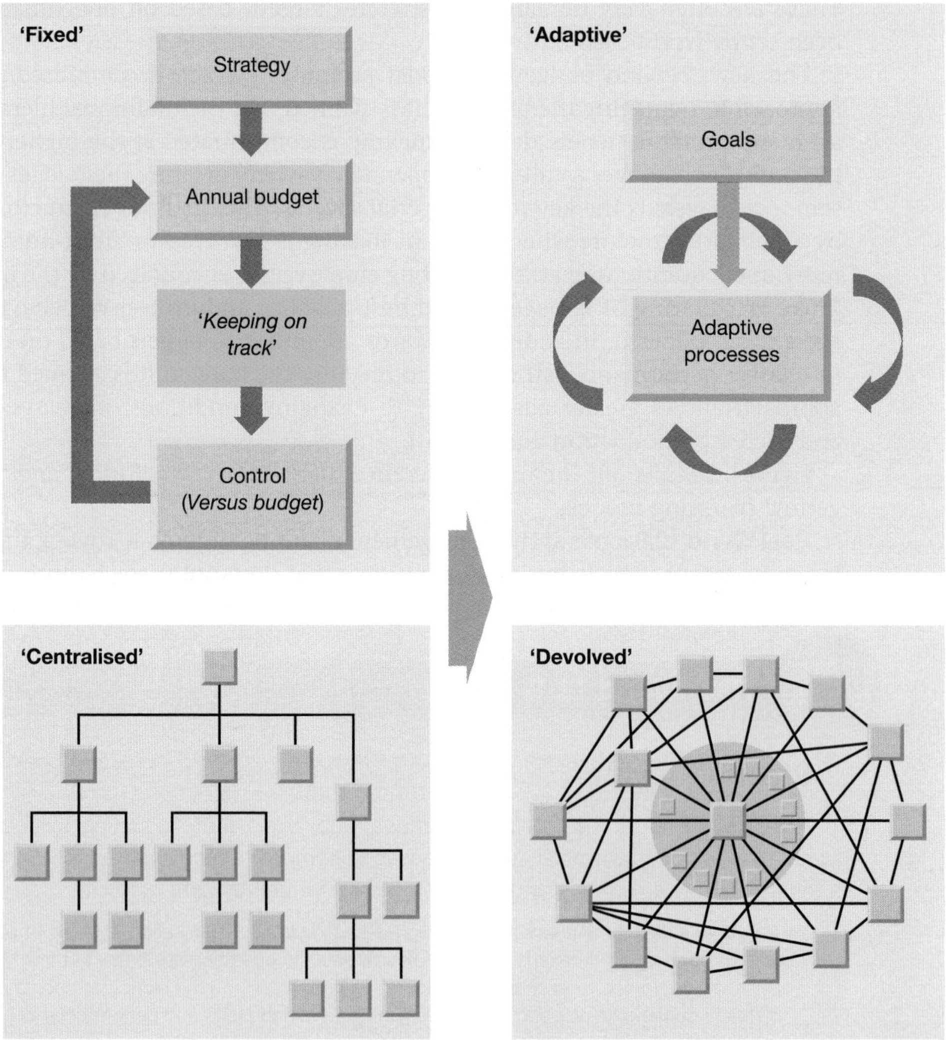

The traditional model is based on the use of fixed targets, which determine the future actions of managers. The 'beyond budgeting' model, on the other hand, is based on the use of stretch targets that can be adapted. The traditional hierarchical management structure is replaced by a network structure.

Source: Beyond budgeting, www.bbrt.org.

It is perhaps too early to predict whether or not the trickle of businesses that are now seeking an alternative to budgets will turn into a flood. However, it is clear that in today's highly competitive environment a business must be flexible and responsive to changing conditions. Management systems that in any way hinder these attributes will not survive.

Long live budgets!

It is worth remembering that, despite the criticisms, budgeting remains a very widely used technique. Real World 12.3 provides evidence for this. Furthermore, a glance through the annual report of virtually any well-known business will reveal that budgeting is used and is not, therefore, regarded as an impediment to success. **Real World 12.9** is an account of a round table discussion at a Better Budgeting forum held in London in March 2004. This was attended by representatives of 32 large organisations, including BAA (the airport operator), the BBC, Ford Motors, Sainsbury (the supermarket business) and Unilever (the household goods group).

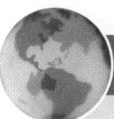

Real World 12.9

Alive and kicking

The report of the forum discussions said:

> If you were to believe all that has been written in recent years, you'd be forgiven for thinking that budgeting is on its way to becoming extinct. Various research reports allude to the widespread dissatisfaction with the bureaucratic exercise in cost cutting that budgeting is accused of having become. Budgets are pilloried as being out of touch with the needs of modern business and accused of taking too long, costing too much and encouraging all sorts of perverse behaviour.
>
> Yet if there was one conclusion to emerge from the day's discussions it was that budgets are in fact alive and well. Not only did all the organisations present operate a formal budget but all bar two had no interest in getting rid of it. Quite the opposite – although aware of the problems it can cause, the participants by and large regarded the budgeting system and the accompanying processes as indispensable.

Later in the report, in what could have been a reference to the use of 'rolling forecasts' among businesses that claim to have abandoned budgeting, it said:

> It quickly became obvious that, as one participant put it, 'one man's budget is another man's rolling forecast'. What people refer to when they talk about budgeting could in reality be very different things.

This presumably meant that businesses that abandon 'budgets' reintroduce them under another name.

Source: Better Budgeting, The Chartered Institute of Management Accountants and The Faculty of Finance and Management, Institute of Chartered Accountants in England and Wales, March 2004.

It can be argued, for example that Toyota's 'Original Business Plan' (see Real World 12.8) is really a budget by another name. The definition of a budget is a business plan, as we saw earlier in the chapter.

Real World 12.10 provides survey evidence of senior finance staff that indicates considerable support for budgets. Nevertheless, many recognised that budgeting is not always well managed and acknowledged some of the criticisms of budgets that were mentioned earlier.

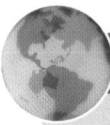

Real World 12.10

Problems with budgets

The survey of the opinions of senior finance staff at 340 businesses of various sizes and operating in a wide range of industries in North America that was mentioned earlier (see Real World 12.4) showed that 86 per cent of those surveyed regarded the budget process as either 'essential' or 'very important'. However:

- 66 per cent thought that budgeting in their business was not agile or flexible enough.
- 59 per cent were not very confident that budget targets would be met in 2008.
- 67 per cent felt that their business devoted inappropriate amounts of time to budgeting (51 per cent felt it was too much and 16 per cent too little).
- 76 per cent felt that their businesses used inappropriate software in the budgeting process (generally using a spreadsheet rather than custom designed software).

Source: 'Perfect how you project', BPM Forum, 2008.

In the next chapter we shall look in some detail at how budgets can be adapted for use as devices for exercising management control.

Summary

The main points of this chapter may be summarised as follows:

A budget is a short-term business plan, mainly expressed in financial terms.

- Budgets are the short-term means of working towards the business's objectives.
- They are usually prepared for a one-year period with sub-periods of a month.
- There is usually a separate budget for each key area.

Uses of budgets

- Promote forward thinking.
- Help co-ordinate the various aspects of the business.
- Motivate performance.
- Provide the basis of a system of control.
- Provide a system of authorisation.

The budget-setting process

- Establish who will take responsibility.
- Communicate guidelines.

- Identify key factor.
- Prepare budget for key factor area.
- Prepare draft budgets for all other areas.
- Review and co-ordinate.
- Prepare master budgets (income statement and statement of financial position (balance sheet)).
- Communicate the budgets to interested parties.
- Monitor performance relative to budget.

Preparing budgets

- There is no standard style – practicality and usefulness are the key issues.
- They are usually prepared in columnar form, with a column for each month (or similarly short period).
- Each budget must link (co-ordinate) with others.

Criticisms of budgets

- Cannot deal with rapid change.
- Focus on short-term financial targets, rather than value creation.
- Encourage a 'top-down' management style.
- Time-consuming.
- Based around traditional business functions and do not cross boundaries.
- Encourage incremental thinking (last year's figure, plus x per cent).
- Protect rather than lower costs.
- Promote 'sharp' practice among managers.
- Budgeting is very widely regarded as useful and extensively practised despite the criticisms.

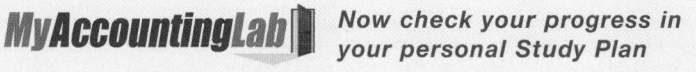

Key terms

mission statement p. 440	**management by exception** p. 448
budget p. 440	**budget committee** p. 450
control p. 441	**budget officer** p. 450
limiting factor p. 443	**incremental budgeting** p. 456
forecast p. 443	**budget holder** p. 456
periodic budget p. 444	**discretionary budget** p. 456
continual budget p. 444	**zero-base budgeting (ZBB)** p. 457
rolling budget p. 444	**activity-based budgeting (ABB)**
master budget p. 445	p. 465

References

1 **Perfect How You Project**, *BPM Forum*, 2008.

2 **Beyond Budgeting**, www.bbrt.org.

Further reading

If you would like to explore the topics covered in this chapter in more depth, we recommend the following books:

Management Accounting, *Atkinson A., Banker R., Kaplan R. and Young S. M.*, 5th edn, Prentice Hall, 2007, chapter 11.

Management and Cost Accounting, *Drury C.*, 7th edn, Cengage Learning, 2007, chapter 15.

Cost Accounting: A Managerial Emphasis, *Horngren C., Foster G., Datar S., Rajan M. and Ittner C.*, 13th edn, Prentice Hall International, 2008, chapter 6.

Managerial Accounting, *Hilton R.*, 6th edn, McGraw-Hill Irwin, 2005, chapter 9.

Review questions

Answers to these questions can be found at the back of the book on pages 747–8.

12.1   Define a budget. How is a budget different from a forecast?

12.2   What were the five uses of budgets that were identified in the chapter?

12.3   What do budgets have to do with control?

12.4   What is a budget committee? What purpose does it serve?

Exercises

Exercises 12.5 to 12.8 are more advanced than 12.1 to 12.4. Those with **coloured numbers** have answers at the back of the book, starting on page 785.

If you wish to try more exercises, visit the students' side of the Companion Website and MyAccountingLab.

12.1   Daniel Chu Ltd, a new business, will start production on 1 April, but sales will not start until 1 May. Planned sales for the next nine months are as follows:

	Sales Units
May	500
June	600
July	700
August	800
September	900
October	900
November	900
December	800
January	700

The selling price of a unit will be a consistent £100 and all sales will be made on one month's credit. It is planned that sufficient finished goods inventories for each month's sales should be available at the end of the previous month.

Raw materials purchases will be such that there will be sufficient raw materials inventories available at the end of each month precisely to meet the following month's planned production. This planned policy will operate from the end of April. Purchases of raw materials will be on one month's credit. The cost of raw material is £40 a unit of finished product.

The direct labour cost, which is variable with the level of production, is planned to be £20 a unit of finished production. Production overheads are planned to be £20,000 each month, including £3,000 for depreciation. Non-production overheads are planned to be £11,000 a month, of which £1,000 will be depreciation.

Various non-current (fixed) assets costing £250,000 will be bought and paid for during April.

Except where specified, assume that all payments take place in the same month as the cost is incurred.

The business will raise £300,000 in cash from a share issue in April.

Required:
Draw up the following for the six months ending 30 September:

(a) A finished inventories budget, showing just physical quantities.
(b) A raw materials inventories budget showing both physical quantities and financial values.
(c) A trade payables budget.
(d) A trade receivables budget.
(e) A cash budget.

12.2 You have overheard the following statements:

(a) 'A budget is a forecast of what is expected to happen in a business during the next year.'
(b) 'Monthly budgets must be prepared with a column for each month so that you can see the whole year at a glance, month by month.'
(c) 'Budgets are OK but they stifle all initiative. No manager worth employing would work for a business that seeks to control through budgets.'
(d) 'Activity-based budgeting is an approach that takes account of the planned volume of activity in order to deduce the figures to go into the budget.'
(e) 'Any sensible person would start with the sales budget and build up the other budgets from there.'

Required:
Critically discuss these statements, explaining any technical terms.

12.3 A nursing home, which is linked to a large hospital, has been examining its budgetary control procedures, with particular reference to overhead costs.

The level of activity in the facility is measured by the number of patients treated in the budget period. For the current year, the budget stands at 6,000 patients and this is expected to be met.

For months 1 to 6 of this year (assume 12 months of equal length), 2,700 patients were treated. The actual variable overhead costs incurred during this six-month period are as follows:

Expense	£
Staffing	59,400
Power	27,000
Supplies	54,000
Other	8,100
Total	148,500

The hospital accountant believes that the variable overhead costs will be incurred at the same rate during months 7 to 12 of the year.

Fixed overheads are budgeted for the whole year as follows:

Expense	£
Supervision	120,000
Depreciation/financing	187,200
Other	64,800
Total	372,000

Required:
(a) Present an overheads budget for months 7 to 12 of the year. You should show each expense, but should not separate individual months. What is the total overheads cost for each patient that would be incorporated into any statistics?

(b) The home actually treated 3,800 patients during months 7 to 12, the actual variable over-heads were £203,300, and the fixed overheads were £190,000. In summary form, examine how well the home exercised control over its overheads.

(c) Interpret your analysis and point out any limitations or assumptions.

12.4 Linpet Ltd is to be incorporated on 1 June. The opening statement of financial position (balance sheet) of the business will then be as follows:

Assets	£
Cash at bank	60,000
Share capital	
£1 ordinary shares	60,000

During June, the business intends to make payments of £40,000 for a leasehold property, £10,000 for equipment and £6,000 for a motor vehicle. The business will also purchase initial trading inventories costing £22,000 on credit.

The business has produced the following estimates:

(1) Sales revenue for June will be £8,000 and will increase at the rate of £3,000 a month until September. In October, sales revenue will rise to £22,000 and in subsequent months will be maintained at this figure.

(2) The gross profit percentage on goods sold will be 25 per cent.

(3) There is a risk that supplies of trading inventories will be interrupted towards the end of the accounting year. The business therefore intends to build up its initial level of inventories (£22,000) by purchasing £1,000 of inventories each month in addition to the monthly purchases necessary to satisfy monthly sales requirements. All purchases of inventories (including the initial inventories) will be on one month's credit.

(4) Sales revenue will be divided equally between cash and credit sales. Credit customers are expected to pay two months after the sale is agreed.

(5) Wages and salaries will be £900 a month. Other overheads will be £500 a month for the first four months and £650 thereafter. Both types of expense will be payable when incurred.

(6) 80 per cent of sales revenue will be generated by salespeople who will receive 5 per cent commission on sales revenue. The commission is payable one month after the sale is agreed.

(7) The business intends to purchase further equipment in November for £7,000 cash.

(8) Depreciation will be provided at the rate of 5 per cent a year on property and 20 per cent a year on equipment. (Depreciation has not been included in the overheads mentioned in 5 above.)

Required:

(a) State why a cash budget is required for a business.

(b) Prepare a cash budget for Linpet Ltd for the six-month period to 30 November.

12.5 Lewisham Ltd manufactures one product line – the Zenith. Sales of Zeniths over the next few months are planned to be as follows:

(1) *Demand*

	Units
July	180,000
August	240,000
September	200,000
October	180,000

Each Zenith sells for £3.

(2) *Receipts from sales*. Credit customers are expected to pay as follows:

- 70 per cent during the month of sale
- 28 per cent during the following month.

The remaining trade receivables are expected to go bad (that is, to be uncollectable). Credit customers who pay in the month of sale are entitled to deduct a 2 per cent discount from the invoice price.

(3) *Finished goods inventories*. Inventories of finished goods are expected to be 40,000 units at 1 July. The business's policy is that, in future, the inventories at the end of each month should equal 20 per cent of the following month's planned sales requirements.

(4) *Raw materials inventories*. Inventories of raw materials are expected to be 40,000 kg on 1 July. The business's policy is that, in future, the inventories at the end of each month should equal 50 per cent of the following month's planned production requirements. Each Zenith requires 0.5 kg of the raw material, which costs £1.50/kg. Raw materials purchases are paid in the month after purchase.

(5) *Labour and overheads*. The direct labour cost of each Zenith is £0.50. The variable overhead element of each Zenith is £0.30. Fixed overheads, including depreciation of £25,000, total £47,000 a month. All labour and overheads are paid during the month in which they arise.

(6) *Cash in hand*. At 1 August the business plans to have a bank balance (in funds) of £20,000.

Required:

Prepare the following budgets:

(a) Finished inventories budget (expressed in units of Zenith) for each of the three months July, August and September.

(b) Raw materials inventories budget (expressed in kilograms of the raw material) for the two months July and August.

(c) Cash budget for August and September.

12.6 Newtake Records Ltd owns a chain of 14 shops selling compact discs. At the beginning of June the business had an overdraft of £35,000 and the bank had asked for this to be eliminated by the end of November. As a result, the directors have recently decided to review their plans for the next six months.

The following plans were prepared for the business some months earlier:

	May £000	June £000	July £000	Aug £000	Sept £000	Oct £000	Nov £000
Sales revenue	180	230	320	250	140	120	110
Purchases	135	180	142	94	75	66	57
Administration expenses	52	55	56	53	48	46	45
Selling expenses	22	24	28	26	21	19	18
Taxation payment				22			
Finance payments	5	5	5	5	5	5	5
Shop refurbishment	–	–	14	18	6	–	–

Notes:

(1) The inventories level at 1 June was £112,000. The business believes it is preferable to maintain a minimum inventories level of £40,000 of goods over the period to 30 November.

(2) Suppliers allow one month's credit. The first three months' purchases are subject to a contractual agreement, which must be honoured.

(3) The gross profit margin is 40 per cent.

(4) Cash from all sales is received in the month of sale. However, 50 per cent of customers pay with a credit card. The charge made by the credit card business to Newtake Records Ltd is 3 per cent of the sales revenue value. These charges are in addition to the selling expenses identified above. The credit card business pays Newtake Records Ltd in the month of sale.

(5) The business has a bank loan, which it is paying off in monthly instalments of £5,000. The interest element represents 20 per cent of each instalment.

(6) Administration expenses are paid when incurred. This item includes a charge of £15,000 each month in respect of depreciation.

(7) Selling expenses are payable in the following month.

Required (working to the nearest £1,000):

(a) Prepare a cash budget for the six months ending 30 November which shows the cash balance at the end of each month.

(b) Compute the inventories levels at the end of each month for the six months to 30 November.

(c) Prepare a budgeted income statement for the whole of the six months period ending 30 November. (A monthly breakdown of profit is *not* required.)

(d) What problems is Newtake Records Ltd likely to face in the next six months? Can you suggest how the business might deal with these problems?

12.7 Prolog Ltd is a small wholesaler of high-specification personal computers. It has in recent months been selling 50 machines a month at a price of £2,000 each. These machines cost £1,600 each. A new model has just been launched and this is expected to offer greatly enhanced performance. Its selling price and cost will be the same as for the old model. From the beginning of January, sales are planned to increase at a rate of 20 machines each month until the end of June, when sales will amount to 170 units a month. They are planned to continue at that level thereafter. Operating costs including depreciation of £2,000 a month are planned as follows:

	January	February	March	April	May	June
Operating costs (£000)	6	8	10	12	12	12

Prolog expects to receive no credit for operating costs. Additional shelving for storage will be bought, installed and paid for in April, costing £12,000. Tax of £25,000 is due at the end of March. Prolog anticipates that trade receivables will amount to two months' sales revenue. To give its customers a good level of service, Prolog plans to hold enough inventories at the end of each month to fulfil anticipated demand from customers in the following month. The computer manufacturer, however, grants one month's credit to Prolog. Prolog Ltd's statement of financial position (balance sheet) appears below.

Statement of financial position at 31 December

ASSETS	£000
Non-current assets	80
Current assets	
Inventories	112
Trade receivables	200
Cash	–
	312
Total assets	392
EQUITY AND LIABILITIES	
Equity	
Share capital (25p ordinary shares)	10
Retained profit	177
	187
Current liabilities	
Trade payables	112
Taxation	25
Overdraft	68
	205
Total equity and liabilities	392

Required:

(a) Prepare a cash budget for Prolog Ltd showing the cash balance or required overdraft for the six months ending 30 June.

(b) State briefly what further information a banker would require from Prolog Ltd before granting additional overdraft facilities for the anticipated expansion of sales.

12.8 Brown and Jeffreys, a West Midlands business, makes one standard product for use in the motor trade. The product, known as the Fuel Miser, for which the business holds the patent, when fitted to the fuel system of production model cars has the effect of reducing petrol consumption.

Part of the production is sold direct to a local car manufacturer, which fits the Fuel Miser as an optional extra to several of its models, and the rest of the production is sold through various retail outlets, garages, and so on.

Brown and Jeffreys assemble the Fuel Miser, but all three components are manufactured by local engineering businesses. The three components are codenamed A, B and C. One Fuel Miser consists of one of each component.

The planned sales for the first seven months of the forthcoming accounting period, by channels of distribution and in terms of Fuel Miser units, are as follows:

	Jan	Feb	Mar	Apr	May	June	July
Manufacturers	4,000	4,000	4,500	4,500	4,500	4,500	4,500
Retail, and so on	2,000	2,700	3,200	3,000	2,700	2,500	2,400
	6,000	6,700	7,700	7,500	7,200	7,000	6,900

The following further information is available:

(1) There will be inventories of finished units at 1 January of 7,000 Fuel Misers.

(2) The inventories of raw materials at 1 January will be:
A   10,000 units
B   16,500 units
C   7,200 units

(3) The selling price of Fuel Misers is to be £10 each to the motor manufacturer and £12 each to retail outlets.

(4) The maximum production capacity of the business is 7,000 units a month. There is no possibility of increasing this output.

(5) Assembly of each Fuel Miser will take 10 minutes of direct labour. Direct labour is paid at the rate of £7.20 an hour during the month of production.

(6) The components are each expected to cost the following:

    A £2.50

    B £1.30

    C £0.80

(7) Indirect costs are to be paid at a regular rate of £32,000 each month.

(8) The cash at the bank at 1 January will be £2,620.

The planned sales volumes must be met and the business intends to pursue the following policies for as many months as possible, consistent with meeting the sales targets:

● Finished inventories at the end of each month are to equal the following month's total sales to retail outlets, and half the total of the following month's sales to the motor manufacturer.

● Raw materials at the end of each month are to be sufficient to cover production requirements for the following month. The production for July will be 6,800 units.

● Suppliers of raw materials are to be paid during the month following purchase. The payment for January will be £21,250.

● Customers will pay in the month of sale, in the case of sales to the motor manufacturer, and the month after sale, in the case of retail sales. Retail sales during December were 2,000 units at £12 each.

Required:

Prepare the following budgets in monthly columnar form, both in terms of money and units (where relevant), for the six months of January to June inclusive:

(a) Sales budget.*

(b) Finished inventories budget (valued at direct cost).[†]

(c) Raw materials inventories budget (one budget for each component).[†]

(d) Production budget (direct costs only).*

(e) Trade receivables budget.[†]

(f) Trade payables budget.[†]

(g) Cash budget.[†]

* The sales and production budgets should merely state each month's sales or production in units and in money terms.

[†] The other budgets should all seek to reconcile the opening balance of inventories, trade receivables, trade payables or cash with the closing balance through movements of the relevant factors over the month.

CHAPTER 13

Accounting for control

Introduction

This chapter deals with the role of budgets in management control. In its 2008 annual report, Associated British Foods Group plc, the food processor, stated:

> Performance against budget is monitored at operational level and centrally, with variances being reported promptly.

How is performance monitored? What are variances? Why does the business identify and report variances? These are some of the questions that we shall seek to answer in this chapter. As we shall see later, the practice at AB Foods is typical of businesses of all sizes.

In this chapter, we shall continue some of the themes that we discussed in Chapter 12. We shall consider how a budget can be used to help control a business, and we shall see that, by collecting information on actual performance and comparing it with a revised budget, it is possible to identify those activities that are in control and those that are not.

Budgets are designed to influence the behaviour of managers and we shall explore some of the issues relating to budgets and management behaviour. We shall also take a look at standard costing and its relationship with budgeting. We shall see that standards provide the building blocks for budgets.

Learning outcomes

When you have completed this chapter, you should be able to:

- Discuss the role and limitations of budgets for performance evaluation and control.
- Undertake variance analysis and discuss possible reasons for the variances calculated.
- Discuss the issues that should be taken into account when designing an effective system of budgetary control.
- Explain the nature, role and limitations of standard costing.

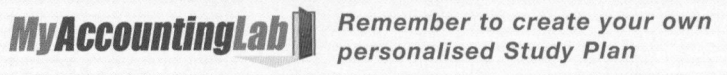

MyAccountingLab Remember to create your own personalised Study Plan

Budgeting for control

In Chapter 12, we saw that budgets provide a useful basis for exercising control over a business. Control involves making events conform to a plan and, since the budget is a short-term plan, making events conform to it is an obvious way to try to control the business. We also saw that, for most businesses, the routine is as shown in Figure 13.1.

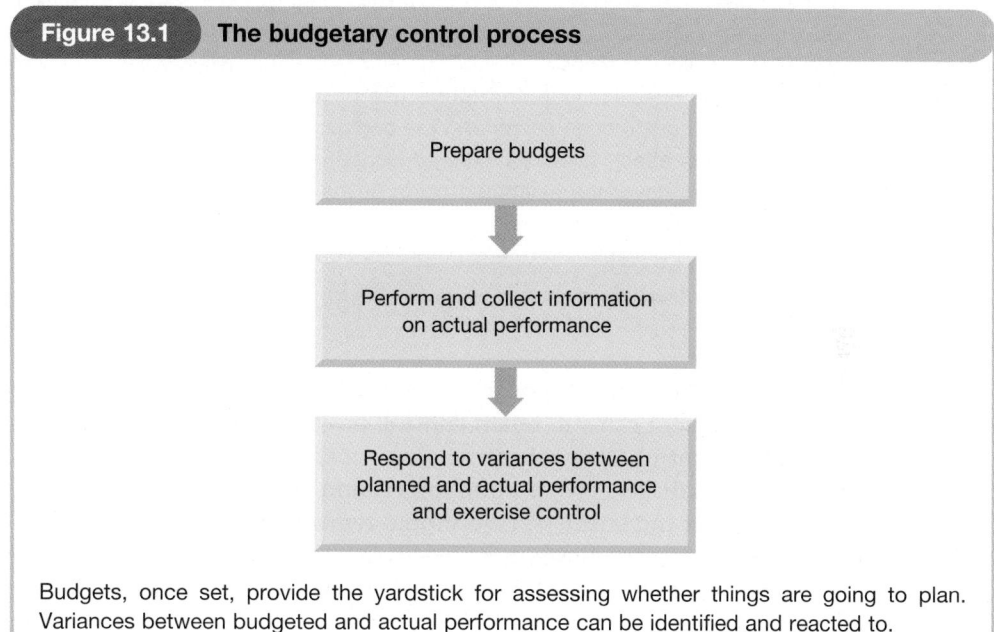

Figure 13.1   The budgetary control process

> Prepare budgets
>
> Perform and collect information on actual performance
>
> Respond to variances between planned and actual performance and exercise control

Budgets, once set, provide the yardstick for assessing whether things are going to plan. Variances between budgeted and actual performance can be identified and reacted to.

If plans are drawn up sensibly, we have a basis for exercising control over the business. We must, however, measure actual performance in the same terms as those in which the budget is stated. If they are not in the same terms, proper comparison will not be possible.

Exercising control involves finding out where and why things did not go according to plan and then seeking ways to put them right for the future. One reason why things may not have gone according to plan is that the budget targets were unachievable. In this case, it may be necessary to revise the budgets for future periods so that targets become achievable.

This last point should not be taken to mean that budget targets can simply be ignored if the going gets tough; rather that they should be adaptable. Unrealistic budgets cannot form a basis for exercising control and little can be gained by sticking with them.

Real World 13.1 reveals how one important budget had to be dramatically revised because it had become unrealistic.

Real World 13.1

No medals for budgeting

FT

The government's dramatic increase this spring in the budget for the 2012 Olympic games, almost tripling the £3.3bn cost to the taxpayer estimated at the time of winning the 2005 bid, has put the event on a 'firmer financial footing', says a report by the National Audit Office (NAO).

Nevertheless, the revised £9.3bn London Olympics budget contains 'significant areas of uncertainty' that could drive costs up, unless effective controls are exercised. Sir John Bourn, head of the NAO, warned the government it still had to 'work to contain funding and achieve value for money'. He highlighted areas of uncertainty affecting costs, including the design specifications and future use of the Olympic venues, the level of price inflation in the construction sector and the contracts negotiated by suppliers.

The NAO, in effect, gives the revised budget its seal of approval, saying it 'should be sufficient' to cover the estimated costs of the games, provided – a 'most important proviso' – the assumptions on which the budget is based hold good. But its report calls for action by the government to ensure proper controls over the huge project.

Source: Adapted from 'Watchdog warns on Olympic costs', Jean Eaglesham, FT.com, 20 July 2007.

Decision making and responsibility can be delegated to junior management, yet senior management can still retain control, provided that there is an adequate system of budgetary control. This is because senior managers can use the system to find out which junior managers are meeting targets and therefore working towards achieving the objectives of the business. (We should remember that budgets are the short-term plans for achieving the business's objectives.) This enables a *management-by-exception* environment to be created where senior management can focus on areas where things are *not* going according to plan (the exceptions – it is to be hoped). Junior managers who are performing to budget can be left to get on with their jobs.

Types of control

→ The control process just outlined is known as **feedback control**. Its main feature is that steps are taken to get operations back on track as soon as there is a signal that they have gone wrong. This is similar to the thermostatic control that is a feature of most central heating systems. The thermostat incorporates a thermometer that senses when the temperature has fallen below a preset level (analogous to the budget). The thermostat then takes action to correct matters by activating the heating device that restores the required minimum temperature. Figure 13.2 depicts the stages in a feedback control system using budgets.

→ There is an alternative type of control, known as **feedforward control**. Here predictions are made as to what can go wrong and steps taken to avoid any undesirable outcome. The preparation of budgets, which we discussed in Chapter 12, provides an example of this type of control. Preparing a particular budget may reveal a problem that will arise unless the business changes its plans. For example, preparing the cash budget may reveal that if the original plans are followed, there will be a negative cash balance for part of the budget period. Having identified the problem, the plans can then be revised to deal with it.

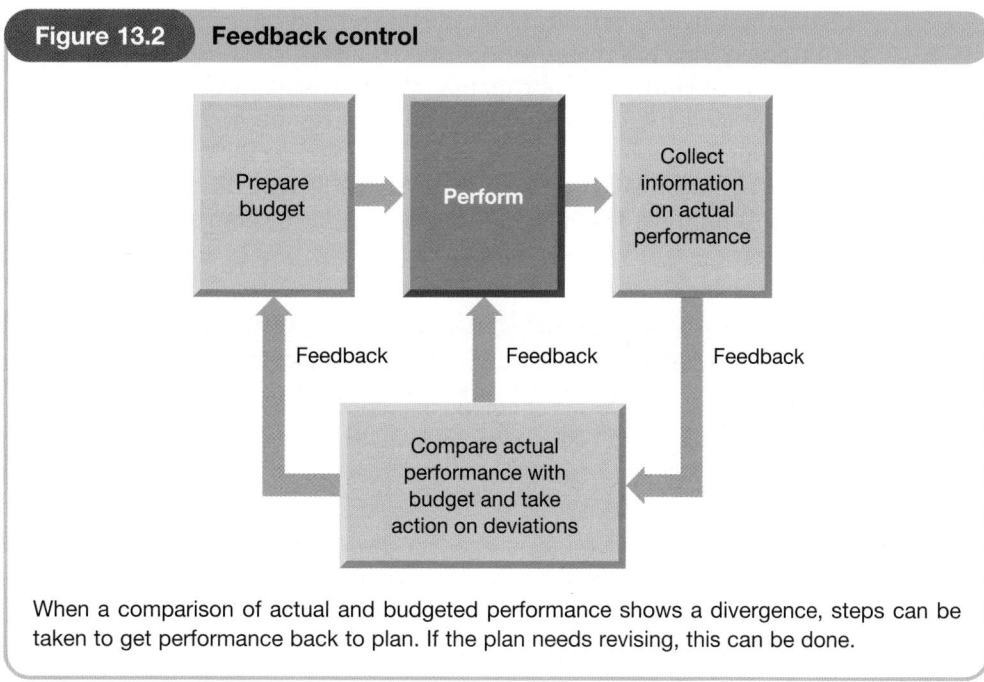

Figure 13.2 **Feedback control**

When a comparison of actual and budgeted performance shows a divergence, steps can be taken to get performance back to plan. If the plan needs revising, this can be done.

We can see that feedforward controls try to anticipate future problems, whereas feedback controls react to problems that have already occurred. Budgeting embraces both forms of control. Preparing a budget is a form of feedforward control while comparing the budget with actual results is a form of feedback control. Generally speaking, feedforward controls are preferable; things are less likely to go wrong in the first place if steps have been taken to anticipate problems and plan accordingly. It is not always possible, however, to establish effective feedforward controls.

Variances from budget

We saw in Chapter 1 that the key financial objective of a business is to increase the wealth of its owners (shareholders). Since profit is the net increase in wealth from business operations, the most important budget target to meet is the profit target. We shall therefore take this as our starting point when comparing the budget with the actual results. Example 13.1 shows the budgeted and actual income statements for Baxter Ltd for the month of May.

Example 13.1

The following are the budgeted and actual income statements for Baxter Ltd, a manufacturing business, for the month of May:

	Budget	Actual
Output (production and sales)	1,000 units	900 units
	£	£
Sales revenue	100,000	92,000
Raw materials	(40,000) (40,000 metres)	(36,900) (37,000 metres)
Labour	(20,000) (2,500 hours)	(17,500) (2,150 hours)
Fixed overheads	(20,000)	(20,700)
Operating profit	20,000	16,900

From these figures, it is clear that the budgeted profit was not achieved. As far as May is concerned, this is a matter of history. However, the business (or at least one aspect of it) is out of control. Senior management must discover where things went wrong during May and try to ensure that these mistakes are not repeated in later months. It is not enough to know that things went wrong overall. We need to know where and why. The approach taken is to compare the budgeted and actual figures for the various items (sales revenue, raw materials and so on) in the above statement.

Activity (13.1)

Can you see any problems in comparing the various items (sales revenue, raw materials and so on) for the budget with the actual performance of Baxter Ltd in an attempt to draw conclusions as to which aspects were out of control?

The problem is that the actual level of output was not as budgeted. The actual level of output was 10 per cent less than budget. This means that we cannot, for example, say that there was a labour cost saving of £2,500 (that is, £20,000 – £17,500) and conclude that all is well in that area.

Flexing the budget

One practical way to overcome our difficulty is to 'flex' the budget to what it would have been had the planned level of output been 900 units rather than 1,000 units. **Flexing the budget** simply means revising it, assuming a different volume of output.

Here, the budget is usually flexed to reflect the volume that actually occurred, where this is higher or lower than that originally planned. This means that we need to know which revenues and costs are fixed and which are variable relative to the volume of output. Once we know this, flexing is a simple operation. We shall assume that sales revenue, material cost and labour cost vary strictly with volume. Fixed overheads, by definition, will not. Whether, in real life, labour cost does vary with the volume of output is not so certain, but it will serve well enough as an assumption for our purposes. Were labour actually fixed, we should simply take this into account in the flexing process.

On the basis of our assumptions regarding the behaviour of revenues and costs, the flexed budget would be as follows:

	Flexed budget
Output (production and sales)	<u>900</u> units
	£
Sales revenue	90,000
Raw materials	(36,000) (36,000 metres)
Labour	(18,000) (2,250 hours)
Fixed overheads	<u>(20,000)</u>
Operating profit	<u>16,000</u>

This is simply the original budget, with the sales revenue, raw materials and labour cost figures scaled down by 10 per cent (the same factor as the actual output fell short of the budgeted one).

Putting the original budget, the flexed budget and the actual for May together, we obtain the following:

	Original budget	Flexed budget	Actual
Output (production and sales)	1,000 units	900 units	900 units
	£	£	£
Sales revenue	100,000	90,000	92,000
Raw materials	(40,000)	(36,000) (36,000 m)	(36,900) (37,000 m)
Labour	(20,000)	(18,000) (2,250 hr)	(17,500) (2,150 hr)
Fixed overheads	(20,000)	(20,000)	(20,700)
Operating profit	20,000	16,000	16,900

→   **Flexible budgets** allow us to make a more valid comparison between the budget (using the flexed figures) and the actual results. Key differences, or variances, between budgeted and actual results for each aspect of the business's activities can then be calculated. In the rest of this section we consider some of the variances that may be calculated.

Sales volume variance

Let us begin by dealing with the shortfall in sales volume. It may seem as if we are saying that this does not matter, because we just revise the budget and carry on as if all is well. It is clearly not true that losing sales volume does not matter because a sales volume shortfall normally means losing profit. The first point we must pick up, therefore, is the profit shortfall arising from the loss of sales of 100 units of the product.

Activity (13.2)

What will be the loss of profit arising from the sales volume shortfall, assuming that everything except sales volume was as planned?

The answer is simply the difference between the original and flexed budget profit figures. The only difference between these two profit figures is the volume of sales; everything else was the same. (That is to say that the flexing was carried out assuming that the per-unit sales revenue, raw material cost and labour cost were all as originally budgeted.) This means that the figure for the loss of profit due to the volume shortfall, taken alone, is £4,000 (that is, £20,000 – £16,000).

When we considered the relationship between cost, volume and profit in Chapter 9, we saw that selling one unit less will result in one less contribution to profit. The contribution is sales revenue less variable cost. We can see from the original budget that the unit sales revenue is £100 (that is, £100,000/1,000), raw material cost is £40 a unit (that is, £40,000/1,000) and labour cost is £20 a unit (that is, £20,000/1,000). Thus the contribution is £40 a unit (that is, £100 – (£40 + £20)).

If, therefore, 100 units of sales are lost, £4,000 (that is, 100 × £40) of contributions and therefore profit are forgone. Incidentally, this would be an alternative means of finding the sales volume variance, instead of taking the difference between the original and flexed budget profit figures. Once we have produced the flexed budget, however, it is generally easier to compare the two profit figures.

The difference between the original and flexed budget profit figures is called the **sales volume variance**.

In this case, it is an **adverse variance** because, taken alone, it has the effect of making the actual profit lower than the budgeted profit. A variance that has the effect of increasing profit beyond the budgeted profit is known as a **favourable variance**. We can therefore say that a **variance** is the effect of that factor (taken alone) on the budgeted profit. Later we shall consider other forms of variance, some of which may be favourable and some adverse. The difference between the sum of all the various favourable and adverse variances will represent the difference between the budgeted and actual profit. This is shown in Figure 13.3.

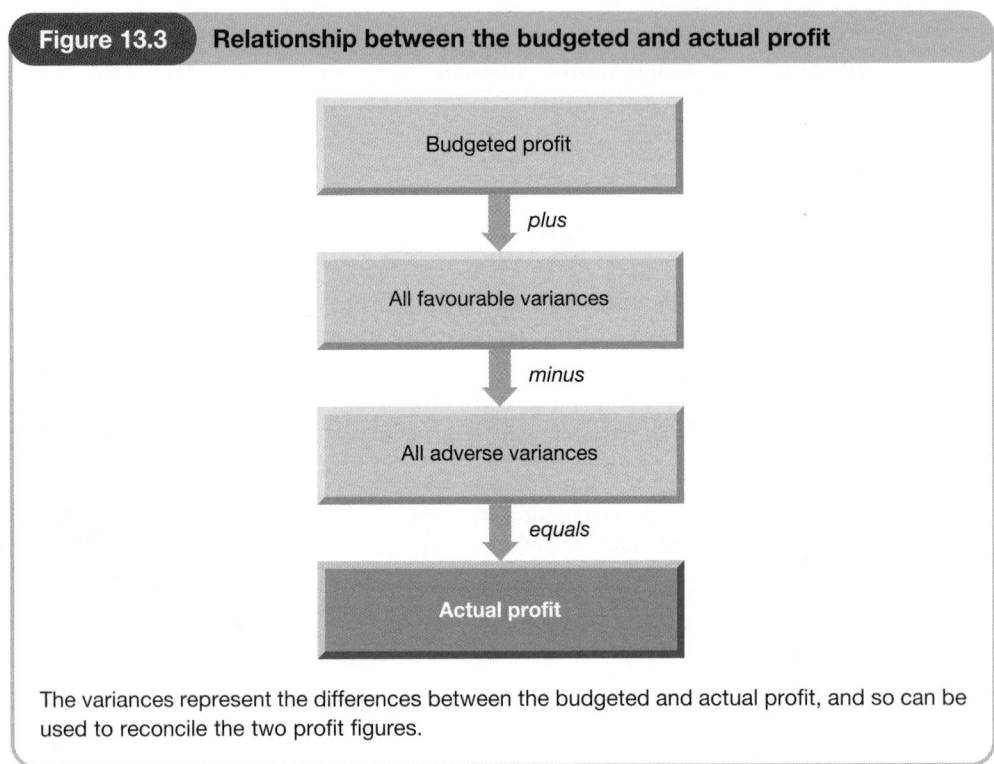

Figure 13.3 **Relationship between the budgeted and actual profit**

The variances represent the differences between the budgeted and actual profit, and so can be used to reconcile the two profit figures.

When calculating a particular variance, such as sales volume, we assume that all other factors went according to plan.

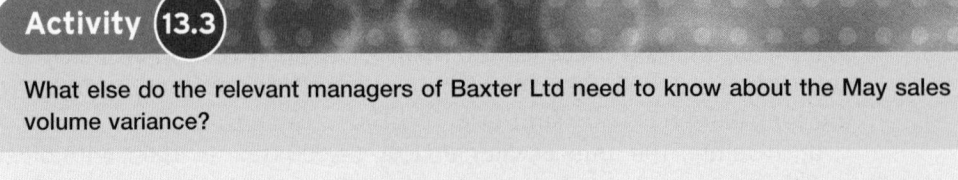

Activity 13.3

What else do the relevant managers of Baxter Ltd need to know about the May sales volume variance?

They need to know why the volume of sales fell below the budgeted figure. Only by discovering this information will they be in a position to try to ensure that it does not occur again.

Who should be held accountable for this sales volume variance? The answer is probably the sales manager, who should know precisely why this has occurred. This is not the same as saying, however, that it was the sales manager's fault. The problem may have been that the business failed to produce the budgeted quantities so that not enough items were available to sell. Nevertheless, the sales manager should know the reason for the problem.

The budget and actual figures for Baxter Ltd for *June* are given in Activity 13.4 and will be used as the basis for a series of activities that provide an opportunity to calculate and assess the variances. We shall continue to use the *May* figures for explaining the variances.

Note that the business had budgeted for a higher level of output for *June* than it did for *May*.

Activity 13.4

	Budget for June	Actual for June
Output (production and sales)	1,100 units	1,150 units
	£	£
Sales revenue	110,000	113,500
Raw materials	(44,000) (44,000 metres)	(46,300) (46,300 metres)
Labour	(22,000) (2,750 hours)	(23,200) (2,960 hours)
Fixed overheads	(20,000)	(19,300)
Operating profit	24,000	24,700

Try flexing the June budget, comparing it with the original June budget, and so find the sales volume variance.

	Flexed budget
Output (production and sales)	1,150 units
	£
Sales revenue	115,000
Raw materials	(46,000) (46,000 metres)
Labour	(23,000) (2,875 hours)
Fixed overheads	(20,000)
Operating profit	26,000

The sales volume variance is £2,000 (favourable) (that is, £26,000 – £24,000). It is favourable because the original budget profit was lower than the flexed budget profit. This arises from more sales actually being made than were budgeted.

For the month of May, we have already identified one reason why the budgeted profit of £20,000 was not achieved and that the actual profit was only £16,900. This was the £4,000 loss of profit (adverse variance) that arose from the sales volume shortfall. Now that the budget is flexed, we can compare like with like and reach further conclusions about May's trading.

The fact that the sales revenue, raw materials, labour and fixed overheads figures differ between the flexed budget and the actual results (see page 487) suggests that the adverse sales volume variance was not the only problem area. To identify those relating to each of the revenue and cost items mentioned, we need to calculate further variances. This is done in the sections below.

Sales price variance

Starting with the sales revenue figure, we can see that, for *May*, there is a difference of £2,000 (favourable) between the flexed budget and the actual figures. This can only arise from higher prices being charged than were envisaged in the original budget, because any variance arising from the volume difference has already been 'stripped out' in the flexing process. This price difference is known as the **sales price variance**. Higher sales prices will, all other things being equal, mean more profit. So there is a favourable variance.

When senior management is trying to identify the reason for a sales price variance, it would normally be the sales manager who should be able to offer an explanation. As we shall see later in the chapter, favourable variances of significant size will normally be investigated.

Activity (13.5)

Using the figures in Activity 13.4, what is the sales price variance for June?

The sales price variance for *June* is £1,500 (adverse) (that is, £115,000 − £113,500). Actual sales prices, on average, must have been lower than those budgeted. The actual price averaged £98.70 (that is, £113,500/1,150) whereas the budgeted price was £100. Selling output at a lower price than that budgeted will have an adverse effect on profit, hence an adverse variance.

Let us now move on to look at the cost variances, starting with materials variances.

Materials variances

In *May*, there was an overall or **total direct materials variance** of £900 (adverse) (that is, £36,900 − £36,000). It is adverse because the actual material cost was higher than the budgeted one, which has an adverse effect on operating profit.

Who should be held accountable for this variance? The answer depends on whether the difference arises from excess usage of the raw material, in which case it is the production manager, or whether it is a higher-than-budgeted cost per metre being paid, in which case it is the responsibility of the buying manager. Fortunately, we can go beyond this total variance to examine the effect of changes in both usage and cost. We can see from the figures that in *May* there was a 1,000 metre excess usage of the raw material (that is, 37,000 metres − 36,000 metres). All other things being equal, this alone would have led to a profit shortfall of £1,000, since clearly the budgeted cost per metre is £1. The £1,000 (adverse) variance is known as the **direct materials usage variance**. Normally, this variance would be the responsibility of the production manager.

Activity (13.6)

Using the figures in Activity 13.4, what was the direct material usage variance for June?

The direct material usage variance for *June* was £300 (adverse) (that is, (46,300 metres − 46,000 metres) × £1). It is adverse because more material was used than was budgeted, for an output of 1,150 units. Excess usage of material will tend to reduce profit.

→ The other aspect of direct materials is their cost. The **direct materials price variance** simply takes the actual cost of materials used and compares it with the cost that was allowed, given the quantity used. In *May* the actual cost of direct materials used was £36,900, whereas the allowed cost of the 37,000 metres was £37,000. Thus we have a favourable variance of £100. Paying less than the budgeted cost will have a favourable effect on profit, hence a favourable variance.

Activity 13.7

Using the figures in Activity 13.4, what was the direct materials price variance for June?

The direct materials price variance for *June* was zero (that is, £46,300 − (46,300 × £1)).

As we have just seen, the total direct materials variance is the sum of the usage variance and the price variance. The relationship between the direct materials variances for May is shown in Figure 13.4.

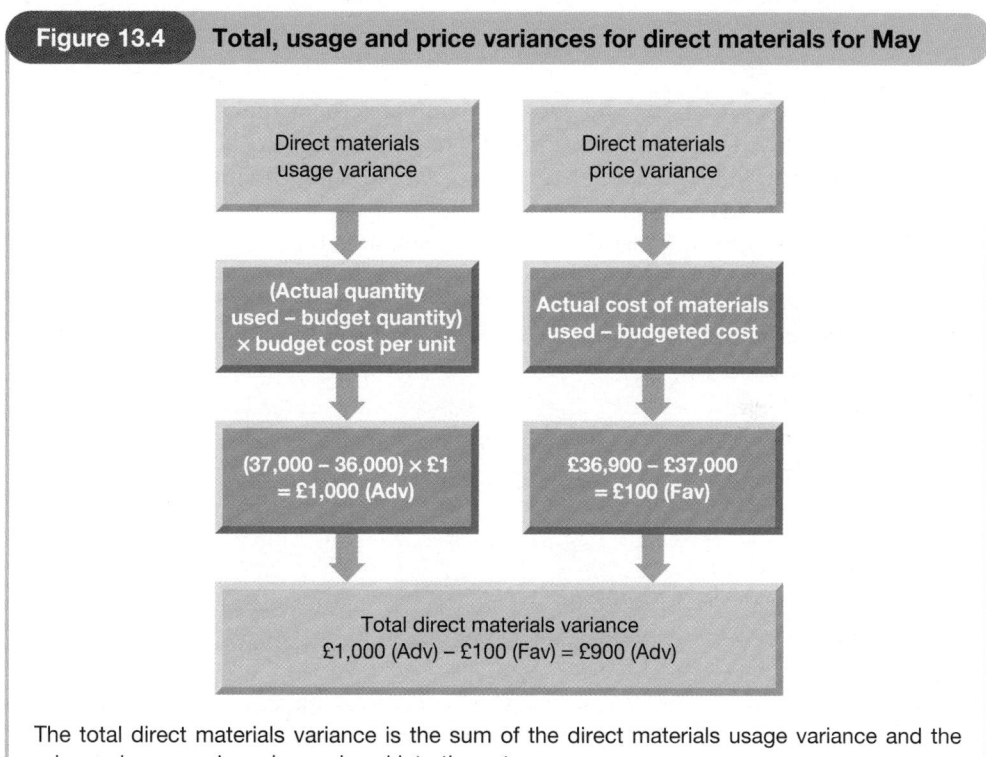

Figure 13.4 — **Total, usage and price variances for direct materials for May**

The total direct materials variance is the sum of the direct materials usage variance and the price variance, and can be analysed into those two.

Labour variances

→ Direct labour variances are similar in form to those for direct materials. The **total direct labour variance** for *May* was £500 (favourable) (that is, £18,000 − £17,500). It is favourable because £500 less was spent on labour than was budgeted for the actual level of output achieved.

Again, this total variance is not particularly helpful and needs to be analysed further into its usage and cost elements. We should bear in mind that the number of hours used to complete a particular quantity of output is the responsibility of the production manager, whereas the responsibility for the rate of pay lies primarily with the human resources manager.

→ The **direct labour efficiency variance** compares the number of hours that would be allowed for the achieved level of production with the actual number of hours taken. It then costs this difference at the allowed hourly rate. Thus, for *May*, it was (2,250 hours – 2,150 hours) × £8 = £800 (favourable). We know that the budgeted hourly rate is £8 because the original budget shows that 2,500 hours were budgeted to cost £20,000. The variance is favourable because fewer hours were used than would have been allowed for the actual level of output. Working more quickly would tend to lead to higher profit.

Activity (13.8)

Using the figures in Activity 13.4, what was the direct labour efficiency variance for June?

The direct labour efficiency variance for *June* was £680 (adverse) (that is, (2,960 hours – 2,875 hours) × £8). It is adverse because the work took longer than the budget allowed and so will have an adverse effect on profit.

→ The **direct labour rate variance** compares the actual cost of the hours worked with the allowed cost. For 2,150 hours worked in *May*, the allowed cost would be £17,200 (that is, 2,150 × £8). So, the direct labour rate variance is £300 (adverse) (that is, £17,500 – £17,200).

The relationship between the direct labour variances for May is shown in Figure 13.5.

Figure 13.5 Total, efficiency and rate variances for direct labour for May

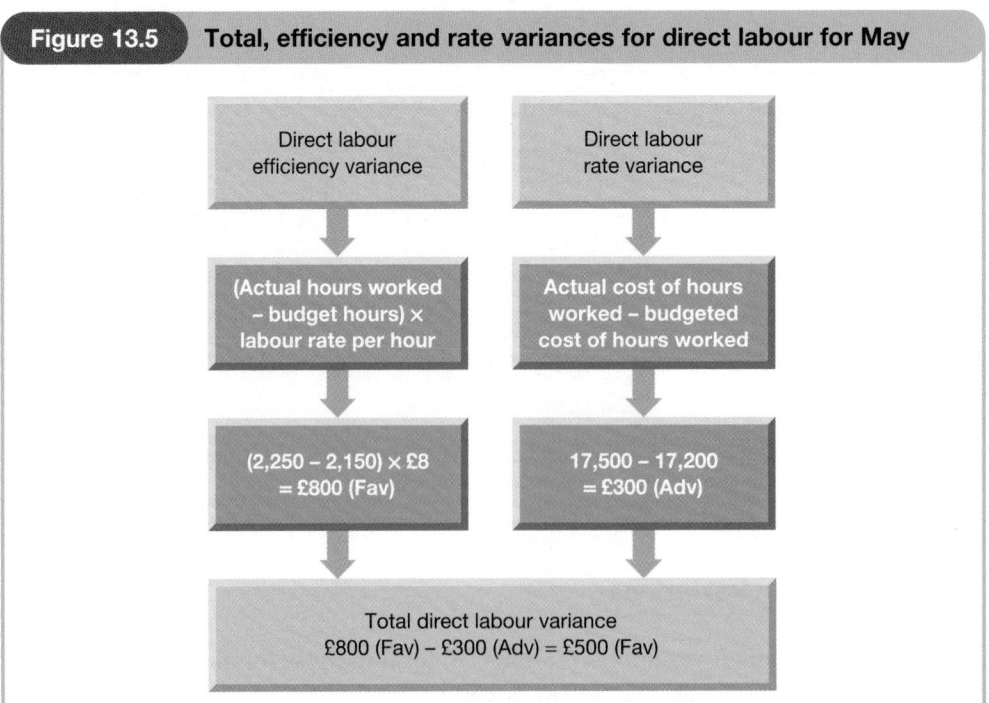

The total direct labour variance is the sum of the direct labour efficiency variance and the rate variance, and can be analysed into those two.

Activity 13.9

Using the figures in Activity 13.4, what was the direct labour rate variance for June?

The direct labour rate variance for *June* was £480 (favourable) (that is, (2,960 × £8) − £23,200). It is favourable because a lower rate was paid than the budgeted one. Paying a lower wage rate will have a favourable effect on profit.

Fixed overhead variance

The final area is that of overheads. In our example, we have assumed that all of the overheads are fixed. Variable overheads certainly exist in practice, but they have been omitted here simply to restrict the amount of detailed coverage. Variances involving variable overheads are similar in style to labour and material variances.

The **fixed overhead spending variance** is simply the difference between the flexed (or original – they will be the same) budget and the actual figures. For *May*, this was £700 (adverse) (that is, £20,700 − £20,000). It is adverse because more overheads cost was actually incurred than was budgeted. This would tend to lead to less profit. In theory, this is the responsibility of whoever controls overheads expenditure.

In practice, overheads tend to be a very slippery area, and one that is notoriously difficult to control. Of course fixed overheads (and variable ones) are usually made up of more than one type of cost. Typically, they would include such things as rent, administrative costs, salaries of managerial staff, cleaning, electricity and so on. These could be individually budgeted and the actuals recorded. This would enable individual spending variances to be identified for each element of overheads, which in turn would enable managers to identify any problem areas.

Activity 13.10

Using the figures in Activity 13.4, what was the fixed overhead spending variance for June?

The fixed overhead spending variance for *June* was £700 (favourable) (that is, £20,000 − £19,300). It was favourable because less was spent on overheads than was budgeted, thereby having a favourable effect on profit.

We are now in a position to reconcile the original *May* budgeted operating profit with the actual operating profit, as follows:

	£	£
Budgeted operating profit		20,000
Add **Favourable variances**		
Sales price	2,000	
Direct materials price	100	
Direct labour efficiency	800	2,900
		22,900
Less **Adverse variances**		
Sales volume	4,000	
Direct materials usage	1,000	
Direct labour rate	300	
Fixed overhead spending	700	6,000
Actual operating profit		16,900

Activity (13.11)

If you were the chief executive of Baxter Ltd, what attitude would you take to the overall difference between the budgeted profit and the actual one?

How would you react to the individual variances that are the outcome of the analysis shown above?

You would probably be concerned about how large the variances are and their direction (favourable or adverse). In particular you may have thought of the following:

- The overall adverse profit variance is £3,100 (that is £20,000 – £16,900). This represents 15.5 per cent of the budgeted profit (that is £3,100/£20,000 × 100%) and you (as chief executive) would almost certainly see it as significant and worrying.
- The £4,000 adverse sales volume variance represents 20 per cent of budgeted profit and would be a particular cause of concern.
- The £2,000 favourable sales price variance represents 10 per cent of budgeted profit. Since this is favourable it might be seen as a cause for celebration rather than concern. On the other hand it means that Baxter Ltd's output was, on average, sold at prices 10 per cent above the planned price. This could have been the cause of the worrying adverse sales volume variance. The business may have sold fewer units because it charged higher prices.
- The £100 favourable direct materials price variance is very small in relation to budgeted profit – only 0.5 per cent. It would be unrealistic to expect the actual figures to hit the precise budgeted figures each month and so this is unlikely to be regarded as significant. The direct materials usage variance, however, represents 5 per cent of the budgeted profit. The chief executive may feel this is cause for concern.
- The £800 favourable direct labour efficiency variance represents 4 per cent of budgeted profit. Although it is a favourable variance, the reasons for it may be worth investigating. The £300 adverse direct labour rate variance represents only 1.5 per cent of the budgeted profit and may not be regarded as significant .
- The £700 fixed overhead adverse variance represents 3.5 per cent of budgeted profit. The chief executive may feel that this is too low to cause real concern.

The chief executive will now need to ask some questions as to why things went so badly wrong in several areas and what can be done to improve future performance.

We shall shortly come back to the dilemma as to which variances to investigate and which to accept.

Activity (13.12)

Using the figures in Activity 13.4, try reconciling the original operating profit figure for June with the actual June figure.

	£	£
Budgeted operating profit		24,000
Add **Favourable variances**		
Sales volume	2,000	
Direct labour rate	480	
Fixed overhead spending	700	3,180
		27,180

Less **Adverse variances**		
Sales price	1,500	
Direct materials usage	300	
Direct labour efficiency	680	2,480
Actual operating profit		24,700

Activity 13.13

The following are the budgeted and actual income statements for Baxter Ltd for the month of July:

	Budget	Actual
Output (production and sales)	1,000 units	1,050 units
	£	£
Sales revenue	100,000	104,300
Raw materials	(40,000) (40,000 metres)	(41,200) (40,500 metres)
Labour	(20,000) (2,500 hours)	(21,300) (2,600 hours)
Fixed overheads	(20,000)	(19,400)
Operating profit	20,000	22,400

Produce a reconciliation of the budgeted and actual operating profit, going into as much detail as possible with the variance analysis.

The original budget, the flexed budget and the actual are as follows:

	Original budget	Flexed budget	Actual
Output (production and sales)	1,000 units	1,050 units	1,050 units
	£	£	£
Sales revenue	100,000	105,000	104,300
Raw materials	(40,000)	(42,000) (42,000 m)	(41,200) (40,500 m)
Labour	(20,000)	(21,000) (2,625 hrs)	(21,300) (2,600 hrs)
Fixed overheads	(20,000)	(20,000)	(19,400)
Operating profit	20,000	22,000	22,400

Reconciliation of the budgeted and actual operating profits for July

	£	£
Budgeted operating profit		20,000
Add **Favourable variances:**		
Sales volume (22,000 − 20,000)	2,000	
Direct materials usage [(42,000 − 40,500) × £1]	1,500	
Direct labour efficiency [(2,625 − 2,600) × £8]	200	
Fixed overhead spending (20,000 − 19,400)	600	4,300
		24,300
Less **Adverse variances:**		
Sales price (105,000 − 104,300)	700	
Direct materials price [(40,500 × £1) − 41,200]	700	
Direct labour rate [(2,600 × £8) − 21,300]	500	1,900
Actual operating profit		22,400

Real World 13.2 shows how two UK-based businesses, Next plc, the retailer, and British Airways, the airline business, use variance analysis to exercise control over their operations. Many businesses explain in their annual reports how they operate systems of budgetary control.

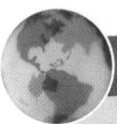

Real World 13.2

Variance analysis in practice

What Next?

According to its annual report Next has the following arrangements:

> The Board is responsible for approving semi-annual Group budgets. Performance against budget is reported to the Board monthly and any substantial variances are explained.

BA at the controls

BA makes it clear that it too uses budgets and variance analysis to help keep control over its activities. The annual report says:

> A comprehensive management accounting system is in place providing management with financial and operational performance measurement indicators. Detailed management accounts are prepared monthly to cover each major area of the business. Variances from plan are analysed, explained and acted on in a timely manner.

> The board of directors of neither of these businesses will seek explanations of variances arising at each branch/flight/department, but they will be looking at figures for the businesses as a whole or the results for major divisions of them.

> Equally certainly, branch/department managers will receive a monthly (or perhaps more frequent) report of variances arising within their area of responsibility alone.

Sources: Next plc Annual Report 2008 (p. 24) and British Airways plc Annual Report 2008 (p. 58).

Real World 13.3 gives some indication of the importance of flexible budgeting in practice.

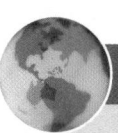

Real World 13.3

Flexing the budgets

A recent study of the UK food and drinks industry by Abdel-Kader and Luther provides us with some insight as to the importance attached by management accountants to flexible budgeting. The study asked those in charge of the management accounting function to rate the importance of flexible budgeting by selecting one of three possible categories – 'not important', 'moderately important' or 'important'. Figure 13.6 sets out the results, from the sample of 117 respondents.

Respondents were also asked to state the frequency with which flexible budgeting was used within the business, using a five-point scale ranging from 1 (never) through to 5 (very often). Figure 13.7 sets out the results.

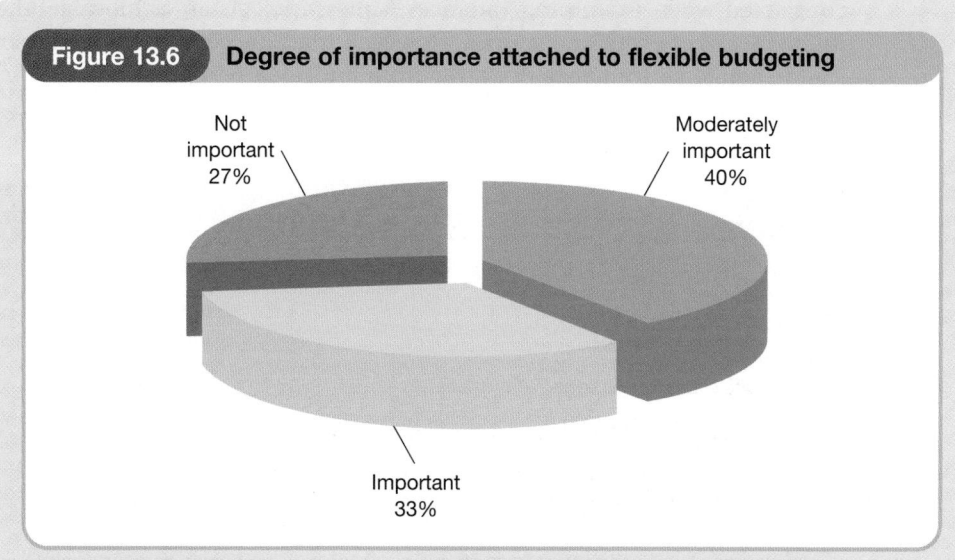

Figure 13.6 Degree of importance attached to flexible budgeting

Not important 27%
Moderately important 40%
Important 33%

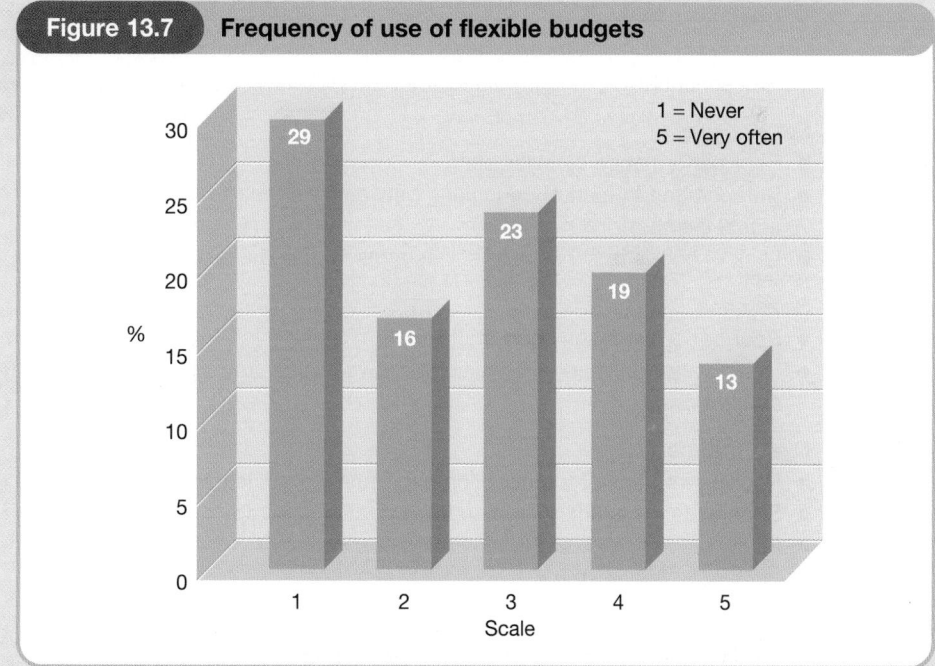

Figure 13.7 Frequency of use of flexible budgets

1 = Never
5 = Very often

%

Scale

We can see that, whilst flexible budgeting is regarded as important by a significant proportion of management accountants and is being used in practice, not all businesses use it.

Source: Taken from information appearing in *An Empirical Investigation of the Evolution of Management Accounting Practices*, M. Abdel-Kader and R. Luther, Working paper No. 04/06, University of Essex, October 2004.

Reasons for adverse variances

One reason that adverse variances may occur is that the budgets against which performance is being measured are unachievable. This possibility should always be

considered when examining variances. Unless budgets are achievable, they are not a useful means of exercising control. However, there are certainly other reasons that may lead to actual performance deviating from budgeted performance.

Activity (13.14)

The variances that we have considered are:

- sales volume
- sales price
- direct materials usage
- direct materials price
- direct labour efficiency
- direct labour rate
- fixed overhead spending.

Assuming that the budget targets are reasonable, jot down some possible reasons for adverse variances for each of the above occurring.

The reasons that we thought of included the following:

Sales volume
- Poor performance by sales staff.
- Deterioration in market conditions between the time that the budget was set and the actual event.
- Lack of goods or services to sell as a result of some production problem.

Sales price
- Poor performance by sales staff.
- Deterioration in market conditions between the time of setting the budget and the actual event.

Direct materials usage
- Poor performance by production department staff, leading to high rates of scrap.
- Substandard materials, leading to high rates of scrap.
- Faulty machinery, causing high rates of scrap.

Direct materials price
- Poor performance by the buying department staff.
- Using higher quality material than was planned.
- Change in market conditions between the time that the budget was set and the actual event.

Labour efficiency
- Poor supervision.
- A low skill grade of worker taking longer to do the work than was envisaged for the correct skill grade.
- Low-grade materials, leading to high levels of scrap and wasted labour time.
- Problems with a customer for whom a service is being rendered.
- Problems with machinery, leading to labour time being wasted.
- Dislocation of materials supply, leading to workers being unable to proceed with production.

Labour rate
- Poor performance by the human resources department.
- Using a higher grade of worker than was planned.
- Change in labour market conditions between the time of setting the budget and the actual event.

Fixed overheads
- Poor supervision of overheads.
- General increase in costs of overheads not taken into account in the budget.

Note that different variances may have the same underlying cause. For example, the purchase of low quality, cheaper materials may result in an unfavourable direct materials usage variance, a favourable direct materials price variance and an unfavourable direct labour efficiency variance.

Variance analysis in service industries

Although we have tended to use the example of a manufacturing business to explain variance analysis, this should not be taken to imply that variance analysis is not relevant and useful to service sector businesses. It is simply that manufacturing businesses tend to have all of the variances found in practice. Service businesses, for example, may not have material variances.

Real World 13.2 earlier shows that BA, a very well-known service provider, uses budgets and variance analysis to help it to manage this complex organisation.

Non-operating-profit variances

There are many areas of business that have a budget but where a failure to meet the budget does not have a direct effect on profit. Frequently, however, it has an indirect effect and, sometimes, a profound one. For example, the cash budget sets out the planned receipts, payments and resultant cash balance for the period. If the person responsible for the cash budget gets things wrong, or is forced to make unplanned expenditures, this could lead to unplanned cash shortages and accompanying costs. These costs might be limited to lost interest on possible investments, which could otherwise have been made, or to the need to pay overdraft interest. If the cash shortage cannot be covered by some form of borrowing, the consequences could be more profound, such as the loss of profits on business that was not able to be undertaken because of the lack of funds.

It is clearly necessary that control be exercised over areas such as cash management as well as over those like production and sales in an attempt to avoid adverse **non-**
 operating profit variances.

Investigating variances

It is unreasonable to expect budget targets to be met precisely each month and so variances will usually arise. Whatever the reason for a variance, finding out what went wrong can be costly. Reports and other information will have to be scrutinised and discussions with individuals and groups may have to be carried out. In some cases, activities may have to be stopped to discover what went wrong. Since small variances are almost inevitable, and investigating variances can be expensive, management needs to establish a policy concerning which variances to investigate and which to accept.

Activity

What broad approach do you feel should be taken as to whether to spend money investigating a particular variance?

The general approach to this policy must be concerned with cost and benefit. The benefit likely to be gained from knowing why a variance arose needs to be balanced against the cost of obtaining that knowledge.

The issue of balancing the benefit of having information against its cost was discussed in Chapter 1, on pages 9–10. Unfortunately, however, both the cost of investigation and the value of the benefit are often difficult to assess in advance of the investigation.

Knowing the reason for a variance is valuable only insofar that it helps management to bring things back under control, thereby enabling future targets to be met. It should be borne in mind that variances should be either zero, or very close to zero. In other words, achieving targets, give or take small variances, should be the norm.

Broadly, we suggest the following approach to investigating variances:

- Significant *adverse* variances should be investigated because the continuation of the fault that they represent could be very costly. Management must decide what 'significant' means. A certain amount of science, in the form of statistical models, can be used in making this decision. Ultimately, however, it must be a matter of managerial judgement as to what is significant. Perhaps variances above a threshold of around 5 per cent of the budgeted figure would be considered significant.
- Significant *favourable* variances should probably be investigated as well as those that are unfavourable. Though such variances would not cause such immediate management concern as adverse ones, they still represent things not going according to plan. If actual performance is significantly better than target, it may well mean that the target is unrealistically low.
- Insignificant variances, though not triggering immediate investigation, should be kept under review. For each aspect of operations, the cumulative sum of variances, over a series of control periods, should be zero, with small adverse variances in some periods being compensated for by small favourable ones in others. This is because small variances caused by random factors will not necessarily recur.

Where a variance is caused by systemic (non-random) factors, which will recur over time, the cumulative sum of the periodic variances will not be zero but an increasing figure. Even though the individual variances may be insignificant, the cumulative effect of these variances may not. Thus, an investigation may well be worthwhile, particularly if the variances are adverse.

To illustrate the cumulative effect of relatively small systemic variances, let us consider Example 13.2.

Example 13.2

Indisurers Ltd finds that the variances for direct labour efficiency for processing motor insurance claims, since the beginning of the year, are as follows:

	£		£
January	25 (adverse)	July	20 (adverse)
February	15 (favourable)	August	15 (favourable)
March	5 (favourable)	September	23 (adverse)
April	20 (adverse)	October	15 (favourable)
May	22 (adverse)	November	5 (favourable)
June	8 (favourable)	December	26 (adverse)

The average total cost of labour performing this task is about £1,200 a month. Management believes that none of these variances, taken alone, is significant given the monthly labour cost. The question is, are they significant when taken together? If we add them together, taking account of the signs, we find that we have a net adverse variance for the year of £73. Of itself this, too, is probably not significant, but we should expect the cumulative total to be close to zero where the variances are random. We might feel that a pattern is developing and, given long enough, a net adverse variance of significant size might build up.

Investigating the labour efficiency might be worth doing. Finding the cause of the variance would put management in a position to correct a systemic fault, which could lead to future cost savings. (Note that 12 periods are probably not enough to reach a statistically sound conclusion on whether the variances are random or not, but it provides an illustration of the point.)

Plotting the cumulative variances, from month to month, as in Figure 13.8, makes it clear what is happening as time proceeds.

It is important to emphasise that the guidelines proposed for investigating variances are subject to the cost–benefit issues discussed at the beginning of this section. Thus, where the cost of investigating a variance, or where the cost of correcting the underlying problem, is expected to be very high, managers may decide against investigating even a significant variance. They may calculate that it would be cheaper to live with the problem and so adjust the budget.

Real World 13.4 provides some insights into how managers determine whether to investigate variances in practice.

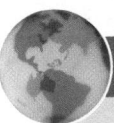

Real World 13.4

Deciding whether to investigate

The table shows the methods used by respondents to decide whether to investigate a particular variance. It is based on a research survey of UK manufacturing businesses by Drury and others.

Real World 13.4 continued

	% 'Often' or 'Always'
Decisions based on managerial judgement	75
Variance exceeds a specific monetary amount	41
Variance exceeds a given percentage of the budgeted figure	36
Statistical models	3

Source: Reproduced from *A Survey of Management Accounting Practices in UK Manufacturing Companies*, C. Drury, S. Braund, P. Osborne and M. Tayles, Chartered Association of Certified Accountants, 1993, p. 39, table 5.7.

Figure 13.8   **The cumulative variances for labour efficiency in motor insurance claim handling at Indisurers Ltd**

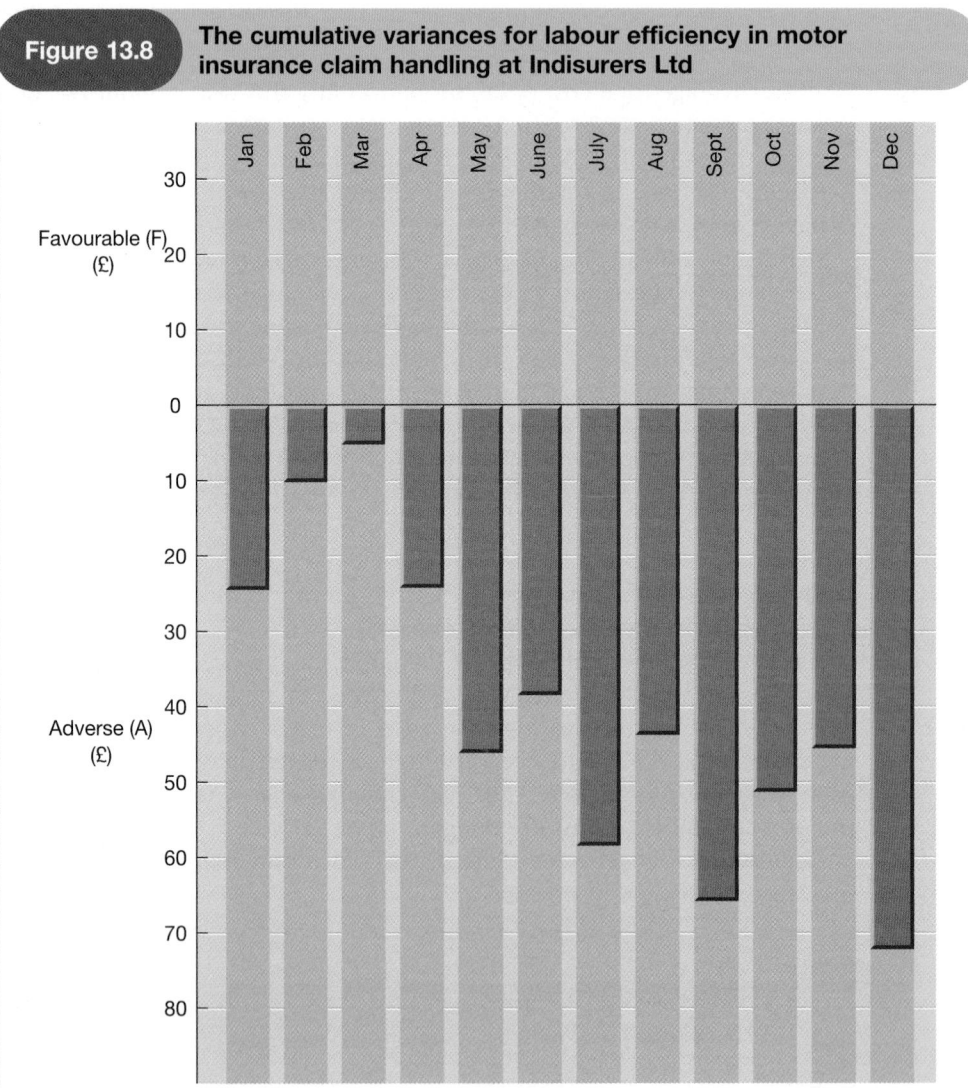

Starting at zero at the beginning of January, each month the cumulative variance is plotted. This is the sum taking account of positive and negative signs. The January figure is £25 (A). The February one is £10 (A) (that is £25 (A) plus £15 (F)) and so on. The graph seems to show an overall trend of adverse variances, but with several favourable variances involved.

It is interesting to note the large extent, revealed by this survey, to which decisions on whether to investigate variances are made on the basis of some, presumably subjective, judgement. We might have expected businesses to adopt a more systematic approach. The survey is not very recent, but it may well give an impression of current practice.

Compensating variances

→ There can be superficial appeal in the idea of **compensating variances**. This involves trading off linked favourable and adverse variances against each other, without further consideration. For example, a sales manager may believe that it would be possible to sell more of a particular service if prices were lowered, and that this would feed through to increased operating profit. This would lead to a favourable sales volume variance, but also to an adverse sales price variance. On the face of it, provided that the former is greater than the latter, all would be well.

Activity (13.16)

What possible reason is there why the sales manager mentioned above should not go ahead with the price reduction?

The change in policy will have ramifications for other areas of the business, including the following:

● The need for more provision of the service to be available to sell. Staff and other resources may not be available to supply this increase.
● Increased sales volumes would involve an increased need for finance to pay for increased activity, for example to pay additional staff costs.

Thus 'trading off' variances is not automatically acceptable, without a more far-reaching consultation and revision of plans.

Making budgetary control effective

→ It should be clear from what we have seen of **budgetary control** that a system, or a set of routines, must be put in place to enable the potential benefits to be gained. Most businesses that operate successful budgetary control systems tend to share some common features. These include the following:

● *A serious attitude taken to the system.* This should apply to all levels of management, right from the very top. For example, senior managers need to make clear to junior managers that they take notice of the monthly variance reports and base some of their actions and decisions upon them.
● *Clear demarcation between areas of managerial responsibility.* It needs to be clear which manager is responsible for each business area so that accountability can more easily be ascribed for any area that seems to be going out of control.

- *Budget targets that are challenging yet achievable.* Setting unachievable targets is likely to have a demotivating effect. There may be a case for getting managers to participate in establishing their own targets to help create a sense of ownership. This, in turn, can increase the managers' commitment and motivation. We shall consider this in more detail shortly.
- *Established data collection, analysis and reporting routines.* These should take the actual results and the budget figures and use them to calculate and report the variances. This should be part of the business's regular accounting information system, so that the required reports are automatically produced each month.
- *Reports aimed at individual managers, rather than general-purpose documents.* This avoids managers having to read through many pages of reports to find the part that is relevant to them.
- *Fairly short reporting periods.* These would typically be one month long, so that things cannot go too far wrong before they are picked up.
- *Timely variance reports.* Reports should be produced and made available to managers shortly after the end of the relevant reporting period. If it is not until the end of June that a manager is informed that the performance in May was below the budgeted level, it is quite likely that the performance for June will be below target as well. Reports on the performance in May ideally need to emerge in early June.
- *Action being taken to get operations back under control if they are shown to be out of control.* The report will not change things by itself. Managers need to take action to try to ensure that the reporting of significant adverse variances leads to action to put things right for the future.

Behavioural issues

Budgets are prepared with the objective of affecting the attitudes and behaviour of managers. The point was made in Chapter 12 that budgets are intended to motivate managers; research evidence generally shows that budgets can be effective in achieving this. More specifically, the research shows:

- The existence of budgets can improve job satisfaction and performance. Where a manager's role is ill-defined or ambiguous, budgets can help bring structure and certainty. Budgets provide clear, quantifiable, targets that must be pursued. This can be reassuring to managers and can increase their level of commitment.
- Demanding, yet achievable, budget targets tend to motivate better than less demanding targets. It seems that setting the most demanding targets that are acceptable to managers is a very effective way to motivate them.
- Unrealistically demanding targets tend to have an adverse effect on managers' performance. Once managers begin to view the budget targets as being too difficult to achieve, their level of motivation and performance declines. The relationship between the level of performance and the perceived degree of budget difficulty is shown in Figure 13.9 below.
- The participation of managers in setting their targets tends to improve motivation and performance. This is probably because those managers feel a sense of commitment to the targets and a moral obligation to achieve them.

It has been suggested that allowing managers to set their own targets will lead to slack (that is, easily achievable) targets being introduced. This would make achievement of the target that much easier. On the other hand, in an effort to impress, a manager may

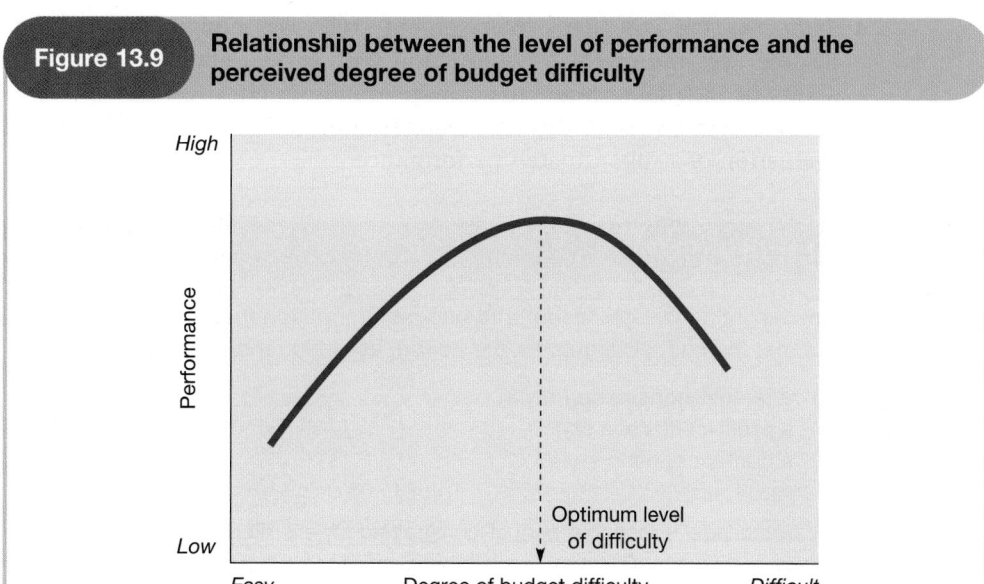

Figure 13.9 Relationship between the level of performance and the perceived degree of budget difficulty

At a low level of budget difficulty, performance also tends to be low as managers do not find the targets sufficiently motivating. However, as the degree of difficulty starts to increase, managers rise to the challenge and improve their performance. Beyond a certain point, the budgets are seen by managers as being too difficult to achieve and so motivation and performance decline.

select a target that is not really achievable. These points imply that care must be taken in the extent to which managers have unfettered choice of their own targets.

Conflict can occur in the budget-setting process, as different groups may well have different agendas. For example, junior managers may be keen to build slack into their budgets while their senior managers may seek to impose unrealistically demanding budget targets. Sometimes, such conflict can be constructive and can result in better decisions being made. To resolve the conflict over budget targets, negotiations may have to take place and other options may have to be explored. This may lead to a better understanding by all parties of the issues involved and final agreement may result in demanding, yet achievable, targets.

The impact of management style

There has been a great deal of discussion among experts on the way in which managers use information generated by the budgeting system and the impact of its use on the attitudes and behaviour of subordinates (that is, the staff). A pioneering study by Hopwood (see reference 1 at the end of the chapter) examined the way that managers, working within a manufacturing environment, used budget information to evaluate the performance of subordinates. He argued that three distinct styles of management could be observed. These are:

● *Budget-constrained style.* This management style focuses rigidly on the ability of subordinates to meet the budget. Other factors relating to the performance of subordinates are not given serious consideration even though they might include improving the long-term effectiveness of the area for which the subordinate has responsibility,

- *Profit-conscious style*. This management style uses budget information in a more flexible way and often in conjunction with other data. The main focus is on the ability of each subordinate to improve long-term effectiveness.
- *Non-accounting style*. In this case, budget information plays no significant role in the evaluation of a subordinate's performance.

Activity (13.17)

How might a manager respond to budget information that indicates a subordinate has not met the budget targets for the period, assuming the manager adopts:

(a) a budget-constrained style?
(b) a profit-conscious style?
(c) a non-accounting style?

(a) A manager adopting a budget-constrained style is likely to take the budget information very seriously. This may result in criticism of the subordinate and, perhaps, some form of sanction.
(b) A manager adopting a profit-conscious style is likely to take a broader view when examining the budget information and so will take other factors into consideration (for example, factors that could not have been anticipated at the time of preparing the budgets), before deciding whether criticism or punishment is justified.
(c) A manager adopting a non-accounting style will regard the failure to meet the budget as being relatively unimportant and so no action may be taken.

Hopwood found that subordinates working for a manager who adopts a budget-constrained style had unfortunate experiences. They suffered higher levels of job-related stress and had poorer working relationships, with both their colleagues and their manager, than those subordinates whose manager adopted one of the other two styles. Hopwood also found that the subordinates of a budget-constrained style of manager were more likely to manipulate the budget figures, or to take other undesirable actions, to ensure the budgets were met.

Reservations about the Hopwood study

Though Hopwood's findings are interesting, subsequent studies have cast doubt on their universal applicability. Later studies confirm that human attitudes and behaviour are complex and can vary according to the particular situation. For example, it has been found that the impact of different management styles on such factors as job-related stress and the manipulation of budget figures seems to vary. The impact is likely to depend on such factors as the level of independence enjoyed by the subordinates and the level of uncertainty associated with the tasks to be undertaken.

It seems that where there is a high level of interdependence between business divisions, subordinate managers are more likely to feel that they have less control over their performance, because the performance of staff in other divisions could be an important influence on the final outcome. In such a situation, rigid application of the budget could be viewed as being unfair and may lead to undesirable behaviour. However, where managers have a high degree of independence, the application of budgets as a measure of performance is likely to be more acceptable. In this case, the managers are likely to feel that the final outcome is much less dependent on the performance of others.

Later studies have also shown that where a subordinate is undertaking a task that has a high degree of uncertainty concerning the outcome (for example, developing a new product), budget targets are unlikely to be an adequate measure of performance. In such a situation, other factors and measures should be taken into account in order to derive a more complete assessment of performance. However, where a task has a low degree of uncertainty concerning the outcome (for example, producing a standard product using standard equipment and an experienced workforce), budget measures may be regarded as more reliable indicators of performance. Thus, it appears that a budget-constrained style is more likely to work where subordinates enjoy a fair amount of independence and where the tasks set have a low level of uncertainty concerning their outcomes.

Failing to meet the budget

The existence of budgets gives senior managers a ready means to assess the performance of their subordinates (that is, junior managers). If a junior manager fails to meet a budget, this must be handled carefully by the relevant senior manager. Adverse variances may imply that the manager needs help. If this is the case, a harsh, critical approach would have a demotivating effect and would be counterproductive.

 Real World 13.5 gives some indication of the effects of the **behavioural aspects of budgetary control** in practice.

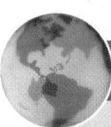

Real World 13.5

Behavioural problems

The survey by Drury *et al.* referred to earlier indicates that there is a large degree of participation in setting budgets by those who will be expected to perform to the budget (the budget holders). It also indicates that senior managers have greater influence in setting the targets than their junior manager budget holders.

Where there is a conflict between the cost estimates submitted by the budget holders and their senior managers, in 40 per cent of respondent businesses the senior manager's view would prevail without negotiation. In nearly 60 per cent of cases, however, a reduction would be negotiated between the budget holder and the senior manager. The general philosophy of the businesses that responded to the survey, regarding budget holders influencing the setting of their own budgets, is:

- 23 per cent of respondents believe that budget holders should not have too much influence since they will seek to obtain easy budgets (build in slack) if they do;
- 69 per cent of respondents take an opposite view.

The general view on how senior managers should judge their subordinates is:

- 46 per cent of respondent businesses think that senior managers should judge junior managers mainly on their ability to achieve the budget;
- 40 per cent think otherwise.

Though this research is not very recent (1993), in the absence of more recent evidence it provides some feel for budget setting in practice.

Source: A Survey of Management Accounting Practices in UK Manufacturing Companies, C. Drury, S. Braund, P. Osborne and M. Tayles, Chartered Association of Certified Accountants, 1993.

Self-assessment question (13.1)

Toscanini Ltd makes a standard product, which is budgeted to sell at £4.00 a unit, in a competitive market. It is made by taking a budgeted 0.4 kg of material, budgeted to cost £2.40/kg, and having it worked on by hand by an employee, paid a budgeted £8.00/hour, for a budgeted 6 minutes. Monthly fixed overheads are budgeted at £4,800. The output for May was budgeted at 4,000 units.

The actual results for May were as follows:

	£
Sales revenue (3,500 units)	13,820
Materials (1,425 kg)	(3,420)
Labour (345 hours)	(2,690)
Fixed overheads	(4,900)
Actual operating profit	2,810

No inventories of any description existed at the beginning or end of the month.

Required:

(a) Deduce the budgeted profit for May and reconcile it, through variances, with the actual profit in as much detail as the information provided will allow.

(b) State which manager should be held accountable, in the first instance, for each variance calculated.

(c) Assuming that the budget was well set and achievable, suggest at least one feasible reason for each of the variances that you identified in (a), given what you know about the business's performance for May.

(d) If it were discovered that the actual total world market demand for the business's product was 10 per cent lower than estimated when the May budget was set, explain how and why the variances that you identified in (a) could be revised to provide information that would be potentially more useful.

The answer to this question appears at the back of the book on pages 734–5.

Standard quantities and costs

We have already seen that a budget is a business plan for the short term – typically one year – that is expressed mainly in financial terms. A budget is often constructed from standards. **Standard quantities and costs** (or revenues) are those planned for an individual unit of input or output and provide the building blocks for budgets.

We can say about Baxter Ltd's operations (see Example 13.1 on page 485) that:

- the standard selling price is £100 for one unit of output;
- the standard marginal cost for one manufactured unit is £60;
- the standard raw materials cost is £40 for one unit of output;
- the standard raw materials usage is 40 metres for one unit of output;
- the standard raw materials price is £1 a metre (that is, for one unit of input);
- the standard labour cost is £20 for one unit of output;
- the standard labour time is 2.50 hours for one unit of output;
- the standard labour rate is £8 an hour (that is, for one unit of input).

Standards, like the budgets to which they are linked, represent targets against which actual performance is measured. To maintain their usefulness for planning and control purposes, they should be subject to frequent review and, where necessary, revision.

Standards provide the basis for variance analysis, which, as we have seen, helps managers to identify where deviations from planned, or standard, performance have occurred and the extent of those deviations.

Standard costs may be helpful to derive the planned cost for units of output (products or services) that are much larger than those produced by Baxter Ltd (mentioned above). For example, a firm of accountants may find standard costing useful. It may set standard costs for each grade of staff (audit manager, audit senior, trainee and so on). When planning a particular audit of a client business, it can assess how many hours each grade of staff should spend on the audit and, using the standard cost per hour for each grade, it can derive a standard cost or 'budget' for the job as a whole. These standards can subsequently be compared with the actual hours and hourly rates.

Setting standards

When setting standards various points have to be considered. We shall now explore some of the more important of these.

Who sets the standards?

Standards often result from the collective effort of various individuals including management accountants, industrial engineers, human resource managers, production managers and other employees. The manager responsible for meeting a particular standard will usually be involved and may be relied on to provide specialised knowledge. The manager may, therefore, have some influence over the final decision, which brings with it the risk that 'slack' may be built into the standard in order to make it easier to achieve. The same problem was mentioned earlier in relation to budgets.

How is information gathered?

Setting standards involves gathering information concerning how much material should be used, how much machine time should be required, how much direct labour time should be spent and so on. Two possible ways of collecting information for standard setting are available.

Activity 13.18

Can you think what these might be?

The first is to examine the particular processes and tasks involved in producing the product or service and to develop suitable estimates. Standards concerning material usage, machine time and direct labour hours may be established by carrying out dummy production runs, time-and-motion studies and so on. This will require close collaboration between the management accountant, industrial engineers and those involved in the production process.

The second approach is to collect information relating to past costs, times and usage for the same, or similar, products and to use this information as a basis for predicting the future. This information may have to be adjusted to reflect changes in price, changes in the production process and so on.

Where the product or service is entirely new or involves entirely new processes, the first approach will probably have to be used, even though it is usually more costly.

What kind of standards should be used?

→ There are basically two types of standards that may be used: **ideal standards** and
→ **practical standards**. Ideal standards, as the name suggests, assume perfect operating conditions where there is no inefficiency due to lost production time, defects and so on. The objective of setting ideal standards, which are attainable in theory at least, is to encourage employees to strive towards excellence. Practical standards, also as the name suggests, do not assume ideal operating conditions. Although they demand a high level of efficiency, account is taken of possible lost production time, defects and so on. They are designed to be challenging yet achievable.

There are two major difficulties with using the ideal standards.

- They do not provide a useful basis for exercising control. Unless the standards set are realistic, any variances computed are extremely difficult to interpret.
- They may not achieve their intended purpose of motivating managers: indeed, the opposite may occur. We saw earlier that the evidence suggests that where managers regard a target as beyond their grasp, it is likely to have a demotivating effect.

Given these problems, it is not surprising that practical standards seem to enjoy more widespread support than ideal standards.

Real World 13.6 provides some evidence on the use of ideal standards in practice.

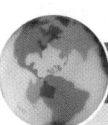

Real World 13.6

Setting the standard

The study of UK manufacturers by Drury and others showed that only 5 per cent of respondents to the survey set standards at a level that could be achieved if everything went perfectly all of the time. Although the study is rather dated now (1993), it represents the most recent survey and is worth noting.

Source: A Survey of Management Accounting Practices in UK Manufacturing Companies, C. Drury, S. Braund, P. Osborne and M. Tayles, Chartered Association of Certified Accountants, 1993.

The learning-curve effect

Where an activity undertaken by direct workers has been unchanged for some time, and the workers are experienced at performing it, the standard labour time will normally stay unchanged. However, where a new activity is introduced, or new workers are
→ involved with performing an existing activity, a **learning-curve** effect will normally occur. This is shown in Figure 13.10.

The first unit of output takes a relatively long time to produce. As experience is gained, the worker takes less time to produce each unit of output. The rate of reduction in the time taken will, however, decrease as experience is gained. Thus, for example, the reduction in time taken between the first and second unit produced will be much bigger than the reduction between, say, the ninth and the tenth. Eventually, the rate

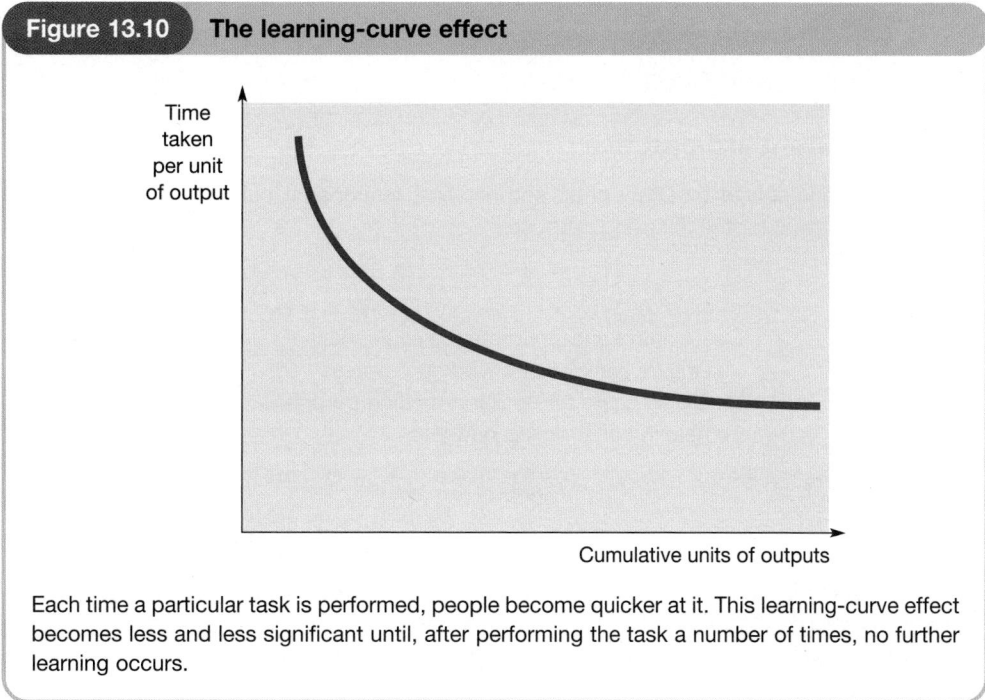

Figure 13.10   The learning-curve effect

Time taken per unit of output

Cumulative units of outputs

Each time a particular task is performed, people become quicker at it. This learning-curve effect becomes less and less significant until, after performing the task a number of times, no further learning occurs.

of reduction in time taken will reduce to zero so that each unit will take as long as the preceding one. At this point, the point where the curve in Figure 13.10 becomes horizontal (the bottom right of the graph), the learning-curve effect will have been eliminated and a steady, long-term standard time for the activity will have been established.

The learning-curve effect seems to have little to do with whether workers are skilled or unskilled; if they are unfamiliar with the task, the learning-curve effect will arise. Practical experience shows that learning curves show remarkable regularity and, therefore, predictability from one activity to another.

The learning-curve effect applies equally well to activities involved with providing a service (such as dealing with an insurance claim, in an insurance business) as to manufacturing-type activities (like upholstering an armchair by hand, in a furniture-making business).

Clearly, the learning-curve effect must be taken into account when setting standards, and when interpreting any adverse labour efficiency variances, where a new process and/or new staff are involved.

Other uses for standard costing

We have seen that standards can play a valuable role in performance evaluation and control. However, standards that relate to costs, usages, selling prices and so on, can also be used for other purposes. In particular, they can be used to determine the cost of inventories and work in progress for income measurement purposes and the cost of items for use in pricing decisions.

Real World 13.7 provides some information on the use of standards in practice.

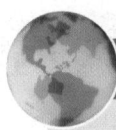

Real World 13.7

Standard practice

The survey by Drury *et al.* showed that respondent businesses found standards to be useful for the following purposes:

	Percentage of respondents
Cost control and performance evaluation	72
Valuing inventories and work in progress	80
Deducing costs for decision-making purposes	62
To help in constructing budgets	69

Source: A Survey of Management Accounting Practices in UK Manufacturing Companies, C. Drury, S. Braund, P. Osborne and M. Tayles, Chartered Association of Certified Accountants, 1993.

Some problems . . .

Although standards and variances may be useful for decision-making purposes, they have limited application. Many business and commercial activities do not have direct relationships between inputs and outputs, as is the case with, say, the number of direct labour hours worked and the number of products manufactured. Many expenses of modern business are in areas such as human resource development and advertising, where the expense is discretionary and there is no direct link to the level of output.

There are also potential problems when applying standard costing techniques. These include the following:

- Standards can quickly become out of date as a result of both changes in the production process and price changes. Standards should, therefore, be frequently monitored and updated where necessary. Although this can be costly, it is essential if standards are to be effective for control purposes. When standards become outdated, performance can be adversely affected. For example, a human resources manager who recognises that it is impossible to meet targets on rates of pay for labour, because of general labour cost rises, may have less incentive to minimise costs.
- Factors may affect a variance for which a particular manager is accountable but over which the manager has no control. When assessing the manager's performance, these uncontrollable factors should be taken into account but there is always a risk that they will not.
- In practice, creating clear lines of demarcation between the areas of responsibility of various managers may be difficult. In this case, one of the prerequisites of effective standard costing is lost.
- Once a standard has been met, there is no incentive for employees to improve the quality or quantity of output further. There are usually no additional rewards for doing so; only additional work. Indeed, employees may have a disincentive for exceeding a standard as it may then be viewed by managers as too loose and therefore in need of tightening. However, simply achieving a standard, and no more, may not be enough in highly competitive and fast-changing markets. To compete effectively, a business may need to strive for continuous improvement and standard costing techniques may impede this *kaizen* process.

● Standard costing may create incentives for managers and employees to act in undesirable ways. It may, for example, encourage the build up of excess inventories, leading to significant storage and financing costs. This problem can arise, for example, where there are opportunities for discounts on bulk purchases of materials, which the purchasing manager then exploits to achieve a favourable direct materials price variance. One way to avoid this problem might be to impose limits on the level of inventories held.

Activity (13.19)

Can you think of another example of how a manager may achieve a favourable direct materials price variance but in doing so would create problems for a business?

A manager may buy cheaper, but lower quality, materials. Although this may lead to a favourable price variance, it may also lead to additional inspection and re-working costs, and perhaps lost sales.

To avoid this problem, the manager may be required to buy material of a particular quality or from particular sources.

A final example of the perverse incentives created by standard costing relates to labour efficiency variances. Where these variances are calculated for individual employees, and form the basis for their rewards, there is little incentive for them to work cooperatively. Cooperative working may be in the best interests of the business, however. To avoid this problem, some businesses calculate labour efficiency variances for groups of employees rather than individual employees. This, however, creates the risk that some individuals will become 'free riders' and will rely on the more conscientious employees to carry the load.

Activity (13.20)

How might the business try to eliminate the 'free-rider' problem just mentioned?

One way would be to carry out an evaluation, perhaps by the group members themselves, of individual contributions to group output, as well as evaluating group output as a whole.

The new business environment

The traditional standard costing approach was developed during an era when business operations were characterised by few product lines, long production runs and heavy reliance on direct labour. More recently, the increasingly competitive environment and the onward march of technology have changed the business landscape. Now, many business operations are characterised by a wide range of different products, shorter product life cycles (leading to shorter production runs) and automated production processes. The effect of these changes has resulted in:

● more frequent development of standards to deal with frequent changes to the product range;

● a change in the focus for control – where manufacturing systems are automated, for example, direct labour becomes less important than direct materials;

● a decline in the importance of monitoring from cost and usage variances – where manufacturing systems are automated, deviations from standards relating to costs and usage become less frequent and less significant.

Thus, where a business has highly automated production systems, traditional standard costing, with its emphasis on costs and usage, is likely to take on less importance. Other elements of the production process such as quality, production levels, product cycle times, delivery times and the need for continuous improvement become the focus of attention. This does not mean, however, that a standards-based approach is not useful for the new manufacturing environment. It can still provide valuable control information and there is no reason why standard costing systems cannot be redesigned to reflect a concern for some of the elements mentioned earlier. Nevertheless, other measures, including non-financial ones, may help to augment the information provided by the standard costing system.

Real World 13.8 indicates that, despite the problems mentioned above, standard costing is used by businesses. However, the extent to which particular standard costing variances are calculated and considered appears to vary.

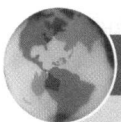

Real World 13.8

Standard use

Senior financial managers of 33 businesses were asked about their businesses' practice. It emerged that standard costing was used by 30 of the businesses concerned, which represented most of the businesses that might be expected to use this method. The popularity among these businesses of standards for each of the main cost items is set out in Figure 13.11.

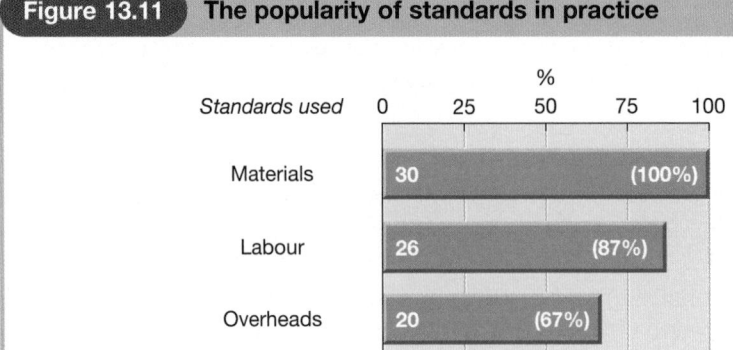

Figure 13.11   **The popularity of standards in practice**

Standards for materials were used by all businesses in the survey and standards for labour were used by nearly all businesses.

Despite the universal use of materials standards, the study found that four businesses calculated the total direct materials variance only and that only two thirds of businesses calculated both the direct materials price and usage variances. For labour standards, the variance analysis is even less complete. The study found that 15 businesses calculated the total direct labour variance only and only one third of businesses calculated both the direct labour and efficiency variances. It seems, therefore, that standard costing was not extensively employed by the businesses.

Source: Figure based on information in *Contemporary Management Accounting Practices in UK Manufacturing*, D. Dugdale, C. Jones and S. Green, CIMA Publication, Elsevier, 2006.

Summary

The main points of this chapter may be summarised as follows:

Controlling through budgets

- Budgets act as a system of both feedback and feedforward control.
- To exercise control, budgets can be flexed to match actual volume of output.

Variance analysis

- Variances may be favourable or adverse according to whether they result in an increase to, or a decrease from, the budgeted profit figure.
- Budgeted profit plus all favourable variances less all adverse variances equals actual profit.
- Commonly calculated variances:
  - Sales volume variance = difference between the original budget and the flexed budget profit figures.
  - Sales price variance = difference between actual sales revenue and actual volume at the standard sales price.
  - Total direct materials variance = difference between the actual direct materials cost and the direct materials cost according to the flexed budget.
  - Direct materials usage variance = difference between actual usage and budgeted usage, for the actual volume of output, multiplied by the standard materials cost.
  - Direct materials price variance = difference between the actual materials cost and the actual usage multiplied by the standard materials cost.
  - Total direct labour variance = difference between the actual direct labour cost and the direct labour cost according to the flexed budget.
  - Direct labour efficiency variance = difference between actual labour time and budgeted time, for the actual volume of output, multiplied by the standard labour rate.
  - Direct labour rate variance = difference between the actual labour cost and the actual labour time multiplied by the standard labour rate.
  - Fixed overhead spending variance = difference between the actual and budgeted spending on fixed overheads.
- Significant and/or persistent variances should normally be investigated to establish their cause. However, the costs and benefits of investigating variances must be considered.

- Trading off favourable variances against linked adverse variances should not be automatically acceptable.

- Not all activities can usefully be controlled through traditional variance analysis.

Effective budgetary control

- Good budgetary control requires establishing systems and routines to ensure such things as a clear distinction between individual managers' areas of responsibility; prompt, frequent and relevant variance reporting; and senior management commitment.

- There are behavioural aspects of control relating to management style, participation in budget setting and the failure to meet budget targets that should be taken into account by senior managers.

Standard costing

- Standards = budgeted physical quantities and financial values for one unit of inputs and outputs.

- Two types of standards: ideal standards and practical standards.

- Information necessary for developing standards can be gathered by analysing the task or by using past data.

- There tends to be a learning-curve effect: routine tasks are performed more quickly with experience.

- Standards are useful in providing data for income measurement and pricing decisions.

- Standards have their limitations, particularly in modern manufacturing environments; however, they are still widely used.

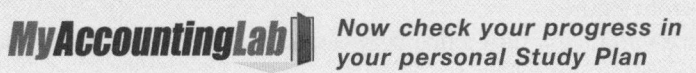

MyAccountingLab Now check your progress in your personal Study Plan

Key terms

feedback control   p. 484
feedforward control   p. 484
flexing the budget   p. 486
flexible budget   p. 487
sales volume variance   p. 488
adverse variance   p. 488
favourable variance   p. 488
variance   p. 488
sales price variance   p. 490
total direct materials variance   p. 490
direct materials usage variance
  p. 490
direct materials price variance
  p. 491
total direct labour variance   p. 491

direct labour efficiency variance
  p. 492
direct labour rate variance   p. 492
fixed overhead spending variance
  p. 493
non-operating-profit variances
  p. 499
compensating variances   p. 503
budgetary control   p. 503
behavioural aspects of budgetary
  control   p. 507
standard quantities and costs   p. 508
ideal standards   p. 510
practical standards   p. 510
learning curve   p. 510

Reference

1 'An empirical study of the role of accounting data in performance evaluation', *Hopwood A. G.*, **Empirical Research in Accounting**, a supplement to the **Journal of Accounting Research**, 1972, pp. 156–82.

Further reading

If you would like to explore the topics covered in this chapter in more depth, we recommend the following books:

Management Accounting, *Atkinson A., Kaplan R., Young S. M. and Matsumura E.*, 5th edn, Prentice Hall, 2007, chapter 12.

Management and Cost Accounting, *Bhimani A., Horngren C., Datar S. and Foster G.*, 4th edn, Financial Times Prentice Hall, 2008, chapters 14 to 16.

Management and Cost Accounting, *Drury C.*, 7th edn, Cengage Learning, 2007, chapters 16 to 18.

Managerial Accounting, *Hilton R.*, 6th edn., McGraw-Hill Irwin, 2005, chapter 10.

Review questions

Answers to these questions can be found at the back of the book on pages 748–9.

13.1 Explain what is meant by feedforward control and distinguish it from feedback control.

13.2 What is meant by a variance? What is the point in analysing variances?

13.3 What is the point in flexing the budget in the context of variance analysis? Does flexing imply that differences between budget and actual in the volume of output are ignored in variance analysis?

13.4 Should all variances be investigated to find their cause? Explain your answer.

Exercises

Exercises 13.4 to 13.8 are more advanced than 13.1 to 13.3. Those with **coloured numbers** have answers at the back of the book, starting on page 791.

If you wish to try more exercises, visit the students' side of the Companion Website and MyAccountingLab.

13.1 You have recently overheard the following remarks:

(a) 'A favourable direct labour rate variance can only be caused by staff working more efficiently than budgeted.'
(b) 'Selling more units than budgeted, because the units were sold at less than standard price, automatically leads to a favourable sales volume variance.'
(c) 'Using below-standard materials will tend to lead to adverse materials usage variances but cannot affect labour variances.'
(d) 'Higher-than-budgeted sales could not possibly affect the labour rate variance.'
(e) 'An adverse sales price variance can only arise from selling a product at less than standard price.'

Required:
Critically assess these remarks, explaining any technical terms.

13.2 Pilot Ltd makes a standard product, which is budgeted to sell at £5.00 a unit. It is made by taking a budgeted 0.5 kg of material, budgeted to cost £3.00 a kilogram, and working on it by hand by an employee, paid a budgeted £10.00 an hour, for a budgeted 7½ minutes. Monthly fixed overheads are budgeted at £6,000. The output for March was budgeted at 5,000 units.

The actual results for March were as follows:

	£
Sales revenue (5,400 units)	26,460
Materials (2,830 kg)	(8,770)
Labour (650 hours)	(6,885)
Fixed overheads	(6,350)
Actual operating profit	4,455

No inventories existed at the start or end of March.

Required:

(a) Deduce the budgeted profit for March and reconcile it with the actual profit in as much detail as the information provided will allow.

(b) State which manager should be held accountable, in the first instance, for each variance calculated.

13.3 Antonio plc makes Product X, the standard costs of which are:

	£
Sales revenue	31
Direct labour (1 hour)	(11)
Direct materials (1 kg)	(10)
Fixed overheads	(3)
Standard profit	7

The budgeted output for March was 1,000 units of Product X; the actual output was 1,100 units, which was sold for £34,950. There were no inventories at the start or end of March.

The actual production costs were:

	£
Direct labour (1,075 hours)	12,210
Direct materials (1,170 kg)	11,630
Fixed overheads	3,200

Required:

Calculate the variances for March as fully as you are able from the available information, and use them to reconcile the budgeted and actual profit figures.

13.4 You have recently overheard the following remarks:

(a) 'When calculating variances, we in effect ignore differences of volume of output, between original budget and actual, by flexing the budget. If there were a volume difference, it is water under the bridge by the time that the variances come to be calculated.'

(b) 'It is very valuable to calculate variances because they will tell you what went wrong.'

(c) 'All variances should be investigated to find their cause.'

(d) 'Research evidence shows that the more demanding the target, the more motivated the manager.'

(e) 'Most businesses do not have feedforward controls of any type, just feedback controls through budgets.'

Required:

Critically assess these remarks, explaining any technical terms.

13.5 Bradley-Allen Ltd makes one standard product. Its budgeted operating statement for May is as follows:

		£	£
Sales (volume and revenue):	800 units		64,000
Direct materials:	Type A	(12,000)	
	Type B	(16,000)	
Direct labour:	Skilled	(4,000)	
	Unskilled	(10,000)	
Overheads:	(All fixed)	(12,000)	
			(54,000)
Budgeted operating profit			10,000

The standard costs were as follows:

Direct materials:	Type A	£50/kg
	Type B	£20/m
Direct labour:	Skilled	£10/hour
	Unskilled	£8/hour

During May, the following occurred:

(1) 950 units were sold for a total of £73,000.
(2) 310 kilos (costing £15,200) of type A material were used in production.
(3) 920 metres (costing £18,900) of type B material were used in production.
(4) Skilled workers were paid £4,628 for 445 hours.
(5) Unskilled workers were paid £11,275 for 1,375 hours.
(6) Fixed overheads cost £11,960.

There were no inventories of finished production or of work in progress at either the beginning or end of May.

Required:
(a) Prepare a statement that reconciles the budgeted to the actual profit of the business for May, through variances. Your statement should analyse the difference between the two profit figures in as much detail as you are able.
(b) Explain how the statement in (a) might be helpful to managers.

13.6 Mowbray Ltd makes and sells one product, the standard costs of which are as follows:

	£
Direct materials (3 kg at £2.50/kg)	(7.50)
Direct labour (15 minutes at £9.00/hr)	(2.25)
Fixed overheads	(3.60)
	(13.35)
Selling price	20.00
Standard profit margin	6.65

The monthly production and sales are planned to be 1,200 units.
The actual results for May were as follows:

	£	
Sales revenue	18,000	
Direct materials	(7,400)	(2,800 kg)
Direct labour	(2,300)	(255 hr)
Fixed overheads	(4,100)	
Operating profit	4,200	

There were no inventories at the start or end of May. As a result of poor sales demand during May, the business reduced the price of all sales by 10 per cent.

Required:
Calculate the budgeted profit for May and reconcile it to the actual profit through variances, going into as much detail as is possible from the information available.

13.7 Varne Chemprocessors is a business that specialises in plastics. It uses a standard costing system to monitor and report its purchases and usage of materials. During the most recent month, accounting period six, the purchase and usage of chemical UK194 were as follows:

Purchases/usage:	28,100 litres
Total price:	£51,704

Because of fire risk and the danger to health, no inventories are held by the business.

UK194 is used solely in the manufacture of a product called Varnelyne. The standard cost specification shows that, for the production of 5,000 litres of Varnelyne, 200 litres of UK194 are needed at a total standard cost of £392. During period six, 637,500 litres of Varnelyne were produced.

Price variances, over recent periods, for two other raw materials used by the business are:

Period	UK500		UK800	
	£		£	
1	301	F	298	F
2	251	A	203	F
3	102	F	52	A
4	202	A	98	A
5	153	F	150	A
6	103	A	201	A

where F = favourable variance and A = adverse variance.

Required:
(a) Calculate the price and usage variances for UK194 for period six.
(b) The following comment was made by the production manager:
   'I knew at the beginning of period six that UK194 would be cheaper than the standard cost specification, so I used rather more of it than normal; this saved £4,900 on other chemicals.'
   What changes do you need to make in your analysis for (a) as a result of this comment?
(c) Calculate, for both UK500 and UK800, the cumulative price variances and comment briefly on the results.

13.8 Brive plc has the following standards for its only product:

Selling price:	£110/unit
Direct labour:	1 hour at £10.50/hour
Direct material:	3 kg at £14.00/kg
Fixed overheads:	£27.00/unit, based on a budgeted output of 800 units/month

During May, there was an actual output of 850 units and the operating statement for the month was as follows:

	£
Sales revenue	92,930
Direct labour (890 hours)	(9,665)
Direct materials (2,410 kg)	(33,258)
Fixed overheads	(21,365)
Operating profit	28,642

There were no inventories of any description at the beginning and end of May.

Required:
Prepare the original budget and a budget flexed to the actual volume. Use these to compare the budgeted and actual profits of the business for the month, going into as much detail with your analysis as the information given will allow.

PART 3

Financial management

Part 3 is concerned with the area of accounting and finance usually known as 'business finance' or 'financial management'. Broadly, we shall be looking at decisions concerning the raising and investment of finance. Businesses can be seen, from a purely economic perspective, as organisations that raise money from investors and others (broadly, shareholders and lenders) and that use those funds to make investments (typically in plant and other assets) that will make the business and its owners wealthier. Clearly, these are important decision-making areas typically involving large amounts of money and relatively long-term commitments.

Chapter 14 considers how businesses make decisions about what represents a worthwhile investment. We shall be looking particularly at investments in such things as factories, offices and plant, which might enable businesses to provide some product or service for which a profitable market is seen. The decision-making techniques that we shall consider could equally well be applied to making investments in the shares of a business, or any other type of 'financial' investment, which individuals might make using their own money.

Chapter 15 deals with the other side of the investment: where the investment finance comes from. Here we shall be reviewing the various types of funding used by businesses of various sizes, including raising funds from

➔ the owners of the business (the shareholders in the case of limited companies).

Chapter 16 looks at a particular area of fundraising and investment: the management of working capital. Working capital consists of the short-term assets and claims of the business: inventories, trade receivables, cash and trade payables. These items typically involve large amounts of finance and need to be managed carefully. The chapter considers how working capital can be managed effectively.

CHAPTER 14

Making capital investment decisions

Introduction

This chapter looks at how proposed investments in new plant, machinery, buildings and other long-term assets should be evaluated. This is a very important area for businesses; expensive and far-reaching consequences can flow from bad investment decisions.

We shall also consider the problem of risk and how this may be taken into account when evaluating investment proposals. Finally, we shall discuss the ways that managers can oversee capital investment projects and how control may be exercised throughout the life of the project.

Learning outcomes

When you have completed this chapter, you should be able to:

- Explain the nature and importance of investment decision making.

- Identify the four main investment appraisal methods found in practice.

- Discuss the strengths and weaknesses of various techniques for dealing with risk in investment appraisal.

- Explain the methods used to monitor and control investment projects.

 **Remember to create your own personalised Study Plan**

The nature of investment decisions

The essential feature of investment decisions is *time*. Investment involves making an outlay of something of economic value, usually cash, at one point in time, which is expected to yield economic benefits to the investor at some other point in time. Usually, the outlay precedes the benefits. Also, the outlay is typically one large amount and the benefits arrive as a series of smaller amounts over a fairly protracted period.

Investment decisions tend to be of profound importance to the business because:

- *Large amounts of resources are often involved.* Many investments made by businesses involve laying out a significant proportion of their total resources (see Real World 14.2). If mistakes are made with the decision, the effects on the businesses could be significant, if not catastrophic.
- *It is often difficult and/or expensive to bail out of an investment once it has been undertaken.* Investments made by a business are often specific to its needs. For example, a hotel business may invest in a new, custom-designed hotel complex. The specialist nature of this complex will probably lead to its having a rather limited second-hand value to another potential user with different needs. If the business found, after having made the investment, that room occupancy rates were not as buoyant as was planned, the only possible course of action might be to close down and sell the complex. This would probably mean that much less could be recouped from the investment than it had originally cost, particularly if the costs of design are included as part of the cost, as they logically should be.

Real World 14.1 gives an illustration of a major investment by a well-known business operating in the UK.

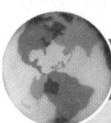

Real World 14.1

Brittany Ferries launches an investment

Brittany Ferries, the cross-Channel ferry operator, recently had a new ship built, to be named *Amorique*. The ship cost the business about €120 million and has been used on the Plymouth to Roscoff route since Spring 2009. Although Brittany Ferries is a substantial business, this level of expenditure was significant. Clearly, the business believed that acquisition of the new ship would be profitable for it, but how would it have reached this conclusion? Presumably the anticipated future cash flows from passengers and freight operators will have been major inputs to the decision. The ship was specifically designed for Brittany Ferries, so it would be difficult for the business to recoup a large proportion of its €81m should these projected cash flows not materialise.

Source: 'New €81m passenger cruise-ferry to be named Amorique', www.brittany-ferries.co.uk.

The issues raised by Brittany Ferries' investment will be the main subject of this chapter.

Real World 14.2 indicates the level of annual net investment for a number of randomly selected, well-known UK businesses. It can be seen that the scale of investment varies from one business to another. (It also tends to vary from one year to the next for a particular business.) In nearly all of these businesses the scale of investment is very significant.

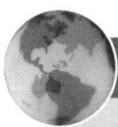

Real World 14.2

The scale of investment by UK businesses

	Expenditure on additional non-current assets as a percentage of:	
	Annual sales revenue	*End-of-year non-current assets*
BT plc (telecommunications)	15.9	17.5
Babcock International Group plc (support services)	6.8	20.6
Tesco plc (supermarkets)	5.5	11.6
J D Wetherspoon plc (pub operator)	12.5	9.0
Marks and Spencer plc (stores)	7.6	14.4
National Grid plc (utilities)	48.0	19.8
J Sainsbury plc (supermarkets)	4.0	8.9
First Group plc (passenger transport)	5.7	13.1

Source: Annual reports of the businesses concerned for the financial year ending in 2007.

Real World 14.2 is limited to considering the non-current asset investment, but most non-current asset investment also requires a level of current asset investment to support it (additional inventories, for example), meaning that the real scale of investment is even greater, typically considerably so, than indicated above.

Activity 14.1

When managers are making decisions involving capital investments, what should the decision seek to achieve?

Investment decisions must be consistent with the objectives of the particular business. For a private-sector business, maximising the wealth of the owners (shareholders) is usually assumed to be the key financial objective.

Investment appraisal methods

Given the importance of investment decisions, it is essential that there is proper screening of investment proposals. An important part of this screening process is to ensure that the business uses appropriate methods of evaluation.

Research shows that there are basically four methods used in practice by businesses throughout the world to evaluate investment opportunities. They are:

- accounting rate of return (ARR)
- payback period (PP)

- net present value (NPV)
- internal rate of return (IRR).

It is possible to find businesses that use variants of these four methods. It is also possible to find businesses, particularly smaller ones, that do not use any formal appraisal method but rely instead on the 'gut feeling' of their managers. Most businesses, however, seem to use one (or more) of these four methods.

We are going to assess the effectiveness of each of these methods and we shall see that only one of them (NPV) is a wholly logical approach. The other three all have flaws. We shall also see how popular these four methods seem to be in practice.

To help us to examine each of the methods, it might be useful to consider how each of them would cope with a particular investment opportunity. Let us consider the following example.

Example 14.1

Billingsgate Battery Company has carried out some research that shows that the business could provide a standard service that it has recently developed.

Provision of the service would require investment in a machine that would cost £100,000, payable immediately. Sales of the service would take place throughout the next five years. At the end of that time, it is estimated that the machine could be sold for £20,000.

Inflows and outflows from sales of the service would be expected to be as follows:

Time		£000
Immediately	Cost of machine	(100)
1 year's time	Operating profit before depreciation	20
2 years' time	Operating profit before depreciation	40
3 years' time	Operating profit before depreciation	60
4 years' time	Operating profit before depreciation	60
5 years' time	Operating profit before depreciation	20
5 years' time	Disposal proceeds from the machine	20

Note that, broadly speaking, the operating profit before deducting depreciation (that is, before non-cash items) equals the net amount of cash flowing into the business. Broadly, apart from depreciation, all of this business's expenses cause cash to flow out of the business. Sales revenues tend to lead to cash flowing in. Expenses tend to lead to it flowing out. For the time being, we shall assume that inventories, trade receivables and trade payables remain constant, and so operating profit before depreciation will tend to equal the net cash inflow.

To simplify matters, we shall assume that the cash from sales and for the expenses of providing the service are received and paid, respectively, at the end of each year. This is clearly unlikely to be true in real life. Money will have to be paid to employees (for salaries and wages) on a weekly or a monthly basis. Customers will pay within a month or two of buying the service. On the other hand, making the assumption probably does not lead to a serious distortion. It is a simplifying assumption, that is often made in real life, and it will make things more straightforward for us now. We should be clear, however, that there is nothing about any of the four methods that *demands* that this assumption is made.

Having set up the example, we shall now go on to consider how each of the appraisal methods works.

Accounting rate of return (ARR)

→ The **accounting rate of return (ARR)** method takes the average accounting operating profit that the investment will generate and expresses it as a percentage of the average investment made over the life of the project. Thus:

$$\text{ARR} = \frac{\text{Average annual operating profit}}{\text{Average investment to earn that profit}} \times 100\%$$

We can see from the equation that, to calculate the ARR, we need to deduce two pieces of information about the particular project:

- the annual average operating profit; and
- the average investment.

In our example, the average annual operating profit *before depreciation* over the five years is £40,000 (that is, in £000: (20 + 40 + 60 + 60 + 20)/5). Assuming 'straight-line' depreciation (that is, equal annual amounts), the annual depreciation charge will be £16,000 (that is, £(100,000 − 20,000)/5). Thus the average annual operating profit *after depreciation* is £24,000 (that is, £40,000 − £16,000).

The average investment over the five years can be calculated as follows:

$$\text{Average investment} = \frac{\text{Cost of machine} + \text{Disposal value}}{2}$$

$$= \frac{£100,000 + £20,000}{2}$$

$$= £60,000$$

Thus, the ARR of the investment is:

$$\text{ARR} = \frac{£24,000}{£60,000} \times 100\% = 40\%$$

Users of ARR should apply the following decision rules:

- For any project to be acceptable it must achieve a target ARR as a minimum.
- Where there are competing projects that all seem capable of exceeding this minimum rate (that is, where the business must choose between more than one project), the one with the higher (or highest) ARR would normally be selected.

To decide whether the 40 per cent return is acceptable, we need to compare this percentage return with the minimum rate required by the business.

Activity (14.2)

Chaotic Industries is considering an investment in a fleet of ten delivery vans to take its products to customers. The vans will cost £15,000 each to buy, payable immediately. The annual running costs are expected to total £50,000 for each van (including the driver's salary). The vans are expected to operate successfully for six years, at the end of which period they will all have to be sold, with disposal proceeds expected to be about £3,000 a van. At present, the business uses a commercial carrier for all of its deliveries. It is expected that this carrier will charge a total of £530,000 each year for the next six years to undertake the deliveries.

What is the ARR of buying the vans? (Note that cost savings are as relevant a benefit from an investment as are net cash inflows.)

The vans will save the business £30,000 a year (that is, £530,000 – (£50,000 × 10)), before depreciation, in total. Thus, the inflows and outflows will be:

Time		£000
Immediately	Cost of vans (10 × £15,000)	(150)
1 year's time	Net saving before depreciation	30
2 years' time	Net saving before depreciation	30
3 years' time	Net saving before depreciation	30
4 years' time	Net saving before depreciation	30
5 years' time	Net saving before depreciation	30
6 years' time	Net saving before depreciation	30
6 years' time	Disposal proceeds from the vans (10 × £3,000)	30

The total annual depreciation expense (assuming a straight-line method) will be £20,000 (that is, (£150,000 – £30,000)/6). Thus, the average annual saving, after depreciation, is £10,000 (that is, £30,000 – £20,000).

The average investment will be

$$\text{Average investment} = \frac{£150,000 + £30,000}{2}$$

$$= £90,000$$

and the ARR of the investment is

$$\text{ARR} = \frac{£10,000}{£90,000} \times 100\%$$

$$= 11.1\%$$

ARR and ROCE

We should note that ARR and the return on capital employed (ROCE) ratio take the same approach to performance measurement, in that they both relate accounting profit to the cost of the assets invested to generate that profit. ROCE is a popular means of assessing the performance of a business, as a whole, *after* it has performed. ARR is an approach that assesses the potential performance of a particular investment, taking the same approach as ROCE, but *before* it has performed.

As we have just seen, managers using ARR will require that any investment undertaken should achieve a target ARR as a minimum. Perhaps the minimum target ROCE would be based on the rate that previous investments had actually achieved (as measured by ROCE). Perhaps it would be the industry-average ROCE.

Since private sector businesses are normally seeking to increase the wealth of their owners, ARR may seem to be a sound method of appraising investment opportunities. Operating profit can be seen as a net increase in wealth over a period, and relating it to the size of investment made to achieve it seems a logical approach.

ARR is said to have a number of advantages as a method of investment appraisal. ROCE seems to be a widely used measure of business performance. Shareholders seem to use this ratio to evaluate management performance, and sometimes the financial objective of a business will be expressed in terms of a target ROCE. It therefore seems sensible to use a method of investment appraisal that is consistent with this overall approach to measuring business performance. It also gives the result expressed as a percentage. It seems that many managers feel comfortable using measures expressed in percentage terms.

Problems with ARR

Activity 14.3

ARR suffers from a very major defect as a means of assessing investment opportunities. Can you reason out what this is? Consider the three competing projects whose profits are shown below. All three involve investment in a machine that is expected to have no residual value at the end of the five years. Note that all of the projects have the same total operating profits over the five years.

Time		Project A £000	Project B £000	Project C £000
Immediately	Cost of machine	(160)	(160)	(160)
1 year's time	Operating profit after depreciation	20	10	160
2 years' time	Operating profit after depreciation	40	10	10
3 years' time	Operating profit after depreciation	60	10	10
4 years' time	Operating profit after depreciation	60	10	10
5 years' time	Operating profit after depreciation	20	160	10

(*Hint*: The defect is not concerned with the ability of the decision maker to forecast future events, although this too can be a problem. Try to remember the essential feature of investment decisions, which we identified at the beginning of this chapter.)

The problem with ARR is that it almost completely ignores the time factor. In this example, exactly the same ARR would have been computed for each of the three projects.

Since the same total operating profit over the five years (£200,000) arises in all three of these projects, and the average investment in each project is £80,000 (that is, £160,000/2), this means that each case will give rise to the same ARR of 50 per cent (that is, £40,000/£80,000).

Given a financial objective of maximising the wealth of the owners of the business, any rational decision maker faced with a choice between the three projects set out in Activity 14.3 would strongly prefer Project C. This is because most of the benefits from the investment arise within twelve months of investing the £160,000 to establish the project. Project A would rank second and Project B would come a poor third. Any appraisal technique that is not capable of distinguishing between these three situations is seriously flawed. We shall look at why timing is so important later in the chapter.

There are further problems associated with the use of ARR. One of these problems concerns the approach taken to derive the average investment in a project.

Example 14.2 illustrates the daft result that ARR can produce.

Example 14.2

George put forward an investment proposal to his boss. The business uses ARR to assess investment proposals using a minimum 'hurdle' rate of 27 per cent. Details of the proposal were as follows:

Cost of equipment	£200,000
Estimated residual value of equipment	£40,000
Average annual operating profit before depreciation	£48,000
Estimated life of project	10 years
Annual straight-line depreciation charge	£16,000 (that is, (£200,000 – £40,000)/10)

The ARR of the project will be:

$$\text{ARR} = \frac{48,000 - 16,000}{(200,000 + 40,000)/2} \times 100\% = 26.7\%$$

The boss rejected George's proposal because it failed to achieve an ARR of at least 27 per cent. Although George was disappointed, he realised that there was still hope. In fact, all that the business had to do was to give away the piece of equipment at the end of its useful life rather than to sell it. The residual value of the equipment then became zero and the annual depreciation charge became ([£200,000 – £0]/10) = £20,000 a year. The revised ARR calculation was then as follows:

$$\text{ARR} = \frac{48,000 - 20,000}{(200,000 + 0)/2} \times 100\% = 28\%$$

ARR is based on the use of accounting profit. When measuring performance over the whole life of a project, however, it is cash flows rather than accounting profits that are important. Cash is the ultimate measure of the economic wealth generated by an investment. This is because it is cash that is used to acquire resources and for distribution to owners. Accounting profit, on the other hand is more appropriate for reporting achievement on a periodic basis. It is a useful measure of productive effort for a relatively short period, such as a year or half year. It is really a question of 'horses for courses'. Accounting profit is fine for measuring performance over a short period but cash is the appropriate measure when considering the performance over the life of a project.

The ARR method can also create problems when considering competing investments of different size.

Activity (14.4)

Sinclair Wholesalers plc is currently considering opening a new sales outlet in Coventry. Two possible sites have been identified for the new outlet. Site A has an area of 30,000 sq m. It will require an average investment of £6m, and will produce an average operating profit of £600,000 a year. Site B has an area of 20,000 sq m. It will require an average investment of £4m, and will produce an average operating profit of £500,000 a year.

What is the ARR of each investment opportunity? Which site would you select, and why?

The ARR of Site A is £600,000/£6m = 10 per cent. The ARR of Site B is £500,000/£4m = 12.5 per cent. Thus, Site B has the higher ARR. However, in terms of the absolute operating profit generated, Site A is the more attractive. If the ultimate objective is to increase the wealth of the shareholders of Sinclair Wholesalers plc, it might be better to choose Site A even though the percentage return is lower. It is the absolute size of the return rather than the relative (percentage) size that is important. This is a general problem of using comparative measures, such as percentages, when the objective is measured in absolute ones, like an amount of money. If businesses were seeking through their investments to generate a percentage rate of return on investment, ARR would be more helpful. The problem is that most businesses seek to achieve increases in their absolute wealth (measured in pounds, euros, dollars and so on), through their investment decisions.

Real World 14.3 illustrates how using percentage measures can lead to confusion.

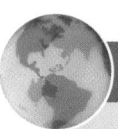

Real World 14.3

Increasing road capacity by sleight of hand

During the 1970s, the Mexican government wanted to increase the capacity of a major four-lane road. It came up with the idea of repainting the lane markings so that there were six narrower lanes occupying the same space as four wider ones had previously done. This increased the capacity of the road by 50 per cent (that is, $2/4 \times 100$). A tragic outcome of the narrower lanes was an increase in deaths from road accidents. A year later the Mexican government had the six narrower lanes changed back to the original four wider ones. This reduced the capacity of the road by 33 per cent (that is, $2/6 \times 100$). The Mexican government reported that, overall, it had increased the capacity of the road by 17 per cent (that is, 50% − 33%), despite the fact that its real capacity was identical to that which it had been originally. The confusion arose because the two percentages (50 per cent and 33 per cent) are based on different bases (four and six).

Source: Reckoning with Risk, G. Gigerenzer, Penguin, 2002.

Payback period (PP)

→ The **payback period (PP)** is the length of time it takes for an initial investment to be repaid out of the net cash inflows from a project. Since it takes time into account, the PP method seems to go some way to overcoming the timing problem of ARR – or at first glance it does.

Let us consider PP in the context of the Billingsgate Battery example. We should recall that essentially the project's cash flows are:

Time		£000
Immediately	Cost of machine	(100)
1 year's time	Operating profit before depreciation	20
2 years' time	Operating profit before depreciation	40
3 years' time	Operating profit before depreciation	60
4 years' time	Operating profit before depreciation	60
5 years' time	Operating profit before depreciation	20
5 years' time	Disposal proceeds	20

Note that all of these figures are amounts of cash to be paid or received (we saw earlier that operating profit before depreciation is a rough measure of the cash flows from the project).

As the payback period is the length of time it takes for the initial investment to be repaid out of the net cash inflows, it will be three years before the £100,000 outlay is covered by the inflows. This is still assuming that the cash flows occur at year ends. The payback period can be derived by calculating the cumulative cash flows as follows:

Time		Net cash flows £000	Cumulative cash flows £000	
Immediately	Cost of machine	(100)	(100)	
1 year's time	Operating profit before depreciation	20	(80)	(–100 + 20)
2 years' time	Operating profit before depreciation	40	(40)	(–80 + 40)
3 years' time	Operating profit before depreciation	60	20	(–40 + 60)
4 years' time	Operating profit before depreciation	60	80	(20 + 60)
5 years' time	Operating profit before depreciation	20	100	(80 + 20)
5 years' time	Disposal proceeds	20	120	(100 + 20)

We can see that the cumulative cash flows become positive at the end of the third year. (Had we assumed that the cash flows arise evenly over the year, the precise payback period would be:

$$2 \text{ years} + (^{40}/_{60}) \text{ years} = 2^{2}/_{3} \text{ years}$$

where 40 represents the cash flow still required at the beginning of the third year to repay the initial outlay, and 60 is the projected cash flow during the third year.

We must now ask how to decide whether three years is an acceptable payback period.

The decision rule for using PP is:

- For a project to be acceptable it would need to have a payback period shorter than a maximum payback period set by the business.
- If there were two (or more) competing projects whose payback periods were all shorter than the maximum payback period requirement, the project with the shorter (or shortest) payback period should be selected.

If, for example, Billingsgate Battery had a maximum acceptable payback period of four years, the project would be undertaken. A project with a longer payback period than four years would not be acceptable.

Activity 14.5

What is the payback period of the Chaotic Industries project from Activity 14.2?

The inflows and outflows are expected to be:

Time		Net cash flows £000	Cumulative net cash flows £000	
Immediately	Cost of vans	(150)	(150)	
1 year's time	Net saving before depreciation	30	(120)	(−150 + 30)
2 years' time	Net saving before depreciation	30	(90)	(−120 + 30)
3 years' time	Net saving before depreciation	30	(60)	(−90 + 30)
4 years' time	Net saving before depreciation	30	(30)	(−60 + 30)
5 years' time	Net saving before depreciation	30	0	(−30 + 30)
6 years' time	Net saving before depreciation	30	30	(0 + 30)
6 years' time	Disposal proceeds from the machine	30	60	(30 + 30)

The payback period here is five years; that is, it is not until the end of the fifth year that the vans will pay for themselves out of the savings that they are expected to generate.

The PP method has certain advantages. It is quick and easy to calculate, and can be easily understood by managers. The logic of using PP is that projects that can recoup their cost quickly are economically more attractive than those with longer payback periods, that is, it emphasises liquidity. PP is probably an improvement on ARR in respect of the timing of the cash flows. PP is not, however, the whole answer to the problem.

Problems with PP

Activity 14.6

In what respect is PP not the whole answer as a means of assessing investment opportunities? Consider the cash flows arising from three competing projects:

Activity 14.6 continued

Time		Project 1 £000	Project 2 £000	Project 3 £000
Immediately	Cost of machine	(200)	(200)	(200)
1 year's time	Operating profit before depreciation	70	20	70
2 years' time	Operating profit before depreciation	60	20	100
3 years' time	Operating profit before depreciation	70	160	30
4 years' time	Operating profit before depreciation	80	30	200
5 years' time	Operating profit before depreciation	50	20	440
5 years' time	Disposal proceeds	40	10	20

(*Hint*: Again, the defect is not concerned with the ability of the manager to forecast future events. This is a problem, but it is a problem whatever approach we take.)

The PP for each project is three years and so the PP method would regard the projects as being equally acceptable. It cannot distinguish between those projects that pay back a significant amount early in the three-year payback period and those that do not.

In addition, this method ignores cash flows after the payback period. A decision maker concerned with increasing owners' wealth would prefer Project 3 because the cash flows come in earlier (most of the initial cost of making the investment has been repaid by the end of the second year) and they are greater in total.

The cumulative cash flows of each project in Activity 14.6 are set out in Figure 14.1.

Figure 14.1   **The cumulative cash flows of each project in Activity 14.6**

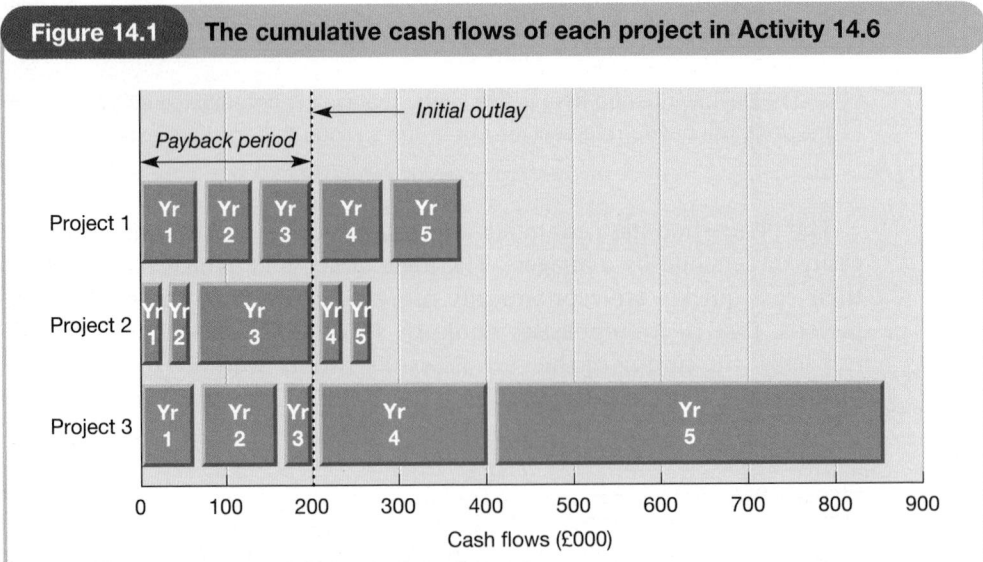

The payback method of investment appraisal would view Projects 1, 2 and 3 as being equally attractive. In doing so, the method completely ignores the fact that Project 3 provides most of the payback cash earlier in the three-year period and goes on to generate large benefits in later years.

We can see that the PP method is not concerned with the profitability of projects; it is concerned simply with their payback period. Thus cash flows arising beyond the payback period are ignored. While this neatly avoids the practical problems of forecasting cash flows over a long period, it means that relevant information could be ignored.

We may feel that, by favouring projects with a short payback period, the PP method does at least provide a means of dealing with the problems of risk and uncertainty. However, this is a fairly crude approach to the problem. It looks only at the risk that the project will end earlier than expected. However, this is only one of many risk areas. What, for example, about the risk that the demand for the product may be less than expected? There are more systematic approaches to dealing with risk that can be used and we shall look at these later in the chapter.

PP takes some note of the timing of the costs and benefits from the project. Its key deficiency, however, is that it is not linked to promoting increases in the wealth of the business and its owners. PP will tend to recommend undertaking projects that pay for themselves quickly.

The PP method requires the managers of a business to select a maximum acceptable payback period. This maximum period, in practice, will vary from one business to the next. **Real World 14.4** provides some evidence of the length of payback period required by small to medium size businesses when investing in new forms of energy generation.

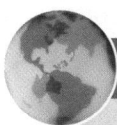 **Real World 14.4**

Payback time

When it comes to self-generation of renewable energy, UK SMEs (small and medium size enterprises) want an unrealistically quick return on investment according to research carried out by energy consultancy energyTEAM. Nearly three-quarters would need payback within three years in order to justify introducing such measures. Only 4 per cent are prepared for this process to take over five years despite growing concern over commercial energy usage. EnergyTEAM's study revealed that 40 per cent of enterprises with 50 to 500 employees would have to be convinced of a return on investment in just one year before they would proceed down the route of self-generation.

When asked which method of self-generation they would be most inclined to choose, over half of respondents highlighted solar power as the preferred method. This is despite the fact that solar has one of the largest payback times, at around ten years.

Brian Rickerby, joint Managing Director of energyTEAM, said 'I can understand that seeking a quick return is a pragmatic, business-like approach, but unfortunately this is not realistic when it comes to energy issues. Self-generation technologies must be viewed as a long-term strategy that will have a significant positive impact for many years to come.'

Source: 'SMEs' unrealistic demands on renewables', *Sustain*, vol. 8, issue 5, 2007, p. 74.

Net present value (NPV)

From what we have seen so far, it seems that to make sensible investment decisions, we need a method of appraisal that both:

- considers *all* of the costs and benefits of each investment opportunity; and
- makes a logical allowance for the *timing* of those costs and benefits.

→ The **net present value (NPV)** method provides us with this.

Consider the Billingsgate Battery example's cash flows, which we should recall can be summarised as follows:

Time		£000
Immediately	Cost of machine	(100)
1 year's time	Operating profit before depreciation	20
2 years' time	Operating profit before depreciation	40
3 years' time	Operating profit before depreciation	60
4 years' time	Operating profit before depreciation	60
5 years' time	Operating profit before depreciation	20
5 years' time	Disposal proceeds	20

Given that the principal financial objective of the business is to increase owners' wealth, it would be very easy to assess this investment if all of the cash inflows and outflows were to occur now (all at the same time). All that we should need to do would be to add up the cash inflows (total £220,000) and compare them with the cash outflows (£100,000). This would lead us to the conclusion that the project should go ahead because the business, and its owners, would be better off by £120,000. Of course, it is not as easy as this because time is involved. The cash outflow (payment) will occur immediately if the project is undertaken. The inflows (receipts) will arise at a range of later times.

The time factor is an important issue because people do not normally see £100 paid out now as equivalent in value to £100 receivable in a year's time. If we were to be offered £100 in 12 months' time in exchange for paying out £100 now, we should not be prepared to do so unless we wished to do someone a favour.

Activity (14.7)

Why would you see £100 to be received in a year's time as not equal in value to £100 to be paid immediately? (There are basically three reasons.)

The reasons are:

- interest lost
- risk
- effects of inflation.

We shall now take a closer look at these three reasons in turn.

Interest lost

If we are to be deprived of the opportunity to spend our money for a year, we could equally well be deprived of its use by placing it on deposit in a bank or building society. In this case, at the end of the year we could have our money back and have interest as well. Thus, by investing the funds in some other way, we shall be incurring an *opportunity cost*. We should remember from Chapter 8 that an opportunity cost occurs where one course of action, for example making an investment, deprives us of the opportunity to derive some benefit from an alternative action, for example putting the money in the bank and earning interest.

From this we can see that any investment opportunity must, if it is to make us wealthier, do better than the returns that are available from the next best opportunity. Thus, if Billingsgate Battery Company sees putting the money in the bank on deposit as the alternative to investment in the machine, the return from investing in the machine must be better than that from investing in the bank. If the bank offered a better return, the business, and its owners, would become wealthier by putting the money on deposit.

Risk

→ All investments expose their investors to **risk**. For example, buying a machine to manufacture a product or to provide a service, to be sold in the market, on the strength of various estimates made in advance of buying the machine, exposes the business to risk. Things may not turn out as expected.

Activity 14.8

Can you suggest some areas where things could go other than according to plan in the Billingsgate Battery Company example (basically, buying a machine and using it to render a service for five years)?

We have come up with the following:

- The machine might not work as well as expected; it might break down, leading to loss of the business's ability to provide the service.
- Sales of the service may not be as buoyant as expected.
- Labour costs may prove to be higher than expected.
- The sale proceeds of the machine could prove to be less than were estimated.

It is important to remember that the decision whether to invest in the machine must be taken *before* any of these things are known. For example, it is only after the machine has been purchased that we could discover that the level of sales which had been estimated before the event is not going to be achieved. It is not possible to wait until we know for certain whether the market will behave as we expected before we buy the machine. We can study reports and analyses of the market. We can commission sophisticated market surveys, and these may give us more confidence in the likely outcome. We can advertise widely and try to promote sales. Ultimately, however, we have to decide whether to jump off into the dark and accept the risk if we want the opportunity to make profitable investments.

Real World 14.5 gives some impression of the extent to which businesses believe that investment outcomes turn out as expected.

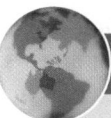

Real World 14.5

Size matters

Senior finance managers of 99 Cambridgeshire manufacturing businesses were asked how their investments were performing compared to expectations at the time of making the investment decision. The results, broken down according to business size, are set out below.

Real World 14.5 continued

Actual performance relative to expectations	Size of business			
	Large %	Medium %	Small %	All %
Under-performed	8	14	32	14
Performed as expected	82	72	68	77
Over-performed	10	14	0	9

It seems that smaller businesses are much more likely to get it wrong than medium-size or larger businesses. This may be because small businesses are often younger and, therefore, less experienced both in the techniques of forecasting and in managing investment projects. They are also likely to have less financial expertise. It also seems that small businesses have a distinct bias towards over-optimism and do not take full account of the possibility that things will turn out worse than expected.

Source: Unpacking the Black Box: An Econometric Analysis of Investment Strategies in Real World Firms, M. Baddeley, CEPP Working Paper No. 08/05, 2006, University of Cambridge, p. 14.

Normally, people expect to receive greater returns where they perceive risk to be a factor. Examples of this in real life are not difficult to find. One such example is that banks tend to charge higher rates of interest to borrowers whom the bank perceives as more risky. Those who can offer good security for a loan, and who can point to a regular source of income, tend to be charged lower rates of interest.

Going back to Billingsgate Battery Company's investment opportunity, it is not enough to say that we should advise making the investment provided that the returns from it are as high as those from investing in a bank deposit. Clearly we should want returns above the level of bank deposit interest rates, because the logical equivalent of investing in the machine is not putting the money on deposit but making an alternative investment that is risky.

We have just seen that investors tend to expect a higher rate of return from investment projects where the risk is perceived as being higher. How risky a particular project is, and therefore how large this **risk premium** should be, are, however, matters that are difficult to handle. It is usually necessary to make some judgement on these questions. We shall come back to the size of the risk premium later in the chapter when we consider how the level of risk can be assessed.

Inflation

If we are to be deprived of £100 for a year, when we come to spend that money it will not buy as many goods and services as it would have done a year earlier. Generally, we shall not be able to buy as many tins of baked beans or loaves of bread or bus tickets as we could have done a year earlier. This is because of the loss in the purchasing power of money, or **inflation**, which occurs over time. Clearly, the investor needs compensating for this loss of purchasing power if the investment is to be made. This compensation is on top of a return that takes account of what could have been gained from an alternative investment of similar risk.

In practice, interest rates observable in the market tend to take inflation into account. Rates that are offered to potential building society and bank depositors include an allowance for the rate of inflation that is expected in the future.

What will logical investors do?

As we have seen, logical investors who are seeking to increase their wealth will only be prepared to make investments that will compensate for the loss of interest and purchasing power of the money invested and for the fact that the returns expected may not materialise (risk). This is usually assessed by seeing whether the proposed investment will yield a return that is greater than the basic rate of interest (which would include an allowance for inflation) plus a risk premium.

These three factors (interest lost, risk and inflation) are set out in Figure 14.2.

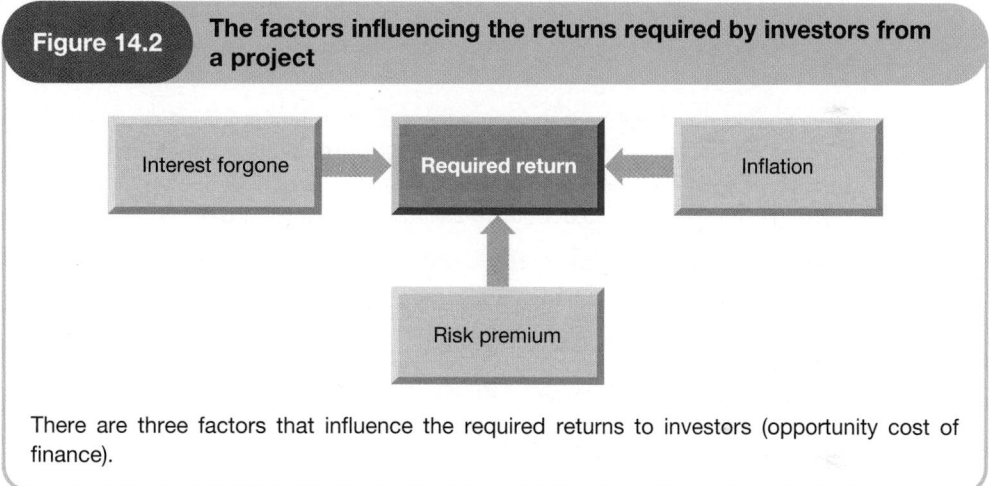

| Figure 14.2 | The factors influencing the returns required by investors from a project |

There are three factors that influence the required returns to investors (opportunity cost of finance).

Naturally, investors need at least the minimum returns before they are prepared to invest. However, it is in terms of the effect on their wealth that they should logically assess an investment project. Usually it is the investment with the highest percentage return that will make the investor most wealthy, but we shall see later in this chapter that this is not always the case. For the time being, therefore, we shall concentrate on wealth.

Let us now return to the Billingsgate Battery Company example. We should recall that the cash flows expected from this investment are:

Time		£000
Immediately	Cost of machine	(100)
1 year's time	Operating profit before depreciation	20
2 years' time	Operating profit before depreciation	40
3 years' time	Operating profit before depreciation	60
4 years' time	Operating profit before depreciation	60
5 years' time	Operating profit before depreciation	20
5 years' time	Disposal proceeds	20

We have already seen that it is not sufficient just to compare the basic cash inflows and outflows for the investment. It would be useful if we could express each of these cash flows in similar terms, so that we could make a direct comparison between the sum of the inflows over time and the immediate £100,000 investment. Fortunately, we can do this.

Let us assume that, instead of making this investment, the business could make an alternative investment with similar risk and obtain a return of 20 per cent a year.

Activity (14.9)

We know that Billingsgate Battery Company could alternatively invest its money at a rate of 20 per cent a year. How much do you judge the present (immediate) value of the expected first year receipt of £20,000 to be? In other words, if instead of having to wait a year for the £20,000, and being deprived of the opportunity to invest it at 20 per cent, you could have some money now, what sum to be received now would you regard as exactly equivalent to getting £20,000 but having to wait a year for it?

We should obviously be happy to accept a lower amount if we could get it immediately than if we had to wait a year. This is because we could invest it at 20 per cent (in the alternative project). Logically, we should be prepared to accept the amount that, with a year's income, will grow to £20,000. If we call this amount PV (for present value) we can say:

$$PV + (PV \times 20\%) = £20,000$$

that is, the amount plus income from investing the amount for the year equals the £20,000.
   If we rearrange this equation we find:

$$PV \times (1 + 0.2) = £20,000$$

(Note that 0.2 is the same as 20 per cent, but expressed as a decimal.) Further re-arranging gives:

$$PV = £20,000/(1 + 0.2) = £16,667$$

Thus, rational investors who have the opportunity to invest at 20 per cent a year would not mind whether they have £16,667 now or £20,000 in a year's time. In this sense we can say that, given a 20 per cent alternative investment opportunity, the present value of £20,000 to be received in one year's time is £16,667.

If we derive the present value (PV) of each of the cash flows associated with Billingsgate's machine investment, we could easily make the direct comparison between the cost of making the investment (£100,000) and the various benefits that will derive from it in years 1 to 5.

We can make a more general statement about the PV of a particular cash flow. It is:

PV of the cash flow of year n = actual cash flow of year n divided by $(1 + r)^n$

where n is the year of the cash flow (that is, how many years into the future) and r is the opportunity investing rate expressed as a decimal (instead of as a percentage).

We have already seen how this works for the £20,000 inflow for year 1 for the Billingsgate project. For year 2 the calculation would be:

PV of year 2 cash flow (that is, £40,000) = £40,000/$(1 + 0.2)^2$ = £40,000/$(1.2)^2$
= £40,000/1.44 = £27,778

Thus the present value of the £40,000 to be received in two years' time is £27,778.

Activity (14.10)

See if you can show that an investor would find £27,778, receivable now, as equally acceptable to receiving £40,000 in two years' time, assuming that there is a 20 per cent investment opportunity.

The reasoning goes like this:

	£
Amount available for immediate investment	27,778
Add Income for year 1 (20% × 27,778)	5,556
	33,334
Add Income for year 2 (20% × 33,334)	6,667
	40,001

(The extra £1 is only a rounding error.)

This is to say that since the investor can turn £27,778 into £40,000 in two years, these amounts are equivalent. We can say that £27,778 is the present value of £40,000 receivable after two years (given a 20 per cent rate of return).

Now let us calculate the present values of all of the cash flows associated with the Billingsgate machine project and from them the *net present value (NPV)* of the project as a whole.

The relevant cash flows and calculations are as follows:

Time	Cash flow £000	Calculation of PV	PV £000
Immediately (time 0)	(100)	(100)/$(1 + 0.2)^0$	(100.00)
1 year's time	20	20/$(1 + 0.2)^1$	16.67
2 years' time	40	40/$(1 + 0.2)^2$	27.78
3 years' time	60	60/$(1 + 0.2)^3$	34.72
4 years' time	60	60/$(1 + 0.2)^4$	28.94
5 years' time	20	20/$(1 + 0.2)^5$	8.04
5 years' time	20	20/$(1 + 0.2)^5$	8.04
Net present value (NPV)			24.19

Note that $(1 + 0.2)^0 = 1$.

Once again, we must ask how we can decide whether the machine project is acceptable to the business. In fact, the decision rule for NPV is simple:

- If the NPV is positive the project should be accepted; if it is negative the project should be rejected.
- If there are two (or more) competing projects that have positive NPVs, the project with the higher (or highest) NPV should be selected.

In this case, the NPV is positive, so we should accept the project and buy the machine. The reasoning behind this decision rule is quite straightforward. Investing in the machine will make the business, and its owners, £24,190 better off than they would be by taking up the next best opportunity available to it. The gross benefits from investing in this machine are worth a total of £124,190 today, and since the business can 'buy' these benefits for just £100,000 today, the investment should be made. If, however, the present value of the gross benefits were below £100,000, it would be less than the cost of 'buying' those benefits and the opportunity should, therefore, be rejected.

Activity (14.11)

What is the *maximum* the Billingsgate Battery Company would be prepared to pay for the machine, given the potential benefits of owning it?

The business would logically be prepared to pay up to £124,190 since the wealth of the owners of the business would be increased up to this price – although the business would prefer to pay as little as possible.

Using discount tables

Deducing the present values of the various cash flows is a little laborious using the approach that we have just taken. To deduce each PV we took the relevant cash flow and multiplied it by $1/(1 + r)^n$. There is a slightly different way to do this. Tables exist that show values of this **discount factor** for a range of values of r and n. Such a table appears in at the end of this book, in Appendix F. Take a look at it.

Look at the column for 20 per cent and the row for one year. We find that the factor is 0.833. This means that the PV of a cash flow of £1 receivable in one year is £0.833. So the present value of a cash flow of £20,000 receivable in one year's time is £16,660 (that is, 0.833 × £20,000), the same result as we found doing it in longhand.

Activity (14.12)

What is the NPV of the Chaotic Industries project from Activity 14.2, assuming a 15 per cent opportunity cost of finance (discount rate)? (Use the discount table in Appendix F.)

Remember that the inflows and outflow are expected to be:

Time		£000
Immediately	Cost of vans	(150)
1 year's time	Net saving before depreciation	30
2 years' time	Net saving before depreciation	30
3 years' time	Net saving before depreciation	30
4 years' time	Net saving before depreciation	30
5 years' time	Net saving before depreciation	30
6 years' time	Net saving before depreciation	30
6 years' time	Disposal proceeds from the machine	30

The calculation of the NPV of the project is as follows:

Time	Cash flows £000	Discount factor (15%)	Present value £000
Immediately	(150)	$1/(1 + 0.15)^0$	(150.00)
1 year's time	30	$1/(1 + 0.15)^1$	26.10
2 years' time	30	$1/(1 + 0.15)^2$	22.68
3 years' time	30	$1/(1 + 0.15)^3$	19.74
4 years' time	30	$1/(1 + 0.15)^4$	17.16
5 years' time	30	$1/(1 + 0.15)^5$	14.91
6 years' time	30	$1/(1 + 0.15)^6$	12.96
6 years' time	30	$1/(1 + 0.15)^6$	12.96
		NPV	(23.49)

Activity 14.13

How would you interpret this result?

The fact that the project has a negative NPV means that the present values of the benefits from the investment are worth less than the cost of entering into it. Any cost up to £126,510 (the present value of the benefits) would be worth paying, but not £150,000.

The discount table in Appendix F shows how the value of £1 diminishes as its receipt goes further into the future. Assuming an opportunity cost of finance of 20 per cent a year, £1 to be received immediately, obviously, has a present value of £1. However, as the time before it is to be received increases, the present value diminishes significantly, as is shown in Figure 14.3.

The discount rate and the cost of capital

We have seen that the appropriate discount rate to use in NPV assessments is the opportunity cost of finance. This is, in effect, the cost to the business of the finance needed to fund the investment. It will normally be the cost of a mixture of funds (shareholders' funds and borrowings) employed by the business and is often referred to as the **cost of capital**.

Why NPV is better

From what we have seen, NPV seems to be a better method of appraising investment opportunities than either ARR or PP. This is because it fully takes account of each of the following:

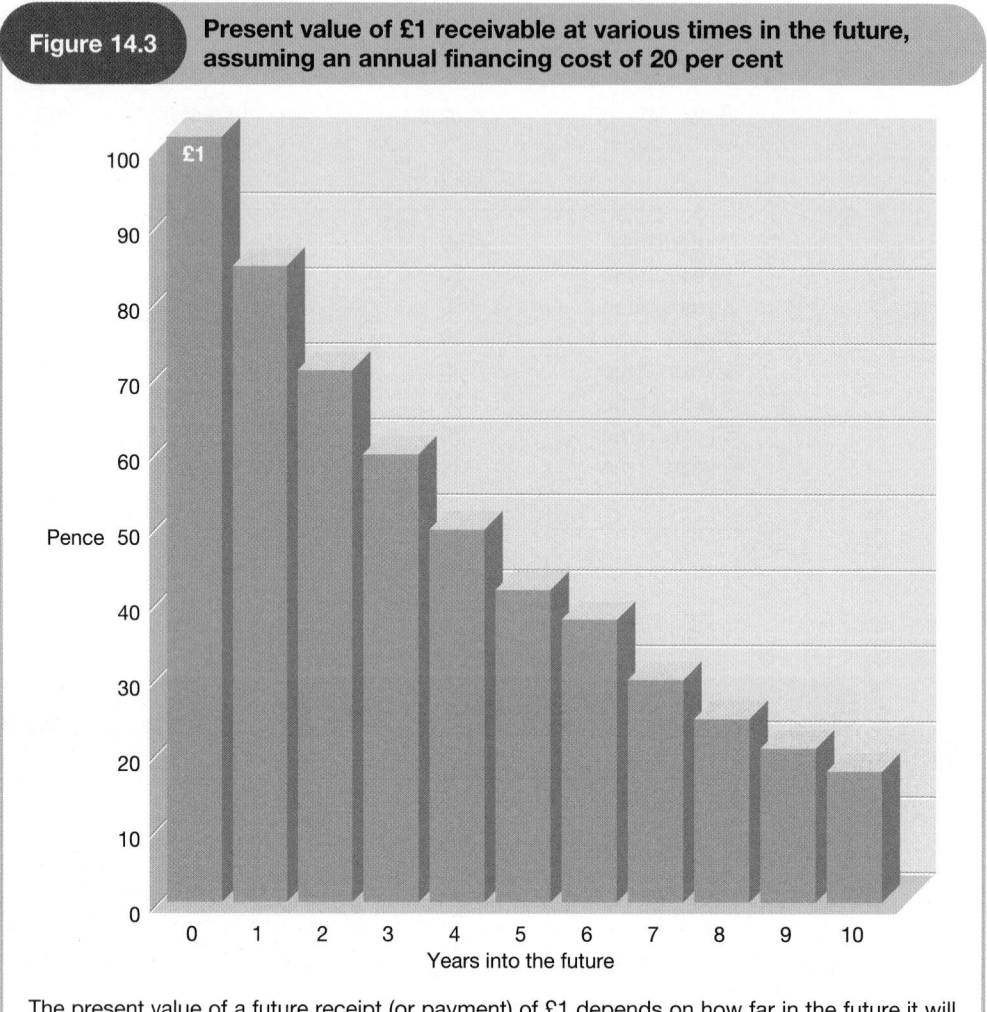

Figure 14.3 **Present value of £1 receivable at various times in the future, assuming an annual financing cost of 20 per cent**

The present value of a future receipt (or payment) of £1 depends on how far in the future it will occur. Those that will occur in the near future will have a larger present value than those whose occurrence is more distant in time.

- *The timing of the cash flows.* By discounting the various cash flows associated with each project according to when each one is expected to arise, NPV takes account of the time value of money. Associated with this is the fact that by discounting, using the opportunity cost of finance (that is, the return that the next best alternative opportunity would generate), the net benefit *after* financing costs have been met is identified (as the NPV of the project).
- *The whole of the relevant cash flows.* NPV includes *all* of the relevant cash flows irrespective of when they are expected to occur. It treats them differently according to their date of occurrence, but they are all taken into account in the NPV, and they all have an influence on the decision.
- *The objectives of the business.* NPV is the only method of appraisal in which the output of the analysis has a direct bearing on the wealth of the owners of the business (with a limited company, the shareholders). Positive NPVs enhance wealth; negative ones reduce it. Since we assume that private sector businesses seek to increase owners' wealth, NPV is superior to the other two methods (ARR and PP) that we have already discussed.

We saw earlier that a business should take on all projects with positive NPVs, when their cash flows are discounted at the opportunity cost of finance. Where a choice has to be made between projects, the business should normally select the one with the higher or highest NPV.

NPV's wider application

NPV is considered the most logical approach to making business decisions about investments in productive assets. The same logic makes NPV equally valid as the best approach to take when trying to place a value on any economic asset, that is, an asset that seems capable of yielding financial benefits. This would include a share in a limited company and a loan. In fact, when we talk of *economic value*, we mean a value that has been derived by adding together the discounted (present) values of all future cash flows from the asset concerned.

Real World 14.6 provides an estimate of the NPV that is expected from one interesting project.

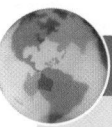

Real World 14.6

A real diamond geezer

Alan Bond, the disgraced Australian businessman and America's Cup winner, is looking at ways to raise money in London for an African diamond mining project. Lesotho Diamond Corporation (LDC) is a private company in which Mr Bond has a large interest. LDC's main asset is a 93 per cent stake in the Kao diamond project in the southern African kingdom of Lesotho.

Mr Bond says, on his personal website, that the Kao project is forecast to yield 5m carats of diamonds over the next 10 years and could become Lesotho's biggest foreign currency earner.

SRK, the mining consultants, have estimated the net present value of the project at £129m.

It is understood that Mr Bond and his family own about 40 per cent of LDC. Mr Bond has described himself as 'spearheading' the Kao project.

Source: Adapted from 'Bond seeks funds in London to mine African diamonds', Rebecca Bream, FT.com, 22 April 2007.

Internal rate of return (IRR)

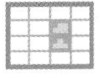

This is the last of the four major methods of investment appraisal that are found in practice. It is quite closely related to the NPV method in that, like NPV, it also involves discounting future cash flows. The **internal rate of return (IRR)** of a particular investment is the discount rate that, when applied to its future cash flows, will produce an NPV of precisely zero. In essence, it represents the yield from an investment opportunity.

Activity (14.14)

We should recall that, when we discounted the cash flows of the Billingsgate Battery Company machine investment opportunity at 20 per cent, we found that the NPV was a positive figure of £24,190 (see page 544). What does the NPV of the machine project tell us about the rate of return that the investment will yield for the business (that is, the project's IRR)?

The fact that the NPV is positive when discounting at 20 per cent implies that the rate of return that the project generates is more than 20 per cent. The fact that the NPV is a pretty large figure implies that the actual rate of return is quite a lot above 20 per cent. We should expect increasing the size of the discount rate to reduce NPV, because a higher discount rate gives a lower discounted figure.

It is somewhat laborious to deduce the IRR by hand, since it cannot usually be calculated directly. Iteration (trial and error) is the approach that must usually be adopted. Fortunately, computer spreadsheet packages can deduce the IRR with ease. The package will also use a trial and error approach, but at high speed.

Despite it being laborious, we shall now go on and derive the IRR for the Billingsgate project by hand.

Let us try a higher rate, say 30 per cent, and see what happens.

Time	Cash flow £000	Discount factor (30%)	PV £000
Immediately (time 0)	(100)	1.000	(100.00)
1 year's time	20	0.769	15.38
2 years' time	40	0.592	23.68
3 years' time	60	0.455	27.30
4 years' time	60	0.350	21.00
5 years' time	20	0.269	5.38
5 years' time	20	0.269	5.38
		NPV	(1.88)

In increasing the discount rate from 20 per cent to 30 per cent, we have reduced the NPV from £24,190 (positive) to £1,880 (negative). Since the IRR is the discount rate that will give us an NPV of exactly zero, we can conclude that the IRR of Billingsgate Battery Company's machine project is very slightly below 30 per cent. Further trials could lead us to the exact rate, but there is probably not much point, given the likely inaccuracy of the cash flow estimates. It is probably good enough, for practical purposes, to say that the IRR is about 30 per cent.

The relationship between the NPV method discussed earlier and the IRR is shown graphically in Figure 14.4 using the information relating to the Billingsgate Battery Company.

We can see in Figure 14.4 that, where the discount rate is zero, the NPV will be the sum of the net cash flows. In other words, no account is taken of the time value of money. However, as the discount rate increases there is a corresponding decrease in the NPV of the project. When the NPV line crosses the horizontal axis there will be a zero NPV, and that represents the IRR.

Figure 14.4   The relationship between the NPV and IRR methods

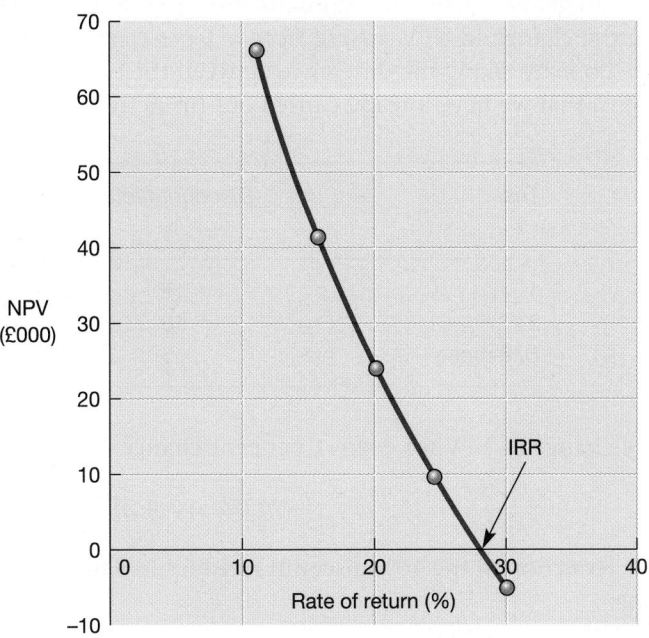

If the discount rate were zero, the NPV would be the sum of the net cash flows. In other words, no account would be taken of the time value of money. However, if we assume increasing discount rates, there is a corresponding decrease in the NPV of the project. When the NPV line crosses the horizontal axis there will be a zero NPV, and the point where it crosses is the IRR.

Activity 14.15

What is the internal rate of return of the Chaotic Industries project from Activity 14.2?
   (*Hint*: Remember that you already know the NPV of this project at 15 per cent – from Activity 14.12.)

Since we know that, at a 15 per cent discount rate, the NPV is a relatively large negative figure, our next trial is using a lower discount rate, say 10 per cent:

Time	Cash flows £000	Discount factor (10% – from the table)	Present value £000
Immediately	(150)	1.000	(150.00)
1 year's time	30	0.909	27.27
2 years' time	30	0.826	24.78
3 years' time	30	0.751	22.53
4 years' time	30	0.683	20.49
5 years' time	30	0.621	18.63
6 years' time	30	0.564	16.92
6 years' time	30	0.564	16.92
		NPV	(2.46)

   This figure is close to zero NPV. However, the NPV is still negative and so the precise IRR will be a little below 10 per cent.

We could undertake further trials in order to derive the precise IRR. If, however, we have to derive the IRR manually, further trials can be time-consuming.

We can get an acceptable approximation to the answer fairly quickly by first calculating the change in NPV arising from a 1 per cent change in the discount rate. This can be done by taking the difference between the two trials (that is, 15 per cent and 10 per cent) that we have already carried out (in Activities 14.12 and 14.15):

Trial	Discount factor %	Net present value £000
1	15	(23.49)
2	10	(2.46)
Difference	5	21.03

The change in NPV for every 1 per cent change in the discount rate will be:

$$(21.03/5) = 4.21$$

The reduction in the 10% discount rate required to achieve a zero NPV would therefore be:

$$[(2.46)/4.21] \times 1\% = 0.58\%$$

The IRR is therefore:

$$(10.00 - 0.58) = 9.42\%$$

However to say that the IRR is about 9 or 10 per cent is near enough for most purposes.

Note that this approach assumes a straight-line relationship between the discount rate and NPV. We can see from Figure 14.4 that this assumption is not strictly correct. Over a relatively short range, however, this simplifying assumption is not usually a problem and so we can still arrive at a reasonable approximation using the approach that we took in deriving the 9.42 per cent IRR.

In practice, most businesses have computer software packages that will derive a project's IRR very quickly. Thus, in practice it is not usually necessary either to make a series of trial discount rates or to make the approximation that we have just considered.

Users of the IRR method should apply the following decision rules:

- For any project to be acceptable, it must meet a minimum IRR requirement. This is often referred to as the *hurdle rate* and, logically, this should be the opportunity cost of finance.
- Where there are competing projects (that is, the business can choose only one of two or more viable projects), the one with the higher (or highest) IRR should be selected.

IRR has certain attributes in common with NPV. All cash flows are taken into account, and their timing is logically handled.

Real World 14.7 provides some idea of the IRR for one form of renewable energy.

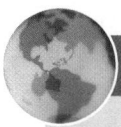

Real World 14.7

The answer is blowin' in the wind

FT

'Wind farms are practically guaranteed to make returns once you have a licence to operate,' says Bernard Lambilliotte, chief investment officer at Ecofin, a financial group that runs Ecofin Water and Power Opportunities, an investment trust.

'The risk is when you have bought the land and are seeking a licence,' says Lambilliotte. 'But once it is built and you are plugged into the grid it is risk-free. It will give an internal rate of return in the low to mid-teens.' Ecofin's largest investment is in Sechilienne, a French company that operates wind farms in northern France and generates capacity in the French overseas territories powered by sugar cane waste.

Source: 'A hot topic, but poor returns', Charles Batchelor, FT.com, 27 August 2005.

Real World 14.8 gives some examples of IRRs sought in practice.

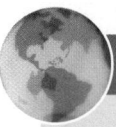

Real World 14.8

Rates of return

IRR rates for investment projects can vary considerably. Here are a few examples of the expected or target returns from investment projects of large businesses.

● Forth Ports plc, a port operator, concentrates on projects that generate an IRR of at least 15 per cent.
● Rok plc, the builder, aims for a minimum IRR of 15 per cent from new investments.
● Hutchison Whampoa, a large telecommunications business, requires an IRR of at least 25 per cent from its telecom projects.
● Airbus, the plane maker, expects an IRR of 13 per cent from the sale of its A380 super-jumbo aircraft.
● Signet Group plc, the jewellery retailer, requires an IRR of 20 per cent over five years when appraising new stores.

Sources: 'FAQs, Forth Ports plc' (www.forthports.co.uk); Numis Broker Research Report, p. 31 (www.rokgroup.com), 17 August 2006; 'Hutchison Whampoa', FT.com, Lex column, 31 March 2004; 'Airbus hikes A380 break-even target', FT.com, 20 October 2006; and 'Risk and other factors', Signet Group plc (www.signetgroupplc.com), 2006.

Problems with IRR

The main disadvantage of IRR, relative to NPV, is the fact that it does not directly address the question of wealth generation. It could therefore lead to the wrong decision being made. This is because the IRR approach will always rank a project with, for example, an IRR of 25 per cent above that of a project with an IRR of 20 per cent, assuming an opportunity cost of finance of, say, 15 per cent. Although accepting the project with the higher percentage return will often generate more wealth, this may not always be the case. This is because IRR completely ignores the *scale of investment*.

With a 15 per cent cost of finance, £15 million invested at 20 per cent for one year will make us wealthier by £0.75 million (that is, $15 \times (20 - 15)\% = 0.75$). With the same cost of finance, £5 million invested at 25 per cent for one year will make us only £0.5 million (that is, $5 \times (25 - 15)\% = 0.50$). IRR does not recognise this. It should be acknowledged that it is not usual for projects to be competing where there is such a large difference in scale. Even though the problem may be rare and so, typically, IRR will give the same signal as NPV, a method that is always reliable (NPV) must be better to use than IRR. This problem with percentages is another example of the one illustrated by the Mexican road discussed in Real World 14.3.

A further problem with the IRR method is that it has difficulty handling projects with unconventional cash flows. In the examples studied so far, each project has a negative cash flow arising at the start of its life and then positive cash flows thereafter. However, in some cases, a project may have both positive and negative cash flows at future points in its life. Such a pattern of cash flows can result in there being more than one IRR, or even no IRR at all. This would make the IRR method difficult to use, although it should be said that this is also quite rare in practice. This is never a problem for NPV, however.

Some practical points

When undertaking an investment appraisal, there are several practical points that we should bear in mind:

→ - *Past costs.* As with all decisions, we should take account only of **relevant costs** in our analysis. This means that only costs that vary with the decision should be considered. Thus, all past costs should be ignored as they cannot vary with the decision. A business may incur costs (such as development costs and market research costs) *before* the evaluation of an opportunity to launch a new product. As those costs have already been incurred, they should be disregarded, even though the amounts may be substantial. Costs that have already been committed but not yet paid should also be disregarded. Where a business has entered into a binding contract to incur a particular cost, it becomes in effect a past cost even though payment may not be due until some point in the future.

- *Common future costs.* It is not only past costs that do not vary with the decision; some future costs may also be the same. For example, the cost of raw materials may not vary with the decision whether to invest in a new piece of manufacturing plant or to continue to use existing plant.

- *Opportunity costs.* Opportunity costs arising from benefits forgone must be taken into account. Thus, for example, when considering a decision concerning whether or not to continue to use a machine already owned by the business, the realisable value of
→ the machine might be an important **opportunity cost**.

- *Taxation.* Owners will be interested in the after-tax returns generated from the business, and so taxation will usually be an important consideration when making an investment decision. The profits from the project will be taxed, the capital investment may attract tax relief and so on. Tax is levied at significant rates. This means that, in real life, unless tax is formally taken into account, the wrong decision could easily be made. The timing of the tax outflow should also be taken into account when preparing the cash flows for the project.

- *Cash flows not profit flows.* We have seen that for the NPV, IRR and PP methods, it is cash flows rather than profit flows that are relevant to the assessment of investment projects. In an investment appraisal requiring the application of any of these methods we may be given details of the profits for the investment period. These need to be adjusted in order to derive the cash flows. We should remember that the operating profit *before* non-cash items (such as depreciation) is an approximation to the cash flows for the period, and so we should work back to this figure.

When the data are expressed in profit rather than cash flow terms, an adjustment in respect of working capital may also be necessary. Some adjustment should be made to take account of changes in working capital. For example, launching a new product may give rise to an increase in the net investment made in trade receivables and inventories less trade payables, requiring an immediate outlay of cash. This outlay for additional working capital should be shown in the NPV calculations as an initial cash outflow. However, at the end of the life of the project, the additional working capital will be released. This divestment results in an effective inflow of cash at the end of the project; it should also be taken into account at the point at which it is received.

- *Year-end assumption.* In the examples and activities that we have considered so far in this chapter, we have assumed that cash flows arise at the end of the relevant year. This is a simplifying assumption that is used to make the calculations easier. (However, it is perfectly possible to deal more precisely with the cash flows.) As we saw earlier, this assumption is clearly unrealistic, as money will have to be paid to employees on a weekly or monthly basis, credit customers will pay within a month or two of buying the product or service and so on. Nevertheless, it is probably not a serious distortion. We should be clear, however, that there is nothing about any of the four appraisal methods that demands that this assumption be made.

- *Interest payments.* When using discounted cash flow techniques (NPV and IRR), interest payments should not be taken into account in deriving the cash flows for the period. The discount factor already takes account of the costs of financing, and so to take account of interest charges in deriving cash flows for the period would be double counting.

- *Other factors.* Investment decision making must not be viewed as simply a mechanical exercise. The results derived from a particular investment appraisal method will be only one input to the decision-making process. There may be broader issues connected to the decision that have to be taken into account but which may be difficult or impossible to quantify.

The reliability of the forecasts and the validity of the assumptions used in the evaluation will also have a bearing on the final decision.

Activity (14.16)

The directors of Manuff (Steel) Ltd are considering closing one of the business's factories. There has been a reduction in the demand for the products made at the factory in recent years, and the directors are not optimistic about the long-term prospects for these products. The factory is situated in the north of England, in an area where unemployment is high.

The factory is leased, and there are still four years of the lease remaining. The directors are uncertain whether the factory should be closed immediately or at the end of the period of the lease. Another business has offered to sublease the premises from Manuff (Steel) Ltd at a rental of £40,000 a year for the remainder of the lease period.

Activity 14.16 continued

The machinery and equipment at the factory cost £1,500,000, and have a value on the statement of financial position (balance sheet) of £400,000. In the event of immediate closure, the machinery and equipment could be sold for £220,000. The working capital at the factory is £420,000, and could be liquidated for that amount immediately, if required. Alternatively, the working capital can be liquidated in full at the end of the lease period. Immediate closure would result in redundancy payments to employees of £180,000.

If the factory continues in operation until the end of the lease period, the following operating profits (losses) are expected:

	Year 1 £000	Year 2 £000	Year 3 £000	Year 4 £000
Operating profit (loss)	160	(40)	30	20

The above figures include a charge of £90,000 a year for depreciation of machinery and equipment. The residual value of the machinery and equipment at the end of the lease period is estimated at £40,000.

Redundancy payments are expected to be £150,000 at the end of the lease period if the factory continues in operation. The business has an annual cost of capital of 12 per cent. Ignore taxation.

Required:

(a) Determine the relevant cash flows arising from a decision to continue operations until the end of the lease period rather than to close immediately.

(b) Calculate the net present value of continuing operations until the end of the lease period, rather than closing immediately.

(c) What other factors might the directors take into account before making a final decision on the timing of the factory closure?

(d) State, with reasons, whether or not the business should continue to operate the factory until the end of the lease period.

Your answer should be as follows:

(a) Relevant cash flows

	Years				
	0 £000	1 £000	2 £000	3 £000	4 £000
Operating cash flows (Note 1)		250	50	120	110
Sale of machinery (Note 2)	(220)				40
Redundancy costs (Note 3)	180				(150)
Sublease rentals (Note 4)		(40)	(40)	(40)	(40)
Working capital invested (Note 5)	(420)				420
	(460)	210	10	80	380

Notes:

(1) Each year's operating cash flows are calculated by adding back the depreciation charge for the year to the operating profit for the year. In the case of the operating loss, the depreciation charge is deducted.

(2) In the event of closure, machinery could be sold immediately. Thus an opportunity cost of £220,000 is incurred if operations continue.

(3) By continuing operations, there will be a saving in immediate redundancy costs of £180,000. However, redundancy costs of £150,000 will be paid in four years' time.

(4) By continuing operations, the opportunity to sublease the factory will be forgone.

(5) Immediate closure would mean that working capital could be liquidated. By continuing operations this opportunity is forgone. However, working capital can be liquidated in four years' time.

(b)

Discount rate 12 per cent	1.000	0.893	0.797	0.712	0.636
Present value	(460)	187.5	8.0	57.0	241.7
Net present value	34.2				

(c) Other factors that may influence the decision include:

- *The overall strategy of the business*. The business may need to set the decision within a broader context. It may be necessary to manufacture the products at the factory because they are an integral part of the business's product range. The business may wish to avoid redundancies in an area of high unemployment for as long as possible.
- *Flexibility*. A decision to close the factory is probably irreversible. If the factory continues, however, there may be a chance that the prospects for the factory will brighten in the future.
- *Creditworthiness of sub-lessee*. The business should investigate the creditworthiness of the sub-lessee. Failure to receive the expected sublease payments would make the closure option far less attractive.
- *Accuracy of forecasts*. The forecasts made by the business should be examined carefully. Inaccuracies in the forecasts or any underlying assumptions may change the expected outcomes.

(d) The NPV of the decision to continue operations rather than close immediately is positive. Hence, shareholders would be better off if the directors took this course of action. The factory should therefore continue in operation rather than close down. This decision is likely to be welcomed by employees and would allow the business to maintain its flexibility.

Investment appraisal in practice

Many surveys have been conducted in the UK into the methods of investment appraisal used by businesses. They have shown the following features:

- Businesses tend to use more than one method to assess each investment decision.
- The discounting methods (NPV and IRR) have become increasingly popular over time, with these two becoming the most popular in recent years.
- The continued popularity of PP, and to a lesser extent ARR, despite their theoretical shortcomings.
- A tendency for larger businesses to rely more heavily on discounting methods than smaller businesses.

Real World 14.9 shows the results of a fairly recent survey conducted of UK manufacturing businesses regarding their use of investment appraisal methods.

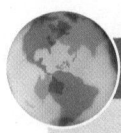

Real World 14.9

A survey of UK business practice

Senior financial managers at 83 of the UK's largest manufacturing businesses were asked about the investment appraisal methods used to evaluate both strategic and non-strategic projects. Strategic projects usually aim to increase or change the competitive capabilities of a business, such as introducing a new manufacturing process.

Method	Non-strategic projects Mean score	Strategic projects Mean score
Net present value	3.6829	3.9759
Payback	3.4268	3.6098
Internal rate of return	3.3293	3.7073
Accounting rate of return	1.9867	2.2667

Response scale 1= never, 2 = rarely, 3 = often, 4 = mostly, 5 = always

We can see that, both for non-strategic and for strategic investments, the NPV method is the most popular. As the sample consists of large businesses (nearly all with total sales revenue in excess of £100 million), a fairly sophisticated approach to evaluation might be expected. Nevertheless, for non-strategic investments, the payback method comes second in popularity. It drops to third place for strategic projects.

The survey also found that 98 per cent of respondents used more than one method and 88 per cent used more than three methods of investment appraisal.

Source: Based on information in 'Strategic capital investment decision-making: a role for emergent analysis tools? A study of practice in large UK manufacturing companies', F. Alkaraan and D. Northcott, *The British Accounting Review*, 38, 2006, p. 159.

A survey of US businesses also shows considerable support for the NPV and IRR methods. There is less support, however, for the payback method and ARR. **Real World 14.10** sets out some of the main findings.

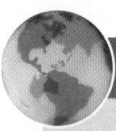

Real World 14.10

A survey of US practice

A survey of the chief financial officers (CFOs) of 392 US businesses examined the popularity of various methods of investment appraisal. Figure 14.5 shows the percentage of businesses surveyed that always, or almost always, used the four methods discussed in this chapter.

Source: Based on information in 'How do CFOs make capital budgeting and capital structure decisions?', R. Graham and C. Harvey, *Journal of Applied Corporate Finance*, vol. 15, no. 1, 2002.

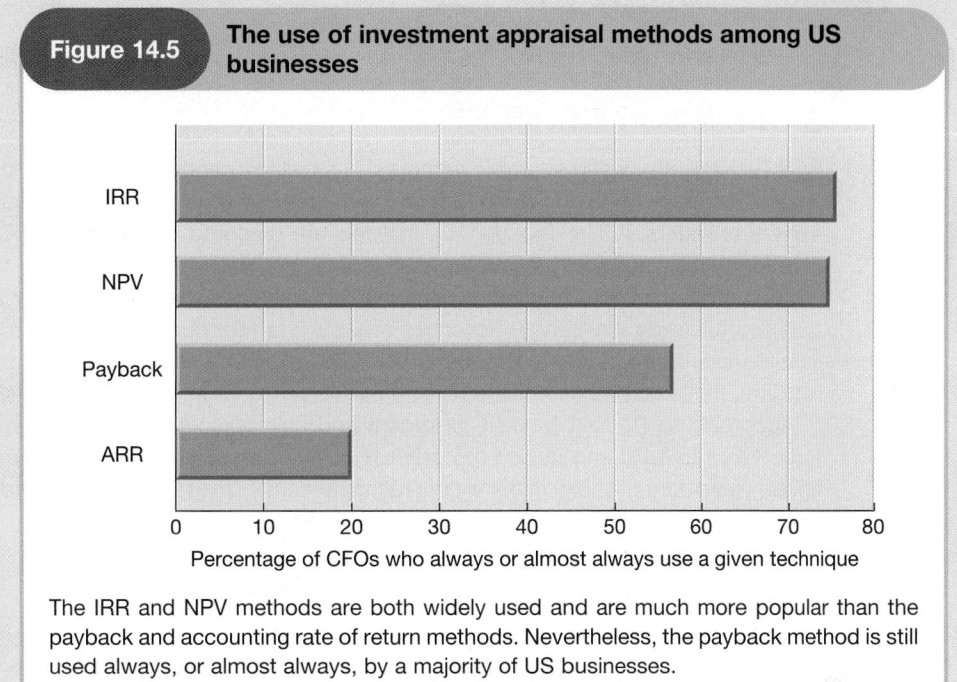

Figure 14.5

The use of investment appraisal methods among US businesses

Percentage of CFOs who always or almost always use a given technique

The IRR and NPV methods are both widely used and are much more popular than the payback and accounting rate of return methods. Nevertheless, the payback method is still used always, or almost always, by a majority of US businesses.

Source: Based on information in 'How do CFOs make capital budgeting and capital structure decisions?', R. Graham and C. Harvey, *Journal of Applied Corporate Finance*, vol. 15, no. 1, 2002.

Activity (14.17)

Earlier in the chapter we discussed the theoretical limitations of the PP method. Can you explain the fact that it still seems to be a popular method of investment appraisal among businesses?

A number of possible reasons may explain this finding:

● PP is easy to understand and use.
● It can avoid the problems of forecasting far into the future.
● It gives emphasis to the early cash flows when there is greater certainty concerning the accuracy of their predicted value.
● It emphasises the importance of liquidity. Where a business has liquidity problems, a short payback period for a project is likely to appear attractive.

PP can provide a convenient, though rough and ready, assessment of the profitability of a project, in the way that it is used in **Real World 14.11**.

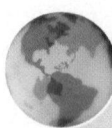

Real World 14.11

An investment lifts off

FT

SES Global is the world's largest commercial satellite operator. This means that it rents satellite capacity to broadcasters, governments, telecommunications groups and Internet service providers. It is a risky venture that few are prepared to undertake. As a result, a handful of businesses dominates the market.

Launching a satellite requires a huge initial outlay of capital, but relatively small cash outflows following the launch. Revenues only start to flow once the satellite is in orbit. A satellite launch costs around €250m. The main elements of this cost are the satellite (€120m), the launch vehicle (€80m), insurance (€40m) and ground equipment (€10m).

According to Romain Bausch, president and chief executive of SES Global, it takes three years to build and launch a satellite. However, the average lifetime of a satellite is fifteen years during which time it is generating revenues. The revenues generated are such that the payback period is around four to five years.

Source: 'Satellites need space to earn', Tim Burt, FT.com, 14 July 2003.

The popularity of PP may suggest a lack of sophistication by managers, concerning investment appraisal. This criticism is most often made against managers of smaller businesses. This point is borne out by both of the surveys discussed above which have found that smaller businesses are much less likely to use discounted cash flow methods (NPV and IRR) than are larger ones. Other surveys have tended to reach a similar conclusion.

IRR may be popular because it expresses outcomes in percentage terms rather than in absolute terms. This form of expression appears to be more acceptable to managers, despite the problems of percentage measures that we discussed earler. This may be because managers are used to using percentage figures as targets (for example, return on capital employed).

Real World 14.12 shows extracts from the 2008 annual report of a well-known business: Rolls-Royce plc, the builder of engines for aircraft and other purposes.

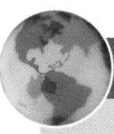

Real World 14.12

The use of NPV at Rolls-Royce

In its 2008 annual report and accounts, Rolls-Royce plc stated that:

> The Group continues to subject all investments to rigorous examination of risks and future cash flows to ensure that they create shareholder value. All major investments require Board approval.
> The Group has a portfolio of projects at different stages of their life cycles. Discounted cash flow analysis of the remaining life of projects is performed on a regular basis.

Source: Rolls-Royce plc, Annual Report 2008, p. 59.

Rolls-Royce makes clear that it uses NPV (the report refers to creating shareholder value and to discounted cash flow, which strongly imply NPV). It is interesting to note that Rolls-Royce not only assesses new projects but also reassesses existing ones. This must be a sensible commercial approach. Businesses should not continue with existing projects unless those projects have a positive NPV based on future cash flows. Just because a project seemed to have a positive NPV before it started does not mean that this will persist, in the light of changing circumstances. Activity 14.16 (pages 553–5) considered a decision to close down a project.

Self-assessment question 14.1

Beacon Chemicals plc is considering buying some equipment to produce a chemical named X14. The new equipment's capital cost is estimated at £100,000. If its purchase is approved now, the equipment can be bought and production can commence by the end of this year. £50,000 has already been spent on research and development work. Estimates of revenues and costs arising from the operation of the new equipment appear below:

	Year 1	Year 2	Year 3	Year 4	Year 5
Sales price (£/litre)	100	120	120	100	80
Sales volume (litres)	800	1,000	1,200	1,000	800
Variable cost (£/litre)	50	50	40	30	40
Fixed cost (£000)	30	30	30	30	30

If the equipment is bought, sales of some existing products will be lost, and this will result in a loss of contribution of £15,000 a year over its life.

The accountant has informed you that the fixed cost includes depreciation of £20,000 a year on the new equipment. They also include an allocation of £10,000 for fixed overheads. A separate study has indicated that if the new equipment were bought, additional overheads, excluding depreciation, arising from producing the chemical would be £8,000 a year. Production would require additional working capital of £30,000.

For the purposes of your initial calculations ignore taxation.

Required:
(a) Deduce the relevant annual cash flows associated with buying the equipment.
(b) Deduce the payback period.
(c) Calculate the net present value using a discount rate of 8 per cent.

(*Hint*: You should deal with the investment in working capital by treating it as a cash outflow at the start of the project and an inflow at the end.)

The answer to this question can be found at the back of the book on page 735.

Investment appraisal and strategic planning

So far, we have tended to view investment opportunities as if they are unconnected, independent, entities. In practice, however, successful businesses are those that set out a clear framework for the selection of investment projects. Unless this framework is in place, it may be difficult to identify those projects that are likely to generate a positive NPV. The best investment projects are usually those that match the business's internal strengths (for example, skills, experience, access to finance) with the opportunities available. In areas where this match does not exist, other businesses, for which the match does exist, are likely to have a distinct competitive advantage. This advantage means that they are likely to be able to provide the product or service at a better price and/or quality.

Establishing what is the best area or areas of activity and style of approach for the business is popularly known as *strategic planning*. Strategic planning tries to identify the direction in which the business needs to go, in terms of products, markets, financing and so on, to best place it to generate profitable investment opportunities. In practice, strategic plans seem to have a time span of around five years and generally tend to ask the question: where do we want our business to be in five years' time and how can we get there?

Real World 14.13 shows how easyJet had made an investment that fitted its strategic objectives.

Real World 14.13

easyFit

FT

EasyJet, the UK budget airline, bought a small rival airline, GB Airways Ltd (GB) in late 2007 for £103m. According to an article in the *Financial Times*:

> GB is a good strategic fit for easyJet. It operates under a British Airways franchise from Gatwick, which happens to be easyJet's biggest base. The deal makes easyJet the single largest passenger carrier at the UK airport. There is plenty of scope for scale economies in purchasing and back office functions. Moreover, easyJet should be able to boost GB's profitability by switching the carrier to its low-cost business model … easyJet makes an estimated £4 a passenger, against GB's £1. Assuming easyJet can drag up GB to its own levels of profitability, the company's value to the low-cost carrier is roughly four times its standalone worth.

The article makes the point that this looks like a good investment for easyJet, because of the strategic fit. For a business other than easyJet, the lack of strategic fit may well have meant that buying GB for exactly the same price of £103 million would not have been a good investment.

Source: 'Easy ride', C. Hughes, FT.com, 26 October 2007.

Dealing with risk

As we discussed earlier all investments are risky. This means that consideration of risk is an important aspect of financial decision making. Risk, in this context, is the extent and likelihood that what is projected to occur will not actually happen. It is a particularly important issue in the context of investment decisions, because of:

● *The relatively long timescales involved.* There tends to be more time for things to go wrong between the decision being made and the end of the project, in comparison with many business decisions.
● *The scale of funds involved.* Many investment projects involve very large amounts of finance. If things go wrong, the impact can be both significant and lasting.

Various approaches to dealing with risk have been proposed. These fall into two categories: assessing the level of risk and reacting to the level of risk. We now consider formal methods of dealing with risk that fall within each category.

Assessing the level of risk

Sensitivity analysis

→ One popular way of attempting to assess the level of risk is to carry out a **sensitivity analysis** on the proposed project. This involves an examination of the key input values affecting the project to see how changes in each input might influence the viability of the project.

Firstly, the investment is appraised, using the best estimates for each of the input factors (for example, labour cost, material cost, discount rate and so on). Assuming that the NPV is positive, each input value is then examined to see how far the estimated figure could be changed before the project becomes unviable for that reason alone. Let us suppose that the NPV for an investment in a machine to provide a particular service is a positive value. If we were to carry out a sensitivity analysis on this project, we should consider in turn each of the key input factors:

- initial outlay for the machine;
- sales volume and selling price;
- relevant operating costs;
- life of the project; and
- financing costs (to be used as the discount rate).

We should seek to find the value that each of them could have before the NPV figure would become negative (that is, the value for the factor at which NPV would be zero). The difference between the value for that factor at which the NPV would equal zero and the estimated value represents the margin of safety for that particular input. The process is set out in Figure 14.6.

Figure 14.6 Factors affecting the sensitivity of NPV calculations

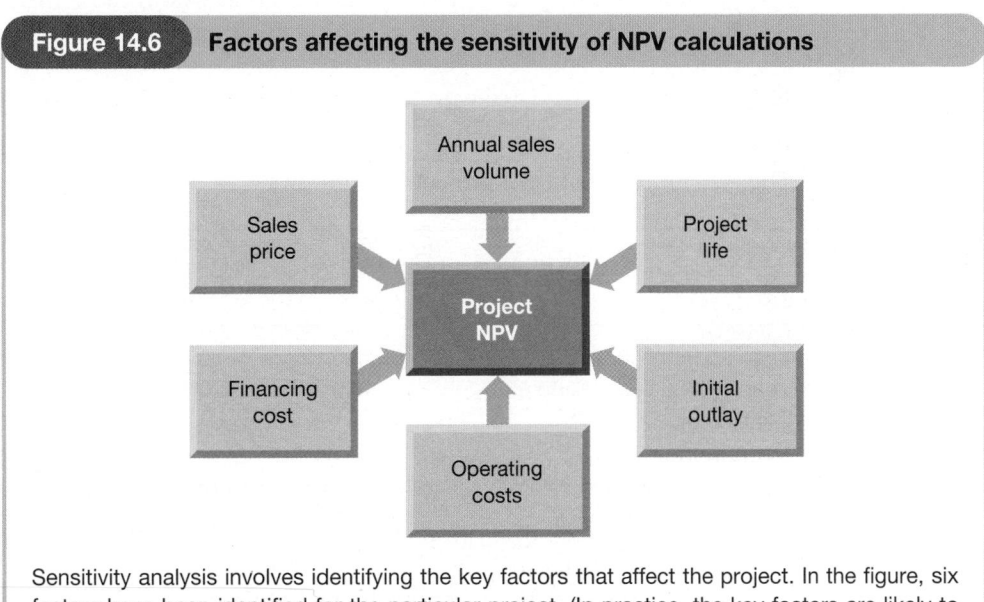

Sensitivity analysis involves identifying the key factors that affect the project. In the figure, six factors have been identified for the particular project. (In practice, the key factors are likely to vary between projects.) Once identified, each factor will be examined in turn to find the value it should have for the project to have a zero NPV.

A computer spreadsheet model of the project can be extremely valuable for this exercise because it then becomes a very simple matter to try various values for the input data and to see the effect of each. As a result of carrying out a sensitivity analysis, the decision maker is able to get a 'feel' for the project, which otherwise might not be possible. Example 14.3, which illustrates a sensitivity analysis, is, however, straightforward and can be undertaken without recourse to a spreadsheet.

Example 14.3

S. Saluja (Property Developers) Ltd intends to bid at an auction, to be held today, for a manor house that has fallen into disrepair. The auctioneer believes that the house will be sold for about £450,000. The business wishes to renovate the property and to divide it into flats, to be sold for £150,000 each. The renovation will be in two stages and will cover a two-year period. Stage 1 will cover the first year of the project. It will cost £500,000 and the six flats completed during this stage are expected to be sold for a total of £900,000 at the end of the first year. Stage 2 will cover the second year of the project. It will cost £300,000 and the three remaining flats are expected to be sold at the end of the second year for a total of £450,000. The cost of renovation will be the subject of a binding contract with local builders, were the property to be bought. There is, however, some uncertainty over the remaining input values. The business estimates its cost of capital at 12 per cent a year.

Required
(a) What is the NPV of the proposed project?
(b) Assuming none of the other inputs deviates from the best estimates provided:
    (1) What auction price would have to be paid for the manor house to cause the project to have a zero NPV?
    (2) What cost of capital would cause the project to have a zero NPV?
    (3) What is the sale price of each of the flats that would cause the project to have a zero NPV? (Each flat is projected to be sold for the same price: £150,000.)
(c) Is the level of risk associated with the project high or low? Discuss your findings.

Solution
(a) The NPV of the proposed project is as follows:

	Cash flows £	Discount factor 12%	Present value £
Year 1 (£900,000 – £500,000)	400,000	0.893	357,200
Year 2 (£450,000 – £300,000)	150,000	0.797	119,550
Initial outlay			(450,000)
Net present value			26,750

(b) (1) To obtain a zero NPV, the auction price would have to be £26,750 higher than the current estimate – that is, a total price of £476,750. This is about 6 per cent above the current estimated price.
    (2) As there is a positive NPV, the cost of capital that would cause the project to have a zero NPV must be higher than 12 per cent. Let us try 20 per cent.

	Cash flows £	Discount factor 20%	Present value £
Year 1 (£900,000 − £500,000)	400,000	0.833	333,200
Year 2 (£450,000 − £300,000)	150,000	0.694	104,100
Initial outlay			(450,000)
Net present value			(12,700)

As the NPV using a 20 per cent discount rate is negative, the 'break-even' cost of capital lies somewhere between 12 per cent and 20 per cent. A reasonable approximation is obtained as follows:

	Discount rate %	Net present value £
	12	26,750
	20	(12,700)
Difference	8	39,450

The change in NPV for every 1 per cent change in the discount rate will be:

$$39,450/8 = £4,931$$

The reduction in the 20 per cent discount rate required to achieve a zero NPV would therefore be:

$$12,700/4,931 = 2.6\%$$

The cost of capital (that is, the discount rate) would, therefore, have to be 17.4 per cent (20.0 − 2.6) for the project to have a zero NPV.

This calculation is, of course, the same as that used earlier in the chapter, when calculating the IRR of the project. In other words, 17.4 per cent is the IRR of the project.

(3) To obtain a zero NPV, the sale price of each flat must be reduced so that the NPV is reduced by £26,750. In year 1, six flats are sold (in year 2, three flats are sold). The discount factor at the 12 per cent rate for year 1 is 0.893 and for year 2 is 0.797. We can derive the fall in price per flat (Y) to give a zero NPV by using the equation:

$$(6Y \times 0.893) + (3Y \times 0.797) = £26,750$$

$$Y = £3,452$$

The sale price of each flat necessary to obtain a zero NPV is therefore:

$$£150,000 − £3,452 = £146,548$$

This represents a fall in the estimated price of 2.3 per cent.

(c) These calculations indicate that the auction price would have to be about 6 per cent above the estimated price before a zero NPV is obtained. The margin of safety is, therefore, not very high for this factor. In practice this should not represent a real risk because the business could withdraw from the bidding if the price rises to an unacceptable level.

The other two factors represent more real risks. Only after the project is at a very late stage can the business be sure as to what actual price per flat will prevail. The same may be true for the cost of capital, though it may be possible to raise finance for the project at a rate fixed before the auction of the house. It would be unusual to be able to have fixed contracts for sale of all of the flats before the auction. The calculations reveal that the price of the flats would only have to fall by 2.3 per cent from the estimated price before the NPV is reduced to zero. Hence, the margin of safety for this factor is very small. However, even if the funding cost cannot be fixed in advance, the cost of capital is less sensitive to changes and there would have to be an increase from 12 per cent to 17.4 per cent before the project produced a zero NPV. It seems from the calculations that the sale price of the flats is the key sensitive factor to consider. A careful re-examination of the market value of the flats seems appropriate before a final decision is made.

There are two major drawbacks with the use of sensitivity analysis:

● It does not give managers clear decision rules concerning acceptance or rejection of the project and so they must rely on their own judgement.
● It is a static form of analysis. Only one input is considered at a time, while the rest are held constant. In practice, however, it is likely that more than one input value will differ from the best estimates provided. Even so, it would be possible to deal with changes in various inputs simultaneously, were the project data put onto a spreadsheet model. This approach, where more than one variable is altered at a time,

is known as **scenario building**.

Real World 14.14 describes the evaluation of a mining project that incorporated sensitivity analysis to test the robustness of the findings.

Real World 14.14

Golden opportunity

In 2006, Eureka Mining plc undertook an evaluation of the opportunity to mine copper and gold deposits at Miheevskoye, which is located in the Southern Urals region of the Russian Federation. Using three investment appraisal methods, the business came up with the following results:

IRR	Pre-tax NPV	Payback period
%	US$m	Years
20.4	178.8	3.8

Sensitivity analysis was carried out on four key variables – the price of copper, the price of gold, operating costs and capital outlay costs – to help assess the riskiness of the project. This was done by assessing the IRR, NPV and PP, making various assumptions regarding the prices of copper and gold and about the percentage change in both the operating and the capital costs. The following table sets out the findings.

			IRR	Pre-tax NPV	Payback period
Copper price		Average spot* copper price $US/lb	%	US$m	Years
		1.10	8.8	(18.4)	8.1
		1.20	14.8	80.2	5.0
		1.40	25.7	277.3	3.0
		1.50	30.8	375.9	2.7
Gold price		Average spot* gold price $US/oz			
		450	18.9	152.0	4.0
		500	19.6	165.4	3.9
		600	21.2	192.2	3.6
		650	21.9	205.6	3.5
Operating costs	Percentage change	Average total costs (lb copper equivalent)			
	−20	$0.66	26.68	298.5	3.0
	−10	$0.72	23.7	238.6	3.3
	+10	$0.83	17.1	118.9	4.4
	+20	$0.88	13.6	59.0	5.3
Capital costs		Initial capital (US$m)			
	−20	360	28.6	261.8	2.8
	−10	405	24.1	220.3	3.2
	+10	495	17.3	137.2	4.4
	+20	540	14.7	95.7	5.1

* The spot price is the price for immediate delivery of the mineral.

In its report, the business stated:

> This project is most sensitive to percentage changes in the copper price which have the largest impact, whereas movements in the gold price have the least. The impact of changes in operating costs is more significant than capital costs.

Source: Adapted from 'Eureka Mining PLC – Drilling Report', 26 July 2006 (www.citywire.co.uk).

Expected net present value

Another means of assessing risk is through the use of statistical probabilities. It may be possible to identify a range of feasible values for each of the items of input data and to assign a probability of occurrence to each of these values. Using this information, we can derive an **expected net present value (ENPV)**, which is, in effect, a weighted average of the possible outcomes where the probabilities are used as weights. To illustrate this method, let us consider Example 14.4.

Example 14.4

C. Piperis (Properties) Ltd has the opportunity to acquire a lease on a block of flats that has only two years remaining before it expires. The cost of the lease would be £100,000. The occupancy rate of the block of flats is currently around 70 per cent and the flats are let almost exclusively to naval personnel. There is a large naval base located nearby, and there is little other demand for the flats. The occupancy rate of the flats will change in the remaining two years of the lease, depending on the outcome of a defence review. The navy is currently considering three options for the naval base. These are:

- *Option 1.* Increase the size of the base by closing one in another region and transferring the personnel to the one located near the flats.
- *Option 2.* Close the naval base near to the flats and leave only a skeleton staff there for maintenance purposes. The personnel would be moved to a base in another region.
- *Option 3.* Leave the base open but reduce staffing levels by 20 per cent.

The directors of Piperis have estimated the following net cash flows for each of the two years under each option and the probability of their occurrence:

	£	Probability
Option 1	80,000	0.6
Option 2	12,000	0.1
Option 3	40,000	0.3
		1.0

Note that the sum of the probabilities is 1.0 (in other words it is certain that one of the possible options will arise). The business has a cost of capital of 10 per cent. Should the business purchase the lease on the block of flats?

Solution
To calculate the expected NPV of the proposed investment, we must first calculate the weighted average of the expected outcomes for each year where the probabilities are used as weights, by multiplying each cash flow by its probability of occurrence. Thus, the expected annual net cash flows will be:

	Cash flows £	Probability	Expected cash flows £
	(a)	(b)	(a × b)
Option 1	80,000	0.6	48,000
Option 2	12,000	0.1	1,200
Option 3	40,000	0.3	12,000
Expected cash flows in each year			61,200

Having derived the expected annual cash flows, we can now discount these using a rate of 10 per cent to reflect the cost of capital:

Year	Expected cash flows £	Discount rate 10%	Expected present value £
1	61,200	0.909	55,631
2	61,200	0.826	50,551
			106,182
Initial investment			(100,000)
Expected NPV			6,182

We can see that the expected NPV is positive. Hence, the wealth of shareholders is expected to increase by purchasing the lease.

The expected NPV approach has the advantage of producing a single numerical outcome and of having a clear decision rule to apply. If the expected NPV is positive, we should invest; if it is negative, we should not.

However, the approach produces an average figure that may not be capable of occurring. This point was illustrated in Example 14.4 where the expected annual cash flow (£61,200) does not correspond to any of the stated options.

Perhaps more importantly, using an average figure can obscure the underlying risk associated with the project. Simply deriving the ENPV, as in Example 14.4, can be misleading. Without some idea of the individual possible outcomes and their probability of occurring, the decision maker is in the dark. In Example 14.4, were either of Options 2 and 3 to occur, the investment would be adverse (wealth destroying). It is 40 per cent probable that one of these two options will occur, so this is a significant risk. Only should Option 1 arise (60 per cent probable) would investing in the flats represent a good decision. Of course, in advance of making the investment, which option will actually occur is not known.

None of this should be taken to mean that the investment in the flats should not be made, simply that the decision maker is better placed to make a judgement where information on the possible outcomes is available. Activity 14.18 further illustrates this point.

Activity 14.18

Qingdao Manufacturing Ltd is considering two competing projects. Details are as follows:

- Project A has a 0.9 probability of producing a negative NPV of £200,000 and a 0.1 probability of producing a positive NPV of £3.8m.
- Project B has a 0.6 probability of producing a positive NPV of £100,000 and a 0.4 probability of producing a positive NPV of £350,000.

What is the expected net present value of each project?

The expected NPV of Project A is:

$$[(0.1 \times £3.8m) - (0.9 \times £200,000)] = £200,000$$

The expected NPV of Project B is:

$$[(0.6 \times £100,000) + (0.4 \times £350,000)] = £200,000$$

Although the expected NPV of each project in Activity 14.18 is identical, this does not mean that the business will be indifferent about which project to undertake. We can see from the information provided that Project A has a high probability of making a loss whereas Project B is not expected to make a loss under either possible outcome. If we assume that the shareholders dislike risk – which is usually the case – they will prefer the directors to take on Project B as this provides the same level of expected return as Project A but for a lower level of risk.

It can be argued that the problem identified above may not be significant where the business is engaged in several similar projects. This is because a worse than expected outcome on one project may well be balanced by a better than expected outcome on another project. However, in practice, investment projects may be unique events and this argument will not then apply. Also, where the project is large in relation to other projects undertaken, the argument loses its force. There is also the problem that a factor that might cause one project to have an adverse outcome could also have adverse effects on other projects. For example, a large, unexpected increase in the price of oil may have a simultaneous adverse effect on all of the investment projects of a particular business.

Where the expected NPV approach is being used, it is probably a good idea to make known to managers the different possible outcomes and the probability attached to each outcome. By so doing, the managers will be able to gain an insight to the *downside risk* attached to the project. The information relating to each outcome can be presented in the form of a diagram if required. The construction of such a diagram is illustrated in Example 14.5.

Example 14.5

Zeta Computing Services Ltd has recently produced some software for a client organisation. The software has a life of two years and will then become obsolete. The cost of producing the software was £10,000. The client has agreed to pay a licence fee of £8,000 a year for the software if it is used in only one of its two divisions, and £12,000 a year if it is used in both of its divisions. The client may use the software for either one or two years in either division but will definitely use it in at least one division in each of the two years.

Zeta believes there is a 0.6 chance that the licence fee received in any one year will be £8,000 and a 0.4 chance that it will be £12,000. There are, therefore, four possible outcomes attached to this project (where *p* denotes probability):

- *Outcome 1.* Year 1 cash flow £8,000 ($p = 0.6$) and Year 2 cash flow £8,000 ($p = 0.6$). The probability of both years having cash flows of £8,000 will be:

$$0.6 \times 0.6 = 0.36$$

- *Outcome 2.* Year 1 cash flow £12,000 ($p = 0.4$) and Year 2 cash flow £12,000 ($p = 0.4$). The probability of both years having cash flows of £12,000 will be:

$$0.4 \times 0.4 = 0.16$$

- *Outcome 3.* Year 1 cash flow £12,000 ($p = 0.4$) and Year 2 cash flow £8,000 ($p = 0.6$). The probability of this sequence of cash flows occurring will be:

$$0.4 \times 0.6 = 0.24$$

- *Outcome 4.* Year 1 cash flow £8,000 ($p = 0.6$) and Year 2 cash flow £12,000 ($p = 0.4$). The probability of this sequence of cash flows occurring will be:

$$0.6 \times 0.4 = 0.24$$

The information in Example 14.5 can be displayed in the form of a diagram (Figure 14.7).

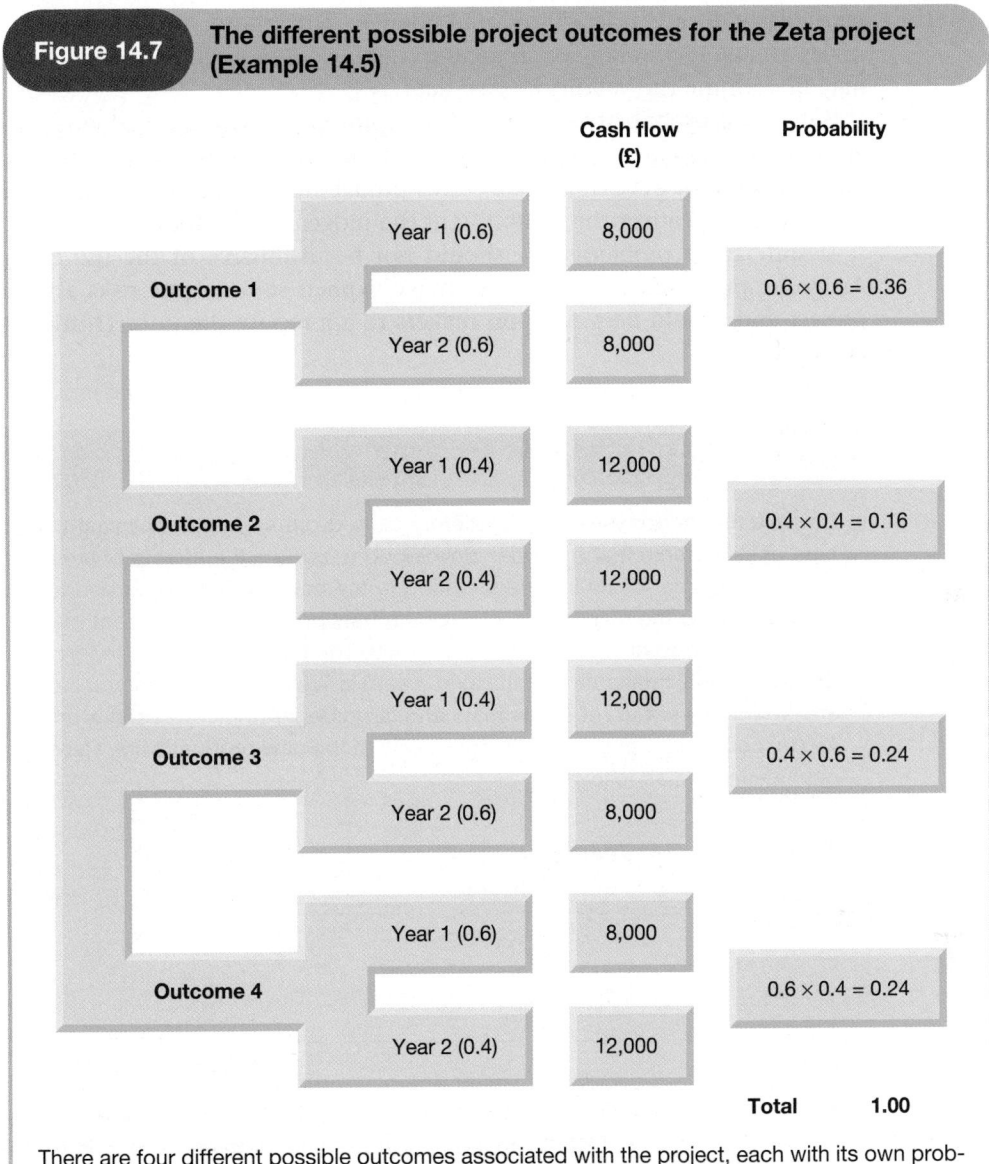

Figure 14.7 The different possible project outcomes for the Zeta project (Example 14.5)

There are four different possible outcomes associated with the project, each with its own probability of occurence. The sum of the probabilities attached to each outcome must equal 1.00, in other words it is certain that one of the possible outcomes will occur. For example, outcome 1 would occur where only one division uses the software in each year.

The source of probabilities

As we might expect, assigning probabilities to possible outcomes can often be a problem. There may be many possible outcomes arising from a particular investment project, and to identify each outcome and then assign a probability to it may prove to be an impossible task. When assigning probabilities to possible outcomes, an objective or a subjective approach may be used. **Objective probabilities** are based on information gathered from past experience. Thus, for example, the transport manager of a business operating a fleet of motor vans may be able to provide information concerning the possible life of a new motor van purchased based on the record of similar vans acquired in the past. From the information available, probabilities may be developed for different possible lifespans. However, the past may not always be a reliable guide to the future, particularly during a period of rapid change. With motor vans, for example, changes in design and technology or changes in the purpose for which the vans are being used may undermine the validity of past data.

→ **Subjective probabilities** are based on opinion and will be used where past data are either inappropriate or unavailable. The opinions of independent experts may provide a useful basis for developing subjective probabilities, though even these may contain bias, which will affect the reliability of the judgements made.

Despite these problems, we should not be dismissive of the use of probabilities. Assigning probabilities can help to make explicit some of the risks associated with a project and should help decision makers to appreciate the uncertainties that have to be faced.

Activity (14.19)

Devonia (Laboratories) Ltd has recently carried out successful clinical trials on a new type of skin cream that has been developed to reduce the effects of ageing. Research and development costs incurred relating to the new product amounted to £160,000. In order to gauge the market potential of the new product, independent market research consultants were hired at a cost of £15,000. The market research report submitted by the consultants indicates that the skin cream is likely to have a product life of four years and could be sold to retail chemists and large department stores at a price of £20 per 100 ml container. For each of the four years of the new product's life, sales demand has been estimated as follows:

Number of 100 ml containers sold	Probability of occurrence
11,000	0.3
14,000	0.6
16,000	0.1

If the business decides to launch the new product, it is possible for production to begin at once. The equipment necessary to produce it is already owned by the business and originally cost £150,000. At the end of the new product's life, it is estimated that the equipment could be sold for £35,000. If the business decides against launching the new product, the equipment will be sold immediately for £85,000, as it will be of no further use.

The new product will require one hour's labour for each 100 ml container produced. The cost of labour is £8.00 an hour. Additional workers will have to be recruited to produce the new product. At the end of the product's life, the workers are unlikely to be offered further work with the business and redundancy costs of £10,000 are expected. The cost of the ingredients for each 100 ml container is £6.00. Additional overheads arising from production of the new product are expected to be £15,000 a year.

The new skin cream has attracted the interest of the business's competitors. If the business decides not to produce and sell the skin cream, it can sell the patent rights to a major competitor immediately for £125,000.

Devonia has a cost of capital of 12 per cent. Ignore taxation.

Required:

(a) Calculate the expected net present value (ENPV) of the new product.

(b) State, with reasons, whether or not Devonia should launch the new product.

Your answer should be as follows:

(a) Expected sales volume per year = $(11,000 \times 0.3) + (14,000 \times 0.6) + (16,000 \times 0.1)$

$\qquad\qquad\qquad\qquad\qquad\qquad = 13,300$ units

Expected annual sales revenue $= 13,300 \times £20$

$\qquad\qquad\qquad\qquad\qquad\quad = £266,000$

Annual labour $\qquad\qquad\quad = 13,300 \times £8$

$\qquad\qquad\qquad\qquad\qquad\quad = £106,400$

Annual ingredient costs $\qquad = 13,300 \times £6$

$\qquad\qquad\qquad\qquad\qquad\quad = £79,800$

Incremental cash flows:

			Years		
	0	*1*	*2*	*3*	*4*
	£	£	£	£	£
Sale of patent rights	(125.0)				
Sale of equipment	(85.0)				35.0
Sales revenue		266.0	266.0	266.0	266.0
Cost of ingredients		(79.8)	(79.8)	(79.8)	(79.8)
Labour costs		(106.4)	(106.4)	(106.4)	(106.4)
Redundancy					(10.0)
Additional overheads		(15.0)	(15.0)	(15.0)	(15.0)
	(210.0)	64.8	64.8	64.8	89.8
Discount factor (12%)	1.000	0.893	0.797	0.712	0.636
	(210.0)	57.9	51.6	46.1	57.1
ENPV	2.7				

(b) The ENPV of the project is positive, and this may be seen as a signal that the project should be undertaken. However, the ENPV is very low in relation to the size of the project and careful checking of the key estimates and assumptions would be advisable. A relatively small downward revision of sales (volume and/or price) or upward revision of costs could make the project ENPV negative.

   It would be helpful to derive the NPV for each of the three possible outcomes regarding sales levels. This would enable the decision maker to have a clearer view of the risk involved with the investment.

Reacting to the level of risk

Demanding a higher rate of return is the logical reaction to a risky project. Clear observable evidence shows that there is a relationship between risk and the return required by investors. It was mentioned earlier, for example, that a bank would normally ask for a higher rate of interest on a loan where it perceives the borrower to be less likely to be able to repay the amount borrowed.

When assessing investment projects, it is normal to increase the NPV discount rate in the face of increased risk – that is, to demand a risk premium: the higher the level of risk, the higher the risk premium that will be demanded. The risk premium is added to the 'risk-free' rate of return to derive the total return required (the **risk-adjusted discount rate**). The risk-free rate is normally taken to be equivalent to the rate of return from government loan notes. In practice, a business may divide projects into low-, medium- and high-risk categories and then assign a risk premium to each category. The cash flows from a particular project will then be discounted using a rate based on the risk-free rate plus the appropriate risk premium. Since all investments are risky to some extent, all projects will have a risk premium linked to them.

The relationship between risk and return is illustrated in Figure 14.8.

Figure 14.8   **Relationship between risk and return**

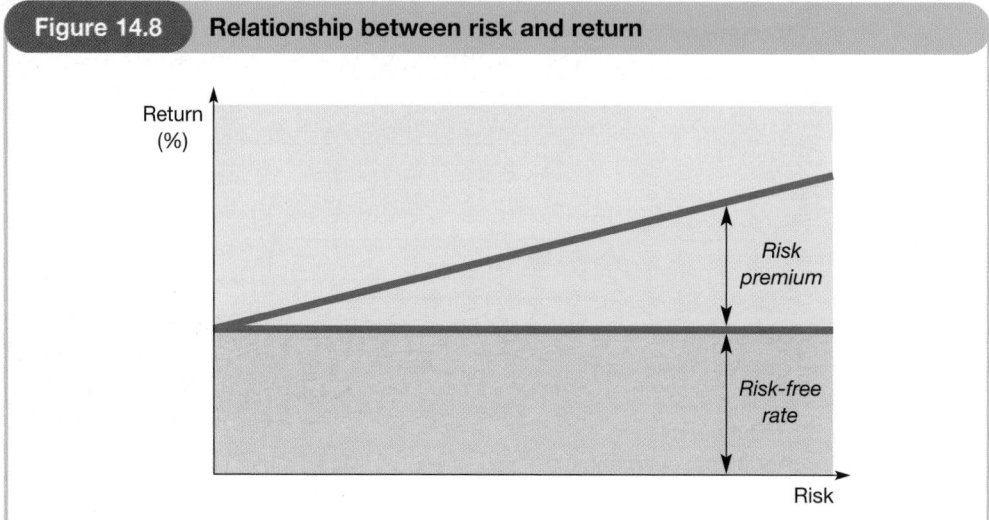

It is logical to take account of the riskiness of projects by changing the discount rate. A risk premium is added to the risk-free rate to derive the appropriate discount rate. A higher return will normally be expected from projects where the risks are higher; thus, the riskier the project, the higher the risk premium.

Activity 14.20

Can you think of any practical problems with estimating an appropriate value for the risk premium for a particular project?

Subjective judgement tends to be required when assigning an investment project to a particular risk category and then in assigning a risk premium to each category. The choices made will reflect the personal views of the managers responsible and this may differ from the views of the shareholders they represent. The choices made can, nevertheless, make the difference between accepting and rejecting a particular project.

Managing investment projects

So far, we have been concerned with the process of carrying out the necessary calculations that enable managers to select among already identified investment opportunities. Though the assessment of projects is undoubtedly important, we must bear in mind that it is only *part* of the process of investment decision making. There are other important aspects that managers must also consider.

It is possible to see the investment process as a sequence of five stages, each of which managers must consider. The five stages are set out in Figure 14.9 and described below.

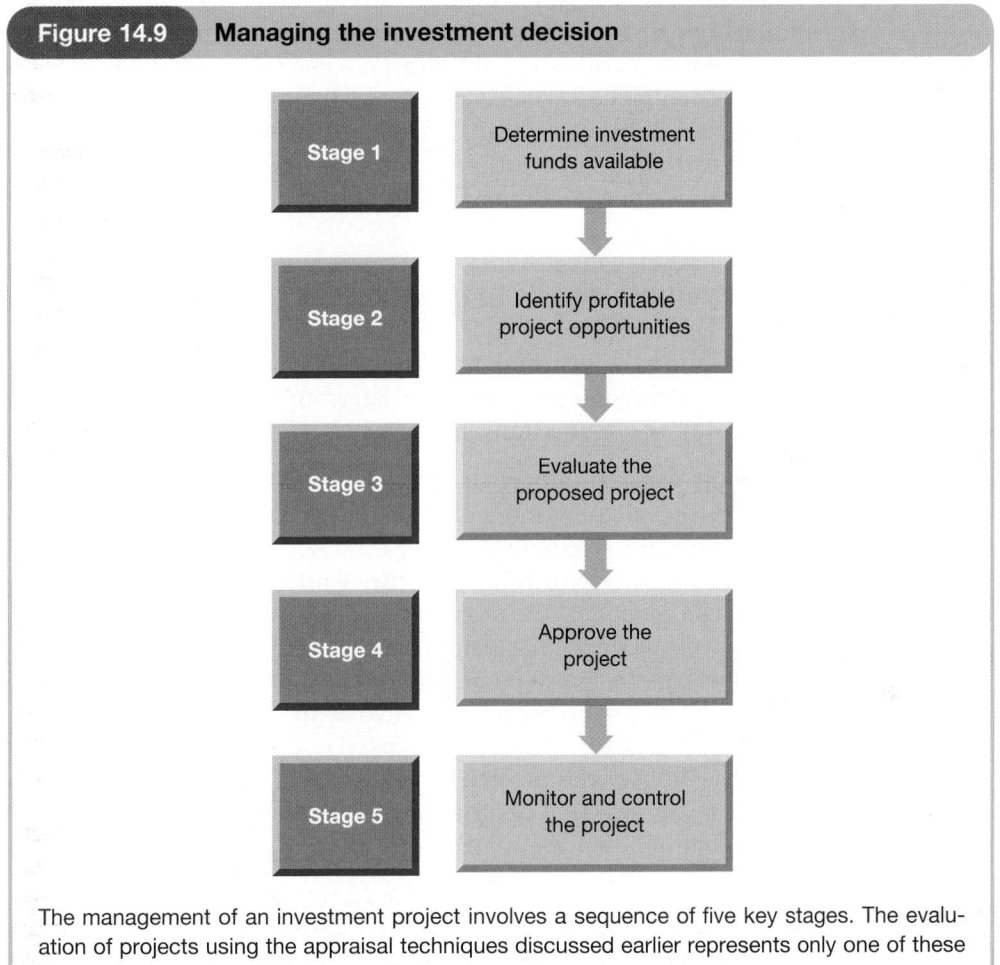

Figure 14.9   Managing the investment decision

Stage 1	Determine investment funds available
Stage 2	Identify profitable project opportunities
Stage 3	Evaluate the proposed project
Stage 4	Approve the project
Stage 5	Monitor and control the project

The management of an investment project involves a sequence of five key stages. The evaluation of projects using the appraisal techniques discussed earlier represents only one of these stages.

Stage 1: Determine investment funds available

The amount of funds available for investment may be limited by the external market for funds or by internal management. In practice, it is often the business's own senior managers that restrict the amount available, perhaps because they lack confidence in the business's ability to handle high levels of investment. In either case, it may mean that the funds will not be sufficient to finance all of the apparently profitable

investment opportunities available. This shortage of investment funds is known as
→ **capital rationing**. When it arises managers are faced with the task of deciding on the
most profitable use of those funds available.

Stage 2: Identify profitable project opportunities

A vital part of the investment process is the search for profitable investment opportunities. The business should carry out methodical routines for identifying feasible
projects. This may be done through a research and development department or by
some other means. Failure to do so will inevitably lead to the business losing its competitive position with respect to product development, production methods or market
penetration. To help identify good investment opportunities, some businesses provide
financial incentives to members of staff who come forward with good investment proposals. The search process will, however, usually involve looking outside the business
to identify changes in technology, customer demand, market conditions and so on.
Information will need to be gathered and this may take some time, particularly for
unusual or non-routine investment opportunities.

Stage 3: Evaluate the proposed project

If management is to agree to the investment of funds in a project, that project's proposal must be rigorously screened. For larger projects, this will involve providing
answers to a number of questions, including:

- What are the nature and purpose of the project?
- Does the project align with the overall strategy and objectives of the business?
- How much finance is required?
- What other resources (such as expertise, work space and so on) are required for
  successful completion of the project?
- How long will the project last and what are its key stages?
- What is the expected pattern of cash flows?
- What are the major problems associated with the project and how can they be
  overcome?
- What is the NPV of the project? If capital is rationed, how does the NPV of this
  project compare with that of other opportunities available?
- Have risk and inflation been taken into account in the appraisal process and, if so,
  what are the results?

The ability and commitment of those responsible for proposing and managing the
project will be vital to its success. This means that, when evaluating a new project, one
consideration will be the quality of those proposing it. Senior managers may decide
not to support a project that appears profitable on paper if they lack confidence in the
ability of key managers to see it through to completion.

Stage 4: Approve the project

Once the managers responsible for investment decision making are satisfied that the
project should be undertaken, formal approval can be given. However, a decision on a

project may be postponed if senior managers need more information from those proposing the project, or if revisions are required to the proposal. Proposals may be rejected if they are considered unprofitable or likely to fail. Before rejecting a proposal, however, the implications of not pursuing the project for such areas as market share, staff morale and existing business operations must be carefully considered.

Stage 5: Monitor and control the project

Making a decision to invest in, say, the plant needed to provide a new service does not automatically cause the investment to be made and provision of the service to go smoothly ahead. Managers will need to manage the project actively through to completion. This, in turn, will require further information-gathering exercises.

Management should receive progress reports at regular intervals concerning the project. These reports should provide information relating to the actual cash flows for each stage of the project, which can then be compared against the forecast figures provided when the proposal was submitted for approval. The reasons for significant variations should be ascertained and corrective action taken where possible. Any changes in the expected completion date of the project or any expected variations in future cash flows from budget should be reported immediately; in extreme cases, managers may even abandon the project if circumstances appear to have changed dramatically for the worse. We saw in Real World 14.12, on page 558, that Rolls-Royce undertakes this kind of reassessment of existing projects.

Project management techniques (for example, critical path analysis) should be employed wherever possible and their effectiveness reported to senior management.

An important part of the control process is a **post-completion audit** of the project. This is, in essence, a review of the project performance to see if it lived up to expectations and whether any lessons can be learned from the way that the investment process was carried out. In addition to an evaluation of financial costs and benefits, non-financial measures of performance such as the ability to meet deadlines and levels of quality achieved should also be reported. We should recall that total life-cycle costing, which we discussed in Chapter 11, is based on similar principles.

The fact that a post-completion audit is an integral part of the management of the project should also encourage those who submit projects to use realistic estimates. **Real World 14.15** provides some evidence of a need for greater realism.

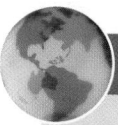

Real World 14.15

Looking on the bright side

McKinsey and Co, the management consultants, surveyed 2,500 senior managers worldwide during the spring of 2007. The managers were asked their opinions on investments made by their businesses in the previous three years. The general opinion is that estimates for the investment decision inputs had been too optimistic. For example sales levels had been overestimated in about 50 per cent of cases, but underestimated in less than 20 per cent of cases. It is not clear whether the estimates were sufficiently inaccurate to call into question the decision that had been made.

Real World 14.15 continued

The survey goes on to ask about the extent that investments made seemed, in the light of the actual outcomes, to have been mistakes. Managers felt that 19 per cent of investments that had been made should not have gone ahead. On the other hand, they felt that 31 per cent of rejected projects should have been taken up. Managers also felt that 'good money was thrown after bad' in that existing investments that were not performing well were continuing to be supported in a significant number of cases.

Source: 'How companies spend their money', A McKinsey Global Survey, www.theglobalmarketer.com 2007.

Other studies confirm a tendency among managers to use over-optimistic estimates when preparing investment proposals. (See reference 1 at the end of the chapter.) It seems that sometimes this is done deliberately in an attempt to secure project approval. Where over-optimistic estimates are used, the managers responsible may well find themselves accountable at the post-completion audit stage. Such audits, however, can be difficult and time-consuming to carry out, and so the likely benefits must be weighed against the costs involved. Senior management may feel, therefore, that only projects above a certain size should be subject to a post-completion audit.

Real World 14.16 describes how two large retailers, Tesco plc and Kingfisher plc, use post-completion audit approaches to evaluating past investment projects.

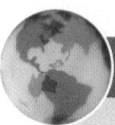

Real World 14.16

Looking back

In its 2008 corporate governance report, Tesco plc, the supermarket chain, stated:

> All major initiatives require business cases to be prepared, normally covering a minimum period of five years. Post-investment appraisals, carried out by management, determine the reasons for any significant variance from expected performance.

In its 2007/8 financial review, Kingfisher plc, the home-improvement retailer, stated:

> An annual post-investment review process will continue to review the performance of all projects above £0.75 million which were completed in the prior year. The findings of this exercise will be considered by both the new Retail Board and the main Board and directly influence the assumptions for similar project proposals going forward.

Sources: www.tescocorporate.com and www.kingfisher.co.uk.

As a footnote to our discussion of business investment decision making, **Real World 14.17** looks at one of the world's biggest investment projects which has proved to be a commercial disaster, despite being a technological success.

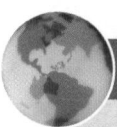

Real World 14.17

Wealth lost in the chunnel

The tunnel, which runs for 31 miles between Folkestone in the UK and Sangatte in northern France, was started in 1986 and opened for public use in 1994. From a technological and social perspective it has been a success, but from a financial point of view it has been a disaster. The tunnel was purely a private sector venture for which a new business, Eurotunnel plc, was created. Relatively little public money was involved. To be a commercial success the tunnel needed to cover all of its costs, including interest charges, and leave sufficient to enhance the shareholders' wealth. In fact the providers of long-term finance (lenders and shareholders) have lost virtually all of their investment. Though the main losers were banks and institutional investors, many individuals, particularly in France, bought shares in Eurotunnel.

Key inputs to the pre-1986 assessment of the project were the cost of construction and creating the infrastructure, the length of time required to complete construction and the level of revenue that the tunnel would generate when it became operational.

In the event:

- construction cost was £10 billion – it was originally planned to cost £5.6 billion
- construction time was seven years – it was planned to be six years
- revenues from passengers and freight have been well below projected – for example, 21 million annual passenger journeys on Eurostar trains were projected; the numbers have consistently remained at around 7 million.

The failure to generate revenues at the projected levels has probably been the biggest contributor to the problem. When preparing the projection pre 1986, planners failed to take adequate account of two crucial factors:

- fierce competition from the ferry operators. At the time many thought that the ferries would roll over and die; and
- the rise of no-frills, cheap air travel between the UK and the continent.

The commercial failure of the tunnel means that it will be very difficult in future for projects of this nature to be funded by private funds.

Source: Annual reports of Eurotunnel plc; and 'How Eurotunnel went wrong', J. Randall, BBC news, www.newsvote.bbc.co.uk.

Summary

The main points of this chapter may be summarised as follows:

Accounting rate of return (ARR) is the average accounting profit from the project expressed as a percentage of the average investment.

- Decision rule – projects with an ARR above a defined minimum are acceptable; the greater the ARR, the more attractive the project becomes.
- Conclusion on ARR:
  - does not relate directly to shareholders' wealth – can lead to illogical conclusions;
  - takes almost no account of the timing of cash flows;
  - ignores some relevant information and may take account of some irrelevant;
  - relatively simple to use;
  - much inferior to NPV.

Payback period (PP) is the length of time that it takes for the cash outflow for the initial investment to be repaid out of resulting cash inflows.

- Decision rule – projects with a PP up to a defined maximum period are acceptable; the shorter the PP, the more attractive the project.

- Conclusion on PP:
  - does not relate to shareholders' wealth;
  - ignores inflows after the payback date;
  - takes little account of the timing of cash flows;
  - ignores much relevant information;
  - does not always provide clear signals and can be impractical to use;
  - much inferior to NPV, but it is easy to understand and can offer a liquidity insight, which might be the reason for its widespread use.

Net present value (NPV) is the sum of the discounted values of the net cash flows from the investment.

- Money has a time value.
- Decision rule – all positive NPV investments enhance shareholders' wealth; the greater the NPV, the greater the enhancement and the greater the attractiveness of the project.
- PV of a cash flow = cash flow $\times 1/(1 + r)^n$, assuming a constant discount rate.
- Discounting brings cash flows at different points in time to a common valuation basis (their present value), which enables them to be directly compared.
- Conclusion on NPV:
  - relates directly to shareholders' wealth objective;
  - takes account of the timing of cash flows;
  - takes all relevant information into account;
  - provides clear signals and is practical to use.

Internal rate of return (IRR) is the discount rate that, when applied to the cash flows of a project, causes it to have a zero NPV.

- Represents the average percentage return on the investment, taking account of the fact that cash may be flowing in and out of the project at various points in its life.
- Decision rule – projects that have an IRR greater than the cost of capital are acceptable; the greater the IRR, the more attractive the project.
- Cannot normally be calculated directly; a trial and error approach is often necessary.
- Conclusion on IRR:
  - does not relate directly to shareholders' wealth. Usually gives the same signals as NPV but can mislead where there are competing projects of different size;
  - takes account of the timing of cash flows;
  - takes all relevant information into account;
  - problems of multiple IRRs when there are unconventional cash flows;
  - inferior to NPV.

Use of appraisal methods in practice:

- all four methods identified are widely used;
- the discounting methods (NPV and IRR) show a steady increase in usage over time;
- many businesses use more than one method;
- larger businesses seem to be more sophisticated in their choice and use of appraisal methods than smaller ones.

Investment appraisal and strategic planning

It is important that businesses invest in a strategic way so as to play to their strengths.

Dealing with risk

- Sensitivity analysis (SA) is an assessment, taking each input factor in turn, of how much each one can vary from estimate before a project is not viable.
  - Provides useful insights to projects.
  - Does not give a clear decision rule, but provides an impression.
  - It can be rather static, but scenario building solves this problem.
- Expected net present value (ENPV) is the weighted average of the possible outcomes for a project, based on probabilities for each of the inputs:
  - Provides a single value and a clear decision rule.
  - The single ENPV figure can hide the real risk.
  - Useful for the ENPV figure to be supported by information on the range and dispersion of possible outcomes.
  - Probabilities may be subjective (based on opinion) or objective (based on evidence).
- Reacting to the level of risk:
  - Logically, high risk should lead to high returns.
  - Using a risk-adjusted discount rate, where a risk premium is added to the risk-free rate, is a logical response to risk.

Managing investment projects

- Determine investment funds available – dealing, if necessary, with capital rationing problems.
- Identify profitable project opportunities.
- Evaluate the proposed project.
- Approve the project.
- Monitor and control the project – using a post-completion audit approach.

MyAccountingLab Now check your progress in your personal Study Plan

Key terms

accounting rate of return (ARR)
  p. 529
payback period (PP)   p. 534
net present value (NPV)   p. 538
risk   p. 539
risk premium   p. 540
inflation   p. 540
discount factor   p. 544
cost of capital   p. 545
internal rate of return (IRR)   p. 547
relevant costs   p. 552

opportunity cost   p. 552
sensitivity analysis   p. 561
scenario building   p. 564
expected net present value (ENPV)
  p. 565
objective probabilities   p. 569
subjective probabilities   p. 570
risk-adjusted discount rate
  p. 572
capital rationing   p. 574
post-completion audit   p. 575

Reference

1 **Fifty Years of Research on Accuracy of Capital Expenditure Project Estimates: A Review of the Findings and Their Validity**, *Linder S.*, Otto Beisham Graduate School of Management, April 2005.

Further reading

If you would like to explore the topics covered in this chapter in more depth, we recommend the following books:

Business Finance: Theory and Practice, *McLaney E.*, 8th edn, Financial Times Prentice Hall, 2009, chapters 4, 5 and 6.

Corporate Finance and Investment, *Pike R. and Neale B.*, 5th edn, Prentice Hall, 2006, chapters 5, 6 and 7.

Corporate Financial Management, *Arnold G.*, 3rd edn, Financial Times Prentice Hall, 2005, chapters 2, 3 and 4.

Management and Cost Accounting, *Drury C.*, 7th edn, Cengage Learning, 2008, chapters 13 and 14.

Review questions

Answers to these questions can be found at the back of the book on pages 749–50.

14.1 Why is the net present value method of investment appraisal considered to be theoretically superior to other methods that are found in practice?

14.2 The payback method has been criticised for not taking the time value of money into account. Could this limitation be overcome? If so, would this method then be preferable to the NPV method?

14.3 Research indicates that the IRR method is extremely popular even though it has shortcomings when compared to the NPV method. Why might managers prefer to use IRR rather than NPV when carrying out discounted cash flow evaluations?

14.4 Why are cash flows rather than profit flows used in the IRR, NPV and PP methods of investment appraisal?

Exercises

Exercises 14.3 to 14.8 are more advanced than 14.1 and 14.2. Those with **coloured numbers** have answers at the back of the book, starting on page 795.

If you wish to try more exercises, visit the students' side of the Companion Website and MyAccountingLab.

14.1 The directors of Mylo Ltd are currently considering two mutually exclusive investment projects. Both projects are concerned with the purchase of new plant. The following data are available for each project:

	Project 1 £000	Project 2 £000
Cost (immediate outlay)	100	60
Expected annual operating profit (loss):		
Year 1	29	18
2	(1)	(2)
3	2	4
Estimated residual value of the plant	7	6

The business has an estimated cost of capital of 10 per cent, and uses the straight-line method of depreciation for all non-current (fixed) assets when calculating operating profit. Neither project would increase the working capital of the business. The business has sufficient funds to meet all capital expenditure requirements.

Required:

(a) Calculate for each project:
   (1) The net present value.
   (2) The approximate internal rate of return.
   (3) The payback period.

(b) State which, if any, of the two investment projects the directors of Mylo Ltd should accept, and why.

14.2 C. George (Controls) Ltd manufactures a thermostat that can be used in a range of kitchen appliances. The manufacturing process is, at present, semi-automated. The equipment used cost £540,000, and has a carrying value of £300,000. Demand for the product has been fairly stable, and output has been maintained at 50,000 units a year in recent years.

The following data, based on the current level of output, have been prepared in respect of the product:

	Per unit £	Per unit £
Selling price		12.40
Labour	(3.30)	
Materials	(3.65)	
Overheads: Variable	(1.58)	
Fixed	(1.60)	
		(10.13)
Operating profit		2.27

Although the existing equipment is expected to last for a further four years before it is sold for an estimated £40,000, the business has recently been considering purchasing new equipment that would completely automate much of the production process. The new equipment would cost £670,000 and would have an expected life of four years, at the end of which it would be sold for an estimated £70,000. If the new equipment is purchased, the old equipment could be sold for £150,000 immediately.

The assistant to the business's accountant has prepared a report to help assess the viability of the proposed change, which includes the following data:

	Per unit £	Per unit £
Selling price		12.40
Labour	(1.20)	
Materials	(3.20)	
Overheads: Variable	(1.40)	
Fixed	(3.30)	
		(9.10)
Operating profit		3.30

Depreciation charges will increase by £85,000 a year as a result of purchasing the new machinery; however, other fixed costs are not expected to change.

In the report the assistant wrote:

The figures shown above that relate to the proposed change are based on the current level of output and take account of a depreciation charge of £150,000 a year in respect of the new equipment. The effect of purchasing the new equipment will be to increase the operating profit to sales revenue ratio from 18.3% to 26.6%. In addition, the purchase of the new equipment will enable us to reduce our inventories level immediately by £130,000.

In view of these facts, I recommend purchase of the new equipment.

The business has a cost of capital of 12 per cent. Ignore taxation.

Required:

(a) Prepare a statement of the incremental cash flows arising from the purchase of the new equipment.

(b) Calculate the net present value of the proposed purchase of new equipment.

(c) State, with reasons, whether the business should purchase the new equipment.

(d) Explain why cash flow forecasts are used rather than profit forecasts to assess the viability of proposed capital expenditure projects.

14.3 The accountant of your business has recently been taken ill through overwork. In his absence his assistant has prepared some calculations of the profitability of a project, which are to be discussed soon at the board meeting of your business. His workings, which are set out below, include some errors of principle. You can assume that the statement below includes no arithmetical errors.

	Year 1 £000	Year 2 £000	Year 3 £000	Year 4 £000	Year 5 £000	Year 6 £000
Sales revenue		450	470	470	470	470
Less Costs						
Materials		126	132	132	132	132
Labour		90	94	94	94	94
Overheads		45	47	47	47	47
Depreciation		120	120	120	120	120
Working capital	180					
Interest on working capital		27	27	27	27	27
Write-off of development costs		30	30	30		
Total costs	180	438	450	450	420	420
Operating profit/(loss)	(180)	12	20	20	50	50

$$\frac{\text{Total profit (loss)}}{\text{Cost of equipment}} = \frac{(£28,000)}{£600,000} = \text{Return on investment (4.7\%)}$$

You ascertain the following additional information:

● The cost of equipment contains £100,000, being the carrying value of an old machine. If it were not used for this project it would be scrapped with a zero net realisable value. New equipment costing £500,000 will be purchased on 31 December Year 0. You should assume that all other cash flows occur at the end of the year to which they relate.

● The development costs of £90,000 have already been spent.

● Overheads have been costed at 50 per cent of direct labour, which is the business's normal practice. An independent assessment has suggested that incremental overheads are likely to amount to £30,000 a year.

● The business's cost of capital is 12 per cent.

Ignore taxation in your answer.

Required:

(a) Prepare a corrected statement of the incremental cash flows arising from the project. Where you have altered the assistant's figures you should attach a brief note explaining your alterations.

(b) Calculate:

(1) The project's payback period.

(2) The project's net present value as at 31 December Year 0.

(c) Write a memo to the board advising on the acceptance or rejection of the project.

14.4 Arkwright Mills plc is considering expanding its production of a new yarn, code name X15. The plant is expected to cost £1m and have a life of five years and a nil residual value. It will be bought, paid for and ready for operation on 31 December Year 0. £500,000 has already been spent on development costs of the product, and this has been charged in the income statement in the year it was incurred.

The following results are projected for the new yarn:

	Year 1 £m	Year 2 £m	Year 3 £m	Year 4 £m	Year 5 £m
Sales revenue	1.2	1.4	1.4	1.4	1.4
Costs, including depreciation	(1.0)	(1.1)	(1.1)	(1.1)	(1.1)
Profit before tax	0.2	0.3	0.3	0.3	0.3

Tax is charged at 50 per cent on annual profits (before tax and after depreciation) and paid one year in arrears. Depreciation of the plant has been calculated on a straight-line basis. Additional working capital of £0.6m will be required at the beginning of the project and released at the end of Year 5. You should assume that all cash flows occur at the end of the year in which they arise.

Required:

(a) Prepare a statement showing the incremental cash flows of the project relevant to a decision concerning whether or not to proceed with the construction of the new plant.

(b) Compute the net present value of the project using a 10 per cent discount rate.

(c) Compute the payback period to the nearest year. Explain the meaning of this term.

14.5 Newton Electronics Ltd has incurred expenditure of £5 million over the past three years researching and developing a miniature hearing aid. The hearing aid is now fully developed, and the directors are considering which of three mutually exclusive options should be taken to exploit the potential of the new product. The options are as follows:

1 The business could manufacture the hearing aid itself. This would be a new departure, since the business has so far concentrated on research and development projects. However, the business has manufacturing space available that it currently rents to another business for £100,000 a year. The business would have to purchase plant and equipment costing £9 million and invest £3 million in working capital immediately for production to begin.

A market research report, for which the business paid £50,000, indicates that the new product has an expected life of five years. Sales of the product during this period are predicted as follows:

	Predicted sales for the year ended 30 November				
	Year 1	Year 2	Year 3	Year 4	Year 5
Number of units (000s)	800	1,400	1,800	1,200	500

The selling price per unit will be £30 in the first year but will fall to £22 in the following three years. In the final year of the product's life, the selling price will fall to £20. Variable production costs are predicted to be £14 a unit, and fixed production costs (including depreciation) will be £2.4 million a year. Marketing costs will be £2 million a year.

The business intends to depreciate the plant and equipment using the straight-line method and based on an estimated residual value at the end of the five years of £1 million. The business has a cost of capital of 10 per cent a year.

2 Newton Electronics Ltd could agree to another business manufacturing and marketing the product under licence. A multinational business, Faraday Electricals plc, has offered to undertake the manufacture and marketing of the product, and in return will make a royalty payment to Newton Electronics Ltd of £5 per unit. It has been estimated that the annual

number of sales of the hearing aid will be 10 per cent higher if the multinational business, rather than if Newton Electronics Ltd, manufactures and markets the product.

3 Newton Electronics Ltd could sell the patent rights to Faraday Electricals plc for £24 million, payable in two equal instalments. The first instalment would be payable immediately and the second at the end of two years. This option would give Faraday Electricals the exclusive right to manufacture and market the new product.

Ignore taxation.

Required:

(a) Calculate the net present value (as at Year 1) of each of the options available to Newton Electronics Ltd.

(b) Identify and discuss any other factors that Newton Electronics Ltd should consider before arriving at a decision.

(c) State what you consider to be the most suitable option, and why.

14.6 Chesterfield Wanderers is a professional football club that has enjoyed considerable success in both national and European competitions in recent years. As a result, the club has accumulated £10 million to spend on its further development. The board of directors is currently considering two mutually exclusive options for spending the funds available.

The first option is to acquire another player. The team manager has expressed a keen interest in acquiring Basil ('Bazza') Ramsey, a central defender, who currently plays for a rival club. The rival club has agreed to release the player immediately for £10 million if required. A decision to acquire 'Bazza' Ramsey would mean that the existing central defender, Vinnie Smith, could be sold to another club. Chesterfield Wanderers has recently received an offer of £2.2 million for this player. This offer is still open but will only be accepted if 'Bazza' Ramsey joins Chesterfield Wanderers. If this does not happen, Vinnie Smith will be expected to stay on with the club until the end of his playing career in five years' time. During this period, Vinnie will receive an annual salary of £400,000 and a loyalty bonus of £200,000 at the end of his five-year period with the club.

Assuming 'Bazza' Ramsey is acquired, the team manager estimates that gate receipts will increase by £2.5 million in the first year and £1.3 million in each of the four following years. There will also be an increase in advertising and sponsorship revenues of £1.2 million for each of the next five years if the player is acquired. At the end of five years, the player can be sold to a club in a lower division and Chesterfield Wanderers will expect to receive £1 million as a transfer fee. During his period at the club, 'Bazza' will receive an annual salary of £800,000 and a loyalty bonus of £400,000 after five years.

The second option is for the club to improve its ground facilities. The west stand could be extended and executive boxes could be built for businesses wishing to offer corporate hospitality to clients. These improvements would also cost £10 million and would take one year to complete. During this period, the west stand would be closed, resulting in a reduction of gate receipts of £1.8 million. However, gate receipts for each of the following four years would be £4.4 million higher than current receipts. In five years' time, the club has plans to sell the existing grounds and to move to a new stadium nearby. Improving the ground facilities is not expected to affect the ground's value when it comes to be sold. Payment for the improvements will be made when the work has been completed at the end of the first year. Whichever option is chosen, the board of directors has decided to take on additional ground staff. The additional wages bill is expected to be £350,000 a year over the next five years.

The club has a cost of capital of 10 per cent. Ignore taxation.

Required:

(a) Calculate the incremental cash flows arising from each of the options available to the club.

(b) Calculate the net present value of each of the options.

(c) On the basis of the calculations made in (b) above, which of the two options would you choose and why?

(d) Discuss the validity of using the net present value method in making investment decisions for a professional football club.

14.7 Simtex Ltd has invested £120,000 to date in developing a new type of shaving foam. The shaving foam is now ready for production and it has been estimated that the new product will sell 160,000 cans a year over the next four years. At the end of four years, the product will be discontinued and replaced by a new product.

The shaving foam is expected to sell at £6 a can and the variable cost is estimated at £4 per can. Fixed cost (excluding depreciation) is expected to be £300,000 a year. (This figure includes £130,000 in fixed cost incurred by the existing business that will be apportioned to this new product.)

To manufacture and package the new product, equipment costing £480,000 must be acquired immediately. The estimated value of this equipment in four years' time is £100,000. The business calculates depreciation using the straight-line method, and has an estimated cost of capital of 12 per cent.

Required:

(a) Deduce the net present value of the new product.
(b) Calculate by how much each of the following must change before the new product is no longer profitable:
   (1) the discount rate;
   (2) the initial outlay on new equipment;
   (3) the net operating cash flows;
   (4) the residual value of the equipment.
(c) Should the business produce the new product?

14.8 Kernow Cleaning Services Ltd provides street-cleaning services for local councils in the far south west of England. The work is currently labour intensive and few machines are used. However, the business has recently been considering the purchase of a fleet of street-cleaning vehicles at a total cost of £540,000. The vehicles have a life of four years and are likely to result in a considerable saving of labour costs. Estimates of the likely labour savings and their probability of occurrence are set out below:

	Estimated savings £	Probability of occurrence
Year 1	80,000	0.3
	160,000	0.5
	200,000	0.2
Year 2	140,000	0.4
	220,000	0.4
	250,000	0.2
Year 3	140,000	0.4
	200,000	0.3
	230,000	0.3
Year 4	100,000	0.3
	170,000	0.6
	200,000	0.1

Estimates for each year are independent of other years. The business has a cost of capital of 10 per cent.

Required:

(a) Calculate the expected net present value (ENPV) of the street-cleaning machines.
(b) Calculate the net present value (NPV) of the worst possible outcome and the probability of its occurrence.

CHAPTER 15

Financing a business

Introduction

In this chapter we shall examine various aspects of financing a business. We begin by considering the main sources of finance available. Some of these sources have already been touched upon when we discussed the financing of limited companies in Chapter 4. In this chapter, we shall look at these in more detail as well as discuss other sources of finance that have not yet been mentioned. The factors to be taken into account when choosing an appropriate source of finance are also considered.

Following our consideration of the main sources of finance, we shall go on to examine various aspects of the capital markets, including the role of the Stock Exchange, the financing of smaller businesses and the ways in which share capital may be issued.

Learning outcomes

When you have completed this chapter, you should be able to:

- Identify the main sources of finance available to a business and explain the advantages and disadvantages of each.

- Outline the ways in which share capital may be issued.

- Explain the role and nature of the Stock Exchange.

- Discuss the ways in which smaller businesses may seek to raise finance.

MyAccountingLab Remember to create your own personalised Study Plan

Sources of finance

When considering the various sources of finance available to a business, it is useful to distinguish between *internal* and *external* sources of finance. By internal sources we mean sources that do not require the agreement of anyone beyond the directors and managers of the business. Thus, retained profits are considered an internal source because the directors of the business have power to retain profits without the agreement of the shareholders, whose profits they are. Finance from an issue of new shares, on the other hand, is an external source because it requires the compliance of potential shareholders.

Within each of the two categories just described, we can further distinguish between *long-term* and *short-term* sources of finance. There is no agreed definition concerning each of these terms but, for the purpose of this chapter, long-term sources of finance are defined as those that are expected to provide finance for at least one year. Short-term sources typically provide finance for a shorter period. As we shall see, sources that are seen as short-term when first used by the business often end up being used for quite long periods.

We shall begin the chapter by considering the various sources of internal finance available. We shall then go on to consider the various sources of external finance. This is probably an appropriate order since, in practice, businesses tend to look first to internal sources before going outside for new funds.

Sources of internal finance

Internal sources of finance usually have the advantage that they are flexible. They may also be obtained quickly – particularly from working capital sources – and need not require the compliance of other parties. The main sources of internal funds are described below and are summarised in Figure 15.1.

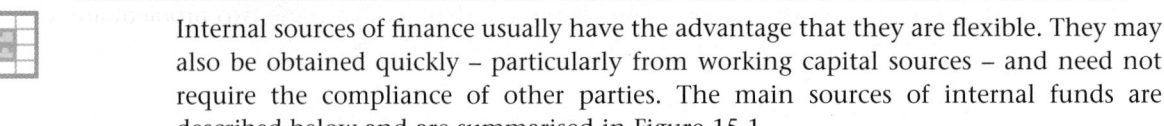

Figure 15.1 **The major sources of internal finance**

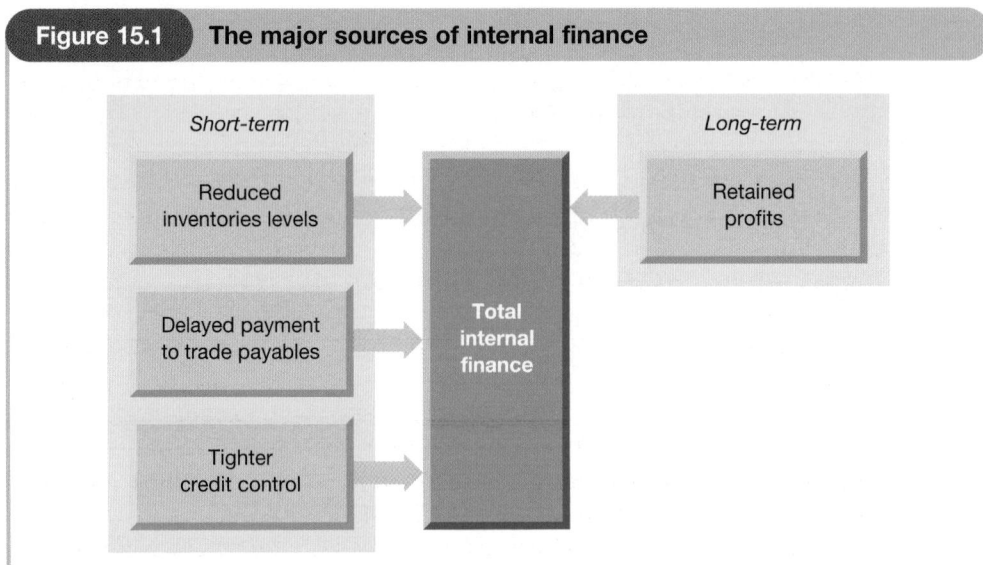

The major long-term source of internal finance is the profits that are retained rather than distributed to shareholders. The major short-term sources of internal finance involve reducing the level of trade receivables and inventories and increasing the level of trade payables.

Long-term sources of internal finance

Retained profits

Retained profits are an important source of finance for most businesses. If profits are retained within the business rather than being distributed to shareholders in the form of dividends, the funds of the business are increased.

Activity (15.1)

Are retained profits a free source of finance to the business?

It is tempting to think that retained profits are a cost-free source of funds for a business. However, this is not the case. If profits are reinvested rather than distributed to share-holders in cash, those shareholders cannot invest this cash in other forms of investment. They will therefore expect a rate of return from the profits reinvested that is equivalent to what they would have received had the funds been invested in another opportunity with the same level of risk.

The reinvestment of profits can be a useful way of raising capital from ordinary share investors.

An obvious alternative way to increase equity investment is to issue new shares. When issuing new shares, however, the issue costs may be substantial and there may be uncertainty over the success of the issue. We shall look at these two problem areas later in the chapter. There are no issue costs associated with retaining profits, and the amount raised is certain, once the profits have been made.

Retaining profits will have no effect on the extent to which existing shareholders control the business, whereas when new shares are issued to outside investors there will be some dilution of control.

The decision to retain profits rather than pay them out as dividends to the share-holders is made by the directors. They may find it easier simply to retain profits rather than ask investors to subscribe to a new share issue. Retained profits are already held by the business, and so it does not have to wait to receive the funds. Moreover, there is often less scrutiny when profits are being retained for reinvestment purposes than when new shares are being issued. Investors and their advisers will closely examine the reasons for any new share issue. A problem with the use of profits as a source of finance, however, is that the timing and level of future profits cannot always be reliably predicted.

Some shareholders may prefer profits to be retained by the business, rather than be distributed in the form of dividends. By ploughing back profits, it may be expected that the business will expand, and that share values will increase as a result. An important reason for preferring profits to be retained is the effect of taxation on the shareholder. In the UK, dividends are treated as income for tax purposes and therefore attract income tax. Gains on the sale of shares attract capital gains tax. Generally speaking, capital gains tax bites less hard than income tax. A further advantage of capital gains over dividends is that the shareholder has a choice as to when to sell the shares and realise the gain. In the UK, it is only when the gain is realised that capital gains tax comes into play. Research indicates that investors may be attracted to particular businesses according to the dividend/retention policies that they adopt.

It would be wrong to get the impression that all businesses either retain all of their profits or pay them all out as dividends. Where businesses pay dividends, and most of the larger ones do pay dividends, they typically pay no more than 50 per cent of the profit, retaining the remainder to fund expansion.

Retained profits are much the most important source of new finance for UK businesses, on average, in terms of value of funds raised.

Short-term sources of internal finance

Tighter credit control

By exerting tighter control over amounts owed by credit customers, it may be possible for a business to reduce the proportion of assets held in this form and so release funds for other purposes. Having funds tied up in trade receivables represents an opportunity cost in that those funds could be used for profit-generating activities. It is important, however, to weigh the benefits of tighter credit control against the likely costs in the form of lost customer goodwill and lost sales. To remain competitive, a business must take account of the needs of its customers and the credit policies adopted by rival businesses within the industry. We shall consider this further in Chapter 16.

Activity (15.2)

Rusli Ltd provides a car valet service for car-hire businesses when their cars are returned from hire. Details of the service costs are as follows:

	Per car £
Car valet charge	20
Variable costs	(14)
Fixed costs	(4)
Profit	2

Sales revenue is £10 million a year and is all on credit. The average credit period taken by Rusli Ltd's customers is 45 days, although the terms of credit state that payment should be made within 30 days. Bad debts are currently £100,000 a year. Trade receivables are financed by a bank overdraft costing 10 per cent a year.

Rusli Ltd's credit control department believes it can completely eliminate bad debts and can reduce the average credit period to 30 days if new credit control procedures are implemented. These will cost £50,000 a year and are likely to result in a loss of business leading to a reduction in sales revenue of 5 per cent a year.

Should Rusli Ltd implement the new credit control procedures? (*Hint*: To answer this activity it is useful to compare the current cost of trade credit with the costs under the proposed approach.)

The current annual cost of trade credit is:

	£
Bad debts	100,000
Overdraft interest ((£10m × 45/365) × 10%)	123,288
	223,288

The annual cost of trade credit under the new policy will be:

	£
Overdraft interest ((95% × (£10m) × (30/365)) × 10%)	78,082
Cost of control procedures	50,000
Net cost of lost sales ((£(10m/20) × 5%) × (20 − 14*))	150,000
	278,082

* The loss will be the contribution per unit (that is, the difference between the selling price and the variable costs).

These calculations show that the business will be worse off if the new policies are adopted.

Reducing inventories levels

Reducing the level of inventories is an internal source of funds that may prove attractive to a business. If the business has a proportion of its assets in the form of inventories there is an opportunity cost, as the funds tied up cannot be used for other purposes. If inventories are reduced, funds become available for those opportunities. However, a business must try to ensure that there are sufficient inventories available to meet likely future sales demand. Failure to do so will result in lost customer goodwill and lost sales revenue.

The nature and condition of the inventories held will determine whether it is possible to exploit this form of finance. A business may have excess inventories as a result of poor buying decisions. This may mean that a significant proportion of the inventories held are slow-moving or obsolete and cannot, therefore, be reduced easily. These issues will be picked up again in Chapter 16.

Delaying payment to trade payables

By providing a period of credit, suppliers are in effect offering a business an interest-free loan. If the business delays payment, the period of the 'loan' is extended and funds can be retained within the business. This can be a cheap form of finance for a business, though this is not always the case. If a business fails to pay within the agreed credit period, there may be significant costs. For example, the business may find it difficult to buy on credit when it has a reputation as a slow payer.

These so-called short-term sources are short-term to the extent that they can be reversed at short notice. For example, a reduction in the level of trade receivables can be reversed within a couple of weeks. Typically, however, once a business has established a reduced receivable collection period, a reduced inventories turnover period and/or an expanded payables payment period, it will tend to maintain these new levels.

As we shall see in Chapter 16, for the typical business, the level of funds involved with the working capital items is vast. This means that substantial amounts of funds can be raised through exercising tighter control of trade receivables and inventories and by exploiting opportunities to delay payment to trade payables.

Sources of external finance

Figure 15.2 summarises the main sources of long-term and short-term external finance.

Long-term sources of external finance

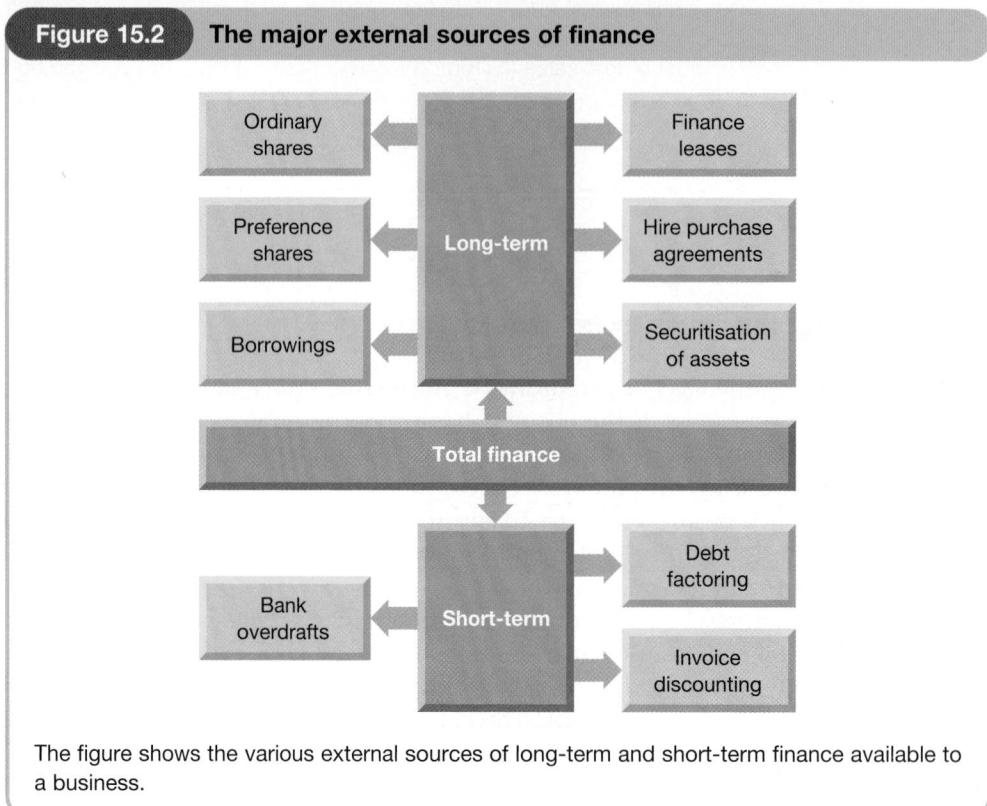

Figure 15.2 **The major external sources of finance**

The figure shows the various external sources of long-term and short-term finance available to a business.

As Figure 15.2 shows, the major forms of long-term external finance are

- ordinary shares
- preference shares
- borrowings
- finance leases, including sale-and-leaseback arrangements
- hire-purchase agreements
- securitisation of assets.

We shall now discuss each of the sources identified.

Ordinary shares

As we saw in Chapter 4, ordinary shares form the backbone of the financial structure of the business. Ordinary share capital represents the business's risk capital. There is no fixed rate of dividend and ordinary shareholders can receive a dividend only if profits available for distribution still remain after other investors (preference shareholders and lenders, if any) have received their dividend or interest payments. If the business is wound up, the ordinary shareholders will receive any proceeds from asset disposals only after any lenders (including trade payables) and preference shareholders have received their entitlements. Because of the high risks associated with this form of investment, ordinary shareholders will normally require a comparatively high rate of return.

Although ordinary shareholders have a potential loss liability that is limited to the amount that they have invested or agreed to invest, the potential returns from their investment are unlimited. In other words, their downside risk is limited whereas their upside potential is not. Ordinary shareholders have control over the business, through their voting rights. This gives them the power both to elect the directors and to remove them from office.

From the business's (directors') perspective, ordinary shares can be an attractive form of financing, relative to borrowing. At times, it can be useful to be able to avoid paying a dividend. It is not usually possible to avoid paying interest on borrowings.

Activity (15.3)

Under what circumstances might a business find it useful to avoid paying a dividend?

We feel that there are two main situations where this would apply:

● An expanding business may prefer to retain funds to help fuel future growth.
● A business in difficulties may need the funds to meet its operating costs and so may find making a dividend payment a real burden.

Real World 15.1 looks at the attitude of one well-known businessman to paying dividends.

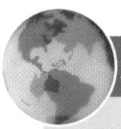

Real World 15.1

No frills, no dividends and no brains

Michael O'Leary, the colourfully-spoken chief executive of the 'no-frills' airline Ryanair Holdings plc, was very clear on his attitude to dividends. He said,

> We are never paying a dividend as long as I live and breathe and as long as I'm the largest share-holder. If you are stupid enough to invest in an airline for its dividend flow you should be put back in the loony bin where you came from.

It is not necessarily the case that Ryanair is expanding at a rate that eats up all available finances. According to its 2008 balance sheet, the business has a vast amount of cash.

Sources: 'Ryanair blunted by Buzz takeover', A. Osborne, *Daily Telegraph*, 6 August 2004; and Ryanair Holdings plc 2008 annual report.

Although a business financed by ordinary shares can avoid making cash payments to shareholders when it is not prudent to do so, the market value of the shares may go down. The cost to the business of financing through ordinary shares may become higher if shareholders feel uncertain about future dividends. On the other hand, for a business like Ryanair, which is clearly expanding its operations in a profitable way, share prices are likely to reflect this despite the lack of dividends.

It is also worth pointing out that the business does not obtain any tax relief on dividends paid to shareholders, whereas interest on borrowings is tax-deductible. This makes it more expensive to the business to pay £1 of dividend than £1 of interest on borrowings.

Preference shares

Preference shares offer investors a lower level of risk than ordinary shares. Provided there are sufficient profits available, preference shares will normally be given a fixed rate of dividend each year, and preference shareholders will be paid the first slice of any dividend paid. Should the business be wound up, preference shareholders may be given priority over the claims of ordinary shareholders. (The business's own particular documents of incorporation will state the precise rights of preference shareholders in this respect.)

Activity (15.4)

Would you expect the returns on preference shares to be higher or lower than those of ordinary shares?

Preference shareholders will expect to receive a lower level of return than ordinary shareholders. This is because of the lower level of risk associated with this form of investment (preference shareholders have priority over ordinary shareholders regarding dividends).

Preference shares are no longer an important source of new finance. A major reason for this is that dividends paid to preference shareholders, like those paid to ordinary shareholders, are not allowable against taxable profits, whereas interest on borrowings is an allowable expense. From the business's point of view, preference shares and borrowings are quite similar, so the tax-deductibility of interest on borrowings is an important issue.

Activity (15.5)

Would you expect the market price of ordinary shares or of preference shares to be the more volatile? Why?

The share price, which reflects the expected future returns from the share, will normally be less volatile for preference shares than for ordinary shares. The dividends of preference shares tend to be fairly stable over time, and there is usually an upper limit on the returns that can be received.

Both preference shares and ordinary shares are, in effect, *redeemable*. The business is allowed to buy back the shares from shareholders at any time.

Borrowings

Most businesses rely on borrowings as well as equity to finance operations. Lenders enter into a contract with the business in which the rate of interest, dates of interest payments, capital repayments and security for the borrowings are clearly stated. In the event that the interest payments or capital repayments are not made on the due dates, the lender will usually have the right, under the terms of the contract, to seize the assets on which their loan is secured and sell them in order to repay the amount outstanding. Security for a loan may take the form of a fixed charge on particular assets of the borrowing business (land and buildings are often favoured by lenders) or a floating charge on the whole of its assets. A floating charge will 'float' over the assets and will only fix on particular assets in the event that the business defaults on its borrowing obligations.

Activity 15.6

What do you think is the advantage for the business of having a floating charge rather than a fixed charge on its assets?

A floating charge on assets allows the managers greater flexibility in their day-to-day operations than a fixed charge. Individual assets can be sold without reference to the lenders.

Term loans

A **term loan** is a type of borrowing offered by banks and other financial institutions, which is usually tailored to the needs of the client business. The amount borrowed, the time period, the repayment terms and the interest payable are all open to negotiation and agreement, which can be very useful. For example, where all of the funds to be borrowed are not required immediately, a business may agree with the lender that funds are drawn only as and when required. This means that interest will be paid only on amounts drawn and so the business will not have to pay interest on amounts borrowed that are temporarily surplus to requirements. Term loans tend to be cheap to set up (from the borrower business's perspective) and can be quite flexible as to conditions. For these reasons they tend to be popular in practice.

Loan notes (or loan stock)

Another form of long-term borrowing is through **loan notes** (or **loan stock**). Loan notes are frequently divided into units (rather like share capital), and investors are invited to purchase the number of units they require. They may be redeemable or irredeemable. Loan notes of public limited companies are often traded on the Stock Exchange, and their listed value will fluctuate according to the fortunes of the business, movements in interest rates and so on.

Loan notes are usually referred to as *bonds* in the US and, increasingly so, in the UK.

Real World 15.2 describes the plans of one well-known business to make a very large bond issue.

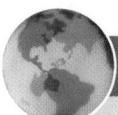

Real World 15.2

Flexi-bond

FT

British Sky Broadcasting plans to raise $600m in a bond issue to institutional investors in order to refinance its debt pile and boost its firepower for acquisitions. The pay-TV broadcaster is issuing 10-year bonds at 9.5 per cent interest which will mature in November 2018. One analyst said: 'BSkyB has a facility to be repaid next year and is also looking to spend money on a deal with Tiscali. The company needs flexibility.'

Real World 15.2 continued

BSkyB must repay about £800m ($1.18bn) of maturing bonds between February and July next year including $600m in February and $650m in July. The company is also locked in exclusive talks with Tiscali, the struggling Italian telecommunications group, over its UK assets. The proposed £450m deal would see the combined company of BSkyB and Tiscali UK becoming the country's largest provider of residential broadband by the end of next year.

The broadcaster said the proceeds of the bond offering would be used for 'general corporate purposes' as well as refinancing debt and acquisitions.

The company had net debt of £1.9bn at the end of September representing a healthy two times earnings before interest, tax, depreciation and amortisation.

Source: 'BSkyB to raise $600m in bond issue', Salamander Davoudi, FT.com, 21 November 2008.

Eurobonds

Eurobonds are unsecured loan notes denominated in a currency other than the home currency of the business that issued them. Eurobonds are issued by businesses (and other large organisations) in various countries, and the finance is raised on an international basis. They are often denominated in US dollars, but many are issued in other major currencies. Interest is normally paid annually. Eurobonds are part of an ever-expanding international capital market, and they are not subject to regulations imposed by authorities in particular countries. Numerous financial institutions throughout the world have created a market for eurobonds, where holders of eurobonds are able to sell them to would-be holders. The business issuing the eurobonds usually makes them available to large banks and other financial institutions, which may either retain them as an investment or sell them to their clients.

The extent of borrowing, by UK businesses, in currencies other than sterling has expanded massively in recent years. Businesses are often attracted to issuing eurobonds because of the size of the international capital market. Access to a large number of international investors is likely to increase the chances of a successful issue. In addition, the lack of regulation in the eurobond market means that national restrictions regarding loan notes issues may be overcome.

Real World 15.3 provides an example of a eurobond issue by a well known healthcare business.

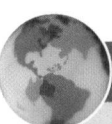

Real World 15.3

Banking on eurobonds

In January 2009, Commerzbank, Germany's second biggest bank, made a eurobond issue equivalent to 5 billion euros. This was guaranteed by the German government and is an attempt to free up the flow of credit in the wake of the credit crunch that hit the world in 2008.

Source: Information taken from 'Commerzbank hails oversubscribed five-billion eurobond issue', www.eurobusines.com, 9 January 2009.

Activity (15.7)

Would you expect the returns to lenders to be higher or lower than those of preference shareholders?

Lenders are usually prepared to accept a lower rate of return. This is because they will normally view loans as being less risky than preference shares. Lenders have priority over any claims from preference shareholders, and will usually have security for their loans.

The risk/return characteristics of borrowing, preference share financing and ordinary share financing (from the investor's point of view) are shown graphically in Figure 15.3. Note that, from the viewpoint of the business (the existing shareholders), the level of risk associated with each form of finance is in reverse order. Thus, borrowing is the most risky because it exposes shareholders to the legally enforceable obligation to make regular interest payments and, usually, repayment of the amount borrowed.

Figure 15.3   The risk/return characteristics of long-term financing

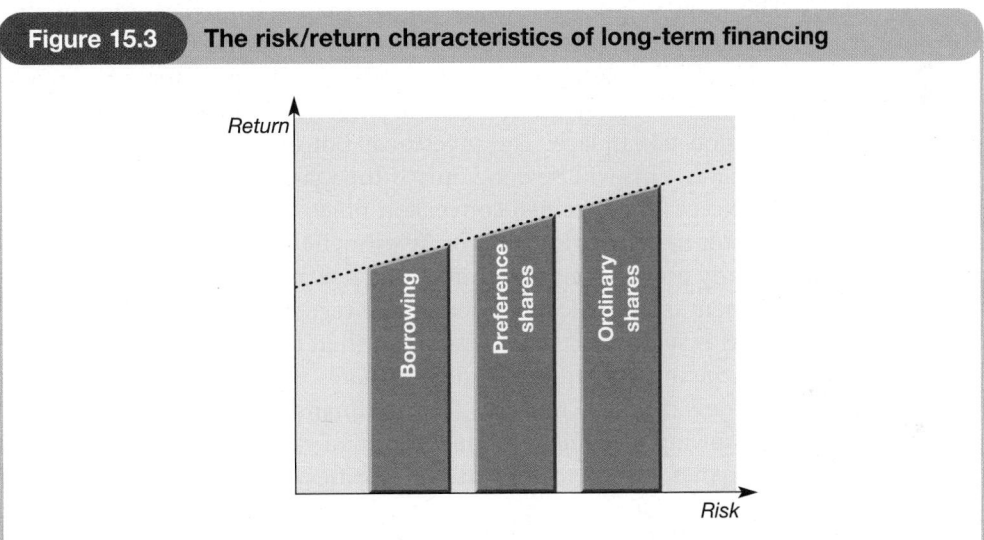

The higher the level of risk associated with a particular form of long-term finance, the higher will be the returns expected by investors. From the investor's point of view, ordinary shares are the most risky and have the highest expected return, and, as a general rule, borrowing is the least risky and has the lowest expected return.

Interest rates and deep discount bonds

Interest rates on borrowings may be either floating or fixed. A floating rate means that the rate of return required by lenders will rise and fall with market rates of interest. However, the market value of the lender's investment in the business is likely to remain fairly stable over time. The converse will normally be true for fixed-interest borrowings. The interest payments will remain unchanged with rises and falls in market rates of interest, but the value of the lender's investment will fall when interest rates rise and will rise when interest rates fall.

A business may issue redeemable loan notes that offer a rate of interest below the market rate. In some cases, the loan notes may even have a zero rate of interest. Such loan notes are issued at a discount to their redeemable value and are often referred to as **deep discount bonds**. Thus loan notes may be issued at, say, £80 for every £100 of nominal value. Although lenders will receive little or no interest during the period of their loan, they will receive a £20 gain when the loan is finally redeemed at the full £100. The redemption yield (that is, the effective rate of return to lenders over the life of their loan) is often quite high and, when calculated on an annual basis, may compare favourably with returns from other forms of lending with the same level of risk. Deep discount bonds may have particular appeal to businesses with short-term cash flow problems. Such businesses receive an immediate injection of cash when the bonds are issued and there are no significant cash outflows associated with the borrowing until the maturity date. Deep discount bonds are likely to appeal to investors who do not have short-term cash flow needs, since they must wait for the loan to mature before receiving a cash return.

Convertible loan notes

Convertible loan notes (or convertible bonds) give investors the right, but not the obligation, to exchange the loan notes for ordinary shares in the business at a specified price (the 'exercise' price) on a given future specified date or within a range of specified dates. The exercise price is usually higher than the market price of those ordinary shares at the time of issue of the convertible loan notes. In effect, the investor swaps the loan notes for a particular number of shares. The investor remains a lender to the business, and will receive interest on the amount of the loan notes, until such time as the conversion takes place. The investor is not obliged to convert the loan notes to ordinary shares. This will be done only if the market price of the shares at the conversion date exceeds the specified conversion price.

An investor may find this form of investment a useful hedge against risk. This may be particularly useful when investment in a new business is being considered. Initially, the investment is in the form of a loan and regular interest payments will be made. If the business is successful, the investor can then decide to benefit from the success by converting the investment into ordinary shares.

The business may also find this form of financing useful. If the business is successful, the borrowings become self-liquidating (no cash payment is required), as investors will exercise their option to convert. The business may also be able to offer a lower rate of interest to investors because they expect future benefits to arise from conversion. There will be, however, some dilution of both control and earnings for existing shareholders if holders of convertible loan notes exercise their option to convert.

Real World 15.4 outlines one particular convertible loan notes (bonds) issue.

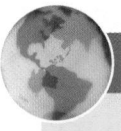

Real World 15.4

Property conversion

Mapeley Limited is a Guernsey-based business that owns and manages 1,670 commercial properties in the UK. Its tenants include the UK tax authority, HM Revenue and Customs. The business issued £45m of convertible bonds (loan notes) in early 2009. The cash was used to help repay £60m borrowing that fell due for repayment in April 2009.

The bonds will be converted into ordinary shares in the business at a rate of one share per £0.86 of bonds in 2014.

Source: Information taken from 'Talk of Workspace cash call', A. Lee and N. Hulme, *Financial Times*, 27 January 2009.

Warrants

→ Holders of **warrants** have the right, but not the obligation, to buy newly issued ordinary shares in a particular business, from that business, at a given price (the exercise price). As with convertible loan notes, the price at which shares may eventually be bought is usually higher than the market price of those shares at the time of the issue of the warrants. The warrant will usually state the number of shares that the holder may buy and the time limit within which the option to buy them can be exercised. Occasionally, perpetual warrants are issued that have no set time limits. Warrants do not confer voting rights or entitle the holders to make any claims on the assets of the business. Warrants are neither shares nor loan notes.

Share warrants are often sold to investors by the business concerned. In some cases, they are given away 'free' as a 'sweetener' to accompany an issue of loan notes, that is, as an incentive to potential lenders. The issue of warrants in this way may enable the business to offer lower rates of interest on the borrowings or to negotiate less restrictive borrowing conditions. Sometimes, businesses sell share warrants without there being a link to a loan notes issue. Warrants enable investors to benefit from any future increases in the business's ordinary share price without having to buy the shares themselves. On the other hand, if the share price remains below the exercise price, the warrant will not be used and the investor will lose out as a result.

Activity 15.8

Under what circumstances will the holders of share warrants exercise their option to purchase?

Holders will exercise this option only if the market price of the shares exceeds the exercise price within the time limit specified. If the exercise price were higher than the market price, it would be cheaper for the investor to buy the shares in the market.

To the business issuing the warrants, warrants represent a source of funds (the proceeds of selling them). Alternatively, they represent an encouragement for the issue of another source of funds (a loan notes issue) to be successful.

Share warrants issued with loan notes may be *detachable*, which means that they can be sold separately from the loan notes. The warrants of businesses whose shares are listed on the Stock Exchange are often themselves listed, providing a ready market for buying and selling the warrants.

It is probably worth mentioning the difference in status within a business between holders of convertible loan notes and holders of loan notes with share warrants attached, if both groups decide to exercise their right to convert. Convertible loan notes holders become ordinary shareholders and are no longer lenders to the business. They will have used the value of the loan notes to 'buy' the shares. Warrant holders become ordinary shareholders by paying cash for the shares. If the warrant holders hold loan notes, their position as lenders will be unaffected by them exercising their right to buy the shares bestowed by the warrant.

→ Both convertibles and warrants are examples of **financial derivatives**. These are any form of financial instrument, based on equity or loans/borrowings, that can be used by investors to increase their returns or reduce risk.

Mortgages

→ A **mortgage** is a form of borrowing that is secured on an asset, typically land. Financial institutions such as banks, insurance businesses and pension funds are often prepared to lend to businesses on this basis. The mortgage may be over a long period (twenty years or more).

Loan covenants

Lenders often impose certain obligations and restrictions on borrowers in an attempt to protect their loan. **Loan covenants** (as they are called) often form part of a loan agreement, and may deal with such matters as:

● *Financial statements.* The lender may require access to the financial statements of the borrowing business on a regular basis.
● *Other borrowings.* The lender may require the business to ask the lender's permission before borrowing further from other sources.
● *Dividend payments.* The lender may require dividend payments to be limited during the period of the loan.
● *Liquidity.* The lender may require the business to maintain a certain level of liquidity during the period of the loan. This would typically be a requirement that the borrower business's current ratio is maintained at, or above, a specified level.

Any breach of these restrictive covenants can have serious consequences for the business. The lender may require immediate repayment of the loan in the event of a material breach.

Real World 15.5 relates to Wolseley plc, the UK builders' merchants with more than 5,000 branches worldwide. It shows how, in early 2009, Wolseley was fighting to avoid breaching the loan covenants imposed by its lenders. The business was particularly hard hit by the recession and by the fact that much of its borrowings were in US$ and in euros.

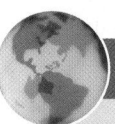

Real World 15.5

Capital problems

FT

Shares in Wolseley lost almost a third of their value yesterday after the building materials group warned that its debt pile, denominated mostly in euros, had swollen by a fifth to £3bn as sterling crumbled.

The rising debt, together with falling profits, stoked fears that Wolseley will breach its banking covenants this year, forcing the company into costly debt renegotiations or a dilutive rights issue.*

UBS, its broker, said Wolseley was 'highly likely' to break its covenants when they are tested in July. The bank said an equity issue of as much as £750m was 'virtually unavoidable'.

Chip Hornsby, chief executive, said: 'Our attention and efforts remain resolutely focused on achieving compliance with our banking covenants.' The company said it was expected to be compliant when the covenant is next tested on January 31.

Wolseley's covenants require its net debt to be no higher than 3.5 times earnings before interest, tax, depreciation and amortisation (ebitda). The figure for the full year to July 2008 was 2.7 times. UBS estimates Wolseley's ebitda in July 2009 will be £608m against net debt of £2.56bn.

In an attempt to keep within the 3.5 figure, Wolseley has over the past five months reduced working capital, cut jobs and set up a receivables funding arrangement to raise cash from its pending invoices. The company cut 7,500 jobs over the period, bringing the total to 66,000, and said the receivables arrangement had reduced net debt by £72m.

However, it has become more difficult to meet the net debt covenant as the slide in the pound has caused Wolseley's foreign currency debt to rise in sterling terms. The effect of currency movements has increased net debt over the period by £557m, a 22 per cent jump.

In an attempt to mitigate this, Wolseley moved a total of £1bn of euro and dollar-denominated debt into sterling and set up a currency hedge against further falls in the pound against the euro.

At the end of July, 75 per cent of Wolseley's debt was denominated in euros and 25 per cent in dollars. By the end of December, 48 per cent was in euros, 14 per cent in dollars and the remainder in sterling. Currency movements also flattered Wolseley's trading figures, but the downturns in Europe and the US still caused trading profit for the five months ending in December to fall 45 per cent, or 52 per cent in constant currency terms.

Profit before amortisation and exceptional items dropped 66 per cent, or 75 per cent in constant currency. Revenue rose in the same period by 3 per cent, but in constant currency dropped 10 per cent.

* We may recall from Chapter 4 that a rights issue is an issue of shares to existing shareholders. We shall discuss rights issues in some detail later in this chapter.

Source: 'Wolseley shares plunge as net debt increases', Robert Cookson and David Fickling, *Financial Times*, 27 January 2009.

Activity (15.9)

Both preference shares and loan notes are forms of finance whose holders expect the business to provide a particular rate of return. What are the factors that may be taken into account by a business when deciding between these two sources of finance?

The main factors are as follows:

- Preference shares tend to have a higher rate of return than loan notes. From the investor's point of view, preference shares are more risky. The amount invested cannot be secured, and the return is paid after the returns paid to lenders.
- A business has a legal obligation to pay interest and, typically, make capital repayments on loan notes at the agreed dates. It will usually make every effort to meet its obligations because failure to do so can have serious consequences. (These consequences have been mentioned earlier.) Failure to pay a preference dividend, on the other hand, is less important. There is no legal obligation to pay if profits are not available for distribution. Failure to pay a preference dividend may prove an embarrassment for the business, however, because it may make it difficult to persuade investors to take up future preference share issues.
- It was mentioned above that the taxation system in the UK permits interest on borrowing to be allowable against profits for taxation, whereas preference dividends are not. As a result, the cost of servicing borrowings is, £ for £, usually much lower for a business than the cost of servicing preference shares.
- The issue of loan notes may result in the management of a business having to accept some restrictions on its freedom of action. We saw earlier that borrowing agreements often contain covenants that can be onerous. Preference shareholders can impose no such restrictions.

A further point is that preference shares issued form part of the permanent capital base of the business. If they are redeemed, the law requires that they be replaced, either by a new issue of shares or by a transfer from revenue reserves, so that the business's capital base stays intact. Borrowings, however, are not viewed in law as part of the business's permanent capital base, and therefore there is no legal requirement to replace any loan notes that have been redeemed.

Finance leases and sale-and-leaseback arrangements

When a business needs a particular asset (for example, an item of plant), instead of buying it direct from a supplier, the business may decide to arrange for another business (typically a bank) to buy it and then lease it to the first business. The business that owns the asset and leases it out is known as a 'lessor'. The one that uses it is known as the 'lessee'.

→ A **finance lease**, as such an arrangement is known, is, in essence, a form of lending. This is because, had the lessee borrowed the funds and then used them to buy the asset itself, the effect would be much the same. The lessee would have use of the asset, but have a financial obligation to the lender – much the same position as the leasing arrangement would lead to.

With finance leasing, legal ownership of the asset rests with the financial institution (the lessor); however, the lease agreement transfers to the user (the lessee) virtually all the rewards and risks that are associated with the item being leased. The finance lease agreement covers a significant part of the life of the item being leased, and often cannot be cancelled.

Finance leasing is a very important source of finance for UK businesses. The Finance and Leasing Association estimates that 27 per cent of finance for non-current assets (excluding land and buildings) comes from finance leasing.

Real World 15.6 gives an example of the use of finance leasing in a leading airline business.

Real World 15.6

BA's leased assets are taking off

Many airline businesses use finance leasing as a means of acquiring new aeroplanes. The financial statements for British Airways plc (BA) for the year ended 31 March 2008 show that almost 29 per cent (totalling £1,728m) of the net carrying amount of its fleet of aircraft had been acquired through this method.

Source: British Airways plc Annual Report and Accounts 2008, p. 98.

→ A finance lease can be contrasted with an **operating lease**, where the rewards and risks of ownership stay with the owner and where the lease is short-term. An example of an operating lease is where a builder hires some earthmoving equipment for a week to carry out a particular job.

Finance leasing greatly grew in popularity in the UK during the 1970s and 1980s. At that time, there were some important benefits associated with finance leasing. These were a favourable tax treatment and the fact that such financing arrangements did not have to be disclosed on the statement of financial position (balance sheet). More recently these benefits have disappeared. Changes in UK tax law no longer make it such a tax-efficient form of financing, and changes in accounting disclosure requirements no longer make it possible to conceal this form of 'borrowing' from investors. Nevertheless, the popularity of finance leases has continued. Other reasons must therefore exist for businesses to adopt this form of financing. These reasons are said to include the following:

- *Ease of borrowing.* Leasing may be obtained more easily than other forms of long-term finance. Lenders normally require some form of security and a profitable track record before making advances to a business. However, a lessor may be prepared to lease assets to a new business without a track record, and to use the leased assets as security for the amounts owing.
- *Cost.* Leasing agreements may be offered at reasonable cost. As the asset leased is used as security, standard lease arrangements can be applied and detailed credit checking of lessees may be unnecessary. This can reduce administrative costs for the lessor and, thereby, help in providing competitive lease rentals.
- *Flexibility.* Leasing can help provide flexibility where there are rapid changes in technology. If an option to cancel can be incorporated into the lease, the business may be able to exercise this option and invest in new technology as it becomes available. This will help the business to avoid the risk of obsolescence.
- *Cash flows.* Leasing, rather than purchasing an asset outright, means that large cash outflows can be avoided. The leasing option allows cash outflows to be smoothed out over the asset's life. In some cases, it is possible to arrange for low lease payments to be made in the early years of the asset's life, when cash inflows may be low, and for these to increase over time as the asset generates positive cash flows.

Real World 15.7 provides some impression of the importance of finance leasing over recent years.

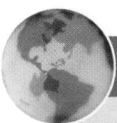

Real World 15.7

A new lease. . . .

The amount of asset finance provided through finance leasing by FLA members over the five-year period has remained fairly stable (see Figure 15.4).

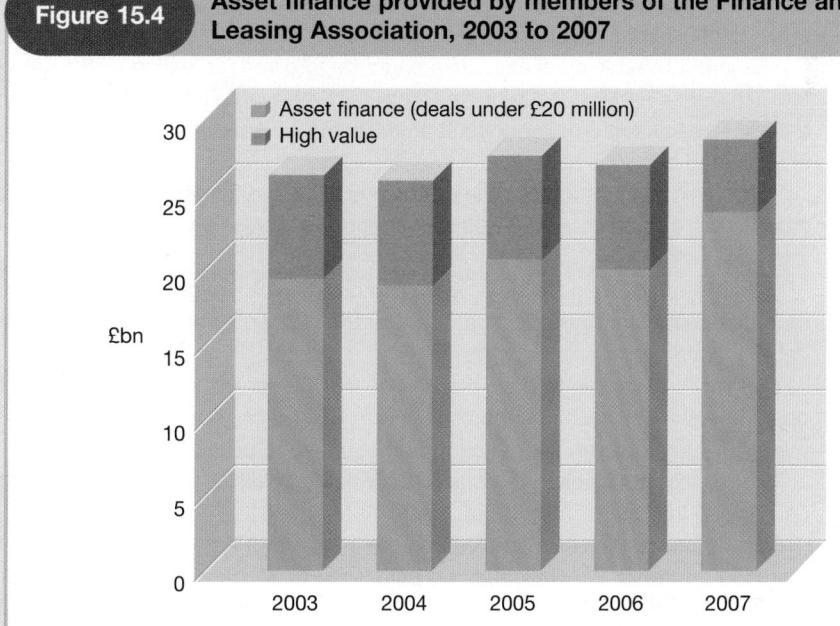

| Figure 15.4 | Asset finance provided by members of the Finance and Leasing Association, 2003 to 2007 |

Source: *Finance and Leasing Association Annual Review 2008* (www.fla.org.uk), p. 10. Copyright © 2008 Finance and Leasing Association.

A **sale-and-leaseback** arrangement involves a business raising finance by selling an asset to a financial institution. The sale is accompanied by an agreement to lease the asset back to the business to allow it to continue to use the asset. The lease payment is allowable against profits for taxation purposes. There are usually reviews at regular intervals throughout the period of the lease, and the amounts payable in future years may be difficult to predict. At the end of the lease agreement, the business must try either to renew the lease or to find an alternative asset. Although the sale of the asset will result in an immediate injection of cash for the business, the business will lose benefits from any future capital appreciation on the asset. Where a capital gain arises on the sale of the asset to the financial institution, a liability for taxation may also arise. Freehold property is often the asset that is the subject of such an arrangement. Many of the well-known UK high street retailers (for example, Boots, Debenhams, Marks and Spencer, Sainsbury, Tesco and the ill-fated Woolworths) have recently sold off their store sites under sale-and-leaseback arrangements.

A sale-and-leaseback agreement can be used to help a business focus on its core areas of competence. In recent years, many hotel businesses have entered into sale-and-leaseback agreements to enable them to become purely hotel operators rather than a combination of hotel operators and owners.

Real World 15.8 is a *Financial Times* article that explains how Woolworths' sale and leaseback arrangements contributed to the collapse of the business.

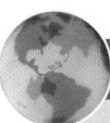

Real World 15.8

The wonder of Woolworths' sale-and-leaseback arrangements

FT

At Woolworths' annual meeting this summer a perennially cheerful Trevor Bish-Jones cut a rather forlorn figure as he told his audience that making '£3bn of [group] sales for £30m of net profit is hard work this side of the fence'.

The imperturbable chief executive could be forgiven for feeling a little sorry for himself: Mr Bish-Jones had just been ousted from the variety retailer having laboured for six-and-a-half years to keep Woolworths afloat under the weight of rising rents, shabby stores and an outdated business model.

This week the fight to save the much-loved but very under-shopped Woolworths chain finally drew to a close as the 800 stores and the wholesale distribution arm were placed into administration.

Having limped along for seven years, with the profit line gradually shifting from black to red, the directors finally called it a day after the retailer, labouring under £385m ($591m) of debt, succumbed to a cash crisis.

But how did it come to pass that the near 100-year-old chain, which in its heyday was opening a store a week and was still selling £1.7bn of goods a year through its stores at the time of its collapse, should end up in such a dire predicament?

Those close to Woolworths place this week's collapse firmly at the feet of those who de-merged the retailer from Kingfisher in August 2001.

They argue that the decision to carry out a sale-and-leaseback deal for 182 Woolworths stores in return for £614m of cash – paid back to Kingfisher shareholders – crippled the chain.

For in return for the princely price tag, Woolworths was saddled with onerous leases that guaranteed the landlords a rising income stream.

One person who knows Woolworths well says the rent bill rose from £70m a decade ago to £160m today.

'There is no doubt that back in 2001, with the de-merger and the sale of these stores, the company was saddled with a huge amount of quasi debt in terms of these leases,' says one former adviser. 'I think probably that is really where this goes back to. If Woolworths had more financial flexibility they might have been able to do more of the stuff they needed to. ... To build a sustainable business requires investment but they were not in a position to incur more costs,' the former adviser adds.

Tony Shiret, analyst at Credit Suisse, says Woolworths' lease-adjusted debt was the highest in the retail sector. 'They didn't really have enough cash flow to cover debt repayments.'

Source: 'Seeds of Woolworths' demise sown long ago', Elizabeth Rigby, *Financial Times*, 29 November 2008.

Hire purchase

Hire purchase is a form of credit used to acquire an asset. Under the terms of a hire purchase (HP) agreement, a customer pays for an asset by instalments over an agreed period. Normally, the customer will pay an initial deposit (down payment) and then make instalment payments at regular intervals (perhaps monthly) until the balance outstanding has been paid. The customer will usually take possession of the asset after payment of the initial deposit, although legal ownership of the asset will not be transferred until the final instalment has been paid.

Hire-purchase agreements will often involve three parties:

● the supplier
● the customer
● a financial institution.

Although the supplier will deliver the asset to the customer, the financial institution will buy the asset from the supplier and then enter into a hire purchase agreement with the customer. This intermediary role played by the financial institution enables the supplier to receive immediate payment for the asset but allows the customer a period of extended credit.

Real World 15.9 describes how one well-known airline operator uses hire purchase to help finance its assets.

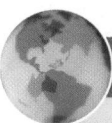

Real World 15.9

Flying by instalments

British Airways plc finances some of its aircraft by hire purchase. At 31 March 2008, nearly 26 per cent (£1,549 million) of the carrying value of its fleet was financed in this way.

Source: British Airways plc Annual Report 2008, p. 98.

Hire purchase is probably a more common source of finance among smaller businesses; however, the British Airways plc example shows that larger businesses also use this source. Hire-purchase agreements are similar to finance leases in so far that they allow a customer to obtain immediate possession of the asset without paying its full cost. Under the terms of an agreement, however, the customer will eventually become the legal owner of the asset, whereas under the terms of a finance lease, ownership will stay with the lessor.

Securitisation (asset-backed finance)

Where a business expects to receive a stream of positive future cash flows, it effectively owns an asset (whose value is the (discounted) present value of those cash flows). An example of such a stream is the monthly repayments, made by those who borrowed money to buy their homes, to a mortgage lender. It is possible for the mortgage lender to raise funds on the basis of these expected future cash receipts by bundling them together to provide asset backing for the issue of bonds to investors (a process known → as **securitisation**).

Securitising mortgage loan repayments became popular among US mortgage lenders during the early years of the 2000s. The monthly repayments were 'securitised' and sold to many of the major banks, particularly in the US. Unfortunately, many of the mortgage loans were made to people on low incomes who were not good credit risks (sub-prime loans). When the borrowers started to default on their obligations, it became clear that the securities, now owned by the banks, were worth much less than the banks had paid the mortgage lenders for them. This led to the, so-called, 'sub-prime' crisis that triggered the worldwide economic problems that emerged during 2008.

There is no inherent reason for securitisation to be a problem and it is unfortunate that the practice is linked with the sub-prime crisis. It is a perfectly legitimate and practical way for a business to raise finance.

Real World 15.10 shows that securitisation of household mortgage loans is not restricted to the US. It is generally believed, however, that the UK securitised mortgage loans are not quite as toxic as some of their US counterparts.

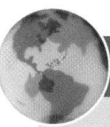 **Real World 15.10**

Banking on bonds

Securitisation of mortgage loans has become an important means of raising finance by UK banks. However, there is a wide variation in the use of this form of finance between the leading banks.

At one end of the scale, HSBC, RBS and Barclays have issued relatively few mortgage-backed bonds. But HBOS, the biggest mortgage lender, funds 17 per cent of all lending with securitisation. Abbey National uses securitisation for 22 per cent of its mortgage lending. Northern Rock used securitisation to fund 57 per cent of its loan book, according to Deutsche Bank data. Following a crisis in the money markets in August 2007, banks found it almost impossible to sell any mortgage-backed bonds. It is clear, however, that some banks will have suffered more than others as a result.

Source: Based on information taken from 'King fails to soothe lenders', Delphine Strauss, FT.com, 23 January 2008.

Gearing and the long-term financing decision

In Chapter 7 we saw that financial gearing (known as 'leverage' in the US) occurs when a business is financed, at least in part, by contributions from fixed-charge capital (preference shares and borrowings). We also saw that the level of gearing associated with a business is often an important factor in assessing the risk and returns to ordinary shareholders. In Example 15.1, we consider the implications of making a choice between a geared and an ungeared approach to raising long-term finance.

Example 15.1

The following are the summarised financial statements of Woodhall Engineers plc:

Woodhall Engineers plc
Income statement for the year ended 31 December

	Year 1 £m	Year 2 £m
Revenue	47	50
Operating costs	(42)	(48)
Operating profit	5	2
Interest payable	(1)	(1)
Profit before tax	4	1
Taxation	–	–
Profit for the year	4	1

Statement of financial position as at 31 December

	Year 1 £m	Year 2 £m
ASSETS		
Non-current assets (less depreciation)	21	20
Current assets		
Inventories	10	18
Receivables	16	17
Cash at bank	3	1
	29	36
Total assets	50	56
EQUITY AND LIABILITIES		
Equity		
Called-up share capital (25p ordinary shares)	16	16
Retained earnings	4	4
	20	20
Non-current liabilities		
Borrowings – Long-term loans (secured)	15	15
Current liabilities		
Trade payables	10	10
Short-term borrowings	5	11
	15	21
Total equity and liabilities	50	56

→

The business is making plans to expand its premises. New plant will cost £8 million, and an expansion in output will increase working capital by £4 million. Over the 15 years' life of the project, incremental operating profit arising from the expansion will be £2 million a year. In addition, Year 3's operating profit from its existing activities is expected to return to Year 1 levels.

Two possible methods of financing the expansion have been discussed by Woodhall's directors. The first is the issue of £12 million of 10 per cent loan notes repayable in Year 18. The second is an issue of 40 million 25p ordinary shares, which will give the business cash of 30p per share after expenses.

The business has substantial tax losses, which can be offset against future profits, so taxation can be ignored in the calculations. The Year 3 total dividend is expected to be £1.0 million if the expansion is financed by loan notes and £1.6 million if the share issue is made.

Prepare Woodhall's projected income statement (excluding revenue and operating costs) for the year ended 31 December Year 3, and a statement of its equity and number of shares in issue at that date, assuming that the business issues:

(a) loan notes
(b) ordinary shares.

The projected income statements under each financing option will be as follows:

Projected income statements for the year ended 31 December Year 3

	Loan notes issue	Share issue
	£m	£m
Operating profit (5.0 + 2.0)	7.0	7.0
Loan notes interest	(2.2)	(1.0)
Profit before tax	4.8	6.0
Taxation	–	–
Profit for the year	4.8	6.0

The equity of the business and number of shares in issue under each option as at the end of Year 3 will be as follows:

	Loan notes issue	Share issue
	£m	£m
Equity		
Share capital (25p ordinary shares)	16.0	26.0
Share premium account*	–	2.0
Retained earnings†	7.8	8.4
	23.8	36.4
Number of shares in issue (25p shares)	64 million	104 million

* This represents the amount received from the issue of shares that is above the nominal value of the shares. The amount is calculated as follows:

$$40\text{m shares} \times (30\text{p} - 25\text{p}) = £2\text{m}$$

† This is the retained profit figure after deducting the dividend paid.

Activity (15.10)

Compute Woodhall's interest cover and earnings per share for the year ended 31 December Year 3 and its gearing on that date, assuming that the business issues:

(a) loan notes;
(b) ordinary shares.

Your answer should be as follows:

	(a) Loan notes issue	(b) Share issue
Interest cover ratio		
$\dfrac{\text{Operating profit}}{\text{Interest payable}}$	$= \dfrac{7.0}{2.2}$	$= \dfrac{7.0}{1.0}$
	$= 3.2$ times	$= 7.0$ times
Earnings per share		
$\dfrac{\text{Earnings available to ordinary shareholders}}{\text{Number of ordinary shares}}$	$= \dfrac{£4.8m}{64m}$	$= \dfrac{£6.0m}{104m}$
	$= 7.5p$	$= 5.8p$
Gearing ratio		
$\dfrac{\text{Non-current liabilities}}{\text{Share capital + Reserves + Non-current liabilities}}$	$= \dfrac{£27m}{£23.8m + £27m}$	$= \dfrac{£15m}{£36.4m + £15m}$
	$= 53.1\%$	$= 29.2\%$

Activity (15.11)

What would your views of the proposed schemes be in each of the following circumstances?

(a) If you were an investor who had been asked to take up some of the loan notes.
(b) If you were an ordinary shareholder in Woodhall and you were asked to subscribe to a share issue.

(a) Investors may be unenthusiastic about lending money to the business. The gearing ratio of 53.1 per cent is rather high, and would leave the loan notes holders in an exposed position. Their existing loan is already secured on the business's assets, and it is not clear whether the business is in a position to offer an attractive form of security for the new loan. The interest cover ratio of 3.2 times is also rather low. If the business is unable to achieve the expected returns from the new project, or if it is unable to restore profits from the remainder of its operations to Year 1 levels, this ratio would be even lower.

(b) Ordinary share investors may need some convincing that it would be worthwhile to make further investments in the business. The return on ordinary shareholders' funds in Year 1 was 20 per cent (£4 million/£20 million). The incremental profit from the new project is £2 million and the investment required is £12 million, which represents a return of 16.7 per cent. Thus, the returns from the project are expected to be lower than for existing operations. In making their decision, investors should discover whether the new investment is of a similar level of risk to their existing investment and how the returns from the investment compare with those available from other opportunities with similar levels of risk.

Share issues

A business may issue shares in a number of ways. These may involve direct appeals to investors or the use of financial intermediaries. The most common methods of share issues for cash are:

● rights issues;
● offers for sale and public issues;
● private placings.

We shall now discuss these methods.

Rights issues

→ As we saw in Chapter 4, **rights issues** are made when businesses that have been established for some time seek to raise additional funds by issuing new shares to their existing shareholders. The funds may be used for expansion, or even to solve a liquidity problem (cash shortage), as we saw in Real World 15.5 (page 600). Company law gives existing shareholders the first right of refusal to buy any new shares issued by a company, so the new shares would be offered to shareholders in proportion to their existing holding. Only where the existing shareholders agree to waive their right could the shares be offered to the investing public generally. Rights issues are a relatively popular form of share issue. Over the period 2000 to 2008, for established businesses listed on the London Stock Exchange, about 40 per cent of funds raised from new share issues are from rights issues, with the exact proportion varying from one year to the next (see reference 1 at the end of the chapter). The business (in effect, the existing shareholders) would typically prefer that existing shareholders buy the shares through a rights issue, irrespective of the legal position. This is for two reasons:

● The ownership (and, therefore, control) of the business remains in the same hands; there is no 'dilution' of control.
● The costs of making the issue (advertising, complying with various company law requirements) tend to be less if the shares are to be offered to existing shareholders. It is estimated that the average cost of making a rights issue are 5.8 per cent of the funds raised. Since a lot of the cost is fixed, this percentage will be greater or lesser for smaller and larger rights issues, respectively (see reference 2 at the end of the chapter). This compares with up to 11 per cent for an issue to the public (see reference 3 at the end of the chapter).

To encourage existing shareholders to take up their 'rights' to buy some new shares, those shares are always offered at a price below the current market price of the existing ones. The evidence shows that shares are typically offered at 31 per cent below the current pre-rights price (see reference 2 at the end of the chapter).

Activity (15.12)

In Chapter 4 (Example 4.2, page 139) the point was made that issuing new shares at below their current worth was to the advantage of the new shareholders at the expense of the old ones. In view of this, does it matter that rights issues are always made at below the current value of the shares?

The answer is that it does not matter *in these particular circumstances*, because, in a rights issue, the existing shareholders and the new shareholders are exactly the same people. Moreover, the shareholders will hold the new shares in the same proportion as they currently hold the existing shares. Thus, shareholders will gain on the new shares exactly as much as they lose on the existing ones: in the end, no one is better or worse off as a result of the rights issue being made at a discount.

Calculating the value of the rights offer received by shareholders is quite straightforward, as shown in Example 15.2.

Example 15.2

Shaw Holdings plc has 20 million ordinary shares of 50p in issue. These shares are currently valued on the Stock Exchange at £1.60 per share. The directors have decided to make a one-for-four issue (that is, one new share for every four shares held) at £1.30 per share.

The first step in the valuation process is to calculate the price of a share following the rights issue. This is known as the *ex-rights price*, and is simply a weighted average of the price of shares before the issue of rights and the price of the rights shares. In this example, we have a one-for-four rights issue. The theoretical ex-rights price is therefore calculated as follows:

	£
Price of four shares before the rights issue (4 × £1.60)	6.40
Price of taking up one rights share	1.30
	7.70

$$\text{Theoretical ex-rights price} = \frac{£7.70}{5} \qquad = £1.54$$

As the price of each share, in theory, should be £1.54 following the rights issue and the price of a rights share is £1.30, the value of the rights offer will be the difference between the two:

$$£1.54 - £1.30 = £0.24 \text{ per share}$$

Market forces will usually ensure that the actual and theoretical price of rights shares will be fairly close.

Activity 15.13

An investor with 2,000 shares in Shaw Holdings plc (see Example 15.2) has contacted you for investment advice. She is undecided whether to take up the rights issue, sell the rights or allow the rights offer to lapse.

Calculate the effect on the net wealth of the investor of each of the options being considered.

Before the rights issue the position of the investor was:

	£
Value of shares (2,000 × £1.60)	3,200

Activity 15.13 continued

If she takes up the rights issue, she will be in the following position:

	£
Value of holding after rights issue ((2,000 + 500) × £1.54)	3,850
Cost of buying the rights shares (500 × £1.30)	(650)
	3,200

If the investor sells the rights, she will be in the following position:

	£
Value of holding after rights issue (2,000 × £1.54)	3,080
Sale of rights (500 × £0.24)	120
	3,200

If the investor lets the rights offer lapse, she will be in the following position:

	£
Value of holding after rights issue (2,000 × £1.54)	3,080

As we can see, the first two options should leave her in the same position concerning net wealth as before the rights issue. Before the rights issue she had 2,000 shares worth £1.60 each, or £3,200 in total. However, she will be worse off if she allows the rights offer to lapse than under the other two options.

In practice, businesses will typically sell the rights on behalf of those investors who seem to be allowing them to lapse. It will then pass on the proceeds in order to ensure that they are not worse off as a result of the issue.

When considering a rights issue, the directors must first consider the amount of funds needing to be raised. This will depend on the future plans and needs of the business. The directors must then decide on the issue price of the rights shares. Normally, this decision is not critical. In Example 15.2, the business made a one-for-four issue with the price of the rights shares set at £1.30. However, it could have raised the same amount by making a one-for-two issue and setting the rights price at £0.65, a one-for-one issue and setting the price at £0.325, and so on. The issue price that is finally decided upon will not affect the value of the underlying assets of the business or the proportion of the underlying assets and earnings to which each shareholder is entitled. The directors must ensure that the issue price is not above the current market price of the shares, however, or the issue will be unsuccessful.

Real World 15.11 describes how Centrica plc, the UK energy generator and supplier, made a rights issue to fund the acquisition of another business.

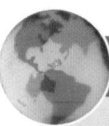

Real World 15.11

Lots of energy

In late 2008, Centrica made a three-for-eight rights issue that raised £2.2 billion. Share-holders took up 91 per cent of the issue. The remaining 9 per cent of the shares were placed with other investors. The rights price was at a discount of 48 per cent to the pre-rights announcement price. This was an unusually large discount.

> The new finance was used, along with some cash raised from loan note issues, to fund the acquisition of 25 per cent of the shares in British Energy Group plc, the UK nuclear energy generator, from its parent business, Electricité de France, the French energy business, in early 2009.
>
> *Source*: Based on information taken from 'Cenrtica looks to US in quest for further acquisitions', E. Crooks, *Financial Times*. 30 January 2009.

Offers for sale and public issues

→ An **offer for sale** usually involves a business that trades as a public limited company selling a new issue of shares to a financial institution known as an *issuing house*. However, shares that are already in issue may also be sold to an issuing house. In this case, existing shareholders agree to sell all or some of their shares to the issuing house. The issuing house will, in turn, sell the shares, purchased from either the business or its shareholders, to the public. The issuing house will publish a prospectus that sets out details of the business and the type of shares to be sold, and investors will be invited to apply for shares. The advantage of this type of issue, from the business's viewpoint, is that the sale proceeds of the shares are certain.

→ A **public issue** involves the business making a direct invitation to the public to purchase its shares. Typically, this is done through a newspaper advertisement. The shares may, once again, be either a new issue or those already in issue. An offer for sale and a public issue will both result in a widening of share ownership in the business.

In practical terms, the net effect on the business is much the same whether there is an offer for sale or a public issue. As we have seen, the administrative costs of a public issue can be very large. Some share issues by Stock Exchange listed businesses arise from the initial listing of the business, often known as an *initial public offering (IPO)*. Other share issues are undertaken by businesses that are already listed and that are seeking additional finance from investors; usually such issues are known as a *seasoned equity offering (SEO)*. IPOs are very popular, but SEOs are rather less so (see reference 1 at the end of the chapter).

Issue by tender

When making an issue of shares, the business or the issuing house will usually set a price for the shares. Establishing this may not be an easy task, however, particularly where the market is volatile or where the business has unique characteristics. One

→ way of dealing with this issue-price problem is to make a **tender issue** of shares. This involves the investors determining the price at which the shares are issued. Although the business (or issuing house) may publish a reserve price to help guide investors, it will be up to the individual investor to determine the number of shares to be purchased and the price the investor is prepared to pay. Once the offers from investors have all been received and recorded, a price at which all the shares can be sold will be established (known as the *striking price*). Investors who have made offers at, or above, the striking price will be issued shares at the striking price; offers received below the striking price will be rejected. Note that all of the shares will be issued at the same price irrespective of the prices actually offered by individual investors.

Although this form of issue is adopted occasionally, it is not popular with investors, and is therefore not in widespread use.

Private placings

→ A **private placing** does not involve an invitation to the public to subscribe for shares. Instead the shares are 'placed' with selected investors, such as large financial institutions. This can be a quick and relatively cheap form of raising funds, because savings can be made in advertising and legal costs. However, it can result in the ownership of the business being concentrated in a few hands. Sometimes, unlisted businesses seeking relatively small amounts of cash will make this form of issue.

Real World 15.12 describes how JJB Sports plc, the sportswear and accessories business, used a placing to raise finance. Though, typically, placings tend to involve shares being issued to a number of different investors, in this case all of the shares were taken up by another similar business.

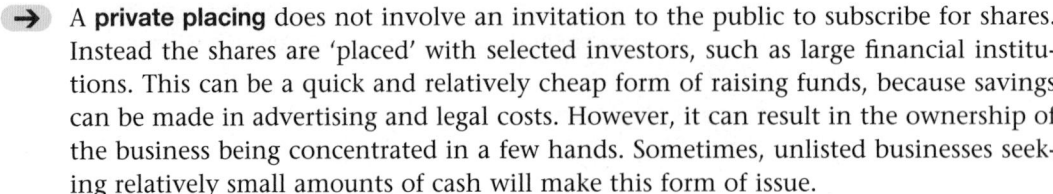

Real World 15.12

Wigan Athletic 0 – 1 Newcastle United

In October 2008, JJB Sports plc issued shares equivalent to 5 per cent of their share capital through a placing. The shares were all taken up by Sports Direct International plc.

JJB was, in effect, founded by the former professional footballer Dave Whelan. He is the owner of Wigan Athletic Football Club, though he had recently sold off his large shareholding in JJB.

Sports Direct's founder and largest shareholder (72.2 per cent of the shares) is Mike Ashley, who also owns Newcastle United Football Club.

Source: Information taken from 'JJB agrees stake deal with Sports Direct', E. Rigby, *Financial Times*, 18 October 2008.

Placings are now a very popular way of issuing new shares, both by newly listed and more seasoned listed businesses. They probably account for more than 50 per cent of new shares issued (see reference 1 at the end of the chapter).

Bonus issues

We should recall from Chapter 4 that a bonus issue is not a means of raising finance. It is simply converting one part of the equity (reserves) into another (ordinary shares). No cash changes hands; this benefits neither the business nor the shareholders.

The role of the Stock Exchange

Earlier we considered the various forms of long-term capital that are available to a busi-
→ ness. In this section we examine the role that the **Stock Exchange** plays in providing finance for businesses. The Stock Exchange acts as both an important *primary* and *secondary* capital market for businesses. As a primary market, its function is to enable businesses to raise new finance. As a secondary market, its function is to enable investors to sell their securities (including shares and loan notes) with ease. Thus, it provides a 'second-hand' market where shares and loan notes already in issue may be bought and sold.

To enable it to issue shares or loan notes through the Stock Exchange, a business must be 'listed'. Similarly, it must also be Stock Exchange listed before its existing shares and loan notes can be bought and sold there. Listing means that the business must meet fairly stringent requirements concerning size, profit history, information disclosure and so on.

Real World 15.13 describes how two of the owners of moneysupermarket.com, a business that provides online financial information, benefited from its IPO (initial public offering).

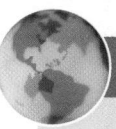

Real World 15.13

Cashing in

Paul Doughty, the CFO (chief financial officer) of moneysupermarket.com, is nearly £3 million richer after his company's IPO despite a below-par fundraising.

The internet broker, which helps consumers to find the cheapest financial products, completed its float last week but ended up with an offer price of £1.70 a share, at the foot of the £1.70 to £2.10 range.

A company spokesperson confirmed that Doughty had cashed in 1.6 million shares, but even with the disappointing showing, the CFO of the UK's leading price-comparison website made himself close to £3 million.

If the IPO offer price had been set at the top end of the range, Doughty would have earned close to £3.5 million. But his windfall was dwarfed by chief executive, Simon Nixon, who cashed in £60.3 million shares, netting £100 million. He still holds more than 57 per cent of the company, which is worth more than £800 million.

Source: 'Internet FD is in the money after floatation', David Jetuah, *Accountancy Age*, 2 August 2007, p. 3.

Real World 15.14 explains how new issues are not always good investments for those who take up the shares concerned.

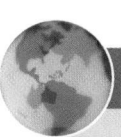

Real World 15.14

New issues but old problems
FT

It seems that we should be cautious when invited to subscribe to a new issue of shares arising from an initial listing on the Stock Exchange. The following extract from the *Financial Times* tells us why investing in new business flotations may be bad for our wealth.

Back in 1940 Benjamin Graham and David Dodd, the fathers of security analysis, wrote: 'the odds are so strongly against the man who buys into these new flotations that he might as well throw three-quarters of the money out the window and keep the rest in the bank.'

Now confirmation of the poor record of recent new issues comes from an Ernst and Young survey. The accountancy group looked at the records of 200 companies that floated on the UK market between 1998 and 2002. It found that only 39% of the sample had increased profits since flotation (although 82% had seen their sales grow).

Real World 15.14 continued

This should not come as too much of a surprise. Companies are most likely to float on the market when their recent trading record is impressive. But periods of rapid growth can be very dangerous for a company – costs and management ambitions can get out of hand. Furthermore, no business can grow rapidly forever, and there is a risk that the flotation occurs just at the moment when the decline is beginning.

And, as Ernst and Young points out, the very act of flotation incurs significant costs and can divert management focus from the business. The money raised can also burn a hole in the management's pockets, leading to a flurry of spending that would disgrace a football manager.

All this is slightly discouraging, given that the primary role of the stock market is to allow growing businesses to raise capital. But perhaps a certain amount of investor greed (and gullibility) is necessary if industry is to gain access to finance. New issue investors have been fooled before; they will be fooled again.

Source: 'Greed and gullibility keep new issues afloat', *Financial Times*, 8 August 2003, p. 22.

Despite the problems with IPOs they have been quite popular in terms of the value of funds raised over recent years (see reference 1 at the end of the chapter). There are signs that the recession, which began in 2008, is leading to a reduction in IPOs. This is not necessarily the case with seasoned businesses, many of whom are seeking to raise additional share capital to shore up their finances and to reduce their levels of borrowing.

Advantages of a listing

The secondary market role of the Stock Exchange means that shares and other financial claims are easily transferable. Furthermore, their prices are constantly under scrutiny by investors and skilled analysts. This helps to promote the tendency for the price quoted for a particular business's shares to reflect their true worth at that particular time. These factors can bring real benefits to a business.

Activity 15.14

What kinds of benefits might a business gain from its shares being listed?

If it is generally accepted that shares can easily be sold for prices that tend to reflect their true worth, investors will have more confidence to invest. The business may benefit from this greater investor confidence by finding it easier to raise long-term finance and by obtaining this finance at a lower cost, as investors will view their investment as being less risky.

It is worth pointing out that investors are not obliged to use the Stock Exchange as the means of transferring shares in a listed business. However, it is usually the most convenient way of buying or selling shares.

The Stock Exchange can be a useful vehicle for a successful entrepreneur wishing to realise the value of the business that has been built up. By floating (listing) the shares on the Stock Exchange, and thereby making the shares available to the public, the entrepreneur will usually benefit from a gain in the value of the shares held and will be able to realise that gain easily, if required, by selling some shares.

Disadvantages of a listing

A Stock Exchange listing can have certain disadvantages for a business. These include:

- Strict rules are imposed on listed businesses, including requirements for levels of financial disclosure additional to those already imposed by International Financial Reporting Standards (for example, the listing rules require that half-yearly financial reports are published).
- Financial analysts, financial journalists and others tend to monitor closely the activities of listed businesses, particularly larger ones. Such scrutiny may not be welcome, particularly if the business is dealing with sensitive issues or is experiencing operational problems.
- It is often suggested that listed businesses are under pressure to perform well over the short term. This pressure may detract from undertaking projects that will yield benefits only in the longer term. If the market becomes disenchanted with the business, and the price of its shares falls, this may make it vulnerable to a takeover bid from another business.
- The costs of obtaining a listing are huge and this may be a real deterrent for some businesses.

To make an initial public offering, a business will rely on the help of various specialists such as lawyers, accountants and bankers. As we have seen, this represents a significant cost to the business.

Though there are over 1,000 UK businesses listed on the London Stock Exchange, in terms of equity market value, the market is dominated by just a few large ones, as is shown in **Real World 15.15**.

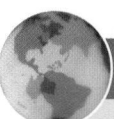

Real World 15.15

Listing to one side

At 31 December 2008 there were 1,080 businesses that had a London Stock Exchange listing. Just 82 of them (8 per cent) accounted for 84 per cent of their total equity market value.

A total of 205 businesses (19 per cent of listed businesses) accounted for 94 per cent of total equity market value.

Source: Main Market Fact Sheet, London Stock Exchange, December 2008, Table 8.

Real World 15.16 provides an analysis of the ownership of shares in UK listed businesses at the end of 2006.

Real World 15.16

Ownership of UK listed shares

At the end of 2006, the proportion of shares of UK listed businesses held by UK investors was as shown in Figure 15.5.

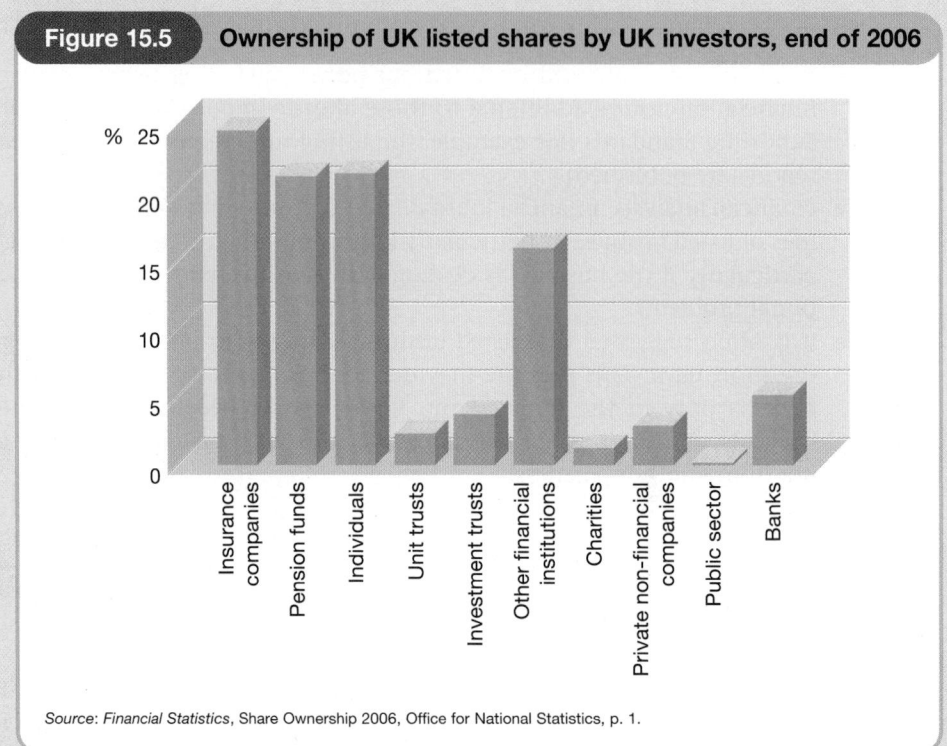

Figure 15.5 Ownership of UK listed shares by UK investors, end of 2006

Source: *Financial Statistics*, Share Ownership 2006, Office for National Statistics, p. 1.

A striking feature of the ownership of UK shares is the extent of overseas ownership. At the end of 2006 this accounted for 40 per cent of the total; in 1963 it was 7 per cent and has grown fairly steadily ever since. This is broadly mirrored by the extent to which UK investors own shares of businesses based elsewhere in the world. It reflects increasing levels of globalisation of business.

Another striking feature is the extent to which large financial institutions now dominate the ownership of UK listed shares. In 1963, 58 per cent of those UK shares owned by UK investors were owned by individuals. At the end of 2006 it was only 21 per cent.

Of course, ultimately individuals own all of the shares. This may be through having a life insurance or pension policy, by investing through unit and investment trusts and so on.

Going private

Such are the disadvantages of a stock market listing that many businesses have 'delisted'. This has obviously denied them the advantages of a listing, but it has avoided the disadvantages.

The Alternative Investment Market

→ The **Alternative Investment Market (AIM)** was established in June 1995 by the London Stock Exchange for smaller, young and growing businesses. AIM is similar in style to the main London Stock Exchange but it is cheaper for the business to enter. Obtaining an AIM listing and raising funds costs the typical business about £500,000. Many AIM listed businesses are family-based ones. AIM has proved to be a very successful market where new equity finance can be raised and shares can be traded. Businesses listed on AIM tend to have market values in the range £1 million to £250 million, with none of them being greater than £1,000 million, as is shown by **Real World 15.17**.

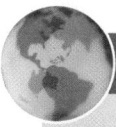

Real World 15.17

Take AIM

At 31 January 2009, there were 1,529 businesses that had an AIM listing. Their distribution according to market value is shown in Figure 15.6.

Figure 15.6 Distribution of AIM listed companies by equity market value (January 2009)

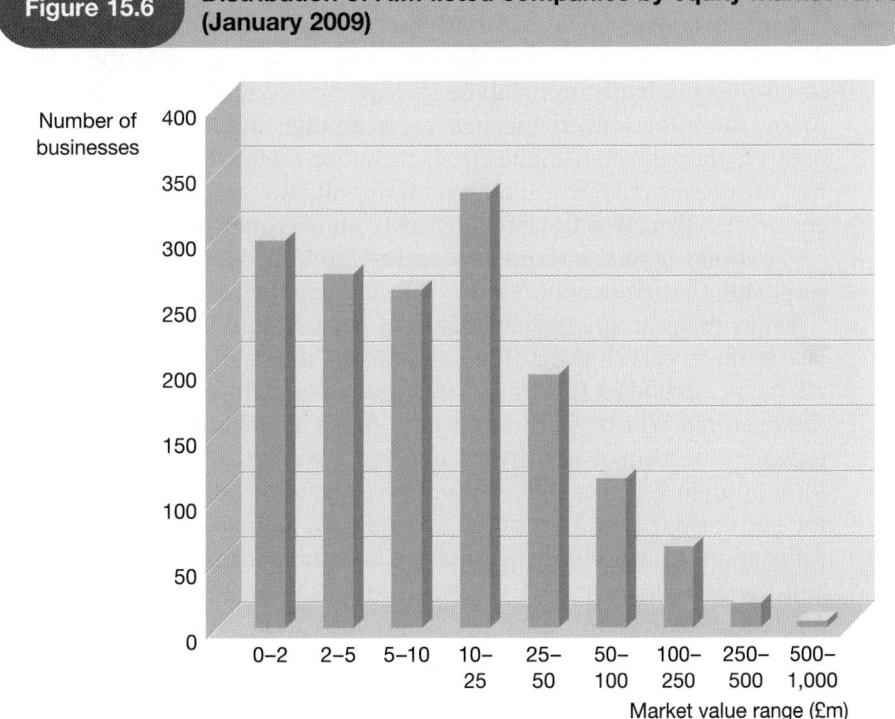

It seems that few AIM listed businesses (only about one in eight) have a market capitalisation greater than £50 million. The most popular range is £10 million to £25 million.

Source: AIM Market Statistics, London Stock Exchange, January 2009.

The listing requirements of AIM are less stringent than those of a full listing. However AIM listed businesses tend to be more risky than fully listed ones, which can make AIM listed shares less attractive.

AIM listed companies include Majestic Wine plc, the wine retailer, and the football clubs Millwall and Preston North End. Also AIM listed is LiDCO Group plc, the heart monitoring equipment developer that we met in Real World 6.3 when dealing with the statement of cash flows.

Short-term sources of external finance

Short-term, in this context, is usually taken to mean up to one year. Figure 15.2 indicated that the major sources of short-term external finance are

- bank overdrafts
- debt factoring
- invoice discounting.

These are discussed below.

Bank overdrafts

→ A **bank overdraft** enables a business to maintain a negative balance on its bank account. It represents a very flexible form of borrowing as the size of the overdraft can (subject to bank approval) be increased or decreased more or less instantaneously. An overdraft is relatively inexpensive to arrange and interest rates are often very competitive, though often higher than those for a term loan. As with all borrowing, the rate of interest charged on an overdraft will vary according to how creditworthy the customer is perceived to be by the bank. An overdraft is normally fairly easy to arrange – sometimes by a telephone call to the bank. In view of these advantages, it is not surprising that an overdraft is an extremely popular form of short-term finance.

Banks prefer to grant overdrafts that are self-liquidating, that is, the funds applied will result in cash inflows that will extinguish the overdraft balance. The banks may ask for a cash budget (projected statement of cash flows) from the business to see when the overdraft will be repaid and how much finance is required. The bank may also require some form of security on amounts advanced. One potential drawback with this form of finance is that the overdraft is repayable on demand. This may pose problems for a business that is short of funds. However, many businesses operate for many years using an overdraft, simply because the bank remains confident of their ability to repay and the arrangement suits the business. Thus the bank overdraft, though in theory regarded as short-term, often becomes a long-term source of finance.

Debt factoring

→ **Debt factoring** is a service offered by a financial institution (known as a *factor*). Many of the large factors are subsidiaries of commercial banks. Debt factoring involves the factor taking over the business's debt collection. In addition to operating normal credit control procedures, a factor may offer to undertake credit investigations and to provide protection for approved credit sales. The factor is usually prepared to make an advance to the business of a maximum of 80 per cent of approved trade receivables. The charge made for the factoring service is based on total sales revenue, and is often 2 to 3 per cent of sales revenue. Any advances made to the business by the factor will attract a rate of interest similar to the rate charged on bank overdrafts.

Debt factoring is, in effect, outsourcing the trade receivables control to a specialist subcontractor. Many businesses find a factoring arrangement very convenient. It can result in savings in credit management and create more certainty with the cash flows. It can also release the time of key personnel for more profitable activities. This may be extremely important for smaller businesses that rely on the talent and skills of a few key individuals. However, there is a possibility that a factoring arrangement will be seen as an indication that the business is experiencing financial difficulties. This may have an adverse effect on the confidence of customers, suppliers and staff. For this reason, some businesses try to conceal the factoring arrangement by collecting debts on behalf of the factor. When considering a factoring agreement, the costs and likely benefits arising must be identified and carefully weighed.

Figure 15.7 shows the factoring process diagrammatically.

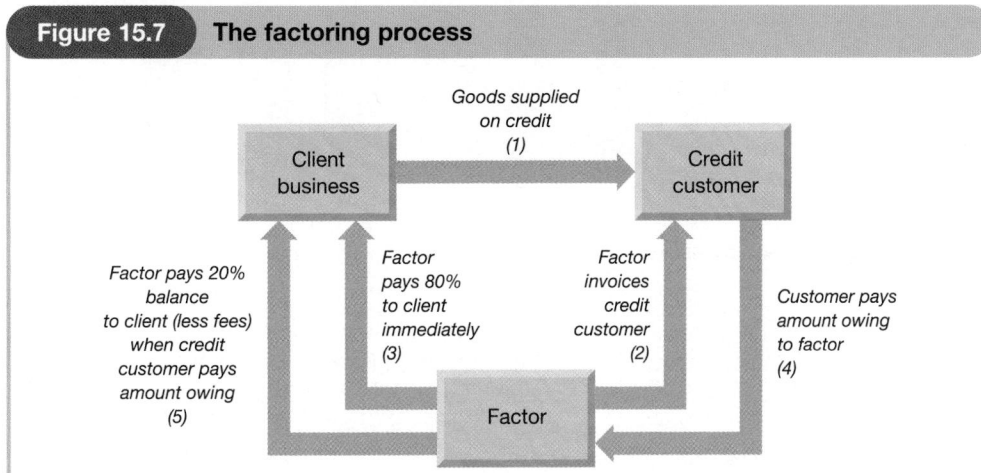

Figure 15.7   The factoring process

There are three main parties to the factoring agreement. The client business will sell goods or services on credit and the factor will take responsibility for invoicing the customer and collecting the amount owing. The factor will then pay the client business the invoice amount, less fees and interest, in two stages. The first stage typically represents 80 per cent of the invoice value and will be paid immediately after the goods or services have been delivered to the customer. The second stage will represent the balance outstanding and will usually be paid when the customer has paid the factor the amount owing.

Invoice discounting

Invoice discounting involves a factor or other financial institution providing a loan based on a proportion of the face value of a business's credit sales outstanding (that is, the trade receivables). The amount advanced is usually 75 to 80 per cent of the value of the approved sales invoices outstanding. The business must agree to repay the advance within a relatively short period, perhaps 60 or 90 days. The responsibility for collecting the trade receivables outstanding remains with the business, and repayment of the advance is not dependent on the trade receivables being collected. Invoice discounting will not result in such a close relationship developing between the business and the financial institution as results with factoring. It may be a short-term arrangement, whereas debt factoring usually involves a longer-term relationship.

Real World 15.18 shows the relative importance of invoice discounting and factoring.

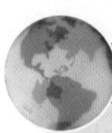

Real World 15.18

The popularity of invoice discounting and factoring

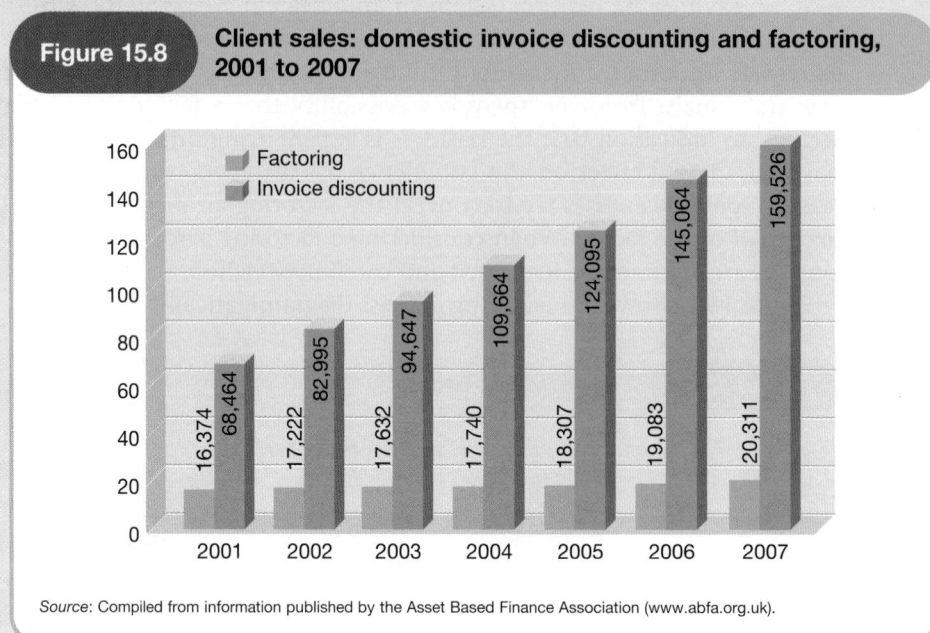

Figure 15.8   Client sales: domestic invoice discounting and factoring, 2001 to 2007

Source: Compiled from information published by the Asset Based Finance Association (www.abfa.org.uk).

In recent years, client use of invoice discounting has been much more popular and has risen much more sharply than client use of factoring. During 2007, for example, client use of factoring grew by 6 per cent whereas invoice discounting grew by 10 per cent (see Figure 15.8). Client sales using invoice discounting in 2007 were nearly eight times the client sales using factoring.

There are three main reasons for the relative popularity of invoice discounting:

- It is a confidential form of financing that the business's customers will know nothing about.
- The service charge for invoice discounting is generally only 0.2 to 0.3 per cent of sales revenue, compared with 2.0 to 3.0 per cent for factoring.
- Many businesses are unwilling to relinquish control of their customers' records. Customers are an important resource of the business, and many wish to retain control over all aspects of their relationship with their customers.

→   Factoring and invoice discounting are forms of **asset-based financing**, as the asset of trade receivables is in effect used as security for the cash advances received by the business.

Long-term versus short-term borrowing

Having decided that some form of borrowing is required to finance the business, managers must then decide whether it should be long-term or short-term in form. There are many issues that should be taken into account when making this decision. These include the following:

● *Matching.* The business may attempt to match the type of borrowing with the nature of the assets held. Thus, long-term borrowing might finance assets that form part of the permanent operating base of the business, including non-current assets and a certain level of current assets. This leaves assets held for a short period, such as current assets held to meet seasonal increases in demand (for example, inventories), to be financed by short-term borrowing, because short-term borrowing tends to be more flexible in that funds can be raised and repaid at short notice. Figure 15.9 shows this funding division graphically.

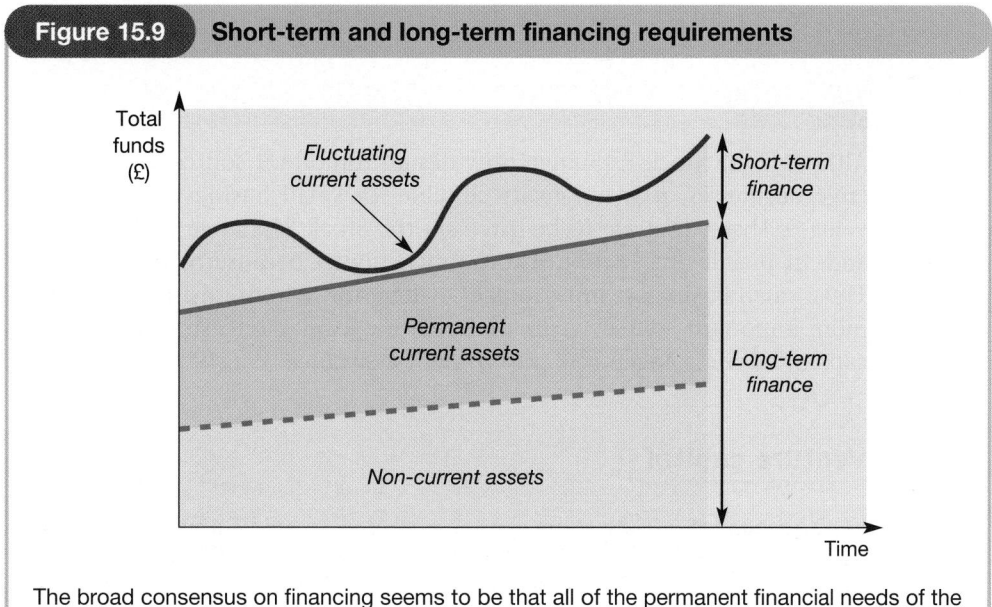

| Figure 15.9 | Short-term and long-term financing requirements |

The broad consensus on financing seems to be that all of the permanent financial needs of the business should come from long-term sources. Only that part of current assets that fluctuates on a short-term, probably a seasonal, basis should be financed from short-term sources.

A business may wish to match the asset life exactly with the period of the related borrowing; however, this may not be possible because of the difficulty of predicting the life of many assets.

● *Flexibility.* Short-term borrowing may be a useful means of postponing a commitment to taking on long-term borrowing. This may be seen as desirable if interest rates are high and it is forecast that they will fall in the future. Short-term borrowing does not usually incur penalties if there is early repayment of the amount outstanding, whereas some form of financial penalty may arise if long-term borrowing is repaid early.

● *Refunding risk.* Short-term borrowing has to be renewed more frequently than long-term borrowing. This may create problems for the business if it is already in financial difficulties or if there is a shortage of funds available for lending.

● *Interest rates.* Interest payable on long-term borrowing is often higher than for short-term borrowing, as lenders require a higher return where their funds are locked up for a long period. This fact may make short-term borrowing a more attractive source of finance for a business. However, there may be other costs associated with borrowing (arrangement fees, for example) to be taken into account. The more frequently borrowings must be renewed, the higher these costs will be.

Activity (15.15)

Some businesses may take up a less cautious financing position than that shown in Figure 15.9, and others may take up a more cautious one. How would the diagram differ under each of these options?

A less cautious position would mean relying on short-term finance to help fund part of the permanent capital base. A more cautious position would mean relying on long-term finance to help finance the fluctuating assets of the business.

Providing long-term finance for the small business

Although the Stock Exchange provides an important source of long-term finance for large businesses, it is not really suitable for small businesses. The aggregate market value of shares that are to be listed on the Stock Exchange must be at least £700,000 and, in practice, the amounts are much higher because of the high costs of listing. Thus, small businesses must look elsewhere for help in raising long-term finance. The more important sources of finance that are available to small businesses are venture capital, business angels and government assistance. We shall now consider these.

Venture capital

→ **Venture capital** is long-term capital provided to small and medium-sized businesses that wish to grow but do not have ready access to stock markets because of the prohibitively large costs of obtaining a listing. The businesses of interest to the venture capitalist will have higher levels of risk than would normally be acceptable to traditional providers of finance, such as the major clearing banks. The attraction for the venture capitalist of investing in higher-risk businesses is the prospect of higher returns.

Many small businesses are designed to provide the owners with a particular lifestyle and with job satisfaction. These kinds of businesses are not of interest to venture capitalists, as they are unlikely to provide the desired financial returns. Instead, venture capitalists look for businesses where the owners are seeking significant sales revenue and profit growth and need some outside help in order to achieve this.

The risks associated with the business can vary in practice. They are often due to the nature of the products or the fact that it is a new business that either lacks a trading record or has new management or both of these.

Venture capitalists provide long-term capital in the form of share and loan finance for different situations, including:

- *Start-up capital.* This is available to businesses that are not fully developed. They may need finance to help refine the business concept or to engage in product development or initial marketing. They have not yet reached the stage where they are trading.
- *Early-stage capital.* This is available for businesses that are ready to start trading.
- *Expansion capital.* This is aimed at providing additional funding for existing, growing businesses.

- *Buy-out or buy-in capital.* This is used to fund the acquisition of a business either by the existing management team ('buy-out') or by a new management team ('buy-in'). Management buy-outs (MBOs) and buy-ins (MBIs) often occur where a large business wishes to divest itself of one of its operating units or where a family business wishes to sell out because of succession problems.
- *Rescue capital.* To help turn around businesses that are in difficulties.

The venture capitalist will often make a substantial investment in the business (usually more than £100,000), and this will often take the form of ordinary shares. However, some of the funding may be in the form of preference shares or loans. To keep an eye on the sum invested, the venture capitalist will usually require a representative on the board of directors as a condition of the investment. The venture capitalist may not be looking for a very quick return, and may well be prepared to invest in a business for five years or more. The return may take the form of a capital gain on the realisation of the investment (typically selling the shares).

Though venture capital is extremely important for some small businesses, the vast majority of small businesses obtain their finance from other sources. **Real World 15.19** shows the main sources of finance for small businesses in the UK.

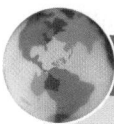

Real World 15.19

Small business funding

Bank finance, such as overdrafts and loans, is the main source of external finance for small businesses, as the pie chart in Figure 15.10 shows.

Figure 15.10   Financing small businesses, 2002 to 2004

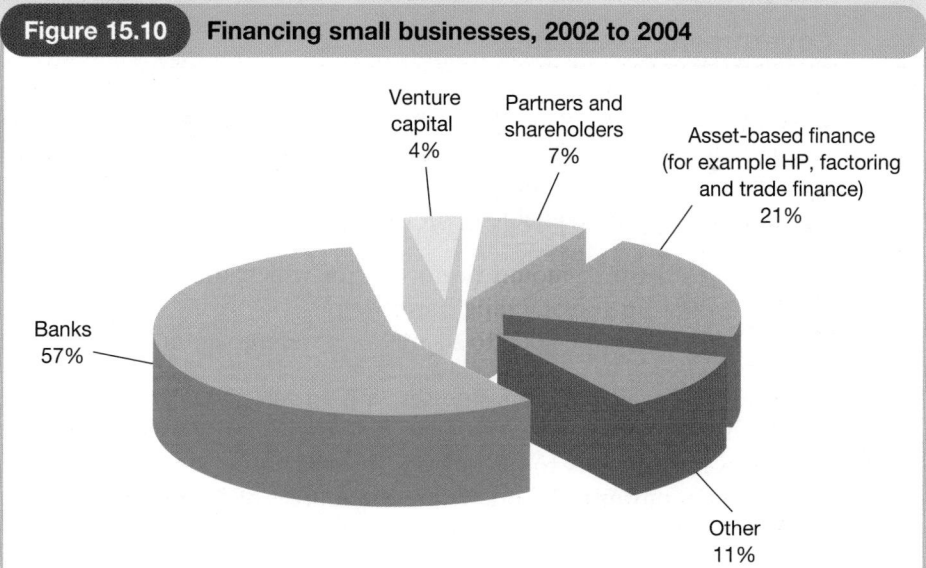

Venture capital, though very important to some small businesses, represents a very small part of the total finance raised. Bank finance remains the most important source of external finance, followed by asset-based finance, such as hire purchase, factoring and trade finance.

Source: British Enterprise: Thriving or Surviving?, A. Cosh and A. Hughes, Centre for Business Research, University of Cambridge, 2007.

Business angels

→ **Business angels** are often wealthy individuals who have been successful in business. They are usually willing to invest, through a shareholding, between £10,000 and £750,000 in a start-up business or in a business that is wishing to expand. If larger amounts are required, a syndicate of business angels may be formed to raise the money. Business angels typically make one or two investments over a three-year period and will usually be prepared to invest for a period of between three and five years. They normally have a minority stake in the business, and although they do not usually become involved in its day-to-day management, they tend to take an interest, more generally, in the way that the business is managed.

Business angels fill an important gap in the market as the size and nature of investments they find appealing are often not so appealing to venture capitalists. They can be attractive to small businesses because they may

● make investment decisions quickly, particularly if they are familiar with the industry in which the new business operates;
● offer useful skills, experience and business contacts;
● accept lower financial returns than those required from venture capitalists in order to have the opportunity to become involved in a new and interesting project.

Business angels offer an informal source of share finance and it is not always easy for owners of small businesses to identify a suitable angel. However, numerous business angel networks have now developed to help owners of small businesses find their 'perfect partner'.

The panellists on the BBC TV programme *Dragons' Den* are business angels.

Government assistance

One of the most effective ways in which the UK government assists small businesses is through the Enterprise Finance Guarantee Scheme (formerly the Small Firms Loan Guarantee Scheme). This aims to help small businesses that have viable business plans but lack the security to enable them to borrow. The scheme guarantees:

● 75 per cent of the amount borrowed, for which the borrower pays a premium of 2 per cent on the outstanding borrowing
● loans ranging from £1,000 to £1 million for a maximum period of ten years.

The scheme is available for businesses with annual sales revenue of up to £25 million.

In addition to other forms of financial assistance, such as government grants and tax incentives for investors to buy shares in small businesses, the government also helps by providing information concerning the sources of finance available.

Self-assessment question 15.1

Helsim Ltd is a wholesaler and distributor of electrical components. The most recent draft financial statements of the business revealed the following:

Income statement for the year

	£m	£m
Sales revenue		14.2
Opening inventories	3.2	
Purchases	8.4	
	11.6	
Closing inventories	(3.8)	(7.8)
Gross profit		6.4
Administration expenses		(3.0)
Distribution expenses		(2.1)
Operating profit		1.3
Finance costs		(0.8)
Profit before taxation		0.5
Taxation		(0.2)
Profit for the year		0.3

Statement of financial position as at the end of the year

ASSETS	£m
Non-current assets	
Property, plant and equipment	
Land and buildings	3.8
Equipment	0.9
Motor vehicles	0.5
	5.2
Current assets	
Inventories	3.8
Trade receivables	3.6
Cash at bank	0.1
	7.5
Total assets	12.7
EQUITY AND LIABILITIES	
Equity	
Share capital	2.0
Retained earnings	1.8
	3.8
Non-current liabilities	
Loan notes (secured on land and buildings)	3.5
Current liabilities	
Trade payables	1.8
Short-term borrowings	3.6
	5.4
Total equity and liabilities	12.7

→

Self-assessment question 15.1 continued

Notes:
(1) Land and buildings are shown at their current market value. Equipment and motor vehicles are shown at their written-down values (that is, cost less accumulated depreciation).
(2) No dividends have been paid to ordinary shareholders for the past three years.

In recent months, trade payables have been pressing for payment. The managing director has therefore decided to reduce the level of trade payables to an average of 40 days outstanding. To achieve this, he has decided to approach the bank with a view to increasing the overdraft (the short-term borrowings comprise only a bank overdraft). The business is currently paying 10 per cent a year interest on the overdraft.

Required:
(a) Comment on the liquidity position of the business.
(b) Calculate the amount of finance required to reduce trade payables, from the level shown on the statement of financial position, to an average of 40 days outstanding.
(c) State, with reasons, how you consider the bank would react to the proposal to grant an additional overdraft facility.
(d) Identify four sources of finance (internal or external, but excluding a bank overdraft) that may be suitable to finance the reduction in trade payables, and state, with reasons, which of these you consider the most appropriate.

The answer to this question can be found at the back of the book on pages 736–7.

Summary

The main points of this chapter may be summarised as follows.

Sources of finance

- Internal sources of finance do not require the agreement of anyone beyond the directors and managers of the business, whereas external sources of finance do require the compliance of 'outsiders'.
- Long-term sources of finance are not due for repayment within one year whereas short-term sources are due for repayment within one year.
- The higher the level of risk associated with investing in a particular form of finance, the higher the level of return that will be expected by investors.

Internal sources of finance

- The major internal source of long-term finance is retained profit.
- The main short-term sources of internal finance are tighter credit control of receivables, reducing inventories levels and delaying payments to trade payables.

External sources of finance

- The main external, *long-term* sources of finance are ordinary shares, preference shares, borrowing, leases, hire purchase agreements and securitisation.

- Ordinary shares are, from the investor's point of view, normally considered to be the most risky form of investment and, therefore, provide the highest expected returns. Lending is normally the least risky and provides the lowest expected returns to investors.

- Leases and hire-purchase agreements allow a business to obtain immediate possession of an asset without having to pay the cost of acquiring the asset.

- The level of gearing associated with a business is often an important factor in assessing the level of risk and returns to ordinary shareholders.

- The main sources of external *short-term* finance are bank overdrafts, debt factoring and invoice discounting.

- When considering the choice between long-term and short-term sources of borrowing, factors such as matching the type of borrowing with the nature of the assets held, the need for flexibility, refunding risk and interest rates should be taken into account.

Share issues

- Share issues that involve the payment of cash by investors can take the form of a rights issue, public issue, offer for sale or a private placing.

- A rights issue is made to existing shareholders. Most share issues are of this type as the law requires that shares that are to be issued for cash must first be offered to existing shareholders.

- A public issue involves a direct issue to the public and an offer for sale involves an indirect issue to the public.

- A private placing is an issue of shares to selected investors.

The Stock Exchange

- The Stock Exchange is an important primary and secondary market in capital for large businesses. However, obtaining a Stock Exchange listing can have certain drawbacks for a business.

The Alternative Investment Market (AIM)

- AIM is another important primary and secondary market managed by the London Stock Exchange for smaller, growing businesses. It tends to be a cheaper way for a business to become listed.

Small businesses

- Venture capital is long-term capital for small or medium-sized businesses that are not listed on the Stock Exchange. These businesses often have higher levels of risk but provide the venture capitalist with the prospect of higher levels of return.

- Business angels are wealthy individuals who are willing to invest in businesses at either an early stage or expansion stage of development.

- The government assists small businesses through guaranteeing loans and by providing grants and tax incentives.

MyAccountingLab **Now check your progress in your personal Study Plan**

Key terms

term loan   p. 595
loan notes   p. 595
loan stock   p. 595
eurobond   p. 596
deep discount bond   p. 598
convertible loan notes   p. 598
warrants   p. 599
financial derivatives   p. 599
mortgage   p. 599
loan covenant   p. 600
finance lease   p. 602
operating lease   p. 602
sale and leaseback   p. 604
hire purchase   p. 605
securitisation   p. 606

rights issue   p. 610
offer for sale   p. 613
public issue   p. 613
tender issue   p. 613
private placing   p. 614
Stock Exchange   p. 614
Alternative Investment Market
    (AIM)   p. 619
bank overdraft   p. 620
debt factoring   p. 620
invoice discounting   p. 621
asset-based financing   p. 622
venture capital   p. 624
business angel   p. 626

References

1   **London Stock Exchange Main Market Statistics**, December 2008.

2   'The direct costs of UK rights issues and open offers', Armitage S., **European Financial Management**, March 2000.

3   **The Cost of Capital: An International Comparison**, London Stock Exchange, 2006.

Further reading

If you would like to explore the topics covered in this chapter in more depth, we recommend the following books:

Business Finance: Theory and Practice *McLaney E.*, 8th edn, Financial Times Prentice Hall, 2009, chapter 8.

Corporate Finance *Brealey R., Myers S. and Allen F.*, 8th edn, McGraw-Hill, 2005, chapters 14, 25 and 26.

Corporate Finance and Investment *Pike R. and Neale B.*, 5th edn, Prentice Hall International, 2005, chapters 15 and 16.

Corporate Financial Management *Arnold G.*, 3rd edn, Financial Times Prentice Hall, 2005, chapters 9 to 12.

Review questions

Answers to these questions can be found at the back of the book on pages 749–50.

15.1 What are the benefits to a business of issuing share warrants?

15.2 Why might a business that has a Stock Exchange listing revert to being unlisted?

15.3 Distinguish between an offer for sale and a public issue of shares.

15.4 Distinguish between invoice discounting and factoring.

Exercises

Exercises 15.3 to 15.8 are more advanced than Exercises 15.1 to 15.2. Those with **coloured numbers** have answers at the back of the book, starting on page 800.

If you wish to try more exercises, visit the students' side of the Companion Website and MyAccountingLab.

15.1 H. Brown (Portsmouth) Ltd produces a range of central heating systems for sale to builders' merchants. As a result of increasing demand for the business's products, the directors have decided to expand production. The cost of acquiring new plant and machinery and the increase in working capital requirements are planned to be financed by a mixture of long-term and short-term borrowing.

Required:
(a) Discuss the major factors that should be taken into account when deciding on the appropriate mix of long-term and short-term borrowing necessary to finance the expansion programme.
(b) Discuss the major factors that a lender should take into account when deciding whether to grant a long-term loan to the business.
(c) Identify three conditions that might be included in a long-term loan agreement.

15.2 Devonian plc has the following equity as at 30 November Year 4:

	£m
Ordinary shares 25p fully paid	50.0
General reserve	22.5
Retained earnings	25.5
	98.0

The business has no long-term borrowings.

In the year to 30 November Year 4, the operating profit (profit before interest and taxation) was £40m and it is expected that this will increase by 25 per cent during the forthcoming year. The business is listed on the London Stock Exchange and the share price as at 30 November Year 4 was £2.10.

The business wishes to raise £72m in order to re-equip one of its factories and is considering two possible financing options. The first option is to make a 1-for-5 rights issue at a discount price of £1.80 per share. The second option is to borrow long-term at an interest rate of 10 per cent a year. If the first option is taken, it is expected that the price/earnings (P/E) ratio will remain the same for the forthcoming year. If the second option is taken, it is estimated that the P/E ratio will fall by 10 per cent by the end of the forthcoming year.

Assume a tax rate of 30 per cent.

Required:
(a) Assuming a rights issue of shares is made, calculate:
 (1) the theoretical ex-rights price of an ordinary share in Devonian plc; and
 (2) the value of the rights for each original ordinary share.
(b) Calculate the price of an ordinary share in Devonian plc in one year's time assuming:
 (1) a rights issue is made; and
 (2) the required funds are borrowed.
 Comment on your findings.
(c) Explain why rights issues are usually made at a discount.
(d) From the business's viewpoint, how critical is the pricing of a rights issue likely to be?

15.3 Brocmar plc has 10 million ordinary £0.50 shares in issue. The market price of the shares is £1.80. The board of directors of the business wishes to finance a major project at a cost of £2.88 million. Forecasts suggest that the implementation of the project will add £0.4 million to after-tax earnings available to ordinary shareholders in the coming year. After-tax earnings for the year just completed were £2 million, but this figure is expected to decline to £1.8 million in the coming year if the project proposed is not undertaken. A rights issue at a 20 per cent discount on the existing market price is proposed. Issue expenses can be ignored.

Required:
(a) To assist the board in coming to a final decision, you are required to present information in the following format:
 ● Project not undertaken
  (1) earnings per share for the coming year.
 ● Project undertaken and financed by a rights issue
  (2) rights issue price per share
  (3) number of shares to be issued
  (4) earnings per share for the coming year
  (5) the theoretical ex-rights price per share.
 All workings should be shown separately.
(b) What information, other than that provided in the question, is needed before the board can make the investment decision?

15.4 Raphael Ltd is a small engineering business that has annual sales revenue of £2.4 million, all of which is on credit. In recent years, the business has experienced credit control problems. The average collection period for trade receivables has risen to 50 days even though the stated policy of the business is for payment to be made within 30 days. In addition, 1.5 per cent of sales are written off as bad debts each year.

The business has recently been in talks with a factor, which is prepared to make an advance to the business equivalent to 80 per cent of trade receivables, based on the assumption that customers will, in future, adhere to a 30-day payment period. The interest rate for the advance will be 11 per cent a year. The trade receivables are currently financed through a bank overdraft, which has an interest rate of 12 per cent a year. The factor will take over the credit control procedures of the business and this will result in a saving to the business of £18,000 a year. However, the factor will make a charge of 2 per cent of sales revenue for this service. The use of the factoring service is expected to eliminate the bad debts incurred by the business.

Required:

Calculate the net cost of the factor agreement to the business and state whether the business should take advantage of the opportunity to factor its trade receivables.

[*Hint*: To answer this question, compare the cost of existing trade credit policies (cost of investment in trade receivables and cost of bad debts) with the cost of using a factor (interest and other charges less the credit control savings.)]

15.5 Russell Ltd installs and services heating and ventilation systems for commercial premises. The business's most recent statement of financial position and income statement are as follows:

Statement of financial position

ASSETS	£000	£000
Non-current assets		
Property, plant and equipment		
Machinery and equipment at cost	883.6	
Accumulated depreciation	(328.4)	555.2
Motor vehicles at cost	268.8	
Accumulated depreciation	(82.2)	186.6
		741.8
Current assets		
Inventories at cost		293.2
Trade receivables		510.3
		803.5
Total assets		1,545.3
EQUITY AND LIABILITIES		
Equity		
£1 ordinary shares		400.0
General reserve		50.2
Retained earnings		382.2
		832.4
Non-current liabilities		
Borrowings – 12% loan notes (repayable in 5 years' time)		250.0
Current liabilities		
Trade payables		199.7
Taxation		128.0
Borrowings – Bank overdraft		135.2
		462.9
Total equity and liabilities		1,545.3

Income statement for the year

	£000
Sales revenue	5,207.8
Operating profit	542.0
Interest payable	(30.0)
Profit before taxation	512.0
Taxation (25%)	(128.0)
Profit for the year	384.0

Note:

Dividend paid during the year	153.6

The business wishes to invest in more machinery and equipment in order to cope with an upsurge in demand for its services. An additional operating profit of £120,000 a year is expected if an investment of £600,000 is made in plant and machinery.

The directors are considering an offer from venture capitalists to finance the expansion programme. The finance will be made available immediately through either:

- an issue of £1 ordinary shares at a premium on par of £3 a share; or
- an issue of £600,000 10 per cent loan notes at par.

The directors wish to maintain the same dividend payout ratio in future years as in past years whichever method of finance is chosen.

Required:
(a) For each of the financing schemes:
  (1) prepare a projected income statement for next year;
  (2) calculate the projected earnings per share for next year;
  (3) calculate the projected level of gearing as at the end of next year.
(b) Briefly assess both of the financing schemes under consideration from the viewpoint of the existing shareholders.

15.6 Carpets Direct plc wishes to increase the number of its retail outlets in the south of England. The board of directors has decided to finance this expansion programme by raising the funds from existing shareholders through a 1-for-4 rights issue. The most recent income statement of the business is as follows:

Income statement for the year ended 30 April

	£m
Sales revenue	164.5
Operating profit	12.6
Interest	(6.2)
Profit before taxation	6.4
Taxation	(1.9)
Profit for the year	4.5

A £2 million ordinary dividend had been paid in respect of the year.

The share capital consists of 120 million ordinary shares with a nominal value of £0.50 a share. These are currently being traded on the Stock Exchange at a price/earnings ratio of 22 times and the board of directors has decided to issue the new shares at a discount of 20 per cent on the current market value.

Required:
(a) Calculate the theoretical ex-rights price of an ordinary share in Carpets Direct plc.
(b) Calculate the price at which the rights in Carpets Direct plc are likely to be traded.
(c) Identify and evaluate, at the time of the rights issue, each of the options arising from the rights issue to an investor who holds 4,000 ordinary shares before the rights announcement.

(*Hint*: To answer part (a), first calculate the earnings per share and then use this and the P/E ratio to calculate the marker value per share.)

15.7 Gainsborough Fashions Ltd operates a small chain of fashion shops in North Wales. In recent months the business has been under pressure from its suppliers to reduce the average credit period taken from three months to one month. As a result, the directors have approached the bank to ask for an increase in the existing overdraft for one year to be able to comply with the suppliers' demands. The most recent financial statements of the business are as follows:

Statement of financial position as at 31 May

ASSETS	£	£
Non-current assets		
Property, plant and equipment		
Fixtures and fittings at cost	90,000	
Accumulated depreciation	(23,000)	67,000
Motor vehicles at cost	34,000	
Accumulated depreciation	(27,000)	7,000
		74,000
Current assets		
Inventories at cost		198,000
Trade receivables		3,000
		201,000
Total assets		275,000
EQUITY AND LIABILITIES		
Equity		
£1 ordinary shares		20,000
General reserve		4,000
Retained earnings		17,000
		41,000
Non-current liabilities		
Borrowings – loan notes repayable in just over one year's time		40,000
Current liabilities		
Trade payables		162,000
Accrued expenses		10,000
Borrowings – bank overdraft		17,000
Taxation		5,000
		194,000
Total equity and liabilities		275,000

Abbreviated income statement for the year ended 31 May

	£
Sales revenue	740,000
Operating profit	38,000
Interest charges	(5,000)
Profit before taxation	33,000
Taxation	(10,000)
Profit for the year	23,000

A dividend of £23,000 was paid for the year.

Notes:
(1) The loan notes are secured by personal guarantees from the directors.
(2) The current overdraft bears an interest rate of 12 per cent a year.

Required:
(a) Identify and discuss the major factors that a bank would take into account before deciding whether to grant an increase in the overdraft of a business.
(b) State whether, in your opinion, the bank should grant the required increase in the overdraft for Gainsborough Fashions Ltd. You should provide reasoned arguments and supporting calculations where necessary.

15.8 Telford Engineers plc, a medium-sized Midlands manufacturer of automobile components, has decided to modernise its factory by introducing a number of robots. These will cost £20 million and will reduce operating costs by £6 million a year for their estimated useful life of ten years starting next year (Year 10). To finance this scheme, the business can raise £20 million by issuing either

- 20 million ordinary shares at 100p; or
- loan notes at 7 per cent interest a year with capital repayments of £3m a year commencing at the end of Year 11.

Extracts from Telford Engineers' financial statements appear below.

Summary of statement of financial position as at 31 December

	Year 6 £m	Year 7 £m	Year 8 £m	Year 9 £m
ASSETS				
Non-current assets	48	51	65	64
Current assets	55	67	57	55
Total assets	103	118	122	119
EQUITY AND LIABILITIES				
Equity	48	61	61	63
Non-current liabilities	30	30	30	30
Current liabilities				
Trade payables	20	27	25	18
Short-term borrowings	5	–	6	8
	25	27	31	26
Total equity and liabilities	103	118	122	119
Number of issued 25p shares	80m	80m	80m	80m
Share price	150p	200p	100p	145p

Note that the short-term borrowings consisted entirely of bank overdrafts.

Summary of income statements for years ended 31 December

	Year 6 £m	Year 7 £m	Year 8 £m	Year 9 £m
Sales revenue	152	170	110	145
Operating profit	28	40	7	15
Interest payable	(4)	(3)	(4)	(5)
Profit before taxation	24	37	3	10
Taxation	(12)	(16)	(0)	(4)
Profit for the period	12	21	3	6
Dividends paid during each year	6	8	3	4

You should assume that the tax rate for Year 10 is 30 per cent, that sales revenue and operating profit will be unchanged from Year 9 except for the £6 million cost saving arising from the introduction of the robots, and that Telford Engineers will pay the same dividend per share in Year 10 as in Year 9.

Required:

(a) Prepare, for each financing arrangement, Telford Engineers' projected income statement for the year ending 31 December Year 10 and a statement of its share capital, reserves and borrowings on that date.

(b) Calculate Telford's projected earnings per share for Year 10 for both schemes.

(c) Which scheme would you advise the business to adopt? You should give your reasons and state what additional information you would require.

CHAPTER 16

Managing working capital

Introduction

This chapter considers the factors that must be taken into account when managing the working capital of a business. Each element of working capital will be identified and the major issues surrounding them will be discussed. Working capital represents a significant investment for many businesses and so its proper management and control can be vital. We saw in Chapter 14 that an investment in working capital is typically an important aspect of new investment proposals. Some useful tools in the management of working capital are financial ratios, which were considered in Chapter 7, budgets, which we examined in Chapter 12, and NPV, which we considered in Chapter 14.

Learning outcomes

When you have completed this chapter, you should be able to:

- Identify the main elements of working capital.

- Discuss the purpose of working capital and the nature of the working capital cycle.

- Explain the importance of establishing policies for the control of working capital.

- Explain the factors that have to be taken into account when managing each element of working capital.

 Remember to create your own personalised Study Plan

What is working capital?

→ **Working capital** is usually defined as current assets less current liabilities. The major elements of current assets are:

- inventories
- trade receivables
- cash (in hand and at bank).

The major elements of current liabilities are:

- trade payables
- bank overdrafts.

The size and composition of working capital can vary between industries. For some types of business, the investment in working capital can be substantial. For example, a manufacturing business will typically invest heavily in raw material, work in progress and finished goods, and will normally sell its goods on credit, giving rise to trade receivables. A retailer, on the other hand, will hold only one form of inventories (finished goods), and will usually sell goods for cash. Many service businesses hold no inventories.

Most businesses buy goods and/or services on credit, giving rise to trade payables. Few, if any, businesses operate without a cash balance, though in some cases it is a negative one (a bank overdraft).

Working capital represents a net investment in short-term assets. These assets are continually flowing into and out of the business and are essential for day-to-day operations. The various elements of working capital are interrelated and can be seen as part of a short-term cycle. For a manufacturing business, the working capital cycle can be depicted as shown in Figure 16.1.

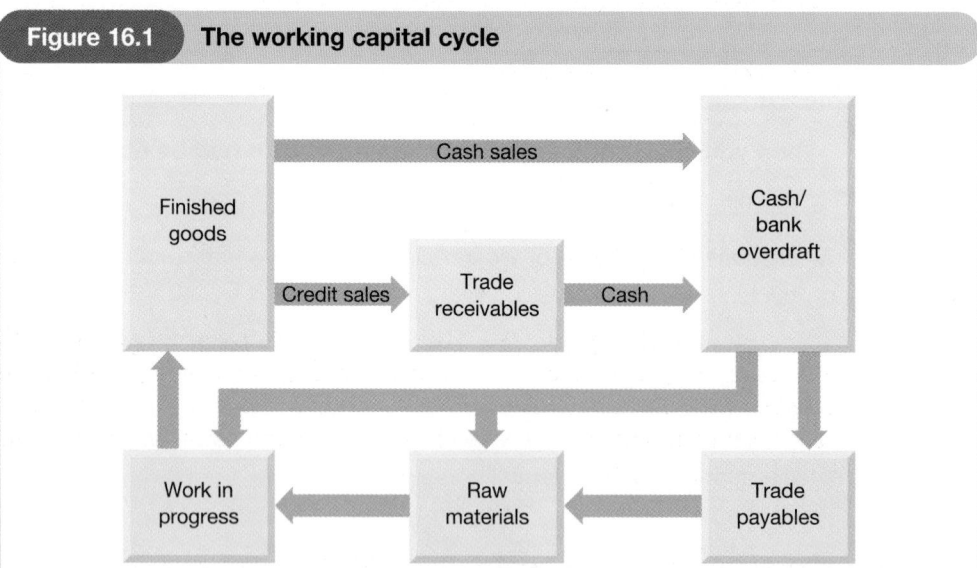

Figure 16.1 The working capital cycle

Cash is used to pay trade payables for raw materials, or raw materials are bought for immediate cash settlement. Cash is also spent on labour and other items that turn raw materials into work in progress and, finally, into finished goods. The finished goods are sold to customers either for cash or on credit. In the case of credit customers, there will be a delay before the cash is received from the sales. Receipt of cash completes the cycle.

For a retailer the situation would be as in Figure 16.1 except that there would be only inventories of finished goods and no work in progress or raw materials. For a purely service business, the working capital cycle would also be similar to that depicted in Figure 16.1 except that there would be no inventories of finished goods or raw materials. There may well be work in progress, however, since many services, for example a case handled by a firm of solicitors, will take some time to complete and costs will build up before the client is billed for them.

Managing working capital

The management of working capital is an essential part of the business's short-term planning process. It is necessary for management to decide how much of each element should be held. As we shall see later in this chapter, there are costs associated with holding either too much or too little of each element. Management must be aware of these costs, which include opportunity costs, in order to manage effectively. Hence, potential benefits must be weighed against likely costs in an attempt to achieve the optimum investment.

The working capital needs of a business are likely to vary over time as a result of changes in the business environment. Managers must try to identify these changes to ensure that the level of investment in working capital is appropriate. This means that working capital decisions are frequently being made.

Activity 16.1

What kinds of changes in the business environment might lead to a decision to change the level of investment in working capital? Try to identify four possible changes that could affect the working capital needs of a business.

These may include the following:

- changes in interest rates
- changes in market demand
- changes in the seasons
- changes in the state of the economy.

You may have thought of others.

In addition to changes in the external environment, changes arising within the business could alter the required level of investment in working capital. Such internal changes might include using different production methods (resulting, perhaps, in a need to hold less inventories) and changes in the level of risk that managers are prepared to take.

The scale of working capital

We might imagine that, compared with the scale of investment in non-current assets by the typical business, the amounts involved with working capital are pretty trivial. However, this is not the case – the scale of the working capital elements for most businesses is vast.

Real World 16.1 gives some impression of the working capital investment for five UK businesses that are either very well known by name, or whose products are everyday commodities for most of us. These businesses were randomly selected, except that each one is high profile and from a different industry. For each business the major items appearing on the statement of financial position (balance sheet) are expressed as a percentage of the total investment by the providers of long-term finance (equity and non-current liabilities).

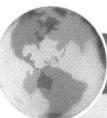

Real World 16.1

A summary of the statements of financial position (balance sheets) of five UK businesses

Business:	Next	BA	Babcock	Tesco	Severn Trent
Statement of financial position date:	26.1.08	31.3.08	31.12.08	23.2.08	31.3.08
Non-current assets	111	101	102	120	97
Current assets					
Inventories	54	1	9	13	1
Trade receivables	81	8	13	–	3
Other receivables	21	7	30	7	4
Cash and near cash	10	24	25	11	11
	166	40	77	31	19
Total assets	277	141	179	151	116
Equity and non-current liabilities	100	100	100	100	100
Current liabilities					
Trade payables	30	8	18	20	1
Taxation	25	1	5	4	1
Other short-term liabilities	81	27	38	15	7
Overdrafts and short-term borrowings	41	5	18	12	7
	177	41	79	51	16
Total equity and liabilities	277	141	179	151	116

The non-current assets, current assets and current liabilities are expressed as a percentage of the total net long-term investment (equity plus non-current liabilities) of the business concerned. Next plc is a major retail and home shopping business. British Airways plc (BA) is a major airline. Babcock International Group plc is a major engineering and support business. Tesco plc is one of the major UK supermarkets. Severn Trent plc is a major supplier of water, sewerage services and waste management, mainly in the UK.

Source: Table constructed from information appearing in the financial statements for the year ended in 2008 for each of the five businesses concerned.

The totals for current assets are pretty large when compared with the total long-term investment. This is particularly true of Next and Babcock. The amounts vary considerably from one type of business to the next. When we look at the nature of working capital held we can see that Next, Babcock and Tesco, which produce and/or sell goods, are the only ones that hold significant amounts of inventories. The other two businesses are service providers and so inventories are not a significant item. We can see from the table that Tesco does not sell on credit and very few of BA's and Severn Trent's sales are on credit as these businesses have little invested in trade receivables. It is interesting to note that Tesco's trade payables are fairly large compared to its inventories. Since most of this money will be due to suppliers of inventories, it means that the business is able, on average, to have much of the cash from a typical trolley load of groceries in the bank before it needs to pay the suppliers for the goods concerned.

These types of variation in the amounts and types of working capital elements are typical of other businesses.

In the sections that follow, we shall consider each element of working capital separately and how they might be properly managed. It seems from the evidence presented in **Real World 16.2** that there is much scope for improvement in working capital management among European businesses.

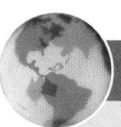 **Real World 16.2**

Working capital not working hard enough!

According to a survey of 1,000 of Europe's largest businesses, working capital is not as well managed as it could be. The survey, conducted in 2008 by REL Consultancy Group and CFO Europe, suggests that larger European businesses have €865 billion tied up in working capital that could be released through better management of inventories, trade receivables and trade payables. The potential for savings represents a total of 36 per cent of the total working capital invested and is calculated by comparing the results for a particular industry with the results for businesses within the upper quartile of that industry.

The overall working capital invested by large European businesses as a percentage of sales for the five-year period ending in 2007 is shown shown in Figure 16.2 below.

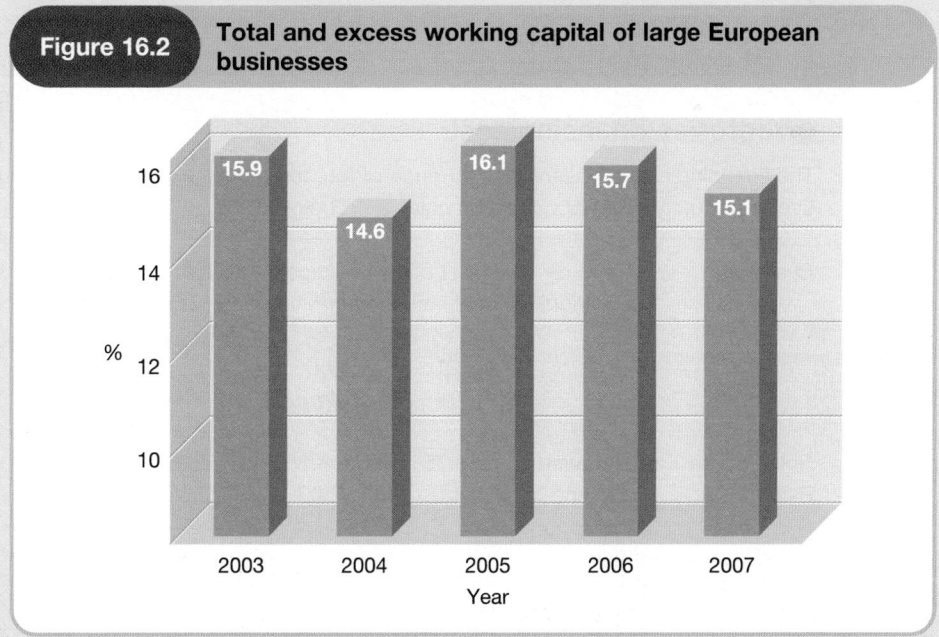

Figure 16.2 Total and excess working capital of large European businesses

The figure shows that there has been little variation in this percentage over time.

Source: Compiled from information in *Europe Working Capital Survey*, REL/CFO Europe, 2008, www.relconsult.com.

Managing inventories

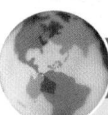

A business may hold inventories for various reasons, the most common of which is to meet the immediate day-to-day requirements of customers and production. However, a business may hold more than is necessary for this purpose if there is a risk that future supplies may be interrupted or scarce. Similarly, if there is a risk that the cost of inventories will rise in the future, a business may decide to stockpile.

For some types of business, the inventories held may represent a substantial proportion of the total assets held. For example, a car dealership that rents its premises may have nearly all of its total assets in the form of inventories. Inventories levels of manufacturers tend to be higher than in many other types of business as it is necessary to hold three kinds of inventories: raw materials, work in progress and finished goods. Each form of inventories represents a particular stage in the production cycle.

For some types of business, the level of inventories held may vary substantially over the year owing to the seasonal nature of the industry. An example of such a business is a greetings card manufacturer. For other businesses, inventories levels may remain fairly stable throughout the year.

Where a business holds inventories simply to meet the day-to-day requirements of its customers and for production, it will normally seek to minimise the amount of inventories held. This is because there are significant costs associated with holding inventories. These include:

● storage and handling costs
● the cost of financing the inventories
● the cost of pilferage and obsolescence
● the cost of opportunities forgone in tying up funds in this form of asset.

To gain some impression of the level of cost involved in holding inventories **Real World 16.3** estimates the *financing* cost of inventories for five large businesses.

Real World 16.3

Inventories financing cost

The financing cost of inventories for each of four large businesses, based on their respective opportunity costs of capital, is calculated below.

Business	Type of operations	Cost of capital (a) %	Average inventories held* (b) £m	Cost of holding inventories (a) × (b) £m	Profit before tax £m	Cost as a % of profit before tax %
Rolls-Royce	Engineering	12.75	2,402	306	1,892	16.2
Rexam	Packaging	11.0	503	55	240	22.9
Carphone Warehouse	Mobile phone retailer	6.6	187	12.3	124.1	9.9
Kingfisher	Home improvement retailer	7.6	1,702	129.4	395	32.8

* Based on opening and closing inventories for the relevant financial period.

We can see that for all of these four businesses, inventories financing costs are significant in relation to the profits generated. These figures do not take account of other costs of inventories holding mentioned above, like the cost of providing a secure store for the inventories. Clearly, the efficient management of inventories is an important issue for many businesses.

These businesses were not selected because they have particularly high inventories costs but simply because they are among the relatively few businesses that publish their costs of capital.

Source: Annual reports of the businesses for the financial year ended in 2008.

As we have just seen, the cost of holding inventories can be very large. A business must also recognise, however, that, if the level of inventories held is too low, there will also be associated costs.

Activity 16.2

What costs might a business incur as a result of holding too low a level of inventories? Try to jot down at least three types of cost.

In answering this activity you may have thought of the following costs:

- loss of sales, from being unable to provide the goods required immediately;
- loss of customer goodwill, for being unable to satisfy customer demand;
- high transport costs incurred to ensure that inventories are replenished quickly;
- lost production due to shortage of raw materials;
- inefficient production scheduling due to shortages of raw materials;
- purchasing inventories at a higher price than might otherwise have been possible in order to replenish inventories quickly.

Before dealing with the various approaches that can be taken to managing inventories, let us consider **Real World 16.4**, which describes how one large international business has sought to reduce its inventories level.

Real World 16.4

Back to basics

FT

Wal-Mart has said it will seek further reductions in the levels of backroom inventory it holds at its US stores, in a drive to improve its performance. . . . John Menzer, vice chairman and head of Wal-Mart's US operations, made the retailer's efforts to cut inventory one of the key elements of remarks to reporters this week when he outlined current strategy. Wal-Mart, he said, currently 'has a real focus on reducing our inventory. Inventory that's on trailers behind our stores, in backrooms and on shelves in our stores.' Cutting back on inventory, he said, reduced 'clutter' in the retailer's stores, gave a better return on invested capital, reduced the need to cut prices on old merchandise, and increased the velocity at which goods moved through the stores.

Real World 16.4 continued

Eduardo Castro-Wright, chief executive of Wal-Mart's US store network, said the inventory reduction marked a return to basics for the retailer, which would be 'getting more disciplined'. Earlier this year, he said Wal-Mart would link inventory reduction to incentive payments to its officers and managers. Wal-Mart is already regarded as one of the most efficient logistical operations in US retailing. It is currently rolling out to all its US stores and distribution centres a new parallel distribution system that speeds the delivery to stores of 5,000 high turnover items. It is also discussing with its suppliers how new RFID radio frequency tagging could be used to further reduce the volume of goods in transit to its stores. But further reductions in its inventory turnover would release working capital that could fund investment in its ongoing initiatives to improve its stores.

Adrienne Shapira, retail analyst at Goldman Sachs, has estimated that the retailer could reduce its annual inventory by 18 per cent, which would lead to a $6bn reduction in working capital needs on a trailing 12-month basis.

Source: 'Wal-Mart aims for further inventory cuts', Jonathan Birchall, FT.com, 19 April 2006.

To try to ensure that the inventories are properly managed, a number of procedures and techniques may be used. These are reviewed below.

Budgeting future demand

One of the best ways to ensure that there will be inventories available to meet future production and sales requirements is to make appropriate plans and budgets. Budgets should deal with each product that the business makes and/or sells. It is important that every attempt is made to ensure that budgets are realistic, as they will determine future ordering and production levels. The budgets may be derived in various ways. They may be developed using statistical techniques such as time series analysis, or they may be based on the judgement of the sales and marketing staff. We considered inventories budgets and their link to production and sales budgets in Chapter 12.

Financial ratios

One ratio that can be used to help monitor inventories levels is the average inventories turnover period, which we examined in Chapter 7. This ratio is calculated as follows:

$$\text{Average inventories turnover period} = \frac{\text{Average inventories held}}{\text{Cost of sales}} \times 365$$

This will provide a picture of the average period for which inventories are held, and can be useful as a basis for comparison. It is possible to calculate the average inventories turnover period for individual product lines as well as for inventories as a whole.

Recording and reordering systems

A sound system of recording inventories movements is a key element in managing inventories. There must be proper procedures for recording inventories purchases and usages. Periodic checks would normally be made in an attempt to ensure that the amount of physical inventories actually held is consistent with what is indicated by the inventories records.

There should also be clear procedures for the reordering of inventories. Authorisation for both the purchase and the issue of inventories should be confined to a few senior staff. This should avoid problems of duplication and lack of co-ordination. To determine the point at which inventories should be reordered, information will be required concerning the **lead time** (that is, the time between the placing of an order and the receipt of the goods) and the likely level of demand.

Activity (16.3)

An electrical retailer stocks a particular type of light switch. The annual demand for the light switch is 10,400 units, and the lead time for orders is four weeks. Demand for the light switch is steady throughout the year. At what level of inventories of the light switch should the business reorder, assuming that it is confident of the information given above?

The average weekly demand for the switch is 10,400/52 = 200 units. During the time between ordering new switches and receiving them, the quantity sold will be 4 × 200 units = 800 units. So the business should reorder no later than when the level held reaches 800 units, in order to avoid running out of inventories.

In most businesses, there will be some uncertainty surrounding the above factors and so a buffer or safety inventories level may be maintained in case problems occur. The amount of the buffer to be held is really a matter of judgement. This judgement will depend on:

- the degree of uncertainty concerning the above factors;
- the likely costs of running out of the item concerned;
- the cost of holding the buffer inventories.

The effect of holding a buffer will be to raise the inventories level (the reorder point) at which an order for new inventories is placed.

Activity (16.4)

Assume the same facts as in Activity 16.3. However, we are also told that the business maintains buffer inventories of 300 units. At what level should the business reorder?

Reorder point = expected level of demand during the lead time plus the level of buffer inventories
= 800 + 300
= 1,100 units

Carrying buffer inventories will increase the cost of holding inventories; however, this must be weighed against the cost of running out of inventories, in terms of lost sales, production problems and so on.

Real World 16.5 provides an example of how small businesses can use technology in inventories reordering to help compete against their larger rivals.

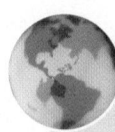

Real World 16.5

Taking on the big boys

The use of technology in inventories recording and reordering may be of vital importance to the survival of small businesses that are being threatened by larger rivals. One such example is that of small independent bookshops. Technology can come to their rescue in two ways. First, electronic point-of-sale (EPOS) systems can record books as they are sold and can constantly update records of inventories held. Thus, books that need to be reordered can be quickly and easily identified. Second, the reordering process can be improved by using web-based technology, which allows books to be ordered in real time. Many large book wholesalers provide free web-based software to their customers for this purpose and try to deliver books ordered during the next working day. This means that a small bookseller, with limited shelf space, may keep one copy only of a particular book but maintain a range of books that competes with that of a large bookseller.

Source: Information taken from 'Small stores keep up with the big boys', FT.com, 5 February 2003.

Levels of control

Senior managers must make a commitment to the management of inventories. However, the cost of controlling inventories must be weighed against the potential benefits. It may be possible to have different levels of control according to the nature of the inventories held. The **ABC system of inventories control** is based on the idea of selective levels of control.

A business may find that it is possible to divide its inventories into three broad categories: A, B and C. Each category will be based on the value of inventories held, as is illustrated in Example 16.1.

Example 16.1

Alascan Products plc makes door handles and door fittings. It makes them in brass, in steel and in plastic. The business finds that brass fittings account for 10 per cent of the physical volume of the finished inventories that it holds, but these represent 65 per cent of its total value. These are treated as Category A inventories. There are sophisticated recording procedures, tight control is exerted over inventories movements and there is a high level of security where the brass inventories are stored. This is economic because the inventories represent a relatively small proportion of the total volume.

The business finds that steel fittings account for 30 per cent of the total volume of finished inventories and represent 25 per cent of its total value. These are treated as Category B inventories, with a lower level of recording and management control being applied.

The remaining 60 per cent of the volume of inventories is plastic fittings, which represent the least valuable items, that account for only 10 per cent of the total value of finished inventories held. These are treated as Category C inventories, so the level of recording and management control would be lower still. Applying to these inventories the level of control that is applied to Category A or even Category B inventories would be uneconomic.

Categorising inventories in this way seeks to direct management effort to the most important areas, and tries to ensure that the costs of controlling inventories are appropriate to its importance.

Figure 16.3 shows the nature of the ABC approach to inventories control.

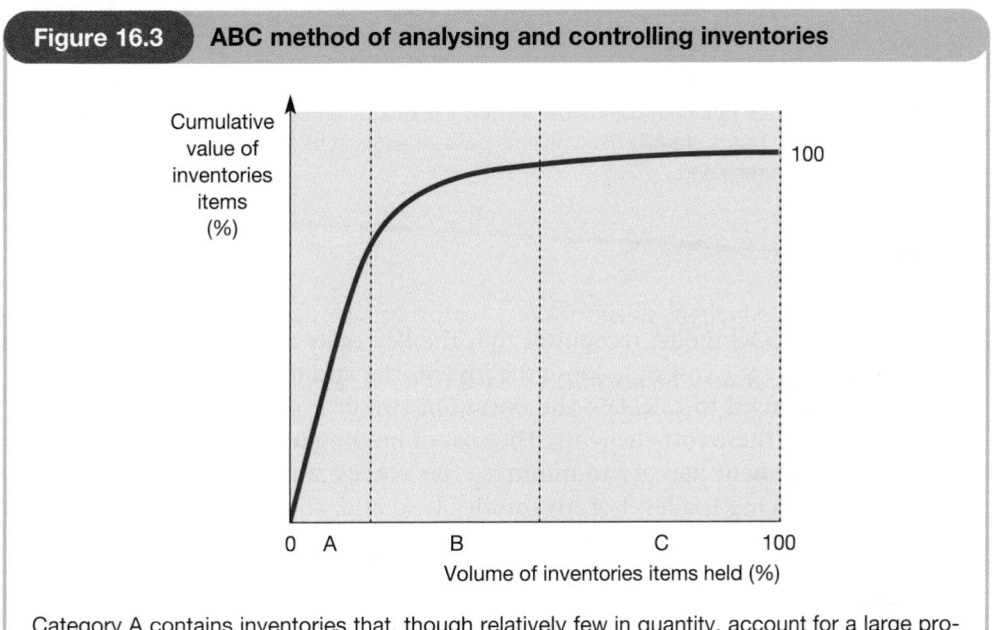

Figure 16.3   ABC method of analysing and controlling inventories

Category A contains inventories that, though relatively few in quantity, account for a large proportion of the total value. Category B inventories consists of those items that are less valuable but more numerous. Category C comprises those inventories items that are very numerous but relatively low in value. Different inventories control rules would be applied to each category. For example, only Category A inventories would attract the more expensive and sophisticated controls.

Inventories management models

Economic order quantity

It is possible to use decision models to help manage inventories. The **economic order quantity (EOQ)** model is concerned with answering the question 'How much inventories should be ordered?' In its simplest form, the EOQ model assumes that demand is constant, so that inventories will be depleted evenly over time, and replenished just at the point that they run out. These assumptions would lead to a 'saw-tooth' pattern to represent inventories movements, as shown in Figure 16.4.

> **Figure 16.4** **Patterns of inventories movements over time**
>
>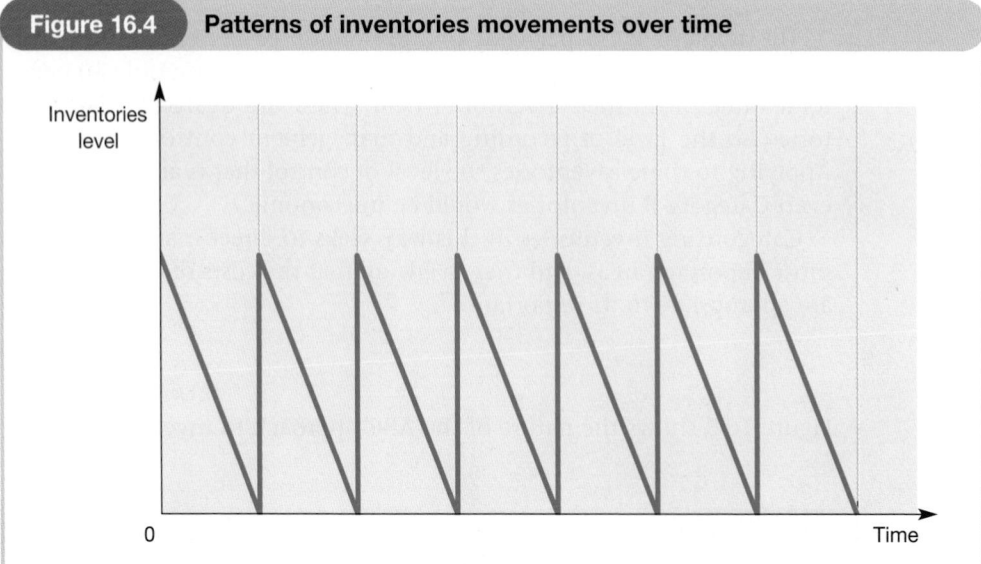
>
> Here we assume that there is a constant rate of usage of the inventories item, and that inventories are reduced to zero just as new inventories arrive. At time 0 there is a full level of inventories. This is steadily used as time passes; and just as it falls to zero it is replaced. This pattern is then repeated.

The EOQ model recognises that the key costs associated with inventories management are the cost of holding the inventories and the cost of ordering them. The model can be used to calculate the optimum size of a purchase order by taking account of both of these cost elements. The cost of holding inventories can be substantial, and so management may try to minimise the average amount of inventories held. However, by reducing the level of inventories held and, therefore, the holding costs, there will be a need to increase the number of orders during the period and so ordering costs will rise.

Figure 16.5 shows how, as the level of inventories and the size of inventories orders increase, the annual costs of placing orders will decrease because fewer orders will be placed. However, the cost of holding inventories will increase, as there will be higher average inventories levels. The total costs curve, which is based on the sum of holding costs and ordering costs, will fall until the point E, which represents the minimum total cost. Thereafter, total costs begin to rise. The EOQ model seeks to identify point E at which total costs are minimised. This will represent half of the optimum amount that should be ordered on each occasion. Assuming, as we are doing, that inventories are used evenly over time and that they fall to zero before being replaced, the average inventories level equals half of the order size.

The EOQ model, which can be used to derive the most economic order quantity, is:

$$\text{EOQ} = \sqrt{\frac{2DC}{H}}$$

where: D = the annual demand for the inventories item (expressed in units of the inventories item);

C = the cost of placing an order;

H = the cost of holding one unit of inventories for one year.

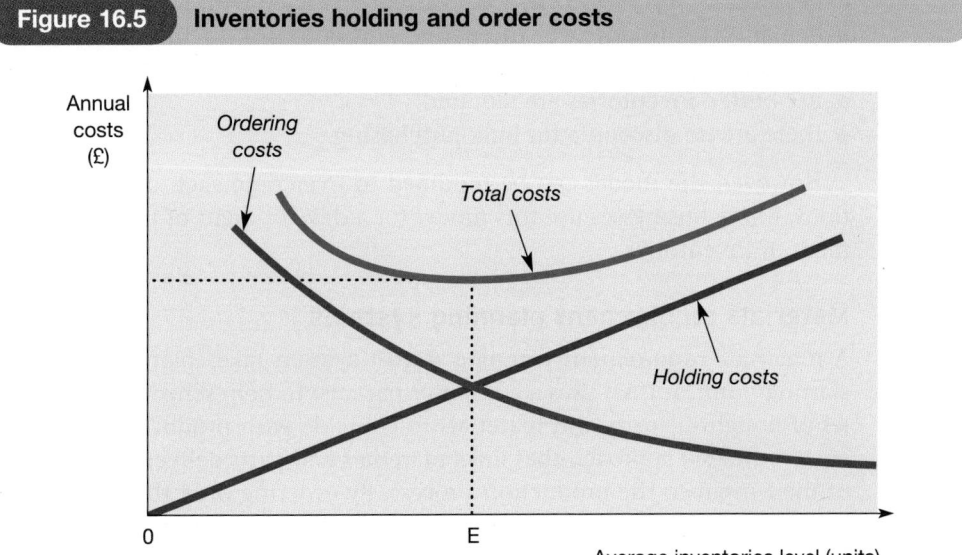

| Figure 16.5 | Inventories holding and order costs |

Small inventories levels imply frequent reordering and high annual ordering costs. Small inventories levels also imply relatively low inventories holding costs. High inventories levels imply exactly the opposite. There is, in theory, an optimum order size that will lead to the sum of ordering and holding costs (total costs) being at a minimum.

Activity (16.5)

HLA Ltd sells 2,000 bags of cement each year. It has been estimated that the cost of holding one bag of cement for a year is £4. The cost of placing an order for new inventories is estimated at £250.

Calculate the EOQ for bags of cement.

Your answer to this activity should be as follows:

$$\text{EOQ} = \sqrt{\frac{2 \times 2,000 \times 250}{4}} = 500 \text{ bags}$$

This will mean that the business will have to order bags of cement four times each year (that is 2,000/500) in batches of 500 bags so that sales demand can be met.

Note that the cost of the inventories concerned, which is the price paid to the supplier, does not directly impact on the EOQ model. The EOQ model is concerned only with the administrative costs of placing each order and the costs of looking after the inventories. Where the business operates an ABC system of inventories control, however, more expensive inventories items will have greater holding costs. For example, Category A inventories would tend to have a lower EOQ than Category B ones. Also, higher-cost inventories tie up more finance than cheaper ones, again leading to higher holding cost. So the cost of the inventories may have an indirect effect on the economic order size that the model recommends.

The basic EOQ model has a number of limiting assumptions. In particular, it assumes that:

- demand for an inventories item can be predicted with accuracy;
- demand is constant over the period and does not fluctuate through seasonality or for other reasons;
- no 'buffer' inventories are required;
- there are no discounts for bulk purchasing.

However, the model can be modified to overcome each of these limiting assumptions. Many businesses use this model (or a development of it) to help in the management of inventories.

Materials requirement planning systems

→ A **materials requirement planning (MRP) system** takes planned sales demand as its starting point. It then uses a computer package to help schedule the timing of deliveries of bought-in parts and materials to coincide with production requirements. It is a co-coordinated approach that links materials and parts deliveries to the scheduled time of their input to the production process. By ordering only those items that are necessary to ensure the flow of production, inventories levels are likely to be reduced. MRP is really a 'top-down' approach to inventories management, which recognises that inventories ordering decisions cannot be viewed as being independent of production decisions. In recent years, this approach has been extended to provide a fully integrated approach to production planning. The approach also takes account of other manufacturing resources such as labour and machine capacity.

Just-in-time inventories management

In recent years, many businesses have tried to eliminate the need to hold inventories → by adopting **just-in-time (JIT) inventories management**. This approach was originally used in the US defence industry during the Second World War, but was first used on a wide scale by Japanese manufacturing businesses. The essence of JIT is, as the name suggests, to have supplies delivered to the business just in time for them to be used in the production process or in a sale. By adopting this approach the inventories holding costs rest with suppliers rather than with the business itself. On the other hand, a failure by a particular supplier to deliver on time could cause enormous problems and costs to the business. Thus JIT can save cost, but it tends to increase risk.

For JIT to be successful, it is important that the business informs suppliers of its inventories requirements in advance. Also suppliers, in their turn, must deliver materials of the right quality at the agreed times. Failure to do so could lead to a dislocation of production or supply to customers and could be very costly. Thus a close relationship is required between the business and its suppliers. This close relationship enables suppliers to schedule their own production to that of their customers. This should mean that between supplier and customer there will be a net saving in the amount of inventories that need to be held, relative to that that would apply were JIT not in operation.

Adopting JIT may well require re-engineering a business's production process. To ensure that orders are quickly fulfilled, factory production must be flexible and responsive. This may require changes both to the production layout and to working practices. Production flows may have to be redesigned and employees may have to be given greater responsibility to allow them to deal with unanticipated problems and to encourage greater commitment. Information systems must also be installed that facilitate an uninterrupted production flow.

Although a business that applies JIT will not have to hold inventories, there may be other costs associated with this approach. As the suppliers may need to hold inventories for the customer, they may try to recoup this additional cost through increased prices. On the other hand, the close relationship between customer and supplier should enable the supplier to predict its customers' inventories needs. This means that suppliers can tailor their own production to that of the customer. The close relationship necessary between the business and its suppliers may also prevent the business from taking advantage of cheaper sources of supply if they become available.

Many people view JIT as more than simply an inventories control system. The philosophy underpinning this approach is concerned with eliminating waste and striving for excellence. There is an expectation that suppliers will always deliver inventories on time and that there will be no defects in the items supplied. There is also an expectation that, for manufacturers, the production process will operate at maximum efficiency. This means that there will be no production breakdowns and the queuing and storage times of products manufactured will be eliminated, as only that time spent directly on processing the products is seen as adding value. While these expectations may be impossible to achieve, they do help to create a culture that is dedicated to the pursuit of excellence and quality.

Real Worlds 16.6 and **16.7** show how two very well-known businesses operating in the UK (one a retailer, the other a manufacturer) use JIT to advantage.

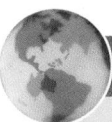

Real World 16.6

JIT at Boots

The Boots Company plc, the UK's largest healthcare retailer, has improved inventories management at its stores. The business is working towards a JIT system where delivery from its one central warehouse in Nottingham will be made every day to each retail branch, with nearly all of the inventories lines being placed directly on to the sales shelves, not into a store room at the branch. The business says that this will bring significant savings of stores staff time and lead to significantly lower levels of inventories being held, without any lessening of the service offered to customers. The new system is expected to lead to major economic benefits for the business.

Source: Information taken from The Boots Company plc Annual Report and Accounts 2005.

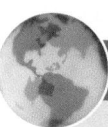

Real World 16.7

JIT at Nissan

Nissan Motors UK Limited, the UK manufacturing arm of the world famous Japanese car business, has a plant in Sunderland in the north east of England. Here it operates a fairly well-developed JIT system. For example, Sommer supplies carpets and soft interior trim from a factory close to the Nissan plant. It makes deliveries to Nissan once every 20 minutes on average, so as to arrive exactly as they are needed in production. This is fairly typical of all of the 200 suppliers of components and materials to the Nissan plant.

The business used to have a complete JIT system. More recently, however, Nissan has drawn back from its total adherence to JIT. By using only local suppliers it has cut itself off from the opportunity to exploit low-cost suppliers, particularly some located in China. This has led the business to feel the need to hold buffer inventories of certain inventories items to guard against disruption of supply arising from transport problems of sourcing parts from the Far East.

Source: Information taken from Partnership Sourcing Best Practice Case Study (www.pslcbi.com/studies/docnissan.htm) and 'Nissan reviews just-in-time parts policy', C. Tighe, *Financial Times*, 23 October 2006.

Managing receivables

Selling goods or services on credit will result in costs being incurred by a business. These costs include credit administration costs, bad debts and opportunities forgone to use the funds for more profitable purposes. However, these costs must be weighed against the benefits of increased sales resulting from the opportunity for customers to delay payment.

Selling on credit is very widespread and is the norm outside the retail industry. When a business offers to sell its goods or services on credit, it must have clear policies concerning:

- which customers should receive credit;
- how much credit should be offered;
- what length of credit it is prepared to offer;
- whether discounts will be offered for prompt payment;
- what collection policies should be adopted;
- how the risk of non-payment can be reduced.

In this section, we shall consider each of these issues.

Which customers should receive credit and how much should they be offered?

A business offering credit runs the risk of not receiving payment for goods or services supplied. Thus, care must be taken over the type of customer to whom credit facilities are offered and how much credit is allowed. When considering a proposal from a customer for the supply of goods or services on credit, the business must take a number of factors into account. The following **five Cs of credit** provide a business with a useful checklist.

- *Capital*. The customer must appear to be financially sound before any credit is extended. Where the customer is a business, its financial statements should be examined. Particular regard should be given to the customer's likely future profitability and liquidity. In addition, any major financial commitments (for example, capital expenditure, contracts with suppliers) must be taken into account.
- *Capacity*. The customer must appear to have the capacity to pay amounts owing. Where possible, the payment record of the customer to date should be examined. If the customer is a business, the type of business operated and the physical resources of the business will be relevant. The value of goods that the customer wishes to buy on credit must be related to the customer's total financial resources.
- *Collateral*. On occasions, it may be necessary to ask for some kind of security for goods supplied on credit. When this occurs, the business must be convinced that the customer is able to offer a satisfactory form of security.
- *Conditions*. The state of the industry in which the customer operates, and the general economic conditions of the particular region or country, may have an important influence on the ability of a customer to pay the amounts outstanding on the due date.
- *Character*. It is important for a business to make some assessment of the customer's character. The willingness to pay will depend on the honesty and integrity of the individual with whom the business is dealing. Where the customer is a business, this will mean assessing the characters of its senior managers. The selling business must feel satisfied that the customer will make every effort to pay any amounts owing.

It is clear from the above that the business will need to gather information concerning the ability and willingness of the customer to pay the amounts owing at the due dates.

Activity 16.6

Assume that you are the credit manager of a business and that a limited company approaches you with a view to buying goods on credit. What sources of information might you decide to use to help assess the financial health of the potential customer?

There are various possibilities. You may have thought of some of the following:

- *Trade references*. Some businesses ask potential customers to supply them with references from other suppliers who have made sales on credit to them. This may be extremely useful provided that the references supplied are truly representative of the opinions of a customer's suppliers. There is a danger that a potential customer will be selective when giving details of other suppliers, in an attempt to create a more favourable impression than is deserved.
- *Bank references*. It is possible to ask the potential customer for a bank reference. Although banks are usually prepared to supply references, the contents of such references are not always very informative. If customers are in financial difficulties, the bank may be unwilling to add to their problems by supplying poor references. It is worth remembering that the bank's loyalty is likely to be with the customer rather than the enquirer. The bank will usually charge a fee for providing a reference.
- *Published financial statements*. A limited company is obliged by law to file a copy of its annual financial statements with the Registrar of Companies. These financial statements are available for public inspection and provide a useful source of information. Apart from the information contained in the financial statements, company law requires public limited companies to state in the directors' report the average time taken to pay suppliers. The annual reports of many companies are available on their own websites or on computer-based information systems (for example, FAME).
- *The customer*. Interviews with the directors of the customer business and visits to its premises may be carried out to gain an impression of the way that the customer conducts its business. Where a significant amount of credit is required, the business may ask the customer for access to internal budgets and other unpublished financial information to help assess the level of risk involved.
- *Credit agencies*. Specialist agencies exist to provide information that can be used to assess the creditworthiness of a potential customer. The information that a credit agency supplies may be gleaned from various sources, including the financial statements of the customer and news items relating to the customer from both published and unpublished sources. The credit agencies may also provide a credit rating for the business. Agencies will charge a fee for their services.
- *Register of County Court Judgments*. Any money judgments given against the business or an individual in a county court will be maintained on the register for six years. This register is available for inspection by any member of the public for a small fee.
- *Other suppliers*. Similar businesses will often be prepared to exchange information concerning slow payers or defaulting customers through an industry credit circle. This can be a reliable and relatively cheap way of obtaining information.

Length of credit period

A business must determine what credit terms it is prepared to offer its customers. The length of credit offered to customers can vary significantly between businesses. It may be influenced by such factors as:

- the typical credit terms operating within the industry;
- the degree of competition within the industry;
- the bargaining power of particular customers;
- the risk of non-payment;
- the capacity of the business to offer credit;
- the marketing strategy of the business.

The last point identified may require some explanation. If, for example, a business wishes to increase its market share, it may decide to be more generous in its credit policy in an attempt to stimulate sales. Potential customers may be attracted by the offer of a longer credit period. However, any such change in policy must take account of the likely costs and benefits arising.

To illustrate this point, consider Example 16.2.

Example 16.2

Torrance Ltd produces a new type of golf putter. The business sells the putter to wholesalers and retailers and has an annual sales revenue of £600,000. The following data relate to each putter produced.

	£
Selling price	40
Variable costs	(20)
Fixed cost apportionment	(6)
Profit	14

The business's cost of capital is estimated at 10 per cent a year.

Torrance Ltd wishes to expand the sales volume of the new putter. It believes that offering a longer credit period can achieve this. The business's average receivables collection period is currently 30 days. It is considering three options in an attempt to increase sales revenue. These are as follows:

	Option		
	1	*2*	*3*
Increase in average collection period (days)	10	20	30
Increase in sales revenue (£)	30,000	45,000	50,000

To enable the business to decide on the best option to adopt, it must weigh the benefits of the options against their respective costs. The benefits arising will be represented by the increase in profit from the sale of additional putters. From the cost data supplied we can see that the contribution (that is, selling price (£40) less variable costs (£20)) is £20 a putter, that is, 50 per cent of the selling price. So, whatever increase there may be in sales revenue, the additional contributions will be half of that figure. The fixed costs can be ignored in our calculations, as they will remain the same whichever option is chosen.

The increase in contribution under each option will therefore be:

	Option		
	1	2	3
50% of the increase in sales revenue (£)	15,000	22,500	25,000

The increase in trade receivables under each option will be as follows:

	Option		
	1	2	3
	£	£	£
Projected level of trade receivables			
40 × £630,000/365 (Note 1)	69,041		
50 × £645,000/365		88,356	
60 × £650,000/365			106,849
Current level of trade receivables			
30 × £600,000/365	(49,315)	(49,315)	(49,315)
Increase in trade receivables	19,726	39,041	57,534

The increase in receivables that results from each option will mean an additional finance cost to the business.

The net increase in the business's profit arising from the projected change is:

	Option		
	1	2	3
	£	£	£
Increase in contribution (see above)	15,000	22,500	25,000
Increase in finance cost (Note 2)	(1,973)	(3,904)	(5,753)
Net increase in profits	13,027	18,596	19,247

The calculations show that Option 3 will be the most profitable one.

Notes:

(1) If the annual sales revenue totals £630,000 and 40 days' credit is allowed (both of which will apply under Option 1), the average amount that will be owed to the business by its customers, at any point during the year, will be the daily sales revenue (that is, £630,000/365) multiplied by the number of days that the customers take to pay (that is 40).

Exactly the same logic applies to Options 2 and 3 and to the current level of trade receivables.

(2) The increase in the finance cost for Option 1 will be the increase in trade receivables (£19,726) × 10 per cent. The equivalent figures for the other options are derived in a similar way.

Example 16.2 illustrates the way that a business should assess changes in credit terms. However, if there is a risk that, by extending the length of credit, there will be an increase in bad debts, this should also be taken into account in the calculations, as should any additional trade receivable collection costs that will be incurred.

Real World 16.8 shows how the length of credit taken varies greatly from one well-known UK business to the next.

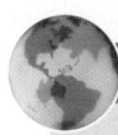

Real World 16.8

Credit where it's due

The following are the lengths of time taken on average for each business to pay its credit suppliers (trade payables).

	Days taken
EasyJet plc (airline operation)	9
Marks and Spencer Group plc (retail)	15
Domino's Pizza UK and Ireland plc (restaurants)	21
National Express Group plc (passenger transport)	22
Prudential plc (insurance)	22
GlaxoSmithKline plc (pharmaceuticals)	24
Next plc (retail)	24
Wm Morrison Supermarkets plc (retail)	32
Stagecoach Group plc (passenger transport)	33
Arriva plc (passenger transport)	40
W H Smith plc (retail)	45
Carphone Warehouse Group plc (retail and telecommunications)	48
Carpetright plc (retail)	53
Debenhams plc (retail)	57
British Energy Group plc (energy supply)	60
Greene King plc (regional brewing and pub management)	68
AstraZeneca plc (pharmaceuticals)	81

These are all based on information in the financial statements of the businesses concerned for the year ended 2007 or 2008.

It is striking how much the days taken to pay suppliers varies from one business to another. Industry differences do not seem to explain this. Debenhams takes nearly four times as long to pay as fellow retailer Marks and Spencer. Among the pharmaceuticals, AstraZeneca takes nearly three and a half times as long as GlaxoSmithKline.

Source: 'The payment league tables', Credit Management Research Centre, 2008, www.paymentleague.com.

An alternative approach to evaluating the credit decision

It is possible to view the credit decision as a capital investment decision. Granting trade credit involves an opportunity outlay of resources in the form of cash (which has been temporarily forgone) in the expectation that future cash flows will be increased (through higher sales) as a result. A business will usually have choices concerning the level of investment to be made in credit sales and the period over which credit is granted. These choices will result in different returns and different levels of risk. There is no reason in principle why the NPV investment appraisal method, which we considered in Chapter 14, should not be used to evaluate these choices. We have seen that the NPV method takes into account both the time value of money and the level of risk involved.

Approaching the problem as an NPV assessment is not different in principle from the way that we dealt with the decision in Example 16.2. In both approaches the time value of money is considered, but in Example 16.2 we did it by charging a financing cost on the outstanding trade receivables.

Cash discounts

In an attempt to encourage prompt payment from its credit customers, a business may decide to offer a **cash discount** (or discount for prompt payment). The size of any discount will be an important influence on whether a customer decides to pay promptly.

From the business's viewpoint, the cost of offering discounts must be weighed against the likely benefits in the form of a reduction both in the cost of financing receivables and in the amount of bad debts.

In practice, there is always the danger that a customer may be slow to pay and yet may still take the discount offered. Where the customer is important to the business, it may be difficult to insist on full payment. An alternative to allowing the customer to take discounts by reducing payment is to agree in advance to provide discounts for prompt payment through quarterly credit notes. As credit notes will be given only for those debts paid on time, the customer will often make an effort to qualify for the discount.

Self-assessment question 16.1

Williams Wholesalers Ltd at present asks its credit customers to pay by the end of the month after the month of delivery. In practice, customers take rather longer to pay; on average 70 days. Sales revenue amounts to £4m a year and bad debts to £20,000 a year.

It is planned to offer customers a cash discount of 2 per cent for payment within 30 days. Williams estimates that 50 per cent of customers will accept this facility but that the remaining customers, who tend to be slow payers, will not pay until 80 days after the sale. At present the business has an overdraft facility at an interest rate of 13 per cent a year. If the plan goes ahead, bad debts will be reduced to £10,000 a year and there will be savings in credit administration expenses of £6,000 a year.

Required:
Should Williams Wholesalers Ltd offer the new credit terms to customers? You should support your answer with any calculations and explanations that you consider necessary.

The answer to this question can be found at the back of the book on page 737.

Debt factoring and invoice discounting

Trade receivables can, in effect, be turned into cash by either factoring them or having sales invoices discounted. Both are forms of asset-based finance, which involves a financial institution providing a business with an advance up to 80 per cent of the value of the trade receivables outstanding. Both of these methods seem to be fairly popular approaches to managing receivables.

Credit insurance

It is possible for a supplier to insure its entire trade receivables, individual accounts (customers) or the outstanding balance relating to a particular transaction.

Collection policies and reducing the risk of non-payment

A business offering credit must ensure that amounts owing are collected as quickly as possible so that the risk of non-payment is minimised. Various steps can be taken to achieve this, including the following.

Develop customer relationships

For major customers it is often useful to cultivate a relationship with the key staff responsible for paying sales invoices. By so doing, the chances of prompt payment may be increased. For less important customers, the business should at least identify key staff responsible for paying invoices, who can be contacted in the event of a payment problem.

Publicise credit terms

The credit terms of the business should be made clear in all relevant correspondence, such as order acknowledgements, invoices and statements. In early negotiations with the prospective customer, credit terms should be openly discussed and an agreement reached.

Issue invoices promptly

An efficient collection policy requires an efficient accounting system. Invoices (bills) must be sent out promptly to customers, as must monthly statements. Reminders must also be despatched promptly to customers who are late in paying. If a customer fails to respond to a reminder, the accounting system should alert managers so that a stop can be placed on further deliveries.

Monitor outstanding debts

Management can monitor the effectiveness of collection policies in a number of ways. One method is to calculate the **average settlement period for trade receivables** ratio, which we met in Chapter 7. This ratio is calculated as follows:

$$\text{Average settlement period for trade receivables} = \frac{\text{Average trade receivables}}{\text{Credit sales}} \times 365$$

Although this ratio can be useful, it is important to remember that it produces an *average* figure for the number of days for which debts are outstanding. This average may be badly distorted by a few large customers who are very slow or very fast payers.

Produce an ageing schedule of trade receivables

A more detailed and informative approach to monitoring receivables may be to produce an **ageing schedule of trade receivables**. Receivables are divided into categories according to the length of time they have been outstanding. An ageing schedule can be produced, on a regular basis, to help managers see the pattern of outstanding receivables. An example of an ageing schedule is set out in Example 16.3.

Ageing schedule of trade receivables at 31 December

Customer	Days outstanding				Total
	1 to 30 days	31 to 60 days	61 to 90 days	More than 90 days	
	£	£	£	£	£
A Ltd	20,000	10,000	–	–	30,000
B Ltd	–	24,000	–	–	24,000
C Ltd	12,000	13,000	14,000	18,000	57,000
Total	32,000	47,000	14,000	18,000	111,000

This shows a business's trade receivables figure at 31 December, which totals £111,000. Each customer's balance is analysed according to how long the amount has been outstanding. (This business has just three credit customers.)

Thus we can see from the schedule, for example, that A Ltd has £20,000 outstanding for 30 days or fewer (that is, arising from sales during December) and £10,000 outstanding for between 31 and 60 days (broadly, arising from November sales). This information can be very useful for credit control purposes.

Many accounting software packages now include this ageing schedule as one of the routine reports available to managers. Such packages often have the facility to put customers 'on hold' when they reach their credit limits. Putting a customer on hold means that no further credit sales will be made to that customer until amounts owing from past sales have been settled.

Answer queries quickly

It is important for relevant staff to deal with customer queries on goods and services supplied quickly and efficiently. Payment is unlikely to be made by customers until their queries have been dealt with.

Deal with slow payers

It is almost inevitably the case that a business making significant sales on credit will be faced with customers who do not pay. When this occurs, there should be agreed procedures for dealing with the situation. However, the cost of any action to be taken against delinquent credit customers must be weighed against the likely returns. For example, there is little point in taking legal action against a customer, incurring large legal expenses, if there is evidence that the customer does not have the necessary resources to pay. Where possible, an estimate of the cost of bad debts should be taken into account when setting prices for products or services.

Real World 16.9 shows that businesses are not always as efficient as they might be with their management of trade receivables.

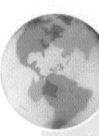

Real World 16.9

Would you credit it?

According to a recent survey of 6,500 UK businesses, 44 per cent of businesses leave it a fortnight, or longer, after the due date for payment before sending reminders to their credit customers, while 13 per cent leave it for a month or more. In other words, many businesses are very slow to react to their customers failing to pay on time.

Intrum Justitia UK, who conducted the survey, said: 'A clear credit policy, consistent checks on overdue payments and robust credit management systems are just some of the critical measures that businesses need to adopt.'

Source: Information taken from 'Late reminders lead to late payments', Jonathon Moules, *Financial Times*, 12 July 2004.

As a footnote to our consideration of managing receivables, **Real World 16.10** outlines some of the excuses that long-suffering credit managers must listen to when chasing payment for outstanding debts.

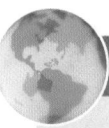

Real World 16.10

It's in the post

The Atradius Group provides trade credit insurance and trade receivables collections services worldwide, and has a presence in 42 countries. Its products and services aim to reduce its customers' exposure to buyers who cannot pay for the products and services customers purchase.

In a recent press release Atradius said:

Although it happens rarely, some debtors (credit customers) still manage to surprise even us. These excuses have actually been used by credit customers:

- It's not a valid debt as my vindictive ex-wife ran off with the company credit card.
- I just got back from my luxury holiday, it cost more than I thought so I no longer have the funds to pay.
- I wanted to pay but all the invoices were in my briefcase, which was stolen on the street.
- My wife has been kidnapped, and I need the money to get her back.

Source: www.atradius.us/news/press-releases, 13 August 2008.

Managing cash

Why hold cash?

Most businesses hold a certain amount of cash. The amount of cash held tends to vary considerably between businesses.

Activity (16.7)

Why do you think a business may decide to hold at least some of its assets in the form of cash? (*Hint*: There are broadly three reasons.)

The three reasons are:

1 To meet day-to-day commitments, a business requires a certain amount of cash. Payments for wages, overhead expenses, goods purchased and so on must be made at the due dates. Cash has been described as the lifeblood of a business. Unless it circulates through the business and is available for the payment of claims as they become due, the survival of the business will be at risk. Profitability is not enough; a business must have sufficient cash to pay its debts when they fall due.

2 If future cash flows are uncertain for any reason, it would be prudent to hold a balance of cash. For example, a major customer that owes a large sum to the business may be in financial difficulties. Given this situation, the business can retain its capacity to meet its obligations by holding a cash balance. Similarly, if there is some uncertainty concerning future outlays, a cash balance will be required.

3 A business may decide to hold cash to put itself in a position to exploit profitable opportunities as and when they arise. For example, by holding cash, a business may be able to acquire a competitor's business that suddenly becomes available at an attractive price.

How much cash should be held?

Although cash can be held for each of the reasons identified, doing so may not always be necessary. If a business is able to borrow quickly, the amount of cash it needs to hold can be reduced. Similarly, if the business holds assets that can easily be converted to cash (for example, marketable securities such as shares in Stock Exchange listed businesses or government bonds), the amount of cash held can be reduced.

The decision as to how much cash a particular business should hold is a difficult one. Different businesses will have different views on the subject.

Activity (16.8)

What do you think are the major factors that influence how much cash a business will hold? See if you can think of five possible factors.

You may have thought of the following:

● *The nature of the business*. Some businesses, such as utilities (for example, water, electricity and gas suppliers), may have cash flows that are both predictable and reasonably certain. This will enable them to hold lower cash balances. For some businesses, cash balances may vary greatly according to the time of year. A seasonal business may accumulate cash during the high season to enable it to meet commitments during the low season.

● *The opportunity cost of holding cash*. Where there are profitable opportunities it may not be wise to hold a large cash balance.

Activity 16.8 continued

- *The level of inflation*. Holding cash during a period of rising prices will lead to a loss of purchasing power. The higher the level of inflation, the greater will be this loss.
- *The availability of near-liquid assets*. If a business has marketable securities or inventories that may easily be liquidated, high cash balances may not be necessary.
- *The availability of borrowing*. If a business can borrow easily (and quickly) there is less need to hold cash.
- *The cost of borrowing*. When interest rates are high, the option of borrowing becomes less attractive.
- *Economic conditions*. When the economy is in recession, businesses may prefer to hold cash so that they can be well placed to invest when the economy improves. In addition, during a recession, businesses may experience difficulties in collecting trade receivables. They may therefore hold higher cash balances than usual in order to meet commitments.
- *Relationships with suppliers*. Too little cash may hinder the ability of the business to pay suppliers promptly. This can lead to a loss of goodwill. It may also lead to discounts being forgone.

Controlling the cash balance

Several models have been developed to help control the cash balance of the business. One such model proposes the use of upper and lower control limits for cash balances and the use of a target cash balance. The model assumes that the business will invest in marketable investments that can easily be liquidated. These investments will be purchased or sold, as necessary, in order to keep the cash balance within the control limits.

The model proposes two upper and two lower control limits (see Figure 16.6). If the business exceeds an *outer* limit, the managers must decide whether the cash balance is likely to return to a point within the *inner* control limits set, over the next few days. If this seems likely, then no action is required. If, on the other hand, it does not seem likely, management must change the cash position of the business by either buying or selling marketable investments.

In Figure 16.6 we can see that the lower outer control limit has been breached for four days. If a four-day period is unacceptable, managers must sell marketable investments to replenish the cash balance.

The model relies heavily on management judgement to determine where the control limits are set and the period within which breaches of the control limits are acceptable. Past experience may be useful in helping managers decide on these issues. There are other models, however, that do not rely on management judgement. Instead, these use quantitative techniques to determine an optimal cash policy. One model proposed, for example, is the cash equivalent of the inventories economic order quantity model, discussed earlier in the chapter.

Cash budgets and managing cash

To manage cash effectively, it is useful for a business to prepare a cash budget. This is a very important tool for both planning and control purposes. Cash budgets were

Figure 16.6   Controlling the cash balance

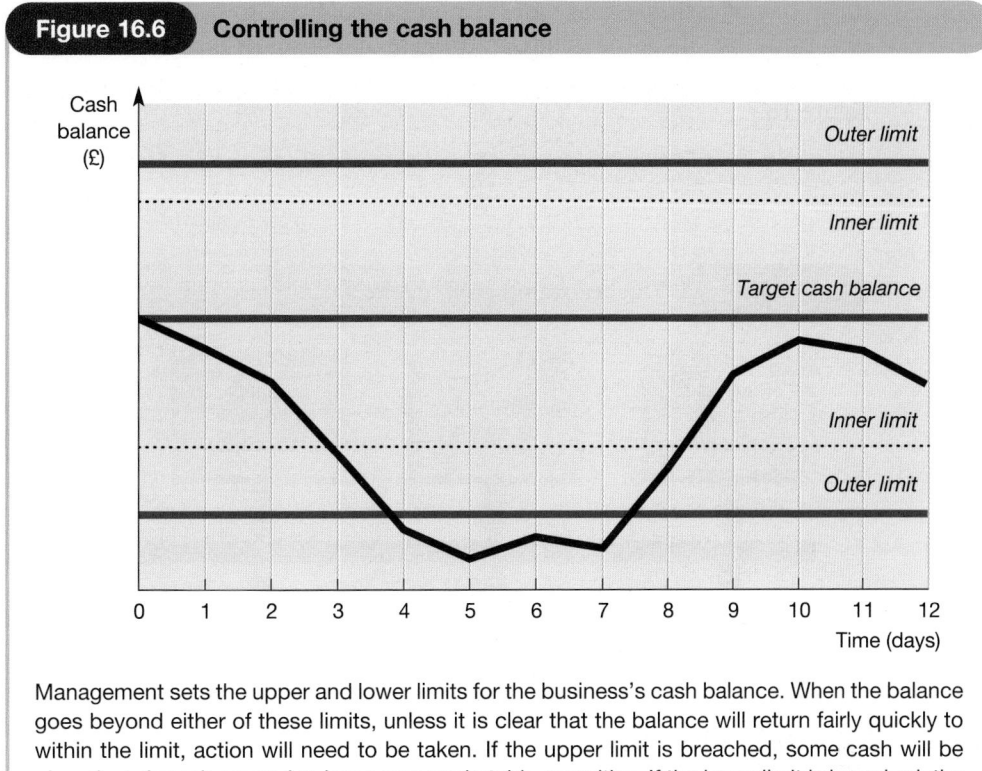

Management sets the upper and lower limits for the business's cash balance. When the balance goes beyond either of these limits, unless it is clear that the balance will return fairly quickly to within the limit, action will need to be taken. If the upper limit is breached, some cash will be placed on deposit or used to buy some marketable securities. If the lower limit is breached, the business will need to borrow some cash or sell some securities.

considered in Chapter 12, and so we shall not consider them again in detail. However, it is worth repeating that these statements enable managers to see how planned events are expected to affect the cash balance. The projected cash budget will identify periods when cash surpluses and cash deficits are expected.

When a cash surplus is expected to arise, managers must decide on the best use of the surplus funds. When a cash deficit is expected, managers must make adequate provision by borrowing, liquidating assets or rescheduling cash payments or receipts to deal with this. Cash budgets are useful in helping to control the cash held. The actual cash flows can be compared with the planned cash flows for the period. If there is a significant divergence between the projected, or forecast, cash flows and the actual cash flows, explanations must be sought and corrective action taken where necessary.

To refresh your memory on cash budgets, it would probably be worth looking back at Chapter 12, pages 458–60.

Although cash budgets are prepared primarily for internal management purposes, prospective lenders sometimes require them when a loan to a business is being considered.

Operating cash cycle

When managing cash, it is important to be aware of the **operating cash cycle (OCC)** of the business. For a retailer, for example, this may be defined as the period between the outlay of cash necessary for the purchase of inventories and the ultimate receipt of cash from the sale of the goods. In the case of a business that purchases goods on credit for subsequent resale on credit (for example, a wholesaler), the OCC is as shown in Figure 16.7.

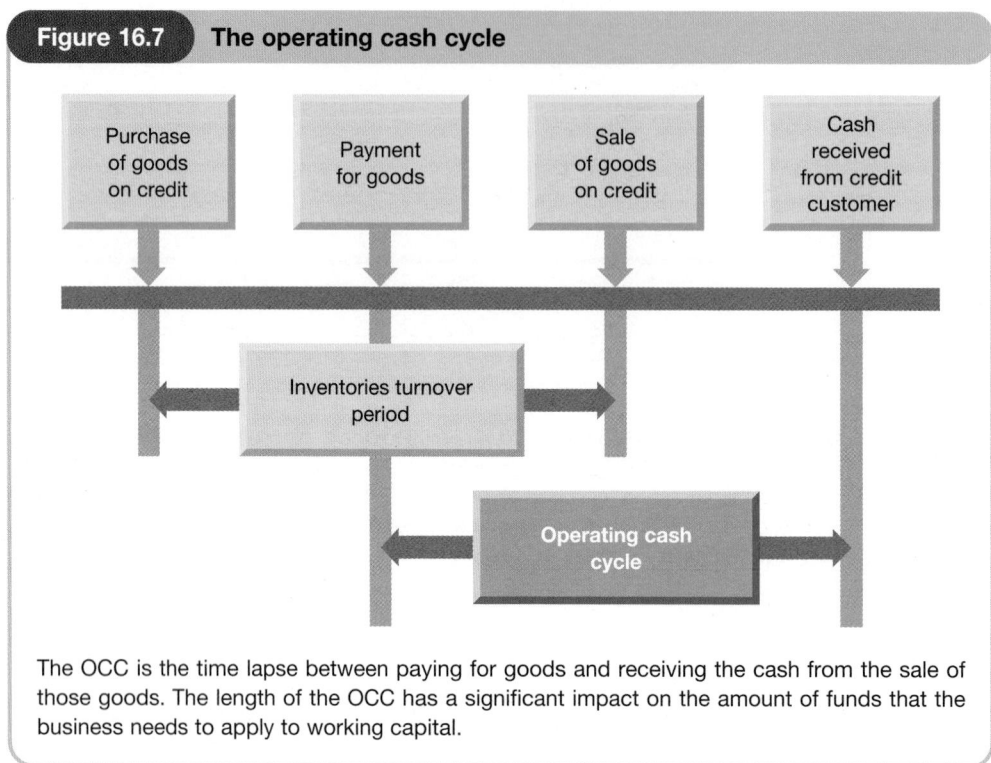

Figure 16.7 **The operating cash cycle**

The OCC is the time lapse between paying for goods and receiving the cash from the sale of those goods. The length of the OCC has a significant impact on the amount of funds that the business needs to apply to working capital.

Figure 16.7 shows that payment for inventories acquired on credit occurs some time after those inventories have been purchased and, therefore, no immediate cash outflow arises from the purchase. Similarly, cash receipts from credit customers will occur some time after the sale is made and so there will be no immediate cash inflow as a result of the sale. The OCC is the period between the payment made to the supplier for goods concerned and the cash received from the credit customer. Although Figure 16.7 depicts the position for a wholesaling business, the precise definition of the OCC can easily be adapted for other types of business.

The OCC is important because it has a significant influence on the financing requirements of the business. Broadly, the longer the cycle, the greater the financing requirements of the business and the greater the financial risks. For this reason, the business is likely to want to reduce the OCC to the minimum possible period.

For the type of business mentioned above, which buys and sells on credit, the OCC can be calculated from the financial statements by the use of certain ratios. It is calculated as shown in Figure 16.8.

Figure 16.8	Calculating the operating cash cycle

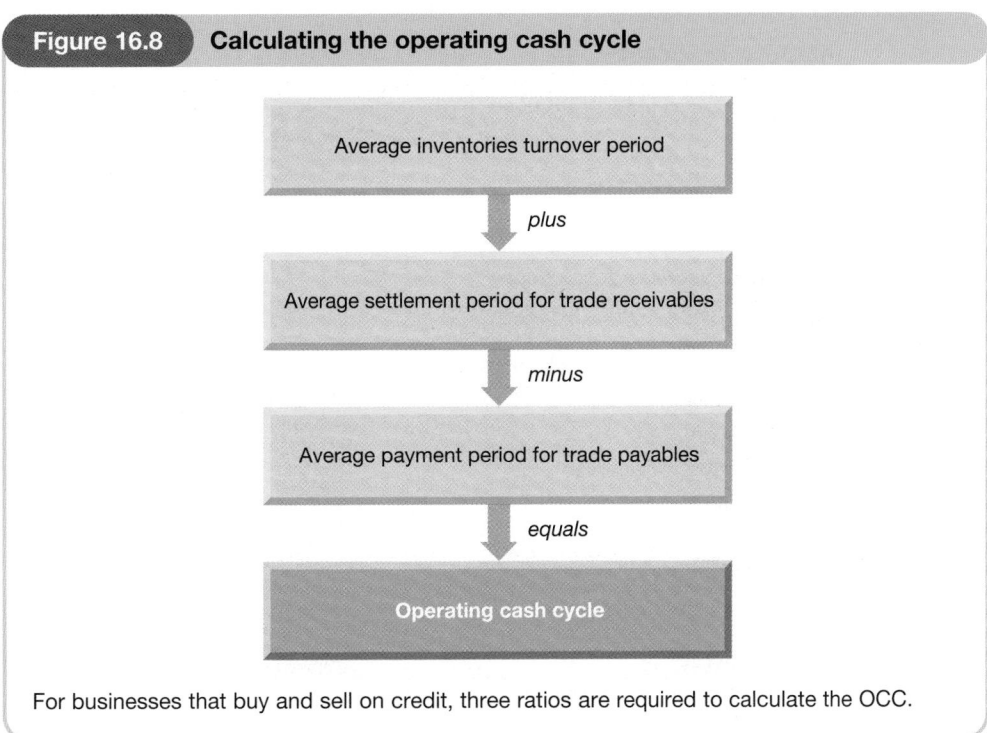

For businesses that buy and sell on credit, three ratios are required to calculate the OCC.

Activity 16.9

The financial statements of Freezeqwik Ltd, a distributor of frozen foods, are set out below for the year ended 31 December last year.

Income statement for the year ended 31 December last year

	£000	£000
Sales revenue		820
Cost of sales		
Opening inventories	142	
Purchases	568	
	710	
Closing inventories	(166)	(544)
Gross profit		276
Administration expenses		(120)
Distribution expenses		(95)
Operating profit		61
Financial expenses		(32)
Profit before taxation		29
Taxation		(7)
Profit for the year		22

Activity 16.9 continued

Statement of financial position (balance sheet) as at 31 December last year

ASSETS	£000
Non-current assets	
Property, plant and equipment	
Premises at valuation	180
Fixtures and fittings at cost less depreciation	82
Motor vans at cost less depreciation	102
	364
Current assets	
Inventories	166
Trade receivables	264
Cash	24
	454
Total assets	818
EQUITY AND LIABILITIES	
Equity	
Ordinary share capital	300
Retained earnings	352
	652
Current liabilities	
Trade payables	159
Taxation	7
	166
Total equity and liabilities	818

All purchases and sales are on credit. There has been no change in the level of trade receivables or payables over the period.

Calculate the length of the OCC for the business and go on to suggest how the business may seek to reduce this period.

The OCC may be calculated as follows:

Number of days

Average inventories turnover period:

$$\frac{(\text{Opening inventories} + \text{Closing inventories})/2}{\text{Cost of sales}} \times 365 = \frac{(142 + 166)/2}{544} \times 365 \qquad 103$$

Average settlement period for trade receivables:

$$\frac{\text{Trade receivables}}{\text{Credit sales}} \times 365 = \frac{264}{820} \times 365 \qquad 118$$

Average settlement period for trade payables:

$$\frac{\text{Trade payables}}{\text{Credit purchases}} \times 365 = \frac{159}{568} \times 365 \qquad (102)$$

OCC ___119___

The business can reduce the length of the OCC in a number of ways. The average inventories turnover period seems quite long. At present, average inventories held represent more than three months' sales requirements. Lowering the level of inventories held will reduce this. Similarly, the average settlement period for trade receivables seems long, at nearly four months' sales. Imposing tighter credit control, offering discounts, charging interest on overdue accounts and so on may reduce this. However, any policy decisions concerning inventories and trade receivables must take account of current trading conditions.

Extending the period of credit taken to pay suppliers could also reduce the OCC. However, for reasons that will be explained later, this option must be given careful consideration.

Real World 16.11 shows the average operating cash cycle for large European businesses.

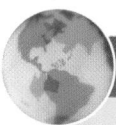

Real World 16.11

Cycling along

The annual survey of working capital by REL Consultancy Group and CFO Europe (see Real World 16.2 above) calculates the average operating cash cycle for the top 1,000 European businesses (excluding the financial sector). Comparative figures for the five-year period ending in 2007 are shown in Figure 16.9.

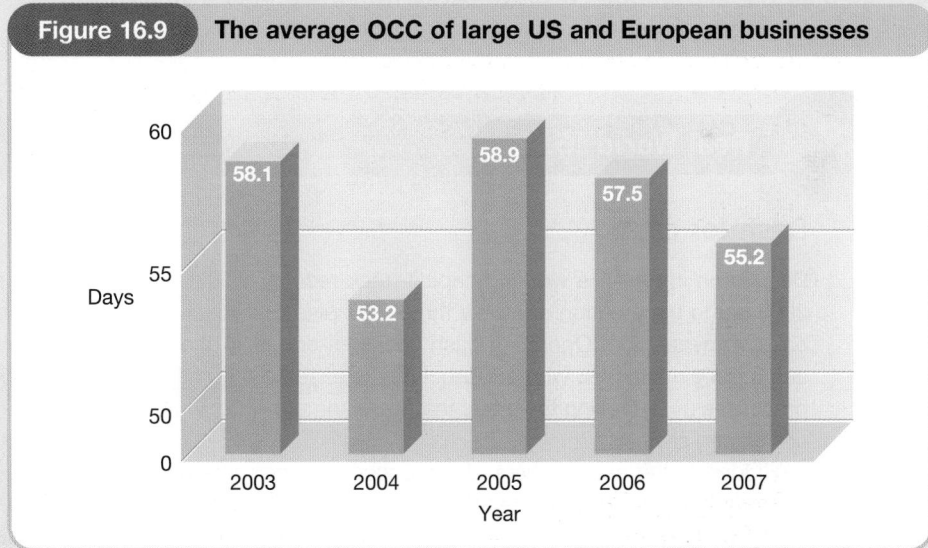

Figure 16.9 **The average OCC of large US and European businesses**

The survey calculates the operating cash cycle using year-end figures for trade receivables, inventories and trade payables. We can see that there has been a slight improvement in 2007 compared to the two previous years.

Source: Compiled from information in *Europe Working Capital Survey*, REL/CFO Europe, 2008, www.relconsult.com.

Cash transmission

A business will normally wish to benefit from receipts from customers at the earliest opportunity. The benefit is immediate where payment is made in cash. However, when payment is made by cheque, there is normally a delay of three to four working days before the cheque can be cleared through the banking system. The business must therefore wait for this period before it can benefit from the amount paid in. In the case of a business that receives large amounts in the form of cheques, the opportunity cost of this delay can be significant.

To avoid this cost, a business could require payments to be made in cash. This is not usually very practical, mainly because of the risk of theft and/or the expense of conveying cash securely. Another option is to ask for payment to be made by standing order or by direct debit from the customer's bank account. This should ensure that the amount owing is always transferred from the bank account of the customer to the bank account of the business on the day that has been agreed.

It is also possible for funds to be transferred directly to a business's bank account. Customers can pay for items by using debit cards, which results in the appropriate account being instantly debited and seller's bank account being instantly credited with the required amount. This method of payment is widely used by large retail businesses, and can be extended to other types of business.

Bank overdrafts

Bank overdrafts are simply bank current accounts that have a negative balance. They are a type of bank loan and can be a useful tool in managing the business's cash flow requirements.

Real World 16.12 shows how Indesit, a large white-goods manufacturer, managed to improve its cash flows through better working capital management.

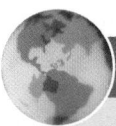

Real World 16.12

Dash for cash

Despite an impressive working capital track record, a 50% plunge in profit at Indesit in 2005 led to the creation of a new three-year plan that meant an even stronger emphasis on cash generation. Operating cash flow was added to the incentive scheme for senior and middle managers, who subsequently released more cash from Indesit's already lean processes by 'attacking the areas that were somehow neglected,' Crenna (the chief financial officer) says.

Hidden in the dark corners of the accounts-receivable department in the UK's after-sales service operation, for example, were a host of delinquent, albeit small, payments – in some cases overdue by a year or more. 'If you don't put a specific focus on these receivables, it's very easy for them to become neglected,' Crenna says. 'In theory, nobody worries about collecting £20. In reality, we were sitting on a huge amount of receivables, though each individual bill was for a small amount.'

More trapped cash was found in the company's spare-parts inventory. The inventory is worth around €30m today compared with around €40m three years ago. 'This was a good result that came just from paying the same level of attention to spare parts as to finished products,' Crenna says. In general, Indesit has been able to improve working capital performance through 'fine-tuning rather than launching epic projects.' Over the past two years, according to REL, Indesit has released €115m from its working capital processes.

Source: 'Dash for Cash', J. Karaian, *CFO Europe Magazine*, 8 July 2008, www.CFO.com. Reprinted with permission from CFO.

Managing trade payables

Trade credit arises from the fact that most businesses buy their goods and service requirements on credit. In effect, suppliers are lending the business money, interest free, on a short-term basis. Trade payables are the other side of the coin from trade receivables. One business's trade payable is another one's trade receivable, in respect of a particular transaction. Trade payables are an important source of finance for most businesses. They have been described as a 'spontaneous' source, as they tend to increase in line with the increase in the level of activity achieved by a business. Trade credit is widely regarded as a 'free' source of finance and, therefore, a good thing for a business to use. There may be real costs, however, associated with taking trade credit.

First, customers who take credit may not be as well treated as those who pay immediately. For example, when goods are in short supply, credit customers may receive lower priority when allocating the goods available. In addition, credit customers may be less favoured in terms of delivery dates or the provision of technical support services. Sometimes, the goods or services provided may be more costly if credit is required. However, in most industries, trade credit is the norm. As a result, the above costs will not apply except, perhaps, to customers that abuse the credit facilities. A business that purchases supplies on credit will normally have to incur additional administration and accounting costs in dealing with the scrutiny and payment of invoices, maintaining and updating payables' accounts and so on.

These points are not meant to imply that taking credit represents a net cost to a business. There are, of course, real benefits that can accrue. Provided that trade credit is not abused, it can represent a form of interest-free loan. It can be a much more convenient method of paying for goods and services than paying by cash, and during a period of inflation there will be an economic gain by paying later rather than sooner for goods and services purchased. For most businesses, these benefits will exceed the costs involved.

In some cases, delaying payment to payables can be a sign of financial problems. One such example is given in **Real World 16.13**.

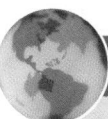 **Real World 16.13**

NHS waiting times

 FT

The National Health Service is delaying paying bills and cutting orders for supplies as it tries to balance its books, according to the trade associations whose members supply the service with everything from scanners to diagnostic tests.

Real World 16.13 continued

Ray Hodgkinson, director-general of the British Healthcare Trades Association, said that while the picture was highly variable 'some of our members are having real trouble getting money out of NHS trusts'.

Most had standing orders that said bills should be paid within 30 days, Mr Hodgkinson said. 'But some are not paying for 60 or 90 days and even longer. They are in breach of their standing orders and for a lot of our members who are small businesses this is creating problems with cash flow. There is no doubt there is slow payment on a significant scale.'

Doris-Ann Williams, director-general of the British In-Vitro Diagnostics Association, whose members provide diagnostics supplies and tests, said: 'We are starting to see invoices not being paid and orders not being closed until the start of the new financial year [in April]. . . . All sorts of measures are being taken to try not to spend money in this financial year.'

Having seen orders dry up and bills not paid this time last year as the NHS headed for a £500m-plus financial deficit, she added that this was 'starting to seem like an annual event'.

Source: 'NHS paying bills late in struggle to balance books, say suppliers', Nicholas Timmins, FT.com, 13 February 2007.

Taking advantage of cash discounts

Where a supplier offers a discount for prompt payment, the business should give careful consideration to the possibility of paying within the discount period. An example may be useful to illustrate the cost of forgoing possible discounts.

Example 16.4

Hassan Ltd takes 70 days to pay for goods from its supplier. To encourage prompt payment, the supplier has offered the business a 2 per cent discount if payment for goods is made within 30 days.

Hassan Ltd is not sure whether it is worth taking the discount offered.

If the discount is taken, payment could be made on the last day of the discount period (that is, the 30th day). However, if the discount is not taken, payment will be made after 70 days. This means that, by not taking the discount, the business will receive an extra 40 days' (that is, 70 – 30) credit. The cost of this extra credit to the business will be the 2 per cent discount forgone. If we annualise the cost of this discount forgone, we have:

$$365/40 \times 2\% = 18.3\%*$$

We can see that the annual cost of forgoing the discount is very high, and so it may be profitable for the business to pay the supplier within the discount period, even if it means that it will have to borrow to enable it to do so.

* This is an approximate annual rate. For the more mathematically minded, the precise rate is:

$$\{[(1 + 2/98)^{9.125}] - 1\} \times 100\% = 20.2\%$$

Controlling trade payables

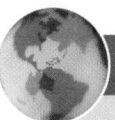 To help monitor the level of trade credit taken, management can calculate the **average settlement period for trade payables**. As we saw in Chapter 7, this ratio is:

$$\text{Average settlement period for trade payables} = \frac{\text{Average trade payables}}{\text{Credit purchases}} \times 365$$

Once again, this provides an average figure, which could be misleading. A more informative approach would be to produce an ageing schedule for payables. This would look much the same as the ageing schedule for receivables described earlier in Example 16.3.

We saw earlier that delaying payment to suppliers may create problems for a business. **Real World 16.14**, however, describes how cash-strapped businesses may delay payments and still retain the support of their suppliers.

Real World 16.14

Credit stretch

According to Gavin Swindell, European managing director of REL, a research and consulting firm, there are 'win-win' ways of extending credit terms. He states: 'A lot of businesses aren't worried about getting paid in 40 or 45 days, but are more interested in the certainty of payment on a specific date.'

Jas Sahota, a partner in Deloitte's UK restructuring practice, says that three-month extensions are common, 'as long as the supplier can see that there is a plan.' In times of stress, he says, it's important to negotiate with only a handful of the most important partners – squeezing suppliers large and small only generates grief and distracts employees with lots of calls.

More fundamentally, the benefits of pulling the payables lever in isolation is 'questionable,' notes Andrew Ashby, director of the working capital practice at KPMG in London, 'especially as the impact on the receivables balance is typically a lot more than the payables balance.'

Improving collections, such as achieving longer payment terms, relies on the strength of relationships built over time, notes Robert Hecht, a London-based managing director of turnaround consultancy AlixPartners. 'You can't wait for a crisis, and then expect suppliers to step up and be your best friends.'

Source: 'Dash for Cash', J. Karaian, *CFO Europe Magazine*, 8 July 2008, www.CFO.com. Reprinted with permission from CFO.

Working capital problems of the small business

We saw earlier (Real World 16.1, page 640) that the amounts invested by businesses in working capital are often high in proportion to the total assets employed. It is, therefore, important that these amounts are properly managed. Although this point applies to businesses of all sizes, it may be of particular importance to small businesses. It is often claimed that many small businesses suffer from a lack of capital and, where this is the case, tight control over working capital investment becomes critical. There is evidence, however, that small businesses are not very good in managing their working capital and this has been cited as a major cause of their high failure rate compared to that of large businesses. In this section, we consider the working capital management problems associated with small businesses.

Managing inventories

A lack of financial management skills within a small business often creates problems in managing inventories in an efficient and effective way. The owners of small businesses are not always aware that there are costs involved in holding too much inventories and that there are also costs involved in holding too little. These costs, which were discussed earlier, may be very high in certain industries such as manufacturing and wholesaling, where inventories account for a significant proportion of the total assets held.

It was mentioned earlier in the chapter that the starting point for an effective inventories management system is good planning and budgeting systems. In particular, there should be reliable budgets, that can help with inventories ordering. Not all small businesses prepare these budgets, however. A survey by Chittenden and others (see reference 1 at the end of the chapter) of small and medium-size businesses indicated that only 78 per cent of those replying prepare a sales budget. Inventories management can also benefit from good reporting systems and the application of quantitative techniques (for example, the Economic Order Quantity model) to try to optimise inventories levels. However, the same survey found that more than one-third of small businesses rely on manual methods of inventories control and the majority do not use inventories optimisation techniques. Though the Chittenden survey is now rather old (1998) it represents the most recent reliable evidence available. There is no reason to believe that practices of small businesses have changed much since this evidence was gathered.

Credit management

Small businesses often lack the resources to manage their trade receivables effectively. It is not unusual for a small business to operate without a separate credit control department. This tends to mean that both the expertise and the information required to make sound judgements concerning terms of sale and so on may not be available. A small business may also lack proper debt-collection procedures, such as prompt invoicing and sending out regular statements. This will increase the risks of late payment and defaulting credit customers.

These risks probably tend to increase where there is an excessive concern for growth. In an attempt to increase sales, small businesses may be too willing to extend credit to customers that are poor credit risks. Whilst this kind of problem can occur in businesses of all sizes, small businesses seem particularly susceptible.

Another problem faced by small businesses is their lack of market power. They will often find themselves in a weak position when negotiating credit terms with larger businesses. Moreover, when a large customer exceeds the terms of credit, the small supplier may feel inhibited from pressing the customer for payment in case future sales are lost.

The reason for the delay suffered by small businesses probably relates to one of the factors mentioned above, namely the bargaining power of customers. The customers of small businesses may well be larger ones, which can use a threat, perhaps an implied one, of withdrawing custom, to force small businesses to accept later trade receivable settlement.

In the UK, the government has intervened to help deal with this problem and the law now permits small businesses to charge interest on overdue accounts. In addition, large companies are now required to disclose in their published financial statements the payment policy adopted towards suppliers in the hope that this will improve the behaviour of those that delay payments. However, it is unlikely that legislation alone will make a significant improvement. Whilst small businesses may be able to charge interest on overdue accounts, they will often avoid doing so because they fear that large customers would view this as a provocative act. What is really needed to help small businesses is a change in the payment culture.

We saw in Chapter 15 that one way of dealing with the credit management problem is to factor the outstanding trade receivables. Under this kind of arrangement, the factor will take over the sales records of the business and will take responsibility for the prompt collection of trade receivables. However, some businesses are too small to take advantage of this facility. The set-up costs of a factoring arrangement often make businesses with a low sales revenue (say, £100,000 a year or less) an uneconomic proposition for the factor.

Managing cash

The management of cash raises similar issues to those relating to the management of inventories. There are costs involved in holding both too much and too little cash. Thus, there is a need for careful planning and monitoring of cash flows over time. The Chittenden survey found, however, that only 63 per cent of those replying prepared a cash budget. It was also found that cash balances are generally proportionately higher for smaller businesses than for larger ones. More than half of those in the survey held surplus cash balances on a regular basis. (See reference 1 at the end of the chapter). Though this may reflect a more conservative approach to liquidity among the owners of smaller businesses, it may suggest a failure to recognise the opportunity costs of cash balances.

Managing credit suppliers

In practice, small businesses often try to cope with the late payment of credit customers by delaying payments to their credit suppliers. We saw earlier in the chapter, however, that this can be an expensive option. Where discounts are forgone, the annual cost of this financing option compares unfavourably with most other forms of short-term financing. Nevertheless, the vast majority of small and medium-size businesses are unaware of the very high cost of delaying payment, according to the Chittenden survey (see reference 1 at the end of the chapter).

Summary

The main points of this chapter may be summarised as follows.

Working capital

- Working capital is the difference between current assets and current liabilities.
- That is, working capital = inventories + trade receivables + cash − trade payables − bank overdrafts.
- An investment in working capital cannot be avoided in practice − typically large amounts are involved.

Inventories

- There are costs of holding inventories, which include:
  - lost interest
  - storage cost
  - insurance cost
  - obsolescence.
- There are also costs of not holding sufficient inventories, which include:
  - loss of sales and customer goodwill
  - production dislocation
  - loss of flexibility − cannot take advantage of opportunities
  - reorder costs − low inventories imply more frequent ordering.
- Practical points on inventories management include:
  - identify optimum order size − models can help with this
  - set inventories reorder levels
  - use forecasts
  - keep reliable inventories records
  - use accounting ratios (for example, inventories turnover period ratio)
  - establish systems for security of inventories and authorisation
  - consider just-in-time (JIT) inventories management.

Trade receivables

- When assessing which customers should receive credit, the five Cs of credit can be used:
  - capital
  - capacity
  - collateral
  - condition
  - character.
- The costs of allowing credit include:
  - lost interest
  - lost purchasing power
  - costs of assessing customer creditworthiness
  - administration cost
  - bad debts
  - cash discounts (for prompt payment).

- The costs of denying credit include:
  - loss of customer goodwill.
- Practical points on receivables management:
  - establish a policy
  - assess and monitor customer creditworthiness
  - establish effective administration of receivables
  - establish a policy on bad debts
  - consider cash discounts
  - use financial ratios (for example, average settlement period for trade receivables ratio)
  - use ageing summaries.

Cash

- The costs of holding cash include:
  - lost interest
  - lost purchasing power.
- The costs of holding insufficient cash include:
  - loss of supplier goodwill if unable to meet commitments on time
  - loss of opportunities
  - inability to claim cash discounts
  - costs of borrowing (should an obligation need to be met at short notice).
- Practical points on cash management:
  - establish a policy
  - plan cash flows
  - make judicious use of bank overdraft finance – it can be cheap and flexible
  - use short-term cash surpluses profitably
  - bank frequently
  - operating cash cycle (for a wholesaler) = length of time from buying inventories to receiving cash from receivables less payables payment period (in days)
  - transmit cash promptly.
- An objective of working capital management is to limit the length of the operating cash cycle (OCC), subject to any risks that this may cause.

Trade payables

- The costs of taking credit include:
  - higher price than purchases for immediate cash settlement
  - administrative costs
  - restrictions imposed by seller.
- The costs of not taking credit include:
  - lost interest-free borrowing
  - lost purchasing power
  - inconvenience – paying at the time of purchase can be inconvenient.
- Practical points on payables management:
  - establish a policy
  - exploit free credit as far as possible
  - use accounting ratios (for example, average settlement period for trade payables ratio).

Working capital and the small business

- Small businesses often lack the skills and resources to manage working capital effectively.
- Small businesses often suffer from large businesses delaying payments for goods and services supplied.
- Changes in the law designed to help small businesses have had limited success.

MyAccountingLab **Now check your progress in your personal Study Plan**

 Key terms

working capital   p. 638
lead time   p. 645
ABC system of inventories control
   p. 646
economic order quantity (EOQ)   p. 647
materials requirement planning (MRP)
   system   p. 650
just-in-time (JIT) inventories
   management   p. 650

five Cs of credit   p. 652
cash discount   p. 657
average settlement period for trade
   receivables   p. 658
ageing schedule of trade receivables
   p. 658
operating cash cycle (OCC)   p. 663
average settlement period for trade
   payables   p. 671

Reference

1 **Financial Management and Working Capital Practices in UK SMEs**, *Chittenden F., Poutziouris P. and Michaelas N.*, Manchester Business School, 1998.

Further reading

If you would like to explore the topics covered in this chapter in more depth, we recommend the following books:

Business Finance: Theory and Practice, *McLaney E.*, 8th edn, Financial Times Prentice Hall, 2009, chapter 13.

Corporate Finance, *Brealey B., Myers S. and Allen F.*, 9th edn, McGraw-Hill, 2008, chapters 30 and 31.

Corporate Finance and Investment, *Pike R. and Neale B.*, 5th edn, Prentice Hall, 2006, chapters 13 and 14.

Corporate Financial Management, *Arnold G.*, 3rd edn, Financial Times Prentice Hall, 2005, chapter 13.

Review questions

Answers to these questions can be found at the back of the book on page 751.

16.1 Tariq is the credit manager of Heltex plc. He is concerned that the pattern of monthly cash receipts from credit sales shows that credit collection is poor compared with budget. Heltex's sales director believes that Tariq is to blame for this situation, but Tariq insists that he is not. Why might Tariq not be to blame for the deterioration in the credit collection period?

16.2 How might each of the following affect the level of inventories held by a business?
(a) An increase in the number of production bottlenecks experienced by the business.
(b) A rise in the level of interest rates.
(c) A decision to offer customers a narrower range of products in the future.
(d) A switch of suppliers from an overseas business to a local business.
(e) A deterioration in the quality and reliability of bought-in components.

16.3 What are the reasons for holding inventories? Are these reasons different from the reasons for holding cash?

16.4 Identify the costs of holding:
(a) too little cash;
(b) too much cash.

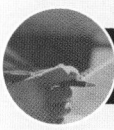

Exercises

Exercises 16.4 to 16.8 are more advanced than 16.1 to 16.3. Those with **coloured numbers** have answers at the back of the book, starting on page 804.

If you wish to try more exercises, visit the students' side of the Companion Website and MyAccountingLab.

16.1 Hercules Wholesalers Ltd has been particularly concerned with its liquidity position in recent months. The most recent income statement and statement of financial position (balance sheet) of the business are as follows:

Income statement for the year ended 31 December last year

	£000	£000
Sales revenue		452
Cost of sales		
Opening inventories	125	
Purchases	341	
	466	
Closing inventories	(143)	(323)
Gross profit		129
Expenses		(132)
Loss for the year		(3)

**Statement of financial position (balance sheet) as at
31 December last year**

	£000
Non-current assets	
Property, plant and equipment	
Premises at valuation	280
Fixtures and fittings at cost less depreciation	25
Motor vehicles at cost less depreciation	52
	357
Current assets	
Inventories	143
Trade receivables	163
	306
Total assets	663
Equity	
Ordinary share capital	100
Retained earnings	158
	258
Non-current liabilities	
Borrowings – Loans	120
Current liabilities	
Trade payables	145
Borrowings – Bank overdraft	140
	285
Total equity and liabilities	663

The trade receivables and payables were maintained at a constant level throughout the year.

Required:
(a) Explain why Hercules Wholesalers Ltd is concerned about its liquidity position.
(b) Calculate the operating cash cycle for Hercules Wholesalers Ltd based on the information above.
(c) State what steps may be taken to improve the operating cash cycle of the business.

16.2 International Electric plc at present offers its customers 30 days' credit. Half the customers, by value, pay on time. The other half takes an average of 70 days to pay. The business is considering offering a cash discount of 2 per cent to its customers for payment within 30 days.

The credit controller anticipates that half of the customers who now take an average of 70 days to pay (that is, a quarter of all customers) will pay in 30 days. The other half (the final quarter) will still take an average of 70 days to pay. The scheme will also reduce bad debts by £300,000 a year.

Annual sales revenue of £365 million is made evenly throughout the year. At present the business has a large overdraft (£60 million) with its bank at an interest cost of 12 per cent a year.

Required:
(a) Calculate the approximate equivalent annual percentage cost of a discount of 2 per cent, which reduces the time taken by credit customers to pay from 70 days to 30 days. (*Hint*: This part can be answered without reference to the narrative above.)
(b) Calculate the value of trade receivables outstanding under both the old and new schemes.
(c) How much will the scheme cost the business in discounts?
(d) Should the business go ahead with the scheme? State what other factors, if any, should be taken into account.
(e) Outline the controls and procedures that a business should adopt to manage the level of its trade receivables.

16.3 The managing director of Sparkrite Ltd, a trading business, has just received summary sets of financial statements for last year and this year:

Sparkrite Ltd
Income statements for years ended 30 September last year and this year

	Last year		This year	
	£000	£000	£000	£000
Sales revenue		1,800		1,920
Cost of sales				
Opening inventories	160		200	
Purchases	1,120		1,175	
	1,280		1,375	
Closing inventories	(200)		(250)	
		(1,080)		(1,125)
Gross profit		720		795
Expenses		(680)		(750)
Profit for the year		40		45

Statements of financial position (balance sheets) as at 30 September last year and this year

	Last year	This year
	£000	£000
Non-current assets	950	930
Current assets		
Inventories	200	250
Trade receivables	375	480
Bank	4	2
	579	732
Total assets	1,529	1,662
Equity		
Fully paid £1 ordinary shares	825	883
Retained earnings	509	554
	1,334	1,437
Current liabilities	195	225
Total equity and liabilities	1,529	1,662

The finance director has expressed concern at the increase in inventories and trade receivables levels.

Required:
(a) Show, by using the data given, how you would calculate ratios that could be used to measure inventories and trade receivables levels during last year and this year.
(b) Discuss the ways in which the management of Sparkrite Ltd could exercise control over:
  (1) inventories levels;
  (2) trade receivables levels.

16.4 Your superior, the general manager of Plastics Manufacturers Limited, has recently been talking to the chief buyer of Plastic Toys Limited, which manufactures a wide range of toys for young children. At present, Plastic Toys is considering changing its supplier of plastic granules and has offered to buy its entire requirement of 2,000 kg a month from you at the going market rate, provided that you will grant it three months' credit on its purchases. The following information is available:

(1) Plastic granules sell for £10 a kg, variable costs are £7 a kg, and fixed costs £2 a kg.
(2) Your own business is financially strong, and has sales revenue of £15 million a year. For the foreseeable future it will have surplus capacity, and it is actively looking for new outlets.
(3) Extracts from Plastic Toys' financial statements:

	Year 1 £000	Year 2 £000	Year 3 £000
Sales revenue	800	980	640
Profit before interest and tax	100	110	(150)
Capital employed	600	650	575
Current assets			
Inventories	200	220	320
Trade receivables	140	160	160
	340	380	480
Current liabilities			
Trade payables	180	190	220
Overdraft	100	150	310
	280	340	530
Working capital	60	40	(50)

Required:

(a) Write some short notes suggesting sources of information that you would use to assess the creditworthiness of potential customers who are unknown to you. You should critically evaluate each source of information.

(b) Describe the accounting controls that you would use to monitor the level of your business's trade receivables.

(c) Advise your general manager on the acceptability of the proposal. You should give your reasons and do any calculations you consider necessary. (*Hint*: To answer this question you must weigh the costs of administration and cash discounts against the savings in bad debts and interest charges.)

16.5　Mayo Computers Ltd has annual sales of £20 million. Bad debts amount to £0.1 million a year. All sales made by the business are on credit and, at present, credit terms are negotiable by the customer. On average, the settlement period for trade receivables is 60 days. Trade receivables are financed by an overdraft bearing a 14 per cent rate of interest per year. The business is currently reviewing its credit policies to see whether more efficient and profitable methods could be employed. Only one proposal has so far been put forward concerning the management of trade credit.

The credit control department has proposed that customers should be given a $2\frac{1}{2}$ per cent discount if they pay within 30 days. For those who do not pay within this period, a maximum of 50 days' credit should be given. The credit department believes that 60 per cent of customers will take advantage of the discount by paying at the end of the discount period. The remainder will pay at the end of 50 days. The credit department believes that bad debts can be effectively eliminated by adopting the above policies and by employing stricter credit investigation procedures, which will cost an additional £20,000 a year. The credit department is confident that these new policies will not result in any reduction in sales revenue.

Required:
Calculate the net annual cost (savings) to the business of abandoning its existing credit policies and adopting the proposals of the credit control department. (*Hint*: To answer this question you must weigh the costs of administration and cash discounts against the savings in bad debts and interest charges.)

16.6　Boswell Enterprises Ltd is reviewing its trade credit policy. The business, which sells all of its goods on credit, has estimated that sales revenue for the forthcoming year will be £3m under the existing policy. Credit customers representing 30 per cent of trade receivables are expected to pay one month after being invoiced and 70 per cent are expected to pay two months after being invoiced. These estimates are in line with previous years' figures.

At present, no cash discounts are offered to customers. However, to encourage prompt payment, the business is considering giving a $2^1/_2$ per cent cash discount to credit customers who pay in one month or less. Given this incentive, the business expects credit customers accounting for 60 per cent of trade receivables to pay one month after being invoiced and those accounting for 40 per cent of trade receivables to pay two months after being invoiced. The business believes that the introduction of a cash discount policy will prove attractive to some customers and will lead to a 5 per cent increase in total sales revenue.

Irrespective of the trade credit policy adopted, the gross profit margin of the business will be 20 per cent for the forthcoming year and three months' inventories will be held. Fixed monthly expenses of £15,000 and variable expenses (excluding discounts), equivalent to 10 per cent of sales revenue, will be incurred and will be paid one month in arrears. Trade payables will be paid in arrears and will be equal to two months' cost of sales. The business will hold a fixed cash balance of £140,000 throughout the year, whichever trade credit policy is adopted. Ignore taxation.

Required:
(a) Calculate the investment in working capital at the end of the forthcoming year under:
   (1) the existing policy;
   (2) the proposed policy.
(b) Calculate the expected profit for the forthcoming year under:
   (1) the existing policy;
   (2) the proposed policy.
(c) Advise the business as to whether it should implement the proposed policy.

   (*Hint*: The investment in working capital will be made up of inventories, trade receivables and cash, *less* trade payables and any unpaid expenses at the year end.)

16.7 Delphi plc has recently decided to enter the expanding market for minidisc players. The business will manufacture the players and sell them to small TV and hi-fi specialists, medium-sized music stores and large retail chain stores. The new product will be launched next February and predicted sales revenue for the product from each customer group for February and the expected rate of growth for subsequent months are as follows:

Customer type	February sales revenue (£000)	Monthly compound sales revenue growth (%)	Credit sales months
TV and hi-fi specialists	20	4	1
Music stores	30	6	2
Retail chain stores	40	8	3

The business is concerned about the financing implications of launching the new product, as it is already experiencing liquidity problems. In addition, it is concerned that the credit control department will find it difficult to cope. This is a new market for the business and there are likely to be many new customers who will have to be investigated for creditworthiness.

Workings should be in £000 and calculations made to one decimal place only.

Required:
(a) Prepare an ageing schedule of the monthly trade receivables balance relating to the new product for each of the first four months of the new product's life, and comment on the results. The schedule should analyse the trade receivables outstanding according to customer type. It should also indicate, for each customer type, the relevant percentage outstanding in relation to the total amount outstanding for each month.

(b) Identify and discuss the factors that should be taken into account when evaluating the credit-worthiness of the new business customers.

16.8 Goliath plc is a retail business operating in Wales. The most recent financial statements of the business are as follows:

Income statement for the year to 31 May

	£000	£000
Sales revenue		2,400.0
Cost of sales		
Opening inventories	550.0	
Purchases	1,450.0	
	2,000.0	
Closing inventories	(560.0)	(1,440.0)
Gross profit		960.0
Administration expenses		(300.0)
Selling expenses		(436.0)
Operating profit		224.0
Interest payable		(40.0)
Profit before taxation		184.0
Taxation (25%)		(46.0)
Profit for the period		138.0

Statement of financial position (balance sheet) as at 31 May

	£000	£000
Non-current assets		
Property, plant and equipment		
Machinery and equipment at cost	424.4	
Accumulated depreciation	(140.8)	283.6
Motor vehicles at cost	308.4	
Accumulated depreciation	(135.6)	172.8
		456.4
Current assets		
Inventories at cost		560.0
Trade receivables		565.0
Cash at bank		36.4
		1,161.4
Total assets		1,617.8
Equity		
£1 ordinary shares		200.0
Retained earnings		520.8
		720.8
Non-current liabilities		
Borrowings – Loan notes		400.0
Current liabilities		
Trade payables		451.0
Taxation		46.0
		497.0
Total equity and liabilities		1,617.8

All sales and purchases are made on credit.

The business is considering whether to grant extended credit facilities to its customers. It has been estimated that increasing the settlement period for trade receivables by a further 20 days will increase the sales revenue of the business by 10 per cent. However, inventories will have to be increased by 15 per cent to cope with the increased demand. It is estimated that purchases will have to rise to £1,668,000 during the next year as a result of these changes. To finance the increase in inventories and trade receivables, the business will increase the settlement period taken for suppliers by 15 days and use a loan facility bearing a 10 per cent rate of interest for the remaining balance.

If the policy is implemented, bad debts are likely to increase by £120,000 a year and administration costs will rise by 15 per cent.

Required:

(a) Calculate the increase or decrease to each of the following that will occur in the forthcoming year if the proposed policy is implemented:

   (1) operating cash cycle (based on year-end figures);

   (2) net investment in inventories, trade receivables and trade payables;

   (3) net profit after taxation.

(b) Should the business implement the proposed policy? Give reasons for your conclusion.

PART 4

Supplementary information

Part 4 provides information that is supplementary to the main text of the book.

Appendix A takes the format of a normal textual chapter and describes the way in which financial transactions are recorded in books of account. Generally, this is by means of the 'double-entry' system, described in basic terms in the appendix.

Appendix B gives definitions of the key terms highlighted throughout the main text and listed at the end of each chapter. The aim of the appendix is to provide a single location to check on the meanings of the major accounting terms used in this book and in the world of finance.

Appendices C, D and E give answers to some of the questions set in the course of the main text. Appendix C gives answers to the self-assessment questions, Appendix D gives the answers to the review questions and Appendix E gives answers to those of the exercises that are marked as having their answers provided in the book.

Appendix F is a table of present value factors that can be used to discount future cash flows.

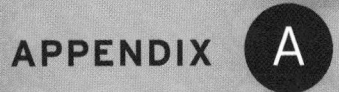

Recording financial transactions

Introduction

In Chapters 2 and 3, we saw how the financial transactions of a business may be recorded by making a series of entries on the statement of financial position (balance sheet) and/or the income statement. Each of these entries had its corresponding 'double', meaning that both sides of the transaction were recorded. However, adjusting the financial statements, by hand, for each transaction can be very messy and confusing. With a reasonably large number of transactions it is pretty certain to result in mistakes.

For businesses whose accounting systems are on a computer, this problem is overcome because suitable software can deal with a series of 'plus' and 'minus' entries very reliably. Where the accounting system is not computerised, however, it would be helpful to have some more practical way of keeping accounting records. Such a system not only exists but, before the advent of the computer, was the routine way of keeping accounting records. It is this system that is explained in this appendix. We should be clear that the system we are going to consider follows exactly the same rules as those that we have already met. Its distinguishing feature is its ability to provide those keeping accounting records by hand with a methodical approach that allows each transaction to be clearly identified and errors to be minimised.

Learning outcomes

When you have completed this appendix, you should be able to:

● Explain the basic principles of double-entry bookkeeping.

● Write up a series of business transactions and balance the accounts.

● Extract a trial balance and explain its purpose.

● Prepare a set of financial statements from the underlying double-entry accounts.

The basics of double-entry bookkeeping

→ When we record accounting transactions by hand, we use a recording system known as **double-entry bookkeeping**. This system does not use plus and minus entries on the face of a statement of financial position and income statement to record a particular transaction, in the way described in Chapters 2 and 3. Instead, these are recorded in

→ accounts. An **account** is simply a record of one or more transactions relating to a particular item, such as cash, fixtures and fittings, borrowings, sales revenue, rent payable and equity. A business may keep few or many accounts, depending on the size and complexity of its operations. Broadly, businesses tend to keep a separate account for each item that appears in either the income statement or the statement of financial position.

An example of an account, in this case the cash account, is as follows:

Cash

£		£

We can see that an account has three main features:

- A title indicating the item to which it relates
→ - A left-hand side, known as the **debit** side
→ - A right-hand side, known as the **credit** side.

One side of an account will record increases in the particular item and the other will record decreases. This, of course, is slightly different from the approach we used when adjusting the financial statements. When adjusting the statement of financial position, for example, we put a reduction in an asset or claim in the same column as any increases, but with a minus sign against it. However, when accounts are used, a reduction is shown on the opposite side of the account.

The side on which an increase or decrease is shown will depend on the nature of the item to which the account relates. For example, an account for an asset, such as cash, will show increases on the left-hand (debit) side of the account and decreases on the right-hand (credit) side. However, for claims (that is, equity and liabilities) it is the other way around. An increase in the account for equity or for a liability will be shown on the right-hand (credit) side and a decrease will be shown on the left-hand (debit) side.

To understand why this difference exists, we should recall from Chapter 2 that the accounting equation is:

$$\text{Assets} = \text{Equity} + \text{Liabilities}$$

We can see that assets appear on one side of the equation and equity and liabilities appear on the other. Recording transactions in accounts simply expresses this difference in the recording process. Increases in assets are shown on the left-hand side of an account and increases in equity and liabilities are shown on the right-hand side of the account. We should recall the point made in Chapter 2 that each transaction has two aspects. Thus, when we record a particular transaction, two separate accounts will be affected. Recording transactions in this way is known as double-entry bookkeeping.

It is worth going through a simple example to see how transactions affecting statement of financial position items would be recorded under the double-entry bookkeeping system. Suppose a new business started on 1 January with the owner putting £5,000 into a newly opened business bank account, as initial equity. This entry would appear in the cash account as follows:

Cash

	£		£
1 January Equity	5,000		

The corresponding entry would be made in the equity account as follows:

Equity

	£		£
		1 January Cash	5,000

It is usual to show, in each account by way of note, where the other side of the entry will be found. Thus, someone looking at the equity account will know that the £5,000 arose from a receipt of cash. This provides potentially useful information, partly because it establishes a 'trail' that can be followed when checking for errors. Including the date of the transaction provides additional information to the reader of the accounts.

Now suppose that, on 2 January, £600 of the cash is used to buy some inventories. This would affect the cash account as follows:

Cash

	£		£
1 January Equity	5,000	2 January Inventories	600

This cash account, in effect, shows 'positive' cash of £5,000 and 'negative' cash of £600, a net amount of £4,400.

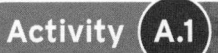

Activity A.1

As you know, we must somehow record the other side of the transaction involving the acquisition of the inventories for £600. See if you can work out what to do in respect of the inventories.

We must open an account for inventories. Since inventories are assets, an increase in it will appear on the left-hand side of the account, as follows:

Inventories

	£		£
2 January Cash	600		

What we have seen so far highlights the key rule of double-entry bookkeeping: each left-hand entry must have a right-hand entry of equal size. Using the jargon, we can say that *every debit must have a credit.*

It might be helpful at this point to make clear that the words 'debit' and 'credit' are no more than accounting jargon for left and right, respectively. Generally, in English, (that is, when not referring to accounting), people tend to use credit to imply something good and debit something undesirable. Debit and credit have no such implication in accounting. Each transaction requires both a debit entry and a credit one. This is equally true whether the transaction is a 'good' one, like being paid by a credit customer, or a 'bad' one, like having to treat a credit customer's balance as worthless because that customer has gone bankrupt.

Recording trading transactions

The rules of double entry also extend to 'trading' transactions, that is, making revenue (sales and so on) and incurring expenses. To understand how these transactions are recorded, we should recall that in Chapter 3 the extended accounting equation was set out as follows:

$$\text{Assets} = \text{Equity} + (\text{Revenues} - \text{Expenses}) + \text{Liabilities}$$

This equation can be rearranged so that:

$$\text{Assets} + \text{Expenses} = \text{Equity} + \text{Revenues} + \text{Liabilities}$$

We can see that increases in expenses are shown on the same side as assets and this means that they will be dealt with in the same way for recording purposes. Thus, an increase in an expense, such as wages, will be shown on the left-hand (debit) side of the wages account and a decrease will be shown on the right-hand (credit) side. Increases in revenues are shown on the same side as equity and liabilities and so will be dealt with in the same way as them. Thus, an increase in revenue, such as sales, will be shown on the right-hand (credit) side and a decrease will be shown on the left-hand (debit) side.

To summarise, therefore, we can say that:

- Debits (left-hand entries) represent increases in assets and expenses and decreases in claims and revenues.
- Credits (right-hand entries) represent increases in claims and revenues and decreases in assets and expenses.

Let us continue with our example by assuming that, on 3 January, the business paid £900 to rent business premises for the three months to 31 March. To record this transaction, we should normally open a 'rent account' and make entries in this account and in the cash account as follows:

Rent

		£			£
3 January	Cash	900			

Cash

		£			£
1 January	Equity	5,000	2 January	Inventories	600
			3 January	Rent	900

The fact that assets and expenses are dealt with in the same way should not be altogether surprising since assets and expenses are closely linked. Assets transform into expenses as they are 'used up'. Rent, which, as here, is usually paid in advance, is an asset when it is first paid. It represents the value to the business of being entitled to occupy the premises for the forthcoming period (until 31 March in this case). As the three months progress, this asset becomes an expense; it is 'used up'. We need to remember that the debit entry in the rent account does not necessarily represent either an asset or an expense; it could be a mixture of the two. Strictly, by the end of the day on which it was paid (3 January), £30 would have represented an expense for the three days; the remaining £870 would have been an asset. As each day passes, an additional £10 (that is, £900/90 (there are 90 days in January, February and March altogether)) will transform from an asset into an expense. As we have already seen, it is not necessary for us to make any adjustment to the rent account as the days pass.

Assume, now, that on 5 January the business sold inventories costing £200 for £300 on credit. As usual, when we are able to identify the cost of the inventories sold at the time of sale, we need to deal with the sale and the cost of sales as two separate issues, each having its own set of debits and credits.

First, let us deal with the sale. We now need to open accounts for both 'sales revenue' and 'trade receivables' – which do not, as yet, exist. The sale gives rise to an increase in revenue and so there is a credit entry in the sales revenue account. The sale also creates an asset of trade receivables and so there is debit entry in trade receivables:

Sales revenue

	£			£
		5 January	Trade receivables	300

Trade receivables

		£		£
5 January	Sales revenue	300		

Let us now deal with the inventories sold. Since the inventories sold have become the expense 'cost of sales', we need to reduce the figure on the inventories account by making a credit entry and to make the corresponding debit in a 'cost of sales' account, opened for the purpose:

Inventories

		£			£
2 January	Cash	600	5 January	Cost of sales	200

Cost of sales

		£		£
5 January	Inventories	200		

We shall now look at the other transactions for our hypothetical business for the remainder of January. These can be taken to be as follows:

8 January	Bought some inventories on credit costing £800
11 January	Bought some office furniture for £600 cash
15 January	Sold inventories costing £600 for £900, on credit
18 January	Received £800 from trade receivables
21 January	Paid trade payables £500
24 January	Paid wages for the month £400
27 January	Bought inventories on credit for £800
31 January	Borrowed £2,000 from the Commercial Finance Company

Naturally, we shall have to open several additional accounts to enable us to record all of these transactions in any meaningful way. By the end of January, the set of accounts would appear as follows:

Cash

		£			£
1 January	Equity	5,000	2 January	Inventories	600
18 January	Trade receivables	800	3 January	Rent	900
31 January	Comm. Fin. Co.	2,000	11 January	Office furniture	600
			21 January	Trade payables	500
			24 January	Wages	400

Equity

		£			£
			1 January	Cash	5,000

Inventories

		£			£
2 January	Cash	600	5 January	Cost of sales	200
8 January	Trade payables	800	15 January	Cost of sales	600
27 January	Trade payables	800			

Rent

		£		£
3 January	Cash	900		

Sales revenue

	£			£
		5 January	Trade receivables	300
		15 January	Trade receivables	900

Trade receivables

		£			£
5 January	Sales revenue	300	18 January	Cash	800
15 January	Sales revenue	900			

Cost of sales

		£		£
5 January	Inventories	200		
15 January	Inventories	600		

Trade payables

		£			£
21 January	Cash	500	8 January	Inventories	800
			27 January	Inventories	800

Office furniture

		£			£
11 January	Cash	600			

Wages

		£			£
24 January	Cash	400			

Borrowings – Commercial Finance Company

	£			£
		31 January	Cash	2,000

All of the transactions from 8 January onwards are quite similar in nature to those up to that date, which we discussed in detail, and so we should be able to follow them using the date references as a guide.

Balancing accounts and the trial balance

Businesses keeping their accounts in the way shown would find it helpful to summarise their individual accounts periodically – perhaps weekly or monthly – for two reasons:

- To be able to see at a glance how much is in each account (for example, to see how much cash the business has left).
- To help to check the accuracy of the bookkeeping so far.

Let us look at the cash account again:

Cash

		£			£
1 January	Equity	5,000	2 January	Inventories	600
18 January	Trade receivables	800	3 January	Rent	900
31 January	Comm. Fin. Co.	2,000	11 January	Office furniture	600
			21 January	Trade payables	500
			24 January	Wages	400

Does this account tell us how much cash the business has at 31 January? The answer is partly yes and partly no.

We do not have a single figure showing the cash **balance** but we can fairly easily deduce this by adding up the debit (receipts) column and deducting the sum of the credit (payments) column. However, it would be better if a cash balance were provided for us.

To summarise or balance this account, we add up the column with the largest amount (in this case, the debit side) and put this total on *both* sides of the account. We then put in, on the credit side, the figure that will make that side add up to the total that appears in the account. We cannot put in this balancing figure only once, as the double-entry rule would be broken. Thus, to preserve the double entry, we also put it in on the other side of the same account below the totals, as follows:

Cash

		£			£
1 January	Equity	5,000	2 January	Inventories	600
18 January	Trade receivables	800	3 January	Rent	900
31 January	Borrowings	2,000	11 January	Office furniture	600
			21 January	Trade payables	500
			24 January	Wages	400
			31 January	Balance carried down	4,800
		7,800			7,800
1 February	Balance brought down	4,800			

Note that the balance carried down (usually abbreviated to 'c/d') at the end of one period becomes the balance brought down ('b/d') at the beginning of the next. Now we can see at a glance what the present cash position is, without having to do any mental arithmetic.

Activity (A.2)

Try balancing the inventories account and then say what we know about the inventories position at the end of January.

The inventories account will be balanced as follows:

Inventories

		£			£
2 January	Cash	600	5 January	Cost of sales	200
8 January	Trade payables	800	15 January	Cost of sales	600
27 January	Trade payables	800	31 January	Balance c/d	1,400
		2,200			2,200
1 February	Balance b/d	1,400			

We can see at a glance that the business held inventories that had cost £1,400 at the end of January. We can also see quite easily how this situation arose.

We can balance all of the other accounts in a similar fashion. However, there is no point in formally balancing accounts that have only one entry at the moment (for example, the equity account) because we cannot summarise one figure; it is already in as summarised a form as it can be. After balancing, the remaining accounts will be as follows:

Equity

	£			£
	£	1 January	Cash	5,000

Rent

		£			£
3 January	Cash	900			

Sales revenue

		£			£
31 January	Balance c/d	1,200	5 January	Trade receivables	300
			15 January	Trade receivables	900
		1,200			1,200
			1 February	Balance b/d	1,200

Trade receivables

		£			£
5 January	Sales revenue	300	18 January	Cash	800
15 January	Sales revenue	900	31 January	Balance c/d	400
		1,200			1,200
1 February	Balance b/d	400			

Cost of sales

		£			£
5 January	Inventories	200	31 January	Balance c/d	800
15 January	Inventories	600			
		800			800
1 February	Balance b/d	800			

Trade payables

		£			£
21 January	Cash	500	8 January	Inventories	800
31 January	Balance c/d	1,100	27 January	Inventories	800
		1,600			1,600
			1 February	Balance b/d	1,100

Office furniture

		£			£
11 January	Cash	600			

Wages

		£			£
24 January	Cash	400			

Borrowings – Commercial Finance Company

		£			£
			31 January	Cash	2,000

Activity A.3

If we now separately total the debit balances and the credit balances, what should we expect to find?

We should expect to find that these two totals are equal. This must, in theory be true since every debit entry was matched by an equally-sized credit entry.

Let us see if our expectation in Activity A.3 works in our example, by listing the debit and credit balances as follows:

	Debits	Credits
	£	£
Cash	4,800	
Inventories	1,400	
Equity		5,000
Rent	900	
Sales revenue		1,200
Trade receivables	400	
Cost of sales	800	
Trade payables		1,100
Office furniture	600	
Wages	400	
Borrowings		2,000
	9,300	9,300

→   This statement is known as a **trial balance**. The fact that it agrees gives us *some* indication that we have not made bookkeeping errors.

This does not, however, give us total confidence that no error could have occurred. Consider, for example, the transaction that took place on 3 January (paid rent for the month of £900). In each of the following cases, all of which would be a wrong treatment of the transaction, the trial balance would still have agreed:

- The transaction was completely omitted from the accounts, that is, no entries were made at all.
- The amount was misread as £9,000 but then (correctly) debited to the rent account and credited to cash.
- The correct amount was (incorrectly) debited to cash and credited to rent.

Nevertheless, a trial balance that agrees does give some confidence that accounts have been correctly written up.

Activity A.4

Why do you think the words 'debtor' and 'creditor' are used to describe those who owe money or are owed money by a business?

The answer simply is that debtors have a debit balance (that is, a balance brought down on the debit side) in the books of the business, whereas creditors have a credit balance.

Preparing the financial statements (final accounts)

If the trial balance agrees and we are confident that there are no errors in recording, the next stage is to prepare the income statement and statement of financial position. Preparing the income statement is simply a matter of going through the individual accounts, identifying those amounts that represent revenue and expenses of the period, and transferring them to the income statement, which is itself also part of the double-entry system.

We shall now do this for the example we have been using. The situation is complicated slightly for three reasons:

- As we know, the £900 rent paid during January relates to the three months January, February and March.
- The business's owner estimates that the electricity used during January is about £110. There is no bill yet from the electricity supply business because it normally bills customers only at the end of each three-month period.
- The business's owner believes that the office furniture should be depreciated by 20% each year (straight-line).

These three factors need to be taken into account. As we shall see, however, the end-of-period adjustments of these types are very easily handled in double-entry accounts. Let us deal with these three areas first.

The rent account will appear as follow, after we have completed the transfer to the income statement:

Rent

		£			£
3 January	Cash	900	31 January	Income statement	300
				Balance c/d	600
		900			900
1 February	Balance b/d	600			

At 31 January, because two months' rent is still an asset, this is carried down as a debit balance. The remainder (representing January's rent) is credited to the rent account and debited to a newly opened income statement. As we shall see shortly, the £600 debit balance remaining will appear in the 31 January statement of financial position.

Now let us deal with the electricity. The electricity account will be as follows after the transfer to the income statement:

Electricity

	£			£
		31 January	Income statement	110

Because there has been no cash payment or other transaction recorded so far for electricity, we do not already have an account for it. It is necessary to open one. We need to debit the income statement with the £110 of electricity used during January and credit the electricity account with the same amount. At 31 January, this credit balance reflects the amount owed by this business to the electricity supplier. Once again, we shall see shortly that this balance will appear on the statement of financial position.

Next we shall consider what is necessary regarding the office furniture. The depreciation for the month will be 20% × £600 × $^1/_{12}$, that is £10. Normal accounting practice is to charge (debit) this to the income statement, with the corresponding credit going to a 'provision for depreciation of office furniture' account. The latter entry will appear as follows:

Provision for depreciation of office furniture account

	£			£
		31 January	Income statement	10

This £10 balance will be reflected in the statement of financial position at 31 January by being deducted from the office furniture itself, as we shall see.

The balances on the following accounts represent straightforward revenue and expenses for the month of January:

- Sales revenue
- Cost of sales
- Wages.

The balances on these accounts will simply be transferred to the income statement.

To transfer balances to the income statement, we simply debit or credit the account concerned, such that any balance amount is eliminated, and make the corresponding credit or debit in the income statement. Take sales revenue, for example. This has a credit balance (because the balance represents a revenue). We must debit the sales revenue account with £1,200 and credit the income statement with the same amount. So a credit balance on the sales revenue account becomes a credit entry in the income statement. For the three accounts, then, we have the following:

Sales revenue

		£			£
31 January	Balance c/d	1,200	5 January	Trade receivables	300
			15 January	Trade receivables	900
		1,200			1,200
31 January	Income statement	1,200	1 February	Balance b/d	1,200

Cost of sales

		£			£
5 January	Inventories	200	31 January	Balance c/d	800
15 January	Inventories	600			
		800			800
1 February	Balance b/d	800	31 January	Income statement	800

Wages

		£			£
24 January	Cash	400	31 January	Income statement	400

The income statement will now look as follows:

Income statement

		£			£
31 January	Cost of sales	800	31 January	Sales revenue	1,200
31 January	Rent	300			
31 January	Wages	400			
31 January	Electricity	110			
31 January	Depreciation	10			

We must now transfer the balance on the income statement (a debit balance of £420).

Activity A.5

What does the balance on the income statement represent, and to where should it be transferred?

The balance is either the profit or the loss for the period. In this case it is a loss as the total expenses exceed the total revenue. This loss must be borne by the owner, and it must therefore be transferred to the equity account.

The two accounts would now appear as follows:

Income statement

		£			£
31 January	Cost of sales	800	31 January	Sales revenue	1,200
31 January	Rent	300			
31 January	Wages	400			
31 January	Electricity	110			
31 January	Depreciation	10	31 January	Equity (loss)	420
		1,620			1,620

Equity

		£			£
31 January	Income statement (loss)	420	1 January	Cash	5,000
31 January	Balance c/d	4,580			
		5,000			5,000
			1 February	Balance b/d	4,580

The last thing done was to balance the equity account.

Now all of the balances remaining on accounts represent either assets or claims as at 31 January. These balances can now be used to produce a statement of financial position, as follows:

Statement of financial position as at 31 January

	£
ASSETS	
Non-current assets	
Property, plant and equipment	
Office furniture: cost	600
depreciation	(10)
	590
Current assets	
Inventories	1,400
Prepaid expense	600
Trade receivables	400
Cash	4,800
	7,200
Total assets	7,790
EQUITY AND LIABILITIES	
Owners' equity	4,580
Non-current liability	
Borrowings	2,000
Current liabilities	
Accrued expense	110
Trade payables	1,100
	1,210
Total equity and liabilities	7,790

The income statement could be written in a more stylish manner, for reporting to users, as follows:

Income statement for the month ended 31 January

	£
Sales revenue	1,200
Cost of sales	(800)
Gross profit	400
Rent	(300)
Wages	(400)
Electricity	(110)
Depreciation	(10)
Loss for the month	(420)

The ledger and its division

→ The book in which the accounts are traditionally kept is known as the **ledger**, and 'accounts' are sometimes referred to as 'ledger accounts', even where they are computerised.

In a handwritten accounting system, the ledger is often divided into various sections. This tends to be for three main reasons:

- Having all of the accounts in one book means that it is only possible for one person at a time to use the accounts, either to make entries or to extract useful information.
- Dividing the ledger along logical grounds can allow specialisation, so that various individual members of the accounts staff can look after their own part of the system. This can lead to more efficient record keeping.

- It can also lead to greater security, that is, less risk of error and fraud, by limiting an individual's access to only part of the entire set of accounts.

There are no clear, universal rules on the division of the ledger, but the following division is fairly common:

- *The cash book.* This tends to be all of the accounts relating to cash either loose or in the bank.
- *The sales (or trade receivables) ledger.* This contains the accounts of all of the business's individual trade receivables.
- *The purchases (or trade payables) ledger.* This consists of the accounts of all of the business's individual trade payables.
- *The nominal ledger.* These accounts tend to be those of expenses and revenue, for example, sales revenue, wages, rent, and so on.
- *The general ledger.* This contains the remainder of the business's accounts, mainly those to do with non-current assets and long-term finance.

Summary

The main points in this appendix may be summarised as follows.

Double-entry bookkeeping = a system for keeping accounting records by hand, such that a relatively large volume of transactions can be handled effectively and accurately.

- There is a separate account for each asset, claim, expense and revenue that needs to be separately identified.
- Each account looks like a letter T.
- Left-hand (debit) side of the account records increases in assets and expenses and decreases in revenues and claims.
- Right-hand (credit) side records increases in revenues and claims and decreases in assets and expenses.
- There is an equal credit entry in one account for a debit entry in another.
- Double-entry bookkeeping can be used to record day-to-day transactions.
- It can also follow through to generate the income statement.
- The statement of financial position is a list of the net figure (the 'balance') on each of the accounts after appropriate transfers have been made to the income statement.
- The accounts are traditionally kept in a 'ledger', a term that persists even with computerised accounting.
- The ledger is traditionally broken down into several sections, each containing particular types of account.

 Key terms

double-entry bookkeeping p. 688	**balance** p. 693
account p. 688	**trial balance** p. 697
debit p. 688	**ledger** p. 700
credit p. 688	

Further reading

If you would like to explore the topics covered in this appendix in more depth, we recommend the following books:

An Introduction to Financial Accounting, *Thomas A.*, 5th edn, McGraw-Hill, 2005, chapters 3 to 8.

Financial Accounting, *Bebbington J., Gray R. and Laughlin R.*, 3rd edn, Thomson Learning, 2001, chapters 2 to 7.

Foundations of Business Accounting, *Dodge R.*, 2nd edn, Thomson Business Press, 1997, chapter 3.

Practical Accounting, *Benedict A. and Elliott B.*, Financial Times Prentice Hall, 2008, chapters 2 to 5.

Exercises

The answers to all three of these exercises are at the back of the book, starting on page 808. If you wish to try more exercises, visit the students' side of the Companion Website.

A.1   In respect of each of the following transactions, state in which two accounts an entry must be made and whether the entry is a debit or a credit. (For example, if the transaction were buying inventories for cash, the answer would be debit the inventories account and credit the cash account.)

(a)   Bought inventories on credit.
(b)   Owner made cash drawings.
(c)   Paid interest on business borrowings.
(d)   Bought inventories for cash.
(e)   Received cash from a credit customer.
(f)   Paid wages to employees.
(g)   The owner received some cash from a credit customer, which was taken as drawings rather than being paid into the business's bank account.
(h)   Paid a credit supplier.
(i)   Paid electricity bill.
(j)   Made cash sales.

A.2   (a)   Record the following transactions in a set of double-entry accounts:

1 February	Lee (the owner) put £6,000 into a newly-opened business bank account to start a new business
3 February	Bought inventories for £2,600 for cash
5 February	Bought some equipment (non-current asset) for cash for £800
6 February	Bought inventories costing £3,000 on credit
9 February	Paid rent for the month of £250
10 February	Paid fuel and electricity for the month of £240
11 February	Paid general expenses of £200
15 February	Sold inventories for £4,000 in cash; the inventories had cost £2,400
19 February	Sold inventories for £3,800 on credit; the inventories had cost 2,300
21 February	Lee withdrew £1,000 in cash for personal use
25 February	Paid £2,000 to trade payables
28 February	Received £2,500 from trade receivables

(b)   Balance the relevant accounts and prepare a trial balance (making sure that it agrees).
(c)   Prepare an income statement for the month and a statement of financial position at the month end. Assume that there are no prepaid or accrued expenses at the end of the month and ignore any possible depreciation.

A.3 The following is the statement of financial position of David's business at 1 January of last year.

ASSETS		£
Non-current assets		
Property, plant and equipment		
Buildings		25,000
Fittings: cost	10,000	
dep'n	(2,000)	8,000
		33,000
Current assets		
Inventories of stationery		140
Trading inventories		1,350
Prepaid rent		500
Trade receivables		1,840
Cash		2,180
		6,010
Total assets		39,010
EQUITY AND LIABILITIES		£
Owners' equity		25,050
Non-current liability		
Borrowings		12,000
Current liabilities		
Trade payables		1,690
Accrued electricity		270
		1,960
Total equity and liabilities		39,010

The following is a summary of the transactions that took place during the year:

(1) Inventories were bought on credit for £17,220.
(2) Inventories were bought for £3,760 cash.
(3) Credit sales revenue amounted to £33,100 (cost £15,220).
(4) Cash sales revenue amounted to £10,360 (cost £4,900).
(5) Wages of £3,770 were paid.
(6) Rent of £3,000 was paid. The annual rental amounts to £3,000.
(7) Electricity of £1,070 was paid.
(8) General expenses of £580 were paid.
(9) Additional fittings were purchased on 1 January for £2,000. The cash for this was raised from additional borrowings of this amount. The interest rate is 10% a year, the same as for the existing borrowings.
(10) £1,000 of the borrowing was repaid on 30 June.
(11) Cash received from trade receivables amounted to £32,810.
(12) Cash paid to trade payables amounted to £18,150.
(13) The owner withdrew £10,400 cash and £560 inventories for private use.

At the end of the year it was found that:

- The electricity bill for the last quarter of the year for £290 had not been paid.
- Trade receivables amounting to £260 were unlikely to be received.
- The value of stationery remaining was estimated at £150. Stationery is included in general expenses.
- The borrowings carried interest of 10% a year and were unpaid at the year end.
- Depreciation to be taken at 20% on the cost of the fittings owned at the year end. Buildings are not depreciated.

Required:

(a) Open ledger accounts and bring down all of the balances in the opening statement of financial position.

(b) Make entries to record the transactions 1 to 13 (above), opening any additional accounts as necessary.

(c) Open an income statement (part of the double entry, remember). Make the necessary entries for the bulleted list above and the appropriate transfers to the income statement.

(d) List the remaining balances in the same form as the opening statement of financial position (above).

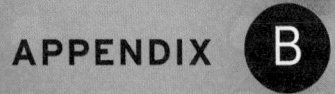

Glossary of key terms

ABC system of inventories control A method of applying different levels of inventories control, based on the value of each category of inventories. *p. 646*

Absorption costing A method of costing in which a 'fair share' of all manufacturing overhead costs is included when calculating the cost of a particular product or service. *p. 354*

Account A section of a double-entry bookkeeping system that deals with one particular asset, claim, expense or revenue. *p. 688*

Accounting The process of identifying, measuring and communicating information to permit informed judgements and decisions by users of the information. *p. 2*

Accounting conventions Accounting rules that have evolved over time in order to deal with practical problems rather than to reflect some theoretical ideal. *p. 58*

Accounting information system The system used within a business to identify, record, analyse and report accounting information. *p. 11*

Accounting period The time span for which a business prepares its financial statements. *p. 79*

Accounting rate of return (ARR) The average profit from an investment, expressed as a percentage of the average investment made. *p. 529*

Accruals accounting The system of accounting that follows the accruals convention. This is the system followed in drawing up the statement of financial position and the income statement. *p. 92*

Accruals convention The convention of accounting that asserts that profit is the excess of revenue over expenses, not the excess of cash receipts over cash payments. *p. 92*

Accrued expense An expense that is outstanding at the end of an accounting period. *p. 89*

Acid test ratio A liquidity ratio that relates the current assets (less inventories) to the current liabilities. *p. 251*

Activity-based budgeting (ABB) A system of budgeting based on the philosophy of activity-based costing (ABC). *p. 465*

Activity-based costing (ABC) A technique for more accurately relating overheads to specific production or provision of a service. It is based on acceptance of the fact that overheads do not just occur but are caused by activities, such as holding products in stores, which 'drive' the costs. *p. 397*

Adverse variance A difference between planned and actual performance, usually where the difference will cause the actual profit to be lower than the budgeted one. *p. 488*

Ageing schedule of trade receivables A report dividing trade receivables into categories, depending on the length of time outstanding. *p. 658*

Allotted share capital *See* Issued share capital.

Allowance for trade receivables An amount set aside out of profit to provide for anticipated losses arising from debts (trade receivables) that may prove irrecoverable. *p. 108*

Alternative Investment Market A stock market for the shares of smaller, young and growing businesses. AIM is similar in style to the main London Stock Exchange, but is cheaper for a business to enter and has a lighter regulatury regime. *p. 619*

Asset-based financing A form of financing where assets are used as security for cash advances to the business. Factoring and invoice discounting, where the security is trade receivables, are examples of asset-based financing. *p. 622*

Assets Resources held by a business, that have certain characteristics. *p. 43*

Auditors Professionals whose main duty is to make a report as to whether, in their opinion, the financial statements of a company do what they are supposed to do, namely show a true and fair view and comply with statutory, and financial reporting standard, requirements. *p. 177*

Average inventories turnover period ratio An efficiency ratio that measures the average period for which inventories are held by a business. *p. 243*

Average settlement period for trade payables ratio The average time taken for a business to pay its trade payables. *pp. 246, 671*

Average settlement period for trade receivables ratio The average time taken for trade receivables to pay the amounts owing. *pp. 244, 658*

Bad debt An amount owed to the business that is considered to be irrecoverable. *p. 107*

Balance The net of the debit and credit totals in an account in a double-entry book-keeping system. *p. 693*

Balanced scorecard A framework for translating the aims and objectives of a business into a series of key performance measures and targets. *p. 418*

Bank overdraft A flexible form of borrowing that allows an individual or business to have a negative current account balance. *p. 620*

Batch costing A technique for identifying full cost, where the production of many types of goods and services – particularly goods – involves producing in a batch of identical or nearly identical units of output, but where each batch is distinctly different from other batches. *p. 375*

Behavioural aspects of budgetary control The effect on people's attitudes and behaviour of using budgets as the basis for planning and controlling a business. *p. 507*

Benchmarking Identifying a successful business, or part of a business, and measuring the effectiveness of one's own business by comparison with this standard. *p. 414*

Bonus issue *See* Bonus shares.

Bonus shares Reserves that are converted into shares and given 'free' to shareholders. *p. 140*

Break-even analysis Deducing the break-even point of some activity through analysing costs and revenue. *p. 314*

Break-even chart A graphical representation of the costs and revenue of some activity, at various levels of output, that enables the break-even point to be identified. *p. 315*

Break-even point (BEP) The level of activity at which total revenue will equal total cost, so that there is neither profit nor loss. *p. 315*

Budget A financial plan for the short term, typically one year or less. *p. 440*

Budget committee A group of managers formed to supervise and take responsibility for the budget-setting process. *p. 450*

Budget holder An individual responsible for a particular budget. *p. 456*

Budget officer An individual, often an accountant, appointed to carry out the technical tasks of the budget committee. *p. 450*

Budgetary control Using the budget as a yardstick against which the effectiveness of actual performance may be assessed. *p. 503*

Business angel An individual who supplies finance (usually equity finance) and advice to a small business. Usually the amount of finance supplied falls between £10,000 and £100,000. *p. 626*

Business entity convention The convention that holds that, for accounting purposes, the business and its owner(s) are treated as quite separate and distinct. *p. 58*

Business review Part of the directors' report, which helps shareholders to assess how well the directors have performed. It provides an analysis of financial performance and position and also sets out the principal risks and uncertainties facing the business. *p. 178*

Called-up share capital That part of a company's share capital for which the shareholders have been asked to pay the agreed amount. It is part of the claim of the owners against the business. *p. 142*

Capital rationing Limiting the long-term funds available for investment during a period. *p. 574*

Capital reserves Reserves that arise from unrealised 'capital' profits or gains rather than from normal realised trading activities. *p. 138*

Carrying amount The difference between the cost (or fair value) of a non-current asset and the accumulated depreciation relating to the asset. The carrying value is also referred to as the written-down value (WDV) and the net book value (NBV). *p. 96*

Cash discount A reduction in the amount due for goods or services sold on credit in return for prompt payment. *p. 657*

Cash generated from operations per ordinary share ratio An investment ratio that relates the cash generated from operations and available to ordinary shareholders to the number of ordinary shares. *p. 261*

Cash generated from operations to maturing obligations ratio A liquidity ratio that compares the cash generated from operations to the current liabilities of the business. *p. 252*

Claims Obligations on the part of a business to provide cash or some other benefit to outside parties. *p. 43*

Combined Code A code of practice for companies listed on the London Stock Exchange that deals with corporate governance matters. *p. 130*

Committed cost A cost that has been incurred but not yet paid, but which must, under some contract or obligation, be paid. *p. 298*

Common costs   Another name for indirect costs or overheads. These are costs that do not relate directly to, and are not measurable in respect of, particular units of output, but relate to all output. *p. 352*

Comparability   The requirement that items, which are basically the same, should be treated in the same manner for measurement and reporting purposes. Lack of comparability will limit the usefulness of accounting information. *p. 8*

Compensating variances   The situation where two variances, one adverse, the other favourable, are of equal size and therefore cancel each other out. *p. 503*

Consistency convention   The accounting convention that holds that, when a particular method of accounting is selected to deal with a transaction, this method should be applied consistently over time. *p. 107*

Consolidated financial statements   *See* Group financial statements.

Consolidating   Changing the nominal value of shares issued to a higher figure (from, say, £0.50 to £1.00) and then reducing the number of shares in issue so that each shareholder has the same total nominal value of shares as before. *p. 137*

Continual budget   A budgeting system that continually updates budgets so that there is always a budget for a full planning period. (Also known as a rolling budget.) *p. 444*

Contribution margin ratio   The contribution from an activity expressed as a percentage of the sales revenue. *p. 320*

Contribution per unit   Sales revenue per unit less variable costs per unit. *p. 319*

Control   Compelling events to conform to a plan. *p. 441*

Convertible loan notes   Long-term borrowings that can be converted into equity share capital at the option of the holders. *p. 598*

Corporate governance   Matters concerned with directing and controlling a company. *p. 129*

Corporation tax   Taxation that a limited company is liable to pay on its profits. *p. 128*

Cost   The amount of resources, usually measured in monetary terms, sacrificed to achieve a particular objective. *p. 292*

Cost allocation   Assigning costs to cost centres according to the amount of cost that has been incurred in each centre. *p. 367*

Cost apportionment   Dividing costs between cost centres on a basis that is considered to reflect fairly the costs incurred in each centre. *p. 368*

Cost behaviour   The manner in which costs alter with changes in the level of activity. *p. 355*

Cost centre   Some area, object, person or activity for which costs are separately collected. *p. 366*

Cost driver   An activity that causes costs. *p. 397*

Cost of capital   The rate of return required by investors in the business. It is used as the criterion for rate of return when evaluating investment proposals using the NPV and IRR methods of investment appraisal. *p. 545*

Cost of sales   The cost of the goods sold during a period. Cost of sales can be derived by adding the opening inventories held to the inventories purchases for the period and then deducting the closing inventories held. *p. 81*

Cost-plus pricing   An approach to pricing output that is based on full cost, plus a percentage profit loading. *p. 378*

Cost pool The sum of the overhead costs that are seen as being caused by the same cost driver. *p. 398*

Cost unit The objective for which the cost is being deduced, usually a product or service. *p. 351*

Creative accounting Adopting accounting policies to achieve a particular view of performance and position that preparers would like users to see rather than what is a true and fair view. *p. 188*

Credit An entry made in the right-hand side of an account in double-entry book-keeping. *p. 688*

Current assets Assets that are held for the short term. They include cash itself and other assets that are held for sale or consumption in the normal course of a business's operating cycle. *p. 51*

Current liabilities Claims against the business which are expect to be settled within the normal course of the business's operating cycle or within 12 months of the statement of financial positon date, or which are held primarily for trading purposes, or for which the business does not have the right to defer settlement beyond 12 months of the statement of financial positon date. *p. 54*

Current ratio A liquidity ratio that relates the current assets of the business to the current liabilities. *p. 251*

Debit An entry made in the left-hand side of an account in double-entry bookkeeping. *p. 688*

Debt factoring A service offered by a financial institution (a factor) that involves the factor taking over the management of the trade receivables of the business. The factor is often prepared to make an advance to the business, based on the amount of trade receivables outstanding. *p. 620*

Deep discount bonds Redeemable loan notes (bonds) offering a rate of interest below the market rate and issued at a discount to their redeemable value. *p. 598*

Depreciation A measure of that portion of the cost (or fair value) of a non-current asset that has been consumed during an accounting period. *p. 93*

Direct costs Costs that can be identified with specific cost units, to the extent that the effect of the cost can be measured in respect of each particular unit of output. *p. 352*

Direct labour efficiency variance The difference between the actual direct labour hours worked and the number of direct labour hours according to the flexed budget (budgeted direct labour hours for the actual output). This figure is multiplied by the budgeted direct labour rate for one hour. *p. 492*

Direct labour rate variance The difference between the actual cost of the direct labour hours worked and the direct labour cost allowed (actual direct labour hours worked at the budgeted labour rate). *p. 492*

Direct materials price variance The difference between the actual cost of the direct material used and the direct materials cost allowed (actual quantity of material used at the budgeted direct material cost). *p. 491*

Direct materials usage variance The difference between the actual quantity of direct materials used and the quantity of direct materials according to the flexed budget (budgeted usage for actual output). This quantity is multiplied by the budgeted direct materials cost for one unit of the direct materials. *p. 490*

Direct method An approach to deducing the cash flows from operating activities, in a statement of cash flows, by analysing the business's cash records. *p. 209*

Directors Individuals who are appointed (normally by being elected) to act as the most senior level of management of a company. *p. 129*

Directors' report A report containing information of a financial and non-financial nature that the directors must produce as part of the annual financial report to shareholders. *p. 178*

Discount factor The rate applied to future cash flows to derive the present value of those cash flows. *p. 544*

Discretionary budget A budget based on a sum allocated at the discretion of senior management. *p. 456*

Discriminate function A boundary line, produced by multiple discriminate analysis, which can be used to identify those businesses that are likely to suffer financial distress and those that are not. *p. 273*

Dividend The transfer of assets (usually cash) made by a company to its shareholders. *p. 136*

Dividend cover ratio An investment ratio that relates the earnings available for dividends to the dividend announced, to indicate how many times the former covers the latter. *p. 259*

Dividend payout ratio An investment ratio that relates the dividends announced for the period to the earnings available for dividends that were generated in that period. *p. 259*

Dividend per share An investment ratio that relates the dividends announced for a period to the number of shares in issue. *p. 260*

Dividend yield ratio An investment ratio that relates the cash return from a share to its current market value. *p. 260*

Double-entry bookkeeping A system for recording financial transactions where each transaction is recorded twice, once as a debit and once as a credit. *p. 688*

Dual aspect convention The accounting convention that holds that each transaction has two aspects and that each aspect must be recorded in the financial statements. *p. 60*

Earnings per share An investment ratio that relates the earnings generated by the business during a period, and available to shareholders, to the number of shares in issue. *p. 261*

Economic order quantity (EOQ) The quantity of inventories that should be bought in each order so as to minimise total inventories costs. *p. 647*

Economic value added (EVA®) A measure of business performance that concentrates on wealth generation. It is based on economic profit rather than accounting profit and takes full account of the costs of financing. *p. 426*

Economies of scale Cost savings per unit that result from undertaking a large volume of activities; they are due to factors such as division and specialisation of labour and discounts from bulk buying. *p. 326*

Equity The owner(s) claim of a business. In the case of a company the sum of the share capital and reserves. *p. 45*

Eurobond A form of long-term borrowing where the finance is raised on an international basis. Eurobonds are issued in a currency that is not that of the country in which the bonds are issued. *p. 596*

Expected net present value (ENPV) A weighted average of the possible present value outcomes, where the probabilities associated with each outcome are used as weights. *p. 565*

Expense A measure of the outflow of assets (or increase in liabilities) incurred as a result of generating revenue. *p. 78*

Fair values The values ascribed to assets as an alternative to historic cost. They are usually the current market value (that is, the exchange values in an arm's-length transaction). *p. 65*

Favourable variance A difference between planned and actual performance, where the difference will cause the actual profit to be higher than the budgeted one. *p. 488*

Feedback control A control device where actual performance is compared with planned and where action is taken to try to avoid future divergences between these. *p. 484*

Feedforward control A control device where forecast future performance is compared with planned performance and where action is taken to deal with divergences between these. *p. 484*

Final accounts The income statement, statement of cash flows and statement of financial position taken together. *p. 42*

Finance The study of how businesses raise funds and select appropriate investments. *p. 2*

Finance lease A financial arrangement where the asset title remains with the owner (the lessor) but the lease agreement transfers virtually all the rewards and risks to the business (the lessee). *p. 602*

Financial accounting The measuring and reporting of accounting information for external users (those users other than the managers of the business). *p. 13*

Financial derivative Any form of financial instrument, based on share capital or borrowings, which can be used by investors either to increase their returns or to decrease their exposure to risk. *p. 599*

Financial gearing The existence of fixed payment-bearing sources of finance (for example, borrowings) in the capital structure of a business. *p. 253*

Financial management *See* Finance. *p. 2*

First in, first out (FIFO) A method of inventories costing which assumes that the earliest acquired inventories are used (in production or sales) first. *p. 103*

Five Cs of credit A checklist of factors to be taken into account when assessing the creditworthiness of a customer. *p. 652*

Fixed cost A cost that stays the same when changes occur to the volume of activity. *p. 310*

Fixed overhead spending variance The difference between the actual fixed overhead cost and the fixed overhead cost according to the flexed (and the original) budget. *p. 493*

Flexible budget A budget that is adjusted to reflect the actual level of output achieved. *p. 487*

Flexing the budget Revising the budget to what it would have been had the planned level of output been different. *p. 486*

Forecast A prediction of future outcomes, or of the future state of the environment. *p. 443*

Framework of principles The main principles that underpin accounting, which can help in identifying best practice and in developing accounting rules. *p. 176*

Full cost The total amount of resources, usually measured in monetary terms, sacrificed to achieve a particular objective. *p. 350*

Full costing Deducing the total direct and indirect (overhead) costs of pursuing some activity or objective. *p. 351*

Fully paid shares Shares on which the shareholders have paid the full issue price. *p. 142*

Gearing ratio A ratio that relates the contribution of finance that required a fixed return (such as borrowings) to the total long-term finance of the business. *p. 256*

Going concern convention The accounting convention that holds that it is assumed that the business will continue operations for the foreseeable future, unless there is reason to believe otherwise. In other words, there is no intention, or need, to liquidate the business. *p. 60*

Gross profit The amount remaining (if positive) after trading expenses (for example, cost of sales) have been deducted from trading revenue. *p. 80*

Gross profit margin ratio A profitability ratio relating the gross profit to the sales revenue for a period. *p. 279*

Group financial statements Sets of financial accounting statements that combine the performance and position of a group of companies under common control. *p. 152*

Hire purchase A method of acquiring an asset by paying the purchase price by instalments over a period. Normally, control of the asset will pass as soon as the hire-purchase contract is signed and the first instalment is paid, whereas ownership will pass on payment of the final instalment. *p. 605*

Historic cost What was paid for an asset when it was originally acquired. *p. 292*

Historic cost convention The accounting convention that holds that assets should be recorded at their historic (acquisition) cost. *p. 58*

Holding company *See* Parent company.

Ideal standards Standards that assume perfect operating conditions, where there is no inefficiency due to lost production time, defects and so on. The objective of setting ideal standards is to encourage employees to strive towards excellence. *p. 510*

Income statement A financial statement (also known as profit and loss account) that measures and reports the profit (or loss) the business has generated during a period. It is derived by deducting from total revenue for a period, the total expenses associated with that revenue. *pp. 39, 79*

Incremental budgeting Constructing budgets on the basis of what happened in the previous period, with some adjustment for expected changes in the forthcoming budget period. *p. 456*

Indirect costs (or overheads) All of those costs that cannot be directly measured in respect of each particular unit of output, that is all costs except direct costs. *p. 352*

Indirect method An approach to deducing the cash flows from operating activities, in a cash flow statement, by analysing the business's financial statements. *p. 209*

Inflation   An increase in the general prices of goods and services resulting in a corresponding decline in the purchasing power of money. *p. 540*

Intangible assets   Assets that do not have a physical substance (for example, patents, goodwill and trade receivables). *p. 45*

Interest cover ratio   A gearing ratio that divides the operating profit (that is, profit before interest and taxation) by the interest payable for a period. *p. 257*

Internal rate of return (IRR)   The discount rate for an investment that will have the effect of producing a zero NPV. *p. 547*

International Accounting Standards   *See* International Financial Reporting Standards.

International Financial Reporting Standards   Transnational accounting rules that have been adopted, or developed, by the International Accounting Standards Board and which should be followed in preparing the published financial statements of listed limited companies. *p. 167*

Invoice discounting   A loan provided by a financial institution based on a proportion of the face value of credit sales outstanding. *p. 621*

Irrelevant cost   A cost that is not relevant to a particular decision. *p. 293*

Issued share capital   That part of the share capital that has been issued to shareholders. Also known as allotted share capital. *p. 142*

Job costing   A technique for identifying the full cost per unit of output, where that output is not similar to other units of output. *p. 354*

Just-in-time (JIT) inventories management   A system of inventories management that aims to have supplies delivered, to production or sales, just in time for their required use. *p. 650*

***Kaizen* costing**   An approach to cost control where an attempt is made to control costs by trying continually to make cost savings, often only small ones, from one time period to the next during the production stage of the product life cycle. *p. 412*

Last in, first out (LIFO)   A method of inventories costing which assumes that the most recently acquired inventories are used (in production or sales) first. *p. 103*

Lead time   The time lag between placing an order for goods or services and their delivery to the required location. *p. 645*

Learning curve   A graph that represents the tendency for people to carry out tasks more quickly as they become more experienced in doing them. *p. 510*

Ledger   The book in which accounts are traditionally kept. *p. 700*

Liabilities   Claims of individuals and organisations, apart from the owner, that have arisen from past transactions or events such as supplying goods or lending money to the business. *p. 46*

Limited company   An artificial legal person that has an identity separate from that of those who own and manage it. *pp. 21, 122*

Limited liability   The restriction of the legal obligation of shareholders to meet all of the company's debts. *p. 125*

Limiting factor   Some aspect of the business (for example, lack of sales demand) that will prevent it achieving its objectives to the maximum extent. *p. 443*

Loan covenant   A condition contained within a loan agreement that is designed to help protect the lenders. *p. 600*

Loan notes   Long-term borrowings usually made by limited companies. *pp. 143, 595*

Loan stock   *See* Loan notes.

Management accounting   The measuring and reporting of accounting information for the managers of a business. *p. 13*

Management by exception   A system of control, based on a comparison of planned and actual performance, that allows managers to focus on areas of poor performance rather than dealing with areas where performance is satisfactory. *p. 448*

Margin of safety   The extent to which the planned level of output, or sales, lies above the break-even point. *p. 320*

Marginal analysis   The activity of decision making through analysing variable costs and revenues, ignoring fixed costs. *p. 332*

Marginal cost   The additional cost of producing one more unit. This is often the same as the variable cost. *p. 332*

Master budget   A summary of the individual budgets, usually consisting of a budgeted income statement, a budgeted statement of financial position and a cash budget. *p. 445*

Matching convention   The accounting convention that holds that, in measuring income, expenses should be matched to revenue which they helped generate in the same accounting period as that revenue was realised. *p. 88*

Materiality   The requirement that material information should be disclosed to users in financial statements. *p. 8*

Materiality convention   The accounting convention that states that, where the amounts involved are immaterial, only what is expedient should be considered. *p. 92*

Materials requirement planning (MRP) system   A computer-based system of inventories control that schedules the timing of deliveries of bought-in parts and materials to coincide with production requirements to meet demand. *p. 650*

Mission statement   A brief statement setting out the aims of the business. *p. 440*

Mortgage   A loan secured on property. *p. 599*

Multiple discriminate analysis   A statistical technique that can be used to predict financial distress; it involves using an index based on a combination of financial ratios. *p. 273*

Net book value   *See* Carrying amount.

Net present value (NPV)   A method of investment appraisal based on the present value of all relevant cash flows associated with an investment. *p. 538*

Nominal value   The face value of a share in a company. (Also called par value.) *p. 135*

Non-controlling interests   That part of the net assets of a subsidiary company that is financed by shareholders other than the parent company. (Formerly known as 'minority interests'.) *p. 153*

Non-current assets   Assets held that do not meet the criteria of current assets. They are held for the long-term operations of the business rather than continuously circulating within the business. Non-current assets can be seen as the tools of the business. (Also known as fixed assets.) *p. 52*

Non-current liabilities   Those amounts due to other parties that are not current liabilities. *p. 54*

Non-operating-profit variances Differences between budgeted and actual performance that do not lead directly to differences between budgeted and actual operating profit. *p. 499*

Objective probabilities Probabilities based on information gathered from past experience. *p. 569*

Offer for sale An issue of shares that involves a public limited company (or its shareholders) selling the shares to a financial institution that will, in turn, sell the shares to the public. *p. 613*

Operating cash cycle (OCC) The period between the outlay of cash to buy supplies and the ultimate receipt of cash from the sale of goods. *p. 663*

Operating gearing The relationship between the total fixed and the total variable costs for some activity. *p. 323*

Operating lease An arrangement where a business hires an asset, usually for a short time. Hiring an asset under an operating lease tends to be seen as an operating, rather than a financing, decision. *p. 602*

Operating profit The profit achieved during a period after all operating expenses have been deducted from revenues from operations. Financing expenses are deducted after the calculation of operating profit. *p. 81*

Operating profit margin ratio A profitability ratio relating the operating profit to the sales revenue for the period. *p. 239*

Operational gearing *See* Operating gearing.

Opportunity cost The cost incurred when one course of action prevents an opportunity to derive some benefit from another course of action. *pp. 292, 552*

Ordinary shares Shares of a company owned by those who are due the benefits of the company's activities after all other stakeholders have been satisfied. *p. 136*

Outlay cost A cost that involves the spending of money or some other transfer of assets. *p. 294*

Outsourcing Subcontracting activities to (sourcing goods or services from) outside organisations. *p. 337*

Overhead absorption (recovery) rate The rate at which overheads are charged to cost units (jobs), usually in a job costing system. *p. 357*

Overheads (or indirect cost) Any cost except a direct cost; a cost which cannot be directly measured in respect of each particular cost objective. *p. 352*

Overtrading The situation arising when a business is operating at a level of activity which cannot be supported by the amount of finance that has been committed. *p. 267*

Paid-up share capital That part of the share capital of a company that has been called and paid. *p. 142*

Par value *See* Nominal value.

Parent company A company that has a controlling interest in another company. *p. 152*

Partnership A form of business unit where there are at least two individuals, but usually no more than twenty, carrying on a business with the intention of making a profit. *p. 20*

Past cost A cost that has been incurred in the past. *p. 294*

Payback period (PP) The time taken for the initial outlay for an investment to be repaid from its future net cash inflows. *p. 534*

Periodic budget A budget developed on a one-off basis to cover a particular planning period. *p. 444*

Post-completion audit A review of the performance of an investment project to see whether actual performance matched planned performance and whether any lessons can be drawn from the way in which the investment was appraised and carried out. *p. 575*

Practical standards Standards that do not assume perfect operating conditions. Although they demand a high level of efficiency, account is taken of possible lost production time, defects and so on. They are designed to be challenging, yet achievable. *p. 510*

Preference shares Shares of a company owned by those who are entitled to the first part of any dividend that the company may pay. *p. 137*

Prepaid expenses Expenses that have been paid in advance at the end of the accounting period. *p. 91*

Price/earnings ratio An investment ratio that relates the market value of a share to the earnings per share. *p. 262*

Private limited company A limited company for which the directors can restrict the ownership of its shares. *p. 127*

Private placing An issue of shares that involves a limited company arranging for the shares to be sold to the clients of particular issuing houses or stockbrokers, rather than to the general investing public. *p. 614*

Process costing A technique for deriving the full cost per unit of output, where the units of output are the same or it is reasonable to treat them as being so. *p. 352*

Product cost centre Some area, object, person or activity for which costs are separately collected, in which cost units have costs added. *p. 367*

Profit The increase in wealth attributable to the owners of a business that arises through business operations. *p. 77*

Profit before taxation The result when all of the appropriately matched expenses of running a business have been deducted from the revenue for the year, but before the taxation charge is deducted. *p. 150*

Profit for the year The result when all of the appropriately matched expenses of running a business have been deducted from the revenue for the year and then, in the case of a limited company, the taxation charge deducted. *pp. 81, 150*

Profit–volume (PV) chart A graphical representation of the contributions (revenue less variable costs) of some activity, at various levels, which enables the break-even point and the profit at various activity levels to be identified. *p. 325*

Property, plant and equipment Those non-current assets that have a physical substance (for example, plant and machinery, motor vehicles). *p. 65*

Prudence convention The accounting convention that holds that financial statements should err on the side of caution. *p. 59*

Public limited company A limited company for which the directors cannot restrict the ownership of its shares. *p. 125*

Public issue   An issue of shares that involves a public limited company (plc) making a direct invitation to the public to buy shares in the company. *p. 613*

Quality costs   The cost of establishing procedures that promote the quality of output, either by preventing quality problems in the first place or by dealing with them when they occur. *p. 411*

Reducing-balance method   A method of calculating depreciation that applies a fixed percentage rate of depreciation to the carrying amount of an asset in each period. *p. 96*

Relevance   The ability of accounting information to influence decisions; regarded as a key characteristic of useful accounting information. *p. 7*

Relevant cost   A cost that is relevant to a particular decision. *pp. 293, 552*

Relevant range   The range of output within which a particular business is expected to operate. *p. 327*

Reliability   The requirement that accounting information should be free from significant errors or bias and should represent what it purports to represent. Reliability is regarded as a key characteristic of useful accounting information. *p. 7*

Reserves   Part of the owners' claim (equity) of a limited company that has arisen from profits and gains, to the extent that these have not been distributed to the shareholders or reduced by losses. *p. 135*

Residual value   The amount for which a non-current asset is sold when the business has no further use for it. *p. 94*

Return on capital employed ratio (ROCE)   A profitability ratio expressing the relationship between the operating profit (that is, profit before interest and taxation) and the long-term funds (equity and borrowings) invested in the business. *p. 238*

Return on ordinary shareholders' funds ratio (ROSF)   A profitability ratio that compares the amount of profit for the period available to the ordinary shareholders with their stake in the business. *p. 237*

Revenue   A measure of the inflow of assets (for example, cash or amounts owed to a business by credit customers), or a reduction in liabilities, arising as a result of trading operations. *p. 77*

Revenue reserve   Part of the owners' claim (equity) of a company that arises from realised profits and gains, including after-tax trading profits and gains from disposals of non-current assets. *p. 136*

Rights issue   An issue of shares for cash to existing shareholders on the basis of the number of shares already held. *p. 610*

Risk   The extent and likelihood that what is projected to occur will not actually occur. *p. 539*

Risk-adjusted discount rate   A discount rate applied to investment projects that is increased (decreased) in the face of increased (decreased) risk. *p. 572*

Risk premium   The additional return required from an investment, owing to a perceived level of risk: the greater the perceived risk, the larger the required risk premium. *p. 540*

Rolling budget   *See* Continual budget.

Sale and leaseback   An agreement to sell an asset (usually property) to another party and simultaneously to lease the asset back in order to continue using the asset. *p. 604*

Sales price variance   The difference between the actual sales revenue figure for the period and the sales revenue figure as shown in the flexed budget. *p. 490*

Sales revenue per employee ratio   An efficiency ratio that relates the sales revenue generated during a period to the average number of employees of the business. *p. 248*

Sales revenue to capital employed ratio   An efficiency ratio that relates the sales revenue generated during a period to the capital employed. *p. 247*

Sales volume variance   The difference between the operating profit, as shown in the original budget, and the operating profit, as shown in the flexed budget for the period. *p. 488*

Scenario building   Creating a model of a business decision, usually on a computer spreadsheet, enabling the decision maker to look at the effect of different assumptions on the decision outcome. *p. 564*

Securitisation   Bundling together illiquid physical or financial assets of the same type to provide backing for issuing interest-bearing securities, such as bonds. *p. 606*

Segmental financial report   A report that breaks down the operating results of a business according to its business or geographical segments. *p. 180*

Semi-fixed (semi-variable) cost   A cost that has an element of both fixed and variable cost. *p. 313*

Sensitivity analysis   An examination of the key variables affecting a decision (for example an investment project), to see how changes in each input might influence the outcome. *p. 561*

Service cost centre   Some area, object, person or activity for which costs are collected separately, in which cost units do not have cost added, because service cost centres only render services to product cost services and to other service cost centres. *p. 367*

Share premium account   A capital reserve reflecting any amount, above the nominal value of shares, that is paid for those shares when issued by a company. *p. 139*

Shares   Portions of the ownership, or equity, of a company. *pp. 6, 122*

Sole proprietorship   An individual in business on his or her own account. *p. 19*

Splitting   Changing the nominal value of shares issued to a lower figure (from, say, £1.00 to £0.50) and then issuing sufficient shares so that each shareholder has the same total nominal value of shares as before. *p. 137*

Standard quantities and costs   Planned quantities and costs (or revenue) for individual units of input or output. Standards are the building blocks used to produce the budget. *p. 508*

Statement of cash flows   A statement that shows the sources and uses of cash for a period. *p. 39*

Statement of changes in equity   A financial statement, required by IAS 1, which shows the effect of gains/losses and capital injections/withdrawals on the equity base of a company. *p. 174*

Statement of comprehensive income   A financial statement that extends the conventional income statement to include other gains and losses that affect shareholders' equity. *p. 171*

Statement of financial position   A financial statement that shows the assets of a business and the claims against those assets (also known as a balance sheet). *p. 39*

Stepped fixed cost A fixed cost that does not remain fixed over all levels of output but which changes in steps as a threshold level of output is reached. *p. 312*

Stock Exchange A market where 'second-hand' shares may be bought and sold and new capital raised. *p. 614*

Straight-line method A method of accounting for depreciation that allocates the amount to be depreciated evenly over the useful life of the asset. *p. 95*

Strategic management The process of setting a course to achieve the business's objectives, taking account of the commercial and economic environment in which the business operates. *p. 24*

Subjective probabilities Probabilities that are based on opinion rather than past data. *p. 570*

Summary financial statements A summarised version of the complete annual financial statements, which shareholders may receive as an alternative to the complete statements. *p. 188*

Sunk cost A cost that has been incurred in the past; the same as a past cost. *p. 298*

Takeover The acquisition of control of one company by another, usually as a result of acquiring a majority of the ordinary shares of the former. *p. 153*

Tangible assets Those assets that have a physical substance (for example, plant and machinery, motor vehicles). *p. 45*

Target costing An approach to deriving product costs where the business starts with the projected selling price and from it deduces the target cost per unit that must be met to enable the business to meet its profit objectives. *p. 410*

Tender issue A public issue of shares or loan notes (by a public limited company) where potential investors are invited to place bids for the securities concerned, rather than the company setting the price itself. *p. 613*

Term loan Finance provided by financial institutions, like banks and insurance companies, under a contract with the borrowing business that indicates the interest rate and dates of payments of interest and repayment of the loan. The loan is not normally transferable from one lender to another. *p. 595*

Total cost The sum of the variable and fixed costs of pursuing some activity. *p. 356*

Total direct labour variance The difference between the actual direct labour cost and the direct labour cost according to the flexed budget (budgeted direct labour hours for the actual output). *p. 491*

Total direct materials variance The difference between the actual direct materials cost and the direct materials cost according to the flexed budget. *p. 490*

Total life-cycle costing Paying attention to all of the costs that will be incurred during the entire life of a product or service. *p. 408*

Transfer price The price at which goods or services are sold, or transferred, between divisions of the same business. *p. 181*

Trial balance A totalled list of the balances on each of the accounts in a double-entry bookkeeping system. *p. 697*

Understandability The requirement that accounting information should be understood by those for whom the information is primarily compiled. Lack of understandability will limit the usefulness of accounting information. *p. 8*

Univariate analysis A method that can be used to help predict financial distress, which involves the use of a single ratio as a predictor. *p. 273*

Value chain analysis Analysing each activity undertaken by a business to identify any that do not add value to the output of goods or services. *p. 412*

Value driver A factor that creates wealth, such as employee satisfaction, customer loyalty and level of product innovation. *p. 415*

Variable cost A cost that varies according to the volume of activity. *p. 310*

Variable costing An approach to costing in which only those costs that vary with the level of output are included in the product cost. *p. 382*

Variance The financial effect, usually on the budgeted profit, of the particular factor under consideration being more, or less, than budgeted. *p. 488*

Venture capital Long-term finance provided by certain institutions to small and medium-sized businesses to exploit relatively high-risk opportunities. *p. 624*

Warrant A document giving the holder the right, but not the obligation, to acquire ordinary shares in a company at an agreed price. *p. 599*

Weighted average cost (AVCO) A method of inventories costing, which assumes that inventories entering the business lose their separate identity and any issues of inventories reflect the weighted average cost of the inventories held. *p. 103*

Working capital Current assets less current liabilities. *pp. 209, 638*

Written-down value (WDV) *See* Carrying amount.

Zero-base budgeting (ZBB) An approach to budgeting, based on the philosophy that all spending needs to be justified annually and that each budget should start as a clean sheet. *p. 457*

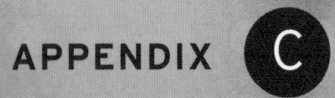

Solutions to self-assessment questions

Chapter 2

2.1 Simonson Engineering

The statement of financial position you prepare should be set out as follows:

Simonson Engineering
Statement of financial position as at 30 September 2009

ASSETS	£
Non-current assets	
Property, plant and equipment	
Property	72,000
Plant and machinery	25,000
Motor vehicles	15,000
Fixtures and fittings	9,000
	121,000
Current assets	
Inventories	45,000
Trade receivables	48,000
Cash in hand	1,500
	94,500
Total assets	215,500
EQUITY AND LIABILITIES	
Equity	
Closing balance*	120,500
Non-current liabilities	
Long-term borrowings	51,000
Current liabilities	
Trade payables	18,000
Short-term borrowings	26,000
	44,000
Total equity and liabilities	215,500
*The equity is calculated as follows:	
Opening balance	117,500
Profit	18,000
	135,500
Drawings	(15,000)
Closing balance	120,500

Chapter 3

3.1 TT and Co.

Statement of financial position as at 31 December 2008

	£
ASSETS	
Delivery van	
(12,000 − 2,500)	9,500
Inventories (143,000 +	
12,000 − 74,000 − 16,000)	65,000
Trade receivables	
(152,000 − 132,000 − 400)	19,600
Cash at bank (50,000 − 25,000	
− 500 − 1,200 − 12,000 −	
33,500 − 1,650 − 12,000	
+ 35,000 + 132,000	
− 121,000 − 9,400)	750
Prepaid expenses	
(5,000 + 300)	5,300
Total assets	100,150
EQUITY AND LIABILITIES	
Equity (50,000 + 26,900)	76,900
Trade payables (143,000 − 121,000)	22,000
Accrued expenses (630 + 620)	1,250
Total equity and liabilities	100,150

Income statement for the year ended 31 December 2008

	£
Sales revenue (152,000 + 35,000)	187,000
Cost of goods sold (74,000 + 16,000)	(90,000)
Gross profit	97,000
Rent	(20,000)
Rates (500 + 900)	(1,400)
Wages (33,500 + 630)	(34,130)
Electricity (1,650 + 620)	(2,270)
Bad debts	(400)
Van depreciation [(12,000 − 2,000)/4]	(2,500)
Van expenses	(9,400)
Profit for the year	26,900

The statement of financial position could now be rewritten in a more stylish form as follows:

Statement of financial position as at 31 December 2008

ASSETS	£
Non-current assets	
Property, plant and equipment	
Delivery van at cost	12,000
Accumulated depreciation	(2,500)
	9,500
Current assets	
Inventories	65,000
Trade receivables	19,600
Prepaid expenses	5,300
Cash	750
	90,650
Total assets	100,150
EQUITY AND LIABILITIES	
Equity	
Closing balance	76,900
Current liabilities	
Trade payables	22,000
Accrued expenses	1,250
	23,250
Total equity and liabilities	100,150

Chapter 4

4.1 Dev Ltd

(a) The summarised statement of financial position of Dev Ltd, immediately following the rights and bonus issue, is as follows:

Statement of financial position as at 31 December 2009

	£000
Net assets [235 + 40 (cash from the rights issue)]	275
Equity	
Share capital: 180,000 shares @ £1 [(100 + 20) + 60]	180
Share premium account (30 + 20 – 50)	–
Revaluation reserve (37 – 10)	27
Retained earnings	68
Total equity	275

Note that the bonus issue of £60,000 is taken from capital reserves (reserves unavailable for dividends) as follows:

	£000
Share premium account	50
Revaluation reserve	10
	60

More could have been taken from the revaluation reserve and less from the share premium account without making any difference to dividend payment possibilities.

(b) There may be pressure from a potential lender for the business to limit its ability to pay dividends. This would place lenders in a more secure position because the maximum buffer or safety margin between the value of the assets and the amount owed by the business is maintained. It is not unusual for potential lenders to insist on some measure to lock up shareholders' funds in this way as a condition of granting the loan.

(c) The summarised statement of financial position of Dev Ltd, immediately following the rights and bonus issue, assuming a minimum dividend potential objective, is as follows:

Statement of financial position as at 31 December 2009

	£000
Net assets [235 + 40 (cash from the rights issue)]	275
Equity	
Share capital: 180,000 shares @ £1 [(100 + 20) + 60]	180
Share premium account (30 + 20)	50
Revaluation reserve	37
Retained earnings (68 − 60)	8
Total equity	275

(d) Before the bonus issue, the maximum dividend was £68,000. Now it is £8,000. Thus the bonus issue has had the effect of locking up an additional £60,000 of the business's assets in terms of the business's ability to pay dividends.

(e) Before the issues, Lee had 100 shares worth £2.35 (that is, £235,000/100,000) each or £235 in total. Lee would be offered 20 shares in the rights issue at £2 each or £40 in total. After the rights issue, Lee would have 120 shares worth £2.2917 (that is, £275,000/120,000) each or £275 in total.

The bonus issue would give Lee 60 additional shares. After the bonus issue, Lee would have 180 shares worth £1.5278 (that is, £275,000/180,000) each or £275 in total.

None of this affects Lee's wealth. Before the issues, Lee had £235 worth of shares and £40 more in cash. After the issues, Lee has the same total wealth but all £275 is in the value of the shares.

(f) The things that we know about the company are as follows:

(1) It is a private (as opposed to a public) limited company, for it has 'Ltd' (limited) as part of its name, rather than plc (public limited company).

(2) It has made an issue of shares at a premium, almost certainly after it had traded successfully for a period. (There is a share premium account. It is very unlikely that the original shares, issued when the company was first formed, would have been issued at a premium.)

(3) Certain of the assets in the balance sheet have been upwardly revalued by at least £37,000. (There is a revaluation reserve of £37,000. This may just be what is left after a previous bonus issue had taken part of the balance.)

(4) The company has traded at an aggregate profit (though there could have been losses in some years), net of tax and any dividends paid. (There is a positive balance on retained earnings.)

Chapter 5

5.1 **Turner plc**

We can see from the table below that the software segment generates the highest revenue, but also generates the lowest profit. We shall be considering financial ratios in detail in Chapter 7. However, we can use some simple ratios at this point to help evaluate segmental performance. We can start by considering the profit generated in relation to the sales revenue for each operating segment. We can see from the table below that the engineering segment generates the most profit in relation to sales revenue. Around 23%, or £0.23 in every £1, of profit is derived from the sales revenue generated. However, for the software segment, only 4%, or £0.04 in every £1, of profit is derived from the sales revenue generated.

We can also compare the profit generated with the net assets employed (that is, total assets – total liabilities) for each segment. We can see from the table below that the electronics segment produces the best return on net assets employed: around £0.65 for every £1 invested. Once again, the software segment produces the worst results.

The reasons for the relatively poor results from the software segment need further investigation. There may be valid reasons; for example, it may be experiencing severe competitive pressures. The results for this segment, however, are not disastrous: it is making a profit. Nevertheless, the business may wish to re-evaluate its long-term presence in this market.

It is interesting to note that the software segment benefited most from the investment in non-current assets during the period – as much as the other two segments combined. The reason for such a large investment in such a relatively poorly performing segment needs to be justified. It is possible that the business will reap rewards for the investment in the future; however, we do not have enough information to understand the reasons for the investment decision.

Depreciation charges in the software segment are significantly higher than for the other operating segments. This may be because the segment has more non-current assets, although we do not have a figure for the non-current assets held. The depreciation charge as a percentage of segment assets is also higher and the reasons for this should be investigated.

Table of key results

	Software	Electronics	Engineering
Total revenue	£250m	£230m	£52m
Segment profit	£10m	£34m	£12m
Net assets (assets – liabilities)	£85m	£52m	£30m
Segment profit as a percentage of sales revenue	4.0%	14.8%	23.1%
Segment profit as a percentage of net assets employed	11.8%	65.4%	40.0%
Expenditure on non-current assets	£22m	£12m	£10m
Depreciation as a percentage of segment assets	42.9%	38.9%	29.4%

Chapter 6

6.1   Touchstone plc

Touchstone plc
Statement of cash flows for the year ended 31 December 2009

	£m
Cash flows from operating activities	
Profit before taxation (after interest)	
(see Note 1 below)	60
Adjustments for:	
Depreciation	16
Interest expense (Note 2)	4
	80
Increase in trade receivables (26 − 16)	(10)
Decrease in trade payables (38 − 37)	(1)
Decrease in inventories (25 − 24)	1
Cash generated from operations	70
Interest paid	(4)
Taxation paid (Note 3)	(12)
Dividend paid	(18)
Net cash from operating activities	36
Cash flows from investing activities	
Payments to acquire tangible non-current assets (Note 4)	(41)
Net cash used in investing activities	(41)
Cash flows from financing activities	
Issue of loan notes (40 − 20)	20
Net cash used in financing activities	20
Net increase in cash and cash equivalents	15
Cash and cash equivalents at 1 January 2009	
Cash	4
Cash and cash equivalents at 31 December 2009	
Cash	4
Treasury bills	15
	19

To see how this relates to the cash of the business at the beginning and end of the year it can be useful to provide a reconciliation as follows:

Analysis of cash and cash equivalents during the year ended 31 December 2009

	£m
Cash and cash equivalents at 1 January 2009	4
Net cash inflow	15
Cash and cash equivalents at 31 December 2009	19

Notes:

(1) This is simply taken from the income statement for the year.

(2) Interest payable expense must be taken out, by adding it back to the profit before taxation figure. We subsequently deduct the cash paid for interest payable during the year. In this case the two figures are identical.

(3) Companies pay 50% of their tax during their accounting year and the other 50% in the following year. Thus the 2009 payment would have been half the tax on the 2008 profit (that is, the figure that would

have appeared in the current liabilities at the end of 2008), plus half of the 2009 tax charge (that is, 4 + ($\frac{1}{2} \times 16$) = 12).

(4) Since there were no disposals, the depreciation charges must be the difference between the start and end of the year's non-current asset values, adjusted by the cost of any additions:

	£m
Carrying amount at 1 January 2009	147
Add Additions (balancing figure)	41
	188
Less Depreciation (6 + 10)	16
Carrying amount at 31 December 2009	172

Chapter 7

7.1 Financial ratios

In order to answer this question you may have used the following ratios:

	Ali plc	Bhaskar plc
Current ratio	$\frac{853.0}{422.4} = 2.0$	$\frac{816.5}{293.1} = 2.8$
Acid test ratio	$\frac{(853.0 - 592.0)}{422.4} = 0.6$	$\frac{(816.5 - 403.0)}{293.1} = 1.4$
Gearing ratio	$\frac{190}{(687.6 + 190)} \times 100 = 21.6\%$	$\frac{250}{(874.6 + 250)} \times 100 = 22.2\%$
Interest cover ratio	$\frac{151.3}{19.4} = 7.8$ times	$\frac{166.9}{27.5} = 6.1$ times
Dividend payout ratio	$\frac{135.0}{99.9} \times 100 = 135\%$	$\frac{95.0}{104.6} \times 100 = 91\%$
Price/earnings ratio	$\frac{£6.50}{31.2p} = 20.8$ times	$\frac{£8.20}{41.8p} = 19.6$ times

Ali plc has a much lower current ratio and acid test ratio than Bhaskar plc. The reasons for this may be partly due to the fact that Ali plc has a lower average settlement period for receivables. The acid test ratio of Ali plc is substantially below 1.0: this may suggest a liquidity problem.

The gearing ratio of each business is quite similar. Neither business seems to have excessive borrowing. The interest cover ratio for each business is also similar. The ratios indicate that both businesses have good profit coverage for their interest charges.

The dividend payout ratio for each business seems very high. In the case of Ali plc, the dividends announced for the year are considerably higher than the profit for the year that is available for dividend. As a result, part of the dividend was paid out of retained profits from previous years. This is an unusual occurrence; although it is quite legitimate, such action may nevertheless suggest a lack of prudence on the part of the directors.

The P/E ratios for both businesses seem high, which indicates market confidence in their future prospects.

Chapter 8

8.1 JB Limited

(a)

	£	
Material M1		
400 × 3 @ £5.50	6,600	The original cost is irrelevant since any inventories used will need to be replaced
Material P2		
400 × 2 @ £2.00 (that is, £3.60 – £1.60)	1,600	The best alternative use of this material is as a substitute for P4 – an effective opportunity cost of £2.00/kg
Part no. 678		
400 × 1 @ £50	20,000	
Labour		
Skilled 400 × 5 @ £12	24,000	The effective cost is £12/hour
Unskilled 400 × 5 @ £10	20,000	
Overheads	3,200	It is only the additional cost that is relevant; the method of apportioning total overheads is not relevant
Total relevant cost	75,400	
Potential revenue		
400 @ £200	80,000	

Clearly, on the basis of the information available it would be beneficial for the business to undertake the contract.

(b) There is an almost infinite number of possible answers to this part of the question, including:

- If material P2 had not already been held, it may be that it would not be possible to buy it in and still leave the contract as a beneficial one. In this case the business may be unhappy about accepting a price under the particular conditions that apply, which could not be accepted under other conditions.
- Will the replacement for the skilled worker be able to do the normal work of that person to the necessary standard?
- Is JB Limited confident that the additional unskilled employee can be made redundant at the end of this contract without cost to itself?

Chapter 9

9.1 Khan Ltd

(a) The break-even point if only the Alpha service were rendered would be:

$$\frac{\text{Fixed costs}}{\text{Sales revenue per unit} - \text{Variable cost per unit}} = \frac{£40,000}{£30 - £(15 + 6)} = 4,445 \text{ units (a year)}$$

(Strictly it is 4,444.44 but 4,445 is the smallest number of units of the service that must be rendered to avoid a loss.)

(b)

	Alpha £/unit	Beta £/unit	Gamma £/unit
Selling price	30	39	20
Variable materials	(15)	(18)	(10)
Variable production costs	(6)	(10)	(5)
Contribution	9	11	5
Staff time (hr/unit)	2	3	1
Contribution/staff hour	£4.50	£3.67	£5.00
Order of priority	2nd	3rd	1st

(c)

	Hours		Contribution £
Render:			
5,000 Gamma using	5,000	generating (that is, 5,000 × £5 =)	25,000
2,500 Alpha using	5,000	generating (that is, 2,500 × £9 =)	22,500
	10,000		47,500
		Less Fixed costs	40,000
		Operating profit	7,500

This leaves a demand for 500 units of Alpha and 2,000 units of Beta unsatisfied.

Chapter 10

10.1 Hector and Co. Ltd

Job-costing basis:

			£
Materials:	Metal wire	1,000 × 2 × £2.20*	4,400
	Fabric	1,000 × 0.5 × £1.00*	500
Labour:	Skilled	1,000 × (10/60) × £12.00	2,000
	Unskilled	1,000 × (5/60) × £7.50	625
Overheads		1,000 × (15/60) × (50,000/12,500)	1,000
Total cost			8,525
Add Profit loading		12.5% thereof	1,066
Total tender price			9,591

* In the traditional approach to full costing, historic costs of materials tend to be used. It would not necessarily have been incorrect to have used the 'relevant' (opportunity) costs here.

Minimum contract price (relevant cost basis):

			£
Materials:	Metal wire	1,000 × 2 × £2.50 (replacement cost)	5,000
	Fabric	1,000 × 0.5 × £0.40 (scrap value)	200
Labour:	Skilled	(there is no effective cost of skilled staff)	–
	Unskilled	1,000 × (5/60) × £7.50	625
Minimum tender price			5,825

The difference between the two prices is partly that the relevant costing approach tends to look to the future, partly that it considers opportunity costs, and partly that the job-costing basis total has a profit loading.

Chapter 11

11.1 Psilis Ltd

(a) *Full cost (present basis)*

	Basic		Super	
	£		£	
Direct labour (all £10/hour)	40.00	(4 hours)	60.00	(6 hours)
Direct material	15.00		20.00	
Overheads	18.20	(£4.55* × 4)	27.30	(£4.55* × 6)
	73.20		107.30	

* Total direct labour hours worked = (40,000 × 4) + (10,000 × 6) = 220,000 hours. Overhead recovery rate = £1,000,000/220,000 = £4.55 per direct labour hour.

Thus the selling prices are currently:

Basic: £73.20 + 25% = £91.50
Super: £107.30 + 25% = £134.13

(b) *Full cost (activity cost basis)*
Here, the cost of each cost-driving activity is apportioned between total production of the two products.

Activity	Cost £000	Basis of apportionment	Basic £000		Super £000	
Machine set-ups	280	Number of set-ups	56	(20/100)	224	(80/100)
Quality inspection	220	Number of inspections	55	(500/2,000)	165	(1,500/2,000)
Sales order processing	240	Number of orders processed	72	(1,500/5,000)	168	(3,500/5,000)
General production	260	Machine hours	182	(350/500)	78	(150/500)
Total	1,000		365		635	

The overheads per unit are:

$$\text{Basic:} \quad \frac{£365,000}{40,000} = £9.13$$

$$\text{Super:} \quad \frac{£635,000}{10,000} = £63.50$$

Thus, on an activity basis, the full costs are as follows:

	Basic £	Super £
Direct labour (all £10/hour)	40.00 (4 hours)	60.00 (6 hours)
Direct material	15.00	20.00
Indirect cost	9.13	63.50
Full cost	64.13	143.50
Current selling price	£91.50	£134.13

(c) It seems that the Supers are being sold for less than they cost to produce. If the price cannot be increased, there is a very strong case for abandoning this product. At the same time, the Basics are very profitable to the extent that it may be worth considering lowering the price to attract more sales revenue.

The fact that the overhead costs can be related to activities and, more specifically, to products does not mean that abandoning Super production would lead to immediate overhead cost savings. For example, it may not be possible or desirable to dismiss machine-setting staff overnight. It would certainly rarely be possible to release factory space occupied by machine setters and make immediate cost savings. Nevertheless, in the medium term, these costs can be avoided and it may be sensible to do so.

Chapter 12

12.1 Antonio Ltd

(a) (1) The raw materials inventories budget for the six months ending 31 December (physical quantities):

	July Units	Aug Units	Sept Units	Oct Units	Nov Units	Dec Units
Opening inventories (Current month's production)	500	600	600	700	750	750
Purchases (Balance figure)	600	600	700	750	750	750
	1,100	1,200	1,300	1,450	1,500	1,500
Issues to production (From question)	(500)	(600)	(600)	(700)	(750)	(750)
Closing inventories (Next month's production)	600	600	700	750	750	750

The raw materials inventories budget for the six months ending 31 December (in financial terms), that is, the physical quantities × £8 is:

	July £	Aug £	Sept £	Oct £	Nov £	Dec £
Opening inventories	4,000	4,800	4,800	5,600	6,000	6,000
Purchases	4,800	4,800	5,600	6,000	6,000	6,000
	8,800	9,600	10,400	11,600	12,000	12,000
Issues to production	(4,000)	(4,800)	(4,800)	(5,600)	(6,000)	(6,000)
Closing inventories	4,800	4,800	5,600	6,000	6,000	6,000

(2) The trade payables budget for the six months ending 31 December:

	July £	Aug £	Sept £	Oct £	Nov £	Dec £
Opening balance (Current month's payment)	4,000	4,800	4,800	5,600	6,000	6,000
Purchases (From raw materials inventories budget)	4,800	4,800	5,600	6,000	6,000	6,000
	8,800	9,600	10,400	11,600	12,000	12,000
Payments	(4,000)	(4,800)	(4,800)	(5,600)	(6,000)	(6,000)
Closing balance (Next month's payment)	4,800	4,800	5,600	6,000	6,000	6,000

(3) The cash budget for the six months ending 31 December:

	July £	Aug £	Sept £	Oct £	Nov £	Dec £
Inflows						
Receipts:						
Trade receivables (40% of sales revenue of two months previous)	2,800	3,200	3,200	4,000	4,800	5,200
Cash sales revenue (60% of current month's revenue)	4,800	6,000	7,200	7,800	8,400	9,600
Total inflows	7,600	9,200	10,400	11,800	13,200	14,800
Outflows						
Trade payables (from trade payables budget)	(4,000)	(4,800)	(4,800)	(5,600)	(6,000)	(6,000)
Direct costs	(3,000)	(3,600)	(3,600)	(4,200)	(4,500)	(4,500)
Advertising	(1,000)	–	–	(1,500)	–	–
Overheads: 80%	(1,280)	(1,280)	(1,280)	(1,280)	(1,600)	(1,600)
20%	(280)	(320)	(320)	(320)	(320)	(400)
New plant			(2,200)	(2,200)	(2,200)	
Total outflows	(9,560)	(10,000)	(12,200)	(15,100)	(14,620)	(12,500)
Net inflows (outflows)	(1,960)	(800)	(1,800)	(3,300)	(1,420)	2,300
Balance c/f	5,540	4,740	2,940	(360)	(1,780)	520

The balances carried forward are deduced by deducting the deficit (net outflows) for the month from (or adding the surplus for the month to) the previous month's balance.

Note how budgets are linked; in this case the inventories budget to the trade payables budget and the trade payables budget to the cash budget.

(b) The following are possible means of relieving the cash shortages revealed by the budget:

- Make a higher proportion of sales on a cash basis.
- Collect the money from trade receivables more promptly, for example during the month following the sale.
- Hold lower inventories, both of raw materials and of finished goods.
- Increase the trade payables payment period.
- Delay the payments for advertising.
- Obtain more credit for the overhead costs; at present only 20% are on credit.
- Delay the payments for the new plant.

Chapter 13

13.1 Toscanini Ltd

(a) and (b)

	Budget		Actual
	Original	Flexed	
Output (units) (prod'n and sales)	4,000	3,500	3,500
	£	£	£
Sales revenue	16,000	14,000	13,820
Raw materials	(3,840)	(3,360) (1,400 kg)	(3,420) (1,425 kg)
Labour	(3,200)	(2,800) (350 hr)	(2,690) (345 hr)
Fixed overheads	(4,800)	(4,800)	(4,900)
Operating profit	4,160	3,040	2,810

	£		Manager accountable
Sales volume variance (4,160 – 3,040)	(1,120)	(A)	Sales
Sales price variance (14,000 – 13,820)	(180)	(A)	Sales
Materials price variance (1,425 × 2.40) – 3,420	0	–	
Materials usage variance [(3,500 × 0.4) – 1,425] × £2.40	(60)	(A)	Production
Labour rate variance (345 × £8) – 2,690	70	(F)	Personnel
Labour efficiency variance [(3,500 × 0.10) – 345] × £8	40	(F)	Production
Fixed overhead spending variance (4,800 – 4,900)	(100)	(A)	Various depending on the nature of the overheads
Total net variances	(1,350)	(A)	
Budgeted profit	4,160		
Total net variance	(1,350)		
Actual profit	2,810		

(c) Feasible explanations include the following:

● Sales volume – unanticipated fall in world demand would account for 400 × £2.24 = £896 of this variance (£2.24 is the budgeted contribution per unit). Ineffective marketing probably caused the remainder, though a lack of availability of the finished product to sell may be a reason.

● Sales price – ineffective selling seems the only logical reason.

● Materials usage – inefficient usage of materials, perhaps because of poor performance by labour or substandard materials.

● Labour rate – less overtime worked or lower production bonuses paid as a result of lower volume of activity.

● Labour efficiency – more effective working.

● Overheads – ineffective control of overheads.

(d) Clearly, not all of the sales volume variance can be attributed to poor marketing, given a 10% reduction in demand.

It will probably be useful to distinguish between that part of the variance that arose from the shortfall in general demand (a planning variance) and a volume variance, which is more fairly attributable to the manager concerned. Thus accountability will be more fairly imposed.

	£
Planning variance (10% × 4,000) × £2.24	896
'New' sales volume variance	
[4,000 − (10% × 4,000) − 3,500] × £2.24	224
Original sales volume variance	1,120

Chapter 14

14.1 Beacon Chemicals plc

(a) Relevant cash flows are as follows:

	Year 0 £000	Year 1 £000	Year 2 £000	Year 3 £000	Year 4 £000	Year 5 £000
Sales revenue	–	80	120	144	100	64
Loss of contribution		(15)	(15)	(15)	(15)	(15)
Variable costs		(40)	(50)	(48)	(30)	(32)
Fixed costs (Note 1)		(8)	(8)	(8)	(8)	(8)
Operating cash flows		17	47	73	47	9
Working capital	(30)					30
Capital cost	(100)					
Net relevant cash flows	(130)	17	47	73	47	39

Notes:
1 Only the fixed costs that are incremental to the project (existing only because of the project) are relevant. Depreciation is irrelevant because it is not a cash flow.
2 The research and development cost is irrelevant since it has been spent irrespective of the decision on X14 production.

(b) The payback period is deduced as follows:

	Year 0 £000	Year 1 £000	Year 2 £000	Year 3 £000
Cumulative cash flows	(130)	(113)	(66)	7

Thus the equipment will have repaid the initial investment by the end of the third year of operations. The payback period is, therefore, three years.

(c) The net present value is calculated as follows:

	Year 0 £000	Year 1 £000	Year 2 £000	Year 3 £000	Year 4 £000	Year 5 £000
Discount factor	1.00	0.926	0.857	0.794	0.735	0.681
Present value	(130)	15.74	40.28	57.96	34.55	26.56
NPV	45.09	(that is, the sum of the present values for years 0 to 5)				

Chapter 15

15.1 **Helsim Ltd**

(a) The liquidity position may be assessed by using the liquidity ratios discussed in Chapter 7:

$$\text{Current ratio} = \frac{\text{Current assets}}{\text{Current liabilities}}$$

$$= \frac{£7.5\text{m}}{£5.4\text{m}}$$

$$= 1.4$$

$$\text{Acid test ratio} = \frac{\text{Current assets (excluding inventories)}}{\text{Current liabilities}}$$

$$= \frac{£3.7\text{m}}{£5.4\text{m}}$$

$$= 0.7$$

These ratios reveal a fairly weak liquidity position. The current ratio seems quite low and the acid test ratio very low. This latter ratio suggests that the business does not have sufficient liquid assets to meet its maturing obligations. It would, however, be useful to have details of the liquidity ratios of similar businesses in the same industry in order to make a more informed judgement. The bank overdraft represents 67% of the current liabilities and 40% of the total liabilities of the business. The continuing support of the bank is therefore important to the ability of the business to meet its commitments.

(b) The finance required to reduce trade payables to an average of 40 days outstanding is calculated as follows:

	£m
Trade payables at statement of financial position date	1.80
Trade payables outstanding based on 40 days' credit 40/365 × £8.4m (that is, credit purchases)	(0.92)
Finance required	0.88 (say £0.9m)

(c) The bank may not wish to provide further finance to the business. The increase in overdraft will reduce the level of trade payables but will increase the risk exposure of the bank. The additional finance invested by the bank will not generate further funds and will not therefore be self-liquidating. The question does not make it clear whether the business has sufficient security to offer the bank for the increase in overdraft facility. The profits of the business will be reduced and the interest cover ratio, based on the profits generated last year, would reduce to about 1.6* times if the additional overdraft were granted (based on interest charged at 10% each year). This is very low and means that only a small decline in profits would leave interest charges uncovered.

* Existing bank overdraft (3.6) + extension of overdraft to cover reduction in trade payables (0.9) + loan notes (3.5) = £8.0m. Assuming a 10% interest rate means a yearly interest payment of £0.8m. The operating profit was £1.3m (that is, 6.4 − 3.0 − 2.1). Interest cover would be 1.63 (that is, 1.3/0.8).

(d) A number of possible sources of finance might be considered. Four possible sources are as follows:

- *Issue equity shares.* This option may be unattractive to investors. The return on equity is fairly low at 7.9% (that is, profit for the year (0.3)/equity (3.8)) and there is no evidence that the profitability of the business will improve. If profits remain at their current level the effect of issuing more equity will be to reduce further the returns to equity.
- *Make other borrowings.* This option may also prove unattractive to investors. The effect of making further borowings will have a similar effect to that of increasing the overdraft. The profits of the business will be reduced and the interest cover ratio will decrease to a low level. The gearing ratio of the business is already quite high at 48% (that is, loan notes (3.5)/(loan notes + equity (3.5 + 3.8)) and it is not clear what security would be available for the loan. The gearing ratio would be much higher if the overdraft were to be included.
- *Chase trade receivables.* It may be possible to improve cash flows by reducing the level of credit outstanding from customers. At present, the average settlement period is 93 days (that is, (trade receivables (3.6)/sales revenue (14.2)) × 365), which seems quite high. A reduction in the average settlement period by approximately one-quarter would generate the funds required. However, it is not clear what effect this would have on sales.
- *Reduce inventories.* This appears to be the most attractive of the four options. At present, the average inventories holding period is 178 days (that is, (closing inventories (3.8)/cost of sales (7.8)) × 365), which seems very high. A reduction in this period by less than one-quarter would generate the funds required. However, if the business holds a large amount of slow-moving and obsolete items, it may be difficult to reduce inventories levels.

Chapter 16

16.1 Williams Wholesalers Ltd

	£	£
Existing level of trade receivables (£4m × 70/365)		767,123
New level of trade receivables: £2m × 80/365	438,356	
£2m × 30/365	164,384	602,740
Reduction in trade receivables		164,383
Costs and benefits of policy		
Cost of discount (£2m × 2%)		40,000
Less		
Interest saved on the reduction in		
trade receivables (£164,384* × 13%)	21,370	
Administration cost saving	6,000	
Cost of bad debts saved (20,000 − 10,000)	10,000	37,370
Net cost of policy		2,630

* It could be argued that the interest should be based on the amount expected to be received, that is the value of the trade receivables *after* taking account of the discount.

The above calculations reveal that the business will be worse off by offering the discounts.

Solutions to review questions

Chapter 1

1.1 The objective of providing accounting information is to enable users to make more informed decisions and judgements about the organisation concerned. Unless it fulfils this objective, there is no point in providing it.

1.2 The main users of financial information for a university and the way in which they are likely to use this information may be summed up as follows:

Students	Whether to enrol on a course of study. This would probably involve an assessment of the university's ability to continue to operate and to fulfil students' needs.
Other universities and colleges	How best to compete against the university. This might involve using the university's performance in various aspects as a 'benchmark' when evaluating their own performance.
Employees	Whether to take up or to continue in employment with the university. Employees might assess this by considering the ability of the university to continue to provide employment and to reward employees adequately for their labour.
Government/ funding authority	How efficient the university is in undertaking its various activities. Possible funding needs that the university may have.
Local community representatives	Whether to allow/encourage the university to expand its premises. To assess this, the university's ability to continue to provide employment for the community, to use community resources and to help fund environmental improvements might be considered.
Suppliers	Whether to continue to supply the university at all; also whether to supply on credit. This would involve an assessment of the university's ability to pay for any goods and services supplied.
Lenders	Whether to lend money to the university and/or whether to require repayment of any existing loans. To assess this, the university's ability to meet its obligations to pay interest and to repay the principal would be considered.
Board of governors and other managers (Faculty deans and so on)	Whether the performance of the university requires improvement. Here performance to date would be compared with earlier plans or some other 'benchmark' to decide whether action needs to be taken. Whether there should be a change in the university's future direction. In making such decisions, management will need to look at the university's ability to perform and at the opportunities available to it.

We can see that the users of accounting information and their needs are similar to those of a private sector business.

1.3 Most businesses are far too large and complex for managers to be able to see and assess everything that is going on in their own areas of responsibility merely by personal observation. Managers need information on all aspects within their control. Management accounting reports can provide them with this information, to a greater or lesser extent. These reports can be seen, therefore, as acting as the eyes and ears of the managers, providing insights not necessarily obvious without them.

1.4 Since we can never be sure what is going to happen in the future, the best that we can do is to make judgements on the basis of past experience. Thus information concerning flows of cash and of wealth in the recent past is likely to be a useful source on which to base judgements about possible future outcomes.

Chapter 2

2.1 The confusion arises because the owner seems unaware of the business entity convention in accounting. This convention requires a separation of the business from the owner(s) of the business for accounting purposes. The business is regarded as a separate entity and the statement of financial position is prepared from the perspective of the business rather than that of the owner. As a result, funds invested in the business by the owner will be regarded as a claim that the owner has on the business. In the statement of financial position, this claim will be shown alongside other claims on the business from outsiders.

2.2 A statement of financial position does not show what a business is worth, for two major reasons:

- Only those items which can be measured reliably in monetary terms are shown on the statement of financial position. Thus, things of value such as the reputation for product quality, skills of employees and so on will not normally appear in the statement of financial position.
- The historic cost convention results in assets being recorded at their outlay cost rather than their current value. In the case of certain assets, the difference between historic cost and current value may be significant.

2.3 The accounting equation is simply the relationship between a business's assets, liabilities and capital. In the horizontal layout it is:

Assets (current and non-current) = Equity + Liabilities (current and non-current)

For the alternative layout mentioned in the chapter, the equation is:

Assets (current and non-current) – Liabilities (current and non-current) = Equity

2.4 Some object to the idea of humans being treated as assets for inclusion on the statement of financial position. It can be seen as demeaning for humans to be listed alongside inventories, plant and machinery and other assets. However, others argue that humans are often the most valuable resource of a business and that placing a value on this resource will help bring to the attention of managers the importance of nurturing and developing this 'asset'. There is a saying in management that 'the things that count are the things that get counted'. As the value of the 'human assets' is not stated in the financial statements, there is a danger that managers will treat these 'assets' less favourably than other assets that are on the statement of financial position.

Humans are likely to meet the first criterion of an asset listed in the chapter, that is, a probable future benefit exists. There would be little point in employing people if this were not the case. The second criterion concerning exclusive right of control is more problematic.

Clearly a business cannot control humans in the same way as most other assets. However, a business can have the exclusive right to the employment services that a person provides. This distinction between control over the services provided and control over the person makes it possible to argue that the second criterion can be met.

Humans usually sign a contract of employment with the business and so the third criterion is normally met. The difficulty, however, is with the fourth criterion, that is, whether the value of humans (or their services) can be measured with any degree of reliability. To date, none of the measurement methods proposed enjoy widespread acceptance.

Chapter 3

3.1 At the time of preparing the income statement, it is not always possible to determine accurately the expenses that need to be matched to the sales revenue figure for the period. It will only be at some later point in time that the true position becomes clear. However, it is still necessary to try to include all relevant expenses in the income statement and so estimates of the future will have to be made. Examples of estimates that may have to be made include:

- expenses accrued at the end of the period such as the amount of telephone expenses incurred since the last quarter's bill.
- the amount of depreciation based on estimates of the life of the non-current asset and future residual value.
- the amount of bad and doubtful debts incurred.

3.2 Depreciation attempts to allocate the cost, or fair value, (less any residual value) of the asset over its useful life. Depreciation does not attempt to measure the fall in value of the asset during a particular accounting period. Thus, the carrying amount of the asset appearing on the statement of financial position normally represents the unexpired cost of the asset rather than its current market value.

3.3 The convention of consistency is designed to provide a degree of uniformity concerning the application of accounting policies. We have seen that, in certain areas, there may be more than one method of accounting for an item, for example inventories. The convention of consistency states that, having decided on a particular accounting policy, a business should continue to apply the policy in successive periods. While this policy helps to ensure that users can make valid comparisons concerning business performance *over time*, it does not ensure that valid comparisons can be made *between businesses*. This is because different businesses may consistently apply different accounting policies.

3.4 An expense is that element of the cost incurred that is used up during the accounting period. An asset is that element of cost which is carried forward on the statement of financial position and which will normally be used up in future periods. Thus, both assets and expenses arise from costs being incurred. The major difference between the two is the period over which the benefits (resulting from the costs incurred) accrue.

Chapter 4

4.1 It does not differ. In both cases they are required to meet their debts to the full extent that there are assets available. To this extent they both have a liability that is limited to the extent of their assets. This is a particularly important fact for the shareholders of a limited company because they know that those owed money by the company cannot demand that the shareholders contribute additional funds to help meet debts. Thus the liability of the shareholders is limited to the amount that they have paid for their shares, or have agreed to pay in the case of partially unpaid shares. This contrasts with the position of the owner or part owner of an unincorporated (non-company) business. Here all of the individual's assets could be required to meet the unsatisfied liabilities of the business.

4.2 A private limited company may place restrictions on the transfer of its shares, that is, the directors can veto an attempt by a shareholder to sell his or her shares to another person to whom the directors object. Thus, in effect, the majority can avoid having as a shareholder someone that they would prefer not to have. A public company cannot do this.

A public limited company must have authorised share capital of at least £50,000. There is no minimum for a private limited company.

The main advantage of being a public limited company is that the company may offer its shares and loan notes to the general public; a private company cannot make such an offer.

4.3 A reserve is that part of the equity (owners' claim) of a company that is not share capital. Reserves represent gains or surpluses that enhance the claim of the shareholders above the nominal value of their shares. For example, the share premium account is a reserve that represents the excess over the nominal value of shares that is paid for them on a share issue. The retained earnings balance is a reserve that arises from ploughed-back profits earned by the company. Revenue reserves arise from realised profits and gains. Capital reserves arise from unrealised profits and gains (for example, the upward revaluation of a non-current asset) or from issuing shares at a premium (share premium).

4.4 A preference share represents part of the ownership of a company. Preference shares entitle their owners to the first part of any dividend paid by the company, up to a maximum amount. The maximum is usually expressed as a percentage of the nominal or par value of the preference shares.

(a) They differ from ordinary shares to the extent that they only entitle their holders to dividends to a predetermined maximum value. Dividends to ordinary shareholders have no predetermined maximum. Were the company to be liquidated, the preference shareholders would normally receive a maximum of the nominal value of their shares, whereas the ordinary shareholders receive the residue after all other claimants, including the preference shareholders.

(b) They differ from loan notes in that these represent borrowings for the company, where normally holders have a contract with the company that specifies the rate of interest, interest payment dates and redemption date. They are often secured on the company's assets. Preference shareholders have no such contract.

Chapter 5

5.1 Accounting is an evolving subject. It is not static and so the principles that are laid down at any particular point in time may become obsolete as a result of changes in our understanding of the nature of accounting information and its impact on users and changes in the economic environment within which accounting is employed. We must accept, therefore, that accounting principles will continue to evolve and that existing principles must be regularly reviewed.

5.2 Apart from increases in accounting regulation, financial reports have increased because of:

- increasing demands by influential user groups, such as shareholders and financial analysts, for financial information relating to the company;
- the increasing sophistication of influential user groups, such as financial analysts, to deal with financial information;

- the increasing complexity of business operations requiring greater explanation;
- increasing recognition of the need for greater accountability towards certain user groups (such as employees and community groups) requiring the need for additional reports, such as environmental reports and social reports.

5.3 There are various problems associated with the measurement of business segments. These include:

- the definition of a segment;
- the treatment of inter-segmental transactions, such as sales;
- the treatment of common costs.

There is no single correct method of dealing with these problems and variations will arise in practice. This, in turn, will hinder comparisons between businesses.

5.4 Preparing a business review may present a problem for accountants. For information to be credible to all interested parties, accountants should be as neutral as possible in measuring and reporting the financial performance and position of the business. The business review requires some interpretation of results and there is always a risk of bias, or at least the perception of bias among some users, in what items are reported and how they reflect on business performance. The business review is not normally audited and so comments made are not subject to independent scrutiny. The board of directors is charged with running the business and it is logical that the directors accept full responsibility for preparing the review. This should be made clear to users.

Chapter 6

6.1 Cash is normally required in the settlement of claims. Thus, employees and contractors want to be paid for their work in cash. A supplier of non-current assets or inventories will normally expect to be paid in cash, perhaps after a short period of credit. When businesses fail, it is their inability to find the cash to pay claimants that actually drives them under. These factors lead to cash being the pre-eminent business asset and, therefore, the one that analysts and others watch carefully in trying to assess the ability of the business to survive and/or to take advantage of commercial opportunities.

6.2 With the direct method, the business's cash records are analysed for the period concerned. The analysis reveals the amounts of cash, in total, which have been paid and received in respect of each category of the cash flow statement. This is not difficult in principle, or in practice if it is done by computer as a matter of routine.

The indirect method takes the approach that, while the profit (loss) for the year is not equal to the net inflow (outflow) of cash from operations, they are fairly closely linked to the extent that appropriate adjustment of the profit (loss) for the year figure will produce the correct cash flow one. The adjustment is concerned with depreciation charge for, and movements in relevant working capital items over, the period.

6.3 (a) *Cash flows from operating activities*. This would normally be positive, even for a business with small profits or even losses. The fact that depreciation is not a cash flow tends to lead to positive cash flows in this area in most cases.

(b) *Cash flows from investing activities*. Normally this would be negative in cash flow terms since assets become worn out and need to be replaced in the normal course of business. This means that, typically, old items of property, plant and equipment are generating less cash on their disposal than is having to be paid out to replace them.

(c) *Cash flows from financing activities*. There is a tendency for businesses either to expand or to fail. In either case, this is likely to mean that, over the years, more finance will be raised than will be redeemed or retired.

6.4 There are several reasons for this, including the following:

- Changes in inventories, trade receivables and trade payables. For example, an increase in trade receivables during an accounting period would mean that the cash received from credit sales would be less than the credit sales revenue for the same period.
- Cash may have been spent on new non-current assets or received from disposals of old ones; these would not directly affect profit.
- Cash may have been spent to redeem or repay a financial claim or received as a result of the creation or the increase of a claim. These would not directly affect profit.
- The taxation charged in the income statement would not be the same tax that is paid during the same accounting period.

Chapter 7

7.1 The fact that a business operates on a low operating profit margin indicates that only a small operating profit is being produced for each £1 of sales revenue generated. However, this does not necessarily mean that the ROCE will be low. If the business is able to generate a large amount of sales revenue during a period, the operating profit may be very high even though the operating profit per £1 of sales revenue is low. If the overall operating profit is high, this can lead, in turn, to a high ROCE, since it is the total operating profit that is used as the numerator (top part of the fraction) in this ratio. Many businesses (including supermarkets) pursue a strategy of 'low margin, high turnover'.

7.2 The statement of financial position is drawn up at a single point in time – the end of the financial period. As a result, the figures shown on the statement represent the position at that single point in time and may not be representative of the position during the period. Wherever possible, average figures (perhaps based on monthly figures) should be used. However, an external user may only have access to the opening and closing balance sheets for the year and so a simple average based on these figures may be all that it is possible to calculate. Where a business is seasonal in nature or is subject to cyclical changes, this simple averaging may not be sufficient.

7.3 Three possible reasons for a long inventories turnover period are:

- poor inventories controls, leading to excessive investment in inventories;
- inventories hoarding in anticipation of price rises or shortages;
- inventories building in anticipation of increased future sales.

A short inventories turnover period may be due to:

- tight inventories controls, thereby reducing excessive investment in inventories and/or the amount of obsolete and slow-moving inventories;
- an inability to finance the required amount of inventories to meet sales demand;
- a difference in the mix of inventories carried by similar businesses (for example, greater investment in perishable goods which are held for a short period only).

7.4 The P/E ratio may vary between businesses within the same industry for the following reasons:

- *Accounting policies*. Differences in the methods used to compute profit (for example, inventories valuation and depreciation) can lead to different profit figures and, therefore, different P/E ratios.
- *Different prospects*. One business may be regarded as having a much brighter future owing to factors such as the quality of management, the quality of products, location. This will

affect the market price that investors are prepared to pay for the share and, hence, it will also affect the P/E ratio.

● *Different asset structure.* One business's underlying asset base may be much higher than the other's and this may affect the market price of its shares.

Chapter 8

8.1   The two attributes are:

● They must relate to the objective(s) that the decision is intended to work towards. In most businesses this is taken to be wealth enhancement. This means that any information relating to the decision that does not impact on wealth enhancement is irrelevant, where wealth enhancement is the sole objective. In practice a business may have more than one objective.

● The costs must differ between the options under consideration. Where a cost will be the same irrespective of the outcome of the decision that is to be taken, that cost is irrelevant. It is only on the basis of things that differ from one outcome to another that decisions can be made.

8.2   A sunk cost is a past and, therefore, an irrelevant cost in the context of any decision about the future. Thus, for example, the cost of an item of inventories already bought is a sunk cost. It is irrelevant, in any decision involving the use of the inventories, because this cost will be the same irrespective of the decision made.

An opportunity cost is the cost of being deprived of the next best option to the one under consideration. For example, where using an hour of a worker's time on activity A deprives the business of the opportunity to use that time in a profitable activity B, the benefit lost from activity B is an opportunity cost of pursuing activity A.

8.3   Cost may be defined as the amount of resources, usually measured in monetary terms, sacrificed to achieve a particular objective.

8.4   A committed cost is like a past cost in that an irrevocable decision has been made to incur the cost. This might be because the business has entered into a binding contract, for example to rent some premises for the next two years. Thus it is effectively a past cost though the payment (for rent, in our example) has yet to be made. Since the business cannot avoid a committed cost, committed costs cannot be relevant costs.

Chapter 9

9.1   A fixed cost is one that is the same irrespective of the level of activity or output. Typical examples of costs that are fixed, irrespective of the level of production or provision of a service, include rent of business premises, salaries of supervisory staff, and insurance.

A variable cost is one that varies with the level of activity or output. Examples include raw materials and labour, where labour is rewarded in proportion to the level of output.

Note particularly that it is relative to the level of activity that costs are fixed or variable. Fixed costs will be affected by inflation and they will be greater for a longer period than for a shorter one.

For a particular product or service, knowing which costs are fixed and which variable enables managers to predict the total cost for any particular level of activity. It also enables them to concentrate only on the variable costs in circumstances where a decision will not alter the fixed costs.

9.2 The BEP or break-even point is the level of activity, measured either in physical units or in value of sales revenue, at which the sales revenues exactly cover all of the costs, both fixed and variable.

Break-even point is calculated as:

$$\text{Fixed costs}/(\text{Sales revenue per unit} - \text{Variable costs per unit})$$

which may alternatively be expressed as:

$$\text{Fixed costs}/\text{Contribution per unit}$$

Thus break-even will occur when the contributions for the period are sufficient to cover the fixed costs for the period.

The break-even point tends to be useful as a comparison with planned level of activity in an attempt to assess the riskiness of the activity.

9.3 Operating (or operational) gearing refers to the extent of fixed costs relative to variable costs in the total costs of some activity. Where the fixed costs form a relatively high proportion of the total, we say that the activity has high operating gearing.

Typically, high operating gearing is present in environments where there is a relatively high level of mechanisation (that is, they are capital intensive). This is because such environments tend simultaneously to involve relatively high fixed costs of depreciation, maintenance and so on and relatively low variable costs.

High operating gearing tends to mean that the effects of increases or decreases in the level of activity have an accentuated effect on operating profit. For example, a 20% decrease in output of a particular service will lead to a greater than 20% decrease in operating profit, assuming no cost or price changes.

9.4 In the face of a restricting scarce resource, profit will be maximised by using the scarce resource on output where the contribution per unit of the scarce resource is maximised.

This means that the contribution per unit of the scarce resource (for example, hour of scarce labour, unit of scarce raw material and so on) for each competing product or service needs to be identified. It is then a question of allocating the scarce resource to the product or service that provides the highest contribution per unit of the particular scarce resource.

The logic of this approach is that the scarce resource is allocated to the activity that uses it most effectively in terms of contribution and, therefore, profit.

Chapter 10

10.1 In process costing, the total production costs for a period are divided by the number of completed units of output for the period to deduce the full cost per unit. Where there is work in progress at the beginning and/or the end of the period complications arise.

The problem is that some of the completed output incurred costs in the preceding period. Similarly, some of the costs incurred in the current period lead to completed production in the subsequent period. Account needs to be taken of these facts if reliable full cost information is to be obtained.

10.2 The only reason for distinguishing between direct and indirect costs is to help to deduce the full cost of a unit of output in a job-costing environment. In an environment where all units of output are identical, or can reasonably be regarded as being so, a process-costing approach will be taken. This avoids the need for identifying direct and indirect costs separately.

Direct cost forms that part of the total cost of pursuing some activity that can, unequivocally, be associated with it. Examples of direct cost items in the typical job-costing environment include direct labour and direct materials.

Indirect cost is the remainder of the cost of pursuing some activity.

In practice, knowledge of the direct cost tends to provide the basis used to charge overheads to jobs.

The distinction between direct and indirect cost is irrelevant for any other purpose.

Directness and indirectness is dictated by the nature of that which is being costed, as much as the nature of the cost.

10.3   The notion of direct and indirect cost is concerned only with the extent to which particular elements of cost can unequivocally be related to and measured in respect of a particular cost unit, usually a product or service. The distinction between direct and indirect costs is made exclusively for the purpose of deducing the full cost of some cost unit, in an environment where each cost unit is not identical, or close enough to being identical for it to be treated as such. Thus, it is typically in the context of job costing, or some variant of it, that the distinction between direct and indirect costs is usefully made.

The notion of variable and fixed costs is concerned entirely with how costs behave in the face of changes in the volume of output. The benefit of being able to distinguish between fixed and variable cost is that predictions can be made of what total cost will be at particular levels of volume and/or what reduction or addition to cost will occur if the volume of output is reduced or increased.

Thus the notion of direct and indirect cost, on the one hand, and that of variable and fixed cost, on the other, are not linked to one another, though it is true that, in most contexts, some elements of direct costs are variable, some are fixed. Similarly, indirect cost might be fixed or variable.

10.4   The full cost includes all of the costs of pursuing the cost objective, including a 'fair' share of the overheads. Generally the full cost represents an average cost of the various elements, rather than a cost that arises because the business finds itself in a particular situation.

The fact that the full cost reflects all aspects of cost should mean that, were the business to sell its output at a price exactly equal to the full cost (manufacturing and non-manufacturing), the sales revenue for the period would exactly cover all of the costs and the business would break even, that is, make neither profit nor loss.

Chapter 11

11.1   ABC is a means of dealing with charging overheads to units of output to derive full costs in a multi-product (job- or batch-costing) environment.

The traditional approach tends to accept that once identifiable direct costs, normally labour and materials, have been taken out, all of the remaining costs (overheads) must be treated as common costs and applied to jobs using the same formula, typically on the basis of direct labour hours.

ABC takes a much more enquiring approach to overheads. It follows the philosophy that overheads do not occur for no reason, but they must be driven by activities. For example, a particular type of product may take up a disproportionately large part of supervisors' time. If that product were not made, in the long run, supervision costs could be cut (fewer supervisors would be needed). Whereas the traditional approach would just accept that supervisory salaries are an overhead which needs to be apportioned along with other overheads, ABC would seek to charge to a particular product that part of the supervisors' salaries that is driven by it.

11.2 One criticism is on the issue of the cost–benefit balance. It is claimed that the work necessary to analyse activities and identify the cost drivers tends to be more expensive than is justified by the increased quality of the full cost information that emerges.

Linked to this is the belief of many that full cost information is of rather dubious value for most purposes, irrespective of how the full costs are deduced. Many argue that full cost information is flawed by the fact that it takes no account of opportunity cost.

ABC enthusiasts would probably argue that deducing better quality full cost information is not the only benefit that is available, if the overhead cost drivers can be identified. Knowing what drives costs can enable management to exercise more control over them. This benefit needs to be taken into account when assessing the cost–benefit balance of using ABC.

11.3 The four main areas in the balanced scorecard are:

(1) *Financial*. Here targets for measures such as return on capital employed will be stated.
(2) *Customer*. Here the market/customers that the business will aim for is established, as will be targets for such things as measures of customer satisfaction and rate of growth in customer numbers.
(3) *Internal business process*. Here the processes that are vital to the business will be established. This might include levels of innovation, types of operation and after-sales service.
(4) *Learning and growth*. In this area issues relating to growing the business and development of staff are identified and targets set.

11.4 Three non-financial measures might include:

- turnover of staff during period
- new clients obtained during period
- level of client satisfaction during period.

Chapter 12

12.1 A budget can be defined as a financial plan for a future period of time. Thus it sets out the intentions which management has for the period concerned. Achieving the budget plans should help to achieve the long-term plans of the business. Achievement of the long-term plans should mean that the business is successfully working towards its objectives.

A budget differs from a forecast in that a forecast is a statement of what is expected to happen without the intervention of management, perhaps because managers cannot intervene (as with a weather forecast). A plan is an intention to achieve.

Normally, management would take account of reliable forecasts when making its plans.

12.2 The five uses of budgets are:

- They tend to promote forward thinking and the possible identification of short-term problems. Managers must plan and the budgeting process tends to force them to do so. In doing so, they are likely to encounter potential problems. If the potential problems can be identified early enough, solutions might be easily found.
- They can be used to help co-ordination between various sections of the business. It is important that the plans of one area of the business fit in with those of other areas; a lack of co-ordination could have disastrous consequences. Having formal statements of plans for each aspect of the business enables a check to be made that plans are complementary.

- They can motivate managers to better performance. It is believed that people are motivated by having a target to aim for. Provided that the inherent goals are achievable, budgets can provide an effective motivational device.
- They can provide a basis for a system of control. Having a plan against which actual performance can be measured provides a potentially useful tool of control.
- They can provide a system of authorisation. Many managers have 'spending' budgets for research and development, staff training and so on. For these people, the size of their budget defines their authority to spend.

12.3 Control can be defined as 'compelling things to occur as planned'. This implies that control can be achieved only if a plan exists. Budgets are financial plans. This means that, if actual performance can be compared with the budget (plan) for each aspect of the business, divergences from plan can be spotted. Steps can then be taken to bring matters back under control where they are going out of control.

12.4 A budget committee is a group of senior staff that is responsible for the budget preparation process within an organisation. The existence of the committee places the budget responsibility clearly with an identifiable group of people. This group can focus on the tasks involved.

Chapter 13

13.1 Feedforward controls try to anticipate what is likely to happen in the future and then assist in making the actual outcome match the desired outcome. They contrast with feedback controls, which simply compare actual to planned outcomes after the event. Feedforward controls are therefore more pro-active.

13.2 A variance is the effect on budgeted profit of the particular cost or revenue item being considered. It represents the difference between the budgeted profit and the actual profit assuming everything, except the item under consideration, had gone according to budget. From this, it must be the case that:

> Budgeted profit + Favourable variances − Unfavourable variances = Actual profit.

The purpose of analysing variances is to identify whether, and if so where, things are not going according to plan. If this can be done, it may be possible to find out the cause of things going out of control. If this can be discovered, it may then be possible to put things right for the future.

13.3 Where the budgeted and actual volumes of output do not coincide, it is impossible to make a valid comparison of 'allowed' and actual costs and revenues. Flexing the original budget to reflect the actual output level enables a more informative comparison to be made.

Flexing certainly does not mean that output volume differences do not matter. Flexing will show (as the difference between flexed and original budget profits) the effect on profit of output volume differences.

13.4 Deciding whether variances should be investigated involves the use of judgement. Often management will set a threshold of significance, for example 5% of the budgeted figure for each variance relating to revenue or cost items. All variances above this threshold would then be investigated. Even where variances are below the threshold, any sign of a systemic variance, shown, for example, by an increasing cumulative total for the factor, should be investigated.

Knowledge of the cause of a particular variance may well put management in a position to take actions that will be beneficial to the business in the future. Investigating variances, however, is likely to be relatively expensive in staff time. A judgement needs to be made on whether the value or benefit of knowing the cause of the variance will be justified by the cost of this knowledge. As with most investigations of this type, it is difficult to judge the value of the knowledge until after the variance has been investigated.

Chapter 14

14.1 NPV is usually considered the best method of assessing investment opportunities because it takes account of:

- *The timing of the cash flows.* By *discounting* the various cash flows associated with each project according to when it is expected to arise, it recognises the fact that cash flows do not all occur simultaneously. Associated with this is the fact that, by discounting, using the opportunity cost of finance (that is, the return that the next best alternative opportunity would generate), the net benefit after financing costs have been met is identified (as the NPV).
- *The whole of the relevant cash flows.* NPV includes all of the relevant cash flows irrespective of when they are expected to occur. It treats them differently according to their date of occurrence, but they are all taken account of in the NPV and they all have, or can have, an influence on the decision.
- *The objectives of the business.* NPV is the only method of appraisal where the output of the analysis has a direct bearing on the wealth of the owners of the business. (Positive NPVs enhance wealth; negative ones reduce it.) Since most private-sector businesses seek to increase their owners' wealth, NPV clearly is the best approach to use.

NPV provides clear decision rules concerning acceptance/rejection of projects and the ranking of projects. It is fairly simple to use, particularly with the availability of modern computer software that takes away the need for routine calculations to be done manually.

14.2 The payback method, in its original form, does not take account of the time value of money. However, it would be possible to modify the payback method to accommodate this requirement. Cash flows arising from a project could be discounted, using the cost of finance as the appropriate discount rate, in the same way as in the NPV and IRR methods. The discounted payback approach is used by some businesses and represents an improvement on the original approach described in the chapter. However, it still retains the other flaws of the original payback approach that were discussed. For example, it ignores relevant data after the payback period. Thus, even in its modified form, the PP method cannot be regarded as superior to NPV.

14.3 The IRR method does appear to be preferred to the NPV method among practising managers. The main reasons for this appear to be as follows:

- A preference for a percentage return ratio rather than an absolute figure as a means of expressing the outcome of a project. This preference for a ratio may reflect the fact that other financial goals of the business are often set in terms of ratios, for example return on capital employed.
- A preference for ranking projects in terms of their percentage return. Managers feel it is easier to rank projects on the basis of percentage returns (though NPV outcomes should be just as easy for them). We saw in the chapter that the IRR method could provide misleading advice on the ranking of projects and the NPV method was preferable for this purpose.

14.4 Cash flows are preferred to profit flows because cash is the ultimate measure of economic wealth. Cash is used to acquire resources and for distribution to shareholders. When cash is invested in a project, an opportunity cost is incurred, as the cash cannot be used in other investment projects. Similarly, when positive cash flows are generated by the project, the cash can be used to reinvest in other projects.

Profit, on the other hand, is relevant to reporting the productive effort for a period. This measure of effort may have only a tenuous relationship to cash flows for a period. The conventions of accounting may lead to the recognition of gains and losses in one period and the relevant cash inflows and outflows occurring in another period.

Chapter 15

15.1 Share warrants may be particularly useful for young expanding businesses that wish to attract new investors. They can help provide a 'sweetener' for the issue of loan notes. By attaching warrants it may be possible to agree a lower rate of interest or less restrictive loan covenants. If the business is successful, the warrants will provide a further source of finance. Investors will exercise their option to acquire shares if the market price of the shares exceeds the exercise price of the warrant. However, this will have the effect of diluting the control of existing shareholders.

15.2 A listed business may wish to revert to unlisted status for a number of possible reasons. These include:

- *Cost.* A Stock Exchange listing can be costly, as the business must adhere to certain administrative regulations and financial disclosures.
- *Scrutiny.* Listed companies are subject to close scrutiny by analysts and this may not be welcome if the business is engaged in sensitive negotiations or controversial business activities.
- *Takeover risk.* The shares of the business may be purchased by an unwelcome bidder and this may result in a takeover.
- *Investor profile.* If the business is dominated by a few investors who wish to retain their interest in the business and do not wish to raise further equity by public issues, the benefits of a listing are few.

15.3 An offer for sale involves an issuing house buying the shares in the business and then, in turn, selling the shares to the public. The issue will be advertised by the publication of a prospectus, which will set out details of the business and the issue price of the shares (or reserve price if a tender issue is being made). The shares issued by the issuing house may be either new shares or shares that have been purchased from existing shareholders. A public issue is where the business undertakes direct responsibility for issuing shares to the public. If an issuing house is employed it will usually be in the role of adviser and administrator of the issue. However, the issuing house may also underwrite the issue. A public issue runs the risk that the shares will not be taken up and is a less popular form of issue for businesses.

15.4 Invoice discounting is a service offered to businesses by a financial institution whereby the institution is prepared to advance a sum equivalent to 75% to 80% of outstanding trade receivables. The amount advanced is usually payable within 60 to 90 days. The business will retain responsibility for collecting the amounts owing from credit customers and the advance must be repaid irrespective of whether the trade receivables have been collected. Factoring is a service that is also offered to businesses by financial institutions. In this case, the factor will take over the business's sales and trade receivables records and will undertake to collect trade receivables on behalf of the client business. The factor will also be prepared to make an advance of up to 80% of approved trade receivables that is repayable from the amounts received from customers. The service charge for invoice discounting is up to 0.5%

of turnover, whereas the service charge for factoring is up to 3% of turnover. This difference explains, in part, why businesses have shown a preference for invoice discounting rather than factoring in recent years. However, the factor provides additional services, as explained.

Chapter 16

16.1 Although the credit manager is responsible for ensuring that receivables pay on time, Tariq may be right in denying blame. Various factors may be responsible for the situation described which are beyond the control of the credit manager. These include:

- a downturn in the economy leading to financial difficulties among receivables;
- a decision made by other managers within the business to liberalise credit policy in order to stimulate sales;
- an increase in competition among suppliers offering credit that is being exploited by customers;
- disputes with customers over the quality of goods or services supplied; and
- problems in the delivery of goods leading to delays.

You may have thought of others.

16.2 Inventories levels will be affected in the following ways:

(a) An increase in production bottlenecks is likely to result in an increase in raw materials and work in progress being processed within the plant. Therefore, inventories levels should rise.

(b) A rise in interest rates will make holding inventories more expensive (if they are financed by debt). This may, in turn, lead to a decision to reduce inventories levels.

(c) The decision to reduce the range of products should result in less inventories being held. It would no longer be necessary to hold certain items in order to meet customer demand.

(d) Switching to a local supplier may reduce the lead time between ordering an item and receiving it. This should, in turn, reduce the need to carry such high levels of the particular item.

(e) A deterioration in the quality of bought-in items may result in the purchase of higher quantities of inventories in order to take account of the defective element in inventories acquired and, perhaps, an increase in the inspection time for items received. This would lead to a rise in inventories levels.

16.3 Inventories are held:

- to meet customer demand,
- to avoid the problems of running out of inventories, and
- to take advantage of profitable opportunities (for example, buying a product that is expected to rise steeply in price in the future).

The first reason may be described as transactionary, the second precautionary and the third speculative. They are, in essence, the same reasons why a business holds cash.

16.4 (a) The costs of holding too little cash are:

- failure to meet obligations when they fall due which can damage the reputation of the business and may, in the extreme, lead to the business being wound up;
- having to borrow and thereby incur interest charges; and
- an inability to take advantage of profitable opportunities.

(b) The costs of holding too much cash are:

- failure to use the funds available for more profitable purposes; and
- loss of value during a period of inflation.

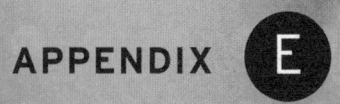
Solutions to selected exercises

Chapter 2

2.1 Paul

Statement of cash flows for Thursday

	£
Opening balance (from Wednesday)	59
Cash from sale of wrapping paper	47
	106
Cash paid to purchase wrapping paper	(53)
Closing balance	53

Income statement for Thursday

	£
Sales revenue	47
Cost of goods sold	(33)
Profit	14

Statement of financial position as at Thursday evening

	£
Cash	53
Inventories of goods for resale (23 + 53 − 33)	43
Total assets	96
Equity	96

2.2 Paul (continued)

Equity	£
Cash introduced by Paul on Monday	40
Profit for Monday	15
Profit for Tuesday	18
Profit for Wednesday	9
Profit for Thursday	14
	96

Thus the equity of the business, all of which belongs to Paul as sole owner, consists of the cash he put in to start the business plus the profit earned each day.

2.3 **Helen**

Income statement for day 1

	£
Sales revenue (70 × £0.80)	56
Cost of sales (70 × £0.50)	(35)
Profit	21

Statement of cash flows for day 1

	£
Opening balance	40
Cash from sales	56
Cash for purchases (80 × £0.50)	(40)
Closing balance	56

Statement of financial position as at end of day 1

	£
Cash balance	56
Inventory of unsold goods (10 × £0.50)	5
Helen's business wealth	61
Equity	61

Income statement for day 2

	£
Sales revenue (65 × £0.80)	52.0
Cost of sales (65 × £0.50)	(32.5)
Profit	19.5

Statement of cash flows for day 2

	£
Opening balance	56.0
Cash from sales	52.0
Cash for purchases (60 × £0.50)	(30.0)
Closing balance	78.0

Statement of financial position as at end of day 2

	£
Cash balance	78.0
Inventory of unsold goods (5 × £0.50)	2.5
Total assets	80.5
Equity	80.5

Income statement for day 3

	£
Sales revenue (20 × £0.80) + (45 × £0.40)	34.0
Cost of sales (65 × £0.50)	(32.5)
Profit	1.5

Statement of cash flows for day 3

	£
Opening balance	78.0
Cash from sales	34.0
Cash for purchases (60 × £0.50)	(30.0)
Closing balance	82.0

Statement of financial position as at end of day 3

	£
Cash balance	82.0
Inventory of unsold goods	–
Total assets	82.0
Equity	82.0

2.5 Crafty Engineering Ltd

(a)

Crafty Engineering Ltd
Statement of financial position as at 30 June last year

	£000
ASSETS	
Non-current assets	
Property, plant and equipment	
Property	320
Equipment and tools	207
Motor vehicles	38
	565
Current assets	
Inventories	153
Trade receivables	185
	338
Total assets	903
EQUITY AND LIABILITIES	
Equity (which is the missing figure)	441
Non-current liabilities	
Long-term borrowings (Loan Industrial Finance Co.)	260
Current liabilities	
Trade payables	86
Short-term borrowings	116
	202
Total equity and liabilities	903

(b) The statement of financial position reveals a high level of investment in non-current assets. In percentage terms, we can say that more than 60% of the total investment in assets (565/903) has been in non-current assets. The nature of the business may require a heavy investment in non-current assets. The investment in current assets exceeds the current liabilities by a large amount (approximately 1.7 times). As a result, there is no obvious sign of a liquidity problem. However, the statement of financial position reveals that the business has no cash balance and is therefore dependent on the continuing support of short-term borrowing in order to meet obligations when they fall due. When considering the long-term financing of the business, we can see that about 37% (that is, 260/(260 + 441)) of the total long-term finance for the business has been supplied by borrowings and about 63% (that is, 441/(260 + 441)) by the owners. This level of long-term borrowing seems quite high but not excessive. However, we would need to know more about the ability of the business to service the borrowing (that is, make interest payments and repayments of the amount borrowed) before a full assessment could be made.

2.8

(a) The income statement shows the increase in wealth, as a result of trading, generated during the period (revenue), the decrease in wealth caused by the generation of that revenue (expenses) and the resulting net increase (profit) or decrease (loss) in wealth for the period. Though most businesses hold some of their wealth in cash, wealth is held in many other forms: non-current assets, receivables and so on.

(b) Assets, to be included in a statement of financial position, must be judged as likely to produce future economic benefits. The economic benefit may come from selling the asset in the short term, in which case the statement is broadly true for those assets that it is the intention of the business to liquidate (turn into cash) in the short term. Many assets have an economic benefit that is not related to liquidation value but to use – for example, in production. For these types of asset, the statement is certainly not true.

There are other conditions that must be met in order for an item to be included in the statement of financial position. These are:

- the business must have an exclusive right to control the asset;
- the benefit must arise from some past transaction or event; and
- the asset must be measurable in monetary terms.

(c) The accounting equation is:

$$\text{Assets} = \text{Equity} + \text{Liabilities}$$

(d) Non-current assets are assets that do not meet the criteria for current assets. They are normally held for the long-term operations of the business. Some non-current assets may be immovable (for example, property) but others are not (for example, motor vans).

(e) Goodwill may or may not have an infinite life – it will depend on the nature of the goodwill. There are no hard and fast rules that can be applied. Where this asset has a finite life, it should be amortised. Where it is considered to have an infinite life, it should not be amortised but should be tested annually for impairment.

Chapter 3

3.1 (a) Equity does increase as a result of the owners introducing more cash into the business, but it will also increase as a result of introducing other assets (for example, a motor car) and by the business generating revenue by trading. Similarly, equity decreases not only as a result of withdrawals of cash by owners but also by withdrawals of other assets (for example, inventories for the owners' personal use) and through trading expenses being incurred. For the typical business in a typical accounting period, equity will alter much more as a result of trading activities than for any other reason.

(b) An accrued expense is not one that relates to next year. It is one that needs to be matched with the revenue of the accounting period under review, but that has yet to be met in terms of cash payment. As such, it will appear on the statement of financial position as a current liability.

(c) The purpose of depreciation is not to provide for asset replacement. Rather, it is an attempt to allocate the cost, or fair value, of the asset (less any residual value) over its useful life. Depreciation is an attempt to provide a measure of the amount of the non-current asset that has been consumed during the period. This amount will then be charged as an expense for the period in deriving the profit figure. Depreciation is a book entry (the outlay of cash occurs when the asset is purchased) and does not normally entail setting aside a separate amount of cash for asset replacement. Even if this were done, there would be no guarantee that sufficient funds would be available at the end of the asset's life for its replacement. Factors such as inflation and technological change may mean that the replacement cost is higher than the original cost of the asset.

(d) In the short term, it is possible for the current value of a non-current asset to exceed its original cost. However, nearly all non-current assets will wear out over time as a result of being used to generate wealth for the business. This will be the case for freehold buildings. As a result, some measure of depreciation should be calculated to take account of the fact that the asset is being consumed. Some businesses revalue their freehold buildings where the current value is significantly different from the original cost. Where this occurs, the depreciation charged should be based on the revalued amount (fair value). This will normally result in higher depreciation charges than if the asset remained at its historic cost.

3.3 The existence of profit and downward movement in cash may be for various reasons, which include the following:

- The purchase of assets for cash during the period (for example, motor cars and inventories), which were not all consumed during the period and are therefore not having as great an effect on expenses as they are on cash.
- The payment of an outstanding liability (for example, borrowings), which will have an effect on cash but not on expenses in the income statement.
- The withdrawal of cash by the owners from the capital invested, which will not have an effect on the expenses in the income statement.
- The generation of revenue on credit where the cash has yet to be received. This will increase the sales revenue for the period but will not have a beneficial effect on the cash balance until a later period.

3.5
(a)	Rent payable – expense for period	£9,000
(b)	Rates and insurance – expense for period	£6,000
(c)	General expenses – paid in period	£7,000
(d)	Interest (on borrowings) payable – prepaid	£500
(e)	Salaries – paid in period	£6,000
(f)	Rent receivable – received during period	£3,000

3.7 WW Associates

WW Associates
Statement of financial position as at 31 December 2009

ASSETS	£
Machinery (25,300 + 6,000 + 9,000 – 13,000 + 3,900 – 9,360)	21,840*
Inventories (12,200 + 143,000 + 12,000 – 127,000 – 25,000)	15,200
Trade receivables (21,300 + 211,000 – 198,000)	34,300
Cash at bank (overdraft) (8,300 – 23,000 – 25,000 – 2,000 – 6,000	
– 23,800 – 2,700 – 12,000 + 42,000 + 198,000 – 156,000 – 17,500)	(19,700)
Prepaid expenses (400 – 400 + 5,000 + 500)	5,500
Total assets	57,140
EQUITY AND LIABILITIES	
Equity (owner's capital) (48,900 – 23,000 + 26,480)	52,380
Trade payables (16,900 + 143,000 – 156,000)	3,900
Accrued expenses (1,700 – 1,700 + 860)	860
Total equity and liabilities	57,140

* Cost less accumulated depreciation at 31 December 2008	25,300
Carrying amount of machine disposed of (£13,000 – £3,900)	(9,100)
Cost of new machine	15,000
Depreciation for 2009 (£31,200 × 30%)	(9,360)
Carrying amount (written-down value) of machine at 31 December 2009	21,840

Income statement for the year ended 31 December 2009

	£
Sales revenue (211,000 + 42,000)	253,000
Cost of goods sold (127,000 + 25,000)	(152,000)
Gross profit	101,000
Rent (20,000)	(20,000)
Rates (400 + 1,500)	(1,900)
Wages (– 1,700 + 23,800 + 860)	(22,960)
Electricity (2,700)	(2,700)
Machinery depreciation (9,360)	(9,360)
Loss on disposal of the old machinery (13,000 – 3,900 – 9,000)	(100)
Van expenses (17,500)	(17,500)
Profit for the year	26,480

The loss on disposal of the old machinery is the carrying amount (cost less depreciation) less the disposal proceeds. Since the machinery had only been owned for one year, with a depreciation rate of 30%, the depreciation on it so far is £3,900 (that is, £13,000 × 30%). The effective disposal proceeds were £9,000 because, as a result of trading it in, the business saved £9,000 on the new asset.

The depreciation expense for 2009 is based on the cost less accumulated depreciation of the assets owned at the end of 2009. Accumulated depreciation must be taken into account because the business uses the reducing-balance method.

The statement of financial position could now be rewritten in a more stylish form as follows:

WW Associates
Statement of financial position as at 31 December 2009

	£
ASSETS	
Non-current assets	
Property, plant and equipment	
Machinery at cost less depreciation	21,840
Current assets	
Inventories	15,200
Trade receivables	34,300
Prepaid expenses	5,500
	55,000
Total assets	76,840
EQUITY AND LIABILITIES	
Equity	
Closing balance	52,380
Current liabilities	
Trade payables	3,900
Accrued expenses	860
Borrowings – Bank overdraft	19,700
	24,460
Total equity and liabilities	76,840

3.8   **Nikov and Co.**

An examination of the income statements for the two years reveals a number of interesting points, which include:

- An increase in sales revenue and gross profit of 9.9% in 2009.
- The gross profit expressed as a percentage of sales revenue remaining at 70%.
- An increase in salaries of 7.2%.
- An increase in selling and distribution costs of 31.2%.
- An increase in bad debts of 392.5%.
- A decline in profit for the year of 39.3%.
- A decline in the profit for the year as a percentage of sales revenue from 13.3% to 7.4%.

Thus, the business has enjoyed an increase in sales revenue and gross profits, but this has failed to translate to an increase in profit for the year because of the significant rise in overheads. The increase in selling costs during 2009 suggests that the increase in sales revenue was achieved by greater marketing effort, and the huge increase in bad debts suggests that the increase in sales revenue may be attributable to selling to less creditworthy customers or to a weak debt-collection policy. There appears to have been a change of policy in 2009 towards sales, and this has not been successful overall as the profit for the year has shown a dramatic decline.

Chapter 4

4.1 Limited companies can no more set a limit on the amount of debts they will meet than can human beings. They must meet their debts up to the limit of their assets, just as we as individuals must. In the context of owners' claim, 'reserves' mean part of the owners' claim against the assets of the company. These assets may or may not include cash. The legal ability of the company to pay dividends is not related to the amount of cash that it has.

Preference shares do not carry a guaranteed dividend. They simply guarantee that the preference shareholders have a right to the first slice of any dividend that is paid. Shares of many companies can, in effect, be bought by one investor from another through the Stock Exchange. Such a transaction has no direct effect on the company, however. These are not new shares being offered by the company, but existing shares that are being sold 'second-hand'.

4.2 (a) The first part of the quote is incorrect. Bonus shares should not, of themselves, increase the value of the shareholders' wealth. This is because reserves, belonging to the shareholders, are used to create bonus shares. Thus, each shareholder's stake in the company has not increased.

(b) This statement is incorrect. Shares can be issued at any price, provided that it is not below the nominal value of the shares. Once the company has been trading profitably for a period, the shares will not be worth the same as they were (the nominal value) when the company was first formed. In such circumstances, issuing shares at above their nominal value would not only be legal, but essential to preserve the wealth of the existing shareholders relative to any new ones.

(c) This statement is incorrect. From a legal perspective, the company is limited to a maximum dividend of the current extent of its revenue reserves. This amounts to any after-tax profits or gains realised that have not been eroded through, for example, payments of previous dividends. Legally, cash is not an issue; it would be perfectly legal for a company to borrow the funds to pay a dividend – although whether such an action would be commercially prudent is another question.

(d) This statement is partly incorrect. Companies do indeed have to pay tax on their profits. Depending on their circumstances, shareholders might also have to pay tax on their dividends.

4.4 Iqbal Ltd

Year	Maximum dividend £	
2005	0	No profit exists out of which to pay a dividend.
2006	0	There remains a cumulative loss of £7,000. Since the revaluation represents a gain that has not been realised, it cannot be used to justify a dividend.
2007	13,000	The cumulative net realised gains are derived as (−£15,000 + £8,000 + £15,000 + £5,000).
2008	14,000	The realised profits and gains for the year.
2009	22,000	The realised profits and gains for the year.

4.6 Pear Limited

Statement of financial position as at 30 September 2009

	£000
ASSETS	
Non-current assets	
Property, plant and equipment	
Cost (1,570 + 30)	1,600
Depreciation (690 + 12)	(702)
	898
Current assets	
Inventories	207
Receivables (182 + 18 − 4)	196
Cash at bank	21
	424
Total assets	1,322
EQUITY AND LIABILITIES	
Equity	
Share capital	300
Share premium account	300
Retained earnings (104 + 41 − 25)	120
	720
Non-current liabilities	
Borrowings – 10% loan (repayable 2012)	300
Current liabilities	
Trade payables	88
Other payables (20 + 30 + 15 + 2)	67
Taxation	17
Dividend approved	25
Borrowings – Bank overdraft	105
	302
Total equity and liabilities	1,322

Income statement for the year ended 30 September 2009

	£000
Revenue (1,456 + 18)	1,474
Cost of sales	(768)
Gross profit	706
Salaries	(220)
Depreciation (249 + 12)	(261)
Other operating costs [131 + (2% × 200) + 2]	(137)
Operating profit	88
Interest payable (15 + 15)	(30)
Profit before taxation	58
Taxation (58 × 30%)	(17)
Profit for the year	41

4.7 **Chips Limited**

Statement of financial position as at 30 June 2009

	Cost £000	Depreciation £000	£000
ASSETS			
Non-current assets			
Property, plant and equipment			
Buildings	800	(112)	688
Plant and equipment	650	(367)	283
Motor vehicles (102 − 8); (53 − 5 + 19)	94	(67)	27
	1,544	(546)	998
Current assets			
Inventories			950
Trade receivables (420 − 16)			404
Cash at bank (16 + 2)			18
			1,372
Total assets			2,370
EQUITY AND LIABILITIES			
Equity			
Ordinary shares of £1, fully paid			800
Reserves at 1 July 2008			248
Retained profit for year			60
			1,108
Non-current liabilities			
Borrowings − secured 10% loan			700
Current liabilities			
Trade payables (361 + 23)			384
Other payables (117 + 35)			152
Taxation			26
			562
Total equity and liabilities			2,370

Income statement for the year ended 30 June 2009

	£000
Revenue (1,850 − 16)	1,834
Cost of sales (1,040 + 23)	(1,063)
Gross profit	771
Depreciation [220 − 2 − 5 + 8 + (94 × 20%)]	(240)
Other operating costs	(375)
Operating profit	156
Interest payable (35 + 35)	(70)
Profit before taxation	86
Taxation (86 × 30%)	(26)
Profit for the year	60

Chapter 5

5.1 Some believe that the annual reports of companies are becoming too long and contain too much information. A few examples of the length of the 2008 accounts of large companies are as follows:

Marks and Spencer plc	104 pages
Tesco plc	112 pages
National Grid plc	196 pages
3i Group plc	128 pages

There is a danger that users will suffer from information overload if they are confronted with an excessive amount of information and that they will be unable to cope with it. This may, in turn, lead them to:

- fail to distinguish between important and less important information;
- fail to approach the analysis of information in a logical and systematic manner;
- feel a sense of confusion and avoid the task of analysing the information.

Lengthy annual reports are likely to be a problem for the less sophisticated user. This problem has been recognised and many companies publish summarised accounts for private investors, which include only the key points. However, for sophisticated users the problem may be that the annual reports are still not long enough. They often wish to glean as much information as possible from the company in order to make investment decisions.

5.3 **I. Ching (Booksellers) plc**

I. Ching (Booksellers) plc
Statement of comprehensive income for the year ended 31 December 2009

	£000
Revenue	943
Cost of sales	(460)
Gross profit	483
Distribution expenses	(110)
Administration expenses	(212)
Other expenses	(25)
Operating profit	136
Finance charges	(40)
Profit before tax	96
Taxation	(24)
Profit for the period	72
Other comprehensive income	
Revaluation of property, plant and equipment	20
Foreign currency translation differences for foreign operations	(15)
Tax on other comprehensive income	(1)
Other comprehensive income for the year, net of tax	4
Total comprehensive income for the year	76

5.4 **Manet plc**

Manet plc
Statement of changes in equity for the year ended 31 December 2009

	Share capital £m	Share premium £m	Revaluation reserve £m	Translation reserve £m	Retained earnings £m	Total £m
Balance as at 1 January 2009	250	50	120	15	380	815
Changes in equity for the year ended 31 December 2009						
Dividends (Note 1)					(80)	(80)
Total comprehensive income for the year (Note 2)	—	—	30	(5)	160	185
Balance at 31 December 2009	250	50	150	10	460	920

Notes:
1. Dividends have been shown in the statement rather than in the notes. Either approach, however, is acceptable.
2. The effect of each component of comprehensive income on each component of shareholder equity must be shown. The revaluation gain and loss on exchange translation are each transferred to a specific reserve and the profit for the year is transferred to retained earnings.

5.5 Here are some points that might be made concerning accounting regulation and accounting measurement:

For

- It seems reasonable that companies, particularly given their limited liability, should be required to account to their members and to the general public and that rules should prescribe how this should be done – including how particular items should be measured. It also seems sensible that these rules should try to establish some uniformity of practice. Investors could be misled if the same item appeared in the financial statements of two separate companies but had been measured in different ways.
- Companies would find it difficult to attract finance, credit and possibly employees without publishing credible information about themselves. An important measure of performance is profit, and investors often need to make judgements concerning relative performance within an industry sector. Without clear benchmarks by which to judge performance, investors may not invest in a company.

Against

- It could be argued that it is up to the companies to decide whether or not they can survive and prosper without publishing information about themselves. If they can, then so much the better for them as they will have saved large amounts of money by not doing so. If it is necessary for a company to provide financial information in order to be able to attract investment finance and other necessary factors, then the company can make the necessary judgement of how much information is necessary and what forms of measurement are required.
- Not all company managements view matters in the same way. Allowing companies to select their own approaches to financial reporting enables them to reflect their personalities. Thus, a conservative management will adopt conservative accounting policies, such as writing off research and development expenditure quickly, whereas more adventurous management may adopt less conservative accounting policies, such as writing off research and development expenditure over several years. The impact of these different views will have an effect on profit and will give the reader an insight to the approach adopted by the management team.

5.8 **Dali plc**

A striking feature of the segmental reports is that the car parts segment generates the highest revenue – more than the other two segments combined. Nevertheless, it is the aircraft parts segment that generates the highest profit. Although we shall be considering financial ratios in detail in Chapter 7, we can use some simple ratios at this point to help evaluate performance.

We can start by considering the profit generated in relation to the sales revenue for each operating segment. We can see from the table below that the boat parts segment generates the most profit in relation to sales revenue. Around 21%, or £0.21 in every £1, of profit is derived from the sales revenue generated. The total revenue for this segment, however, is much lower than for the other two segments. Although the car parts segment generates the most revenue, less than 6%, or £0.06 in every £1, of profit is derived from the sales revenue generated. It is worth noting that the aircraft parts segment suffered a large impairment charge during the year, which had a significant effect on profits. The reasons for this impairment charge should be investigated.

We can also compare the profit generated with the net assets employed (that is, total assets – total liabilities) for each segment. We can see from the table below that the boat parts segment produces the best return on net assets employed by far: around 82%, that is, £0.82 for every £1 invested. Once again, the car parts segment produces the worst results with a return of less than 24%.

The relatively poor results from the car parts segment may simply reflect the nature of the market in which it operates. Compared with car parts segments of other businesses, it may be doing very well. Nevertheless, the business may still wish to consider whether future investment would not be better directed to those areas where greater profits can be found.

The investment in non-current assets during the period in relation to the total assets held is much higher for the boat parts segment. This may reflect the faith of the directors in the potential of this segment.

The depreciation charge as a percentage of segment assets seems to be high for all of the operating segments – but particularly for the car parts division. This should be investigated as it may suggest poor buying decisions.

Table of key results

	Car	Aircraft	Boat
Total revenue	£360m	£210m	£85m
Segment profit	£20m	£24m	£18m
Net assets (assets – liabilities)	£85m	£58m	£22m
Segment profit as a percentage of sales revenue	5.6%	11.4%	21.2%
Segment profit as a percentage of net assets employed	23.5%	41.4%	81.8%
Expenditure on non-current assets	£28m	£23m	£26m
Depreciation as a percentage of segment assets	47.1%	44.0%	34.1%

Chapter 6

6.1   (a) An increase in the level of inventories would, ultimately, have an adverse effect on cash.

(b) A rights issue of ordinary shares will give rise to a positive cash flow, which will be included in the 'financing' section of the statement of cash flows.

(c) A bonus issue of ordinary shares has no cash flow effect.

(d) Writing off some of the value of the inventories has no cash flow effect.

(e) A disposal for cash of a large number of shares by a major shareholder has no cash flow effect as far as the business is concerned.

(f) Depreciation does not involve cash at all. Using the indirect method of deducing cash flows from operating activities involves the depreciation expense in the calculation, but this is simply because we are trying to find out from the profit before taxation (after depreciation) figure what the profit before taxation *and* depreciation must have been.

6.3 **Torrent plc**

Torrent plc
Statement of cash flows for the year ended 31 December 2009

	£m
Cash flows from operating activities	
Profit before taxation (after interest) (see Note 1 below)	170
Adjustments for:	
Depreciation (Note 2)	78
Interest expense (Note 3)	26
	274
Decrease in inventories (41 − 35)	6
Increase in trade receivables (145 − 139)	(6)
Decrease in trade payables (54 − 41)	(13)
Cash generated from operations	261
Interest paid	(26)
Taxation paid (Note 4)	(41)
Dividend paid	(60)
Net cash from operating activities	134
Cash flows from investing activities	
Payments to acquire plant and machinery	(67)
Net cash used in investing activities	(67)
Cash flows from financing activities	
Redemption of loan notes (250 − 150) (Note 5)	(100)
Net cash used in financing activities	(100)
Net decrease in cash and cash equivalents	(33)
Cash and cash equivalents at 1 January 2009	
Bank overdraft	(56)
Cash and cash equivalents at 31 December 2009	
Bank overdraft	(89)

To see how this relates to the cash of the business at the beginning and end of the year it can be useful to provide a reconciliation as follows:

Analysis of cash and cash equivalents during the year ended 31 December 2009

	£m
Cash and cash equivalents at 1 January 2009	(56)
Net cash outflow	(33)
Cash and cash equivalents at 31 December 2009	(89)

Notes:

(1) This is simply taken from the income statement for the year.

(2) Since there were no disposals, the depreciation charges must be the difference between the start and end of the year's plant and machinery values, adjusted by the cost of any additions.

	£m
Carrying amount at 1 January 2009	325
Add Additions	67
	392
Less Depreciation (balancing figure)	78
Carrying amount at 31 December 2009	314

(3) Interest payable expense must be taken out, by adding it back to the profit before taxation figure. We subsequently deduct the cash paid for interest payable during the year. In this case the two figures are identical.

(4) Companies pay 50% of their tax during their accounting year and 50% in the following year. Thus the 2009 payment would have been half the tax on the 2008 profit (that is, the figure that would

have appeared in the current liabilities at the end of 2008), plus half of the 2009 tax charge (that is, 23 + (½ × 36) = 41).

(5) It is assumed that the cash payment to redeem the debentures was simply the difference between the two statement of financial position figures.

It seems that there was a bonus issue of ordinary shares during the year. These increased by £100m. At the same time, the share premium account balance reduced by £40m (to zero) and the revaluation reserve balance fell by £60m.

6.6 Blackstone plc

Blackstone plc
Statement of cash flows for the year ended 31 March 2009

	£m
Cash flows from operating activities	
Profit before taxation (after interest)	
(see Note 1 below)	1,853
Adjustments for:	
Depreciation (Note 2)	1,289
Interest expense (Note 3)	456
	3,598
Increase in inventories (2,410 – 1,209)	(1,201)
Increase in trade receivables (1,173 – 641)	(532)
Increase in trade payables (1,507 – 931)	576
Cash generated from operations	2,441
Interest paid	(456)
Taxation paid (Note 4)	(300)
Dividend paid	(400)
Net cash from operating activities	1,285
Cash flows from investing activities	
Proceeds of disposals	54
Payment to acquire intangible non-current asset	(700)
Payments to acquire property, plant and equipment	(4,578)
Net cash used in investing activities	(5,224)
Cash flows from financing activities	
Bank borrowings	2,000
Net cash from financing activities	2,000
Net decrease in cash and cash equivalents	(1,939)
Cash and cash equivalents at 1 April 2008	
Cash at bank	123
Cash and cash equivalents at 31 March 2009	
Bank overdraft	(1,816)

To see how this relates to the cash of the business at the beginning and end of the year it can be useful to provide a reconciliation as follows:

Analysis of cash and cash equivalents during the year ended 31 March 2009

	£m
Cash and cash equivalents at 1 April 2008	123
Net cash outflow	(1,939)
Cash and cash equivalents at 31 March 2009	1,816

Notes:

(1) This is simply taken from the income statement for the year.

(2) The full depreciation charge was that stated in Note 2 to the question (£1,251m), plus the deficit on disposal of the non-current assets. According to Note 2, these non-current assets had originally

cost £581m and had been depreciated by £489m, that is a net carrying amount of £92m. They were sold for £54m, leading to a deficit on disposal of £38m. Thus the full depreciation expense for the year was £1,289m (that is, £1,251m + £38m).

(3) Interest payable expense must be taken out, by adding it back to the profit before taxation figure. We subsequently deduct the cash paid for interest payable during the year. In this case the two figures are identical.

(4) Companies pay tax at 50% during their accounting year and the other 50% in the following year. Thus the 2009 payment would have been half the tax on the 2008 profit (that is, the figure that would have appeared in the current liabilities at 31 March 2008), plus half of the 2009 tax charge (that is, $105 + (\frac{1}{2} \times 390) = 300$).

6.7 **York plc**

York plc
Statement of cash flows for the year ended 30 September 2009

	£m
Cash flows from operating activities	
Profit before taxation (after interest)	
(see Note 1 below)	10.0
Adjustments for:	
Depreciation (Note 2)	9.8
Interest expense (Note 3)	3.0
	22.8
Increase in inventories and trade receivables	
(122.1 − 119.8)	(2.3)
Increase in trade payables (82.5 − 80.0)	2.5
Cash generated from operations	23.0
Interest paid	(3.0)
Taxation paid (Note 4)	(2.3)
Dividend paid	(3.5)
Net cash from operating activities	14.2
Cash flows from investing activities	
Proceeds of disposals (Note 2)	5.2
Payments to acquire non-current assets	(20.0)
Net cash used in investing activities	(14.8)
Cash flows from financing activities	
Increase in long-term borrowings	3.0
Share issue (Note 5)	5.0
Net cash from financing activities	8.0
Net increase in cash and cash equivalents	7.4
Cash and cash equivalents at 1 October 2008	
Cash at bank	9.2
Cash and cash equivalents at 30 September 2009	
Cash at bank	16.6

To see how this relates to the cash of the business at the beginning and end of the year it can be useful to provide a reconciliation as follows:

Analysis of cash and cash equivalents
during the year ended 30 September 2009

	£m
Cash and cash equivalents at 1 October 2008	9.2
Net cash inflow	7.4
Cash and cash equivalents at 30 September 2009	16.6

Notes:

(1) This is simply taken from the income statement for the year.

(2) The full depreciation charge was the £13.0m, less the surplus on disposal (£3.2m), both stated in Note 1 to the question. (According to the table in Note 4 to the question, the non-current assets disposed of had a net carrying value of £2.0m. To produce a surplus of £3.2m, they must have been sold for £5.2m.)

(3) Interest payable expense must be taken out, by adding it back to the profit before taxation figure. We subsequently deduct the cash paid for interest payable during the year. In this case the two figures are identical.

(4) Companies pay 50% of their tax during their accounting year and the other 50% in the following year. Thus the 2009 payment would have been half the tax on the 2008 profit (that is, the figure that would have appeared in the current liabilities at 30 September 2008), plus half of the 2009 tax charge (that is, $1.0 + (\frac{1}{2} \times 2.6) = 2.3$).

(5) This issue must have been for cash since it could not have been a bonus issue – the share premium is untouched and 'Reserves' had altered over the year only by the amount of the 2009 retained profit (profit for the year, less the dividend). The shares seem to have been issued at par (that is, at their nominal value). This is a little surprising since the business has assets that seem to be above that value. On the other hand, were this a rights issue, the low issue price would not have disadvantaged the existing shareholders since they were also the beneficiaries of the advantage of the low issue price.

6.8 Axis plc

Axis plc
Statement of cash flows for the year ended 31 December 2009

	£m
Cash flows from operating activities	
Profit before taxation (after interest) (see Note 1 below)	34
Adjustments for:	
Depreciation (Note 2)	19
Interest expense (Note 3)	2
	55
Decrease in inventories (25 – 24)	1
Increase in trade receivables (26 – 16)	(10)
Increase in trade payables (36 – 31)	5
Cash generated from operations	51
Interest paid	(2)
Taxation paid (Note 4)	(15)
Dividend paid	(14)
Net cash from operating activities	20
Cash flows from investing activities	
Proceeds of disposals (Note 2)	4
Payments to acquire non-current assets	(25)
Net cash used in investing activities	(21)
Cash flows from financing activities	
Issue of loan notes	20
Net cash from financing activities	20
Net increase in cash and cash equivalents	19
Cash and cash equivalents at 1 January 2009	
Cash at bank	nil
Short-term investments	nil
	nil
Cash and cash equivalents at 31 December 2009	
Cash at bank	7
Short-term investments	12
	19

To see how this relates to the cash of the business at the beginning and end of the year it can be useful to provide a reconciliation as follows:

Analysis of cash and cash equivalents during the year ended 31 December 2009

	£m
Cash and cash equivalents at 1 January 2009	nil
Net cash inflow	19
Cash and cash equivalents at 31 December 2009	19

Notes:

(1) This is simply taken from the income statement for the year.

(2) The full depreciation charge for the year is the sum of two figures labelled 'depreciation' and the deficit on disposal of non-current assets (that is, £2m + £16m + £1m = £19m). These were detailed in the income statement.

According to the note in the question, the non-current assets disposed of had a net carrying amount of £5.0m (that is, £15m – £10m). To produce a deficit of £1m, they must have been sold for £4m.

(3) Interest payable expense must be taken out, by adding it back to the profit before taxation figure. We subsequently deduct the cash paid for interest payable during the year. In this case the two figures are identical.

(4) Companies pay 50% of their tax during their accounting year and the other 50% in the following year. Thus the 2009 payment would have been half the tax on the 2008 profit (that is, the figure that would have appeared in the current liabilities at 31 December 2008), plus half of the 2009 tax charge (that is, $7 + (1/2 \times 16) = 15$).

Chapter 7

7.1 I. Jiang (Western) Ltd

The effect of each of the changes on ROCE is not always easy to predict.

1 On the face of it, an increase in the gross profit margin would tend to lead to an increase in ROCE. An increase in the gross profit margin may, however, lead to a decrease in ROCE in particular circumstances. If the increase in the margin resulted from an increase in sales prices, which in turn led to a decrease in sales revenue, a fall in ROCE can occur. A fall in sales revenue can reduce the operating profit (the numerator (top part of the fraction) in ROCE) if the overheads of the business did not decrease correspondingly.

2 A reduction in sales revenue can reduce ROCE for the reasons mentioned above.

3 An increase in overhead expenses will reduce the operating profit and this in turn will result in a reduction in ROCE.

4 An increase in inventories held would increase the amount of capital employed by the business (the denominator [bottom part of the fraction] in ROCE) where long-term funds are employed to finance the inventories. This will, in turn, reduce ROCE.

5 Repayment of the borrowings at the year end will reduce the capital employed and this will increase the ROCE, assuming that the year-end capital employed figure has been used in the calculation. Since the operating profit was earned during a period in which the borrowings existed, there is a strong argument for basing the capital employed figure on what was the position during the year, rather than at the end of it.

6 An increase in the time taken for credit customers to pay will result in an increase in capital employed if long-term funds are employed to finance the trade receivables. This increase in long-term funds will, in turn, reduce ROCE.

7.2   Amsterdam Ltd and Berlin Ltd

The ratios for Amsterdam Ltd and Berlin Ltd reveal that the trade receivables turnover ratio for Amsterdam Ltd is three times that for Berlin Ltd. Berlin Ltd is therefore much quicker in collecting amounts outstanding from customers. On the other hand, there is not much difference between the two businesses in the time taken to pay trade payables.

It is interesting to compare the difference in the trade receivables and payables collection periods for each business. As Amsterdam Ltd allows an average of 63 days' credit to its customers, yet pays suppliers within 50 days, it will require greater investment in working capital than Berlin Ltd, which allows an average of only 21 days to its customers but takes 45 days to pay its suppliers.

Amsterdam Ltd has a much higher gross profit margin than Berlin Ltd. However, the operating profit margin for the two businesses is identical. This suggests that Amsterdam Ltd has much higher overheads (as a percentage of sales revenue) than Berlin Ltd. The inventories turnover period for Amsterdam Ltd is more than twice that of Berlin Ltd. This may be due to the fact that Amsterdam Ltd maintains a wider range of inventories in an attempt to meet customer requirements. The evidence therefore suggests that Amsterdam Ltd is the one that prides itself on personal service. The higher average settlement period for trade receivables is consistent with a more relaxed attitude to credit collection (thereby maintaining customer goodwill) and the high overheads are consistent with incurring the additional costs of satisfying customers' requirements. Amsterdam Ltd's high inventories levels are consistent with maintaining a wide range of inventories, with the aim of satisfying a range of customer needs.

Berlin Ltd has the characteristics of a more price-competitive business. Its gross profit margin is much lower than that of Amsterdam Ltd, that is, a much lower gross profit for each £1 of sales revenue. However, overheads have been kept low, the effect being that the operating percentage is the same as Amsterdam Ltd's. The low inventories turnover period and average collection period for trade receivables are consistent with a business that wishes to minimise investment in current assets, thereby reducing costs.

7.6   Bradbury Ltd

(a)

	2008	2009
1 Operating profit margin	$\dfrac{914}{9,482} \times 100\% = 9.6\%$	$\dfrac{1,042}{11,365} \times 100\% = 9.2\%$
2 ROCE	$\dfrac{914}{11,033} \times 100 = 8.3\%$	$\dfrac{1,042}{13,943} \times 100\% = 7.5\%$
3 Current ratio	$\dfrac{4,926}{1,508} = 3.3{:}1$	$\dfrac{7,700}{5,174} = 1.5{:}1$
4 Gearing ratio	$\dfrac{1,220}{11,033} \times 100\% = 11.1\%$	$\dfrac{3,675}{13,943} \times 100\% = 26.4\%$
5 Days trade receivables	$\left(\dfrac{2,540}{9,482}\right) \times 365 = 98$ days	$\left(\dfrac{4,280}{11,365}\right) \times 365 = 137$ days
6 Sales revenue to capital employed	$\dfrac{9,482}{(9,813 + 1,220)} = 0.9$ times	$\dfrac{11,365}{(10,268 + 3,675)} = 0.8$ times

(b) The operating profit margin was slightly lower in 2009 than in 2008. Although there was an increase in sales revenue in 2009, this could not prevent a slight fall in ROCE in that year. The lower operating margin and increases in sales revenue may well be due to the new contract. The capital employed by the company increased in 2009 by a larger percentage than the increase in revenue. Hence, the sales revenue to capital employed ratio decreased over the period. The increase in capital during 2009 is largely due to an increase in borrowing. However, the gearing ratio is probably still low in comparison with other businesses. Comparison of the premises and borrowings figures indicates possible unused borrowing (debt) capacity.

The major cause for concern has been the dramatic decline in liquidity during 2009. The current ratio has more than halved during the period. There has also been a similar decrease in the acid test ratio, from 1.7:1 in 2008 to 0.8:1 in 2009. The balance sheet shows that the business now has a large overdraft and the trade payables outstanding have nearly doubled in 2009.

The trade receivables outstanding and inventories have increased much more than appears to be warranted by the increase in sales revenue. This may be due to the terms of the contract that has been negotiated and may be difficult to influence. If this is the case, the business should consider whether it is overtrading. If the conclusion is that it is, increasing its long-term funding may be a sensible policy.

7.7 **Harridges Ltd**

(a)

	2008	2009
ROCE	$\dfrac{310}{1,600} = 19.4\%$	$\dfrac{350}{1,700} = 20.6\%$
ROSF	$\dfrac{155}{1,100} = 14.1\%$	$\dfrac{175}{1,200} = 14.6\%$
Gross profit margin	$\dfrac{1,040}{2,600} = 40\%$	$\dfrac{1,150}{3,500} = 32.9\%$
Operating profit margin	$\dfrac{310}{2,600} = 11.9\%$	$\dfrac{350}{3,500} = 10\%$
Current ratio	$\dfrac{735}{400} = 1.8$	$\dfrac{660}{485} = 1.4$
Acid test ratio	$\dfrac{485}{400} = 1.2$	$\dfrac{260}{485} = 0.5$
Trade receivables settlement period	$\dfrac{105}{2,600} \times 365 = 15$ days	$\dfrac{145}{3,500} \times 365 = 15$ days
Trade payables settlement period	$\dfrac{300}{1,560} \times 365 = 70$ days	$\dfrac{375}{2,350^*} \times 365 = 58$ days
Inventories turnover period	$\dfrac{250}{1,560} \times 365 = 58$ days	$\dfrac{400}{2,350} \times 365 = 62$ days
Gearing ratio	$\dfrac{500}{1,600} = 31.3\%$	$\dfrac{500}{1,700} = 29.4\%$
EPS	$\dfrac{155}{490} = 31.6\text{p}$	$\dfrac{175}{490} = 35.7\text{p}$

* Used because the credit purchases figure is not available.

(b) There has been a considerable decline in the gross profit margin during 2009. This fact, combined with the increase in sales revenue by more than one-third, suggests that a price-cutting policy has been adopted in an attempt to stimulate sales. The resulting increase in sales revenue, however, has led to only a small improvement in ROCE and ROSF. Similarly, there has only been a small improvement in EPS.

Despite a large cut in the gross profit margin, the operating profit margin has fallen by less than 2%. This suggests that overheads have been tightly controlled during 2009. Certainly, overheads have not risen in proportion to sales revenue.

The current ratio has fallen and the acid test ratio has fallen by more than half. Even though liquidity ratios are lower in retailing than in manufacturing, the liquidity of the business should now be a cause for concern. However, this may be a passing problem. The business is investing heavily in non-current assets and is relying on internal funds to finance this growth. When this investment ends, the liquidity position may improve quickly.

The trade receivables period has remained unchanged over the two years, and there has been no significant change in the inventories turnover period in 2009. The gearing ratio seems quite low and provides no cause for concern given the profitability of the business.

Overall, the business appears to be financially sound. Although there has been rapid growth during 2009, there is no real cause for alarm provided that the liquidity of the business can be improved in the near future. In the absence of information concerning share price, it is not possible to say whether an investment should be made.

7.8   **Genesis Ltd**

(a) and (b) These parts have been answered in the text of the chapter and you are referred to it for a discussion on overtrading and its consequences.

(c)

$$\text{Current ratio} = \frac{232}{550} = 0.42$$

$$\text{Acid test ratio} = \frac{104}{550} = 0.19$$

$$\text{Inventories turnover period} = \frac{128}{1,248} \times 365 = 37 \text{ days}$$

$$\text{Average settlement period for trade receivables} = \frac{104}{1,640} \times 365 = 23 \text{ days}$$

$$\text{Average settlement period for trade payables} = \frac{184}{1,260} \times 365 = 53 \text{ days}$$

(d) Overtrading must be dealt with either by increasing the level of funding to match the level of activity or by reducing the level of activity to match the funds available. The latter option may result in a reduction in operating profit in the short term but may be necessary to ensure long-term survival.

Chapter 8

8.1 **Lombard Ltd**

Relevant costs of undertaking the contract are:

	£
Equipment costs	200,000
Component X (20,000 × 4 × £5)	400,000
Component Y (20,000 × 3 × £8)	480,000
Additional costs (20,000 × £8)	160,000
	1,240,000
Revenue from the contract (20,000 × £80)	1,600,000

Thus, from a purely financial point of view the project is acceptable. (Note that there is no relevant labour cost since the staff concerned will be paid irrespective of whether the contract is undertaken.)

8.2 **The local authority**

(a) *Net benefit of accepting the touring company proposal*

	£
Net reduction in ticket revenues (see workings below)	(20,000)
Savings on: Costumes	5,600
Scenery	3,300
Casual staff	3,520
Net deficit	(7,580)

Since there is a net deficit, on financial grounds the touring company's proposal should be rejected.

Note that all of the following are irrelevant, because they will occur irrespective of the decision:

- non-performing staff salaries
- artistes' salaries
- heating and lighting
- administration costs
- refreshment revenues and costs
- programme advertising.

Workings		£	£
Normal ticket sales revenue:	200 @ £24 =	4,800	
	500 @ £16 =	8,000	
	300 @ £12 =	3,600	
		16,400	
Ticket revenue at 50 per cent capacity for 20 performances:			
(£16,400 × 50% × 20)			164,000

Touring company ticket sales:

Total revenue for each performance for a full house:

		£	
	200 @ £22 =	4,400	
	500 @ £14 =	7,000	
	300 @ £10 =	3,000	
		14,400	
Ticket revenues	(£14,400 × 10 × 50%)		72,000
	(£14,400 × 15 × $^2/_3$ × 50%)		72,000
			144,000
Net loss of revenue	(£164,000 − £144,000)		20,000

(b) Other possible factors to consider include:
- The reliability of the estimations, including the assumption that the level of occupancy will not alter programme and refreshment sales revenue.
- A desire to offer theatregoers the opportunity to see another group of players.
- Dangers of loss of morale of staff not employed, or employed to do other than their usual work.

8.3 Andrews and Co. Ltd

Minimum contract price:

			£
Materials	Steel core:	10,000 × £2.10	21,000
	Plastic:	10,000 × 0.10 × £0.10	100
Labour	Skilled:		–
	Unskilled:	10,000 × 5/60 × £7.50	6,250
Minimum tender price			27,350

8.6 The local education authority

(a) *One-off financial net benefits of closing:*

	D only	A and B	A and C
Capacity reduction	800	700	800
	£m	£m	£m
Property developer (A)	–	14.0	14.0
Shopping complex (B)	–	8.0	–
Property developer (D)	9.0	–	–
Safety (C)	–	–	3.0
Adapt facilities	(1.8)	–	–
Total	7.2	22.0	17.0
Ranking based on total one-off benefits	3	1	2

(Note that all past costs of buying and improving the schools are irrelevant.)

Recurrent financial net benefits of closing:

	D only £m	A and B £m	A and C £m
Rent (C)	–	–	0.3
Administrators	0.2	0.4	0.4
Total	0.2	0.4	0.7
Ranking based on total of recurrent benefits	3	2	1

On the basis of the financial figures alone, closure of either A and B or A and C looks best. It is not possible to add the one-off and the recurring costs directly, but the large one-off cost saving associated with closing Schools A and B makes this option look attractive. (In Chapter 14 we shall see that it is possible to combine one-off and recurring costs in a way that should lead to sensible conclusions.)

(b) The costs of acquiring and improving the schools in the past are past costs or sunk costs and, therefore, irrelevant. The costs of employing the chief education officer is a future cost, but irrelevant because it is not dependent on outcomes, it is a common cost.

(c) There are many other factors, some of a non-quantifiable nature. These include:
- accuracy of projections of capacity requirements;
- location of existing schools relative to where potential pupils live;

- political acceptability of selling schools to property developers;
- importance of purely financial issues in making the final decision;
- the quality of the replacement sporting facilities compared with those at School D;
- political acceptability of staff redundancies;
- possible savings/costs of employing fewer teachers, which might be relevant if economies of scale are available by having fewer schools;
- staff morale.

8.7 **Rob Otics Ltd**

(a) The minimum price for the proposed contract would be:

	£
Materials	
Component X (2 × 8 × £180)	2,880
If the 16 units of this component are used on the proposed contract, the business will need to buy an additional 16 units at the new price	
Component Y	0
The history of the components held in inventories is irrelevant because it applies irrespective of the decision made on this contract. Since the alternative to using the units on this contract is to scrap them, the relevant cost is zero.	
Component Z [(75 + 32) × £20] – (75 × £25)	265
The relevant cost here is how much extra the business will pay the supplier as a result of undertaking the contract	
Other miscellaneous items	250
Labour	
Assembly (25 + 24 + 23 + 22 + 21 + 20 + 19 + 18) × £48	8,256
The assembly labour cost is irrelevant because it will be incurred irrespective of which work the members of staff do. The relevant cost is based on the sales revenue per hour lost if the other orders are lost less the material cost per hour saved; that is £60 – £12 = £48	
Inspection (8 × 6 × £12 × 150%)	864
Total	12,515

Thus the minimum price is £12,515.

(b) Other factors include:
- competitive state of the market;
- the fact that the above figure is unique to the particular circumstances at the time – for example, having component Y in available but having no use for it. Any subsequent order might have to take account of an outlay cost;
- breaking even (that is, just covering the costs) on a contract will not fulfil the business's objective;
- charging a low price may cause marketing problems. Other customers may resent the low price for this contract. The current enquirer may expect a similar price in future.

Chapter 9

9.4 **Motormusic Ltd**

(a) Break-even point = fixed cost/contribution per unit

$$= (80,000 + 60,000)/[60 – (20 + 14 + 12 + 3)] = 12,727 \text{ radios}$$

These would have a sales value of £763,620 (that is, 12,727 × £60).

(b) The margin of safety is 7,273 radios (that is, 20,000 – 12,727). This margin would have a sales value of £436,380 (that is, 7,273 × £60).

9.5 **Products A, B and C**

(a) Total time required on cutting machines is:

$$(2,500 \times 1.0) + (3,400 \times 1.0) + (5,100 \times 0.5) = 8,450 \text{ hours}$$

Total time available on cutting machines is 5,000 hours. Therefore, this is a limiting factor.
Total time required on assembling machines is:

$$(2,500 \times 0.5) + (3,400 \times 1.0) + (5,100 \times 0.5) = 7,200 \text{ hours}$$

Total time available on assembling machines is 8,000 hours. Therefore, this is not a limiting factor.

	A (per unit) £	B (per unit) £	C (per unit) £
Selling price	25	30	18
Variable materials	(12)	(13)	(10)
Variable production cost	(7)	(4)	(3)
Contribution	6	13	5
Time on cutting machines	1.0 hour	1.0 hour	0.5 hour
Contribution per hour on cutting machines	£6	£13	£10
Order of priority	3rd	1st	2nd

Therefore, produce:

3,400 product B using	3,400 hours
3,200 product C using	1,600 hours
	5,000 hours

(b) Assuming that the business would make no saving in variable production costs by subcontracting, it would be worth paying up to the contribution per unit (£5) for product C, which would therefore be £5 × (5,100 − 3,200) = £9,500 in total.
   Similarly it would be worth paying up to £6 per unit for product A, that is, £6 × 2,500 = £15,000 in total.

9.6 **Darmor Ltd**

(a) Contribution per hour of skilled labour of product X is:

$$\frac{£(30 - 6 - 2 - 12 - 3)}{(6/12)} = £14$$

Given the scarcity of skilled labour, if the management is to be indifferent between the products, the contribution per skilled labour hour must be the same. Thus for product Y the selling price must be:

$$£[14 \times (9/12)] + 9 + 4 + 25 + 7 = £55.50$$

(that is, the contribution plus the variable cost), and for product Z the selling price must be:

$$£[14 \times (3/12)] + 3 + 10 + 14 + 7 = £37.50$$

(b) The business could pay up to £26 an hour (£12 + £14) for additional hours of skilled labour. This is the potential contribution per hour, before taking account of the labour rate of £12 an hour.

9.7 **Intermediate Products Ltd**

(a)

	A £	B £	C £	D £
Total costs per unit	(65)	(41)	(36)	(46)
Less Fixed cost	20	8	8	12
Variable cost per unit	(45)	(33)	(28)	(34)
Buying/selling price per unit	70	45	40	55
Contribution per unit	25	12	12	21
Hours on special machine	0.5	0.4	0.5	0.3
Contribution per hour	50	30	24	70
Order of preference	2nd	3rd	4th	1st

Optimum use of hours on special machine	*Balance of hours*
D 3,000 × 0.3 = 900	5,100 (that is, 6,000 − 900)
A 5,000 × 0.5 = 2,500	2,600 (that is, 5,100 − 2,500)
B 6,000 × 0.4 = 2,400	200 (that is, 2,600 − 2,400)
C 400 × 0.5 = 200	−
6,000	

Therefore, make all of the demand for Ds, As and Bs plus 400 (of 4,000) Cs.

(b) The contribution per hour from Cs is £24, and so this is the maximum amount per hour that it would be worth paying to rent the machine, for a maximum of 1,800 hours (that is, 3,600 × 0.5, the time necessary to make the remaining demand for Cs).

(c) Other possible actions to overcome the shortage of machine time include:
- Alter the design of the products to avoid the use of the special machine.
- Increase the selling price of the product so that the demand will fall, making the available machine time sufficient but making production more profitable.

9.8 **Gandhi Ltd**

(a) Given that the spare capacity could not be used by other services, the standard service should continue to be offered. This is because it renders a positive contribution.

(b) The standard service renders a contribution per unit of £15 (that is, £80 − £65), or £30 during the time it would take to render one unit of the nova service. The nova service would provide a contribution of only £25 (that is, £75 − £50). The nova service should, therefore, not replace the standard service.

(c) Under the original plans, the following contributions would be rendered by the basic and standard services:

		£
Basic	11,000 × (£50 − £25) =	275,000
Standard	6,000 × (£80 − £65) =	90,000
		365,000

If the basic were to take the standard's place, 17,000 units (that is, 11,000 + 6,000) of them could be produced in total. To generate the same total contribution, each unit of the standard service would need to provide £21.47 (that is, £365,000/17,000) of contribution. Given the basic's variable cost of £25, this would mean a selling price of £46.47 each (that is £21.47 + £25.00).

Chapter 10

10.4 Promptprint Ltd

(a) The plan (budget) may be summarised as:

	£	
Sales revenue	196,000	
Direct materials	(38,000)	
Direct labour	(32,000)	
Total indirect cost	(77,000)	(2,400 + 3,000 + 27,600 + 36,000 + 8,000)
Profit	49,000	

The job may be priced on the basis that both indirect costs and profit should be apportioned to it on the basis of direct labour cost, as follows:

	£	
Direct materials	4,000	
Direct labour	3,600	
Overheads	8,663	(£77,000 × 3,600/32,000)
Profit	5,513	(£49,000 × 3,600/32,000)
	21,776	

This answer assumes that variable overheads vary in proportion to direct labour cost.

Various other bases of charging overheads and profit loading the job could have been adopted. For example, materials cost could have been included (with direct labour) as the basis for profit loading, or even apportioning overheads.

(b) This part of the question is, in effect, asking for comments on the validity of 'full cost-plus' pricing. This approach can be useful as an indicator of the effective long-run cost of doing the job. On the other hand, it fails to take account of relevant opportunity costs as well as the state of the market and other external factors. For example, it ignores the price that a competitor printing business may quote.

(c) Revised estimates of direct material costs for the job:

	£	
Paper grade 1	1,500	(£1,200 × 125%; this item of inventories needs to be replaced)
Paper grade 2	0	(it has no opportunity cost value)
Card	510	(£640 – £130: using the card on another job would save £640, but cost £130 to achieve that saving)
Inks and so on	300	(this item of inventories needs to be replaced)
	2,310	

10.5 Bookdon plc

(a) To answer this question, we need first to allocate and apportion the overheads to product cost centres, as follows:

Cost	Basis of apportionment	Total	Department			
			Machine shop	Fitting section	Canteen	Machine main'ce section
		£	£	£	£	£
Allocated items:	Specific	90,380	27,660	19,470	16,600	26,650
Rent, rates, heat, light	Floor area	17,000	9,000	3,500	2,500	2,000
			(3,600/ 6,800)	(1,400/ 6,800)	(1,000/ 6,800)	(800/ 6,800)
Dep'n and insurance	Book value	25,000	12,500	6,250	2,500	3,750
			(150/300)	(75/300)	(30/300)	(45/300)
		132,380	49,160	29,220	21,600	32,400
Canteen	Number of employees	–	10,800	8,400	(21,600)	2,400
			(18/36)	(14/36)		(4/36)
		132,380	59,960	37,620	–	34,800
Machine main'ce section	Specified %	–	24,360	10,440	–	(34,800)
			(70%)	(30%)		
		132,380	84,320	48,060	–	–

Note that the canteen overheads were reapportioned to the other cost centres first because the canteen renders a service to the machine maintenance section but does not receive a service from it.

Calculation of the overhead absorption (recovery) rates can now proceed:

(1) Total budgeted machine hours are:

	Hours
Product X (4,200 × 6)	25,200
Product Y (6,900 × 3)	20,700
Product Z (1,700 × 4)	6,800
	52,700

Overhead absorption rate for the machine shop is:

$$\frac{£84,320}{52,700} = £1.60/\text{machine-hour}$$

(2) Total budgeted direct labour cost for the fitting section is:

	£
Product X (4,200 × £12)	50,400
Product Y (6,900 × £3)	20,700
Product Z (1,700 × £21)	35,700
	106,800

Overhead absorption rate for the fitting section is:

$$\frac{£48,060}{£106,800} \times 100\% = 45\% \quad \text{or } £0.45 \text{ per } £ \text{ of direct labour cost}$$

(b) The cost of one unit of product X is calculated as follows:

	£
Direct materials	11.00
Direct labour:	
Machine shop	6.00
Fitting section	12.00
Overheads:	
Machine shop (6 × £1.60)	9.60
Fitting section (£12 × 45%)	5.40
	44.00

Therefore, the cost of one unit of Product X is £44.00.

10.6 Products A, B and C

Allocation and apportionment of overheads to product cost centres

	Basis of apportionment	Department				
		Cutting £	Machining £	Pressing £	Engineering £	Personnel £
Total		154,482	64,316	58,452	56,000	34,000
Personnel	Specified	18,700 (55%)	3,400 (10%)	6,800 (20%)	5,100 (15%)	(34,000)
		173,182	67,716	65,252	61,100	–
Engineering	Specified	12,220 (20%)	27,495 (45%)	21,385 (35%)	(61,100)	
		185,402	95,211	86,637	–	–

Note that the personnel overheads were reapportioned to the other cost centres first because the canteen renders a service to the engineering department section, but does not receive a service from it.

Calculation of the overhead absorption (recovery) rates
In both the cutting and pressing departments no machines seem to be used, and so a direct labour hour basis of overhead absorption seems reasonable.

In the machining department, machine hours are far in excess of labour hours and the overheads are probably machine related. In this department, machine hours seem a fair basis for cost units to absorb overheads.

Total planned direct labour hours for the cutting department are thus:

Product A [4,000 × (3 + 6)]	36,000
Product B [3,000 × (5 + 1)]	18,000
Product C [6,000 × (2 + 3)]	30,000
	84,000

The overhead absorption rate for the cutting department = £185,402/84,000 = £2.21 per direct labour hour.

Total planned machine hours for the machining department are thus:

Product A (4,000 × 2.0)	8,000
Product B (3,000 × 1.5)	4,500
Product C (6,000 × 2.5)	15,000
	27,500

The overhead absorption rate for the machining department = £95,211/27,500 = £3.46 per machine hour.

Total planned direct labour hours for the pressing department are:

Product A (4,000 × 2)	8,000
Product B (3,000 × 3)	9,000
Product C (6,000 × 4)	24,000
	41,000

The overhead absorption rate for the cutting department = £86,637/41,000 = £2.11 per direct labour hour.

(a) Cost of one completed unit of Product A

		£
Direct materials		7.00
Direct labour:		
Cutting department: Skilled	(3 × £16)	48.00
Unskilled	(6 × £10)	60.00
Machining department	(0.5 × £12)	6.00
Pressing department	(2 × £12)	24.00
Overheads:		
Cutting department	(9 × £2.21)	19.89
Machining department	(2 × £3.46)	6.92
Pressing department	(2 × £2.11)	4.22
		176.03

(b) Cost of one uncompleted unit of Product B

		£
Direct materials		4.00*
Direct labour:		
Cutting department: Skilled	(5 × £16)	80.00
Unskilled	(1 × £10)	10.00
Machining department	(0.25 × £12)	3.00
Overheads:		
Cutting department	(6 × £2.21)	13.26
Machining department	(1.5 × £3.46)	5.19
		115.45

* This assumes that all of the materials are added in the cutting or machining departments.

10.7

Offending phrase	Explanation
'Necessary to divide up the business into departments'	This can be done but it will not always be of much benefit. Only in quite restricted circumstances will it give significantly different job costs.
'Fixed costs (or overheads)'	This implies that fixed costs and overheads are the same thing. They are not really connected with one another. 'Fixed' is to do with how costs behave as the level of output is raised or lowered; 'overheads' are to do with the extent to which costs can be directly measured in respect of a particular unit of output. Although it is true that many overheads are fixed, not all are. Also, direct labour is usually a fixed cost. All of the other references to fixed and variable costs are wrong. The person should have referred to indirect and direct costs.
'Usually this is done on the basis of area'	Where overheads are apportioned to departments, they will be apportioned on some logical basis. For certain costs – for example, rent – the floor area may be the most logical; for others, such as machine maintenance costs, the floor area would be totally inappropriate.
'When the total fixed costs for each department have been identified, this will be divided by the number of hours that were worked'	Where overheads are dealt with on a departmental basis, they may be divided by the number of direct labour hours to deduce a recovery rate. However, this is only one basis of applying overheads to jobs. For example, machine hours or some other basis may be more appropriate to the particular circumstances involved.
'It is essential that this approach is taken in order to deduce a selling price'	It is relatively unusual for the 'job cost' to be able to dictate the price at which the manufacturer can price its output. For many businesses, the market dictates the price.

10.8 (a) Charging overheads to jobs on a departmental basis means that overheads are collected 'product' cost centre (department) by 'product' cost centre. This involves picking up the overheads that are direct to each department and adding to them a share of overheads that are general to the business as a whole. The overheads of 'service' cost centres must then be apportioned to the product cost centres. At this point, all of the overheads for the whole business are divided between the 'product' cost centres, such that the sum of the 'product' cost centre overheads equals those for the whole business.

Dealing with overheads departmentally is believed to provide more fair and useful information to decision makers, because different departments may have rather different overheads, and applying overheads departmentally can take account of that and reflect it in the derived job cost.

In theory, dealing with overheads on a departmental basis is more costly than on a business-wide basis. In practice, it possibly does not make too much difference to the cost of collecting the information. This is because, normally, businesses are divided into departments, and the costs are collected departmentally, as part of the normal routine for exercising control over the business.

(b) In order to make any difference to the job cost that will emerge as a result of dealing with overheads departmentally, as compared with a business-wide basis, the following *both* need to be the case:

- The overheads per unit of the basis of charging (for example direct labour hours) need to be different from one department to the next; and
- The proportion (but not the actual amounts) of total overheads that are charged to jobs must differ from one job to the next.

Assume, for the sake of argument, that direct labour hours are used as the basis of charging overheads in all departments. Also assume that there are three departments, A, B and C.

There will be no difference in the overheads charged to a particular job if the rate of overheads per direct labour hour is the same for all departments. Obviously, if the charging rate is the same in all departments, that same rate must also apply to the business taken as a whole.

Also, even where overheads per direct labour hour differ significantly from one department to another – if all jobs spend, say, about 20% of their time in Department A, 50% in Department B and 30% in Department C – it will not make any difference whether overheads are charged departmentally or overall.

These conclusions are not in any way dependent on the basis of charging overheads or even that overheads are charged on the same basis in each department.

The statements above combine to mean that, probably in many cases in practice, departmentalising overheads is not providing information that is significantly different from that which would be provided by charging overheads to jobs on a business-wide basis.

Chapter 11

11.1 Aires plc

The EVA® approach to determining shareholder value will be as follows:

Year	Opening capital invested (C) £m	Capital charge (12% × C) £m	Operating profit after tax £m	EVA® £m
1	64.0	7.7	12.0	4.3
2	48.0	5.8	12.0	6.2
3	32.0	3.8	12.0	8.2
4	16.0	1.9	12.0	10.1

11.2 The balanced scorecard

(a) The balanced scorecard has nothing to do with the statement of financial position. The former is a framework that translates the aims and objectives of a business into a series of key performance measures and targets. The latter is a statement of the assets of a business and the claims against it; it is sometimes known as the 'balance sheet'.

(b) The finance area of the balanced scorecard specifies financial targets for the future and is usually expressed in terms of financial ratios, such as return on capital employed. The income statement is an historical statement of revenues, the expenses matched against them and the resulting profit or loss.

(c) The balanced scorecard approach does not prescribe a particular set of objectives and targets. It is up to the business concerned to establish its own set of parameters.

(d) The balanced scorecard in no way downplays financial objectives and measures. Financial aspects are key issues in all areas of the balanced scorecard.

11.3 Kaplan plc

(a) The business makes each model of suitcase in a batch. The direct cost (materials and labour) will be recorded in respect of each batch. To this cost will be added a share of the overheads of the business for the period in which production of the batch takes place. The basis of the batch absorbing overheads is a matter of managerial judgement. A popular method is direct labour hours spent working on the batch, relative to total direct labour hours worked during the period. This is not the 'correct' way, however. There is no correct way. If the activity is capital intensive, some machine hour basis of dealing with overheads might be more appropriate, though still not 'correct'. Overheads might be collected, cost centre by cost centre (department by department), and charged to the batch as it passes through each product cost centre. Alternatively, all of the overheads for the entire production facility might be totalled and the overheads dealt with more globally. It is only in restricted circumstances that overheads charged to batches will be affected by a decision to deal with them by cost centres, rather than globally.

Once the 'full cost' (direct cost plus a share of indirect cost) has been ascertained for the batch, the cost per suitcase can be established by dividing the batch cost by the number in the batch.

(b) Whereas the traditional approach to dealing with overheads is just to accept that they exist and deal with them in a fairly broad manner, ABC takes a much more enquiring approach. ABC takes the view that overheads do not just 'occur', but that they are caused or 'driven' by 'activities'. It is a matter of finding out which activities are driving the cost and how much cost they are driving.

For example, a significant part of the cost of making suitcases of different sizes might be resetting machinery to cope with a batch of a different size from its predecessor batch. Where a particular model is made in very small batches, because it has only a small market, ABC would advocate that this model is charged directly with its machine-setting cost. The traditional approach would be to treat machine setting as a general overhead that the individual suitcases (irrespective of the model) might bear equally. ABC, it is claimed, leads to more accurate costing and thus to more accurate assessment of profitability.

(c) The other advantage of pursuing an ABC philosophy and identifying cost drivers is that, once the drivers have been identified, they are likely to become much more susceptible to being controlled. Thus the ability of management to assess the benefit of certain activities against their cost becomes more feasible.

11.6 Badger Ltd

(a) *Price using absorption costing*

Overhead absorption rate = Total overheads/total direct labour hours = £280,000/4,000 = £70 per direct labour hour.

	Largeflo	Smallflo
	£	£
Direct materials	16.00	15.00
Direct labour	8.00	8.00
Overheads: ½ × £70	35.00	35.00
Total cost	59.00	58.00
Mark-up at 35%	20.65	20.30
Price	79.65	78.30

(b) *Price using activity based costing*

Cost driver rates:

Large machine	£96,000/480	=	£200 per hour
Small machine	£44,800/1,280	=	£35 per hour
Set-ups	£32,500/260	=	£125 per set up
Ordering	£10,800/120	=	£90 per part
Handling	£45,600/380	=	£120 per movement
Other overheads	£50,300/4,000	=	£12.58 per direct labour hour

Prices for the two products

		Largeflo		*Smallflo*
		£		£
Direct materials		16.00		15.00
Direct labour		8.00		8.00
Large machine	(100 × £200)/1,000	20.00		–
Small machine			(25 × £35)/50	17.50
Set-ups	£125/1,000	0.13	(2 × £125)/50	5.00
Ordering		–	(3 × £90)/50	5.40
Handling	£120/1,000	0.12	(5 × £120)/50	12.00
Other overheads	½ × £12.58	6.29	½ × £12.58	6.29
Total cost		50.54		70.19
35% mark up		17.69		24.57
Price		68.23		94.76

(c) *Points for the management*

- Under the traditional approach, the prices are quite similar because the direct costs are quite similar, which also leads to a similar allocation of overheads (because these are absorbed on the basis of direct labour hours).
- With ABC, the prices are quite different between the products. This is because the Smallflo product causes much more overhead cost than the Largeflo one and ABC reflects this fact.
- Management must seriously consider its pricing policy. If the traditionally-based price is, in fact, the current selling price, the Smallflo product is earning only a small margin.
- If the market will not bear a higher price for Smallflo products, management may consider dropping them and concentrating its efforts on the Largeflo ones. Projected market demand for the two products will obviously have a major bearing on these considerations.

(d) *Practical problems of using ABC*

- Identifying the cost-driving activities and determining cost driver rates can be difficult and expensive. It is sometimes necessary to use arbitrary approaches to certain parts of the overheads, as with 'other overheads' in the Largeflo/Smallflo example above.
- The costs of introducing ABC may outweigh the benefits.
- Changing the culture in the way necessary to introduce ABC may pose difficulties. There may be resistance to a new approach.
- On a positive note, ABC may have benefits beyond cost determination and pricing. Careful analysis of costs and what drives them can provide a basis for exercising better control over costs.

11.7 Sillycon Ltd

(a) *Overhead analysis*

	Electronics £000	Testing £000	Service £000
Variable overheads	1,200	600	700
Apportionment of service dept (800:600)	400	300	(700)
	1,600	900	–
Direct labour hours ('000)	800	600	
Variable overheads per direct labour hour	£2.00	£1.50	

	Electronics £000	Testing £000	Service £000
Fixed overheads	2,000	500	800
Apportionment of service dept (equally)	400	400	(800)
	2,400	900	–
Direct labour hours	800	600	
Fixed overheads per direct labour hour	£3.00	£1.50	

Product cost (per unit)

		£	
Direct materials		7.00	
Direct labour:	electronics	40.00	(2 × £20.00)
	testing	18.00	(1.5 × £12.00)
Variable overheads:	electronics	4.00	(2 × £2.00)
	testing	2.25	(1.5 × £1.50)
Total variable cost		71.25	(assuming direct labour to be variable)
Fixed overheads:	electronics	6.00	(2 × £3.00)
	testing	2.25	(1.5 × £1.50)
Total 'full' cost		79.50	
Add Mark-up, say 30%		23.85	
		103.35	

On the basis of the above, the business could hope to compete in the market at a price that reflects normal pricing practice.

(b) At this price, and only taking account of incremental fixed overheads, the break-even point (BEP) would be given by:

$$\text{BEP} = \frac{\text{Fixed costs}}{\text{Contribution per unit}} = \frac{£150,000^*}{£103.35 - £71.25} = 4,673 \text{ units}$$

* (£13,000 + £100,000 + £37,000) namely the costs specifically incurred.

As the potential market for the business is around 5,000 to 6,000 units a year, the new product looks viable.

Chapter 12

12.3 Nursing Home

(a) The rates per patient for the variable overheads, on the basis of experience during months 1 to 6, are as follows:

Expense	Amount for 2,700 patients	Amount per patient
	£	£
Staffing	59,400	22
Power	27,000	10
Supplies	54,000	20
Other	8,100	3
	148,500	55

Since the expected level of activity for the full year is 6,000, the expected level of activity for the second six months is 3,300 (that is, 6,000 – 2,700).

Thus the budget for the second six months will be:

	£	
Variable element:		
Staffing	72,600	(3,300 × £22)
Power	33,000	(3,300 × £10)
Supplies	66,000	(3,300 × £20)
Other	9,900	(3,300 × £3)
	181,500	(3,300 × £55)
Fixed element:		
Supervision	60,000 ⎫	
Depreciation/finance	93,600 ⎬ 6/12 of the annual figure	
Other	32,400 ⎭	
	186,000	(per patient = £56.36 (= £186,000/3,300))
Total (second six months)	367,500	(per patient = £111.36 (= £56.36 + £55.00))

(b) For the second six months the actual activity was 3,800 patients. For a valid comparison with the actual outcome, the budget will need to be revised to reflect this activity.

	Actual costs	Budget (3,800 patients)	Difference
	£	£	£
Variable element	203,300	209,000 (3,800 × £55)	5,700 (saving)
Fixed element	190,000	186,000	4,000 (overspend)
Total	393,300	395,000	1,700 (saving)

(c) Relative to the budget, there was a saving of nearly 3% on the variable element and an overspend of about 2% on fixed costs. Without further information, it is impossible to deduce much more than this.

The differences between the budget and the actual may be caused by some assumptions made in framing the budget for 3,800 patients in the second part of the year. There may be some element of economies of scale in the variable costs, that is, the costs may not be strictly linear. If this were the case, basing a relatively large activity budget on the experience of a relatively small activity period would tend to overstate the large activity budget. The fixed-cost budget was deduced by dividing the budget for 12 months by 2. In fact, there could be seasonal factors or inflationary pressures at work that might make such a crude division of the fixed-cost element unfair.

12.4 **Linpet Ltd**

(a) Cash budgets are extremely useful for decision-making purposes. They allow managers to see the likely effect on the cash balance of the plans that they have set in place. Cash is an important asset and it is necessary to ensure that it is properly managed. Failure to do so can have disastrous consequences for the business. Where the cash budget indicates a surplus balance, managers must decide whether this balance should be reinvested in the business or distributed to the owners. Where the cash budget indicates a deficit balance, managers must decide how this deficit should be financed or how it might be avoided.

(b) The cash budget for the six months to 30 November is:

	June £	July £	Aug £	Sept £	Oct £	Nov £
Receipts						
Cash sales revenue						
(Note 1)	4,000	5,500	7,000	8,500	11,000	11,000
Credit sales revenue						
(Note 2)	–	–	4,000	5,500	7,000	8,500
	4,000	5,500	11,000	14,000	18,000	19,500
Payments						
Purchases						
(Note 3)	–	29,000	9,250	11,500	13,750	17,500
Overheads	500	500	500	500	650	650
Wages	900	900	900	900	900	900
Commission						
(Note 4)	–	320	440	560	680	880
Equipment	10,000					7,000
Motor vehicle	6,000					
Leasehold	40,000					
	57,400	30,720	11,090	13,460	15,980	26,930
Cash flow	(53,400)	(25,220)	(90)	540	2,020	(7,430)
Opening balance	60,000	6,600	(18,620)	(18,710)	(18,170)	(16,150)
Closing balance	6,600	(18,620)	(18,710)	(18,170)	(16,150)	(23,580)

Notes:
(1) 50% of the current month's sales revenue.
(2) 50% of sales revenue of two months previous.
(3) To have sufficient inventories to meet each month's sales will require purchases of 75% of the month's sales inventories figures (25% is profit). In addition, each month the business will buy £1,000 more inventories than it will sell. In June, the business will also buy its initial inventories of £22,000. This will be paid for in the following month. For example, June's purchases will be (75% × £8,000) + £1,000 + £22,000 = £29,000, paid for in July.
(4) This is 5% of 80% of the month's sales revenue, paid in the following month. For example, June's commission will be 5% × 80% × £8,000 = £320, payable in July.

12.5 Lewisham Ltd

(a) The finished goods inventories budget for the three months ending 30 September (in units of production) is:

	July '000 units	Aug '000 units	Sept '000 units
Opening inventories (Note 1)	40	48	40
Production (Note 2)	188	232	196
	228	280	236
Inventories sold (Note 3)	(180)	(240)	(200)
Closing inventories	48	40	36

(b) The raw materials inventories budget for the two months ending 31 August (in kg) is:

	July '000 kg	Aug '000 kg
Opening inventories (Note 1)	40	58
Purchases (Note 2)	112	107
	152	165
Production (Note 4)	(94)	(116)
Closing inventories	58	49

(c) The cash budget for the two months ending 30 September is:

	Aug £	Sept £
Inflows		
Receivables: Current month (Note 5)	493,920	411,600
Preceding month (Note 6)	151,200	201,600
Total inflows	645,120	613,200
Outflows		
Payments to trade payables (Note 7)	168,000	160,500
Labour and overheads (Note 8)	185,600	156,800
Fixed overheads	22,000	22,000
Total outflows	375,600	339,300
Net inflows/(outflows)	269,520	273,900
Balance c/f	289,520	563,420

Notes:

(1) The opening balance is the same as the closing balance from the previous month.

(2) This is a balancing figure.

(3) This figure is given in the question.

(4) This figure derives from the finished inventories budget (July, $188,000 \times 0.5 = 94,000$).

(5) This is 98% of 70% of the current month's sales revenue.

(6) This is 28% of the previous month's sales revenue.

(7) This figure derives from the raw materials inventories budget (July, $112,000 \times £1.50 = £168,000$).

(8) This figure derives from the finished inventories budget (July, $232,000 \times £0.80 = £185,600$).

12.6 Newtake Records

(a) The cash budget for the period to 30 November is:

	June £000	July £000	Aug £000	Sept £000	Oct £000	Nov £000
Cash receipts						
Sales revenue (Note 1)	227	315	246	138	118	108
Cash payments						
Administration (Note 2)	(40)	(41)	(38)	(33)	(31)	(30)
Goods purchased	(135)	(180)	(142)	(94)	(75)	(66)
Repayments of borrowings	(5)	(5)	(5)	(5)	(5)	(5)
Selling expenses	(22)	(24)	(28)	(26)	(21)	(19)
Tax paid			(22)			
Shop refurbishment		(14)	(18)	(6)		
	(202)	(264)	(253)	(164)	(132)	(120)
Cash surplus (deficit)	25	51	(7)	(26)	(14)	(12)
Opening balance	(35)	(10)	41	34	8	(6)
Closing balance	(10)	41	34	8	(6)	(18)

Notes:

(1) (50% of the current month's sales revenue) + (97% × 50% of that sales revenue). For example, the June cash receipts = (50% × £230,000) + (97% × 50% × £230,000) = £226,550.

(2) The administration expenses figure for the month, *less* £15,000 for depreciation (a non-cash expense).

(b) The inventories budget for the six months to 30 November is:

	June £000	July £000	Aug £000	Sept £000	Oct £000	Nov £000
Opening balance	112	154	104	48	39	33
Inventories purchased	180	142	94	75	66	57
	292	296	198	123	105	90
Cost of inventories sold (60% sales revenue)	(138)	(192)	(150)	(84)	(72)	(66)
Closing balance	154	104	48	39	33	24

(c) The budgeted income statement for the six months ending 30 November is:

	£000
Sales revenue	1,170
Cost of goods sold	(702)
Gross profit	468
Selling expenses	(136)
Admin. expenses	(303)
Credit card charges	(18)
Interest payable	(6)
Profit for the period	5

(d) We are told that the business is required to eliminate the bank overdraft by the end of November. However, the cash budget reveals that this will not be achieved. There is a decline in the overdraft of nearly 50% over the period, but this is not enough and ways must be found to comply with the bank's requirements. It may be possible to delay the refurbishment programme that is included in the forecasts or to obtain an injection of funds from the owners or other investors. It may also be possible to stimulate sales in some way. However, there has been a decline in the sales revenue since the end of July and the November sales revenue is approximately one-third of the July sales revenue. The reasons for this decline should be sought.

The inventories levels will fall below the preferred minimum level for each of the last three months. However, to rectify this situation it will be necessary to purchase more inventories, which will, in turn, exacerbate the cash flow problems of the business.

The budgeted income statement reveals a very low profit for the period. For every £1 of sales revenue, the business is managing to generate only 0.4p in profit. The business should look carefully at its pricing policies and its overhead expenses. The administration expenses, for example, absorb more than one-quarter of the total sales revenue. Any reduction in overhead expenses will have a beneficial effect on cash flows.

12.7 Prolog Ltd

(a) The cash budget for the six months to 30 June is:

	Jan £000	Feb £000	Mar £000	Apr £000	May £000	June £000
Receipts						
Credit sales revenue (Note 1)	100	100	140	180	220	260
Payments						
Trade payables (Note 2)	112	144	176	208	240	272
Operating expenses	4	6	8	10	10	10
Shelving				12		
Tax paid			25			
	116	150	209	230	250	282
Cash flow	(16)	(50)	(69)	(50)	(30)	(22)
Opening balance	(68)	(84)	(134)	(203)	(253)	(283)
Closing balance	(84)	(134)	(203)	(253)	(283)	(305)

Notes:

(1) Sales receipts will equal the month's sales revenue, but will be received two months later. For example, the January sales revenue = £2,000 × (50 + 20) = £140,000, to be received in March.

(2) Payments to suppliers will equal the next month's sales requirements, payable the next month. For example, January purchases = £1,600 × (50 + 40) = £144,000, payable in February.

(b) A banker may require various pieces of information before granting additional overdraft facilities. These may include:
- Security available for the loan.
- Details of past profit performance.
- Profit projections for the next 12 months.
- Cash projections beyond the next six months to help assess the prospects of repayment.
- Details of the assumptions underlying projected figures supplied.
- Details of the contractual commitment between Prolog Ltd and its supplier.
- Details of management expertise. Can they manage the expansion programme?
- Details of the new machine and its performance in relation to competing models.
- Details of funds available from owners to finance the expansion.

Chapter 13

13.1 True or False

(a) A favourable direct labour rate variance can only be caused by something that leads to the rate per hour paid being less than standard. Normally, this would not be linked to efficient working. Where, however, the standard envisaged some overtime working, at premium rates, the actual labour rate may be below standard if efficiency has removed the need for the overtime.

(b) The statement is true. The action will lead to an adverse sales price variance and may well lead to problems elsewhere, but the sales volume variance must be favourable.

(c) It is true that below-standard material could lead to adverse materials usage variances because there may be more than a standard amount of scrap. This could also cause adverse labour efficiency variances because working on materials that would not form part of the output would waste labour time.

(d) Higher-than-budgeted sales volumes could well lead to an adverse labour rate variance because producing the additional work may require overtime working at premium rates.

(e) The statement is true. Nothing else could cause such a variance.

13.2 Pilot Ltd

(a) and (b)

	Budget			Actual	
	Original	Flexed			
Output (units)					
(production and sales)	5,000	5,400		5,400	
	£	£		£	
Sales revenue	25,000	27,000		26,460	
Raw materials	(7,500)	(8,100)	(2,700 kg)	(8,770)	(2,830 kg)
Labour	(6,250)	(6,750)	(675 hr)	(6,885)	(650 hr)
Fixed overheads	(6,000)	(6,000)		(6,350)	
Operating profit	5,250	6,150		4,455	

	£		Manager accountable
Sales volume variance (5,250 − 6,150)	900	(F)	Sales
Sales price variance (27,000 − 26,460)	(540)	(A)	Sales
Materials price variance (2,830 × 3) − 8,770	(280)	(A)	Buyer
Materials usage variance [(5,400 × 0.5) − 2,830] × £3	(390)	(A)	Production
Labour rate variance (650 × 10) − 6,885	(385)	(A)	Personnel
Labour efficiency variance [(5,400 × 7.5/60) − 650] × £10	250	(F)	Production
Fixed overhead spending variance (6,000 − 6,350)	(350)	(A)	Various – depends on the nature of the overheads
Total net variances	(795)	(A)	

	£
Budgeted profit	5,250
Less Total net variance	(795)
Actual profit	4,455

13.4 **Overheard remarks**

(a) Flexing the budget identifies what the profit would have been had the only difference between the original budget and the actual figures been concerned with the difference in volume of output. Comparing this profit figure with that in the original budget reveals the profit difference (variance) arising solely from the volume difference (sales volume variance). Thus, flexing the budget does not mean at all that volume differences do not matter. Flexing the budget is the means of discovering the effect on profit of the volume difference.

In one sense, all variances are 'water under the bridge', to the extent that the past cannot be undone, and so it is impossible to go back to the last control period and put in a better performance. Identifying variances can, however, be useful in identifying where things went wrong, which should enable management to take steps to ensure that the same things do not go wrong in the future.

(b) Variances will not tell you what went wrong. They should, however, be a great help in identifying the manager within whose sphere of responsibility things went wrong. That manager should know why it went wrong. In this sense, variances identify relevant questions, but not answers.

(c) Identifying the reason for variances may well cost money, usually in terms of staff time. It is a matter of judgement in any particular situation, of balancing the cost of investigation against the potential benefits. As is usual in such judgements, it is difficult, before undertaking the investigation, to know either the cost or the likely benefit.

In general, significant variances, particularly adverse ones, should be investigated. Persistent (over a period of months) smaller variances should also be investigated. It should not automatically be assumed that favourable variances can be ignored. They indicate that things are not going according to plan, possibly because the plans (budgets) are flawed.

(d) Research evidence does not show this. It seems to show that managers tend to be most motivated by having as a target the most difficult goals that they find acceptable.

(e) Budgets normally provide the basis of feedforward and feedback control. During a budget preparation period, potential problems (for example, a potential inventories shortage) might be revealed. Steps can then be taken to revise the plans in order to avoid the potential problem. This is an example of a feedforward control: potential problems are anticipated and eliminated before they can occur.

Budgetary control is a very good example of feedback control, where a signal that something is going wrong triggers steps to take corrective action for the future.

13.5 Bradley-Allen Ltd

(a)

	Budget			Actual	
	Original	Flexed			
Output (units) (production and sales)	800	950		950	
	£	£		£	
Sales revenue	64,000	76,000		73,000	
Raw materials – A	(12,000)	(14,250)	(285 kg)	(15,200)	(310 kg)
– B	(16,000)	(19,000)	(950m)	(18,900)	(920m)
Labour – skilled	(4,000)	(4,750)	(475 hr)	(4,628)	(445 hr)
– unskilled	(10,000)	(11,875)	(1,484.375 hr)	(11,275)	(1,375 hr)
Fixed overheads	(12,000)	(12,000)		(11,960)	
Profit	10,000	14,125		11,037	

Sales variances
  Volume: 10,000 – 14,125 = £4,125 (F)
  Price: 76,000 – 73,000 = £3,000 (A)
Direct materials A variances
  Usage: [(950 × 0.3) – 310] × £50 = £1,250 (A)
  Price: (310 × £50) – £15,200 = £300 (F)
Direct materials B variances
  Usage: [(950 × 1) – 920] × £20 = £600 (F)
  Price: (920 × £20) – £18,900 = £500 (A)
Skilled direct labour variances
  Efficiency: [(950 × 0.5) – 445] × £10 = £300 (F)
  Rate: (445 × £10) – £4,628 = £178 (A)
Unskilled direct labour variances
  Efficiency: [(950 × 1.5625) – 1,375] × £8 = £875 (F)
  Rate: (1,375 × £8) – £11,275 = £275 (A)
Fixed overhead variances
  Spending: (12,000 – 11,960) = £40 (F)

		£		£
Budgeted profit				10,000
Sales:	Volume	4,125	(F)	
	Price	(3,000)	(A)	1,125
Direct material A:	Usage	(1,250)	(A)	
	Price	300	(F)	(950)
Direct material B:	Usage	600	(F)	
	Price	(500)	(A)	100
Skilled labour:	Efficiency	300	(F)	
	Rate	(178)	(A)	122
Unskilled labour:	Efficiency	875	(F)	
	Rate	(275)	(A)	600
Fixed overheads:	Expenditure			40
Actual profit				11,037

(b) The statement in (a) is useful to management because it enables them to see where there have been failures to meet the original budget and to quantify the extent of such failures. This means that junior managers can be held accountable for the performance of their particular area of responsibility.

13.7 Varne Chemprocessors

(a) The standard usage rate of UK194 (per litre of Varnelyne) is $200/5,000 = 0.04$.

The standard price $= £392/200 = £1.96$ per litre of UK194.

Materials usage variance (UK194) is

$$[(637,500 \times 0.04) - 28,100] \times £1.96 = £5,096 \ (A)$$

Materials price variance is

$$(28,100 \times £1.96) - £51,704 = £3,372 \ (F)$$

(b) The net variance on UK194 was, from the calculations in (a), £1,724 (A) (that is £5,096 – £3,372). This seems to have led directly to savings elsewhere of £4,900, giving a net cost saving of over £3,000 for the month.

Unfortunately things may not be quite as simple as the numbers suggest. Will the non-standard mix to make the Varnelyne lead to a substandard product, which could have very wide-ranging ramifications in terms of potential loss of market goodwill?

There is also the possibility that the material for which the UK194 was used as a substitute was already held in inventories. If this were the case, is there any danger that this material may deteriorate and, ultimately, prove to be unusable?

Other possible adverse outcomes of the non-standard mix could also arise.

The question is raised by the analysis in part (a) (and by the production manager's comment) of why the cost standard for UK194 had not been revised to take account of the lower price prevailing in the market.

(c) The variances, period by period and cumulatively, for each of the two materials are given as follows:

Period	UK500			UK800			
	Period £		Cumulative £		Period £		Cumulative £
1	301	(F)	301	(F)	298	(F)	298 (F)
2	(251)	(A)	50	(F)	203	(F)	501 (F)
3	102	(F)	152	(F)	(52)	(A)	449 (F)
4	(202)	(A)	(50)	(A)	(98)	(A)	351 (F)
5	153	(F)	103	(F)	(150)	(A)	201 (F)
6	(103)	(A)	zero		(201)	(A)	zero

Without knowing the scale of these variances relative to the actual costs involved, it is not possible to be too dogmatic about how to interpret the above information.

UK500 appears to show a fairly random set of data, with the period variances fluctuating from positive to negative and giving a net variance of zero. This is what would be expected from a situation that is basically under control.

UK800 also shows a zero cumulative figure over the six periods, *but* there seems to be a more systematic train of events, particularly the four consecutive adverse variances from period 3 onwards. This looks as if it may be out of control and worthy of investigation.

Chapter 14

14.1 Mylo Ltd

(a) The annual depreciation of the two projects is:

$$\text{Project 1:} \quad \frac{(£100,000 - £7,000)}{3} = £31,000$$

$$\text{Project 2:} \quad \frac{(£60,000 - £6,000)}{3} = £18,000$$

Project 1

(1)

	Year 0 £000	Year 1 £000	Year 2 £000	Year 3 £000
Operating profit/(loss)		29	(1)	2
Depreciation		31	31	31
Capital cost	(100)			
Residual value				7
Net cash flows	(100)	60	30	40
10% discount factor	1.000	0.909	0.826	0.751
Present value	(100.00)	54.54	24.78	30.04
Net present value	9.36			

(2) Clearly the IRR lies above 10%. Try 15%:

15% discount factor	1.000	0.870	0.756	0.658
Present value	(100.00)	52.20	22.68	26.32
Net present value	1.20			

Thus the IRR lies a little above 15%, perhaps around 16%.

(3) To find the payback period, the cumulative cash flows are calculated:

Cumulative cash flows	(100)	(40)	(10)	30

Thus the payback will occur after three years if we assume year-end cash flows.

Project 2

(1)

	Year 0 £000	Year 1 £000	Year 2 £000	Year 3 £000
Operating profit/(loss)		18	(2)	4
Depreciation		18	18	18
Capital cost	(60)			
Residual value				6
Net cash flows	(60)	36	16	28
10% discount factor	1.000	0.909	0.826	0.751
Present value	(60.00)	32.72	13.22	21.03
Net present value	6.97			

(2) Clearly the IRR lies above 10%. Try 15%:

15% discount factor	1.000	0.870	0.756	0.658
Present value	(60.00)	31.32	12.10	18.42
Net present value	1.84			

Thus the IRR lies a little above 15%, perhaps around 17%.

(3) The cumulative cash flows are:

Cumulative cash flows	(60)	(24)	(8)	20

Thus, the payback will occur after three years (assuming year-end cash flows).

(b) Assuming that Mylo Ltd is pursuing a wealth-enhancement objective, Project 1 is preferable since it has the higher net present value. The difference between the two net present values is not significant, however.

14.5 Newton Electronics Ltd

(a) **Option 1**

	Year 0 £m	Year 1 £m	Year 2 £m	Year 3 £m	Year 4 £m	Year 5 £m
Plant and equipment	(9.0)					1.0
Sales revenue		24.0	30.8	39.6	26.4	10.0
Variable cost		(11.2)	(19.6)	(25.2)	(16.8)	(7.0)
Fixed cost (ex. dep'n)		(0.8)	(0.8)	(0.8)	(0.8)	(0.8)
Working capital	(3.0)					3.0
Marketing cost		(2.0)	(2.0)	(2.0)	(2.0)	(2.0)
Opportunity cost		(0.1)	(0.1)	(0.1)	(0.1)	(0.1)
	(12.0)	9.9	8.3	11.5	6.7	4.1
Discount factor 10%	1.000	0.909	0.826	0.751	0.683	0.621
Present value	(12.0)	9.0	6.9	8.6	4.6	2.5
Net present value	19.6					

Option 2

	Year 0 £m	Year 1 £m	Year 2 £m	Year 3 £m	Year 4 £m	Year 5 £m
Royalties	–	4.4	7.7	9.9	6.6	2.8
Discount factor 10%	1.000	0.909	0.826	0.751	0.683	0.621
Present value	–	4.0	6.4	7.4	4.5	1.7
Net present value	24.0					

Option 3

	Year 0	Year 2
Instalments	12.0	12.0
Discount factor 10%	1.000	0.826
Present value	12.0	9.9
Net present value	21.9	

(b) Before making a final decision, the board should consider the following factors:
- The long-term competitiveness of the business may be affected by the sale of the patents.
- At present, the business is not involved in manufacturing and marketing products. Would a change in direction be desirable?
- The business will probably have to buy in the skills necessary to produce the product itself. This will involve costs, and problems will be incurred. Has this been taken into account?
- How accurate are the forecasts made and how valid are the assumptions on which they are based?

(c) Option 2 has the highest net present value and is therefore the most attractive to shareholders. However, the accuracy of the forecasts should be checked before a final decision is made.

14.6 Chesterfield Wanderers

(a) and (b)

Player option

	Year 0 £000	Year 1 £000	Year 2 £000	Year 3 £000	Year 4 £000	Year 5 £000
Sale of player	2,200					1,000
Purchase of Bazza	(10,000)					
Sponsorship and so on		1,200	1,200	1,200	1,200	1,200
Gate receipts		2,500	1,300	1,300	1,300	1,300
Salaries paid		(800)	(800)	(800)	(800)	(1,200)
Salaries saved		400	400	400	400	600
	(7,800)	3,300	2,100	2,100	2,100	2,900
Discount factor 10%	1.000	0.909	0.826	0.751	0.683	0.621
Present values	(7,800)	3,000	1,735	1,577	1,434	1,801
Net present value	1,747					

Ground improvement option

	Year 1 £000	Year 2 £000	Year 3 £000	Year 4 £000	Year 5 £000
Ground improvements	(10,000)				
Increased gate receipts	(1,800)	4,400	4,400	4,400	4,400
	(11,800)	4,400	4,400	4,400	4,400
Discount factor 10%	0.909	0.826	0.751	0.683	0.621
Present values	(10,726)	3,634	3,304	3,005	2,732
Net present value	1,949				

(c) The ground improvement option provides the higher net present value and is therefore the preferable option, based on the objective of shareholder wealth enhancement.

(d) A professional football club may not wish to pursue an objective of shareholder wealth enhancement. It may prefer to invest in quality players in an attempt to enjoy future sporting success. If this is the case, the net present value approach will be less appropriate because the club is not pursuing a strict wealth-related objective.

14.7　Simtex Ltd

(a) Net operating cash flows each year will be:

	£000
Sales revenue (160 × £6)	960
Variable cost (160 × £4)	(640)
Relevant fixed costs	(170)
	150

The estimated net present value of the new product can then be calculated:

	£000
Annual cash flows (150 × 3.038*)	456
Residual value of equipment (100 × 0.636)	64
	520
Initial outlay	(480)
Net present value	40

* This is the sum of the discount factors over four years (that is 0.893 + 0.797 + 0.712 + 0.636 = 3.038). Where the cash flows are constant, it is a quicker procedure than working out the present value of cash flows for each year and then adding them together.

(b) (1) Assume the discount rate is 18%. The net present value of the project would be:

	£000
Annual cash flows (150 × 2.690*)	404
Residual value of equipment (100 × 0.516)	52
	456
Initial outlay	(480)
Net present value	(24)

* That is 0.847 + 0.718 + 0.609 + 0.516 = 2.690.

Thus an increase of 6%, from 12% to 18%, in the discount rate causes a fall from +40 to −24 in the net present value: a fall of 64, or 10.67 (that is, 64/6) for each 1% rise in the discount rate. So a zero net present value will occur with a discount rate approximately equal to 12 + (40/11.67) = 15.4%. (This is, of course, the internal rate of return.)

This higher discount rate represents an increase of about 28% on the existing cost of capital figure.

(2) The initial outlay on equipment is already expressed in present-value terms and so, to make the project no longer viable, the outlay will have to increase by an amount equal to the net present value of the project (that is, £40,000) – an increase of 8.3% on the stated initial outlay.

(3) The change necessary in the annual net cash flows to make the project no longer profitable can be calculated as follows.

Let Y = change in the annual operating cash flows. Then (Y × cumulative discount rates for a four-year period) − NPV = 0. This can be rearranged as:

$$Y \times \text{cumulative discount rates for a four-year period} = \text{NPV}$$

$$Y \times 3.038 = £40,000$$
$$Y = £40,000/3.038$$
$$= £13,167$$

In percentage terms, this is a decrease of 8.8% on the estimated cash flows.

(4) The change in the residual value required to make the new product no longer profitable can be calculated as follows.

Let V = change in the residual value. Then (V × discount factor at end of four years) − NPV of product = 0. This can be rearranged as:

$$V \times \text{discount factor at end of four years} = \text{NPV of product}$$

$$V \times 0.636 = £40,000$$
$$V = £40,000/0.636$$
$$= £62,893$$

This is a decrease of 62.9% in the residual value of the equipment.

(c) The net present value of the product is positive and so it will increase shareholder wealth. Thus, it should be produced. The sensitivity analysis suggests the initial outlay and the annual cash flows are the most sensitive variables for managers to consider.

14.8 Kernow Cleaning Services Ltd

(a) The first step is to calculate the expected annual cash flows:

Year 1	£	Year 2	£
£80,000 × 0.3	24,000	£140,000 × 0.4	56,000
£160,000 × 0.5	80,000	£220,000 × 0.4	88,000
£200,000 × 0.2	40,000	£250,000 × 0.2	50,000
	144,000		194,000
Year 3		Year 4	
£140,000 × 0.4	56,000	£100,000 × 0.3	30,000
£200,000 × 0.3	60,000	£170,000 × 0.6	102,000
£230,000 × 0.3	69,000	£200,000 × 0.1	20,000
	185,000		152,000

The expected net present value (ENPV) can now be calculated as follows:

Period	Expected cash flow £	Discount rate 10%	Expected PV £
0	(540,000)	1.000	(540,000)
1	144,000	0.909	130,896
2	194,000	0.826	160,244
3	185,000	0.751	138,935
4	152,000	0.683	103,816
ENPV			(6,109)

(b) The *worst possible outcome* can be calculated by taking the lowest values of savings each year, as follows:

Period	Cash flow £	Discount rate 10%	PV £
0	(540,000)	1.000	(540,000)
1	80,000	0.909	72,720
2	140,000	0.826	115,640
3	140,000	0.751	105,140
4	100,000	0.683	68,300
NPV			(178,200)

The probability of occurrence can be obtained by multiplying together the probability of *each* of the worst outcomes above, that is $0.3 \times 0.4 \times 0.4 \times 0.3 = 0.014$.

Thus, the probability of occurrence is 1.4%, which is very low.

Chapter 15

15.1 H. Brown (Portsmouth) Ltd

(a) The main factors to take into account are:

Risk. If a business borrows, there is a risk that at the maturity date for the repayment of the funds the business will not have sufficient funds to repay the amount owing and will be unable to find a suitable form of replacement borrowing. With short-term borrowingss, the maturity dates will arrive more quickly and the type of risk outlined will occur at more frequent intervals.

Matching. A business may wish to match the life of an asset with the maturity date of the borrowing. In other words, long-term assets will be purchased with long-term borrowed funds. A certain level of current assets, which form part of the long-term asset base of the business, may also be funded by long-term borrowing. Those current assets that fluctuate owing to seasonality and so on will be funded by short-term borrowing. This approach to funding assets will help reduce risks for the business.

Cost. Interest rates for long-term borrowings may be higher than for short-term ones as investors may seek extra compensation for having their funds locked up for a long period. However, issue costs may be higher for short-term borrowings as there will be a need to refund at more frequent intervals.

Flexibility. Short-term borrowings may be more flexible. It may be difficult to repay long-term ones before the maturity period.

(b) When deciding to grant a loan, a lender should consider the following factors:
security
purpose of the loan
ability of the borrower to repay
loan period
availability of funds
character and integrity of the senior managers.

(c) Loan conditions may include:
the need to obtain permission before issuing further loans
the need to maintain a certain level of liquidity during the loan period
a restriction on the level of dividends and directors' pay.

15.2 **Devonian plc**

(a) (1) *Ex-rights price*

	£
5 original shares @ £2.10 per share	10.50
1 rights share @ £1.80	1.80
	12.30
Theoretical ex-rights price (£12.30/6)	£2.05

(2) *Value of rights*

	£
Value of a share after the rights issue	2.05
Cost of a rights share	1.80
Value of rights	0.25
Value of rights attached to each original share = £0.25/5 =	£0.05

(b) (1) *Share price in one year's time*
Rights issue
We must first calculate the existing P/E ratio in order to determine the share price in one year's time. This can be done as follows:

	£m
Operating profit (Year 4)	40.0
Taxation (30%)	(12.0)
Profit for the year (available to shareholders)	28.0
Earnings per share (EPS) (£28.0m/200m)	= £0.14
P/E ratio	$= \dfrac{\text{Share price}}{\text{EPS}}$
	= £2.10/£0.14
	= 15 times

	£m
Operating profit (Year 5)	50.0
Taxation (30%)	(15.0)
Profit for the year (available to ordinary shareholders)	35.0
Earnings per share (£35m/240m)	= £0.146
Share price (Year 5)	= EPS × P/E ratio
	= £0.146 × 15
	= £2.19

(2) *Borrowing*

	£m
Operating profit (Year 5)	50.0
Interest payable (£72m @ 10%)	(7.2)
	42.8
Taxation (30%)	(12.8)
Profit for the year (available to ordinary shareholders)	30.0
Earnings per share (£30m/200m)	= £0.15
Share price (Year 5)	= EPS × P/E ratio
	= £0.15 × 13.5
	= £2.03

These calculations reveal that in one year's time the share price is expected to rise by more than 4% above the current share price if a rights issue is made, whereas the share price will fall by more than 3% if the business borrows the money. Given the additional financial risks attached to borrowing, it seems that a rights issue offers the better option – at least in the short term.

(c) By issuing shares at a discount in a rights issue, pressure is put on the shareholders either to take up the shares or to sell the right to someone that will. Failure to do one of these will lead to a loss of wealth for the shareholder.

(d) The price at which rights issues are made is not critical. It needs to be sufficiently low to put pressure on shareholders to take them up or sell the rights. It also needs to be low enough to make it unlikely that, between setting the issue price and the date of the issue, the current market price of the existing share will have fallen below the rights issue price. Since the discount does not represent a real bonus to the shareholders, it can be quite large.

15.3 Brocmar plc

(a) (1) EPS = £1.8m/10m   = £0.180

    (2) Rights price = £1.80 – (20% × £1.80)   = £1.44

    (3) Number of shares issued = £2.88m/£1.44   = 2m

    (4) EPS for next year = (£1.8m + £0.4m)/(10m + 2m) = £0.183

    (5) Ex-rights price: 5 shares @ £1.80   = £9.00

                       1 share @ £1.44   = £1.44

                       6   £10.44

      Theoretical ex-rights price per share = £10.44/6   = £1.74

(b) Additional information should include:
- future cash flows from the project
- the degree of risk associated with the project
- the cost of capital required to undertake the project
- the NPV of the project
- the extent to which the project fits with the strategy of the business.

15.4 Raphael Ltd

The existing credit policies have the following costs:

	£
Cost of investment in trade receivables [(50/365) × £2.4m × 12%]	39,452
Cost of bad debts (1.5% × £2.4m)	36,000
Total cost	75,452

Employing a factor will result in the following costs and savings:

	£
Charges of the factor (2% × £2.4m)	48,000
Interest charges on advance [(30/365) × (80% × £2.4m) × 11%]	17,359
Interest charges on overdraft [(30/365) × (20% × £2.4m) × 12%]	4,734
Total cost	70,093
Less Credit control savings	(18,000)
Net cost	52,093

We can see the net cost of factoring is lower than the existing costs, and so there would be a benefit gained from entering into an agreement with the factor.

15.6 Carpets Direct plc

(a) The earnings per share (EPS) is:

$$\frac{\text{Profit after taxation}}{\text{Number of ordinary shares}} = \frac{£4.5m}{120m} = £0.0375$$

The current market value per share is:

$$\text{Earnings per share} \times \text{P/E} = £0.0375 \times 22 = £0.825$$

The rights issue price will be £0.825, less 20% discount = £0.66.
The theoretical ex-rights price is:

	£
Original shares (4 @ £0.825)	3.30
Rights share (1 @ £0.66)	0.66
Value of five shares following rights issue	3.96

Therefore, the value of one share following the rights issue is:

$$\frac{£3.96}{5} = 79.2p$$

(b)

Value of one share after rights issue	79.2p
Cost of a rights share	(66.0p)
Value of rights to shareholder	13.2p

(c) (1) *Taking up rights issue*

	£
Shareholding following rights issue [(4,000 + 1,000) × 79.2p]	3,960
Less Cost of rights shares (1,000 × 66p)	(660)
Shareholder wealth	3,300

(2) *Selling the rights*

	£
Shareholding following rights issue (4,000 × 79.2p)	3,168
Add Proceeds from sale of rights (1,000 × 13.2p)	132
Shareholder wealth	3,300

(3) *Doing nothing*
As the rights are neither purchased nor sold, the shareholder wealth following the rights issue will be:

Shareholding (4,000 × 79.2p)	3,168

We can see that the investor will have the same wealth under the first two options. However, by the investor doing nothing, the rights offer will lapse and so the investor will lose the value of the rights and will be worse off.

Chapter 16

16.1 **Hercules Wholesalers Ltd**

(a) The business is probably concerned about its liquidity position because:

- it has a substantial overdraft, which together with its non-current borrowings means that it has borrowed an amount roughly equal to its equity (according to statement of financial position (balance sheet) values);
- it has increased its investment in inventories during the past year (as shown by the income statement); and
- it has a low current ratio (ratio of current assets to current liabilities).

(b) The operating cash cycle can be calculated as follows:

Number of days

Average inventories holding period:

$$\frac{[(\text{Opening inventories} + \text{Closing inventories})/2] \times 365}{\text{Cost of inventories}} = \frac{[(125 + 143)/2] \times 365}{323} \qquad 151$$

Add Average settlement period for trade receivables:

$$\frac{\text{Trade receivables} \times 365}{\text{Credit sales revenue}} = \frac{163}{452} \times 365 \qquad \underline{132}$$
$$283$$

Less Average settlement period for trade payables:

$$\frac{\text{Trade payables} \times 365}{\text{Credit purchases}} = \frac{145}{341} \times 365 \qquad \underline{155}$$
$$\underline{128}$$

(c) The business can reduce the operating cash cycle in a number of ways. The average inventories holding period seems quite long. At present, average inventories held represent almost five months' sales. This period can be shortened by reducing the level of inventories held. Similarly, the average settlement period for trade receivables seems long at more than four months' sales revenue. Imposing tighter credit control, offering discounts, charging interest on overdue accounts and so on, may reduce this. However, any policy decisions concerning inventories and trade receivables must take account of current trading conditions.

Extending the period of credit taken to pay suppliers would also reduce the operating cash cycle. However, for the reasons mentioned in the chapter, this option must be given careful consideration.

16.5

Mayo Computers Ltd
New proposals from credit control department

	£000	£000
Current level of investment in trade receivables		
[£20m × (60/365)]		3,288
Proposed level of investment in trade receivables		
[(£20m × 60%) × (30/365)]	(986)	
[(£20m × 40%) × (50/365)]	(1,096)	(2,082)
Reduction in level of investment		1,206

The reduction in overdraft interest as a result of the reduction in the level of investment will be £1,206,000 × 14% = £169,000.

	£000	£000
Cost of cash discounts offered (£20m × 60% × 2½%)		300
Additional cost of credit administration		20
		320
Bad debt savings	(100)	
Interest charge savings (see above)	(169)	(269)
Net cost of policy each year		51

These calculations show that the business would incur additional annual costs if it implemented this proposal. It would therefore be cheaper to stay with the existing credit policy.

16.6 Boswell Enterprises Ltd

(a) The investment in working capital will be:

	Current policy		New policy	
	£000	£000	£000	£000
Receivables				
[(£3m × $^1/_{12}$ × 30%) + (£3m × $^2/_{12}$ × 70%)]		425.0		
[(£3.15m × $^1/_{12}$ × 60%) + (£3.15m × $^2/_{12}$ × 40%)]				367.5
Inventories				
[£3m − (£3m × 20%)] × $^3/_{12}$]		600.0		
{[£3.15m − (£3.15m × 20%)] × $^3/_{12}$}				630.0
Cash (fixed)		140.0		140.0
		1,165.0		1,137.5
Trade payables				
[[£3m − (£3m × 20%)] × $^2/_{12}$]	(400.0)			
{[£3.15m − (£3.15m × 20%)] × $^2/_{12}$}			(420.0)	
Accrued variable expenses				
[£3m × $^1/_{12}$ × 10%]	(25.0)			
[£3.15m × $^1/_{12}$ × 10%]			(26.3)	
Accrued fixed expenses	(15.0)	(440.0)	(15.0)	(461.3)
Investment in working capital		725.0		676.2

(b) The expected profit for the year will be:

	Current policy		New policy	
	£000	£000	£000	£000
Sales revenue		3,000.0		3,150.0
Cost of goods sold		(2,400.0)		(2,520.0)
Gross profit (20%)		600.0		630.0
Variable expenses (10%)	(300.0)		(315.0)	
Fixed expenses	(180.0)		(180.0)	
Discounts (£3.15m × 60% × 2.5%)	–	(480.0)	(47.3)	(542.3)
Profit for the year		120.0		87.7

(c) Under the proposed policy we can see that the investment in working capital will be slightly lower than under the current policy. However, profit will be substantially lower as a result of offering discounts. The increase in sales revenue resulting from the discounts will not be sufficient to offset the additional costs of making the discounts to customers. It seems that the business should, therefore, stick with its current policy.

16.7   **Delphi plc**

(a) The receivables ageing schedule is:

	1 month or less		1 to 2 months		2 to 3 months		Total receivables	
	£000	%	£000	%	£000	%	£000	%
February								
TV and hi-fi	20.0	(22.2)					20.0	(22.2)
Music	30.0	(33.3)					30.0	(33.3)
Retail	40.0	(44.5)					40.0	(44.5)
	90.0	(100.0)					90.0	(100.0)
March								
TV and hi-fi	20.8	(12.5)					20.8	(12.5)
Music	31.8	(19.2)	30.0	(18.1)			61.8	(37.3)
Retail	43.2	(26.1)	40.0	(24.1)			83.2	(50.2)
	95.8	(57.8)	70.0	(42.2)			165.8	(100.0)
April								
TV and hi-fi	21.6	(10.0)					21.6	(10.0)
Music	33.7	(15.6)	31.8	(14.7)			65.5	(30.2)
Retail	46.7	(21.5)	43.2	(19.9)	40.0	(18.4)	129.9	(59.7)
	102.0	(47.0)	75.0	(34.6)	40.0	(18.4)	217.0	(100.0)
May								
TV and hi-fi	22.5	(9.7)					22.5	(9.7)
Music	35.7	(15.4)	33.7	(14.5)			69.4	(29.9)
Retail	50.4	(21.7)	46.7	(20.1)	43.2	(18.6)	140.3	(60.4)
	108.6	(46.8)	80.4	(34.6)	43.2	(18.6)	232.2	(100.0)

Number of months outstanding

We can see that the trade receivables figure will increase substantially in the first four months. The retail chains will account for about 60% of the total trade receivables outstanding by May as this group has the fastest rate of growth. There is also a significant decline in the proportion of total receivables outstanding from TV and hi-fi shops over this period.

(b) In answering this part of the question, you should refer to the 'five Cs of credit' that were discussed in detail in the chapter.

16.8 **Goliath plc**

(a) (1)   The existing operating cash cycle can be calculated as follows:

Number of days

Inventories holding period $= \dfrac{\text{Inventories at year end}}{\text{Cost of sales}} \times 365$

$= \dfrac{560}{1,440} \times 365$ 142

Receivables settlement period

$= \dfrac{\text{Receivables at year end}}{\text{Sales revenue}} \times 365$

$= \dfrac{565}{2,400} \times 365$ <u>86</u>

228

Payables settlement period

$= \dfrac{\text{Payables at year end}}{\text{Purchases}} \times 365$

$= \dfrac{451}{1,450} \times 365$ <u>(114)</u>

Operating cash cycle   <u>114</u>

The new operating cash cycle is:

Number of days

Inventories holding period $= \dfrac{(560 \times 1.15)}{(2,400 \times 1.10) \times 0.60^*} \times 365$ 148

Receivables settlement period $= 86 + 20$ <u>106</u>

254

Payables settlement period $= 114 + 15$ <u>(129)</u>

<u>125</u>

New operating cash cycle   125

Existing operating cash cycle   (114)

Increase in operating cash cycle (days)   <u>11</u>

* Cost of sales is 60% of sales revenue (see the income statement).

(2)

	£000
Increase (decrease) in inventories held [(560 × 1.15) − 560]	84.0
Increase (decrease) in receivables {[(2,400 × 1.1) × (106/365)] − 565}	201.7
	285.7
(Increase) decrease in payables [1,668 × (129/365) − 451]	(138.5)
Increase (decrease) in net investment	147.2

(3)

	£000	£000
Gross profit increase [(2,400 × 0.1) × 0.40]		96.0
Adjust for:		
Administration expenses increase (15%)	(45.0)	
Bad debts increase	(120.0)	
Interest (10%) on borrowing for increased net investment in working capital (147.2)	(14.7)	(179.7)
Increase (decrease) in profit before tax		(83.7)
Decrease in tax charge for the period (25% × 83.7)		20.9
Increase (decrease) in profit for the year		(62.8)

(b) There would be an increase in the operating cash cycle and this will have an adverse effect on liquidity. The existing trade payables and inventories holding periods already appear to be quite high. Any increase in either of these must be justified. The planned increase in the trade payables period must also be justified because it may risk the loss of goodwill from suppliers. Although there is an expected increase in sales revenue of £240,000 from adopting the new policy, the profit for the year will decrease by £62,800. This represents a substantial decrease when compared with the previous year. (The increase in bad debts is a major reason why the profit is, for the period, adversely affected.) There is also a substantial increase in the net investment in inventories, trade receivables and trade payables, which seem high in relation to the expected increase in sales revenue. The new policy requires a significant increase in investment and is expected to generate lower profit than is currently being enjoyed. It should, therefore, be rejected.

Appendix A

A.1   *Account to be debited*   *Account to be credited*
   (a) Inventories   Trade payables
   (b) Equity (or a separate drawings account)   Cash
   (c) Interest on borrowings   Cash
   (d) Inventories   Cash
   (e) Cash   Trade receivables
   (f) Wages   Cash
   (g) Equity (or a separate drawings account)   Trade receivables
   (h) Trade payables   Cash
   (i) Electricity (or heat and light)   Cash
   (j) Cash   Sales revenue

Note that the precise name given to an account is not crucial so long as it is clear to those who are using the information what each account deals with.

A.2 (a) and (b)

Cash

		£			£
1 Feb	Equity	6,000	3 Feb	Inventories	2,600
15 Feb	Sales revenue	4,000	5 Feb	Equipment	800
28 Feb	Trade receivables	2,500	9 Feb	Rent	250
			10 Feb	Fuel and electricity	240
			11 Feb	General expenses	200
			21 Feb	Equity	1,000
			25 Feb	Trade payables	2,000
			28 Feb	Balance c/d	5,410
		12,500			12,500
1 Mar	Balance b/d	5,410			

Equity

		£			£
21 Feb	Cash	1,000	1 Feb	Cash	6,000
28 Feb	Balance c/d	5,000			
		6,000			6,000
			28 Feb	Balance b/d	5,000
28 Feb	Balance c/d	7,410	28 Feb	Income statement	2,410
		7,410			7,410
			1 Mar	Balance b/d	7,410

Inventories

		£			£
3 Feb	Cash	2,600	15 Feb	Cost of sales	2,400
6 Feb	Trade payables	3,000	19 Feb	Cost of sales	2,300
			28 Feb	Balance c/d	900
		5,600			5,600
1 Mar	Balance b/d	900			

Equipment

		£			£
5 Feb	Cash	800			

Trade payables

		£			£
25 Feb	Cash	2,000	6 Feb	Inventories	3,000
28 Feb	Balance c/d	1,000			
		3,000			3,000
			1 Mar	Balance b/d	1,000

Rent

		£			£
9 Feb	Cash	250	28 Feb	Income statement	250

Fuel and electricity

		£			£
10 Feb	Cash	240	28 Feb	Income statement	240

General expenses

		£			£
11 Feb	Cash	200	28 Feb	Income statement	200

Sales revenue

		£				£
28 Feb	Balance c/d	7,800	15 Feb	Cash		4,000
			19 Feb	Trade receivables		3,800
		7,800				7,800
28 Feb	Income statement	7,800	28 Feb	Balance b/d		7,800

Cost of sales

		£			£
15 Feb	Inventories	2,400	28 Feb	Balance c/d	4,700
19 Feb	Inventories	2,300			
		4,700			4,700
28 Feb	Balance b/d	4,700	28 Feb	Income statement	4,700

Trade receivables

		£			£
19 Feb	Sales revenue	3,800	28 Feb	Cash	2,500
			28 Feb	Balance c/d	1,300
		3,800			3,800
1 Mar	Balance b/d	1,300			

Trial balance as at 28 February

	Debits	Credits
	£	£
Cash	5,410	
Equity		5,000
Inventories	900	
Equipment	800	
Trade payables		1,000
Rent	250	
Fuel and electricity	240	
General expenses	200	
Sales revenue		7,800
Cost of sales	4,700	
Trade receivables	1,300	
	13,800	13,800

(c)

Income statement

			£			£
28 Feb	Cost of sales		4,700	28 February	Sales revenue	7,800
28 Feb	Rent		250			
28 Feb	Fuel and electricity		240			
28 Feb	General expenses		200			
28 Feb	Equity (profit)		2,410			
			7,800			7,800

Statement of financial position as at 28 February

	£
ASSETS	
Non-current assets	
Equipment	800
Current assets	
Inventories	900
Trade receivables	1,300
Cash	5,410
	7,610
Total assets	8,410
EQUITY AND LIABILITIES	
Owners' equity	7,410
Current liabilities	
Trade payables	1,000
Total equity and liabilities	8,410

Income statement for the month ended 28 February

	£
Sales revenue	7,800
Cost of sales	(4,700)
Gross profit	3,100
Rent	(250)
Fuel and electricity	(240)
General expenses	(200)
Profit for the month	2,410

A.3

Buildings

		£			£
1 Jan	Balance brought down	25,000			

Fittings – cost

		£			£
1 Jan	Balance brought down	10,000	31 Dec	Balance carried down	12,000
	Cash	2,000			
		12,000			12,000
1 Jan	Balance brought down	12,000			

Fittings – depreciation

		£				£
31 Dec	Balance carried down	4,400	1 Jan	Balance brought down		2,000
			31 Dec	Income statement		
				(£12,000 × 20%)		2,400
		4,400				4,400
			1 Jan	Balance brought down		4,400

General expenses

		£			£
1 Jan	Balance brought down	140	31 Dec	Income statement	570
	Cash	580		Balance carried down	150
		720			720
1 Jan	Balance brought down	150			

Inventories

		£			£
1 Jan	Balance brought down	1,350	31 Dec	Cost of sales	15,220
31 Dec	Trade payables	17,220		Cost of sales	4,900
	Cash	3,760		Equity	560
				Balance carried down	1,650
		22,330			22,330
1 Jan	Balance brought down	1,650			

Cost of sales

		£			£
31 Dec	Inventories	15,220	31 Dec	Income statement	20,120
	Inventories	4,900			
		20,120			20,120

Rent

		£			£
1 Jan	Balance brought down	500	31 Dec	Income statement	3,000
31 Dec	Cash	3,000		Balance carried down	500
		3,500			3,500
1 Jan	Balance brought down	500			

Trade receivables

		£			£
1 Jan	Balance brought down	1,840	31 Dec	Cash	32,810
31 Dec	Sales revenue	33,100		Income statement (bad debt)	260
				Balance carried down	1,870
		34,940			34,940
1 Jan	Balance brought down	1,870			

Cash

		£			£
1 Jan	Balance brought down	2,180	31 Dec	Inventories	3,760
31 Dec	Sales revenue	10,360		Wages	3,770
	Borrowings	2,000		Rent	3,000
	Trade receivables	32,810		Electricity	1,070
				General expenses	580
				Fittings	2,000
				Borrowings	1,000
				Trade payables	18,150
				Equity	10,400
				Balance carried down	3,620
		47,350			47,350
1 Jan	Balance brought down	3,620			

Equity

		£			£
31 Dec	Inventories	560	1 Jan	Balance brought down	25,050
	Cash	10,400		Income statement (profit)	10,900
	Balance carried down	24,990			
		35,950			35,950
			1 Jan	Balance brought down	24,990

Borrowings

		£			£
30 June	Cash	1,000	1 Jan	Balance brought down	12,000
31 Dec	Balance carried down	13,000		Cash	2,000
		14,000			14,000
			1 Jan	Balance brought down	13,000

Trade payables

		£			£
31 Dec	Cash	18,150	1 Jan	Balance brought down	1,690
	Balance carried down	760	31 Dec	Inventories	17,220
		18,910			18,910
			1 Jan	Balance brought down	760

Electricity

		£			£
31 Dec	Cash	1,070	1 Jan	Balance brought down	270
31 Dec	Balance carried down	290	31 Dec	Income statement	1,090
		1,360			1,360
			1 Jan	Balance brought down	290

Sales revenue

		£			£
31 Dec	Income statement	43,460	31 Dec	Trade receivables	33,100
				Cash	10,360
		43,460			43,460

Wages

	£			£
31 Dec Cash	3,770	31 Dec	Income statement	3,770

Interest on borrowings

	£			£
		31 Dec	Income statement	
			[(6/12 × 14,000) +	
			(6/12 × 13,000)] × 10%	1,350

Income statement for the year to 31 December

		£			£
31 Dec	Cost of sales	20,120	31 Dec	Sales revenue	43,460
	Depreciation	2,400			
	General expenses	570			
	Rent	3,000			
	Bad debts (Trade receivables)	260			
	Electricity	1,090			
	Wages	3,770			
	Interest on borrowings	1,350			
	Profit (Equity)	10,900			
		43,460			43,460

Statement of financial position as at 31 December last year

ASSETS		£
Non-current assets		
Property, plant and equipment		
Buildings		25,000
Fittings: cost	12,000	
depreciation	(4,400)	7,600
		32,600
Current assets		
Inventories of stationery		150
Inventories		1,650
Prepaid rent		500
Trade receivables		1,870
Cash		3,620
		7,790
Total assets		40,390
EQUITY AND LIABILITIES		£
Owners' equity		24,990
Non-current liabilities		
Borrowings		13,000
Current liabilities		
Trade payables		760
Accrued electricity		290
Accrued interest on borrowings		1,350
		2,400
Total equity and liabilities		40,390

Present value table

Present value of £1, that is, $1/(1 + r)^n$

where r = discount rate

n = number of periods until payment

					Discount rates (r)						
Periods (n)	1%	2%	3%	4%	5%	6%	7%	8%	9%	10%	
1	0.990	0.980	0.971	0.962	0.952	0.943	0.935	0.926	0.917	0.909	1
2	0.980	0.961	0.943	0.925	0.907	0.890	0.873	0.857	0.842	0.826	2
3	0.971	0.942	0.915	0.889	0.864	0.840	0.816	0.794	0.772	0.751	3
4	0.961	0.924	0.888	0.855	0.823	0.792	0.763	0.735	0.708	0.683	4
5	0.951	0.906	0.863	0.822	0.784	0.747	0.713	0.681	0.650	0.621	5
6	0.942	0.888	0.837	0.790	0.746	0.705	0.666	0.630	0.596	0.564	6
7	0.933	0.871	0.813	0.760	0.711	0.665	0.623	0.583	0.547	0.513	7
8	0.923	0.853	0.789	0.731	0.677	0.627	0.582	0.540	0.502	0.467	8
9	0.914	0.837	0.766	0.703	0.645	0.592	0.544	0.500	0.460	0.424	9
10	0.905	0.820	0.744	0.676	0.614	0.558	0.508	0.463	0.422	0.386	10
11	0.896	0.804	0.722	0.650	0.585	0.527	0.475	0.429	0.388	0.350	11
12	0.887	0.788	0.701	0.625	0.557	0.497	0.444	0.397	0.356	0.319	12
13	0.879	0.773	0.681	0.601	0.530	0.469	0.415	0.368	0.326	0.290	13
14	0.870	0.758	0.661	0.577	0.505	0.442	0.388	0.340	0.299	0.263	14
15	0.861	0.743	0.642	0.555	0.481	0.417	0.362	0.315	0.275	0.239	15

(continued over)

Periods (n)	Discount rates (r)										
	11%	12%	13%	14%	15%	16%	17%	18%	19%	20%	
1	0.901	0.893	0.885	0.877	0.870	0.862	0.855	0.847	0.840	0.833	1
2	0.812	0.797	0.783	0.769	0.756	0.743	0.731	0.718	0.706	0.694	2
3	0.731	0.712	0.693	0.675	0.658	0.641	0.624	0.609	0.593	0.579	3
4	0.659	0.636	0.613	0.592	0.572	0.552	0.534	0.516	0.499	0.482	4
5	0.593	0.567	0.543	0.519	0.497	0.476	0.456	0.437	0.419	0.402	5
6	0.535	0.507	0.480	0.456	0.432	0.410	0.390	0.370	0.352	0.335	6
7	0.482	0.452	0.425	0.400	0.376	0.354	0.333	0.314	0.296	0.279	7
8	0.434	0.404	0.376	0.351	0.327	0.305	0.285	0.266	0.249	0.233	8
9	0.391	0.361	0.333	0.308	0.284	0.263	0.243	0.225	0.209	0.194	9
10	0.352	0.322	0.295	0.270	0.247	0.227	0.208	0.191	0.176	0.162	10
11	0.317	0.287	0.261	0.237	0.215	0.195	0.178	0.162	0.148	0.135	11
12	0.286	0.257	0.231	0.208	0.187	0.168	0.152	0.137	0.124	0.112	12
13	0.258	0.229	0.204	0.182	0.163	0.145	0.130	0.116	0.104	0.093	13
14	0.232	0.205	0.181	0.160	0.141	0.125	0.111	0.099	0.088	0.078	14
15	0.209	0.183	0.160	0.140	0.123	0.108	0.095	0.084	0.074	0.065	15

Index